SAXON® ALGEBRA 2

Solution Manual

www.SaxonPublishers.com
800-531-5015

ISBN 13: 978-1-6027-7525-1
ISBN 10: 1-6027-7525-7

Printed in the United States of America

3 4 5 6 7 8 1421 15 14 13 12 11
4500295908

LESSON 1

Warm Up 1

1. negative
2. $12 + (-12) = 0$
3. $\frac{2}{3} \cdot \frac{3}{2} = \frac{6}{6} = 1$
4. $10 - 9.85 = 0.15$

Lesson Practice 1

a. $\sqrt{3}$ is a real number and an irrational number.

b. $-\frac{2}{3}$ is a real number and a rational number.

c. 1 is a real number, a rational number, an integer, a whole number, and a natural number.

d. Distributive Property

e. Associative Property of Multiplication

f. Commutative Property of Addition

g. $(43 + 21) + 9$
$= 43 + (21 + 9)$ Associative Property of Addition.
$= 43 + 30$ Add.
$= 73$ Add.

h. $(4 \cdot 16) \cdot 4$
$= (16 \cdot 4) \cdot 4$ Commutative Property of Multiplication.
$= 16 \cdot (4 \cdot 4)$ Associative Property of Multiplication.
$= 16 \cdot 16$ Multiply.
$= 256$ Multiply.

i. The additive inverse of $\frac{3q}{2}$ is $-\frac{3q}{2}$ since $\frac{3q}{2} + -\frac{3q}{2} = 0$.

j. The multiplicative inverse is the reciprocal of -4, which is $-\frac{1}{4}$.
$-4 \cdot \left(-\frac{1}{4}\right) = 1$

k. The distance traveled is speed times time, or $55 \cdot 4$, which can be written using the Commutative Property of Multiplication as $4 \cdot 55$. Now, think of 55 as $50 + 5$.
$4(50 + 5)$
$= 4(50) + 4(5)$ Distributive Property
$= 200 + 20$ Multiply.
$= 220$ Add.
The distance is 220 miles.

Practice 1

1. $-3 - 6 + 1 = -9 + 1 = -8$
2. $-4 + 6 - 8 = 2 - 8 = -6$
3. $-2[(5 - 7 - 2) - (-2 - 7) - 2]$
$= -2[5 - 7 - 2 + 2 + 7 - 2]$ Distributive Prop.
$= -2[5 - 7 - 2 + 7 + 2 - 2]$ Com. Prop. of Add.
$= -2[5 - 7 - 2 + 7]$ Subtract.
$= -2[5 - 7 + 7 - 2]$ Com. Prop. of Add.
$= -2[5 - 2]$ Add.
$= -2(5) + (-2)(-2)$ Distributive Prop.
$= -10 + 4$ Multiply.
$= -6$ Add.
4. $4[3 - (-2)] + 5(-2 + 1)$
$= 4[3 + 2] + 5(-2 + 1)$ Multiply.
$= 4(3) + 4(2) + 5(-2) + 5(1)$ Distributive Prop.
$= 12 + 8 + (-10) + 5$ Multiply.
$= 15$ Add.
5. $14.6 - 9.03 = 5.57$
6. $39.75 + 49.2 = 88.95$
7. 2.09, 2.1, 2.3
8. $\frac{1}{2}, \frac{4}{7}, \frac{3}{5}$
9. distance = rate · time
$d = 40 \frac{\text{miles}}{\text{hour}} \cdot 3\frac{1}{2} \text{ hours}$
$= \frac{40 \text{ miles}}{1 \text{ hour}} \cdot \frac{7 \text{ hours}}{2}$
$= 140$ miles
10. distance = rate · time
$d = 55 \text{ mi/h} \cdot 0.5 \text{ h} = 27.5$ miles

11. First subtract 28 − 19. Then multiply by −2. Finally, add 6.

$$\begin{aligned}-2(28-19)+6 &= -2(9)+6\\ &= -18+6\\ &= -12\end{aligned}$$

12. $2 \cdot 3 \cdot 6$

$= 2 \cdot (3 \cdot 6)$	Associative Property of Mult.
$= 2 \cdot (18)$	Multiply.
$= 36$	Multiply.

13. Mount Hood has the lowest elevation.

14. Area = length · width

Length = 120 yd

$\text{Width} = 160 \text{ ft} = \frac{160}{3} \text{ yd}$

$$A = \frac{120 \text{ yd}}{1} \times \frac{160 \text{ yd}}{3}$$

$$= 6400 \text{ yd}^2$$

The area of the football field is 6400 square yards.

15. $(6 \cdot 5) \cdot 2$

$= 6 \cdot (5 \cdot 2)$	Associative Property of Mult.
$= 6 \cdot 10$	Multiply.
$= 60$	Multiply.

$(6 \cdot 5) \cdot 2$

$= (5 \cdot 6) \cdot 2$	Commutative Property of Mult.
$= 5 \cdot (6 \cdot 2)$	Associative Property of Mult.
$= 5 \cdot 12$	Multiply.
$= 60$	Multiply.

16. 7 is a real number, a rational number, an integer, and a whole number. It is not an irrational number

Answer Choice **A**

17. a. Suzy reads 12 pages in 4 minutes or, $\frac{12 \text{ pages}}{4 \text{ min}} = \frac{3 \text{ pages}}{1 \text{ min}}$

Jonas reads 9 pages in 3 minutes or, $\frac{9 \text{ pages}}{3 \text{ min}} = \frac{3 \text{ pages}}{1 \text{ min}}$

b. $\frac{3 \text{ pages}}{1 \text{ min}} = \frac{3 \text{ pages}}{1 \text{ min}}$. The rates are the same.

18. Distributive Property

Answer Choice **D**

19. a. Circumference $= 2\pi r$

$$9 = 2\pi r$$

$$r = \frac{9}{2\pi}$$

$$\approx 1.43 \text{ in.}$$

b. Surface Area $= 4\pi r^2$

$$= 4\pi(1.43)^2$$

$$\approx 25.68 \text{ in}^2$$

20.

$\text{Average} = \frac{6+13+14}{3}$	
$\text{Average} = \frac{6+14+13}{3}$	Comm. Prop. of Add.
$\text{Average} = \frac{(6+14)+13}{3}$	Assoc. Prop. of Add.
$\text{Average} = \frac{20+13}{3}$	Add.
$\text{Average} = \frac{33}{3}$	Add.
$\text{Average} = 11$	Divide.

The average annual home runs is 11.

21. The annual rate is 19% or 0.19. Think of 0.19 as 0.20 − 0.01

$$\begin{aligned}500(0.20-0.01) &= 500(0.20) - 500(0.01)\\ &= 100 - 5 = 95\end{aligned}$$

The interest is $95.

22. a. 2 weeks = 14 days, so the bamboo grows 1 m · 14, or 14 m in 14 days. The bamboo was already 2 m tall, so it is now 2 m + 14 m = 16 m tall.

b. The bamboo will grow (50 m − 2 m) or 48 m. At 1 m per day, this will take 48 days.

23. $\frac{1}{2}\left(\frac{1}{m} \cdot m\right)$ is the Inverse Property of Multiplication.

$\frac{1}{2} \cdot 1$ is the Identity Property of Multiplication.

24. a. An angle and its complement total 90°. $90° - 35° = x$. Therefore, $x = 55°$.

b. An angle and its supplement total 180°. $180° - 55° = x$. Therefore, $x = 125°$.

25. Negative numbers are not whole numbers, they are integers. The statement should be: −7 is a real number, a rational number, and an integer.

26. The amounts rounded to the nearest ten-thousand are as follows:

Year	2003	2004	2005	2006
Cars Sold	50,000	80,000	210,000	250,000

a. The estimated total is 50,000 + 80,000 + 210,000 + 250,000 = 590,000

b. The sales increase from 2003 to 2006 is 250,000 − 50,000 = 200,000.

27. $12(18) = 18(10 + 2)$
$= 18(10) + 18(2)$
$= 216$

28. Student B is correct. Student A did not distribute the 3 to 0.05.

29. a. Surface area $= 6s^2$
$= 6(5)^2$
$= 150 \text{ cm}^2$

b. Volume $= s^3$
$= 5^3$
$= 125 \text{ cm}^3$

30. 44% of 100 people chose dogs.
$44\% \times 100 = 0.44(100) = 44$

LESSON 2

Warm Up 2

1. coefficient
2. $23 + 2(4) = 23 + 8 = 31$
$5(6) + 7 = 30 + 7 = 37$
$31 \neq 37$
So, $23 + 2(4) = 5(6) + 7$ is false.
3. $8 + 12 \div 4 - 5 = 8 + 3 - 5$
$= 11 - 5$
$= 6$

Lesson Practice 2

a. $2x - 5x^2y$
$= 2(3) - 5(3)^2(-2)$ Replace x with 3 and y with −2
$= 2(3) - 5(9)(-2)$ Perform operations with exponents
$= 6 - (-90)$ Multiply.
$= 96$ Subtract.

b. $4xy^2 + x^2$
$= 4(-3)(-1)^2 + (-3)^2$ Replace x with −3 and y with −1.
$= 4(-3)(1) + 9$ Perform operations with exponents.
$= -12 + 9$ Multiply.
$= -3$ Add.

c. $\dfrac{2(a + b) + 4}{4} - a$
$= \dfrac{2(-4 + 6) + 4}{4} - (-4)$ Replace a with −4 and b with 6.
$= \dfrac{2(2) + 4}{4} - (-4)$ Perform operation inside parentheses.
$= \dfrac{4 + 4}{4} - (-4)$ Multiply.
$= \dfrac{8}{4} - (-4)$ Add.
$= 2 - (-4)$ Divide.
$= 6$ Subtract.

d. $-3ab - b(4 - a)$
$= -3(-2)(7) - 7(4 - (-2))$ Replace a with −2 and b with 7.
$= -3(-2)(7) - 7(6)$ Perform operation inside parentheses.
$= 42 - 42$ Multiply.
$= 0$ Subtract.

e. $p(-p + 1) - m$ Replace m with 5 and p with −3.
$-3(-(-3) + 1) - 5$
Enter this expression into the calculator as shown
$-3(- -3 + 1) - 5$
Press ENTER to find the answer is −17.

f. $-xy + 9 - 7x - 9xy + 7$
$= -xy - 9xy - 7x + 9 + 7$
$= -10xy - 7x + 16$

g. First find the individual costs:
1 notebook cost $1 \cdot 7x = 7x$ dollars
2 pens cost $2 \cdot 2x = 4x$ dollars
3 folders cost $3 \cdot 3x = 9x$ dollars

1 highlighter cost $1 \cdot 4x$ dollars

Now add to find the total cost.

$7x + 4x + 9x + 4x = 24x$ dollars

Practice 2

1. $V = lwh$

$= 2 \text{ in.} \cdot 4 \text{ in.} \cdot 9 \text{ in.}$

$= 72 \text{ in.}^3$

2. $V = lwh$

$= 0.5 \text{ cm} \cdot 1.2 \text{ cm} \cdot 6 \text{ cm}$

$= 3.6 \text{ cm}^3$

3. $4(68) = 4(60) + 4(8)$

$= 240 + 32$

$= 272$

4. a. A child ticket costs \$30 and an adult ticket costs \$40 when rounded. a adult tickets cost $40a$ and c child tickets cost $30c$. The total is $40a + 30c$.

b. A family with 1 adult and 4 children pays $40(1) + 30(4) = \$160$. A family with 3 adults and 1 child pays $40(3) + 30(1) = \$150$. The family with 1 adult and 4 children pays more.

5. $x - xy^2 - xy$

$= (-2) - (-2)(-3)^2 - (-2)(-3)$ Replace x with -2 and y with -3.

$= (-2) - (-2)(9) - (-2)(-3)$ Perform operations with exponents.

$= (-2) - (-18) - (6)$ Multiply.

$= 10$ Subtract.

6. $(x - y) - x(-y)$

$= (-5 - 3) - (-5)(-3)$ Replace x with -5 and y with 3.

$= -8 - (-5)(-3)$ Perform operations in parentheses.

$= -8 - 15$ Multiply.

$= -23$ Subtract.

7. $x^2(x - xy)$

$= (-2)^2(-2 - (-2)(3))$ Replace x with -2 and y with 3.

$= 4(-2 - (-2)(3))$ Perform operations with exponents.

$= 4(-2 - (-6))$ Perform multiplication in parentheses.

$= 4(4)$ Perform subtraction in parentheses.

$= 16$ Multiply.

8. $x^2 - y(x - y)$

$= \left(-\frac{1}{2}\right)^2 - \frac{1}{4}\left(-\frac{1}{2} - \frac{1}{4}\right)$ Replace x with $-\frac{1}{2}$ and y with $\frac{1}{4}$.

$= \frac{1}{4} - \frac{1}{4}\left(-\frac{1}{2} - \frac{1}{4}\right)$ Perform operations with exponents.

$= \frac{1}{4} - \frac{1}{4}\left(-\frac{3}{4}\right)$ Perform operations inside parentheses.

$= \frac{1}{4} - \left(-\frac{3}{16}\right)$ Multiply.

$= \frac{7}{16}$ Subtract.

9. $xy(1 - y)$

$= \frac{1}{5}(-10)(1 - (-10)$ Replace x with $\frac{1}{5}$ and y with -10.

$= \frac{1}{5}(-10)(11)$ Perform operations in parentheses.

$= -22$ Multiply.

10. $xy - (x^2 - y)$

$= \left(-\frac{1}{3}\right)\left(\frac{1}{2}\right) - \left(\left(-\frac{1}{3}\right)^2 - \frac{1}{2}\right)$ Replace x with $-\frac{1}{3}$ and y with $\frac{1}{2}$.

$= \left(-\frac{1}{3}\right)\left(\frac{1}{2}\right) - \left(\frac{1}{9} - \frac{1}{2}\right)$ Perform operations with exponents.

$= \left(-\frac{1}{3}\right)\left(\frac{1}{2}\right) - \left(-\frac{7}{18}\right)$ Perform operations in parentheses.

$= -\frac{1}{6} - \left(-\frac{7}{18}\right)$ Multiply.

$= \frac{4}{18}$ Subtract.

$= \frac{2}{9}$ Simplify.

11. $\sqrt{8}$ is a real number and an irrational number.

12. -3 is a real number, a rational number, and an integer.

13. $\frac{2}{3}$ is a real number and a rational number.

14. There are 5 weekdays so the budget for weekdays is 5(12), or \$60. There are 2 weekend days, so the budget for the weekend is 2(15) = \$30. The total budget for the week is \$60 + \$30 = \$90. For w weeks the budget is \$90(w) or 90w.

15. a. $2qr(3 + r)$

$= 2(2)(-1)(3 + (-1))$ Replace q with 2 and r with -1.

$= 2(2)(-1)(2)$ Perform operations inside parentheses.

$= -8$ Multiply.

b. $2qr(3 + r)$ If q is doubled the result will double. To check, replace q with 4 and r with -1. The result is $2(4)(-1)(3 + (-1)) = -16$.

c. $2qr(3 + r)$

$= 2(4)(-1)(3 +(-1))$ Replace q with 4 and r with -1.

$= 2(4)(-1)(2)$ Perform operations inside parentheses.

$= -16$ Multiply.

16. $-16t^2 + 48t$

$= -16(2)^2 + 48(2)$ Replace t with 2.

$= -16(4) + 48(2)$ Perform operations with exponents.

$= -64 + 96$ Multiply.

$= 32$ Add.

The height is 32 feet.

17. The angle and its complement total 90°.
90° − 35° = 55°.

18. The angle and its complement total 90°.
90° − 68° = 22°.

19. The angle and its complement total 90°.
90° − 5° = 85°.

20. The angle and its complement total 90°.
90° − 89° = 1°.

21. $4x^2 + 7y$

$= 4(3)^2 + 7(-2)$ Replace x with 3 and y with -2.

$= 4(9) + 7(-2)$ Perform operations with exponents.

$= 36 + (-14)$ Multiply.

$= 22$ Add.

Answer Choice **D**

22. Student A is correct. Student B did not distribute the negative sign when multiplying −13 by 2.

23. $A = lw$

The area of the first rectangle is $c \cdot 2d$ or $2cd$.

The area of the second rectangle is $4(5 - c) = 4(5) - 4c$ or $20 - 4c$. The combined area is $2cd + 20 - 4c$, or $2cd - 4c + 20$.

24. Substitute values for a and b to see if the equation is true. If a is 2 and b is 3, then $a^2 + b^2 = (a + b)^2$ becomes $2^2 + 3^2 = (2 + 3)^2$, or $13 = 25$, which is not true. So $a^2 + b^2 \neq (a + b)^2$.

25. Ten lunches cost 6(10), and with the \$5 discount the ten lunches cost 6(10) − 5 = \$55.

26. No. The multiplicative inverse would be $\frac{1}{0}$, but division by zero is undefined.

27. $fg^2 - (2f - g^2)$ Replace f with 1 and g with -2.

$(1)(-2)^2 - (2(1) - (-2)^2)$

Enter this expression into the calculator as shown

$(1)(-2)x^2 - (2(1) - (-2)x^2)$

Press ENTER to find the answer is 6.

Verify: $fg^2 - (2f - g^2)$

$= (1)(-2)^2 - (2(1) - (-2)^2)$ Replace f with 1 and g with -2.

$= (1)(-2)^2 - (2(1) - 4)$ Perform operations with exponents in parentheses.

$= (1)(-2)^2 - (2 - 4)$ Perform multiplication in parentheses.

$= (1)(-2)^2 - (-2)$ Perform subtraction in parentheses.

$= (1)(4) - (-2)$ Perform operations with exponents.

$= 4 - (-2)$ Multiply.

$= 6$ Subtract.

28. $5ab + 7a - 3ab + 4b$
$= 5ab - 3ab + 7a + 4b$
$= 2ab + 7a + 4b$

29. $y - 9x^2y + 4 + 3x^2y + 12$
$= y - 9x^2y + 3x^2y + 12 + 4$
$= y - 6x^2y + 16$
$= -6x^2y + y + 16$

30. $2(x + 3) - x$
$= 2x + 2(3) - x$
$= 2x + 6 - x$
$= 2x - x + 6$
$= x + 6$

LESSON 3

Warm Up 3

1. exponent
2. $5^4 = 5 \cdot 5 \cdot 5 \cdot 5 = 625$
$5 + 5 + 5 + 5 = 20$
So, $5^4 = 5 + 5 + 5 + 5$ is false.
3. $n \cdot n \cdot n \cdot n$
$= -3 \cdot -3 \cdot -3 \cdot -3$ Replace n with -3.
$= 81$

Lesson Practice 3

a. $\frac{1}{2^{-3}} = 2^3 = 8$

b. $2^{-4} = \frac{1}{2^4} = \frac{1}{16}$

c. $-2^{-2} = -\frac{1}{2^2} = -\frac{1}{4}$

d. $(-2)^{-3} = \frac{1}{(-2)^3} = \frac{1}{-8} = -\frac{1}{8}$

e. $-(-2)^{-4} = -\frac{1}{(-2)^4} = -\frac{1}{16}$

f. $x^9y^{-1}x^{-2}y^3y^{-7}$
$= x^9x^{-2}y^{-1}y^3y^{-7}$
$= x^{(9+(-2))}y^{(-1+3+(-7))}$
$= x^7y^{-5}$ or $\frac{x^7}{y^5}$

g. $\frac{xx^6y^8x^{-11}y^{-3}}{x^{-5}yy^2x^{-4}}$
$= \frac{x^{1+6+(-11)}y^{8+(-3)}}{x^{-5+(-4)}y^{1+2}}$
$= \frac{x^{-4}y^5}{x^{-9}y^3}$
$= x^{-4} \cdot x^9 \cdot y^5 \cdot y^{-3}$
$= x^5y^2$

h. $\frac{(y^2)^{-3}\, x^4(xy^{-2})^{-2}}{xy^4}$
$= \frac{y^{-6}x^4x^{-2}y^4}{xy^4}$
$= \frac{y^{-2}x^2}{xy^4}$
$= xy^{-6}$ or $\frac{x}{y^6}$

i. $\frac{(x^b)^{a-1}(xy^{-a})^{-b}}{y^{-1}}$
$= \frac{x^{ab-b}x^{-b}y^{ab}}{y^{-1}}$
$= \frac{x^{ab-2b}y^{ab}}{y^{-1}}$
$= x^{ab-2b}y^{ab}y^1$
$= x^{ab-2b}y^{ab+1}$

j. $\frac{(0.004)(600 \times 10^9)}{(30000 \times 10^{-12})(0.0001 \times 10^3)}$
$= \frac{(4 \times 10^{-3})(6 \times 10^{11})}{(3 \times 10^{-8})(1 \times 10^{-1})}$
$= \frac{4 \cdot 6}{3 \cdot 1} \times \frac{10^8}{10^{-9}}$
$= 8 \times 10^{8+9}$
$= 8 \times 10^{17}$

k. Divide the amount of garbage produced by the population.

$$\frac{4.78 \times 10^{11}}{2.99 \times 10^{8}} = \frac{4.78}{2.99} \times \frac{10^{11}}{10^{8}}$$
$$\approx 1.60 \times 10^{3}$$

The average American produced about 1.60×10^3 pounds of garbage.

Practice 3

1. $-b^2 - b(a - b^2)$

$= -(-3)^2 - (-3)((4) - (-3)^2)$ Replace a with 4 and b with -3.

$= -(-3)^2 - (-3)(-5)$ Perform operations with exponents then subtraction in parentheses.

$= -9 - (-3)(-5)$ Perform operations with exponents.

$= -24$ Multiply and Subtract.

2. $a^2 - b^3(a - b)$

$= (-2)^2 - (-3)^3(-2 - (-3))$ Replace a with -2 and b with -3.

$= (-2)^2 - (-3)^3(1)$ Perform operations inside parentheses.

$= 4 - (-27)(1)$ Perform operations with exponents.

$= 31$ Multiply and Subtract.

3. Commutative Property

4. Distributive Property

5. $$\frac{(2x^2)^{-3}(xy^0)^{-2}}{2xx^0x^1xxy^2} = \frac{2^{-3}x^{-6}x^{-2}y^0}{2xx^0x^1xxy^2}$$
$$= \frac{2^{-3}x^{-8}y^0}{2x^4y^2}$$
$$= 2^{-4}x^{-12}y^{-2}$$
$$= \frac{1}{2^4x^{12}y^2}$$
$$= \frac{1}{16x^{12}y^2}$$

6. $$\frac{a^0bc^0(a^{-1}b^{-1})^2}{ab(ab^0)abc} = \frac{a^0bc^0a^{-2}b^{-2}}{abab^0abc}$$
$$= \frac{a^{-2}b^{-1}c^0}{a^3b^2c}$$
$$= a^{-5}b^{-3}c^{-1}$$
$$= \frac{1}{a^5b^3c}$$

7. $$\frac{(2x^2y^3)^{-3}y}{(4xy)^{-2}(x^{-2}y)^3y} = \frac{2^{-3}x^{-6}y^{-9}y}{4^{-2}x^{-2}y^{-2}x^{-6}y^3y}$$
$$= \frac{2^{-3}x^{-6}y^{-8}}{4^{-2}x^{-8}y^2}$$
$$= \frac{4^2x^2}{2^3y^{10}}$$
$$= \frac{2x^2}{y^{10}}$$

8. $$\frac{xx^{-2}y(x^{-3})^2xy^0}{(2xy)^{-2}x^2(y^{-3})^2} = \frac{xx^{-2}yx^{-6}xy^0}{2^{-2}x^{-2}y^{-2}x^2y^{-6}}$$
$$= \frac{x^{-6}y}{2^{-2}x^0y^{-8}}$$
$$= \frac{2^2y^9}{x^6}$$
$$= \frac{4y^9}{x^6}$$

9. $A = \pi r^2 = \pi(3)^2 = 9\pi \text{ m}^2$

10. Vertical angles have the same measure. So, angle a measures 74°.

11. Multiply 1.4×10^{-3} by 3×10^7 by using the Commutative Property of Multiplication.

$1.4 \times 3 \times 10^{-3} \times 10^7 = 4.2 \times 10^4$.

12. a. $10\% = 0.1$

$0.1 \times 18 = 0.1(10 + 8)$
$= 0.1(10) + 0.1(8)$
$= 1 + 0.8$
$= 1.8$ or \$1.80

b. A 15% tip is the 10% tip plus one-half the 10% tip. So a 15% tip is \$1.80 + \$0.90 = \$2.70.

13. $(8 \cdot 9) + (4 \cdot 9)$ is the Distributive Property, and $72 + 36$ is Multiplication.

14. a. $1 - (3x^2 - 2y)$

$= 1 - (3(2)^2 - 2(3))$ Replace x with 2 and y with 3.

$= 1 - 6$ Perform operation with exponent, then multiplication, then subtraction in parentheses.

$= -5$ Subtract.

b. The result would increase by $2y$.

c. $1 - (3x^2 - 2y)$

$= 1 - (3(2)^2 - 2(6))$ Replace x with 2 and y with 6.

$= 1 - 0$ Perform operation with exponent, then multiplication, then subtraction in parentheses.

$= 1$ Subtract.

Since $1 - (-5) = 6$ and $2y = 2(3) = 6$, this verifies that the result will increase by $2y$ if y is doubled.

15. There is 3 times the amount of calcium in $\frac{3}{4}$ cup of cereal than in $\frac{1}{4}$, and 2 times the amount in $\frac{1}{2}$ cup of milk than in $\frac{1}{4}$.

So, $3(33) + 2(75) = 99 + 150 = 249$ mg of calcium.

16. For the given segments of both squares, the y values are the same, so each slope is zero representing horizontal lines. For the first square, the distance between the points $(u, 1)$ and $(5u, 1)$ is $5u - u$ or $4u$, which is the length of the side of the square. Since the side of the square is $4u$, the area is $(4u)^2$, or $16u^2$ square units. For the second square, the distance between the points $(2u, 1)$ and $(4u, 1)$ is $4u - 2u$ or $2u$, which is the length of the side of this square. Since the side of the square is $2u$, the area is $(2u)^2$, or $4u^2$ square units. The combined total is $16u^2 + 4u^2 = 20u^2$ square units.

17. $x + 2 = 19, x = 17$

$y + 5 = 19, y = 14$

The point is (17, 14).

18. $3g - 2f + fg^2 - 5g + 4fg^2 + 6f$

$= 3(-1) - 2(1) + (1)(-1)^2 - 5(-1) + 4(1)(-1)^2 + 6(1)$ Replace f with 1 and g with -1.

$= 3(-1) - 2(1) + (1)(1) - 5(-1) + 4(1)(1) + 6(1)$ Perform operations with exponents.

$= -3 - 2 + 1 - (-5) + 4 + 6$

$= 11$ Subtract and Add.

Verify: $3g - 2f + fg^2 - 5g + 4fg^2 + 6f$

$= -2g + 4f + 5fg^2$

$= -2(-1) + 4(1) + 5(1)(-1)^2$

Replace f with 1 and g with -1.

$= -2(-1) + 4(1) + 5(1)(1)$

Perform operations with exponents.

$= 2 + 4 + 5$ Multiply.

$= 11$ Add.

19. $\frac{y^{-3}xy^2x^{-4}x^5}{x^3y^{-1}} = \frac{x^2y^{-1}}{x^3y^{-1}}$

$= x^{-1}y^0$

$= \frac{1}{x}$

Answer choice **A**

20. $1^{10000000}$ means 1 multiplied by itself 10000000 times. A number times 1 is the number itself. So, 1 times 1 is always 1, no matter how many times 1 is multiplied by itself.

21. Student A placed a negative on 2 when evaluating $\frac{2^{-3}}{12}$,

$\frac{2^{-3}}{12} \neq \frac{1}{12(-2)^3}$

Student B added the exponents in the parentheses.

$2(2^2 + 2) \neq 2(2^3)$

22. $4200 \text{ m} + 590 \text{ m} = 4790 \text{ m}$

23. Atlantic: $V = 3.93 \times 10^3 \times 8.24 \times 10^{13}$

$= 32.3832 \times 10^{16}$

$\doteq 3.24 \times 10^{17} \text{m}^3$

Pacific: $V = 3.93 \times 10^3 \times 1.66 \times 10^{14}$

$= 6.52 \times 10^{17} \text{ m}^3$

$3.24 \times 10^{17} \times 2 = 6.48 \times 10^{17}$

6.48×10^{17} is approx. the same as 6.52×10^{17}

24. $1 \text{ mile} = 5280 \text{ feet}$
$1770 \text{ miles} = 1770 \times 5280$
$= 9{,}345{,}600 \text{ feet}$

25. Divide the volume by the area to find the height.

$$\frac{x^3y^2x^{-2}}{y^{-3}x^2y} \div \frac{x^{-2}y^3x^{-1}}{y^{-4}x^{-2}y^2}$$
$$= \frac{xy^2}{y^{-2}x^2} \div \frac{x^{-3}y^3}{y^{-2}x^{-2}}$$
$$= \frac{y^4}{x} \div \frac{y^5}{x}$$
$$= \frac{y^4}{x} \times \frac{x}{y^5}$$
$$= \frac{1}{y}$$

26. Rita can rent 8 movies for \$35 at the first store because the 8th one is free (7 × \$5). She can rent 8 movies for \$42 at the second store because the 4th and 8th ones are free (6 × \$7). Rita should consider the cost of renting each movie.

27. $\frac{2^{-3}}{8^{-2}} = \frac{8^2}{2^3} = \frac{64}{8} = 8$

28. The driver multiplied the highway fuel efficiency by the city mileage. The city fuel efficiency, 50, should be multiplied by the number of gallons in the city. Then this should be added to the highway fuel efficiency times the number of gallons on the highway. If 4 gallons are used in the city, then (15 − 4) gallons are left to be used on the highway.
$50(4) + 61(15 - 4) = 871$ miles

29. Associative Property of Multiplication
The property is useful because it results in a multiplication of two 1-digit numbers in the final step, which is easier to multiply than a 1-digit number and a 2-digit number.

30. **a.** $2.24 + x$
b. \$2.24 + \$5.97 = \$8.21

LAB 1

Lab Practice

a.

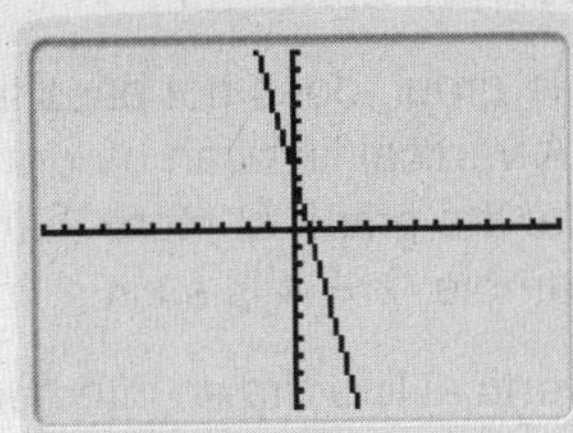

b. x-intercept = (2, 0)
y-intercept = (0, 4)

c.

X	Y1
1	5
3	-1
5	-7
7	-13
9	-19
11	-25
13	-31

X=1

d.

x	y
0	−6
0.5	−4
1	−2
1.5	0
2	2

LESSON 4

Warm Up 4

1. coordinate
2. $5x^3 - 3x$

$= 5(2)^3 - 3(2)$	Replace x with 2.
$= 5(8) - 3(2)$	Perform operation with exponent.
$= 40 - 6$	Multiply.
$= 34$	Subtract.

3. The x-coordinate is the first coordinate in each pair. They are −2, 0, 2.

Lesson Practice 4

a. This is not a function. The domain is 2, 3, 6. The range is 4, 5, 7, 9.

b. This is a function. The domain is *m*, *n*. The range is *p*.

c. Function. Every vertical line drawn intersects the graph no more than once.

d. Not a function. The graph does not pass the vertical line test. A vertical line can be drawn so that it intersects the graph at more than one point. For example, $x = 4$ is such a line.

e. Function. Every vertical line drawn intersects the graph no more than once.

f. Substitute 2 for *x* in $v(x) = 9x + 3x^2$ (do not use $a(x) = 9 + 6x$).

$v(2) = 9(2) + 3(2)^2$ Replace *x* with 2.

$v(2) = 9(2) + 3(4)$ Perform operation with exponent.

$v(2) = 18 + 12$ Multiply.

$v(2) = 30$ Add.

g. Two tickets will cost \$25 + \$20 = \$45.

Three tickets will cost \$25 + \$20 + \$20 = \$65.

Four tickets will cost \$25 + \$20 + \$20 + \$20 = \$85. The ordered pairs in set notation are: {(2, 45), (3, 65), (4, 85)}

The domain is 2, 3, 4. The range is 45, 65, 85.

The set of ordered pairs represent a function since for every value of *x* there is exactly one *y*-value.

h. Two shirts will cost \$15.50, three shirts will cost \$31.00, four shirts will cost \$31.00, five shirts will cost \$46.50, and six shirts will cost \$46.50. The ordered pairs in set notation are: {(2, 15.5), (3, 31), (4, 31), (5, 46.5), (6, 46.5)}

The domain is 2, 3, 4, 5, 6. The range is 15.5, 31, 46.5.

The set of ordered pairs represent a function since for every value of *x* there is exactly one *y*-value.

Practice 4

1. $3p$; since $-3p + 3p = 0$

2. -50; since $50 + (-50) = 0$

3. $2m - 4n(3m - 4)$

$= 2(1) - 4(-3)(3(1) - 4)$ Replace *m* with 1 and *n* with -3.

$= 2(1) - 4(-3)(-1)$ Perform operations in parentheses.

$= 2 - 12$ Multiply.

$= -10$ Subtract.

4. $-m^3 + mn^2(n - m)$

$= -(-2)^3 + (-2)(-3)^2((-3) - (-2))$ Replace *m* with -2 and *n* with -3.

$= -(-2)^3 + (-2)(-3)^2(-1)$ Perform operation in parentheses.

$= -(-8) + (-2)(9)(-1)$ Perform operations with exponents.

$= 8 + 18$ Multiply.

$= 26$ Add.

5. $\dfrac{(m^3n^{-1})^{-4}}{(3mn)^{-2}} = \dfrac{m^{-12}n^4}{3^{-2}m^{-2}n^{-2}}$

$= \dfrac{3^2n^6}{m^{10}}$

$= \dfrac{9n^6}{m^{10}}$

6. $\dfrac{-a^3(a^3b^{-2})^3}{ab(ab)^{-4}} = \dfrac{-a^3a^9b^{-6}}{aba^{-4}b^{-4}}$

$= \dfrac{-a^{12}b^{-6}}{a^{-3}b^{-3}}$

$= -\dfrac{a^{15}}{b^3}$

7. This is not a function, since an *x*-value has more than one unique *y*-value. For example when $x = 4$, then $y = 2$ or $y = -2$.

8. This is a function. The domain is the set of real numbers.

Since *x* is squared, *y* has the least value when *x* is 0; that is when $y = 3(0) - 2$, or -2. So, the range is the values of *y* that are equal to or greater than -2. Range is $y \geq -2$.

9. Student A is correct.

Student B added the exponents for a power to a power, instead of multiplying them.

10. $C = 2\pi r$

$16\pi = 2\pi r$ Replace C with 16π.

$8 = r$ Divide both sides of the equation by 2π.

The radius is 8 ft.

11. a. The domain is the x-values. The domain is 2, 3, 5, 7.

b. The range is the y-values. The range is 4, 7, 9, 11.

c. This is not a function. For instance, when $x = 2$, y can have two different values.

12. $y = 3x^2 + 4$

A $10 = 3(1)^2 + 4$ $10 = 7$ Not true

B $31 = 3(3)^2 + 4$ $31 = 31$ True

C $229 = 3(5)^2 + 4$ $229 = 79$ Not True

D $24 = 3(2)^2 + 4$ $24 = 16$ Not True

Answer choice **B** is the only one that is true.

13. She will save 75(12) in twelve months.

12 can be written as 10 + 2. Using the Distributive Property:

$75(12) = 75(10 + 2)$

$= 75(10) + 75(2)$

$= 750 + 150 = 900$

She will save $900.

14. Yes, it is a function. Each radius has only one value for the area. So the relationship from the radius to the area is a function.

15. Divide the height by the speed of light.

$$\frac{1.02 \times 10^4}{3 \times 10^8} = \frac{1.02}{3} \times \frac{10^4}{10^8}$$

$= 0.34 \times 10^{-4}$

$= 3.4 \times 10^{-5}$

It will take about 3.4×10^{-5} seconds.

16. $ab + 3b - a - 5ab + 2b$

$= (-3)(2) + 3(2) - (-3) - 5(-3)(2) + 2(2)$ Replace a with -3 and b with 2.

$= -6 + 6 + 3 + 30 + 4$ Multiply.

$= 37$ Add.

17. $$\frac{a^3b^{-2}c^{-3}b^6c^{-1}a^{-1}}{b^2c^4b^{-1}a^{-5}} = \frac{a^2b^4c^{-4}}{a^{-5}bc^4}$$

$$= \frac{a^7b^3}{c^8}$$

Answer choice **C**

18. Commutative Property. The total is found by 2 + 22 + 58. Changing the order to 2 + 58 + 22 makes it easier to add. 2 + 58 + 22 = 60 + 22 = 88.

19. a. The sales rep receives $9 for each hour she works, so she will receive 9(8) for 8 hours. She receives $30 for each computer she sells, or $30c$ for an unknown number of computers (c) during that time. She receives $20 for each printer she sells, or $20p$ for an unknown number of printers (p) during that time. The total is $9(8) + 30c + 20p$.

b. $9(8) + 30c + 20p$

$= 9(8) + 30(10) + 20(4)$ Replace c with 10 and p with 4.

$= 72 + 300 + 80$ Multiply.

$= 452$ Add.

She will earn $452.

20. The additive inverse is the opposite of the number. And the product of a number and its opposite is equal to the opposite of the square of the number.

21. If h represents the number of gallons used on the highway, then $15 - h$ represents the number of gallons left to be used in the city. So, $61h$ miles can be traveled on the highway, and $50(15 - h)$ will be traveled in the city. The total is $61h + 50(15 - h) = 61h + 750 - 50h = 11h + 750$.

22. If the discount is 15% or 0.15 off the original price, then a customer pays 85% or 0.85 of the original price. The rebate subtracts 200. So, $f(r) = 0.085r - 200$ is correct. $g(r)$ calculates the total discount from the original price, not the final price.

23. If $a = 2$, then the relation is not a function since 2 would have more than one y-value.

If $a = 3$ and $b \neq 8$, then the relation is not a function since 3 would have more than one associated y-value.

24. 1.14×10^2 cm $= 1.14 \times 10^2 \div 10^2$ m $= 1.14 \times 10^0$ m

The volume is $1.14 \times 10^0 \times 8.02 \times 10^8 = 1.14 \times 8.02 \times 10^0 \times 10^8 = 9.14 \times 10^8$ m^3.

25. $f(x) = 3x^2 + x$

$f(-1) = 3(-1)^2 + (-1)$ Replace x with -1.

$f(-1) = 3(1) + (-1)$ Peform operation with exponent.

$f(-1) = 2$ Add.

26. $f(x) = 3x^2 + x$

$f(0) = 3(0)^2 + 0$ Substitute.

$f(0) = 0$ Simplify.

27. $f(x) = 3x^2 + x$

$f\left(\frac{3}{2}\right) = 3\left(\frac{3}{2}\right)^2 + \left(\frac{3}{2}\right)$ Replace x with $\frac{3}{2}$.

$f\left(\frac{3}{2}\right) = 3\left(\frac{9}{4}\right) + \left(\frac{3}{2}\right)$ Perform operation with exponent.

$f\left(\frac{3}{2}\right) = \frac{27}{4} + \left(\frac{3}{2}\right)$ Multiply.

$f\left(\frac{3}{2}\right) = \frac{33}{4}$ or $8\frac{1}{4}$ Add.

28. $-36 + (36 + 17)$

$= (-36 + 36) + 17$ Associative Property of Addition.

$= 0 + 17$ Additive Inverse

$= 17$ Identify Property of Addition

29. Enter this expression into the calculator as shown to find $f(-2.8)$

$(-2.8)x^2$

Press ENTER to find the answer is 7.84.

Enter this expression into the calculator as shown to find $f(2.8)$

$2.8x^2$

Press ENTER to find the answer is 7.84.

To evaluate $f(-2.8)$, parentheses are used since the value is negative. However parentheses are not needed to evaluate $f(2.8)$ since the value is positive.

30. Divide $\frac{2.8 \times 10^8}{2.8 \times 10^5} = \frac{2.8}{2.8} \times \frac{10^8}{10^5}$

$= 10^3$

$= 1000$

1000 people will likely be struck this year.

LAB 2

Lab Practice

a. $A \times B = \begin{bmatrix} -2 & 10 \\ -2 & -35 \end{bmatrix}$

b. $B^{-1} = \begin{bmatrix} 0 & -\frac{1}{3} \\ -\frac{1}{5} & -\frac{1}{15} \end{bmatrix}$

c. Determinant of $A = -6$.

d. $C = \begin{bmatrix} 1 & 0 & 0 & 10 \\ 0 & 1 & 0 & -3 \\ 0 & 0 & 1 & -1 \end{bmatrix}$

LESSON 5

Warm Up 5

1. Inverse

2. $16.5 - (-24.8) = 16.5 + 24.8 = 41.3$

3. $4 - 3y = 16$

$-3y = 16 - 4$

$-3y = 12$

$y = -4$

4. $j - k = j + (-k) = -k + j$

So, $j - k = k - j$ is false.

5. $-4(x + 1) + 3(2x - 7)$

$= -4x - 4 + 6x - 21$

$= 2x - 25$

Lesson Practice 5

a. $W = \begin{bmatrix} 13 & 4 & 8 \\ 1 & 6 & 2 \end{bmatrix}$ $E = \begin{bmatrix} 0 & 11 & 3 \\ 4 & 2 & 5 \end{bmatrix}$

$W + E = \begin{bmatrix} 13 + 0 & 4 + 11 & 8 + 3 \\ 1 + 4 & 6 + 2 & 2 + 5 \end{bmatrix}$

$$W + E = \begin{bmatrix} 13 & 15 & 11 \\ 5 & 8 & 7 \end{bmatrix}$$

b. $-1 + 1 = 0, 1 + -1 = 0, -5 + 5 = 0$

The inverse is $\begin{bmatrix} -1 \\ 1 \\ -5 \end{bmatrix}$

c. $\begin{bmatrix} -1 & 0 \\ 6 & -8 \\ 5 & 3 \end{bmatrix} - \begin{bmatrix} 2 & -4 \\ 2 & -1 \\ 5 & -3 \end{bmatrix}$

$$= \begin{bmatrix} -1 & 0 \\ 6 & -8 \\ 5 & 3 \end{bmatrix} + \begin{bmatrix} -2 & 4 \\ -2 & 1 \\ -5 & 3 \end{bmatrix}$$

$$= \begin{bmatrix} -1 + (-2) & 0 + 4 \\ 6 + (-2) & -8 + 1 \\ 5 + (-5) & 3 + 3 \end{bmatrix}$$

$$= \begin{bmatrix} -3 & 4 \\ 4 & -7 \\ 0 & 6 \end{bmatrix}$$

d. Add $\begin{bmatrix} 2 & -4 \\ -4 & 8 \end{bmatrix}$ to both sides.

$$Y + \begin{bmatrix} 2 & -4 \\ -4 & 8 \end{bmatrix} - \begin{bmatrix} 2 & -4 \\ -4 & 8 \end{bmatrix}$$

$$= \begin{bmatrix} 6 & 5 \\ -10 & 2 \end{bmatrix} + \begin{bmatrix} 2 & -4 \\ -4 & 8 \end{bmatrix}$$

$$Y = \begin{bmatrix} 8 & 1 \\ -14 & 10 \end{bmatrix}$$

e. Equal matrices have equal elements in matching positions. Therefore, $x = 25$ and $z = -5$. Also, $x - y = 18$, and after substituting 25 for x, to get $25 - y = 18$, we find that $y = 7$. We could also use $x + z = 20$, and after substituting 25 for x, to get $25 + z = 20$, we find that $z = -5$.

f. $A = \begin{bmatrix} 0 \\ 4.50 \\ 8.50 \\ 5.50 \end{bmatrix}$ and $B = \begin{bmatrix} 0 \\ 5.00 \\ 9.00 \\ 6.00 \end{bmatrix}$

$0.80A = \begin{bmatrix} 0 \\ 3.60 \\ 6.80 \\ 4.40 \end{bmatrix}$ and $0.70B = \begin{bmatrix} 0 \\ 3.50 \\ 6.30 \\ 4.20 \end{bmatrix}$

$$0.80A - 0.70B = \begin{bmatrix} 0 \\ 3.60 \\ 6.80 \\ 4.40 \end{bmatrix} - \begin{bmatrix} 0 \\ 3.50 \\ 6.30 \\ 4.20 \end{bmatrix}$$

$$= \begin{bmatrix} 0 \\ 0.10 \\ 0.50 \\ 0.20 \end{bmatrix}$$

The differences range from \$0 to \$0.50. Theater A is more expensive than Theater B for all ticket categories for next Saturday.

Practice 5

1. The multiplicative inverse is the reciprocal of $-\frac{2}{3}$, which is $-\frac{3}{2}$.

2. The multiplicative inverse is the reciprocal of 6, which is $\frac{1}{6}$.

3. $x^2y(x + 3y)$

$= 0^2(-6)(0 + 3(-6))$	Replace x with 0 and y with -6.
$= 0^2(-6)(-18)$	Perform operations in parentheses.
$= 0$	Multiply.

4. $4x^2(x^{-2}y^{-4})^{-1}$
$= 4x^2x^2y^4$
$= 4x^4y^4$

5. The graph is not a function. The graph does not pass the vertical line test. A vertical line can be drawn so that it intersects the graph at more than one point. For example, the line $x = 1$ is such a line.

6. $4\begin{bmatrix} 2 & 1 \\ -6 & 3.5 \end{bmatrix} - 3\begin{bmatrix} 0 & 0.4 \\ 8 & -2 \end{bmatrix}$

$$= \begin{bmatrix} 8 & 4 \\ -24 & 14 \end{bmatrix} - \begin{bmatrix} 0 & 1.2 \\ 24 & -6 \end{bmatrix}$$

$$= \begin{bmatrix} 8 & 4 \\ -24 & 14 \end{bmatrix} + \begin{bmatrix} 0 & -1.2 \\ -24 & 6 \end{bmatrix}$$

$$= \begin{bmatrix} 8 & 2.8 \\ -48 & 20 \end{bmatrix}$$

7. $\frac{1}{4}\begin{bmatrix}2 & 4\\6 & 8\end{bmatrix} + \begin{bmatrix}-2 & 1\\-\frac{1}{2} & 5\end{bmatrix} = \begin{bmatrix}\frac{1}{2} & 1\\\frac{3}{2} & 2\end{bmatrix} + \begin{bmatrix}-2 & 1\\-\frac{1}{2} & 5\end{bmatrix}$

$= \begin{bmatrix}-1\frac{1}{2} & 2\\1 & 7\end{bmatrix}$

8. $A = \frac{1}{2}bh = \frac{1}{2}(10)(2) = 10 \text{ cm}^2$

9. $A = \frac{1}{2}bh = \frac{1}{2}(18)\left(\frac{1}{2}\right) = 3 \text{ ft}^2$

10. Alternate interior angles formed by parallel lines cut by a transversal are congruent. If $y = 32°$, then $x = 32°$.

11. The score is 4(72). Think of 72 as 70 + 2, so using the Distributive Property, $4(72) = 4(70 + 2) = 4(70) + 4(2) = 280 + 8 = 288$.

12. a. Sometimes true. This is true only when a and b have the same value; $a = b$. It is not true when a and b have different values.

b. Always true. Rational numbers are a subset of real numbers, so if a and b are rational they are also real. Therefore, by the Closure Property of Addition, $a + b$ is a real number.

13. The total is the cost for each student to view the exhibit, \$3, times the number of students for the two days $(9v + 7v)$, which is $3(9v + 7v)$, or $27v + 21v = 48v$.

14. a. The orbit is a circle, and the distance around a circle is the circumference. The distance between the Sun and Jupiter is the radius of the circle. So, the radius is 7.786×10^{11} m or $7.786 \times 10^{11} \div 10^3 \text{ km} = 7.786 \times 10^8 \text{ km}$.

$C = 2\pi r$

$C = 2\pi(7.786 \times 10^8)$

$= 48.89608 \times 10^8$

$= 4.890 \times 10^9$ km.

b. 4333 days $= 4333 \times 24 \times 60 \times 60$

$= 3.747 \times 10^8$ seconds.

$\text{Rate} = \frac{\text{distance}}{\text{time}} = \frac{4.89 \times 10^9}{3.747 \times 10^8}$

$= 1.31 \times 10 = 13.1$ km/s

15. No, there is more than one y-value for the same x-value.

16. a. $C = 2\pi r$ so the matrix is $2\pi\begin{bmatrix}3 & 3.5\\4 & 4.5\end{bmatrix}$.

b. No. Since $A = \pi r^2$, each radius has to be squared and there is no scalar multiplication or addition that squares the radius.

17. $\frac{1 \times 10^{22}}{1 \times 10^{20}} = 10^2 = 100$

$r = 100s$

18. The matrices have different dimensions and cannot be added.

19. If the vertical line intercepts the graph more than once, it results in more than one y-value, and it is not a function. If every vertical line intercepts the graph only once, it results in a single y-value, and it is a function.

20. $P = 4s = 4(2x + 5) = 4(2x) + 4(5) = 8x + 20$

21. Round 4.8 to 5 and the matrix to $\begin{bmatrix}3 & 3\\-\frac{1}{8} & 0.5\end{bmatrix}$.

$5\begin{bmatrix}3 & 3\\-\frac{1}{8} & 0.5\end{bmatrix} = \begin{bmatrix}15 & 15\\-\frac{5}{8} & 2.5\end{bmatrix}$

22. $x(xy + 2y^2)$

$= (4)((4)(-1) + 2(-1)^2)$ Replace x with 4 and y with -1.

$= (4)(-2)$ Perform operations in parentheses.

$= -8$ Multiply.

Answer Choice **C**

23. a. The subscript tells the row and column for the element. So, a_{21} is the element in row 2 column 1. So matrix A is $\begin{bmatrix}4 & 6\\0 & -1\end{bmatrix}$

b. $\begin{bmatrix}-4 & -6\\0 & 1\end{bmatrix}$

24. $\sqrt{48}$ can be written as $4\sqrt{3}$, and $\sqrt{3}$ is an irrational number, so $\sqrt{48}$ is a real number, but not a rational number.

25. $uv + 8v - u - 4uv + 7u$

$= (-1)(-1) + 8(-1) - (-1) - 4(-1)(-1) + 7(-1)$ Replace u with -1 and v with -1.

$= 1 + (-8) - (-1) - 4 + (-7)$ Multiply.

$= -17$ Add and Subtract.

Verify: $uv + 8v - u - 4uv + 7u$

$= -3uv + 8v + 6u$

$= -3(-1)(-1) + 8(-1) + 6(-1)$

Replace u with -1 and v with -1.

$= -3 + (-8) + (-6)$ Multiply.

$= -17$ Add.

26. $f(x) = x + 2$

$f(16) = 16 + 2$ Replace x with 16.

$f(16) = 18$ Add.

27. Each y-value is 1 greater than -2 times the x-value, so $f(x) = -2x + 1$.

28. Since 1 USD = 0.49 pounds and 1 USD = 115.84 yen, then 0.49 pounds = 115.84 yen.

So, 1 yen $= \frac{0.49}{115.84}$ pounds. Therefore

$f(y) = \frac{0.49y}{115.84}$.

29. No, for example

$\begin{bmatrix} 4 & 5 \\ 1 & 0 \end{bmatrix} - \begin{bmatrix} 3 & 2 \\ 0 & 4 \end{bmatrix} = \begin{bmatrix} 1 & 3 \\ 1 & -4 \end{bmatrix}$ but

$\begin{bmatrix} 3 & 2 \\ 0 & 4 \end{bmatrix} - \begin{bmatrix} 4 & 5 \\ 1 & 0 \end{bmatrix} = \begin{bmatrix} -1 & -3 \\ -1 & 4 \end{bmatrix}$.

30. Divide the number of pennies that fill the Sears Tower by the number of pennies in a cubic foot.

$\frac{2.6 \times 10^{12}}{4.9 \times 10^4} = \frac{2.6}{4.9} \times \frac{10^{12}}{10^4}$

$= 0.53 \times 10^8$

$= 5.3 \times 10^7 \text{ ft}^3$

LESSON 6

Warm Up 6

1. hundred
2. 30% of 40 = $0.30 \times 40 = 12$
3. $\frac{5}{8} = 5 \div 8 = 0.625$
4. $25\% = \frac{25}{100} = \frac{1}{4}$
5. 20% of 60 $= \frac{20}{100} \times \frac{60}{1} = 12$

Lesson Practice 6

a. $1.65 \times 100 = 165$, so $1.65 = 165\%$

b. $0.2 \times 100 = 20$, so $0.2 = 20\%$

c. $7 \div 4 = 1.75 = 175\%$

d. $3 \div 5 = 0.6 = 60\%$

e. The change is an increase.

percent change $= \frac{\text{amount of increase}}{\text{original amount}}$

amount of increase $= 11 - 10$, so percent change

$= \frac{1}{10}$

$= 0.1 = 10\%$

The percent change is a 10% increase.

f. The change is a decrease.

percent change $= \frac{\text{amount of decrease}}{\text{original amount}}$

Amount of decrease $= 50 - 12$. So percent change

$= \frac{38}{50}$

$= 0.76 = 76\%$

The percent change is a 76% decrease.

g. Find the percent increase.

$3\% \times 700$ Write the percent as a decimal and multiply.

$0.03 \times 700 = 21$

Add the amount of increase to the original amount to find the new amount.

$700 + 21 = 721$

h. Find the percent decrease.

$90\% \times 6.2$ Write the percent as a decimal and multiply.

$0.90 \times 6.2 = 5.58$

Subtract the amount of decrease from the original amount to find the new amount.

$6.2 - 5.58 = 0.62$

i. Understand: The amount Ethan pays is the original cost, $230, minus the discount, which is 10% of $230.

Plan: Translate the sentence into algebra.

The amount he pays is (original price − discount).

The amount he pays is 230 − (10% of 230).

$a = 230 - 0.10(230)$

Solve: $a = 230 - 23$

$a = 207$

Ethan will pay $207 for the printer.

j. Understand: The marked up price is the price before mark up, $60, plus the mark up, which is 45% of $60.

Plan: Translate the sentence into algebra.

The mark up price is price before mark up + mark up.

The mark up price is 60 + (45% of 60).

$m = 60 + 0.45(60)$

Solve: $m = 60 + 27$

$m = 87$

The new price of the card is $87.

Practice 6

1. $\sqrt{225} = 15$ Rational

2. π Not rational

3. $\frac{xy(x^2)}{2x}$

$= \frac{(-1)(4)((-1)^2)}{2(-1)}$ Replace x with −1 and y with 4.

$= \frac{(-1)(4)(1)}{2(-1)}$ Perform operation with exponent.

$= 2$ Multiply and Divide.

4. $x^5y(2x^{-5}y^4)^3 = x^5y(2^3x^{-15}y^{12})$

$= 2^3x^{-10}y^{13}$

$= \frac{8y^{13}}{x^{10}}$

5. $\begin{bmatrix} 1 & 5 \\ 2 & -3.2 \end{bmatrix} + 2\begin{bmatrix} 1 & 0 \\ -1 & 4 \end{bmatrix}$

$= \begin{bmatrix} 1 & 5 \\ 2 & -3.2 \end{bmatrix} + \begin{bmatrix} 2 & 0 \\ -2 & 8 \end{bmatrix}$

$= \begin{bmatrix} 3 & 5 \\ 0 & 4.8 \end{bmatrix}$

6. The net has six rectangles and three pairs are congruent. The net is a rectangular prism.

7. The change is an increase.

percent change $= \frac{\text{amount of increase}}{\text{original amount}}$

amount of increase = 4.5 − 3, so percent change

$= \frac{1.5}{3}$

$= 0.5 = 50\%$

The percent change is a 50% increase.

8. The change is an increase.

percent change $= \frac{\text{amount of increase}}{\text{original amount}}$

amount of increase = 2.74 − 0.8, so percent change

$= \frac{1.94}{0.8}$

$= 2.425 = 242.5\%$

The percent change is a 242.5% increase.

9. $y^2 = x + 1$ is not a function, since there is more than one value of y for each value of x. For instance, when x is 24, y is 5 or −5.

10. $y = x^2 - 2$ is a function. The domain is all real numbers. The range is $y \geq -2$.

11. Student A made errors. The first step in Student A's work should be Distributive Property, and the second step should be Multiply.

12. a. The sale price is the original price minus the discount.

For the notebook, the discount is 30% of \$3.20 = 0.30(3.20) = 0.96. The sale price is 3.20 − 0.96 = 2.24.

For the calculator, the discount is 10% of \$78 = 0.10(78) = 7.8. The sale price is 78 − 7.8 = 70.2.

The total is 2.24 + 70.2 = 72.44

The student spent \$72.44.

b. The total of the items is \$3.20 + \$78 = \$81.20. 40% of 81.20 = 0.40(81.20) = 32.48. The sale price is 81.20 − 32.48 = 48.72.

\$72.44 ≠ \$48.72

13. $-x^2 + 6y$

$= -(2)^2 + 6(0)$ Replace x with 2 and y with 0.

$= -4 + 6(0)$ Perform operation with exponent.

$= -4$ Multiply and Add.

Answer Choice **B**

14. $g(x) = 0.5 + 0.2(x - 1)$

$g(10) = 0.5 + 0.2(10 - 1)$ Replace x with 10.

$g(10) = 0.5 + 1.8$

$g(10) = 2.3$

A 10-minute call costs \$2.30.

15. percent change $= \dfrac{\text{amount of increase}}{\text{original amount}}$

amount of increase = 6,080,485 − 5,544,159 so percent change

$= \dfrac{536326}{5544159}$

$= 0.0967 = 9.67\%$

16. −5 is a real number, a rational number, and an integer. It is not a whole number.

Answer Choice **C**

17. a. $LY = \begin{bmatrix} 27 & 33 & 51 \\ 29 & 42 & 41 \\ 25 & 29 & 60 \end{bmatrix}$

$TY = \begin{bmatrix} 18 & 45 & 47 \\ 34 & 33 & 62 \\ 35 & 31 & 54 \end{bmatrix}$

b. $\begin{bmatrix} 18 & 45 & 47 \\ 34 & 33 & 62 \\ 35 & 31 & 54 \end{bmatrix} - \begin{bmatrix} 27 & 33 & 51 \\ 29 & 42 & 41 \\ 25 & 29 & 60 \end{bmatrix}$

$= \begin{bmatrix} 18 & 45 & 47 \\ 34 & 33 & 62 \\ 35 & 31 & 54 \end{bmatrix} + \begin{bmatrix} -27 & -33 & -51 \\ -29 & -42 & -41 \\ -25 & -29 & -60 \end{bmatrix}$

$= \begin{bmatrix} -9 & 12 & -4 \\ 5 & -9 & 21 \\ 10 & 2 & -6 \end{bmatrix}$

18. a. $-5vw(-2 + w)$

$= -5(3)(-4)(-2 + (-4))$ Replace v with 3 and w with −4.

$= -5(3)(-4)(-6)$ Perform operation in parentheses.

$= -360$ Multiply.

b. The result would triple.

c. $-5vw(-2 + w)$

$= -5(9)(-4)(-2 + (-4))$ Replace v with 9 and w with −4.

$= -5(9)(-4)(-6)$ Perform operation in parentheses.

$= -1080$

−1080 is three times −360.

19. If the original is 75 and the new amount is 0, the amount of the decrease is 75, since 75 − 75 = 0. The percent decrease is $\frac{\text{amount of decrease}}{\text{original amount}}$ or $\frac{75}{75}$ = 1 = 100%.

20. a. Divide distance by rate to find time.

$\dfrac{4.437 \times 10^{12}}{3 \times 10^8} = \dfrac{4.437}{3} \times \dfrac{10^{12}}{10^8}$

$= 1.479 \times 10^4$

It would take about 14,790 seconds.

b. Divide distance by rate to find time.

$\dfrac{7.376 \times 10^{12}}{3 \times 10^8} = \dfrac{7.376}{3} \times \dfrac{10^{12}}{10^8}$

$= 2.4587 \times 10^4$

It would take about 24,587 seconds.

21. Mark up and discounts are both percent changes, and can be used to find the new price of an item. A mark up is a percent increase, while a discount is a percent decrease. A mark up is added to the original price and a discount is subtracted from the original price.

22. The original area is $A = lw = 2(7) = 14$. The area when the dimensions are tripled is $A = lw = 6(21) = 126$. The increase is $126 - 14 = 112$. The percent increase is $\frac{112}{14} = 8 = 800\%$.
The area of the rectangle increased by 800%.

23. $(2 + 3) + 1$
$= 2 + (3 + 1)$ Associative Property of Addition
$= 2 + 4$
$= 6$
$(2 + 3) + 1$
$= (3 + 2) + 1$ Commutative Property of Addition
$= 3 + (2 + 1)$, Associative Property of Addition
$= 3 + 3 = 6$

24. a. Since 1 USD = 119 yen and 1 euro = 157 yen, then 1 USD to 1 euro is 119 yen to 157 yen. So, 1 USD = $\frac{157}{119}$ euros. Therefore
$d = \frac{157e}{119}$

b. $d = \frac{157e}{119}$
$d = \frac{157(5)}{119} = 6.60$
On that day 5 euros was the same as \$6.60 USD.

25. $a^2b^3 - (5a - b^2)$
$= (1)^2(3)^3 - (5(1) - (3)^2)$ Replace with $a = 1$ and $b = 3$.
$= 27 - (-4)$
$= 31$

26. a. The additive inverse and $\frac{-4x}{7}$ equals zero. $\frac{-4x}{7} + \frac{4x}{7} = 0$. So, the additive inverse of $\frac{-4x}{7}$ is $\frac{4x}{7}$.

b. The multiplicative inverse times $\frac{-4x}{7}$ equals 1. $\frac{-4x}{7} \times -\frac{7x}{4} = 1$. Therefore, the multiplicative inverse of $\frac{-4x}{7}$ is $\frac{-7x}{4}$.

27. a.

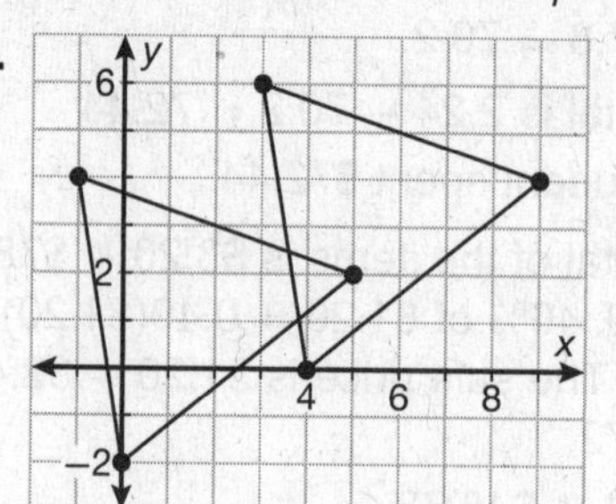

Triangle has vertices at $(-1, 4)$, $(0, -2)$, and $(5, 2)$.

b. The new triangle has vertices at $(3, 6)$, $(4, 0)$, and $(9, 4)$.

28. $\begin{bmatrix} -2 \\ -4 \\ 5 \end{bmatrix}$

29. Use multiplication.
$4.9 \times 10^4 \times 6.45 \times 10^7$
$= 4.9 \times 6.45 \times 10^4 \times 10^7$
$= 31.605 \times 10^{11}$
$= 3.1605 \times 10^{12}$, which is about 3.2×10^{12}

30. In both, you multiply a group of objects by one outside object. In the Distributive Property, the factor that everything is multiplied by can be a constant or a variable expression. In Scalar Multiplication, that factor is a constant.

LESSON 7

Warm Up 7

1. Commutative
2. $5(x - 3) = 5x - 5(3) = 5x - 15$
3. $3x + 4y - 8x - 4y = 3x - 8x + 4y - 4y$
$= -5x$

Lesson Practice 7

a. $8t - 21 = 11$

$+21 = +21$ Add 21 to both sides.

$8t = 32$

$\frac{8t}{8} = \frac{32}{8}$ Divide both sides by 8.

$t = 4$

Check in the original equation.

$8t - 21 = 11$

$8(4) - 21 \stackrel{?}{=} 11$

$32 - 21 \stackrel{?}{=} 11$

$11 = 11$

b. $5r - 12 = -4r - 30$

$+12 = +12$ Add 12 to both sides.

$5r = -4r - 18$

$+4r = +4r$ Add $4r$ to both sides.

$9r = -18$

$\frac{9r}{9} = \frac{-18}{9}$ Divide both sides by 9.

$r = -2$

Check in the original equation.

$5r - 12 = -4r - 30$

$5(-2) - 12 \stackrel{?}{=} -4(-2) - 30$

$-10 - 12 \stackrel{?}{=} 8 - 30$

$-22 = -22$

c. $6(y - 5) + 4y = 5(y + 2)$

$6y - 30 + 4y = 5y + 10$

$10y - 30 = 5y + 10$

$+30 = +30$

$10y = 5y + 40$

$-5y = -5y$

$5y = 40$

$\frac{5y}{5} = \frac{40}{5}$

$y = 8$

Check in the original equation.

$6(y - 5) + 4y = 5(y + 2)$

$6(8 - 5) + 4(8) \stackrel{?}{=} 5(8 + 2)$

$6(3) + 32 \stackrel{?}{=} 5(10)$

$18 + 32 = 50$

d. $-\frac{3}{4}s - 3 = \frac{1}{3}s + \frac{1}{4}$

$12\left(-\frac{3}{4}s - 3\right) = 12\left(\frac{1}{3}s + \frac{1}{4}\right)$

$-9s - 36 = 4s + 3$

$+36 = +36$

$-9s = 4s + 39$

$-4s = -4s$

$-13s = 39$

$\frac{-13s}{-13} = \frac{39}{-13}$

$s = -3$

e. Let d represent the distance in miles between Cortex and Rock Springs.

The equation is

$410 + d + 180 = 955$.

$410 + d + 180 = 955$

$d + 590 = 955$

$-590 = -590$

$d = 365$

The distance between Cortez and Rock Springs is 365 miles.

Practice 7

1. Two supplementary angles total 180°. The angle supplementary to a 65° angle is 180° − 65° = 115°.

2. Two supplementary angles total 180°. The angle supplementary to a 138° angle is 180° − 138° = 42°.

3. $3xy^3 + x - y$

$3(-2)(-2)^3 + (-2) - (-2)$ Replace x with −2 and y with −2.

$= 3(-2)(-8) + (-2) - (-2)$ Perform operation with exponent.

$= 48 + (-2) - (-2)$ Multiply.

$= 48$ Add and subtract.

4. $\frac{3}{4}\begin{bmatrix} 8 & -4 \\ 2 & 0 \end{bmatrix} - \begin{bmatrix} 1 & -6 \\ -7 & -2 \end{bmatrix}$

$= \begin{bmatrix} 6 & -3 \\ \frac{3}{2} & 0 \end{bmatrix} - \begin{bmatrix} 1 & -6 \\ -7 & -2 \end{bmatrix}$

$$= \begin{bmatrix} 6 & -3 \\ 1\frac{1}{2} & 0 \end{bmatrix} + \begin{bmatrix} -1 & 6 \\ 7 & 2 \end{bmatrix}$$

$$= \begin{bmatrix} 5 & 3 \\ 8\frac{1}{2} & 2 \end{bmatrix}$$

5. $A = lw$

$A = 2(1.3) = 2.6 \text{ in}^2$

6. $A = lw$

$A = 4(3) = 12 \text{ cm}^2$

7. percent change $= \frac{\text{amount of increase}}{\text{original amount}}$

amount of increase $= 6.1 - 5$, so percent change

$= \frac{1.1}{5} = 0.22 = 22\%$

8. $3(x + 2) = 2x - 1$

$3x + 6 = 2x - 1$ Distributive Property

$-6 \quad -6$ Subtract 6 from both sides.

$3x = 2x - 7$

$-2x = -2x$ Subtract $2x$ from both sides.

$x = -7$

9. $\frac{1}{2}x + 8 = 24$

$2\left(\frac{1}{2}x + 8\right) = 2(24)$ Multiply by 2.

$x + 16 = 48$

$-16 = -16$ Subtract 16 from both sides.

$x = 32$

10. a. The domain is the x-values 0, 1, 2, 3.

b. The range is the y-values 9, 7, 5, 3.

c. This is a function since each domain value has exactly one range value.

11. Multiply $5 \times 6.5 \times 10^2$.

$5 \times 6.5 \times 10^2 = 32.5 \times 10^2 = 3.25 \times 10^3 = 3250$

The diameter of Ganymede is about 3250 miles.

12. $3 \cdot 5 \cdot \frac{1}{3}$

$= 3 \cdot \frac{1}{3} \cdot 5$ Commutative Property of Mult.

$= \left(3 \cdot \frac{1}{3}\right) \cdot 5$ Associative Property of Mult.

$= 1 \cdot 5$ Multiplicative Inverse Property

$= 5$ Identity Property of Multiplication

13. $P(d) = \frac{1}{33}d + 1$

$P(50) = \frac{1}{33}(50) + 1$ Replace d with 50.

$P(50) \approx 2.5$

The pressure on the diver is about 2.5 atmospheres.

14. The discount on the \$85 pair of shoes is $40\% \times 85 = 0.40 \times 85 = 34$. So the new cost is $\$85 - \$34 = \$51$.

The discount on the \$68 pair of shoes is $15\% \times 68 = 0.15 \times 68 = 10.20$. So the new cost is $\$65 - \$10.20 = \$57.80$.

The \$85 pair of shoes with 40% discount is less expensive by $\$57.80 - \$51 = \$6.80$.

15. a. Let s represent Sandra's age, then $s + 6$ represents Sandra's brother's age, $s - 2$ represents Sandra's sister's age, and $3s$ represents Sandra's mother's age.

$(s + 6) + (s - 2) + (3s) = 64$

b. $(s + 6) + (s - 2) + (3s) = 64$

$s + 6 + s - 2 + 3s = 64$

$5s + 4 = 64$ Combine like terms.

$-4 = -4$ Subtract 4.

$5s = 60$

$\frac{5s}{5} = \frac{60}{5}$ Divide by 5.

$s = 12$

16. a. Divide the height by the speed of sound.

$\frac{1.02 \times 10^4}{3.44 \times 10^2} = \frac{1.02}{3.44} \times \frac{10^4}{10^2}$

$\approx 0.297 \times 10^2 = 2.97 \times 10 = 29.7$

It would take about 30 seconds.

b. From the peak to sea level is

$(1.02 \times 10^4) - (5.96 \times 10^3) = 10{,}200 - 5{,}960 = 4{,}240$ or 4.24×10^3.

Divide this height by the speed of sound.

$\frac{4.24 \times 10^3}{3.44 \times 10^2} \approx 1.23 \times 10 = 12.3$

It would take about 12 seconds.

17. $9x - \frac{2}{7} = 8x + \frac{11}{14}$

$9\left(\frac{1}{14}\right) - \frac{2}{7} \stackrel{?}{=} 8\left(\frac{1}{14}\right) + \frac{11}{14}$ Replace x with $\frac{1}{14}$.

$\frac{9}{14} - \frac{2}{7} \stackrel{?}{=} \frac{8}{14} + \frac{11}{14}$ Multiply.

$\frac{5}{14} \neq \frac{19}{14}$ Subtract and Add.

No, $\frac{1}{14}$ is not the solution to $9x - \frac{2}{7} = 8x + \frac{11}{14}$.

18. A circle on a coordinate grid does not represent a function. At a given value of x, two y-values will result—a point along the top of the circle and a point along the bottom of the circle. This can be demonstrated by drawing a vertical line through the circle.

19. For females:

percent change $= \frac{\text{amount of increase}}{\text{original amount}}$

amount of increase $= 60{,}733 - 40{,}172$, so

percent change $= \frac{20561}{40172} \approx 0.51 = 51\%$

For males:

percent change $= \frac{\text{amount of increase}}{\text{original amount}}$

amount of increase $= 78{,}092 - 54{,}626$, so

percent change $= \frac{23466}{54626} \approx 0.43 = 43\%$

Females had a greater percent increase, by about $51\% - 43\% = 8\%$.

20. The student added 6 to each element instead of multiplying. The result should be:

$$6\begin{bmatrix} 2 & 5 \\ 9 & -2 \end{bmatrix} = \begin{bmatrix} 12 & 30 \\ 54 & -12 \end{bmatrix}$$

21. a_{13} is the element in A that is in the 1st row and 3rd column, -6. b_{21} is the element in B that is in the 2nd row and 1st column, 8.

$a_{13} + b_{21} = -6 + 8 = 2$

22. The percent change is the amount of change as a percent of the original number, not as a percent of the new number. Since the amount of change is 15, and 15 divided by 15 is 1, the percent change is 100%.

23. a. Let r represent the amount of regular coffee sold, then $r - 5$ is the amount of decaffeinated coffee sold, and $2r$ is the amount of flavored coffee sold.

$r + (r - 5) + 2r = 115$

b. $r + (r - 5) + 2r = 115$

$r + r - 5 + 2r = 115$ Distributive Property

$4r - 5 = 115$ Combine like terms.

$+5 = +5$ Add 5.

$4r = 120$

$\frac{4r}{4} = \frac{120}{4}$ Divide by 4.

$r = 30$

24. The discount is $20\% \times 14 = 0.20 \times 14 = 2.8$, or \$2.80.

Answer Choice **A**

25. $-5x^2 + 2y$

$= -5(1)^2 + 2(-1)$ Replace x with 1 and y with -1.

$= -5(1) + 2(-1)$ Perform operation with exponent.

$= -7$ Add.

Answer Choice **A**

26. Each y-value is 7 greater than x.

$f(x) = x + 7$

27. Subtract to find the difference between the two amounts, $50.4 - 28 = 22.4$. Divide this result by the original amount,

$\frac{22.4}{28} = 0.8$ or 80%

28. $(3y - 2) + 9 + 8 = 8y$

$3y + 15 = 8y$ Combine like terms.

$-15 = -15$ Subtract 15.

$3y = 8y - 15$

$-8y = -8y$ Subtract $8y$.

$-5y = -15$

$\frac{-5y}{-5} = \frac{-15}{-5}$ Divide by −5.

$y = 3$

29. a. $6st(6 + t)$

$= 6(6)(-2)(6 + (-2)$ Replace s with 6 and t with −2.

$= 6(6)(-2)(4)$ Perform operation in parentheses.

$= -288$ Multiply.

b. If s is doubled the result would double.

c. $6st(6 + t)$

$= 6(12)(-2)(6 + (-2)$ Replace s with 12 and t with −2.

$= 6(12)(-2)(4)$ Perform operation in parentheses.

$= -576$ Multiply.

30. Let c represent the sales tax in Colorado. Then $c + 1.1$ represents the sales tax in Louisiana, and $c + 3.6$ represents the sales tax in Nevada.

$c + (c + 1.1) + (c + 3.6) = 13.4$

$c + c + 1.1 + c + 3.6 = 13.4$

$3c + 4.7 = 13.4$

$-4.7 = -4.7$

$3c = 8.7$

$\frac{3c}{3} = \frac{8.7}{3}$

$c = 2.9$

The sales tax rate for Colorado is 2.9%.

LESSON 8

Warm Up 8

1. constant

2. $42 = 6k$

$\frac{42}{6} = \frac{6k}{6}$ Divide by 6.

$7 = k$

Therefore $k = 7$.

3. $\frac{3}{x} = \frac{4}{12}$

$3(12) = 4x$ Cross multiply.

$36 = 4x$ Multiply.

$\frac{36}{4} = \frac{4x}{4}$ Divide by 4.

$9 = x$

Therefore $x = 9$.

Lesson Practice 8

a. $I = kF$ Write a direct variation.

$(36) = k(3)$ Substitute the given variation.

$k = 12$ Solve for k.

$I = 12F$ Replace k with its value.

$(60) = 12F$ Substitute for I.

$\frac{60}{12} = \frac{12F}{12}$ Divide.

$F = 5$

The board measures 5 feet.

b. $C = kO$ Write a direct variation.

$(5) = k(40)$ Substitute the given variation.

$k = \frac{1}{8}$ Solve for k.

$C = \frac{1}{8}O$ Replace k with its value.

$C = \frac{1}{8}(64)$ Substitute for O.

$C = 8$

There are 8 cups.

c. $\frac{C_1}{C_2} = \frac{G_1}{G_2}$ Write a proportion.

$\frac{25}{C_2} = \frac{10}{15}$ Substitute the given values.

$25 \cdot 15 = 10C_2$ Cross multiply.

$\frac{25 \cdot 15}{10} = \frac{10C_2}{10}$ Divide by 10.

$37.5 = C_2$

15 gallons would cost $37.50.

d. $\frac{D_1}{D_2} = \frac{A_1}{A_2}$ Write a proportion.

$\frac{2}{D_2} = \frac{54}{135}$ Substitute the given values.

$2 \cdot 135 = 54D_2$ Cross multiply.

$\frac{2 \cdot 135}{54} = \frac{54D_2}{54}$ Divide by 54.

$5 = D_2$

5 bags are needed to cover 135 square feet.

e. $V = kL$

$(30) = k(20)$

$k = \frac{3}{2}$

$V = \frac{3}{2}L$

$V = \frac{3}{2}(40)$

$V = 60$

The volume is 60 gallons.

f. Plot length on the x-axis and volume on the y-axis. The points are (20, 30), (30, 45), and (40, 60).

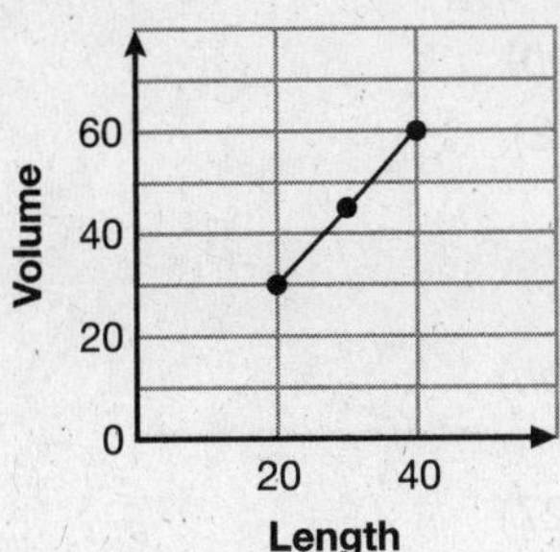

g. $V = \frac{3}{2}L$

$V = \frac{3}{2}(100)$ Replace L with 100.

$V = 150$

The volume of the pipe at a length of 100 feet is 150 gallons.

Practice 8

1. $(-7 + 3) - |-2 + 9| - 2[1 - (-5)]$
$= (-4) - |7| - 2[6]$
$= (-4) - 7 - 12$
$= -23$

2. $\frac{3x}{y} - 7x^2x^{-1}y^{-1} + 2y^2y^{-1}x^{-1}$
$= \frac{3x}{y} - 7xy^{-1} + 2yx^{-1}$
$= \frac{3x}{y} - \frac{7x}{y} + \frac{2y}{x}$
$= -\frac{4x}{y} + \frac{2y}{x}$
or $2yx^{-1} - 4xy^{-1}$

3. $\frac{xy^2}{x^0x^{-3}}\left(\frac{xy^{-2}}{x(y^2)^0} - \frac{3y^{-2}}{x^4}\right)$
$= \frac{xy^2}{x^0x^{-3}}\left(\frac{xy^{-2}}{xy^0} - \frac{3y^{-2}}{x^4}\right)$
$= x^4y^2(y^{-2} - 3y^{-2}x^{-4})$
$= x^4y^2(y^{-2}) - x^4y^2(3y^{-2}x^{-4})$
$= x^4 - 3$

4. $A = \pi r^2$
$= \pi(1.5)^2$
$\approx 7.07 \text{ in}^2$

5. percent change $= \frac{\text{amount of increase}}{\text{original amount}}$
$= \frac{12.8 - 10}{10} = 0.28 = 28\%$

6. $15(4 - 5b) = 16(4 - 6b) + 10$
$60 - 75b = 64 - 96b + 10$
$60 - 75b = 74 - 96b$
$-60 \quad = -60$
$-75b = 14 - 96b$
$+96b = \quad +96b$
$21b = 14$
$\frac{21b}{21} = \frac{14}{21}$
$b = \frac{14}{21} = \frac{2}{3}$

7. $-2(2x - 3) - 2^3 - 3 = -x - (-4)$
$-4x + 6 - 8 - 3 = -x + 4$
$-4x - 5 = -x + 4$
$-4x = -x + 9$
$-3x = 9$
$x = -3$

8. $x = ky$
$12 = k(3)$
$k = 4$

9. $x = ky$
$4 = k(16)$
$k = \frac{4}{16} = \frac{1}{4}$

10. $5x^2 - 2(x - 3x^2)$
$= 5x^2 - 2x + 6x^2$
$= 11x^2 - 2x$

11. The rate is 19% or 0.19. Think of 0.19 as 0.20 − 0.01.

$600(0.20 - 0.01)$
$= 600(0.20) - (600)0.01$
$= 120 - 6 = 114$

The interest is \$114.

12. a. The discount is 15% of 12
$= 0.15(12)$
$= 1.8$, or \$1.80.

b. Students pay \$12 − \$1.80 = \$10.20.

13. a. $\begin{bmatrix} 315 & 511 \\ 631 & 826 \end{bmatrix}$

b. $\begin{bmatrix} 484 & 562 \\ 709 & 914 \end{bmatrix}$

c. $\begin{bmatrix} 315 & 511 \\ 631 & 826 \end{bmatrix} + \begin{bmatrix} 484 & 562 \\ 709 & 914 \end{bmatrix}$

$= \begin{bmatrix} 799 & 1073 \\ 1340 & 1740 \end{bmatrix}$

14. $S = kP$

$1\frac{1}{2} = k(2)$

$k = \frac{3}{4}$

Answer Choice **C**

15. Round 6.89×10^{-2} to 7×10^{-2} and round 13.9 to 14, and then multiply $14 \times 7 \times 10^{-2}$. $14 \times 7 \times 10^{-2} = 98 \times 10^{-2} = 9.8 \times 10^{-1}$ inches. The answer seems reasonable because the answer is 0.98 which is about an inch. An inch seems reasonable for the diameter of a quarter.

16. Find the average for the first test.

$\frac{75 + 82 + 93 + 81 + 64 + 78 + 80}{7}$

$= \frac{553}{7} = 79$

Find the average for the second test.

$\frac{65 + 72 + 100 + 83 + 68 + 55 + 40}{7}$

$= \frac{483}{7} = 69$

The percent change is $\frac{79 - 69}{79} = \frac{10}{79} = 0.13 = 13\%$.

This is a 13% decrease in the average score from the first to the second test.

17. $P = kO$

$12 = k(192)$

$k = \frac{12}{192} = \frac{1}{16}$

$P = \frac{1}{16}(240) = 15$ lb

18. $1 = z + 2$, so $z = -1$

$y + 4 = 16$, so $y = 12$

$x^2 = 25$, so $x = 5$ or -5

$x + 1 = \frac{y}{2} = \frac{12}{2} = 6$

So $x = 5$.

19. $A = k(bh)$

$6 = k(12)$

$k = \frac{1}{2}$

$A = \frac{1}{2}(bh)$

$A = \frac{1}{2}(27)$

$A = 13.5 \text{ cm}^2$

20. The new price is 100% of the original price plus 150% mark up, for a total of 250% or 2.5 times the original price. Multiplying each price by 2.5 gives the marked up prices.

Ticket Service Prices

Day	Floor	Balcony
Friday	\$150	\$87.50
Saturday	\$200	\$112.50

21. $-10x + 6 = 4x + 34$

$-10(2) + 6 \stackrel{?}{=} 4(2) + 34$ Replace x with 2.

$-14 \neq 42$

Therefore $x = 2$ is not a solution to the equation $-10x + 6 = 4x + 34$.

22. $6x + 3 - 8x = 13$

$-2x + 3 = 13$

$-2x = 10$

$x = -5$

23. Two ads cost \$400 + \$300 = \$700, three ads cost \$400 + \$300 + \$300 = \$1000, and four ads cost $400 + $300 + $300 + $300 = $1300. The ordered pairs in set notation are {(2, 700), (3, 1000), (4, 1300)}.

24. Yes, $(x^2)^3 = (x^3)^2$ because of the Commutative Property of Multiplication.

$(x^2)^3 = (x^3)^2$

$x^6 = x^6$

25. A percent change equals 0% when there is no change between the old and new amounts. For example, from 20 to 20.

26.

$V = kR^3$

$2144.768 = 4.189(8)^3$

$2144.768 = 2144.768$

$V = kR^3$

$20{,}580.557 = 4.189(17)^3$

$20{,}580.557 = 20{,}580.557$

$V = kR^3$

$65{,}453.125 = 4.189(25)^3$

$65{,}453.125 = 65{,}453.125$

So, the constant of variation is 4.189.

27. The matrix has one row and four columns, so it is a 1×4 matrix.

Answer Choice **B**

28. If e is the level of exports in 2005, then exports in 2004 are $e - 125{,}820$, and exports in 2006 are $e + 162{,}633$.

$e + (e - 125{,}820) + (e + 162{,}633) = 3{,}886{,}023$

$e + e - 125{,}820 + e + 162{,}633 = 3{,}886{,}023$

$3e + 36{,}813 = 3{,}886{,}023$

$3e = 3{,}849{,}210$

$e = 1{,}283{,}070$

The total exports in millions of dollars in 2005 was 1,283,070.

29. $v(x) = 5x + 2x^2$

$v(4) = 5(4) + 2(4)^2$ Replace x with 4.

$v(4) = 20 + 32 = 52$

30. 3 is not an irrational number because it can be written as $\frac{3}{1}$. The statement should read, "3 is a rational number and an integer."

LESSON 9

Warm Up 9

1. elements

2. $2(-5) + 2(6) + (-1)(-5) + (-1)(6) + 3(-5) + 3(-6)$

$= -10 + 12 + 5 + (-6) + (-15) + (-18)$

$= -32$

3. The matrix has 1 row and 4 columns, so it is a 1×4 matrix.

Lesson Practice 9

a. Yes, the "inside" numbers are equal. The number of columns of A, 1, equals the number of rows of B, 1. AB is a 5×4 matrix.

b. No, the "inside" numbers are not equal. The number of columns of A, 7, does not equal the number of rows of B, 4. AB is undefinded.

c. Yes, the "inside" numbers are equal. The number of columns of A, 9, equals the number of rows of B, 9. AB is a 3×3 matrix.

d. $\begin{bmatrix} 4 & 2 \\ 1 & 6 \\ 3 & 9 \end{bmatrix} \begin{bmatrix} 0 & 3 \\ 5 & 8 \end{bmatrix}$

$= \begin{bmatrix} 4(0) + 2(5) & 4(3) + 2(8) \\ 1(0) + 6(5) & 1(3) + 6(8) \\ 3(0) + 9(5) & 3(3) + 9(8) \end{bmatrix}$

$= \begin{bmatrix} 10 & 28 \\ 30 & 51 \\ 45 & 81 \end{bmatrix}$

e. $\begin{bmatrix} -1 \\ 3 \\ -6 \end{bmatrix} \begin{bmatrix} 4 & -2 & 10 \end{bmatrix}$

$= \begin{bmatrix} -1(4) & -1(-2) & -1(10) \\ 3(4) & 3(-2) & 3(10) \\ -6(4) & -6(-2) & -6(10) \end{bmatrix}$

$= \begin{bmatrix} -4 & 2 & -10 \\ 12 & -6 & 30 \\ -24 & 12 & -60 \end{bmatrix}$

f. $AB = \begin{bmatrix} 4 & -2 \\ 2 & 0 \end{bmatrix}\begin{bmatrix} 1 & 0 \\ 4 & -2 \end{bmatrix} = \begin{bmatrix} 4(1)+(-2)(4) & 4(0)+(-2)(-2) \\ 2(1)+0(4) & 2(0)+0(-2) \end{bmatrix} = \begin{bmatrix} -4 & 4 \\ 2 & 0 \end{bmatrix}$

$BA = \begin{bmatrix} 1 & 0 \\ 4 & -2 \end{bmatrix}\begin{bmatrix} 4 & -2 \\ 2 & 0 \end{bmatrix} = \begin{bmatrix} 1(4)+(0)(2) & 1(-2)+(0)(0) \\ 4(4)+(-2)(2) & 4(-2)+(-2)(0) \end{bmatrix} = \begin{bmatrix} 4 & -2 \\ 12 & -8 \end{bmatrix}$

$AB \neq BA$

g. $AI = \begin{bmatrix} -1 & 4 & 2 \\ 0 & 5 & -3 \\ 1 & -2 & 10 \end{bmatrix}\begin{bmatrix} 1 & 0 & 0 \\ 0 & 1 & 0 \\ 0 & 0 & 1 \end{bmatrix}$

$= \begin{bmatrix} -1(1)+4(0)+2(0) & -1(0)+4(1)+2(0) & -1(0)+4(0)+2(1) \\ 0(1)+5(0)+-3(0) & 0(0)+5(1)+-3(0) & 0(0)+5(0)+-3(1) \\ 1(1)+-2(0)+10(0) & 1(0)+-2(1)+10(0) & 1(0)+-2(0)+10(1) \end{bmatrix}$

$= \begin{bmatrix} -1 & 4 & 2 \\ 0 & 5 & -3 \\ 1 & -2 & 10 \end{bmatrix}$

h. $\begin{bmatrix} 1 & 2 & 1 \\ 2 & 0 & 1 \\ 1 & 2 & 2 \end{bmatrix}\begin{bmatrix} 3 \\ 2 \\ 1 \end{bmatrix} = \begin{bmatrix} 1(3)+2(2)+1(1) \\ 2(3)+0(2)+1(1) \\ 1(3)+2(2)+2(1) \end{bmatrix} = \begin{bmatrix} 8 \\ 7 \\ 9 \end{bmatrix}$

Alana spends \$8, Maurice spends \$7, and Jon spends \$9.

Practice 9

1. $0.24 = \frac{24}{100} = \frac{24 \div 4}{100 \div 4} = \frac{6}{25}$

2. $0.82 = \frac{82}{100} = \frac{82 \div 2}{100 \div 2} = \frac{41}{50}$

3. $0.32 = \frac{32}{100} = \frac{32 \div 4}{100 \div 4} = \frac{8}{25}$

4. The measure of each interior angle of a regular polygon can be found using the formula $\frac{180(n-2)}{n}$, where n is the number of sides of the polygon. A pentagon has 5 sides.

$\frac{180(n-2)}{n} = \frac{180(5-2)}{5} = \frac{540}{5} = 108°$

5. $y^2 = 8x$ is not a function, since for every x-value there is more than one possible y-value. For example when $x = 2$, $y = 4$ or -4.

6. $2\begin{bmatrix} 1 & 0 \\ 0 & 1 \end{bmatrix} + \begin{bmatrix} -3 & -2 \\ -4 & 0 \end{bmatrix} = \begin{bmatrix} 2 & 0 \\ 0 & 2 \end{bmatrix} + \begin{bmatrix} -3 & -2 \\ -4 & 0 \end{bmatrix} = \begin{bmatrix} -1 & -2 \\ -4 & 2 \end{bmatrix}$

7. $m = kn$

$8 = k(2)$ Substitute the values.

$k = 4$

8. $\begin{bmatrix} 2 & -1 \\ 3 & 0 \\ 1 & 4 \end{bmatrix} \times \begin{bmatrix} 1 & 1 & -3 \\ 6 & -5 & 0 \end{bmatrix}$

$$= \begin{bmatrix} 2(1)+(-1)(6) & 2(1)+(-1)(-5) & 2(-3)+(-1)(0) \\ 3(1)+(0)(6) & 3(1)+(0)(-5) & 3(-3)+(0)(0) \\ 1(1)+(4)(6) & 1(1)+(4)(-5) & 1(-3)+(4)(0) \end{bmatrix} = \begin{bmatrix} -4 & 7 & -6 \\ 3 & 3 & -9 \\ 25 & -19 & -3 \end{bmatrix}$$

9. $\begin{bmatrix} -1 & -1 & -1 \\ 2 & 5 & 3 \\ -5 & 4 & -2 \end{bmatrix} \times \begin{bmatrix} 0 \\ 1 \\ 0 \end{bmatrix} = \begin{bmatrix} -1(0) + (-1)(1) + (-1)(0) \\ 2(0) + 5(1) + 3(0) \\ -5(0) + 4(1) + (-2)(0) \end{bmatrix} = \begin{bmatrix} -1 \\ 5 \\ 4 \end{bmatrix}$

10. $A + B = \begin{bmatrix} -3 & 7 \\ 12 & -1 \end{bmatrix} + \begin{bmatrix} 9 & 17 \\ 3 & -1 \end{bmatrix} = \begin{bmatrix} -3+9 & 7+17 \\ 12+3 & -1+(-1) \end{bmatrix} = \begin{bmatrix} 6 & 24 \\ 15 & -2 \end{bmatrix}$

$B + A = \begin{bmatrix} 9 & 17 \\ 3 & -1 \end{bmatrix} + \begin{bmatrix} -3 & 7 \\ 12 & -1 \end{bmatrix} = \begin{bmatrix} 9+(-3) & 17+7 \\ 3+12 & -1+(-1) \end{bmatrix} = \begin{bmatrix} 6 & 24 \\ 15 & -2 \end{bmatrix}$

So, $A + B = B + A$

11. Sample: The Associative Property of Addition. Adding the numbers in order would result in (9 + 18) + 22 = 27 + 22, which is more difficult to add mentally than 9 + (18 + 22) = 9 + 40.

12. Divide the area of the Earth by the area of New York.

$\frac{1.488 \times 10^{14}}{1.272 \times 10^{11}} = \frac{1.488}{1.272} \times \frac{10^{14}}{10^{11}} \approx 1.170 \times 10^3$ times.

13. $AB = \begin{bmatrix} -3 & 1 & -1 \\ -4 & 6 & 2 \\ -1 & -1 & 4 \end{bmatrix} \begin{bmatrix} -7 & 0 & 1 \\ -8 & -2 & -1 \\ 0 & 3 & -3 \end{bmatrix}$

$$= \begin{bmatrix} -3(-7) + 1(-8) + (-1)(0) & -3(0) + 1(-2) + (-1)(3) & -3(1) + 1(-1) + (-1)(-3) \\ -4(-7) + 6(-8) + 2(0) & -4(0) + 6(-2) + 2(3) & -4(1) + 6(-1) + 2(-3) \\ -1(-7) + (-1)(-8) + 4(0) & -1(0) + (-1)(-2) + 4(3) & -1(1) + (-1)(-1) + 4(-3) \end{bmatrix}$$

$$= \begin{bmatrix} 13 & -5 & -1 \\ -20 & -6 & -16 \\ 15 & 14 & -12 \end{bmatrix}$$

Answer Choice **B**

14. $J = \begin{bmatrix} 34{,}950 & 7800 & 12{,}300 \\ 6400 & 2100 & 970 \end{bmatrix}$

$T = \begin{bmatrix} 28{,}900 & 10{,}450 & 11{,}950 \\ 7200 & 3600 & 4860 \end{bmatrix}$

15. Since $a^{-1} = \frac{1}{a}$, if a is a number greater than 1, then $\frac{1}{a}$ is a fraction, which is less than 1.

16. Percent change $= \frac{\text{amount of increase}}{\text{original amount}}$

$= \frac{626{,}932 - 550{,}043}{550{,}043} = \frac{76{,}889}{550{,}043} \approx 0.1398 = 13.98\%$

The percent increase is 13.98%.

17. a. $\begin{bmatrix} 650 \\ 890 \\ 940 \end{bmatrix}$

b. The increase is the original price plus the mark up, or 100% + 10% = 110% = 1.1

$$1.1\begin{bmatrix}650\\890\\940\end{bmatrix}=\begin{bmatrix}715\\979\\1034\end{bmatrix}$$

18. $\begin{bmatrix}-14 & -6\\-6 & -1\end{bmatrix}+\begin{bmatrix}15 & 0\\0 & 5\end{bmatrix}$

$=\begin{bmatrix}-14+15 & -6+0\\-6+0 & -1+5\end{bmatrix}=\begin{bmatrix}1 & -6\\-6 & 4\end{bmatrix}$

19. Distributive Property

20. $S = kE$

$1.86 = k(2)$ Substitute the values.

$k = 0.93$

$S = 0.93E$

$S = 0.93(85)$

$S = 79.05$

An object that weighs 85 kg on Earth weighs 79.05 kg on Saturn.

21. Both sets of ordered pairs are functions, since for every x-value there is a different y-value. Britan reversed the coordinates in (7, 9) to read (9, 7) so that the x-values in (9, 4) and (9, 7) are paired with different y-values. Sara may not have understood that the y-values can be the same, it's only the same x-values that cannot be paired with different y-values.

22. Since this is a percent increase from 2001 to 2002, the salary in 2002 is greater than the salary in 2001. Let x represent the salary in 2001.

$$\text{Percent change} = \frac{\text{amount of increase}}{\text{original amount}}$$

$$15.6\% = \frac{\text{Salary in 2002} - \text{Salary in 2001}}{\text{Salary in 2002}}$$

$$0.156 = \frac{76{,}252 - x}{76{,}252}$$

$0.156(76{,}252) = 76{,}252 - x$

$11{,}895.31 = 76{,}252 - x$

$x \approx 64{,}356.69$

The average annual salary in 2001 is about $64,357.

23. a. It is sometimes true. It is true when $a = b$, and a and b are not equal to zero. For example, when $a = b = 2$, $2 \cdot \left(\frac{1}{2}\right) = 2 \cdot \left(\frac{1}{2}\right)$. However, when $a \neq b$ the statement is false. For example, when $a = 2$ and $b = 3$, $2 \cdot \left(\frac{1}{3}\right) \neq 3 \cdot \left(\frac{1}{2}\right)$.

b. Sometimes true. If a and b are both irrational and $a = b$, sometimes ab is rational. For example, $\sqrt{2}$ is irrational, but $\sqrt{2} \cdot \sqrt{2} = 4$, which is a rational number. However, if $a = b = \pi$, $\pi \cdot \pi = \pi^2$, which is still irrational.

24. $$\begin{bmatrix}2 & 4 & 3\\1 & 6 & 6\\3 & 3 & 3\end{bmatrix}\begin{bmatrix}2\\3\\\frac{1}{2}\end{bmatrix}=\begin{bmatrix}2(2)+4(3)+3\left(\frac{1}{2}\right)\\1(2)+6(3)+6\left(\frac{1}{2}\right)\\3(2)+3(3)+3\left(\frac{1}{2}\right)\end{bmatrix}$$

$$=\begin{bmatrix}17\frac{1}{2}\\23\\16\frac{1}{2}\end{bmatrix}$$

The new perimeter of Triangle 1 is $17\frac{1}{2}$cm, the perimeter of Triangle 2 is 23 cm, and the perimeter of Triangle 3 is $16\frac{1}{2}$ cm. Triangle 2 has the greatest perimeter.

25. The mark up amount is 200% of $4.25, or $2 \times 4.25 = \$8.50$.

The new price is $4.25 + $8.50 = $12.75.

The customer paid $12.75 for the part.

With a 5% coupon, the discount amount for 5% off $12.75 is $0.05 \times 12.75 = \$0.64$.

The new price is $12.75 − $0.64 = $12.11

A customer would pay $12.11 with a 5% coupon.

26.

$3x - 5 = 2 - 4x$

$+5 = +5$ Add 5.

$3x = 7 - 4x$

$+4x = +4x$ Add $4x$.

$7x = 7$

$\frac{7x}{7} = \frac{7}{7}$ Divide by 7.

$x = 1$

27. $\frac{3}{4}x - \frac{1}{5}x = 2\frac{3}{4}$

$$20\left(\frac{3}{4}x - \frac{1}{5}x\right) = 20\left(\frac{11}{4}\right)$$
$$15x - 4x = 55$$
$$11x = 55$$
$$\frac{11x}{11} = \frac{55}{11}$$
$$x = 5$$

28. $5x - 2 = 7 + 2x$

$+2 = +2$ Add 2.

$5x = 9 + 2x$

$-2x = -2x$ Subtract $2x$.

$3x = 9$

$$\frac{3x}{3} = \frac{9}{3}$$
$$x = 3$$

29. a. $\begin{bmatrix} -3 & 6 & 2 \\ 7 & 8 & -3 \end{bmatrix}$

b. $\begin{bmatrix} -3 & 6 & 2 \\ 7 & 8 & -3 \end{bmatrix} + \begin{bmatrix} -2 & -2 & -2 \\ 3 & 3 & 3 \end{bmatrix}$

$= \begin{bmatrix} -3 + (-2) & 6 + (-2) & 2 + (-2) \\ 7 + 3 & 8 + 3 & -3 + 3 \end{bmatrix}$

$= \begin{bmatrix} -5 & 4 & 0 \\ 10 & 11 & 0 \end{bmatrix}$

c. $A(-5, 10)$, $B(4, 11)$, $C(0, 0)$

30. a. $T = kt$

$80 = k120$

$k = \frac{2}{3}$

b. $T = \frac{2}{3}t$

$T = \frac{2}{3}(240)$

$T = 160°$

c. $T = \frac{2}{3}t$

$T = \frac{2}{3}(360)$

$T = 240°$

LESSON 10

Warm Up 10

1. equation
2. $3x - 4 = -12$

   $3x = -8$

   $x = -\frac{8}{3}$
3. $-(-5) - 2 \stackrel{?}{=} -3$

   $5 - 2 \stackrel{?}{=} -3$

   $3 \neq -3$

   False, -5 is not a solution.
4. $0.25 = \frac{25}{100} = \frac{1}{4}$. Therefore, $0.25 = \frac{1}{4}$
5. $6.5 > 6.38$

Lesson Practice 10

a. $3y + 2 > 8$

$3y + 2 - 2 > 8 - 2$ Subtraction Property of Equality

$3y > 6$ Simplify.

$\frac{3y}{3} > \frac{6}{3}$ Division Property

$y > 2$ Simplify.

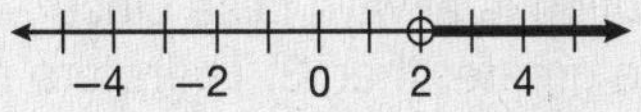

The solution is all values of y greater than 2. Check: substitute 2 in the original inequality and then substitute a number greater than 2.

Let $y = 2$

$3(2) + 2 > 8$

$8 \not> 8$ 2 is not in the solution set.

Let $y = 4$

$3(4) + 2 > 8$

$14 > 8$ 4 is in the solution set.

b. $2(5 + a) \leq 5 - a$

$10 + 2a \leq 5 - a$ Distributive Property

$10 - 10 + 2a \leq 5 - 10 - a$ Subtraction Property of Equality

$2a \leq -5 - a$ Simplify.

$2a + a \leq -5 - a + a$ Addition Property of Equality

$3a \le -5$ Simplify.

$\frac{3a}{3} \le \frac{-5}{3}$ Division Property

$a \le \frac{-5}{3}$ Simplify.

$-\frac{10}{3}$ $-\frac{5}{3}$ 0 $\frac{5}{3}$ $\frac{10}{3}$

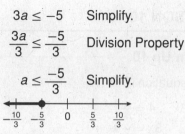

The solution is all values of a equal to or less than $\frac{-5}{3}$.

Check: substitute $\frac{-5}{3}$ and a number less than $\frac{-5}{3}$ into the original inequality.

Let $a = \frac{-5}{3}$.

$2\left(5 + \frac{-5}{3}\right) \le 5 - \frac{-5}{3}$

$\frac{20}{3} = \frac{20}{3}$ $\frac{-5}{3}$ is in the solution set.

Let $a = -3$

$2(5 + (-3)) \le 5 - (-3)$

$4 < 8$ -3 is in the solution set.

c. $4(x - 1) > 4x + 3$

$4x - 4 > 4x + 3$ Distributive Property

$4x - 4x - 4 > 4x - 4x + 3$ Subtraction Property of Equality

$-4 > 3$

The solution is always false since -4 will never be greater than 3. There are no values of x that will make this statement true. Therefore, there is no solution.

d. $2w < -1 + 2(w + 3)$

$2w < -1 + 2w + 6$ Distributive Property

$2w < 2w + 5$ Simplify.

$2w - 2w < 2w - 2w + 5$ Subtraction Property of Equality

$0 < 5$

The solution is always true since 0 is always less than 5. Any value of x will make the statement true. The solution is all real numbers.

e. $8 \le 5x + 3 \le 23$

$8 - 3 \le 5x + 3 - 3 \le 23 - 3$

$5 \le 5x \le 20$

$\frac{5}{5} \le \frac{5x}{5} \le \frac{20}{5}$

$1 \le x \le 4$

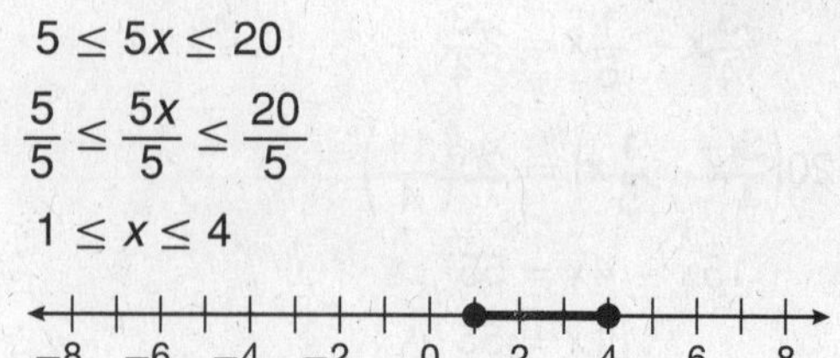

f. For this problem consider:

David and Alannah may kick the ball in the same direction. In this case the distance between the balls is $10 - 6 = 4$ feet. This is the least distance.

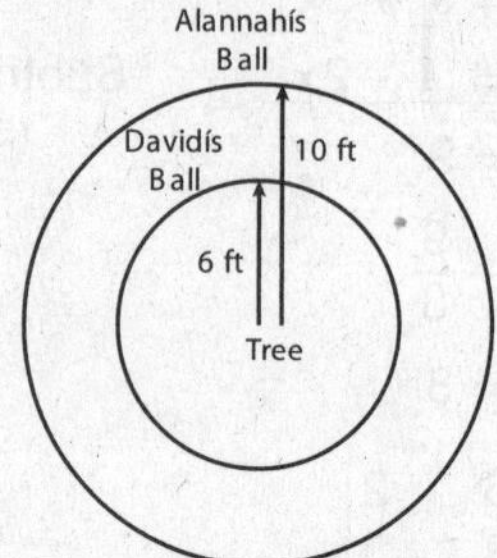

David and Alannah may kick the ball in the opposite directions. In this case the distance between the balls is $10 + 6 = 16$ feet. This is the greatest distance.

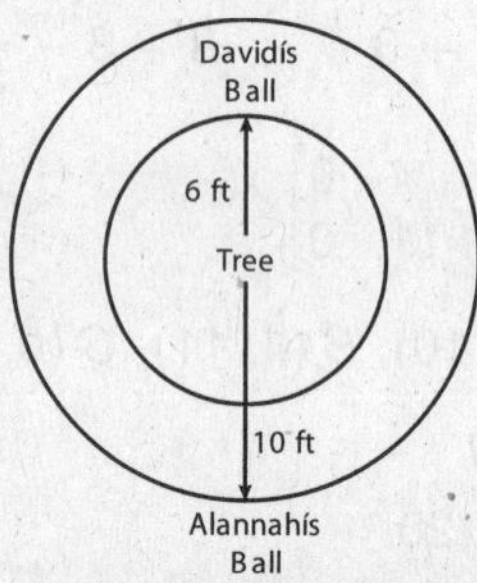

David and Alannah may kick the ball in a direction other than described above.

Based on the information, the distance between David's and Alannah's ball is $4 \le x \le 16$.

Practice 10

1. The figure has one square base and four triangular faces, so the figure is a square pyramid.

2. $y = -2x^2$ is a function, since every x-value has a different y-value. The domain is all real numbers. The range is $y \le 0$.

3. $\frac{(2x^{-2}y^0)^{-2}yx^{-2}}{xxxy^2(y^{-2})^2} = \frac{2^{-2}x^4y^0yx^{-2}}{xxxy^2y^{-4}}$

$= \frac{2^{-2}x^2y^1}{x^3y^{-2}} = \frac{y^3}{4x}$

4. $\frac{(m^2n^{-5})^{-2}m(n^0)^2}{(m^2n^{-2})^{-3}m^2} = \frac{m^{-4}n^{10}mn^0}{m^{-6}n^6m^2}$

$= \frac{m^{-3}n^{10}}{m^{-4}n^6} = mn^4$

5. $0.003x + 0.02x - 0.03 = 0.177$

$0.023x - 0.03 = 0.177$

$0.023x - 0.03 + 0.03 = 0.177 + 0.03$

$0.023x = 0.207$

$\frac{0.023x}{0.023} = \frac{0.207}{0.023}$

$x = 9$

6. $4\frac{1}{3}x - \frac{1}{2} = 3\frac{2}{5}$

$30\left(\frac{13}{3}x - \frac{1}{2}\right) = 30\left(\frac{17}{5}\right)$

$130x - 15 = 102$

$130x - 15 + 15 = 102 + 15$

$130x = 117$

$\frac{130x}{130} = \frac{117}{130}$

$x = \frac{9}{10}$

7. $3(x - 4) > 6$

$3x - 12 > 6$ Distributive Property

$3x - 12 + 12 > 6 + 12$ Addition Property

$3x > 18$ Simplify.

$\frac{3x}{3} > \frac{18}{3}$

$x > 6$

−8 −6 −4 −2 0 2 4 6 8

8. $2x + 3 \geq 4x - 5$

$2x + 3 - 3 \geq 4x - 5 - 3$ Subtraction Prop.

$2x \geq 4x - 8$ Simplify.

$2x - 4x \geq 4x - 4x - 8$ Subtraction Prop.

$-2x \geq -8$ Simplify.

$\frac{-2x}{-2} \leq \frac{-8}{-2}$ Division Prop.

$x \leq 4$

−8 −6 −4 −2 0 2 4 6 8

9. a. $W = kM$

$11.25 = k(100)$

$k = 0.1125$

b. $W = 0.1125M$

$W = 0.1125(240)$

$W = 27$

27 pints of water are needed for 240 lb of dry mortar mix.

10. $4[3(x + 9) + 2] = 4[3x + 27 + 2]$

$= 12x + 108 + 8$

$= 12x + 116$

11. $\begin{bmatrix} 1 & 0 \\ 0 & 1 \end{bmatrix} \times \begin{bmatrix} -1 & 2 \\ 3 & -2 \end{bmatrix}$

$= \begin{bmatrix} 1(-1) + 0(3) & 1(2) + 0(-2) \\ 0(-1) + 1(3) & 0(2) + 1(-2) \end{bmatrix}$

$= \begin{bmatrix} -1 & 2 \\ 3 & -2 \end{bmatrix}$

12. $\begin{bmatrix} 0 & -1 \\ -1 & 0 \end{bmatrix} \times \begin{bmatrix} 4 & -1 \\ -2 & -6 \end{bmatrix}$

$= \begin{bmatrix} 0(4) + (-1)(-2) & 0(-1) + (-1)(-6) \\ -1(4) + 0(-2) & -1(-1) + 0(-6) \end{bmatrix}$

$= \begin{bmatrix} 2 & 6 \\ -4 & 1 \end{bmatrix}$

13. percent change $= \frac{\text{amount of change}}{\text{original amount}}$

$\frac{318 - 265}{265} = \frac{53}{265} = 0.2 = 20\%$

This is a 20% increase.

14. percent change $= \frac{\text{amount of change}}{\text{original amount}}$

$\frac{17 - 14.45}{17} = \frac{2.55}{17} = 0.15 = 15\%$

This is a 15% decrease.

15. The volume of the cube is

$$(2.73 \times 10^4)^3 = (2.73)^3 \times 10^{12}$$
$$\approx 20.35 \times 10^{12} \text{ ft}^3$$
$$\approx 2.035 \times 10^{13} \text{ ft}^3$$

Multiply the number of cubic feet, 2.035×10^{13} by the number of pennies in a cubic foot, 4.9×10^4.

$$2.035 \times 10^{13} \times 4.9 \times 10^4$$
$$\approx 2.035 \times 4.9 \times 10^{13} \times 10^4$$
$$\approx 9.9715 \times 10^{17}$$

This is the same as 0.99715×10^{18} or about 1×10^{18}. Therefore, there are about 1×10^{18} pennies in the cube.

16. The explanation is not correct. The symbol $\leq$ tells you to draw a closed circle, not an open circle.

17. a. You need 0.76 times the number of dollars you have to find the number of euros you have. So $e = 0.76d$. Then, $f = 1.22d$, so $e = \frac{0.76f}{1.22}$.

b. $e = \frac{0.76(5)}{1.22} \approx 3$, which represents that on that day, 5 francs was equivalent to about 3 euros.

c. The answer makes sense since there are fewer euros for a greater number of Swiss francs.

18. a. percent change $= \frac{\text{amount of change}}{\text{original amount}}$

$$\frac{60 - 50}{50} = \frac{10}{50} = 0.2 = 20\%$$
$$\frac{60 - 50}{60} = \frac{10}{60} \approx 0.17 = 17\%$$

From 50 to 60 is a greater percent change.

b. Compare the amount of change over the original amount for each. Since the numerators are the same, the fraction with the denominator that is less is the greater fraction.

19. In the first line of the solution 14 is added to the left side of the equation, but subtracted from the right side. 14 should be added to both sides.

$$7x - 14 = -9 + 12x$$
$$7x - 14 + 14 = -9 + 14 + 12x$$
$$7x = 5 + 12x$$
$$7x - 12x = 5 + 12x - 12x$$
$$-5x = 5$$
$$\frac{-5x}{-5} = \frac{5}{-5}$$
$$x = -1$$

20. Steps $2(x + 4) + 2(5) = 2(x + 4 + 5)$ and $2(x + 9) = 2x + 18$ show the Distributive Property. Step $2(x + 4 + 5) = 2(x + 9)$ shows the Associative Property

21. Let x represent the missing value.

$$\frac{12 + 15 + 8 + x + 20}{5} = 11.8$$
$$\frac{55 + x}{5} = 11.8$$
$$11 + \frac{1}{5}x = 11.8 \text{ or}$$
$$55 + x = 59$$

Therefore, $x = 4$.

22. 12 g, since 10 g on Earth is twice 5 g on Earth, therefore 12 g on Neptune is twice 6 g on Neptune.

23. Divide the circumference of Earth by the average height of a boy.

1.737×10^3 mm $= (1.737 \times 10^3) \div 10^6$ km $= 1.737 \times 10^{-3}$ km

$$\frac{4.0076 \times 10^4}{1.737 \times 10^{-3}} = \frac{4.0076}{1.737} \times \frac{10^4}{10^{-3}}$$
$$\approx 2.307 \times 10^7$$

It would take about 2.307×10^7 boys.

24. $C = kr$

$$(12.566) = (6.283)(2)$$
$$12.566 = 12.566$$
$$(94.245) = (6.283)(15)$$
$$94.245 = 94.245$$
$$(232.471) = (6.283)(37)$$
$$232.471 = 232.471$$

So, the constant of variation is 6.283.

25. $\begin{bmatrix} 4 & 1 & 4 \\ 3 & 2 & 3 \\ 5 & 0 & 5 \end{bmatrix}\begin{bmatrix} 6 \\ 3 \\ 1 \end{bmatrix} = \begin{bmatrix} 4(6)+1(3)+4(1) \\ 3(6)+2(3)+3(1) \\ 5(6)+0(3)+5(1) \end{bmatrix}$

$= \begin{bmatrix} 31 \\ 27 \\ 35 \end{bmatrix}$

The team scored the most points in game 12.

26. Let x represent the number of meals. The number of meals, x, has to be less than or equal to $\frac{300}{2.35}$. The inequality is $x \leq 133$.

27. a. $[0.75 \quad 1.20 \quad 1.60]$ or $\begin{bmatrix} 0.75 \\ 1.20 \\ 1.60 \end{bmatrix}$

b. $200\begin{bmatrix} 0.75 \\ 1.20 \\ 1.60 \end{bmatrix} = \begin{bmatrix} 150 \\ 240 \\ 320 \end{bmatrix}$

c. The new cost with a 5% discount is the original cost, 100%, minus the discount 5%. 100% − 5% = 95% = 0.95 of the original price.

$0.95\begin{bmatrix} 0.75 \\ 1.20 \\ 1.60 \end{bmatrix} = \begin{bmatrix} 0.7125 \\ 1.14 \\ 1.52 \end{bmatrix}$

28. percent change $= \frac{\text{amount of change}}{\text{original amount}}$

$\frac{35 - 31.5}{35} = \frac{3.5}{35} = 0.1 = 10\%$

Answer Choice **A**

29. a. $AB = \begin{bmatrix} 6 & -3 \\ 1 & 4 \end{bmatrix}\begin{bmatrix} 0 & 4 \\ -2 & 6 \end{bmatrix}$

$= \begin{bmatrix} 6(0)+(-3)(-2) & 6(4)+(-3)(6) \\ 1(0)+(4)(-2) & 1(4)+(4)(6) \end{bmatrix}$

$= \begin{bmatrix} 6 & 6 \\ -8 & 28 \end{bmatrix}$

$BA = \begin{bmatrix} 0 & 4 \\ -2 & 6 \end{bmatrix}\begin{bmatrix} 6 & -3 \\ 1 & 4 \end{bmatrix}$

b. $= \begin{bmatrix} 0(6)+(4)(1) & 0(-3)+(4)(4) \\ -2(6)+(6)(1) & -2(-3)+(6)(4) \end{bmatrix}$

$= \begin{bmatrix} 4 & 16 \\ -6 & 30 \end{bmatrix}$

c. $AB \neq BA$

30. For two matrices to be multiplied there needs to be a one-to-one correspondence between the number of columns in matrix A and the number of rows in matrix B.

INVESTIGATION 1

1. Since $p \rightarrow q$ is false only when p is true and q is false, the truth table for $p \rightarrow q$ is true when p and q are both true, when p and q are both false, and when p is false and q is true.

p	q	$p \rightarrow q$
T	T	T
T	F	F
F	T	T
F	F	T

2. Switch the "if" and "then" parts of the statement.

"If an organism eats fish, then it is an eagle." The converse is not true, since many organisms, such as people, eat fish and they are not eagles.

3. $q \rightarrow p$ is false only when q is true and p is false. $q \rightarrow p$ is true when p and q are both true, when p and q are both false, and when p is true and q is false.

p	q	$p \rightarrow q$	$q \rightarrow p$
T	T	T	T
T	F	F	T
F	T	T	F
F	F	T	T

4. $\neg q \rightarrow \neg p$ is false only when p is true and q is false. $\neg q \rightarrow \neg p$ is true when p and q are both true, when p and q are both false, and when p is false and q is true.

p	q	$p \rightarrow q$	$\neg q \rightarrow \neg p$
T	T	T	T
T	F	F	F
F	T	T	T
F	F	T	T

5. In all cases $p \vee \neg p$ is true.

p	$\neg p$	$p \vee \neg p$
T	F	T
T	F	T
F	T	T
F	T	T

6. In all cases $p \wedge \neg p$ is false.

p	$\neg p$	$p \wedge \neg p$
T	F	F
T	F	F
F	T	F
F	T	F

7.

p	q	$p \leftrightarrow q$
T	T	T
T	F	F
F	T	F
F	F	T

8. a. Let p = an organism has flight feathers and q = it can fly. The logic statement is $p \rightarrow q$. "If an organism has flight feathers, then it can fly.

b. The converse is $q \rightarrow p$. "If an organism can fly, then it has flight feathers. The converse of the statement is not true, since there are organisms, such as bats, that fly and do not have feathers.

c. The contrapositive is $\neg q \rightarrow \neg p$. "If an organism cannot fly, then it does not have flight feathers. The contrapositive is true, since any organism that cannot fly doesn't have flight feathers.

d. It is not correct to conclude $q \leftrightarrow p$, since the converse is not true. Therefore, the statement is not bidirectional.

9. a. Let p = has contour feathers, q = has flight feathers, and r = it can fly. The logic statement is $(p \wedge q) \rightarrow r$.

b.

p	q	r	$(p \wedge q) \rightarrow r$
T	T	T	T
T	T	F	F
T	F	T	T
T	F	F	T
F	T	T	T
F	F	T	T
F	T	F	T
F	F	F	T

c. The statement is neither a tautology nor a contradiction.

10. a. Let p = has contour feathers, q = has flight feathers, and r = it is a bird. The logic statement is $(p \vee q) \rightarrow r$.

b.

p	q	r	$(p \vee q) \rightarrow r$
T	T	T	T
T	T	F	F
T	F	T	T
T	F	F	F
F	T	T	T
F	F	T	T
F	T	F	F
F	F	F	T

c. The statement is neither a tautology nor a contradiction.

11. If $p \rightarrow q \leftrightarrow \neg p \lor q$ is a tautology, then $p \rightarrow q$ and $\neg p \lor q$ are logically equivalent.

Investigation Practice 1

a. 1. If $\neg p \rightarrow \neg q$ is true, $q \rightarrow p$ is true.

2. This is because the statement is the contrapositive of the original statement.

b. 1. $(\neg p \land p) \rightarrow \neg q$ is neither a tautology nor a contradiction.

2. $(\neg p \land p) \rightarrow \neg p$ is a tautology.

3. $(\neg p \land p) \rightarrow (\neg q \land q)$ is a tautology.

c. 1. The statements are logically equivalent.

2. The statements are not logically equivalent.

LESSON 11

Warm Up 11

1. variable

2. $-5(6x - 2)$
$= -5(6x) - 2(-5)$
$= -30x + 10$

3. $6 + 3x - 5x + 4y + 17 - 2y$
$= 6 + 17 + 3x - 5x + 4y - 2y$
$= 23 + -2x + 2y$
$= -2x + 2y + 23$

4. $g(x) = 2x + 7$ and $f(x) = x - 5$
$f(g(x)) = (2x + 7) - 5 = 2x + 2$

5. The function $f(x) = 3x^2 + 4$ is not linear, since there are two different inputs for x that will give the same value for $f(x)$.

Lesson Practice 11

a. $3x - 1 + 4x^4 + x$
$= 4x^4 + 3x + x - 1$
$= 4x^4 + 4x - 1$
Leading coefficient is 4, constant is -1

b. $-x^3$ has a degree of 3, so it is cubic. It has 1 term so it is a monomial.

c. $x^2 + 40x + 10 - 9x^2 - 1$
$= -9x^2 + x^2 + 40x + 10 - 1$
$= -8x^2 + 40x + 9$
$-8x^2 + 40x + 9$ has a degree of 2, so it is quadratic. It has 3 terms so it is a trinomial.

d. $(2x^2 - 3x^5) + (2x^5 - x^2 + 1)$
$= 2x^2 - 3x^5 + 2x^5 - x^2 + 1$
$= -3x^5 + 2x^5 + 2x^2 - x^2 + 1$
$= -x^5 + x^2 + 1$

e. $(1 - x - x^3) - (x^3 + 2x^2 - x)$
$= 1 - x - x^3 - x^3 - 2x^2 + x$
$= -x^3 - x^3 - 2x^2 + x - x + 1$
$= -2x^3 - 2x^2 + 1$

f. Understand: Sales in each sector is modeled by a quadratic function.
Plan: To find a model for how much higher the average was in the residential sector than the industrial sector, subtract the polynomials.

Solve:
$$\begin{array}{r} 0.041x^2 + 0.009x + 8.334 \\ -\ 0.028x^2 + 0.037x + 4.756 \\ \hline 0.013x^2 - 0.028x + 3.578 \end{array}$$

$f(x) = 0.013x^2 - 0.028x + 3.578$ is a model for how much higher the retail price was in the residential sector than in the industrial sector.
Check: The answer makes sense because the polynomial $0.013x^2 - 0.028x + 3.578$ is the difference of the two polynomials.

Practice 11

1. a. $x + 5.354x + 0.683x = 3{,}736{,}275$

b. $x + 5.354x + 0.683x = 3{,}736{,}275$
$7.037x = 3{,}736{,}275$
$\frac{7.037x}{7.037} = \frac{3{,}736{,}275}{7.037}$
$= 530{,}946 \approx 530{,}900$

2. Let x represent the number.
$4(2x - 9) = 10x - 8$
$8x - 36 = 10x - 8$
$8x = 10x + 28$
$-2x = 28$
$x = -14$

3. $x^6(2x^2) = 2x^2x^6 = 2x^8$

4. $2(2x^2)^6 = 2(2^6x^{12}) = 2^7x^{12} = 128x^{12}$

5. $\frac{x^2}{2x^6} = \frac{x^{-4}}{2} = \frac{1}{2x^4}$

6. Let x represent the first angle, then $2x$ represents the second angle, and $3x$ represents the third angle. The sum of the three angles is 180°.

$x + 2x + 3x = 180$
$6x = 180$
$x = 30$
$2x = 2(30) = 60$
$3x = 3(30) = 90$

Therefore, the first angle is 30°, the second angle is 60°, and the third angle is 90°.

7. $-7 \le -2x + 3 < 9$
$-7 - 3 \le -2x + 3 - 3 < 9 - 3$
$-10 \le -2x < 6$
$\frac{-10}{-2} \ge \frac{-2x}{-2} > \frac{6}{-2}$
$5 \ge x > -3$
$-3 < x \le 5$

8. $\frac{3}{2}x + 2 < \frac{1}{2}x + 5$
$2\left(\frac{3}{2}x + 2\right) < 2\left(\frac{1}{2}x + 5\right)$
$3x + 4 < x + 10$
$3x + 4 - 4 < x + 10 - 4$
$3x < x + 6$
$3x - x < x - x + 6$
$2x < 6$
$x < 3$

9. $(a - b) - a(-b)$
$= (-5 - 3) - (-5)(-3)$ Replace a with -5 and b with 3.
$= (-8) - 15$ Simplify.
$= -23$ Simplify.

10. $(a - x)(x - a)$
$= (-2 - 4)(4 - (-2))$ Replace a with -2 and x with 4.
$= (-6)(6)$ Simplify.
$= -36$ Simplify.

11. $a^2 - y^3(a - y^2)y$
$= (-2)^2 - (-3)^3(-2 - (-3)^2)(-3)$
Replace a with -2 and y with -3.
$= 4 - (-27)(-11)(-3)$ Simplify.
$= 4 - (-891)$
$= 895$

12. $0.05 = 0.05 \times 100\% = 5\%$

13. $\frac{3}{10} = 0.3 = 30\%$

14. $\frac{4}{5} = 0.8 = 80\%$

15. $0.37 = 37\%$

16. Scientist B solved the problem using the correct steps. The second ratio shows $\frac{\text{amount of other constituents}}{\text{total amount of sulfuric acid}}$, so the first ratio should also show the same quantities. The amount of other constituents for the first ratio is $49 - 16 = 33$, where the total acid is 49.Therefore, the first ratio should be $\frac{33}{49}$.

17. Let x represent the other components.

$\frac{x_1}{\text{Compound}_1} = \frac{x_2}{\text{Compound}_2}$
$\frac{160 - 20}{160} = \frac{x}{640}$
$\frac{140}{160} = \frac{x}{640}$
$140(640) = 160x$
$x = 560$

560 kg of other components were needed.

18. Neither a tautology nor a contradiction

p	q	$\neg p \rightarrow q$
T	T	T
T	F	T
F	T	T
F	F	F

19. Neither a tautology nor a contradiction

p	q	$\neg p \vee q$
T	T	T
T	F	F
F	T	T
F	F	T

20. Let m represent the number of miles she can travel. The least remaining distance she can drive is 380 − 45 and the greatest remaining distance she can drive is 410 − 45.

$380 - 45 \leq m \leq 410 - 45$

$335 \leq m \leq 365$

21. $t = \frac{d}{r}$

$= \frac{1.321 \times 10^{12}}{3 \times 10^8} = \frac{1.321}{3} \times \frac{10^{12}}{10^8}$

$= 0.4403 \times 10^4 = 4403$

It will take about 4403 seconds.

22. Divide Earth's circumference by the length of a snake.

$\frac{4.0076 \times 10^4}{6 \times 10^{-4}} = \frac{4.0076}{6} \times \frac{10^4}{10^{-4}}$

$= 0.66793 \times 10^8$

$= 6.6793 \times 10^7$

It would take about 6.6793×10^7 snakes.

23. $5x^2 + 3x^4 + 2$ is a polynomial.
Standard form: $3x^4 + 5x^2 + 2$

24. This is not a polynomial because it is a radical.

25. $7x^3 + 3x^2 + 5x$ has a degree of 3, so it is cubic. It has 3 terms so it is a trinomial.

26. $x^1 + 5x^0$ has a degree of 1, so it is linear. It has 2 terms so it is a binomial.

27. $(7x^3 + 3x^2 + 5x) - (3x^3 + x)$

$= 7x^3 + 3x^2 + 5x - 3x^3 - x$

$= 7x^3 - 3x^3 + 3x^2 + 5x - x$

$= 4x^3 + 3x^2 + 4x$

28. $y = \frac{1}{2}x + 4$

A $4 \stackrel{?}{=} \frac{1}{2}(2) + 4$ Replace x with 2 and y with 4.

$4 \neq 5$

B $6 \stackrel{?}{=} \frac{1}{2}(6) + 4$ Replace x with 6 and y with 6.

$6 \neq 7$

C $6 \stackrel{?}{=} \frac{1}{2}(4) + 4$ Replace x with 4 and y with 6.

$6 = 6$

D $8 \stackrel{?}{=} \frac{1}{2}(4) + 4$ Replace x with 4 and y with 8.

$8 \neq 6$

Choice **C** is correct.

29. $\begin{bmatrix} 2 & -3 & 4 \\ 5 & 8 & -1 \\ 7 & 0 & 9 \end{bmatrix} \cdot \begin{bmatrix} -4 & 7 \\ 0 & 1 \\ 3 & 6 \end{bmatrix}$

$$= \begin{bmatrix} 2(-4) + (-3)(0) + 4(3) & 2(7) + (-3)(1) + 4(6) \\ 5(-4) + 8(0) + (-1)(3) & 5(7) + 8(1) + (-1)(6) \\ 7(-4) + 0(0) + 9(3) & 7(7) + 0(1) + 9(6) \end{bmatrix} = \begin{bmatrix} 4 & 35 \\ -23 & 37 \\ -1 & 103 \end{bmatrix}$$

30. $\begin{bmatrix} 4 & -1 \\ 6 & -2 \end{bmatrix} \cdot \begin{bmatrix} -1 & \frac{1}{2} & 0 \\ -2 & 4 & -3 \end{bmatrix}$

$$= \begin{bmatrix} 4(-1) + (-1)(-2) & 4\left(\frac{1}{2}\right) + (-1)(4) & 4(0) + (-1)(-3) \\ 6(-1) + (-2)(-2) & 6\left(\frac{1}{2}\right) + (-2)(4) & 6(0) + (-2)(-3) \end{bmatrix} = \begin{bmatrix} -2 & -2 & 3 \\ -2 & -5 & 6 \end{bmatrix}$$

LESSON 12

Warm Up 12

1. constant

2. $3x - 7y = 15$

$3(3) - 7(-3) \stackrel{?}{=} 15$ Replace x with 3 and y with -3.

$9 - (-21) \stackrel{?}{=} 15$ Simplify.

$30 \neq 15$ Simplify.

Therefore, $(3, -3)$ is not a solution to $3x - 7y = 15$.

3. An equation in the form $y = mx + b$ has a slope of m and y-intercept of b. Rewrite the equation in this form.

$5x + 4y = 20$

$4y = -5x + 20$ Subtract $5x$ from both sides.

$y = -\frac{5}{4}x + 5$ Divide both sides by 4.

The y-intercept is 5 and the slope is $-\frac{5}{4}$.

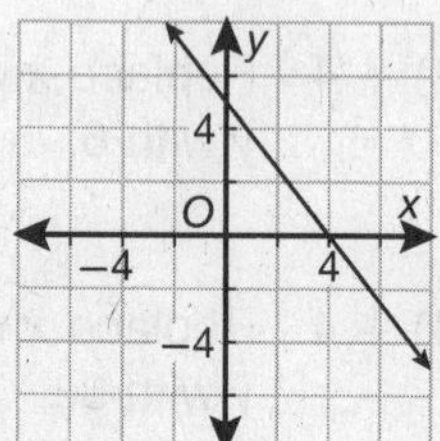

Lesson Practice 12

a. Multiply each xy pair to see if they equal the same constant, k.

b. $3(0.5) = 1.5$, $4(0.375) = 5(0.3)$ $= 1.5$, $6(0.25) = 1.5$

xy for the values in the table is 1.5, not 3.5. Therefore, the data set has a constant of variation $k = 1.5$.

c. $\left(-\frac{1}{2}\right)\left(-\frac{1}{2}\right) = \frac{1}{4}$; $(3)\left(\frac{1}{12}\right) = \frac{1}{4}$;

$(5)\left(\frac{1}{20}\right) = \frac{1}{4}$; $(9)\left(\frac{1}{36}\right) = \frac{1}{4}$;

inverse; $k = \frac{1}{4}$; $y = \frac{1}{4x}$

d. As x increases, the value of y also increases. This could be a direct variation. If it is a direct variation, then $\frac{y}{x}$ is a constant.

$$\frac{-9}{-2} = 4.5, \frac{36}{8} = 4.5, \frac{45}{10} = 4.5, \frac{90}{20} = 4.5$$

This is a direct variation. The constant of variation is $k = 4.5$, and the equation is $y = 4.5x$.

e. As x increases, the value of y also increases. This could be a direct variation. If it is a direct variation, then $\frac{y}{x}$ is a constant.

$$\frac{2}{1} = 2, \frac{6}{2} = 3, \frac{8}{3} = 2.67, \frac{10}{4} = 2.5$$

This is neither a direct nor an inverse variation.

f. Yes. Voltage is dependent on two variables, current and resistant. The ratio of voltage and current × resistance is a constant.

g. As S decreases P increases, and as S increases P decreases. Since PS is a constant, this is an inverse variation. $PS = k$, so $S = \frac{k}{P}$.

h. Calculate the ratio $\frac{PE}{mh}$ for each set of data points to see if they equal a constant value.

$$\frac{196}{2(10)} = 9.8, \frac{588}{3(20)} = 9.8, \frac{1176}{4(30)} = 9.8, \frac{1960}{5(40)} = 9.8$$

In each case, the ratio is the same value, 9.8. So this is a joint variation, with constant of variation 9.8. The equation is $PE = 9.8mh$.

i. Since there are two variables inversely proportional, this is an inverse variation. The equation is $I = \frac{k}{d^2}$.

j. F is proportional to the product of q_1 and q_2. Since there are three variables (two for q and one for F), this is a joint variation. The equation is $F = kq_1q_2$, where k is the constant of variation.

k. The direct proportion can be written as $F_e = kq_1q_2$. The inverse proportion is $F_e = \frac{k}{d^2}$.

The combined equation is $F_e = k\frac{q_1q_2}{d^2}$, where k is the constant of variation.

Practice 12

1. This is a fraction so it is not a polynomial.

2. $28x^2 - x^9 + 12x^7$
   $= -x^9 + 12x^7 + 28x^2$
   This is a polynomial.

3. Scientist A used the correct steps, since each ratio should show the amount of other components to the amount of compound. The first ratio should be $\frac{2400 - 900}{2400}$. Scientist B found the amount of acetylene required instead.

4. An isosceles triangle has two angles of equal measure. Let x represent the measure of each angle. Then $1.75x$ represents the measure of the third angle.
   The sum of the angles of a triangle is 180°.
   $x + x + 1.75x = 180$
   $3.75x = 180$
   $x = 48$
   So, $1.75x = 1.75(48) = 84$.
   The angles measure 48°, 48°, and 84°.

5. $RT = k$
   $120(40) = k$
   $k = 4800$
   $R(30) = 4800$
   $R = 160$
   The RPM would be 160.

6. $S = kB$
   $8 = k2$
   $k = 4$
   $S = 4(7)$
   $S = 28$
   There are 28 students.

7. $k = \frac{R}{BW}$
   $k = \frac{100}{4(5)} = 5$
   $5 = \frac{20}{B(2)}$
   $5B = 10$
   $B = 2$
   There would be 2 bicyclists.

8. $5x^7(3^3xy^2)$
   $= 5 \cdot 3^3x^7xy^2$
   $= 135x^8y^2$

9. $\left(\frac{5xy^3}{2x^3y^2z^{-4}}\right)^2 = \left(\frac{5yz^4}{2x^2}\right)^2$
   $= \frac{5^2y^2z^8}{2^2x^4}$
   $= \frac{25y^2z^8}{4x^4}$

10. $\frac{2^{-2}}{x^{-6}} = \frac{x^6}{2^2}$
    $= \frac{x^6}{4}$
    $= \frac{1}{4}x^6$

11. Divide Earth's diameter by the length of a green frog.
    $\frac{1.2753 \times 10^4}{7.5 \times 10^{-5}} = \frac{1.2753}{7.5} \times \frac{10^4}{10^{-5}}$
    $\approx 0.17004 \times 10^9$
    $= 1.7004 \times 10^8$
    It would take about 1.7004×10^8 frogs.

12. $-8 - 3^2 - (-2)^2 - 3(-2) + 2$
    $= -8 - 9 - 4 - (-6) + 2$
    $= -13$

13. $-\{-[-5(-3 + 2)7]\}$
    $= -\{-[-5(-1)7]\}$
    $= -\{-[35]\}$
    $= 35$

14. $-p^2 - p(a - p^2)$
    $= -(-3)^2 - (-3)(4 - (-3)^2)$ Replace a with 4 and p with −3.
    $= -(-3)^2 - (-3)(4 - 9)$ Simplify.
    $= -(-3)^2 - (-3)(-5)$ Simplify.
    $= -(9) - (-3)(-5)$ Simplify.
    $= -(9) - 15$ Simplify.
    $= -24$

15. $$-9 \le 2x - 5 < 9$$
$$-9 + 5 \le 2x - 5 + 5 < 9 + 5$$
$$-4 \le 2x < 14$$
$$\frac{-4}{2} \le \frac{2x}{2} < \frac{14}{2}$$
$$-2 \le x < 7$$

16. $$-\frac{1}{2}x + 7 \ge 15$$
$$-\frac{1}{2}x + 7 - 7 \ge 15 - 7$$
$$-\frac{1}{2}x \ge 8$$
$$(-2)(-\frac{1}{2}x) \le (8)(-2)$$
$$x \le -16$$

17. a. $x + 0.336x + 0.151x = 2{,}185{,}816$
$1.487x = 2{,}185{,}816$

b. $1.487x = 2{,}185{,}816$
$x = 1{,}469{,}950$ Divide both sides by 1.487.

The population of Phoenix in 2005 rounded to the nearest thousand is about 1,470,000.

18. Let d represent the number of ducks at the beginning. Then $3d$ represent the number when the new flock landed, $3d + 11$ when 11 more came, and $4d - 13$ represent the resulting number.
$$3d + 11 = 4d - 13$$
$$3d + 24 = 4d$$
$$24 = d$$
There were 24 ducks at the beginning.

19. $1.3 = 1.3 \times 100\% = 130\%$

20. $\frac{5}{8} = 0.625 = 62.5\%$

21. $\frac{13}{20} = 0.65 = 65\%$

22. $0.4 = 40\%$

23. Let x represent the amount of other materials.
$$\frac{x_1}{\text{Compound}_1} = \frac{x_2}{\text{Compound}_2}$$
$$\frac{3000 - 500}{3000} = \frac{x}{6000}$$
$$\frac{2500}{3000} = \frac{x}{6000}$$
$$3000x = 2500(6000)$$
$$3000x = 2500(6000)$$
$$3000x = 15{,}000{,}000$$
$$x = 5000$$
5000 kg of other materials are needed.

24. Substitute each x- and y-value into the equation $y = \frac{3}{4}x - 1$ to determine which is true.

A $-5 \stackrel{?}{=} \frac{3}{4}(8) - 1$
$-5 \ne 5$

B $-7 \stackrel{?}{=} \frac{3}{4}(-8) - 1$
$-7 = -7$

C $-2 \stackrel{?}{=} \frac{3}{4}(4) - 1$
$-2 \ne 2$

D $7 \stackrel{?}{=} \frac{3}{4}(-8) - 1$
$7 \ne -7$

Choice **B** is correct.

25. $$\begin{bmatrix} -2 & 3 & -4 \\ 0 & -3 & -1 \\ 5 & 0 & 2 \end{bmatrix} \cdot \begin{bmatrix} 4 & 7 \\ -6 & 1 \\ 3 & 6 \end{bmatrix}$$
$$= \begin{bmatrix} -2(4) + 3(-6) + (-4)(3) & -2(7) + 3(1) + (-4)(6) \\ 0(4) + (-3)(-6) + (-1)(3) & 0(7) + (-3)(1) + (-1)(6) \\ 5(4) + 0(-6) + 2(3) & 5(7) + 0(1) + 2(6) \end{bmatrix}$$
$$= \begin{bmatrix} -38 & -35 \\ 15 & -9 \\ 26 & 47 \end{bmatrix}$$

26. $\begin{bmatrix} -2 & -1 \\ 6 & 4 \end{bmatrix} \cdot \begin{bmatrix} -1 & 0 & 1 \\ 0 & 1 & 0 \end{bmatrix}$

$= \begin{bmatrix} -2(-1) + (-1)(0) & -2(0) + (-1)(1) & -2(1) + (-1)(0) \\ 6(-1) + 4(0) & 6(0) + 4(1) & 6(1) + 4(0) \end{bmatrix}$

$= \begin{bmatrix} 2 & -1 & -2 \\ -6 & 4 & 6 \end{bmatrix}$

27. $t = \frac{d}{r}$

$= \frac{1.35 \times 10^{12}}{3 \times 10^{8}}$

$= 0.45 \times 10^{4}$

$= 4.5 \times 10^{3}$

It would take about 4500 seconds.

28. Neither a tautology nor a contradiction.

p	q	$(p \wedge q)$	$(p \wedge q) \rightarrow \neg p$
T	T	T	F
T	F	F	T
F	T	F	T
F	F	F	T

29. Neither a tautology nor a contradiction.

p	q	$(p \vee q)$	$(p \vee q) \vee q$
T	T	T	T
T	F	T	T
F	T	T	T
F	F	F	F

30. No, matrix subtraction is not commutative. For example, if

$A = \begin{bmatrix} 3 & 5 \\ 9 & 0 \end{bmatrix}$ and $B = \begin{bmatrix} 1 & 0 \\ 2 & 6 \end{bmatrix}$, then

$A - B = \begin{bmatrix} 3 & 5 \\ 9 & 0 \end{bmatrix} - \begin{bmatrix} 1 & 0 \\ 2 & 6 \end{bmatrix} = \begin{bmatrix} 2 & 5 \\ 7 & -6 \end{bmatrix}$ and

$B - A = \begin{bmatrix} 1 & 0 \\ 2 & 6 \end{bmatrix} - \begin{bmatrix} 3 & 5 \\ 9 & 0 \end{bmatrix} = \begin{bmatrix} -2 & -5 \\ -7 & 6 \end{bmatrix}$

LAB 3

Graphing Calculator Practice

a. $x = 3$

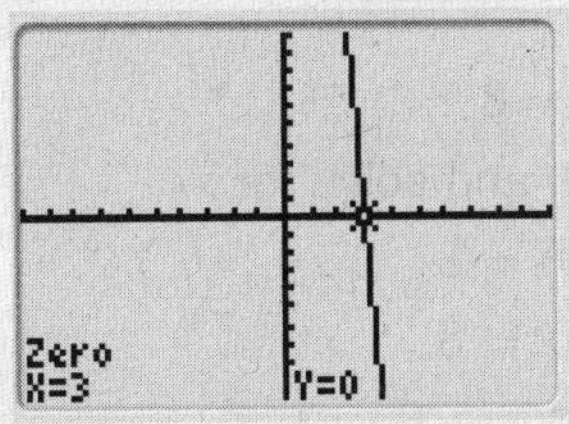

b. $x = -2$, $y = 9$

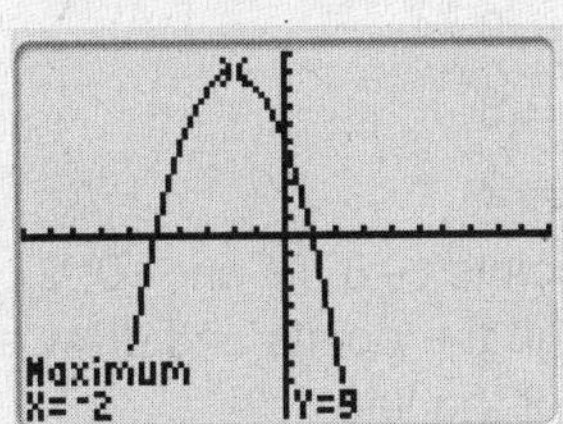

c. $x = -0.75$, $y = 2.75$

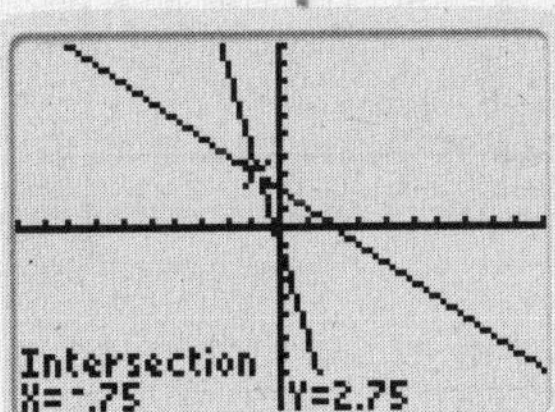

LESSON 13

Warm Up 13

1. vertical

2. $-8 - (-6) = -8 + 6 = -2$

3. $-5x + 3y$

$= -5(-2) + 3(-3)$ Replace x with -2 and y with -3.

$= 10 - 9$

$= 1$

Lesson Practice 13

a. If $x = 2$, $y = -\frac{1}{2}(2) + 3 = 2$

If $x = 4$, $y = -\frac{1}{2}(4) + 3 = 1$

If $x = 6$, $y = -\frac{1}{2}(6) + 3 = 0$

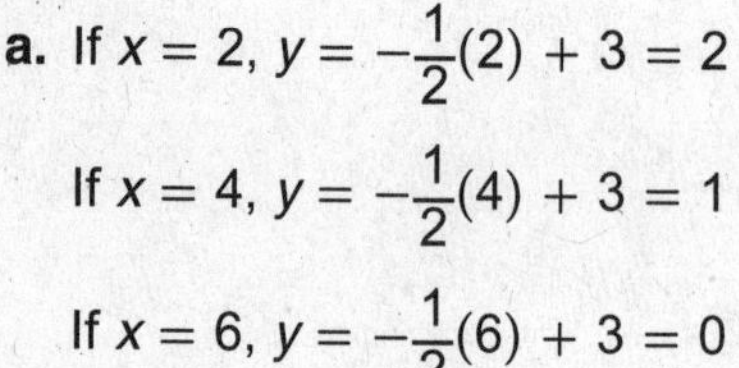

x	y
2	2
4	1
6	0

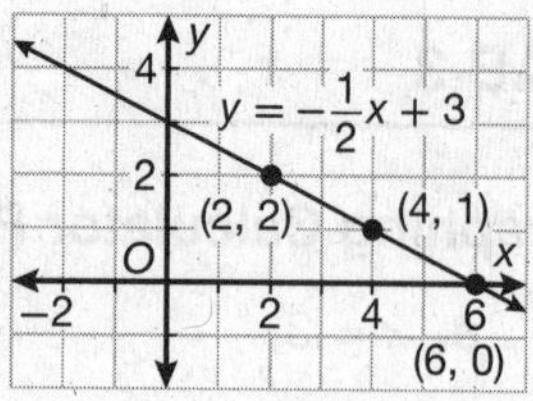

b. $-x + 4y = 8$

Let $y = 0$, and solve for x.

$-x + 4(0) = 8$

$-x = 8$

$x = -8$

Let $x = 0$, and solve for y.

$-0 + 4y = 8$

$4y = 8$

$y = 2$

Plot the points $(-8, 0)$ and $(0, 2)$. Extend the line through the points and draw arrows on the ends of the line.

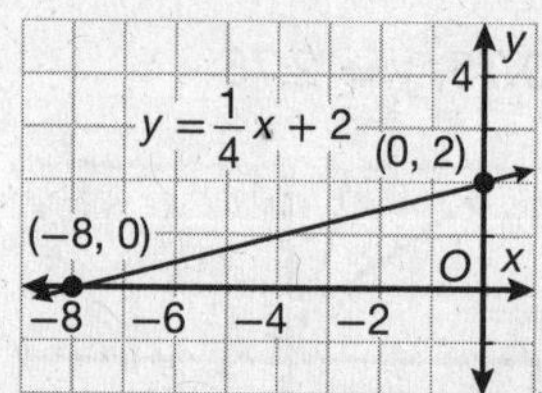

c. $m = \frac{-6 - 5}{5 - (-3)} = \frac{-11}{8} = -\frac{11}{8}$

Because m is negative, the line falls.

d. $m = \frac{0 - 4}{-2 - 0} = \frac{-4}{-2} = 2$

Because m is positive, the line rises.

e. $m = \frac{3 - 3}{8 - (-4)} = \frac{0}{12} = 0$

Because $m = 0$, the line is horizontal.

f. The equation is in the form $y = mx + b$. The slope of the line is $m = \frac{1}{3}$ and the y-intercept is $b = 2$, or $(0, 2)$.

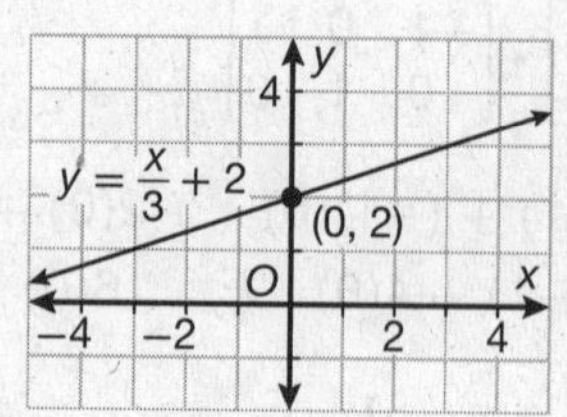

g. The slope can be calculated using

$m = \frac{\text{rise}}{\text{run}} = \frac{24 \text{ ft}}{50 \text{ ft}} = \frac{12}{25}$.

Practice 13

1. $k = \frac{ED}{A}$

$k = \frac{75(85)}{15} = 425$

$425 = \frac{20D}{30}$

$20D = 425(30)$

$D = 637.5$

There are 638 deer.

2. $k = \frac{DS}{R}$

$k = \frac{65(3)}{15} = 13$

$13 = \frac{5S}{100}$

$13(100) = 5S$

$S = 260$

There are 260 sunflowers.

3. Sample: If $x = -4$, $y = -\frac{3}{4}(-4) + 1 = 4$

If $x = 0$, $y = -\frac{3}{4}(0) + 1 = 1$

If $x = 4$, $y = -\frac{3}{4}(4) + 1 = -2$

x	y
−4	4
0	1
4	−2

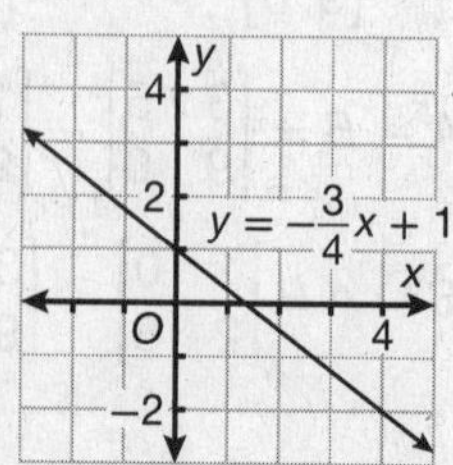

4. $-2x - y = 3$

Let $y = 0$, and solve for x.

$-2x - 0 = 3$

$$-2x = 3$$
$$x = -\frac{3}{2}$$

Let $x = 0$, and solve for y.

$$-2(0) - y = 3$$
$$-y = 3$$
$$y = -3$$

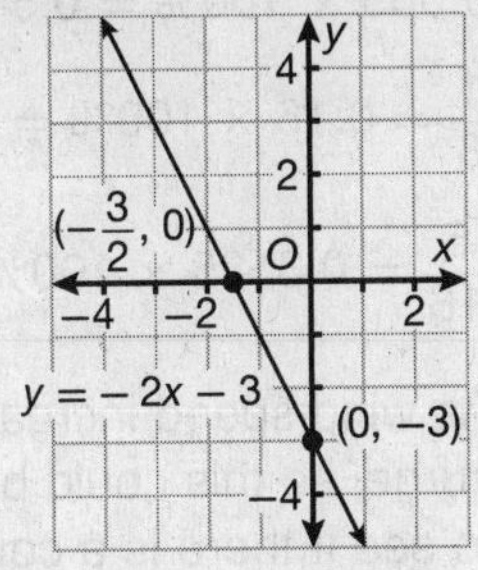

5. Farmer A solved the problem using the correct steps. Farmer B solved the problem as if it involved both direct and inverse variation.

6. $m = \frac{-5 - 0}{7 - (-2)} = \frac{-5}{9} = -\frac{5}{9}$

Because m is negative, the line falls.

7. $m = \frac{0 - 4}{-2 - 0} = \frac{-4}{-2} = 2$

Because m is positive, the line rises.

8. The equation is in the form $y = mx + b$. The slope of the line is $m = -\frac{5}{4}$ and the y-intercept is $b = 2$, or $(0, 2)$.

9. $25x^3 + x^{-7} + 2xy$ is not a polynomial since there is a negative exponent.

10. $0.25x^4 + 5x^{\frac{4}{2}} = 0.25x^4 + 5x^2$

This is a polynomial.

11. **a.** $5.879x + 1.704x + x = 1{,}775{,}721$
$8.583x = 1{,}775{,}721$

b. $8.583x = 1{,}775{,}72$
$x = 206{,}888$

The population of Modesto in 2005 rounded to the nearest thousand is 207,000.

12. $-2 - 3(-2 - 2) - 5(-5 + 7)$
$= -2 - 3(-4) - 5(2)$
$= -2 - (-12) - 10$
$= 0$

13. $-[-2(-5 + 2) - (-2 - 3)]$
$= -[-2(-3) - (-5)]$
$= -[6 - (-5)]$
$= -[11]$
$= -11$

14. $a^2 - y^3(a - y^2)y^2$
$= (-2)^2 - (3)^3((-2) - (3)^2)(3)^2$

Replace a with −2 and y with 3.

$= (-2)^2 - (3)^3(-11)(3)^2$
$= 4 - (27)(-11)(9)$
$= 4 - (-2673)$
$= 2677$

15. Since two sides are congruent, the base angles are congruent. Therefore, $x = 45°$ The sum of the angles is 180°, so $45 + 45 + y = 180$. Therefore, $y = 90°$

16. $3x - 5 \geq 3(x + 7)$
$3x - 5 \geq 3x + 21$
$3x - 3x - 5 \geq 3x - 3x + 21$
$-5 \geq 21$

But −5 is never greater than 21, so the inequality has no solution.

17. $7x - 5 < 7(x + 5) + 2$
$7x - 5 < 7x + 35 + 2$
$7x - 5 < 7x + 37$
$7x - 7x - 5 < 7x - 7x + 37$
$-5 < 37$

Since 37 is always greater than −5, there are infinitely many solutions.

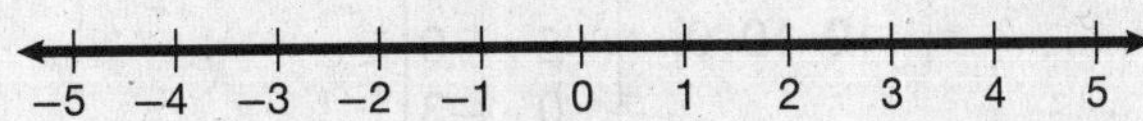

18. Divide the number of pennies that fit in the Empire State Building by the number of pennies in one cubic foot.

$$\frac{1.8 \times 10^{12}}{4.9 \times 10^4} = \frac{1.8}{4.9} \times \frac{10^{12}}{10^4}$$
$$= 0.3673 \times 10^8$$
$$= 3.7 \times 10^7$$

The approximate volume of the building is 3.7×10^7 cubic feet.

19. $(7p - 6) + 3p - (-2 - p) = 73$
$$7p - 6 + 3p + 2 + p = 73$$
$$7p + 3p + p - 6 + 2 = 73$$
$$11p - 4 = 73$$
$$11p = 77$$
$$p = 7$$

20. $$\frac{7(p+3)}{2} = 21$$
$$2\left(\frac{7(p+3)}{2}\right) = 21(2)$$
$$7(p+3) = 42$$
$$7p + 21 = 42$$
$$7p = 21$$
$$p = 3$$

21. $4p + (p - 4)(2) = 8p - 7$
$$4p + 2p - 8 = 8p - 7$$
$$6p - 8 = 8p - 7$$
$$-2p = 1$$
$$p = -\frac{1}{2}$$

22. $AB = [-1\ \ 2] \times \begin{bmatrix} 4 & 0 & 2 \\ -3 & 5 & 1 \end{bmatrix}$
$= [-1(4) + 2(-3)\ \ -1(0) + 2(5)$
$-1(2) + 2(1)]$
$= [-10\ \ 10\ \ 0]$

23. $ABC = [-1\ \ 2] \cdot \begin{bmatrix} 4 & 0 & 2 \\ -3 & 5 & 1 \end{bmatrix} \cdot \begin{bmatrix} 7 & 1 \\ -2 & 0 \\ 0 & -3 \end{bmatrix}$

$[-10\ \ 10\ \ 0] \cdot \begin{bmatrix} 7 & 1 \\ -2 & 0 \\ 0 & -3 \end{bmatrix}$
$= [-10(7) + 10(-2) + 0(0)$
$-10(1) + 10(0) + 0(-3)]$
$= [-90\ \ -10]$

24. Oranges $= f(x) = -0.044x^3 + 0.258x^2$
$- 0.657x + 12.883$

Grapefruits $= g(x) = 0.004x^3 - 0.065x^2$
$- 0.040x + 2.695$

The combined oranges and grapefruits is
$f(x) + g(x) = (-0.044x^3 + 0.258x^2$
$- 0.657x + 12.883)$
$+ (0.004x^3 - 0.065x^2$
$- 0.040x + 2.695)$
$= -0.044x^3 + 0.004x^3 + 0.258x^2 - 0.065x^2$
$- 0.657x - 0.040x + 2.695 + 12.883$
$= -0.04x^3 + 0.193x^2 - 0.697x + 15.578$

25. $0.005 \times 100\% = 0.5\%$

26. $\frac{1}{6} = 0.1\overline{6} \times 100\% = 16.\overline{6}\%$

27. $\frac{5}{16} = 0.3125 \times 100\% = 31.25\%$

28. As wind speed increases, so does storm surge, so this could be a direct variation. Test to see if there is a constant ratio.
$\frac{74}{4} = 18.5, \frac{96}{6} = 16, \frac{111}{9} = 12.3.$
The ratio of wind speed and storm surge is not a constant, so the relationship is not a direct variation.

29. **A** This is not a function, since the same x-value, -7, is paired with different y-values, 6 and 3.

B This is not a function since the same x-value, -2, is paired with different y-values, 5 and 7.

C This is a function since each x-value is paired with a different y-value.

D This is not a function, since the same x-value, 0, is paired with different y-values, 1, 2, and 3.

Choice **C** is correct.

30. The slope can be calculated using
$$m = \frac{\text{rise}}{\text{run}} = \frac{268\text{ ft}}{1000\text{ ft}} = \frac{67}{250}.$$

LESSON 14

Warm Up 14

1. matrix

2.

$4x + 6 = 22$	
$4x + 6 - 6 = 22 - 6$	Subtract 6 on both sides.
$4x = 16$	Simplify.
$\frac{4x}{4} = \frac{16}{4}$	Divide by 4 on both sides.
$x = 4$	Simplify.

3. $\begin{bmatrix} 3 & 2 \\ -1 & 7 \end{bmatrix} \times \begin{bmatrix} 4 & -3 \\ 6 & 8 \end{bmatrix}$

$= \begin{bmatrix} 3(4)+(2)(6) & 3(-3)+(2)(8) \\ -1(4)+(7)(6) & -1(-3)+(7)(8) \end{bmatrix}$

$= \begin{bmatrix} 24 & 7 \\ 38 & 59 \end{bmatrix}$

Lesson Practice 14

a. $\begin{bmatrix} 1 & -6 \\ 0 & 8 \end{bmatrix} = 1(8) - (0)(-6) = 8 - 0 = 8$

b. $\begin{vmatrix} x-7 & 8 \\ -1 & -5 \end{vmatrix} = 23$

$(-5)(x-7) - (-1)(8) = 23$

$-5x + 35 + 8 = 23$

$-5x + 43 = 23$

$-5x = -20$

$x = 4$

c. $\begin{vmatrix} 5 & -9 & -5 \\ -5 & -3 & 8 \\ 2 & -8 & -1 \end{vmatrix}$

$= 5\begin{vmatrix} -3 & 8 \\ -8 & -1 \end{vmatrix} - (-9)\begin{vmatrix} -5 & 8 \\ 2 & -1 \end{vmatrix}$

$+ (-5)\begin{vmatrix} -5 & -3 \\ 2 & -8 \end{vmatrix}$

$= 5[(-3)(-1) - (-8)(8)] - (-9)$
$[(-5)(-1) - (2)(8)] + (-5)[(-5)(-8)$
$- (2)(-3)]$

$= 5[(3 - (-64)] - (-9)[(5 - 16]$
$+ (-5)[40 - (-6)]$

$= 5[67] - (-9)[-11] + (-5)[46]$

$= 5[67] - (-9)[-11] + (-5)[46]$

$= 335 - 99 - 230$

$= 6$

d. $\begin{vmatrix} -4 & 2 & 7 \\ 9 & 3 & -4 \\ 7 & -1 & -2 \end{vmatrix}$

$= \begin{vmatrix} -4 & 2 & 7 & -4 & 2 \\ 9 & 3 & -4 & 9 & 3 \\ 7 & -1 & -2 & 7 & -1 \end{vmatrix}$

$= [(-4)(3)(-2) + (2)(-4)(7)$
$+ (7)(9)(-1)] - [(7)(3)(7) + (-1)$
$(-4)(-4) + (-2)(9)(2)]$

$= [(24 + (-56) + (-63)] - [147$
$+ (-16) + (-36)]$

$= [-95] - [95] = -190$

e. Store the data in a matrix.

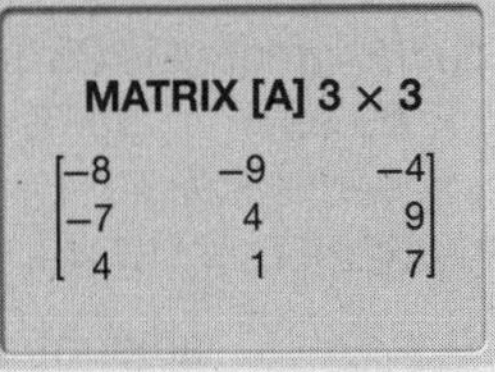

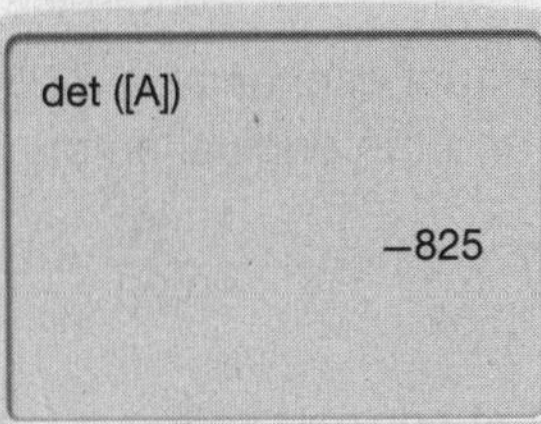

Use expansion by minors to check the calculator answer.

$-8\begin{vmatrix} 4 & 9 \\ 1 & 7 \end{vmatrix} - (-9)\begin{vmatrix} -7 & 9 \\ 4 & 7 \end{vmatrix} + (-4)\begin{vmatrix} -7 & 4 \\ 4 & 1 \end{vmatrix}$

$= (-8)[(4)(7) - (1)(9)] - (-9)[(-7)(7)$
$- (4)(9)] + (-4)[(-7)(1) - (4)(4)]$

$= (-8)[28 - 9] - (-9)[-49 - 36]$
$+ (-4)[-7 - 16]$

$= (-8)[19] - (-9)[-85] + (-4)[-23]$

$= -152 - 765 + 92$

$= -825$

f. $\frac{1}{2}\begin{vmatrix} -2 & -3 & 3 \\ 3 & 2 & 1 \\ 1 & 1 & 1 \end{vmatrix}$

$= \frac{1}{2}\left[-2\begin{vmatrix} 2 & 1 \\ 1 & 1 \end{vmatrix} - (-3)\begin{vmatrix} 3 & 1 \\ 1 & 1 \end{vmatrix} + 3\begin{vmatrix} 3 & 2 \\ 1 & 1 \end{vmatrix}\right]$

$= \frac{1}{2}[-2[(2)(1) - (1)(1)] - (-3)[(3)(1)$
$- (1)(1)] + 3[(3)(1) - (1)(2)]]$

$= \frac{1}{2}[(-2)[2 - 1] - (-3)[3 - 1] + 3[3 - 2]]$

$= \frac{1}{2}[-2[1] - (-3)[2] + 3[1]]$

$= \frac{1}{2}[-2 - [-6] + [3]]$

$= \frac{1}{2}[7]$

$= 3.5$

The area is 3.5 square units.

Practice 14

1. a. The reduced amount is 25% of \$89.99, or $0.25 \times 89.99 = 22.50$. Therefore, the amount saved is \$22.50. The new price is \$89.99 − \$22.50 = \$67.49.

   b. $\text{percent change} = \frac{\text{amount of change}}{\text{original amount}}$

   The amount of change is $22.50 + 15 = 37.50$ and the original amount is 89.99.

   $\text{percent change} = \frac{37.50}{89.99} \approx 0.417$, or about 42%

2. Student A is correct. As the quantity decreases the price increases, which suggests an inverse variation. Student A multiplied to find a constant. Although Student B multiplied correctly, this student labeled the results as a quotient and therefore incorrectly concluded that the relationship is a direct variation, instead of an inverse variation.

3. $\frac{y}{x} = 3$, direct variation

4. $\frac{y}{x} = \frac{1}{2}$, direct variation

5. $yx = 20$, inverse variation

6. Sample: If $x = -3$, $y = -\frac{2}{3}(-3) + 4 = 6$

   If $x = 0$, $y = -\frac{2}{3}(0) + 4 = 4$

   If $x = 3$, $y = -\frac{2}{3}(3) + 4 = 2$

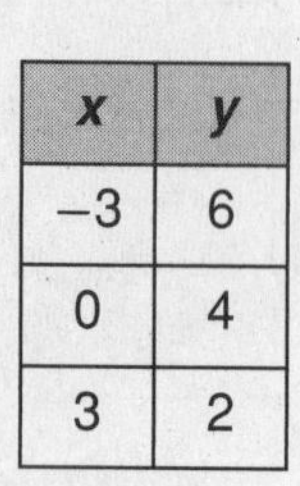

x	y
−3	6
0	4
3	2

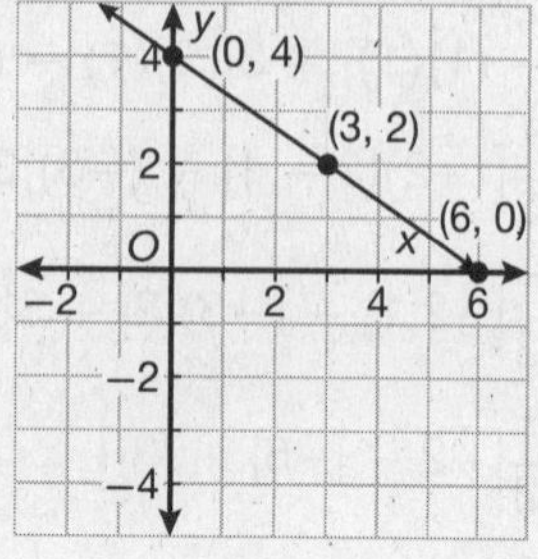

7. $y = \frac{5}{4}x + 1$

   Let $y = 0$, and solve for x.

   $$0 = \frac{5}{4}x + 1$$
   $$-\frac{5}{4}x = 1$$
   $$\left(-\frac{5}{4}\right)\left(-\frac{4}{5}\right)x = (1)\left(-\frac{4}{5}\right)$$
   $$x = -\frac{4}{5}$$

   Let $x = 0$, and solve for y.

   $$y = \frac{5}{4}(0) + 1$$
   $$y = 1$$

   The intercepts are $\left(-\frac{4}{5}, 0\right)$ and $(0, 1)$.

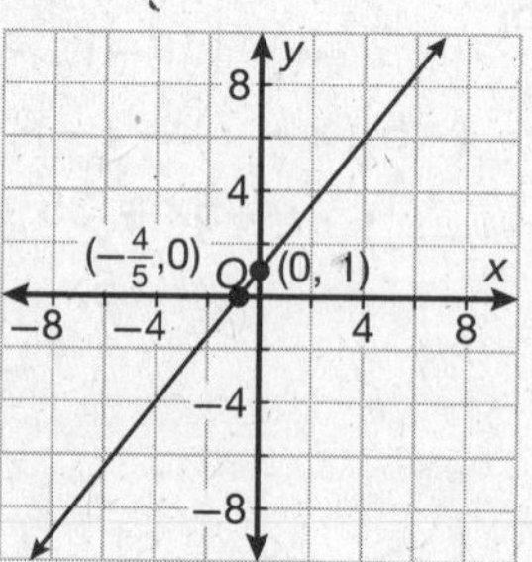

8. $m = \frac{-1 - 2}{3 - (-8)} = -\frac{3}{11} = -\frac{3}{11}$

   Because m is negative, the line falls.

9. $m = \frac{-2 - 4}{-5 - 6} = \frac{-6}{-11} = \frac{6}{11}$

   Because m is positive, the line rises.

10. $m = \frac{2 - 2}{-5 - 6} = \frac{0}{-11} = 0$

    Because m is zero, the line is horizontal.

11. $\begin{vmatrix} -1 & 2 \\ 3 & 5 \end{vmatrix} = (-1)(5) - (3)(2) = -5 - 6$

    $= -11$

12. $\begin{vmatrix} 3 & 5 \\ -2x + 1 & -7 \end{vmatrix} = 24$

    $$(3)(-7) - (-2x + 1)(5) = 24$$
    $$-21 - (-10x + 5) = 24$$
    $$-21 + 10x - 5 = 24$$
    $$-26 + 10x = 24$$
    $$10x = 50$$
    $$x = 5$$

13. a. $\begin{vmatrix} 7 & -1 & 2 \\ -3 & 0 & -2 \\ 4 & 3 & 5 \end{vmatrix}$

$= 7\begin{vmatrix} 0 & -2 \\ 3 & 5 \end{vmatrix} - (-1)\begin{vmatrix} -3 & -2 \\ 4 & 5 \end{vmatrix}$

$+ 2\begin{vmatrix} -3 & 0 \\ 4 & 3 \end{vmatrix}$

$= 7[(0)(5) - (3)(-2)] - (-1)$
$[(-3)(5) - (4)(-2)] + 2\,[(-3)(3)$
$- (4)(0)]$

$= 7[0 - (-6)] - (-1)[(-15) - (-8)]$
$+ 2[(-9) - 0]$

$= 7[6] - (-1)[-7] + 2[-9]$

$= 42 - 7 + (-18)$

$= 17$

b. $\begin{vmatrix} 7 & -1 & 2 & 7 & -1 \\ -3 & 0 & -2 & -3 & 0 \\ 4 & 3 & 5 & 4 & 3 \end{vmatrix}$

$= [(7)(0)(5) + (-1)(-2)(4) + (2)$
$(-3)(3)] - [(4)(0)(2) + (3)(-2)(7)$
$+ (5)(-3)(-1)]$

$= [0 + 8 + (-18)] - [0 + (-42) + 15]$

$= (-10) - (-27)$

$= 17$

14. Store the data in a matrix.

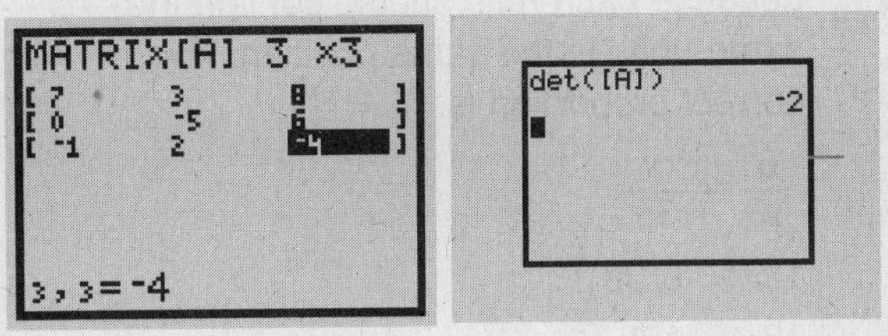

15. $\frac{1}{2}\begin{vmatrix} -2 & 7 & -4 \\ 5 & 3 & -3 \\ 1 & 1 & 1 \end{vmatrix}$

$= \frac{1}{2}\left[-2\begin{vmatrix} 3 & -3 \\ 1 & 1 \end{vmatrix} - 7\begin{vmatrix} 5 & -3 \\ 1 & 1 \end{vmatrix}\right.$

$\left. + (-4)\begin{vmatrix} 5 & 3 \\ 1 & 1 \end{vmatrix}\right]$

$= \frac{1}{2}[-2[(3)(1) - (1)(-3)] - 7[(5)(1)$
$- (1)(-3)] + (-4)[(5)(1) - (1)(3)]]$

$= \frac{1}{2}[-2[3 - (-3)] - 7[5 - (-3)]$
$+ (-4)[5 - 3]]$

$= \frac{1}{2}[-2[6] - 7[8] + (-4)[2]]$

$= \frac{1}{2}[-12 - 56 + [-8]]$

$= \frac{1}{2}[-76]$

$= \frac{1}{2}(76) = 38$

The area of the triangle is 38 square units.

16. a. $A = \begin{bmatrix} 71.4 & 71.5 & 72.0 & 72.5 & 73.7 & 75.1 \\ 71.7 & 71.1 & 72.7 & 73.9 & 75.4 & 77.7 \end{bmatrix}$

b. $\frac{5}{9}\left[\begin{bmatrix} 71.4 & 71.5 & 72.0 & 72.5 & 73.7 & 75.1 \\ 71.7 & 71.1 & 72.7 & 73.9 & 75.4 & 77.7 \end{bmatrix} + \begin{bmatrix} -32 & -32 & -32 & -32 & -32 & -32 \\ -32 & -32 & -32 & -32 & -32 & -32 \end{bmatrix}\right]$

$= \frac{5}{9}\begin{bmatrix} 39.4 & 39.5 & 40.0 & 40.5 & 41.7 & 43.1 \\ 39.7 & 39.1 & 40.7 & 41.9 & 43.4 & 45.7 \end{bmatrix}$

$= \begin{bmatrix} 21.9 & 21.9 & 22.2 & 22.5 & 23.2 & 23.9 \\ 22.1 & 21.7 & 22.6 & 23.3 & 24.1 & 25.4 \end{bmatrix}$

17. Josh set up the proportion incorrectly because each ratio should contain the same units in the same position. The correct proportion is $\frac{6}{18} = \frac{x}{33}$.

$$\frac{6}{18} = \frac{x}{33}$$
$$18x = 6(33)$$
$$18x = 198$$
$$x = 11$$

The rope measures 11 yards.

18. Let x represent the number of newspapers that she will have to deliver.

The inequality is $0.25x \geq 500$.

$$0.25x \geq 500$$
$$\frac{0.25x}{0.25} \geq \frac{500}{0.25}$$
$$x \geq 2000$$

She will have to deliver at least 2000 newspapers.

19. $-1.9 < 2(x - 0.25) \leq 2.5$

$$-1.9 < 2x - 0.50 \leq 2.5$$
$$-1.9 + 0.50 < 2x - 0.50 + 0.50$$
$$\leq 2.5 + 0.50$$
$$-1.4 < 2x \leq 3$$
$$\frac{-1.4}{2} < \frac{2x}{2} \leq \frac{3}{2}$$
$$-0.7 < x \leq 1.5$$

20. $-2 < \frac{2(x-7)}{3} \leq 5$

$$-2 \cdot 3 < 3\left(\frac{2(x-7)}{3}\right) \leq 5 \cdot 3$$
$$-6 < 2(x - 7) \leq 15$$
$$-6 < 2x - 14 \leq 15$$
$$-6 + 14 < 2x - 14 + 14 \leq 15 + 14$$
$$8 < 2x \leq 29$$
$$\frac{8}{2} < \frac{2x}{2} \leq \frac{29}{2}$$
$$4 < \frac{2x}{2} \leq \frac{29}{2}$$
$$4 < x \leq 14.5$$

21. $A = \begin{bmatrix} 2 & 1 & 1 \\ 1 & 1 & 1 \\ 2 & 3 & 0 \end{bmatrix}$

$B = \begin{bmatrix} 3 \\ 2 \\ 1 \end{bmatrix}$

22. $AB = \begin{bmatrix} 2 & 1 & 1 \\ 1 & 1 & 1 \\ 2 & 3 & 0 \end{bmatrix} \cdot \begin{bmatrix} 3 \\ 2 \\ 1 \end{bmatrix}$

$$= \begin{bmatrix} 2(3) + 1(2) + 1(1) \\ 1(3) + 1(2) + 1(1) \\ 2(3) + 3(2) + 0(1) \end{bmatrix}$$

$$= \begin{bmatrix} 9 \\ 6 \\ 12 \end{bmatrix}$$

Lan scored 9.
Stacy scored 6.
Robert scored 12.

23. $y = mx + b$

$\frac{y}{x} = m + \frac{b}{x}$ There is no variation.

24. $y = mx + 0$

$\frac{y}{x} = m$ This is a direct variation.

25. 0.33 is a real number and a rational number.

26. 0 is a real number, a rational number, an integer, and a whole number.

27. $\sqrt{5}$ is a real number and an irrational number.

28. There are two variables and as wind speed increases storm surge also increases. This could be a direct variation. So determine if the ratio is a constant.

$$\frac{95}{5} \neq \frac{100}{8} \neq \frac{130}{12} \neq \frac{155}{18} \neq \frac{155}{19}$$

The ratios are not equivalent, so the relationship is not a direct variation.

29. A polynomial that is in standard form has its terms in descending order of degree. Choice **A** is correct.

30. a. $500x^4 + 1000x^3 + 600x^2 + 500x$
$+ 1000x^4 + 200x^3 + 200x^2 + 200x$
$= 500x^4 + 1000x^4 + 1000x^3 + 200x^3$
$+ 600x^2 + 200x^2 + 500x + 200x$
$= 1500x^4 + 1200x^3 + 800x^2 + 700x$

b. $1500x^4 + 1200x^3 + 800x^2 + 700x$ and $x = 1 + r$, so $x = 1 + 5\% = 1 + 0.05$
$= 1.05$
Replace x with 1.05.
$1500(1.05)^4 + 1200(1.05)^3$
$+ 800(1.05)^2 + 700(1.05)$
$\approx 1823.26 + 1389.15 + 882 + 735$
$= 4829.41$
The total value of both accounts is $4829.41.

LESSON 15

Warm Up 15

1. slope
2. In the form $y = mx + b$ the slope is m and the y-intercept is b. For the equation $y = -3x + 5$, the slope is -3 and the y-intercept is 5.
3. $y = 3x - 5$
   $1 \stackrel{?}{=} 3(2) - 5$ Replace x with 2 and y with 1.
   $1 \stackrel{?}{=} 6 - 5$
   $1 = 1$
   $y = x + 3$
   $1 \stackrel{?}{=} 2 + 3$ Replace x with 2 and y with 1.
   $1 \neq 5$
   (2, 1) satisfies $y = 3x - 5$, but it does not satisfy $y = x + 3$.

Lesson Practice 15

a. Solve each equation for y to get the slope-intercept form.
$2x - y = 6$
$-y = 6 - 2x$
$y = 2x - 6$
$y + 2x = -10$
$y = -2x - 10$

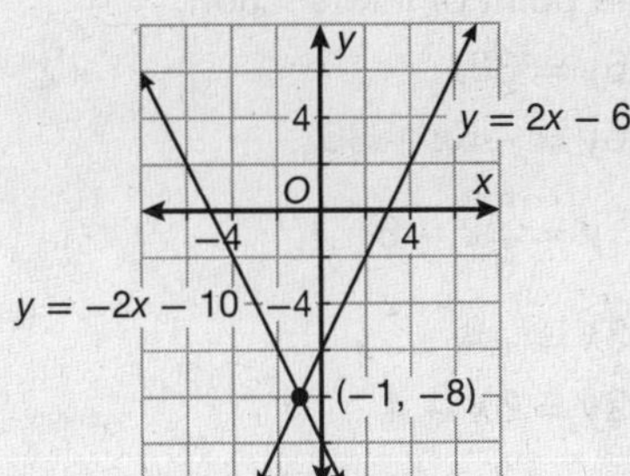

The solution is (−1, −8).

b. $2x - y = 6$
$y = 2x - 6$
$y = 2(-2) - 6$ Replace x with −2.
$y = -10$
$y = 2(-1) - 6$ Replace x with −1.
$y = -8$
$y = 2(0) - 6$ Replace x with 0.
$y = -6$
$y = 2(1) - 6$ Replace x with 1.
$y = -4$
$y + 2x = -10$
$y = -2x - 10$
$y = -2(-2) - 10$ Replace x with −2.
$y = -6$
$y = -2(-1) - 10$ Replace x with −1.
$y = -8$
$y = -2(0) - 10$ Replace x with 0.
$y = -10$
$y = -2(1) - 10$ Replace x with 1.
$y = -12$

$2x - y = 6$

x	y
−2	−10
−1	−8
0	−6
1	−4

$y + 2x = -10$

x	y
−2	−6
−1	−8
0	−10
1	−12

When $x = -1$, the y-values are the same for both equations. The solution to the system is (−1, −8).

c. Solve each equation for y to get the slope-intercept form. Then graph the equations and find the point of intersection.

$5x - 6y = 36$
$-6y = -5x + 36$
$y = \frac{5}{6}x - 6$

$2y - 3x = -4$
$2y = 3x - 4$
$y = \frac{3}{2}x - 2$

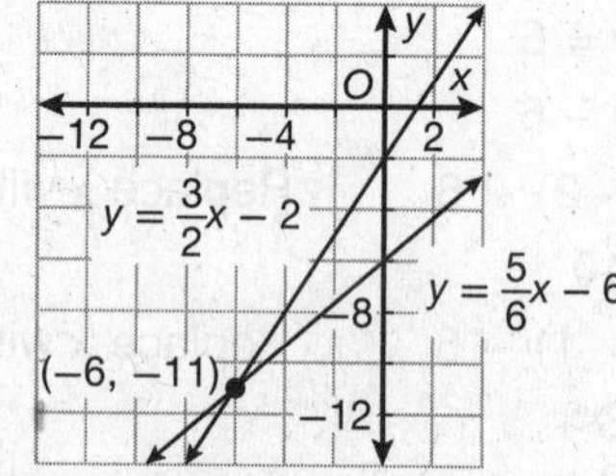

The lines intersect at $(-6, -11)$, so $(-6, -11)$ is the solution of the system.

d. The lines intersect at one point. The system is consistent and independent. The lines intersect at $(-3, 3)$, so $(-3, 3)$ is the solution to the system.

e. The lines are parallel and do not intersect. The system is inconsistent. There are no common points, so there is no solution.

f. The lines coincide. The system is consistent and dependent. There are an infinite number of solutions, so the solution is an infinite set of ordered pairs.

g. Let x represent the number of fitness classes.
Nonmembers: $y = 20x$
Members: $y = 5x + 75$

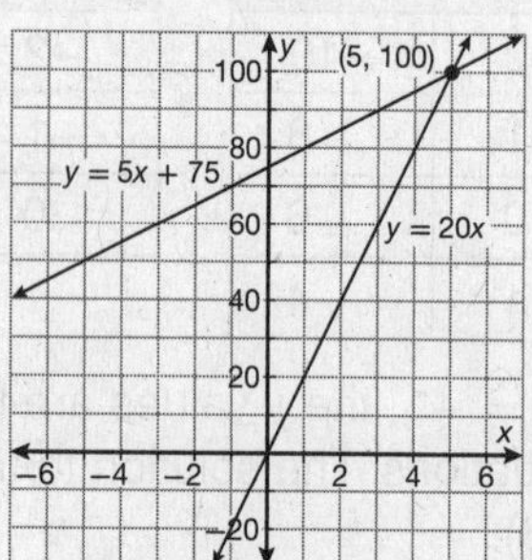

When x is 5, the y-values are the same for both equations, so this is the solution.

Therefore, after 5 fitness classes the total cost will be the same for members and nonmembers.

Practice 15

1. $p(x) = 2x^2 - x$
$p(-5) = 2(-5)^2 - (-5)$ Replace x with -5.
$p(-5) = 50 - (-5)$
$p(-5) = 55$

2. $h(x) = 6x + 3$
$h\left(\frac{1}{2}\right) = 6\left(\frac{1}{2}\right) + 3$ Replace x with $\frac{1}{2}$.
$h\left(\frac{1}{2}\right) = 3 + 3$
$h\left(\frac{1}{2}\right) = 6$

3. $\frac{1}{3}y = x$
$\frac{x}{y} = \frac{1}{3}$, or $\frac{y}{x} = 3$
This is a direct variation.

4. $y = \frac{1}{2}xz$
$\frac{y}{xz} = \frac{1}{2}$
This is a joint variation.

5. $xy = 10$
This is an inverse variation.

6. $\frac{C}{2r} = \pi$
The ratio is a constant, so this is a direct variation.

7. $\frac{A}{r^2} = \pi$
The ratio is a constant, so this is a direct variation.

8. The price reduction is 75% of \$39.99, or $75\% \times 39.99 = 0.75 \times 39.99 = 29.99$. The price reduction is \$29.99. The new price is \$39.99 − \$29.99 = \$10.00 without the sales tax. The sales tax is 5% of \$10.00 = $0.05 \times 10 = 0.5$ or \$0.50. Therefore, the new price with sales tax is \$10.00 + \$0.50 = \$10.50.

9. Only square matrices have determinants. This is not a square matrix so it does not have a determinant.

Choice **D** is correct.

10. In the form $y = mx + b$, m is the slope and b is the y-intercept. So rewrite the equation in this form.

$8x - 2y = -10$

$-2y = -8x - 10$

$y = 4x + 5$

Therefore, the slope is 4 and the y-intercept is 5.

b.

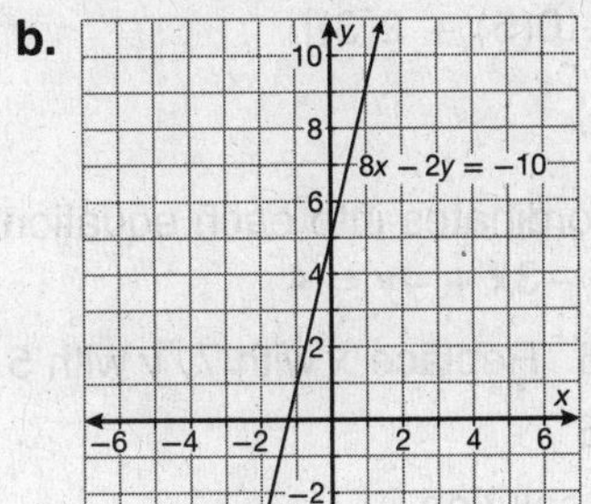

11. $m = \dfrac{y_2 - y_1}{x_2 - x_1}$

$\dfrac{4}{9} = \dfrac{y - 8}{-6 - 3}$

$4(-6 - 3) = 9(y - 8)$

$-36 = 9y - 72$

$36 = 9y$

$y = 4$

12. $m = \dfrac{y_2 - y_1}{x_2 - x_1}$

$-\dfrac{7}{3} = \dfrac{3 - (-4)}{x - 4}$

$-7(x - 4) = 3(3 + 4)$

$-7x + 28 = 21$

$-7x = -7$

$x = 1$

13. The student found the correct decrease, \$3, but divided the amount of change by the new price instead of the original price when finding the percent change.

14. $\begin{vmatrix} -5 & 2 \\ 1 & -3 \end{vmatrix} = (-5)(-3) - (1)(2)$

$= 15 - 2 = 13$

15. $\begin{vmatrix} 2x & 3 \\ -x - 4 & -1 \end{vmatrix} = 10$

$(2x)(-1) - (-x - 4)(3) = 10$

$-2x - (-3x - 12) = 10$

$-2x + 3x + 12 = 10$

$x = -2$

16. Write each equation in slope-intercept form $y = mx + b$ to graph.

$2x - y = -2$

$-y = -2x - 2$

$y = 2x + 2$

The slope is 2 and the y-intercept is 2.

$2y = 4x - 4$

$y = 2x - 2$

The slope is 2 and the y-intercept is -2.

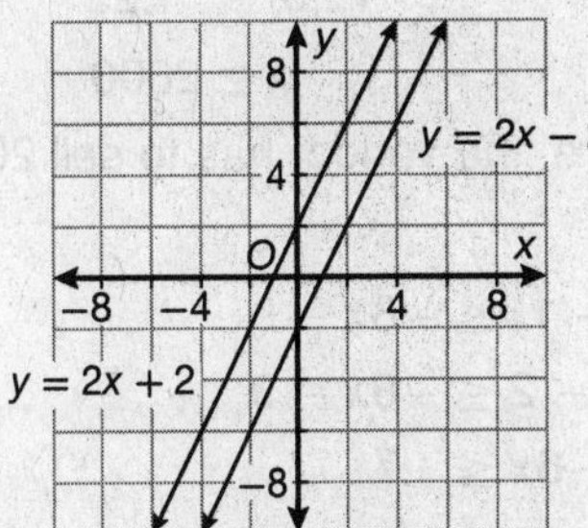

The lines are parallel. There are no points in common, so the system has no solution. The system is inconsistent.

17. The volume of the prism is $2x \cdot 2x \cdot h = 4x^2h$. The radius of the cylinder is x, so the volume of the cylinder is $\pi x^2 h$.

The amount to cut is $4x^2h - \pi x^2 h$ or $x^2h(4 - \pi)$ cubic units.

18. $CR = k$

$0.01(1200) = k$ Substitute the value of the current and resistance to find the constant, k.

$k = 12$

$0.1R = 12$ Substitute the value of the current and the constant to find the resistance.

$R = 120$

The resistance is 120 ohms.

19. Let d represent the number of miles between Cortez and Rock Springs.

The equation is $410 + d + 180 = 955$.

$$410 + d + 180 = 955$$
$$d + 590 = 955$$
$$d = 365$$

The distance between Cortez and Rock Springs is 365 miles.

20. Each x-value is squared to get the y-value.

$f(x) = x^2$.

21. Let x represent the number of snow cones the vendor has to sell.

The inequality is $1.25x \geq 2500$.

$$1.25x \geq 2500$$
$$\frac{1.25x}{1.25} \geq \frac{2500}{1.25}$$
$$x \geq 2000$$

Therefore, the vendor has to sell 2000 snow cones.

22. $-2(7x + 1) \leq -8x - 9$

$$-14x - 2 \leq -8x - 9$$
$$-6x \leq -7$$
$$\frac{-6x}{-6} \geq \frac{-7}{-6}$$
$$x \geq \frac{7}{6}$$

Check.

$-2(7(2) + 1) \leq -8(2) - 9$ Replace x with 2.

$$-2(15) \leq -16 - 9$$
$$-30 \leq -25$$

The solution is correct.

23. $\begin{bmatrix} 7 & 5 & 4 \\ 6 & 7 & 3 \\ 7 & 4 & 5 \end{bmatrix} \cdot \begin{bmatrix} 3 \\ 5 \\ 10 \end{bmatrix}$

$$= \begin{bmatrix} 7(3) + 5(5) + 4(10) \\ 6(3) + 7(5) + 3(10) \\ 7(3) + 4(5) + 5(10) \end{bmatrix}$$

$$= \begin{bmatrix} 86 \\ 83 \\ 91 \end{bmatrix}$$

Gracie scored the greatest number of points.

24. $AB = \begin{bmatrix} -1 \\ 5 \\ 3 \end{bmatrix} \cdot [-2 \;\; 0 \;\; 2]$

$$= \begin{bmatrix} (-1)(-2) & -1(0) & -1(2) \\ 5(-2) & 5(0) & 5(2) \\ 3(-2) & 3(0) & 3(2) \end{bmatrix}$$

$$= \begin{bmatrix} 2 & 0 & -2 \\ -10 & 0 & 10 \\ -6 & 0 & 6 \end{bmatrix}$$

25. $BA = [-2 \;\; 0 \;\; 2] \cdot \begin{bmatrix} -1 \\ 5 \\ 3 \end{bmatrix}$

$$= [-2(-1) + 0(5) + 2(3)]$$
$$= [8]$$

26. Substitute the coordinates into each equation: $-x + 2y = 6$ and $-3x + 4y = 4$

A $-7 + 2(5) \stackrel{?}{=} 6$ Replace x with 7, y with 5.

$3 \neq 6$

(7, 5) is not a solution.

$-3(7) + 4(5) \stackrel{?}{=} 4$ Replace x with 7, y with 5.

$-12 \neq 4$

(7, 5) is not a solution.

B $-8 + 2(7) \stackrel{?}{=} 6$ Replace x with 8, y with 7.

$6 = 6$

(8, 7) is a solution.

$-3(8) + 4(7) \stackrel{?}{=} 4$ Replace x with 8, y with 7.

$4 = 4$

(8, 7) is a solution.

C $-0 + 2(0) \stackrel{?}{=} 6$ Replace x with 0, y with 0.

$0 \neq 6$

(0, 0) is not a solution.

$-3(0) + 4(0) \stackrel{?}{=} 4$ Replace x with 0, y with 0.

$0 \neq 4$

(0, 0) is not a solution.

D $-(-16) + 2(-11) \stackrel{?}{=} 6$ Replace x with -16, y with -11.

$-6 \stackrel{?}{=} 6$

(−16, −11) is not a solution.

$-3(-16) + 4(-11) \stackrel{?}{=} 4$ Replace x with −16, y with −11.

$4 = 4$

(−16, −11) is a solution.

Only choice **B** has a solution to both equations.

27. Write the equations in slope-intercept form to graph.

$-2x - y = 2$

$-y = 2x + 2$

$y = -2x - 2$

The slope is −2 and the y-intercept is −2.

$3x + 2y = 1$

$2y = -3x + 1$

$y = -\frac{3}{2}x + \frac{1}{2}$

The slope is $-\frac{3}{2}$ and the y-intercept is $\frac{1}{2}$.

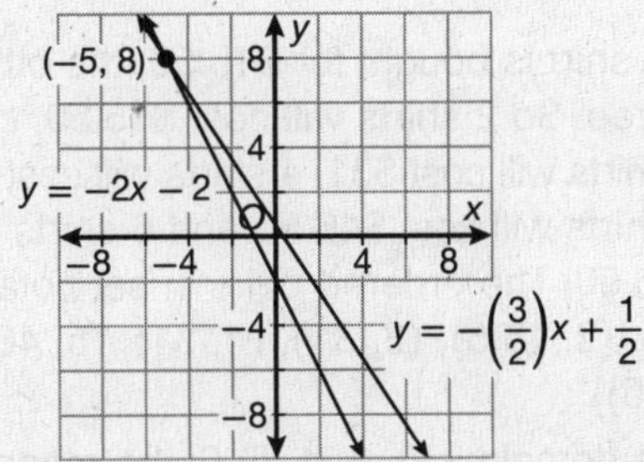

28. The graph consists of two lines intersecting at exactly one point. Since there is exactly one solution, which is the point of intersection, the system is consistent and independent.

29. $S = kF$

$3 = k(8)$ Substitute the values to find the constant, k.

$k = \frac{3}{8}$

$S = \frac{3}{8}(12)$ Replace k and F with their values.

$S = 4.5$

4.5 cups of sugar are used.

30. Divide the amount of garbage by the population.

$$\frac{4.78 \times 10^{11}}{2.99 \times 10^{8}} = \frac{4.78}{2.99} \times \frac{10^{11}}{10^{8}}$$

$$\approx 1.60 \times 10^{3}$$

The average American produced about 1.60×10^3 pounds of garbage.

LESSON 16

Warm Up 16

1. determinant

2. $\begin{vmatrix} 4 & -3 \\ 5 & 2 \end{vmatrix} = 4(2) - (5)(-3)$

$= 8 - (-15) = 23$

3. A table of values for the two equations can solve the system.

Write each equation in the form $y = mx + b$, then substitute values for x and solve for y.

$2x + y = 2$

$y = -2x + 2$

x	y
−1	4
0	2
1	0
2	−2

$4x - y = 10$

$-y = -4x + 10$

$y = 4x - 10$

x	y
−1	−14
0	−10
1	−6
2	−2

When $x = 2$ the y-values are the same for both equations. The solution to the system is (2, −2).

Lesson Practice 16

a. $2x + 2y = 3$

$3x + 8y = 7$

$$x = \frac{\begin{vmatrix} 3 & 2 \\ 7 & 8 \end{vmatrix}}{\begin{vmatrix} 2 & 2 \\ 3 & 8 \end{vmatrix}} = \frac{3(8) - 7(2)}{2(8) - 3(2)}$$

$$= \frac{24 - 14}{16 - 6} = 1$$

$$y = \frac{\begin{vmatrix} 2 & 3 \\ 3 & 7 \end{vmatrix}}{\begin{vmatrix} 2 & 2 \\ 3 & 8 \end{vmatrix}} = \frac{2(7) - 3(3)}{2(8) - 3(2)}$$

$$= \frac{14 - 9}{16 - 6} = \frac{5}{10} = \frac{1}{2}$$

The solution is $\left(1, \frac{1}{2}\right)$.

b. $2y - x = 6$ or $-x + 2y = 6$
$2y - x = -2$ or $-x + 2y = -2$

$$x = \frac{\begin{vmatrix} 6 & 2 \\ -2 & 2 \end{vmatrix}}{\begin{vmatrix} -1 & 2 \\ -1 & 2 \end{vmatrix}} = \frac{6(2) - (-2)(2)}{-1(2) - (-1)(2)}$$

$$= \frac{12 - (-4)}{-2 - (-2)} = \frac{16}{0}$$

$$y = \frac{\begin{vmatrix} -1 & 6 \\ -1 & -2 \end{vmatrix}}{\begin{vmatrix} -1 & 2 \\ -1 & 2 \end{vmatrix}} = \frac{-1(-2) - (-1)(6)}{-1(2) - (-1)(2)}$$

$$= \frac{2 - (-6)}{-2 - (-2)} = \frac{8}{0}$$

Both denominators contain zero and there is no zero in the numerator, so there is no solution.

c. $x + 2y = -4$
$3x + 6y = -12$

$$x = \frac{\begin{vmatrix} 4 & 2 \\ -12 & 6 \end{vmatrix}}{\begin{vmatrix} 1 & 2 \\ 3 & 6 \end{vmatrix}} = \frac{4(6) - (-12)(2)}{1(6) - (3)(2)}$$

$$= \frac{24 - (-24)}{6 - 6} = \frac{48}{0}$$

$$y = \frac{\begin{vmatrix} 1 & -4 \\ 3 & -12 \end{vmatrix}}{\begin{vmatrix} 1 & 2 \\ 3 & 6 \end{vmatrix}} = \frac{1(-12) - (3)(-4)}{1(6) - (3)(2)}$$

$$= \frac{-12 - (-12)}{6 - 6} = \frac{0}{0}$$

Both denominators contain zero, and there is a zero in one numerator, so there is an infinite number of solutions.

d. Using N and O as variables, the equations are
$2N + 4O = 92$
$2N + O = 44$

$$N = \frac{\begin{vmatrix} 92 & 4 \\ 44 & 1 \end{vmatrix}}{\begin{vmatrix} 2 & 4 \\ 2 & 1 \end{vmatrix}} = \frac{92(1) - (44)(4)}{2(1) - (2)(4)}$$

$$= \frac{92 - 176}{2 - 8} = 14$$

$$O = \frac{\begin{vmatrix} 2 & 92 \\ 2 & 44 \end{vmatrix}}{\begin{vmatrix} 2 & 4 \\ 2 & 1 \end{vmatrix}} = \frac{2(44) - (2)(92)}{2(1) - (2)(4)}$$

$$= \frac{88 - 184}{2 - 8} = 16$$

The atomic weight of nitrogen is 14 amu and the atomic weight of oxygen is 16 amu.

Practice 16

1. If 1 shirt is bought for \$15.50, the other is free. So 2 shirts will cost \$15.50, 3 shirts will cost \$31, 4 shirts will cost \$31, 5 shirts will cost \$46.50 and 6 shirts will cost \$46.50. The ordered pairs in set notation are {(2, 15.5), (3, 31), (4, 31), (5, 46.5), (6, 46.5)}

The domain is 2, 3, 4, 5, 6; the range is 15.5, 31, 46.5.

The set of ordered pairs represents a function since for every x-value there is exactly one y-value.

2. a. Equations are inconsistent if they have no solution. The student incorrectly assumed that the equations are inconsistent because there are no matching values in the table.

b. This error can be avoided by graphing the system and determining if the lines intersect.

c. 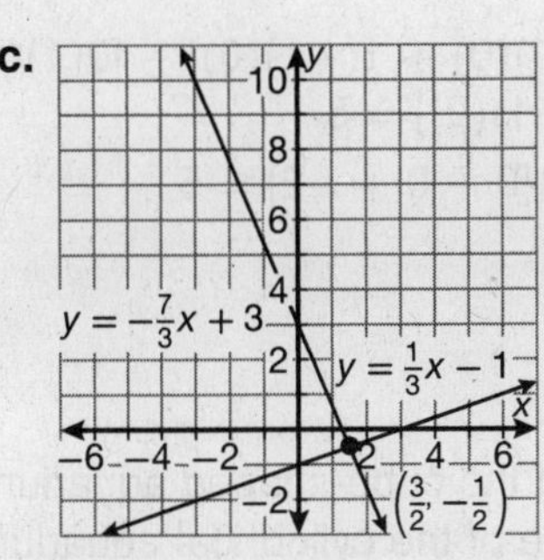

3. 1 USD = 0.77 euro and 1 USD = 1.24 CDN, so 0.77 euros = 1.24 CDN, or 1 euro = $\frac{0.77\text{ CDN}}{1.24}$. Therefore, $f(c) = \frac{0.77c}{1.24}$.

4. Plot the lines by plotting the x- and y-intercepts of each.

$x - 2y = 6$

For the x-intercept let $y = 0$.

$x - 2(0) = 6$, $x = 6$

For the y-intercept let $x = 0$.

$0 - 2y = 6$, $y = -3$

$-6x + 3y = 1$

For the x-intercept let $y = 0$.

$-6x + 3(0) = 1$, $x = -\frac{1}{6}$

$-6x + 3y = 1$

For the y-intercept let $x = 0$.

$-6(0) + 3y = 1$, $y = \frac{1}{3}$

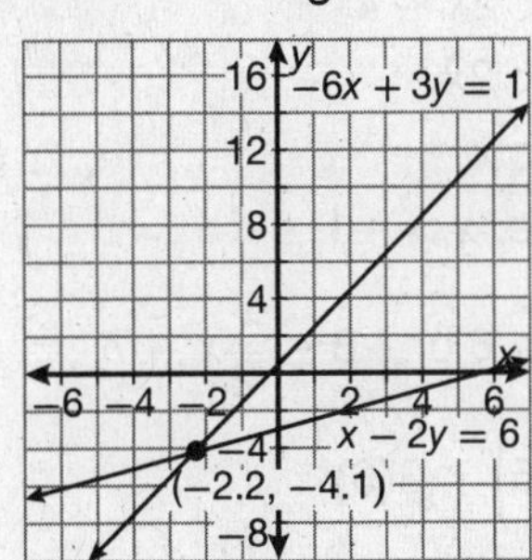

The solution is $(-2.2, -4.1)$

5. a. percent change = $\frac{\text{amount of change}}{\text{original amount}}$

The amount of change is about 500 and the original is about 2000.

$\frac{500}{2000} = \frac{1}{4} = 25\%$

b. $\frac{2080 - 1575}{2080} = \frac{505}{2080}$

$= 0.243 = 24\%$

The actual percent change is a 24% decrease.

6. This is a function, since it passes the vertical line test. The domain is all real numbers equal to and greater than zero, $x \geq 0$. The range is all real numbers equal to and greater than zero, $y \geq 0$.

7. This is not a function, since the same x-value has different y-values. The domain is 2, the range is $-1, 3, 7$.

8. The surface area of the sphere with radius x is $\frac{1}{2}(4\pi x^2) = 2\pi x^2$, since it is half the sphere. The surface area of the cylinder with radius x and height h is

$(2\pi x^2 + 2\pi xh) - \pi x^2 = \pi x^2 + 2\pi xh$,

since the top circle is not included.

The total is $2\pi x^2 + (\pi x^2 + 2\pi xh) = 3\pi x^2 + 2\pi xh$.

9. The number of columns in C does not equal the number of rows in A so it is not possible to multiply.

10. $AB = \begin{vmatrix} 1 & 1 \\ 2 & 3 \end{vmatrix} \cdot \begin{vmatrix} 3 & 2 \\ -1 & 1 \end{vmatrix}$

$= \begin{bmatrix} 1(3) + 1(-1) & 1(2) + 1(1) \\ 2(3) + 3(-1) & 2(2) + 3(1) \end{bmatrix}$

$= \begin{bmatrix} 2 & 3 \\ 3 & 7 \end{bmatrix}$

11. $BC = \begin{bmatrix} 3 & 2 \\ -1 & 1 \end{bmatrix} \cdot \begin{bmatrix} 0 & 2 & 0 \\ 3 & 1 & 4 \end{bmatrix}$

$= \begin{bmatrix} 3(0) + 2(3) & 3(2) + 2(1) & 3(0) + 2(4) \\ -1(0) + 1(3) & -1(2) + 1(1) & -1(0) + 1(4) \end{bmatrix}$

$= \begin{bmatrix} 6 & 8 & 8 \\ 3 & -1 & 4 \end{bmatrix}$

12. $\frac{4}{7} + \frac{x + 2}{3} = \frac{5}{3}$

$21\left(\frac{4}{7} + \frac{x + 2}{3}\right) = 21\left(\frac{5}{3}\right)$

$12 + 7(x + 2) = 35$

$12 + 7x + 14 = 35$

$$7x + 26 = 35$$
$$7x = 9$$
$$x = \frac{9}{7} \text{ or } 1\frac{2}{7}$$

13. $\frac{5}{3} - \frac{x-4}{2} = \frac{1}{2}$

$$6\left(\frac{5}{3} - \frac{x-4}{2}\right) = 6\left(\frac{1}{2}\right)$$
$$10 - 3(x - 4) = 3$$
$$10 - 3x + 12 = 3$$
$$-3x + 22 = 3$$
$$-3x = -19$$
$$x = \frac{19}{3} \text{ or } 6\frac{1}{3}$$

14. $x - 7 + \frac{x}{4} = -\frac{1}{3}$

$$12\left(x - 7 + \frac{x}{4}\right) = 12\left(-\frac{1}{3}\right)$$
$$12x - 84 + 3x = -4$$
$$15x - 84 = -4$$
$$15x = 80$$
$$x = \frac{80}{15} = \frac{16}{3} \text{ or } 5\frac{1}{3}$$

15. a. Find the value of x, which is the number of years after 2005, by making the two populations equal and solving for x.

$2038x + 451{,}743 = 17{,}427x + 386{,}619$

$2038x + 451{,}743 - 451{,}743 = 17{,}427x + 386{,}619 - 451{,}743$

$2038x = 17{,}427x - 65{,}124$

$2038x - 17{,}427x = 17{,}427x - 17{,}427x - 65{,}124$

$-15{,}389x = -65{,}124$

$x \approx 4.2$

Therefore, about 4 years after 2005, or in 2009, the populations will be the same.

b. Replace x with 4 in one of the equations and solve for y.

$y = 2038(4) + 451{,}743 = 459{,}895$

Therefore, the population will be about 460,000.

16. $\begin{vmatrix} x & 2 & 1 & x & 2 \\ -1 & 1 & 0 & -1 & 1 \\ 0 & 0 & 1 & 0 & 0 \end{vmatrix} = 5$

$[x(1)(1) + 2(0)(0) + 1(-1)(0)] - [0(1)(1) + 0(0)(x) + 1(-1)(2)] = 5$

$[x + 0 + 0] - [0 + 0 + -2] = 5$

$x - (-2) = 5$

$x + 2 = 5$

$x = 3$

17. The volume of the cube-shaped aquarium is x^3. The volume of the cylindrical aquarium is $\pi\left(\frac{1}{2}x\right)^2 x = \frac{1}{4}\pi x^2 x = \frac{1}{4}\pi x^3$.

The difference is

$x^3 - \frac{1}{4}\pi x^3$

or

$x^3\left(1 - \frac{1}{4}\pi\right)$

or

$x^3\left(1 - \frac{\pi}{4}\right)$

18. A number cannot be greater than -1 and at the same time be less than -10.

19. $3x + 1 > -2$ or $6 < 2x - 4$

$3x + 1 > -2$

$3x > -3$

$x > -1$

or

$6 < 2x - 4$

$10 < 2x$

$5 < x$

Therefore, $x > -1$

20. $\frac{1}{3}x + 5 \leq 6$ or $-8 \leq \frac{1}{2}x - 7$

$3\left(\frac{1}{3}x + 5\right) \leq 3(6)$

$x + 15 \leq 18$

$x \leq 3$

or

$-8 \leq \frac{1}{2}x - 7$

$2(-8) \leq 2\left(\frac{1}{2}x - 7\right)$

$-16 \leq x - 14$

$-2 \leq x$

Therefore, $-2 \leq x \leq 3$

21. Let l be the cost of the large tiles and s be the cost of the small tiles.

$416l + 256s = 233.6$

$400l + 512s = 251.2$

Next, solve the systems.

$$l = \frac{\begin{vmatrix} 233.6 & 256 \\ 251.2 & 512 \end{vmatrix}}{\begin{vmatrix} 416 & 256 \\ 400 & 512 \end{vmatrix}}$$

$$= \frac{233.6(512) - 251.2(256)}{416(512) - 400(256)}$$

$$= \frac{119{,}603.2 - 64{,}307.2}{212{,}992 - 102{,}400}$$

$$= \frac{55{,}296}{110{,}592} = 0.5$$

$$s = \frac{\begin{vmatrix} 416 & 233.6 \\ 400 & 251.2 \end{vmatrix}}{\begin{vmatrix} 416 & 256 \\ 400 & 512 \end{vmatrix}}$$

$$= \frac{416(251.2) - 400(233.6)}{416(512) - 400(256)}$$

$$= \frac{104{,}499.2 - 93{,}440}{212{,}992 - 102{,}400}$$

$$= \frac{11{,}059.2}{110{,}592} = 0.1$$

Each large tile cost \$0.50 and each small tile cost \$0.10.

22. $$x = \frac{\begin{vmatrix} 8 & 4 \\ 4 & 4 \end{vmatrix}}{\begin{vmatrix} -3 & 4 \\ 1 & 4 \end{vmatrix}} = \frac{8(4) - 4(4)}{-3(4) - 1(4)}$$

$$= \frac{32 - 16}{-12 - 4} = \frac{16}{-16} = -1$$

$$y = \frac{\begin{vmatrix} -3 & 8 \\ 1 & 4 \end{vmatrix}}{\begin{vmatrix} -3 & 4 \\ 1 & 4 \end{vmatrix}} = \frac{-3(4) - 1(8)}{-3(4) - 1(4)}$$

$$= \frac{-12 - 8}{-12 - 4} = \frac{-20}{-16} = 1.25$$

The solution is $(-1, 1.25)$.

23. $$x = \frac{\begin{vmatrix} 8 & 5 \\ 4 & 5 \end{vmatrix}}{\begin{vmatrix} -3 & 5 \\ -3 & 5 \end{vmatrix}} = \frac{8(5) - 4(5)}{-3(5) - (-3)(5)}$$

$$= \frac{40 - 20}{-15 - (-15)} = \frac{20}{0}$$

$$y = \frac{\begin{vmatrix} -3 & 8 \\ -3 & 4 \end{vmatrix}}{\begin{vmatrix} -3 & 5 \\ -3 & 5 \end{vmatrix}} = \frac{-3(4) - (-3)(8)}{-3(5) - (-3)(5)}$$

$$= \frac{-12 - (-24)}{-15 - (-15)} = \frac{12}{0}$$

The denominators are zeros, so there is no solution.

24. $$x = \frac{\begin{vmatrix} 10 & 4 \\ -25 & -10 \end{vmatrix}}{\begin{vmatrix} 2 & 4 \\ -5 & -10 \end{vmatrix}} = \frac{10(-10) - (-25)(4)}{2(-10) - (-5)(4)}$$

$$= \frac{-100 - (-100)}{-20 - (-20)} = \frac{0}{0}$$

$$y = \frac{\begin{vmatrix} 2 & 10 \\ -5 & -25 \end{vmatrix}}{\begin{vmatrix} 2 & 4 \\ -5 & -10 \end{vmatrix}} = \frac{2(-25) - (-5)(10)}{2(-10) - (-5)(4)}$$

$$= \frac{-50 - (-50)}{-20 - (-20)} = \frac{0}{0}$$

Both the denominators and numerators are zero, so there are infinitely many solutions.

25. For the equations in the form $ax + by = e$ and $cx + dy = f$, the solution is

$$x = \frac{\begin{vmatrix} e & b \\ f & d \end{vmatrix}}{\begin{vmatrix} a & b \\ c & d \end{vmatrix}} \text{ and } y = \frac{\begin{vmatrix} a & e \\ c & f \end{vmatrix}}{\begin{vmatrix} a & b \\ c & d \end{vmatrix}}$$

Choice **C** is correct.

26. The system could be consistent and the lines parallel. Or the system could be dependent and consistent, and the lines coincide.

27. $$A = \frac{1}{4}\begin{vmatrix} 2 & 8 & 8 & 4 \\ 2 & 2 & 6 & 8 \\ 1 & 1 & 1 & 1 \\ -1 & 1 & -1 & 1 \end{vmatrix}$$

$$= \frac{1}{4}(104) = 26 \text{ square units}$$

28. $3x - \frac{1}{2}y = 6$

For the x-intercept, let $y = 0$.

$$3x - \frac{1}{2}(0) = 6$$
$$3x = 6$$
$$x = 2$$

For the y-intercept, let $x = 0$.

$$3(0) - \frac{1}{2}y = 6$$
$$-\frac{1}{2}y = 6$$
$$y = -12$$

The x-intercept is (2, 0) and the y-intercept is (0, −12).

29. a. $A = \begin{bmatrix} 29.7 & 29.9 & 32.6 & 37.3 & 43.5 & 49.2 \\ 21.9 & 24.8 & 29.8 & 37.7 & 45.8 & 52.2 \end{bmatrix}$

b. $\frac{5}{9}\left(\begin{bmatrix} 29.7 & 29.9 & 32.6 & 37.3 & 43.5 & 49.2 \\ 21.9 & 24.8 & 29.8 & 37.7 & 45.8 & 52.2 \end{bmatrix} + \begin{bmatrix} -32 & -32 & -32 & -32 & -32 & -32 \\ -32 & -32 & -32 & -32 & -32 & -32 \end{bmatrix}\right)$

$= \frac{5}{9}\begin{bmatrix} -2.3 & -2.1 & 0.6 & 5.3 & 11.5 & 17.2 \\ -10.1 & -7.2 & -2.2 & 5.7 & 13.8 & 20.2 \end{bmatrix}$

$= \begin{bmatrix} -1.3 & -1.2 & 0.3 & 2.9 & 6.4 & 9.6 \\ -5.6 & -4 & -1.2 & 3.2 & 7.7 & 11.2 \end{bmatrix}$

30. a. $m = \frac{\text{rise}}{\text{run}} = \frac{15}{25} = \frac{3}{5}$

b. $\frac{3}{5} = \frac{450}{x}$

$$3x = 2250$$
$$x = 750 \text{ ft}$$

LAB 4

Graphing Calculator Practice

1.

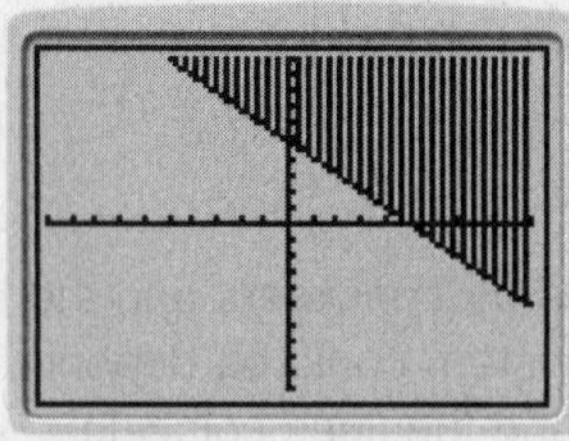

2.

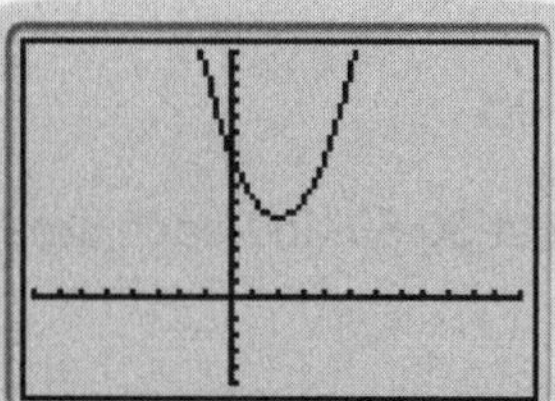

3.

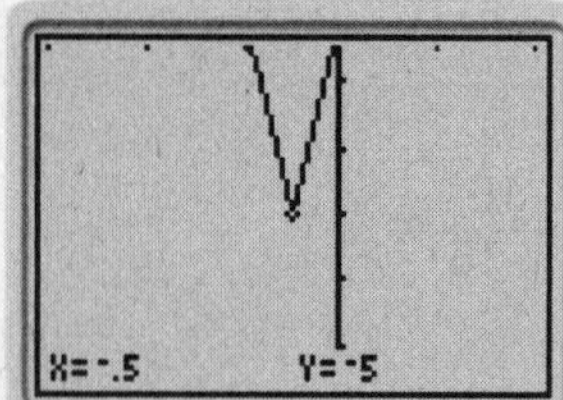

LESSON 17

Warm Up 17

1. conjunction
2. The solution is the overlap for $x \geq -1$ and $x \leq 4$. The solution is $-1 \leq x \leq 4$.

3. The solution includes both $x \geq -1$ and $x \leq 4$. The solution is all real numbers.

Lesson Practice 17

a. $|x + 3| = 7$

$x + 3 = 7$ or $x + 3 = -7$

$x + 3 = 7$

$x = 4$

or

$x + 3 = -7$

$x = -10$

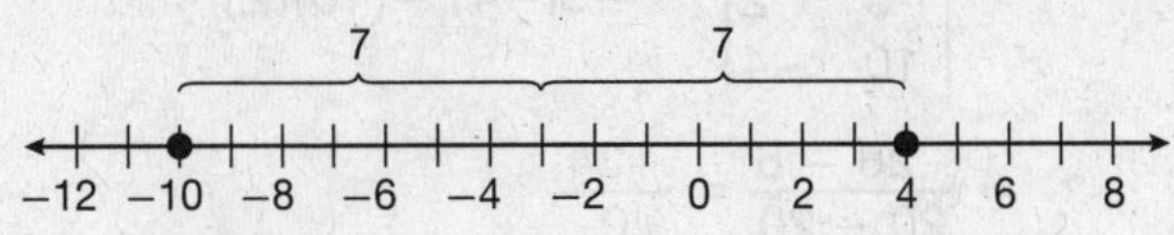

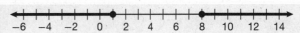

Check.

$|4 + 3| = |7| = 7$

$|-10 + 3| = |-7| = 7$

The solutions are 4 and −10.

b. $|3x - 3| + 5 = 8$

$|3x - 3| = 3$

$3x - 3 = 3$ or $3x - 3 = -3$

$3x - 3 = 3$

$3x = 6$

$x = 2$

$3x - 3 = -3$

$3x = 0$

$x = 0$

Check.

$|3(2) - 3| + 5 \stackrel{?}{=} 8$

$|6 - 3| \stackrel{?}{=} 3$

$3 = 3$

$|3(0) - 3| + 5 \stackrel{?}{=} 8$

$|0 - 3| \stackrel{?}{=} 3$

$3 = 3$

The solutions are 2 and 0.

c. $|7x - 2| = -8$

There is no solution. The absolute value of a number is never negative, as it represents distance.

d. $|4x - 1| = 2x$

$4x - 1 = 2x$ or $4x - 1 = -2x$

$4x - 1 = 2x$

$-1 = -2x$

$\frac{1}{2} = x$ or

$4x - 1 = -2x$

$-1 = -6x$

$\frac{1}{6} = x$

Check.

Evaluate $|4x - 1| = 2x$ for $x = \frac{1}{2}$ and $x = \frac{1}{6}$.

$\left|4\left(\frac{1}{2}\right) - 1\right| \stackrel{?}{=} 2\left(\frac{1}{2}\right)$

$|2 - 1| \stackrel{?}{=} 1$

$1 = 1$

$\left|4\left(\frac{1}{6}\right) - 1\right| \stackrel{?}{=} 2\left(\frac{1}{6}\right)$

$\left|\frac{2}{3} - 1\right| \stackrel{?}{=} \frac{1}{3}$

$\frac{1}{3} = \frac{1}{3}$

The solutions are $\frac{1}{2}$ and $\frac{1}{6}$.

e. $|x + 2| < 8$

$x + 2 < 8$ and $x + 2 > -8$

$x < 6$ and $x > -10$

$-10 < x < 6$

−12 −10 −8 −6 −4 −2 0 2 4 6 8

f. $3|5x| - 6 \leq 6$

$3|5x| \leq 12$

$|5x| \leq 4$

$5x \leq 4$ and $5x \geq -4$

$x \leq \frac{4}{5}$ and $x \geq -\frac{4}{5}$

g. $|-2x + 9| \geq 7$

$-2x + 9 \geq 7$ or $-2x + 9 \leq -7$

$-2x \geq -2$

$x \leq 1$ or

$-2x + 9 \leq -7$

$-2x \leq -16$

$x \geq 8$

$x \leq 1$ or $x \geq 8$

−6 −4 −2 0 2 4 6 8 10 12 14

h. $-|2x + 3| \le 5$

$|2x + 3| \ge -5$

Since the absolute value of an expression is always greater than or equal to zero, all real numbers satisfy the inequality.

i. Let t represent temperature.

$|t - (-333)| = 13$

$|t + 333| = 13$

$t + 333 = 13$ or $t + 333 = -13$

$t = -320$ or $t = -346$

−350 −345 −340 −335 −330 −325 −320 −315 −310 −305 −300

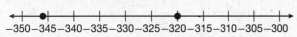

The least temperature is −346°F and the greatest temperature is −320°F.

Practice 17

1. Let t represent thickness of the rope.

$$\left|t - 1\frac{3}{4}\right| = \frac{3}{8}$$

$$t - 1\frac{3}{4} = \frac{3}{8} \text{ or } t - 1\frac{3}{4} = -\frac{3}{8}$$

$$t = 2\frac{1}{8} \text{ or } t = 1\frac{3}{8}$$

The minimum safe thickness is $1\frac{3}{8}$ inches.

2. $m = \dfrac{5 - (-7)}{3 - 3} = \dfrac{12}{0}$

The denominator results in zero when the coordinates are substituted into the slope formula. These points lie on a vertical line.

3. Isolating the absolute value expression results in $|x - 7| \ge -4$. This absolute value expression is greater than a negative number. Since absolute value is always positive, x can be replaced with any number and the inequality will be true.

4. $$x = \frac{\begin{vmatrix} 6 & -2 \\ 15 & -5 \end{vmatrix}}{\begin{vmatrix} 4 & -2 \\ 10 & -5 \end{vmatrix}} = \frac{6(-5) - (15)(-2)}{4(-5) - (10)(-2)}$$

$$= \frac{-30 - (-30)}{-20 - (-20)} = \frac{0}{0}$$

$$y = \frac{\begin{vmatrix} 4 & 6 \\ 10 & 15 \end{vmatrix}}{\begin{vmatrix} 4 & -2 \\ 10 & -5 \end{vmatrix}} = \frac{4(15) - (10)(6)}{4(-5) - (10)(-2)}$$

$$= \frac{60 - 60}{-20 - (-20)} = \frac{0}{0}$$

The denominators are zeros, and there are zeros in the numerators, so there are infinitely many solutions.

5. $$x = \frac{\begin{vmatrix} 7 & 2 \\ 3 & -4 \end{vmatrix}}{\begin{vmatrix} -5 & 2 \\ 10 & -4 \end{vmatrix}} = \frac{7(-4) - (3)(2)}{-5(-4) - (10)(2)}$$

$$= \frac{-28 - 6}{20 - 20} = \frac{-34}{0}$$

$$y = \frac{\begin{vmatrix} -5 & 7 \\ 10 & 3 \end{vmatrix}}{\begin{vmatrix} -5 & 2 \\ 10 & -4 \end{vmatrix}} = \frac{-5(3) - (10)(7)}{-5(-4) - (10)(2)}$$

$$= \frac{-15 - 70}{20 - 20} = \frac{-85}{0}$$

The denominators are zeros. Therefore, there is no solution.

6. $$x = \frac{\begin{vmatrix} 4 & 2 \\ 10 & 2 \end{vmatrix}}{\begin{vmatrix} -3 & 2 \\ 1 & 2 \end{vmatrix}} = \frac{4(2) - (10)(2)}{-3(2) - (1)(2)}$$

$$= \frac{-12}{-8} = \frac{3}{2} \text{ or } 1.5$$

$$y = \frac{\begin{vmatrix} -3 & 4 \\ 1 & 10 \end{vmatrix}}{\begin{vmatrix} -3 & 2 \\ 1 & 2 \end{vmatrix}} = \frac{-3(10) - (1)(4)}{-3(2) - (1)(2)}$$

$$= \frac{-34}{-8} = \frac{17}{4} \text{ or } 4.25$$

The solution is (1.5, 4.25).

7. Replace the variables in the system with the coordinates to determine the solution.

A Replace x with 1 and y with 1.

$2(1) - 5(1) \stackrel{?}{=} -3$

$-3 = -3$

$-10(1) + 25(1) \stackrel{?}{=} 15$

$15 = 15$

(1, 1) is a solution.

B Replace x with 0 and y with 0.

$2(0) - 5(0) \stackrel{?}{=} -3$

$0 \neq -3$

$-10(0) + 25(0) \stackrel{?}{=} 15$

$0 \neq 15$

(0, 0) is not a solution.

C Replace x with 6 and y with 3.

$2(6) - 5(3) \stackrel{?}{=} -3$

$-3 = -3$

$-10(6) + 25(3) \stackrel{?}{=} 15$

$15 = 15$

(6, 3) is a solution.

D Choice **B**, (0, 0), is not a solution, so this answer is incorrect.

Choice **B** is the correct choice.

8. $\begin{bmatrix} 1 & 0 & -2 \\ 0 & 3 & -1 \\ 2 & 0 & 4 \end{bmatrix} \cdot \begin{bmatrix} 4 & -3 \\ 1 & 2 \\ 0 & -1 \end{bmatrix}$

$$= \begin{bmatrix} 1(4) + 0(1) + (-2)(0) & 1(-3) + 0(2) + (-2)(-1) \\ 0(4) + 3(1) + (-1)(0) & 0(-3) + 3(2) + (-1)(-1) \\ 2(4) + 0(1) + 4(0) & 2(-3) + 0(2) + 4(-1) \end{bmatrix} = \begin{bmatrix} 4 & -1 \\ 3 & 7 \\ 8 & -10 \end{bmatrix}$$

9. $[2 \quad -3 \quad 1 \quad -2]$ g $\begin{bmatrix} 0 & 1 \\ -3 & 2 \\ 1 & 0 \\ 4 & 6 \end{bmatrix}$

$= [2(0) + (-3)(-3) + 1(1) + (-2)(4) \quad 2(1) + (-3)(2) + 1(0) + (-2)(6)]$

$= [2 \quad -16]$

10. a. Let T represent temperature and t represent time.

$T = kt$

$80 = k(120)$

$k = \frac{80}{120} = \frac{2}{3}$

b. $T = \frac{2}{3}(240)$

$T = 160$

The temperature is 160 degrees when time = 240 seconds.

c. $T = \frac{2}{3}(360)$

$T = 240$

The temperature is 240 degrees when time = 360 seconds

11. The slope is m when the equation is in the form $y = mx + b$.

$2x + 9y = 18$

$9y = -2x + 18$

$y = -\frac{2}{9} + 2$

The slope is $-\frac{2}{9}$.

Choice **D** is correct.

12. a. For Pitcher A:

$$1620 = k(90)^2$$
$$1620 = 8100k$$
$$k = 0.2$$

For Pitcher B:

$$2025 = k(90)^2$$
$$2025 = 8100k$$
$$k = 0.25$$

b. The force for Pitcher B was greater to produce the same ball speed, so Pitcher B was throwing the ball harder.

c. Sample: The weather could be a factor in wind resistance.

13. $x = \dfrac{\begin{vmatrix} 0 & 3 \\ 6 & 3 \end{vmatrix}}{\begin{vmatrix} -2 & 3 \\ 1 & 3 \end{vmatrix}} = \dfrac{0(3) - (6)(3)}{-2(3) - (1)(3)}$

$= \dfrac{0 - 18}{-6 - 3} = \dfrac{-18}{-9} = 2$

$y = \dfrac{\begin{vmatrix} -2 & 0 \\ 1 & 6 \end{vmatrix}}{\begin{vmatrix} -2 & 3 \\ 1 & 3 \end{vmatrix}} = \dfrac{-2(6) - (1)(0)}{-2(3) - (1)(3)}$

$= \dfrac{-12 - 0}{-6 - 3} = \dfrac{-12}{-9} = \dfrac{4}{3}$

The solution is $\left(2, \frac{4}{3}\right)$.

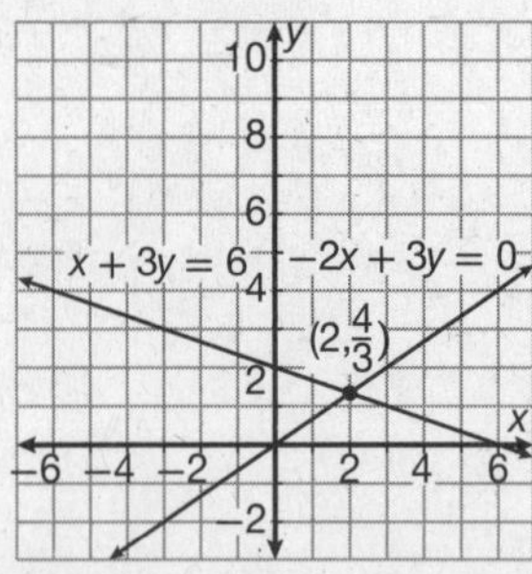

14. The polynomials have the same degree, 5. The monomial with the greatest degree in the first polynomial is ab^4, which has a degree of 5. The monomial with the greatest degree in the second polynomial is a^2b^3, which also has a degree of 5.

15. $\dfrac{y-2}{4} = 7y - 2 - 6(y + 1)$

$\dfrac{y-2}{4} = 7y - 2 - 6y - 6$

$\dfrac{y-2}{4} = y - 8$

$4\left(\dfrac{y-2}{4}\right) = 4(y - 8)$

$y - 2 = 4y - 32$

$-3y = -30$

$y = 10$

The solution is $y = 10$.

16. $2 + \frac{1}{3}x \le 1\frac{2}{3}$ and $-2x - 5 \le 7$

$\frac{1}{3}x \le -\frac{1}{3}$ $\quad$ $-2x \le 12$

$x \le -1$ $\quad$ $x \ge -6$

The solution is $-6 \le x \le -1$.

17. $-\frac{1}{3} - \frac{2x}{3} > \frac{1}{3}$ and $-7x - \frac{1}{2} < 6\frac{1}{2}$

$-\frac{2x}{3} > \frac{2}{3}$ $\quad$ $-7x < 7$

$x < -1$ $\quad$ $x > -1$

Since x cannot be greater than -1 and less than -1, there is no solution.

18. $|-2x + 7| - 3 = 10$

$|-2x + 7| = 13$

$-2x + 7 = 13$ or $-2x + 7 = -13$

$-2x + 7 = 13$

$-2x = 6$

$x = -3$

or

$-2x + 7 = -13$

$-2x = -20$

$x = 10$

The solution is $x = -3$ or $x = 10$.

19. $|8x - 3| = 16x$

$8x - 3 = 16x$ or $8x - 3 = -16x$

$8x - 3 = 16x$

$-3 = 8x$

$x = -\frac{3}{8}$

or

$8x - 3 = -16x$

$-3 = -24x$

$x = \dfrac{-3}{-24} = \dfrac{1}{8}$

Check.
Evaluate $|8x-3| = 16x$ for $x = -\frac{3}{8}$ and $x = \frac{1}{8}$.

$$\left|8\left(-\frac{3}{8}\right) - 3\right| \stackrel{?}{=} 16\left(-\frac{3}{8}\right)$$
$$|-3-3| \stackrel{?}{=} -6$$
$$|6| \neq -6$$
$$\left|8\left(\frac{1}{8}\right) - 3\right| \stackrel{?}{=} 16\left(\frac{1}{8}\right)$$
$$|1-3| \stackrel{?}{=} 2$$
$$|-2| = 2$$

The solution is $x = \frac{1}{8}$; $-\frac{3}{8}$ is extraneous.

20. $|3x+2| \leq 14$

$3x + 2 \leq 14$ and $3x + 2 \geq -14$

$$3x + 2 \leq 14$$
$$3x \leq 12$$
$$x \leq 4$$

and

$$3x + 2 \geq -14$$
$$3x \geq -16$$
$$x \geq -\frac{16}{3}$$
$$-\frac{16}{3} \leq x \leq 4$$

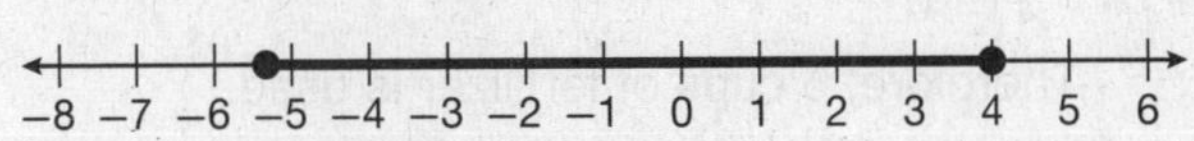

21. a. Find the x- and y-intercepts to graph each equation.

$3x - 2y = 2$

$3x - 2(0) = 2$ For the x-intercept, let $y = 0$.

$3x = 2$

$x = \frac{2}{3}$

$3(0) - 2y = 2$ For the y-intercept, let $x = 0$.

$-2y = 2$

$y = -1$

$-3x - 2y = -34$

$-3x - 2(0) = -34$ For the x-intercept, let $y = 0$.

$-3x = -34$

$x = \frac{34}{3} = 11\frac{1}{3}$

$-3(0) - 2y = -34$ For the y-intercept, let $x = 0$.

$-2y = -34$

$y = 17$

$x - 2y = 6$

$x - 2(0) = 6$ For the x-intercept, let $y = 0$.

$x = 6$

$0 - 2y = 6$ For the y-intercept, let $x = 0$.

$-2y = 6$

$y = -3$

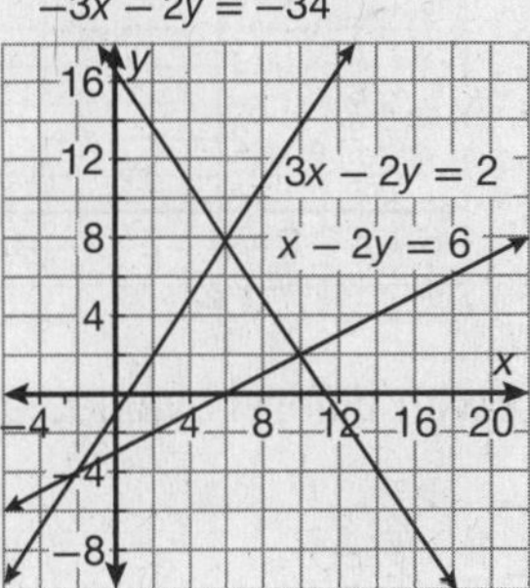

The lines enclose a triangle.

b. The vertices are the points of intersection of the lines. The vertices are (6, 8), (10, 2), and (–2, –4).

22. $\frac{1}{2}\begin{vmatrix} 1 & 1 & 4 \\ 2 & -4 & -4 \\ 1 & 1 & 1 \end{vmatrix}$

$= \frac{1}{2}\left[1\begin{vmatrix} -4 & -4 \\ 1 & 1 \end{vmatrix} - 1\begin{vmatrix} 2 & -4 \\ 1 & 1 \end{vmatrix} + 4\begin{vmatrix} 2 & -4 \\ 1 & 1 \end{vmatrix}\right]$

$= \frac{1}{2}[1[(-4)(1) - (1)(-4)] - 1[(2)(1) - (1)(-4)] + 4[(2)(1) - (1)(-4)]$

$= \frac{1}{2}[1(0)] - 1[6] + 4[6]$

$= \frac{1}{2}[18]$

$= 9$

The area of the triangle is 9 square units.

23. Replace x with different values and solve for y.

$y = -\frac{5}{3}x - 2$

For $x = -3$, $y = -\frac{5}{3}(-3) - 2 = 3$

For $x = 0$, $y = -\frac{5}{3}(0) - 2 = -2$

For $x = 3$, $y = -\frac{5}{3}(3) - 2 = -7$

x	y
−3	3
0	−2
3	−7

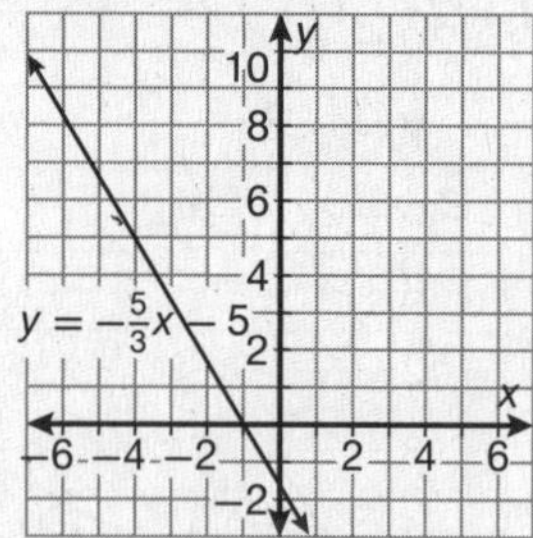

24. Replace x with different values and solve for y.

$y = -\frac{1}{2}x + 5$

For $x = -2$, $y = -\frac{1}{2}(-2) + 5 = 6$

For $x = 0$, $y = -\frac{1}{2}(0) + 5 = 5$

For $x = 2$, $y = -\frac{1}{2}(2) + 5 = 4$

x	y
−2	6
0	5
2	4

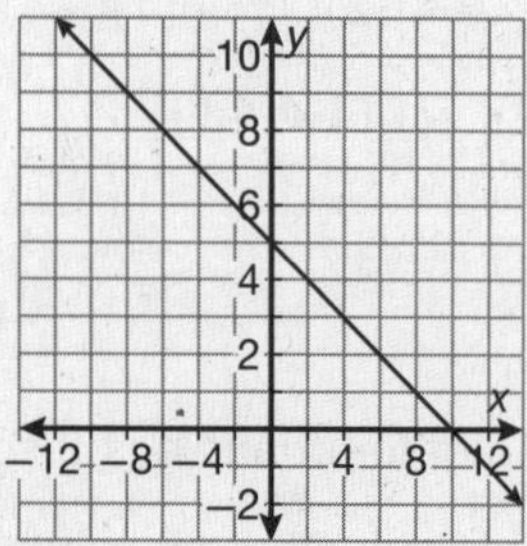

25. Use a graphing calculator to find the determinant. The determinant is −1005.

26. The earth travels once around the sun in one year. This orbit is a circle, and the distance around a circle is the circumference. The distance between the sun and the earth is the radius of the circle. So the radius is about 1.495×10^{11} m or $1.495 \times 10^{11} \div 10^3$ km = 1.495×10^8 km.

$C = 2\pi r$

$C = 2\pi(1.495 \times 10^8)$

$= 9.39 \times 10^8$ km

b. $365.25 \text{ day} \times \frac{24 \text{ hr}}{\text{day}} \times \frac{60 \text{ min}}{\text{hr}} \times \frac{60 \text{ s}}{\text{min}}$

$= 3.156 \times 10^7$ s

$\text{rate} = \frac{\text{distance}}{\text{time}} = \frac{9.39 \times 10^8}{3.156 \times 10^7}$

$= 2.975 \times 10$

The average speed is about 29.75 km/s.

27. $m = \frac{1 - (-7)}{2 - (-2)} = \frac{8}{4} = 2$

The slope is positive, so the line rises.

28. $F = kW$

$(2) = k(16)$

$k = \frac{1}{8}$

$F = \frac{1}{8}(48)$

$F = 6$

Therefore, 6 cups of fertilizer is used.

29. If a, b, $c \neq 0$, there is no constant, and no variation.

30. If b and $c = 0$, then $y = ax^2$ and this is a direct variation.

If a and $c = 0$, then $y = bx$ and this is also a direct variation.

LESSON 18

Warm Up 18

1. equivalent

2. $\frac{x^4 \times x^2}{x^3} = \frac{x^{4+2}}{x^3} = \frac{x^6}{x^3} = x^6 \times x^{-3} = x^{6+(-3)} = x^3$

3. $\frac{6}{7} \times \frac{5}{6} \times \frac{3}{5} \times \frac{2}{3} = \frac{2}{7}$

Lesson Practice 18

a. Put 720 in. over 1.

$\frac{720 \text{ in.}}{1}$

There are 12 inches in a foot, so

$$\frac{720 \cancel{\text{in.}}}{1} \times \frac{1 \text{ ft}}{12 \cancel{\text{in.}}} = 60 \text{ ft.}$$

b. Put 6 hr over 1.

$$\frac{6 \text{ hr}}{1}$$

There are 60 minutes in an hour, so

$$\frac{6 \cancel{\text{hr}}}{1} \times \frac{60 \text{ min}}{1 \cancel{\text{hr}}} = 360 \text{ min.}$$

c. Put 52 yd^2 over 1.

$$\frac{52 \text{ yd}^2}{1}$$

There are 3 feet in a yard and 12 inches in a foot, so

$$\frac{52 \cancel{\text{yd}^2}}{1} \times \frac{3 \cancel{\text{ft}}}{1 \cancel{\text{yd}}} \times \frac{3 \cancel{\text{ft}}}{1 \cancel{\text{yd}}} \times \frac{12 \text{ in.}}{1 \cancel{\text{ft}}} \times \frac{12 \text{ in.}}{1 \cancel{\text{ft}}}$$

$$= 67{,}392 \text{ in}^2$$

d. Put 2700 s over 1.

$$\frac{2700 \text{ s}}{1}$$

There are 60 seconds in a minute and 60 minutes in an hour, so

$$\frac{2700 \text{ s}}{1} \times \frac{1 \text{ min}}{60 \text{ s}} \times \frac{1 \text{ hr}}{60 \text{ min}} = \frac{3}{4} \text{ hr or } 0.75 \text{ hr.}$$

e. Write 80 feet per second as a fraction.

$$\frac{80 \text{ ft}}{1 \text{ s}}$$

Convert feet to miles and seconds to hours. There are 5280 feet in a mile. There are 60 seconds in a minute and 60 minutes in an hour, so

$$\frac{80 \cancel{\text{ft}}}{1 \text{ s}} \times \frac{1 \text{ mi}}{5280 \cancel{\text{ft}}} \times \frac{60 \text{ s}}{1 \cancel{\text{min}}} \times \frac{60 \cancel{\text{min}}}{1 \text{ hr}}$$

$$= \frac{80(60)(60) \text{ mi}}{5280 \text{ hr}} = 54.54 \frac{\text{mi}}{\text{hr}} \approx 55 \frac{\text{mi}}{\text{hr}}$$

f. Add the three distances.

6.21 mi + 3.672 mi + 0.8 mi = 10.682 mi

Since 0.8 has one decimal place the answer must be rounded to one decimal place, resulting in 10.7 mi.

g. Multiply the three lengths.

$8.08 \text{ ft} \times 0.020 \text{ ft} \times 407 \text{ ft} = 65.7712 \text{ ft}^3$

Since 0.020 has only two significant digits, the answer can only have two significant digits, resulting in 66 ft^3.

h. Write the given speed as a fraction.

$$\frac{24 \text{ ft}}{1 \text{ s}}$$

One of the conversion factors needs to have ft in its denominator and the other needs s in its numerator.

$$\frac{24 \cancel{\text{ft}}}{1 \cancel{\text{s}}} \times \frac{1 \text{ mi}}{5280 \cancel{\text{ft}}} \times \frac{3600 \cancel{\text{s}}}{1 \text{ hr}}$$

$$= \frac{24(3600) \text{ mi}}{5280 \text{ hr}} \approx 16.4 \frac{\text{mi}}{\text{hr}}$$

The speed is about 16.4 $\frac{\text{mi}}{\text{hr}}$, or 16.4 mph.

Practice 18

1. Write the equations in standard form:

$x - y = 1$

$3x + 2y = 8$

$$x = \frac{\begin{vmatrix} 1 & -1 \\ 8 & 2 \end{vmatrix}}{\begin{vmatrix} 1 & -1 \\ 3 & 2 \end{vmatrix}} = \frac{1(2) - (8)(-1)}{1(2) - (3)(-1)}$$

$$= \frac{2 - (-8)}{2 - (-3)} = \frac{10}{5} = 2$$

$$y = \frac{\begin{vmatrix} 1 & 1 \\ 3 & 8 \end{vmatrix}}{\begin{vmatrix} 1 & -1 \\ 3 & 2 \end{vmatrix}} = \frac{1(8) - (3)(1)}{1(2) - (3)(-1)}$$

$$= \frac{8 - 3}{2 - (-3)} = \frac{5}{5} = 1$$

The solution is (2, 1).

2. $$x = \frac{\begin{vmatrix} 22 & -1 \\ -11 & 3 \end{vmatrix}}{\begin{vmatrix} 3 & -1 \\ 2 & 3 \end{vmatrix}} = \frac{22(3) - (-11)(-1)}{3(3) - (2)(-1)}$$

$$= \frac{66 - 11}{9 - (-2)} = \frac{55}{11} = 5$$

$$y = \frac{\begin{vmatrix} 3 & 22 \\ 2 & -11 \end{vmatrix}}{\begin{vmatrix} 3 & -1 \\ 2 & 3 \end{vmatrix}} = \frac{3(-11) - (2)(22)}{3(3) - (2)(-1)}$$

$$= \frac{-33 - 44}{9 - (-2)} = \frac{-77}{11} = -7$$

The solution is (5, –7).

3. $x = \dfrac{\begin{vmatrix} 20 & 1 \\ 200 & 10 \end{vmatrix}}{\begin{vmatrix} 1 & 1 \\ 5 & 10 \end{vmatrix}} = \dfrac{20(10) - (200)(1)}{1(10) - (5)(1)}$

$= \dfrac{200 - 200}{10 - 5} = \dfrac{0}{5} = 0$

$y = \dfrac{\begin{vmatrix} 1 & 20 \\ 5 & 200 \end{vmatrix}}{\begin{vmatrix} 1 & 1 \\ 5 & 10 \end{vmatrix}} = \dfrac{1(200) - (5)(20)}{1(10) - (5)(1)}$

$= \dfrac{200 - 100}{10 - 5} = \dfrac{100}{5} = 20$

The solution is (0, 20).

4. $-5|2x - 7| - 4 = -34$

$-5|2x - 7| = -30$

$|2x - 7| = 6$

$2x - 7 = 6$ or $2x - 7 = -6$

$2x - 7 = 6$

$2x = 13$

$x = 6.5$

or

$2x - 7 = -6$

$2x = 1$

$x = 0.5$

The solution is $x = 6.5$ or $x = 0.5$.

5. The absolute value of a number cannot be less than a negative number, so there is no solution.

$\left|\frac{1}{2}x + 1\right| \le -\frac{1}{2}$

$\frac{1}{2}x + 1 \le -\frac{1}{2}$ and $\frac{1}{2}x + 1 \ge \frac{1}{2}$

$\frac{1}{2}x \le -1\frac{1}{2}$ $\qquad \frac{1}{2}x \ge -\frac{1}{2}$

$x \le -3$ $\qquad x \ge -1$

There is no solution.

6. $|8 - 3x| > 9$

$8 - 3x > 9$ or $8 - 3x < -9$

$-3x > 1$

$x < -\frac{1}{3}$

$8 - 3x < -9$

$-3x < -17$

$x > \frac{17}{3}$ or $5\frac{2}{3}$

The solution is $x < -\frac{1}{3}$ or $x > 5\frac{2}{3}$.

7. In a direct variation, $\frac{y}{x} = k$, where k is the constant. Since $\frac{y}{x} = \sqrt{2}$, this is a direct variation, and the constant is $\sqrt{2}$.

8. In an inverse variation, $xy = k$, where k is the constant. Since $xy = 15$, this is an inverse variation and the constant is 15.

9. **a.** Let x represent 10% iodine and y represent 50% iodine. Then write an equation for the number of milliliters of each solution in the mixture, and an equation using the percent of each solution in the mixture.

$x + y = 100$

$0.1x + 0.5y = 0.2(100)$

b. The system of equations is

$x + y = 100$

$0.1x + 0.5y = 0.2(100)$

$x = 75,\ y = 25$

Therefore 75 milliliters of 10% iodine and 25 milliliters of 50% iodine are used.

10. As x increases, y decreases. This could be an inverse variation. Check to determine if there is a constant.

$xy = k$

$(1)(4) = 4,\ (2)(2) = 4,\ (3)\left(1\frac{1}{3}\right) = 4,$
$(4)(1) = 4$

The constant of variation is 4. Therefore, this is an inverse variation.

Choice **C** is correct.

11. **a.** Let x represent the number of baskets you make, and y represent the number of baskets your friend makes. Then write an equation for the number of points you have, and an equation for the number of points your friend has.

$2x - y = 16$

$2y - x = 10$

b. Solve the system of equations.

The solution is $x = 14$ and $y = 12$. Therefore, you made 14 baskets and your friend made 12 baskets.

12. As one quantity increases the other increases and as one decreases the other decreases. There is a constant of variation. Therefore, this is direct variation. The equation is $C = \pi d$.

13. The upper right product was subtracted from the lower left product, instead of the other way. The correct determinant is

$$\begin{vmatrix} -2 & 6 \\ 3 & -1 \end{vmatrix} = -2(-1) - 3(6) = 2 - 18$$
$$= -16.$$

14. Put 0.075 hr over 1.

$$\frac{0.075 \text{ hr}}{1}$$

There are 60 minutes in an hour and 60 seconds in a minute, so there are 3600 seconds in an hour.

$$\frac{0.075 \cancel{\text{hr}}}{1} \times \frac{3600 \text{ s}}{1 \cancel{\text{hr}}} = 0.075(3600) \text{ s}$$
$$= 270 \text{ s}$$

15. Put 1224 in^2 over 1.

$$\frac{1224 \text{ in}^2}{1}$$

There are 3 feet in a yard and 12 inches in a foot, so

$$\frac{1224 \cancel{\text{in}^2}}{1} \times \frac{1 \cancel{\text{ft}}}{12 \cancel{\text{in}}} \times \frac{1 \cancel{\text{ft}}}{12 \cancel{\text{in}}} \times \frac{1 \text{ yd}}{3 \cancel{\text{ft}}} \times \frac{1 \text{ yd}}{3 \cancel{\text{ft}}}$$
$$= \frac{1224 \text{ yd}^2}{12(12)(3)(3)} = \frac{17}{18} \text{ yd}^2$$

16. Write 0.26 miles per hour as a fraction.

$$\frac{0.26 \text{ mi}}{1 \text{ hr}}$$

Convert miles to feet and hours to minutes. There are 5280 feet in a mile. There are 60 minutes in an hour, so

$$\frac{0.26 \cancel{\text{mi}}}{1 \cancel{\text{hr}}} \times \frac{5280 \text{ ft}}{1 \cancel{\text{mi}}} \times \frac{1 \cancel{\text{hr}}}{60 \text{ min}}$$
$$= \frac{0.26(5280) \text{ ft}}{60 \text{ min}} = 22.88 \frac{\text{ft}}{\text{min}}$$

17. Write 27,404 feet per second as a fraction. Convert feet to miles, and miles to kilometers; convert seconds to hours. There are 5280 feet in a mile and 1.61 kilometers in a mile. There are 60 minutes in an hour, and 60 seconds in a minute, so there are 3600 seconds in an hour.

$$\frac{27{,}404 \cancel{\text{ft}}}{1 \cancel{\text{s}}} \times \frac{1 \cancel{\text{mi}}}{5280 \cancel{\text{ft}}} \times \frac{1.61 \text{ km}}{1 \cancel{\text{mi}}} \times \frac{3600 \cancel{\text{s}}}{1 \text{ hr}}$$
$$= \frac{27{,}404(1.61)(3600) \text{ km}}{5280 \text{ hr}} \approx 30{,}082 \frac{\text{km}}{\text{hr}}$$

$$\frac{27{,}404 \cancel{\text{ft}}}{1 \cancel{\text{s}}} \times \frac{1 \text{ mi}}{5280 \cancel{\text{ft}}} \times \frac{3600 \cancel{\text{s}}}{1 \text{ hr}}$$
$$= \frac{27{,}404 (3600) \text{ mi}}{5280 \text{ hr}} = 18{,}685 \frac{\text{mi}}{\text{hr}}$$

18. $|2x + 3| = 16x$

$2x + 3 = 16x$ or $2x + 3 = -16x$

$3 = 14x \qquad 3 = -18x$

$x = \frac{3}{14} \qquad x = -\frac{1}{6}$

Check.

$$\left|2\left(\frac{3}{14}\right) + 3\right| \stackrel{?}{=} 16\left(\frac{3}{14}\right)$$
$$3\frac{3}{7} = 3\frac{3}{7}$$

$$\left|2\left(-\frac{1}{6}\right) + 3\right| \stackrel{?}{=} 16\left(-\frac{1}{6}\right)$$
$$2\frac{2}{3} \neq -2\frac{2}{3}$$

Therefore, the solution is $\frac{3}{14}$; $-\frac{1}{6}$ is extraneous.

19. $|-3x + 5| \geq x$

$|-3x + 5| \leq -x$

$-3x + 5 \geq |x|$

$-(-3x + 5) \leq |x|$, which is $3x - 5 \leq |x|$

20. **a.** Let t represent temperature.

$|t - (-332.925)| = 35.845$

$|t + 332.925| = 35.845$

b. $t + 332.925 = 35.845$ or

$t + 332.925 = -35.845$

$t = -297.08$ or $t = -368.77$

The least temperature is −368.77°F and the greatest temperature is −297.08°F.

21. First, find the x-intercept, by replacing y with 0 in the equation and solving for x. Next, find the y-intercept, by replacing x with 0 in the equation and solving for y. Then plot the points for the two intercepts and extend a line through the points with arrowheads at the ends of the line.

22. Sample: $a^6 + a^5 + a^4$ and $a^3 + a^2 + a$
The sum of the two trinomials is
$a^6 + a^5 + a^4 + a^3 + a^2 + a$.

23. $$\begin{vmatrix} \frac{x}{2} & 4 \\ 3 & -10 \end{vmatrix} = -(-x + 7)$$

$$\frac{x}{2}(-10) - (3)(4) = x - 7$$
$$-5x - 12 = x - 7$$
$$-6x = 5$$
$$x = -\frac{5}{6}$$

24. $$\begin{vmatrix} -3 & 2 \\ 4x - 1 & 2x - \frac{1}{3} \end{vmatrix} = -16x + 7$$

$$-3\left(2x - \frac{1}{3}\right) - (4x - 1)(2) = -16x + 7$$
$$-6x + 1 - 8x + 2 = -16x + 7$$
$$2x = 4$$
$$x = 2$$

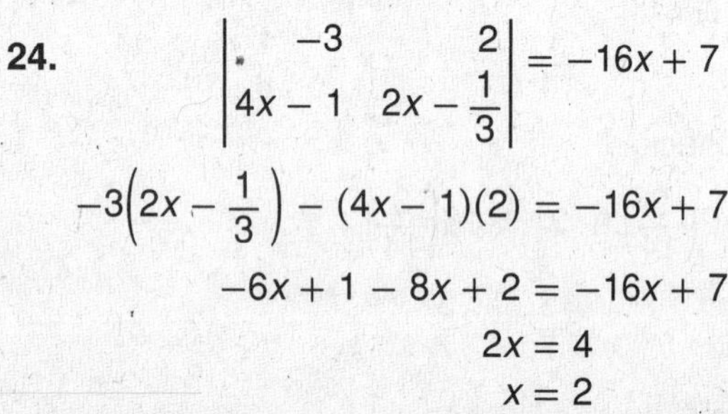

25. Write the equation of the line by replacing the slope and point in the general formula for slope. When the equation of the line is in the form $y = mx + b$, b is the y-intercept.

$$\frac{5}{3} = \frac{y - 1}{x - (-3)}$$
$$3(y - 1) = 5(x + 3)$$
$$3y - 3 = 5x + 15$$
$$3y = 5x + 18$$
$$y = \frac{5}{3}x + 6$$

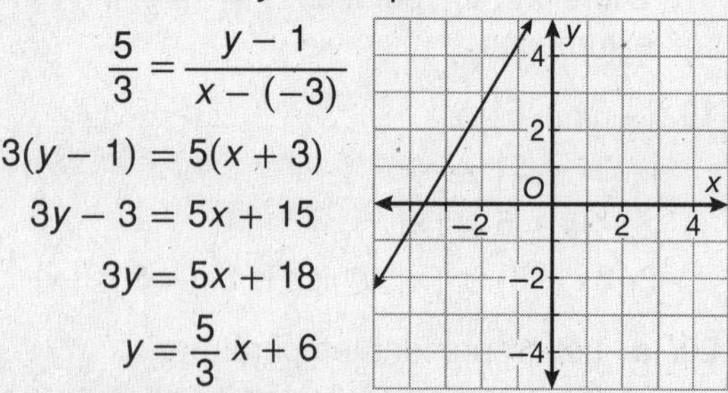

The y-intercept is 6, or (0, 6).

26. Write the equation of the line by replacing the slope and point in the general formula for slope. When the equation of the line is in the form $y = mx + b$, b is the y-intercept.

$$-\frac{4}{5} = \frac{y - (-5)}{x - 5}$$
$$5(y + 5) = -4(x - 5)$$
$$5y + 25 = -4x + 20$$
$$5y = -4x - 5$$
$$y = -\frac{4}{5}x - 1$$

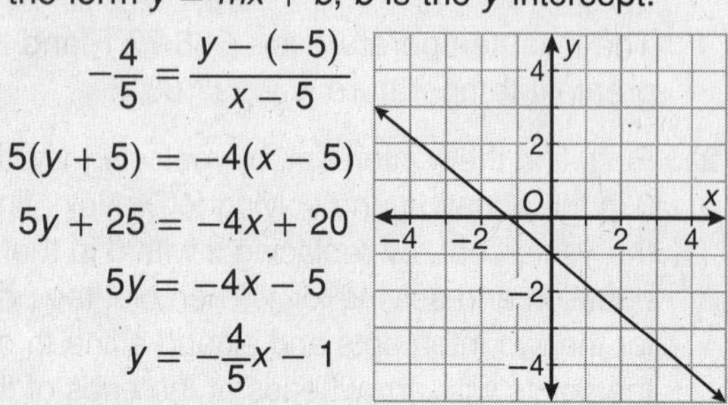

The y-intercept is −1, or (0, −1).

27. Write 29.8 kilometers per second as a fraction.

$$\frac{29.8 \text{ km}}{1 \text{ s}}$$

Convert kilometers to meters and seconds to hours. There are 1000 meters in a kilometer. There are 3600 seconds in an hour, so

$$\frac{29.8 \text{ km}}{1 \text{ s}} \times \frac{1000 \text{ m}}{1 \text{ km}} \times \frac{3600 \text{ s}}{1 \text{ hr}}$$
$$= \frac{29.8(1000)(3600) \text{ m}}{1 \text{ hr}} = 1.073 \times 10^8 \frac{\text{m}}{\text{hr}}$$

28. $$AB = \begin{bmatrix} 6 & -3 \\ 1 & 4 \end{bmatrix} \times \begin{bmatrix} 0 & 4 \\ -2 & 6 \end{bmatrix}$$
$$= \begin{bmatrix} 6(0) + (-3)(-2) & 6(4) + (-3)(6) \\ 1(0) + 4(-2) & 1(4) + 4(6) \end{bmatrix}$$
$$= \begin{bmatrix} 6 & 6 \\ -8 & 28 \end{bmatrix}$$

29. $$BA = \begin{bmatrix} 0 & 4 \\ -2 & 6 \end{bmatrix} \times \begin{bmatrix} 6 & -3 \\ 1 & 4 \end{bmatrix}$$
$$= \begin{bmatrix} 0(6) + 4(1) & 0(-3) + 4(4) \\ -2(6) + 6(1) & -2(-3) + 6(4) \end{bmatrix}$$
$$= \begin{bmatrix} 4 & 16 \\ -6 & 30 \end{bmatrix}$$

30. $$A^2 = \begin{bmatrix} 6 & -3 \\ 1 & 4 \end{bmatrix} \times \begin{bmatrix} 6 & -3 \\ 1 & 4 \end{bmatrix}$$
$$= \begin{bmatrix} 6(6) + (-3)(1) & 6(-3) + (-3)(4) \\ 1(6) + 4(1) & 1(-3) + 4(4) \end{bmatrix}$$
$$= \begin{bmatrix} 33 & -30 \\ 10 & 13 \end{bmatrix}$$

LESSON 19

Warm Up 19

1. coefficient

2. $5(3 + 4) = 5(3) + 5(4) = 15 + 20 = 35$

3. $3x^2 + 5x - 8x^2 - x$
$= 3x^2 - 8x^2 + 5x - x$
$= -5x^2 + 4x$

4. $2a^3 \cdot 3a^3$
$= 2 \cdot 3 \cdot a^3 \cdot a^3$
$= 6a^{3+3}$
$= 6a^6$

Lesson Practice 19

a. $(a + 7)(a - 4)$

F: $a \cdot a = a^2$

O: $a \cdot (-4) = -4a$

I: $7 \cdot a = 7a$

L: $7 \cdot (-4) = -28$

$a^2 - 4a + 7a - 28$ Combine like terms.

$a^2 + 3a - 28$

b. $(4x + 5)(3x - 2)$

F: $4x \cdot 3x = 12x^2$

O: $4x \cdot (-2) = -8x$

I: $5 \cdot 3x = 15x$

L: $5 \cdot (-2) = -10$

$= 12x^2 - 8x + 15x - 10$ Combine like terms.

$= 12x^2 + 7x - 10$

c. $(a + 9)(2a^2 - 6a + 5)$

$= a(2a^2) + a(-6a) + a(5) + 9(2a^2) + 9(-6a) + 9(5)$

$= 2a^3 + (-6a^2) + 5a + 18a^2 + (-54a) + 45$

$= 2a^3 + 12a^2 - 49a + 45$

d. $[(r + 3)(r - 6)](r + 2)$

$(r + 3)(r - 6)$

$= r(r) + r(-6) + 3(r) + 3(-6)$

$= r^2 - 6r + 3r - 18$

$= r^2 - 3r - 18$

$(r + 2)(r^2 - 3r - 18)$

$= r(r^2) + r(-3r) + r(-18) + 2(r^2) + 2(-3r) + 2(-18)$

$= r^3 - 3r^2 - 18r + 2r^2 - 6r - 36$

$= r^3 - r^2 - 24r - 36$

$(r + 3)[(r - 6)(r + 2)]$

$(r - 6)(r + 2)$

$= r(r) + r(2) + (-6)(r) + (-6)(2)$

$= r^2 + 2r - 6r - 12$

$= r^2 - 4r - 12$

$(r + 3)(r^2 - 4r - 12)$

$= r(r^2) + r(-4r) + r(-12) + 3(r^2) + 3(-4r) + 3(-12)$

$= r^3 - 4r^2 - 12r + 3r^2 - 12r - 36$

$= r^3 - r^2 - 24r - 36$

e. $(4y + 3)^2$

$= (4y + 3)(4y + 3)$

$= (4y)^2 + 2(4y)(3) + 3^2$

$= 16y^2 + 24y + 9$

f. $(7a + 3b)(7a - 3b)$

$= (7a)^2 - (3b)^2$

$= 49a^2 - 9b^2$

g. $(5q + 4r)^2$

$= (5q + 4r)(5q + 4r)$

$= (5q)^2 + 2(5q)(4r) + (4r)^2$

$= 25q^2 + 40qr + 16r^2$

h. The area of a rectangle is equal to length times width. The area of the food court is $(x - 15)(x - 12)$.

$(x - 15)(x - 12)$

$x(x) + x(-12) + (-15)x + (-15)(-12)$

$x^2 - 12x - 15x + 180$

$x^2 - 27x + 180$

The area of the food court is $x^2 - 27x + 180$ square yards.

Practice 19

1. Add the three lengths.

25 yd + 7.6 yd + 0.58 yd = 10.43 yd

Since 7.6 has one decimal place the answer must be rounded to one decimal place, resulting in 10.4 yd.

2. Multiply the three lengths.

2.08 ft × 0.033 ft × 15.5 ft = 1.06392 ft^3

Since 0.033 has only two significant digits, the answer can only have two significant digits, resulting in 1.1 ft^3.

3. For a fixed area, such as 120, the length and width can be 1 × 120, 2 × 60, 3 × 40, and so on. As the length increases, the width decreases, or as the length decreases, the width increases. Since $l \times w = A$ and A is a constant, this is an inverse variation. The constant of variation when $A = 25$ is 25.

4. If $r \times t = d$, and d is held constant, then this is an inverse variation.

If $r \times t = d$ and r is held constant, then

$\frac{d}{t} = r$ and this is a direct variation.
If $r \times t = d$ and t is held constant, then
$\frac{d}{r} = t$ and this is a direct variation.

5. Add the three distances.
2.25 mi + 3.2 mi + 2.31 mi = 7.76 mi
Since 3.2 has one decimal place, the answer must be rounded to one decimal place, resulting in 7.8 mi.
Kellie walked 7.8 miles.

6. $|2x + 1| < 4$
$2x + 1 < 4$ and $2x + 1 > -4$
$2x + 1 < 4$
$2x < 3$
$x < \frac{3}{2}$ and
$2x + 1 > -4$
$2x > -5$
$x > -\frac{5}{2}$
The solution is $-\frac{5}{2} < x < \frac{3}{2}$.
Choice **A** is correct.

7. Let x represent the length of each side of the original box. Then its volume is $V = x^3$.
The new box has a base with sides $(x + 1)$ and height $(x - 2)$. Its volume is $V = (x + 1)^2(x - 2)$.
$(x - 2)(x + 1)^2$
$= (x - 2)\left(x^2 + 2(1)(x) + 1^2\right)$
$= (x - 2)(x^2 + 2x + 1)$
$= x(x^2) + x(2x) + x(1) + (-2)x^2$
$+ (-2)(2x) + (-2)(1)$
$= x^3 + 2x^2 + x - 2x^2 - 4x - 2$
$= x^3 - 3x - 2$
The difference between the two volumes:
$x^3 - (x^3 - 3x - 2)$
$= x^3 - x^3 + 3x + 2$
$= 3x + 2$
For any value greater than 2, x^3 is greater than $3x + 2$, therefore the volume decreases for $x > 2$.

8. In the form $y = mx + b$, m is the slope and b is the y-intercept.
$x + 2y = 2$
$2y = -x + 2$
$y = -\frac{1}{2}x + 1$
Graph the equation with y-intercept (0, 1) and slope $-\frac{1}{2}$.
$y = -\frac{1}{2}x - 3$
Graph the equation with y-intercept (0, −3) and slope $-\frac{1}{2}$.

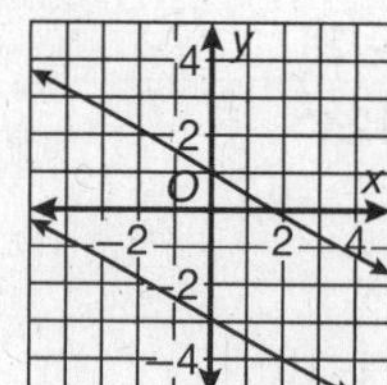

The lines are parallel so they do not intersect. Therefore, the system has no solution.

9. There are 3600 seconds in an hour and 5280 feet in a mile. Convert feet per second to feet per hour, and then feet per hour to miles per hour.
$$\frac{x \text{ ft}}{\text{s}} \times \frac{3600 \text{ s}}{1 \text{ hr}} \times \frac{1 \text{ mi}}{5280 \text{ ft}} = \frac{x(3600) \text{ mi}}{5280 \text{ hr}}$$

10. a. Let x represent water that is 3.5% salt and y represent water that is 25% salt. Then write an equation for the amount of each solution in the mixture, and an equation using the percent of each solution in the mixture.
$x + y = 1600$
$0.035x + 0.25y = 0.15(1600)$

b. The system of equations is
$x + y = 100$
$0.035x + 0.25y = 0.15(1600)$
$x = 744,\ y = 856$
Therefore, the chemist will use about 744 mL of ocean water.

11. a. As x increases, y increases. This could be a direct variation. The constant of variation is $\frac{y}{x} = k$.
$\frac{1.5}{1} = 1.5,\ \frac{3}{2} = 1.5,\ \frac{4.5}{3} = 1.5,\ \frac{6}{4}$
$= 1.5,\ \frac{7.5}{5} = 1.5$

This is a direct variation, and the constant of variation is 1.5.

b. As x increases, y decreases. This could be an inverse variation. The constant of variation is $xy = k$:

$1(4) = 4, (2)(2) = 4, 3\left(\frac{4}{3}\right)$

$= 4, 4(1) = 4, 5\left(\frac{4}{5}\right) = 4.$

This is an inverse variation, and the constant of variation is 4.

c. As x increases, y increases. This could be a direct variation. The constant of variation is $\frac{y}{x} = k$.

$\frac{\frac{4}{3}}{2} = \frac{2}{3}, \frac{2}{3} = \frac{2}{3}, \frac{\frac{8}{3}}{4} = \frac{2}{3}, \frac{\frac{10}{3}}{5} = \frac{2}{3}$

This is a direct variation, and the constant of variation is $\frac{2}{3}$.

12. The product of P and V for different values of each variable would need to be a constant. The equation would be $PV = k$.

13. $(8x + 6)(7x - 9)$

$= 8x(7x) + 8x(-9) + 6(7x) + 6(-9)$ Use FOIL.

$= 56x^2 - 72x + 42x - 54$ Multiply.

$= 56x^2 - 30x - 54$ Combine like terms.

14. $(y - 3)(y^2 + 2y - 5)$

$= y(y^2) + y(2y) + y(-5) + (-3)(y^2) + (-3)(2y) + (-3)(-5)$ Use FOIL.

$= y^3 + 2y^2 - 5y - 3y^2 - 6y + 15$ Multiply.

$= y^3 - y^2 - 11y + 15$ Combine like terms.

15. Student B is correct. Student A used the wrong conversion factor for the number of seconds in one hour. There are 3600 seconds in one hour.

16. There are 36 inches in a yard.

$\frac{8 \text{ yd}^2}{1} \times \frac{36 \text{ in.}}{1 \text{ yd}} \times \frac{36 \text{ in.}}{1 \text{ yd}}$

$= \frac{8(36)(36) \text{ in}^2}{1}$

$= 10{,}368 \text{ in}^2$

17. There are 3600 seconds in an hour.

$\frac{72 \text{ hr}}{1} \times \frac{3600 \text{ s}}{1 \text{ hr}}$

$= \frac{(72)(3600) \text{ s}}{1}$

$= 259{,}200 \text{ s}$

18. Since the system is consistent and dependent the lines coincide. The slope of each line in the system is $m = \frac{2 - (-1)}{2 - 0} = \frac{3}{2}$ and the equation is $\frac{3}{2} = \frac{y - 2}{x - 2}$.

$2(y - 2) = 3(x - 2)$

$2y - 4 = 3x - 6$

$2y = 3x - 2$

$y = \frac{3}{2}x - 1$

The coordinates of the system are given for $x = 0, 2,$ and 4: $(0, -1), (2, 2), (4, 5)$.
When $x = 6$, $y = \frac{3}{2}(6) - 1 = 8$

x	0	2	4	6
y	−1	2	5	8

19. a. Each rate is distance divided by time, and the average is the rates divided by the number of rates, 4. The average rate is

$\frac{\frac{6}{0.5} + \frac{12}{1} + \frac{18}{1.5} + \frac{36}{3}}{4}$

$= \frac{12 + 12 + 12 + 12}{4}$

$= 12$

The average rate is 12 miles per hour.

b. There are 5280 feet in one mile and 3600 seconds in one hour.

$\frac{12 \text{ mi}}{1 \text{ hr}} \times \frac{5280 \text{ ft}}{1 \text{ mi}} \times \frac{1 \text{ hr}}{3600 \text{ s}}$

$= \frac{12(5280) \text{ ft}}{3600 \text{ s}} = 17.6 \frac{\text{ft}}{\text{s}}$

Jess's speed is 17.6 feet per second.

c. $t = \frac{d}{r} = \frac{500 \text{ ft}}{17.6 \frac{\text{ft}}{\text{s}}} \approx 28.4 \text{ s}$

It would take about 28.4 seconds.

20. $\frac{5x^2y}{7y^5} \times \frac{28z}{115x^{-2}y^{-3}} = \frac{5x^2y}{115} \times \frac{28z}{7x^{-2}y^{5+(-3)}}$
$= \frac{x^2y}{23} \times \frac{4z}{x^{-2}y^2}$
$= \frac{x^2y}{23} \times 4zx^2y^{-2}$
$= \frac{x^{2+2}y^{1+(-2)}}{23} \times 4z$
$= \frac{x^4y^{-1}}{23} \times 4z$
$= \frac{4x^4z}{23y}$

21. $\frac{3x^2yz^{-4}}{18xy^{-2}} \div \frac{9y^4}{54x^6z^8} = \frac{3x^2yz^{-4}}{18xy^{-2}} \times \frac{54x^6z^8}{9y^4}$
$= \frac{x^{2+6}yz^{-4+8}}{xy^{-2+4}}$
$= \frac{x^8yz^4}{xy^2}$
$= x^8yz^4 \times x^{-1}y^{-2}$
$= x^{8+(-1)}y^{1+(-2)}z^4$
$= x^7y^{-1}z^4$
$= \frac{x^7z^4}{y}$

22. **a.** Let t represent temperature.
$|t - (-454.9065)| = 3.0935$
$|t + 454.9065| = 3.0935$

b. $t + 454.9065 = 3.0935$ or
$t + 454.9065 = -3.0935$
$t = -451.813$ or $t = -458$
The least temperature is −458°F and the greatest temperature is −451.813°F.

23. **a.** (5, 0) is located 5 units to the right of the origin, (0, 0).
$|5| = 5$

b. (−7, 0) is located 7 units to the left of the origin, (0, 0).
$|-7| = 7$

c. (0, 9) is located 9 units above the origin, (0, 0).
$|9| = 9$

d. (0, −8) is located 8 units below the origin, (0, 0).
$|-8| = 8$

24. $(-3y + 7)^2$
$= (-3y + 7)(-3y + 7)$
$= (-3y)^2 + 2(-3y)(7) + (7)^2$
$= 9y^2 - 42y + 49$

25. $(4a + 6b)(4a - 6b)$
$= (4a)^2 - (6b)^2$
$= 16a^2 - 36b^2$

26. $P_1 + P_2 = (2x^5 + x^3)$
$+ (-2x^5 - x^3 + x) = x$
$P_1 + P_2$ has one term.
$P_1 + P_3 = (2x^5 + x^3) + x^2$
$= 2x^5 + x^3 + x^2$
$P_1 + P_3$ has three terms.
$P_1 + P_4 = (2x^5 + x^3) + x^5 = 3x^5 + x^3$
$P_1 + P_4$ has two terms.
The sum of two polynomials can have more terms than any of the addends, fewer terms than any of the addends, or the same number of terms as any of the addends.

27. Divide the mass of Earth by the mass of the moon.
$\frac{5.9736 \times 10^{24}}{7.3477 \times 10^{22}}$
$= \frac{5.9736}{7.3477} \times \frac{10^{24}}{10^{22}}$
$\approx 0.813 \times 10^2$
$= 8.13 \times 10$
The mass of Earth is about 81.3 times greater than the mass of the moon.

28. **a.** $A = lw = (x + 2)(3x^2 - 5x + 8)$

b. $(x + 2)(3x^2 - 5x + 8)$
$= x(3x^2) + x(-5x) + x(8) +$
$2(3x^2) + 2(-5x) + 2(8)$
$= 3x^3 - 5x^2 + 8x + 6x^2 - 10x + 16$
$= 3x^3 + x^2 - 2x + 16$

c. The area is $3x^3 + x^2 - 2x + 16$.

$3(3)^3 + (3)^2 - 2(3) + 16$ Replace x with 3.

$= 81 + 9 - 6 + 16$

$= 100$

The area is 100 ft^2.

29. $m = \dfrac{\frac{3}{4} - \frac{1}{2}}{-\frac{1}{2} - \left(-\frac{1}{2}\right)} = \dfrac{\frac{1}{4}}{0}$

The slope is undefined. This is a vertical line.

30. $m = \dfrac{\frac{1}{2} - \frac{1}{2}}{3 - (-1)} = \dfrac{0}{4}$

The slope is 0. This is a horizontal line.

LESSON 20

Warm Up 20

1. function
2. $f(x) = 3x + 5$

   $f(-1) = 3(-2) + 5$ Replace x with -2.

   $f(-1) = -6 + 5$

   $f(-1) = -1$
3. False. The x-value, 1, has two different y-values, 7 and -2. Therefore, the points do not represent a function.

Lesson Practice 20

a. Replace x with 6 to find the value of each function, and then add the values.

$f(6) = 3(6) - 5 = 13$

$g(6) = 6 - 3 = 3$

$(f + g)(6) = 13 + 3 = 16$

b. $f(x) = 3x - 5$

$\underline{g(x) = x - 3}$

$(f + g)(x) = 4x - 8$

c. Replace x with 3 to find the value of each function, and then subtract the values.

$f(3) = 7(3) - 8 = 13$

$g(3) = 3 + 5 = 8$

$(f - g)(3) = 13 - 8 = 5$

d. $f(x) = 7x - 8$

$\underline{g(x) = x + 5}$

$(f - g)(x) = 7x - 8 - (x + 5)$

$= 7x - 8 - x - 5$

$= 6x - 13$

e. Step 1: Write $(f + g)(x)$ as $(f(x) + g(x))$ and replace both notations with y.

Step 2: Graph $f(x) = y = 8$, $g(x) = y = 3x$.

Step 3: Given D for both f and g is {Reals}, let $x = 2$ and $x = -2$.

Step 4: Find the vertical distance from x-axis to the y-coordinates $f(2)$ and $g(2)$. Find (2, 0) on the x-axis and count the units vertically up or down to the y-coordinate of each function, f and g. Add the vertical distances from the x-axis to $f(2)$ and $g(2)$: $8 + 6 = 14$. Plot the point (2, 14).

Step 5: Find the y-coordinate of each function at $x = -2$. Add the vertical distances from the x-axis to $f(-2)$ and $g(-2)$: $8 + (-6) = 2$. Plot the point $(-2, 2)$. Draw a line through (2, 14) and $(-2, 2)$.

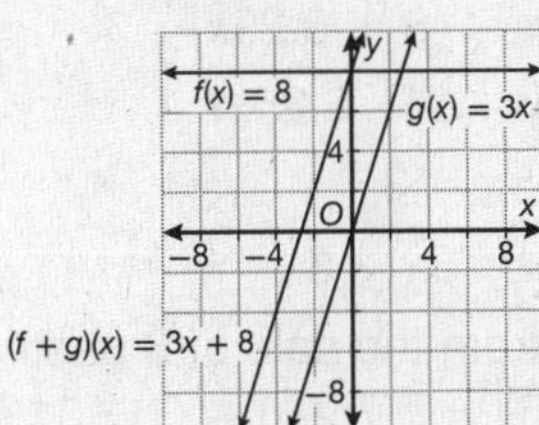

f. Step 1: Write $(f - g)(x)$ as $(f(x) - g(x))$ and replace both notations with y.

Step 2: Graph $f(x) = y = 8$, $g(x) = y = 3x$.

Step 3: Given D for both f and g is {Reals}, let $x = 2$ and $x = -2$.

Step 4: Find the vertical distance from x-axis to the y-coordinates $f(2)$ and $g(2)$. Find (2, 0) on the x-axis and count the units vertically up or down to the y-coordinate of each function, f and g. Subtract the vertical distances from the x-axis to $f(2)$ and $g(2)$: $8 - 6 = 2$. Plot the point (2, 2).

Step 5: Find the y-coordinate of each function at $x = -2$. Subtract the vertical distances from the x-axis to $f(-2)$ and $g(-2)$: $8 - (-6) = 14$. Plot the point $(-2, 14)$. Draw a line through (2, 2) and $(-2, 14)$.

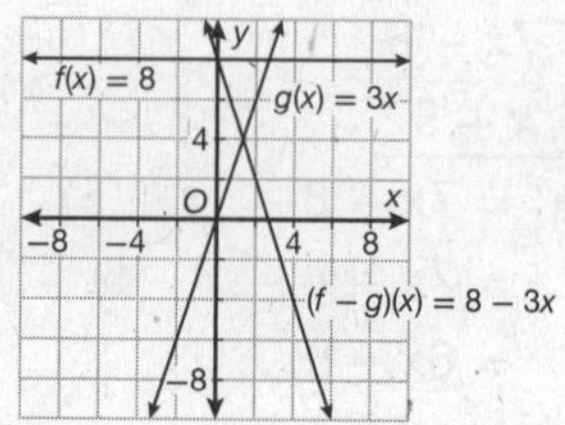

g. Replace x with -4 to find the value of each function, and then multiply the values.

$h(-4) = (-4) + 6 = 2$

$g(-4) = -4 - 5 = -9$

$(hg)(-4) = 2(-9) = -18$

h. The common domain is positive integers only. Therefore, $(fg)(-4)$ cannot be found.

i. Find $f(7)$ and $g(7)$ and divide these answers.

$f(7) = 7 + 3 = 10$

$g(7) = 7 + 5 = 12$

$\frac{f}{g}(7) = \frac{10}{12} = \frac{5}{6}$

j. The profit is represented by

$p(x) = g(x) - f(x)$

$= 12x - (3 + 6.25x)$

$= 12x - 3 - 6.25x$

$= 5.75x - 3$

So $p(x) = 5.75x - 3$

The profit from the sale of 6 pastries is $p(6)$. $p(6) = 5.75(6) - 3 = 31.5$

Patty's profit on 6 pastries is $31.50.

Practice 20

1. First add the lengths together.

12.65 in. + 30.1 in. + 15.843 in. = 58.593 in.

Then round the sum to one decimal place, since there is only one decimal place in 30.1. The result is 58.6 in.

2. a. $x = \frac{\begin{vmatrix} 5 & 1 \\ -4 & q \end{vmatrix}}{\begin{vmatrix} 1 & 1 \\ p & q \end{vmatrix}}, y = \frac{\begin{vmatrix} 1 & 5 \\ p & -4 \end{vmatrix}}{\begin{vmatrix} 1 & 1 \\ p & q \end{vmatrix}}$

b. $3 = \frac{\begin{vmatrix} 5 & 1 \\ -4 & q \end{vmatrix}}{\begin{vmatrix} 1 & 1 \\ p & q \end{vmatrix}}$

$3 = \frac{5q - (-4)}{q - p}$

$3q - 3p = 5q + 4$

$-2q - 3p = 4$

$3p + 2q = -4$

$2 = \frac{\begin{vmatrix} 1 & 5 \\ p & -4 \end{vmatrix}}{\begin{vmatrix} 1 & 1 \\ p & q \end{vmatrix}}$

$2 = \frac{-4 - 5p}{q - p}$

$2q - 2p = -4 - 5p$

$3p + 2q = -4$

The equation is $3p + 2q = -4$.

c. Graph the equation by the intercepts. The intercepts are:

$3(0) + 2q = -4$, or $q = -2$.

$3p + 2(0) = -4$, or $p = -\frac{4}{3}$

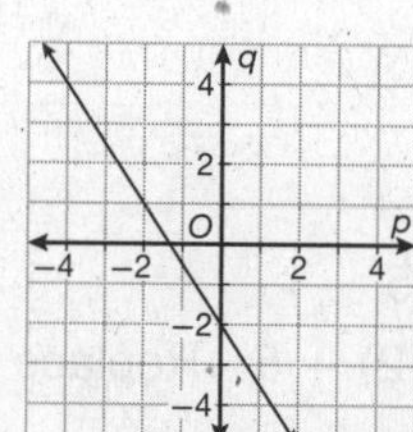

d. A point on the line is $(-2, 1)$, for when $p = -2$, $q = 1$. Substitute $(-2, 1)$.

$x + y = 5$

$-2x + y = -4$

e.

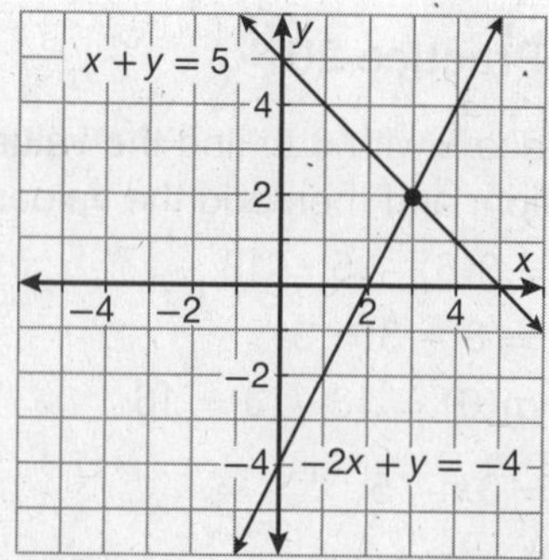

The solution to the system of equations is (3, 2), so the lines should intersect at (3, 2).

3. $3(5r - 10) = 8(2r - 4) + 5r$

$15r - 30 = 16r - 32 + 5r$

$15r - 30 = 21r - 32$

$-6r = -2$

$r = \frac{2}{6} = \frac{1}{3}$

4. $\frac{3}{4}\left(\frac{1}{2}x - 4\right) = (x - 7)$

$\frac{3}{8}x - 3 = x - 7$

$-\frac{5}{8}x = -4$

$x = \frac{32}{5}$

5. $x = \frac{\begin{vmatrix} 54 & 3 \\ 48 & 6 \end{vmatrix}}{\begin{vmatrix} 2 & 3 \\ -1 & 6 \end{vmatrix}} = \frac{54(6) - 48(3)}{2(6) - (-1)(3)}$

$= \frac{324 - 144}{12 + 3} = \frac{180}{15} = 12$

$y = \frac{\begin{vmatrix} 2 & 54 \\ -1 & 48 \end{vmatrix}}{\begin{vmatrix} 2 & 3 \\ -1 & 6 \end{vmatrix}} = \frac{2(48) - (-1)(54)}{2(6) - (-1)(3)}$

$= \frac{96 + 54}{12 + 3} = \frac{150}{15} = 10$

The solution is (12, 10).

6. Area $= \frac{1}{2}bh$

$A = \frac{1}{2}(x + 6)(2x + 4)$

$= \frac{1}{2}(2x^2 + 4x + 12x + 24)$

$= \frac{1}{2}(2x^2 + 16x + 24)$

$= x^2 + 8x + 12$

The area is $x^2 + 8x + 12$ in^2

7. There are 1852 meters in one knot, and 3600 seconds in one hour.

$\frac{20 \text{ knots}}{1 \text{ hr}} \times \frac{1852 \text{ m}}{1 \text{ knot}} \times \frac{1 \text{ hr}}{3600 \text{ s}}$

$= \frac{20(1852) \text{ m}}{3600 \text{ s}} \approx 10.3 \frac{\text{m}}{\text{s}}$

8. There are 5280 feet in one mile and 3600 seconds in one hour.

$\frac{180 \text{ mi}}{1 \text{ hr}} \times \frac{5280 \text{ ft}}{1 \text{ mi}} \times \frac{1 \text{ hr}}{3600 \text{ s}}$

$= \frac{180(5280) \text{ ft}}{3600 \text{ s}} = 264 \frac{\text{ft}}{\text{s}}$

9. Let x represent 10% iodine and y represent 40% iodine. Then write an equation for the number of milliliters of each solution in the mixture, and an equation using the percent of each solution in the mixture.

$x + y = 100$

$0.1x + 0.4y = 0.25(100)$

$x = \frac{\begin{vmatrix} 100 & 1 \\ 25 & 0.4 \end{vmatrix}}{\begin{vmatrix} 1 & 1 \\ 0.1 & 0.4 \end{vmatrix}} = \frac{100(0.4) - 25}{0.4 - 0.1} = \frac{15}{0.3}$

$= 50$

$y = \frac{\begin{vmatrix} 1 & 100 \\ 0.1 & 25 \end{vmatrix}}{\begin{vmatrix} 1 & 1 \\ 0.1 & 0.4 \end{vmatrix}} = \frac{25 - 0.1(100)}{0.4 - 0.1} = \frac{15}{0.3}$

$= 50$

$x = 50$, $y = 50$

Therefore, 50 milliliters of 10% iodine and 50 milliliters of 40% iodine are used.

10. $(x + 7)(x - 9)$

$x(x) + x(-9) + (7)x + (7)(-9)$ Use FOIL.

$x^2 - 9x + 7x - 63$ Multiply.

$x^2 - 2x - 63$ Combine like terms.

11. $(x + 3)^2(x - 2)$

$= \left(x^2 + 2(3)(x) + 3^2\right)(x - 2)$

$= (x - 2)\left(x^2 + 6x + 9\right)$

$= x\left(x^2\right) + x(6x) + x(9) + (-2)x^2 + (-2)(6x) + (-2)(9)$

$= x^3 + 6x^2 + 9x - 2x^2 - 12x - 18$

$= x^3 + 4x^2 - 3x - 18$

12. Multiply the first terms in each binomial $2x(3x)$. Then multiply the outer two terms, $2x(-6)$. Next, multiply the two inner terms, $8(3x)$. Finally, multiply the last two terms $8(-6)$. Combine any like terms to simplify to $6x^2 + 12x - 48$.

13. This is not a joint variation. Since $xyz = 0$, either $x = 0$, $y = 0$, or $z = 0$.
However, the term $\frac{0}{0}$ is not defined.
Therefore, $xyz = 0$ is not a joint variation.

14. a. Set the two equations equal and solve for x.

$$1393x + 381{,}479 = 7088x + 325{,}800$$
$$55{,}679 = 5695x$$
$$x = 9.8$$

x is the number of years after 2005, so $2005 + 9.8 = 2014.8$. The populations will be the same in late 2014.

b. Replace x with its value and solve for y in one of the equations.

$y = 1393(9.8) + 381{,}479$
$y = 395{,}130$

15. Volume of the bottom rectangular prism:
$x(x + 2)(x + 3)$
$= (x^2 + 2x)(x + 3)$
$= x^3 + 3x^2 + 2x^2 + 6x$
$= x^3 + 5x^2 + 6x$
Volume of the trapezoidal prism:
$\frac{1}{2}((x + 2) + (x + 8))x \times x$
$= \frac{1}{2}(2x + 10)x^2$
$= \frac{1}{2}(2x^3 + 10x^2)$
$= x^3 + 5x^2$
Volume of the top rectangular prism:
$x(x)(x + 8)$
$= x^2(x + 8)$
$= x^3 + 8x^2$
The total volume:
$(x^3 + 5x^2 + 6x) + (x^3 + 5x^2) + (x^3 + 8x^2)$
$= 3x^3 + 18x^2 + 6x$

16. percent change $= \frac{\text{amount of change}}{\text{original amount}}$

$\frac{150{,}000 - 135{,}000}{135{,}000} = \frac{15{,}000}{135{,}000}$
$\approx 0.111 = 11.1\%$
This is approximately an 11.1% increase.

17. percent change $= \frac{\text{amount of change}}{\text{original amount}}$

$\frac{2.59 - 2.49}{2.49} = \frac{0.10}{2.49} \approx 0.040 = 4.0\%$
This is approximately a 4.0% increase.

18. percent change $= \frac{\text{amount of change}}{\text{original amount}}$

$\frac{25{,}500 - 22{,}500}{25{,}500} = \frac{3000}{25{,}500} \approx 0.118$
$= 11.8\%$
This is approximately an 11.8% decrease.

19. The equation can be written as $xy = 1$. In an inverse variation $xy = k$; therefore, this is an inverse variation.

20. If $a = 0$, then there are three variables, and $xyz = 1$. This is a joint variation.

21. $\begin{bmatrix} -x & 2 & -2 \\ 0 & -3 & 1 \\ 2x & 8 & -3 \end{bmatrix} = -4x + 10$

$-x\begin{vmatrix} -3 & 1 \\ 8 & -3 \end{vmatrix} - 2\begin{vmatrix} 0 & 1 \\ 2x & -3 \end{vmatrix} + (-2)\begin{vmatrix} 0 & -3 \\ 2x & 8 \end{vmatrix}$
$= -4x + 10$
$-x(9 - 8) - 2(0 - 2x) + (-2)(0 - (-6x))$
$= -4x + 10$
$-x + 4x - 12x = -4x + 10$
Solve for x in the equation.

$$-x + 4x - 12x = -4x + 10$$
$$-9x = -4x + 10$$
$$-5x = 10$$
$$x = -2$$

22. Student A is correct. Student B forgot to distribute the negative through both terms in the second set of parentheses.

23. The shaded area is the entire rectangle minus the unshaded area. The area of a rectangle is length times width. Therefore, the area of the entire rectangle is $2x(x)$, and the area of the unshaded rectangle is $3(x - 5)$.
$2x(x) - [3(x - 5)]$
$2x^2 - 3x + 15$

24. a. The combined amount is
$h(x) = (f + g)(x) = 20x + 100 + (-10x + 400) = 10x + 500.$

b. The amount is $h(3)$.
$h(3) = 10(3) + 500 = 30 + 500 = 530$
In three weeks the girls will have $530.

c. Compare $f(15)$ and $g(15)$.
$f(15) = 20(15) + 100 = 400$
$g(x) = -10(15) + 400 = 250$
Hannah will have $400 and Jess will have $250; therefore, Hannah will have more.

25. $(f + g)(x) = 6x + 13 + (7x - 15)$
$= 13x - 2$

26. Use FOIL to multiply the two binomials; that is, multiply the first terms, the outer terms, the inner terms, and the last terms. Then combine like terms.
$(f \cdot g)(x) = (5x - 9)(9x + 8)$
$= 45x(x) + 5x(8) + (-9)(9x) + (-9)(8)$
$= 45x^2 + 40x - 81x - 72$
$= 45x^2 - 41x - 72$

27. $(f + g)(x) = -2x + 11 + (6x - 1)$
$= 4x + 10$
$(f + g)(8) = 4(8) + 10 = 42$
Choice **A** is correct.

28. $|-3x - 4| \geq 2$
$-3x - 4 \geq 2$ or $-3x - 4 \leq -2$
$-3x - 4 \geq 2$
$-3x \geq 6$
$x \leq -2$ or
$-3x - 4 \leq -2$
$-3x \leq 2$
$x \geq -\frac{2}{3}$

$x = 4$ is included in the graph; therefore, it is a solution.

29. The parent function is an absolute value function $f(x) = |x|$. It has been shifted to the right by 4 units, $f(x) = |x - 4|$. Then shifted up by 2 units, $f(x) = |x - 4| + 2$

30. a. Let t represent temperature.
$|t - (-247.1755)| = 1.2715$
$|t + 247.1755| = 1.2715$

b. $t + 247.1755 = 1.2715$ or
$t + 247.1755 = -1.2715$
$t = -245.904$ or $t = -248.447$
The least temperature is −248.447°C and the greatest temperature is −245.904°C.

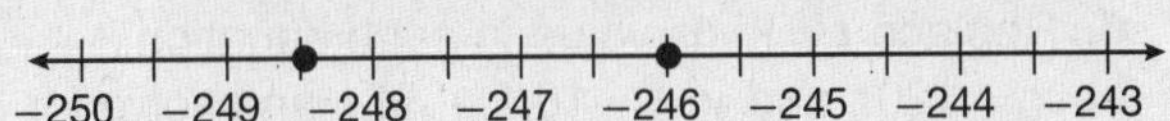

INVESTIGATION 2

1. $x = 200(7) = 1400$
She paints 1400 ft^2.

2. $y = 30t = 30(7) = 210$
She earns $210.

3. Replace t with its value in each equation, $x = 200t$ and $y = 30t$, and solve for x and y to complete the table.

t (hours)	0	1	2	3	4	5
x (square feet)	0	200	400	600	800	1000
y (dollars)	0	30	60	90	120	150

(0, 0), (200, 30), (400, 60), (600, 90), (800, 120), (1000, 150)

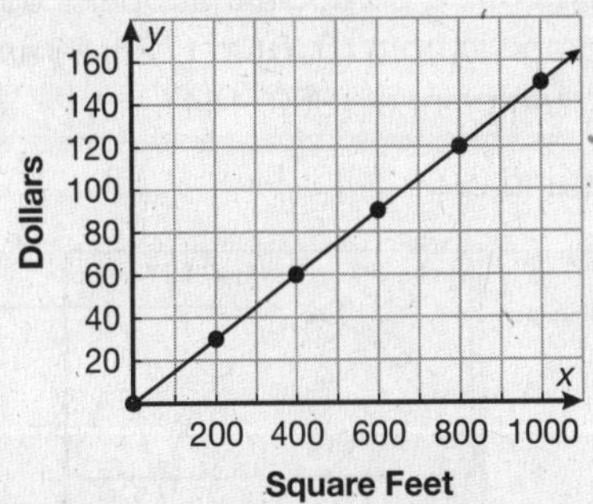

4. The graph is linear, beginning at (0, 0), and rises 30 units for every 200 units, or 3 units for every 20 units. The real-world meaning for (200, 30) is that when the painter paints 200 square feet she earns $30.

5. a., b., and c.

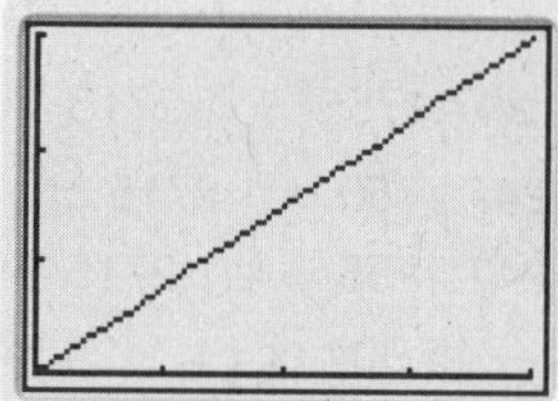

d. The graphs are the same.

6. Replace t with its value in each equation, $x = 120t$, and $y = -16t^2 + 96t$, and solve for x and y to complete the table.

t (seconds)	0	1	2	3	4	5	6
x (feet)	0	120	240	360	480	600	720
y (feet)	0	80	128	144	128	80	0

7. (0. 0), (120, 80), (240, 128), (360, 144), (480, 128), (600, 80), (720, 0)

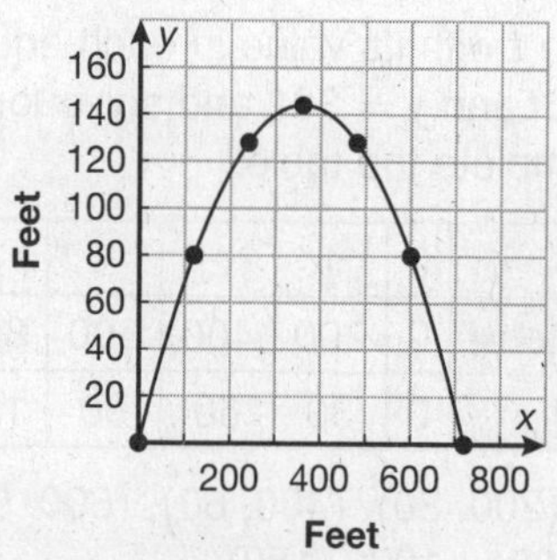

The graph is a parabola that opens downward. The graph is from (0, 0) to (720, 0) and has a maximum point at (360, 144).

8. a., b., and c.

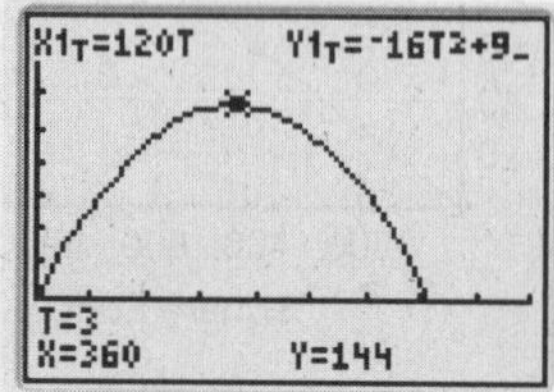

d. The golf ball reaches its highest point at 144 feet in 3 seconds. It takes 6 seconds for the golf ball to reach the ground, and it travels 720 feet horizontally.

Investigation Practice

a. Replace t with its value in each equation, $x = 1.8t + 11.4$ and $y = 10t$, and solve for x and y to complete the table.

t (months)	2	4	6	9	12
x (inches)	15	18.6	22.2	27.6	33
y (pounds)	20	40	60	90	120

b. The coordinates are (15, 20), (18.6, 40), (22.2, 60), (27.6, 90), (33, 120).

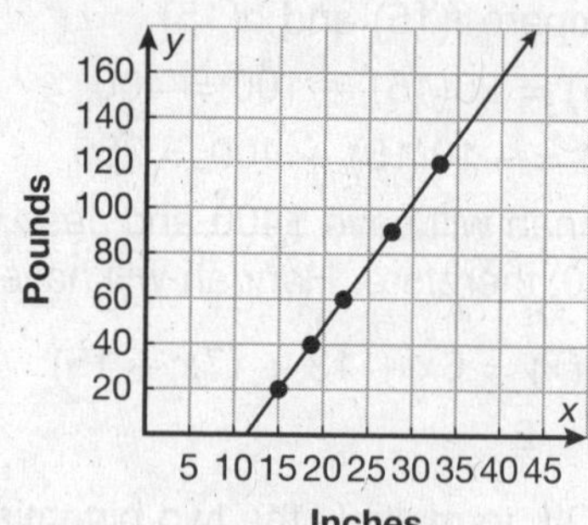

The graph is linear. It rises 20 units for every 3.6 units.

c. On the graph when $x = 24$, $y = 70$ Therefore, a 24-inch tall puppy will weigh 70 pounds.

d. $x = 40t$

$y = 60 - 5t$

e.

t (hours)	0	2	4	6	8
x (miles)	0	80	160	240	320
y (gallons)	60	50	40	30	20

The coordinate pairs are (0, 60), (80, 50), (160, 40), (240, 30), (320, 20).

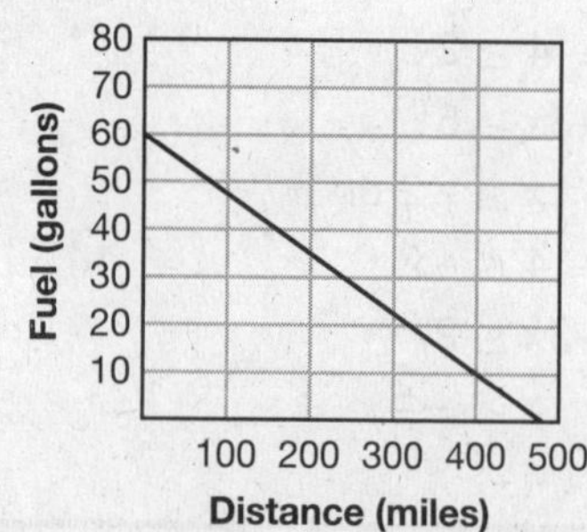

The graph is a linear descending graph (negative slope), starting at (0, 60) and ending at (480, 0).

f. The bus can travel 480 miles on one tank. The bus can be driven for 12 hours before it needs to refuel.

g. $x = 60t$

$y = -16t^2 + 128t$

h.

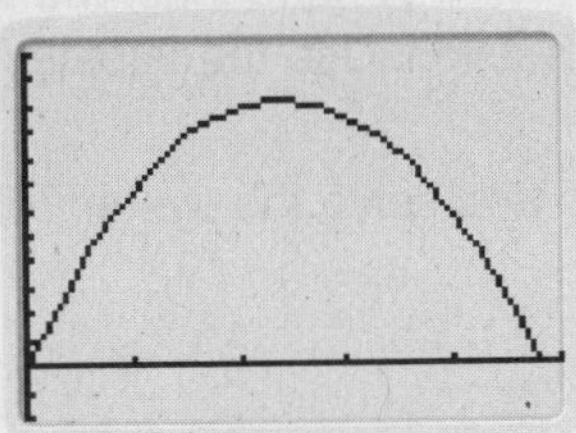

i. The x-coordinate gives the horizontal distance the ball travels at a given time, and the y-coordinate gives the height of the ball at that time.

j. The golf ball reaches its highest point, 256 feet high, in 4 seconds. It takes the golf ball 8 seconds to reach the ground and it travels 480 feet.

k. The second shot had a greater vertical velocity than the first, so it went higher. The first shot had a greater horizontal velocity than the second, so it traveled a greater horizontal distance.

LESSON 21

Warm Up 21

1. solution

2.
$$-6x + 3y = -9$$
$$-6x + 6x + 3y = -9 + 6x$$
$$3y = -9 + 6x$$
$$\frac{3y}{3} = \frac{6x}{3} - \frac{9}{3}$$
$$y = 2x - 3$$

3. $7xy(5x - 3 + 4y)$

$= 7xy(5x) + 7xy(-3) + 7xy(4y)$

$= 35x^2y + (-21xy) + 28xy^2$

$= 35x^2y - 21xy + 28xy^2$

Lesson Practice 21

a. $y + 3x = -4$

$3y - 2x = -2$

Step 1: Solve for y in the first equation.

$y + 3x = -4$

$y = -3x - 4$

Step 2: Substitute the expression for y into the other equation. Solve for x.

$3y - 2x = -2$

$3(-3x - 4) - 2x = -2$ Substitute for y

$-9x - 12 - 2x = -2$

$-9x - 2x = 10$

$-11x = 10$

$\frac{-11x}{-11} = \frac{10}{-11}$

$x = \frac{-10}{11}$ Solve for x

Step 3: Substitute the value of x into either equation to solve for y.

$y + 3\left(-\frac{10}{11}\right) = -4$

$y - \left(\frac{30}{11}\right) = -4$

$y = -\frac{14}{11}$

The solution is $\left(-\frac{10}{11}, -\frac{14}{11}\right)$

b. $3y = 12 - 6x$

$y = -2x + 4$

Step 1: Choose an equation and solve for one of the variables. Use the bottom equation, since it has been solved for y.

$y = -2x + 4.$

Step 2: Substitute the expression for y into the other equation. Solve for x.

$3y = 12 - 6x$

$3(-2x + 4) = 12 - 6x$ Substitute for y

$-6x + 12 = 12 - 6x$

$12 = 12$ True

The substitution produced an equation that is always true. Therefore, these two equations form overlapping lines. Since, all of the coordinates on the line are solutions, write the solution as $\{(x, y) | y = -2x + 4.\}$

c. $y = 6x - 5$

$2y - 10 = 12x$

Step 1: Choose an equation and solve for one of the variables. Use the top equation, since y has been solved for.

$y = 6x - 5$

Step 2: Substitute the expression for y into the other equation. Solve for x.

$2y - 10 = 12x$

$2(6x - 5) - 10 = 12x$ Substitute for y

$12x - 10 - 10 = 12x$

$-10 = 10$ False

The substitution produced an equation that is always false. Therefore, these two equations form parallel lines. Since parallel lines do not intersect, this system has no solution.

d. $3y - 7x = 5$

$4x - 9y = 2$

Choose an equation and solve for one of the variables.

$4x - 9y = 2$

$4x = 9y + 2$

$\frac{4x}{4} = \frac{9y + 2}{4}$

$x = \frac{9y + 2}{4}$

Substitute the expression for x into the other equation.

$3y - 7x = 5$

$3y - 7\left(\frac{9y + 2}{4}\right) = 5$

Eliminate the denominator by multiplying every term on both sides by 4.

$3y(4) - 7\left(\frac{9y + 2}{4}\right)4 = 5(4)$

$12y - 7(9y + 2) = 20$

$12y - 63y - 14 = 20$

$-51y = 34$

$y = -\frac{34}{51} = -\frac{2}{3}$

Substitute the value for y into the other equation.

$4x - 9y = 2$

$4x - 9\left(-\frac{2}{3}\right) = 2$

$4x + 6 = 2$

$4x = -4$

$x = -1$

The solution is $\left(-1, -\frac{2}{3}\right)$.

e. Understand: The number of rushing yards in the two years and the constant increase each year is given for each player. Find the year in which the two players will have the same yardage.

Plan: Set up a system of equations and find the point of intersection. Use the substitution method.

Solve: Formulate and solve the system of equations.

$y = 79x + 812$

$y = 116x + 654$

Step 1: Choose an equation and solve for one of the variables.

$y = 79x + 812$

Step 2: Substitute.

$79x + 812 = 116x + 654$

$158 = 37x$

$x = 4.3$ years after 2006

The players will have the same total rushing yards sometime during the year 2010.

Practice 21

1. $3x + y = 10$

$-2x - 5y = -11$

Choose an equation and solve for one of the variables.

$3x + y = 10$

$y = -3x + 10$

Substitute the expression for y into the other equation.

$-2x - 5(-3x + 10) = -11$

$-2x + 15x - 50 = -11$

$13x = 39$ Solve for x.

$x = 3$

Substitute the value for x into the first equation

$3(3) + y = 10$

$9 + y = 10$

$y = 1$

The solution is (3, 1).

2. $-x + 3y = 10$

$3x + 4y = -4$

Choose an equation and solve for one of the variables.

$-x + 3y = 10$

$3y - 10 = x$

Substitute the expression for x into the other equation.

$$3(3y - 10) + 4y = -4$$
$$9y - 30 + 4y = -4$$
$$13y = 26 \quad \text{Solve for } y.$$
$$y = 2$$

Substitute the value for y into one of the original equations

$$3x + 4(2) = -4$$
$$3x + 8 = -4$$
$$3x = -12$$
$$x = -4$$

The solution is $(-4, 2)$.

3. $|-2x - 1| \geq 3$

$-2x - 1 \geq 3$ or $-2x - 1 \leq -3$

$$-2x - 1 \geq 3$$
$$-2x \geq 4$$
$$x \leq -2 \quad \text{or}$$
$$-2x - 1 \leq -3$$
$$-2x \leq -2$$
$$x \geq 1$$

$x \leq -2$ or $x \geq 1$

−2 −1 0 1 2

4. $f(3) = -(2)(3) + 4 = -2$

$g(3) = -(3^2) = -9$

$f(3) + g(3) = -2 + (-9) = -11$

5. $\begin{bmatrix} 2 & -1 \\ 3 & 1 \\ 1 & 5 \end{bmatrix} \times \begin{bmatrix} 2 & 0 & -1 \\ 1 & 5 & 3 \end{bmatrix}$

$$= \begin{bmatrix} 2(2) + (-1)(1) & 2(0) + (-1)(5) & 2(-1) + (-1)(3) \\ 3(2) + (1)(1) & 3(0) + 1(5) & 3(-1) + 1(3) \\ 1(2) + 5(1) & 1(0) + 5(5) & 1(-1) + 5(3) \end{bmatrix} = \begin{bmatrix} 3 & -5 & -5 \\ 7 & 5 & 0 \\ 7 & 25 & 14 \end{bmatrix}$$

6. a. $2y - 4x = 6$

$y + 5x = -10$

Solve the first equation for y.

$$2y - 4x = 6$$
$$2y = 4x + 6$$
$$y = 2x + 3$$

Substitute the expression for y into the other equation to solve for x.

$$y + 5x = -10$$
$$(2x + 3) + 5x = -10$$
$$2x + 3 + 5x = -10$$
$$7x = -13$$
$$x = -\frac{13}{7}$$

Substitute the value for x into the first equation.

$$2y - 4\left(-\frac{13}{7}\right) = 6$$
$$2y = -\frac{10}{7}$$
$$y = -\frac{10}{14} = -\frac{5}{7}$$

The solution is $\left(-\frac{13}{7}, -\frac{5}{7}\right)$.

b. $2y - 4x = 6$

$y + 5x = -10$

Solve the second equation for y.

$$y + 5x = -10$$
$$y = -5x - 10$$

Substitute the expression for y into the other equation.

$$2(-5x - 10) - 4x = 6$$
$$-10x - 20 - 4x = 6$$
$$-14x = 26$$
$$x = -\frac{26}{14} = -\frac{13}{7}$$

Substitute the value for x into the second equation.

$$y + 5\left(-\frac{13}{7}\right) = -10$$
$$y = -\frac{5}{7}$$

The solution is $\left(-\frac{13}{7}, -\frac{5}{7}\right)$.

7. $|x + 3| = 16$

$x + 3 = 16$ or $x + 3 = -16$

$x = 13$ $\qquad$ $x = -19$

8. $|2x+3| = 2 - x$

$$2x+3 = (2-x) \quad \text{or} \quad 2x+3 = -(2-x)$$
$$2x+3 = 2-x \qquad 2x+3 = -2+x$$
$$3x+3 = 2 \qquad x+3 = -2$$
$$3x = -1 \qquad x = -5$$
$$x = -\frac{1}{3}$$

9. $2|x+6| = 8x$

$$|x+6| = 4x$$
$$x+6 = 4x \quad \text{or} \quad x+6 = -4x$$
$$-3x = -6 \qquad 5x = -6$$
$$x = 2 \qquad x = -\frac{6}{5}$$

10. Student A is correct. Student B forgot to distribute the negative sign through both terms in the second set of parentheses.

11. $A = \frac{1}{2}bh$

$$= \frac{1}{2}(x+3)(4x+2)$$
$$= \frac{1}{2}(4x^2 + 2x + 12x + 6)$$
$$= \frac{1}{2}(4x^2 + 14x + 6)$$
$$= 2x^2 + 7x + 3$$

The area is $2x^2 + 7x + 3$ in.^{2}

12. $\begin{vmatrix} -2 & 6 \\ 1 & 5 \end{vmatrix} = (-2)(5) - 1(6) = -10 - 6$

$$= -16$$

13. If x represents the number of half-dollars and y represents the number of silver dollars, the following system of equations can represent the situation:

$x + y = 192$

$5y = x$, which is $-x + 5y = 0$.

Therefore $y = \dfrac{\begin{vmatrix} 1 & 192 \\ -1 & 0 \end{vmatrix}}{\begin{vmatrix} 1 & 1 \\ -1 & 5 \end{vmatrix}} = \dfrac{\begin{vmatrix} 1 & 192 \\ -1 & 0 \end{vmatrix}}{6}$

Answer choice **C**

14. The inequality is $20x < 170$, so $x < 8.5$. So 8 productions will cost less than \$170.

Answer choice **B**

15. $(f+g)(x) = (4x-1) + (2x-1)$

$$= 4x - 1 + 2x - 1$$
$$= 6x - 2$$

16. Sample: 14.082 is about 14, and 9.68% is about 10%. The increase is 10% of 14 or 1.4, and $1.4 + 14 = 15.4$.

17. distance = rate × time.

Let d represent the distance Makayla travels. Then the distance Bill travels is $(8.25 - d)$.

For Makayla: $d = 3h$

For Bill: $8.25 - d = 8h$

$$d = 8.25 - 8h$$

18. $\begin{vmatrix} 4 & 6 \\ 2 & 3 \end{vmatrix} = 4(3) - 2(6) = 0.$

The transformation squashes the shape to a line segment, which has an area of zero.

19. $3x + 6x^5 - 3x^2 + 43 - 5x^3$

Write the expression with the terms going from greatest to least degree.

$6x^5 - 5x^3 - 3x^2 + 3x + 43$

20. Volume of the cylinder is $\pi x^2 x = \pi x^3$.

Volume of the half sphere is $\frac{1}{2}\left(\frac{4}{3}\right)\pi x^3 = \frac{2}{3}\pi x^3$.

The total volume is $\pi x^3 + \frac{2}{3}\pi x^3 = \frac{5}{3}\pi x^3$ cubic units.

21. No, this is not a joint variation. If $abc = 0$, then either a, b, or c is equal to 0. But the term $\frac{0}{0}$ is not defined. Therefore, $abc = 0$ is not a joint variation.

22. Each field goal is 2 points and each free throw is 1 point.

$$\begin{bmatrix} 1 & 5 & 6 \\ 2 & 5 & 5 \\ 1 & 7 & 1 \end{bmatrix} \cdot \begin{bmatrix} 3 \\ 2 \\ 1 \end{bmatrix}$$

$$= \begin{bmatrix} 1(3) + 5(2) + 6(1) \\ 2(3) + 5(2) + 5(1) \\ 1(3) + 7(2) + 1(1) \end{bmatrix} = \begin{bmatrix} 19 \\ 21 \\ 18 \end{bmatrix}$$

M. Evans scored the most points in the game.

23. $m = \dfrac{138}{115} = 1.2$ m

24. $\dfrac{a^{-3}x}{y^{-3}}\left(\dfrac{xxx^{-2}}{y^{-2}yy} - 3\right) = \dfrac{a^{-3}x}{y^{-3}}(1-3)$

$$= \frac{a^{-3}x}{y^{-3}}(-2)$$

$$= -2a^{-3}xy^3$$
$$= \frac{-2xy^3}{a^3}$$

25. $M = kE$
$57 = k(150)$
$k = \frac{57}{150}$
$M = kE$
$M = \frac{57}{150}(25)$
$M = 9.5$
The object weighs 9.5 pounds on Mercury.

26. Let x represent distance.
10 minutes $= \frac{1}{6}$ hr. She drives $\frac{1}{6}x$ in 10 minutes.
She drives $\frac{1}{2}x$ in $\frac{1}{2}$ hour. Write and solve the equation.
$$\frac{1}{6}x + \frac{1}{2}x + \frac{1}{6}x = 40$$
$$\frac{5}{6}x = 40$$
$$x = 48$$
Her average speed is 48 mph.

27. $15\%(24) = 24(0.1 + 0.05) = 2.4 + 1.2 = 3.6$
The tip is \$3.60.

28. $\begin{bmatrix} 1 & 0 \\ 0 & 1 \\ 1 & 0 \end{bmatrix} \times \begin{bmatrix} -2 & 3 & -4 \\ 0 & -1 & 1 \end{bmatrix}$

$$= \begin{bmatrix} 1(-2)+0(0) & 1(3)+0(-1) & 1(-4)+0(1) \\ 0(-2)+1(0) & 0(3)+1(-1) & 0(-4)+1(1) \\ 1(-2)+0(0) & 1(3)+0(-1) & 1(-4)+0(1) \end{bmatrix} = \begin{bmatrix} -2 & 3 & -4 \\ 0 & -1 & 1 \\ -2 & 3 & -4 \end{bmatrix}$$

29. a. $A = lw$
$= (x + 12)(x - 32)$

b. $= (x + 12)(x - 32)$
$= (82 + 12)(82 - 32)$
$= (94)(50) = 4700$
The area of the court is 4700 ft^2.

30. $-2(x + 3) \leq 4$
$-2x - 6 \leq 4$
$-2x \leq 10$
$x \geq -5$

−8 −6 −4 −2 0 2

LAB 5

Graphing Calculator Practice

1.

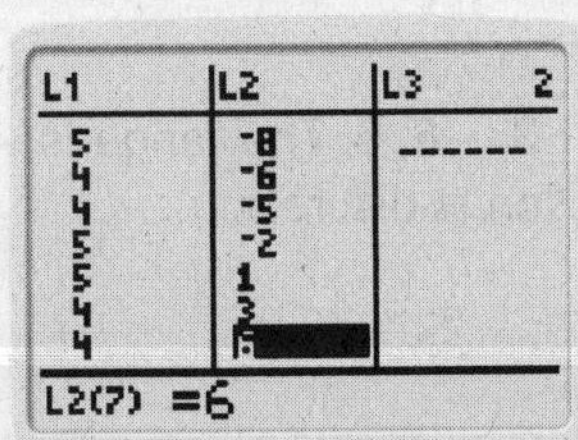

2.

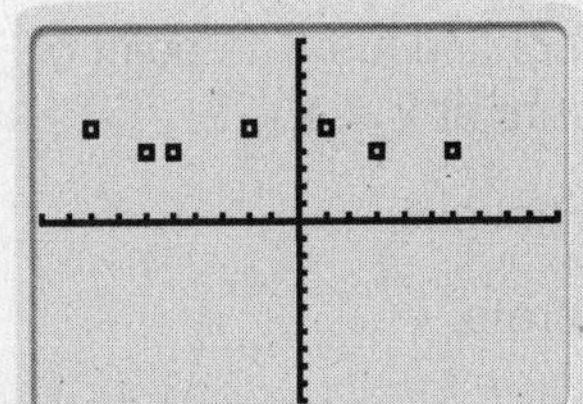

LESSON 22

Warm Up 22

1. once
2. The domain is the x-values and the range is the y-values. The domain is 5, 7, −1, and the range is 2, 0, 9.
3. Find the value of the function for each domain to find the range.
$f(0) = 2(0) + 7 = 7$
$f(3) = 2(3) + 7 = 13$
$f(4) = 2(4) + 7 = 15$
The range is 7, 13, 15.

Lesson Practice 22

a. 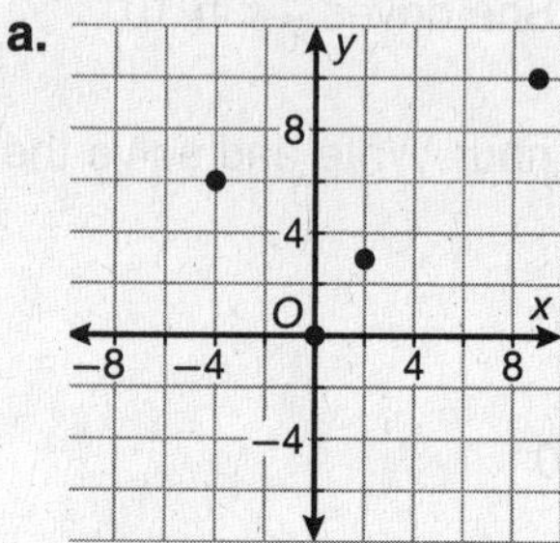

The domain is 0, 2, −4, 9. The range is 0, 3, 6, 10.

b. 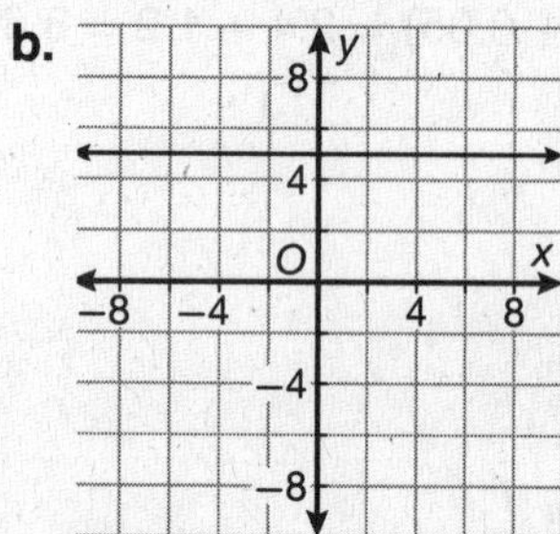

The domain is all real numbers. The range is 5.

c. The graph is discontinuous. The point of discontinuity occurs at $x = 4$.

d. The graph is continuous.

e. The graph is discrete.

f. The graph is continuous. A vertical line will intersect the graph at two different points, so the graph is not a function. The graph is a relation. The domain is $x \geq 0$. The range is all real numbers.

g. The graph is discontinuous. The graph passes the vertical line test, so it is a function. The domain is $0 \leq x < 4$. The range is 0, 2.

h. The graph is discrete. The graph passes the vertical line test, so it is a function. The domain is −2, 0, 1, 6. The range is 5, 0, 3, 7.

i. The points to plot are (1, 2), (2, 0), (3, 3), (4, 3), and (5, 1). The domain is 1, 2, 3, 4, 5. The range is 2, 0, 3, 1.

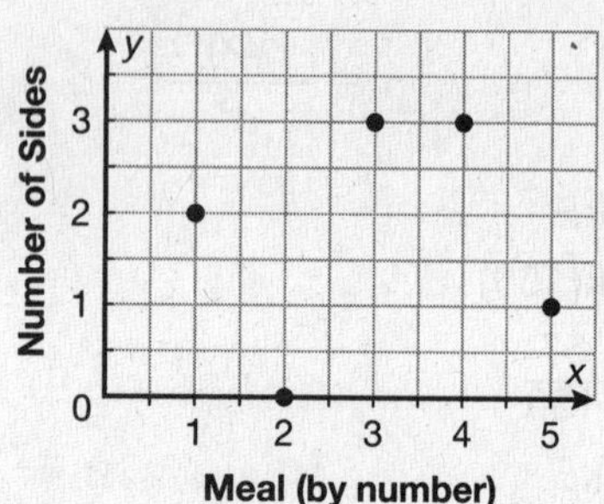

Any vertical line will not intersect the graph more than once, so the relation is a function. Examining the domain and range indicates that for every x-value, there is exactly one y-value.

Practice 22

1. Let the population of California be C, the population of Texas be T, and the population of New York be N.

$C + T + N = 73{,}699{,}925$

$C = T + 13{,}019{,}828$

$N = T - 1{,}875{,}363$

Replace C and N in the first equation with the expressions for C and N.

$C + T + N = 73{,}699{,}925$

$(T + 13{,}019{,}828) + T + (T - 1{,}875{,}363) = 73{,}699{,}925$

$3T + 11{,}144{,}465 = 73{,}699{,}925$

$3T = 62{,}555{,}460$

$T = 20{,}851{,}820$

The population of Texas is 20,851,820.

2. 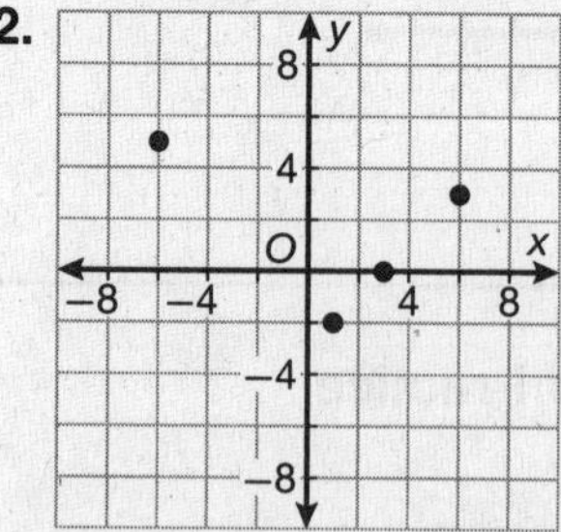

The domain is 1, 3, −6, 6. The range is −2, 0, 5, 3. The function is discrete.

3.

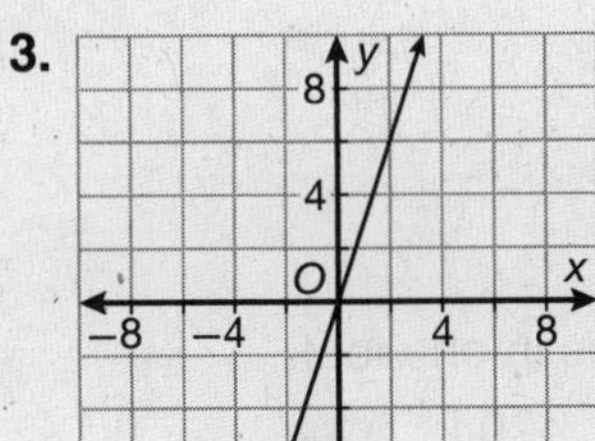

The domain is all real numbers. The range is all real numbers. The function is continuous.

4. $f(-2) = 3(-2) + 1 = -5$

$g(-2) = (-2) + 6 = 4$

$f(-2) \cdot g(-2) = (-5)(4) = -20$

5. $x = \dfrac{\begin{vmatrix} -18 & 7 \\ -37 & 11 \end{vmatrix}}{\begin{vmatrix} 3 & 7 \\ -4 & 11 \end{vmatrix}}$

$= \dfrac{-18(11) - (-37)(7)}{3(11) - (-4)(7)}$

$= \dfrac{-198 - (-259)}{33 - (-28)} = \dfrac{61}{61} = 1$

$y = \dfrac{\begin{vmatrix} 3 & -18 \\ -4 & -37 \end{vmatrix}}{\begin{vmatrix} 3 & 7 \\ -4 & 11 \end{vmatrix}}$

$= \dfrac{3(-37) - (-4)(-18)}{3(11) - (-4)(7)}$

$= \dfrac{-111 - 72}{33 - (-28)} = -\dfrac{183}{61} = -3$

The solution is (1, −3).

6. a. Graphing the equation results in a parabola from $x = 0$ to $x = 6.875$. The rocket takes 6.875 seconds to hit the ground.

b. x is the horizontal distance. Replace $t = 6.875$ in $x = 38t$.

$x = 38(6.875)$

$x = 261.25.$

The rocket travels 261.25 feet.

c. At the halfway point the rocket reaches its highest point. This is about 131 feet.

7. The degree is 7.

8. The degree is 5.

9. $A = s^2 = (4x + 12)^2$

$= (4x)^2 + 2(4x)(12) + 12^2$

$= 16x^2 + 96x + 144$

10. $m = \dfrac{20{,}320}{119{,}727} = 0.170$

11. $\dfrac{(4x)^{-2}y^0(y^{-2})^2y}{32^{-1}x^2(yx^0)^{-3}} = \dfrac{4^{-2}x^{-2}y^0y^{-4}y}{32^{-1}x^2y^{-3}x^0}$

$= \dfrac{32x^{-2}y^{-3}}{4^2x^2y^{-3}}$

$= 2x^{-4}y^0$

$= 2x^{-4}$

12. $\dfrac{9x^{-4}(y^3x^2)^{-2}}{2^{-3}x^2y^3x(x^{-4}y^2)} = \dfrac{9x^{-4}y^{-6}x^{-4}}{2^{-3}x^2y^3xx^{-4}y^2}$

$= \dfrac{9x^{-8}y^{-6}}{2^{-3}y^5x^{-1}}$

$= 9\ 2^3x^{-7}y^{-11}$

$= 72x^{-7}y^{-11}$

13. The graph is discontinuous at the line $x = 0$. The domain is all real numbers, except $x = 0$.

14. Ben is correct.

$32 + \dfrac{|x - 7|}{13} < 7$

$\dfrac{|x - 7|}{13} < -25$

$|x - 7| < -325$

Since the absolute value of a number is always greater than or equal to zero, there is no solution.

15. percent change $= \dfrac{\text{amount of change}}{\text{original amount}}$

$= \dfrac{8.2 - 5}{5} = \dfrac{3.2}{5}$

$= 0.64 = 64\%$

16. percent change $= \dfrac{\text{amount of change}}{\text{original amount}}$

$= \dfrac{9.4 - 5}{5} = \dfrac{4.4}{5}$

$= 0.88 = 88\%$

17. a. x is the horizontal distance the ball travels. Replace x with 41 in the equation $x = 11t$.

$41 = 11t$

so $t \approx 3.73$

It takes about 3.73 seconds for the ball to reach the field goal post.

b. Yes. In 3.73 seconds the ball travels $-4.9(3.73)^2 + 23(3.73)$ or 17.6 meters above the ground, enabling the ball to be high enough to go through the field goal posts.

18. a. Let p represent the number of pages and m represent the number of minutes. Kate will read $p = \frac{1}{3}m + 70$ pages and Riley will read $p = \frac{3}{4}m + 30$ pages.

Solve the equations. Replace p with its expression in one equation and solve for m.

$$p = \frac{1}{3}m + 70$$

$$p = \frac{3}{4}m + 30$$

$$\frac{1}{3}m + 70 = \frac{3}{4}m + 30$$

$$40 = \frac{5}{12}m$$

$$96 = m$$

Substitute for m and solve for p.

$$p = \frac{1}{3}(96) + 70$$

$$p = 102$$

Riley will catch up to Kate on page 102.

b. Since $m = 96$, they will have read 96 minutes or 1 hr 36 min when Riley catches up.

19. a. The proportion is

$$\frac{\text{Gallons of gasoline}_1}{\text{Gallons of gasoline}_2} = \frac{\text{Ounces of oil}_1}{\text{Ounces of oil}_2}$$

$$\frac{3}{5} = \frac{19.2}{x}$$

b. $\frac{3}{5} = \frac{19.2}{x}$

$$3x = 5(19.2)$$

$$3x = 96$$

$$x = 32$$

32 ounces of oil is needed.

c. $\frac{3}{5} = \frac{19.2}{32}$

$$3(32) = 5(19.2)$$

$$96 = 96$$

20. There are 12 inches in one foot.

$$\frac{420 \text{ in.}}{1} \times \frac{1 \text{ ft}}{12 \text{ in.}} = \frac{420 \text{ ft}}{12} = 35 \text{ ft}$$

21. $V = \begin{vmatrix} 1 & 3 & 4 \\ -3 & 2 & 1 \\ 4 & -2 & 3 \end{vmatrix}$

$$= 1\begin{vmatrix} 2 & 1 \\ -2 & 3 \end{vmatrix} - 3\begin{vmatrix} -3 & 1 \\ 4 & 3 \end{vmatrix} + 4\begin{vmatrix} -3 & 2 \\ 4 & -2 \end{vmatrix}$$

$$= 1[(2)(3) - (-2)(1)] - 3[(-3)(3) - 4(1)] + 4[(-3)(-2) - 4(2)]$$

$$= 1[8] - 3[-13] + 4[(-2)]$$

$$= 8 - (-39) + (-8)$$

$$= 39$$

The volume is 39 cubic units.

22. **A** $\begin{bmatrix} 6 & -1 \end{bmatrix}\begin{bmatrix} 3 \\ 1 \end{bmatrix} = [6(3) + (-1)(1)]$

$$= [17]$$

B $\begin{bmatrix} 3 \\ 1 \end{bmatrix}\begin{bmatrix} 6 & -1 \end{bmatrix} = \begin{bmatrix} 3(6) & 3(-1) \\ 1(6) & 1(-1) \end{bmatrix} = \begin{bmatrix} 18 & -3 \\ 6 & -1 \end{bmatrix}$

C $\begin{bmatrix} 1 & 0 & 3 \end{bmatrix}\begin{bmatrix} 4 \\ -2 \\ 5 \end{bmatrix} = [1(4) + 0(-2) + 3(5)]$

$$= [19]$$

D $\begin{bmatrix} 4 \\ -2 \\ 5 \end{bmatrix}\begin{bmatrix} 1 & 0 & 3 \end{bmatrix} = \begin{bmatrix} 4(1) & 4(0) & 4(3) \\ -2(1) & -2(0) & -2(3) \\ 5(1) & 5(0) & 5(3) \end{bmatrix}$

$$= \begin{bmatrix} 4 & 0 & 12 \\ -2 & 0 & -6 \\ 5 & 0 & 15 \end{bmatrix}$$

Answer choice **C**

23. No, this is not an inverse variation. If $xy = 0$, then either x is 0 or y is 0, but $\frac{0}{0}$ is not defined. Therefore, $xy = 0$ is not an inverse variation.

24. $-x + y = -2$

$x + y = 8$

Solve for y in $-x + y = -2$.

$$y = x - 2$$

Replace y with its expression in $x + y = 8$, and solve for x.

$x + y = 8$
$x + (x - 2) = 8$
$x + x - 2 = 8$
$2x = 10$
$x = 5$

Replace x with 5 in the other equation and solve for y.

$-x + y = -2$
$-(5) + y = -2$
$y = 3$

The solution is (5, 3).

25. $3x + y = 4$
$-3x + y = 8$

Solve for y in $-3x + y = 8$.

$y = 3x + 8$

Replace y with its expression in $3x + y = 4$, and solve for x.

$3x + y = 4$
$3x + (3x + 8) = 4$
$3x + 3x + 8 = 4$
$6x = -4$
$x = -\frac{4}{6} = -\frac{2}{3}$

Replace x with $-\frac{2}{3}$ in the other equation and solve for y.

$-3x + y = 8$
$-3\left(-\frac{2}{3}\right) + y = 8$
$2 + y = 8$
$y = 6$

The solution is $\left(-\frac{2}{3}, 6\right)$.

26. Sample: $2 < x < 5$ is a compound inequality using "and." $x > 5$ or $x < 2$ is a compound inequality using "or." Compound inequalities with "and" represent the intersection of the solutions, while compound inequalities with "or" represent the union of the solutions.

27. $x = ky$
$28 = k(7)$
$k = 4$

28. $\text{percent change} = \frac{\text{amount of change}}{\text{original amount}}$
$= \frac{5.15 - 0.75}{0.75}$
$= \frac{4.4}{0.75}$
$\approx 5.87 = 587\%$

29. Sample:
$3 \cdot 4 \cdot 7$
$= (3 \cdot 4) \cdot 7$ Assoc. Prop. of Mult.
$= 12 \cdot 7$ Multiply.
$= 84$ Multiply.

30. a. $m = \frac{-8 - (-3)}{1 - (-8)} = -\frac{5}{9}$

b. The slope is negative, so the line is falling.

c.

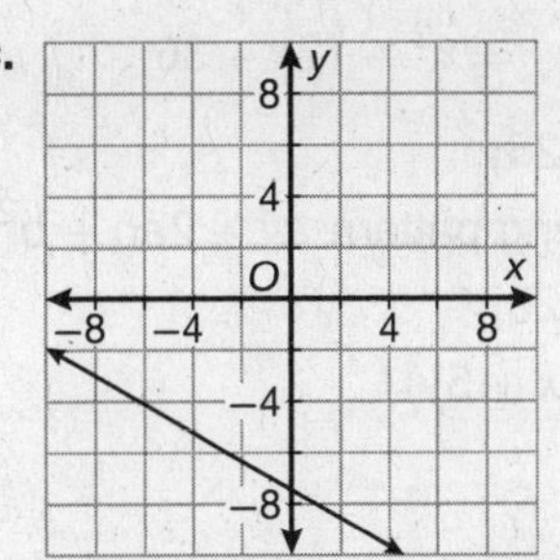

d. The slope goes down as it goes from left to right on the graph, so the line is falling.

LESSON 23

Warm Up 23

1. factors
2. Since $1 \times 15 = 15$, $3 \times 5 = 15$, the factor pairs are 1 and 15, and 3 and 5.
3. The factors of −35 are the integers that multiply together to get 35. The factor pairs are 1 and −35, −1 and 35, −5 and 7, 5 and −7.
4. The factors of 16 are the integers that multiply together to get 16. The factor pairs are 1 and 16, 2 and 8, 4 and 4, −1 and −16, −2 and −8, −4 and −4.

Lesson Practice 23

a. $12x^2 + 4x + 8$
$= 4 \cdot 3 \cdot x \cdot x + 4 \cdot x + 4 \cdot 2$ 4 is the GCF
$= 4(3x^2 + x + 2)$
Check $4(3x^2 + x + 2) = 12x^2 + 4x + 8$

b. $-20x^3 + 5x^2$
$= -5 \cdot 4 \cdot x \cdot x \cdot x + -5 \cdot x \cdot x$ $-5x^2$ is the GCF.
$= -5x^2(4x - 1)$ Factor out $-5x^2$ so $(4x - 1)$ has a positive leading coefficient.

c. $x^2 + 12x + 36$
Use the factoring pattern $a^2 + 2ab + b^2$.
$x^2 + 12x + 36 = (x + 6)(x + 6) = (x + 6)^2$
Check. $(x + 6)^2 = (x + 6)(x + 6)$
$= x^2 + 12x + 36$

d. $9x^2 + 30xy + 25y^2$
Use the factoring pattern $a^2 + 2ab + b^2$.
$9x^2 + 30xy + 25y^2$
$= (3x + 5y)(3x + 5y)$
$= (3x + 5y)^2$
Check.
$(3x + 5y)^2 = (3x + 5y)(3x + 5y)$
$= 9x^2 + 30xy + 25y^2$

e. $x^2 - 1 = x^2 - 1^2$ so it is a difference of squares.
$x^2 - 1 = (x + 1)(x - 1)$
Check. $(x + 1)(x - 1) = x^2 - 1x + 1x - 1$
$= x^2 - 1$

f. $x^2 - 10x + 21 = 0$
Factor $x^2 - 10x + 21$ by finding two numbers whose product is 21 and whose sum is -10. The factor pairs for 21 are (1)(21), (3)(7), $(-1)(-21)$, and $(-3)(-7)$. The factor pair whose sum is -10 is $(-3)(-7)$. So, the factored expression for $x^2 - 10x + 21$ is $(x - 3)(x - 7)$. Now use the Zero Product Property to solve the equation.
$x^2 - 10x + 21 = 0$ Original equation
$(x - 3)(x - 7) = 0$ Factor.
$(x - 3) = 0$ or $(x - 7) = 0$ Zero Product Prop.
$x = 3$ or $x = 7$ Solve each equation.

Check.
$(3)^2 - 10(3) + 21 \stackrel{?}{=} 0$
$0 = 0$
$(7)^2 - 10(7) + 21 \stackrel{?}{=} 0$
$0 = 0$
The solutions are 3 and 7 because they both make the original equation true.

g. The original area is 40(50) or 2000. The increase in area is 50% of 2000, or 1000. So the new area will be 2000 + 1000 = 3000. The increase in dimensions is $(x + 40)$ and $(x + 50)$. So, the equation for the new area is $(x + 40)(x + 50) = 3000$. Solve this equation.
$(x + 40)(x + 50) = 3000$
$x^2 + 50x + 40x + 2000 = 3000$ Use FOIL.
$x^2 + 90x - 1000 = 0$ Simplify.
$(x - 10)(x + 100) = 0$ Factor.
$(x - 10) = 0$ or $(x + 100) = 0$ Zero Product Property
$x = 10$ or $x = -100$
Use the positive solution, since length cannot be negative. The increase should be 10 feet.

Practice 23

1. $-a(a - b)$
$= -\left(-\frac{1}{2}\right)\left(-\frac{1}{2} - \frac{1}{3}\right)$ Replace a with $-\frac{1}{2}$ and b with $\frac{1}{3}$.
$= -\left(-\frac{1}{2}\right)\left(-\frac{5}{6}\right)$
$= -\frac{5}{12}$

2. $-xy(-x^2 - y)$
$-\left(-\frac{1}{2}\right)\left(\frac{1}{4}\right)\left(-\left(-\frac{1}{2}\right)^2 - \frac{1}{4}\right)$ Replace x with $-\frac{1}{2}$ and y with $\frac{1}{4}$.
$= -\left(-\frac{1}{2}\right)\left(\frac{1}{4}\right)\left(-\frac{1}{4} - \frac{1}{4}\right)$
$= \left(\frac{1}{8}\right)\left(-\frac{1}{2}\right) = -\frac{1}{16}$

3. This is a function since for every x-value, there is a different y-value.

4. There are 12 inches in one foot, and 60 seconds in one minute.

$$\frac{120\text{ in.}}{1\text{ s}} \times \frac{1\text{ ft}}{12\text{ in.}} \times \frac{60\text{ s}}{1\text{ min}} = \frac{120(60)\text{ ft}}{12\text{ min}}$$
$$= 600\ \frac{\text{ft}}{\text{min}}$$

5. $\frac{-3^{-2}x}{y}\left(\frac{9y^0x}{-x} - \frac{3x}{y}\right)$

$= \frac{-3^{-2}x}{y}\left(\frac{-9y^0x^{1-1}}{1} - \frac{3x}{y}\right)$

$= \frac{-3^{-2}x}{y}\left(\frac{-(3)^2}{1} - \frac{3x}{y}\right)$

$= \left(\frac{-3^{-2}x}{y} \cdot \frac{-(3)^2}{1}\right) - \left(\frac{-3^{-2}x}{y} \cdot \frac{3x}{y}\right)$

$= \frac{x}{y} - \frac{-3^{-1}x^2}{y^2}$

$= \frac{x}{y} + \frac{x^2}{3y^2}$

6. $0.003x + 0.02x - 0.03 = 0.177$

$0.023x = 0.207$

$x = 9$

7. $2\frac{1}{3}x + 1\frac{3}{5} = 7\frac{2}{5}$

$2\frac{1}{3}x = 5\frac{4}{5}$

$x = \frac{29}{5} \cdot \frac{3}{7}$

$= \frac{87}{35}$

8. $\frac{1}{2}x + 4 = 6\frac{1}{5}$

$\frac{1}{2}x = 2\frac{1}{5}$

$x = \frac{11}{5} \cdot 2$

$= \frac{22}{5}$

9.

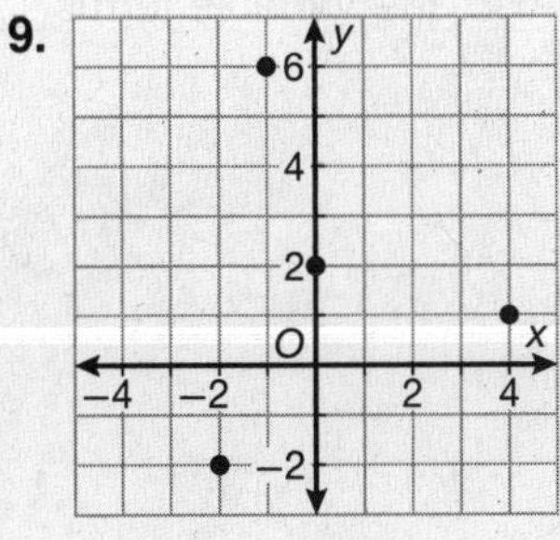

The domain is −2, 4, −1, 0. The range is −2, 1, 6, 2.

10. $-3x^3 + 6x^2 + 3x$

Factor out the common factor $-3x$

$= -3x(x^2 - 2x - 1)$

11. $-2x^2 + 5x + 3$

$= -(2x^2 - 5x - 3)$

Factor out the common factor -1

$= -(2x + 1)(x - 3)$

12. $x^2 - 5x + 6$

Find the numbers whose product is 6 and whose sum is −5.

$= (x - 3)(x - 2)$

13. $x^2 = x(x)$ and $25 = 5(5) = 5^2$, so this is a Difference of Two Squares.

14. The perimeter is $2(l + w) = 2[f(x) + g(x)]$.

$= 2(2x + 5 + 5x + 4)$

$= 2(7x + 9)$

$= 14x + 18$

15. Replace x with −1 in the equation to determine if the equation is true.

$5(4x - 1) = -7(9 + 4x) + 8 - 2x$

$5(4(-1) - 1) \stackrel{?}{=} -7(9 + 4(-1)) + 8 - 2(-1)$

$5(-5) \stackrel{?}{=} -7(5) + 8 - (-2)$

$-25 \stackrel{?}{=} -35 + 8 + 2$

$-25 = -25$

Therefore, $x = -1$ is a solution.

16. First, find the x-intercept by letting $y = 0$ and solving for x. Then find the y-intercept, by letting $x = 0$ and solving for y. Plot the x- and y-intercepts and connect the points, extending the line with arrowheads at each end.

17. a. There are 16 ounces in pound, so there are 80 ounces in 5 pounds. If w represents the weight, then the maximum weight is $80 + y$, or $80 + y \geq w$ and the minimum weight is $80 - y$ or $80 - y \leq w$.

$80 + y \geq w$ $\qquad$ $80 - y \leq w$

$y \geq w - 80$ $\qquad$ $-y \leq w - 80$

Therefore, $|w - 80| \leq y$.

b.

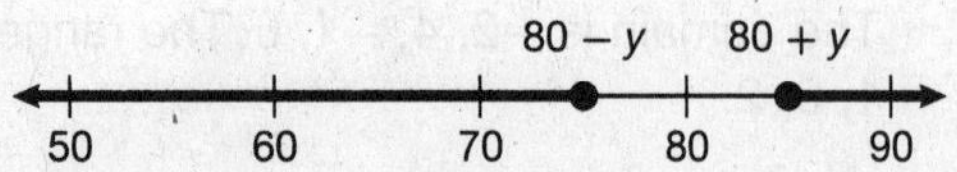

18. a. $x = \dfrac{\begin{vmatrix} 0 & 2 \\ 6 & 3 \end{vmatrix}}{\begin{vmatrix} 1 & 2 \\ 1 & 3 \end{vmatrix}} = \dfrac{0(3) - 6(2)}{1(3) - 1(2)} = \dfrac{-12}{1} = -12$

$y = \dfrac{\begin{vmatrix} 1 & 0 \\ 1 & 6 \end{vmatrix}}{\begin{vmatrix} 1 & 2 \\ 1 & 3 \end{vmatrix}} = \dfrac{1(6) - 1(0)}{1(3) - 1(2)} = \dfrac{6}{1} = 6$

The solution is $(-12, 6)$.

b. Write the equations in the form $y = mx + b$ to plot.

$x + 2y = 0$

$2y = -x + 0$

$y = -\frac{1}{2}x + 0$

The y-intercept is 0 and the slope is $-\frac{1}{2}$.

$x + 3y = 6$

$3y = -x + 6$

$y = -\frac{1}{3}x + 2$

The y-intercept is 6 and the slope is $-\frac{1}{3}$.

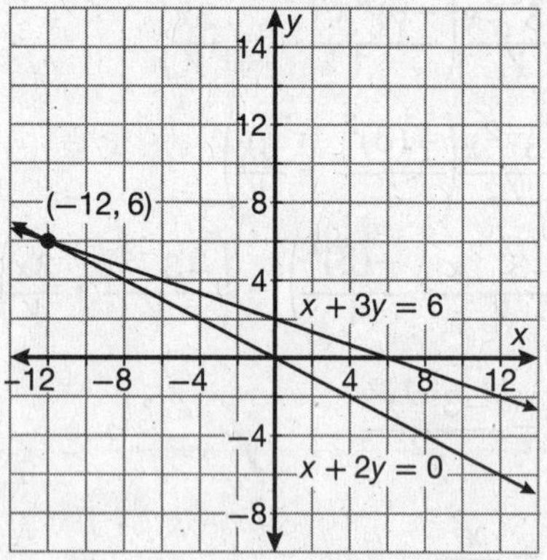

19. $\begin{bmatrix} 1 & 0 \\ 0 & 1 \\ 1 & 0 \end{bmatrix} \times \begin{bmatrix} -1 & 4 & -8 \\ 0 & -3 & 1 \end{bmatrix}$

$= \begin{bmatrix} 1(-1) + 0(0) & 1(4) + 0(-3) & 1(-8) + 0(1) \\ 0(-1) + 1(0) & 0(4) + 1(-3) & 0(-8) + 1(1) \\ 1(-1) + 0(0) & 1(4) + 0(-3) & 1(-8) + 0(1) \end{bmatrix} = \begin{bmatrix} -1 & 4 & -8 \\ 0 & -3 & 1 \\ -1 & 4 & -8 \end{bmatrix}$

20. $3x$ and $2x$ both have a degree of 1. Therefore the expression has a degree of 1.
Answer choice **B**

21. The first equation can be written as $-3y = -x + 12$ and the second as $by = -3x + c$.

a. If the system is consistent and dependent, then the lines coincide, so the slope and intercepts are the same. Compared to the first equation, the x-value in the second equation is multiplied by 3, so each coefficient in the second equation is also multiplied by 3. Therefore, $b = -9$, and $c = 36$.

b. If the system is inconsistent then the lines are parallel, so the slopes are the same and the y-intercept is different. Therefore the value of $b = -9$ and $c \neq 36$.

c. If the system is consistent and independent then the lines intersect at one point, so the slopes cannot be the same. Therefore $b \neq -9$.

22. When isolating the variable, 3 was subtracted from −2 instead of added. Also, the variable terms were not combined correctly. The solution should be

$4x - 3 > x - 2$

$4x > x + 1$

$3x > 1$

$x > \frac{1}{3}$

23. $AB = \begin{bmatrix} 5 & 2 & 14 \\ 9 & 11 & 18 \\ 3 & 7 & 6 \end{bmatrix} \times \begin{bmatrix} 15 & 6 \\ 7 & 13 \\ 10 & 16 \end{bmatrix}$

Multiply each element of the first row in the first matrix by the corresponding element in the first column of the second matrix to get the first element of the product. Then multiply the first row of the first matrix by the second column of the second matrix to get the next element in the first row of the product. Then repeat the process for the second row of the first matrix, and so on.

$$AB = \begin{bmatrix} 5(15) + 2(7) + 14(10) & 5(6) + 2(13) + 14(16) \\ 9(15) + 11(7) + 18(10) & 9(6) + 11(13) + 18(16) \\ 3(15) + 7(7) + 6(10) & 3(6) + 7(13) + 6(16) \end{bmatrix}$$

Simplify the addition.

$$AB = \begin{bmatrix} 229 & 280 \\ 392 & 485 \\ 154 & 205 \end{bmatrix}$$

24. $S = kE$

$336 = k(12)$

$k = 28$

$S = 28(7)$

$S = 196$

The object weighs 196 ounces on the Sun.

25. a. Convert the time into a 24-hour clock. Graph the points (1, 83), (6, 75), (10, 90), (14, 101), (16, 105), (20, 99), (23, 90).

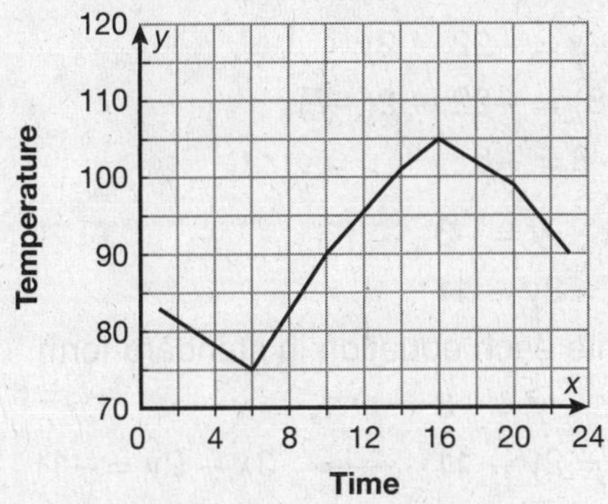

b. The temperature data creates a continuous relation because given a specific time of day, the temperature can always be measured and it does not immediately switch from one temperature to another. Therefore the graph of the temperature is continuous.

c. Yes, the graph is a function. For every time given, there is exactly one temperature. The graph also passes the vertical line test.

26. Write a system of equations.

$48.7r + 28.6p = 85$

$9.1r + 16.5p = 50$

Solve the system.

$$r = \frac{\begin{vmatrix} 85 & 28.6 \\ 50 & 16.5 \end{vmatrix}}{\begin{vmatrix} 48.7 & 28.6 \\ 9.1 & 16.5 \end{vmatrix}} = \frac{85(16.5) - 50(28.6)}{48.7(16.5) - 9.1(28.6)}$$

$$= \frac{-27.5}{543.29} \approx -0.05$$

$$p = \frac{\begin{vmatrix} 48.7 & 85 \\ 9.1 & 50 \end{vmatrix}}{\begin{vmatrix} 48.7 & 28.6 \\ 9.1 & 16.5 \end{vmatrix}} = \frac{48.7(50) - 9.1(85)}{48.7(16.5) - 9.1(28.6)}$$

$$= \frac{1661.5}{543.29} \approx 3.06$$

This means that 0 cups of fried rice and 3 cups of prawn will give the minimum daily allowance of carbohydrate and protein.

27. $(2x + 1.5)(x + 1) = 69$

$2x^2 + 2x + 1.5x + 1.5 = 69$

$2x^2 + 3.5x - 67.5 = 0$

$(2x + 13.5)(x - 5) = 0$

$2x + 13.5 = 0$ or $x - 5 = 0$

$2x = -13.5$ $\quad x = 5$

$x = -6.75$

The dimensions cannot be negative, so $x = 5$. Therefore, the envelope cannot be greater than 2(5) + 1.5, or 11.5 inches long, and 5 + 1, or 6 inches high.

28. a. Write the x-coordinate for the number of years after 2000.

(0, 1.21), (1, 1.22), (2, 1.23)

b. The slope is $m = \frac{1.22 - 1.21}{1 - 0} = 0.01$

The y-intercept is (0, 1.21), since that point lies on the y-axis.

The equation is $y = 0.01x + 1.21$.

29. $4x^2 - 25$ This is a Difference of Squares.

$4x^2 - 25 = (2x - 5)(2x + 5)$

30. $x^2 + 3x - 18$

Find the two numbers whose sum is 3 and whose product is −18. The two numbers are 6 and −3.

$x^2 + 3x - 18 = (x - 3)(x + 6)$.

LESSON 24

Warm Up 24

1. consistent, dependent
2. Write each equation in $y = mx + b$ form and graph the equation by y-intercept and slope.

$y = x + 1$

$y + 3x = 5$, or $y = -3x + 5$.

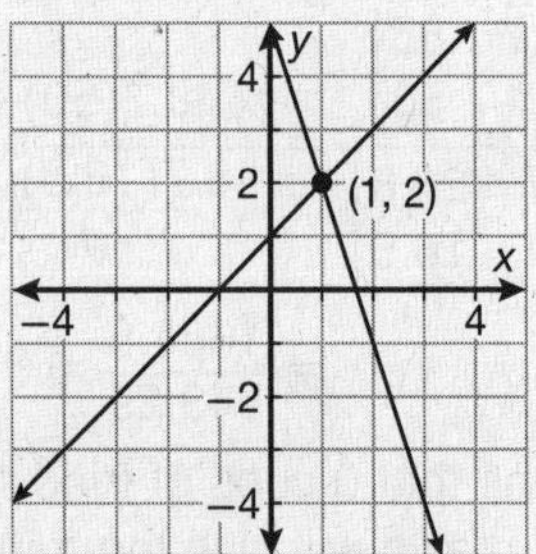

The solution is (1, 2).

3. $y = x + 9$

$2x - y = -13$

Substitute the expression for y in the second equation.

$2x - (x + 9) = -13$

$2x - x - 9 = -13$

$x = -4$

Replace x with −4 in the first equation.

$y = -4 + 9$

$y = 5$

The solution is (−4, 5).

Lesson Practice 24

a. $-2y = -6x + 62$

$-x = -22 - 2y$

Write each equation in standard form.

$-2y = -6x + 62 \longrightarrow 6x - 2y = 62$

$-x = -22 - 2y \longrightarrow -x + 2y = -22$

Add vertically. The y-terms will be eliminated. Solve for x and substitute the value of x into either original equation to find y.

$6x - 2y = 62$

$\underline{-x + 2y = -22}$

$5x \quad = 40$

$x = 8$

$-(8) = -22 - 2y$

$14 = -2y$

$-7 = y$

The solution is (8, −7). The system is consistent and independent.

Check: Substitute 8 for x and −7 for y into both original equations.

$-2y = -6x + 62$

$-2(-7) = -6(8) + 62$

$14 = 14$

$-x = -22 - 2y$

$-(8) = -22 - 2(-7)$

$-8 = -8$

b. $-x - y = -3$

$3x = 2y - 11$

Write each equation in standard form

$-x - y = -3$

$3x = 2y - 11 \longrightarrow 3x - 2y = -11$

Multiply the first equation by −2.

$-2(-x - y = -3)$

$2x + 2y = 6$

Add the equations, and solve for x and y.

$2x + 2y = 6$

$\underline{3x - 2y = -11}$

$5x \quad = -5$

$x = -1$

$-x - y = -3$

$-(-1) - y = -3$

$1 - y = -3$

$$-y = -4$$
$$y = 4$$

The solution is $(-1, 4)$. The system is consistent and independent.

c. $5x + 7y = -36$

$\frac{2}{3}x - 8y = 22$

The equations are in standard form. Multiply the second equation by 3 to clear the fraction.

$$3\left(\frac{2}{3}x - 8y = 22\right)$$
$$2x - 24y = 66$$

Multiply this equation by 5, and the first original equation by -2 to make the x-coefficients opposite integers.

$$5(2x - 24y = 66) \longrightarrow 10x - 120y = 330$$
$$-2(5x + 7y = -36) \longrightarrow -10x - 14y = 72$$

Add the equations, and solve for x and y.

$$\begin{array}{r} 10x - 120y = 330 \\ \underline{-10x - 14y = 72} \\ -134y = 402 \\ y = -3 \end{array}$$

$$5x + 7(-3) = -36$$
$$5x - 21 = -36$$
$$5x = -15$$
$$x = -3$$

The solution is $(-3, -3)$.

d. The equations are already in standard form. Clear fraction by multiplying equation 1 by 2 and equation 2 by 12 (LCM of denominators). Then multiply equation 1 by 2 to make y-terms opposite.

$$\begin{cases} \frac{1}{2}x - y = 15 \\ \frac{1}{4}x + \frac{1}{3}y = 0 \end{cases} \longrightarrow \begin{cases} 2\left(\frac{1}{2}x - y\right) = 2(15) \\ 12\left(\frac{1}{4}x + \frac{1}{3}y\right) = 12(0) \end{cases}$$

$$\longrightarrow \begin{cases} x - 2y = 30 \\ 3x + 4y = 0 \end{cases} \longrightarrow \begin{cases} 2(x - 2y) = 2(30) \\ 3x + 4y = 0 \end{cases}$$

$$\longrightarrow \begin{cases} 2x - 4y = 60 \\ 3x + 4y = 0 \end{cases}$$

Add vertically to eliminate y and solve for x.

$$\begin{array}{r} 2x - 4y = 60 \\ \underline{3x + 4y = 0} \\ 5x \qquad = 60 \end{array}$$

$$\frac{5x}{5} = \frac{60}{5}$$
$$x = 12$$

Substitute for x and solve for y.

$$\frac{1}{2}x - y = 15$$
$$\frac{1}{2}(12) - y = 15$$
$$6 - y = 15$$
$$-15 + 6 - y + y = -15 + 15 + y$$
$$-9 = y$$

Solution is $(12, -9)$.

e. Write in standard form:

$$\begin{cases} -7 = y + 3x \\ 15x = 50 - 5y \end{cases} \longrightarrow \begin{cases} 3x + y = -7 \\ 15x + 5y = 50 \end{cases}$$

Multiply equation 1 by -5 to make opposite y-terms.

$$\begin{cases} 3x + y = -7 \\ 15x + 5y = 50 \end{cases} \longrightarrow \begin{cases} -5(3x + y) = -5(-7) \\ 15x + 5y = 50 \end{cases}$$

$$\longrightarrow \begin{cases} -15x - 5y = 35 \\ 15x + 5y = 50 \end{cases}$$

Add vertically

$$\begin{array}{r} -15x - 5y = 35 \\ \underline{15x + 5y = 50} \\ 0 = 85 \end{array}$$

$0 = 85$ is a false statement.

No solutions; system is inconsistent (lines are parallel)

f. Write in standard form:

$$\begin{cases} 4x = 10 + 2y \\ 5 = 2x - y \end{cases} \longrightarrow \begin{cases} 4x - 2y = 10 \\ 2x - y = 5 \end{cases}$$

Multiply equation 2 by -2 to make opposite y-terms.

$$\begin{cases} 4x - 2y = 10 \\ 2x - y = 5 \end{cases} \longrightarrow \begin{cases} 4x - 2y = 10 \\ -2(2x - y) = -2(5) \end{cases}$$

$$\longrightarrow \begin{cases} 4x - 2y = 10 \\ -4x + 2y = -10 \end{cases}$$

Solve for x and y.

$$\begin{array}{r} 4x - 2y = 10 \\ \underline{-4x + 2y = -10} \\ 0 = 0 \end{array}$$

$0 = 0$ is a true statement.

Infinitely many solutions; system is consistent and dependent (lines coincide)

g. $\begin{cases}10a + 3c = 109\\5a + 3c = 59\end{cases} \longrightarrow \begin{cases}10a + 3c = 109\\-1(5a + 3c) = -1(59)\end{cases}$

$\longrightarrow \begin{cases}10a + 3c = 109\\-5a - 3c = -59\end{cases}$

Solve for a:

$$10a + 3c = 109$$
$$-5a - 3c = -59$$
$$5a = 50$$
$$\frac{5a}{5} = \frac{50}{5}$$
$$a = 10$$

Solve for c:

$$10a + 3c = 109$$
$$10(10) + 3c = 109$$
$$100 + 3c = 109$$
$$-100 + 100 + 3c = -100 + 109$$
$$3c = 9$$
$$\frac{3c}{3} = \frac{9}{3}$$
$$c = 3$$

The cost for each adult is \$10 and the cost for each child is \$3.

Practice 24

1. $\begin{vmatrix}-2 & 1\\1 & x\end{vmatrix} = 16$

$$(-2)(x) - (1)(1) = 16$$
$$-2x - 1 = 16$$
$$-2x = 17$$
$$\frac{-2x}{-2} = \frac{17}{-2}$$
$$x = -\frac{17}{2}$$

2. $\begin{vmatrix}-3 + x & x\\1 & 6\end{vmatrix} = 5$

$$(-3 + x)(6) - (x)(1) = 5$$
$$-18 + 6x - x = 5$$
$$-18 + 5x = 5$$
$$5x = 23$$
$$\frac{5x}{5} = \frac{23}{5}$$
$$x = \frac{23}{5}$$

3. $\begin{vmatrix}4 & -5\\2 & x\end{vmatrix} = 8$

$$(4)(x) - (-5)(2) = 8$$
$$4x + 10 = 8$$
$$4x = -2$$
$$\frac{4x}{4} = \frac{-2}{4}$$
$$x = -\frac{1}{2}$$

4. $\frac{120 \text{ in.}}{1 \text{ s}} \times \frac{1 \text{ ft}}{12 \text{ in.}} \times \frac{60 \text{ s}}{1 \text{ min}} = \frac{120 \cdot 60}{12} \frac{\text{ft}}{\text{min}}$

Rate is 600 ft/min.

5. Using slope formula,

$$m = \frac{y_2 - y_1}{x_2 - x_1}$$
$$= \frac{5 - 1}{0 - 2}$$
$$= \frac{4}{-2} = -2$$

6. $\begin{bmatrix}-5 & 2\\0 & 1\end{bmatrix} \times \begin{bmatrix}3 & 4\\1 & 8\end{bmatrix}$

$$= \begin{bmatrix}(-5)(3) + 2(1) & (-5)(4) + 2(8)\\0(3) + 1(1) & 0(4) + 1(8)\end{bmatrix}$$
$$= \begin{bmatrix}-13 & -4\\1 & 8\end{bmatrix}$$

7. $[-1 \quad 5] \times \begin{bmatrix}6\\8\end{bmatrix} = [(-1)(6) + 5(8)] = [34]$

8. $[-3 \quad 4] \times \begin{bmatrix}1\\7\end{bmatrix} = [(-3)(1) + 4(7)] = [25]$

9. This is a Difference of Squares

$$x^4 - 16 = (x^2)^2 - 4^2$$
$$= (x^2 - 4)(x^2 + 4)$$

The first part of the expression $(x^2 - 4)$ is again a Difference of Squares

$$x^4 - 16 = (x^2 - 2^2)(x^2 + 4)$$
$$= (x - 2)(x + 2)(x^2 + 4)$$

10. The equations are already in standard form. Multiply equation 2 by 5 to make y-terms opposite.

$\begin{cases}2x - 5y = 5\\-5x + y = -1\end{cases} \longrightarrow \begin{cases}2x - 5y = 5\\5(-5x + y) = 5(-1)\end{cases}$

$\longrightarrow \begin{cases}2x - 5y = 5\\-25x + 5y = -5\end{cases}$

Add vertically to eliminate y and solve for x.

$$\begin{aligned} 2x - 5y &= 5 \\ -25x + 5y &= -5 \\ \hline -23x &= 0 \\ x &= 0 \end{aligned}$$

Substitute for x and solve for y.

$$\begin{aligned} -5(0) + y &= -1 \\ y &= -1 \end{aligned}$$

Solution is (0, −1)

11. The equations are already in standard form. Multiply equation 1 by 3 and equation 2 by 4 to make x-terms opposite.

$$\begin{cases} -4x + 7y = -47 \\ 3x - 5y = 34 \end{cases} \longrightarrow \begin{cases} 3(-4x + 7y) = 3(-47) \\ 4(3x - 5y) = 4(34) \end{cases}$$

$$\longrightarrow \begin{cases} -12x + 21y = -141 \\ 12x - 20y = 136 \end{cases}$$

Add vertically to eliminate x and solve for y.

$$\begin{aligned} -12x + 21y &= -141 \\ 12x - 20y &= 136 \\ \hline y &= -5 \end{aligned}$$

Substitute for y and solve for x.

$$\begin{aligned} 3x - 5y &= 34 \\ 3x - 5(-5) &= 34 \\ 3x + 25 &= 34 \\ 3x + 25 - 25 &= 34 - 25 \\ 3x &= 9 \\ \frac{3x}{3} &= \frac{9}{3} \\ x &= 3 \end{aligned}$$

Solution is (3, −5)

12. The equations are already in standard form. Multiply equation 1 by 4 to make y-terms opposite.

$$\begin{cases} 5x + y = 14 \\ -3x - 4y = -5 \end{cases} \longrightarrow \begin{cases} 4(5x + y) = 4(14) \\ -3x - 4y = -5 \end{cases}$$

$$\longrightarrow \begin{cases} 20x + 4y = 56 \\ -3x - 4y = -5 \end{cases}$$

Add vertically to eliminate y and solve for x.

$$\begin{aligned} 20x + 4y &= 56 \\ -3x - 4y &= -5 \\ \hline 17x &= 51 \\ \frac{17x}{17} &= \frac{51}{17} \\ x &= 3 \end{aligned}$$

Substitute for x and solve for y.

$$\begin{aligned} 5x + y &= 14 \\ 5(3) + y &= 14 \\ 15 + y &= 14 \\ -15 + 15 + y &= -15 + 14 \\ y &= -1 \end{aligned}$$

Solution is (3, −1)

13. The equations are already in standard form. Multiply equation 1 by 5 to make x-terms opposite.

$$\begin{cases} 2x - 5y = -3 \\ -10x + 25y = 15 \end{cases} \longrightarrow \begin{cases} 5(2x - 5y) = 5(-3) \\ -10x + 25y = 15 \end{cases}$$

$$\longrightarrow \begin{cases} 10x - 25y = -15 \\ -10x + 25y = 15 \end{cases}$$

Add vertically to eliminate y.

$$\begin{aligned} 10x - 25y &= -15 \\ -10x + 25y &= 15 \\ \hline 0 &= 0 \end{aligned}$$

$0 = 0$ is a true statement: therefore, there are infinitely many solutions.

14.

$$\begin{aligned} V &= 104 \\ lwh &= 104 \\ (x + 8)(x - 1)(2) &= 104 \\ \frac{(x + 8)(x - 1)(2)}{2} &= \frac{104}{2} \\ (x + 8)(x - 1) &= 52 \\ (x)(x) + (x)(-1) + (8)(x) + (8)(-1) &= 52 \\ x^2 - x + 8x - 8 &= 52 \\ x^2 + 7x - 8 &= 52 \\ x^2 + 7x - 8 - 52 &= 52 - 52 \\ x^2 + 7x - 60 &= 0 \end{aligned}$$

$$\begin{aligned} x^2 + 7x - 60 &= 0 \\ (x - 5)(x + 12) &= 0 \end{aligned}$$

$x - 5 = 0$ or $x + 12 = 0$

$x = 5$ or $x = -12$

Since x can't be negative, $x = 5$.

15. Solve equation 2 for y:

$$\begin{aligned} x + y &= 7 \\ y &= 7 - x \end{aligned}$$

Substitute expression for y into equation and solve for x:

$$2x + y = -4$$
$$2x + (7 - x) = -4$$
$$x + 7 = -4$$
$$x + 7 - 7 = -4 - 7$$
$$x = -11$$

Substitute for x into equation 2 to solve for y:

$$x + y = 7$$
$$-11 + y = 7$$
$$y = 18$$

Solution: (–11, 18)

16. First terms: $a \cdot c = ac$
Outer terms: $a \cdot d = ad$
Inner terms: $b \cdot c = bc$
Last terms: $b \cdot d = bd$
Add the terms: $ac + ad + bc + bd$
Combine any like terms at the end.

17. a. $AB = \begin{bmatrix} 5 & 3 \\ 6 & 5 \end{bmatrix}\begin{bmatrix} 7 & 4 \\ 8 & 7 \end{bmatrix}$

$$= \begin{bmatrix} 5(7) + 3(8) & 5(4) + 3(7) \\ 6(7) + 5(8) & 6(4) + 5(7) \end{bmatrix}$$

$$= \begin{bmatrix} 59 & 41 \\ 82 & 59 \end{bmatrix}$$

b. $BA = \begin{bmatrix} 7 & 4 \\ 8 & 7 \end{bmatrix}\begin{bmatrix} 5 & 3 \\ 6 & 5 \end{bmatrix}$

$$= \begin{bmatrix} 7(5) + 4(6) & 7(3) + 4(5) \\ 8(5) + 7(6) & 8(3) + 7(5) \end{bmatrix}$$

$$= \begin{bmatrix} 59 & 41 \\ 82 & 59 \end{bmatrix}$$

c. Yes; $\begin{bmatrix} 59 & 41 \\ 82 & 59 \end{bmatrix} = \begin{bmatrix} 59 & 41 \\ 82 & 59 \end{bmatrix}$

18. $\begin{cases} 5a + 4s = 154 \\ 3a + 8s = 182 \end{cases} \longrightarrow \begin{cases} -2(5a + 4s) = -2(154) \\ 3a + 8s = 182 \end{cases}$

$$\longrightarrow \begin{cases} -10a - 8s = -308 \\ 3a + 8s = 182 \end{cases}$$

Solve for a and s:

$$-10a - 8s = -308$$
$$\underline{3a + 8s = 182}$$
$$-7a = -126$$
$$a = 18$$

Substitute the value for a

$$5a + 4s = 154$$
$$5(18) + 4s = 154$$
$$90 + 4s = 154$$
$$-90 + 90 + 4s = -90 + 154$$
$$4s = 64$$
$$\frac{4s}{4} = \frac{64}{4}$$
$$s = 16$$

The cost per adult is $18 and the cost per senior is $16.

19. Not necessarily; The value of a polynomial is not determined by degree alone; it also depends on the coefficients and the value(s) substituted for the variable(s).
Possible examples; Let $P_1 = x^3$ and $P_2 = x^2$. Then for $x = 3$, the value of P_1 is 27 and the value of P_2 is 9. But for $x = -3$, the value of P_1 is –27 and the value of P_2 is 9.

20. $(fg)(x) = f(x)\,g(x)$

$$= (3x - 9)(x - 3)$$
$$= (3x)(x) + (3x)(-3) + (-9)(x) + (-9)(-3)$$
$$= 3x^2 - 9x - 9x + 27$$
$$= 3x^2 - 18x + 27$$

21. Substituting and using a graphing calculator,

$$\text{Area} = \frac{1}{4}\begin{vmatrix} x_1 & x_2 & x_3 & x_4 \\ y_1 & y_3 & y_3 & y_4 \\ 1 & 1 & 1 & 1 \\ -1 & 1 & -1 & 1 \end{vmatrix}$$

$$= \frac{1}{4}\begin{vmatrix} 1 & 7 & 7 & 3 \\ 2 & 2 & 6 & 8 \\ 1 & 1 & 1 & 1 \\ -1 & 1 & -1 & 1 \end{vmatrix} = \frac{104}{4} = 26$$

Area is 26 square units.

22. a.

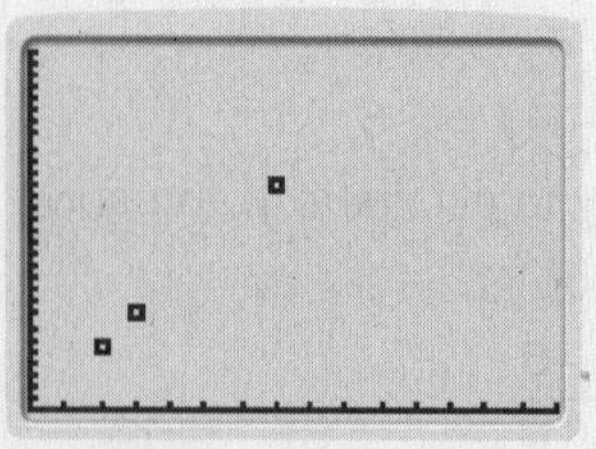

b.

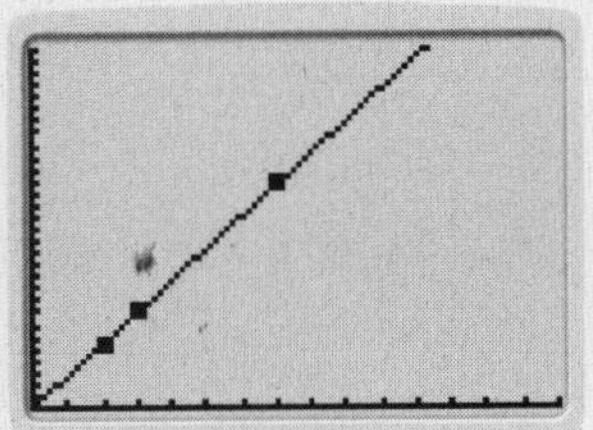

c. Using equation of line calculated in b,

$$\text{predicted \#} = \frac{8}{3}(x) = \frac{8}{3}(10) = \frac{80}{3} = 26\frac{2}{3}$$

23. The student did not multiply the right side of the second equation by −1. Correct solution:

$$\begin{cases} 4x + y = 9 \\ 4x - 3y = 5 \end{cases} \longrightarrow \begin{cases} 4x + y = 9 \\ -4x + 3y = -5 \end{cases}$$

$$\begin{array}{rl} 4x + y = 9 & \longrightarrow 4x + y = 9 \\ \underline{-4x + 3y = -5} & \quad 4x + 1 = 9 \\ 4y = 4 & \quad 4x = 8 \\ y = 1 & \quad x = 2 \end{array}$$

Correct solution is (2, 1).

24. Score of 530 on first 2 games + score x on third game is at least 750 points:

$$530 + x \geq 750$$
$$-530 + 530 + x \geq -530 + 750$$
$$x \geq 220$$

Minimum score: 220 points

25. $\frac{70 \cancel{\text{mi}}}{1 \cancel{\text{h}}} \times \frac{5280 \text{ ft}}{1 \cancel{\text{mi}}} \times \frac{1 \cancel{\text{h}}}{3600 \text{ s}} = \frac{70\ 5280}{3600} \frac{\text{ft}}{\text{s}}$

About 103 ft/s

26. Conjunction. The amount must be greater than or equal to the minimum ***and*** less than or equal to the maximum.

27. $\frac{C_1}{C_2} = \frac{W_1}{W_2}$ Write a proportion.

$\frac{80}{200} = \frac{6}{W_2}$ Substitute.

$80\ W_2 = (200)\ (6)$ Cross multiply.

$W_2 = 15$ pt Simplify.

Answer choice **A**

28. Discrete, since function consists of disconnected points.

29. Discrete, since function consists of disconnected points.

30. Continuous; graph can be drawn without lifting pencil from paper

LAB 6

Graphing Calculator Practice

a.

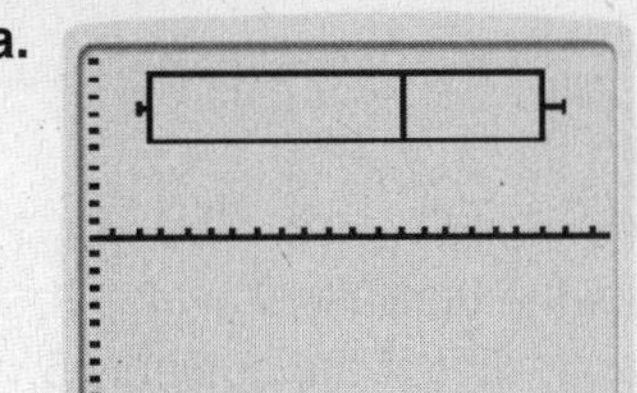

b. 1255

LESSON 25

Warm Up 25

1. discrete

2. $\begin{array}{r} 25.5 \\ -\ 37.75 \\ \hline -12.25 \end{array}$

3. $(-0.25)^2 = (-0.25)(-0.25) = 0.0625$

Lesson Practice 25

a. Mean:

$$\bar{x} = \frac{4.5 + 6.5 + 7 + 5 + 7 + 5 + 7}{7} = \frac{42}{7} = 6$$

Median: Arrange the data in order:
4.5, 5, 5, 6.5, 7, 7, 7
The median is the middle number, 6.5.
Mode: The mode is the number that appears most often, 7.

b. The range is the difference between the largest and smallest data values.

The range is $12 - 2 = 10$.

To find the standard deviation, first calculate the mean.

$$\bar{x} = \frac{11 + 8 + 2 + 7 + 12}{5} = \frac{40}{5} = 8$$

$$\sigma = \sqrt{\frac{(11-8)^2 + (8-8)^2 + (2-8)^2 + (7-8)^2 + (12-8)^2}{5}}$$

$$= \sqrt{\frac{62}{5}} \approx 3.5$$

c. Range = 25 − 8 = 17

$$\bar{x} = \frac{14 + 9 + 19 + 16 + 8 + 17 + 25 + 21 + 15}{9} = \frac{144}{9} = 16$$

$$\sigma = \sqrt{\frac{(14-16)^2 + (9-16)^2 + (19-16)^2 + (16-16)^2 + (8-16)^2 + (17-16)^2 + (25-16)^2 + (21-16)^2 + (15-16)^2}{9}}$$

$$= \sqrt{\frac{233}{9}} \approx 5.1$$

d. The outlier is 47.
The range with the outlier is 47 − 4 = 43.
The range without the outlier is 7 − 4 = 3.
The mode with and without the outlier is 5.
The median with the outlier is 5.5.
The median without the outlier is 5.
The mean with the outlier is

$$\bar{x} = \frac{6 + 4 + 7 + 47 + 5 + 5 + 6 + 5}{8} = \frac{85}{8} \approx 10.625$$

The mean without the outlier is

$$\bar{x} = \frac{6 + 4 + 7 + 5 + 5 + 6 + 5}{8} = \frac{38}{7} \approx 5.429$$

The standard deviation with the outlier is

$$\sigma = \sqrt{\frac{(6-10.6)^2 + (4-10.6)^2 + (7-10.6)^2 + (47-10.6)^2 + (5-10.6)^2 + (5-10.6)^2 + (6-10.6)^2 + (5-10.6)^2}{8}}$$

$$= \sqrt{\frac{1517.88}{8}} \approx 13.8$$

The standard deviation with the outlier is

$$\sigma = \sqrt{\frac{(6-5.4)^2 + (4-5.4)^2 + (7-5.4)^2 + (5-5.4)^2 + (5-5.4)^2 + (6-5.4)^2 + (5-5.4)^2}{8}}$$

$$= \sqrt{\frac{5.72}{7}} \approx 0.9$$

e. Write the data in ascending order: 1, 2, 2, 3, 4, 5, 6
The median of the data is 3.
The lower quartile is the median of the lower half of the data which is 2.
The upper quartile is the median of the upper half of the data which is 5.
The minimum is 1. The maximum is 6.

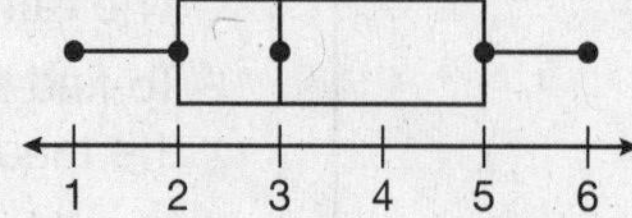

f. The mean is

$$x = \frac{158.7 + 132.4 + 111.3 + 100.9 + 109.1 + 78.2 + 88.9}{7}$$

$$= \frac{779.5}{7} \approx 111.4$$

The standard deviation is

$$\sigma = \sqrt{\frac{(158.7 - 111.4)^2 + (132.4 - 111.4)^2 + (111.3 - 111.4)^2 + (100.9 - 111.4)^2 + (109.1 - 111.4)^2 + (78.2 - 111.4)^2 + (88.9 - 111.4)^2}{7}}$$

$$= \sqrt{\frac{4402.33}{7}} \approx 25.1$$

Practice 25

1. $-5[(2 - 1 - 3) - (5 - 8) - 6]$
$= -5[(-2) - (-3) - 6]$
$= -5[-5] = 25$

2. $2(2 - 6) - (-1 - 1) - 3$
$= 2(-4) - (-2) - 3$
$= -8 - (-2) - 3 = -9$

3. $-3x^6(x^{-1}y^{-8})^{-3}$
$= -3x^6(x^3y^{24}) = -3x^9y^{24}$

4. $3x + 1 > x + 13$
$2x > 12$
$x > 6$

$x > 6$ 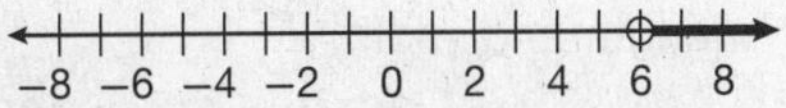

5. $\begin{bmatrix} -2 & 10 \\ 2 & 3 \end{bmatrix} \begin{bmatrix} -1 & 0 \\ 0 & 1 \end{bmatrix}$

$\begin{bmatrix} -2(-1) + 10(0) & -2(0) + 10(1) \\ 2(-1) + 3(0) & 2(0) + 3(1) \end{bmatrix}$

$\begin{bmatrix} 2 & 10 \\ -2 & 3 \end{bmatrix}$

6. $3x^2(2x^2 - 3x) = 6x^4 - 9x^3$

7. $2x^2 + 9x - 5 = (2x - 1)(x + 5)$

8. $4x + y = -11$
$-x + y = 9 \longrightarrow y = x + 9$
Substitute $y = x + 9$ into $4x + y = -11$
$4x + (x + 9) = -11$
$5x = -20$
$x = -4$
Substitute $x = -4$ into $-x + y = 9$
$-(-4) + y = 9$
$y = 5$
The solution is $(-4, 5)$.

9. $x + y = 4$
$x - y = 6 \longrightarrow y = x - 6$
Substitute $y = x - 6$ into $x + y = 4$.
$x + (x - 6) = 4$
$2x = 10$
$x = 5$
Substitute $x = 5$ into $x - y = 6$.
$5 - y = 6$
$y = -1$
The solution is $(5, -1)$.

10. Mean: $\bar{x} = \frac{2 + 2 + 3 + 10 + 11 + 13 + 15}{7}$
$= \frac{56}{7} = 8$
Median is 10.

11. Mean: $\bar{x} = \frac{1 + 2 + 3 + 3}{4}$
$= \frac{9}{4} = 2.25$
Median is $\frac{2+3}{2} = 2.5$.

12. Mean: $\bar{x} = \frac{1 + 1 + 13 + 15 + 14}{5}$
$= \frac{44}{5} = 8.8$
Median is 13.

13. Factor the polynomial.
$x^2 - 24x + 144 = (x - 12)(x - 12)$
Therefore the width is $(x - 12)$ inches and the length is $(x - 12)$ inches.

14. $f(12) = -3(12) + 11 = -25$

$g(12) = 4(12) - 10 = 38$

$f(12) + g(12) = -25 + 38 = 13$

Answer choice **B**

15. Add the equations.

$$\begin{array}{r} 5x + y = 19 \\ -2x - y = -7 \\ \hline 3x \quad = 12 \\ x = 4 \end{array}$$

Substitute $x = 4$ into one of the equations.

$5(4) + y = 19$

$20 + y = 19$

$y = -1$

The solution is $(4, -1)$.

16. $-x + 3y = 12$

$6x - y = -21$

Multiply the first equation by 6.

$6(-x + 3y) = (12)6$

$-6x + 18y = 72$

Add the equations.

$$\begin{array}{r} -6x + 18y = 72 \\ 6x - y = -21 \\ \hline 17y = 51 \\ y = 3 \end{array}$$

Substitute $y = 3$ into one of the original equations

$-x + 3(3) = 12$

$-x + 9 = 12$

$x = -3$

The solution is $(-3, 3)$.

17. Add the equations.

$$\begin{array}{r} 2x + y = 8 \\ x - y = 10 \\ \hline 3x \quad = 18 \\ x = 6 \end{array}$$

Substitute $x = 6$ into one of the equations.

$2(6) + y = 8$

$12 + y = 8$

$y = -4$

The solution is $(6, -4)$.

18. The graph of $P_1 + P_2$ is a vertical translation of the graph of P_1. If P_2 does not equal zero but has a degree of 0, then it is a nonzero constant function. So, $P_1 + P_2$ is the function obtained by adding the nonzero constant P_2 to P_1.

19. a. There are 3600 seconds in one hour.

$$\frac{1247 \text{ singles}}{60 \not{s}} \times \frac{3600 \not{s}}{1 \text{ hr}}$$

$$= \frac{1247(3600) \text{ singles}}{60 \text{ hr}}$$

$$= 74{,}820 \frac{\text{singles}}{\text{hr}}$$

b. There are 60 minutes in one hour.

$$\frac{13{,}222 \text{ singles}}{15 \not{\text{min}}} \times \frac{60 \not{\text{min}}}{1 \text{ hr}}$$

$$= \frac{113{,}222(60) \text{ singles}}{15 \text{ hr}}$$

$$= 52{,}888 \frac{\text{singles}}{\text{hr}}$$

c. $74{,}820 - 52{,}888 = 21{,}932$

Per hour Mike drums 21,932 more singles with his hands than with his feet.

20. a. Let x represent the amount to add to the length and width.

$$(x + 36)(x + 56) = 4800$$
$$x^2 + 36x + 56x + 36(56) = 4800$$
$$x^2 + 92x + 2016 = 4800$$
$$x^2 + 92x - 2784 = 0$$
$$(x - 24)(x + 116) = 0$$
$$x - 24 = 0 \quad \text{or} \quad x + 116 = 0$$
$$x = 24 \qquad\qquad x = -116$$

The amount to add has to be positive. So, 24 inches is added to the length and 24 inches to the width. This means that 12 inches is added to each side. Since each square is 4 inches long, then 3 squares make up 12 inches. Therefore, 3 squares are added to each side.

b. Adding a border of 3 squares to each side is the same as adding 24 inches to to the length and 24 inches to the width. Therefore $(36 + 24)(56 + 24) = 4800$ square inches.

21. a.

Lunch

Person	Drink	Sandwich	Snack
Alea	1	2	2
Cory	2	2	1
Troy	2	1	3

Cost	
Drink	\$1.50
Sandwich	\$4.00
Snack	\$1.00

b. Lunch $= \begin{bmatrix} 1 & 2 & 2 \\ 2 & 2 & 1 \\ 2 & 1 & 3 \end{bmatrix}$ Cost $= \begin{bmatrix} \$1.50 \\ \$4.00 \\ \$1.00 \end{bmatrix}$

c. $\begin{bmatrix} 1 & 2 & 2 \\ 2 & 2 & 1 \\ 2 & 1 & 3 \end{bmatrix} \cdot \begin{bmatrix} 1.50 \\ 4.00 \\ 1.00 \end{bmatrix}$

$$= \begin{bmatrix} 1(1.5) + 2(4) + 2(1) \\ 2(1.5) + 2(4) + 1(1) \\ 2(1.5) + 1(4) + 3(1) \end{bmatrix} = \begin{bmatrix} 11.5 \\ 12 \\ 10 \end{bmatrix}$$

Alea spent \$11.50, Cory spent \$12, and Troy spent \$10. Therefore, Cory spent the most money.

22. a. $\begin{bmatrix} -x & 2 & -2 \\ 0 & -3 & 1 \\ 8 & 2x & 0 \end{bmatrix} = 0$

$$-x\begin{vmatrix} -3 & 1 \\ 2x & 0 \end{vmatrix} - 2\begin{vmatrix} 0 & 1 \\ 8 & 0 \end{vmatrix} + (-2)\begin{vmatrix} 0 & -3 \\ 8 & 2x \end{vmatrix} = 0$$

$-x[-3(0) - 2x(1)] - 2[0(0) - 8(1)]$

$+ (-2)[0(2x) - 8(-3)] = 0$

$2x^2 - (-16) + (-48) = 0$

$2x^2 - 32 = 0$

b. $2x^2 - 32 = 0$

$2(x^2 - 16) = 0$

$2(x + 4)(x - 4) = 0$

$2(x + 4) = 0$ or $(x - 4) = 0$

$x = -4$ or $x = 4$

c. $\begin{vmatrix} -4 & 2 & -2 \\ 0 & -3 & 1 \\ 8 & 2(4) & 0 \end{vmatrix} = 0$

$\begin{vmatrix} -4 & 2 & -2 \\ 0 & -3 & 1 \\ 8 & 8 & 0 \end{vmatrix} = 0$

or

$\begin{vmatrix} -(-4) & 2 & -2 \\ 0 & -3 & 1 \\ 8 & 2(-4) & 0 \end{vmatrix} = 0$

$\begin{vmatrix} 4 & 2 & -2 \\ 0 & -3 & 1 \\ 8 & -8 & 0 \end{vmatrix} = 0$

23. a. Let m represent the number of minutes used over 250 minutes.

The equation is $29.95 + 0.40m + 25 = 114.95$.

b. $29.95 + 0.40m + 25 = 114.95$

$0.40m = 60$

$m = 150$

c. $29.95 + 0.40(150) + 25 \stackrel{?}{=} 114.95$

$29.95 + 60 + 25 \stackrel{?}{=} 114.95$

$114.95 \stackrel{?}{=} 114.95$

d. The total minutes used is $250 + 150 = 400$.

24. Possible answer $5x + 2y = 10$

$3x + 7y = 12$

Multiply the first equation by 3 and the second one by -5 so that the coefficients of the x-terms are 15 and -15. 15 is the LCM of 5 and 3.

25. The area is a square, so square the expression.

$(2x - 5)^2 = (2x - 5)(2x - 5)$

$= 4x^2 - 20x + 25$

26. a. Let x represent the heart rate.

$|x - 147| = 24$

b. $x - 147 = 24$ or $x - 147 = -24$

$x - 147 = 24$

$x = 171$

or

$x - 147 = -24$

$x = 123$

The lowest heart rate is 123 bpm and the highest is 171 bpm.

27. The slope is correct. However, the line does not fall; it rises. Because the slope is positive the line rises.

28. a. The graph is continuous. It is a function since it passes the vertical line test. The domain is all real numbers. The range is $y \geq 0$.

b. The graph is discontinuous. It is a function since it passes the vertical line test. The domain is all real numbers. The range is $-1, 2$.

29. $\bar{x} = \frac{8.2 + 7.2 + 7.8 + 11.6}{4}$

$= \frac{34.8}{4} = 8.7$

$\sigma = \sqrt{\frac{(8.2 - 8.7)^2 + (7.2 - 8.7)^2 + (7.8 - 8.7)^2 + (11.6 - 8.7)^2}{4}}$

$= \sqrt{\frac{11.72}{4}} \approx 1.71$

30. As the pasta amount increases the servings increase. This could be a direct variation.

$y = kx$

$8 = k(4), k = 2$

$26 = k(13), k = 2$

$34 = k(17), k = 2$

$58 = k(29), k = 2$

The constant of variation is 2.

LESSON 26

Warm Up 26

1. vertical

2. $m = \frac{-1 - 3}{4 - (-2)} = \frac{-4}{6} = -\frac{2}{3}$

3. In the form $y = mx + b$, the slope is m and the y-intercept is b. For the equation $y = 2x - 5$, the slope is 2 and the y-intercept is -5.

4. **A** $m = \frac{-2 - (-2)}{7 - (-2)} = \frac{0}{9} = 0$

B $m = \frac{2 - (-2)}{-1 - 4} = \frac{4}{-5} = -\frac{4}{5}$

C $m = \frac{-2 - (-7)}{3 - 5} = \frac{5}{-2} = -\frac{5}{2}$

D $m = \frac{5 - 0}{5 - 0} = \frac{5}{5} = 1$

Answer choice **A**

5. In the form $y = mx + b$, the slope is m. Rewrite the equation in this form.

$2x + 3y = 12$

$3y = -2x + 12$

$y = -\frac{2}{3}x + 4$

The slope is $-\frac{2}{3}$.

Lesson Practice 26

a. $C = \frac{5}{9}(F - 32)$

$9C = 9\left[\frac{5}{9}(F - 32)\right]$ Multiply both sides by 9

$9C = 5(F - 32)$

$9C = 5F - 160$ Use the Distributive Property

$-5F + 9C = -160$

$5F - 9C = 160$ Multiply the equation by -1

b. In the form $y = mx + b$, the slope is m and the y-intercept is b. Substitute $m = -2$ and $b = 15$.

$y = -2x + 15$

c. Substitute the values into the point slope form of the linear equation, then solve the equation for y to write the slope-intercept form.

$y - 0 = 1.5(x - (-24))$

$y = 1.5x + 36$

d. Step 1: Use the slope formula to find the value of m.

$m = \frac{12 - 0}{16 - 10} = \frac{12}{6} = 2$

Step 2: Use the point-slope form using one of the given points, then solve for y to find the equation in slope-intercept form.

$y - 0 = 2(x - 10)$

$y = 2x - 20$

e. Step 1: Use the slope formula to find m.

$m = \frac{500 - 375}{1 - 2} = \frac{125}{-1} = -125$

Step 2: Use the point-slope form using one of the given points, then solve for y to find the equation in slope-intercept form.

$$y - 500 = -125(x - 1)$$
$$y - 500 = -125x + 125$$
$$y = -125x + 625$$

Practice 26

1. The degree is 4 so the polynomial is quartic. There is one term so it is a monomial.

2. The degree is 3 so the polynomial is cubic. There are two terms so it is a binomial.

3. The degree is 2 so the polynomial is quadratic. There are three terms so it is a trinomial.

4. $\begin{bmatrix} 0 & 1 \\ 1 & 0 \end{bmatrix} + 6\begin{bmatrix} 2 & -2 \\ -3 & 1 \end{bmatrix}$

$\begin{bmatrix} 0 & 1 \\ 1 & 0 \end{bmatrix} + \begin{bmatrix} 12 & -12 \\ -18 & 6 \end{bmatrix}$

$= \begin{bmatrix} 0 + 12 & 1 + (-12) \\ 1 + (-18) & 0 + 6 \end{bmatrix}$

$= \begin{bmatrix} 12 & -11 \\ -17 & 6 \end{bmatrix}$

5. There are 3 feet in a yard.

$$\frac{450 \text{ ft}}{1} \times \frac{1 \text{ yd}}{3 \text{ ft}} = \frac{450 \text{ yd}}{3} = 150 \text{ yd}$$

6. Factor out the GCF.

$-15x^2 + 5x = -5x(3x - 1)$

7. Factor the Difference of Squares.

$4x^2 - 9 = (2x - 3)(2x + 3)$

8. $6x^2 + 19x - 7 = (3x - 1)(2x + 7)$

9. The mode occurs most often. The modes are 128 and 130.

10. $m = \frac{-4 - 3}{4 - 0} = -\frac{7}{4}$

The equation is

$$y - 3 = -\frac{7}{4}(x - 0)$$
$$y - 3 = -\frac{7}{4}x$$
$$y = -\frac{7}{4}x + 3$$

11. $m = \frac{2 - 5}{4 - 1} = -\frac{3}{3} = -1$

The equation is

$$y - 5 = -1(x - 1)$$
$$y - 5 = -x + 1$$
$$y = -x + 6$$

12. $m = \frac{0 - 2}{5 - (-3)} = -\frac{2}{8} = -\frac{1}{4}$

The equation is

$$y - 0 = -\frac{1}{4}(x - 5)$$
$$y = -\frac{1}{4}x + \frac{5}{4}$$

13. The Associative Property of Multiplication. The product 6 • 5 is a multiple of 10, and it is easier to multiply 30 • 4, than 24 • 5.

14. a. Use a graphing calculator to graph. This is a parabola.

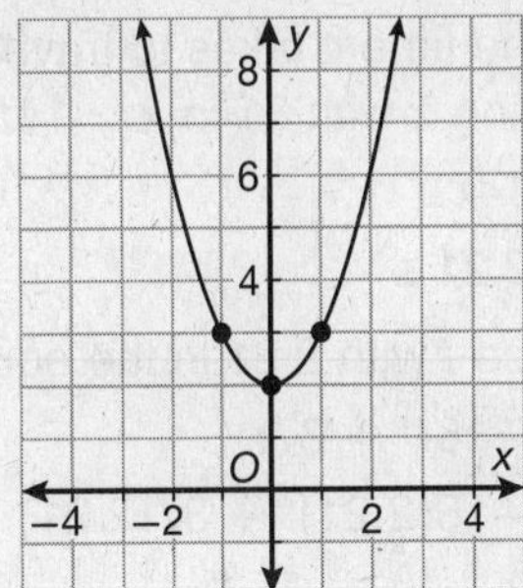

b. The relation is a function since there is one x-value for each y-value, and the graph passes the vertical line test.

c. The graph is continuous.

15. $\frac{2}{5}c + 3 = -5c + \frac{3}{4}$

$$20\left(\frac{2}{5}c + 3\right) = 20\left(-5c + \frac{3}{4}\right)$$
$$8c + 60 = -100c + 15$$
$$108c = -45$$
$$c = -\frac{45}{108} = -\frac{5}{12}$$

Answer choice **D**

16. $4 + 6 > x$

$10 > x$

and

$4 + x > 6$

$x > 2$

and

$6 + x > 4$

$x > -2$, but the length cannot be negative.

Therefore, $2 < x < 10$.

17. a. The new area is $30(20) - 225 = 375$ in.^{2}

b. Let x represent the amount to decrease each dimension by.

$$(30 - x)(20 - x) = 375$$
$$600 - 50x + x^2 = 375$$
$$x^2 - 50x + 225 = 0$$
$$(x - 5)(x - 45) = 0$$
$$x - 5 = 0 \text{ or } x - 45 = 0$$
$$x = 5 \qquad x = 45$$

Since 45 inches is greater than either of the original dimensions, $x = 5$. Therefore, she should decrease each dimension by 5 inches.

18. a. Find the time it takes to travel 31 feet by replacing x with 31 in $x = 14t$.

$$31 = 14t$$
$$t \approx 2.21 \text{ s}$$

b. Replace t with 2.21 in the equation

$$y = -16t^2 + 37t.$$
$$y = -16(2.21)^2 + 37(2.21)$$
$$y \approx 3.6$$

Mia will not make the goal. The ball will reach the goal, but only at a height of about 3.6 feet, which means that the goal will be blocked.

19. a. Use a table to graph each equation.

$f(x) = -4x + 3$		$g(x) = -x + 2$	
x	$f(x)$	x	$g(x)$
0	3	0	2
1	−1	1	1
2	−5	2	0

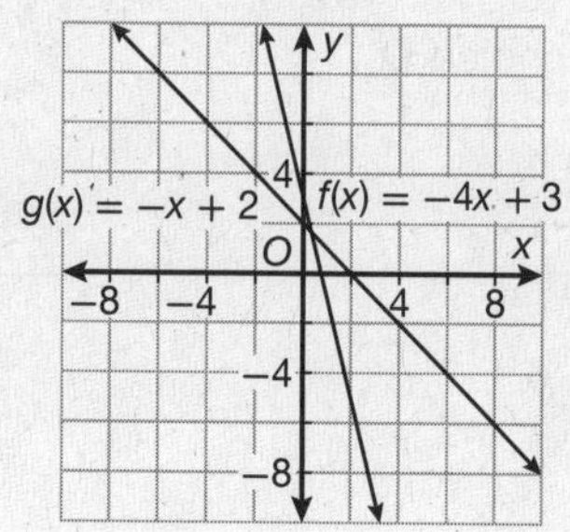

b. Find the difference between points on the graph. At $x = 0$, the difference between the y-values is $3 - 2$, or 1, so plot (0, 1). At $x = 1$, the difference between the y-values is $-1 - 1 = -2$, so plot $(1, -2)$. Draw a straight line through these points.

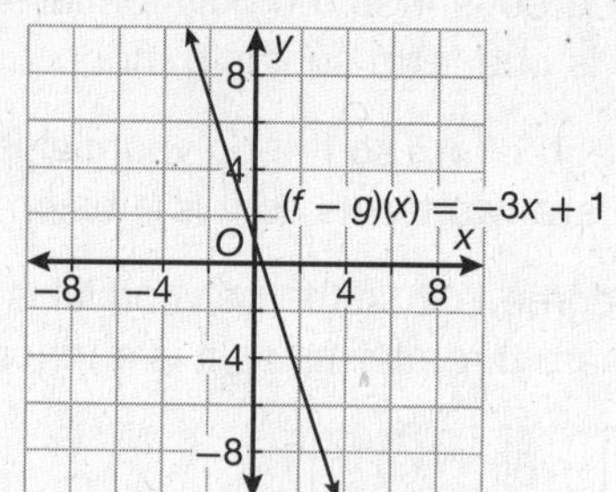

c. $(f - g)(x) = -4x + 3 - (-x + 2)$

$$= -4x + 3 + x - 2$$
$$= -3x + 1$$

20. The solution is not correct. When $3x$ is removed from the left side of the equation, $-2y$ should remain (not $2y$). The correct solution for writing the equation in slope-intercept form should be

$$3x - 2y = 9$$
$$-2y = -3x + 9$$
$$y = \frac{3}{2}x - \frac{9}{2}$$
$$= \frac{3}{2}x - 4\frac{1}{2}$$

The slope is $\frac{3}{2}$, and the y-intercept is $-4\frac{1}{2}$.

21. a. $|x - 21.7| < 3.2$

b. $|x - 21.7| < 3.2$

$x - 21.7 < 3.2$ and $x - 21.7 > -3.2$

$x < 24.9 \qquad x > 18.5$

$18.5 < x < 24.9$

22. There are 60 minutes in one hour.

$$\frac{1 \text{ mi}}{3.719 \not{\text{min}}} \times \frac{60 \not{\text{min}}}{1 \text{ hr}} = \frac{60 \text{ mi}}{3.719 \text{ hr}}$$
$$\approx 16.133 \frac{\text{mi}}{\text{hr}}$$

23. Let s represent the total weight of Sumatra beans and k represent the total weight of Kona beans in the blend. Then the equations are

$$12s + 45k = 30(s + k)$$
$$s + k = 50$$

Solve the equations.

$12s + 45k = 30(s + k)$

$12s + 45k = 30s + 30k$

$15k = 18s$

$\frac{15}{18}k = s$ Solve for s.

$\frac{5}{6}k = s$

Substitute s into the other equation.

$\frac{5}{6}k + k = 50$

$\frac{11}{6}k = 50$

$k \approx 27.3$

Substitute $k = 27.3$ and solve.

$s + k = 50$

$s + 27.3 = 50$

$s = 22.7$

Therefore, there are about 22.7 pounds of Sumatra beans and 27.3 pounds of Kona beans.

24. For both systems, multiply each equation by factors to make either the x- or y-coefficients opposite integers. Add the equations. Both x and y coefficients will result in zero. For systems with infinitely many solutions there will be a true statement remaining, such as $0 = 0$. For systems with no solution there will be a false statement remaining, such as $0 = 20$.

25. $-1\begin{vmatrix} 4 & 1 \\ 1 & -3 \end{vmatrix} - 2\begin{vmatrix} 2 & 1 \\ -1 & -3 \end{vmatrix} + (-2)\begin{vmatrix} 2 & 4 \\ -1 & 1 \end{vmatrix}$

$= -1(-12 - 1) - 2(-6 - -1) + (-2)|2 - -4|$

$= 13 + 10 - 12$

$= 11$

26. Yes. The number π is a real number and a part of the coefficient for x.

27. $\begin{bmatrix} 2 & 3 & 7 \\ 5 & 5 & 4 \\ 9 & 6 & 3 \end{bmatrix}\begin{bmatrix} 4 \\ 6 \\ 8 \end{bmatrix}$

$= \begin{bmatrix} 2(4) + 3(6) + 7(8) \\ 5(4) + 5(6) + 4(8) \\ 9(4) + 6(6) + 3(8) \end{bmatrix}$

$= \begin{bmatrix} 82 \\ 82 \\ 96 \end{bmatrix}$

Ava scored the greatest number of points on the test.

28. a. $a + b = 6$

$0.009a + 0.1b = 0.07(6)$

$0.009a + 0.1b = 0.42$

b. $a = \frac{\begin{vmatrix} 6 & 1 \\ 0.42 & 0.1 \end{vmatrix}}{\begin{vmatrix} 1 & 1 \\ 0.009 & 0.1 \end{vmatrix}} = \frac{6(0.1) - 0.42(1)}{1(0.1) - 0.009(1)}$

$= \frac{0.18}{0.091} \approx 1.98$

$b = \frac{\begin{vmatrix} 1 & 6 \\ 0.009 & 0.42 \end{vmatrix}}{\begin{vmatrix} 1 & 1 \\ 0.009 & 0.1 \end{vmatrix}} = \frac{1(0.42) - 0.009(6)}{1(0.1) - 0.009(1)}$

$= \frac{0.366}{0.091} \approx 4.02$

Therefore, about 2 mL of 0.9% and 4 mL of 10% solution is needed.

29. $y = 3.55x - 79.4$

30. First multiply the first terms in each binomial, $(x)(2x)$ to get $2x^2$. Next, multiply the outer terms $(x)(-1)$ to get $-x$. Then multiply the inner terms $(2)(2x)$ to get $4x$. Finally multiply the last terms $(2)(-1)$ to get -2. Combine the like terms $-x + 4x$ to get $3x$. The product is $2x^2 + 3x - 2$.

LESSON 27

Warm Up 27

1. linear

2. For x-intercepts, let $y = 0$.

$6x - 4(0) = -12$

$6x = -12$

$x = -2$

For y-intercepts, let $x = 0$.

$6(0) - 4y = -12$

$-4y = -12$

$y = 3$

3. The domain is all real numbers. The range is $y \geq 0$.

4. $(x + 8)(x + 8) = (x + 8)^2 = x^2 + 16x + 64$

Lesson Practice 27

a. Isolate y and list the terms in decreasing order.

$$11 - x^2 = y + 7x$$
$$-x^2 - 7x + 11 = y$$
$$y = -x^2 - 7x + 11$$

b. Expand and simplify

$f(x) = -(x + 1)^2 - 5$
$= -(x^2 + 2x + 1) - 5$
$= -x^2 - 2x - 1 - 5$
$= -x^2 - 2x - 6$

c. $f(x) = x^2 - 5x + 4$

Make a table of ordered pairs. Plot the points and connect with a smooth line.

x	$x^2 - 5x + 4$	y
−3	$(-3)^2 - 5(-3) + 4$	28
−2	$(-2)^2 - 5(-2) + 4$	18
−1	$(-1)^2 - 5(-1) + 4$	10
0	$(0)^2 - 5(0) + 4$	4
1	$(1)^2 - 5(1) + 4$	0
2	$(2)^2 - 5(2) + 4$	−2
3	$(3)^2 - 5(3) + 4$	−2
4	$(4)^2 - 5(4) + 4$	0

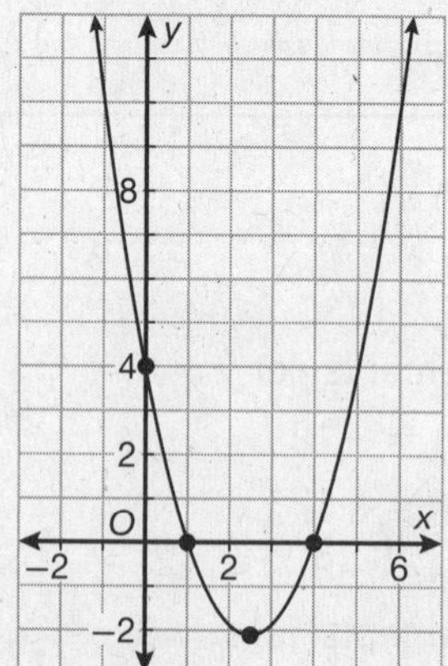

d. The x-intercepts are the x-coordinates of the points where the graph intersects the x-axis at $x = -7$ and $x = -4$. The y-intercept is the y-coordinate of the point where the graph intersects the y-axis at $y = 28$. The vertex is the lowest point on the parabola. Since the graph is symmetric, it occurs midway between the x-intercepts, so the x-coordinate is $\frac{-7 + (-4)}{2} = -5.5$. Plugging $x = -5.5$ into $f(x)$ gives the y-value, -2.25. The coordinates of the vertex is $(-5.5, -2.5)$.
The values are the same when graphed.

e. The domain consists of the values that can be substituted for x. Any real number can be squared so the domain is the set of all real numbers. The range consists of all the possible outputs. The parabola has a vertex at $(0, -4.5)$, which is a maximum, so there are no outputs above the vertex. Therefore the greatest possible value for $f(x)$ is -4.5. The range is all real numbers less than or equal to -4.5.

f. Understand: The question asks for the time it will take for the coin to hit the ground.

Plan: Find the x-intercepts.

Solve: Use a graphing calculator. The x-intercepts are about 1.48 and −1.48. Since time is always positive, it will take 1.48 seconds.

Practice 27

1. Expand and simplify. List the terms in decreasing order.

$f(x) = (2x + 3)^2$
$= 4x^2 + 12x + 9$

2. Expand and simplify. List the terms in decreasing order.

$f(x) = 2(x + 5) + x^2$
$= 2x + 10 + x^2$
$= x^2 + 2x + 10$

3. Expand and simplify. List the terms in decreasing order.

$f(x) = (x - 5)^2$
$= x^2 - 10x + 25$

4. Make a table of ordered pairs. Plot the points and connect with a smooth line. Then use a graphing calculator to check.

x	$(-x+1)^2$	y
−2	$(-(-2)+1)^2$	9
−1	$(-(-1)+1)^2$	4
0	$(-(0)+1)^2$	1
1	$(-(1)+1)^2$	0
2	$(-(2)+1)^2$	1
3	$(-(3)+1)^2$	4
4	$(-(4)+1)^2$	9

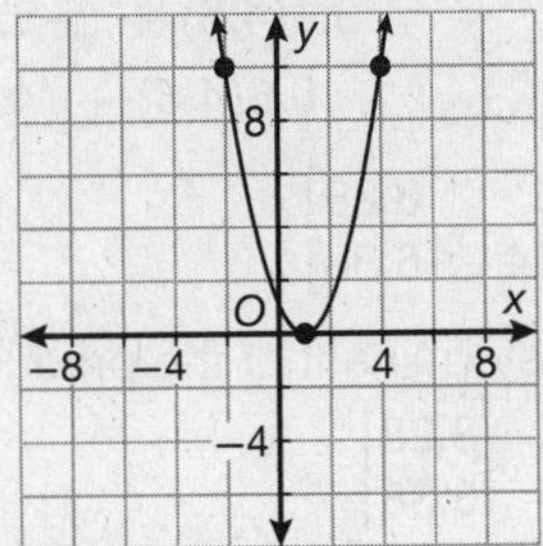

5. Make a table of ordered pairs. Plot the points and connect with a smooth line. Then use a graphing calculator to check.

x	$x^2 - 3$	y
−3	$(-3)^2 - 3$	6
−2	$(-2)^2 - 3$	1
−1	$(-1)^2 - 3$	−2
0	$(0)^2 - 3$	−3
1	$(1)^2 - 3$	−2
2	$(2)^2 - 3$	1
3	$(3)^2 - 3$	6

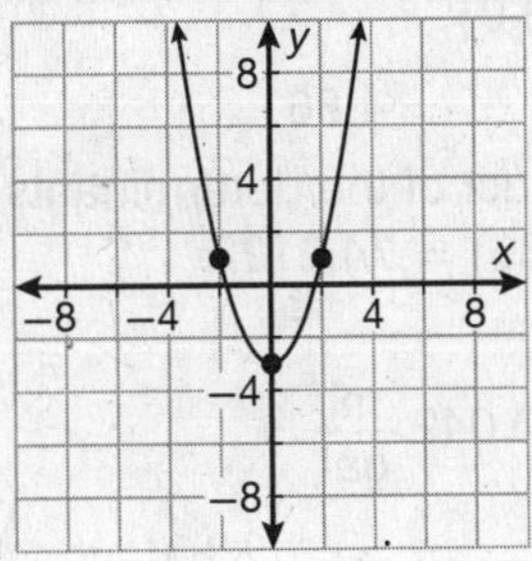

6. $2x^2 - 4x - 30$
$= 2(x^2 - 2x - 15)$
$= 2(x + 3)(x - 5)$

7. $-4x^3 + 20x^2 + 12x$
$= -4x(x^2 - 5x - 3)$

8. There are 1000 milliliters in one liter, and there are 60 seconds in one minute.

$$\frac{3\,\cancel{L}}{1\,\cancel{min}} \times \frac{1000\text{ mL}}{1\,\cancel{L}} \times \frac{1\,\cancel{min}}{60\text{ s}} = \frac{3(1000)\text{ mL}}{60\text{ s}}$$
$$= 50\,\frac{\text{mL}}{\text{s}}$$

9. For y-intercept, let $x = 0$.
$y - 4 = 2(x - 2)$
$y - 4 = 2(0 - 2)$
$y = 0$
The y-intercept is (0, 0).

10. $xy = k$
$3(12) = k$
$36 = k$

11. $xy = k$
$10(5) = k$
$50 = k$

12. $xy = k$
$4(9) = k$
$36 = k$

13. a. The number of dimes, *d*, and the number of nickels, *n*, total 47.
$d + n = 47$

b. The value of each dime is 0.10 and the value of each nickel is 0.05.
$0.10d + 0.05n = 3.20$

c. Solve the system of equations.
$d + n = 47$
$d = 47 - n$
Substitute $d = 47 - n$ into
$0.10d + 0.05n = 3.20$
$0.10(47 - n) + 0.05n = 3.20$
$4.7 - 0.10n + 0.05n = 3.20$
$-0.05n = -1.5$
$n = 30$
Substitute $n = 30$ into $d + n = 47$.
$d + 30 = 47$
$d = 17$
There are 30 nickels and 17 dimes.

14. $3(5r - 10) = 8(2r - 4) + 5r$
$15r - 30 = 16r - 32 + 5r$

$15r - 30 = 21r - 32$
$-6r = -2$
$r = \frac{-2}{-6} = \frac{1}{3}$

Answer choice **B**

15. Sample: The range values will always be greater than or equal to the minimum or less than or equal to the maximum value of the function, which will be a subset of the real numbers.

16. The system has an infinite number of solutions because the lines coincide and have all points in common. Each coefficient in the second equation is twice the coefficient in the first equation. Solving for y in each equation gives the same equation, $y = 3x - 1$.

17. a. There are three variables that can be written in the form $k = \frac{y}{xz}$, where k is the constant of variation. This is joint variation.

b. There are two variables that can be written in the form $k = \frac{y}{x}$. This is direct variation.

18. The graph of $y = -4x + 2$ has x-intercept at $0 = -4x + 2$, or $\left(\frac{1}{2}, 0\right)$, and y-intercept at $y = -4(0) + 2$, or $(0, 2)$.

Answer choice **C**

19. a. The old area is (40)(30) square feet. The new area will be twice the old area, or 2(40)(30) = 2400 square feet.

b. Let x be the increase in the width. Then the increase in length will be $2x$. The new dimensions will be $(2x + 40)$ and $(x + 30)$, and the new area will be

$(2x + 40)(x + 30) = 2400$

Solve the equation.

$(2x + 40)(x + 30) = 2400$
$2x^2 + 100x + 1200 = 2400$
$2x^2 + 100x - 1200 = 0$
$2(x^2 + 50x - 600) = 0$
$2(x + 60)(x - 10) = 0$
$(x + 60) = 0$ or $(x - 10) = 0$
$x = -60$ or $x = 10$

Since length cannot be negative, then the increase will be length: 20 feet; width: 10 feet.

20. Randy is correct. Solving for y in Equation 3 results in $y = -3x + 5$, so Equations 2 and 3 coincide. Solving for y in Equation 1 results in a different equation, $y = -3x + 7$. Equations 1 and 3 are parallel.

21. $\begin{bmatrix} 3.1 & -2.2 \\ 0.6 & 4.5 \end{bmatrix}\begin{bmatrix} -1.9 & 4.8 \\ -2.2 & 3.0 \end{bmatrix}$

$= \begin{bmatrix} 3.1(-1.9) + (-2.2)(-2.2) & 3.1(4.8) + (-2.2)(3.0) \\ 0.6(-1.9) + (4.5)(-2.2) & 0.6(4.8) + (4.5)(3.0) \end{bmatrix}$

$= \begin{bmatrix} -1.05 & 8.28 \\ -11.04 & 16.38 \end{bmatrix}$

So, the determinant of the product is

$\begin{vmatrix} -1.05 & 8.28 \\ -11.04 & 16.38 \end{vmatrix}$

$= -1.05(16.38) - (-11.04)(8.28)$
$= 74.2122$

The determinant of the product of the matrices is 74.2122. Now find the product of the determinants.

The determinant of $\begin{bmatrix} 3.1 & -2.2 \\ 0.6 & 4.5 \end{bmatrix}$ is

$\begin{vmatrix} 3.1 & -2.2 \\ 0.6 & 4.5 \end{vmatrix} = 3.1(4.5) - 0.6(-2.2)$
$= 15.27$

The determinant of $\begin{bmatrix} -1.9 & 4.8 \\ -2.2 & 3.0 \end{bmatrix}$ is

$\begin{vmatrix} -1.9 & 4.8 \\ -2.2 & 3.0 \end{vmatrix} = -1.9(3.0) - (-2.2)(4.8)$
$= 4.86$

The product of the determinants is $15.27(4.86) = 74.2122$.

22. $\frac{\frac{1}{4}\text{ mi}}{6\text{ gal}} \approx 0.042\,\frac{\text{mi}}{\text{gal}}$

$\frac{0.042\text{mi}}{\cancel{\text{gal}}} \times 20\ \cancel{\text{gal}} = 0.84\text{ mi}$

The car will travel 0.84 miles.

23. Let x be the imports in 2005. Then $(x - 228{,}100)$ represents imports in 2005, and $(x + 206{,}784)$ represents imports in 2006. So

$x + (x - 228{,}100) + (x + 206{,}784) =$
$5{,}971{,}007$

$$x + x - 228{,}100 + x + 206{,}784 = 5{,}971{,}007$$
$$3x - 21{,}316 = 5{,}971{,}007$$
$$3x = 5{,}992{,}323$$
$$x = 1{,}997{,}441$$

24. The volume is *lwh*.

$x(x - 3.75)(x - 0.25)$
$= (x^2 - 3.75x)(x - 0.25)$
$= x^3 - 0.25x^2 - 3.75x^2 + 0.9375x$
$= x^3 - 4x^2 + 0.9375x$

25. The polynomials have the same degree, 5. In the first polynomial, ab^4 has a degree of 5. Therefore the greatest degree in the first polynomial is 5. The monomial with the greatest degree in the second polynomial is a^2b^3, which also has a degree of 5.

26. The mean is the sum of the terms divided by 3.

$$m(x) = \frac{35x - 100 + 52x - 60 + 100x - 250}{3}$$
$$= \frac{187x - 410}{3}$$

27. The range is the difference between the greatest and least values.

Range = \$61,156 − \$43,679 = \$17,477

The median is the middle number when the data is listed in ascending order.

The median is \$50,236.

28. $|1 - 3x| = 5x$

so

$$1 - 3x = 5x$$
$$-8x = -1$$
$$x = \frac{1}{8}$$

or

$$1 - 3x = -5x$$
$$2x = -1$$
$$x = -\frac{1}{2}$$

Check:

$$\left|1 - 3\left(\frac{1}{8}\right)\right| \stackrel{?}{=} 5\left(\frac{1}{8}\right)$$
$$\left|1 - \frac{3}{8}\right| \stackrel{?}{=} \frac{5}{8}$$
$$\frac{5}{8} \stackrel{?}{=} \frac{5}{8}$$

or

$$\left|1 - 3\left(-\frac{1}{2}\right)\right| \stackrel{?}{=} 5\left(-\frac{1}{2}\right)$$
$$\left|1 + \frac{3}{2}\right| \stackrel{?}{=} -\frac{5}{2}$$
$$\frac{5}{2} \neq -\frac{5}{2}$$

Therefore $x = -\frac{1}{2}$ is extraneous.

29. Use any of the two points with the slope formula to find the value of *m*.

$$m = \frac{40 - 37}{4 - 3} = \frac{3}{1} = 3$$

Use the point-slope form using one of the given points, then solve for *y* to find the equation in slope-intercept form.

$$y - 37 = 3(x - 3)$$
$$y - 37 = 3x - 9$$
$$y = 3x + 28$$

30. $AB = \begin{bmatrix} -5 & 3 \\ 1 & 2 \end{bmatrix}\begin{bmatrix} -6 & 0 \\ 0 & -6 \end{bmatrix} = \begin{bmatrix} 30 & -18 \\ -6 & -12 \end{bmatrix}$

$BA = \begin{bmatrix} -6 & 0 \\ 0 & -6 \end{bmatrix}\begin{bmatrix} -5 & 3 \\ 1 & 2 \end{bmatrix} = \begin{bmatrix} 30 & -18 \\ -6 & -12 \end{bmatrix}$

Therefore $AB = BA$.

LESSON 28

Warm Up 28

1. polynomial
2. $-4x^2(6x^2y^3 + 2xy^2 - 1)$
   $= (-4x^2)(6x^2y^3) + (-4x^2)(2xy^2) - (-4x^2)(1)$
   $= -24x^4y^3 - 8x^3y^2 + 4x^2$
3. The GCF is $-3x^5$.
   $-12x^6 + 15x^5y = -3x^5(4x - 5y)$
4. Choice **A**: This is the sum of two squares.
   Choice **B**: 8 is a perfect cube, not a square.

Choice **C**: 50 is not a perfect square.
Choice **D**: $(x^{10} - 100) = (x^5)^2 - (10)^2$
Answer choice **D**

Lesson Practice 28

a. $9p^3 \neq 0$

$p \neq 0$

The excluded value is $p = 0$.

$$\frac{3p^8}{9p^3} = \frac{1p^{8-3}}{3} = \frac{p^5}{3}$$

b. $6a^4 \neq 0$

$a \neq 0$

The excluded value is $a = 0$.

$$\frac{a}{6a^4} = \frac{1}{6}a^{1-4} = \frac{1}{6}a^{-3} = \frac{1}{6a^3}$$

c. $6x + 42 \neq 0$

$6x \neq -42$

$x \neq -7$

The excluded value is $x = -7$.

$$\frac{x^2 + 7x}{6x + 42} = \frac{x\cancel{(x+7)}}{6\cancel{(x+7)}} = \frac{x}{6}$$

d. $10x - 10 \neq 0$

$10x \neq 10$

$x \neq 1$

$$\frac{-2x^2 + 2}{10x - 10} = \frac{-2(x^2 - 1)}{10(x - 1)}$$

$$= \frac{-2(x + 1)\cancel{(x - 1)}}{10\cancel{(x - 1)}} = \frac{-(x + 1)}{5}$$

e. $81 - 9a \neq 0$

$-9a \neq -81$

$a \neq 9$

$$\frac{a^2 - 81}{81 - 9a} = \frac{(a + 9)\cancel{(a - 9)}}{-9\cancel{(a - 9)}} = -\frac{(a + 9)}{9}$$

f. $2x^3 - 2x \neq 0$

$2x(x^2 - 1) \neq 0$

$2x(x + 1)(x - 1) \neq 0$

$x \neq -1, 0, 1$

$$\frac{2x^2 - 4x - 6}{2x^3 - 2x} = \frac{2(x^2 - 2x - 3)}{2x(x^2 - 1)}$$

$$= \frac{\cancel{2}(x - 3)\cancel{(x + 1)}}{\cancel{2}x\cancel{(x + 1)}(x - 1)} = \frac{x - 3}{x(x - 1)}$$

g. $V = \frac{4}{3}\pi r^3$; $SA = 4\pi r^2$

$$\frac{4\pi r^2}{\frac{4}{3}\pi r^3} = \frac{\cancel{4} \times \frac{3}{\cancel{4}}\cancel{\pi}}{\cancel{\pi} r^{3-2}} = \frac{3}{r}$$

The diameter is 2160 so the radius will be $r = 2160 \div 2 = 1080$

$$\frac{3}{r} = \frac{3}{1080} = \frac{1}{360}$$

Practice 28

1. $(-x + 1)^2$

$= (-x + 1)(-x + 1)$

$= x^2 - x - x + 1$

$= x^2 - 2x + 1$

2. $16q \neq 0$

$q \neq 0$

$$\frac{-2q^3}{16q} = \frac{-q^{3-1}}{8} = \frac{-q^2}{8}$$

3. $s + 1 \neq 0$

$s \neq -1$

$$\frac{s + 1}{15(s + 1)^2} = \frac{\cancel{(s + 1)}}{15(s + 1)\cancel{(s + 1)}}$$

$$= \frac{1}{15(s + 1)} = \frac{1}{15s + 15}$$

4. $x \neq 0$

$$\frac{x^2}{x} = x^{2-1} = x$$

5. $12x \neq 0$

$x \neq 0$

$$\frac{4x^5}{12x} = \frac{1x^{5-1}}{3} = \frac{x^4}{3}$$

6. $\begin{cases} x + y = 5 \\ x - y = 5 \end{cases}$

$$x = \frac{\begin{vmatrix} 5 & 1 \\ 5 & -1 \end{vmatrix}}{\begin{vmatrix} 1 & 1 \\ 1 & -1 \end{vmatrix}} = \frac{5(-1) - 5(1)}{1(-1) - 1(1)} = \frac{-10}{-2} = 5$$

$$y = \frac{\begin{vmatrix} 1 & 5 \\ 1 & 5 \end{vmatrix}}{\begin{vmatrix} 1 & 1 \\ 1 & -1 \end{vmatrix}} = \frac{1(5) - 1(5)}{1(-1) - 1(1)} = \frac{0}{-2} = 0$$

$x = 5, y = 0$

7. $\begin{cases} -5x + y = 7 \\ x - 3y = 7 \end{cases}$

$$x = \frac{\begin{vmatrix} 7 & 1 \\ 7 & -3 \end{vmatrix}}{\begin{vmatrix} -5 & 1 \\ 1 & -3 \end{vmatrix}} = \frac{7(-3) - 7(1)}{(-5)(-3) - 1(1)}$$

$$= \frac{-21 - 7}{14} = \frac{-28}{14} = -2$$

$$y = \frac{\begin{vmatrix} -5 & 7 \\ 1 & 7 \end{vmatrix}}{\begin{vmatrix} -5 & 1 \\ 1 & -3 \end{vmatrix}}$$

$$= \frac{-5(7) - (1)(7)}{(-5)(-3) - 1(1)}$$

$$= \frac{-35 - 7}{15 - 1} = \frac{-42}{14} = -3$$

8. $x^3y^{-3}x^{-5}y^8y^7 = x^{3-5}y^{-3+8+7} = x^{-2}y^{12} = \frac{y^{12}}{x^2}$

9. $\frac{xx^{-2}y^5x^{-1}y^{-1}}{x^8y^{-3}y^2x^{-4}} = \frac{x^{1-2-1}y^{5-1}}{x^{8-4}y^{-3+2}}$

$$= \frac{x^{-2}y^4}{x^4y^{-1}} = x^{-2-4}y^{4-(-1)} = \frac{y^5}{x^6}$$

10. $\frac{2x^6y^{-4}}{24xy^{-1}} = \frac{1}{12}x^{6-1}y^{-4-(-1)} = \frac{x^5}{12y^3}$

11. $3 \div 5 = 0.60 = 60\%$

12. $0.8 = 80\%$

13. $0.025 = 2.5\%$

14. $9 + 1.50x \leq 45$

$1.50x \leq 36$

$x \leq 24$

He can ride 24 rides.

15. Converting 20 hours into 72,000 seconds.

16. Both properties require that the bases be the same before the exponents can be added or subtracted. In the Product of Powers Property, the exponents are added. In the Quotient of Powers Property, the exponents are subtracted.

17. $-3|4x| - 2 \geq 22$

$-3|4x| \geq 24$

$|4x| \leq -8$

No solution.

Answer choice **D**

18. Each month there are 4500 delays; so in x months there are $4500x$ delays. The equation is $y = 4500x$

19. a. $\bar{x} = (13 + 14 + 65 + 11 + 15 + 14 + 14 + 12 + 13 + 15 + 14 + 12) \div 12$

$= 212 \div 12$

≈ 17.7

b. $$\sigma = \sqrt{\frac{(17.7-13)^2 + (17.7-14)^2 + (17.7-65)^2 + (17.7-11)^2 + (17.7-15)^2 + (17.7-14)^2 + (17.7-14)^2 + (17.7-12)^2 + (17.7-13)^2 + (17.7-15)^2 + (17.7-14)^2 + (17.7-12)^2}{12}}$$

$$= \sqrt{\frac{2460.68}{12}} \approx 14.3$$

c. 65

d. The outlier increases the mean from approximately 13.4 to approximately 17.7, and increases the standard deviation from approximately 1.2 to approximately 14.3.

20. The volume decreases by $-x^2 + 8x + 12$ cubic units. The volume of the cube is x^3. The volume of the other box is $(x + 2)(x + 2)(x - 3) = x^3 + x^2 - 8x - 12$. The difference in volumes is $x^3 - (x^3 + x^2 - 8x - 12)$ $= -x^2 + 8x + 12$.

21. a. $-7x + 14(0) = -84$

$-7x = -84$

$x = 12$

The x-intercept is at (12, 0).

b. $-7(0) + 14y = -84$

$y = -6$

The y-intercept is at (0, −6).

22. $\begin{cases} x + y = 90 \\ x - 2y = 30 \end{cases}$

$$x + y = 90$$
$$\underline{-(x - 2y = 30)}$$
$$3y = 60$$
$$y = 20°$$
$$x + 20° = 90°$$
$$x = 70°$$

23. Student A interchanged columns of the matrix in the numerator instead of replacing the first column with the coefficients of x. Correct solutions may take different approaches, but will produce the same answers as Student B.

24. $(f+g)(x) = 2x-2+x^2 = x^2+2x-2$

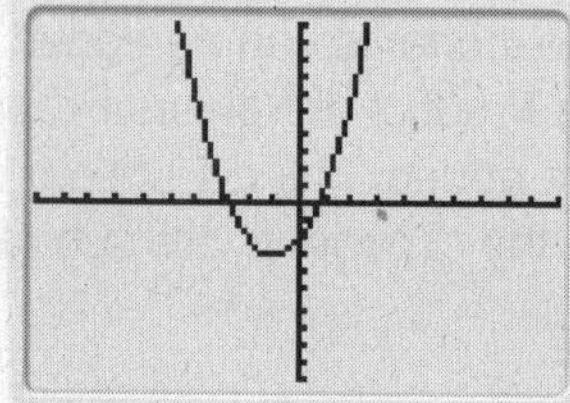

The sum of the functions forms a parabola that opens upward.

25. a. $5 = 2m + b$

b. $-3 = 4m + b$

c. $\begin{cases} 5 = 2m + b \\ -3 = 4m + b \end{cases}$

$$-2(5 = 2m + b)$$
$$-10 = -4m - 2b$$
$$\underline{-3 = 4m + b}$$
$$-13 = -b$$
$$13 = b$$
$$5 = 2m + 13$$
$$-4 = m$$

d. $y = mx + b$

$y = -4x + 13$

26. Florida: $y = -4x + 47$

Wisconsin: $y = x + 27$

$$x + 27 = -4x + 47$$
$$5x = 20$$
$$x = 4$$

The schools will have the same rank after 4 years, in 2010.

27. The graph passes the vertical line test because any vertical line intersects the graph no more than once. The point of discontinuity does not change this fact.

28. $f(-9) = (-9)^2 + 7(-9) - 18$

$= 81 - 63 - 18$

$= 0$

$f(2) = (2)^2 + 7(2) - 18$

$= 4 + 14 - 18$

$= 0$

-9 and 2 are both roots of the function.

29. a. The mean will be greater because the sum is the same for both, and she will divide by 94 rather than 100.

b. The standard deviation will be less because the set of 94 values ranges from 1 to 10 and so is not as spread out as the set of 100 values.

30. a. Let x represent the width of the additional border around the painting. Each dimension will increase by $2x$ (an x increase on each side).

$$(20 + 2x)(16 + 2x) = 1.5(16)(20)$$
$$4x^2 + 72x + 320 = 4800$$
$$4x^2 + 72x - 160 = 0$$

b. $4x^2 + 72x - 160 = 0$

$4(x^2 + 18x - 40) = 0$

$4(x + 20)(x - 2) = 0$

$x = 2$ or $x = -20$

The increase is $x = 2$. So, each dimension should increase by $2x$ or 4 feet. Therefore, the frame will be 24 feet by 20 feet.

LESSON 29

Warm Up 29

1. inconsistent

2. $-2x - 5y$

$-2(-5) - 5(-3)$

$= 10 - (-15)$

$= 25$

3. $x + y = 5$

$\underline{x - y = 1}$

$2x = 6$

$x = 3$

$3 + y = 5$

$y = 2$

The solution is (3, 2).

Lesson Practice 29

a. $\begin{cases} 6x - 3y + 3z = 3 \\ 3x + 3y - z = 5 \\ 5x + 2y - 2z = 4 \end{cases}$

Eliminate one variable using the first and second equations.

$6x - 3y + 3z = 3$

$3x + 3y - z = 5$

$9x + 2z = 8$

Eliminate the same variable using the second and third equations.

$2(3x + 3y - z = 5) \longrightarrow 6x + 6y - 2z = 10$

$-3(5x + 2y - 2z = 4) \longrightarrow -15x - 6y + 6z = -12$

$-9x + 4z = -2$

Solve the system of equations that results.

$9x + 2z = 8$

$-9x + 4z = -2$

$6z = 6$

$z = 1$

$9x + 2(1) = 8$

$9x = 6$

$x = \frac{2}{3}$

Substitute the values of the two variables into one of the original equations to solve for the third variable.

$6\left(\frac{2}{3}\right) - 3y + 3(1) = 3$

$4 - 3y + 3 = 3$

$-3y = -4$

$y = \frac{4}{3}$

$\left(\frac{2}{3}, \frac{4}{3}, 1\right)$

b. $\begin{cases} -3x - y - 4z = 15 \\ 9x + 3y + 12z = -45 \\ -6x + 2y - 8z = -30 \end{cases}$

Eliminate one variable using the second and third equations.

$-2(9x + 3y + 12z = -45) \longrightarrow$

$-18x - 6y - 24z = 90$

$3(-6x + 2y - 8z = -30) \longrightarrow$

$-18x + 6y - 24z = -90$

$-36x \quad -48z = 0$

Eliminate the same variable using the first and third equations.

$2(-3x - y - 4z = 15) \longrightarrow$

$-6x - 2y - 8z = 30$

$-6x + 2y - 8z = -30 \longrightarrow$

$-6x + 2y - 8z = -30$

$-12x \quad -16z = 0$

Solve the system of equations that results.

$-36x - 48z = 0$

$-12x - 16z = 0$

Use elimination to solve for the solution to the system of two equations.

$36x - 48z = 0 \longrightarrow -36x - 48z = 0$

$-3(-12x - 16z = 0) \longrightarrow 36x + 48z = 0$

$0 = 0$

The result is an identity statement. Therefore, there are infinitely many solutions to the system of equations.

c. $\begin{cases} 4x - 2y + z = 2 \\ 2x + 4y - 3z = 0 \\ -12x + 6y - 3z = 6 \end{cases}$

Eliminate one variable from the first and third equations.

$3(4x - 2y + z = 2) \longrightarrow 12x - 6y + 3z = 6$

$-12x + 6y - 3z = 6 \longrightarrow -12x + 6y - 3z = 6$

$0 = 12$

The result is a false statement. Therefore, there is no solution to the system of equations.

d. $\begin{cases} 4x + 9y - 22z = 10 \\ 3x - y + 2z = -3 \\ -15x + 5y - 10z = -15 \end{cases}$

Combine the second and third equations.

$5(3x - y + 2z = -3) \longrightarrow$

$15x - 5y + 10z = -15$

$-15x + 5y - 10z = -15 \longrightarrow$

$-15x + 5y - 10z = -15$

$0 = -30$

The result is a false statement. Therefore, there is no solution. The system of equations is inconsistent.

e. $\begin{cases} 5x - 3y + z = 2 \\ -28x + 24y - 4z = 20 \\ -7x + 6y - z = 5 \end{cases}$

Combine the second and third equations.

$-28x + 24y - 4z = 20 \longrightarrow$

$$-28x + 24y - 4z = 20$$

$-4(-7x + 6y - z = 5) \longrightarrow$

$$\frac{28x - 24y + 4z = -20}{0 = 0}$$

Since the result is a true statement, there are an infinite number of solutions, therefore the system is consistent.

f. Let x represent the amount invested at 12%, y represent the amount invested at 15%, and z represent the amount invested at 18%. Write the system of equations and solve.

$\begin{cases} x + y + z = 5400 \\ 0.12x + 0.15y + 0.18z = 822 \\ x = (y + z) - 2600 \end{cases}$

$$x + y + z = 5400$$

$x = (y + z) - 2600 \longrightarrow \underline{x - y - z = -2600}$

$$2x = 2800$$

$$x = 1400$$

Sub. $x = 1400$ into two of the equations.

$0.12(1400) + 0.15y + 0.18z = 822$

$168 + 0.15y + 0.18z = 822$

$0.15y + 0.18z = 654$

$1400 = (y + z) - 2600$

$4000 = y + z$

Solve the resulting equations, $0.15y + 0.18z = 654$ and $y + z = 4000$.

$100(0.15y + 0.18z = 654) \longrightarrow$

$$15y + 18z = 65{,}400$$

$-15(y + z = 4000) \longrightarrow$

$$\frac{-15y - 15z = -60{,}000}{3z = 5400}$$

$$z = 1800$$

$1400 = (y + 1800) - 2600$

$y = 2200$

Therefore, \$1400 is invested at 12%, \$2200 at 15% and \$1800 at 18%.

Practice 29

1. $\begin{cases} x - 5y + 2z = 2 \\ 2x - y + z = 1 \\ 7x - 3y + z = 8 \end{cases}$

$$-2(x - 5y + 2z = 2)$$
$$\underline{2x - y + z = 1}$$

$$-2x + 10y - 4z = -4$$
$$\frac{2x - y + z = 1}{9y - 3z = -3}$$

$$-7(x - 5y + 2z = 2)$$
$$\underline{7x - 3y + z = 8}$$

$$-7x + 35y - 14z = -14$$
$$\frac{7x - 3y + z = 8}{32y - 13z = -6}$$

$$-13(9y - 3z = -3)$$
$$\underline{3(32y - 13z = -6)}$$

$$-117y + 39z = 39$$
$$\frac{96y - 39z = -18}{-21y = 21}$$

$$y = -1$$

$$9(-1) - 3z = -3$$
$$-3z = 6$$
$$z = -2$$

$$x - 5(-1) + 2(-2) = 2$$
$$x = 1$$

$(1, -1, -2)$

2. $\begin{cases} -4x + 2y - z = 2 \\ 4x + 8y - 6z = 0 \\ 4x - 2y + z = 2 \end{cases}$

$$-4x + 2y - z = 2$$
$$\frac{4x + 8y - 6z = 0}{10y - 7z = 2}$$

$$-4x + 2y - z = 2$$
$$\frac{4x - 2y + z = 2}{0 = 4}$$

No solution

3. $144x^2 - 1$

$(12x + 1)(12x - 1)$

4. $9x^2 - 25$

$(3x + 5)(3x - 5)$

5. $(f - g)(x) = 2x + 1 - x^2$

$= -x^2 + 2x + 1$

$(f - g)(4) = -(4)^2 + 2(4) + 1 = -7$

6. $(f + g)(x) = x^2 + 2x + 1$

$(f + g)(-3) = (-3)^2 + 2(-3) + 1 = 4$

7. $(g + f)(x) = -(x^2 + 3) + (-x - 7)$

$= -x^2 - x - 10$

$(g + f)(0) = -(0)^2 + (0) - 10 = -10$

8. $(g - f)(x) = -(x^2 + 3) - (-x - 7)$

$= -x^2 + x + 4$

$(g - f)(-1) = -(-1)^2 + (-1) + 4 = 2$

9. $x + 3 = 4$ and $x + 3 = -4$

$x = 1$ and $x = -7$

10. $|2x + 6| = -1$

no solution

11. $|1 - 3x| + 5 = 6$

$|1 - 3x| = 1$

$1 - 3x = 1$ and $1 - 3x = -1$

$-3x = 0$ and $-3x = -2$

$x = 0$ and $x = \frac{2}{3}$

12. First terms: $a \cdot a = a^2$

Outer terms: $a \cdot b = ab$

Inner terms: $b \cdot a = ab$

Last terms: $b \cdot b = b^2$

Add the terms: $a^2 + ab + ab + b^2$

The outer and inner terms in this case will always be the same, leaving you with the product: $a^2 + 2ab + b^2$

13. $18\frac{\text{in.}}{\text{hr}} \times \frac{1\text{ ft}}{12\text{ in.}} \times \frac{1\text{ hr}}{60\text{ min}} = 0.025\text{ ft/min}$

14. $144\frac{\text{in.}}{\text{min}} \times \frac{1\text{ ft}}{12\text{ in.}} = 12\text{ ft/min}$

15. $-(-1) + 2 - (-3) = 1 + 2 + 3 = 6$

$-(-1) - 2(2) + 2(-3) = 1 - 4 - 6 = -9$

$3(-1) - 2 + 2(-3) = -3 - 2 - 6 = -11$

Yes, $(-1, 2, -3)$ is a solution of the system.

16. $6x + 3y = -9$

$3y = -6x - 9$

$y = -2x - 3$

slope $= -2$; y-intercept $= -3$

17. Possible answer: The student forgot to change the inequality sign when dividing by -4.

$-4x - 2 \geq 14$

$-4x \geq 16$

$x \leq -4$

18.

```
MATRIX[A] ■ ×3
[ 4    -2    1 ]
[ 3     0    2 ]
[ 2    -1    1 ]
```

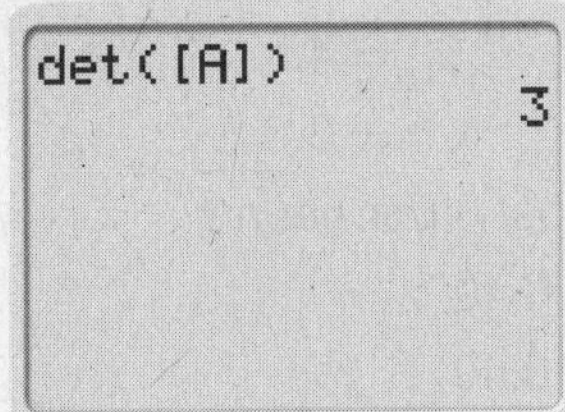

19. $m = \frac{-5 - (-30)}{1 - 3} = \frac{25}{-2} = -12.50$

$y = -12.50x + b$

$-5 = -12.50(1) + b$

$7.5 = b$

$y = -12.50x + 7.5$

Answer choice **C**

20. Possible answer: Factor $v^2 - 7v + 10$ to $(v - 5)(v - 2)$.

Area is length times width, and the side length for the side along the x-axis is the difference between the x values. So, let $v - 5 = x - (4 + v)$. Then, $x = 2v - 1$. Therefore, a possible adjacent vertex is $(2v - 1, 0)$.

21. $x = ky$

$x = (3)(12) = 36$

22. 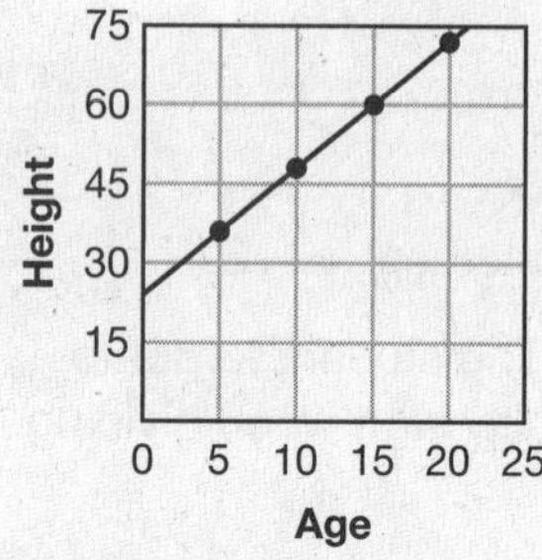

Continuous function; this is a linear function with no holes or points of discontinuity.

23. a. $\begin{cases} 4n + 2r = 37.20 \\ 2n + 4r = 26.40 \end{cases}$

b. Solving the first equation for r,

$r = 18.60 - 2n.$

Substituting into second equation,

$$2n + 4(18.60 - 2n) = 26.40$$
$$2n + 74.4 - 8n = 26.40$$
$$6n = 48$$
$$n = 8$$

So the nuts cost 8 per pound.

$$2(8) + 4r = 26.40$$
$$4r = 10.40$$
$$r = 2.6$$

So the raisins cost \$2.60 per pound. A pound of nuts and a pound of raisins will cost \$8 + \$2.60 = \$10.60.

24. First see if the x- or y-terms are opposites. If they are, add the two equations and solve for the variable that is not eliminated. Then substitute into either original equation to solve for the other variable. If neither of the variable terms are opposites, multiply one or both equations by a constant so that either the x- or y-terms become opposites.

25. $(f + g)(x) = (-2x + 11) + (6x - 1)$
$= 4x + 10$

$(f + g)(8) = 4(8) + 10 = 42$

Answer choice **A**

26. $\frac{100 \cancel{m}}{47.84 \text{ sec}} \times \frac{100 \cancel{cm}}{1 \cancel{m}} \times \frac{1 \cancel{in.}}{2.54 \cancel{cm}} \times \frac{1 \text{ ft}}{12 \cancel{in.}}$

≈ 6.858 feet per second

27. The transformation moves the graph to the right 3 units. The original function equals 1 at $x = -1$ and $x = 1$. The new function equals 1 at $x = 2$ and $x = 4$.

28. $102.2 - 33.9 - 20.9 = 47.4$

$$\begin{cases} N + F + I = 47.4 \\ N - F = 3 \\ F - I = 3.6 \end{cases}$$

$$\begin{aligned} N + F + I &= 47.4 \\ F - I &= 3.6 \\ \hline N + 2F \quad &= 51 \end{aligned}$$

$$\begin{aligned} N + 2F &= 51 \\ 2(N - F &= 3) \end{aligned}$$

$$\begin{aligned} N + 2F &= 51 \\ 2N - 2F &= 6 \\ \hline 3N \quad &= 57 \end{aligned}$$

$$N = 19$$
$$19 - F = 3$$
$$F = 16$$
$$16 - I = 3.6$$
$$I = 12.4$$

29. $x = \frac{\begin{vmatrix} 2 & 1 \\ 7 & -1 \end{vmatrix}}{\begin{vmatrix} 1 & 1 \\ 2 & -1 \end{vmatrix}} = \frac{2(-1) - 7(1)}{1(-1) - 2(1)} = \frac{-2 - 7}{-1 - 2}$

$= \frac{-9}{-3} = 3$

$y = \frac{\begin{vmatrix} 1 & 2 \\ 2 & 7 \end{vmatrix}}{\begin{vmatrix} 1 & 1 \\ 2 & -1 \end{vmatrix}} = \frac{1(7) - 2(2)}{1(-1) - 2(1)} = \frac{7 - 4}{-1 - 2}$

$= \frac{3}{-3} = -1$

$(3, -1)$

30. Area of base $= s^2$

Volume $= \left(\frac{1}{3}\right)s^2 s$

$$\frac{\cancel{s^2}}{\frac{1}{3}(\cancel{s^2})(s)} = \frac{3}{s}$$

LESSON 30

Warm Up 30

1. parabola
2. $f(x) = x^2$

3. $y = 2(x - 3)^2 + 5$
$y = 2(x - 3)(x - 3) + 5$
$y = 2(x^2 - 6x + 9) + 5$
$y = 2x^2 - 12x + 18 + 5$
$y = 2x^2 - 12x + 23$

4. $y = (x - 0)^2 + 0$
The vertex is located at (0, 0).

Lesson Practice 30

a.

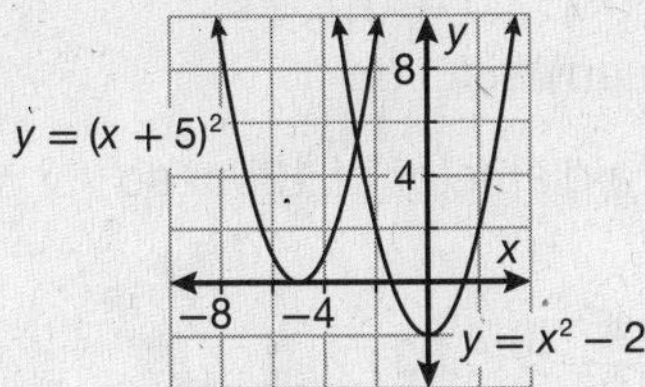

The vertex of $y = (x + 5)^2$ is (−5, 0) and the axis of symmetry is $x = -5$. Relative to the parent function, it is shifted 5 units left. The vertex of $y = x^2 - 2$ is (0, −2) and the axis of symmetry is $x = 0$. Relative to the parent function, it is shifted 2 units down.

b. The vertex is located at (−4, 3) and the axis of symmetry is $x = -4$. Plot a few points on one side of the axis of symmetry.

x	−3	−2	−1
y	4	7	12

Find the reflection of each of those points across the axis of symmetry, then join the points with a smooth line.

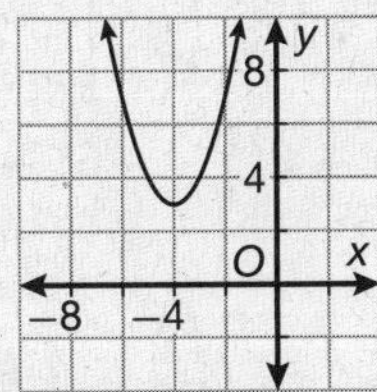

c. Graphs A and C open upward, so the value of a is positive in each. Since Graph A is narrower, the absolute value of a is greater than in Graph C. So, Graph A shows $y = 4x^2$, and Graph c shows $y = 0.25x^2$.
Graphs B and D open downward, so the value of a is negative in each. Since Graph B is wider than Graph D, the absolute value of a is less for Graph B than for Graph D.
Graph B shows $y = -0.25x^2$, and Graph D shows $y = -4x^2$.

d. $y = a(x + 1)^2 - 8$
$-3 = a(4 + 1)^2 - 8$
$5 = 25a \qquad \frac{1}{5} = a$
$y = \frac{1}{5}(x + 1)^2 - 8$

e. The value of a is positive, so the graph opens upward and the function has a minimum. The minimum occurs at the vertex (18, 39.50). It represents the value of the stock at week 18.

Practice 30

1. $y = (x - 0)^2 + 3$
vertex: (0, 3)
axis of symmetry: $x = 0$

2. $y = 2(x - 1)^2 + 3$
vertex: (1, 3)
axis of symmetry: $x = 1$

3. $y = -(x + 2)^2 + 0$
vertex: (−2, 0)
axis of symmetry: $x = -2$

4. $y = 3(x - 0)^2 + 5$
vertex: (0, 5)
axis of symmetry: $x = 0$

5. $\begin{cases} x + 3y - z = 10 \\ 2x + 5y + z = 9 \\ -3x + y - 3z = 8 \end{cases}$

$$\begin{array}{r} x + 3y - z = 10 \\ 2x + 5y + z = 9 \\ \hline 3x + 8y \quad = 19 \end{array}$$

$$\begin{array}{r} 3(2x + 5y + z = 9) \\ -3x + y - 3z = 8 \\ \hline 6x + 15y + 3z = 27 \\ -3x + y - 3z = 8 \\ \hline 3x + 16y \quad = 35 \end{array}$$

$$\begin{array}{r} 3x + 16y = 35 \\ -(3x + 8y = 19) \\ \hline 8y = 16 \\ y = 2 \end{array}$$

$$3x + 16(2) = 35$$
$$3x = 3$$
$$x = 1$$
$$1 + 3(2) - z = 10$$
$$-z = 3$$
$$z = -3$$

(1, 2, −3)

6. Domain: all real numbers
Range: all real numbers greater than or equal to 0.

7. $2x^2(2x - 4) = 4x^4 - 8x^2$

8. $3x^3 \neq 0$
$x \neq 0$
$\frac{4x^2}{3x^3}(x^3 + 9) = \frac{4x^5}{3x^3} + \frac{12x^2}{1x^3} = \frac{4x^2}{3} + \frac{12}{x}$

9. $y = \pm\sqrt{x + 5}$
This is not a function because there is a positive and negative y-value for every x-value.

10. $y = -3x^3 + 2x + 1$

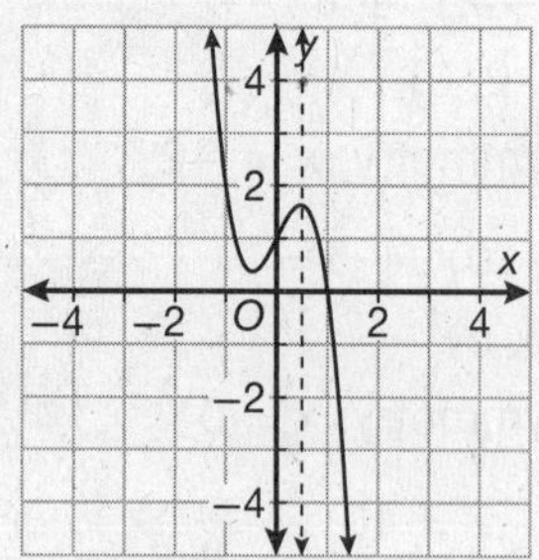

It is a function because it passes the vertical line test.

11. $y = \pm\sqrt{x^2 + 3}$
This is not a function because there is a positive and negative y-value for every x-value.

12. The graph of $y = -5x^2 + 381$ is narrower than the parent function, is shifted vertically 381 units up, and opens downward. The graph of $y = -5x^2 + 442$ is also narrower than the parent function, is shifted vertically 442 units up, and also opens downward. The two graphs have the same width, open downward, and are vertical shifts of each other.

13. a. $\begin{cases} 5x + 9y - z = -4 \\ 15x - 6y + 4z = 12 \\ 20x - 36y + 4z = 16 \end{cases}$

b. Infinitely many solutions; the first and third equations are multiples of each other.

c. $4(-5x + 9y - z = -4)$
$$-20x + 36y - 4z = -16$$
$$\underline{20x - 36y + 4z = 16}$$
$$0 = 0$$
Infinitely many solution

14. The Eye has a diameter of 135m so $r = \left(\frac{135}{2}\right)$m.
$\frac{2\pi r}{\pi r^2} = \frac{2}{r} = \frac{4}{135} \approx 0.03$

15. $y = -\frac{2}{5}x + \frac{7}{5}$
$y = -2x + 3$

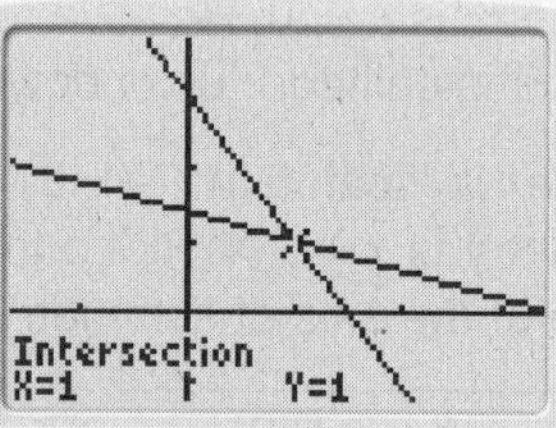

(1, 1)

16. $\begin{bmatrix} \boxed{0} & -2 & 3 \\ 1 & 4 & 2 \\ -3 & -1 & 1 \end{bmatrix} \begin{bmatrix} 0 & \boxed{-2} & 3 \\ 1 & 4 & 2 \\ -3 & -1 & 1 \end{bmatrix} \begin{bmatrix} 0 & -2 & \boxed{3} \\ 1 & 4 & 2 \\ -3 & -1 & 1 \end{bmatrix}$

$0\begin{bmatrix} 4 & 2 \\ -1 & 1 \end{bmatrix} - -2\begin{bmatrix} 1 & 2 \\ -3 & 1 \end{bmatrix} + 3\begin{bmatrix} 1 & 4 \\ -3 & -1 \end{bmatrix}$
$= 0(4 - -2) + 2(1 - -6) + 3(-1 - -12)$
$= 0 + 14 + 33$
$= 47$

17.

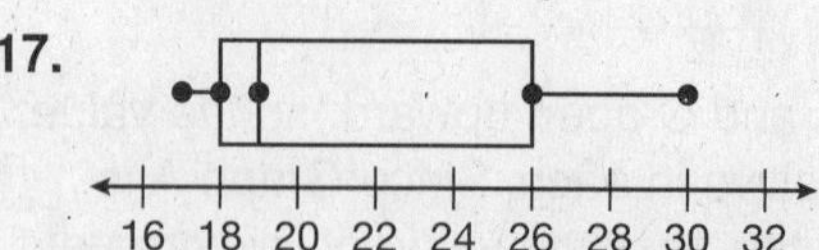

18. The Addition Property of Equality; because both sides of an equation are equivalent expressions, adding an equation to another is like adding equal expressions to both sides of the equation.

19. The student added unlike terms resulting in a linear equation. The student should have factored to solve. The solution should be:

$3x^2 - x - 4 = 0$

$(3x - 4)(x + 1) = 0$

$3x - 4 = 0$ or $x + 1 = 0$

$x = \frac{4}{3}$ or $x = -1$

20. a. The lines intersect at a single point.

b. The lines coincide, sharing all points.

c. The lines are parallel.

21. $|2x + 1| < 4$

$2x + 1 < 4$ and $2x + 1 > -4$

$2x < 3$ and $2x > -5$

$x < \frac{3}{2}$ and $x > -\frac{5}{2}$

Answer choice **A**

22. This is a discontinuous function. The points of discontinuity are at $x = 5, 10, 15$.

23. a. $(x + 24)(x - 10) = x^2 + 14x - 240$

b. $(60)^2 + 14(60) - 240 = 4200 \text{ ft}^2$

24. $2 \text{ mi} \times \frac{5280 \text{ ft}}{1 \text{ mi}} = 10{,}560 \text{ ft}$

25. The distance is from (0, 0). Since one coordinate is 0, the distance will be the absolute value of the other coordinate.

$|3| = 3, |-5| = 5, |-6| = 6$

26. a. $g(x) + h(x) = (x^2 + 1) + (x^2 - 1) = 2x^2$

b. $f(g(x) + h(x)) = (2x^2)^3 - (2x^2)$

$= 8x^6 - 2x^2$

27. $-|2x + 9| \le -3$

$|2x + 9| \ge 3$

$(2x + 9) \ge 3$ or $2x + 9 \le -3$

$2x \ge -6$ or $2x \le -12$

$x \ge -3$ or $x \le -6$

Answer choice **B**

28. Student A is incorrect. The function can be written as $y = -(x - (-4))^2 + 1$, which shows more clearly that $h = -4$. Since the axis of symmetry passes through the vertex $(-4, 1)$. The axis of symmetry is $x = -4$.

29. Domain: all real numbers

Range: all real numbers greater than or equal to -7.

Any number can be substituted in for x, but, because any real number squared is greater than or equal to zero, -7 is the lowest possible output for the function.

30. Since one of the lengths will be the house, $2w + l = 300$.

INVESTIGATION 3

1. $-x + y = 4$

$y = x + 4$

2. The resulting expression is substituted into the other equation; $2x - (x + 4) = -10$

3. Sample: Forming a one-variable equation produces a solvable equation.

4. Solve for x in the equation from step 2.

$2x - (x + 4) = -10$

$2x - x - 4 = -10$

$x - 4 = -10$

$x = -6$

Then substitute the value for x into one of the original the equations. $-(-6) + y = 4$ Then solve this equation to find $y = -2$.

5. Sample: Substitute x and y into each equation. If both values satisfy both original equations, then this verifies the answer.

6. $x - 3y + 2z = 11$

$x - 3y = -2z + 11$

$x = 3y - 2z + 11$

7. $-(3y - 2z + 11) + 4y + 3z = 5$

$-3y + 2z - 11 + 4y + 3z = 5$

$y + 5z - 11 = 5$

$\boxed{y + 5z = 16}$

8. $2(3y - 2z + 11) - 2y - 4z = 2$

$6y - 4z + 22 - 2y - 4z = 2$

$4y - 8z + 22 = 2$

$\boxed{4y - 8z = -20}$

9. two; y and z

10. $y + 5z = 16$

$y = -5z + 16$

Substitute into the second boxed equation.

$4(-5z + 16) - 8z = -20$

$-20z + 64 - 8z = -20$

$-28z + 64 = -20$

$-28z = -84$

$z = 3$

Substitute the value of z into the first boxed equation.

$y = -5(3) + 16$

$y = -15 + 16$

$y = 1$

$y = 1; z = 3$

11. Substitute the y and z values into the first equation that was solved for x.

$x = 3(1) - 2(3) + 11$

$x = 3 - 6 + 11$

$x = 8$

By substituting the other two variables into one of the original equations

12. Set $y = 0$, set $z = 0$, and then solve for x.

13. $2x + 3(0) + 6(0) = 12$

$2x = 12$

$x = 6$

$2(0) + 3y + 6(0) = 12$

$3y = 12$

$y = 4$

$2(0) + 3(0) + 6z = 12$

$6z = 12$

$z = 2$

(6,0,0), (0,4,0), (0,0,2)

14.

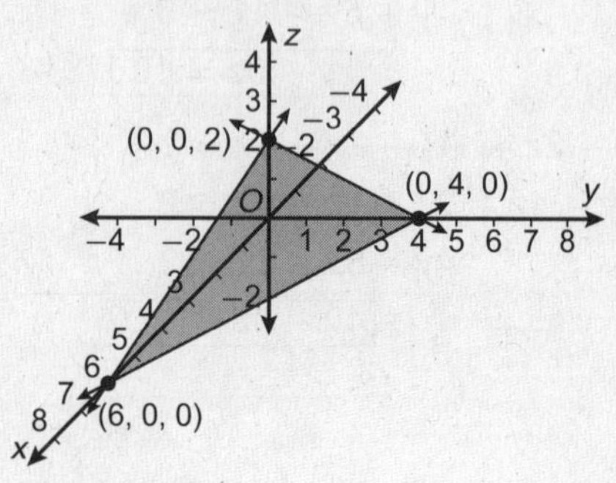

Investigation Practice

a. $x + 4y - 5z = -7$ solve for x.

$x = -4y + 5z - 7$

Substitute into the second equation.

$3(-4y + 5z - 7) + 2y + 3z = 7$

$-12y + 15z - 21 + 2y + 3z = 7$

$-10y + 18z = 28$

Substitute into the third equation.

$2(-4y + 5z - 7) + y + 5z = 8$

$-8y + 10z - 14 + y + 5z = 8$

$-7y + 15z = 22$

$-10y + 18z = 28$ Solve for y.

$-10y = -18z + 28$

$y = 1.8z - 2.8$

$-7(1.8z - 2.8) + 15z = 22$ Substitute and find z.

$-12.6z + 19.6 + 15z = 22$

$2.4z = 2.4$

$z = 1$

$y = 1.8(1) - 2.8$ Enter z, find y.

$y = -1$

$x = -4(-1) + 5(1) - 7$ Enter y and z, find x.

$x = 4 + 5 - 7$

$x = 2$

$(2, -1, 1)$

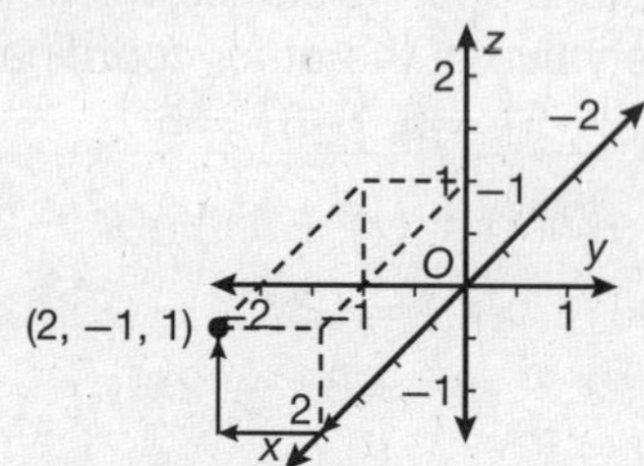

b. $2x - (0) + 3(0) = 6$

$2x = 6$

$x = 3$

$2(0) - y + 3(0) = 6$

$-y = 6$

$y = -6$

$2(0) - (0) + 3z = 6$

$3z = 6$

$z = 2$

$(0, 0, 2), (0, -6, 0), (3, 0, 0)$

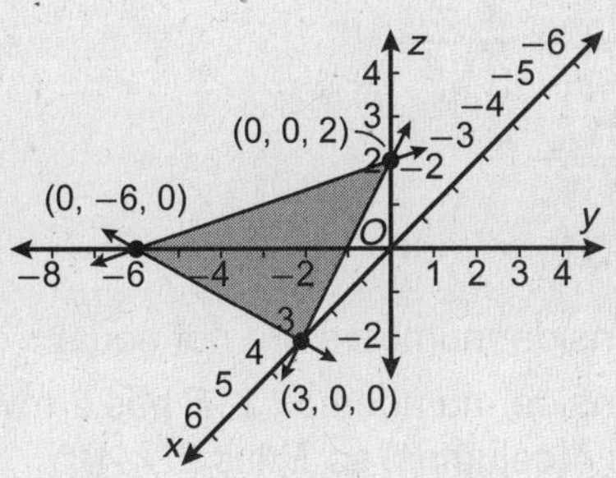

LESSON 31

Warm Up 31

1. undefined

2. $\frac{3}{10} \cdot \frac{5}{9} = \frac{15}{90}$
$= \frac{\cancel{15} \cdot 1}{\cancel{15} \cdot 6}$
$= \frac{1}{6}$

3. $\frac{2}{5} \div \frac{1}{20} = \frac{2}{5} \cdot \frac{20}{1}$
$= \frac{40}{5}$
$= \frac{\cancel{5} \cdot 8}{\cancel{5} \cdot 1}$
$= \frac{8}{1}$
$= 8$

4. $4xy^3 = 4(3)(-2)^3$
$= 4(3)(-8)$
$= -96$

Lesson Practice 31

a. $\frac{4x^2 - 9}{x + 1} \cdot \frac{x^2 + x}{4x^2 + 12x + 9}$
$= \frac{(2x - 3)(2x + 3)}{x + 1} \cdot \frac{x(x + 1)}{(2x + 3)(2x + 3)}$
$= \frac{x\cancel{(x + 1)}\cancel{(2x + 3)}(2x - 3)}{\cancel{(x + 1)}\cancel{(2x + 3)}(2x + 3)}$
$= \frac{x(2x - 3)}{2x + 3}$

$\frac{x(2x - 3)}{2x + 3} = \frac{(5)(2(5) - 3)}{2(5) + 3}$
$= \frac{5(7)}{13}$
$= \frac{35}{13}$

b. $\frac{x^2 + 5x - 14}{x^2 + x - 6} \cdot \frac{x^2 - x - 12}{5x^2 - 20x}$
$= \frac{(x - 2)(x + 7)}{(x - 2)(x + 3)} \cdot \frac{(x - 4)(x + 3)}{5x(x - 4)}$
$= \frac{\cancel{(x - 2)}\cancel{(x - 4)}\cancel{(x + 3)}(x + 7)}{5x\cancel{(x - 2)}\cancel{(x - 4)}\cancel{(x + 3)}}$
$= \frac{x + 7}{5x}$

The given expression is $\frac{x^2 + 5x - 14}{x^2 + x - 6} \cdot \frac{x^2 - x - 12}{5x^2 - 20x}$, which is equivalent to $\frac{(x - 2)(x + 7)}{(x - 2)(x + 3)} \cdot \frac{(x - 4)(x + 3)}{5x(x - 4)}$.

The factors in the denominator are $5x$, $(x - 2)$, $(x - 4)$, and $(x + 3)$. These factors are zero when x is 0, 2, 4, and −3, respectively. So, the values of x that make the given expression undefined are 0, 2, 4, and −3.

c. $\frac{x^2 - 4}{7x^2 + 14x - 56} \cdot \frac{7x - 21}{x + 4} \cdot \frac{x + 4}{x^2 - x - 6}$
$= \frac{(x - 2)(x + 2)}{7(x - 2)(x + 4)} \cdot \frac{7(x - 3)}{x + 4} \cdot \frac{x + 4}{(x - 3)(x + 2)}$
$= \frac{\cancel{7}\cancel{(x - 2)}\cancel{(x - 3)}\cancel{(x + 2)}\cancel{(x + 4)}}{\cancel{7}\cancel{(x - 2)}\cancel{(x - 3)}\cancel{(x + 2)}(x + 4)^{\cancel{2}}}$
$= \frac{1}{x + 4}$

d. $\frac{3x - 9}{6x^2 + 12x} \cdot (x^2 - 4x - 12)$
$= \frac{3(x - 3)}{6x(x + 2)} \cdot (x - 6)(x + 2)$
$= \frac{\cancel{3}(x - 3)(x - 6)\cancel{(x + 2)}}{\cancel{3} \cdot 2x\cancel{(x + 2)}}$
$= \frac{(x - 3)(x - 6)}{2x}$

e. $\frac{3x^2y^5}{7xy^8} \div \frac{9x^8y^2}{14xy^6} = \frac{3x^2y^5}{7xy^8} \cdot \frac{14xy^6}{9x^8y^2}$
$= \frac{42x^3y^{11}}{63x^9y^{10}}$
$= \frac{2 \cdot \cancel{21} \cdot \cancel{x^3} \cdot y \cdot \cancel{y^{10}}}{3 \cdot \cancel{21} \cdot x^6 \cdot \cancel{x^3} \cdot \cancel{y^{10}}}$
$= \frac{2y}{3x^6}$

$$\frac{2y}{3x^6} = \frac{2(-6)}{3(-1)^2}$$
$$= \frac{-12}{3}$$
$$= -4$$

f. $\frac{1}{x^2 + 2x} \div \frac{2x - 1}{x^3 + 7x^2 + 10x}$

$= \frac{1}{x^2 + 2x} \cdot \frac{x^3 + 7x^2 + 10x}{2x - 1}$

$= \frac{1}{x(x + 2)} \cdot \frac{x(x + 2)(x + 5)}{2x - 1}$

$= \frac{\cancel{x}\cancel{(x + 2)}(x + 5)}{\cancel{x}\cancel{(x + 2)}(2x - 1)}$

$= \frac{x + 5}{2x - 1}$

The given expression is $\frac{1}{x^2 + 2x} \div \frac{2x - 1}{x^3 + 7x^2 + 10x}$, which is equivalent to $\frac{1}{x(x + 2)} \cdot \frac{x(x + 2)(x + 5)}{2x - 1}$. The factors in the denominator are x, $(x + 2)$, and $(2x - 1)$. These factors are zero when x is 0, -2, and $\frac{1}{2}$, respectively. So, the values of x that make the given expression undefined are 0, -2, and $\frac{1}{2}$.

g. $\frac{16 - x^2}{4xy} \cdot \frac{x^2y}{x - 4} \div \frac{x + 4}{4}$

$= \frac{16 - x^2}{4xy} \cdot \frac{x^2y}{x - 4} \cdot \frac{4}{x + 4}$

$= \frac{(4 - x)(4 + x)}{4xy} \cdot \frac{x^2y}{x - 4} \cdot \frac{4}{x + 4}$

$= \frac{\cancel{4} \cdot (-1)\cancel{(x - 4)}\cancel{(x + 4)}\cancel{x} \cdot x \cdot \cancel{y}}{\cancel{4} \cdot \cancel{x} \cdot \cancel{y}\cancel{(x - 4)}\cancel{(x + 4)}}$

$= -x$

h. $V_{cube} = V_{cylinder}$

$x^3 = \pi\left(\frac{x}{2}\right)^2 h$

$\frac{1}{x^2}x^3 = \frac{1}{x^2}\pi\left(\frac{x^2}{4}\right)h$ Multiply both sides by the reciprocal of x^2.

$\frac{1}{\cancel{x^2}}\cancel{x^2}x = \frac{1}{\cancel{x^2}}\frac{\pi \cancel{x^2} h}{4}$ Factor and divide out common factors.

$x = \frac{\pi h}{4}$ Multiply both sides by $\frac{4}{\pi}$.

$\frac{4}{\pi}x = \frac{4}{\pi}\frac{\pi h}{4}$ Factor and divide out common factors.

$\frac{4}{\pi}x = \frac{\cancel{4}}{\cancel{\pi}}\frac{\cancel{\pi} h}{\cancel{4}}$

$\frac{4x}{\pi} = h$

Practice 31

1. AB: "inside" numbers are not equal

BA: "inside" numbers = 2. B has 2 rows and A has 4 columns, so BA is 2×4

AC: "inside" numbers = 4. A has 2 rows and C has 2 columns, so AC is 2×2

CA: "inside" numbers = 2. C has 4 rows and A has 4 columns, so CA is 4×4

AD: "inside" numbers = 4. A has 2 rows and D has 4 columns, so AD is 2×4

DA: "inside" numbers are not equal

BC: "inside" numbers are not equal

CB: "inside" numbers = 2. C has 4 rows and B has 2 columns, so CB is 4×2

BD: "inside" numbers are not equal

DB: "inside" numbers are not equal

CD: "inside" numbers are not equal

DC: "inside" numbers = 4. D has 4 rows and C has 2 columns, so DC is 4×2

2. $f(x)\ g(x) = \frac{x^2 - 100}{x^2 + 20x + 100}\ \frac{10x + 100}{3x - 30}$

$= \frac{(x - 10)(x + 10)}{(x + 10)^2}\ \frac{10(x + 10)}{3(x - 10)}$

$= \frac{10\cancel{(x - 10)}\ \cancel{(x + 10)^2}}{3\cancel{(x - 10)}\ \cancel{(x + 10)^2}}$

$= \frac{10}{3}$

3. $\frac{V}{L} = \frac{\cancel{\pi} r^{\cancel{2}} \cancel{h}}{2\cancel{\pi r} h} = \frac{r}{2}$

$r = \frac{d}{2} = \frac{7.6}{2} = 3.8$

$\frac{V}{L} = \frac{r}{2} = \frac{3.8}{2} = 1.9$

4. $\frac{F_1}{F_2} = \frac{W_1}{W_2}$

$\frac{(2)}{F_2} = \frac{(16)}{(48)}$

Cross-multiply and solve:

$2(48) = 16F_2$

$$F_2 = \frac{2(48)}{16}$$

$$F_2 = 6$$

6 cups of fertilizer will be needed.

5. The sum of the lengths of any two sides must be greater than the length of the third side.

$4 + 6 > x$

$4 + x > 6$

$6 + x > 4$

Solve separately:

$4 + 6 > x$ so $x < 10$.

$4 + x > 6$ and $6 + x > 4$

$-4 + 4 + x > -4 + 6$ $\quad -6 + 6 + x > -6 + 4$

$x > 2$ $\quad x > -2$

Length cannot be negative, so $2 < x < 10$

6. Function is $y = a(x - h)^2 + k$ where $h = 4$ (shift 4 right), $k = -6$ (shift 6 down), and $a = 1$ (no compression or stretch):

$y = (x - 4)^2 - 6$

7. Function is $y = a(x - h)^2 + k$ where $a = -1$ (reflection across x-axis), $h = 0$ (no horizontal shift), and $k = 3$ (shift 3 up):

$$y = (-1)(x - 0)^2 + 3$$
$$= -x^2 + 3$$

8. $V_{prism} = (2x)(2x)(h) = 4x^2h$

$V_{cylinder} = \pi x^2 h$

Subtract polynomials:

$$V_{prism} - V_{cylinder} = 4x^2h - \pi x^2 h$$
$$= (4 - \pi)x^2 h$$

9. $$\frac{3a^3b^2}{5a^5} \cdot \frac{10a^3b}{7a^4b^2} = \frac{30a^6b^3}{35a^9b^2}$$

$$= \frac{6 \cdot \cancel{5}\ \cancel{a^6}\ b\ \cancel{b^2}}{7 \cdot \cancel{5}\ a^3\ \cancel{a^6}\ \cancel{b^2}}$$

$$= \frac{6b}{7a^3}$$

10. $$\frac{2xy}{3y^{11}} \cdot \frac{6x^2y}{3xy} = \frac{12x^3y^2}{9xy^{12}}$$

$$= \frac{4 \cdot \cancel{3}\ \cancel{x}\ x^2\ \cancel{y^2}}{3 \cdot \cancel{3}\ \cancel{x}\ y^{10}\ \cancel{y^2}}$$

$$= \frac{4x^2}{3y^{10}}$$

11. $$(x + c)(x + d) = x(x) + c(x) + x(d) + c(d)$$
$$= x^2 + cx + dx + cd$$
$$= x^2 + (c + d)x + cd$$

Therefore $a = c + d$ and $b = cd$.

12. Rise = 14,433 ft, run = 22,105 ft

$$\text{slope} = \frac{\text{rise}}{\text{run}}$$
$$= \frac{14{,}433}{22{,}105}$$
$$\approx 0.653$$

13. Terms must be in descending order by degree. Answer choice **A**

14. There are 12 in. in a foot, so

$$\frac{87\ \cancel{ft^2}}{1} \times \frac{12\text{ in.}}{1\ \cancel{ft}} \times \frac{12\text{ in.}}{1\ \cancel{ft}} = 12{,}528\text{ in.}^2$$

15. Let the integers be n and $n + 2$. The sum is less than or equal to 130:

$n + n + 2 \leq 130$

$2n + 2 \leq 130$

$2n + 2 - 2 \leq 130 - 2$ Add. Prop. of Eq.

$2n \leq 128$

$\frac{2n}{2} \leq \frac{130}{2}$ Mult. Prop.

$n \leq 64$ Simplify

Largest even numbers: $n = 64$ and $n + 2 = 66$

16. The upper-right product was subtracted from the lower-left product, instead of the other way around. Correct answer:

$(-2)(-1) - (6)(3) = 2 - 18 = -16$

17. Solve equations for y:

(1) $2x - 3y = 4$

$$-2x + 2x - 3y = -2x + 4$$
$$-3y = -2x + 4$$
$$\frac{-3y}{-3} = \frac{-2x + 4}{-3}$$
$$y = \frac{2}{3}x - \frac{4}{3}$$

(2) $4x + y = 1$

$$-4x + 4x + y = -4x + 1$$
$$y = -4x + 1$$

Graph both equations and use the Intersect function:

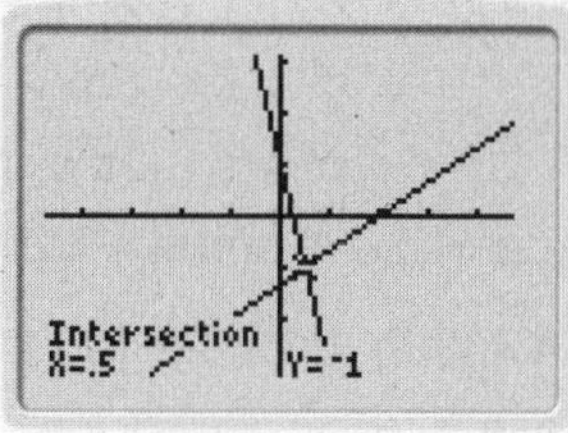

Intersection is at $\left(\frac{1}{2}, -1\right)$, or $x = \frac{1}{2}$, $y = -1$

18. a. $|ax + b| \le c$

$ax + b \le c$ and $ax + b \ge -c$

$ax + b - b \le c - b$ $\quad ax + b - b \ge -c - b$

$ax \le c - b$ $\quad ax \ge -(c + b)$

$\frac{ax}{a} \le \frac{c - b}{a}$ $\quad \frac{ax}{a} \ge \frac{-(c + b)}{a}$

$x \le \frac{c - b}{a}$ $\quad x \ge \frac{-(c + b)}{a}$

Combine inequalities:

$$\frac{-(c + b)}{a} \le x \le \frac{c - b}{a}$$

b. $\frac{-(c + b)}{a} \le x \le \frac{c - b}{a}$

$$\frac{-(5 + 3)}{2} \le x \le \frac{5 - 3}{2}$$

$$\frac{-8}{2} \le x \le \frac{2}{2}$$

$$-4 \le x \le 1$$

19. $x = 3$ and $x = -3$ are vertical lines, $y = -4$ is a horizontal line.

$y = \frac{2}{3}x + 3$ has slope $\frac{2}{3}$ and y-intercept 3. Plot (0, 3), move up 2 and 3 to the right to plot (3, 5), draw line.

$y = -\frac{2}{3}x + 3$ has slope $-\frac{2}{3}$ and y-intercept 3. Plot (0, 3), move down 2 and 3 to the right to plot (3, 1), draw line.

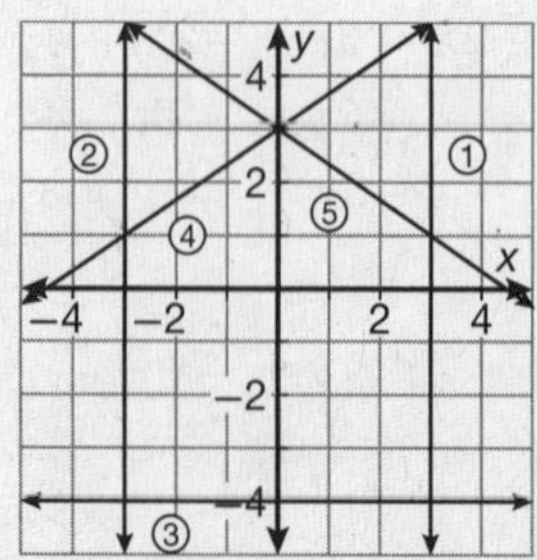

a. No, the pentagon is not regular.

b. (0, 3), (3, 1), (3, –4), (–3, –4), and (–3, 1)

20. The value of h is positive; the minus sign is included in the vertex form of the equation: $y = a(x - h)^2 + k$. So, the graph is a shift 6 units to the right.

21. $(x + 11)(x - 8)$

$= x(x) + x(-8) + 11(x) + 11(-8)$

$= x^2 - 8x + 11x - 88$

$= x^2 + 3x - 88$

Answer choice **B**

22. Equation is of form $y = kx$: direct variation.

23. $y = \frac{20}{x} \rightarrow xy = 20$: inverse variation since product of x, y is a constant.

24. a. The lines intersect at a single point.

b. The lines coincide, sharing all points.

c. The lines are parallel, they do not intersect.

25. Possible answer: Factor $a^2 - 49$ to get $(a + 7)(a - 7)$. Factor $2a^2 + 14a$ to get $2a(a + 7)$. Divide out the common factors a, $(a + 7)$, and $(a - 7)$. The product in simplest form is $\frac{1}{2}$.

26. a. $\frac{4x^2 - 13x + 3}{9 - 6x + x^2} = \frac{(4x - 1)\cancel{(x - 3)}}{(x - 3)^{\cancel{2}}}$

$$= \frac{4x - 1}{x - 3}$$

b. $\frac{4x - 1}{x - 3} = \frac{(4(9) - 1)}{(9) - 3}$

$$= \frac{(36 - 1)}{6}$$

$$= \frac{35}{6}$$

$$= 5\frac{5}{6}$$

27. $\begin{cases} q + d = 157 \\ 0.25q + 0.1d = 26.95 \end{cases}$

$\rightarrow \begin{cases} q + d = 157 \\ -10(0.25q + 0.1d) = -10(26.95) \end{cases}$

$\rightarrow \begin{cases} q + d = 157 \\ -2.5q - d = -269.5 \end{cases}$

Solve for q:

$$q + d = 157$$
$$\frac{-2.5q - d = -269.5}{-1.5q \quad = -112.5}$$
$$\frac{-1.5q}{-1.5} = \frac{-112.5}{-1.5}$$
$$q = 75$$

Substitute and solve for d:

$$q + d = 157$$
$$75 + d = 157$$
$$-75 + 75 + d = -75 + 157$$
$$d = 82$$

75 quarters and 82 dimes

28. $f(3) = 5(3) - 9 = 15 - 9 = 6$ $\quad g(3) = 9(3) + 8 = 27 + 8 = 35$

$(f \cdot g)(3) = (6)(35) = 210$

29. $f(2) = 5(2) - 9 = 10 - 9 = 1$

$g(2) = 9(2) + 8 = 18 + 8 = 26$

$$\left(\frac{f}{g}\right)(2) = \frac{(1)}{(26)} = \frac{1}{26}$$

30. $10x + 3(0) - 8(0) = 12$

$$10x = 12$$
$$x = 1.2$$
$$10(0) + 3y - 8(0) = 12$$
$$3y = 12$$
$$y = 4$$
$$10(0) + 3(0) - 8z = 12$$
$$-8z = 12$$
$$z = -1.5$$

[x: (1.2, 0, 0), y: (0, 4, 0), z: (0, 0, −1.5)]

LESSON 32

Warm Up 32

1. matrix

2. $-2[1 \quad 3 \quad -4] = [-2(1) \quad -2(3) \quad -2(-4)] = [-2 \quad -6 \quad 8]$

3. $\begin{bmatrix} 1 & 2 \\ 2 & 3 \end{bmatrix}\begin{bmatrix} 0 & 4 \\ 1 & 5 \end{bmatrix} = \begin{bmatrix} 0+2 & 4+10 \\ 0+3 & 8+15 \end{bmatrix} = \begin{bmatrix} 2 & 14 \\ 3 & 23 \end{bmatrix}$

Exploration

1. $AB = \begin{bmatrix} -2 & 0 \\ 5 & 1 \end{bmatrix} \cdot \begin{bmatrix} -0.5 & 0 \\ 2.5 & 1 \end{bmatrix}$

$$= \begin{bmatrix} -2(-0.5) + 0(2.5) & -2(0) + 0(1) \\ 5(-0.5) + 1(2.5) & 5(0) + 1(1) \end{bmatrix}$$
$$= \begin{bmatrix} 1 & 0 \\ 0 & 1 \end{bmatrix}$$

$BA = \begin{bmatrix} -0.5 & 0 \\ 2.5 & 1 \end{bmatrix} \cdot \begin{bmatrix} -2 & 0 \\ 5 & 1 \end{bmatrix}$

$$= \begin{bmatrix} -0.5(-2) + 0(5) & -0.5(0) + 0(1) \\ 2.5(-2) + 1(5) & 2.5(0) + 1(1) \end{bmatrix}$$
$$= \begin{bmatrix} 1 & 0 \\ 0 & 1 \end{bmatrix}$$

2. $PQ = \begin{bmatrix} 8 & 5 \\ 6 & 4 \end{bmatrix} \cdot \begin{bmatrix} 2 & -2.5 \\ -3 & 4 \end{bmatrix}$

$$= \begin{bmatrix} 8(2) + 5(-3) & 8(-2.5) + 5(4) \\ 6(2) + 4(-3) & 6(-2.5) + 4(4) \end{bmatrix}$$
$$= \begin{bmatrix} 1 & 0 \\ 0 & 1 \end{bmatrix}$$

$QP = \begin{bmatrix} 2 & -2.5 \\ -3 & 4 \end{bmatrix} \cdot \begin{bmatrix} 8 & 5 \\ 6 & 4 \end{bmatrix}$

$$= \begin{bmatrix} 2(8) + (-2.5)(6) & 2(5) + (-2.5)(4) \\ -3(8) + 4(6) & -3(5) + 4(4) \end{bmatrix}$$
$$= \begin{bmatrix} 1 & 0 \\ 0 & 1 \end{bmatrix}$$

3. $ST = \begin{bmatrix} 3 & 1 \\ 11 & 4 \end{bmatrix} \cdot \begin{bmatrix} 4 & -1 \\ -11 & 3 \end{bmatrix}$

$$= \begin{bmatrix} 3(4) + 1(-11) & 3(-1) + 1(3) \\ 11(4) + 4(-11) & 11(-1) + 4(3) \end{bmatrix}$$
$$= \begin{bmatrix} 1 & 0 \\ 0 & 1 \end{bmatrix}$$

$TS = \begin{bmatrix} 4 & -1 \\ -11 & 3 \end{bmatrix} \cdot \begin{bmatrix} 3 & 1 \\ 11 & 4 \end{bmatrix}$

$$= \begin{bmatrix} 4(3) + (-1)(11) & 4(1) + (-1)(4) \\ -11(3) + 3(11) & -11(1) + 3(4) \end{bmatrix}$$

$$= \begin{bmatrix} 1 & 0 \\ 0 & 1 \end{bmatrix}$$

4. The products are all $\begin{bmatrix} 1 & 0 \\ 0 & 1 \end{bmatrix}$.

5. It is the multiplicative identity matrix.

Lesson Practice 32

a. $QW = \begin{bmatrix} -1 & 2 \\ 1.5 & -2.5 \end{bmatrix} \cdot \begin{bmatrix} 5 & 4 \\ 3 & 2 \end{bmatrix}$

$$= \begin{bmatrix} -1(5) + 2(3) & -1(4) + 2(2) \\ 1.5(5) + (-2.5)(3) & 1.5(4) + (-2.5)(2) \end{bmatrix}$$

$$= \begin{bmatrix} 1 & 0 \\ 0 & 1 \end{bmatrix} = I$$

$$WQ = \begin{bmatrix} 5 & 4 \\ 3 & 2 \end{bmatrix} \cdot \begin{bmatrix} -1 & 2 \\ 1.5 & -2.5 \end{bmatrix}$$

$$= \begin{bmatrix} 5(-1) + 4(1.5) & 5(2) + 4(-2.5) \\ 3(-1) + 2(1.5) & 3(2) + 2(-2.5) \end{bmatrix}$$

$$= \begin{bmatrix} 1 & 0 \\ 0 & 1 \end{bmatrix} = I$$

$QW = I$ and $WQ = I$, so Q and W are inverses.

b. $AB = \begin{bmatrix} 2 & -1 \\ -4 & 3 \end{bmatrix} \cdot \begin{bmatrix} \frac{1}{2} & -1 \\ -\frac{1}{4} & \frac{1}{3} \end{bmatrix}$

$$= \begin{bmatrix} 2\left(\frac{1}{2}\right) + (-1)\left(-\frac{1}{4}\right) & 2(-1) + (-1)\left(\frac{1}{3}\right) \\ -4\left(\frac{1}{2}\right) + 3\left(-\frac{1}{4}\right) & -4(-1) + 3\left(\frac{1}{3}\right) \end{bmatrix}$$

$$= \begin{bmatrix} 1\frac{1}{4} & -2\frac{1}{3} \\ -2\frac{3}{4} & 5 \end{bmatrix} \neq I$$

$AB \neq I$, so A and B are not inverses.

c. $|A| = (5)(1) - (-2)(-3) = 5 - 6 = -1.$

$$A^{-1} = \frac{1}{-1}\begin{bmatrix} 1 & 2 \\ 3 & 5 \end{bmatrix} = \begin{bmatrix} -1 & -2 \\ -3 & -5 \end{bmatrix}$$

d. $|B| = (2)(2) - (0)(0) = 4 - 0 = 4.$

$$B^{-1} = \frac{1}{4}\begin{bmatrix} 2 & 0 \\ 0 & 2 \end{bmatrix} = \begin{bmatrix} \frac{1}{2} & 0 \\ 0 & \frac{1}{2} \end{bmatrix}$$

e.

```
[A]-1
   [[12   -7 3 ]
    [-20 12 -5]
    [1.5 -1 .5]]
```

```
[A]*[A]-1
          [[1 0 0]
           [0 1 0]
           [0 0 1]]
```

```
[A]-1*[A]
           [[1 0 0]
            [0 1 0]
            [0 0 1]]
```

f. $|A| = (3)(4) - (7)(1) = 12 - 7 = 5.$

$$A^{-1} = \frac{1}{5}\begin{bmatrix} 4 & -7 \\ -1 & 3 \end{bmatrix} = \begin{bmatrix} 0.8 & -1.4 \\ -0.2 & 0.6 \end{bmatrix}$$

$$X = A^{-1}B$$

$$= \begin{bmatrix} 0.8 & -1.4 \\ -0.2 & 0.6 \end{bmatrix}\begin{bmatrix} -1 & -8 \\ -3 & -24 \end{bmatrix}$$

$$= \begin{bmatrix} 0.8(-1) + (-1.4)(-3) & 0.8(-8) + (-1.4)(-24) \\ -0.2(-1) + 0.6(-3) & -0.2(-8) + 0.6(-24) \end{bmatrix}$$

$$= \begin{bmatrix} 3.4 & 27.2 \\ -1.6 & -12.8 \end{bmatrix}$$

g. $$\underbrace{\begin{bmatrix} -5 & -1 & 1 \\ 3 & 2 & -1 \\ 1 & 1 & 2 \end{bmatrix}}_{A}\underbrace{\begin{bmatrix} x \\ y \\ z \end{bmatrix}}_{X} = \underbrace{\begin{bmatrix} -16 \\ 12 \\ -10 \end{bmatrix}}_{B}$$

Using a graphing calculator:

$$A^{-1} = \begin{bmatrix} \frac{-5}{17} & \frac{-3}{17} & \frac{1}{17} \\ \frac{7}{17} & \frac{11}{17} & \frac{2}{17} \\ \frac{-1}{17} & \frac{-4}{17} & \frac{7}{17} \end{bmatrix}$$

$$X = A^{-1}B$$

$$= \begin{bmatrix} \frac{-5}{17} & \frac{-3}{17} & \frac{1}{17} \\ \frac{7}{17} & \frac{11}{17} & \frac{2}{17} \\ \frac{-1}{17} & \frac{-4}{17} & \frac{7}{17} \end{bmatrix} \begin{bmatrix} -16 \\ 12 \\ -10 \end{bmatrix}$$

$$= \begin{bmatrix} 2 \\ 0 \\ -6 \end{bmatrix}$$

Solution is $x = 2$, $y = 0$, $z = -6$.

h. masses of ingredients (g):

$b + c + r = 350$

masses of fat in ingredients (g):

$0.03b + 0.2c + 0.02r = 24.7$

masses of protein in ingredients (g):

$0.23b + 0.8c + 0.08r = 115.3$

$$\underbrace{\begin{bmatrix} 1 & 1 & 1 \\ 0.03 & 0.2 & 0.02 \\ 0.23 & 0.8 & 0.08 \end{bmatrix}}_{A} \underbrace{\begin{bmatrix} b \\ c \\ r \end{bmatrix}}_{X} = \underbrace{\begin{bmatrix} 350 \\ 24.7 \\ 115.3 \end{bmatrix}}_{B}$$

Using a graphing calculator:

$$X = A^{-1}B = \begin{bmatrix} 150 \\ 90 \\ 110 \end{bmatrix}$$

Solution is $b = 150$, $c = 90$, $r = 110$. The entrée contains 160 g of beans, 90 g of chicken, and 110 g of rice.

Practice 32

1. First equation:

$$2x + y + 2z = 5$$
$$2(5) + (-3) + 2(-1) \stackrel{?}{=} 5$$
$$10 - 3 - 2 = 5 \quad ✓$$

Second equation:

$$x - 4y + 3z = 14$$
$$(5) - 4(-3) + 3(-1) \stackrel{?}{=} 14$$
$$5 + 12 - 3 = 14 \quad ✓$$

Third equation:

$$-x + 4y - 3z = -6$$
$$-(5) + 4(-3) - 3(-1) \stackrel{?}{=} -6$$
$$-5 + (-12) - (-3) = -6$$
$$-14 \neq -6 \quad \textbf{X}$$

$(5, -3, -1)$ is not a solution.

2. a. $$\bar{x} = \frac{(-4) + (-7) + 12 + (-2) + 8 + 3 + (-1) + 2 + 4 + (-52)}{10}$$
$$= -3.7$$

b. $$\sigma = \sqrt{\frac{(-4-(-3.7))^2 + (-7-(-3.7))^2 + (12-(-3.7))^2 + (-2-(-3.7))^2 + (8-(-3.7))^2 + (3-(-3.7))^2 + (-1-(-3.7))^2 + (2-(-3.7))^2 + (4-(-3.7))^2 + (-52-(-3.7))^2}{10}}$$

$$= \sqrt{\frac{(-0.3)^2 + (-3.3)^2 + (15.7)^2 + (1.7)^2 + (11.7)^2 + (6.7)^2 + (2.7)^2 + (5.7)^2 + (7.7)^2 + (-48.3)^2}{10}}$$

$$\approx \sqrt{\frac{2874}{10}} \approx \sqrt{287.4} \approx 17.0$$

c. -52

d. Without outlier,

$$\bar{x} = \frac{(-4) + (-7) + 12 + (-2) + 8 + 3 + (-1) + 2 + 4}{9} \approx 1.7$$

and

$$\sigma = \sqrt{\frac{(-4-(1.7))^2 + (-7-(1.7))^2 + (12-(1.7))^2 + (-2-(1.7))^2 + (8-(1.7))^2 + (3-(1.7))^2 + (-1-(1.7))^2 + (2-(1.7))^2 + (4-(1.7))^2}{9}}$$

$$= \sqrt{\frac{(-5.7)^2 + (-8.7)^2 + (10.3)^2 + (-3.7)^2 + (6.3)^2 + (1.3)^2 + (-2.7)^2 + (0.3)^2 + (2.3)^2}{9}}$$

$$\approx \sqrt{\frac{282}{9}} \approx \sqrt{31.3} \approx 5.6$$

The outlier decreases the mean from ≈ 1.7 to -3.7, and increases the standard deviation from ≈ 5.6 to ≈ 17.0.

3.
$$\begin{aligned} 3t + 4 &< 2(t + 3) + t \\ 3t + 4 &< 2t + 6 + t \\ 3t + 4 &< 3t + 6 \\ -3t + 3t + 4 &< -3t + 3t + 6 \\ 4 &< 6 \end{aligned}$$

The inequality is always true, so the solution is all real numbers.

4. $\frac{x^2 - 1}{x} \div \frac{3 - x}{2x + 2}$

$= \frac{x^2 - 1}{x} \cdot \frac{2x + 2}{3 - x}$

$= \frac{(x - 1)(x + 1)}{x} \cdot \frac{2(x + 1)}{3 - x}$

The factors in the denominator are x and $(3 - x)$. The denominator of the divisor fraction has factor $(x + 1)$. So, the values of x that make the expression undefined are 0, 3, and -1. Answer choice **A**

5. No; Possible explanation: Any even power of x is nonnegative, and any positive coefficient times any nonnegative value is nonnegative. So, the value of the polynomial is the sum of nonnegative values, and that sum is therefore nonnegative.

6. Write second equation in standard form:

$$\begin{aligned} y &= 2x - 4 \\ -2x + y &= -2x + 2x - 4 \\ -2x + y &= -4 \\ 3x - y &= 5 \\ -2x + y &= -4 \end{aligned}$$

$$\underbrace{\begin{bmatrix} 3 & -1 \\ -2 & 1 \end{bmatrix}}_{A} \underbrace{\begin{bmatrix} x \\ y \end{bmatrix}}_{X} = \underbrace{\begin{bmatrix} 5 \\ -4 \end{bmatrix}}_{B}$$

$|A| = (3)(1) - (-1)(-2) = 3 - 2 = 1.$

$A^{-1} = \begin{bmatrix} 1 & 1 \\ 2 & 3 \end{bmatrix}$

$X = A^{-1}B$

$= \begin{bmatrix} 1 & 1 \\ 2 & 3 \end{bmatrix} \cdot \begin{bmatrix} 5 \\ -4 \end{bmatrix}$

$= \begin{bmatrix} 5 - 4 \\ 10 - 12 \end{bmatrix} = \begin{bmatrix} 1 \\ -2 \end{bmatrix}$

Solution $x = 1$, $y = -2$.

7. The slope of the graph is positive and greater than 1. Answer choice **C**

8. Substitute for x and y:

$$\begin{aligned} 5.3(1.3) - (0.8)(-2.7) &= 9.05 \\ 6.98 + 2.16 &= 9.05 \\ 9.05 &= 9.05 \\ -3.0(1.3) + 1.4(-2.7) &= -7.68 \\ -3.9 - 3.78 &= -7.68 \\ -7.68 &= -7.68 \end{aligned}$$

9. $\frac{36x^5y^{10}}{7y^4} \div \frac{12y^4}{21x^2} = \frac{36x^5y^{10}}{7y^4} \cdot \frac{21x^2}{12y^4}$

$= \frac{756x^7y^{10}}{84y^8}$

$= \frac{9 \cdot \cancel{84} \cdot x^7 \cdot y^2 \cdot \cancel{y^8}}{\cancel{84} \cdot \cancel{y^8}}$

$= 9x^7y^2$

10. a. Graph the function. The vertex is the maximum.

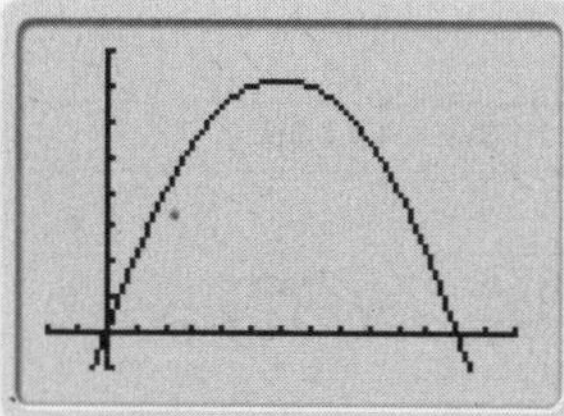

The greatest area is at $x = 6$.

b. $A = -x^2 + 12x$

$= -(6)^2 + 12(6)$

$= -36 + 72 = 36$

The greatest area is 36 m^2.

11. a. 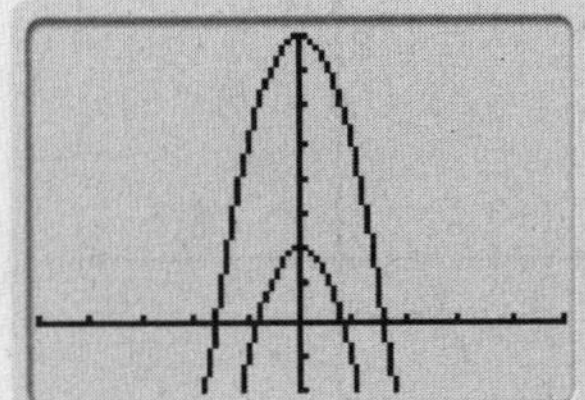

A vertical shift of 30 units down transforms the first graph to the second.

b. Quadrant I; time is positive and the lowest height is ground level. (Quadrant IV could make sense if the scenario involved negative elevations.)

12. $\begin{bmatrix} 2 & 4 & 1 \\ 1 & -5 & 1 \\ 1 & 1 & 1 \end{bmatrix}\begin{bmatrix} x \\ y \\ z \end{bmatrix} = \begin{bmatrix} 16 \\ -5 \\ 7 \end{bmatrix}$

13. $\begin{bmatrix} 3 & 0 & 4 \\ 0 & 15 & -2 \\ 0 & 0 & 6 \end{bmatrix}\begin{bmatrix} x \\ y \\ z \end{bmatrix} = \begin{bmatrix} 13 \\ 20 \\ 6 \end{bmatrix}$

14. Compare $f(x) = -2\left(x - \frac{1}{2}\right)^2 - 5$ with

$f(x) = a(x - h)^2 + k$

$a = -2$, $h = \frac{1}{2}$, and $k = 5$

15. Possible answer: Combine the like terms x, $4x$, and $-x$ to get $4x$, and then write the terms in descending order by degree to get $-5x^2 + 4x + 12$.

16. masses of carbohydrates (g):

$0.06s + 0.09h + 0.77r = 37.4$

masses of fat (g):

$0.64s + 0.48h + 0.11r = 46$

masses of protein (g):

$0.3s + 0.43h + 0.12r = 36.6$

$$\underbrace{\begin{bmatrix} 0.06 & 0.09 & 0.77 \\ 0.64 & 0.48 & 0.11 \\ 0.3 & 0.43 & 0.12 \end{bmatrix}}_{A}\underbrace{\begin{bmatrix} s \\ h \\ r \end{bmatrix}}_{B} = \underbrace{\begin{bmatrix} 37.4 \\ 46 \\ 36.6 \end{bmatrix}}_{C}$$

Using a graphing calculator:

$X = A^{-1}B = \begin{bmatrix} 20 \\ 60 \\ 40 \end{bmatrix}$

So $s = 20$, $h = 60$, $r = 40$. The sandwich contains 20 g of swiss cheese, 60 g of ham, and 40 g of rye bread.

17. The student changed $5 - r$ to $r - 5$ without first factoring out -1. The numerator should be $-2(r - 5)$, making the simplified expression $-\frac{2}{r-5}$.

18. a. A direct variation can be written in the form $\frac{y}{x} = k$, where k is the constant of variation. This is a direct variation because it has the form $A = \pi r^2$ or $\frac{A}{r^2} = \pi$, where π is a constant.

b. A joint variation can be written in the form $\frac{y}{xz} = k$, where k is the constant of variation. This is a joint variation because it has the form $A =$ constant $\times\, l \times w$ or $\frac{A}{lw} = k$.

19. a. $\frac{S_{small}}{V_{small}} = \frac{2\pi r^2 + 2\pi rh}{\pi r^2 h}$

$= \frac{2\cancel{\pi r}(r + h)}{\cancel{\pi r^2} h}$

$= \frac{2(r + h)}{rh}$

b. $\frac{S_{large}}{V_{large}} = \frac{2\pi r^2 + 2\pi r(2h)}{\pi r^2(2h)}$

$= \frac{\cancel{2\pi r}(r + 2h)}{\cancel{\pi r^2 2}h}$

$= \frac{r + 2h}{rh}$

c. Since the denominators of the ratios are the same, the expression with the greater numerator has a greater value.

$2(r + h) > r + 2h$ so $\frac{2(r + h)}{rh} > \frac{r + 2h}{rh}$.

The large container is more economical because its ratio of surface area to volume is smaller.

20. a. $|x - 155| < 25$

b. $x - 155 < 25$

$x - 155 + 155 < 25 + 155$

$x < 180$

and

$x - 155 > -25$

$x - 155 + 155 > -25 + 155$

$x > 130$

Combining: $130 < x < 180$

21. Use power rule, then simplify using product rule:

$$\frac{x^2x^0x^{-1}(x^{-2})^2yx^{-3}}{(x^2y)^{-3}xyx^{-2}x^2} = \frac{x^2x^0x^{-1}x^{-4}yx^{-3}}{x^{-6}y^{-3}xyx^{-2}x^2}$$

$$= \frac{x^{-6}y}{x^{-5}y^{-2}}$$

$$= x^{-6-(-5)}y^{1-(-2)}$$

$$= x^{-1}y^3 = \frac{y^3}{x}$$

22. a. Area = length × width

$= (x + 24)(x - 10)$

$= x(x) + x(-10) + 24(x) + 24(-10)$

$= x^2 - 10x + 24x - 240$

$= x^2 + 14x - 240$

The area is $x^2 + 14x - 240$ square feet.

b. $A = x^2 + 14x - 240$

$= (60)^2 + 14(60) - 240$

$= 3600 + 840 - 240$

$= 4200$

The area is 4200 ft^2.

23. Possible answer: To solve $AX = B$, both sides must be multiplied by A^{-1}. To get $X = BA^{-1}$, A^{-1} would have to be written as a matrix factor on the right of both sides of $AX = B$, and the result would be $AXA^{-1} = BA^{-1}$. But the left side of this equation does not generally equal X.

24. $f(x) = -7x + 4$ and $g(x) = 9x + 2$

Let $x = 0$ and -2.

$(f + g)(0) = f(0) + g(0)$

$= 4 + 2 = 6$

and

$(f + g)(-3) = f(-3) + g(-3)$

$= (-7(-3) + 4) + (9(-3) + 2)$

$= (21 + 4) + (-27 + 2)$

$= 25 - 25 = 0$

Plot points (0, 6) and (−3, 0) and draw line $y = (f + g)(x)$ through them:

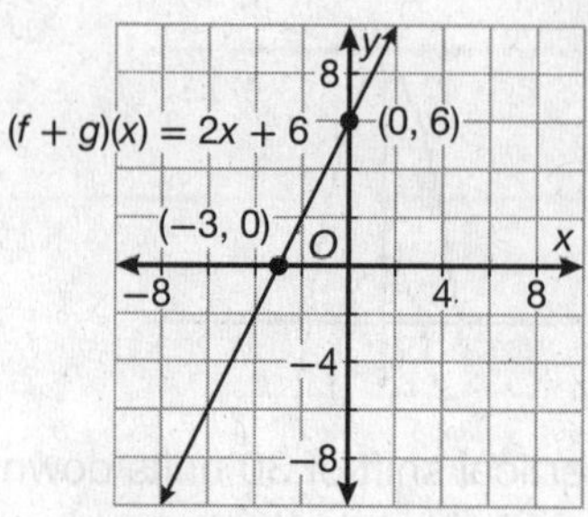

25. There are x red marbles, x blue marbles, and x^2 white marbles.

$$P(\text{red}) = \frac{\#\text{ outcomes (red)}}{\text{total }\#\text{ outcomes}}$$

$$= \frac{x}{x + x + x^2}$$

$$= \frac{x}{2x + x^2}$$

$$= \frac{x}{x(2 + x)} = \frac{1}{2 + x}$$

26. $\begin{cases} \frac{3}{8}x - \frac{1}{3}y = -9 \\ 2x + 4y = 4 \end{cases}$

$\begin{cases} 12\left(\frac{3}{8}x - \frac{1}{3}y\right) = 12(-9) \\ 2x + 4y = 4 \end{cases} \rightarrow \begin{cases} 4.5x - 4y = -108 \\ 2x + 4y = 4 \end{cases}$

Solve for x by eliminating y:

$4.5x - 4y = -108$

$\underline{2x + 4y = 4}$

$6.5x = -104$

$\frac{6.5x}{6.5} = \frac{-104}{6.5}$

$x = -16$

Solve for y:

$2x + 4y = 4$

$2(-16) + 4y = 4$

$-32 + 4y = 4$

$32 - 32 + 4y = 32 + 4$

$4y = 36$

$\frac{4y}{4} = \frac{36}{4}$

$y = 9$

Solution is $x = -16$, $y = 9$.

27. $\frac{-3-x}{2} - \frac{x}{2} = 7$

$2\left(\frac{-3-x}{2} - \frac{x}{2}\right) = 2(7)$

$2\left(\frac{-3-x}{2}\right) + 2\left(-\frac{x}{2}\right) = 14$

$-3 - x - x = 14$

$-3 - 2x = 14$

$3 - 3 - 2x = 3 + 14$

$-2x = 17$

$\frac{-2x}{-2} = \frac{17}{-2}$

$x = \frac{-17}{2}$

28. a. $\begin{cases} 9x = y - 3z - 21 \\ 4y - 6z = 8x + 10 \\ 56x - 28y = 2 - 42z \end{cases}$

$\rightarrow \begin{cases} 9x - y + 3z = -21 \\ -8x + 4y - 6z = 10 \\ 56x - 28y + 42z = 2 \end{cases}$

b. No solution; Equations 2 and 3 have coefficients that are multiples of each other but the constants are not multiples.

c. Multiply equation 2 by 7:

$\begin{cases} 9x - y + 3z = -21 \\ -8x + 4y - 6z = 10 \\ 56x - 28y + 42z = 2 \end{cases}$

$\rightarrow \begin{cases} 9x - y + 3z = -21 \\ 7(-8)x + 7(4)y + 7(-6)z = 7(10) \\ 56x - 28y + 42z = 2 \end{cases}$

$\rightarrow \begin{cases} 9x - y + 3z = -21 \\ -56x + 28y - 42z = 70 \\ 56x - 28y + 42z = 2 \end{cases}$

Eliminate y between equations 2 and 3:

$-56x + 28y - 42z = 70$

$\underline{56x - 28y + 42z = 6}$

$0 = 76$ ✗

No solution

29. Factor pairs for -36: $(1)(-36)$, $(-1)(36)$, $(2)(-18)$, $(-2)(18)$, $(3)(-12)$, $(-3)(12)$, $(4)(-9)$, $(-4)(9)$, $(6)(-6)$. Factor pair with sum -5 is $(4)(-9)$. So the factored expression is $(x + 4)(x - 9)$

$x^2 - 5x - 36 = 0$

$(x + 4)(x - 9) = 0$

$(x + 4) = 0$ or $(x - 9) = 0$

$x = -4$ or $x = 9$

30. Middle term should be subtracted; the determinant is $5 - (-6) + 0 = 11$.

LESSON 33

Warm Up 33

1. median
2. $\overline{x} = \frac{12 + 20 + 20 + 30}{4} = \frac{82}{4} = 20.5$
3. Arrange in order: 10, 20, 30, 32, 38, 40
   Median = mean of middle two numbers
   $= \frac{30 + 32}{2} = 31$

Lesson Practice 33

a. Pair each color T-shirt with jeans and khakis.

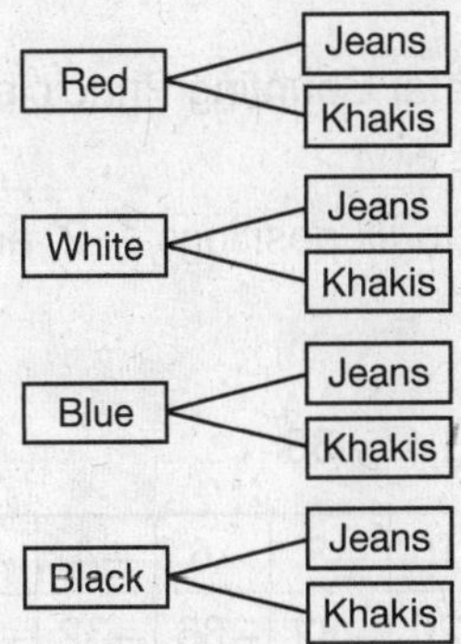

There are 8 different outfits.

b. The events *draw a heart* and *draw a club* are mutually exclusive. There are 13 hearts and 13 clubs.

$13 + 13 = 26$

There are 26 outcomes

c. For whole numbers 21 through 40, events *choose a perfect square, choose a multiple of 8,* and *choose a prime number* are mutually exclusive. There are 2 perfect squares: 25, 36. There are 3 multiples of 8: 24, 32, 40. There are 4 prime numbers: 23, 29, 31, 37.

$2 + 3 + 4 = 9$

So, there are 9 outcomes: 23, 24, 25, 29, 31, 32, 36, 37, 40

d. Digits may be repeated, so there are 10 choices for each digit.

$10 \cdot 10 \cdot 10 \cdot 10 = 10{,}000$

10,000 possible passwords

e. Digits may not be repeated, so there are 10 choices for first digit, 9 choices for second digit, 8 choices for third digit, and 7 choices for fourth digit.

$10 \cdot 9 \cdot 8 \cdot 7 = 5{,}040$

5,040 possible passwords

f. Events are independent because there is a 1 in 5 probability of choosing S second, regardless of what is chosen first.

g. Events are dependent. If W is chosen first, there is a 1 in 4 probability of choosing S second. But if W is not chosen first, then it is possible that S is chosen first, in which case there is zero probability of choosing S second.

h. Fundamental Counting Principle:

$9 \cdot 8 \cdot 7 = 504$

504 ways to fill positions 1, 2, and 3

Practice 33

1. $y = (x + 6)^2 - 36$

x	−12	−10	−8	−6	−4	−2	0	2
y	0	−20	−32	−36	−32	−20	0	28

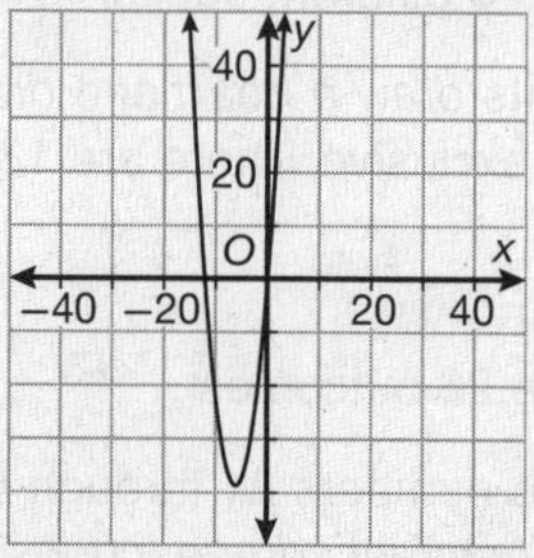

Because width, length, and area can only be positive, the graph only makes sense for values in Quadrant I.

2.
$4 < 2(x - 2) \leq 16$

$4 < 2x - 4 \leq 16$

$4 + 4 < 2x - 4 + 4 \leq 16 + 4$

$8 < 2x \leq 20$

$\frac{8}{2} < \frac{2x}{2} \leq \frac{20}{2}$

$4 < x \leq 10$

3. There are 7 choices for each letter.

$7 \cdot 7 \cdot 7 \cdot 7 \cdot 7 \cdot 7 \cdot 7 = 823{,}543$

There are 823,543 possible passwords.

4. There are 7 choices for first letter, 6 choices for second letter, etc.

$7 \cdot 6 \cdot 5 \cdot 4 \cdot 3 \cdot 2 \cdot 1 = 5040$

There are 5040 possible passwords.

5. Use the slope formula:

$$m = \frac{y_2 - y_1}{x_2 - x_1} = \frac{-5 - (-5)}{4 - (-3)} = \frac{0}{7} = 0$$

Since slope is 0, the line is horizontal with y-intercept $= -5$. Therefore, the equation is $y = -5$.

6. Distance: $x = 210t$

Altitude: $y = 45t$

7. $$\begin{bmatrix} 1 & 1 & 1 \\ 0.4 & 0.5 & 2 \\ 2.2 & 3.4 & 1 \end{bmatrix}\begin{bmatrix} p \\ q \\ r \end{bmatrix} = \begin{bmatrix} 6 \\ 5.7 \\ 12 \end{bmatrix}$$

8. Student A is correct; Student B forgot to distribute the negative through both terms in the second set of parentheses.

9. a. $(f + g + h)(x)$

$= f(x) + g(x) + h(x)$

$= \left(\frac{1}{2}x^2 - 3\right) + (2x^2) + (4x)$

$= \frac{1}{2}x^2 + 2x^2 + 4x - 3$

$= \left(\frac{1}{2} + 2\right)x^2 + 4x - 3$

$= 2\frac{1}{2}x^2 + 4x - 3$

b. $(f \cdot g \cdot h)(x)$

$= (f(x)) \cdot (g(x)) \cdot (h(x))$

$= \left(\frac{1}{2}x^2 - 3\right) \cdot (2x^2) \cdot (4x)$

$= \left(\frac{1}{2}x^2 - 3\right) \cdot (8x^3)$

$=\left(\frac{1}{2}x^2\right)\cdot(8x^3)+(-3)\cdot(8x^3)$
$=4x^5-24x^3$

10. Multiplication is commutative. Division is not commutative. Possible justification for multiplication; Multiplication of real numbers is commutative, and all rational expressions represent real numbers, so multiplication of rational expressions is commutative. Possible justification for division (a counterexample):
$\frac{2x}{y}\div\frac{y}{x}=\frac{2x}{y}\cdot\frac{x}{y}=\frac{2x^2}{y^2}$,
but $\frac{y}{x}\div\frac{2x}{y}=\frac{y}{x}\cdot\frac{y}{2x}=\frac{y^2}{2x^2}$

11. $\frac{2x^4y^5}{3x^2}\cdot\frac{15x^2}{8x^3y^2}=\frac{30x^6y^5}{24x^5y^2}$
$=\frac{5\cdot\cancel{6}\cdot x\cdot\cancel{x^5}\cdot y^3\cdot\cancel{y^2}}{4\cdot\cancel{6}\cdot\cancel{x^5}\cdot\cancel{y^2}}=\frac{5xy^3}{4}$

12. There are 3 choices for the digit, 4 choices for first letter, and 4 choices for second letter.
$3\cdot4\cdot4=48$

13. a. $(x)(4)-(2)(-6)=8$
$4x+12=8$

b. $4x+12=8$
$4x+12-12=8-12$
$4x=-4$
$x=-1$

c. Using a calculator, $\begin{vmatrix}-1 & 2\\ -6 & 4\end{vmatrix}=8$

14. $|M^{-1}|=(4)(6)-(8)(2)=24-16=8.$

$M=\frac{1}{8}\begin{bmatrix}6 & -8\\ -2 & 4\end{bmatrix}=\begin{bmatrix}0.75 & -1\\ -0.25 & 0.5\end{bmatrix}$

15. $y=1.5x+3$
$0=1.5x-y+3$
$-3=1.5x-y$
$1.5x-y=-3$

16. $y=-0.05x+20$
$0.05x+y=0.05x-0.05x+20$
$0.05x+y=20$

17. a. $\begin{cases}c+a=45\\ 10.95c+14.95a=516.75\end{cases}$

b. $c=\frac{\begin{vmatrix}45 & 1\\ 516.75 & 14.95\end{vmatrix}}{\begin{vmatrix}1 & 1\\ 10.95 & 14.95\end{vmatrix}}$
$=\frac{45(14.95)-516.75(1)}{1(14.95)-10.95(1)}$
$=\frac{672.75-516.75}{1(14.95)-10.95(1)}$
$=\frac{156}{4}=39$

$a=\frac{\begin{vmatrix}1 & 45\\ 10.95 & 516.75\end{vmatrix}}{\begin{vmatrix}1 & 1\\ 10.95 & 14.95\end{vmatrix}}$
$=\frac{1(516.75)-10.95(45)}{1(14.95)-10.95(1)}$
$=\frac{516.75-492.75}{1(14.95)-10.95(1)}$
$=\frac{24}{4}=6$

39 children, 6 adults

18. The system has no solutions because the lines are parallel and have no points in common. Solving for *y* in each equation gives the same slope and two different *y*-intercepts.

19. $\frac{(xm^{-2})^0x^0m^0}{xx^2m^0(2x)^{-2}}=\frac{1\cdot1\cdot1}{x^31(2x)^{-2}}$
$=\frac{1}{x^3(2x)^{-2}}\cdot\frac{(2x)^2}{(2x)^2}$
$=\frac{(2x)^2}{x^3(2x)^0}$
$=\frac{4x^2}{x^3\cdot1}$
$=\frac{4\cancel{x^2}}{x\cdot\cancel{x^2}}=\frac{4}{x}$

20. Possible answer: There are 4 choices for first letter in an arrangement, 3 choices for second letter, 2 choices for third letter, and 1 choice for fourth letter. So number of arrangements is
$4\cdot3\cdot2\cdot1=24.$

21. $-12x^4 + 6x^2 + 18x$
$= -6 \cdot 2 \cdot x \cdot x \cdot x \cdot x + 6 \cdot x \cdot x + 6 \cdot 3 \cdot x$
$6x$ is the GCF.
$= -6x(2x^3 - x - 3)$
Factor out $-6x$.
Answer choice **A**

22. 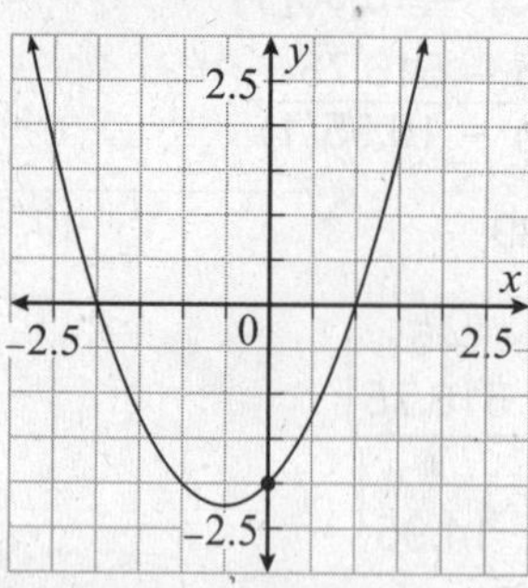

y-intercept $= -2$

23. Fundamental Counting Principle:
$12 \cdot 11 \cdot 10 \cdot 9 \cdot 8 = 95{,}040$
There are 95,040 ways to choose 5 starters (assuming order is important).

24. a. $\begin{cases} x = 25t \\ x = 2 - 10t \end{cases}$

b. $\begin{cases} x = 25t \\ x = 2 - 10t \end{cases} \rightarrow \begin{cases} x - 25t = 0 \\ x + 10t = 2 \end{cases}$

$$t = \frac{\begin{vmatrix} 1 & 0 \\ 1 & 2 \end{vmatrix}}{\begin{vmatrix} 1 & -25 \\ 1 & 10 \end{vmatrix}} = \frac{2 - 0}{10 - (-25)} = \frac{2}{35}$$

The boats meet after $\frac{2}{35}$ h.

25. $A = \frac{1}{2}bh = \frac{1}{2}(3x)(4x) = 6x^2$
Hypotenuse: $c^2 = a^2 + b^2$
$c = \sqrt{(3x)^2 + (4x)^2}$
$= \sqrt{9x^2 + 16x^2}$
$= \sqrt{25x^2}$
$= \sqrt{(5x)^2}$
$= 5x$
$P = a + b + c$
$= 3x + 4x + 5x = 12x$
$\frac{A}{P} = \frac{6x^2}{12x} = \frac{\cancel{6} \cdot x \cdot \cancel{x}}{2 \cdot \cancel{6} \cdot \cancel{x}} = \frac{x}{2}$

26. $40 + 8y - 2z = -5x$
$5x + 8y - 2z = -40$ Convert to standard form.
$5x + 8(0) - 2(0) = -40$
$5x = -40$
$x = -8$
$5(0) + 8y - 2(0) = -40$
$8y = -40$
$y = -5$
$5(0) + 8(0) - 2z = -40$
$-2z = -40$
$z = 20$
[x: $(-8, 0, 0)$, y: $(0, -5, 0)$, z: $(0, 0, 20)$]

27. a. No. Possible reason: the value of the median is between the first and third quartiles.

b. range = max − min
$55 = 93 - \text{min}$
$\text{min} = 93 - 55$
$\text{min} = 38$

c. Range of scores is between first quartile and third quartile, or between 55 and 74.

28. a. $x + y = 73$

b. $2y - x = 2$

c. $\begin{cases} x + y = 73 \\ 2y - x = 2 \end{cases}$
Write in standard form:
$\rightarrow \begin{cases} x + y = 73 \\ -x + 2y = 2 \end{cases}$
Eliminate x and solve for y:
$x + y = 73$
$-x + 2y = 2$
$3y = 75$
$\frac{3y}{3} = \frac{75}{3}$
$y = 25$
Substitute and solve for x:
$x + (25) = 73$
$x + 25 - 25 = 73 - 25$
$x = 48$
Solution is $x = 48$, $y = 25$

29. There are 3 ft in a yard and 12 in. in a foot, so

$$\frac{61\ \cancel{yd^2}}{\cancel{1}} \cdot \frac{3\ \cancel{ft}}{1\ \cancel{yd}} \cdot \frac{3\ \cancel{ft}}{1\ \cancel{yd}} \cdot \frac{12\ \text{in.}}{1\ \cancel{ft}} \cdot \frac{12\ \text{in.}}{1\ \cancel{ft}}$$

$= 79{,}056\ \text{in.}^2$

30. $\begin{vmatrix} 2 & 2 \\ 4 & 5 \end{vmatrix} = (2)(5) - (4)(2) = 10 - 8 = 2$

$$\begin{bmatrix} 2 & 2 \\ 4 & 5 \end{bmatrix}^{-1} = \frac{1}{2}\begin{bmatrix} 5 & -2 \\ -4 & 2 \end{bmatrix} = \begin{bmatrix} 2.5 & -1 \\ -2 & 1 \end{bmatrix}$$

LESSON 34

Warm Up 34

1. slope
2. Equation is in form $y = mx + b$. The y-intercept is 5.
3. Substitute $y = 2$

$$-x + 3y = 4$$
$$-x + 3(2) = 4$$
$$-x + 6 - 6 = 4 - 6$$
$$-x = -2$$
$$x = 2$$

Point is (2, 2)

Lesson Practice 34

a. Rate of change from (0, 2) to (2, 1):

$$\frac{y_2 - y_1}{x_2 - x_1} = \frac{1 - 2}{2 - 0} = \frac{-1}{2} = -\frac{1}{2}$$

Rate of change from (2, 1) to (4, 0):

$$\frac{y_2 - y_1}{x_2 - x_1} = \frac{0 - 1}{4 - 2} = \frac{-1}{2} = -\frac{1}{2}$$

Yes. No vertical line intersects the graph in more than one point, so it represents a function; it is a linear function because the rate of change is constant.

b. No. The vertical line $x = 1$ intersects the graph in two points, (1, 1) and (1, 3), so it does not represent a function.

c.

x	−4	−2	0	2	4
y	−4	−3	−2	−1	0

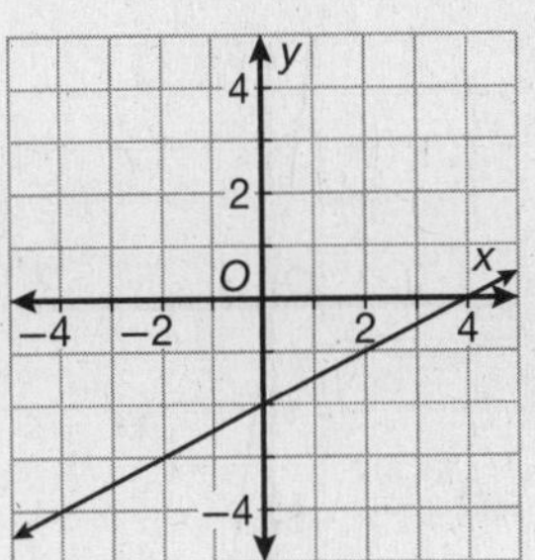

d.

$$2x - 5y = 5$$
$$-2x + 2x - 5y = -2x + 5$$
$$-5y = -2x + 5$$
$$\frac{-5y}{-5} = \frac{-2x + 5}{-5}$$
$$y = \frac{2}{5}x - 1$$

The y-intercept is −1, so the line crosses the y-axis at (0, −1). Plot (0, 1). From (0, −1), count 2 units up and 5 units right to point (5, 1). Plot (5, 1). Draw a straight line through (0, 1) and (5, 1).

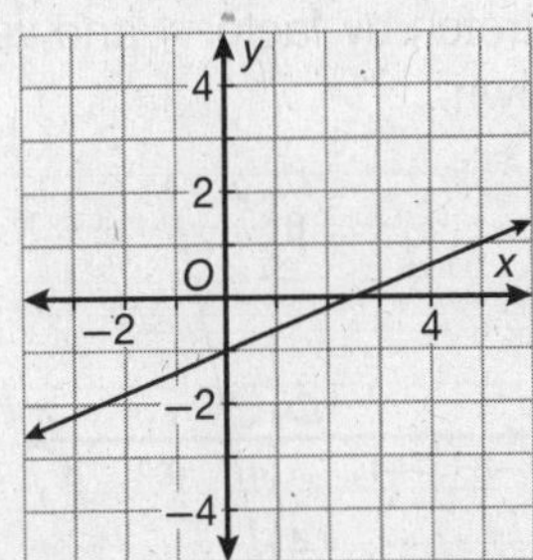

e. The equation is in the point-slope form $y - y_1 = m(x - x_1)$. Slope is $m = \frac{3}{4}$, a point on line is (4, −1). From (4, −1) count 3 up and 4 right to point (8, 2).

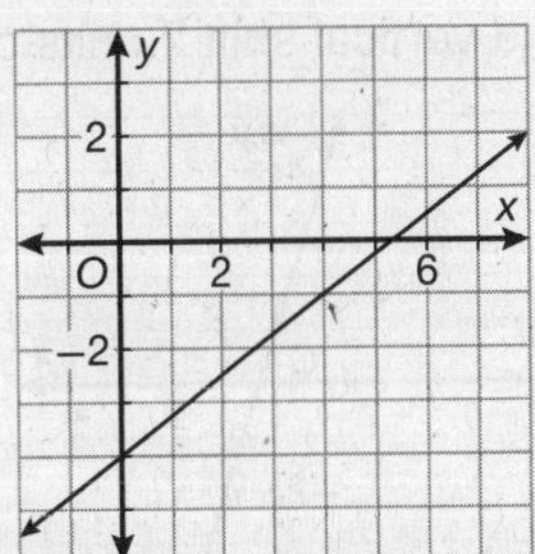

f. $g(x) = -6x = (-6) \cdot f(x)$. This is a vertical stretch by factor 6 and reflection over x-axis.

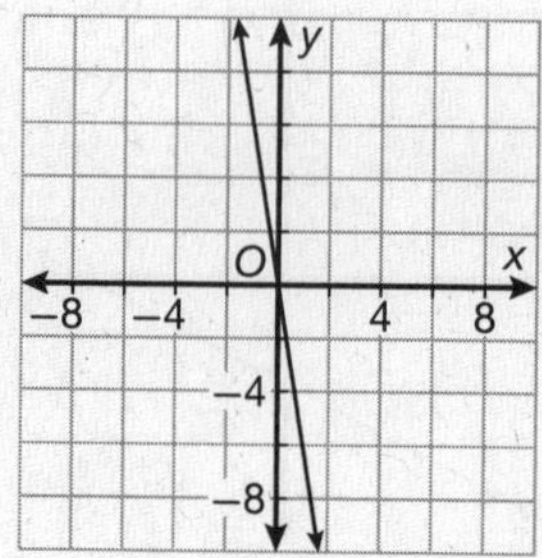

g. $g(x) = x + 5 = f(x) + 5$. This is a vertical shift 5 units up.

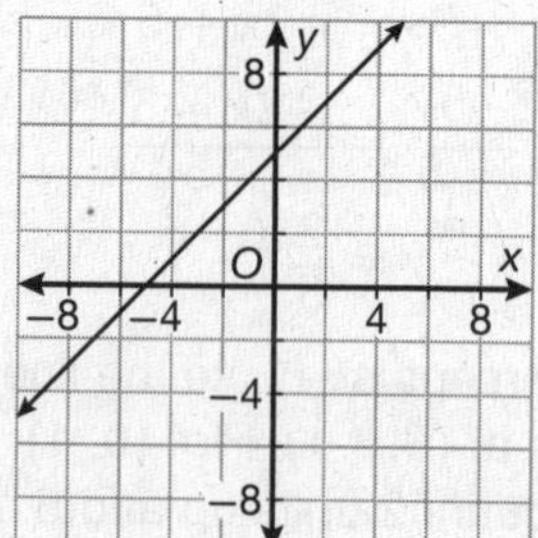

h. $g(x) = 4x - 7 = 4 \cdot f(x) - 7$. This is a vertical stretch by factor 4 and vertical shift 7 units down.

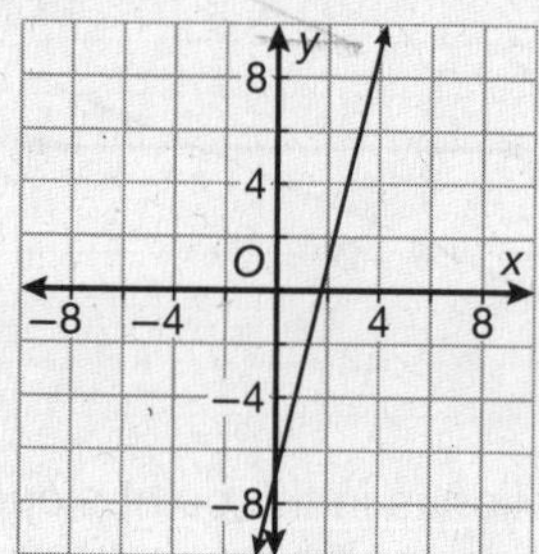

i. $g(x) = -3x + 1 = (-3) \cdot f(x) + 1$. This is a vertical stretch by factor 3, reflection over x-axis, and vertical shift 7 units down

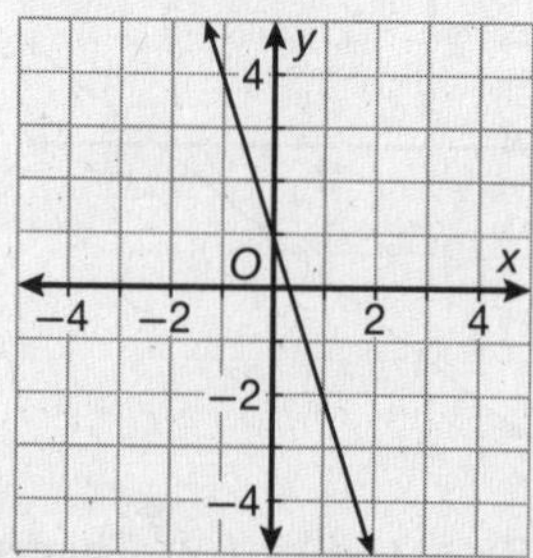

j.

x	4	4	4
y	−2	0	3

Plot the points the points in the table.

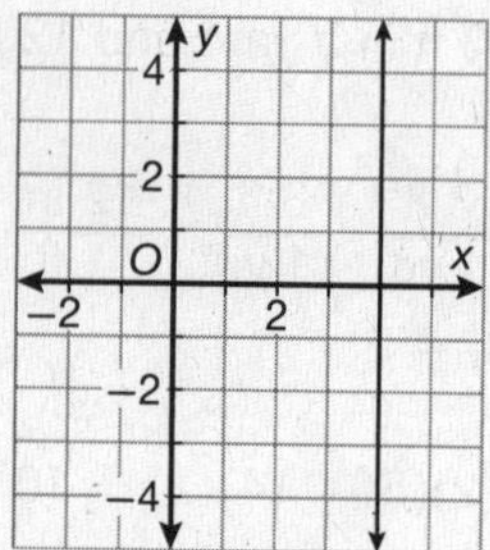

k.

x	−4	0	2
y	−5	−5	−5

Plot the points the points in the table.

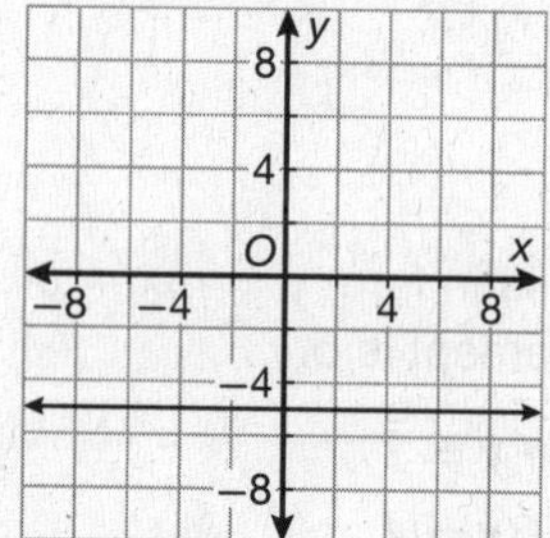

l. Graph line through point P with rise of 3 and run of 5:

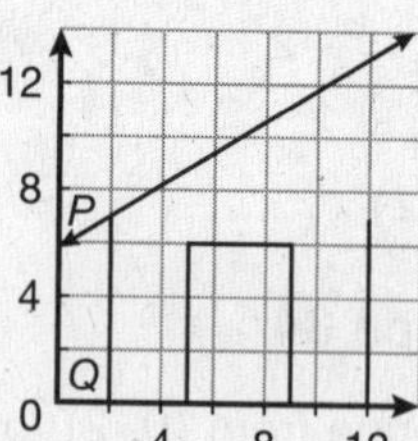

Write equation of line in point-slope form:

$$y - 7 = \frac{3}{5}(x - 2)$$

Solve for y to obtain slope-intercept form:

$$y - 7 = \frac{3}{5}(x - 2)$$

$$y - 7 = \frac{3}{5}x - \frac{6}{5}$$

$$y - 7 + 7 = \frac{3}{5}x - 1\frac{1}{5} + 7$$

$$y = \frac{3}{5}x + 5\frac{4}{5}$$

Practice 34

1. $\begin{cases} c + n = 173 \\ c = n + 11 \end{cases}$

Equation 2 gives an expression for c.

Substitute for c in equation 1:

$$c + n = 173$$
$$(n + 11) + n = 173$$
$$2n + 11 = 173$$
$$2n + 11 - 11 = 173 - 11$$
$$2n = 162$$
$$\frac{2n}{2} = \frac{162}{2}$$
$$n = 81$$

Substitute for n in the second equation:

$c = n + 11 = (81) + 11 = 92$

Chuck = 92 qt, Nikita = 81 qt

2. $-2ab + abx + abx^2$
$= -2 \cdot ab + ab \cdot x + ab \cdot x^2$
$= ab(-2 + x + x^2)$
$= ab(x^2 + x - 2)$

Factor pairs for -2 are $(1)(-2)$ and $(-1)(2)$. Factor pair with sum 1 is $(-1)(2)$, so factored expression for $(x^2 + x - 2)$ is $(x - 1)(x + 2)$. Original expression factors as

$$-2ab + abx + abx^2 = ab(-2 + x + x^2)$$
$$= ab(x - 1)(x + 2)$$

3. $x^2 - y^2(x - y)$
$$= \left(\frac{1}{2}\right)^2 - \left(\frac{1}{3}\right)^2\left(\frac{1}{2} - \frac{1}{3}\right)$$
$$= \frac{1}{4} - \frac{1}{9}\left(\frac{1}{6}\right)$$
$$= \frac{1}{4} - \frac{1}{54} = \frac{25}{108}$$

4. $ax - a(a - x)$
$$= \left(-\frac{1}{2}\right)\left(\frac{1}{4}\right) - \left(-\frac{1}{2}\right)\left[\left(-\frac{1}{2}\right) - \left(\frac{1}{4}\right)\right]$$
$$= -\frac{1}{8} - \left(-\frac{1}{2}\right)\left(-\frac{3}{4}\right)$$
$$= -\frac{1}{8} - \frac{3}{8} = -\frac{1}{2}$$

5. $x + 2y = 5$
$3x - y = 7$

Solve equation 1 for x:

$$x + 2y = 5$$
$$x + 2y - 2y = 5 - 2y$$
$$x = 5 - 2y$$

Substitute expression for x into equation 2 and solve for y:

$$3x - y = 7$$
$$3(5 - 2y) - y = 7$$
$$15 - 6y - y = 7$$
$$15 - 7y = 7$$
$$-15 + 15 - 7y = -15 + 7$$
$$-7y = -8$$
$$\frac{-7y}{-7} = \frac{-8}{-7}$$
$$y = \frac{8}{7}$$

Substitute for y in equation 1:

$$x + 2y = 5$$
$$x + 2\left(\frac{8}{7}\right) = 5$$
$$x = 5 - 2\left(\frac{8}{7}\right)$$
$$x = \frac{7(5) - 2(8)}{7}$$
$$x = \frac{35 - 16}{7} = \frac{19}{7}$$

Solution: $\left(\frac{19}{7}, \frac{8}{7}\right)$

6. $$\frac{4x^{-2}y^{-2}}{z^2}\left(\frac{3x^{\wedge 2}y^{\wedge 2}z^{\wedge 2}}{4} + \frac{2x^{\wedge 0}y^{\wedge -2}}{z^{\wedge 2}y^{\wedge 2}}\right)$$
$$= \frac{4x^{-2}y^{-2}}{z^2} \cdot \frac{3x^2y^2z^2}{4} + \frac{4x^{-2}y^{-2}}{z^2} \cdot \frac{2x^0y^{-2}}{z^2y^2}$$
$$= \frac{12z^2}{4z^2} + \frac{8x^{-2}y^{-4}}{y^2z^4}$$
$$= \frac{3 \cdot \cancel{4} \cdot \cancel{z^2}}{\cancel{4} \cdot \cancel{z^2}} + 8x^{-2}y^{-4}y^{-2}z^{-4}$$
$$= 3 + 8x^{-2}y^{-6}z^{-4}$$

7. $$\frac{(0.0003 \times 10^8)(6000)}{(0.006 \times 10^{15})(2000 \times 10^5)}$$
$$= \frac{(3 \times 10^{-4} \times 10^8)(6 \times 10^3)}{(6 \times 10^{-3} \times 10^{15})(2 \times 10^3 \times 10^5)}$$
$$= \frac{(3 \times 10^4)(6 \times 10^3)}{(6 \times 10^{12})(2 \times 10^8)}$$
$$= \frac{3 \cdot \cancel{6}}{\cancel{6} \cdot 2} \times \frac{10^7}{10^{20}}$$
$$= 1.5 \times 10^{7-20} = 1.5 \times 10^{-13}$$

8. $\frac{3m}{x} - \frac{2x^{-1}}{m^0m^{-1}} + \frac{5x^2m^2}{x^3m}$

$= \frac{3m}{x} - \frac{2x^{-1}}{m^{-1}} + \frac{5x^2m^2}{x^3m}$

$= 3mx^{-1} - 2x^{-1}m + 5x^{-1}m$

$= (3 - 2 + 5)mx^{-1}$

$= 6mx^{-1}$ or $\frac{6m}{x}$

9. $y = \frac{2}{3}x + \frac{4}{5}$

$-\frac{2}{3}x + y = -\frac{2}{3}x + \frac{2}{3}x + \frac{4}{5}$

$-\frac{2}{3}x + y = \left(-\frac{2}{3} + \frac{2}{3}\right)x + \frac{4}{5}$

$-\frac{2}{3}x + y = 0x + \frac{4}{5}$

$-\frac{2}{3}x + y = \frac{4}{5}$

$\frac{2}{3}x - y = -\frac{4}{5}$

10. Subtract $[2 \quad -29 \quad 5]$ from both sides:

$[2 \quad -29 \quad 5] + C = [31 \quad -18 \quad 14]$

$-[2 \quad -29 \quad 5] + [2 \quad -29 \quad 5] + C =$
$-[2 \quad -29 \quad 5] + [31 \quad -18 \quad 14]$

$C = [-2 \quad 29 \quad -5] + [31 \quad -18 \quad 14]$

$C = [-2 + 31 \quad 29 - 18 \quad -5 + 14]$

$C = [29 \quad 11 \quad 9]$

11. Function is linear, so rate of change is constant and = slope = 3. Answer choice **B**

12. $f(x) \cdot g(x) = \frac{3x - 2}{x + 2} \cdot \frac{10x^2 + 20x}{3x^2 - 2x}$

$= \frac{\cancel{3x - 2}}{\cancel{x + 2}} \cdot \frac{10 \cdot \cancel{x} \cdot \cancel{(x + 2)}}{\cancel{x} \cdot \cancel{(3x - 2)}}$

$= 10 = h(x)$

Possible description: They are identical except that $f(x) \cdot g(x)$ is undefined at the values $x = 0$, $x = -2$, and $x = \frac{2}{3}$.

13. a. (0, 6.1), (1, 6.13), (2, 6.16)

b. Slope:

$m = \frac{y_2 - y_1}{x_2 - x_1} = \frac{6.16 - 6.1}{2 - 0}$

$= \frac{0.06}{2} = 0.03$

y-intercept: When $x = 0$, $y = 6.1$

Equation of line:

$y = mx + b$

$y = 0.03x + 6.1$

14. a. $\begin{cases} 0.2x + 0.5y = -1 \\ x - y = 16 \end{cases}$

$\rightarrow \begin{cases} 10(0.2x + 0.5y) = 10(-1) \\ x - y = 16 \end{cases}$

$\rightarrow \begin{cases} 2x + 5y = -10 \\ x - y = 16 \end{cases}$

All the coefficients are now whole numbers.

b. $\begin{cases} 2x + 5y = -10 \\ x - y = 16 \end{cases} \rightarrow \begin{cases} 2x + 5y = -10 \\ 5(x - y) = 5(16) \end{cases}$

$\rightarrow \begin{cases} 2x + 5y = -10 \\ 5x - 5y = 80 \end{cases}$

Add vertically to eliminate *y*, then solve for *x*:

$2x + 5y = -10$

$\underline{5x - 5y = 80}$

$7x = 70$

$\frac{7x}{7} = \frac{70}{7}$

$x = 10$

Substitute for *x* and solve for *y*:

$x - y = 16$

$(10) - y = 16$

$-10 + 10 - y = -10 + 16$

$-y = 6$

$y = -6$

Solution: (10, –6)

15.

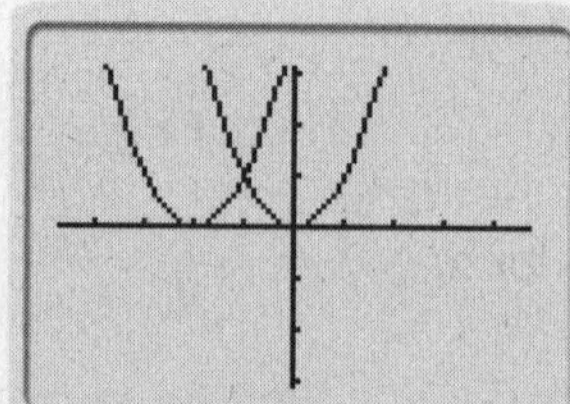

Vertex of graph of $y = (x + 2)^2$ is units further to left.

16. Equations for motion of boat: if x is water speed of boat and y is speed of current,

$$\begin{cases}(x+y)3.3 = 175\\(x-y)4.3 = 175\end{cases} \longrightarrow \begin{cases}x+y = \frac{175}{3.3}\\x-y = \frac{175}{4.3}\end{cases}$$

$$\longrightarrow \begin{cases}y = -x + \frac{175}{3.3}\\-y = -x + \frac{175}{4.3}\end{cases} \longrightarrow \begin{cases}y = -x + \frac{175}{3.3}\\y = x - \frac{175}{4.3}\end{cases}$$

Using a graphing calculator to find the point of intersection of the system:

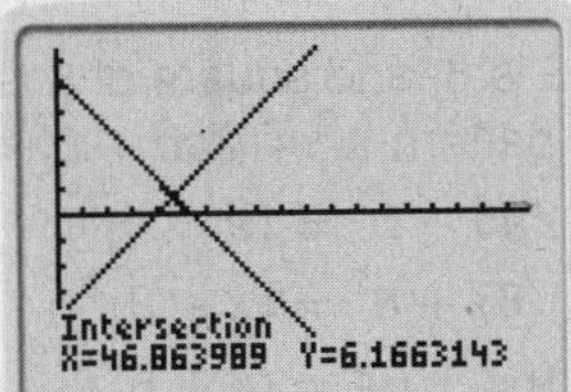

about 6.17 km/h

17. A diagram of the situation is as follows:

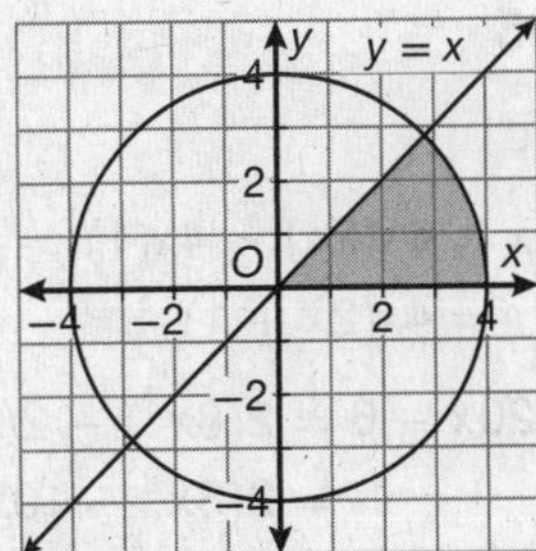

Shaded region is $\frac{1}{8}$ of circle area, so the probability that the chosen point is in Quadrant I and below $y = x$ is $\frac{1}{8}$.

18. An inconsistent solution implies the line is parallel to the original line. Only the opposite side is parallel. so 1 line has an inconsistent solution with the original line.
A consistent solution implies the line is not parallel to original line. Adjacent sides are perpendicular and therefore not parallel, so 2 lines have consistent solutions with the original line.

19. $\det A = \begin{vmatrix}3 & 8\\2 & 4\end{vmatrix} = 3(4) - 8(2) = 12 - 16$

$= -4$

$$A^{-1} = \frac{1}{-4}\begin{bmatrix}4 & -8\\-2 & 3\end{bmatrix} = \begin{bmatrix}-1 & 2\\\frac{1}{2} & -\frac{3}{4}\end{bmatrix}$$

Check that $A^{-1}A = AA^{-1} = I$:

$$A^{-1}A = \begin{bmatrix}-1 & 2\\\frac{1}{2} & -\frac{3}{4}\end{bmatrix}\begin{bmatrix}3 & 8\\2 & 4\end{bmatrix}$$

$$= \begin{bmatrix}-1(3)+2(2) & -1(8)+2(4)\\\frac{1}{2}(3)-\frac{3}{4}(2) & \frac{1}{2}(8)-\frac{3}{4}(4)\end{bmatrix}$$

$$= \begin{bmatrix}-3+4 & -8+8\\\frac{3}{2}-\frac{3}{2} & 4-3\end{bmatrix} = \begin{bmatrix}1 & 0\\0 & 1\end{bmatrix}$$

$$AA^{-1} = \begin{bmatrix}3 & 8\\2 & 4\end{bmatrix}\begin{bmatrix}-1 & 2\\\frac{1}{2} & -\frac{3}{4}\end{bmatrix}$$

$$= \begin{bmatrix}3(-1)+8\left(\frac{1}{2}\right) & 3(2)+8\left(-\frac{3}{4}\right)\\2(-1)+4\left(\frac{1}{2}\right) & 2(2)+4\left(-\frac{3}{4}\right)\end{bmatrix}$$

$$= \begin{bmatrix}-3+4 & 6-6\\-2+2 & 4-3\end{bmatrix} = \begin{bmatrix}1 & 0\\0 & 1\end{bmatrix}$$

20. $(x+7)(x-9)$
$= (x)(x) + (x)(-9) + (7)(x) + (7)(-9)$
$= x^2 - 9x + 7x - 63$
$= x^2 - 2x - 63$
Answer choice **C**

21. Yes :
$6x - 4 = 20$
$6(4) - 4 \stackrel{?}{=} 20$
$24 - 4 \stackrel{?}{=} 20$
$20 = 20$ ✓

22. range = max − min
Measurement 1:
range = 11.875 − 7.5 = 4.375
Measurement 2:
range = 8.5 − 3.375 = 5.125
Measurement 3:
range = 14.375 − 5.5 = 8.875
Measurement 3 had the greatest range; 8.875 inches

23. Graph line through point A with rise of 1 and run of 3:

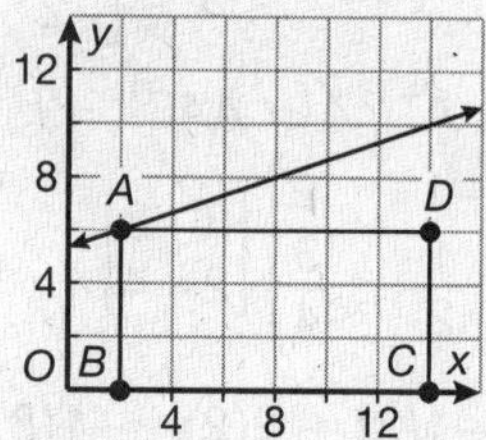

Write equation of line in point-slope form:

$$y - 6 = \frac{1}{3}(x - 2)$$

Solve for y to obtain slope-intercept form:

$$y - 6 = \frac{1}{3}(x - 2)$$

$$y - 6 = \frac{1}{3}x - \frac{2}{3}$$

$$y - 6 + 6 = \frac{1}{3}x - \frac{2}{3} + 6$$

$$y = \frac{1}{3}x + \frac{16}{3}$$

24. There are 26 choices for the letter and 600 choices for the number (000 to 599).

$26 \cdot 600 = 15{,}600$

There are 15,600 different passwords.

25. All related matrices have determinant 0, so the solutions are $\frac{0}{0}$, indicating infinitely many possibilities. The two equations are equivalent, so there are infinitely many solutions.

26. The student used the Addition Counting Principle instead of the Fundamental Counting Principle. The correct answer is $26 \cdot 25 \cdot 24 \cdot 23 = 358{,}800$.

27. It is a basic quadratic polynomial. 7 is the sum of 3 and 4, and 12 is the product of 3 and 4. So, factors are in the form $(x + u)(x + v)$ where $u + v = 7$ and $uv = 12$.

28. Possible answer: Compress graph of $y = x$ vertically by a factor of $\frac{3}{4}$ and then shift resulting graph 3 units down.

29. A solution to a linear system of two equations is an ordered pair, not a single number. Correct solution: add vertically to eliminate y, then solve for x:

$$x + y = 3$$
$$\underline{x - y = 1}$$
$$2x = 4$$
$$\frac{2x}{2} = \frac{4}{2}$$
$$x = 2$$

Substitute for x and solve for y:

$$x + y = 3$$
$$(2) + y = 3$$
$$-2 + 2 + y = -2 + 3$$
$$y = 1$$

The solution is (2, 1).

30. Half of 16 is 8, and square of 8 is 64. Using factoring pattern $a^2 + 2ab + b^2 = (a + b)^2$

$$a^2 + 2ab + b^2 = (a + b)^2$$
$$x^2 + 2(x)(8) + 8^2 = (x + 8)^2$$
$$x^2 + 16x + 64 = (x + 8)^2$$

LESSON 35

Warm Up 35

1. quadratic

2. $8x^2 + 4x = 4x(2x) + 4x(1)$
$= 4x(2x + 1)$

3. $16x^2 - 20x - 6 = 2(8x^2) - 2(10x) - 2(3)$
$= 2(8x^2 - 10x - 3)$

Factor $8x^2 - 10x - 3$. Positive factor pairs for $8x^2$ are $(x)(8x)$ and $(2x)(4x)$; factor pairs for -3 are $(1)(-3)$ and $(-1)(3)$. The sum of product of pairs are:

$x(1) + 8x(-3) = -23x$ ✗

$x(-3) + 8x(1) = 5x$ ✗

$2x(1) + 4x(-3) = 10x$ ✓

Original expression factors as

$16x^2 - 20x - 6 = 2(8x^2 - 10x - 3)$
$= 2(2x - 3)(4x + 1)$

Lesson Practice 35

a. $25x^2 - 1 = 0$

$$(5x)^2 - (1)^2 = 0$$
$$(5x - 1)(5x + 1) = 0$$

$5x - 1 = 0$ or $5x + 1 = 0$

$5x = 1$ $\quad$ $5x = -1$

$$\frac{5x}{5} = \frac{1}{5} \qquad \frac{5x}{5} = \frac{-1}{5}$$

$$x = \frac{1}{5} \qquad x = -\frac{1}{5}$$

Zeros are $\frac{1}{5}$ and $-\frac{1}{5}$.

b.

$$x^2 - 7x = 0$$
$$x \cdot x - 7 \cdot x = 0$$
$$x(x - 7) = 0$$
$$x = 0 \quad \text{or} \quad x - 7 = 0$$
$$x - 7 + 7 = 0 + 7$$
$$x = 7$$

Zeros are 0 and 7.

c.

$$3x^2 - x = 2$$
$$3x^2 - x - 2 = 0$$
$$(3x + 2)(x - 1) = 0$$
$$3x + 2 = 0 \quad \text{or} \quad x - 1 = 0$$
$$3x + 2 - 2 = 0 - 2 \qquad x - 1 + 1 = 0 + 1$$
$$3x = -2 \qquad x = 1$$
$$\frac{3x}{3} = -\frac{2}{3}$$
$$x = -\frac{2}{3}$$

Roots are $-\frac{2}{3}$ and 1.

d.

$$x^2 + 8x + 16 = 0$$
$$x^2 + 2(4)x + (4)^2 = 0$$
$$(x + 4)^2 = 0$$
$$x + 4 = 0$$
$$x + 4 - 4 = 0 - 4$$
$$x = -4$$

-4 is a double Root of the equation, the only zero of the related function, and the only x-intercept of the graph.

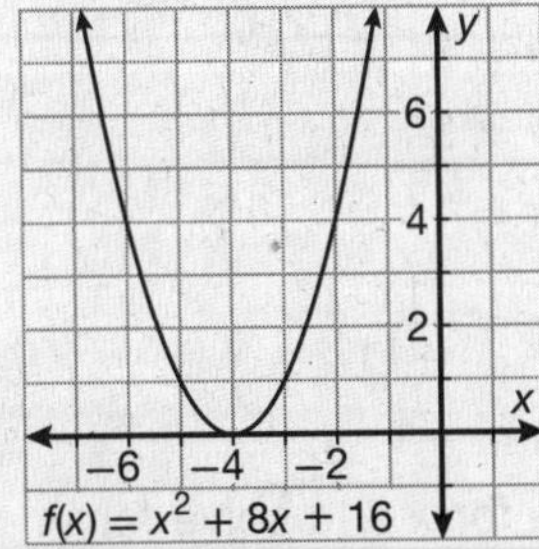

e. Factor pairs for -8 are $(1)(-8)$, $(-1)(8)$, $(2)(-4)$, and $(-2)(4)$. Factor pair $(-2)(4)$ sums to 2.

$$x^2 + 2x - 8 = 0$$
$$(x + 2)(x - 4) = 0$$
$$x + 2 = 0 \quad \text{or} \quad x - 4 = 0$$
$$x = -2 \qquad x = -2 \text{ and}$$

4 are the Roots of the equation, the zeros of the related function and the x-intercepts of the graph.

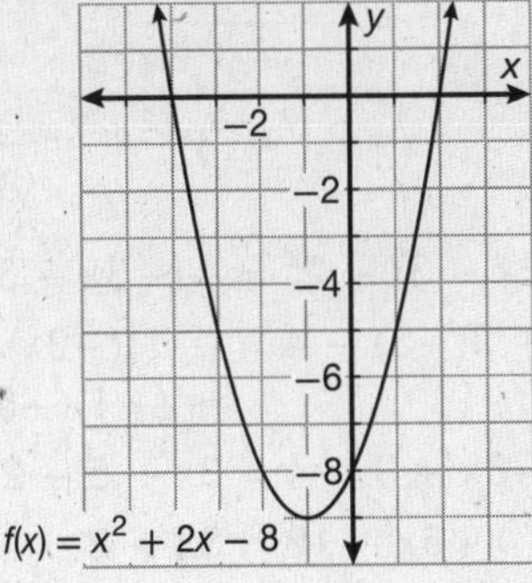

f.

$$(x + 5)\left(x - \frac{3}{4}\right) = 0$$
$$4(x + 5)\left(x - \frac{3}{4}\right) = 4(0)$$
$$(x + 5)(4x - 3) = 0$$
$$(x)(4x) + (x)(-3) + (5)(4x) + (5)(-3) = 0$$
$$4x^2 - 3x + 20x - 15 = 0$$
$$4x^2 + 17x - 15 = 0$$

The quadratic function $f(x) = 4x^2 + 17x - 15$ has zeros -5 and $\frac{3}{4}$.

g. Initial velocity v_0 is $+8$ ft/s.

$$h(t) = -16t^2 + v_0t + h_0$$
$$0 = -16t^2 + 8t + 80$$
$$0 = -8(2t^2 - t - 10)$$
$$0 = -8(2t - 5)(t + 2)$$
$$2t - 5 = 0 \quad \text{or} \quad t + 2 = 0$$
$$2t - 5 + 5 = 0 + 5 \qquad t + 2 - 2 = 0 - 2$$
$$2t = 5 \qquad t = -2$$
$$\frac{2t}{2} = \frac{5}{2}$$
$$t = 2.5$$

Solution cannot be negative, so it takes the object 2.5 s to hit the ground.

Practice 35

1. $$\frac{(b^2c^{-2})^{-3}c^{-3}}{(b^2c^0b^{-2})^4} = \frac{b^{-6}c^6\,c^{-3}}{b^8c^0b^{-8}}$$

$$= \frac{b^{-6}c^3}{b^0c^0}$$

$$= b^{-6}c^3 \text{ or } \frac{c^3}{b^6}$$

2. $\dfrac{(2x^2ya)^{-3}ya^3}{x^2y(ay)^{-2}y} = \dfrac{2^{-3}x^{-6}y^{-3}a^{-3}\ ya^3}{x^2ya^{-2}y^{-2}y}$

$$= \frac{2^{-3}x^{-6}y^{-2}}{x^2a^{-2}}$$

$$= 2^{-3}x^{-8}y^{-2}a^2 = \frac{a^2}{8x^8y^2}$$

3. $3(-2x-3) - 2^2 = -(-3x-5) - 2$

$3(-2x) + 3(-3) - 4 = (-1)(-3x) + (-1)(-5) - 2$

$-6x - 9 - 4 = 3x + 5 - 2$

$-6x - 13 = 3x + 3$

$6x - 6x - 13 - 3 = 6x + 3x + 3 - 3$

$-16 = 9x$

$\dfrac{-16}{9} = \dfrac{9x}{9}$

$\dfrac{-16}{9} = x$

4. Factor pairs for −56 are (1)(−56), (−1)(56), (2)(−28), (−2)(28), (4)(−14), (−4)(14), (7)(−8), and (−7)(8). Factor pair (−2)(28) sums to 26.

$x^2 + 26x - 56 = 0$

$(x-2)(x+28) = 0$

$x - 2 = 0$ or $x + 28 = 0$

$x - 2 + 2 = 0 + 2$ $\quad x + 28 - 28 = 0 - 28$

$x = 2$ $\quad x = -28$

$x = 2$ or $x = -28$

5. Slope is $m = \dfrac{y_2 - y_1}{x_2 - x_1}$

$= \dfrac{-2-4}{3-(-3)}$

$= \dfrac{-6}{6} = -1$

Use point-slope form:

$y - y_1 = m(x - x_1)$

$y - 4 = (-1)(x - (-3))$

$y - 4 = (-1)(x + 3)$

$y - 4 = -x - 3$

$y - 4 + 4 = -x - 3 + 4$

$y = -x + 1$

6. Multiply equation 2 by −2:

$$\begin{cases} 4x - 3y = -1 \\ 2x + 5y = 19 \end{cases}$$

$$\rightarrow \begin{cases} 4x - 3y = -1 \\ -2(2x + 5y) = -2(19) \end{cases}$$

$$\rightarrow \begin{cases} 4x - 3y = -1 \\ -4x - 10y = -38 \end{cases}$$

Add vertically to eliminate x and solve for y:

$4x - 3y = -1$

$\underline{-4x - 10y = -39}$

$-13y = -39$

$\dfrac{-13y}{-13} = \dfrac{-39}{-13}$

$y = 3$

Substitute for y and solve for x:

$2x + 5y = 19$

$2x + 5(3) = 19$

$2x + 15 = 19$

$2x + 15 - 15 = 19 - 15$

$2x = 4$

$\dfrac{2x}{2} = \dfrac{4}{2}$

$x = 2$

The solution is (2, 3).

7. Multiply equation 1 by −2:

$$\begin{cases} 5x + \frac{1}{2}y = -4 \\ -x + y = 3 \end{cases} \rightarrow \begin{cases} -2\left(5x + \frac{1}{2}y\right) = -2(-4) \\ -x + y = 3 \end{cases}$$

$$\rightarrow \begin{cases} -10x - y = 8 \\ -x + y = 3 \end{cases}$$

Add vertically to eliminate y and solve for x:

$-10x - y = 8$

$\underline{-x + y = 3}$

$-11x = 11$

$\dfrac{-11x}{-11} = \dfrac{11}{-11}$

$x = -1$

Substitute for x and solve for y:

$-x + y = 3$

$-(-1) + y = 3$

$1 + y = 3$

$$-1 + 1 + y = -1 + 3$$
$$y = 2$$

The solution is $(-1, 2)$.

8. $\begin{bmatrix} a \\ 64 \end{bmatrix} = \begin{bmatrix} 102 \\ a - b \end{bmatrix} \rightarrow \begin{cases} a = 102 \\ 64 = a - b \end{cases}$

Substitute $a = 102$ into equation 2:

$$64 = a - b$$
$$64 = 102 - b$$
$$-102 + 64 = -102 + 102 - b$$
$$-38 = -b$$
$$38 = b$$

Solution: $a = 102$, $b = 38$

9. $(f \cdot g)(x)$

$= f(x) \cdot g(x)$

$= (4x - 3)(8x + 9)$

$= (4x)(8x) + (4x)(9) + (-3)(8x) + (-3)(9)$

$= 32x^2 + 36x - 24x - 27$

$= 32x^2 + 12x - 27$

10. Possible answer: Trace graph of function with a pencil. If the function can be drawn without lifting the pencil from the paper the function is continuous.

11. Negative factor pairs for 6 are $(-1)(-6)$ and $(-2)(-3)$. Factor pair $(-2)(-3)$ sums to -5. The zeros of $f(x) = x^2 - 5x + 6$ are solutions of

$$x^2 - 5x + 6 = 0$$
$$(x - 2)(x - 3) = 0$$
$$x - 2 = 0 \quad \text{or} \quad x - 3 = 0$$
$$x - 2 + 2 = 0 + 2 \quad x - 3 + 3 = 0 + 3$$
$$x = 2 \quad\quad x = 3$$

Answer choice **C**

12. On each roll, the outcomes for a sum of 11 are $5 + 6$ and $6 + 5$, and the only outcome for a sum of 12 is $6 + 6$. There are $6 \times 6 = 36$ outcomes in total. Therefore,

$$P(\text{sum} > 10 \text{ on one roll}) = \frac{3}{36} = \frac{1}{12}.$$

For two rolls, since events are independent,

P(sum > 10 on both rolls)

$= P(\text{sum} > 10 \text{ on roll 1}) \times P(\text{sum} > 10 \text{ on roll 2})$

$= \frac{1}{12} \times \frac{1}{12} = \frac{1}{144}$

13. The line has no slope, or an undefined slope. It does not have a zero slope. A horizontal line has a zero slope.

14. Degree of the resulting polynomial is equal to the degree of the monomial with greatest degree. The two original polynomials have mononmials with degrees 3 and 4. So the monomial with the greatest degree has degree 4. The only possible degree is 4.

15. $\dfrac{x^2 - 4}{x^2 - 3x - 4} \cdot \dfrac{x - 4}{x + 2}$

is equivalent to

$\dfrac{(x - 2)(x + 2)}{(x - 4)(x + 1)} \cdot \dfrac{x - 4}{x + 2}$

$(x - 4)$ is a factor in the denominator, and is zero when $x = 4$, so the expression is undefined when $x = 4$.

16. Factor the expression for the area:

$A = a^2 - 8a + 16$

$= a^2 - 2(4)a + (4)^2$

$= (a - 4)^2$

So side length is $a - 4$. One vertex $(a - 1, 0)$ lies on the x-axis. Possible adjacent vertices are $a - 4$ units above or below this vertex, and $a - 4$ units to left or right of it. That is, either

$(a - 1, 0) + (0, a - 4) = (a - 1, a - 4)$ or

$(a - 1, 0) - (0, a - 4) = (a - 1, 4 - a)$ and either

$(a - 1, 0) + (a - 4, 0) = (2a - 5, 0)$ or

$(a - 1, 0) - (a - 4, 0) = (3, 0)$

17. Possible answer: The equation $y + 1 = \frac{1}{4}(x - 2)$ is a linear equation in point-slope form $y - y_1 = m(x - x_1)$. So its graph is a line, $(x_1, y_1) = (2, -1)$ is a point on the line, and $m = \frac{1}{4}$ is the slope of the line.

18.

$$4 < 2(x - 2) \leq 16$$
$$4 < 2x - 4 \leq 16$$
$$4 + 4 < 2x - 4 + 4 \leq 16 + 4$$
$$8 < 2x \leq 20$$
$$\frac{8}{2} < \frac{2x}{2} \leq \frac{20}{2}$$
$$4 < x \leq 10$$

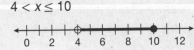

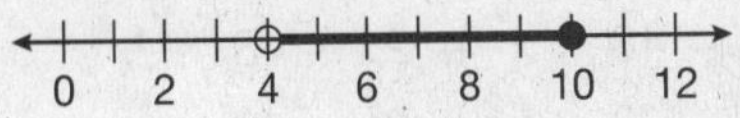

0 2 4 6 8 10 12

19. a. $v_{average} = \frac{s}{t}$

$= \frac{16t^2 + 8t}{t}$

$= \frac{(16t + 8)\cancel{t}}{\cancel{t}}$

$= 16t + 8$

b. $v_{average} = 16t + 8$

$= 16(2.5) + 8$

$= 40 + 8 = 48$

The average velocity is 48 ft/s.

20. $\begin{cases} x + y = 7 \\ 0.15x + 0.35y = 0.2(7) = 1.4 \end{cases}$

Multiply to eliminate a variable:

$\rightarrow \begin{cases} -0.15(x + y) = -0.15(7) \\ 0.15x + 0.35y = 1.4 \end{cases}$

$\rightarrow \begin{cases} -0.15x - 0.15y = -1.05 \\ 0.15x + 0.35y = 1.4 \end{cases}$

Solve for x and y:

$-0.15x - 0.15y = -1.05$

$\underline{0.15x + 0.35y = 1.4}$

$0.2y = 0.35$

$5(0.2y) = 5(0.35)$

$y = 1.75$

$x + y = 7$

$x + 1.75 = 7$

$x = 5.25$

5.25 L of the 15% solution and 1.75 L of the 35% solution will be needed.

21. 0, 1, or 2 real zeros. The number of real zeros is the number of points in which the graph intersects the x-axis.

22. Ratio $\frac{y}{x} = \sqrt{2}$ is constant so this is a direct variation

23. $A = \frac{1}{2}bh$

$24 = \frac{1}{2}(x + 2)(x)$

$2(24) = 2\left(\frac{1}{2}(x + 2)(x)\right)$

$48 = (x + 2)(x)$

$48 = x^2 + 2x$

$48 - 48 = x^2 + 2x - 48$

$0 = x^2 + 2x - 48$

$0 = (x - 6)(x + 8)$

$x - 6 = 0$ or $x + 8 = 0$

$x - 6 + 6 = 0 + 6$ $\quad x + 8 - 8 = 0 - 8$

$x = 6$ $\quad x = -8$

The length cannot be negative, so $x = 6$.

24. Stretch the graph of $y = x$ vertically by a factor of 1.2563.

25. Answer choice **B**

26. Enter data in table using List function. Use linear regression to determine line of best fit, and read slope-intercept form from Y= editor:

Approximate slope-intercept form:
$y = 5.51x - 144.94$

27. Put each set into slope-intercept form:

A $\begin{cases} y = 2x + 4 \\ 2y - 2x = 8 \end{cases} \rightarrow \begin{cases} y = 2x + 4 \\ y - x = 4 \end{cases}$

$\rightarrow \begin{cases} y = 2x + 4 \\ y = x + 4 \end{cases}$

B $\begin{cases} y = 2x + 4 \\ 12 - 3y = -6x \end{cases} \rightarrow \begin{cases} y = 2x + 4 \\ 4 - y = -2x \end{cases}$

$\rightarrow \begin{cases} y = 2x + 4 \\ -y = -2x - 4 \end{cases} \rightarrow \begin{cases} y = 2x + 4 \\ y = 2x + 4 \end{cases}$

C $\begin{cases} 2y = 4x - 12 \\ y = 2x + 6 \end{cases} \rightarrow \begin{cases} y = 2x - 6 \\ y = 2x + 6 \end{cases}$

D $\begin{cases} -4x = 8 - 2y \\ y = 2x + 6 \end{cases} \rightarrow \begin{cases} -2x = 4 - y \\ y = 2x + 6 \end{cases}$

$\rightarrow \begin{cases} y = 2x + 4 \\ y = 2x + 6 \end{cases}$

The graph has parallel, non-coincident lines with positive y-intercepts. Answer choice **D**

28. masses of carbs (g):

$0.81s + 0b + 0.87t = 118.68$

masses of fat (g):

$0.05s + 0.6b + 0.03t = 40.12$

masses of protein (g):

$0.14s + 0.4b + 0.1t = 41.2$

$$\underbrace{\begin{bmatrix} 0.81 & 0 & 0.87 \\ 0.05 & 0.6 & 0.03 \\ 0.14 & 0.4 & 0.1 \end{bmatrix}}_{A} \underbrace{\begin{bmatrix} s \\ b \\ t \end{bmatrix}}_{X} = \underbrace{\begin{bmatrix} 118.68 \\ 40.12 \\ 41.2 \end{bmatrix}}_{B}$$

Using a graphing calculator:

$$X = A^{-1}B = \begin{bmatrix} 110 \\ 56 \\ 34 \end{bmatrix}$$

Solution is $s = 110$, $b = 56$, $t = 34$. The entrée contains 110 g of spaghetti, 56 g of ground beef, and 34 g of tomato sauce.

29.
$$A = lw$$
$$17.1 = x(1.9x)$$
$$17.1 = 1.9x^2$$
$$\frac{17.1}{1.9} = \frac{1.9x^2}{1.9}$$
$$9 = x^2$$
$$\pm 3 = x$$

The length cannot be negative so $x = 3$. The dimensions are 3 ft and $1.9(3) = 5.7$ ft.

30. Perimeter in inches:

10 in. + 8 in. + 10 in. + 8 in. = 36 in.

Convert to feet:

$$\frac{36 \text{ in.}}{1} \times \frac{1 \text{ ft}}{12 \text{ in.}} = \frac{36}{12} \text{ ft} = 3 \text{ ft}$$

The perimeter is 3 ft.

LESSON 36

Warm Up 36

1. point-slope
2. $m = \frac{y_2 - y_1}{x_2 - x_1} = \frac{9 - 4}{5 - 1} = \frac{5}{4} = 1.25$
3.
$$3x - 7y = 28$$
$$-3x + 3x - 7y = -3x + 28$$
$$-7y = -3x + 28$$
$$\frac{-7y}{-7} = \frac{-3x + 28}{-7}$$
$$y = \frac{3}{7}x - 4$$

Lesson Practice 36

a. Slope of line through (1, –4) and (2, –1):

$$m = \frac{y_2 - y_1}{x_2 - x_1} = \frac{-1 - (-4)}{2 - 1} = \frac{3}{1} = 3$$

Slope of line through (3, 19) and (5, 25):

$$m = \frac{y_2 - y_1}{x_2 - x_1} = \frac{25 - 19}{5 - 3} = \frac{6}{2} = 3$$

So the lines are parallel. Are they the same line? Check whether (3, 19) could be on first line:

The slope of line through (3, 19) and (2, –1) is:

$$m = \frac{y_2 - y_1}{x_2 - x_1} = \frac{-1 - 19}{2 - 3} = \frac{-20}{-1} = 20 \neq 3$$

So (3, 19) does not lie on first line. The lines are parallel.

b. Slope of line through (1, 16.88) and (3, 16.63):

$$m = \frac{y_2 - y_1}{x_2 - x_1} = \frac{16.63 - 16.88}{3 - 1}$$
$$= \frac{-0.25}{2} = -0.125$$

Slope of line through (2, 24) and (4, 40):

$$m = \frac{y_2 - y_1}{x_2 - x_1} = \frac{40 - 24}{4 - 2} = \frac{16}{2} = 8$$

Since $-0.125(8) = -1$, the lines are perpendicular.

c. The slopes of the lines are equal: $m = -13$. Use the point-slope formula:

$$m = \frac{y - y_1}{x - x_1}$$
$$-13 = \frac{y - 15}{x - 0}$$
$$-13x = y - 15$$
$$-13x + 15 = y - 15 + 15$$
$$y = -13x + 15$$

d. Find the slope that is the opposite reciprocal of 25: $m = -\frac{1}{25}$

Use the point-slope formula:

$$m = \frac{y - y_1}{x - x_1}$$
$$-\frac{1}{25} = \frac{y - 37}{x - 1}$$
$$-\frac{1}{25}(x - 1) = y - 37$$

$$-\frac{1}{25}x + \frac{1}{25} = y - 37$$
$$-0.04x + 0.04 + 37 = y - 37 + 37$$
$$y = -0.04x + 37.04$$

e. Both equations are in slope-intercept form. The slopes are equal and the y-intercepts are different, so the lines are parallel.

f. Both equations are in slope-intercept form. The product of the slopes is $(-0.125)(8) = -1$, so the lines are perpendicular.

g. The graph of $y = 5$ is horizontal. The line perpendicular to this is vertical, so it has the equation $x = c$. The line with equation $x = 21$ is perpendicular to the graph of $y = 2$ and passes through (21, 1).

h. The graph of $x = 7$ is vertical. The line perpendicular to this is horizontal, so it has the equation $y = c$. The line with equation $y = 5$ is perpendicular to graph of $x = 7$ and passes through (−3, 5).

i. The slope of the tangent is $\frac{4}{3}$. Find the slope of the diameter, which is the line through (−1, 6) and (3, 3). The slope of this line is:

$$m = \frac{y_2 - y_1}{x_2 - x_1} = \frac{3 - 6}{3 - (-1)} = -\frac{3}{4}$$

Since $\left(\frac{4}{3}\right)\left(-\frac{3}{4}\right) = -1$, the tangent is perpendicular to the diameter at the point (−1, 6).

Practice 36

1. $m = \frac{y_2 - y_1}{x_2 - x_1} = \frac{0 - 7}{1 - (-3)} = -\frac{7}{4}$

2. $m = \frac{y_2 - y_1}{x_2 - x_1} = \frac{-6 - (-5)}{0 - 2} = \frac{-1}{-2} = \frac{1}{2}$

3. $y = mx + b$

$$\frac{y}{x} = \frac{mx + b}{x} = m + \frac{b}{x}$$

Since $b \neq 0$, ratio $\frac{y}{x}$ is not a constant. No variation.

4. $y = mx + b$

$$\frac{y}{x} = \frac{mx + b}{x} = m + \frac{b}{x}$$

Ratio $\frac{y}{x}$ is constant only when $b = 0$. Direct variation when $b = 0$.

5.
$$\frac{xx^2(x^0y^{-1})^2}{x^2x^{-5}(y^2)^5} = \frac{xx^2x^0y^{-2}}{x^2x^{-5}y^{10}}$$
$$= \frac{x^3y^{-2}}{x^{-3}y^{10}}$$
$$= x^3y^{-2}x^3y^{-10} = x^6y^{-12}$$

6.
$$\frac{m^2p^0(m^{-2}p)^2}{m^{-2}p^{-1}(m^{-3}p^2)^3} = \frac{m^2p^0m^{-4}p^2}{m^{-2}p^{-1}m^{-9}p^6}$$
$$= \frac{m^{-2}p^2}{m^{-11}p^5}$$
$$= m^{-2}p^2m^{11}p^{-5}$$
$$= m^9p^{-3}$$

7.
$$x^2 + 2 = 4x + 7$$
$$x^2 + 2 - (4x + 7) = 4x + 7 - (4x + 7)$$
$$x^2 - 4x - 5 = 0$$
$$(x - 5)(x + 1) = 0$$
$$x - 5 = 0 \quad \text{or} \quad x + 1 = 0$$
$$x - 5 + 5 = 0 + 5 \quad x + 1 - 1 = 0 - 1$$
$$x = 5 \quad x = -1$$

$x = 5$ or $x = -1$

8. Multiply equation 2 by 3 to make opposite x-terms:

$$\begin{cases} 12x - 5y = 24 \\ 20y - 4x = 3 \end{cases} \rightarrow \begin{cases} 12x - 5y = 24 \\ 3(20y - 4x) = 3(3) \end{cases}$$

$$\rightarrow \begin{cases} 12x - 5y = 24 \\ -12x + 60y = 9 \end{cases}$$

Solve for x and y:

$$12x - 5y = 24$$
$$\underline{-12x + 60y = 9}$$
$$55y = 33$$
$$\frac{55y}{55} = \frac{33}{55}$$
$$y = 0.6$$
$$12x - 5y = 24$$
$$12x - 5(0.6) = 24$$
$$12x - 3 = 24$$
$$12x - 3 + 3 = 24 + 3$$
$$12x = 27$$
$$\frac{12x}{12} = \frac{27}{12}$$

$$x = 2.25$$

The solution is (2.25, 0.6).

9. $y = \frac{1}{11}x + \frac{1}{7}$

$$-y + y - \frac{1}{7} = -y + \frac{1}{11}x + \frac{1}{7} - \frac{1}{7}$$

$$-\frac{1}{7} = -y + \frac{1}{11}x$$

$$\frac{1}{11}x - y = -\frac{1}{7}$$

10. Possible answer: Write denominator as a product of four algebraic expressions so that when each expression is set to zero, the solution is different. For example, excluded values for $\frac{1}{x(x-1)(x+1)(x-2)}$ are 0, 1, −1, and 2.

11. Instead of correctly using $x^2 + bx + c = (x + u)(x + v)$ with $u + v = b$ and $uv = c$, Carmen wrote $u + v = c$ and $uv = b$.

12. The points on the graph of this linear function are connected, which means that the function is continuous.

13. $\begin{vmatrix} -4 & 3 \\ 5 & x \end{vmatrix} = -x$

$$(-4)(x) - (3)(5) = -x$$

$$-4x - 15 = -x$$

$$4x - 4x - 15 = 4x - x$$

$$-15 = 3x$$

$$-\frac{15}{3} = \frac{3x}{3}$$

$$x = -5$$

Verify by graphing calculator:

$5 = -x$, as required.

14. $\frac{x}{15} \cdot \frac{x^7}{2x} \cdot \frac{20}{x^4} = \frac{20x^8}{30x^5}$

$$= \frac{2 \cdot \cancel{10} \cdot x^3 \cdot \cancel{x^5}}{3 \cdot \cancel{10} \cdot \cancel{x^5}}$$

$$= \frac{2x^3}{3}$$

15. $A = lw$

$$1250 = (w + 25)w$$

$$1250 = w^2 + 25w$$

$$0 = w^2 + 25w - 1250$$

$$0 = (w - 25)(w + 50)$$

$(w - 25) = 0$ or $(w + 50) = 0$

$w = 25$ or $w = -50$

The width cannot be negative, so $w = 25$ m, and $l = (25) + 25 = 50$ m.

16. $\begin{cases} x = y + 5 \\ y = 3z - 21 \\ x + y + z = 180 \end{cases} \rightarrow \begin{cases} x - y + 0z = 5 \\ 0x + y - 3z = -21 \\ x + y + z = 180 \end{cases}$

$$\underbrace{\begin{bmatrix} 1 & -1 & 0 \\ 0 & 1 & -3 \\ 1 & 1 & 1 \end{bmatrix}}_{A} \underbrace{\begin{bmatrix} x \\ y \\ z \end{bmatrix}}_{X} = \underbrace{\begin{bmatrix} 5 \\ -21 \\ 180 \end{bmatrix}}_{B}$$

Using a graphing calculator:

$$X = A^{-1}B = \begin{bmatrix} 77 \\ 72 \\ 31 \end{bmatrix}$$

Solution: $x = 77$, $y = 72$, $z = 31$

17. Equation 1:

$$y = ax^2 + bx + c$$

$$124 = a(1)^2 + b(1) + c$$

$$124 = a + b + c$$

Equation 2:

$$y = ax^2 + bx + c$$

$$4476 = a(5)^2 + b(5) + c$$

$$4476 = 25a + 5b + c$$

Equation 3:

$$y = ax^2 + bx + c$$

$$3796 = a(10)^2 + b(10) + c$$

$$3796 = 100a + 10b + c$$

$$\underbrace{\begin{bmatrix} 1 & 1 & 1 \\ 25 & 5 & 1 \\ 100 & 10 & 1 \end{bmatrix}}_{A} \underbrace{\begin{bmatrix} a \\ b \\ c \end{bmatrix}}_{X} = \underbrace{\begin{bmatrix} 124 \\ 4{,}476 \\ 3{,}796 \end{bmatrix}}_{B}$$

Using a graphing calculator:

$$X = A^{-1}B = \begin{bmatrix} -136 \\ 1{,}904 \\ -1{,}644 \end{bmatrix}$$

$a = -136$, $b = 1904$, $c = -1644$

The equation is $y = -136x^2 + 1904x - 1644$.

18. 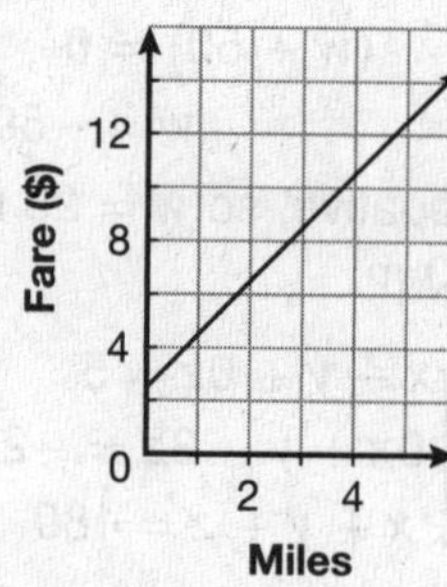

Rate of change $= \frac{\text{rise}}{\text{run}} = \frac{4.50 - 2.90}{1 - 0.2}$

$= \frac{1.6}{0.8} = 2$

Possible description: The fare increases \$2.00 per mile, or \$0.40 for every 0.2 mile.

19. Horizontal equation: $x = 5t$

Vertical equation: $y = 20t$

20. Student B incorrectly transposed coordinates.

21. **A** median = 8, mode = 8

B median = 8, mode = 4

C median $= \frac{4+8}{2} = 6$, mode = 8

D median $= \frac{4+4}{2} = 4$, mode = 4 or 8

Answer choice **B**

22. Determine slope of each side:

Side from (–4, 6) to (4, 4):

$$m = \frac{y_2 - y_1}{x_2 - x_1} = \frac{4 - 6}{4 - (-4)} = \frac{-2}{8} = \frac{-1}{4}$$

Side from (–4, 6) to (1, –8):

$$m = \frac{y_2 - y_1}{x_2 - x_1} = \frac{-8 - 6}{1 - (-4)} = \frac{-14}{-3} = \frac{14}{3}$$

Side from (4, 4) to (1, –8):

$$m = \frac{y_2 - y_1}{x_2 - x_1} = \frac{-8 - 4}{1 - 4} = \frac{-12}{-3} = 4$$

Since $-\frac{1}{4}(4) = -1$, sides (–4, 6)(4, 4) and (4, 4)(1, –8) are perpendicular, so the triangle is a right triangle.

23. Value of a is positive, so graph opens upward and has a minimum. Minimum is –\$840.50, occurring when $x = 22$, i.e. during week 22.

24. $x^2 + 7x + 6 = 0$

$(x + 1)(x + 6) = 0$

$x + 1 = 0$ or $x + 6 = 0$

$x + 1 - 1 = 0 - 1$ $\quad x + 6 - 6 = 0 - 6$

$x = -1$ $\quad x = -6$

Roots are $x = -1$ and $x = -6$.

25. If a were zero, there would be no term raised to the second power, because zero times any number is zero. The function would be linear.

26. There are 8 choices for 1st, 7 choices for 2nd, and 6 choices for 3rd place.

$8 \cdot 7 \cdot 6 = 336$

Answer choice **C**

27. a. 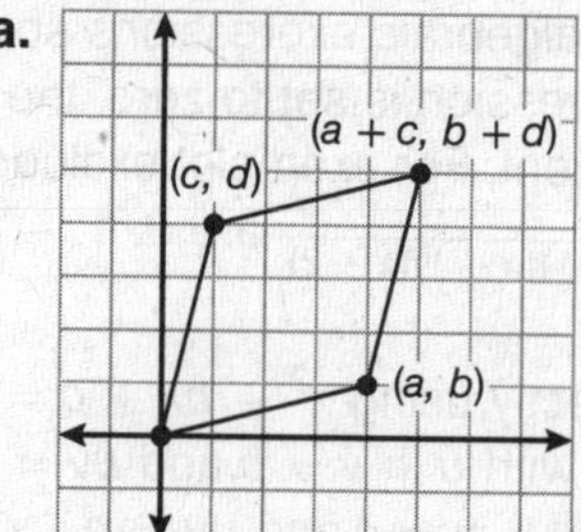

b. 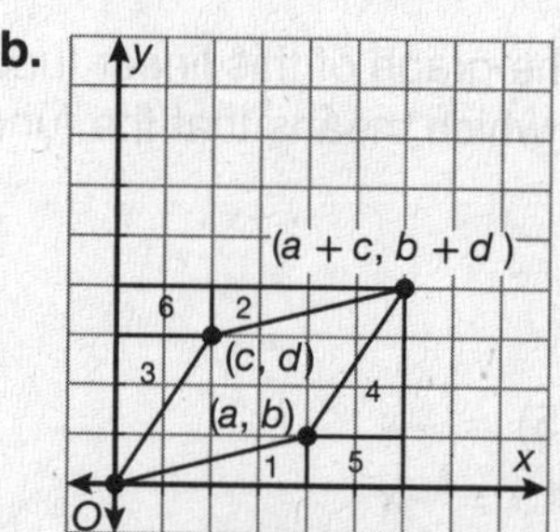

Note that triangles 1 and 2, triangles 3 and 4, and small rectangles 5 and 6 are congruent pairs.

Area of parallelogram

= area of large rectangle – area of triangle 1 – area of triangle 2 – area of triangle 3 – area of triangle 4 – area of small rectangle 5 – area of small rectangle 6

$= (a + c)(b + d)$

$-\frac{1}{2}ab - \frac{1}{2}ab - \frac{1}{2}cd - \frac{1}{2}cd$

$-b[(a + c) - a] - b[(a + c) - a]$

$= (a + c)(b + d) - ab - cd - 2bc$

c. $(a + c)(b + d) - ab - cd - 2bc$

$= ab + ad + bc + cd - ab - cd - 2bc$

$= ad - bc = \begin{vmatrix} a & c \\ b & d \end{vmatrix}$

28. There are 12 choices for 1st, 11 choices for 2nd, and 10 choices for 3rd place.

$12 \cdot 11 \cdot 10 = 1320$

There are 1320 ways that teams can finish in 1st, 2nd, and 3rd place.

29. Plot vertex, which is at $(h, k) = (2, 2)$, find y-values for several x-values that are either all less than 2 or all greater than 2, and plot those ordered pairs. Sketch axis of symmetry $x = 2$, and plot points that are mirror images of points already found.

30. $\frac{x^2 + x}{x^2 - 9} \cdot \frac{3x - x^2}{3x + 3}$

$= \frac{x(x+1)}{(x-3)(x+3)} \cdot \frac{x(3-x)}{3(x+1)}$

$= \frac{x^2 \cdot \cancel{(x+1)} \cdot (-1) \cdot \cancel{(x-3)}}{\cancel{(x-3)} \cdot (x+3) \cdot 3 \cdot \cancel{(x+1)}}$

$= \frac{-x^2}{3(x+3)} = \frac{-(6)^2}{3(6+3)}$

$= \frac{-36}{27} = -\frac{4}{3}$

Answer choice **A**

LESSON 37

Warm Up 37

1. rational

2. $\frac{2}{7} + \frac{4}{5} = \frac{2(5) + 4(7)}{(7)(5)} = \frac{10 + 28}{35} = \frac{38}{35}$

or $1\frac{3}{35}$

3. Positive factor pairs for 12: (1)(12), (2)(6), and (3)(4). Negative factor pairs for 15: $(-1)(-15)$ and $(-3)(-5)$.

Since $(2)(-5) + (6)(-3) = -28$,

$12x^2 - 28x + 15 = (2x - 3)(6x - 5)$

Lesson Practice 37

a. The rational expressions have the same denominators, so add the numerators.

$\frac{7}{5x^3} + \frac{3}{5x^3} = \frac{10}{5x^3} = \frac{2}{x^3}$

b. The rational expressions have the same denominators, so subtract the numerators.

$\frac{x}{x^2 - 1} - \frac{1}{x^2 - 1} = \frac{x - 1}{x^2 - 1}$

The denominators can be factored and the expression further simplified.

$= \frac{x - 1}{(x-1)(x+1)}$

$= \frac{1}{x + 1}$

c. The rational expressions have the same denominators, so add the numerators.

$\frac{4x}{3x^2 + 19x - 14} + \frac{1}{3x^2 + 19x - 14}$

$- \frac{x + 3}{3x^2 + 19x - 14}$

$= \frac{4x + 1 - (x + 3)}{3x^2 + 19x - 14} = \frac{3x - 2}{3x^2 + 19x - 14}$

Factor the denominator to simplify further.

$\frac{3x - 2}{3x^2 + 19x - 14} = \frac{3x - 2}{(x+7)(3x-2)} = \frac{1}{x + 7}$

d. Multiples of $6x^3$ and $7x^2$ are:

$6x^3 \quad 12x^3 \quad \ldots \quad 36x^3 \quad 42x^3$

$7x^2 \quad 14x^2 \quad \ldots$

$7x^3 \quad 14x^3 \quad \ldots \quad 42x^3$

LCD is $42x^3$.

e. Factor each denominator.

$\frac{1}{7x^2 + 32x - 15} = \frac{1}{(x+5)(7x-3)}$

$\frac{1}{2x^2 + 3x - 35} = \frac{1}{(x+5)(2x-7)}$

Multiply numerator and denominator by least number of factors not in common:

$\frac{(2x - 7)}{(x+5)(7x-3)(2x-7)}$,

$\frac{(7x - 3)}{(x+5)(7x-3)(2x-7)}$

LCD is $(x + 5)(7x - 3)(2x - 7)$.

f. Factor the denominator.

$\frac{1}{7x^2 - 66x + 27} = \frac{1}{(x-9)(7x-3)}$

When denominator is zero,

$$x - 9 = 0 \quad \text{or} \quad 7x - 3 = 0$$
$$x - 9 + 9 = 0 + 9 \qquad 7x - 3 + 3 = 0 + 3$$
$$x = 9 \qquad 7x = 3$$
$$\frac{7x}{7} = \frac{3}{7}$$
$$x = \frac{3}{7}$$

g. $\frac{1}{5x^4} + \frac{1}{7x^5} = \frac{1 \cdot 7x}{5x^4 \cdot 7x} + \frac{1 \cdot 5}{7x^5 \cdot 5}$

$$= \frac{7x}{35x^5} + \frac{5}{35x^5} = \frac{7x + 5}{35x^5}$$

h. Factor the first denominator:

$$\frac{1}{8x^2 - 22x + 15} = \frac{1}{(2x - 3)(4x - 5)}$$

Factor the second denominator:

$$\frac{1}{2x^2 + 13x - 24} = \frac{1}{(x + 8)(2x - 3)}$$

Therefore

$$\frac{1}{8x^2 - 22x + 15} - \frac{1}{2x^2 + 13x - 24}$$
$$= \frac{1}{(2x - 3)(4x - 5)} - \frac{1}{(x + 8)(2x - 3)}$$
$$= \frac{(x + 8)}{(2x - 3)(4x - 5)(x + 8)}$$
$$- \frac{(4x - 5)}{(2x - 3)(4x - 5)(x + 8)}$$
$$= \frac{(x + 8) - (4x - 5)}{(2x - 3)(4x - 5)(x + 8)}$$
$$= \frac{13 - 3x}{(2x - 3)(4x - 5)(x + 8)}$$

i. Upstream: $s_1 = \frac{d}{t}$

Downstream: $s_2 = \frac{d}{t + \frac{3}{4}} = \frac{4d}{4t + 3}$

$$s_1 - s_2 = \frac{d}{t} - \frac{4d}{4t + 3}$$
$$= \frac{d(4t + 3)}{t(4t + 3)} - \frac{4dt}{t(4t + 3)} = \frac{3d}{t(4t + 3)}$$

Practice 37

1. y-terms are already opposite. Add vertically to eliminate y and solve for x:

$$5x + 2y = 70$$
$$\underline{3x - 2y = 10}$$
$$8x = 80$$
$$\frac{8x}{8} = \frac{80}{8}$$
$$x = 10$$

Substitute for x and solve for y:

$$5x + 2y = 70$$
$$5(10) + 2y = 70$$
$$-50 + 50 + 2y = -50 + 70$$
$$2y = 20$$
$$y = 10$$

Solution: (10, 10)

2. Use point-slope formula:

$$y - y_1 = m(x - x_1)$$
$$y - 4 = -\frac{3}{8}(x - 4)$$

or in slope-intercept form,

$$y - 4 = -\frac{3}{8}x + \frac{3}{2}$$
$$y - 4 + 4 = -\frac{3}{8}x + \frac{3}{2} + 4$$
$$y = -\frac{3}{8}x + \frac{11}{2}$$

3. $\frac{k^2}{2p} + c - \frac{4}{p^2c}$

$$= \frac{k^2 \cdot pc}{2p \cdot pc} + \frac{c \cdot 2p^2c}{2p^2c} - \frac{4 \cdot 2}{p^2c \cdot 2}$$
$$= \frac{k^2pc + 2p^2c^2 - 8}{2p^2c}$$

4. Slopes of lines are equal: $m = \frac{1}{6}$

Use point-slope formula:

$$m = \frac{y - y_1}{x - x_1}$$
$$\frac{1}{6} = \frac{y - 5}{x - 3}$$
$$\frac{1}{6}(x - 3) = y - 5$$
$$\frac{1}{6}x - \frac{1}{2} + 5 = y - 5 + 5$$
$$y = \frac{1}{6}x + \frac{9}{2}$$

5. $$\frac{x^2y^{-2}}{z^2}\left(\frac{z^2}{y^2(2x^{-2})^{-1}} - \frac{4x^2y^0}{z^{-2}}\right) = \frac{x^2y^{-2}}{z^2}\left(\frac{z^2}{y^2 2^{-1}x^2} - \frac{4x^2y^0}{z^{-2}}\right)$$
$$= \frac{x^2y^{-2}}{z^2}\cdot\frac{z^2}{y^2 2^{-1}x^2} - \frac{x^2y^{-2}}{z^2}\cdot\frac{4x^2y^0}{z^{-2}}$$
$$= 2y^{-4} - 4x^4y^{-2}$$

6. $$\begin{bmatrix}4 & -1\\ 3 & 7\end{bmatrix}\cdot\begin{bmatrix}2 & 4 & 3\\ 1 & 0 & 8\end{bmatrix}$$
$$= \begin{bmatrix}4(2)+(-1)(1) & 4(4)+(-1)(0) & 4(3)+(-1)(8)\\ 3(2)+7(1) & 3(4)+7(0) & 3(3)+7(8)\end{bmatrix}$$
$$= \begin{bmatrix}7 & 16 & 4\\ 13 & 12 & 65\end{bmatrix}$$

7. Factor pairs for -6 are $(1)(-6)$, $(-1)(6)$, $(2)(-3)$, and $(-2)(3)$. Factor pair $(-2)(3)$ sums to 1, so $x^2 + x - 6 = (x - 2)(x + 3)$

8. $$x^3 - 3x = x(x^2) - x(9)$$
$$= x(x^2 - 9)$$
$$= x(x^2 - 3^2)$$
$$= x(x - 3)(x + 3)$$

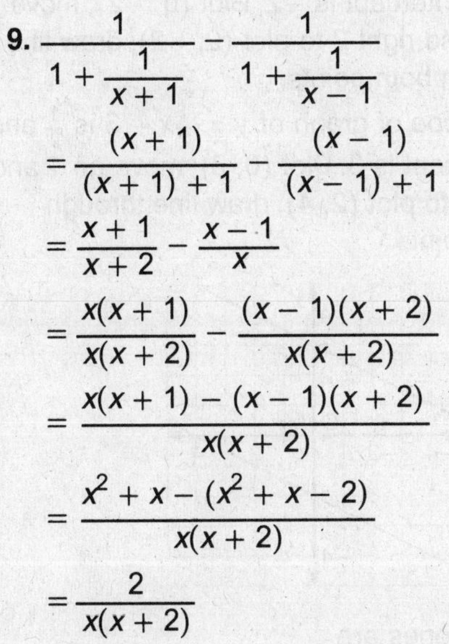

9. $$\frac{1}{1+\frac{1}{x+1}} - \frac{1}{1+\frac{1}{x-1}}$$
$$= \frac{(x+1)}{(x+1)+1} - \frac{(x-1)}{(x-1)+1}$$
$$= \frac{x+1}{x+2} - \frac{x-1}{x}$$
$$= \frac{x(x+1)}{x(x+2)} - \frac{(x-1)(x+2)}{x(x+2)}$$
$$= \frac{x(x+1) - (x-1)(x+2)}{x(x+2)}$$
$$= \frac{x^2 + x - (x^2 + x - 2)}{x(x+2)}$$
$$= \frac{2}{x(x+2)}$$

10. Slope of graph of $f(x)$ is 2 and y-intercept is -7. Plot $(0, -7)$; move up 2 and right 1 to plot $(1, -5)$; draw line through both points. Slope of graph of $g(x)$ is -5 and y-intercept is 8. Plot $(0, 8)$; move down -5 and right 1 to plot $(1, 3)$; draw line through both points.

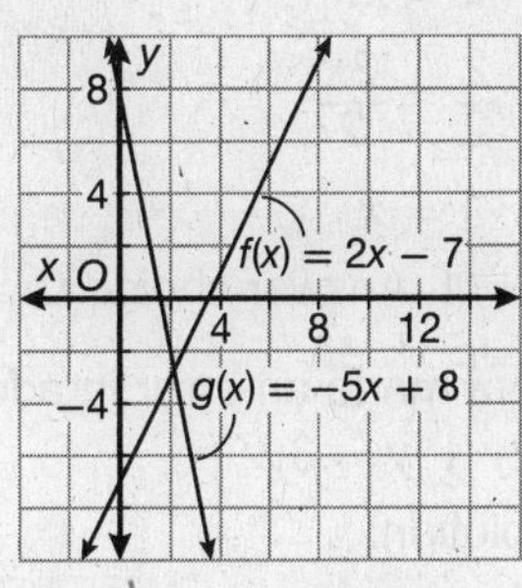

11. If $x \geq 0$, then $|x| = x$, so $|x| > |2 + 7x|$ becomes $x > |2 + 7x|$.
$x > 2 + 7x$ and $-x < 2 + 7x$
$x > -2 - 7x$
If $x < 0$, then $|x| = -x$, so $|x| > |2 + 7x|$ becomes $-x > |2 + 7x|$.
$-x > 2 + 7x$ and $-(-x) < 2 + 7x$
$x < -2 - 7x$ $x < 2 + 7x$

12. **a.** a is coefficient of x^2-term, b is coefficient of linear term, and c is the constant.
b. $f(x) = ax^2 + bx + c$
$f(x) = (-1)x^2 + (-2)x + 3$
$f(x) = -x^2 - 2x + 3$

13. Outbound: $s_1 = \dfrac{d}{t + \frac{1}{2}} = \dfrac{2d}{2t + 1}$

Return: $s_2 = \dfrac{d}{t}$

$$s_2 - s_1 = \frac{d}{t} - \frac{2d}{2t+1}$$
$$= \frac{d(2t+1)}{t(2t+1)} - \frac{2dt}{t(2t+1)}$$
$$= \frac{d}{t(2t+1)}$$

14. The error is in dividing out terms of polynomials. The correct product is

$$\frac{x^2-1}{x^2+2x+1}\cdot\frac{x+1}{x-3}=\frac{(x-1)(x+1)}{(x+1)^2}\cdot\frac{x+1}{x-3}$$
$$=\frac{(x-1)\cancel{(x+1)^2}}{\cancel{(x+1)^2}(x-3)}$$
$$=\frac{x-1}{x-3}$$

15. Substitute for y in Equation 2:

$$y = 3x - 2$$
$$x = 3x - 2$$
$$-x + x + 2 = -x + 3x - 2 + 2$$
$$2 = 2x$$
$$\frac{2}{2} = \frac{2x}{2}$$
$$1 = x$$

So $x = y = 1$. Answer choice **C**

16. The student made an error in adding the y-terms: $2y + y = 3y$.

Correct solution:

$$2x + 2y = 6$$
$$\underline{-2x + y = -12}$$
$$3y = -6$$
$$\frac{3y}{3} = \frac{-6}{3}$$
$$y = -2$$
$$-2x + y = -12$$
$$-2x + (-2) = -12$$
$$-2x = -10$$
$$x = 5$$

The solution is $x = 5$, $y = -2$

17. Up to \$50: $y = 1.377x + 3$

More than \$50: $y = 1.377x + 5$

Lines are parallel.

18. Use the expression for the area of a triangle to solve for x:

$$A = \frac{1}{2}bh$$
$$120 = \frac{1}{2}(x + 14)x$$
$$2(120) = (x + 14)x$$
$$240 = x^2 + 14x$$
$$0 = x^2 + 14x - 240$$
$$0 = (x - 10)(x + 24)$$
$$x - 10 = 0 \quad \text{or} \quad x + 24 = 0$$
$$x = 10 \qquad\qquad x = -24$$

Ignoring the negative solution, the triangle height and base are 10 and $10 + 14 = 24$. Use Pythagorean Theorem to determine hypotenuse:

$$c = \sqrt{a^2 + b^2}$$
$$= \sqrt{(10)^2 + (24)^2}$$
$$= \sqrt{676} = 26$$

Since the hypotenuse is also a diameter of the circle, the radius $r = \frac{c}{2} = \frac{26}{2} = 13$.

The probability that the point is inside the triangle is equal to the area of the triangle divided by the area of the circle:

$$\frac{A_{\triangle}}{A_{\odot}} = \frac{120}{\pi r^2} = \frac{120}{\pi(13)^2} = \frac{120}{169\pi}$$

19. **a.** The slope of graph of $y = \frac{1}{2}x - 2$ is $\frac{1}{2}$ and y-intercept is -2. Plot $(0, -2)$; move up 1 and right 2 to plot $(2, -2)$; draw line through both points.

The slope of graph of $y = \frac{1}{2}x + 3$ is $\frac{1}{2}$ and y-intercept is 3. Plot $(0, 3)$; move up 1 and right 2 to plot $(2, 4)$; draw line through both points.

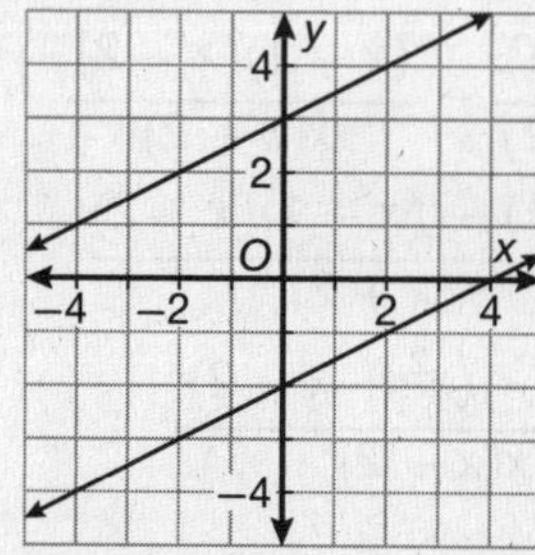

b. Both slopes are $\frac{1}{2}$.

c. Non-vertical lines are parallel if and only if they have the same slope.

20. Denominators $g(x)$ and $i(x)$ have no common factors.

21. 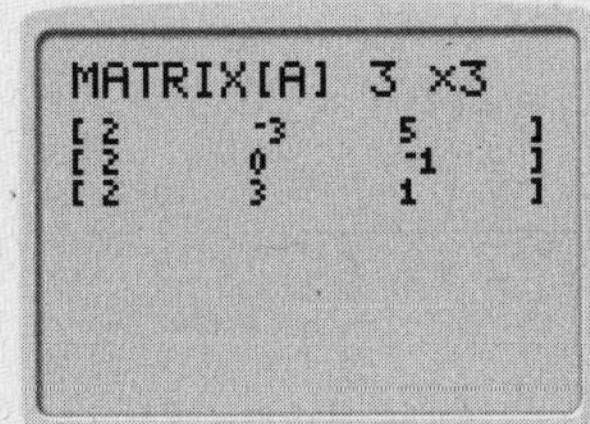

22. The possible choices for pairs are a red card and a face card, a red card and the jack of spades, a red card and a black jack, a face card and the jack of spades, a face card and a black jack, and the jack of spades and a black jack.

Since some face cards are also red, a red card and face cards are not mutually exclusive. Since a jack of spades is black, a red card and the jack of spades are mutually exclusive. Since a black jack is not red, a red card and a black jack are mutually exclusive. Since a jack of spades is a face card, a face card and the jack of spades are not mutually exclusive. Since a black jack is a face card, a face card and a black jack are not mutually exclusive. Since the jack of spades is a black jack, the jack of spades and a black jack are not mutually exclusive. Therefore, there are two pairs of mutually exclusive events, which are choosing a red card and a jack of spades; and choosing a red card and a black jack.

23. **a.** $A = lw$

$= (x + 24)(x - 10)$

$= x^2 + 14x - 240$

b. $A = x^2 + 14x - 240$

$= (60)^2 + 14(60) - 240$

$= 3600 + 840 - 240$

$= 4200$

Area is 4200 ft^2.

24. Since $m_1 = -\frac{1}{m_3}$ and $m_2 = -\frac{1}{m_3}$, then $m_1 = m_2$. Therefore, lines y_1 and y_2 are parallel.

25. Solve equation 1 for y:

$$2y - 3x = -10$$
$$2y - 3x + 3x = -10 + 3x$$
$$2y = 3x - 10$$
$$\frac{2y}{2} = \frac{3x - 10}{2}$$
$$y = \frac{3}{2}x - 5$$

Substitute in equation 2:

$$4x = 7 - y$$
$$4x = 7 - \left(\frac{3}{2}x - 5\right)$$
$$4x = -\frac{3}{2}x + 12$$
$$\frac{3}{2}x + 4x = \frac{3}{2}x - \frac{3}{2}x + 12$$
$$\frac{11}{2}x = 12$$
$$\frac{2}{11}\left(\frac{11}{2}x\right) = \frac{2}{11}(12)$$
$$x = \frac{24}{11}$$

Substitute this value for x:

$$y = \frac{3}{2}x - 5$$
$$= \frac{3}{2}\left(\frac{24}{11}\right) - 5$$
$$= \frac{36}{11} - 5 = -\frac{19}{11}$$

Solution: $\left(\frac{24}{11}, -\frac{19}{11}\right)$

Solve equation 2 for y:

$$4x = 7 - y$$
$$-4x + 4x + y = -4x + 7 - y + y$$
$$y = -4x + 7$$

Substitute in equation 1:

$$2y - 3x = -10$$
$$2(-4x + 7) - 3x = -10$$
$$-11x + 14 - 14 = -10 - 14$$
$$-11x = -24$$
$$\frac{-11x}{-11} = \frac{-24}{-11}$$
$$x = \frac{24}{11}$$

Substitute in expression for y:

$$y = -4x + 7$$
$$= -4\left(\frac{24}{11}\right) + 7$$
$$= -\frac{96}{11} + 7 = -\frac{19}{11}$$

Solution is verified.

26. Monday: $6m + 6b + 6f = 24$
Tuesday: $4m + 12b + 4f = 22.8$
Wednesday: $8m + 12b + 10f = 39.3$

$$\underbrace{\begin{bmatrix} 6 & 6 & 6 \\ 4 & 12 & 4 \\ 8 & 12 & 10 \end{bmatrix}}_{A} \underbrace{\begin{bmatrix} m \\ b \\ f \end{bmatrix}}_{X} = \underbrace{\begin{bmatrix} 24 \\ 22.8 \\ 39.3 \end{bmatrix}}_{B}$$

Using a graphing calculator:

$$X = A^{-1}B = \begin{bmatrix} 1.2 \\ 0.85 \\ 1.95 \end{bmatrix}$$

Solution is $m = 1.2$, $b = 0.85$, $f = 1.95$. Costs are 1.20 per muffin, \$0.85 per bagel, and \$1.95 per fruit cup.

27.

Number of sides of the polygon	Number of triangles
3	1
4	2
5	3
6	4
7	5
8	6

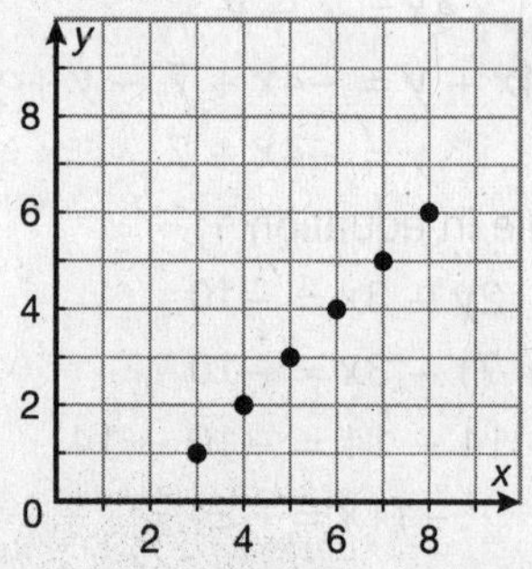

Domain = {3, 4, 5, 6, 7, 8}, range = {1, 2, 3, 4, 5, 6}. The graph is discontinuous and discrete.

28. a. $f(x) \div g(x) = \frac{2x-1}{x+5} \div \frac{14x-7}{14x^2+70x}$

$= \frac{2x-1}{x+5} \cdot \frac{14x^2+70x}{14x-7}$

$= \frac{\cancel{(2x-1)}}{\cancel{(x+5)}} \cdot \frac{\cancel{7} \cdot 2x\,\cancel{(x+5)}}{\cancel{7} \cdot \cancel{(2x-1)}}$

$= 2x$

b. $f(x) \div g(x) = 2x$

$f(10) \div g(10) = 2(10) = 20$

29. $\frac{1}{x^2+x-72} + \frac{1}{x^2-x-56}$

$= \frac{1}{(x-8)(x+9)} + \frac{1}{(x-8)(x+7)}$

$= \frac{(x+7)}{(x-8)(x+9)(x+7)}$

$+ \frac{(x+9)}{(x-8)(x+9)(x+7)}$

$= \frac{x+7+x+9}{(x-8)(x+9)(x+7)}$

$= \frac{2x+16}{(x-8)(x+9)(x+7)}$

$= \frac{2x+16}{(x-8)(x^2+16x+63)}$

$= \frac{2x+16}{x(x^2+16x+63) - 8(x^2+16x+63)}$

$= \frac{2x+16}{x^3+16x^2+63x\ 8x^2 - 128x - 504}$

$= \frac{2x+16}{x^3+8x^2-65x-504}$

Answer choice **D**

30. $\begin{cases} 416l + 256s = 233.6 \\ 400l + 512s = 251.2 \end{cases}$

Use Cramer's rule:

$l = \frac{\begin{vmatrix} 233.6 & 256 \\ 251.2 & 512 \end{vmatrix}}{\begin{vmatrix} 416 & 256 \\ 400 & 512 \end{vmatrix}}$

$= \frac{233.6(512) - 251.2(256)}{416(512) - 400(256)}$

$= \frac{55{,}296}{110{,}592} = 0.5$

$s = \frac{\begin{vmatrix} 416 & 233.6 \\ 400 & 251.2 \end{vmatrix}}{\begin{vmatrix} 416 & 256 \\ 400 & 512 \end{vmatrix}}$

$= \frac{416(251.2) - 400(233.6)}{416(512) - 400(256)}$

$= \frac{11{,}059.2}{110{,}592} = 0.1$

The cost: \$0.50 per large tile and \$0.10 per small tile.

LESSON 38

Warm Up 38

1. inequality
2. $(x+3)(x+7)$
 $= x(x) + x(7) + 3(x) + 3(7)$
 $= x^2 + 7x + 3x + 21$
 $= x^2 + 10x + 21$
3. Substitute -5 for x in the function.
 $f(-5) = 2(-5)^2 - 3(-5)$
 $f(-5) = 50 + 15$
 $f(-5) = 65$

Lesson Practice 38

a.

$$3x\overline{)12x^3 - 9x^2 - 237x + 40}\quad \text{quotient: } 4x^2 - 3x - 79$$
$$-(12x^3)$$
$$0 - 9x^2 - 237x + 40$$
$$-(-9x^2)$$
$$0 - 237x + 40$$
$$+237x$$
$$40$$

$$= 4x^2 - 3x - 79 + \frac{40}{3x}$$

b.

$$x - 3\overline{)6x^4 - 23x^3 - 34x^2 + 207x - 180}\quad \text{quotient: } 6x^3 - 5x^2 - 49x + 60$$
$$-(6x^4 - 18x^3)$$
$$0 - 5x^3 - 34x^2 + 207x - 180$$
$$-(-5x^3 + 15x^2)$$
$$0 - 49x^2 + 207x - 180$$
$$-(-49x^2 + 147x)$$
$$60x - 180$$
$$-(60x - 180)$$
$$0$$

c.

$$x^2 - 5x - 36\overline{)2x^4 + 7x^3 - 241x^2 - 192x + 3024}\quad \text{quotient: } 2x^2 + 17x - 84x$$
$$-(2x^4 - 10x^3 - 72x^2)$$
$$0 + 17x^3 - 169x^2 - 192x + 3024$$
$$-(17x^3 - 85x^2 - 612x)$$
$$0 - 84x^2 + 420x + 3024$$
$$-(-84x^2 + 420x + 3024)$$
$$0$$

d.

$$x - 6\overline{)2x^3 + x^2 - 177x + 594}\quad \text{quotient: } 2x^2 + 13x - 99$$
$$-(2x^3 - 12x^2)$$
$$0 + 13x^2 - 177x + 594$$
$$-(13x^2 - 78x)$$
$$0 - 99x + 594$$
$$-(-99x + 594)$$
$$0$$

$x - 6$ is a factor since the remainder is 0.

e.
$$\begin{array}{r} 7x^2 - 11x + 190 \\ x + 27\overline{)7x^3 + 178x^2 - 107x - 78} \\ \underline{-(7x^3 + 189x^2)} \\ 0 - 11x^2 - 107x - 78 \\ \underline{-(-11x^2 - 297x)} \\ 0 + 190x - 78 \\ \underline{-(190x + 5130)} \\ -5208 \end{array}$$

There is a remainder so $x + 27$ is not a factor.

f. $\frac{\text{volume}}{\text{surface area}}$

$$= \frac{15x(x)(x+5)}{2(15x)(x) + 2(15x)(x+5) + 2(x)(x+5)}$$

$$= \frac{15x^3 + 75x^2}{30x^2 + 30x^2 + 150x + 2x^2 + 10x}$$

$$= \frac{15x^3 + 75x^2}{62x^2 + 160x}$$

$$= \frac{x(15x^2 + 75x)}{x(62x + 160)}$$

$$= \frac{15x^2 + 75x}{62x + 160}$$

Since the numerator and denominator have no factors in common, the expression has a non-zero remainder.

Practice 38

1. The vertex form of an equation is $y = a(x - h)^2 + k$, where the vertex is (h, k). The parent function is $y = x^2$, which has a vertex of $(0, 0)$. If the parent function shifts 10 units to the left, then the vertex becomes $(-10, 0)$, so $a = 1$, $h = -10$ and $k = 0$. The equation is $y = (x - (-10))^2 + 0$, or $y = (x + 10)^2$.

2. The vertex form of an equation is $y = a(x - h)^2 + k$, where the vertex is (h, k). The parent function is $y = x^2$. If the parent function shifts 1 unit to the right and 3 units down, then the vertex becomes $(1, -3)$, so $a = 1$, $h = 1$, and $k = -3$. The equation is $y = (x - 1)^2 + (-3)$, or $y = (x - 1)^2 - 3$.

3.
$$\begin{array}{r} x^2 - 15x + 6 \\ x + 5\overline{)x^3 - 10x^2 - 69x + 30} \\ \underline{-(x^3 + 5x^2)} \\ 0 - 15x^2 - 69x + 30 \\ \underline{-(-15x^2 - 75x)} \\ 0 + 6x + 30 \\ \underline{-(6x + 30)} \\ 0 \end{array}$$

4. $X = A^{-1}B$

$$A^{-1} = \frac{1}{4(4) - 8(-2)}\begin{bmatrix} 4 & 2 \\ -8 & 4 \end{bmatrix} = \frac{1}{32}\begin{bmatrix} 4 & 2 \\ -8 & 4 \end{bmatrix} = \begin{bmatrix} 0.125 & 0.0625 \\ -0.25 & 0.125 \end{bmatrix}$$

$X = A^{-1}B$

$$= \begin{bmatrix} 0.125 & 0.0625 \\ -0.25 & 0.125 \end{bmatrix}\begin{bmatrix} -2 & 0 \\ 0 & -2 \end{bmatrix} = \begin{bmatrix} 0.125(-2) + 0.0625(0) & 0.125(0) + 0.0625(-2) \\ -0.25(-2) + 0.125(0) & -0.25(0) + 0.125(-2) \end{bmatrix}$$

$$= \begin{bmatrix} -0.25 & -0.125 \\ 0.5 & -0.25 \end{bmatrix}$$

5. A number cannot be odd and be a 6. These are mutually exclusive events.

6. 2 is an even number that is less than 3. These are not mutually exclusive events.

7. $\frac{1}{x+3} - \frac{1}{x+2} - \frac{1}{x+1}$

$$= \frac{1}{x+3} \cdot \frac{(x+1)(x+2)}{(x+1)(x+2)} - \frac{1}{x+2} \cdot \frac{(x+1)(x+3)}{(x+1)(x+3)} - \frac{1}{x+1} \cdot \frac{(x+2)(x+3)}{(x+2)(x+3)}$$

$$= \frac{x^2 + 3x + 2}{(x+1)(x+2)(x+3)} - \frac{x^2 + 4x + 3}{(x+1)(x+2)(x+3)} - \frac{x^2 + 5x + 6}{(x+1)(x+2)(x+3)}$$

$$= \frac{x^2 + 3x + 2 - x^2 - 4x - 3 - x^2 - 5x - 6}{(x+1)(x+2)(x+3)} = \frac{-x^2 - 6x - 7}{(x+1)(x+2)(x+3)} = \frac{-x^2 - 6x - 7}{x^3 + 6x^2 + 11x + 6}$$

8. $x = \dfrac{\begin{vmatrix} -15 & -12 \\ 7 & 2 \end{vmatrix}}{\begin{vmatrix} 3 & -12 \\ 1 & 2 \end{vmatrix}} = \dfrac{-15(2) - 7(-12)}{3(2) - 1(-12)}$

$= \dfrac{54}{18} = 3$

$y = \dfrac{\begin{vmatrix} 3 & -15 \\ 1 & 7 \end{vmatrix}}{\begin{vmatrix} 3 & -12 \\ 1 & 2 \end{vmatrix}} = \dfrac{3(7) - 1(-15)}{3(2) - 1(-12)} = \dfrac{36}{18} = 2$

9. $|A| = 2(13) - 7(-12) = 110$

10. $|B| = -1(0.5) - 0.25(-24) = 5.5$

11. In the slope-intercept form, $y = mx + b$, m is the slope and b is the y-intercept. Write the equation in slope-intercept form.

$3x + 10y = -1$

$10y = -3x - 1$

$y = -\frac{3}{10}x - \frac{1}{10}$

Slope $= -\frac{3}{10}$ or -0.3 and y-intercept $= -\frac{1}{10}$ or -0.1.

12. When one variable increases, the other also increases; and when one decreases the other also decreases; and since there is a constant of variation, this is direct variation.

For a direct variation $\frac{y}{x} = k$, so $\frac{C}{d} = \pi$, or $C = \pi d$.

13. 1 and only 1. The graph of a quadratic function is a parabola that opens either up or down and extends without end to the left and to the right. So for any quadratic function, the graph intersects the x-axis in at least one point. And, the graph intersects the y-axis in at most one point because no vertical line can intersect the graph of a function in more than one point.

14. Since $x^2 + ax + bx + ab = (x + a)(x + b)$, then $x + a$ is a factor and the remainder is zero.

15. Let x represent the pay at \$16 per hour, y represent the pay at \$24 per hour, and z represent the rate at \$32 per hour.

$x + y = 10z$

$16x + 24y + 32z = 808$

$x + y + z = 44$

Solve the equations.

Eliminate x using the first and second, and first and third equations.

$-16(x + y - 10z = 0) \longrightarrow$

$-16x - 16y + 160z = 0$

$16x + 24y + 32z = 808 \longrightarrow$

$16x + 24y + 32z = 808$

$8y + 192z = 808$

$x + y = 10z \longrightarrow x + y - 10z = 0$

$-1(x + y + z = 44) \longrightarrow -x - y - z = -44$

$-11z = -44$

$z = 4$

$8y + 192(4) = 808$

$8y = 40$

$y = 5$

Substitute $y = 5$ and $z = 4$ into one of the original equations.

$x + 5 + 4 = 44$

$x = 35$

Therefore 35 hours were worked at \$16 per hour, 5 hours at \$24 per hour, and 4 hours at \$32 per hour.

Student **A** is correct.

16.
$$
\begin{array}{r}
-14x^2 + 18x + 80 \\
x - 2 \overline{) -14x^3 + 46x^2 + 44x - 16} \\
\underline{-(-14x^3 + 28x^2)} \\
0 + 18x^2 + 44x - 16 \\
\underline{-(18x^2 - 36x)} \\
0 + 80x - 16 \\
\underline{-(80x - 160)} \\
144
\end{array}
$$

Student **B** incorrectly subtracts 36 instead of adding.

17. The vertex is the minimum point, which is (2, −6).

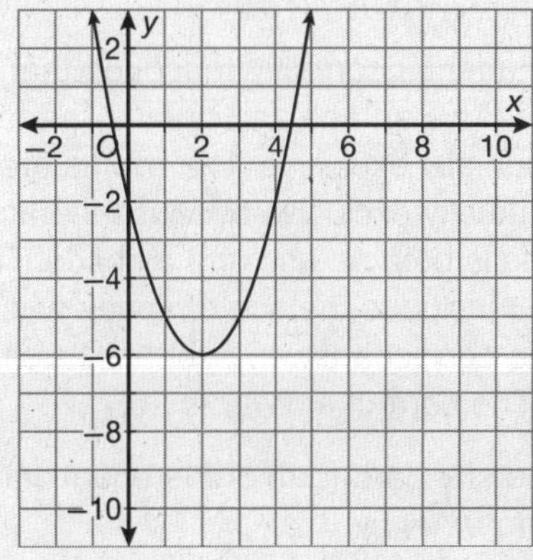

18. The slope of $y = 4x + 10$ is 4, so the slope of the perpendicular line has the opposite reciprocal slope, $-\frac{1}{4}$. Use the point-slope formula and substitute $m = -\frac{1}{4}$ and (1, 1) into the formula.

$$y - 1 = -\frac{1}{4}(x - 1)$$

$$y - 1 = -\frac{1}{4}x + \frac{1}{4}$$

$$y = -\frac{1}{4}x + 1\frac{1}{4}$$

$$= -\frac{1}{4}x + \frac{5}{4}$$

Answer choice **B**

19.

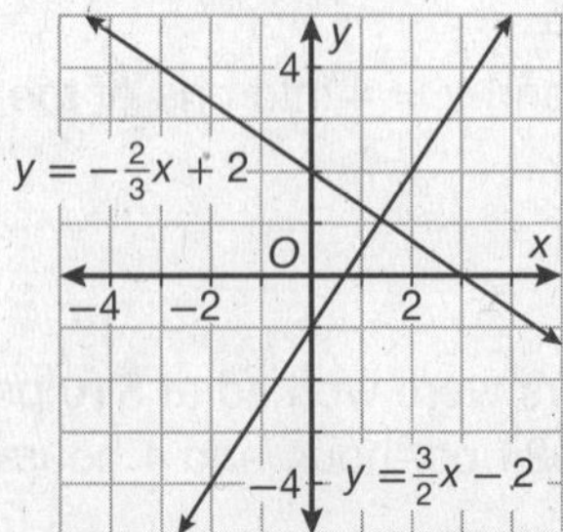

a. The equations are in the form $y = mx + b$ and the slope of each line is m. The slopes are $\frac{3}{2}$ and $-\frac{2}{3}$. The graph confirms the slopes, since the slope $\frac{3}{2}$ has a rise of 3 and a run of 2, while the slope of $-\frac{2}{3}$ has a rise of -2 and a run of 3.

b. The product of the slopes is $\frac{3}{2} \cdot -\frac{2}{3} = -1$.

c. Two non-vertical lines are perpendicular if and only if the product of their slopes is -1.

20. The area is πr^2 and circumference is $2\pi r$. The ratio of area to circumference is $\frac{\pi r^2}{2\pi r} = \frac{r}{2}$. If the radius is about 3 miles, then $\frac{r}{2} = \frac{3}{2} = 1.5$

21. The student incorrectly reasoned that the events draw an ace and draw a spade are mutually exclusive. The events are not mutually exclusive because the ace of spades is both an ace and a spade. The sum $4 + 13$ includes the ace of spade twice. To get the correct answer, subtract 1 from that sum. The correct answer is 16.

22. a. The standard form of the equation is the form $ax + by = c$

$y = 5 - 7x \longrightarrow 7x + y = 5$

$10 = 14x + 2y \longrightarrow 14x + 2y = 10$

b. Infinitely many solutions. All the like terms are opposites if the first equation is multiplied by -2, which means that the solution would be $0 = 0$ indicating that the lines coincide.

c. $-2(7x + y = 5) \longrightarrow -14x - 2y = -10$

$14x + 2y = 10 \longrightarrow \underline{14x + 2y = 10}$

$0 = 0$

There are infinitely many solutions. The systems are consistent and dependent.

23. Let x represent the number of ninth graders, y represent the number of tenth graders, and z represent the number of eleventh graders. The equations are:

$0.2x + 0.3y + 0.25z = 143$

$0.4x + 0.5y + 0.45z = 258$

$0.2x + 0.2y + 0.35z = 142$

The matrix equation is

$$\begin{bmatrix} 0.2 & 0.3 & 0.25 \\ 0.4 & 0.5 & 0.45 \\ 0.2 & 0.2 & 0.35 \end{bmatrix}\begin{bmatrix} x \\ y \\ z \end{bmatrix} = \begin{bmatrix} 143 \\ 258 \\ 142 \end{bmatrix}$$

Solve with a graphing calculator using the inverse matrix.

205 ninth graders, 190 tenth graders, and 180 eleventh graders are surveyed.

24. A change in the value of h shifts the parent function to the right when h is positive and to the left when h is negative. A change in the value of k shifts the parent function up when k is positive and down when k is negative. When the absolute value of a is greater than 1, the graph is stretched away from the x-axis, appearing narrower than the parent function. When the absolute value of a is between 0 and 1, the graph is compressed towards the x-axis, appearing wider than the parent function.

25. When a polynomial is factored and is equal to zero, since the product of the terms equals zero, at least one of its terms equals zero. Setting each term containing a variable equal to zero enables you to solve for a possible value of the variable.

26. If time for the first part of the trip is t and the distance is d, then the speed is $s_1 = \frac{d}{t}$. The time for the return trip is $t + 1.5$, the distance is d, and the speed is $s_2 = \frac{d}{t + 1.5}$.

The difference in speeds is

$$\frac{d}{t} - \frac{d}{t + 1.5} = \frac{d}{t} \cdot \frac{(t + 1.5)}{(t + 1.5)} - \frac{d}{t + 1.5} \cdot \frac{t}{t}$$

$$= \frac{d(t + 1.5)}{t(t + 1.5)} - \frac{dt}{t(t + 1.5)}$$

$$= \frac{dt + 1.5d - dt}{t(t + 1.5)}$$

$$= \frac{1.5d}{t^2 + 1.5t}$$

27.

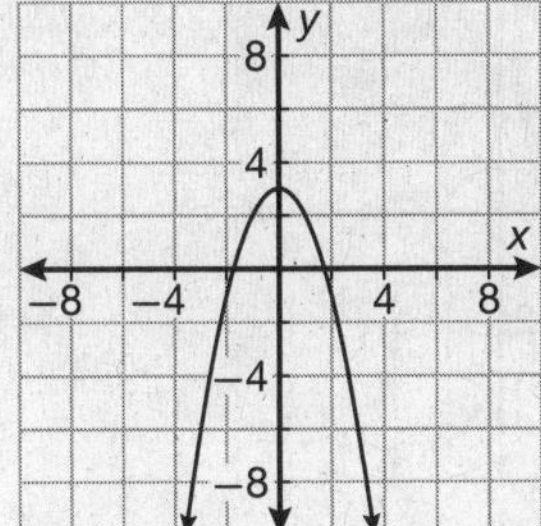

The point (0, 3) is the highest point on the parabola. None of the y-values is above 3.

28. A

$$x + 2\overline{)\,3x^3 + 8x^2 - 31x + 20}$$ quotient: $3x^2 + 2x - 35$

$$-(3x^3 + 6x^2)$$
$$0 + 2x^2 - 31x + 20$$
$$-(2x^2 + 4x)$$
$$0 - 35x + 20$$
$$-(-35x - 70)$$
$$90$$

There is a remainder so $x + 2$ is not a factor.

B

$$3x + 4\overline{)\,3x^3 + 8x^2 - 31x + 20}$$ quotient: $x^2 + 1.\overline{3}x - 12.\overline{1}$

$$-(3x^3 + 4x^2)$$
$$0 + 4x^2 - 31x + 20$$
$$-(4x^2 + 5.\overline{3}x)$$
$$0 - 36.\overline{3}x + 20$$
$$-(-36.\overline{3}x - 48.\overline{4})$$
$$68.\overline{4}$$

There is a remainder so $3x + 4$ is not a factor.

C

$$x - 1\overline{)\,3x^3 + 8x^2 - 31x + 20}$$ quotient: $3x^2 + 11x - 20$

$$-(3x^3 - 3x^2)$$
$$0 + 11x^2 - 31x + 20$$
$$-(11x^2 - 11x)$$
$$0 - 20x + 20$$
$$-(-20x + 20)$$
$$0$$

There is no remainder so $x - 1$ is a factor.

D

$$x + 6\overline{)\,3x^3 + 8x^2 - 31x + 20}$$ quotient: $3x^2 - 10x + 29$

$$-(3x^3 + 18x^2)$$
$$0 - 10x^2 - 31x + 20$$
$$-(-10x^2 - 60x)$$
$$0 + 29x + 20$$
$$-(29x + 174)$$
$$-154$$

There is a remainder so $x + 6$ is not a factor.

Answer choice **C**

29. Use any two points to find the slope. Using (3, 38.5) and (4, 41.5), the slope is $m = \frac{y_2 - y_1}{x_2 - x_1} = \frac{41.5 - 38.5}{4 - 3} = 3$.

Substitute the slope, 3, and any point, such as (5, 44.5) into the point-slope formula, $y - y_1 = m(x - x_1)$.

$$y - 44.5 = 3(x - 5)$$
$$y - 44.5 = 3x - 15$$
$$y = 3x + 29.5$$

30. The only expression that can give the sum of $\frac{1}{x}$ is $\frac{1}{2x} + \frac{1}{2x}$. So, the probability of rolling $\frac{1}{2x}$ on each cube is $\frac{1}{6}$. The probability of rolling $\frac{1}{2x}$ on both cubes is $\frac{1}{6} \cdot \frac{1}{6} = \frac{1}{36}$.

LESSON 39

Warm Up 39

1. slope-intercept

2. The slope is

$$m = \frac{y_2 - y_1}{x_2 - x_1} = \frac{5 - 3}{-7 - 9} = \frac{2}{-16} = -\frac{1}{8}$$

3. undefined

4. In the form $y = mx + b$, b is the y-intercept. The equation in this form is as follows:

$2x - y = -4$

$-y = -2x - 4$

$y = 2x + 4$

Since $b = 4$, the y-intercept is 4. True.

Lesson Practice 39

a. $y \geq 7 - 4x$

$1 \overset{?}{\geq} 7 - 4(-2)$

$1 \geq 15$ False; $(-2, 1)$ is not a solution.

b. $-2y + x < 0$

$-2(0) + (0) \overset{?}{<} 0$

$0 < 0$ False; $(0, 0)$ is not a solution.

c. $4y - 6x > 15$

$4(13) - 6(4) \overset{?}{>} 15$

$28 > 15$ True; $(4, 13)$ is a solution.

d. Step 1: Find ordered pairs that satisfy the equation $2y - 6x \leq -12$. Use the x- and y-intercepts as well as other points.

x	-1	0	2	3
y	-9	-6	0	3

Step 2: Connect the points with a solid line.

Step 3: Use the test point $(0, 0)$ to determine which half-plane to shade.

$2(0) - 6(0) \leq -12$

$0 \leq -12$ False

The point $(0, 0)$ is not a solution. Shade the half of the plane that does not contain $(0, 0)$.

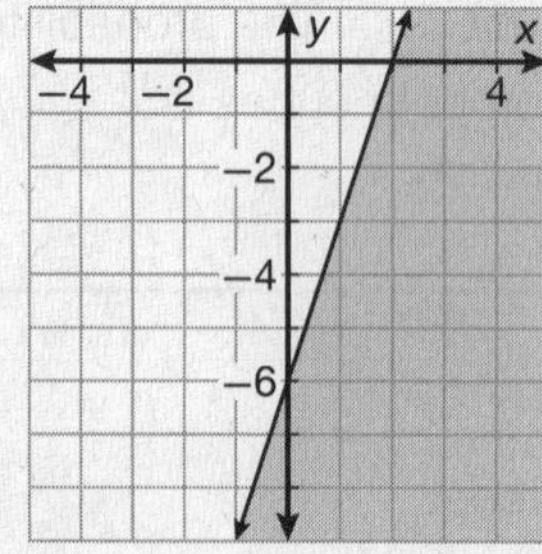

e. Step 1: Write the inequality in slope-intercept form.

$4y + 4 > x$

$4y > x - 4$

$y > \frac{1}{4}x - 1$

Step 2: Graph $y > \frac{1}{4}x - 1$ by plotting $(0, -1)$ and a second point by moving 1 unit up and 4 units right. Connect the points with a dashed line to indicate that the points on the line are not a solution.

Step 3: Shade above the line because the inequality symbol is $>$.

The test point $(0, 0)$ verifies this.

$4y + 4 > x$

$4(0) + 4 > (0)$

$4 > 0$ True

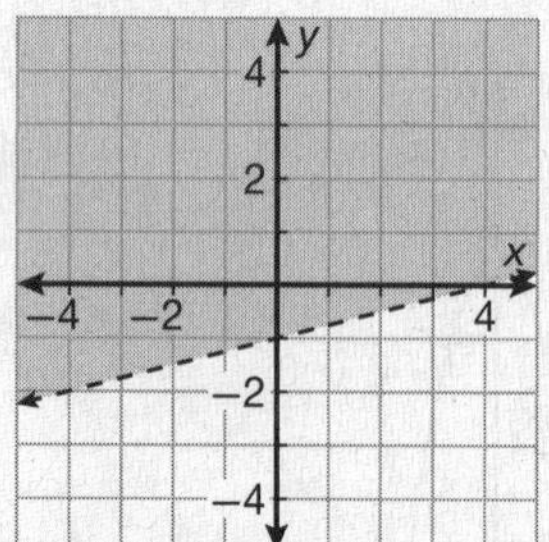

f. Step 1: Write the inequality in slope-intercept form. Don't forget to switch the direction of the inequality sign when multiplying or dividing by a negative number.

$4 - 2y > -x$

$-2y > -x - 4$

$y < \frac{1}{2}x + 2$

Step 2: Graph $y < \frac{1}{2}x + 2$ by plotting $(0, 2)$ and a second point by moving 1 unit up and 2 units right. Connect the points with a dashed line to indicate that the points on the line are not a solution.

Step 3: Shade below the line because the inequality symbol is $<$.

The test point $(0, 0)$ verifies this.

$4 - 2y > -x$

$4 - 2(0) > -(0)$

$4 > 0$ True

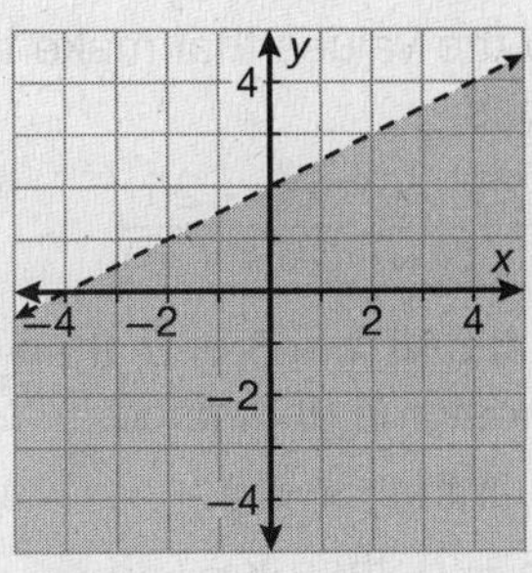

g. In the [Y =] editor, after y enter 0. To indicate shading above the line, use the arrow key to highlight the symbol to the left of Y_1. Press enter until the symbol shows the upper right portion of the square shaded, then graph.

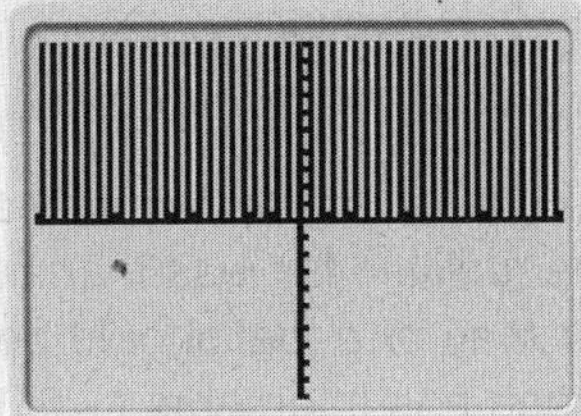

h. First write the inequality in slope-intercept form.

$3y + 9 \geq 3x$

$3y \geq 3x - 9$

$y \geq x - 3$

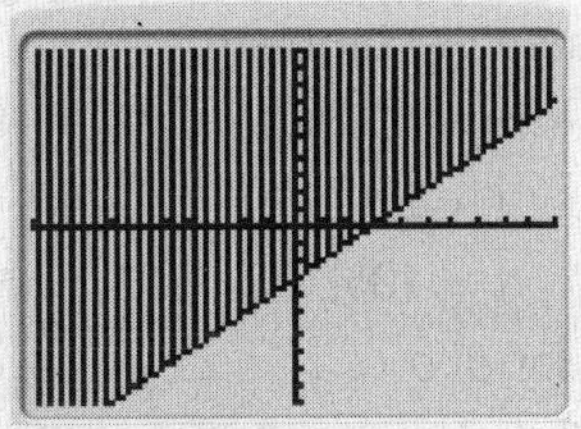

i. Let x represent cups of beans and y represent cups of peas. So $35x + 48y > 840$.

$48y > -35x + 840$

$y > -0.7x + 17.5$

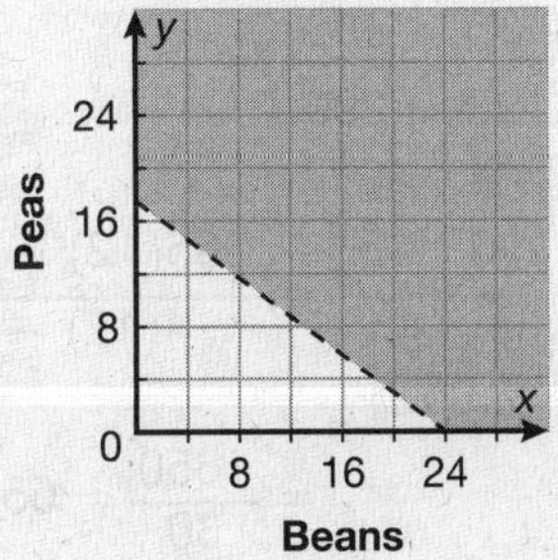

Practice 39

1. $y < 6x - 2$

$18 \overset{?}{<} 6(3) - 2$

$18 < 16$ False; (3, 18) is not a solution.

2. $y + 2x \geq -4$

$(-2) + 2(-1) \overset{?}{\geq} -4$

$-4 \overset{?}{\geq} -4$ True, (−1, −2) is a solution.

3. $m + \frac{x}{c} + \frac{c}{x^2b} = m \cdot \frac{bcx^2}{bcx^2} + \frac{x}{c} \cdot \frac{bx^2}{bx^2} + \frac{c}{x^2b} \cdot \frac{c}{c}$

$= \frac{mbcx^2}{bcx^2} + \frac{bx^3}{bcx^2} + \frac{c^2}{bcx^2}$

$= \frac{mbcx^2 + bx^3 + c^2}{bcx^2}$

4. $-8x - 22 + 2y = 2z \rightarrow -8x + 2y - 2z = 22$

$-6x + 2y = 16 + z \rightarrow -6x + 2y - z = 16$

$6 + 3y + z = -x \rightarrow x + 3y + z = -6$

Eliminate x using the first and second, and second and third equations.

$-8x + 2y - 2z = 22 \rightarrow -8x + 2y - 2z = 22$

$-(-6x + 2y - z = 16) \rightarrow 6x - 2y + z = -16$

$-2x \quad - z = \quad 6$

$3(-6x + 2y - z = 16) \rightarrow$

$-18x + 6y - 3z = 48$

$-2(x + 3y + z = -6) \rightarrow -2x - 6y - 2z = 12$

$-20x \quad -5z = 60$

Use resulting equations to solve for x and z.

$-5(-2x - z = 6) \rightarrow 10x + 5z = -30$

$-20x - 5z = 60 \rightarrow -20x - 5z = 60$

$-10x \quad = 30$

$x \quad = -3$

$-2(-3) - z = 6$

$6 - z = 6$

$z = 0$

Substitute −3 for x and 0 for z in one of the original equations.

$6 + 3y + 0 = -(-3)$

$3y = -3$

$y = -1$

The solution is (−3, −1, 0).

5. Substitute $x = y + 1$ into $3x + 2y = 8$.

$3(y + 1) + 2y = 8$

$3y + 3 + 2y = 8$

$5y = 5$

$y = 1$

Substitute 1 for y in one of the original equations.

$x = 1 + 1$

$x = 2$

The solution is (2, 1).

6. $3x - y = 22 \rightarrow y = 3x - 22$

Substitute $y = 3x - 22$ into $2x + 3y = -11$.

$2x + 3(3x - 22) = -11$

$2x + 9x - 66 = -11$

$11x = 55$

$x = 5$

Substitute 5 for x in one of the original equations.

$3(5) - y = 22$

$y = -7$

The solution is (5, −7).

7. $-7x + y = 8 \rightarrow y = 7x + 8$

Substitute $y = 7x + 8$ into $5x - y = -6$

$5x - (7x + 8) = -6$

$5x - 7x - 8 = -6$

$-2x = 2$

$x = -1$

Substitute −1 for x in one of the original equations.

$-7(-1) + y = 8$

$y = 1$

The solution is (−1, 1).

8.

$$
\begin{array}{r}
2x^2 + 7x - 9 \\
3x + 1 \overline{)6x^3 + 23x^2 - 20x - 9} \\
\underline{-(6x^3 + 2x^2)} \\
0 + 21x^2 - 20x - 9 \\
\underline{-(21x^2 + 7x)} \\
0 - 27x - 9 \\
\underline{-(-27x - 9)} \\
0
\end{array}
$$

9. Identify the values that make the denominator undefined.

$$\frac{x^2 - 25}{3x^2 + 15x} = \frac{x^2 - 25}{3x(x + 5)}$$

If $3x = 0$ or if $x + 5 = 0$, then the denominator is undefined.

If $3x = 0$, then $x = 0$

If $x + 5 = 0$, then $x = -5$.

Therefore the excluded values are 0 and −5.

10. $2x^4 + 4x^3 - 4x = 2x(x^3 + 2x^2 - 2)$

11. Substitute a value (such as 3) for x. If the value of the x's could be divided out then $\frac{\cancel{3} + 2}{\cancel{3} + 5} = \frac{2}{5}$. However, $\frac{3 + 2}{3 + 5} = \frac{5}{8}$, and $\frac{2}{5} \neq \frac{5}{8}$, so the x's cannot be divided out.

12. The inequality is graphed with a solid line, so only inequalities for *less than or equal* and *greater than or equal* should be considered. The graph has intercepts (−6, 0) and (0, −8) and the test point (0, 0) does not make the inequality true since the plane that includes (0, 0) is not shaded. Only answer choice **A** fits these criteria.

Answer choice **A**

13. The following equations can be written to represent the problem:

$l + d + n = 100\%$

$l = 2d$

$n = 10\% \ l$

Solve for d: $d = \frac{l}{2}$

Substitute into the first equation:

$l + \frac{l}{2} + 0.1l = 100\%$

$1.6l = 100\%$

$l = 62.5\%$

14. a. If T = cost of bats and B = the cost of balls, then

$4T + 9B = 355$

$2T + 12B = 290$

b.

$$T = \frac{\begin{vmatrix} 355 & 9 \\ 290 & 12 \end{vmatrix}}{\begin{vmatrix} 4 & 9 \\ 2 & 12 \end{vmatrix}} = \frac{355(12) - 290(9)}{4(12) - 2(9)}$$

$$= \frac{1650}{30} = 55$$

$$B = \frac{\begin{vmatrix} 4 & 355 \\ 2 & 290 \end{vmatrix}}{\begin{vmatrix} 4 & 9 \\ 2 & 12 \end{vmatrix}} = \frac{4(290) - 2(355)}{4(12) - 2(9)}$$
$$= \frac{450}{30} = 15$$

Each bat costs \$55 and each ball costs \$15.

15. Test a point such as (0, 0) in the shaded region.

$y - x < 2$
$0 - 0 \overset{?}{<} 2$
$0 < 2$ True. (0, 0) is in the solution.

Test a point such as (−4, 0) in the unshaded region.

$y - x < 2$
$0 - (-4) \overset{?}{<} 2$
$4 < 2$ False. (−4, 0) is not in the solution.

Therefore the graph is correct.

16.

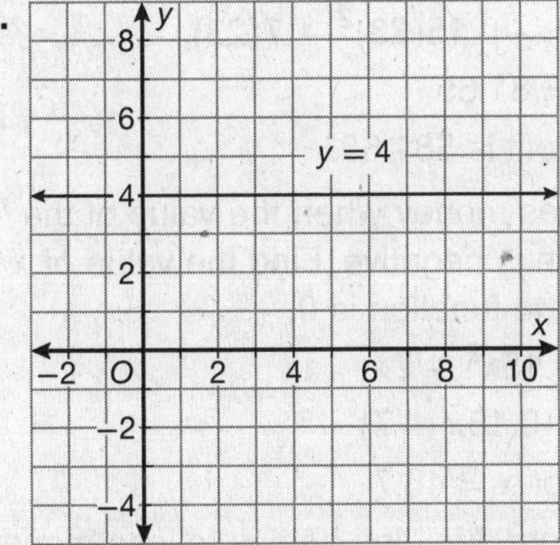

The relation is a function, since for every x-value a unique y-value exists. The graph also passes the vertical line test. The function is continuous.

17. The equation is $x(x + 3) = 180$. Solve for x.

$$x(x + 3) = 180$$
$$x^2 + 3x = 180$$
$$x^2 + 3x - 180 = 0$$
$$(x - 12)(x + 15) = 0$$
$$(x - 12) = \text{ or } (x + 15) = 0$$
$$x = 12 \quad \text{or} \quad x = -15$$

Since the dimension cannot be negative $x = 12$. The maximum length is $12 + 3 = 15$ inches, and the maximum width is 12 inches.

18. a. The factors of −48 are (1)(−48), (2)(−24), (3)(−16), (4)(−12), (6)(−8), (−1)(48), (−2)(24), (−3)(16), (−4)(12), and (−6)(8).

b. $-4 + 12 = 8$

c. $(x - 4)(x + 12)$

19. A reflection over the x-axis produces a graph with the equation $y = -x$. Translating four units up results in $y = -x + 4$.

Answer choice **D**

20. a. $4g + 2f = 22$

$2g + 4f = 26$

b. Solve the systems.

$4g + 2f = 22 \rightarrow \quad 4g + 2f = 22$
$-2(2g + 4f = 26) \rightarrow -4g - 8f = -52$
$-6f = -30$
$f = 5$

$4g + 2(5) = 22$
$4g = 12$
$g = 3$

A pound of granola cost \$3 and a pound of dried fruit cost \$5 individually. Together they cost \$3 + \$5 = \$8.

21.

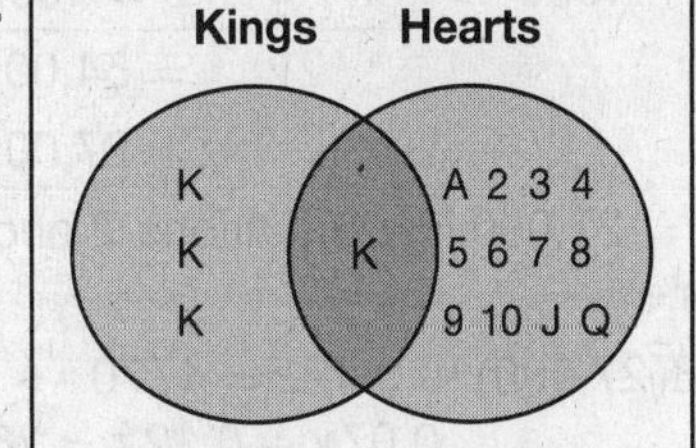

22. $2x = 10$, $3y = 12$, $5z = 50$.

The solution is $x = 5$, $y = 4$, $z = 10$.

23. The student did not multiply by the reciprocal of the divisor. The solution should be

$$\frac{20x^2}{y} \div \frac{y}{x^3} = \frac{20x^2}{y} \cdot \frac{x^3}{y} = \frac{20x^5}{y^2}$$

24. If $2n$ is an even number, then $2n + 1$ is an odd number. The ratio is $\frac{2n+1}{2n}$.

$$\frac{2n+1}{2n} = \frac{2n}{2n} + \frac{1}{2n} = 1 + \frac{1}{2n}$$

25. The equation in vertex form is $y = a(x - h)^2 + k$.

Substituting the values and solving

$200 = a(5 - 3.75)^2 + 225$

$-25 = a(1.5625)$

$-16 = a$

26. Volume $= x(x + 15)(x + 1)$

$= (x^2 + 15x)(x + 1)$

$= x^3 + 16x^2 + 15x.$

Surface area $= 2(x)(x + 15) + 2(x)(x + 1) + 2(x + 15)(x + 1)$

$= 2x^2 + 30x + 2x^2 + 2x + 2x^2 + 32x + 30$

$= 6x^2 + 64x + 30.$

The ratio of volume to surface area is $\frac{x^3 + 16x^2 + 15x}{6x^2 + 64x + 30}$. The numerator and denominator have no factors in common, so the ratio does have a remainder.

27. Let x represent the amount invested at 7%, y represent the amount at 8%, and z represent the amount at 12%. The equations are

$x + y + z = 50{,}000$

$0.07x + 0.08y + 0.12z = 4770$

$y = (x + z) + 4000$

Solve the system.

$x + y + z = 50{,}000 \rightarrow x + y + z = 50{,}000$

$y = (x + z) + 4000 \rightarrow -x + y - z = 4000$

$2y = 54{,}000$

$y = 27{,}000$

Substitute $y = 27{,}000$ into equations 2 and 3 and solve for x.

$0.07x + 0.08(27{,}000) + 0.12z = 4770 \rightarrow 0.07x + 0.12z = 2610$

$27{,}000 = (x + z) + 4000 \rightarrow x + z = 23{,}000$

Solve the resulting equations.

$100(0.07x + 0.12z = 2610) \rightarrow 7x + 12z = 261{,}000$

$-7(x + z = 23{,}000) \rightarrow -7x - 7z = -161{,}000$

$5z = 100{,}000$

$z = 20{,}000$

Substitute $y = 27{,}000$ and $z = 20{,}000$ into one of the original equations.

$x + 27{,}000 + 20{,}000 = 50{,}000$

$x = 3000$

Therefore $3,000 is invested at 7%, $27,000 is invested at 8% and $23,000 is invested at 12%.

28. Convert centimeters to millimeters. There are 10 mm in 1 cm, so there are 150 mm in 15 cm. Let x represent the number of half dollars and y represent the number of dimes.

$2.15x + 1.35y < 150.$

If $x = 30$ and $y = 70$, then

$2.15(30) + 1.35(70) < 150$

$159 < 150$

The statement is false, so 30 half dollars and 70 dimes is not a possibility.

29. a. The maximum is the vertex of the function, and the x-value of the vertex represents the number of animals. The x-value can be found using

$$x = -\frac{b}{2a} = -\frac{7}{2(-0.15)} = 23.\overline{3}$$

He makes the maximum profit for 23 animals.

The profit is $f(x)$, so replace x in the function with 23.

$f(23) = -0.15(23)^2 + 7(23)$

$= 81.65$

The profit is $81.65.

b. He loses money when the value of the function is negative. Find the value of x when the function is 0.

$0 = -0.15x^2 + 7x$

$0 = -x(0.15x - 7)$

$x = 0$ or $x = 46.7$

Therefore, Mr. Jing begins to lose money when he sells 47 animals.

30. The slope of the line parallel to $y = 5x - 3$ has the same slope, 5.

Substitute the slope and point into the slope-intercept equation.

$y - y_1 = m(x - x_1)$

$y - 4 = 5(x - 1)$

$y - 4 = 5x - 5$

$y = 5x - 1$

LESSON 40

Warm Up 40

1. square root

2. $(2x - 5)(2x + 5)$
$= 2x(2x) + 2x(5) + (-5)(2x) + (-5)(5)$
$= 4x^2 + 10x - 10x - 25$
$= 4x^2 - 25$

3. $3x^2 + 5x^3 - 8x^3 + x^2 - 5x^2$
$= -8x^3 + 5x^3 + 3x^2 + x^2 - 5x^2$
$= -3x^3 - x^2$

4. $7^3 \cdot 7^2 = 7^{3+2} = 7^5 = 16{,}807$

5. $(3^2)^3 = 3^{2\times3} = 3^6 = 729$

Lesson Practice 40

a. $\sqrt[3]{-125} = -5$ because $(-5)^3 = -125$.

b. $-\sqrt{9} = -3$ because $-(3^2) = -9$.

c. $\sqrt[5]{-1} = -1$ because $(-1)^5 = -1$.

d. Either multiply and then simplify or simplify and then multiply.
Option 1: $\sqrt{45} \cdot \sqrt{2} = \sqrt{90} = \sqrt{9}\sqrt{10}$
$= 3\sqrt{10}$
Option 2:
$\sqrt{45} \cdot \sqrt{2} = \sqrt{9}\sqrt{5} \cdot \sqrt{2} = 3\sqrt{5} \cdot \sqrt{2}$
$= 3\sqrt{10}$

e. $\sqrt[5]{64} = \sqrt[5]{32} \cdot \sqrt[5]{2}$
Find a factor of 64 that has a root 5.
$= 2\sqrt[5]{2}$
The root of $\sqrt[5]{32}$ is 2.

f. $\sqrt{50} - \sqrt{32} = \sqrt{25} \cdot \sqrt{2} - \sqrt{16} \cdot \sqrt{2}$
$= 5\sqrt{2} - 4\sqrt{2}$
$= \sqrt{2}$

g. $\sqrt{98w^{10}} = \sqrt{49} \cdot \sqrt{2} \cdot w^{\frac{10}{2}} = 7w^5\sqrt{2}$

h. $-\sqrt[4]{y} + 2\sqrt{y} - 7\sqrt[4]{y} - \sqrt{y} = -8\sqrt[4]{y} + \sqrt{y}$

i. $l = \dfrac{8s^2}{\pi^2}$

$l = \dfrac{8\left(\sqrt{2\pi^4} \times \sqrt[4]{2}\right)^2}{\pi^2}$

$l = \dfrac{8 \times 2\pi^4 \times \sqrt{2}}{\pi^2}$

$l = 16\pi^2\sqrt{2}$ feet

Practice 40

1. Solve the inequality for y. Then pick a value for x and solve for y.
$2x - 4y \geq 12$
$-4y \geq -2x + 12$
$y \leq \frac{1}{2}x - 3$
$-4 \leq \frac{1}{2}(-1) - 3$
$-4 \leq -3\frac{1}{2}$ True. $(-1, -4)$ is a solution.
$-3 \leq \frac{1}{2}(0) - 3$
$-3 \leq -3$ True. $(0, -3)$ is a solution.
$-6 \leq \frac{1}{2}(1) - 3$
$-6 \leq -2\frac{1}{2}$ True. $(1, -6)$ is a solution.

x	y
−1	−4
0	−3
1	−6

2. Find the slope of the line. Then substitute the slope and one point into the point-slope formula. Then write in the form $Ax + By = C$.
$m = \dfrac{y_2 - y_1}{x_2 - x_1} = \dfrac{2.5 - 5.5}{-1 - 4} = \dfrac{-3}{-5} = \dfrac{3}{5} = 0.6$
$y - y_1 = m(x - x_1)$
$y - 5.5 = 0.6(x - 4)$
$y - 5.5 = 0.6x - 2.4$
$-0.6x + y = 3.1$
$-10(-0.6x + y) = -10(3.1)$
$6x - 10y = -31$

3. Find the slope of the line. Then substitute the slope and one point into the point-slope formula. Then write in the form $Ax + By = C$.
$m = \dfrac{y_2 - y_1}{x_2 - x_1} = \dfrac{4 - 5}{6 - 3} = -\dfrac{1}{3}$
$y - y_1 = m(x - x_1)$
$y - 5 = -\frac{1}{3}(x - 3)$
$y - 5 = -\frac{1}{3}x + 1$

$\frac{1}{3}x + y = 6$

$3\left(\frac{1}{3}x + y\right) = 3(6)$

$x + 3y = 18$

4. $\sqrt{30} \cdot \sqrt{6} = \sqrt{180} = \sqrt{36} \cdot \sqrt{5} = 6\sqrt{5}$

5. $\sqrt{180} \cdot \sqrt{10} = \sqrt{1800} = \sqrt{900} \cdot \sqrt{2} = 30\sqrt{2}$

6. $5x^2y^2 - 2xy + 10xy^2 = xy(5xy - 2 + 10y)$

7. $x^2y^3m^5 + 12x^3ym^4 - 3x^2y^2m^2 = x^2ym^2(y^2m^3 + 12xm^2 - 3y)$

8. $f(x) \cdot g(x) = \frac{1}{x} \cdot \frac{x^2}{x+4} = \frac{x}{x+4}$

if $x = -2$

$f(x) = \frac{-2}{-2+4} = \frac{-2}{2} = -1$

9. $-x + x^2 = 12$

$x^2 - x - 12 = 0$

$(x - 4)(x + 3) = 0$

$(x - 4) = 0$ or $(x + 3) = 0$

$x = 4$ or $x = -3$

10. $-48x = -2x^2 - x^3$

$x^3 + 2x^2 - 48x = 0$

$x(x^2 + 2x - 48) = 0$

$x(x + 8)(x - 6) = 0$

$x = 0$, $(x + 8) = 0$ or $(x - 6) = 0$

$x = 0 \quad x = -8$, or $\quad x = 6$

11. a. $\sqrt{x \cdot x \cdot x \cdot x \cdot x \cdot x \cdot x \cdot x}$

b. Rewrite each pair of xs as x^2 so the square root can be taken easily: $\sqrt{x^2 \cdot x^2 \cdot x^2 \cdot x^2}$

c. $x \cdot x \cdot x \cdot x = x^4$

12. The student subtracted the exponents in the wrong order. The exponent of the denominator should be subtracted from the exponent in the numerator.

$\frac{x^2}{x^5} = x^{2-5} = x^{-3} = \frac{1}{x^3}$

13. $X = A^{-1}B$

$A^{-1} = \frac{1}{2(4) - 3(3)}\begin{bmatrix} 4 & -3 \\ -3 & 2 \end{bmatrix}$

$= \frac{1}{-1}\begin{bmatrix} 4 & -3 \\ -3 & 2 \end{bmatrix} = \begin{bmatrix} -4 & 3 \\ 3 & -2 \end{bmatrix}$

$A^{-1}B = \begin{bmatrix} -4 & 3 \\ 3 & -2 \end{bmatrix} \cdot \begin{bmatrix} -1 & 2 \\ 5 & 0 \end{bmatrix}$

$= \begin{bmatrix} -4(-1) + 3(5) & -4(2) + 3(0) \\ 3(-1) + (-2)(5) & 3(2) + (-2)(0) \end{bmatrix}$

$= \begin{bmatrix} 19 & -8 \\ -13 & 6 \end{bmatrix}$

Answer choice **A**

14. The original volume is $x(x)(x) = x^3$. The new volume is $x(x)(x + a) = x^3 + ax^2$. The ratio of the new volume to the original volume is $\frac{x^3 + ax^2}{x^3} = \frac{x^2(x + a)}{x^3} = \frac{x + a}{x}$.

15. $\frac{2}{x^2 - 4x - 45} - \frac{1}{x^2 + 9x + 20} = \frac{2}{(x - 9)(x + 5)} - \frac{1}{(x + 4)(x + 5)}$

$= \frac{2}{(x - 9)(x + 5)} \cdot \frac{(x + 4)}{(x + 4)} - \frac{1}{(x + 4)(x + 5)} \cdot \frac{(x - 9)}{(x - 9)}$

$= \frac{2(x + 4)}{(x - 9)(x + 5)(x + 4)} - \frac{1(x - 9)}{(x - 9)(x + 4)(x + 5)} = \frac{2x + 8 - x + 9}{(x - 9)(x + 5)(x + 4)}$

$= \frac{x + 17}{(x - 9)(x^2 + 9x + 20)} = \frac{x + 17}{x^3 - 61x - 180}$

Answer choice **B**

16. Since the outlier is eliminated, there are 9 addends. The denominator should be 9.

$\bar{x} = \frac{12 + 14 + 11 + 15 + 12 + 13 + 15 + 14 + 11}{9} = \frac{117}{9} = 13$

17. Since the slope from the center to (–2, 6) is $-\frac{3}{4}$, the line perpendicular to y_1 crosses (–2, 6). Since a tangent is perpendicular to the circle, then the line crossing (–2, 6) is parallel to y_1.

18. $25x^{12} - 9$. Since the two factors fit the factored form of the difference of two squares, use the formula in reverse by squaring the first and last term of the binomial and using the negative sign.

19. The rate of change (slope) is constant. The slope between points is as follows:

From (−4, 11) to (0, 5), $m = \frac{5 - 11}{0 - (-4)} = -\frac{3}{2}$.

From (0, 5) to (2, 2), $m = \frac{2 - 5}{2 - 0} = -\frac{3}{2}$.

From (2, 2) to (8, −7), $m = \frac{-7 - 2}{8 - 2} = -\frac{3}{2}$.

20. There are $4 \times 3 \times 2 \times 1 = 24$ ways.

21. First write the inequality in slope-intercept form: $y \leq 5x + 1$. Type $5x + 1$ next to *Y*. Move to the left of *Y* and press enter until the symbol shows the lower half of a square shaded. Then press the Graph key. Adjust the viewing window if needed.

22. a. The circumference of the circle is *x*. Substitute *x* for *C* in $C = 2\pi r$ and solve for *r*.

$x = 2\pi r$

$\frac{x}{2\pi} = r$

Substitute $\frac{x}{2\pi}$ for *r* in the area formula for a circle, $A = \pi r^2$.

The expression for area is

$$\pi\left(\frac{x}{2\pi}\right)^2 = \pi\left(\frac{x^2}{4\pi^2}\right) = \frac{x^2}{4\pi}$$

b. The perimeter of the square is *x*. The length of a side is $\frac{x}{4}$. Substitute $\frac{x}{4}$ for *s* in the area formula for a square, $A = s^2$. The expression for area is $\left(\frac{x}{4}\right)^2 = \frac{x^2}{16}$.

c. The numerators of the expressions are the same. The denominator for the area of a circle is less. Therefore the area of the circle is larger. The ratio of the area of the circle to the area of the square is

$$\frac{\frac{x^2}{4\pi}}{\frac{x^2}{16}} = \frac{x^2}{4\pi} \cdot \frac{16}{x^2} = \frac{4}{\pi}.$$

d. The percent is $\frac{4}{\pi} \times 100\% = 127\%$.

23. To find the zero(s) of *f*(*x*), the *x*-intercept(s) of *f*(*x*), and the root(s) of $f(x) = 0$, set the function *f*(*x*) to 0. Therefore all the values are the same.

$0 = x^2 + 12x + 36$

$0 = (x + 6)(x + 6)$

$0 = x + 6$

$-6 = x$

Each value is −6.

24. The vertex is (3, −8).

25. $73\sqrt[4]{625} = 73(5) = 365$

About 365 Calories per day.

26. Let *x* represent the number of hours babysitting and *y* represent the number of hours washing cars. The equations are

$x + y = 20$

$5.50x + 2.75y = 96.25$

Solve the system.

$x + y = 20$

$x = -y + 20$

Substitute $x = -y + 20$ into the second equation

$5.50(-y + 20) + 2.75y = 96.25$

$-5.50y + 110 + 2.75y = 96.25$

$-2.75y = -13.75$

$y = 5$

Substitute $y = 5$ into $x + y = 20$

$x + 5 = 20$

$x = 15$

Angela worked 15 hours babysitting and 5 hours washing cars.

27. Let *x* represent the number of touchdowns with conversions and *y* represent the number of field goals.

$7x + 3y \leq 105$

A solution on the boundary line occurs when $7x + 3y = 105$. So, you can substitute a value for *x* and solve for *y*. A possible solution is 12 touchdowns with conversions and 7 field goals, since $7(12) + 3(7) = 105$.

28. Solve a system of two equations using substitution to calculate the *x*- and *y*-coordinates of one vertex. Repeat with a different pair of equations from the set.

Repeat with the last pair of equations. These will be the three vertices of the triangle.

29. An example can be calculated by choosing a value for x in $-(x^n) = b$, such that x is an odd number and $n > 2$. Examples are $\sqrt[3]{-125} = -5$ and $\sqrt[7]{-1} = -1$.

30. The total delay for x months is $2000x$. Therefore the cumulative delays is $y = 2000x$.

INVESTIGATION 4

1–3.

	A	B	C	D	E
1	A	1		S	=VLOOKUP(D1,$A$1:$B$26,2)
2	B	3		E	
3	C	5		C	
4	D	7		R	
5	E	9		E	
6	F	11		T	
7	G	13		M	
8	H	15		E	
9	I	17		S	
10	J	19		S	
11	K	21		A	
12	L	23		G	
13	M	25		E	
14	N	2			
15	O	4			
16	P	6			
17	Q	8			
18	R	10			
19	S	12			
20	T	14			
21	U	16			
22	V	18			
23	W	20			
24	X	22			
25	Y	24			
26	Z	26			

4. 12 9 5 10 9 14 25 9 12 12 1 13 9

5. a. 8 16 1 7 10 1 14 17 5

b. 1 23 13 9 3 10 1

6. a–c.

	A	B	C	D	E
1	1	A		8	=VLOOKUP(D1,$A$1:$B$26,2)
2	2	N		16	
3	3	B		17	
4	4	O		26	
5	5	C		14	
6	6	P		15	
7	7	D		17	
8	8	Q		12	
9	9	E		11	
10	10	R		10	
11	11	F		17	
12	12	S		7	
13	13	G		1	
14	14	T		24	
15	15	H			
16	16	U			
17	17	I			
18	18	V			
19	19	J			
20	20	W			
21	21	K			
22	22	X			
23	23	L			
24	24	Y			
25	25	M			
26	26	Z			

d. QUIZ THIS FRIDAY

7. 14 4 6 12 9 5 10 9 14 25 9 12 12 1 13 9

8. Write the numbers as columns. Complete the last column with zeros.

$$\begin{bmatrix} 14 & 12 & 10 \\ 4 & 9 & 9 \\ 6 & 5 & 14 \end{bmatrix} \begin{bmatrix} 25 & 12 & 9 \\ 9 & 1 & 0 \\ 12 & 13 & 0 \end{bmatrix}$$

9. $$\begin{bmatrix} 14 & 12 & 10 \\ 4 & 9 & 9 \\ 6 & 5 & 14 \end{bmatrix} \cdot \begin{bmatrix} 1 & -1 & 2 \\ 0 & 0 & -5 \\ 2 & -3 & 2 \end{bmatrix} = \begin{bmatrix} 34 & -44 & -12 \\ 22 & -31 & -19 \\ 34 & -48 & 15 \end{bmatrix}$$

$$\begin{bmatrix} 25 & 12 & 9 \\ 9 & 1 & 0 \\ 12 & 13 & 0 \end{bmatrix} \begin{bmatrix} 1 & -1 & 2 \\ 0 & 0 & -5 \\ 2 & -3 & 2 \end{bmatrix} = \begin{bmatrix} 43 & -52 & 8 \\ 9 & -9 & 13 \\ 12 & -12 & -41 \end{bmatrix}$$

10. Write the numbers in the product matrices as a string of numbers.

34 22 34 −44 −31 −48 −12 −19 15 43 9 12 −52 −9 −12 8 13 −41

11. The matrix product creates a message that cannot be hacked one letter at a time.

12. a. $A = \begin{bmatrix} 1 & -1 & 2 \\ 0 & 0 & -5 \\ 2 & -3 & 2 \end{bmatrix}$

b. $$\begin{bmatrix} 38 & -50 & -8 \\ 39 & -51 & -71 \\ 19 & -20 & -9 \end{bmatrix} \begin{bmatrix} 23 & -28 & -24 \\ 41 & -57 & -10 \\ 37 & -47 & 9 \end{bmatrix} \begin{bmatrix} 9 & -9 & 18 \\ 0 & 0 & 0 \\ 0 & 0 & 0 \end{bmatrix}$$

c. $A^{-1} = \begin{bmatrix} 3 & 0.8 & -1 \\ 2 & 0.4 & -1 \\ 0 & 0.2 & 0 \end{bmatrix}$

$$\begin{bmatrix} 38 & -50 & -8 \\ 39 & -51 & -71 \\ 19 & -20 & -9 \end{bmatrix} \cdot \begin{bmatrix} 3 & 0.8 & -1 \\ 2 & 0.4 & -1 \\ 0 & 0.2 & 0 \end{bmatrix} = \begin{bmatrix} 14 & 12 & 12 \\ 15 & 25 & 12 \\ 17 & 9 & 1 \end{bmatrix}$$

$$\begin{bmatrix} 23 & -28 & -24 \\ 41 & -57 & -10 \\ 37 & -47 & 9 \end{bmatrix} \cdot \begin{bmatrix} 3 & 0.8 & -1 \\ 2 & 0.4 & -1 \\ 0 & 0.2 & 0 \end{bmatrix} = \begin{bmatrix} 13 & 12 & 5 \\ 9 & 12 & 16 \\ 17 & 9 & 10 \end{bmatrix}$$

$$\begin{bmatrix} 9 & -9 & 18 \\ 0 & 0 & 0 \\ 0 & 0 & 0 \end{bmatrix} \cdot \begin{bmatrix} 3 & 0.8 & -1 \\ 2 & 0.4 & -1 \\ 0 & 0.2 & 0 \end{bmatrix} = \begin{bmatrix} 9 & 0 & 0 \\ 0 & 0 & 0 \\ 0 & 0 & 0 \end{bmatrix}$$

d. 14 15 17 12 25 9 12 12 1 13 9 17 12 12 9 5 16 10 9

e. THIS MESSAGE IS SECURE

Investigation Practice

a. $A = \begin{bmatrix} 1 & -1 & 2 \\ 0 & 0 & -5 \\ 2 & -3 & 2 \end{bmatrix}$ and $A^{-1} = \begin{bmatrix} 3 & 0.8 & -1 \\ 2 & 0.4 & -1 \\ 0 & 0.2 & 0 \end{bmatrix}$

Multiply each message matrix by A^{-1}.

$$\begin{bmatrix} 16 & -17 & -30 \\ 25 & -30 & -45 \\ 25 & -29 & -18 \end{bmatrix} \cdot \begin{bmatrix} 3 & 0.8 & -1 \\ 2 & 0.4 & -1 \\ 0 & 0.2 & 0 \end{bmatrix} = \begin{bmatrix} 14 & 12 & 1 \\ 15 & 17 & 5 \\ 17 & 12 & 4 \end{bmatrix}$$

$$\begin{bmatrix} 31 & -43 & -87 \\ 11 & -12 & -25 \\ 33 & -46 & -20 \end{bmatrix} \cdot \begin{bmatrix} 3 & 0.8 & -1 \\ 2 & 0.4 & -1 \\ 0 & 0.2 & 0 \end{bmatrix} = \begin{bmatrix} 7 & 25 & 12 \\ 9 & 9 & 1 \\ 7 & 12 & 13 \end{bmatrix}$$

$$\begin{bmatrix} 9 & -9 & 18 \\ 0 & 0 & 0 \\ 0 & 0 & 0 \end{bmatrix} \cdot \begin{bmatrix} 3 & 0.8 & -1 \\ 2 & 0.4 & -1 \\ 0 & 0.2 & 0 \end{bmatrix} = \begin{bmatrix} 9 & 0 & 0 \\ 0 & 0 & 0 \\ 0 & 0 & 0 \end{bmatrix}$$

Write the partially decrypted message as a string of numbers.

14 15 17 12 17 12 1 5 4 7 9 7 25 9 12 12 1 13 9

Use the decryption spreadsheet to decipher the message.

THIS IS A CODED MESSAGE

b. $A = \begin{bmatrix} 1 & -1 & 2 \\ 0 & 0 & -5 \\ 2 & -3 & 2 \end{bmatrix}$ and $A^{-1} = \begin{bmatrix} 3 & 0.8 & -1 \\ 2 & 0.4 & -1 \\ 0 & 0.2 & 0 \end{bmatrix}$

Multiply each message matrix by A^{-1}.

$$\begin{bmatrix} 38 & -50 & 22 \\ 55 & -75 & 65 \\ 17 & -21 & -34 \end{bmatrix} \cdot \begin{bmatrix} 3 & 0.8 & -1 \\ 2 & 0.4 & -1 \\ 0 & 0.2 & 0 \end{bmatrix} = \begin{bmatrix} 14 & 6 & 12 \\ 15 & 1 & 20 \\ 9 & 12 & 4 \end{bmatrix}$$

$$\begin{bmatrix} 38 & -52 & -12 \\ 27 & -37 & -91 \\ 51 & -68 & 63 \end{bmatrix} \cdot \begin{bmatrix} 3 & 0.8 & -1 \\ 2 & 0.4 & -1 \\ 0 & 0.2 & 0 \end{bmatrix} = \begin{bmatrix} 10 & 12 & 14 \\ 7 & 25 & 10 \\ 17 & 1 & 17 \end{bmatrix}$$

$$\begin{bmatrix} 22 & -22 & 44 \\ 0 & 0 & 0 \\ 0 & 0 & 0 \end{bmatrix} \cdot \begin{bmatrix} 3 & 0.8 & -1 \\ 2 & 0.4 & -1 \\ 0 & 0.2 & 0 \end{bmatrix} = \begin{bmatrix} 22 & 0 & 0 \\ 0 & 0 & 0 \\ 0 & 0 & 0 \end{bmatrix}$$

Write the partially decrypted message as a string of numbers.

14 15 9 6 1 12 12 20 4 10 7 17 12 25 1 14 10 17 22

Use the decryption spreadsheet to decipher the message.

THE PASSWORD IS MATRIX

LESSON 41

Warm Up 41

1. radical
2. $\sqrt{300} = \sqrt{100} \cdot \sqrt{3} = 10\sqrt{3}$
3. $(x-5)^2 = x^2 + (-2)(x)(5) + (-5)^2$
   $= x^2 - 10x + 25$
4. $x^2 + 7x = -10$
   $x^2 + 7x + 10 = 0$
   $(x+5)(x+2) = 0$
   $(x+5) = 0$ or $(x+2) = 0$
   $x = -5$ or $x = -2$

Lesson Practice 41

a. Substitute 14 and 20 for a and b, and 25 for c in $a^2 + b^2 = c^2$.

$a^2 + b^2 = c^2$
$14^2 + 20^2 \stackrel{?}{=} 25^2$
$196 + 400 \stackrel{?}{=} 625$
$596 \neq 625$

The triangle is not a right triangle.

b. Substitute 12 and 16 for a and b, and 20 for c in $a^2 + b^2 = c^2$.

$a^2 + b^2 = c^2$
$12^2 + 16^2 \stackrel{?}{=} 20^2$
$144 + 256 \stackrel{?}{=} 400$
$400 = 400$

The triangle is a right triangle.

c. $a^2 + b^2 = c^2$

$x^2 + 9^2 = 15^2$ Substitute x and 9 for the legs, a and b.
$x^2 + 81 = 225$ Square 9 and 25.
$x^2 = 144$ Subtract 81 from each side.
$x = 12$ Take the square root of both sides.

d. Count the number of units to find the lengths of the legs.

The vertical segment is 15 units long. The horizontal segment is 8 units long.

$a^2 + b^2 = c^2$
$15^2 + 8^2 = y^2$
$225 + 64 = y^2$
$289 = y^2$
$17 = y$

e. The vertical segment is 4 units long. The horizontal segment is 2 units long.

$a^2 + b^2 = c^2$
$4^2 + 2^2 = z^2$
$16 + 4 = z^2$
$20 = z^2$
$\sqrt{20} = z$
$\sqrt{20} = \sqrt{4} \cdot \sqrt{5} = 2\sqrt{5}$

The value of z is exactly $2\sqrt{5}$ units, or about 4.5 units long.

f. Label (6, 9) as (x_1, y_1) and (−18, −1) as (x_2, y_2).

$d = \sqrt{(x_2 - x_1)^2 + (y_2 - y_1)^2}$
$= \sqrt{(-18 - 6)^2 + (-1 - 9)^2}$
$= \sqrt{(-24)^2 + (-10)^2}$
$= \sqrt{576 + 100}$
$= \sqrt{676}$
$= 26$

g. Label (5, −5) as (x_1, y_1) and (9, −11) as (x_2, y_2).

$d = \sqrt{(x_2 - x_1)^2 + (y_2 - y_1)^2}$
$= \sqrt{(9-5)^2 + (-11 - (-5))^2}$
$= \sqrt{4^2 + (-6)^2}$
$= \sqrt{16 + 36}$
$= \sqrt{52}$
$= \sqrt{4}\sqrt{13} = 2\sqrt{13} \approx 7.2$

h. Substitute values into

$d = \sqrt{(x_2 - x_1)^2 + (y_2 - y_1)^2}$
$13 = \sqrt{(6-1)^2 + (-3-k)^2}$
$13 = \sqrt{5^2 + 9 + 6k + k^2}$

$13 = \sqrt{25 + 9 + 6k + k^2}$

$13 = \sqrt{34 + 6k + k^2}$

Solve $13 = \sqrt{34 + 6k + k^2}$ by factoring.

$169 = 34 + 6k + k^2$ Square both sides of the equation.

$0 = k^2 + 6k - 135$ Make one side zero.

$0 = (k - 9)(k + 15)$ Factor the trinomial.

$(k - 9) = 0$ or $(k + 15) = 0$ Solve.

$k = 9$ or $k = -15$

i. $d = \sqrt{(x_2 - x_1)^2 + (y_2 - y_1)^2}$

$= \sqrt{(225 - 200)^2 + (287 - 205)^2}$

$= \sqrt{25^2 + 82^2}$

$= \sqrt{625 + 6724}$

$= \sqrt{7349}$

≈ 86

The distance between Silver City and Los Alamos is about 86 kilometers.

Practice 41

1. $d = \sqrt{(x_2 - x_1)^2 + (y_2 - y_1)^2}$

$= \sqrt{(3 - (-3))^2 + (0 - 8)^2}$

$= \sqrt{6^2 + (-8)^2}$

$= \sqrt{36 + 64}$

$= \sqrt{100}$

$= 10$

2. $d = \sqrt{(x_2 - x_1)^2 + (y_2 - y_1)^2}$

$= \sqrt{(13 - (-1))^2 + (6 - (-1))^2}$

$= \sqrt{14^2 + 7^2}$

$= \sqrt{196 + 49}$

$= \sqrt{245}$

≈ 15.65

3. Perpendicular lines have slopes that are the opposite reciprocal of each another. The line for $y = \frac{1}{3}x - 1$ has slope $\frac{1}{3}$. The line that is perpendicular will have a slope of -3. Substitute the point $(2, -3)$ and slope, -3, into the point-slope formula.

$y - (-3) = -3(x - 2)$

$y + 3 = -3x + 6$

$y = -3x + 3$

4. $3\sqrt{3} \cdot 4\sqrt{12} - 5\sqrt{300}$

$= 12\sqrt{36} - 5\sqrt{300}$

$= 12(6) - 5\sqrt{100}\sqrt{3}$

$= 12(6) - 50\sqrt{3}$

$= 72 - 50\sqrt{3}$

5. $4\sqrt{3}\,(2\sqrt{3} - \sqrt{6})$

$= 4\sqrt{3} \cdot 2\sqrt{3} - 4\sqrt{3} \cdot \sqrt{6}$

$= 24 - 4\sqrt{18}$

$= 24 - 4\sqrt{9}\sqrt{2}$

$= 24 - 12\sqrt{2}$

6. $2 + \frac{1}{x} = 2 \cdot \frac{x}{x} + \frac{1}{x}$

$= \frac{2x}{x} + \frac{1}{x}$

$= \frac{2x + 1}{x}$

7. $\frac{5x^2}{y} + p^2 - \frac{3x}{py} = \frac{5x^2}{y} \cdot \frac{p}{p} + p^2 \cdot \frac{py}{py} - \frac{3x}{py}$

$= \frac{5x^2p}{py} + \frac{p^3y}{py} - \frac{3x}{py}$

$= \frac{5x^2p + p^3y - 3x}{py}$

8. Parallel lines have the same slope. The line for $y = -\frac{3}{7}x + 4$ has slope $-\frac{3}{7}$. The line that is parallel will also have a slope of $-\frac{3}{7}$. Substitute the point $(2, 2)$ and slope, $-\frac{3}{7}$, into the point-slope formula.

$y - 2 = -\frac{3}{7}(x - 2)$

$y - 2 = -\frac{3}{7}x - (-\frac{3}{7})(2)$

$y - 2 = -\frac{3}{7}x + \frac{6}{7}$

$y = -\frac{3}{7}x + \frac{20}{7}$

9. $xy^{-2}\left(\frac{x^0y^2}{x} - \frac{3x^0y^2}{x^2}\right)$

$= xy^{-2} \cdot \frac{x^0y^2}{x} - xy^{-2} \cdot \frac{3x^0y^2}{x^2}$

$= 1 - 3x^{-1}$

10. $\frac{xy^{-2}}{p^2}\left(\frac{p^2y^2}{x}+\frac{5x^2y^3}{p^{-2}}\right)$

$=\frac{xy^{-2}}{p^2}\cdot\frac{p^2y^2}{x}+\frac{xy^{-2}}{p^2}\cdot\frac{5x^2y^3}{p^{-2}}$

$=1+5x^3y$

11. The area is s^2. The perimeter is $4s$. The area to perimeter ratio is

$\frac{s^2}{4s}=\frac{s}{4}$

If the length of each side is 330 miles, then the ratio is

$\frac{s}{4}=\frac{300}{4}=75$

12. The distance from the pier for each boat is the hypotenuse of a right triangle with legs equal to 4 units and 6 units.

$c^2=a^2+b^2$

$=4^2+6^2$

$=16+36$

$=52$

$c=\sqrt{52}=\sqrt{4}\cdot\sqrt{13}=2\sqrt{13}\approx 7.2$

Each boat is $2\sqrt{13}$ units or about 7.2 units from the pier. So, the boats are $2\sqrt{13}+2\sqrt{13}=4\sqrt{13}$ or 14.4 units apart. Since each unit is 2.5 miles, the distance is about $2.5\times 14.4=36$ miles.

13 a. An equation in the form $y=a(x-h)^2+k$ has vertex at (h, k). The given equation in this form is $y=1(x-(-3))^2+(-5)$. Therefore, the vertex is $(-3, -5)$. An equation in standard form $y=ax^2+bx+c$ has its axis of symmetry at $x=-\frac{b}{2a}$. The standard form of the given equation is $y=x^2+6x+4$. The axis of symmetry is $x=-\frac{6}{2(1)}=-3$.

b. Substitute $x=-6$ to find y.

$y=(-6+3)^2-5$

$y=9-5=4$

Substitute $x=-5$ to find y.

$y=(-5+3)^2-5$

$y=4-5=-1$

Substitute $x=-4$ to find y.

$y=(-4+3)^2-5$

$y=1-5=-4$

c. For $x=-2$, $y=-4$, for $x=-1$, $y=-1$, and for $x=0$, $y=4$.

14. $\frac{\sqrt{V}}{\sqrt{\pi h}}=\frac{\sqrt{V}}{\sqrt{\pi h}}\cdot\frac{\sqrt{\pi h}}{\sqrt{\pi h}}=\frac{\sqrt{V\pi h}}{\pi h}$

15. There are 10 possible digits (0 to 9) to occupy each of the three spaces in a three-digit number. Therefore, there are $10\times 10\times 10$, or 1000 possible three-digit passwords. Answer choice **D**

16. If $\frac{f(x)}{g(x)}$ has a zero remainder, then $\frac{f(x)}{g(x)}$ has the degree $m-n$.

17. The student factored incorrectly. The correct solution is as follows:

$(x^2-16)=0$

$(x-4)(x+4)=0$

$(x-4)=0$ or $(x+4)=0$

$x=4$ or $x=-4$

18.

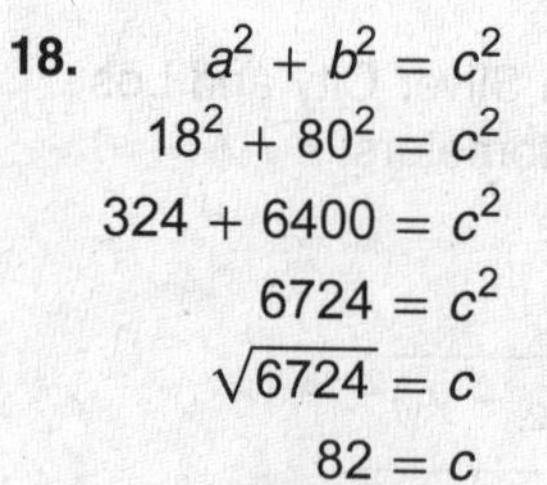

$a^2+b^2=c^2$

$18^2+80^2=c^2$

$324+6400=c^2$

$6724=c^2$

$\sqrt{6724}=c$

$82=c$

The hypotenuse is 82 mm.

Answer choice **B**

19. Plot the points $(-2, -5)$, $(0, -2)$, $(2, 1)$, and $(4, 4)$. Then draw a straight line that continues through the points.

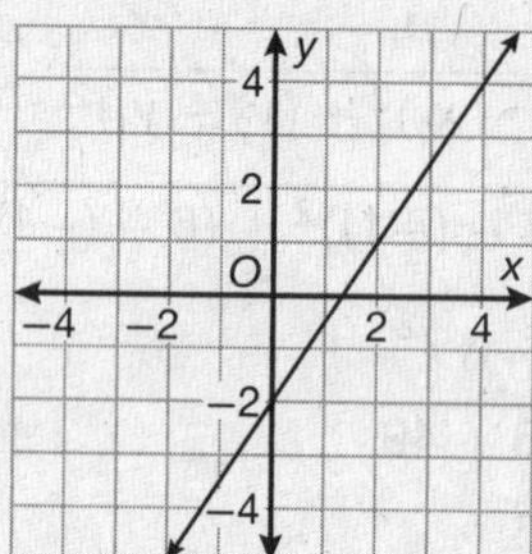

20. It is a good test point because it makes the math quicker and easier, and less prone to errors. It cannot be used when it is on the boundary line.

21. The roots are about −9 and 9.

22. Let x represent the amount of almonds, y represent the amount of cashews, and z represent the amount of pecans in the mix. The equation for the amount of each in the mix is $x + y + z = 1$

The equation for amount of protein is $0.13x + 0.09y + 0.05z = \frac{86}{1000}$

The equation for cost is $15x + 18y + 19z = 17.7$

The simplified system of equations is

$x + y + z = 1$

$0.13x + 0.09y + 0.05z = 0.086$

$15x + 18y + 19z = 17.7$

The system as a matrix equation is

$$\begin{bmatrix} 1 & 1 & 1 \\ 0.13 & 0.09 & 0.05 \\ 15 & 18 & 19 \end{bmatrix} \begin{bmatrix} x \\ y \\ z \end{bmatrix} = \begin{bmatrix} 1 \\ 0.086 \\ 17.7 \end{bmatrix}$$

$$X = A^{-1}B = \begin{bmatrix} 10.125 & -12.5 & -0.5 \\ -21.5 & 50 & 1 \\ 12.375 & -37.5 & -0.5 \end{bmatrix} \begin{bmatrix} 1 \\ 0.056 \\ 17.7 \end{bmatrix}$$

$$= \begin{bmatrix} 0.2 \\ 0.5 \\ 0.3 \end{bmatrix}$$

$x = 0.2$, $y = 0.5$, $z = 0.3$.

There are 0.2 kg of almonds, 0.5 kg of cashews, and 0.3 kg of pecans in the mix.

23. Let x represent the number of \$5 tickets, y represent the number of \$7 tickets, and z represent the number of \$10 tickets.

The equation for the total number of tickets sold is $x + y + z = 350$.

The equation for the income is $5x + 7y + 10z = 2665$.

The equation comparing the number of tickets sold is $6x = y + z$, or $-6x + y + z = 0$.

The system of equations is

$x + y + z = 350$

$5x + 7y + 10z = 2665$

$-6x + y + z = 0$

Eliminate x in the first and second equations, and in the first and third equations.

$-5(x + y + z = 350) \rightarrow$
$$-5x - 5y - 5z = -1750$$

$5x + 7y + 10z = 2665 \rightarrow$
$$\underline{5x + 7y + 10z = 2665}$$
$$2y + 5z = 915$$

$6(x + y + z = 350) \rightarrow 6x + 6y + 6z = 2100$

$-6x + y + z = 0 \rightarrow \underline{-6x + y + z = 0}$
$$7y + 7z = 2100$$

Solve the resulting system.

$-7(2y + 5z = 915) \rightarrow -14y - 35z = -6405$

$2(7y + 7z = 2100) \rightarrow \underline{14y + 14z = 4200}$
$$-21z = -2205$$
$$z = 105$$

Substitute $z = 105$ into $2y + 5z = 915$ to find y.

$2y + 5(105) = 915$

$2y = 390$

$y = 195$

Substitute $z = 105$ and $y = 195$ into $x + y + z = 350$ to find x.

$x + 195 + 105 = 350$

$x + 300 = 350$

$x = 50$

Therefore, 50 \$5 tickets, 195 \$7 tickets, and 105 \$10 tickets are sold.

24. Any number divided by itself is 1, so the expression is really being multiplied by 1. Multiplying the expression by 1 does not change the value of the expression.

$$\frac{3}{\sqrt{5}} \cdot \frac{\sqrt{5}}{\sqrt{5}} = \frac{3}{\sqrt{5}} \cdot 1 = \frac{3}{\sqrt{5}}.$$

25. The acceleration of satellite 1 is $\frac{v^2}{r}$. The acceleration of satellite 2 is $\frac{v^2}{\frac{4}{5}r} = \frac{5v^2}{4r}$.

The difference is

$$\frac{5v^2}{4r} - \frac{v^2}{r}$$
$$= \frac{5v^2}{4r} - \frac{v^2}{r} \cdot \frac{4}{4}$$
$$= \frac{5v^2}{4r} - \frac{4v^2}{4r}$$
$$= \frac{v^2}{4r}$$

26. The mean is

$$\bar{x} = \frac{1.80 + 0.89 + 7.54 + 2.89 + 5.28 + 3.18 + 0.48 + 0.22 + 3.00 + 3.93 + 1.29 + 4.20}{12}$$

$$= \frac{34.7}{12} \approx 2.89$$

The standard deviation is

$$\sigma^2 = \frac{(1.80 - 2.89)^2 + (0.89 - 2.89)^2 + (7.54 - 2.89)^2 + (2.89 - 2.89)^2 + (5.28 - 2.89)^2 + (3.18 - 2.89)^2}{12}$$

$$+ \frac{(0.48 - 2.89)^2 + (0.22 - 2.89)^2 + (3.00 - 2.89)^2 + (3.93 - 2.89)^2 + (1.29 - 2.89)^2 + (4.20 - 2.89)^2}{12}$$

$$\sigma \approx \sqrt{\frac{50.9136}{12}} \approx 2.06$$

27. The student wrote the formula incorrectly. There should be a plus sign between the two quantities that are squared.

$d = \sqrt{(8 - 7)^2 + (-5 - 2)^2}$

$= \sqrt{1^2 + (-7)^2}$

$= \sqrt{1 + 49}$

$= \sqrt{50}$

$= 5\sqrt{2}$

28. The standard form of a linear equation is $Ax + By = C$. The equation is in standard form since π is a real number and a part of the coefficient of x.

29.

s	t	$\neg t$	$s \wedge \neg t$
T	T	F	F
T	F	T	T
F	T	F	F
F	F	T	F

30. The graph is a vertical set of points. Therefore, the graph is discrete and discontinuous.

LAB 7

Lab Practice

a. 3,991,680

b. 9240

c. 792

d. 1540

LESSON 42

Warm Up 42

1. event
2. {1, 2, 3, 4, 5, 6}
3. {HH, HT, TH, TT}
4. The outcome of one does not depend on the other. Therefore, the events are independent.
5. $3 \times 2 \times 4 = 24$ outfits.

Lesson Practice 42

a. $6! = 6 \times 5 \times 4 \times 3 \times 2 \times 1 = 720$

b. $\frac{6!}{4!(6 - 4)!} = \frac{6!}{4!2!} = \frac{6 \times 5 \times \cancel{4!}}{\cancel{4!}2!} = \frac{6 \times 5}{2}$

$= \frac{30}{2} = 15$

c. $7! = 7 \times 6 \times 5 \times 4 \times 3 \times 2 \times 1 = 5040$

d. $P(12,3) = \frac{12!}{(12 - 3)!} = \frac{12!}{9!}$

$= \frac{12 \times 11 \times 10 \times \cancel{9!}}{\cancel{9!}} = 1320$

e. OHIO has 4 letters with O repeated 2 times. Therefore $n = 4$ and $q_1 = 2$.

The distinguishable permutations can be found using $\frac{n!}{q_1!}$.

$\frac{4!}{2!} = \frac{4 \times 3 \times \cancel{2!}}{\cancel{2!}} = 12$

f. $C(10,7) = \frac{10!}{7!(10 - 7)!} = \frac{10!}{7!3!}$

$= \frac{10 \times 9 \times 8 \times \cancel{7!}}{\cancel{7!}3!} = 120$

g. $C(4,1) \times C(4,2) = \frac{4!}{1!(4-1)!} \times \frac{4!}{2!(4-2)!}$

$= \frac{4 \times \cancel{3!}}{1!\cancel{3!}} \times \frac{4 \times 3 \times \cancel{2!}}{2!\cancel{2!}}$

$= \frac{4}{1} \times \frac{12}{2}$

$= 24$

h. This is a combination problem because order does not make a difference. The 4 cards drawn give the same hand no matter what order they are drawn in.

$C(52,4) = \frac{52!}{4!(52-4)!}$

$= \frac{52!}{4!48!} = \frac{52 \times 51 \times 50 \times 49 \times \cancel{48!}}{4!\cancel{48!}}$

$= 270{,}725$

i. This is a permutation problem because order makes a difference. For example, picking and playing an ace before a queen is different than picking and playing a queen before an ace.

$P(52, 4) = \frac{52!}{(52-4)!} = \frac{52!}{48!}$

$= \frac{52 \times 51 \times 50 \times 49 \times \cancel{48!}}{\cancel{48!}} = 6{,}497{,}400$

j. Since order matters this is a permutation problem. There are 10 colors. Blue repeats 3 times, red repeats 2 times, and green repeats 5 times. Therefore $n = 10$ and $q_1 = 3$, $q_2 = 2$, and $q_3 = 5$.
The permutations can be found using $\frac{n!}{q_1!q_2!q_3!}$.

$\frac{10!}{3!2!5!} = \frac{10 \times 9 \times 8 \times 7 \times 6 \times \cancel{5!}}{3!2!\cancel{5!}}$

$= \frac{30{,}240}{12} = 2520$

Practice 42

1. There are 5280 feet in one mile and 12 inches in one foot.

$\frac{32\ \cancel{mi}^3}{1} \times \frac{5280\ \cancel{ft}}{1\ \cancel{mi}} \times \frac{5280\ \cancel{ft}}{1\ \cancel{mi}} \times \frac{5280\ \cancel{ft}}{1\ \cancel{mi}} \times \frac{12\ in.}{1\ \cancel{ft}} \times \frac{12\ in.}{1\ \cancel{ft}} \times \frac{12\ in.}{1\ \cancel{ft}}$

$= \frac{32(5280)(5280)(5280)(12)(12)(12)\ in.^3}{1}$

$\approx 8.14 \times 10^{15}\ in.^3$

2. There are 5280 feet in one mile.

$\frac{10\ \cancel{mi}^2}{1} \times \frac{5280\ ft}{1\ \cancel{mi}} \times \frac{5280\ ft}{1\ \cancel{mi}} = \frac{10(5280)(5280)\ ft^2}{1} = 278{,}784{,}000$

3. Substitute the slope, -1, and point (4,5.5) into the point slope formula, $y - y_1 = m(x - x_1)$, where m is the slope and the coordinates of the point is (x_1, y_1). Then simplify.

$y - 5.5 = -1(x - 4)$

$y - 5.5 = -x + 4$

$y = -x + 9.5$

4. Substitute the slope, 1.8, and point (−10,0) into the point slope formula.

$y - 0 = 1.8(x - (-10)$

$y = 1.8x + 18$

5. $d = \sqrt{(4-(-2))^2 + (6-2)^2}$

$= \sqrt{6^2 + 4^2}$

$= \sqrt{36 + 16}$

$= \sqrt{52}$

$= 2\sqrt{13}$

6. $d = \sqrt{(5 - (-3))^2 + (2 - 2)^2}$
$= \sqrt{8^2 + 0^2} = \sqrt{64}$
$= 8$

7. $P(5,3) = \frac{5!}{(5-3)!} = \frac{5!}{2!} = \frac{5 \times 4 \times 3 \times \cancel{2!}}{\cancel{2!}} = 60$

8. $C(8,4) = \frac{8!}{4!(8-4)!}$
$= \frac{8!}{4!4!} = \frac{8 \times 7 \times 6 \times 5 \times \cancel{4!}}{4!\cancel{4!}} = 70$

9. $11! = 11 \times 10 \times 9 \times 8 \times 7 \times 6 \times 5 \times 4 \times 3 \times 2 \times 1 = 39{,}916{,}800$

10. $\frac{1}{x+1} + \frac{1}{x+2} + \frac{1}{x+3}$
$= \frac{1}{x+1} \cdot \frac{(x+2)(x+3)}{(x+2)(x+3)} + \frac{1}{x+2} \cdot \frac{(x+1)(x+3)}{(x+1)(x+3)} + \frac{1}{x+3} \cdot \frac{(x+1)(x+2)}{(x+1)(x+2)}$
$= \frac{(x+2)(x+3)}{(x+1)(x+2)(x+3)} + \frac{(x+1)(x+3)}{(x+1)(x+2)(x+3)} + \frac{(x+1)(x+2)}{(x+1)(x+2)(x+3)}$
$= \frac{x^2 + 5x + 6}{(x+1)(x+2)(x+3)} + \frac{x^2 + 4x + 3}{(x+1)(x+2)(x+3)} + \frac{x^2 + 3x + 2}{(x+1)(x+2)(x+3)}$
$= \frac{x^2 + 5x + 6 + x^2 + 4x + 3 + x^2 + 3x + 2}{(x+1)(x+2)(x+3)}$
$= \frac{3x^2 + 12x + 11}{(x^2 + 3x + 2)(x+3)} = \frac{3x^2 + 12x + 11}{x^3 + 6x^2 + 11x + 6}$

11. $\frac{1}{1 + \frac{1}{x+1}} + \frac{1}{1 + \frac{1}{x-1}} = \frac{1}{1 \cdot \frac{x+1}{x+1} + \frac{1}{x+1}} + \frac{1}{1 \cdot \frac{x-1}{x-1} + \frac{1}{x-1}}$
$= \frac{1}{\frac{x+1}{x+1} + \frac{1}{x+1}} + \frac{1}{\frac{x-1}{x-1} + \frac{1}{x-1}}$
$= \frac{1}{\frac{x+2}{x+1}} + \frac{1}{\frac{x}{x-1}}$
$= \frac{x+1}{x+2} + \frac{x-1}{x}$
$= \frac{x+1}{x+2} \cdot \frac{x}{x} + \frac{x-1}{x} \cdot \frac{x+2}{x+2}$
$= \frac{x^2 + x + x^2 + x - 2}{x(x+2)} = \frac{2x^2 + 2x - 2}{x(x+2)}$

12. Solve by eliminating x terms.
$-2(2x + 3y = 13) \rightarrow -4x - 6y = -26$
$4x - 9y = -79 \rightarrow \underline{4x - 9y = -79}$
$-15y = -105$
$y = 7$

Substitute for y

$2x + 3(7) = 13$

$2x = -8$

$x = -4$

The solution is $(-4, 7)$.

Solve by eliminating y terms.

$3(2x + 3y = 13) \rightarrow 6x + 9y = 39$

$4x - 9y = -79 \rightarrow 4x - 9y = -79$

$10x = -40$

$x = -4$

Substitute for x

$2(-4) + 3y = 13$

$3y = 21$

$y = 7$

The solution is $(-4, 7)$.

13. Since order matters this is a permutation problem. There are 10 dogs of which beagle repeats 3 times, poodle repeats 2 times, and grey hound repeats 5 times. Therefore $n = 10$, $q_1 = 3$, $q_2 = 2$, and $q_3 = 5$.

The permutations can be found using $\frac{n!}{q_1!q_2!q_3!}$.

$$\frac{10!}{3!2!5!} = \frac{10 \times 9 \times 8 \times 7 \times 6 \times \not{5}!}{3!2!\not{5}!} = \frac{30{,}240}{12}$$

$= 2520$

14. The student used $\frac{1}{ad - cb}\begin{bmatrix} -a & c \\ b & -d \end{bmatrix}$

instead of $\frac{1}{ad - cb}\begin{bmatrix} d & -b \\ -c & a \end{bmatrix}$. The correct inverse is

$$A^{-1} = \frac{1}{1(-3) - 2(1)}\begin{bmatrix} -3 & -1 \\ -2 & 1 \end{bmatrix}$$

$$= \frac{1}{-5}\begin{bmatrix} -3 & -1 \\ -2 & 1 \end{bmatrix}$$

$$= \begin{bmatrix} 0.6 & 0.2 \\ 0.4 & -0.2 \end{bmatrix}$$

15. a. Substitute each value of x in the table into $f(x) = x^3 - 4x - 2$ to find $f(x)$.

$f(x) = (-2)^3 - 4(-2) - 2 = -2$

$f(x) = (-1)^3 - 4(-1) - 2 = 1$

$f(x) = (0)^3 - 4(0) - 2 = -2$

$f(x) = (1)^3 - 4(1) - 2 = -5$

$f(x) = (2)^3 - 4(2) - 2 = -2$

$f(x) = (3)^3 - 4(3) - 2 = 13$

x	−2	−1	0	1	2	3
$f(x)$	−2	1	−2	−5	−2	13

b. The x-intercepts occur when $f(x) = 0$. The table shows that this occurs between $x = -2$ and $x = -1$, between $x = -1$ and $x = 0$, and between $x = 2$ and $x = 3$.

16. In permutations order matters. There are 6 two-letter permutations: AB, BA, AC, CA, BC, and CB. In combinations order does not matter. There are 3 two-letter combinations AB, AC, and BC.

17.

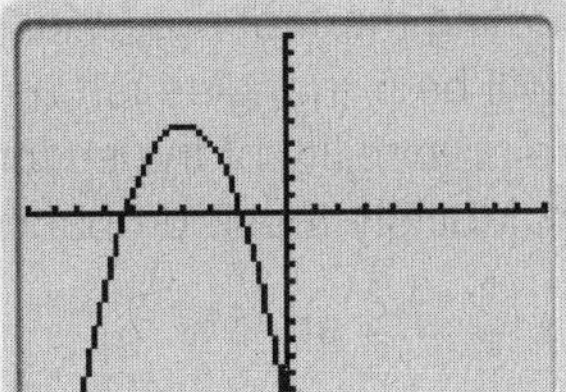

The graph of $f(x) -x^2 - 8x - 11$ opens downward, and it is shifted 4 units to the left and 5 units up compared to the parent function.

18. x-intercept(s) occur when $f(x) = 0$.

$0 = x^2 + 2x + 1$

$0 = (x + 1)(x + 1)$

$x = -1$

Answer choice **A**

19. Substitute values into $a^2 + b^2 = c^2$ to determine which triangles are right triangles

$30^2 + 72^2 \stackrel{?}{=} 78^2$

$900 + 5184 \stackrel{?}{=} 6084$

$6084 = 6084$

The 30, 72, 80 triangle is a right triangle.

$24^2 + 45^2 \stackrel{?}{=} 51^2$

$576 + 2025 \stackrel{?}{=} 2601$

$2601 = 2601$

The 24, 45, 51 triangle is a right triangle.

$12^2 + 18^2 \stackrel{?}{=} 20^2$

$144 + 324 \stackrel{?}{=} 400$

$468 \neq 400$

The 12, 18, 20 triangle is not a right triangle.

$25^2 + 60^2 \stackrel{?}{=} 65^2$

$625 + 3600 \stackrel{?}{=} 4225$

$4225 = 4225$

The 25, 60, 65 triangle is a right triangle.

$9^2 + 40^2 \stackrel{?}{=} 41^2$

$81 + 1600 \stackrel{?}{=} 1681$

$1681 = 1681$

The 9, 40, 41 triangle is a right triangle.

$14^2 + 50^2 \stackrel{?}{=} 54^2$

$196 + 2500 \stackrel{?}{=} 2916$

$2696 \neq 2916$

The 14, 50, 54 triangle is not a right triangle. So, 4 of the 6 are right triangles. The probability of selecting the first right triangle is $\frac{4}{6}$. Then there will be 5 triangles left and 3 are right, so the probability of the second right triangle is $\frac{3}{5}$. Multiply these probabilities.

Probability $= \frac{4}{6} \times \frac{3}{5} = \frac{2}{5}$ or 40%.

20. It indicates whether the boundary line should be solid or dashed. It does not indicate which half of the plane to shade.

21. $\frac{3x^2 + 6x + 3}{x^2 - 3x - 4} = \frac{(3x + 3)\cancel{(x + 1)}}{(x - 4)\cancel{(x + 1)}} = \frac{3(x + 1)}{(x - 4)}$

Answer choice **C**

22. $d = \sqrt{(x_2 - x_1)^2 + (y_2 - y_1)^2}$

$= \sqrt{(146 - 132)^2 + (72 - 4)^2}$

$= \sqrt{14^2 + 68^2}$

$= \sqrt{196 + 4624}$

$= \sqrt{4820}$

≈ 69

The distance between Hamilton and Missoula is about 69 kilometers.

23. a. $\frac{16t^2 + 32t}{t} = \frac{\cancel{t}(16t + 32)}{\cancel{t}} = 16t + 32$

b. Substitute 2 seconds for t.

$16(2) + 32 = 64$

The average velocity is 64 feet per second.

24. Student A incorrectly added the squared terms.

25.

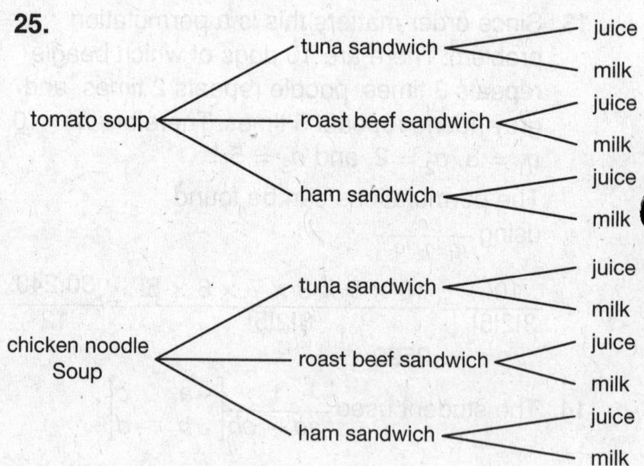

There are 12 possible lunches.

26. a. $y = -5x + 2z - 18 \rightarrow \quad 5x + y - 2z = -18$

$-6x = 2y - 3z + 23 \rightarrow \quad -6x - 2y + 3z = 23$

$z = -10 - 4x + y \rightarrow \quad 4x - y + z = -10$

b. There should be one solution, since no two equations are multiples of each other in any way

c. Eliminate y in the first and second equations, and in the first and third equations.

$2(5x + y - 2z = -18) \rightarrow \quad 10x + 2y - 4z = -36$

$-6x - 2y + 3z = 23 \rightarrow \quad \underline{-6x - 2y + 3z = 23}$

$4x \quad - z = -13$

$5x + y - 2z = -18$

$\underline{4x - y + z = -10}$

$9x \quad - z = -28$

Solve the resulting system.

$$-(4x - z = -13) \rightarrow \quad -4x + z = 13$$
$$9x - z = -28 \rightarrow \quad \underline{9x - z = -28}$$
$$5x \quad = -15$$
$$x = -3$$

Substitute for x

$9(-3) - z = -28$

$z = 1$

Substitute $x = -3$ and $z = 1$ into one of the original equations.

$4(-3) - y + (1) = -10$

$-y = 1$

$y = -1$

The solution is $(-3, -1, 1)$.

27. $F = \frac{9}{5}C + 32$

$F - 32 = \frac{9}{5}C + 32 - 32$

$F - 32 = \frac{9}{5}C$

$\frac{5}{9}(F - 32) = \left(\frac{9}{5} \cdot \frac{5}{9}\right)C$

$\frac{5}{9}(F - 32) = C$

The slope of one graph is $\frac{5}{9}$ and the slope of the other is $\frac{9}{5}$. The slopes are not the same, so the lines are not parallel. The slopes are not the opposite reciprocal of each other, so the lines are not perpendicular.

28. a. Only $-4\sqrt{5}$ and $\sqrt{5}$ have the same number or expression under the radical sign. Therefore $-4\sqrt{5}$ and $\sqrt{5}$ are like radicals.

b. $4\sqrt[3]{5k} - 4\sqrt{5} + \sqrt[3]{4k} + \sqrt{5}$
$= 4\sqrt[3]{5k} - 3\sqrt{5} + \sqrt[3]{4k}$

29. The lines $y = \frac{3}{4}x + 2$ and $y = \frac{3}{4}x - 1$, each have a slope of $\frac{3}{4}$, but different y-intercepts, so they are parallel but do not coincide. They are neither horizontal nor vertical. The lines $y = 6$ and $y = 2$ are both horizontal lines with a slope of zero, but have different y-intercepts, so they are parallel but do not coincide. Therefore, the lines form a quadrilateral that is a parallelogram.

30. Sample answer.

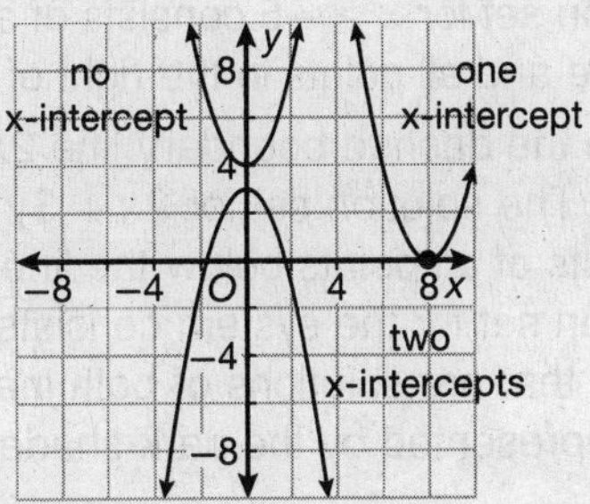

LESSON 43

Warm Up 43

1. solution

2. Substitute 3 for x and 5 for y to determine if the inequality is true.

$2(3) + 5 \overset{?}{>} 10$

$11 > 10$

The inequality is true. Therefore (3, 5) is a solution.

3. Substitute -1 for x and 4 for y to determine if the inequality is true.

$-3(-1) + 2(4) \overset{?}{\leq} 11$

$11 \leq 11$

The inequality is true. Therefore $(-1, 4)$ is a solution.

Lesson Practice 43

a. Substitute the ordered pairs for x and y.

Substitute $(-5, 0)$.

$x \geq -5 \rightarrow \quad -5 \geq -5$ true

$2x + 3y < -3 \rightarrow \quad 2(-5) + 3(0) < -3$

$-10 < -3$ true

Therefore, $(-5, 0)$ is a solution.

Substitute $(-6, 0)$.

$x \geq -5 \rightarrow \quad -6 \geq -5$ false

$2x + 3y < -3 \rightarrow \quad 2(-6) + 3(0) < -3$

$-12 < -3$ true

Therefore, $(-6, 0)$ is not a solution.

Substitute $(1, -2)$.

$x \geq -5 \rightarrow \quad 1 \geq -5$ true

$2x + 3y < -3 \rightarrow \quad 2(1) + 3(-2) < -3$

$-4 < -3$ true

Therefore, $(1, -2)$ is a solution.

b. Graph the solid boundary line $x = -5$. The solution set for $x \geq -5$ consists of all points on the line and all points to the right of the line. Graph the dashed boundary line $2x + 3y = -3$. The solution set for $2x + 3y < -3$ consists of all points below the line. The solution set for the system consists of all points that are solutions of both inequalities. It is represented by the dark shaded region.

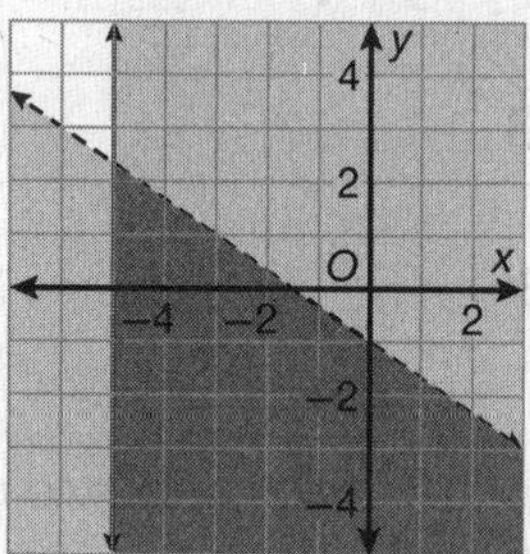

c. Graph the dashed boundary line $y = -x - 2$. The solution set for $y > -x - 2$ consists of all points above the line.
Graph the dashed boundary line $x + y = 3$. The solution set for $x + y < 3$ consists of all points below the line. The boundary lines are parallel. The solution set for the system consists of all points between the boundary lines.

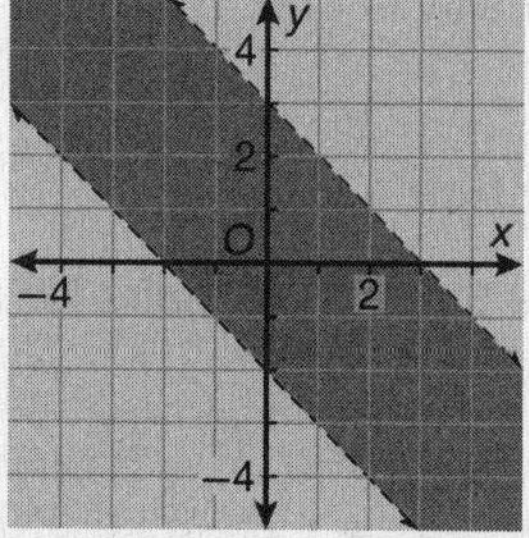

d. The equations of the boundary lines must be entered in the form $y = mx + b$, so solve $3x + 4y \leq 4$ to get $y = -\frac{3}{4}x + 4$ and $y = -\frac{3}{4}x + 1$. Enter these and then use the SHADE feature to shade the appropriate half-plane for each inequality. The graph of $y \geq -\frac{3}{4}x + 4$ consists of all points on the boundary line and all points above the line. The graph of $3x + 4y \leq 4$ consists of all points on the boundary line and all points below the line. The boundary lines are parallel so the graphs do not intersect. The solution set of the system is the empty set.

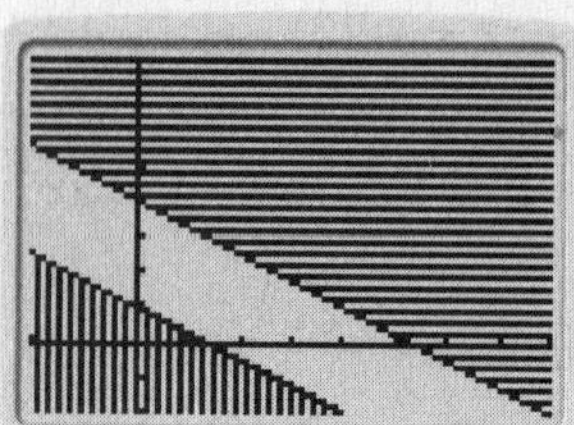

e. Graph the dashed boundary line $y = 4$, and shade below the line. Graph the solid boundary line $2x + y = 4$ and shade above the line. Graph the solid boundary line $x - 2y = -2$ and shade above the line. The solution set consists of all points within the triangle bounded by the three lines, and also includes the points on the part of the lines formed by $2x + y \geq 4$ and $x - 2y \leq -2$.

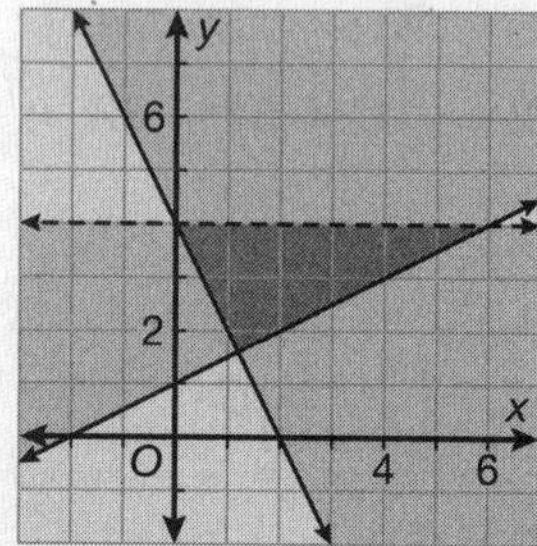

f. $x + y \leq 20$. The maximum number of tickets is 20.
$65x + 12y \leq 500$. The maximum amount to spend is $500.

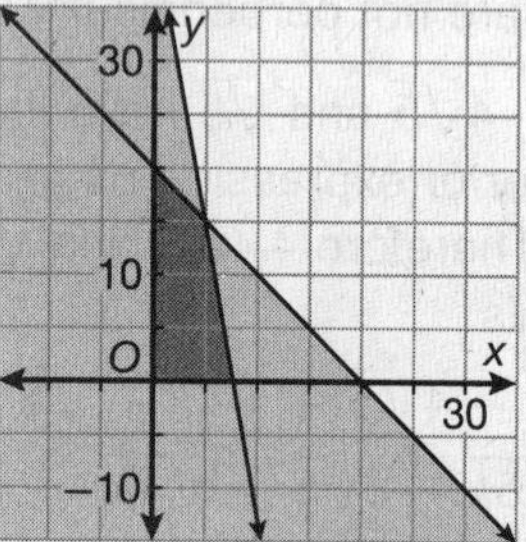

Practice 43

1. $63x^3 + 108x^2 + 81x = 9x(7x^2 + 12x + 9)$

2. This is a Difference of Squares.
$x^{10} - 400 = (x^5 - 20)(x^5 + 20)$

3. The denominator $5x^2 - 20x - 60$ cannot be zero. These excluded values will make the denominator zero:

$$5x^2 - 20x - 60 = 0$$
$$5(x^2 - 4x - 12) = 0$$

$$5(x-6)(x+2)=0$$
$$(x-6)=0 \text{ or } (x+2)=0$$
$$x=6 \text{ or } \quad x=-2$$

4. There are no values that can make the denominator zero, so there are no excluded values.

5.

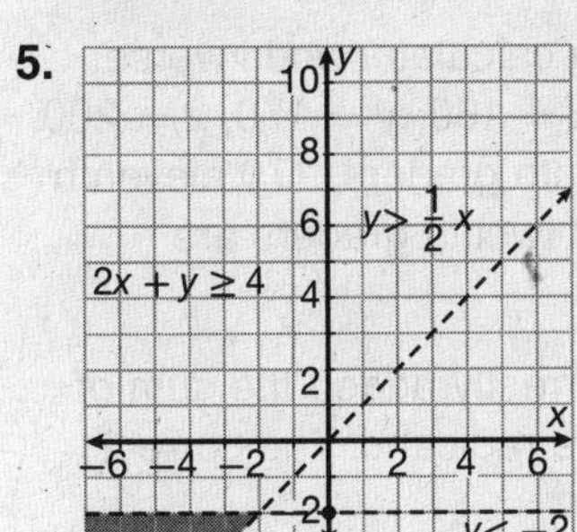

Every solution for $y > \frac{1}{2}x$ lies in quadrants I, II, or III. Every solution for $y < -2$ lies in quadrant III or IV. Therefore, every solution to the system lies in quadrant III.

6. The equation is in the form $y = a(x-h)^2 + k$. Since a is negative the parabola opens downward and the vertex is a maximum. The vertex occurs at (h, k) which is (12, 630). This means that the maximum occurs at week 12 and the value is $630.

7. $x = \dfrac{\begin{vmatrix} -4 & -12 \\ -6 & 18 \end{vmatrix}}{\begin{vmatrix} 4 & -12 \\ -6 & 18 \end{vmatrix}} = \dfrac{-4(18) - (-6)(-12)}{4(18) - (-6)(-12)}$

$= \dfrac{-144}{0}$

$x = \dfrac{\begin{vmatrix} 4 & -4 \\ -6 & -6 \end{vmatrix}}{\begin{vmatrix} 4 & -12 \\ -6 & 18 \end{vmatrix}} = \dfrac{4(-6) - (-6)(-4)}{4(18) - (-6)(-12)}$

$= \dfrac{-48}{0}$

The coefficient matrix has a determinant of 0. The numerator matrices are non-zero, indicating that there are no solutions. The two equations are inconsistent.

8. a. $x + y \leq 15$. The maximum number of tickets is 15.

$45x + 90y \leq 900$. The maximum amount to spend is 900.

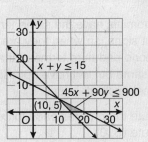

b. The points in the graph of the system that represent all the possible combinations of right field box seats and pavilion box seats you can buy are all the points where both coordinates are nonnegative integers.

c. The point of intersection is (10, 5). It represents 10 right field box seats and 5 pavilion seats for a total cost of $900, the maximum amount that can be spent.

9. $h(x) = f(x) - g(x)$
$= x + 42 - x$
$= 42$ ft

10. The solution is (−1, 3, 2).

11. If $b_1 = b_2$ the y-intercepts are the same, so the lines must intersect at the y-axis.

12.

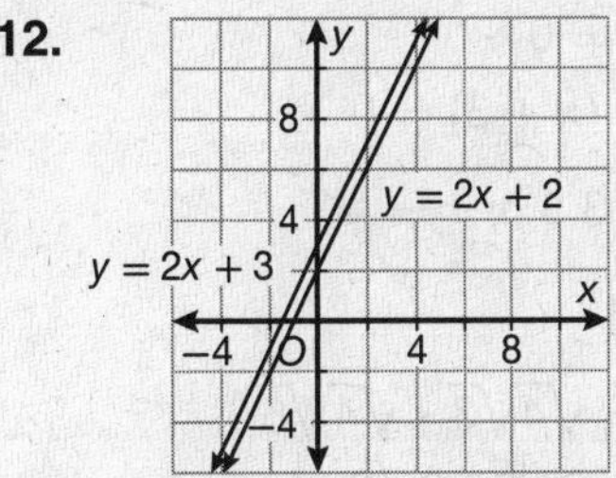

The graph for $y \leq 2x + 2$ is shaded below the line, and $y \geq 2x + 3$ is shaded above the line. This system has no solution.

The graph for $y \leq 2x + 2$ is shaded below the line, and $y \leq 2x + 3$ is shaded below the line. This system has a solution.

The graph for $y \geq 2x + 2$ is shaded above the line, and $y \leq 2x + 3$ is shaded below the line. This system has a solution.

The graph for $y \geq 2x + 2$ is shaded above the line, and $y \geq 2x + 3$ is shaded above the line. This system has a solution.

Answer choice **A**

13. The binomials have the same terms with different signs, so when they are multiplied the second and third terms of the product will be the same but will have opposite signs and so cancel each other out.

14. Substitute the ordered pairs for x and y.
Substitute (6, 0).

$y + x \leq 6 \rightarrow 0 + 6 \leq 6$ true

$2x - 3y > 12 \rightarrow 2(6) - 3(0) > 12$

$12 > 12$ false

Therefore, (6, 0) is not a solution.

15. Substitute the ordered pairs for x and y.
Substitute (1, 3).

$10x + 5y \geq 16 \rightarrow 10(1) + 5(3) \geq 16$

$25 \geq 16$ true

$4x - 6y < 22 \rightarrow 4(1) - 6(3) < 22$

$-14 < 22$ true

Therefore, (1, 3) is a solution.

16. The denominator $2x^2 - x - 21$ cannot be zero. The following excluded values will make the denominator zero:

$2x^2 - x - 21 = 0$

$(2x - 7)(x + 3) = 0$

$(2x - 7) = 0$ or $(x + 3) = 0$

$x = \frac{7}{2} = 3.5$ or $x = -3$

Answer choice **C**

17. a. $\sqrt{12} \cdot \sqrt{24} = \sqrt{4}\sqrt{3} \cdot \sqrt{4}\sqrt{6}$

$= 2\sqrt{3} \cdot 2\sqrt{6}$

$= 4\sqrt{18}$

$= 4\sqrt{9} \cdot \sqrt{2}$

$= 12\sqrt{2}$

b. $\sqrt{12} \cdot \sqrt{24} = \sqrt{288}$

$= \sqrt{144} \cdot \sqrt{2}$

$= 12\sqrt{2}$

18. The quadratic has no real roots and therefore there are no linear polynomials that result in a zero remainder.

19. Let x represent tenth graders, y represent eleventh graders, and z represent twelfth graders. The equations are

$0.3x + 0.2y + 0.16z = 114$

$0.5x + 0.5y + 0.4z = 245$

$0.2x + 0.3y + 0.44z = 171$

The matrix equation is

$$\begin{bmatrix} 0.3 & 0.2 & 0.16 \\ 0.5 & 0.5 & 0.4 \\ 0.2 & 0.3 & 0.44 \end{bmatrix} \begin{bmatrix} x \\ y \\ z \end{bmatrix} = \begin{bmatrix} 114 \\ 245 \\ 171 \end{bmatrix}$$

Using a graphing calculator and inverse matrix to solve, $x = 160$, $y = 170$, $z = 200$. Therefore 160 tenth graders, 170 eleventh graders, and 200 twelfth graders are surveyed.

20. The student incorrectly added the sum of the squares in the radicand. The correct distance is

$d = \sqrt{(0 - (-1))^2 + (2 - 3)^2}$

$= \sqrt{1^2 + (-1)^2}$

$= \sqrt{2}$

21. Let x represent the time in years, and y represent the rank.

The change is the slope on a graph and the rank in 2007 can be used as the y-intercept. The equations can be written in $y = mx + b$ form.

$y = -4x + 43$

$y = x + 28$

Solve the equations to find y.

$-4x + 43 = x + 28$

$-5x = -15$

$x = 3$

$y = 3 + 28 = 31$

Therefore, the two universities will be equal when the rank is 31.

22. $8! = 8 \times 7 \times 6 \times 5 \times 4 \times 3 \times 2 \times 1$

23. $\frac{10!}{3!} = \frac{10 \times 9 \times 8 \times 7 \times 6 \times 5 \times 4 \times \cancel{3!}}{\cancel{3!}}$

$= 10 \times 9 \times 8 \times 7 \times 6 \times 5 \times 4$

24. Let x represent the number of 5 inch by 5 inch squares, and y represent the number of 5 inch by 10 inch squares.

The area of each 5 by 5 inch square is 25 in.^{2} and the area of each 5 inch by 10 inch square is 50 in.^{2}

$25x + 50y < 1500$. The total area must be less than 1500.

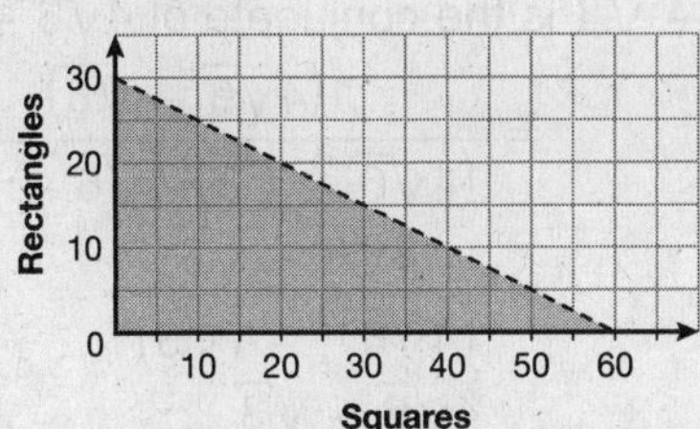

25. a. The surface area of the cube is $6x^2$. The volume of the cube is x^3. The ratio of the surface area to volume is $\frac{6x^2}{x^3} = \frac{6}{x}$.
The surface area of the cylinder is $2\pi\left(\frac{x}{2}\right)^2 + \pi xx = \frac{1}{2}\pi x^2 + \pi x^2 = \frac{3}{2}\pi x^2$.
The volume of the cylinder is $\pi\left(\frac{x}{2}\right)^2 x = \frac{x^2}{4}\pi x = \frac{1}{4}\pi x^3$. The ratio of the surface area to volume is $\frac{\frac{3}{2}\pi x^2}{\frac{1}{4}\pi x^3} = \frac{6}{x}$.

b. For every value of x, the two containers have the same ratio of surface area to volume.

26. The student did not distribute the −2 fully. The correct answer is

$$\begin{aligned} f(x) &= -2(x-4)^2 - 1 \\ &= -2(x^2 - 8x + 16) - 1 \\ &= -2x^2 + 16x - 32 - 1 \\ &= -2x^2 + 16x - 33 \end{aligned}$$

27.

$$\begin{array}{r} 15x^2 - 47x + 28 \\ x+2\overline{)15x^3 - 17x^2 - 66x + 56} \\ \underline{-(15x^3 + 30x^2)} \\ -47x^2 - 66x \\ \underline{-(-47x^2 - 94x)} \\ 28x - 56 \\ \underline{28x - 56} \\ 0 \end{array}$$

To find the roots

$$15x^3 - 17x^2 - 66x + 56 = 0$$
$$(x + 2)(15x^2 - 47x^2 + 28) = 0$$
$$(x + 2)(3x - 7)(5x - 4) = 0$$
$$(x + 2) = 0,\ (3x - 7) = 0, \text{ or } (5x - 4) = 0$$
$$x = -2, \qquad x = \frac{7}{3} \text{ or } \qquad x = \frac{4}{5}$$

The roots are $-2, \frac{7}{3}, \frac{4}{5}$.

28.

$$\begin{array}{r} -8x^2 + 26x - 15 \\ x-3\overline{)-8x^3 + 50x^2 - 93x + 45} \\ \underline{-(-8x^3 + 24x^2)} \\ 26x^2 - 93x \\ \underline{-(26x^2 - 78x)} \\ -15x + 45 \\ \underline{-(-15x + 45)} \\ 0 \end{array}$$

To find the roots

$$-8x^3 + 50x^2 - 93x + 45 = 0$$
$$(x - 3)(-8x^2 + 26x^2 - 15) = 0$$
$$-(x - 3)(8x^2 - 26x^2 + 15) = 0$$
$$-(x - 3)(4x - 3)(2x - 5) = 0$$
$$(x - 3) = 0,\ (4x - 3) = 0, \text{ or } (2x - 5) = 0$$
$$x = 3, \qquad x = \frac{3}{4} \text{ or } \qquad x = \frac{5}{2}$$

The roots are $3, \frac{3}{4}, \frac{5}{2}$.

29. Order is important, so this is a permutation. For seniors:

$$\begin{aligned} P(9,3) &= \frac{9!}{(9-3)!} = \frac{9!}{6!} \\ &= \frac{9 \times 8 \times 7 \times \cancel{6!}}{\cancel{6!}} \\ &= 504 \end{aligned}$$

For juniors:

$$\begin{aligned} P(6,3) &= \frac{6!}{(6-3)!} = \frac{6!}{3!} \\ &= \frac{6 \times 5 \times 4 \times \cancel{3!}}{\cancel{3!}} \\ &= 120 \end{aligned}$$

Because the multiple events must both occur, the number of total possible outcomes is the product, $504 \times 120 = 60{,}480$.

30. a. Area $= (x + 4)(2x^2 - 6x + 10)$

b. $(x + 4)(2x^2 - 6x + 10)$
$= 2x^3 - 6x^2 + 10x + 8x^2 - 24x + 40$
$= 2x^3 + 2x^2 - 14x + 40$

c. Substitute 4 for x
$2(4)^3 + 2(4)^2 - 14(4) + 40$
$= 128 + 32 - 56 + 40$
$= 144$
The area of the garden is 144 ft^2.

LESSON 44

Warm Up 44

1. radicand

2. $\frac{-2x+10}{x^2-25} \cdot \frac{(x+5)}{6}$

$= \frac{-2(x-5)}{(x-5)(x+5)} \cdot \frac{(x+5)}{6} = -\frac{1}{3}$

3. $2\sqrt{3} \cdot 4\sqrt{2} = 8\sqrt{6}$

4. $4\sqrt{5} \cdot \sqrt{5} = 4\sqrt{25} = 4 \cdot 5 = 20$

Lesson Practice 44

a. $\frac{2}{5\sqrt{7}} = \frac{2}{5\sqrt{7}} \cdot \frac{\sqrt{7}}{\sqrt{7}}$ Multiply the numerator and denominator by $\sqrt{7}$ to eliminate radical from the denominator.

$= \frac{2\sqrt{7}}{5\sqrt{7}\sqrt{7}}$

$= \frac{2\sqrt{7}}{5 \cdot 7}$

$= \frac{2\sqrt{7}}{35}$

b. $\sqrt{\frac{3}{20}} = \sqrt{\frac{3}{20} \cdot \frac{5}{5}}$ The radicand is a fraction. Multiply the numerator and denominator of the radicand by 5 to get a perfect square in the denominator.

$= \sqrt{\frac{15}{100}}$

$= \frac{\sqrt{15}}{\sqrt{100}}$

$= \frac{\sqrt{15}}{10}$

c. $\frac{2}{2-\sqrt{7}} = \frac{2}{2-\sqrt{7}} \cdot \frac{2+\sqrt{7}}{2+\sqrt{7}}$

$2+\sqrt{7}$ is the conjugate of $2-\sqrt{7}$.

$= \frac{2(2+\sqrt{7})}{(2-\sqrt{7})(2+\sqrt{7})}$

$= \frac{4+2\sqrt{7}}{(2)^2-(\sqrt{7})^2}$

$= \frac{4+2\sqrt{7}}{4-7}$

$= \frac{4+2\sqrt{7}}{-3}$ or $\frac{-4-2\sqrt{7}}{3}$

d. $\frac{1}{4\sqrt{6}+\sqrt{3}} = \frac{1}{4\sqrt{6}+\sqrt{3}} \cdot \frac{4\sqrt{6}-\sqrt{3}}{4\sqrt{6}-\sqrt{3}}$

$4\sqrt{6}-\sqrt{3}$ is the conjugate of $4\sqrt{6}+\sqrt{3}$.

$= \frac{1(4\sqrt{6}-\sqrt{3})}{(4\sqrt{6}+\sqrt{3})(4\sqrt{6}-\sqrt{3})}$

$= \frac{4\sqrt{6}-\sqrt{3}}{(4\sqrt{6})^2-(\sqrt{3})^2}$

$= \frac{4\sqrt{6}-\sqrt{3}}{96-3}$

$= \frac{4\sqrt{6}-\sqrt{3}}{93}$

e. $\frac{3+\sqrt{5}}{1-\sqrt{5}} = \frac{3+\sqrt{5}}{1-\sqrt{5}} \cdot \frac{1+\sqrt{5}}{1+\sqrt{5}}$

$1+\sqrt{5}$ is the conjugate of $1-\sqrt{5}$.

$= \frac{(3+\sqrt{5})(1+\sqrt{5})}{(1-\sqrt{5})(1+\sqrt{5})}$

$= \frac{3+3\sqrt{5}+\sqrt{5}+(\sqrt{5})^2}{(1)^2-(\sqrt{5})^2}$

$= \frac{3+4\sqrt{5}+5}{1-5}$

$= \frac{8+4\sqrt{5}}{-4}$

$= \frac{2+\sqrt{5}}{-1} = -2-\sqrt{5}$

Practice 44

1. $\frac{5}{3\sqrt{3}} = \frac{5}{3\sqrt{3}} \cdot \frac{\sqrt{3}}{\sqrt{3}}$

$= \frac{5\sqrt{3}}{3\sqrt{3}\sqrt{3}}$

$= \frac{5\sqrt{3}}{3 \cdot 3}$

$= \frac{5\sqrt{3}}{9}$

2. $\frac{4}{2+\sqrt{7}} = \frac{4}{2+\sqrt{7}} \cdot \frac{2-\sqrt{7}}{2-\sqrt{7}}$

$= \frac{4(2-\sqrt{7})}{(2+\sqrt{7})(2-\sqrt{7})}$

$= \frac{8-4\sqrt{7}}{(2)^2-(\sqrt{7})^2}$

$= \frac{8-4\sqrt{7}}{4-7}$

$= \frac{8-4\sqrt{7}}{-3}$ or $-\frac{8-4\sqrt{7}}{3}$

3. $\sqrt{\frac{9}{10}} = \sqrt{\frac{9}{10} \cdot \frac{10}{10}}$

$= \sqrt{\frac{90}{100}}$

$= \frac{\sqrt{90}}{\sqrt{100}}$

$= \frac{\sqrt{9}\sqrt{10}}{\sqrt{100}}$

$= \frac{3\sqrt{10}}{10}$

4. For each hiker the distances walked equal the legs of a right triangle and the distance from the campsite equals the hypotenuse of the triangle.

For the first hiker

$c^2 = a^2 + b^2$

$c^2 = (3)^2 + (4)^2$

$c^2 = 25$

$c = 5$

For the second hiker

$c^2 = a^2 + b^2$

$c^2 = (5)^2 + (7)^2$

$c^2 = 74$

$c \approx 8.6$

The second hiker is $8.6 - 5 = 3.6$ units farther from the campsite. Since each unit is 1.5 miles, then the second hiker is $3.6 \times 1.5 = 5.4$ miles farther.

5. $4x = 12 - 5y \rightarrow 4x + 5y = 12$

$24 = 8x + 10y \rightarrow 8x + 10y = 24$

Multiply the first equation by -2 and add to the second equation.

$-2(4x + 5y = 12) \rightarrow -8x - 10y = -24$

$8x + 10y = 24 \rightarrow \quad 8x + 10y = 24$

$0 = 0$

The lines coincide. There are infinitely many solutions.

6. The student shaded below the boundary line for $2x - y \leq 2$, instead of shading above the line. The solution on the graph is therefore incorrect. The correct graph is as follows.

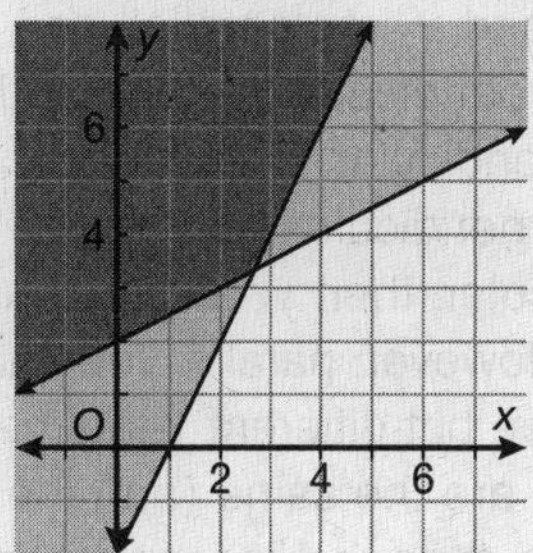

7. Each letter of the alphabet is replaced with a number.

8. If order is not important, then it is a combination. Ten items taken 4 at a time is $C(10,4)$, and 10 items taken 6 at a time is $C(10,6)$.

$C(10,4) = \frac{10!}{4!(10-4)!}$

$= \frac{10!}{4!6!}$

$= \frac{10 \times 9 \times 8 \times 7 \times \cancel{6!}}{4!\cancel{6!}} = 210$

$C(10,6) = \frac{10!}{6!(10-6)!}$

$= \frac{10!}{6!4!}$

$= \frac{10 \times 9 \times 8 \times 7 \times \cancel{6!}}{\cancel{6!}4!} = 210$

The combinations are the same.

9. $\frac{\sqrt{726}}{\sqrt{16}} = \frac{\sqrt{121}\sqrt{6}}{\sqrt{16}} = \frac{11\sqrt{6}}{4} \approx 6.7$

It takes about 6.7 seconds.

10. The boundary line is $x = -2$, and $x = -2$ is not included since the boundary line is dashed. The plane to the left of the boundary line is shaded, so all x values in the solution are less than -2.

Answer choice **B**

11. No. The quadratic has no factors of the form $x + d$. Therefore, dividing by $x + d$ will result in a nonzero remainder.

12. a. No. A triangle can be both obtuse and isosceles.

b. Yes. A triangle cannot be both right and acute.

13. Since y_1 and y_2 are parallel, and y_2 and y_3 are perpendicular then, y_1 and y_3 are also perpendicular. Then since y_1 and y_3 are perpendicular, and y_3 and y_4 are perpendicular, then y_1 and y_4 must be parallel. However, parallel lines have the same slope but different y-intercepts, so if the intercepts are the same (and the slopes are the same), then the lines must be the same line. Therefore, $y_1 = y_4$.

14. $x^3y^2z^3 + x^2yz^2 - 3x^3yz$
$= x^2yz\,(xyz^2 + z - 3x)$

15. Replace (x) in g(x) with f(x).
$$\frac{3}{2\left(\frac{x}{x+1}\right)} = \frac{3}{\frac{2x}{x+1}} = \frac{3(x+1)}{2x}$$

16. $A = \begin{pmatrix} 6 & -2 \\ 4 & 12 \end{pmatrix}$
$$A^{-1} = \frac{1}{|A|}\begin{pmatrix} 12 & 2 \\ -4 & 6 \end{pmatrix}$$
$$= \frac{1}{(6)(12) - (4)(-2)}\begin{pmatrix} 12 & 2 \\ -4 & 6 \end{pmatrix}$$
$$= \frac{1}{80}\begin{pmatrix} 12 & 2 \\ -4 & 6 \end{pmatrix}$$
$$= \begin{pmatrix} 0.15 & 0.025 \\ -0.05 & 0.075 \end{pmatrix}$$

17. For the same x-values, the coefficient 5 makes the y-value in $y = 5x^2$ five times as great as in $y = x^2$. Therefore, the graph of $y = 5x^2$ is narrower than the graph of $y = x^2$.

18. a. $2x + 3y = 2z \rightarrow 2x + 3y - 2z = 0$
$4x = -5y + 4z \rightarrow 4x + 5y - 4z = 0$
$3x + 5z = 2y \rightarrow 3x - 2y + 5z = 0$

b. There should be one solution, since no two equations are multiples of each other in any way.

c. $2x + 3y - 2z = 0$
$4x + 5y - 4z = 0$
$3x - 2y + 5z = 0$
Eliminate the x variable using equations 1 and 2 and equations 1 and 3.

$-2(2x + 3y - 2z = 0) \rightarrow$
$-4x + -6y + 4z = 0$
$4x + 5y - 4z = 0 \rightarrow \quad 4x + 5y - 4z = 0$
$-y = 0$
$y = 0$

$-3(2x + 3y - 2z = 0) \rightarrow$
$-6x + -9y + 6z = 0$
$2(3x - 2y + 5z = 0) \rightarrow$
$6x - 4y + 10z = 0$
$-13y + 16z = 0$

Substitute $y = 0$ into $-13y + 16z = 0$ to find z.
$-13(0) + 16z = 0$
$16z = 0$
$z = 0$

Substitute $y = 0$ and $z = 0$ into one of the original equations.
$2x + 3(0) - 2(0) = 0$
$2x = 0$
$x = 0$

The solution is (0, 0, 0).

19. The distance from the center to the pole is $\frac{150}{2} = 75$ feet. Substitute 75 for x in the function $f(x) = 0.0005x^2 + 35$.
$f(x) = 0.0005(75)^2 + 35$
$f(x) = 2.8125 + 35$
$= 37.8125$
The cable is attached to the poles about 37.8 feet up.

20. The standard form is $ax^2 + bx + c$. The equation can be written as $3x^2 + 0x + 0$, so $a = 3$, $b = 0$, and $c = 0$.

21. There are no real zeros. Since $a < 0$, the graph opens down. Because the graph opens down and the vertex is in Quadrant III, the graph does not intersect the x-axis.

22. Student B is correct. Student A reversed the x- and y-coordinates when substituting the values into the point-slope formula.

23. There are 12 inches in one foot.
$$\frac{36x^2 + 72x + 96 \text{ in.}}{1}$$

$$= \frac{12(3x^2 + 6x + 8) \text{ in.}}{1}$$

$$= \frac{\cancel{12}(3x^2 + 6x + 8)\cancel{\text{in.}}}{1} \times \frac{1 \text{ ft}}{\cancel{12} \text{ in.}}$$

$$= 3x^2 + 6x + 8 \text{ ft}$$

24. $16m^2p^3y - 8y^4mp^3 + 4m^2p^2y^2$
$= 4mp^2y(4mp - 2py^3 + my)$

25.
$$(2x + 1.5)(x + 1) = 69$$
$$2x^2 + 2x + 1.5x + 1.5 = 69$$
$$2x^2 + 3.5x - 67.5 = 0$$
$$(2x + 13.5)(x - 5) = 0$$
$(2x + 13.5) = 0$ or $(x - 5) = 0$

$x = -\frac{13.5}{2} = -6.75$ or $x = 5$

A dimension cannot be negative, so $x = 5$.

The maximum length is $2(5) + 1.5 = 11.5$ inches, and the maximum height is $5 + 1 = 6$ inches.

26.
$$\begin{array}{r} x^3 - x^2 + x - 1 \\ x + 1\overline{)x^4 + 0x^3 + 0x^2 + 0x - 2} \\ \underline{-(x^4 + x^3)} \\ -x^3 + 0x^2 \\ \underline{-(-x^3 - x^2)} \\ x^2 + 0x \\ \underline{-(x^2 + x)} \\ -x - 2 \\ \underline{-(-x - 1)} \\ -1 \end{array}$$

$$= x^3 - x^2 + x - 1 - \frac{1}{x + 1}$$

Check:

$$\left(x^3 - x^2 + x - 1 - \frac{1}{x + 1}\right)(x + 1)$$

$$= \left(\frac{x^3(x + 1)}{x + 1} - \frac{x^2(x + 1)}{x + 1} + \frac{x(x + 1)}{x + 1} - \frac{1(x + 1)}{x + 1} - \frac{1}{x + 1}\right)(x + 1)$$

$$= \left(\frac{x^4 + x^3 - x^3 - x^2 + x^2 + x - x - 1 - 1}{x + 1}\right)(x + 1)$$

$$= \left(\frac{x^4 - 2}{x + 1}\right)(x + 1)$$

$$= x^4 - 2$$

27. One way is to pick a test point, such as (0, 0) and substitute the values into the inequality. If the inequality is true, shade the region that includes the test point. If the inequality is not true, shade the region that does not include the test point. The inequality would not be true with test point (0, 0) so shade the region that does not include (0, 0).

Another way is to write the equation in slope intercept form, and shade above the boundary line, since the inequality has a > sign.

28. a.
$$10 = \sqrt{(x_2 - x_1)^2 + (y_2 - y_1)^2}$$
$$10 = \sqrt{(-2 - 6)^2 + (-7 - k)^2}$$
$$10 = \sqrt{(-8)^2 + (49 + 14k + k^2)}$$
$$10^2 = \left(\sqrt{113 + 14k + k^2}\right)^2$$
$$100 = 113 + 14k + k^2$$
$$0 = 13 + 14k + k^2$$
$$(k + 13)(k + 1) = 0$$
$$k = -13 \text{ or } k = -1$$

b. Substitute the two values of k

$$6.1 \stackrel{?}{=} \sqrt{(0 - 6)^2 + (0 - (-1))^2}$$
$$6.1 \stackrel{?}{=} \sqrt{(-6)^2 + (1)^2}$$
$$6.1^2 \stackrel{?}{=} (\sqrt{37})^2$$
$$37.21 \approx 37$$
$$6.1 \stackrel{?}{=} \sqrt{(0 - 6)^2 + (0 - (-13))^2}$$
$$6.1 \stackrel{?}{=} \sqrt{(-6)^2 + (13)^2}$$
$$6.1^2 \stackrel{?}{=} (\sqrt{205})^2$$
$$37.21 \neq 205$$

Therefore, the biker's coordinates are (6, −1).

29. Order is not important, so this is a combination of 5 objects taken 3 at a time.

$$C(5,3) = \frac{5!}{3!(5 - 3)!} = \frac{5!}{3!2!} = 10.$$

The customer who said there are 10 combinations is correct. The other customer performed a permutation of 5 objects taken 3 at a time.

30.

$$\begin{array}{r} -3x^2 + 6x - 12 \\ -x-2\overline{)3x^3 + 0x^2 + 0x - 3} \\ \underline{-(3x^3 + 6x^2)} \\ -6x^2 + 0x \\ \underline{-(-6x^2 - 12x)} \\ 12x - 3 \\ \underline{-(12x + 24)} \\ -27 \end{array}$$

$$= -3x^2 + 6x - 12 - \frac{27}{-x-2}$$

Check:

$$\left(-3x^2 + 6x - 12 - \frac{27}{-x-2}\right)(-x-2)$$

$$= \left(\frac{-3x^2(-x-2)}{-x-2} + \frac{6x(-x-2)}{-x-2} - \frac{12(-x-2)}{-x-2} - \frac{27}{-x-2}\right)(-x-2)$$

$$= \left(\frac{3x^3 + 6x^2}{-x-2} + \frac{-6x^2 - 12x}{-x-2} - \frac{-12x - 24}{-x-2} - \frac{27}{-x-2}\right)(-x-2)$$

$$= \left(\frac{3x^3 + 6x^2 - 6x^2 - 12x + 12x + 24 - 27}{-x-2}\right)(-x-2)$$

$$= \left(\frac{3x^3 - 3}{-x-2}\right)(-x-2) = 3x^3 - 3$$

LAB 8

Lab Practice

a. $y = -0.48x + 10.69$

b. $y = -0.52x + 11.01$

c.

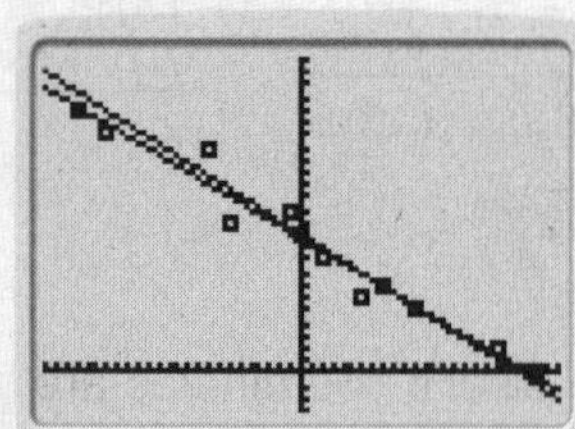

LESSON 45

Warm Up 45

1. y-intercept
2. In the form $y = mx + b$, m is the slope and b is the y-intercept. The equation in this form is

$$2x - 4y = 8$$
$$-4y = -2x + 8$$
$$y = \frac{1}{2}x - 2$$

The slope is $\frac{1}{2}$ and the y-intercept is -2.

3. Substitute x with 90 in the equation.
   $15.5(90) + 70 = 1465$
4. The slope of the line is -4 and the y-intercept is -3. Substitute -4 for m and -3 for b in the equation $y = mx + b$.
   $y = -4x - 3$
5. The line falls so the slope is negative.

Lesson Practice 45

a. Plot the points (minutes, incorrect answers).

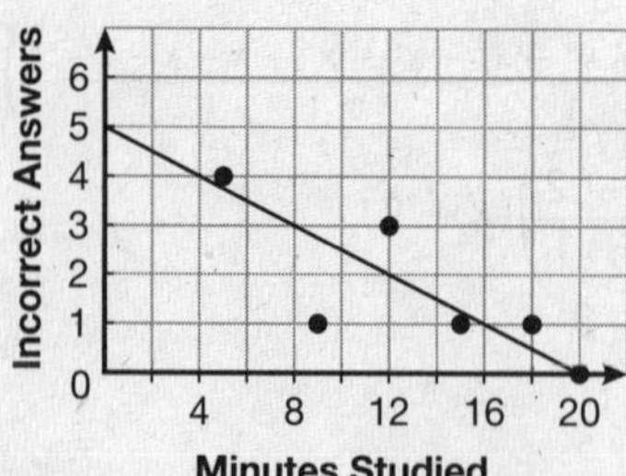

The points tend to fall from left to right. There is a negative correlation. Sketch a line of best fit and use two points on the line to write the equation.

(8, 3), (12, 2): $m = \frac{3-2}{8-12} = -\frac{1}{4}$

$y - y_1 = m(x - x_1)$

$y - 3 = -\frac{1}{4}(x - 8)$

$y - 3 = -\frac{1}{4}x + 2$

$y = -\frac{1}{4}x + 5$

The slope indicates that for every four minutes of study, there is a decrease of one incorrect answer.

b. Plot the points (temperature, bill).

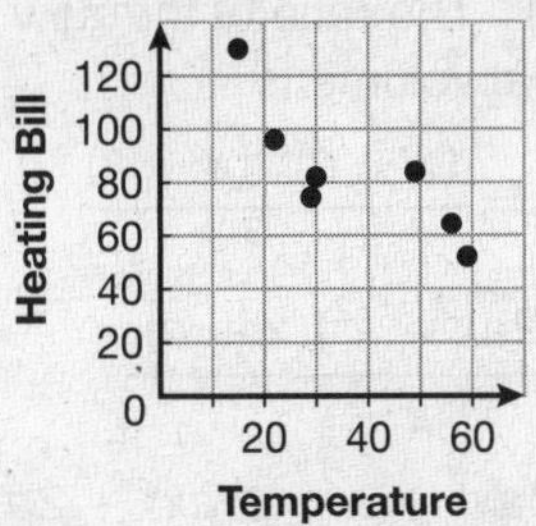

The points fall, so r is negative. The points are fairly close to forming a line so the value is near to -1, but not -1 because the points do not form a line exactly. A good estimate of the r-value would be -0.8. Sketching a line of best fit shows that 78 is a good prediction for the heating bill when the average temperature is 40°F.

c. To avoid a large gap on the x-axis, write the years as the number of years after 2000. Enter the data into a graphing calculator. Choose **LinReg(*ax* + *b*)** from the CALC menu. Then type the list names.

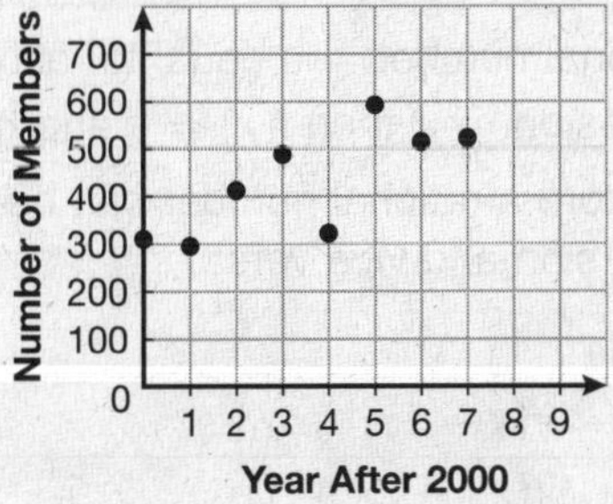

The r-value is about 0.76. The enrollment for 2008 is about 590 members.

Practice 45

1. **a–b.** Plot the points (x, y).

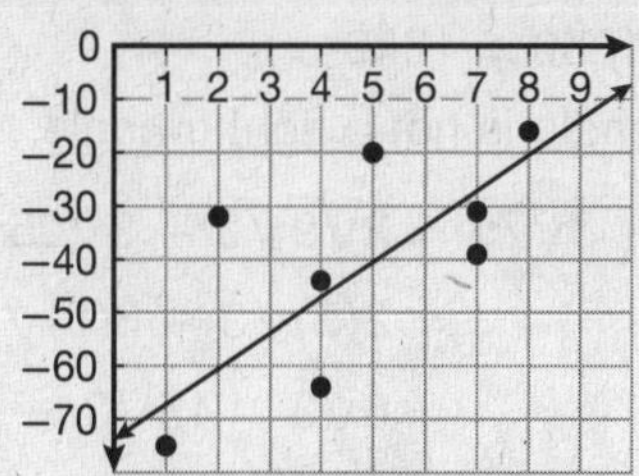

c. The slope of the line is about $\frac{20}{3}$. The y-intercept is about $-73\frac{1}{3}$. The equation is roughly $y = \frac{20}{3}x - 73\frac{1}{3}$.

2. The r-value is about -0.71. This value means that there is a moderate negative correlation between the weight of a bicycle and the price.

3. 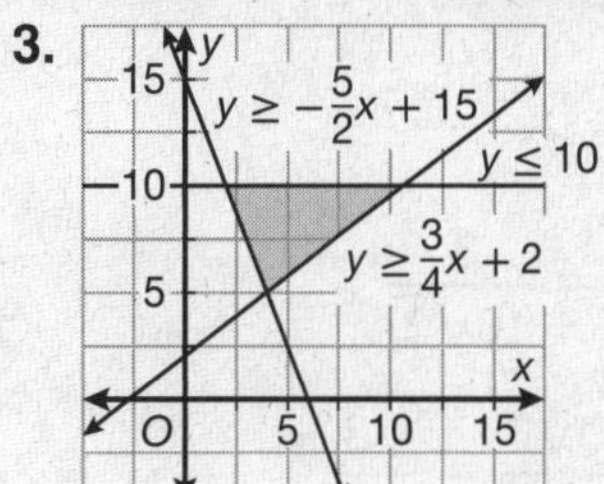

The solution to the system forms a triangle with an area of about $21\frac{2}{3}$ square units.

4. Since order matters this is a permutation problem. There are 9 items of which DVD repeats 4 times, CD repeats 3 times, and hand-held device repeats 2 times. Therefore $n = 9$ and $q_1 = 4$, $q_2 = 3$, and $q_3 = 2$.

The permutations can be found using $\frac{n!}{q_1!q_2!q_3!}$.

$\frac{9!}{4!3!2!} = 1260$

1260 distinguishable displays are possible.

5. Substitute 16 and 40 for a and b, and 43 for c in $a^2 + b^2 = c^2$.

$$a^2 + b^2 = c^2$$
$$16^2 + 40^2 \stackrel{?}{=} 43^2$$
$$256 + 1600 = 1849$$
$$1856 \neq 1849$$

The triangle is not a right triangle.

6. $2\sqrt{27} - 3\sqrt{75} = 2\sqrt{9}\sqrt{3} - 3\sqrt{25}\sqrt{3}$
$= 2(3)\sqrt{3} - 3(5)\sqrt{3}$
$= 6\sqrt{3} - 15\sqrt{3}$
$= -9\sqrt{3}$

7. $3\sqrt{2}\,(2\sqrt{2} - \sqrt{6}) \cdot 4\sqrt{3} + 2$
$= (3\sqrt{2} \cdot 2\sqrt{2} - 3\sqrt{2} \cdot \sqrt{6}) \cdot 4\sqrt{3} + 2$
$= (6\sqrt{4} - 3\sqrt{12}) \cdot 4\sqrt{3} + 2$
$= (12 - 3\sqrt{4}\,\sqrt{3}) \cdot 4\sqrt{3} + 2$
$= (12 - 6\sqrt{3}) \cdot 4\sqrt{3} + 2$
$= 12 \cdot 4\sqrt{3} - 6\sqrt{3} \cdot 4\sqrt{3} + 2$
$= 48\sqrt{3} - 72 + 2$
$= 48\sqrt{3} - 70$

8. $\dfrac{3}{5\sqrt{12}} = \dfrac{3}{5\sqrt{4}\sqrt{3}} = \dfrac{3}{10\sqrt{3}}$

$= \dfrac{3}{10\sqrt{3}} \cdot \dfrac{\sqrt{3}}{\sqrt{3}} = \dfrac{3\sqrt{3}}{30} = \dfrac{\sqrt{3}}{10}$

9. $\dfrac{14}{3\sqrt{75}} = \dfrac{14}{3\sqrt{25}\sqrt{3}} = \dfrac{14}{15\sqrt{3}}$

$= \dfrac{14}{15\sqrt{3}} \cdot \dfrac{\sqrt{3}}{\sqrt{3}} = \dfrac{14\sqrt{3}}{45}$

10. $\dfrac{2}{3\sqrt{6}} = \dfrac{2}{3\sqrt{6}} \cdot \dfrac{\sqrt{6}}{\sqrt{6}} = \dfrac{2\sqrt{6}}{3(6)} = \dfrac{2\sqrt{6}}{18} = \dfrac{\sqrt{6}}{9}$

11. $\sqrt[3]{250} = \sqrt[3]{5 \cdot 5 \cdot 5 \cdot 2} = 5\sqrt[3]{2}$

Answer choice **D**

12. Let a represent the number of adult tickets and c represent the number of child tickets. The equation is $16a + 8c \leq 200$.

Graph the equation.

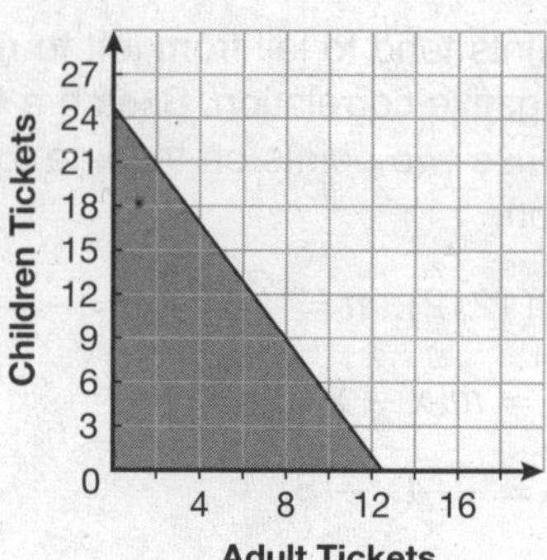

The point (6, 15) is outside the shaded area of the graph. Therefore, they could not buy 6 adult and 15 child tickets.

13. The value of the correlation coefficient cannot be greater than 1.

14. Each original side is x, so the volume is x^3. Each new side is $(x + a)$, so the new volume is $(x + a)^3$. The ratio of the new volume to the original volume is

$$\frac{(x+a)^3}{x^3} = \frac{(x+a)^2\,(x+a)}{x^3}$$
$$= \frac{(x^2 + 2ax + a^2)(x+a)}{x^3}$$
$$= \frac{x^3 + 2ax^2 + a^2x + ax^2 + 2a^2x + a^3}{x^3}$$
$$= \frac{x^3 + 3ax^2 + 3a^2x + a^3}{x^3}$$

15. Roots of negative numbers exist when the index of the radical is an odd number. They are undefined when the index is an even number.

16. Perimeter $= 4s$. Area $= s^2$

Perimeter to area ratio $= \frac{4s}{s^2} = \frac{4}{s}$.

If each side is 10 miles, then the perimeter is $4(10) = 40$ and the area is $10(10) = 100$. The perimeter to area ratio is $\dfrac{4}{s} = \dfrac{4}{10} = \frac{2}{5}$.

17. If rational number $\frac{a}{b}$ is equal to rational expression $\frac{f(x)}{g(x)}$, then $f(x) = a$ and $g(x) = b$. Therefore a rational number can be a rational expression and vice versa.

18. $(x - 1)^3$
$= (x - 1)(x - 1)^2$
$= (x - 1)(x^2 - 2x + 1)$

$= x^3 - 2x^2 + x - x^2 + 2x - 1$
$= x^3 - 3x^2 + 3x - 1$

19. $(x + 5)^3$
$= (x + 5)(x + 5)^2$
$= (x + 5)(x^2 + 10x + 25)$
$= x^3 + 10x^2 + 25x + 5x^2 + 50x + 125$
$= x^3 + 15x^2 + 75x + 125$

20. The line will have the same slope as the given line, $m = -5$, and a y-intercept of 0, $b = 0$. The equation $y = -5x$ satisfies these conditions.
Answer choice **A**

21. The student factored incorrectly.
$4x^2 - 20x + 25 = 0$
$(2x - 5)(2x - 5) = 0$
$(2x - 5) = 0$
$2x = 5$
$x = \frac{5}{2}$

22. $C = \frac{5}{9}(F - 32)$

$C - 0 = \frac{5}{9}(F - 32)$

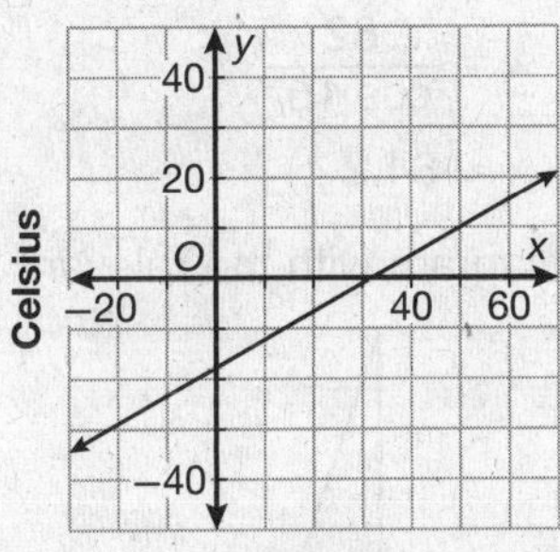

The rate of change is the slope of the graph, $\frac{5}{9}$. It means that for every change in 5 degrees in Celsius, there is a change of 9 degrees Fahrenheit.

23. The outcomes for a vowel are A and E. The outcomes for an odd number are 1, 3, and 5. The outcomes are A1, A3, A5, E1, E3, and E5. There are 6 outcomes.

24. The diameter of the circle is the hypotenuse of the right triangle.
$a^2 + b^2 = c^2$.
$x^2 + x^2 = c^2$
$2x^2 = c^2$
$c = \sqrt{2x^2} = \sqrt{x^2}\sqrt{2} = x\sqrt{2}$

The radius is one-half the diameter. So, the radius of the circle is $\frac{x\sqrt{2}}{2}$.
The area of the circle is $A = \pi r^2$.

$$A = \pi\left(\frac{x\sqrt{2}}{2}\right)^2 = \pi\left(\frac{2x^2}{4}\right) = \frac{2\pi x^2}{4}$$

The area of the right triangle is $A = \frac{1}{2}bh$.

$A = \frac{1}{2}x(x) = \frac{1}{2}x^2$ or $\frac{x^2}{2}$.

The ratio of the area of the circle to the area of the triangle is

$$\frac{\frac{2\pi x^2}{4}}{\frac{x^2}{2}} = \frac{2\pi x^2}{4} \cdot \frac{2}{x^2} = \pi$$

25. Multiply the matrices in both orders. If the product is the identity matrix both times, then the matrices are inverses.

26. $-x + x^2 = 12$
$x^2 - x - 12 = 0$
$(x - 4)(x + 3) = 0$
$(x - 4) = 0$ or $(x + 3) = 0$
$x = 4$ or $x = -3$

27. $-48x = -2x^2 - x^3$
$x^3 + 2x^2 - 48x = 0$
$x(x^2 + 2x - 48) = 0$
$x(x + 8)(x - 6) = 0$
$x = 0$, $(x + 8) = 0$, or $(x - 6) = 0$
$x = 0$, $x = -8$, or $x = 6$

28. The vertex form of an equation is $y = a(x - h)^2 + k$.
Substitute the values into the equation.
$y = -1(x - (-2))^2 + 3$
$y = -(x + 2)^2 + 3$

29. $$\frac{4x}{x + 4} + \frac{6}{x + 2} = \frac{4x}{x + 4} \cdot \frac{x + 2}{x + 2} + \frac{6}{x + 2} \cdot \frac{x + 4}{x + 4}$$
$$= \frac{4x(x + 2)}{(x + 4)(x + 2)} + \frac{6(x + 4)}{(x + 2)(x + 4)}$$
$$= \frac{4x^2 + 8x + 6x + 24}{(x + 4)(x + 2)}$$

$$= \frac{4x^2 + 14x + 24}{(x + 4)(x + 2)}$$

30. $\frac{3m}{m^2 + 3m + 2} - \frac{5m}{m + 1}$

$$= \frac{3m}{(m + 1)(m + 2)} - \frac{5m}{m + 1}$$

$$= \frac{3m}{(m + 1)(m + 2)} - \frac{5m}{m + 1} \cdot \frac{m + 2}{m + 2}$$

$$= \frac{3m}{(m + 1)(m + 2)} - \frac{5m(m + 2)}{(m + 1)(m + 2)}$$

$$= \frac{3m}{(m + 1)(m + 2)} - \frac{5m^2 + 10m}{(m + 1)(m + 2)}$$

$$= \frac{3m - 5m^2 - 10m}{(m + 1)(m + 2)}$$

$$= \frac{-5m^2 - 7m}{(m + 1)(m + 2)}$$

LESSON 46

Warm Up 46

1. hypotenuse

2. $4.2 = \frac{x}{35}$

   $4.2(35) = x$

   $147 = x$

3. $0.06x = 42$

   $\frac{0.06x}{0.06} = \frac{42}{0.06}$

   $x = 700$

4. The reciprocal of $\frac{3}{4}$ is its multiplicative inverse, $\frac{4}{3}$, because $\frac{3}{4} \cdot \frac{4}{3} = 1$.

5. Substitute 20 and 25 for a and b, and 30 for c in $a^2 + b^2 = c^2$.

   $a^2 + b^2 = c^2$

   $20^2 + 25^2 \stackrel{?}{=} 30^2$

   $400 + 625 \stackrel{?}{=} 900$

   $1025 \neq 900$

   The triangle is not a right triangle.

Lesson Practice 46

a. Identify the hypotenuse: $\overline{AB}$

Identify the side opposite $\angle A$: $\overline{BC}$

Identify the side adjacent $\angle A$: $\overline{AC}$

$$\sin A = \frac{\text{opp}}{\text{hyp}} = \frac{15}{39} = \frac{5}{13} \approx 0.3846$$

$$\cos A = \frac{\text{adj}}{\text{hyp}} = \frac{36}{39} = \frac{12}{13} \approx 0.9231$$

$$\tan A = \frac{\text{opp}}{\text{adj}} = \frac{15}{36} = \frac{5}{12} \approx 0.4167$$

b. Identify the hypotenuse: $\overline{AB}$

Identify the side opposite $\angle A$: $\overline{BC}$

Identify the side adjacent $\angle A$: $\overline{AC}$

$$\csc A = \frac{\text{hyp}}{\text{opp}} = \frac{20}{12} = \frac{5}{3} = 1.\overline{6}$$

$$\sec A = \frac{\text{hyp}}{\text{adj}} = \frac{20}{16} = \frac{5}{4} = 1.25$$

$$\cot A = \frac{\text{adj}}{\text{opp}} = \frac{16}{12} = \frac{4}{3} = 1.\overline{3}$$

c. Identify the known and unknown lengths as the hypotenuse and the adjacent side to the given angle. Use a trigonometric function that uses the hypotenuse and adjacent side and substitute the given information.

$\cos 15° = \frac{\text{adj}}{\text{hyp}}$

$\cos 15° = \frac{62}{x}$

$x(\cos 15°) = 62$

$x = \frac{62}{\cos 15°}$

$x \approx 64.2$

d. Draw a diagram with the relevant information.

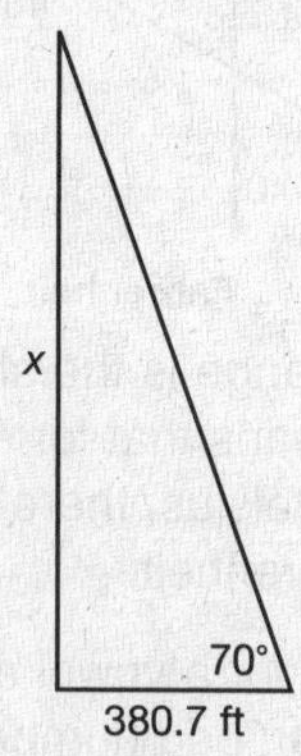

$\tan 70° = \frac{\text{opp}}{\text{adj}}$

$\tan 70° = \frac{x}{380.7}$

$\tan 70°(380.7) = x$

$1045.96 \approx x$

The height of the building is about 1046 feet.

Practice 46

1. In the form $y = mx + b$, m is the slope. Parallel lines have the same slope. Therefore $m = 3$. Substitute the slope, 3, and point (3, 4) into the point-slope formula.
$y - 4 = 3(x - 3)$
$y - 4 = 3x - 9$
$y = 3x - 5$
Perpendicular lines have negative reciprocal slopes. Therefore $m = -\frac{1}{3}$. Substitute the slope, $-\frac{1}{3}$, and point (3, 4) into the point-slope formula.
$y - 4 = -\frac{1}{3}(x - 3)$
$y - 4 = -\frac{1}{3}x + 1$
$y = -\frac{1}{3}x + 5$

2. In the form $y = mx + b$, m is the slope. Parallel lines have the same slope. Therefore $m = -2$. Substitute the slope, -2, and point $(-7, 0)$ into the point-slope formula.
$y - 0 = -2(x - (-7))$
$y - 0 = -2x - 14$
$y = -2x - 14$
Perpendicular lines have negative reciprocal slopes. Therefore $m = \frac{1}{2}$. Substitute the slope, $\frac{1}{2}$, and point $(-7, 0)$ into the point-slope formula.
$y - 0 = \frac{1}{2}(x - (-7))$
$y - 0 = \frac{1}{2}x + \frac{7}{2}$
$y = \frac{1}{2}x + \frac{7}{2}$

3. There are 3600 seconds in one hour.
$\frac{1800 \not{s}}{1} \times \frac{1 \text{ hr}}{3600 \not{s}} = \frac{1800 \text{ hr}}{3600} = \frac{1}{2}$ hr or 0.5 hr

4. There are 36 inches in one yard.
$\frac{16 \not{yd}^2}{1} \times \frac{36 \text{ in.}}{1 \not{yd}} \times \frac{36 \text{ in.}}{1 \not{yd}} = \frac{16(36)(36) \text{ in.}^2}{1}$
$= 20{,}736 \text{ in.}^2$

5. In the form $y = a(x - h)^2 + k$, h is the x-coordinate of the vertex and k is the y-coordinate of the vertex. The parent function is $y = x^2$, where $a = 1$, $h = 0$, and $k = 0$. If the parent function shifts 5 units right from its vertex at (0, 0), then $a = 1$, $h = 5$ and $k = 0$, and the equation is $y = (x - 5)^2$.

6. $\tan(x) = \frac{\text{opp}}{\text{adj}} = \frac{56}{33}$

7. $\csc(x) = \frac{\text{hyp}}{\text{opp}} = \frac{65}{56}$

8. $-12x^4 - 18x^2 - 6$
$= -6(2x^4 + 3x^2 + 1)$

9. $x^2 - 28x + 196$
$= (x - 14)(x - 14)$
$= (x - 14)^2$

10. Substitute the slope, -8, and point $(-2, 9)$ into the point-slope formula.
$y - 9 = -8(x - (-2))$
$y - 9 = -8x - 16$
$y = -8x - 7$

11. Substitute the slope, $\frac{4}{9}$, and point (6, 3) into the point-slope formula.
$y - 3 = \frac{4}{9}(x - 6)$
$y - 3 = \frac{4}{9}x - \frac{24}{9}$
$y = \frac{4}{9}x + \frac{3}{9}$
$y = \frac{4}{9}x + \frac{1}{3}$

12. $\csc M = \frac{\text{hyp}}{\text{opp}} = \frac{10}{8} = \frac{5}{4} = 1.25$
Answer choice **C**

13. $9x + 3y = 21$
$2x - 2y = 2$
$$x = \frac{\begin{vmatrix} 21 & 3 \\ 2 & -2 \end{vmatrix}}{\begin{vmatrix} 9 & 3 \\ 2 & -2 \end{vmatrix}} = \frac{21(-2) - 2(3)}{9(-2) - 2(3)} = \frac{-48}{-24} = 2$$
$$y = \frac{\begin{vmatrix} 9 & 21 \\ 2 & 2 \end{vmatrix}}{\begin{vmatrix} 9 & 3 \\ 2 & -2 \end{vmatrix}} = \frac{9(2) - 2(21)}{9(-2) - 2(3)} = \frac{-24}{-24} = 1$$
The solution is (2, 1).

14. The initial height $h_o = 56$ feet, the initial velocity $v_o = 0$, and the height reached $h(t) = 20$ feet. Substitute the values into the equation and solve for t.

$20 = -16t^2 + 0t + 56$

$0 = -16t^2 + 36$

$0 = -(16t^2 - 36)$

$0 = -(4t - 6)(4t + 6)$

So

$(4t - 6) = 0$ or $(4t + 6) = 0$

$t = \frac{3}{2}$ or $t = -\frac{3}{2}$

Since time cannot be negative, it will take $\frac{3}{2}$ or 1.5 seconds to reach 20 feet.

15. Find the intersection of the boundary lines

$\frac{3}{4}x - 3 = \frac{1}{3}x + 4$

$\frac{5}{12}x = 7$

$x = 16.8$

$y = \frac{1}{3}(16.8) + 4 = 9.6$

The intersection of the boundary lines is (16.8, 9.6).

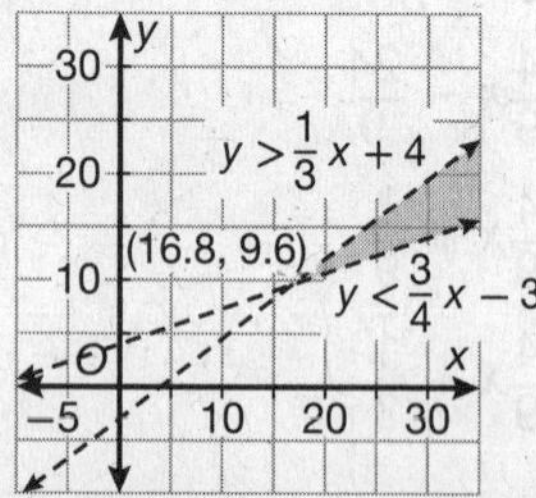

All solutions of the system are above and to the right of (16.8, 9.6), so every solution has an x-coordinate greater than 16.8 and a y-coordinate greater than 9.6. So the least pair of integers, and therefore the least sum, is (17, 10).

16. a. Use two points on the line to write the equation. (30, 40), (90, 90):

$m = \frac{90 - 40}{90 - 30} = \frac{50}{60} = \frac{5}{6}$

$y - 40 = \frac{5}{6}(x - 30)$

$y - 40 = \frac{5}{6}x - 25$

$y = \frac{5}{6}x + 15$

b. Every increase of 6 points on the quiz grade is an increase of 5 points on the test grade.

17. The student replaced the x-value with the y-value and vice versa. The correct answer is

$2y + 3 \leq -4x$

$2(-8) + 3 \leq -4(4)$

$-16 + 3 \leq -16$

$-13 \leq -16$

False, (4, −8) is not a solution.

18. $x^2 - 9x - 36$

$= (x + 3)(x - 12)$

Answer choice **C**

19. a. $\frac{\sqrt[3]{m}}{\sqrt[3]{p}} = \frac{\sqrt[3]{m}}{\sqrt[3]{p}} \cdot \frac{\sqrt[3]{p}\sqrt[3]{p}}{\sqrt[3]{p}\sqrt[3]{p}} = \frac{\sqrt[3]{mp^2}}{p}$

b. $s = \frac{\sqrt[3]{mp^2}}{p} = \frac{\sqrt[3]{1000(88)^2}}{88}$

$= \frac{10\sqrt[3]{(4^3 \cdot 121)}}{88} = \frac{40\sqrt[3]{121}}{88} \approx 2.2$

The side length is about 2.2 cm.

20. The number of inches is always 12 times the number of feet, so all the points lie on the straight line $y = 12x$. A perfectly straight line has correlation of 1.

21. This is a permutation problem since order matters.

$P(5,2) = \frac{5!}{(5-2)!} = \frac{5!}{3!} = \frac{5 \times 4 \times \cancel{3!}}{\cancel{3!}} = 20$

22. The new surface area is

$2(x + 30)(x + 10) + 2(x + 10)(x - 20)$
$+ 2(x + 30)(x - 20)$

$= 2x^2 + 80x + 600 + 2x^2 - 20x - 400 +$
$2x^2 + 20x - 1200$

$= 6x^2 + 80x - 1000$

The original surface area is

$2(x)(x - 10) + 2(x)(x - 10) + 2(x - 10)$
$(x - 10)$

$= 2x^2 - 20x + 2x^2 - 20x + 2x^2 - 40x + 200$

$= 6x^2 - 80x + 200$

The ratio of new surface area to original surface area is

$$\frac{6x^2 + 80x - 1000}{6x^2 - 80x + 200} = \frac{3x^2 + 40x - 500}{3x^2 - 40x + 100}$$

The quotient does not have a zero remainder because there are no common factors for the numerator and denominator.

23. $d = \sqrt{(x_2 - x_1)^2 + (y_2 - y_1)^2}$

$= \sqrt{(225 - 192)^2 + (87 - 232)^2}$

$= \sqrt{1089 + 21{,}025}$

$= \sqrt{22{,}114}$

≈ 149

The distance between Bismarck and Minot is about 149 kilometers.

24. $AX = B$

$X = A^{-1}B$

$$A^{-1}B = \begin{bmatrix} -1 & 0.5 \\ 0.75 & -0.25 \end{bmatrix} \cdot \begin{bmatrix} 10 & 12 \\ 14 & 16 \end{bmatrix}$$

$$= \begin{bmatrix} -3 & -4 \\ 4 & 5 \end{bmatrix}$$

$$X = \begin{bmatrix} -3 & -4 \\ 4 & 5 \end{bmatrix}$$

25. Sample: They are alike because they both use the length of the hypotenuse in the denominator of the ratio. The sine function uses the opposite side in the numerator, and the cosine function uses the adjacent side in the numerator.

26. The student did not include the middle term when squaring the binomial.

$f(x) = -(x + 3)^2 + 14$

$= -(x^2 + 6x + 9) + 14$

$= -x^2 - 6x - 9 + 14$

$= -x^2 - 6x + 5$

27. This is a combination problem, since order does not matter. Choosing Person A and Person B is the same as choosing Person B and Person A. This is a combination of 10 people chosen two at a time, $C(10,2)$.

$$C(10,2) = \frac{10!}{2!(10-2)!} = \frac{10!}{2!8!}$$

$$= \frac{10 \times 9 \times \cancel{8!}}{2!\cancel{8!}} = 45$$

28. The slope is $m = \frac{\text{rise}}{\text{run}} = \frac{15}{10} = 1.5$. The y-intercept, b is 3. Substitute these values into the equation $y = mx + b$.

$y = 1.5x + 3$

29. a. Draw a diagram with the relevant information.

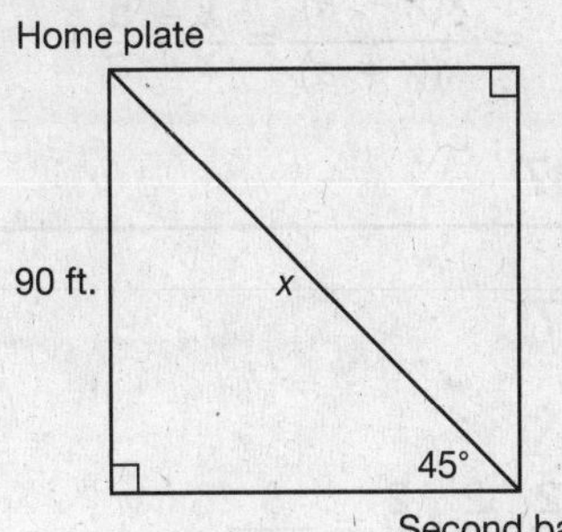

$$\sin 45° = \frac{\text{opp}}{\text{hyp}}$$

$$\sin 45° = \frac{90}{x}$$

$$x = \frac{90}{\sin 45°}$$

$x \approx 127.3$

The distance from home plate to second base is about 127.3 feet.

b. Substitute 90 for both a and b, and 127.3 for c in $a^2 + b^2 = c^2$.

$a^2 + b^2 = c^2$

$90^2 + 90^2 \stackrel{?}{=} 127.3^2$

$8100 + 8100 \stackrel{?}{=} 16{,}205$

$16{,}200 \approx 16{,}205$

30. The unshaded region is the area of the square minus the shaded region (the area of the triangle). Each side of the square is x. The area of the square is x^2.

The height of the triangle is x and the base is $x - a$. The area of the shaded triangle is $\frac{x(x-a)}{2} = \frac{x^2 - ax}{2}$

The unshaded region is

$$x^2 - \frac{x^2 - ax}{2}$$

$$= x^2 \cdot \frac{2}{2} - \frac{x^2 - ax}{2}$$

$$= \frac{2x^2}{2} - \frac{x^2 - ax}{2}$$

$$= \frac{2x^2 - x^2 + ax}{2} = \frac{x^2 + ax}{2}$$

The ratio of the area of the shaded region to the unshaded region is

$$\frac{\frac{x^2 - ax}{2}}{\frac{x^2 + ax}{2}} = \frac{x^2 - ax}{2} \cdot \frac{2}{x^2 + ax}$$

$$= \frac{x(x - a)}{x(x + a)} = \frac{x - a}{x + a}$$

LESSON 47

Warm Up 47

1. base

2. $\left(\frac{2}{5}\right)^3 = \frac{2}{5} \cdot \frac{2}{5} \cdot \frac{2}{5} = \frac{8}{125}$

3. The minimum value occurs at the vertex. If the equation is in the form $y = a(x - h)^2 + k$, the vertex is given by (h, k). The equation in this form is $y = (x - 0)^2 + (-5)$. So, the minimum is (0, −5) and the maximum is −5.

Lesson Practice 47

a. Make a table, plot the ordered pairs, and draw a smooth curve through them.

x	−3	−2	−1	0	1	2	3
$y = \left(\frac{1}{2}\right)^x$	8	4	2	1	$\frac{1}{2}$	$\frac{1}{4}$	$\frac{1}{8}$

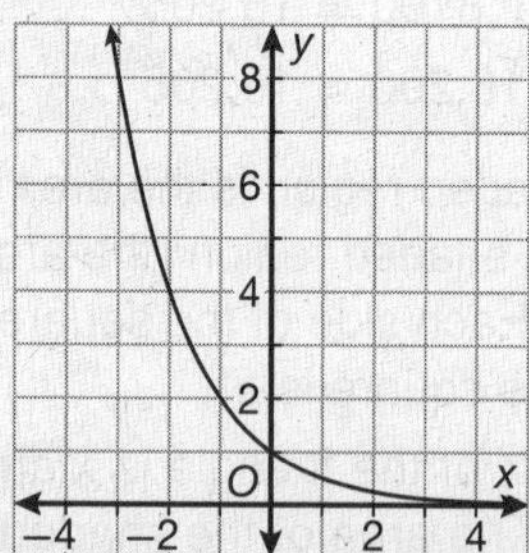

The domain is the set of all real numbers; the graph extends without end to the left and to the right. The asymptote is the line $y = 0$; as x increases without bound, y approaches 0. The range is the set of all positive real numbers; the graph gets closer and closer to the x-axis from above, and it extends up without end.

b. Make a table of values and graph each function.

x	−3	−2	−1	0	1	2	3
$y = \left(\frac{3}{4}\right)^x$	$\frac{64}{27}$	$\frac{16}{9}$	$\frac{4}{3}$	1	$\frac{3}{4}$	$\frac{9}{16}$	$\frac{27}{64}$
$y = \left(\frac{4}{3}\right)^x$	$\frac{27}{64}$	$\frac{9}{16}$	$\frac{3}{4}$	1	$\frac{4}{3}$	$\frac{16}{9}$	$\frac{64}{27}$

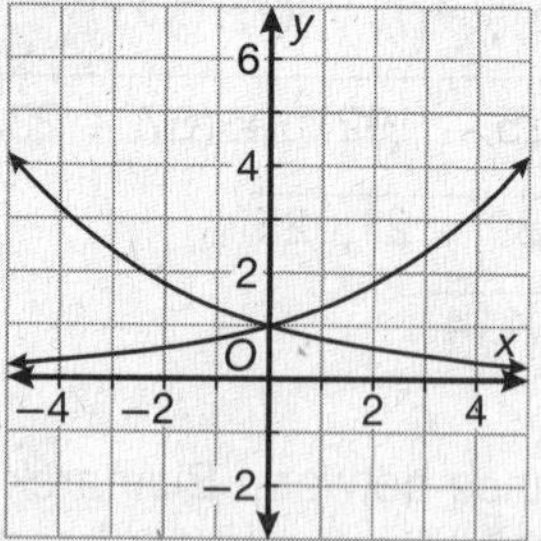

The graphs are reflection images of each other across the y-axis.

c. Make a table of values and graph each function.

x	−2	−1	0	1	2
$y_1 = 2^x$	$\frac{1}{4}$	$\frac{1}{2}$	1	2	4
$y_2 = \frac{1}{2} \cdot 2^x$	$\frac{1}{8}$	$\frac{1}{4}$	$\frac{1}{2}$	1	2
$y_3 = \frac{1}{2} \cdot 2^x + 3$	$3\frac{1}{8}$	$3\frac{1}{4}$	$3\frac{1}{2}$	4	5

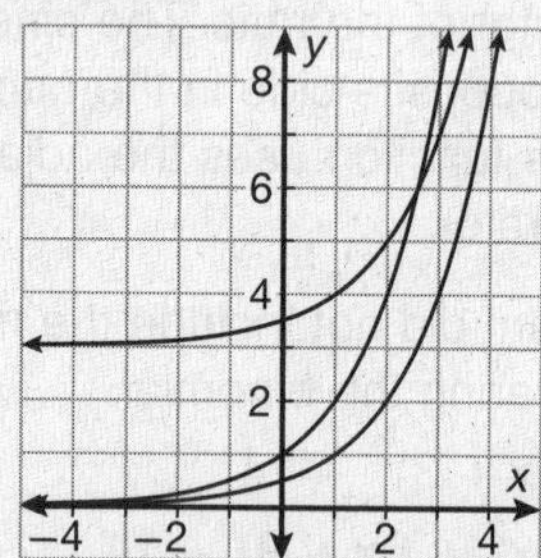

y_1 is the parent function of all exponential functions with base 2. The domain of all the functions is the set of all real numbers. The range of y_1, and y_2 is the set of all positive real numbers. The range of y_3 is the set of all real numbers greater than 3.

The graph of y_2 is a vertical compression of the graph y_1 by a factor of $\frac{1}{2}$.

The graph of y_3 is a vertical shift 3 units up of the graph y_2.

d. 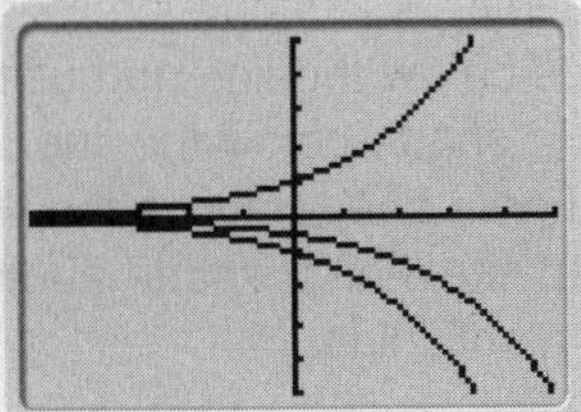

y_1 is the parent function of all exponential functions with base 1.6.

The graph of y_2 is a reflection of the graph of y_1 over the x-axis.

The graph of y_3 is a vertical compression of the graph y_2 by a factor of $\frac{1}{2}$.

e. Understand: Quarterly means 4 times per year. Monthly means 12 times per year.

Plan: Evaluate the function letting $n = 4$ and $n = 12$.

Solve:

Compounded Quarterly:

$$A = P\left(1 + \frac{r}{n}\right)^{nt}$$
$$A = 1000\left(1 + \frac{0.06}{4}\right)^{4(2)}$$
$$A = 1000(1 + 0.015)^8$$
$$A = 1000(1.015)^8$$
$$A = 1126.49$$

Compounded Monthly:

$$A = P\left(1 + \frac{r}{n}\right)^{nt}$$
$$A = 1000\left(1 + \frac{0.06}{12}\right)^{12(2)}$$
$$A = 1000(1.005)^{24}$$
$$A = 1127.16$$

There will be \$1126.49 in the account after 2 years if the interest is compounded quarterly and \$1127.16 if the interest in compounded monthly.

Practice 47

1. The area of the large (total) rectangle is

$(7x + 2)(2x^2 + 3x + 8)$
$= 14x^3 + 21x^2 + 56x + 4x^2 + 6x + 16$
$= 14x^3 + 25x^2 + 62x + 16$

The area of the shaded part is

$(x + 4)(3x + 9)$
$= 3x^2 + 21x + 36$

The probability is

$$\frac{3x^2 + 21x + 36}{14x^3 + 25x^2 + 62x + 16}$$

2.

$$\begin{array}{r} 3x^2 - 19x + 31 \\ x + 1\overline{)3x^3 - 16x^2 + 12x + 16} \\ \underline{-(3x^3 + 3x^2)} \\ -19x^2 + 12x \\ \underline{-(-19x^2 - 19x)} \\ 31x + 16 \\ \underline{-(31x + 31)} \\ -15 \end{array}$$

Answer choice **B**

3. The x-intercepts are equidistant from the line of symmetry, which is a vertical line through the vertex. The x-coordinate of the vertex is therefore the mean of the x-intercepts.

$x = \frac{x_1 + x_2}{2}$.

4. 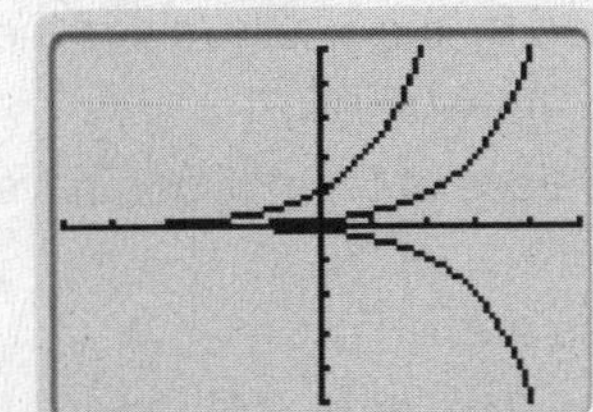

y_1 is the parent function of all exponential functions with base 2.3.

The graph of y_2 is a vertical compression of the graph y_1 by a factor of $\frac{1}{6}$.

The graph of y_3 is a reflection of the graph of y_2 over the x-axis.

5. $\frac{5x^2}{pm} - 4 + \frac{c}{p^2m}$

$$= \frac{5x^2}{pm} \cdot \frac{p}{p} - 4 \cdot \frac{p^2m}{p^2m} + \frac{c}{p^2m}$$
$$= \frac{5x^2p}{p^2m} - \frac{4p^2m}{p^2m} + \frac{c}{p^2m}$$
$$= \frac{5x^2p - 4p^2m + c}{p^2m}$$

6. $3xy^2m + \frac{4}{x}$

$$= 3xy^2m \cdot \frac{x}{x} + \frac{4}{x}$$

$$= \frac{3x^2y^2m}{x} + \frac{4}{x} = \frac{3x^2y^2m + 4}{x}$$

7. There are 60 seconds in one minute.

$$= \frac{120x^2 - 60x - 240 \text{ ft}}{1 \cancel{\text{min}}} \cdot \frac{1 \cancel{\text{min}}}{60 \text{ s}}$$

$$= \frac{120x^2 - 60x - 240 \text{ ft}}{60 \text{ s}}$$

$$= \frac{\cancel{60}(2x^2 - x - 4) \text{ ft}}{\cancel{60} \text{ s}} = 2x^2 - x - 4 \frac{\text{ft}}{\text{s}}$$

8. a. $10x + 15y \geq 240$

$x + y \leq 20$

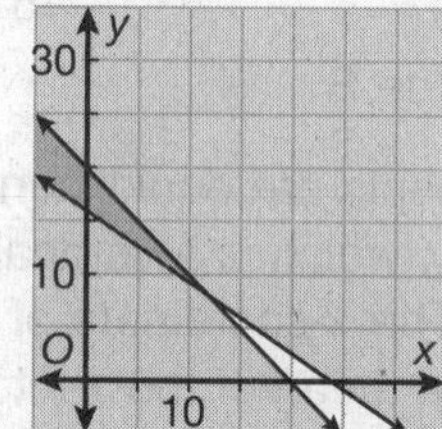

b. The portion that contains meaningful solutions is the area that forms a triangle that is bounded by the y-axis, since the x-values cannot be negative.

c. Two of the vertices of the polygon have x-values of zero.

These vertices are

$10(0) + 15y = 240$, or $(0, 16)$, and

$0 + y = 20$, or $(0, 20)$.

The other vertex is the intersection of the lines.

$10x + 15y = 240 \longrightarrow \quad 10x + 15y = 240$

$x + y = 20 \longrightarrow \quad \underline{-10x - 10y = -240}$

$5y = 40$

$y = 8$

$x + 8 = 20$

$x = 12$

$(0, 20)$, $(0, 16)$, $(12, 8)$; Possible description: $(0, 20)$ represents 0 hours in the library and 20 hours landscaping for total earnings of \$300; $(0, 16)$ represents 0 hours in the library and 16 hours landscaping for total earnings of \$240; $(12, 8)$ represents 12 hours in the library and 8 hours landscaping for total earnings of \$240.

9. Assume the inequality is in slope-intercept form. For $<$ shade below the line and use a dashed line. For $\leq$ shade below the line and use a solid line. For $>$ shade above the line and use a dashed line. For $\geq$ shade above the line and use a solid line.

10. The initial height $h_o = 52$ feet, the initial velocity $v_o = 36$ feet per second, and the height it reached $h(t) = 0$ feet. Substitute the values into the equation and solve for t.

$0 = -16t^2 + 36t + 52$

$0 = -4(4t^2 - 9t - 13)$

$0 = -4(4t - 13)(t + 1)$

so

$-4(4t - 13) = 0 \quad$ or $(t + 1) = 0$

$t = \frac{13}{4} \quad$ or $\quad t = -1$

Since time cannot be negative, it will take $\frac{13}{4}$ or 3.25 seconds.

11.

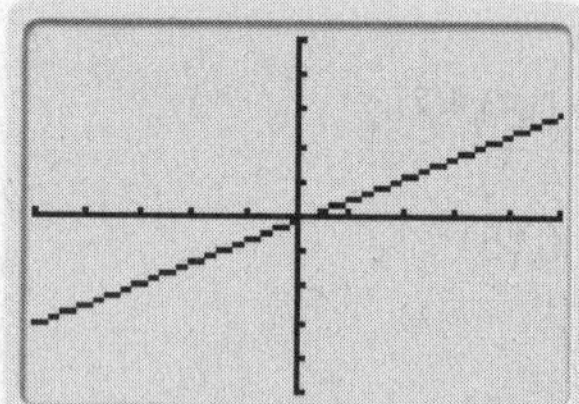

All three lines coincide.

12. Daily means 365 times per year.

$A = P\left(1 + \frac{r}{n}\right)^{nt}$

$A = 3000\left(1 + \frac{0.083}{365}\right)^{365(2)}$

$A = \$3541.65$

13. Substitute 2 for x, -5 for y, and 3 for z in each equation.

$4(2) + 3(-5) + 5(3) \stackrel{?}{=} 8$

$8 = 8$

$-6(2) + 3(-5) + 7(3) \stackrel{?}{=} -6$

$-6 = -6$

$8(2) + (-5) - 2(3) \stackrel{?}{=} 5$

$5 = 5$

$(2, -5, 3)$ is a solution.

14. Substitute 0 for x, 1 for y, and 2 for z in each equation.

$10(0) + 9(1) + 6(2) \stackrel{?}{=} 21$

$$21 = 21$$
$$-(0) + 4(1) - 7(2) \stackrel{?}{=} -10$$
$$-10 = -10$$
$$-9(0) + 5(1) + 2(2) \stackrel{?}{=} 9$$
$$9 = 9$$

(0, 1, 2) is a solution.

15. Multiplying by the conjugate adds and subtracts the same middle terms in the product which contain radicals, thereby eliminating them. Also, multiplying the first terms square the radical, so the first term of the product is no longer a radical. Therefore, all the radical terms are eliminated.

16. $$x = \frac{\begin{vmatrix} -4 & -12 \\ -6 & 18 \end{vmatrix}}{\begin{vmatrix} 4 & -12 \\ -6 & 18 \end{vmatrix}} = \frac{-4(18) - (-6)(-12)}{4(18) - (-6)(-12)}$$
$$= \frac{-144}{0}$$
$$y = \frac{\begin{vmatrix} 4 & -4 \\ -6 & -6 \end{vmatrix}}{\begin{vmatrix} 4 & -12 \\ -6 & 18 \end{vmatrix}} = \frac{4(-6) - (-6)(-4)}{4(18) - (-6)(-12)}$$
$$= \frac{-48}{0}$$

The coefficient matrix has a determinant of 0. The numerator matrices are non-zero, indicating that there are no solutions. The two equations are inconsistent.

17. Substitute 30 for a, 72 for b, and 78 for c in $a^2 + b^2 = c^2$.

$$30^2 + 72^2 \stackrel{?}{=} 78^2$$
$$900 + 5184 \stackrel{?}{=} 6084$$
$$6084 = 6084$$

Therefore, the triangle is a right triangle.

18.

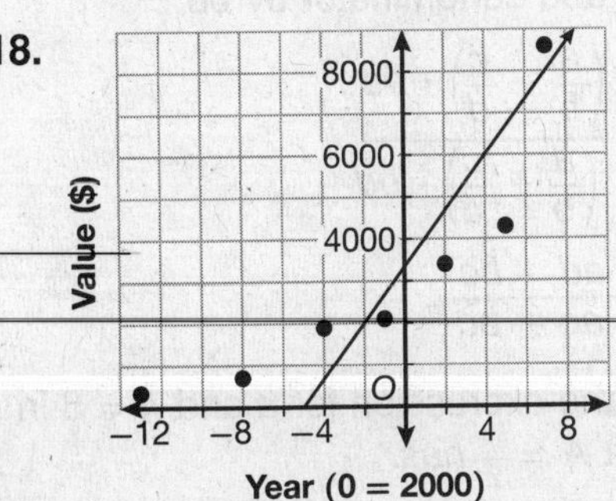

19. The student did not completely simplify the expression because the square root of 12 can be simplified.

$$2\sqrt{12} = 2\sqrt{4}\sqrt{3} = 4\sqrt{3}$$

20. Find the length of the hypotenuse

$$c^2 = (8x)^2 + (15x)^2$$
$$c^2 = 64x^2 + 225x^2$$
$$c^2 = 289x^2$$
$$c = \sqrt{289x^2}$$
$$c = 17x$$

The perimeter is $8x + 15x + 17x = 40x$.

The area is

$$A = \frac{bh}{2} = \frac{8x(15x)}{2} = \frac{120x^2}{2} = 60x^2.$$

The ratio of perimeter to area is $\frac{40x}{60x^2} = \frac{2}{3x}$.

21. The equation for amounts up to \$50 is $y = 2.0284x + 2.5$.

The equation for amounts above \$50 is $y = 2.0284x + 7.5$.

In the form $y = mx + b$ the graphs have the same slope (value for m) and different y-intercepts (value for b) so they are parallel lines and they do not coincide.

22. The graph represents $y = -2$. The y-coordinate of every point on the line is -2.

23. **a.** Yes. When 3 is factored out, it does not cancel out with the 2 in the denominator.

b. No. The denominator will never be 0.

24. Draw a diagram of the problem.

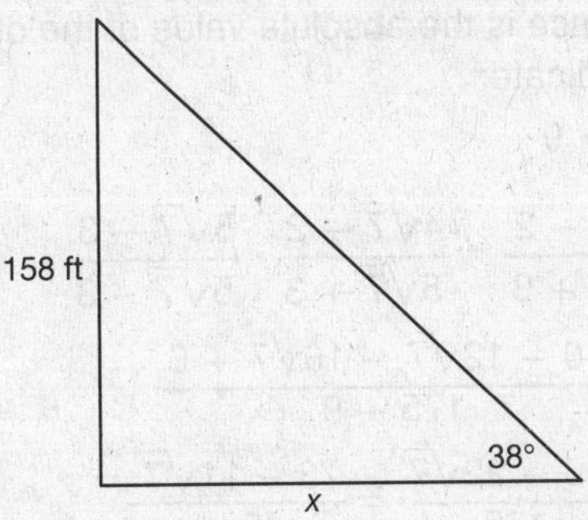

$$\tan A = \frac{\text{opp}}{\text{adj}}$$
$$\tan 38° = \frac{158}{x}$$

$$x = \frac{158}{\tan 38°}$$
$$\approx 202$$

The tourist is about 202 feet from the base of the lighthouse.

25. 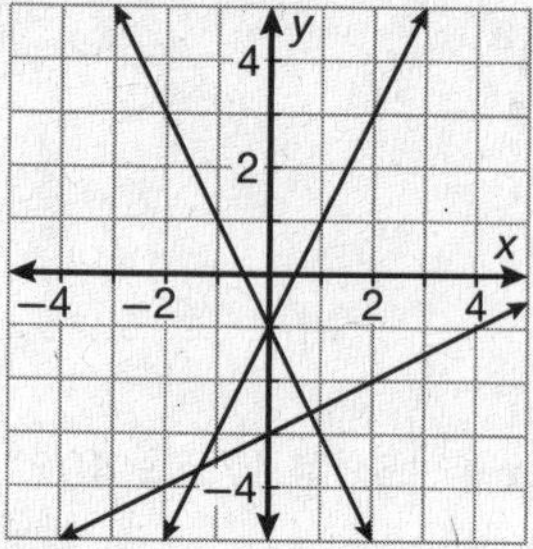

The intersections of the lines form a triangle.

26. This is a combination problem, since order does not matter. This is a combination of 15 people chosen 3 at a time, $C(15,3)$.

$$C(15,3) = \frac{15!}{3!(15-3)!} = \frac{15!}{3!12!}$$
$$= \frac{15 \times 14 \times 13 \times \cancel{12!}}{3!\cancel{12!}} = 455$$

Answer choice **A**

27. Since one of the coordinates is zero, then the distance is the absolute value of the other coordinate.

$|5| = 5$

28. Since one of the coordinates is zero, then the distance is the absolute value of the other coordinate.

$|-7| = 7$

29. Since one of the coordinates is zero, then the distance is the absolute value of the other coordinate.

$|9| = 9$

30. $$\frac{4\sqrt{7}-2}{5\sqrt{7}+3} = \frac{4\sqrt{7}-2}{5\sqrt{7}+3} \cdot \frac{5\sqrt{7}-3}{5\sqrt{7}-3}$$
$$= \frac{140 - 12\sqrt{7} - 10\sqrt{7} + 6}{175 - 9}$$
$$= \frac{146 - 22\sqrt{7}}{166} = \frac{73 - 11\sqrt{7}}{83}$$

Answer choice **A**

LESSON 48

Warm Up 48

1. reciprocal
2. $\frac{3}{10} \div \frac{6}{5} = \frac{3}{10} \times \frac{5}{6} = \frac{1}{4}$
3. The factors of $4x$ are $2(2)x$. The factors of $6x$ are $2(3)x$. The factors of $x + 5$ are $1(x + 5)$. The LCD is $12x(x + 5)$.

Lesson Practice 48

a. Add the terms in the numerator. Add the terms in the denominator

$$\frac{\frac{1}{10} - 1}{\frac{5}{8} + \frac{3}{20}} = \frac{\frac{1}{10} - \frac{10}{10}}{\frac{25}{40} + \frac{6}{40}}.$$

Simplify.

$$= \frac{-\frac{9}{10}}{\frac{31}{40}}$$

To divide by a fraction, multiply by its reciprocal.

$$= -\frac{9}{10} \cdot \frac{40}{31}$$
$$= -\frac{36}{31}$$

b. The LCD of $\frac{5}{x}$ and $\frac{3}{y}$ is xy. Multiply the numerator and denominator by xy.

$$\frac{\frac{5}{x} - 1}{\frac{3}{y} + 1} = \frac{\left(\frac{5}{x} - 1\right) \cdot xy}{\left(\frac{3}{y} + 1\right) \cdot xy} = \frac{5y - xy}{3x + xy}$$

c. The LCD of $\frac{a}{b}$ and $\frac{c}{d}$ is bd. Multiply the numerator and denominator by bd.

$$\frac{\frac{a}{b} - \frac{c}{d}}{\frac{a}{b} + \frac{c}{d}} = \frac{\left(\frac{a}{b} - \frac{c}{d}\right) \cdot bd}{\left(\frac{a}{b} + \frac{c}{d}\right) \cdot bd}$$
$$= \frac{ad - bc}{ad + bc}$$

d. Substitute the expression for a and $n = 5$ in the formula $A = \frac{1}{2}nas$.

$$A = \frac{1}{2}nas$$

$$A = \frac{1}{2}(5)\left(\frac{\frac{s}{2}}{0.727}\right)s$$

$$A = \frac{5}{2}\left(\frac{\frac{s}{2} \cdot 2}{0.727 \cdot 2}\right)s$$

$$A = \frac{5}{2}\left(\frac{s}{1.454}\right)s$$

$$A = \frac{5}{2}\left(\frac{s^2}{1.454}\right)$$

$$A = \frac{5s^2}{2.908} \text{ or } A = 1.719s^2$$

Practice 48

1. $$\frac{\frac{x}{m+p}}{\frac{y}{m+p}} = \frac{\left(\frac{x}{m+p}\right) \cdot (m+p)}{\left(\frac{y}{m+p}\right) \cdot (m+p)} = \frac{x}{y}$$

2. $$\frac{x + \frac{4xy}{x}}{\frac{1}{x} - y} = \frac{\left(x + \frac{4xy}{x}\right) \cdot x}{\left(\frac{1}{x} - y\right) \cdot x} = \frac{x^2 + 4xy}{1 - xy}$$

3. $$\frac{\frac{m}{p} + \frac{3}{xp}}{\frac{y}{p}} = \frac{\left(\frac{m}{p} + \frac{3}{xp}\right) \cdot xp}{\left(\frac{y}{p}\right) \cdot xp} = \frac{mx + 3}{xy}$$

4. $h(x) = f(x) - g(x)$.
$h(x) = (x + 24) - (2x - 90)$
$h(x) = x + 24 - 2x + 90$
$h(x) = -x + 114$ feet

5. In t seconds the plane travels a ground distance of x feet and an altitude of y feet. The parametric equations are
$x = 240t$
$y = 40t$
Substitute 20 for t in the equations.
$x = 240(20) = 4800$
$y = 40(20) = 800$
Therefore the plane is at a ground distance of 4800 feet from the airport and has an altitude of 800 feet.

6. One pair from the three lines must be perpendicular if this is a right triangle. Perpendicular lines have opposite reciprocal slopes.
Slope from $(-3, 6)$ to $(4, 4)$:
$$m = \frac{y_2 - y_1}{x_2 - x_1} = \frac{4 - 6}{4 - (-3)} = \frac{-2}{7} = \frac{-2}{7}$$
Slope from $(4, 4)$ to $(1, -8)$:
$$m = \frac{y_2 - y_1}{x_2 - x_1} = \frac{-8 - 4}{1 - 4} = \frac{-12}{-3} = 4$$
Slope from $(-3, 6)$ to $(1, -8)$:
$$m = \frac{y_2 - y_1}{x_2 - x_1} = \frac{-8 - 6}{1 - (-3)} = \frac{-14}{4} = -\frac{7}{2}$$
None of the slopes are the opposite reciprocal of each other, so none of the pairs of lines are perpendicular. The triangle is not a right triangle.

7. $$A = lw$$
$$30 = l(\sqrt{3} + 1)$$
$$\frac{30}{(\sqrt{3} + 1)} = \frac{l(\sqrt{3} + 1)}{(\sqrt{3} + 1)}$$
$$\frac{30}{(\sqrt{3} + 1)} = l$$
$$\frac{30}{\sqrt{3} + 1} \cdot \frac{\sqrt{3} - 1}{\sqrt{3} - 1} = l$$
$$\frac{30\sqrt{3} - 30}{3 - 1} = l$$
$$\frac{30\sqrt{3} - 30}{2} = l$$
$$15\sqrt{3} - 15 = l$$
So the length of the garden is $15(\sqrt{3} - 1)$ ft.

8. A quadratic function has the form $y = a(x - h)^2 + k$, where the vertex is (h, k). The parent function is $y = x^2$, which can be written as $y = 1(x - 0)^2 + 0$, so its vertex is $(0, 0)$. A shift 5 units right puts the vertex at $(5, 0)$, so the equation is $y = 1(x - 5)^2 + 0$, or $y = (x - 5)^2$.

9. A quadratic function has the form $y = a(x - h)^2 + k$, where the vertex is (h, k). The parent function is $y = x^2$, which can be written as $y = 1(x - 0)^2 + 0$, so its vertex is $(0, 0)$. A shift 2 units left and 7 units up puts the vertex at $(-2, 7)$, so the equation is $y = 1(x - (-2))^2 + 7$, or $y = (x + 2)^2 + 7$.

10. If the absolute value signs were missing, then substituting a negative value for x, such as $x = -2$, would give a false answer, since $\sqrt{(-2)^2} = \sqrt{4} = -2$ is not true, as the radical symbol indicates that only the positive root can be given.

11. This is a discrete, discontinuous function, since the graph consists of four points which are not connected.

12. Once a position is specified, there are only four digits left that can be arranged in any order. $4! = 4 \times 3 \times 2 \times 1 = 24$ arrangements.

13. If the outlier, 65, is eliminated the data in order is 11, 11, 12, 12, 13, 14, 14, 14, 14, 15, 15, and the median is 14. 14 should be marked in the box. The mean is marked instead of the median.

Mean

$$= \frac{11 + 11 + 12 + 12 + 13 + 14 + 14 + 14 + 14 + 15 + 15}{11}$$

$$= \frac{145}{11} \approx 13.2$$

14. $$\frac{\frac{5}{2x} - \frac{2}{x+5}}{\frac{1}{2(x+5)} + \frac{1}{x}} = \frac{\left(\frac{5}{2x} - \frac{2}{x+5}\right) \cdot 2x(x+5)}{\frac{1}{2(x+5)} + \frac{1}{x} \cdot 2x(x+5)}$$

$$= \frac{5(x+5) - 2(2x)}{(x) + 2(x+5)}$$

$$= \frac{5x + 25 - 4x}{x + 2x + 10}$$

$$= \frac{x + 25}{3x + 10}$$

15. a. Pick values for x and solve for $f(x)$ to make a table.

x	$(x-2)^2 + 6$	$f(x)$
−2	$(-2-2)^2 + 6$	22
0	$(0-2)^2 + 6$	10
2	$(2-2)^2 + 6$	6
4	$(4-2)^2 + 6$	10

Plot the values in the table: (−2, 22), (0, 10), (2, 6), (4, 10).

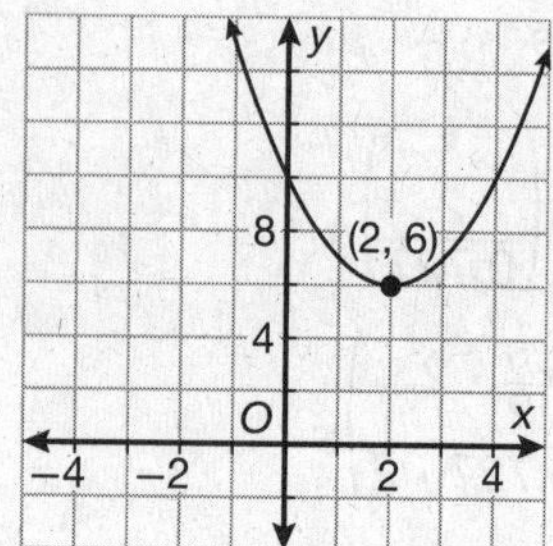

b. The vertex is (h, k) for a function in the form $y = (x - h)^2 + k$.

16. $5\sqrt{18} - 10\sqrt{50} + 3\sqrt{72}$
$= 5\sqrt{9}\sqrt{2} - 10\sqrt{25}\sqrt{2} + 3\sqrt{36}\sqrt{2}$
$= 15\sqrt{2} - 50\sqrt{2} + 18\sqrt{2}$
$= -17\sqrt{2}$

17. $3\sqrt{18}(4\sqrt{2} - 2\sqrt{3}) = 12\sqrt{36} - 6\sqrt{54}$
$= 72 - 6\sqrt{9}\sqrt{6}$
$= 72 - 18\sqrt{6}$

18. $$2\sqrt{\frac{2}{9}} - 3\sqrt{\frac{9}{2}} = 2\frac{\sqrt{2}}{\sqrt{9}} - 3\frac{\sqrt{9}}{\sqrt{2}}$$

$$= 2\frac{\sqrt{2}}{\sqrt{9}} \cdot \frac{\sqrt{9}}{\sqrt{9}} - 3\frac{\sqrt{9}}{\sqrt{2}} \cdot \frac{\sqrt{2}}{\sqrt{2}}$$

$$= 2\frac{3\sqrt{2}}{9} - 3\frac{3\sqrt{2}}{2}$$

$$= \frac{6\sqrt{2}}{9} - \frac{9\sqrt{2}}{2}$$

$$= \frac{6\sqrt{2}}{9} \cdot \frac{2}{2} - \frac{9\sqrt{2}}{2} \cdot \frac{9}{9}$$

$$= \frac{12\sqrt{2}}{18} - \frac{81\sqrt{2}}{18}$$

$$= -\frac{69\sqrt{2}}{18} = -\frac{23\sqrt{2}}{6}$$

19. $$-3\sqrt{\frac{2}{3}} + 2\sqrt{\frac{3}{2}} = -3\frac{\sqrt{2}}{\sqrt{3}} + 2\frac{\sqrt{3}}{\sqrt{2}}$$

$$= -3\frac{\sqrt{2}}{\sqrt{3}} \cdot \frac{\sqrt{3}}{\sqrt{3}} + 2\frac{\sqrt{3}}{\sqrt{2}} \cdot \frac{\sqrt{2}}{\sqrt{2}}$$

$$= -\frac{\cancel{3}\sqrt{6}}{\cancel{3}} + \frac{\cancel{2}\sqrt{6}}{\cancel{2}}$$

$$= -\sqrt{6} + \sqrt{6}$$

$$= 0$$

20. $3\sqrt{24}(2\sqrt{6} - 3\sqrt{12}) = 6\sqrt{144} - 9\sqrt{288}$
$= 72 - 9\sqrt{144}\sqrt{2}$
$= 72 - 108\sqrt{2}$

21. a. The equation is in the form $y = a(x - h)^2 + k$. Since a is positive, the graph has a vertex which is a minimum at $(h, k) = (5, 1)$. The y-intercept is at $y = (0 - 5)^2 + 1 = 26$. Find another point by substituting a value such as 8 for x and solve for y: (8, 10). Plot the points.

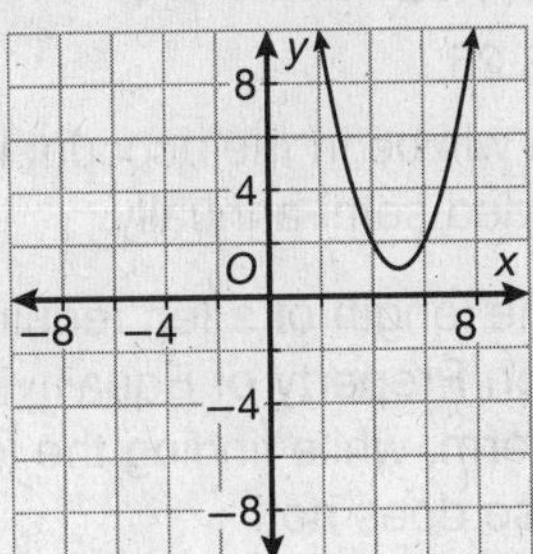

b. Plot each point in the first graph the same distance from the x-axis (on the other side of the x-axis) to sketch the reflection.

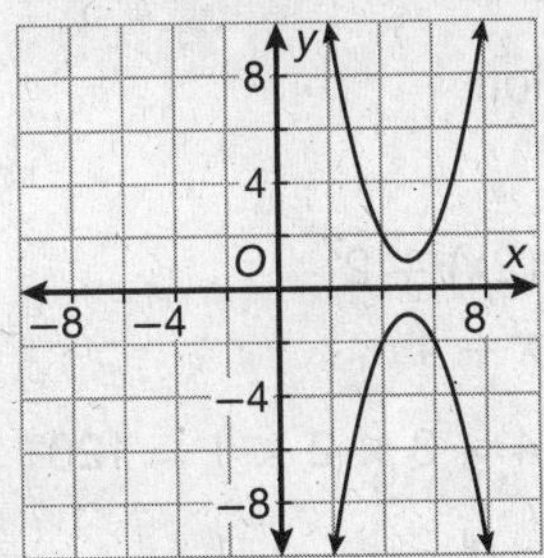

c. The second graph has a maximum so a is negative, and the vertex is at (5, −1). The equation is $y = -(x - 5)^2 - 1$.

22. **A** The coefficients for x are opposite integers in both equations, so they do not need to be multiplied.

B The coefficient of x can be multiplied by −1 in one of the equations to get the opposite of the coefficient in the other equation.

C The second equation can be multiplied by 16 to get opposite coefficients for x.

D Multiply the first equation by 3 and the second equation by −4 to get opposite x-coefficients. Alternatively, multiply the first equation by 5 and the second equation by 4 to get opposite y-coefficients.

Answer choice **D**

23. Student A incorrectly multiplied the numerator in the second term by $(x - 3)$ instead of $(x + 3)$.

24. The graphs of $y = \left(\frac{1}{b}\right)^x$ and $y = bx$ are reflections of each other about the y-axis. $y = bx + k$ shifts $y = bx$ vertically k units. Therefore $y = \left(\frac{1}{5}\right)^x + 3$ must be reflected about the y-axis and translated 2 units down to get the graph of $y = 5x + 1$.

25. Using a graphing calculator, the solution is (1.25, 8.75).

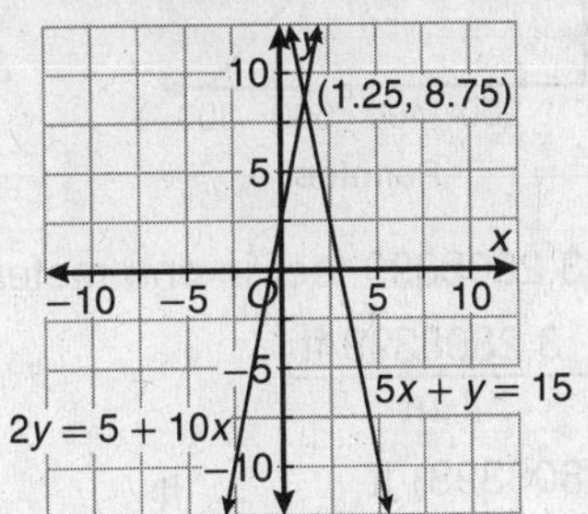

26. $$\frac{\frac{4}{x+2} - \frac{2}{x+3}}{\frac{2}{x+3}}$$

$$= \frac{\left(\frac{4}{x+2} - \frac{2}{x+3}\right)(x+2)(x+3)}{\left(\frac{2}{x+3}\right)(x+2)(x+3)}$$

$$= \frac{4(x+3) - 2(x+2)}{2(x+2)}$$

$$= \frac{4x + 12 - 2x - 4}{2x + 4}$$

$$= \frac{2x+8}{2x+4} = \frac{2(x+4)}{2(x+2)} = \frac{x+4}{x+2}$$

27. There are 1000 grams in one kilogram, so there are 2000 grams in 2 kilograms.

Let x represent the number of pennies, and y represent the number of nickels.

$2.5x + 5y \geq 2000$

Write the inequality as an equation in $y = mx + b$ form to graph.

$2.5x + 5y = 2000$

$5y = -2.5x + 2000$

$y = -0.5x + 400$

Plot the graph with slope −0.5 and y-intercept 400. Use a test point (0, 0) to determine which plane to shade.

2.5(0) + 5(0) ≥ 2000 is false so shade the plane above the line that does not include (0, 0).

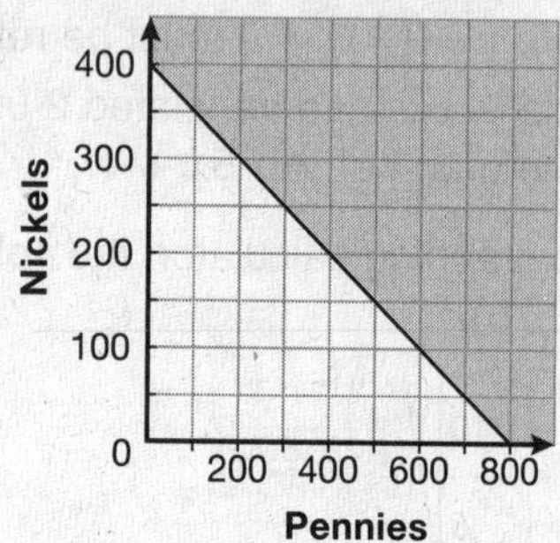

28. a. There are 3.2808399 feet in one meter.

$$\frac{100\ \cancel{m}}{51.59\ s} \times \frac{3.2808399\ ft}{1\ \cancel{m}}$$

$$= \frac{100(3.2808399)\ ft}{51.59\ s} \approx 6.36\ \frac{ft}{s}$$

b. $$\frac{100\ \cancel{m}}{48.62\ s} \times \frac{3.2808399\ ft}{1\ \cancel{m}}$$

$$= \frac{100(3.2808399)\ ft}{48.62\ s} \approx 6.75\ \frac{ft}{s}$$

29. Annually means one time per year. Evaluate $A = P\left(1 + \frac{r}{n}\right)^{nt}$, letting $P = 2800$, $n = 1$, $t = 3$, $r = 0.04$.

$$A = 2800\left(1 + \frac{0.04}{1}\right)^{1(3)}$$

$$= 2800(1.04)^3$$

$$= 3149.62$$

\$3149.62 will be in the account if interest is compounded annually.

Semi-annually means 2 times per year. Evaluate $A = P\left(1 + \frac{r}{n}\right)^{nt}$, letting $P = 2800$, $n = 2$, $t = 3$, $r = 0.04$.

$$A = 2800\left(1 + \frac{0.04}{2}\right)^{2(3)}$$

$$= 2800(1.02)^6$$

$$= 3153.25$$

\$3153.25 will be in the account if interest is compounded semi-annually.

30. Finding the length of a leg requires using the Subtraction Property of Equality to isolate the squared term, while finding the length of the hypotenuse does not.

LESSON 49

Warm Up 49

1. combination

2. $(x + 2)^2$

$= x^2 + 2(2x) + 2^2$

$= x^2 + 4x + 4$

3. $5! = 5 \times 4 \times 3 \times 2 \times 1 = 120$

4. $_nC_r = \frac{n!}{r!(n-r)!}$

$$_6C_2 = \frac{6!}{2!(6-2)!} = \frac{6 \times 5 \times \cancel{4!}}{2!\cancel{4!}} = 15$$

5. $$\frac{2!}{6!} = \frac{\cancel{2!}}{6 \times 5 \times 4 \times 3 \times \cancel{2!}} = \frac{1}{360}$$

Lesson Practice 49

a. Using the third row of Pascal's Triangle to write the coefficients

$(a + b)^3 = 1a^3b^0 + 3a^2b^1 + 3a^1b^2 + 1a^0b^3$

$(2x + 4)^3 = 1(2x)^3 4^0 + 3(2x)^2 4^1 + 3(2x)^1 4^2 + 1(2x)^0 4^3$

$= 8x^3 + 48x^2 + 96x + 64$

b. Use the binomial theorem to expand $(a + b)^n$ where $a = f$, $b = 2$, and $n = 5$.

$(f + 2)^5 = ({_5C_0})f^5 2^0 + ({_5C_1})f^4 2^1 + ({_5C_2})f^3 2^2 + ({_5C_3})f^2 2^3 + ({_5C_4})f^1 2^4 + ({_5C_5})f^0 2^5$

Evaluate the coefficients and simplify.

$(f + 2)^5 = (1)f^5 2^0 + (5)f^4 2^1 + (10)f^3 2^2 + (10)f^2 2^3 + (5)f^1 2^4 + (1)f^0 2^5$

$= f^5 + 10f^4 + 40f^3 + 80f^2 + 80f + 32$

c. Use the binomial theorem to expand $(a + b)^n$ where $a = 1$, $b = -7x$, and $n = 3$.

$(1 - 7x)^3 = ({}_3C_0)1^3(-7x)^0 + ({}_3C_1)1^2(-7x)^1 + ({}_3C_2)1^1(-7x)^2 + ({}_3C_3)1^0(-7x)^3$

Evaluate the coefficients and simplify.

$$(1 - 7x)^3 = (1)1^3(-7x)^0 + (3)1^2(-7x)^1 + (3)1^1(-7x)^2 + (1)1^0(-7x)^3$$
$$= 1 - 21x + 147x^2 - 343x^3$$

d. First use the Binomial Theorem to write the expression in summation notation.

$$(x + 3)^{10} = \sum_{r=0}^{10}({}_{10}C_r)x^{10-r}3^r$$

In the fourth term $r = 3$.

$$({}_{10}C_r)x^{10-3}3^r = ({}_{10}C_3)x^{10-3}3^3$$
$$= \frac{10!}{3!(10-3)!}x^{10-3}3^3$$
$$= \frac{10 \times 9 \times 8 \times \cancel{7!}}{3 \times 2 \times \cancel{7!}}x^7 \cdot 27$$
$$= 3240x^7$$

e. $P(\text{exactly 5 tails}) = ({}_6C_5)p^5q^{6-5}$

$$({}_6C_5)p^5q^1 = (6)\left(\frac{1}{2}\right)^5\left(\frac{1}{2}\right)^1$$
$$= \frac{3}{32}$$

f. $P(\text{at least 1 tail}) = 1 - P(\text{0 tails})$

$$= 1 - ({}_6C_0)p^0q^6$$
$$= 1 - (1)\left(\frac{1}{2}\right)^0\left(\frac{1}{2}\right)^6$$
$$= 1 - \frac{1}{64}$$
$$= \frac{63}{64}$$

g. Understand: The probability of spinning white is $\frac{3}{4}$ and the probability of spinning black is $\frac{1}{4}$.

Plan: Find the probability of spinning white 1 time.

Solve: $P(\text{spinning white 1 time})$

$$= ({}_4C_1)p^1q^3$$
$$= ({}_4C_1)\left(\frac{3}{4}\right)^1\left(\frac{1}{4}\right)^3$$
$$= (4)\left(\frac{3}{4}\right)\left(\frac{1}{64}\right) = \frac{3}{64}$$

Practice 49

1. $\dfrac{4xy + 4x^2y^2}{4xy} = \dfrac{4xy(1 + xy)}{4xy} = 1 + xy$

2. $p^5x^3 + p^4x^2 - p^3x = p^3x(p^2x^2 + px - 1)$

3. $$\frac{ax^2 - \frac{4}{a}}{\frac{x^2}{a} + 6} = \frac{\left(ax^2 - \frac{4}{a}\right)a}{\left(\frac{x^2}{a} + 6\right)a}$$
$$= \frac{a^2x^2 - 4}{x^2 + 6a}$$

4. $$\frac{\frac{m^2p}{x} - 6}{m^2p - \frac{4}{x}} = \frac{\left(\frac{m^2p}{x} - 6\right)x}{\left(m^2p - \frac{4}{x}\right)x}$$
$$= \frac{m^2p - 6x}{m^2px - 4}$$

5. $6\sqrt{18} + 5\sqrt{8} - 3\sqrt{50}$

$$= 6\sqrt{9}\sqrt{2} + 5\sqrt{4}\sqrt{2} - 3\sqrt{25}\sqrt{2}$$
$$= 18\sqrt{2} + 10\sqrt{2} - 15\sqrt{2}$$
$$= 13\sqrt{2}$$

6. $2\sqrt{5}(3\sqrt{15} - 2\sqrt{5})$

$$= 2\sqrt{5} \cdot 3\sqrt{5}\sqrt{3} - 2\sqrt{5} \cdot 2\sqrt{5}$$
$$= 30\sqrt{3} - 20$$

7. $3x - 2y = 10$

$y = -\frac{1}{2}$

Using substitution: Substitute the second equation into the first.

$$3x - 2\left(-\frac{1}{2}\right) = 10$$
$$3x + 1 = 10$$
$$3x = 9$$
$$x = 3$$

$y = -\frac{1}{2}$

The solution is $\left(3, -\frac{1}{2}\right)$.

Using elimination: Write the second equation in standard form and multiply it by 2.

$0x + y = -\frac{1}{2}$

$$2\left(0x + y = -\frac{1}{2}\right) \longrightarrow 0x + 2y = -1$$

Add the resulting equation to the first equation.

$$\begin{aligned} 3x - 2y &= 10 \\ 0x + 2y &= -1 \\ \hline 3x \quad &= 9 \\ x &= 3 \\ y &= -\frac{1}{2} \end{aligned}$$

The solution is $\left(3, -\frac{1}{2}\right)$.

8. Use the binomial theorem to expand $(a + b)^n$ where $a = b$, $b = -2$, and $n = 4$.

$$\begin{aligned}(b-2)^4 &= ({}_4C_0)b^4(-2)^0 + ({}_4C_1)b^3(-2)^1 + ({}_4C_2)b^2(-2)^2 + ({}_4C_3)b^1(-2)^3 + ({}_4C_4)b^0(-2)^4 \\ &= (1)b^4(-2)^0 + (4)b^3(-2)^1 + (6)b^2(-2)^2 + (4)b^1(-2)^3 + (1)b^0(-2)^4 \\ &= b^4 - 8b^3 + 24b^2 - 32b + 16\end{aligned}$$

9. Use the binomial theorem to expand $(a + b)^n$ where $a = 2x$, $b = y$, and $n = 6$.

$$\begin{aligned}(2x+y)^6 &= ({}_6C_0)(2x)^6y^0 + ({}_6C_1)(2x)^5y^1 + ({}_6C_2)(2x)^4y^2 + ({}_6C_3)(2x)^3y^3 + ({}_6C_4)(2x)^2y^4 \\ &\quad + ({}_6C_5)(2x)^1y^5 + ({}_6C_6)(2x)^0y^6 \\ &= (1)(2x)^6y^0 + (6)(2x)^5y^1 + (15)(2x)^4y^2 + (20)(2x)^3y^3 + (15)(2x)^2y^4 + (6)(2x)^1y^5 \\ &\quad + (1)(2x)^0y^6 \\ &= 64x^6 + 192x^5y + 240x^4y^2 + 160x^3y^3 + 60x^2y^4 + 12xy^5 + y^6\end{aligned}$$

10. Find the slope of the line passing through (2, 4) and (−3, −2)

$$m = \frac{y_2 - y_1}{x_2 - x_1} = \frac{-2-4}{-3-2} = \frac{6}{5}$$

The slope of the perpendicular line will be $-\frac{5}{6}$. Substitute the slope, $-\frac{5}{6}$, and point (2, 4) into the point-slope formula and simplify.

$$\begin{aligned} y - y_1 &= m(x - x_1) \\ y - 4 &= -\frac{5}{6}(x-2) \\ y - 4 &= -\frac{5}{6}x + \frac{5}{3} \\ y &= -\frac{5}{6}x + \frac{17}{3} \end{aligned}$$

11. $$\begin{aligned} f(x) \cdot g(x) &= \frac{2x-2}{x} \cdot \frac{x^2+3x}{x-1} \\ &= \frac{2(x-1)}{x} \cdot \frac{x(x+3)}{x-1} \\ &= 2(x+3) = 2x+6 \end{aligned}$$

The excluded values are $x = 0$ and $x - 1 = 0$, or $x = 1$. Therefore $x \neq 0$, or 1.

The graph of the product function is $y = 2x + 6$, except for the points of discontinuity at the x-values 0 and 1.

12. a. $P(\text{exactly 2 hits}) = ({}_4C_2)p^2q^2$

$$\begin{aligned}({}_4C_2)p^2q^2 &= (6)(0.32)^2(0.68)^2 \\ &\approx 0.28\end{aligned}$$

b. $$\begin{aligned}P(\text{at least 1 hit}) &= 1 - P(0 \text{ hits}) \\ &= 1 - ({}_4C_0)p^0q^4 \\ &= 1 - (1)(0.32)^0(0.68)^4 \\ &= 1 - (0.21381376) \\ &\approx 0.79\end{aligned}$$

13. a – b. Plot the points.

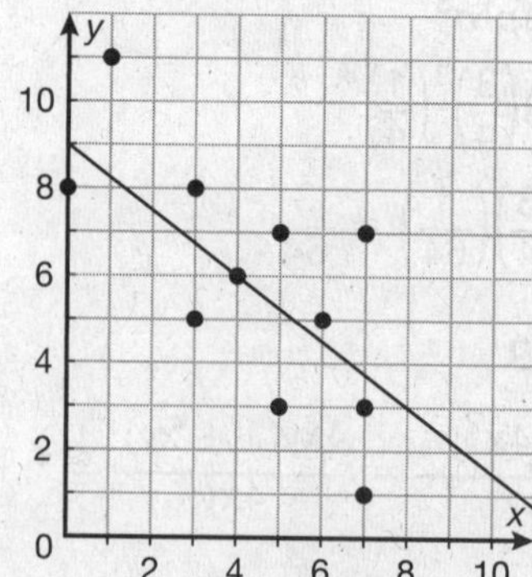

The y-intercept of the line is 9. Pick two points on the line such as (4, 6) and (0, 9) and find the slope.

$m = \frac{9-6}{0-4} = -\frac{3}{4}.$

The equation of the line is $y = -\frac{3}{4}x + 9$.

c. The points fall so r is negative and the points are not clustered on the line. Therefore $r \approx -0.7$.

14. This is a discontinuous function. The points of discontinuity are $x = 5, 10, 15, 20, 25$.

15. a. $x + y \leq 24$

$27x + 45y \leq 720$

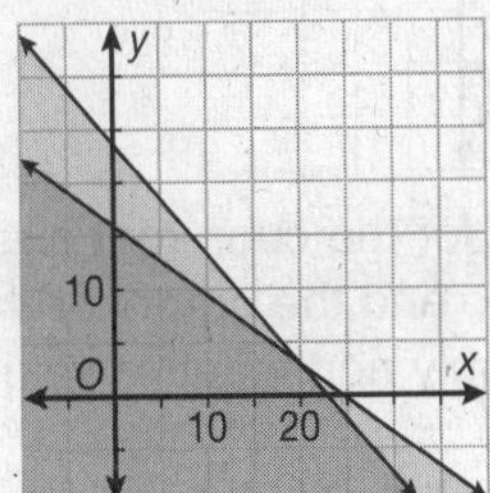

b. The points in the graph of the system that represent all the possible combinations of outfield grandstand seats and right field box seats are all points with both coordinates nonnegative integers.

c. (20, 4). It represents 20 outfield grandstand seats and 4 right field box seats at a total cost of $720, the maximum that can be spent.

16. In a right triangle $a^2 + b^2 = c^2$.

A $21^2 + 72^2 \stackrel{?}{=} 75^2$

$5625 = 5625$

This is a right triangle.

B $30^2 + 35^2 \stackrel{?}{=} 45^2$

$2125 \neq 2025$

This is not a right triangle.

C $35^2 + 48^2 \stackrel{?}{=} 58^2$

$3529 \neq 3364$

This is not a right triangle.

D $41^2 + 82^2 \stackrel{?}{=} 90^2$

$8405 \neq 8100$

This is not a right triangle.

Answer choice **A**

17. $|x - 21.7| = 3.2$

$x - 21.7 = 3.2$

$x = 24.9$

or

$x - 21.7 = -3.2$

$x = 18.5$

The maximum is 24.9 and the minimum is 18.5.

18. Use the fifth row of Pascal's Triangle to get the coefficients 1, 5, 10, 10, 5, and 1. The exponent of y decreases by 1 for each term and the exponent of z increases by 1 for each term.

19. a. Volume of Box 1 $= 11.875(3.375)(13.625)$

$\approx 546 \text{ in.}^3$

Volume of Box 2 $= 11(8.5)(5.5)$

$\approx 514 \text{ in.}^3$

Volume of Box 3 $= 7.5(5.125)(14.375) =$

$\approx 553 \text{ in.}^3$

The range is $553 \text{ in}^3 - 514 \text{ in}^3 = 39 \text{ in.}^3$

b. Sample: The largest and smallest volumes are used to find the range. None of these boxes could be used to ship something with a volume greater than 553 cubic inches.

20. This is a permutation, since order matters. The permutation of 24 items taken 4 at a time is $P(24,4)$.

$$P(24,4) = \frac{24!}{(24-4)!} = \frac{24!}{20!}$$

$$= \frac{24 \times 23 \times 22 \times 21 \times \cancel{20!}}{\cancel{20!}}$$

$$= 255{,}024$$

21. Since the second function opens downward, a is negative. The graph is narrower than the parent function so $|a| > 1$. The value of a is about -3.

22. The student multiplied by the wrong radical conjugate. The student multiplied by the radical conjugate of the numerator and the denominator rather than multiplying both the numerator and the denominator by the radical conjugate of the denominator.

$$\frac{2\sqrt{2}+6}{3\sqrt{2}+\sqrt{5}} \cdot \frac{3\sqrt{2}-\sqrt{5}}{3\sqrt{2}-\sqrt{5}}$$

$$= \frac{12 - 2\sqrt{10} + 18\sqrt{2} - 6\sqrt{5}}{18 - 5}$$

$$= \frac{12 - 2\sqrt{10} + 18\sqrt{2} - 6\sqrt{5}}{13}$$

23. a. Slope from A to B:

$$m = \frac{y_2 - y_1}{x_2 - x_1} = \frac{7-3}{4-0} = 1$$

y-intercept = 3. Substitute slope, 1, and point (0,3) into the point-slope formula.

Equation of line from A to B is $y = x + 3$.

Slope from B to C:

$$m = \frac{y_2 - y_1}{x_2 - x_1} = \frac{7-0}{4-11} = -1$$

Substitute the slope, −1, and point (11, 0) into the point-slope formula.

$y = -x - 11$.

The object starts with an initial speed of 3 and acceleration of 1. After 4 seconds it decelerates and stops at 11 seconds.

b. The slopes indicate that the two lines are perpendicular.

24. Draw a diagram of the situation.

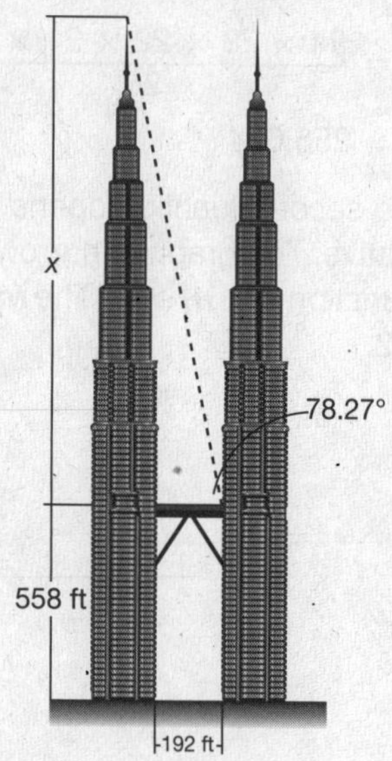

$$\tan 78.27° = \frac{x}{192}$$

$$x = 192(\tan 78.27°)$$

$$x = 925$$

The height is 925 + 558 = 1483 feet.

25. $2x - 7 = -(7 - 2x)$ Given

$= -7 + 2x$ Distributive Property

$= 2x - 7$ Commutative Property

26.

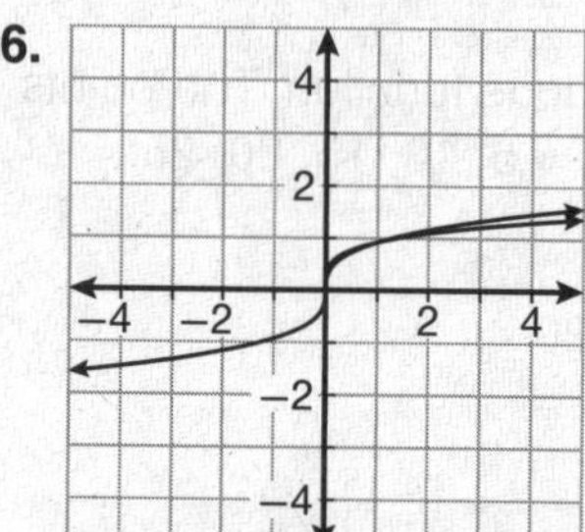

The graph for the cube root exists for all values of x, and the graph for the fourth root exists for only nonnegative values of x.

27. $(y-3)^8 = \sum_{r=0}^{8} ({}_8C_r)y^{8-r}(-3)^r$

In the fifth term $r = 4$.

$({}_8C_4)y^{8-4}(-3)^4$

$= \frac{8!}{4!(8-4)!}y^{8-4}(-3)^4$

$= 70y^4 \cdot 81$

$= 5670y^4$

Answer choice **B**

28. a. Rate of first car is $\frac{3x+60}{2}$.

Rate of second car is $\frac{2x+40}{3}$.

Ratio of rate of first car to second:

$$\frac{\frac{3x+60}{2}}{\frac{2x+40}{3}}$$

b.

$$\frac{\frac{3x+60}{2}}{\frac{2x+40}{3}} = \frac{\frac{3x+60}{2} \cdot 6}{\frac{2x+40}{3} \cdot 6}$$

$$= \frac{3(3x+60)}{2(2x+40)}$$

$$= \frac{9x+180}{4x+80} = \frac{9(x+20)}{4(x+20)}$$

$$= \frac{9}{4}$$

The first car traveled $\frac{9}{4}$ or 2.25 times as fast as the second.

29. The student should have used a dashed line because points on the boundary are not included. Also, the student should have shaded below the line because if −4 is greater than y, then y is less than −4.

30. An exponetial function has the form $y = ab^x$. Only $y = x^3$ does not have that form. Answer choice **B**

LESSON 50

Warm Up 50

1. range

2.
$$2y - 8 = 4x$$
$$2y - 8 + 8 = 4x + 8$$
$$2y = 4x + 8$$
$$\frac{2y}{2} = \frac{4x}{2} + \frac{8}{2}$$
$$y = 2x + 4$$

3. The reflection image is the same distance from the y-axis on the other side of the y-axis. Its coordinates are $(-x, y)$. Therefore, the image is (−2, 6).

Exploration 50

a.

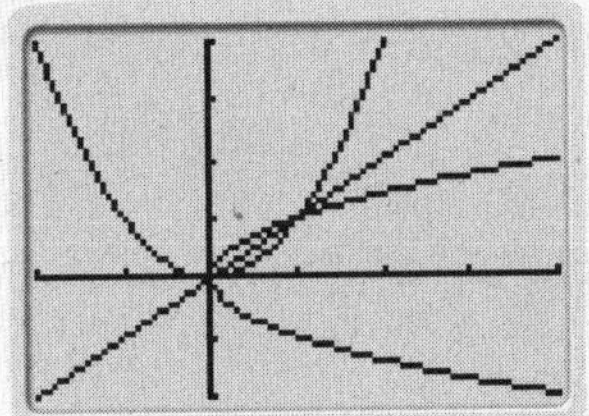

b. The inverse of f is the functions of g and h combined.

c. No; it does not pass the vertical line test.

d. Its graph is the line of reflection.

Lesson Practice 50

a. Reverse the coordinates in each ordered pair.

Domain	x	2	2	1
Range	y	0	3	−3

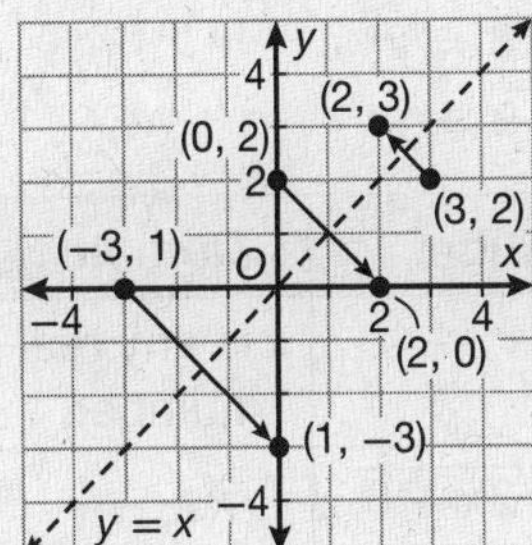

Relation r is a function because each element in the domain is paired with exactly one element in the range. The inverse of r is not a function because the domain element 2 is paired with two different range elements: 0 and 3.

Each point in the graph of the inverse of r is the reflection image of the corresponding point in the relation r. The line of reflection is $y = x$.

b.

$y = -\frac{1}{3}x - 1$ Original equation

$x = -\frac{1}{3}y - 1$ Interchange the variables

$x + 1 = -\frac{1}{3}y$ Solve for y

$-3x - 3 = y$

c.

$y = -\frac{1}{2}x^3 + 1$ Original equation

$x = -\frac{1}{2}y^3 + 1$ Interchange the variables

$x - 1 = -\frac{1}{2}y^3$ Solve for y

$-2x + 2 = y^3$ Multiply each side by −2.

$\sqrt[3]{-2x + 2} = y$ Write the cube root of each side to solve for y.

For every x-value of the domain there is a different value for the range in both the original equation and the inverse. Therefore, both relations are functions.

d.

$y = \frac{1}{2}x^2 - 4$ Original equation

$x = \frac{1}{2}y^2 - 4$ Interchange the variables

$x + 4 = \frac{1}{2}y^2$ Solve for y

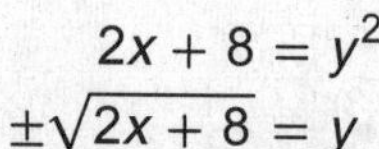

$$2x + 8 = y^2$$
$$\pm\sqrt{2x+8} = y$$

Relation	Domain	Range
$y = \frac{1}{2}x^2 - 4$	x is any real number.	$y \geq -4$
$y = \pm\sqrt{2x+8}$	$x \geq -4$	$y \geq 0$

e. Require that $x \geq 0$ in the function $y = \frac{1}{2}x^2 - 4$, then $f(x) = \frac{1}{2}x^2 - 4$ and $f^{-1} = \sqrt{2x+8}$.

Function	Domain	Range
$f(x) = \frac{1}{2}x^2 - 4$, $x \geq 0$	$x \geq 0$	$y \geq -4$
$f^{-1}(x) = \sqrt{2x+8}$	$x \geq -4$	$y \geq 0$

f. Substitute $2r$ for h.

$V = \pi r^2(2r)$ $r \geq 0$ The domain is naturally restricted because radius cannot be negative.

$V = \pi r^2(2r)$ Solve for r

$$V = 2\pi r^3$$
$$\frac{V}{2\pi} = r^3$$
$$\sqrt[3]{\frac{V}{2\pi}} = r$$

$\sqrt[3]{\frac{1728}{2\pi}} = r$ Substitute 1728 for V since $1 \text{ ft}^3 = 12 \text{ in.} \cdot 12 \text{ in.} \cdot 12 \text{ in.} = 1728 \text{ in.}^3$

$$r \approx 6.5 \text{ in.}$$

Practice 50

1. $(3x^3 - 2x)(2x^2 - x - 4)$
$= 6x^5 - 3x^4 - 12x^3 - 4x^3 + 2x^2 + 8x$
$= 6x^5 - 3x^4 - 16x^3 + 2x^2 + 8x$

2. $(4x + 2)(x^3 - 2x + 4)$
$= 4x^4 - 8x^2 + 16x + 2x^3 - 4x + 8$
$= 4x^4 + 2x^3 - 8x^2 + 12x + 8$

3. Slope of the line passing through $(-3, 0)$ and $(-5, 1)$ is

$$m = \frac{y_2 - y_1}{x_2 - x_1} = \frac{1 - 0}{-5 - (-3)} = -\frac{1}{2}$$

Substitute the slope, $-\frac{1}{2}$, and a point $(-3, 0)$ into the point-slope formula, simplify and write in standard form.

$$y - y_1 = m(x - x_1)$$
$$y - 0 = -\frac{1}{2}(x - (-3))$$
$$y = -\frac{1}{2}x - \frac{3}{2}$$
$$x + 2y = -3$$

4. Slope of the line passing through $(-7, 9)$ and $(-10, 11)$ is

$$m = \frac{y_2 - y_1}{x_2 - x_1} = \frac{11 - 9}{-10 - (-7)} = -\frac{2}{3}$$

Substitute the slope, $-\frac{2}{3}$, and a point $(-10, 11)$ into the point-slope formula, simplify and write in standard form.

$$y - y_1 = m(x - x_1)$$
$$y - 11 = -\frac{2}{3}(x - (-10))$$
$$y - 11 = -\frac{2}{3}x - \frac{20}{3}$$
$$3y - 33 = -2x - 20$$
$$2x + 3y = 13$$

5. Use the binomial theorem to expand $(a + b)^n$ where $a = 2$, $b = -m$, and $n = 7$.

$(2 - m)^7$

$= ({}_7C_0)2^7(-m)^0 + ({}_7C_1)2^6(-m)^1 + ({}_7C_2)2^5(-m)^2 + ({}_7C_3)2^4(-m)^3 + ({}_7C_4)2^3(-m)^4 + ({}_7C_5)2^2(-m)^5 + ({}_7C_6)2^1(-m)^6 + ({}_7C_7)2^0(-m)^7$

$= (1)2^7(-m)^0 + (7)2^6(-m)^1 + (21)2^5(-m)^2 + (35)2^4(-m)^3 + (35)2^3(-m)^4 + (21)2^2(-m)^5 + (7)2(-m)^6 + (1)2^0(-m)^7$

$= 128 - 448m + 672m^2 - 560m^3 + 280m^4 - 84m^5 + 14m^6 - m^7$

$= -m^7 + 14m^6 - 84m^5 + 280m^4 - 560m^3 + 672m^2 - 448m + 128$

6. Use the binomial theorem to expand $(a + b)^n$ where $a = 3g$, $b = 2h$, and $n = 3$.

$$(3g + 2h)^3 = ({}_3C_0)(3g)^3(2h)^0 + ({}_3C_1)(3g)^2(2h)^1 + ({}_3C_2)(3g)^1(2h)^2 + ({}_3C_3)(3g)^0(2h)^3$$
$$= (1)(3g)^3(2h)^0 + (3)(3g)^2(2h)^1 + (3)(3g)^1(2h)^2 + (1)(3g)^0(2h)^3$$
$$= 27g^3 + 54g^2h + 36gh^2 + 8h^3$$

7. $y = 3x^2 - 1$ Original equation

$x = 3y^2 - 1$ Interchange the variables

$x + 1 = 3y^2$ Solve for y

$\frac{x+1}{3} = y^2$

$y = \pm\sqrt{\frac{x+1}{3}} = \pm\frac{\sqrt{3x+3}}{3}$

8. $y = \sqrt{x}$ Original equation

$x = \sqrt{y}$ Interchange the variables

$x^2 = y$ Solve for y

9. $y = \frac{1}{2}x + 6$ Original equation

$x = \frac{1}{2}y + 6$ Interchange the variables

$x - 6 = \frac{1}{2}y$ Solve for y

$2x - 12 = y$

10. Using a graphing calculator $r \approx 0.82$. There is a strong positive correlation between the category of a hurricane and the amount of damage that results.

11. Divide velocity by time to find acceleration.

$\frac{90t}{t+6} \div t$

Simplify.

$\frac{90t}{t+6} \div t = \frac{90t}{t+6} \times \frac{1}{t} = \frac{90}{t+6}$

12. The probability of guessing correctly is $\frac{1}{2}$ and the probability of guessing incorrectly is $\frac{1}{2}$.

$P(\text{exactly 4 correct}) = ({}_{10}C_4)p^4q^6$

$({}_{10}C_4)p^4q^6 = (210)\left(\frac{1}{2}\right)^4\left(\frac{1}{2}\right)^6$

$= \frac{210}{1024} = \frac{105}{512}$

13. $|2x + 1| < 4$

$2x + 1 < 4$ and $2x + 1 > -4$

$2x < 3$ $\quad$ $2x > -5$

$x < \frac{3}{2}$ $\quad$ $x > -\frac{5}{2}$

$-\frac{5}{2} < x < \frac{3}{2}$

Answer choice **A**

14. The student is incorrect.

$P(10,5) = \frac{10!}{(10-5)!}$

$= \frac{10 \times 9 \times 8 \times 7 \times 6 \times 5!}{5!} = 30{,}240$

$C(10,5) = \frac{10!}{5!(10-5)!}$

$= \frac{10 \times 9 \times 8 \times 7 \times 6 \times 5!}{5! \times 5 \times 4 \times 3 \times 2 \times 1} = 252$

$30{,}240 \div 252 = 120$. There are 120 times more permutations than combinations.

15. There are two faces on each box with the following areas:

Box 1: $11.875(3.375) \approx 40$ in.^{2}, $11.875(13.625) \approx 162$ in.^{2}, $13.625(3.375) \approx 46$ in.^{2}

Box 2: $11(8.5) \approx 94$ in.^{2}, $11(5.5) \approx 61$ in.^{2}, $5.5(8.5) \approx 47$ in.^{2}

Box 3: $5.125(7.5) \approx 38$ in.^{2}, $14.375(7.5) \approx 108$ in.^{2}, $5.125(14.375) \approx 74$ in.^{2}

There are two of each side, so the areas in order are 38, 38, 40, 40, 46, 46, 47, 47, 61, 61, 74, 74, 94, 94, 108, 108, 162, 162.

The median is 61. The lower quartile is 46 and the upper quartile is 94. The minimum value is 38 and the maximum is 162.

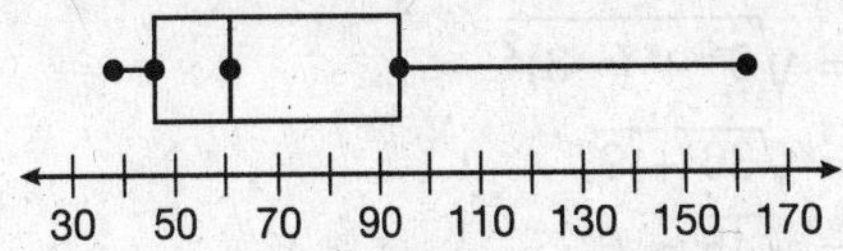

16. Since (5, −12) is lower on the graph than the vertex (2, −3), the graph must open downward and the vertex is a maximum. Therefore a is negative, and $h = 2$ and $k = -3$ in the equation $y = a(x - h)^2 + k$.

The equation is $y = -(x - 2)^2 - 3$.

17. a. Let f represent the number of pounds of food. $24 \le f \le 67$

b. $|f - 45.5| \le 21.5$

$f - 45.5 \le 21.5$ and $f - 45.5 \ge -21.5$

$f \le 67$ $\quad f \ge 24$

$24 \le f \le 67$

18. $\sqrt[4]{16} = 2$ or -2

Answer choice **C**

19. a. The area is $7(5) - x(x) = 35 - x^2$.

A quadratic equation can be written in standard form as $y = ax^2 + bx + c$. The equation in standard form is $y = -x^2 + 35$.

b. $a = -1$, $b = 0$, $c = 35$

20. Student B is correct. Student A forgot to make the 8 negative in the inner multiplication.

21. The boundary lines for the inequalities are parallel because they have the same slope, 3. All solutions of $y > 3x + 1$ are above its boundary line and all solutions of $y < 3x - 1$ are below its boundary line. Also, the boundary line for $y > 3x + 1$ is above the boundary line for $y < 3x - 1$ because it has the greater y-intercept. Therefore, there is no ordered pair that is a solution of both inequalities.

22. $p(x) = b(x) - d(x)$

$= -27x + 4103 - (23x + 2164)$

$= -50x + 1939$

23. The expression can be written as a fraction with a denominator of 1 and 1 is a constant monomial, so the fraction is a quotient of two polynomials.

24. $d = \sqrt{(x_2 - x_1)^2 + (y_2 - y_1)^2}$

$= \sqrt{(6 - 0)^2 + (-3 - 0)^2}$

$= \sqrt{6^2 + (-3)^2}$

$= \sqrt{36 + 9}$

$= \sqrt{45} \approx 6.7$

The distance between the cities is about $6.7 \times 120 = 805$ km.

25. $(g(x))^2 = \left(\frac{1}{x + 2}\right)^2$

$= \frac{1}{(x + 2)^2}$

26. In each ratio, the numerator is a leg length and the denominator is the length of the hypotenuse. Since the hypotenuse is the greatest side of a right triangle, the numerator is never greater than the denominator, making it impossible for the fraction to have a value greater than or equal to 1.

27.

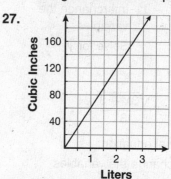

The rate of change is the slope of the graph:

$m = \frac{y_2 - y_1}{x_2 - x_1} = \frac{152.5 - 140.3}{2.5 - 2.3} = 61$

The rate of change means that there are 61 cubic inches in every liter.

28. a. $9x - y + 3z = -21$

$-8x + 4y - 6z = 10$

$56x - 28y + 42z = 2$

b. No solution. The second and third equations have coefficients that are multiples of each other but the constants are not multiples.

c. Use equations 2 and 3

$7(-8x + 4y - 6z = 10) \rightarrow$

$-56x + 28y - 42z = 70$

$56x - 28y + 42z = 2 \rightarrow$

$56x - 28y + 42z = 2$

$0 = 72$

no solution

29. The variables represent the lengths of the sides and the sides of a triangle must have a length greater than 0.

30. The GCF is the greatest common factor, which means that each term in the polynomial can be divided by the GCF with no remainder. So, factoring out the GCF means to divide each polynomial term by the GCF.

INVESTIGATION 5

1. Yes, because the four conditions of a binomial experiment are still met.

2. No, because there are four possible outcomes, so condition 2 is not met.

3. No, because each time there are 6 possible outcomes, so condition 2 is not met.

4.

Binomial Experiment	Does the Test Scenario Comply?
There are *n* trials in the experiment	Yes. There are 15 trials.
Only two possible outcomes per trial	Yes. The sum of the faces on the number cubes is greater than 3 or not.
Each trial is independent	Yes. The result of one trial does not influence the result of any other.
The probability of success is the same from trial to trial	Yes. $P(3 \text{ or less}) = \frac{2}{11}$ and $P(>3) = \frac{9}{11}$

This is a binomial experiment, since all the conditions are met.

There are 11 possible sums from 36 unique combinations.

5. a.

Binomial Experiment	Does the Test Scenario Comply?
1. There are *n* trials in the experiment	Yes. There are 5 trials.
2. Only two possible outcomes per trial	Yes. The result is even or odd.
3. Each trial is independent	Yes. The result of one trial does not influence the result of any other.
4. The probability of success is the same from trial to trial	Yes. $P(\text{even}) = \frac{3}{6}$ and $P(\text{odd}) = \frac{3}{6}$

b. There are 3 possible outcomes for even in each trial. In five trials, expect even 2 or 3 times.

6. Check students' work. Answers will vary.

7. g. Answers will vary. Possible answer: 13 even and 12 odd.

h. Answers will vary. Possible graph:

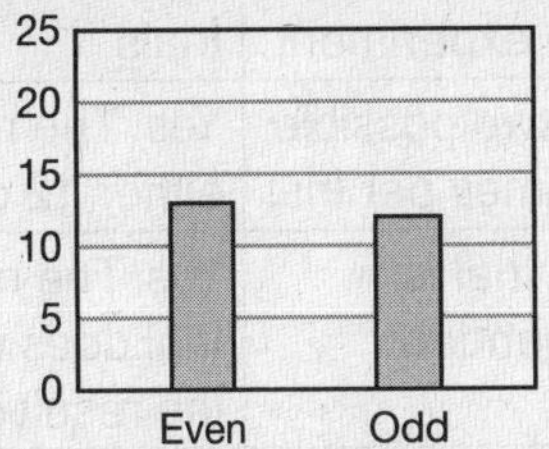

i. The results are similar.

8. a. Answers will vary. Possible graph.

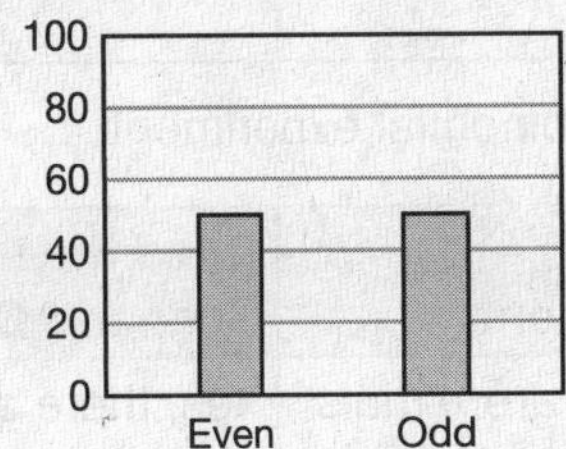

b. The results are similar.

9.

Binomial Experiment	Does the Test Scenario Comply?
a. There are *n* trials in the experiment	Yes. There are 20 questions in the test.
b. Only two possible outcomes per trial	Yes. The guess is either correct or incorrect.
c. Each trial is independent	Yes. The result of one guess does not influence the result of any other guesses.
d. The probability of success is the same from trial to trial	Yes. Each guess has a 1 in 5 (or 20%) chance of success.

10. Answers will vary. Possible answer: 4

11. d. Possible answer: 6 correct.

e. Answers will vary.

f. The results are similar.

Investigation Practice 5

a.

Binomial Experiment	Does the test Scenario Comply?
1. There are n trials in the experiment	Yes, there are 500 trials.
2. Only two possible outcomes per trial	Yes. The result is either 12 or not 12.
3. Each trial is independent	Yes. The result of one trial does not influence the result of any other.
4. The probability of success is the same from trial to trial	Yes.

This is a binomial experiment.

b.

Binomial Experiment	Does the test Scenario Comply?
1. There are n trials in the experiment	Yes, there are 20 trials.
2. Only two possible outcomes per trial	Yes. The result is correct or not.
3. Each trial is independent	Yes. The result of one trial does not influence the result of any other.
4. The probability of success is the same from trial to trial	No. Probability for guess is 1 in 5, which is different for not guessing.

The conditions are different for half the questions, so this is not a binomial experiment.

c. Answers will vary. A 12 results from rolling 6 on each cube. This probability is 1 out of 36. In 50 times this is likely to occur once or twice.

LESSON 51

Warm Up 51

1. divisor

2. $(2x + 1)(x^2 + 2x - 3)$
$= 2x^3 + 4x^2 - 6x + x^2 + 2x - 3$
$= 2x^3 + 5x^2 - 4x - 3$

3. Replace x with 2.
$f(2) = (2)^4 + (2)^3 - 3(2) - 1$
$f(2) = 16 + 8 - 6 - 1$
$f(2) = 17$

4. $\dfrac{6x + 15y}{3} = \dfrac{3(2x + 5y)}{3} = 2x + 5y$

5. $12.18 \div 2.1 = 5.8$

Lesson Practice 51

a.

$$\begin{array}{r} 2x^2 + 3x - 5 \\ x^2 - x + 4 \overline{\smash{)}\, 2x^4 + x^3 + 0x^2 - 5x + 2} \\ \underline{-(2x^4 - 2x^3 + 8x^2)} \\ 0 + 3x^3 - 8x^2 - 5x \\ \underline{-(3x^3 - 3x^2 + 12x)} \\ 0 - 5x^2 - 17x + 2 \\ \underline{-(-5x^2 + 5x - 20)} \\ -22x + 22 \end{array}$$

$= 2x^2 + 3x - 5 + \dfrac{-22x + 22}{x^2 - x + 4}$

b. $x - 3 = x - k$, so $k = 3$

$$\begin{array}{r|rrrr} 3 & -2 & 1 & 5 & -1 \\ & & -6 & -15 & -30 \\ \hline & -2 & -5 & -10 & -31 \end{array}$$

The quotient is $-2x^2 - 5x - 10$ and the remainder is -31.

$\dfrac{-2x^3 + x^2 + 5x - 1}{x - 3} = -2x^2 - 5x - 10 + \dfrac{-31}{x - 3}$

c. Divide $f(x)$ by $x + 2$ to find $f(-2)$.

$$\begin{array}{r|rrrrrr} -2 & 1 & 0 & -2 & -1 & 0 & 10 \\ & & -2 & 4 & -4 & 10 & -20 \\ \hline & 1 & -2 & 2 & -5 & 10 & -10 \end{array}$$

The remainder is -10, so $f(-2) = -10$.

d. Use synthetic division to evaluate $P(7)$.

$$\begin{array}{r|rrrr} 7 & -1 & 12 & -8 & 800 \\ & & -7 & 35 & 189 \\ \hline & -1 & 5 & 27 & 989 \end{array}$$

The predicted enrollment is 989.

Practice 51

1. $x - 2 = x - k$, so $k = 2$

$$\begin{array}{r|rrrrr} 2 & 2 & 0 & 0 & -1 & 0 \\ & & 4 & 8 & 16 & 30 \\ \hline & 2 & 4 & 8 & 15 & 30 \end{array}$$

The quotient is $2x^3 + 4x^2 + 8x + 15$ and the remainder is 30, or $2x^3 + 4x^2 + 8x + 15 + \frac{30}{x-2}$.

2. $-3 + x = x - k$, so $k = 3$

$$\begin{array}{r|rrrr} 3 & 4 & -2 & 4 & 2 \\ & & 12 & 30 & 102 \\ \hline & 4 & 10 & 34 & 104 \end{array}$$

The quotient is $4x^2 + 10x + 34$ and the remainder is 104, or $4x^2 + 10x + 34 + \frac{104}{x-3}$.

3. $d = \sqrt{(x_2 - x_1)^2 + (y_2 - y_1)^2}$

$= \sqrt{(-1-(-3))^2 + (2-5)^2}$

$= \sqrt{4+9} = \sqrt{13}$

4. $d = \sqrt{(x_2 - x_1)^2 + (y_2 - y_1)^2}$

$= \sqrt{(6-2)^2 + (-2-4)^2}$

$= \sqrt{16+36}$

$= \sqrt{52} = 2\sqrt{13}$

5. $d = \sqrt{(x_2 - x_1)^2 + (y_2 - y_1)^2}$

$= \sqrt{(4-(-3))^2 + (-2-5)^2}$

$= \sqrt{49+49}$

$= \sqrt{98} = 7\sqrt{2}$

6. Determinant = $1.5(1.5) - (-0.71)(0.71) = 2.7541$.

7. $\frac{m^2}{x^2a} + \frac{5}{ax} - \frac{m}{a} = \frac{m^2}{x^2a} + \frac{5}{ax} \cdot \frac{x}{x} - \frac{m}{a} \cdot \frac{x^2}{x^2}$

$= \frac{m^2}{ax^2} + \frac{5x}{ax^2} - \frac{mx^2}{ax^2}$

$= \frac{m^2 + 5x - mx^2}{ax^2}$

8. $\frac{a}{x^2} - a - \frac{3x}{2a^4}$

$= \frac{a}{x^2} \cdot \frac{2a^4}{2a^4} - a \cdot \frac{2a^4x^2}{2a^4x^2} - \frac{3x}{2a^4} \cdot \frac{x^2}{x^2}$

$= \frac{2a^5}{2a^4x^2} - \frac{2a^5x^2}{2a^4x^2} - \frac{3x^3}{2a^4x^2}$

$= \frac{2a^5 - 2a^5x^2 - 3x^3}{2a^4x^2}$

9. The box-and-whisker plot shows that the median of the data is 11, the lower quartile is 8, the upper quartile is 13, the minimum value is 6 and the maximum value is 15. The data in answer choice **C** has these values.

Answer Choice **C**

10. $\frac{3}{4\sqrt{15}} = \frac{3}{4\sqrt{15}} \cdot \frac{\sqrt{15}}{\sqrt{15}} = \frac{3\sqrt{15}}{60} = \frac{\sqrt{15}}{20}$

11. $\frac{5\sqrt{3} - \sqrt{2}}{4\sqrt{3} + 3\sqrt{2}} = \frac{5\sqrt{3} - \sqrt{2}}{4\sqrt{3} + 3\sqrt{2}} \cdot \frac{4\sqrt{3} - 3\sqrt{2}}{4\sqrt{3} - 3\sqrt{2}}$

$= \frac{60 - 15\sqrt{6} - 4\sqrt{6} + 6}{48 - 18}$

$= \frac{66 - 19\sqrt{6}}{30}$

12. $\frac{5}{2\sqrt{7} - \sqrt{5}} = \frac{5}{2\sqrt{7} - \sqrt{5}} \cdot \frac{2\sqrt{7} + \sqrt{5}}{2\sqrt{7} + \sqrt{5}}$

$= \frac{10\sqrt{7} + 5\sqrt{5}}{28 - 5} = \frac{10\sqrt{7} + 5\sqrt{5}}{23}$

13. Divide $f(x)$ by $x - 3$ to find $f(3)$.

$$\begin{array}{r|rrrr} 3 & 3 & 0 & -7 & 15 \\ & & 9 & 27 & 60 \\ \hline & 3 & 9 & 20 & 75 \end{array}$$

The remainder is 75, so $f(3) = 75$.

14. Divide $f(x)$ by $x - 6$ to find $f(6)$.

$$\begin{array}{r|rrrrrr} 6 & -3 & -12 & 30 & -16 & -1 & 0 \\ & & -18 & -180 & -900 & -5496 & -32{,}982 \\ \hline & -3 & -30 & -150 & -916 & -5497 & -32{,}982 \end{array}$$

The remainder is $-32{,}982$, so $f(6) = -32{,}982$.

15. a. $\frac{1}{\frac{1}{R_1} + \frac{1}{R_2}} = \frac{1(R_1R_2)}{\left(\frac{1}{R_1} + \frac{1}{R_2}\right)(R_1R_2)}$

$= \frac{R_1R_2}{R_2 + R_1}$

So, $R_t = \frac{R_1R_2}{R_2 + R_1}$

b. $R_t = \frac{R_1R_2}{R_2 + R_1}$

$R_t = \frac{3(6)}{6+3} = 2$

The total resistance is 2 ohms.

16. Pick a coordinate in the shaded region such as (3, 0) and $0 - 3 < 2$ is true. Pick a coordinate in the unshaded region such as (−3, 0) and $0 - (-3) < 2$ is not true. This means that the shading is correct. However, the line should be dashed and not solid, since the inequality does not include "equal to" excluding all points on the boundary line.

17. Both $f(x)$ and $g(x)$ must have a common factor of degree 2.

18. The student distributed the negative sign over the first term only, in the second parentheses. The correct answer should be

$(3x^4 - 2x^3 + 1) - (x^4 - x^3 + 5)$
$= 3x^4 - 2x^3 + 1 - x^4 + x^3 - 5$
$= 2x^4 - x^3 - 4$

19. Using a graphing calculator $r \approx -0.79$ and the line of best fit is $y \approx -0.00434x - 21.6$. The record cold temperature at 5000 ft is $y \approx -0.00434(5000) - 21.6$ or about −43.3°F.

20. The distances for each biker form a right triangle where the hypotenuse is the biker's distance from the parking lot. The distance of the first biker from the parking lot is

$c^2 = a^2 + b^2$
$c^2 = 2^2 + 9^2$
$c = \sqrt{85} \approx 9.2$ units

The distance of the second biker is

$c^2 = 8^2 + 5^2$
$c = \sqrt{89} \approx 9.4$ units

The second biker is $9.4 - 9.2 = 0.2$ units farther, which represents $0.2(3) = 0.6$ miles.

21. The graph crosses the x-axis at about −4.5 and 6.5. These are the x-intercepts. The graph crosses the y-axis at about −4.9. This is the y-intercept.

22. The tangent ratio is $\frac{\text{opposite}}{\text{adjacent}}$ and the cotangent ratio is $\frac{\text{adjacent}}{\text{opposite}}$, so the cotangent ratio is the inverse of the tangent ratio. If the tangent is 0.75, the cotangent is $\frac{1}{0.75} = 1.\overline{3}$.

Answer Choice **D**

23. a. $(500x^4 + 1000x^3 + 600x^2 + 500x)$
$+ (1000x^4 + 200x^3 + 200x^2 + 200x)$
$= 1500x^4 + 1200x^3 + 800x^2 + 700x$

b. $x = 1 + 0.05 = 1.05$. Substitute 1.05 for x in the polynomial that represents the total.
$1500(1.05)^4 + 1200(1.05)^3 + 800(1.05)^2 + 700(1.05) = 1823.26 + 1389.15 + 882 + 735 = 4829.41$

The total value in both accounts is $4829.41.

24. The slope of the line parallel to $y = mx + b$ is m. Substitute the slope m and the point (x_1, y_1) in the point-slope formula, $y - y_1 = m(x - x_1)$ and rewrite.

$y - y_1 = m(x - x_1)$
$y - y_1 = mx - mx_1$
$y = mx + y_1 - mx_1$
$y = mx + (y_1 - mx_1)$

25. Choose some values for x and solve for the corresponding y-values to make the table.

$y = \frac{3}{4}(-1) + 9 = 8.25$

$y = \frac{3}{4}(0) + 9 = 9$

$y = \frac{3}{4}(1) + 9 = 9.75$

Construct a table of values.

x	−1	0	1
y	8.25	9	9.75

Plot each ordered pair on a coordinate grid.

26. There are 4 aces in a deck of 52 cards. The probability of picking an ace is $\frac{4}{52}$. If an ace is selected without replacing, then 51 cards are left and 3 are aces. The probability of an ace is then $\frac{3}{52}$. The compound probability is $\frac{4}{52} \times \frac{3}{51} = \frac{1}{221}$.

27. The last term in the polynomial it is 6. But the product of the last terms in the binomials is $6 \times (-1) = -6$. The factored form should be $(x + 2)(x + 3)$.

28. The volume is $(s + 0.5)^3$.

$$(s + 0.5)^3 = ({}_3C_0)s^3(0.5)^0 + ({}_3C_1)s^2(0.5)^1 + ({}_3C_2)s^1(0.5)^2 + ({}_3C_3)s^0(0.5)^3$$
$$= (1)s^3(0.5)^0 + (3)s^2(0.5)^1 + (3)s^1(0.5)^2 + (1)s^0(0.5)^3$$
$$= s^3 + 1.5s^2 + 0.75s + 0.125$$

29. a. $x + y \leq 16$

$8x + 12y \geq 150$

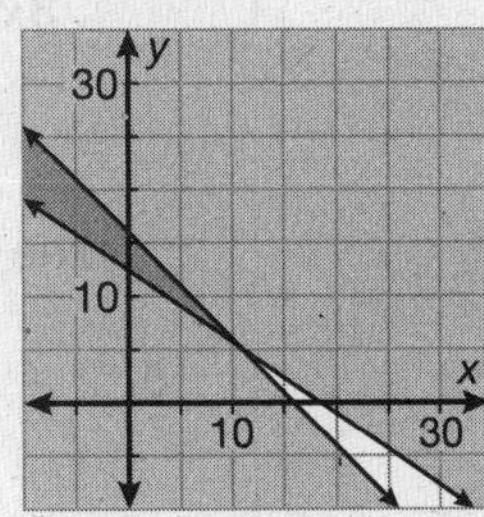

b. All meaningful solutions are the ordered pairs of the solution which are on the boundary and inside the triangle whose left side is the segment from (0, 12.5) to (0, 16).

c. The vertices are (0, 16), (0, 12.5), and (10.5, 5.5). (0, 16) represents 0 hours for the recreation department and 16 hours at the candy store for total earnings of \$192. (0, 12.5) represents 0 hours for the recreation department and 12.5 hours.
at the candy store for total earnings of \$150. (10.5, 5.5) represents 10.5 hours for the recreation department and 5.5 hours at the candy store for total earnings of \$150.

30. $(a + b)^5 = ({}_5C_0)a^5b^0 + ({}_5C_1)a^4b^1 + ({}_5C_2)a^3b^2 + ({}_5C_3)a^2b^3 + ({}_5C_4)a^1b^4 + ({}_5C_5)a^0b^5$

$$= (1)a^5b^0 + (5)a^4b^1 + (10)a^3b^2 + (10)a^2b^3 + (5)a^1b^4 + (1)a^0b^5$$
$$= a^5 + 5a^4b + 10a^3b^2 + 10a^2b^3 + 5ab^4 + b^5$$

The terms that have the same coefficient have exponents that are reversed, as in $10a^3b^2$ and $10a^2b^3$.

LAB 9

Solutions on page 232.

LESSON 52

Warm Up 52

1. tangent

2. $90° + 24° + x = 180°$
$x = 66°$

3. A right triangle has a 90° angle. Answer choice **A**

4. Substitute 12 for a and 13 for c in the Pythagorean Theorem, $a^2 + b^2 = c^2$.

$12^2 + b^2 = 13^2$
$b^2 = 169 - 144$
$b = \sqrt{25} = 5$ cm

Lesson Practice 52

a. The triangles are similar triangles, so the lengths of the sides are proportional. Set up the proportion and solve for x.

$$\frac{x}{10} = \frac{12}{6}$$
$$x = \frac{120}{6}$$
$$x = 20$$

b. The side with length p is opposite a 45° angle, and the length of the hypotenuse is given.

$$\sin 45° = \frac{\text{opposite}}{\text{hypotenuse}} = \frac{\sqrt{2}}{2}$$

Use the two known facts to solve for p.

$$\frac{p}{5\sqrt{2}} = \frac{\sqrt{2}}{2}$$
$$2p = 5\sqrt{2}\sqrt{2}$$
$$2p = 10$$
$$p = 5$$

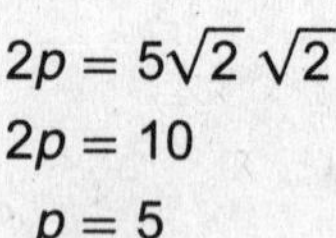

$$2p = 5\sqrt{2}\,\sqrt{2}$$
$$2p = 10$$
$$p = 5$$

c. The sine of a 45° angle is $\frac{\sqrt{2}}{2}$. Let the height from the boy's arm to the kite (the height of the triangle) be x.

$$\frac{x}{18\sqrt{2}} = \frac{\sqrt{2}}{2}$$
$$x = 18$$

The distance from the ground is 18 + 2.4 = 20.4 feet.

Practice 52

1. $3y - x = 3$

$$y = \frac{1}{3}x + 1$$

The slope of the given line is $\frac{1}{3}$, and the slope of any parallel line will also be $\frac{1}{3}$. Substitute the slope, $\frac{1}{3}$, and the point $(2, -1)$ into the point-slope formula.

$$y - y_1 = m(x - x_1)$$
$$y - (-1) = \frac{1}{3}(x - 2)$$
$$y + 1 = \frac{1}{3}x - \frac{2}{3}$$
$$y = \frac{1}{3}x - \frac{5}{3}$$

2. $8y - 3x = 22 \rightarrow 8y - 3x = 22$

$-4(2y + 4x = 34) \rightarrow -8y - 16x = -136$

$$-19x = -114$$
$$x = 6$$
$$8y - 3(6) = 22$$
$$8y = 40$$
$$y = 5$$

The solution is (6, 5).

3. $3x + y = 11 \rightarrow 3x + y = 11$

$-(3x - 2y = 2) \rightarrow -3x + 2y = -2$

$$3y = 9$$
$$y = 3$$
$$3x + (3) = 11$$
$$3x = 8$$
$$x = \frac{8}{3}$$

The solution is $\left(\frac{8}{3}, 3\right)$.

4. $4(3x + 4y = 20) \rightarrow 12x + 16y = 80$

$3(-4x + 3y = 15) \rightarrow -12x + 9y = 45$

$$25y = 125$$
$$y = 5$$
$$3x + 4(5) = 20$$
$$3x = 0$$
$$x = 0$$

The solution is (0, 5).

5. $2 + \frac{a}{2x^2} = 2 \cdot \frac{2x^2}{2x^2} + \frac{a}{2x^2}$

$$= \frac{4x^2}{2x^2} + \frac{a}{2x^2}$$
$$= \frac{4x^2 + a}{2x^2}$$

6. $\frac{4}{cx} + c - \frac{3}{4c^2x}$

$$= \frac{4}{cx} \cdot \frac{4c}{4c} + c \cdot \frac{4c^2x}{4c^2x} - \frac{3}{4c^2x}$$
$$= \frac{16c}{4c^2x} + \frac{4c^3x}{4c^2x} - \frac{3}{4c^2x}$$
$$= \frac{16c + 4c^3x - 3}{4c^2x}$$

7. $\tan 45° = 1$ and $\tan 45° = \frac{x}{4}$

$$\frac{x}{4} = 1$$
$$x = 4$$

$\sin 45° = \frac{\sqrt{2}}{2}$ and $\sin 45° = \frac{4}{y}$

$$\frac{4}{y} = \frac{\sqrt{2}}{2}$$
$$y\sqrt{2} = 8$$
$$y = \frac{8}{\sqrt{2}}$$
$$y = \frac{8}{\sqrt{2}} \cdot \frac{\sqrt{2}}{\sqrt{2}}$$
$$y = 4\sqrt{2}$$

8. $\tan 45° = 1$ and $\tan 45° = \frac{x}{\sqrt{3}}$

$$\frac{x}{\sqrt{3}} = 1$$

$x = \sqrt{3}$

$\cos 45° = \frac{\sqrt{2}}{2}$ and $\cos 45° = \frac{\sqrt{3}}{y}$

$\frac{\sqrt{3}}{y} = \frac{\sqrt{2}}{2}$

$y\sqrt{2} = 2\sqrt{3}$

$y = \frac{2\sqrt{3}}{\sqrt{2}}$

$y = \frac{2\sqrt{3}}{\sqrt{2}} \cdot \frac{\sqrt{2}}{\sqrt{2}}$

$y = \sqrt{6}$

9.

$$\begin{array}{r} 4x^2 + x + 5 \\ x^2 + 5x\overline{)4x^4 + 21x^3 + 10x^2 + 25x} \\ \underline{-(4x^4 + 20x^3)} \\ x^3 + 10x^2 + 25x \\ \underline{-(x^3 + 5x^2)} \\ 5x^2 + 25x \\ \underline{-(5x^2 + 25x)} \\ 0 \end{array}$$

10. Substitute 13,225 for A in $3.56\sqrt{A}$.

$3.56\sqrt{13{,}225} = 3.56 \cdot 115$

$= 409.4$

The distance is about 409 km.

11. $\frac{x+5}{x+2} \cdot \frac{x}{x^3 + 2x^2 + x} = \frac{x+5}{x+2} \cdot \frac{x}{x(x+1)(x+1)}$

The expression is undefined for $x + 2 = 0$, or $x = -2$; $x = 0$; and $x + 1 = 0$, or $x = -1$.

12. The trigonometric ratios associated with the inner angles measuring 45° are the same regardless of the lengths of the sides of the triangles. Since the ratios are the same and the angles are congruent, the corresponding sides of the triangles are proportional.

13. The original surface area is

$2(x - 15)(x - 15) + 2(x)(x - 15) + 2(x)(x - 15)$

$= 2x^2 - 60x + 450 + 2x^2 - 30x + 2x^2 - 30x$

$= 6x^2 - 120x + 450$

The new surface area is

$2(x + 15)(x - 40) + 2(x + 15)(x + 35)$
$+ 2(x + 35)(x - 40)$

$= 2x^2 - 50x - 1200 + 2x^2 + 100x + 1050$
$+ 2x^2 - 10x - 2800$

$= 6x^2 + 40x - 2950$

The ratio of the new surface area to the original is

$\frac{6x^2 + 40x - 2950}{6x^2 - 120x + 450} = \frac{2(3x^2 + 20x - 1475)}{2(3x^2 - 60x + 225)}$

$= \frac{3x^2 + 20x - 1475}{3x^2 - 60x + 225}$

14. Answer Choice **B**

15. a.

$$\begin{array}{r} x^3 - 5x^2 - 2x - 24 \\ x^2 - x - 6\overline{)x^5 + 4x^4 - 13x^3 - 52x^2 + 36x + 144} \\ \underline{-(x^5 - x^4 - 6x^3)} \\ 5x^4 - 7x^3 - 52x^2 + 36x + 144 \\ \underline{-(5x^4 - 5x^3 - 30x^2)} \\ -2x^3 - 22x^2 + 36x + 144 \\ \underline{-(-2x^3 + 2x^2 + 12x)} \\ -24x^2 + 24x + 144 \\ \underline{-(-24x^2 + 24x + 144)} \\ 0 \end{array}$$

b.

$$\begin{array}{r|rrrr} -5 & 1 & 5 & -2 & -24 \\ & & -5 & 0 & 10 \\ \hline & 1 & 0 & -2 & -14 \end{array}$$

The quotient is $x^2 - 2$, and the remainder is -14.

16. Draw a diagram of the situation.

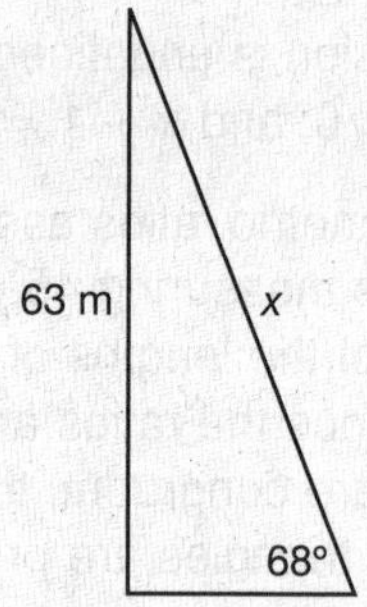

$\sin 68^\circ = \frac{63}{x}$

$x = \frac{63}{\sin 68^\circ}$

$x \approx 67.9$

The rope is about 68 m long.

17. For Step 2, the variable y should be eliminated, not the x variable.

Step 1:

$-9x + 4y + 5z = -16$
$+x - 4y - 6z = 25$
$-8x \qquad - z = 9$

Step 2:

$x - 4y - 6z = 25 \rightarrow x - 4y - 6z = 25$
$4(-x + y - z = -3) \rightarrow -4x + 4y - 4z = -12$
$-3x \quad - 10z = 13$

Step 3:

$-10(-8x - z = 9) \rightarrow 80x + 10z = -90$
$-3x - 10z = 13 \rightarrow -3x - 10z = 13$
$77x \quad = -77$
$x = -1$

$-3(-1) - 10z = 13$
$-10z = 10$
$z = -1$

Step 4:

$-(-1) + y - (-1) = -3$
$y = -5$

The solution is $(-1, -5, -1)$.

18. $\sin 60^\circ = \frac{\sqrt{3}}{2}$ and $\sin 60^\circ = \frac{x}{20}$

$\frac{x}{20} = \frac{\sqrt{3}}{2}$

$x = \frac{20\sqrt{3}}{2}$

$x = 10\sqrt{3}$

$x \approx 17$

The opposite side is about 17 in. long.

19. The vertex form is $y = (x + 0)^2 - 3$, so $h = 0$. Answer Choice **B**

20. First terms $a \cdot a = a^2$

outer terms $a \cdot -b = -ab$

Inner terms $b \cdot a = ab$

Last terms $b \cdot -b = -b^2$

Add the terms: $a^2 - ab + ab - b^2$

The outer and inner terms in this case will always be opposites and cancel out, leaving the product: $a^2 - b^2$.

21. In $y = 0.25(x + 6)^2$, $a < 0$, so the graph is wider than that of the parent function. The vertex is $(-6, 0)$ so the function is shifted 6 units to the left of the parent function, whose vertex is $(0, 0)$.

22. Sketch the lines to find that the boundary lines intersect at points shown in the sketch.

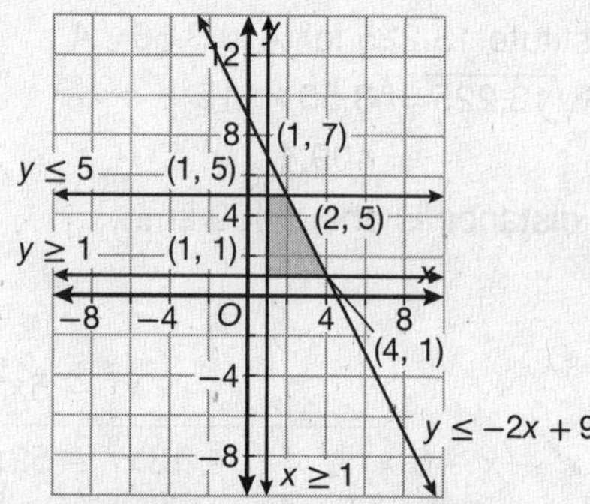

The shape is a trapezoid with $b_1 = 3$, $b_2 = 1$ and $h = 4$. The area is

$A = \frac{(b_1 + b_2)h}{2}$

$= \frac{(3 + 1)4}{2}$

$= 8$

The area is 8 square units.

23. a. The rate is $\frac{d}{t}$, which is the slope. The slope for the first day is $\frac{2 - 0}{2} = 1$ and the y-intercept is 0, so the equation is $d = t$. The slope for the second day is $\frac{5.75 - 8}{2} = -1.125$ and the y-intercept is 8. So, the equation for the second day is $y = -1.125t + 8$.

b.

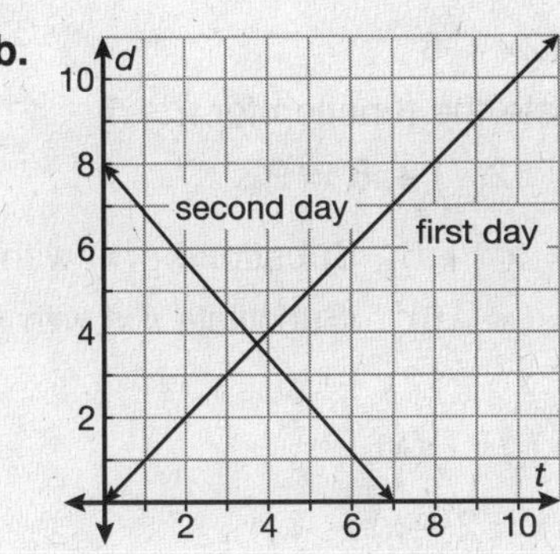

c. Yes. This is the intersection of the graphs at about 3.76 hours and 3.76 miles.

24. The student did not rewrite $(m-2)^3$ as $(m+(-2))^3$. The correct answer should be

$$(m-2)^3 = {}_3C_0m^3(-2)^0 + {}_3C_1m^2(-2)^1 + {}_3C_2m^1(-2)^2 + {}_3C_3m^0(-2)^3$$
$$= m^3 - 6m^2 + 12m - 8$$

25. $V = lwh$, so $lw = \frac{V}{h}$

$$\frac{5x^2+50x-280}{5} = \frac{5(x^2+10x-56)}{5}$$
$$= x^2 + 10x - 56$$
$$x^2 + 10x - 56 = (x-4)(x+14).$$

So, the length is $x + 14$ yd and the width is $x - 4$ yd.

26. a. $y = 3x + 2$

$x = 3y + 2$ Interchange the variables.

$\frac{1}{3}x - \frac{2}{3} = y$ Solve for y.

$$y = \frac{1}{3}x - \frac{2}{3}$$

b.

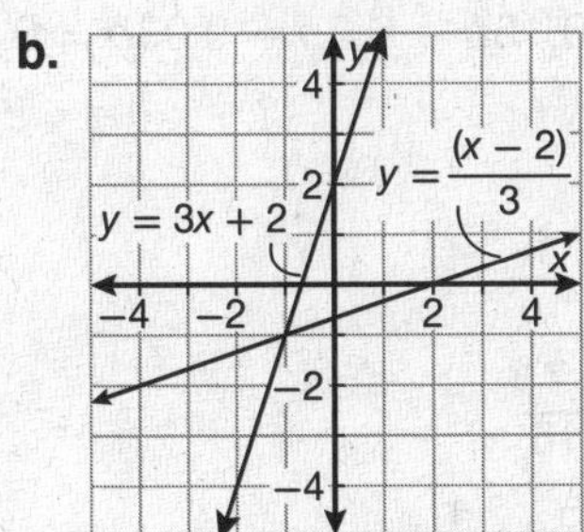

c. The slopes are the reciprocal of each other. Each line is the reflection of the other across the line $y = x$.

27. a. This is a combination since order does not matter.

$${}_{52}C_5 = \frac{52!}{5!(52-5)!} = \frac{52!}{5!47!}$$
$$= \frac{52 \times 51 \times 50 \times 49 \times 48 \times \cancel{47!}}{5 \times 4 \times 3 \times 2 \times 1 \times \cancel{47!}}$$
$$= 2{,}598{,}960$$

b. There are 13 hearts, and if one is dealt there are 12 left. There are 39 cards from the other suits.

$$13 \times 12 \times {}_{39}C_3 = 13 \times 12 \times \frac{39!}{3!36!}$$
$$= 13 \times 12 \times 9139$$
$$= 1{,}425{,}684$$

28. The lengths of the edges in order are 3.375, 3.375, 3.375, 3.375, 5.125, 5.125, 5.125, 5.125, 5.5, 5.5, 5.5, 5.5, 7.5, 7.5, 7.5, 7.5, 8.5, 8.5, 8.5, 8.5, 11, 11, 11, 11, 11.875, 11.875, 11.875, 11.875, 13.625, 13.625, 13.625, 13.625, 14.375, 14.375, 14.375, 14.375.

The median is 8.5, the lower quartile is 5.5, and the upper quartile is 11.875. The minimum value is 3.375 and the maximum value is 14.375.

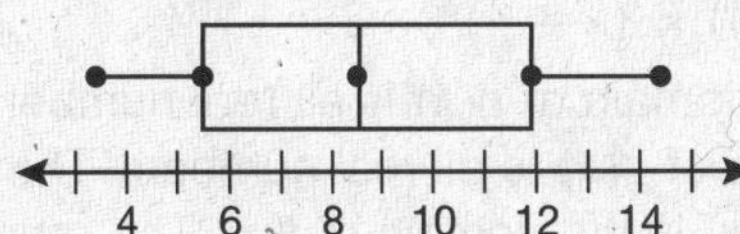

29. Acceleration of satellite 1 is $\frac{v^2}{r}$. Acceleration of satellite 2 is

$$\frac{v^2}{\frac{2r}{3}} = v^2 \cdot \frac{3}{2r} = \frac{3v^2}{2r}$$

The difference is

$$\frac{v^2}{r} - \frac{3v^2}{2r} = \frac{2v^2 - 3v^2}{2r} = \frac{-v^2}{2r}$$

30. Let x = tropical storms and y = hurricanes. Using a graphing calculator: $r \approx 0.99$, and the line of best fit is $y \approx 0.4276x + 1.49$. Substitute 9.5 for x and solve for y.

$y \approx 0.4276(9.5) + 1.49$

$y \approx 5.6$

There were about 5.6 hurricanes per year.

LESSON 53

Warm Up 53

1. function
2. $x(3x - 4) - 2(3x - 4)$
   $= 3x^2 - 4x - 6x + 8$
   $= 3x^2 - 10x + 8$
3. $f(-1) = (-1)^2 - 3(-1) = 4$
4. The domain can be any number, so the domain is $(-\infty, \infty)$. The range cannot be less than -5, so the range is $(-5, \infty)$.
5. $\frac{x^2 - x - 6}{x^2 - 4} = \frac{(x-3)\cancel{(x+2)}}{(x-2)\cancel{(x+2)}} = \frac{x-3}{x-2}$

Lesson Practice 53

a. $f(g(x)) = f((x+1)^2)$ Substitute the output $(x+1)^2$ for $g(x)$.
$= 2(x+1)^2 - 9$ Use the output from $g(x)$ as input for $f(x)$.
$= 2x^2 + 4x + 2 - 9$
$= 2x^2 + 4x - 7$

b. $f(g(x)) = (x - 4)^2 - 2$
The domain of $g(x)$ is all real numbers. The range of $g(x)$ is all real numbers. The range of $g(x)$ is the domain of $f(x)$. The range of the composite function $(f \circ g)(x)$ contains the real numbers greater than or equal to -2.
Therefore, the domain of $(f \circ g)(x)$ is $(-\infty, \infty)$ and the range is $(-2, \infty)$.

c. Method 1
Use 7 for the input for the function $g(x)$.
$g(7) = 4(7) + 5 = 33$
Now take 33 as the input for function $f(x)$.
$f(x) = 3x - 7.$
$f(33) = 3(33) - 7 = 92$
So $(f \circ g)(7) = 92$
Method 2
Replace the function $g(x)$ as the input for the function $f(x)$, then substitute 7 for the value of x.
$f(g(x)) = f(4x + 5)$
$= 3(4x + 5) - 7$
$= 12x + 15 - 7$
$= 12x + 8$
Now evaluate the function for $x = 7$.
$(f \circ g)(7) = 12(7) + 8 = 92.$

d. $(f \circ g)(x) = x^2 + 6$ Substitute $g(x)$ with x^2
$(g \circ f)(x) = (x + 6)^2$ Substitute $f(x)$ with $x + 6$
$= x^2 + 12x + 36$
$(f \circ g)(x) \neq (g \circ f)(x)$

e. $f(g(x)) = 2(-x) - 1$
$= -2x - 1$
$(f \circ g)(-1) = -2(-1) - 1 = 1$
$g(f(x)) = -(2x - 1) = -2x + 1$
$(g \circ f)(-1) = -2(-1) + 1 = 3$

f. $f(x) = -3x + 1$, $g(x) = 9x$, $h(x) = -x^2$
$f(g(h(x))) = f(g(-x^2))$ Substitute $h(x)$ with $-x^2$
$= f(9(-x^2))$ Use $-x^2$ as the input for $g(x)$
$= f(-9x^2)$ Simplify
$= -3(-9x^2) + 1$ Use $-9x^2$ as the input for $f(x)$
$= 27x^2 + 1$

g. The sale function can be written as $s(p) = p - 0.15p$, where p is the original price of an item without discounts. The Saturday morning discount function can be written as $d(p) = p - 0.2p$. Since the two separate discounts are applied to the price p of the item, we need to find the composite function $d(s(p))$.
$d(s(p)) = d(p - 0.15p)$
$= (p - 0.15p) - 0.2(p - 0.15p)$
$= p - 0.15p - 0.2p + 0.03p = 0.68p$

Practice 53

1. $2\frac{1}{4}x - 3\frac{1}{2} = -\frac{1}{16}$
   $2\frac{1}{4}x = 3\frac{7}{16}$
   $x = \frac{55}{16} \times \frac{4}{9}$
   $x = \frac{55}{36}$
2. $0.002x - 0.02 = 6.6$
   $0.002x = 6.62$
   $x = 3310$

3. $\dfrac{3-2x}{4} + \dfrac{x}{3} = 5$

$$12\left(\frac{3-2x}{4} + \frac{x}{3}\right) = 5(12)$$
$$3(3-2x) + 4x = 60$$
$$9 - 6x + 4x = 60$$
$$-2x = 51$$
$$x = -\frac{51}{2}$$

4. $\tan 45° = 1$ and $\tan 45° = \dfrac{\sqrt{5}}{x}$

$$\frac{\sqrt{5}}{x} = 1$$
$$x = \sqrt{5}$$

$\sin 45° = \dfrac{\sqrt{2}}{2}$ and $\sin 45° = \dfrac{\sqrt{5}}{y}$

$$\frac{\sqrt{5}}{y} = \frac{\sqrt{2}}{2}$$
$$y\sqrt{2} = 2\sqrt{5}$$
$$y\sqrt{2} \cdot \sqrt{2} = 2\sqrt{5} \cdot \sqrt{2}$$
$$2y = 2\sqrt{10}$$
$$y = \sqrt{10}$$

5. $\tan 45° = 1$ and $\tan 45° = \dfrac{x}{3}$

$$\frac{x}{3} = 1$$
$$x = 3$$

$\cos 45° = \dfrac{\sqrt{2}}{2}$ and $\cos 45° = \dfrac{3}{y}$

$$\frac{3}{y} = \frac{\sqrt{2}}{2}$$
$$y\sqrt{2} = 6$$
$$y\sqrt{2} \cdot \sqrt{2} = 6 \cdot \sqrt{2}$$
$$2y = 6\sqrt{2}$$
$$y = 3\sqrt{2}$$

6. $3x + 10 > 4y$

$$\frac{3}{4}x + \frac{5}{2} > y$$

The boundary line goes through the intercepts (0, 2.5) and $\left(-\frac{10}{3}, 0\right)$. The solution is all points below the boundary line. A point that is a solution is (1, −2) since $3(1) + 10 > 4(-2)$ is true.

7. All points above the boundary line are not solutions. A point that is not a solution is (−4, 3) since $3(-4) + 10 > 4(3)$ is false.

8. The 17th row of Pascal's Triangle has 18 terms. The binomial has 18 terms.

9. $x(y(t)) = 3$

$$y(x(t)) = -7(3) + 6$$
$$= -15$$

10. $p(q(x)) = 3$

$$q(p(x)) = -(3)^2 + 3(3)$$
$$= 0$$

11. The possible outcomes are ABC, ACB, BAC, BCA, CAB, CBA. There are 6 outcomes.

12. a. The discount function can be written as $d(p) = p - 0.1p$, where p is the original price of an item without discounts. The sales tax function can be written as $s(p) = p + 0.06p$. If the discount is calculated first, find $s(d(p))$.

$$s(d(p)) = (p - 0.1p) + 0.06(p - 0.1p)$$
$$= p - 0.1p + 0.06p - 0.006p$$
$$= 0.954p$$

Therefore you save $1p - 0.954p = 0.046p$.

b. If the sales tax is calculated first, find $d(s(p))$.

$$d(s(p)) = (p + 0.06p) - 0.1(p + 0.06p)$$
$$= p + 0.06p - 0.1p - 0.006p$$
$$= 0.954p$$

Therefore you save $1p - 0.954p = 0.046p$.

c. It doesn't matter whether you calculate the tax or the discount first, you will save the same amount.

13. a. $l = A \div w$

$$l = \frac{60}{\frac{3\sqrt{3}}{2}}$$
$$= \frac{60(2)}{3\sqrt{3}}$$
$$= \frac{20(2)}{\sqrt{3}} \cdot \frac{\sqrt{3}}{\sqrt{3}}$$
$$= \frac{40\sqrt{3}}{3}$$

b. $P = 2(l + w)$

$$P = 2\left(\frac{3\sqrt{3}}{2} + \frac{40\sqrt{3}}{3}\right)$$
$$= 2\left(\frac{3\sqrt{3}}{2} \cdot \frac{3}{3} + \frac{40\sqrt{3}}{3} \cdot \frac{2}{2}\right)$$
$$= 2\left(\frac{9\sqrt{3}}{6} + \frac{80\sqrt{3}}{6}\right)$$
$$= 2\left(\frac{89\sqrt{3}}{6}\right)$$
$$= \frac{89\sqrt{3}}{3}$$

14. The boundary line goes through the intercepts (0, 6) and $\left(\frac{18}{7}, 0\right)$. The solution is all points above the boundary line. A point that is a solution is (3, 0) since $-7(3) + 18 < 3(0)$ is true. A point that is not a solution is (1, 2) since $-7(1) + 18 < 3(2)$ is false.

15. The divisor is $x + 1$, the dividend is $10x^4 + 5x^3 + 4x^2 - 9$, and the quotient is $10x^3 - 5x^2 + 9x - 9$.

16. The student did not multiply the numerator and denominator by the radical that makes the radicand in the denominator a perfect cube. Also, the cube root of 9 is not 3. The student should multiply the numerator and denominator by the cube root of 9. The correct solution is

$$\frac{3}{\sqrt[3]{3}} \cdot \frac{\sqrt[3]{9}}{\sqrt[3]{9}} = \frac{3\sqrt[3]{9}}{\sqrt[3]{27}} = \frac{3\sqrt[3]{9}}{3} = \sqrt[3]{9}.$$

17. $P(x) = 1.2^x + 22$. Using a graphing calculator, if $P(x) = 100$, $x = 24$. Therefore, it will take 24 weeks.

18. $h(k(x)) = (x^{-1})^{-3} + (x^{-1})^3$
$= x^3 + x^{-3}$

$(h \circ k)(2) = (2)^3 + (2)^{-3} = 8\frac{1}{8}$

Answer Choice **C**

19. Draw a diagram of the triangle.

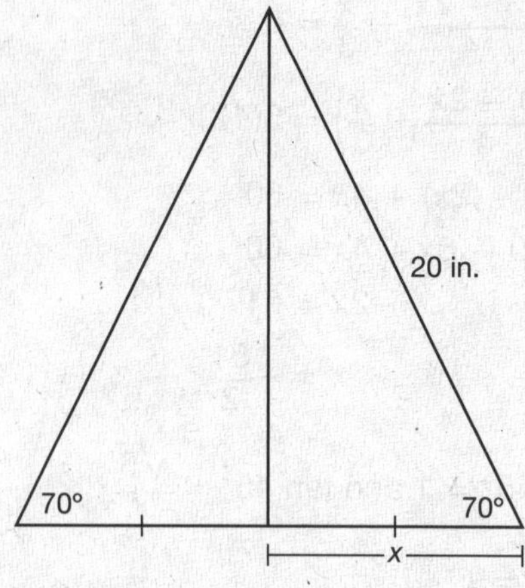

$$\cos 70° = \frac{x}{20}$$
$$20\cos 70° = x$$
$$6.8404 \approx x$$

The base is about $2x = 2(6.84) = 13.68$ in.

20. Substitute 29.4 for h_0, 4.9 for v_0, and 0 for $h(t)$ to solve for t in the equation $h(t) = -4.9t^2 + v_0 t + h_0$.

$$0 = -4.9t^2 + (4.9)t + 29.4$$
$$0 = -4.9(t^2 - t - 6)$$
$$0 = -4.9(t - 3)(t + 2)$$
$$(t - 3) = 0 \text{ or } (t + 2) = 0$$
$$t = 3 \text{ or } t = -2$$

Since time cannot be negative, the only solution is 3. Therefore, it will take 3 s.

21. The composite function is $p(r(u)) = 2(u - 3) + 5 = 2u - 1$. If the domain of $p(u)$ is {4, 6, 8, 10} and the domain of $r(u)$ is {3, 5} the domain of $r(u)$ limits the domain and range of the composite function.

22. $d = \sqrt{(x_2 - x_1)^2 + (y_2 - y_1)^2}$

$$= \sqrt{(125 - 86)^2 + (150 - 220)^2}$$
$$= \sqrt{39^2 + (-70)^2}$$
$$= \sqrt{1521 + 4900}$$
$$= \sqrt{6421}$$
$$\approx 80$$

The distance between Great Falls and Conrad is about 80 km.

23. $P(\text{exactly 2 goals}) = ({}_8C_2)p^2q^6$

$$({}_8C_2)p^2q^6 = (28)\left(\frac{1}{3}\right)^2\left(\frac{2}{3}\right)^6$$

$$= \frac{1792}{6561}$$

24. If $\frac{1}{x^2 + ax + bx + ab} = \frac{1}{x^2 - 1}$, then $\frac{1}{(x + a)(x + b)}$ $= \frac{1}{(x + 1)(x - 1)}$. This means that $|a| = |b| = 1$. One of the terms is positive and the other negative.

25. Draw a diagram of the triangle.

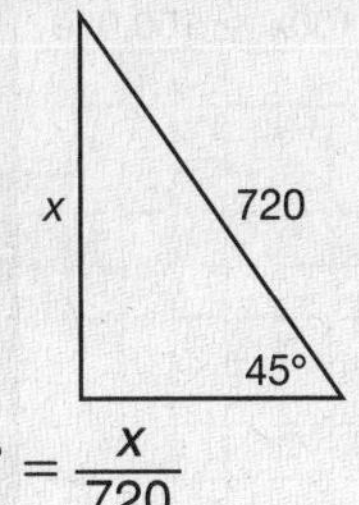

$$\sin 45° = \frac{x}{720}$$

$$720 \sin 45° = x$$

$$509.117 = x$$

The vertical rise is about 509 m.

26. $\frac{1}{1 + 1} = \frac{1}{2}$, $\frac{1}{1 + \frac{1}{1 + 1}} = \frac{1}{1\frac{1}{2}} = \frac{2}{3}$,

$$\frac{1}{1 + \frac{1}{1 + \frac{1}{1 + 1}}} = \frac{1}{1 + \frac{2}{3}} = \frac{3}{5},$$

$$\frac{1}{1 + \frac{1}{1 + \frac{1}{1 + \frac{1}{1 + 1}}}} = \frac{1}{1 + \frac{3}{5}} = \frac{5}{8}$$

$$\frac{1}{1 + \frac{1}{1 + \frac{1}{1 + \frac{1}{1 + \frac{1}{1 + 1}}}}} = \frac{1}{1 + \frac{5}{8}} = \frac{8}{13}$$

The numerators and denominators are consecutive Fibonacci numbers. The next term should be $\frac{13}{21}$.

27. $\frac{8!}{5!} = \frac{8 \times 7 \times 6 \times \cancel{5!}}{\cancel{5!}} = 336$

Answer Choice **B**

28. a. The slope from A to B is $m = \frac{9 - 5}{2 - 0} = 2$ and the y-intercept is 5. The equation of the line from A to B is $y = 2x + 5$. The slope from B to C is $m = \frac{9 - 0}{2 - 20} = -\frac{1}{2}$. The equation is

$$y - 0 = -\frac{1}{2}(x - 20)$$

$$y = -\frac{1}{2} + 10$$

The object starts with an initial speed of 5 and an acceleration of 2. After 2 seconds it has a negative acceleration (or deceleration) of $-\frac{1}{2}$ and stops after 20 seconds.

b. The slopes are the opposite reciprocals, so the lines of the equations are perpendicular.

29. $p = 326{,}000 + 8526t$

$$p - 326{,}000 = 8526t$$

$$t = \frac{p - 326{,}000}{8526}$$

Substitute 450,000 for p.

$$t = \frac{450{,}000 - 326{,}000}{8526}$$

$$t = 14.5$$

Since t is about 15, the year will be 15 years after 1998 or 2013.

30. a. $x + y \leq 15$

$$92x + 54y \leq 1000$$

b. The points in the graph of the system that represent all the possible combinations of field seats and upper view seats you can buy are all points with both coordinates nonnegative integers.

LESSON 54

Warm Up 54

1. inequality
2. Substitute 5 for x and 10 for y.

   $10 \geq 2(5) - 3$

   $10 \geq 7$ True

   Therefore (5, 10) is a solution.
3. Substitute -5 for x.

   $f(-5) = 2(-5)^2 - 3(-5)$

   $= 50 + 15$

   $= 65$

Lesson Practice 54

a. The feasible region is (0, 0), (2, 1), (0, 1.5), (2.5, 3).

x	y	$C = 25x + 30y$
0	0	0
0	1.5	45
2	1	80
2.5	0	62.5

Aside from the trivial solution (0, 0), the minimum value is 45.
The maximum value is 152.5.

b. Let $x =$ the number of chicken dishes.
Let $y =$ the number of seafood dishes.
Objective function: Cost $= 2.50x + 3.75y$
The goal is to find the minimum cost subject to these constraints:
$x \geq 0,\ y \geq 0$
$x + y \leq 1000$
$x = 2y$

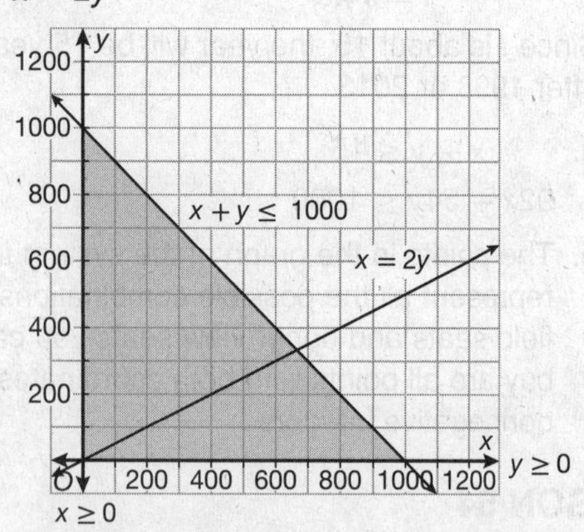

The vertices are (0, 1000), (1000, 0), (667, 333).
Evaluate the objective function for the coordinates of the vertices.

x	y	Cost $= 2.50x + 3.75y$
0	1000	3750
1000	0	2500
667	333	2916.25

The caterer should prepare no more than 667 chicken dishes and no more than 333 seafood dishes.

c. Let $x =$ the number of officers
Objective function: Cost $= 100x$
The goal is to find the minimum and maximum cost subject to these constraints:
$x \geq 0,\ y \geq 0$
$100x \geq 100{,}000$

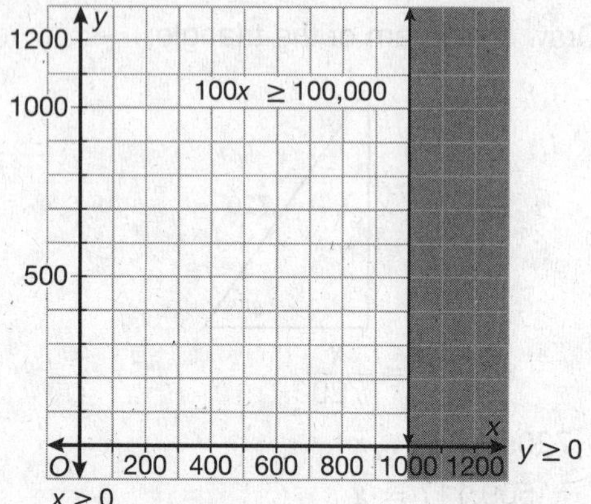

The feasible region is unbounded. Therefore, there is no way to keep costs to a minimum. The organizers will have to impose a limit on spending.

d. Let $x =$ the number of M20 models
Let $y =$ the number of M25 models
Objective function: Profit $= 12x + 7y$
The goal is to find the minimum and maximum profit with these constraints.
$x \geq 0,\ y \geq 0$
$3x + y \leq 720$
$15x + 10y \leq 9000$

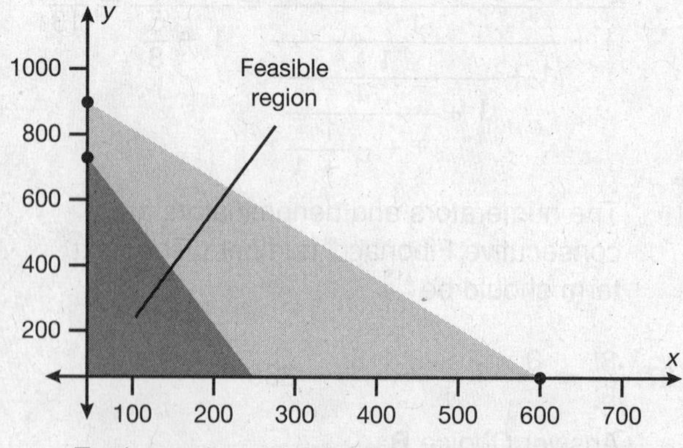

Evaluate the objective function for the coordinates of the vertices.

x	y	Profit = 12x + 7y
0	0	0
0	720	5040
240	0	2880

The company should produce 720 M25 models.

Practice 54

1. 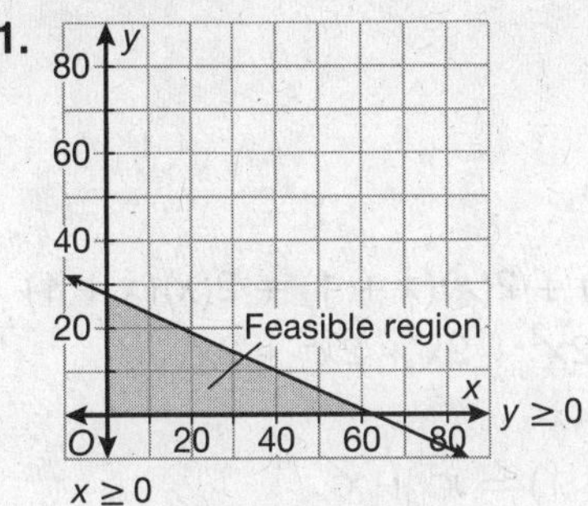

The minimum is where $x = 0$ and $y = 27.8$.
$P = 2(0) + 3(27.8) = 83.4$
The maximum is where $x = 62.5$ and $y = 0$.
$P = 2(62.5) + 3(27.8) = 125$

2. The minimum is where $x = 1$ and $y = 0$
$P = 5(1) + 9(0) = 5$
The maximum is where $x = 0$ and $y = 0.7$
$P = 5(0) + 9(0.7) = 6.3$

3. $$\frac{a^2x - \frac{a}{x}}{ax - \frac{4}{x}} = \frac{\left(a^2x - \frac{a}{x}\right)x}{\left(ax - \frac{4}{x}\right)x} = \frac{a^2x^2 - a}{ax^2 - 4}$$

4. $$\frac{\frac{m}{m+x}}{\frac{x}{m+x}} = \frac{\left(\frac{m}{m+x}\right)m + x}{\left(\frac{x}{m+x}\right)m + x} = \frac{m}{x}$$

5. $$\frac{\frac{s}{a+b} + \frac{x}{b}}{\frac{a}{s+x}} = \frac{\left(\frac{s}{a+b} + \frac{x}{b}\right) b(s+x)(a+b)}{\left(\frac{a}{s+x}\right) b(s+x)(a+b)}$$
$$= \frac{s(b)(s+x) + x(s+x)(a+b)}{a(b)(a+b)}$$
$$= \frac{(s+x)(bs + x(a+b))}{ab(a+b)}$$
$$= \frac{(s+x)(bs + ax + bx)}{ab(a+b)}$$

6. Answer Choice **B**

7. The equation is of the form $y = kx$. This is direct variation.

8. The equation is of the form $xy = k$. This is inverse variation.

9. In the equation as y increases x decreases, and as y decreases, x increases, but xy is not a constant. Therefore this is neither inverse nor direct variation.

10. 300 nickels = 300 × 0.05 = $15.00

11. The feasible region has vertices (0, 5), (2.5, 0), (0, 0).

12. Sample: A profit and loss where loss is represented by negative values.

13. Equation 2 can be written as $6y + 8x = 10$. So, each coefficient in Equation 2 is twice the corresponding coefficient in Equation 1. Therefore, these two lines coincide. Equations 1 and 3 do not coincide and intersect having only one solution. Therefore, Equations 2 and 3 intersect also. Shelby is correct.

14. Volume of cube = x^3.
Volume of cylinder =
$$\pi\left(\frac{1}{2}x\right)^2 x = \frac{1}{4}x^3\pi = \frac{\pi}{4}x^3$$
The difference is
$$x^3 - \frac{\pi}{4}x^3 \text{ or } x^3\left(1 - \frac{\pi}{4}\right)$$

15. Replace each occurrence of x in the function $f(x)$ with the given function for $g(x)$, and then simplify the function.

16. Two radii and the chord form a right triangle, where the chord is the hypotenuse.
Draw a diagram.

4 cm
45°
x

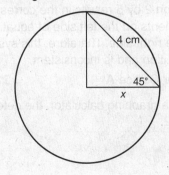

$\sin 45^\circ = \frac{\sqrt{2}}{2}$ and $\sin 45^\circ = \frac{x}{4}$

$$\frac{\sqrt{2}}{2} = \frac{x}{4}$$
$$2x = 4\sqrt{2}$$
$$x = 2\sqrt{2}$$

17. The graph passes the vertical line test, since the graph is discontinuous at $x = 0$. The graph is a function.

18. $1.861 = \frac{2.25 + 2.21 + x + 0.72 + 3.13 + 0.89 + 2.75 + 2.44 + 1.44 + 1.78 + 0.33 + 0.09}{12}$

$$1.861 = \frac{18.03 + x}{12}$$
$$22.332 = 18.03 + x$$
$$4.302 = x$$

19. Jenny is correct. Since $(x - 3)$ is a given divisor, you must divide the polynomial by 3. Haley divided by 3 instead of −3.

20. Because the y-intercept is 13, the point (0, 13) appears on the graph. Use this point and (1, 9) to solve for a.

$$13 = a(0 - 1)^2 + 9$$
$$13 = a + 9$$
$$4 = a$$

The equation in vertex form is $y = 4(x - 1)^2 + 9$. To write it in standard form, square the binomial and simplify:

$$y = 4(x - 1)^2 + 9$$
$$y = 4(x^2 - 2x + 1) + 9$$
$$y = 4x^2 - 8x + 4 + 9$$
$$y = 4x^2 - 8x + 13$$

21. Divide 1 by the tangent value. For example, $\tan A = 0.6$, $\cot A = \frac{1}{0.6} = 1.\overline{6}$

22. Multiplying equation 2 by −2 results in the corresponding coefficients on the left side of equation 1, but not the right side. Multiplying equation 2 by 5 results in the corresponding coefficients on the left side of equation 3, but not the right side. Therefore, this system has no solution and is inconsistent.

Answer Choice **A**

23. Using a graphing calculator, the determinant is 1422.

24. $SA = 2(x)(x) + 2(x)(x + 1) + 2(x)(x + 1)$

$$= 2x^2 + 2x^2 + 2x + 2x^2 + 2x$$
$$= 6x^2 + 4x$$

$$V = x(x)(x + 1) = x^3 + x^2$$

The ratio is $\frac{6x^2 + 4x}{x^3 + x^2} = \frac{2x(3x + 2)}{x^2(x + 1)}$

$$= \frac{2(3x + 2)}{x(x + 1)}$$

25. $a(b(t)) = 3.1t^2 - 2.0t + 4.3$

26. $C(I(t)) = 37 - (-0.006t^2 + 0.733t)$

$$= 0.006t^2 - 0.733t + 37$$

27. Substitute 5 for l.

$$t = 2\pi\sqrt{\frac{5}{9.8}}$$
$$= 2\pi\frac{\sqrt{5}}{\sqrt{9.8}}$$
$$= 2\pi\frac{\sqrt{5}}{\sqrt{9.8}} \cdot \frac{\sqrt{9.8}}{\sqrt{9.8}}$$
$$= 2\pi\frac{\sqrt{49}}{9.8}$$
$$= \frac{14\pi}{9.8} \approx 4.5$$

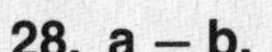

28. a – b.

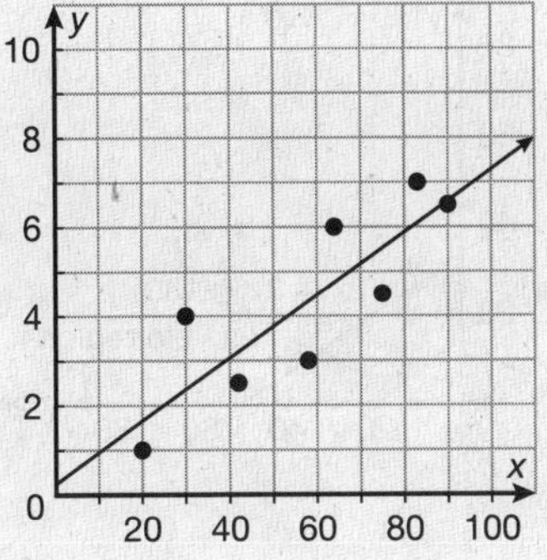

29. $5x^2 + 4x^3 - x^4$
$= -x^2(x^2 - 4x - 5)$
$= -x^2(x - 5)(x + 1)$

30. In a binomial experiment, there are two outcomes. Therefore, even numbers could be successes and odd numbers could be failures.

LESSON 55

Warm Up 55

1. sample space
2. Using the Fundamental Counting Principle, there are $4 \times 3 = 12$ bicycles.
3. $\frac{3}{8} = 0.375 = 37.5\%$

   Answer Choice **C**
4. ${}_3P_2 = \frac{3!}{(3-2)!} = \frac{3 \times 2 \times 1}{1} = 6$
5. ${}_3C_2 = \frac{3!}{2!1!} = \frac{3 \times \cancel{2!}}{\cancel{2!}} = 3$

Lesson Practice 55

a. There are three favorable outcomes (1, 4, 9) and 10 total outcomes.

$P(\text{perfect square}) = \frac{3}{10}$.

b. Base of triangle is $5^2 - 4^2 = b^2$

$b = 3$

$P(\text{shaded region}) = \frac{\text{area of shaded region}}{\text{area of rectangle}}$

$= \frac{\text{area of rectangle} - \text{area of triangle}}{\text{area of rectangle}}$

$= \frac{7(4) - \frac{1}{2}(3)(4)}{7(4)}$

$= \frac{28 - 6}{28}$

$= \frac{11}{14} \approx 0.79$

c. ${}_7P_5 =$ total number of outcomes

$= \frac{7!}{(7-5)!}$

$= \frac{7!}{2!} = 2520$

There is only 1 favorable outcome, so the probability is $\frac{1}{2520} \approx 0.04\%$.

d. ${}_6C_4 =$ total number of outcomes

$= \frac{6!}{4!(6-4)!}$

$= \frac{6!}{4!2!} = 15$

Out of the 15 outcomes, there is 1 way to pick the 4 students. Therefore the probability is $\frac{1}{15} \approx 6.7\%$

e. The events are independent. Multiply individual probabilities.

$P(<10, >50) = \frac{9}{100} \times \frac{50}{100} = \frac{9}{200} = 4.5\%$

f. $P(\text{blue, then blue}) = \frac{10}{25} \times \frac{9}{24} = \frac{3}{20} = 15\%$

g. odds in favor of rolling 6

$= \frac{\text{number of favorable outcomes}}{\text{number of unfavorable outcomes}} = \frac{1}{5}$

h. $P(\text{event}) = \frac{\text{favorable outcomes}}{\text{all outcomes}}$

$10\% = \frac{1}{10}$

Since the favorable outcomes is 1, the unfavorable outcomes must be 9.

odds in favor of event $=$

$\frac{\text{number of favorable outcomes}}{\text{number of unfavorable outcomes}} = \frac{1}{9}$

i. Divide the wins, losses and overtime losses by the total number of games. The total is $53 + 22 + 7 = 82$.

Buffalo Sabres

Wins	Losses	Overtime Losses
53	22	7
0.6463	0.2683	0.0854

Practice 55

1. $\frac{1}{-2\sqrt{24}} = \frac{1}{-2\sqrt{24}} \cdot \frac{\sqrt{24}}{\sqrt{24}}$
$= \frac{2\sqrt{6}}{-48}$
$= -\frac{\sqrt{6}}{24}$

2. $\frac{\sqrt{5}+3}{\sqrt{2}+\sqrt{45}} = \frac{\sqrt{5}+3}{\sqrt{2}+\sqrt{45}} \cdot \frac{\sqrt{2}-\sqrt{45}}{\sqrt{2}-\sqrt{45}}$
$= \frac{\sqrt{10}-\sqrt{225}+3\sqrt{2}-3\sqrt{45}}{2-45}$
$= \frac{\sqrt{10}-15+3\sqrt{2}-9\sqrt{5}}{-43}$

3. $\frac{-1}{\sqrt{12}+3} = \frac{-1}{\sqrt{12}+3} \cdot \frac{\sqrt{12}-3}{\sqrt{12}-3}$
$= \frac{-\sqrt{12}+3}{12-9}$
$= \frac{-2\sqrt{3}+3}{3}$

4. $\sqrt{5}(2\sqrt{5} - 3\sqrt{10}) = 10\sqrt{25} - 15\sqrt{50}$
$= 50 - 75\sqrt{2}$

5. $3\sqrt{200} - 5\sqrt{18} + 7\sqrt{50}$
$= 3\sqrt{100}\sqrt{2} - 5\sqrt{9}\sqrt{2} + 7\sqrt{25}\sqrt{2}$
$= 30\sqrt{2} - 15\sqrt{2} + 35\sqrt{2}$
$= 50\sqrt{2}$

6. $2\sqrt{3} \cdot 2\sqrt{2}(6\sqrt{6} - 3\sqrt{2})$
$= 4\sqrt{6}\,(6\sqrt{6} - 3\sqrt{2})$
$= 24\sqrt{36} - 12\sqrt{12}$
$= 144 - 12\sqrt{4}\sqrt{3}$
$= 144 - 24\sqrt{3}$

7. There are solutions in quadrant I, such as (1, 2). Every solution of the system has a positive x-coordinate because it must satisfy $x \geq 1$. And every solution of the system has a positive y-coordinate because it must satisfy $y > x$. Therefore, both coordinates of every solution of the system are positive, and every solution lies in quadrant I.

8. 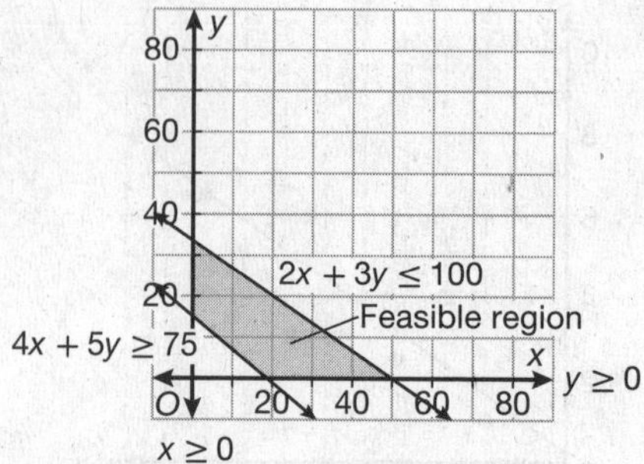

The minimum is at (0, 15). Substitute (0, 15) into the objective function for the minimum.
$P = 7(0) + 8(15) = 120.$
The minimum is 120.
The maximum is at (50, 0). Substitute (50, 0) into the objective function for the maximum.
$P = 7(50) + 8(0) = 350.$
The maximum is 350.

9. Student B for got to distribute the minus sign to the two terms in the numerator.

10. **a.** $(a+b)^n = \sum_{r=0}^{n} ({}_nC_r)a^{n-r}b^r$ For $1716a^7b^6$, $n - r = 7$ and $r = 6$, so $n = 13$. Therefore, $(a + b)$ is raised to the power of 13.
b. $n - r = 7$ in the 7th term.

11. The diagonal is the hypotenuse of a right triangle with 3-ft legs.
$a^2 + b^2 = c^2$
$3^2 + 3^2 = c^2$
$c = \sqrt{18} = 3\sqrt{2}$

12. There are 18 kittens in total.
${}_{18}C_2$ = total number of outcomes
$= \frac{18!}{2!(18-2)!}$
$= \frac{18!}{2!16!}$
$= 153$
The probability is $\frac{2}{153} \approx 1.3\%$.

13. r has a value between 1 and −1. When r is closest to −1 or 1, the strongest correlations occur. 0.22 is farthest from −1 or 1.
Answer Choice **C**

14. Change 6000 feet per minute to miles per hour. There are 5280 feet in one mile and 60 minutes in 1 hour.

$$\frac{6000 \text{ ft}}{1 \text{ min}} \times \frac{1 \text{ mi}}{5280 \text{ ft}} \times \frac{60 \text{ min}}{1 \text{ hr}} = 68.\overline{18} \frac{\text{mi}}{\text{hr}}$$

Substitute 1800 for f_{sr} and 68.2 for v.

$$f_1 = \frac{740(1800)}{740 - 68.2} \approx 1983$$

15. The Star Plan is 0.07((800(10) − 2200) + 25(10) or 656 for each month (except the first month where it is \$656 + \$75 = \$731. The Silver Plan is 0.05((800(10) − 1500) + 30(10) or 625 for each month (except the first month where it is \$625 + \$125 = \$750. Although the Silver Plan has a higher start-up fee, over the long-term it is still the better deal.

16.

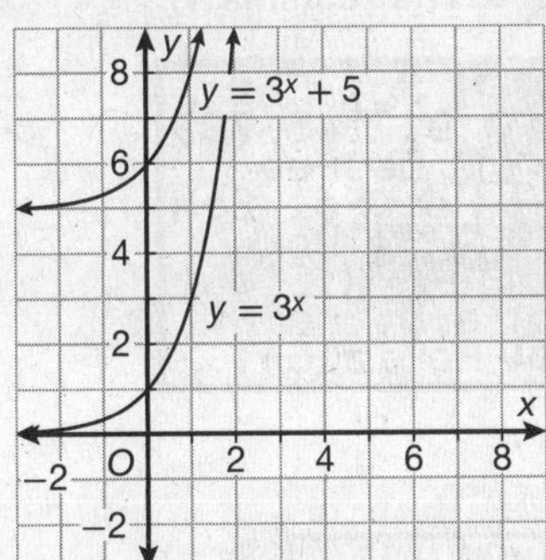

The domain for both functions is the set of all real numbers. The range of the function $y = 3^x$ is the set of real numbers greater than 0, or $\{y \mid y > 0\}$, and the range of $y = 3^x + 5$ is the set of real numbers greater than 5, or $\{y \mid y > 5\}$.

17. a. 6! = 720

b. 5! = 120

c. Yes. To find the answer for part *a* you use 6!. But you use 5! for part *b* since there is only 1 choice for the first letter.

18. AAA, AAB, AAC, ABA, ABB, ABC, ACA, ACB, ACC, BAA, BAB, BAC, BBA, BBB, BBC, BCA, BCB, BCC, CAA, CAB, CAC, CBA, CBB, CBC, CCA, CCB, CCC

There are 27 outcomes.

19. This is a right triangle with legs, $\overline{AC} = 10$ units and $\overline{BC} = 5$ units.

$$\cot \angle B = \frac{\text{adjacent}}{\text{opposite}} = \frac{5}{10} = 0.5$$

20. Student B made the error. The denominator should be the total number of outcomes, both favorable, 3, and unfavorable, 5.

21. a. The amount the account is worth after 2 quarters.

b. $f(f(p)) = 1.01(1.01p) = 1.0201p$

c. There are 4 quarters in a year.

The account is worth $f(f(f(f(p))))$ after a year.

$$\begin{aligned} f(f(f(f(p)))) &= (1.01)(1.01)(1.01)(1.10p) \\ &= (1.01)^4 p = 1.04p \end{aligned}$$

22. a. $\frac{a}{b}$

b. $\frac{b}{a + b}$

c. $\frac{a}{b} = \frac{b}{a + b}$

d. $\frac{a}{b} \cdot b(a + b) = \frac{b}{a + b} \cdot b(a + b)$

$$a(a + b) = b(b)$$

$$a^2 + ab = b^2$$

e. Substitute 1 for *a* and *x* for *b*. The equation is $x^2 - x - 1 = 0$.

$$\begin{aligned} x &= \frac{-b \pm \sqrt{b^2 - 4ac}}{2a} \\ &= \frac{-(-1) \pm \sqrt{(-1)^2 - 4(1)(-1)}}{2(1)} \\ &= \frac{1 \pm \sqrt{5}}{2} \end{aligned}$$

f. You can ignore $\frac{1 - \sqrt{5}}{2}$ since it has a negative value.

g. $\frac{1 + \sqrt{5}}{2} \approx 1.618$, which is the Golden Ratio.

23. $\text{Probability} = \frac{\text{favorable outcomes}}{\text{total outcomes}} = \frac{x}{y}$

$$\text{odds} = \frac{\text{favorable outcomes}}{\text{unfavorable outcomes}} = \frac{x}{(y - x)}$$

Answer Choice **D**

24.

$$C = \frac{5}{9}(F - 32)$$

$$\frac{9}{5}C = F - 32$$

$$\frac{9}{5}C + 32 = F$$

$$F = \frac{9}{5}C + 32$$

25. The trigonometric ratios associated with the inner angles are the same regardless of the lengths of the sides of the triangles. Since the ratios are the same and the angles are congruent, the corresponding sides of the triangles are proportional.

26. $h^2 = (\sqrt{21})^2 - 2^2 = 17$

$h = \sqrt{17}$

$A = \frac{4(\sqrt{17})}{2} = 2\sqrt{17} \text{ in}^2$

27.

$$\begin{array}{r|rrrr} 5 & 1 & 0 & 0 & -2 \\ & & 5 & 25 & 125 \\ \hline & 1 & 5 & 25 & 123 \end{array}$$

The quotient is $x^2 + 5x + 25$ and the remainder is 123, or $x^2 + 5x + 25 + \frac{123}{x - 5}$

28.

$$\begin{array}{r|rrrr} 2 & 2 & 0 & 0 & -1 \\ & & 4 & 8 & 16 \\ \hline & 2 & 4 & 8 & 15 \end{array}$$

The quotient is $2x^2 + 4x + 8$ and the remainder is 15, or $2x^2 + 4x + 8 + \frac{15}{x - 2}$

29. $m = \frac{-3 - 0}{-3 - 6} = \frac{-3}{-9} = \frac{1}{3}$

$y - 0 = \frac{1}{3}(x - 6)$

$y = \frac{1}{3}x - 2$

30. Since the denominator in the remainder is $x - 4$, then the divisor is $x - 4$.

$(x - 4)\left(x^2 - 6x + 8 - \frac{2}{x - 4}\right)$

$= x^2(x - 4) - 6x(x - 4) + 8(x - 4) - \frac{2}{x - 4}(x - 4)$

$= x^3 - 4x^2 - 6x^2 + 24x + 8x - 32 - 2$

$= x^3 - 10x^2 + 32x - 34.$

So, the two polynomials may have been $(x - 4)$ and $x^3 - 10x^2 + 32x - 34$.

LAB 9

Lab Practice 9

a. Press MODE and highlight **radian**. Press COS 2nd ^. The result is −1.

b. Press MODE and highlight **degree**. Press COS 2nd ^. The result is 0.9984971499.

c. Press MODE and highlight **degree**. Press COS **0**. The result is 1.
Press MODE and highlight **radian**. Press COS **0**. The result is 1.

d. 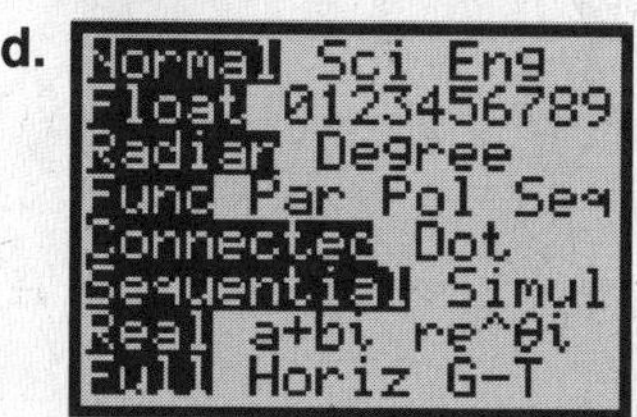

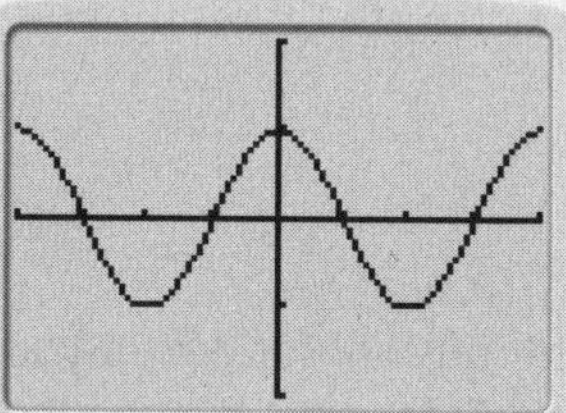

LESSON 56

Warm Up 56

1. Pythagorean Theorem

2. $\sin A = \frac{5}{13} = \frac{o}{h} \rightarrow \csc A = \frac{h}{o} = \frac{13}{5}$

$\cos A = \frac{12}{13} = \frac{a}{h} \rightarrow \sec A = \frac{h}{a} = \frac{13}{12}$

3. $AB = \begin{bmatrix} 2 & 7 \\ 3 & 9 \end{bmatrix} \cdot \begin{bmatrix} 6 \\ 10 \end{bmatrix}$

$= \begin{bmatrix} 2(6) + 7(10) \\ 3(6) + 9(10) \end{bmatrix} = \begin{bmatrix} 82 \\ 108 \end{bmatrix}$

Lesson Practice 56

a.

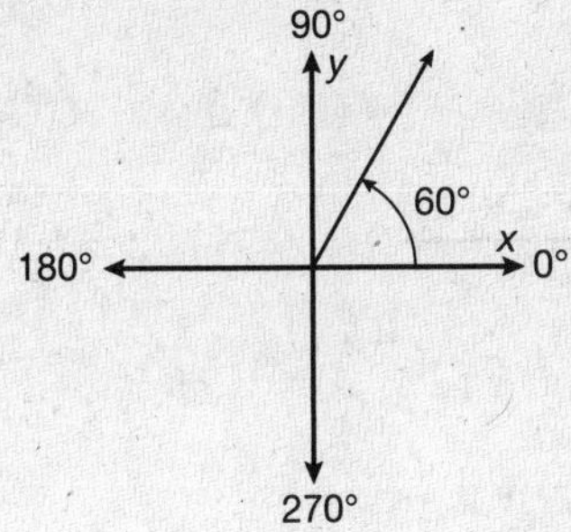

b.

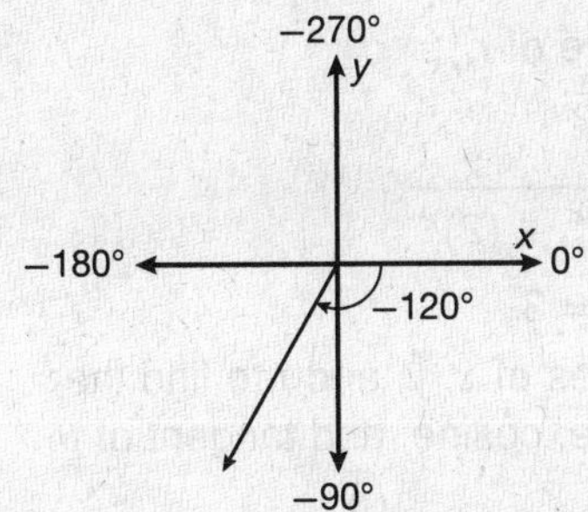

c.

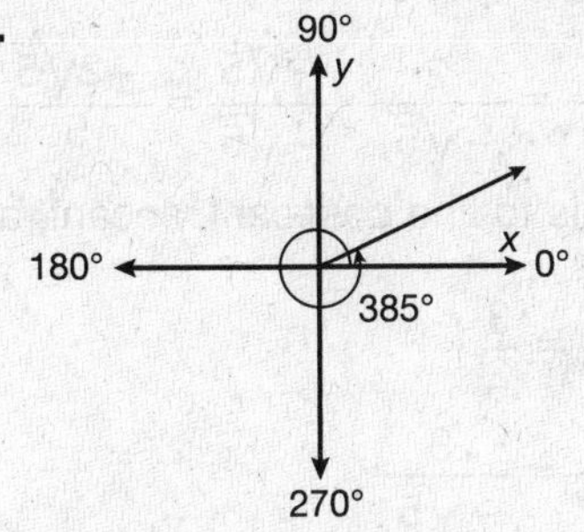

d. $360° + 94° = 454°$

$94° - 360° = -266°$

e. $730 - 2(360°) = 10°$

$360° + 10° = 370°$

$10° - 360° = -350°$

f. $180° - 115° = 65°$

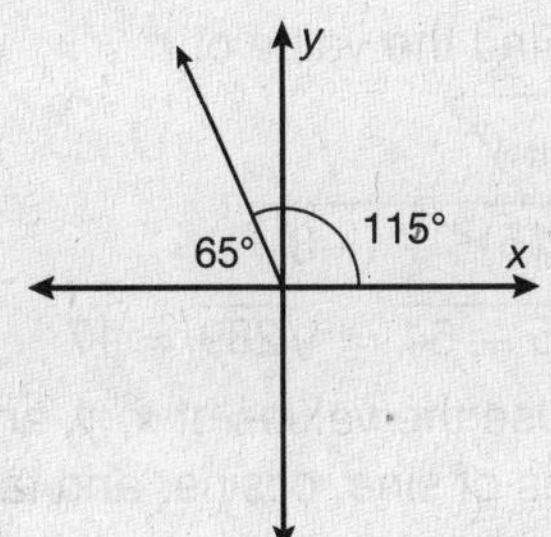

Reference angle for 115° is 65°.

g. $200° - 180° = 20°$

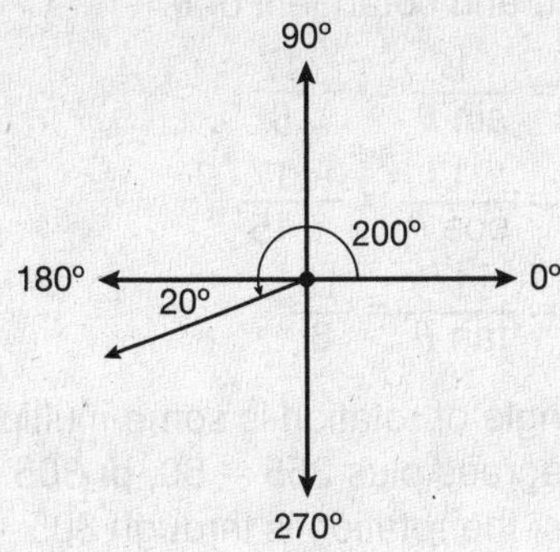

Reference angle for 200° is 20°.

h. $-145° + 360° = 215°$

$215° - 180° = 35°$

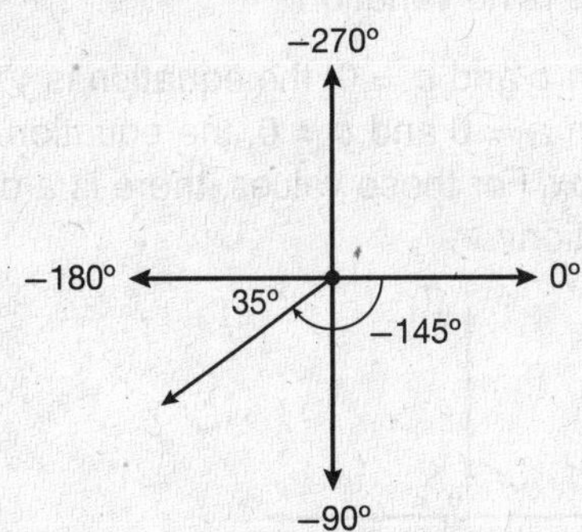

Reference angle for −145° is 35°.

i. Step 1: Plot point *P* and draw the angle in standard form. Then sketch a right triangle.

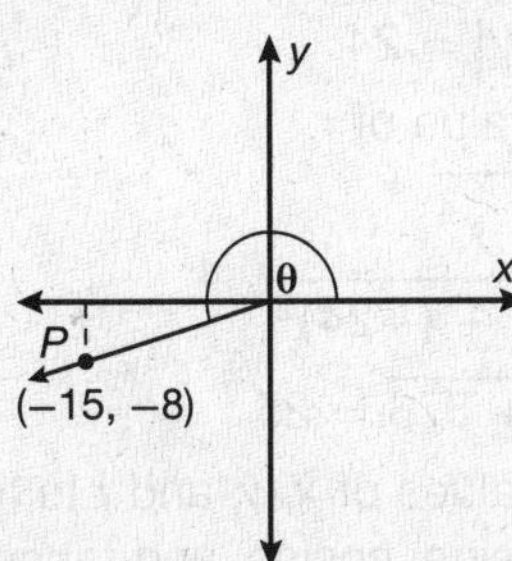

$|x| = 15, |y| = 8$

Step 2: Find the value of r.

$r = \sqrt{x^2 + y^2}$

$r = \sqrt{(-15)^2 + (-8)^2}$

$r = \sqrt{225 + 64} = \sqrt{289} = 17$

Step 3: Use the values of x, y, and r to find the values of sine, cosine, and tangent of θ.

$\sin\theta = \frac{-8}{17}$ $\cos\theta = \frac{-15}{17}$ $\tan\theta = \frac{-8}{-15} = \frac{8}{15}$

Step 4: Use reciprocals to find cosecant, secant, and cotangent of θ.

$\csc\theta = \frac{1}{\sin\theta} = -\frac{17}{8}$

$\sec\theta = \frac{1}{\cos\theta} = -\frac{17}{15}$

$\cot\theta = \frac{1}{\tan\theta} = \frac{15}{8}$

j. The angle of rotation is some multiple of 360 degrees plus 355 − 50, or 305 degrees. That is, the rotation is through 305 + 360n degrees for some integer, n.

Practice 56

1. There is no variation.

2. When b and $c = 0$, the equation is $y = ax^2$. When $a = 0$ and $c = 0$, the equation is $y = bx$. For these values, there is a direct variation.

3.

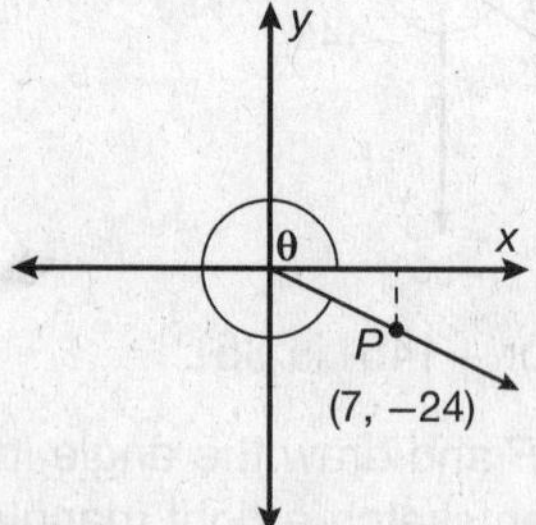

$|x| = 7, |y| = 24$

Find the value of r.

$r = \sqrt{x^2 + y^2}$

$r = \sqrt{(7)^2 + (-24)^2}$

$r = \sqrt{49 + 576} = 25$

Use the values of x, y, and r to find the values of sine, cosine, and tangent of θ.

$\sin\theta = \frac{-24}{25}$ $\cos\theta = \frac{7}{25}$ $\tan\theta = \frac{-24}{7}$

Use reciprocals to find cosecant, secant, and cotangent of θ.

$\csc\theta = \frac{1}{\sin\theta} = -\frac{25}{24}$ $\sec\theta = \frac{1}{\cos\theta} = \frac{25}{7}$

$\cot\theta = \frac{1}{\tan\theta} = -\frac{7}{24}$

4.

$(-\sqrt{5}, 2)$
P
θ

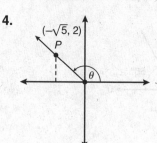

$|x| = \sqrt{5}, |y| = 2$

Find the value of r.

$r = \sqrt{x^2 + y^2}$

$r = \sqrt{(-\sqrt{5})^2 + (2)^2}$

$r = \sqrt{5 + 4} = 3$

Use the values of x, y, and r to find the values of sine, cosine, and tangent of θ.

$\sin\theta = \frac{2}{3}$ $\cos\theta = \frac{-\sqrt{5}}{3}$

$\tan\theta = \frac{2}{-\sqrt{5}} = \frac{2}{-\sqrt{5}} \cdot \frac{-\sqrt{5}}{-\sqrt{5}} = \frac{-2\sqrt{5}}{5}$

Use reciprocals to find cosecant, secant, and cotangent of θ.

$\csc\theta = \frac{1}{\sin\theta} = \frac{3}{2}$

$\sec\theta = \frac{1}{\cos\theta} = \frac{3}{-\sqrt{5}}$

$= \frac{3}{-\sqrt{5}} \cdot \frac{-\sqrt{5}}{-\sqrt{5}} = \frac{-3\sqrt{5}}{5}$

$\cot\theta = \frac{1}{\tan\theta} = \frac{5}{-2\sqrt{5}}$

$= \frac{5}{-2\sqrt{5}} \cdot \frac{\sqrt{5}}{\sqrt{5}}$

$= -\frac{5\sqrt{5}}{10} = -\frac{\sqrt{5}}{2}$

5. The leading coefficient is −1 and the constant term is −2.

6. $({}_9C_5)a^4b^5 = \frac{9!}{5!(9-5)!}a^4b^5 = 126a^4b^5$

7. $(f + g)(x) = (2x - 7) + (-5x + 8)$

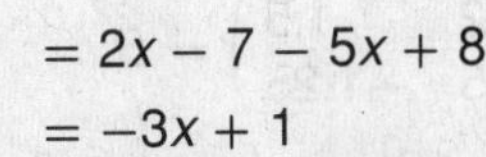

$= 2x - 7 - 5x + 8$

$= -3x + 1$

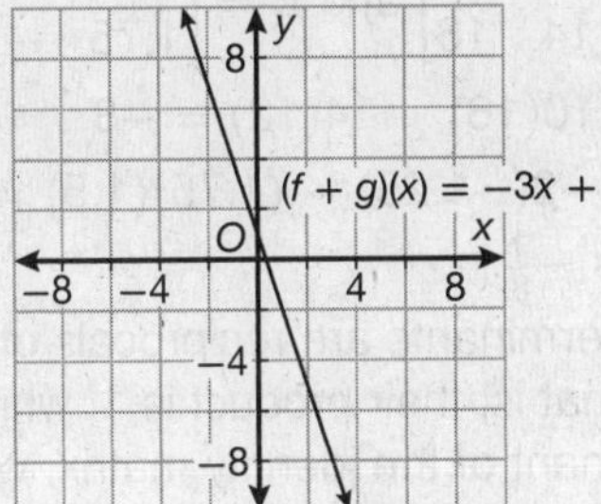

8. Odds in favor $= \dfrac{\text{favorable outcomes}}{\text{unfavorable outcomes}} = \dfrac{4}{12}$

Probability $= \dfrac{\text{favorable outcomes}}{\text{total outcomes}}$

$= \dfrac{4}{4 + 12} = \dfrac{4}{16} = \dfrac{1}{4}$

9. $(x)(x) = 196$

$x^2 = 196$

$x^2 - 196 = 0$

$(x + 14)(x - 14) = 0$

$x + 14 = 0$ or $x - 14 = 0$

$x = -14$ or $x = 14$

Since the dimensions cannot be negative, then −14 is not valid. The dimensions are 14 feet by 14 feet.

10. Donnie is correct. The equation $y = (-5)^x$ is not usually considered an exponential function, since some values of x give complex values.

11. $2.25 + 3.29 + 2.318 = 7.858$

The sum should have two decimal places.

7.86 miles

12. a. There are more peaches than nectarines, so the probability is greater for peaches.

b. $P(\text{2 peaches}) = \dfrac{12}{20} \times \dfrac{11}{19} = 34.7\%$

$P(\text{2 nectarines}) = \dfrac{8}{20} \times \dfrac{7}{19} = 14.7\%$

The difference is $34.7\% - 14.7\% = 20\%$

13. a. Range is all real numbers greater than −5. Answer Choice **C**

14. $({}_{12}C_6)g^6 2^6 = \dfrac{12!}{6!(12 - 6)!} g^6(64) = 924g^6(64)$

$= 59{,}136g^6$

15. Let x represent the distance of the farthest buoy from the base of the observation point, and let y represent the distance of the other buoy.

$\tan(90 - 57)^\circ = \dfrac{y}{435}$

$435 \tan 33^\circ = y$

$y \approx 282.5$

$\tan(90 - 13)^\circ = \dfrac{x}{435}$

$435 \tan 77^\circ = x$

$x \approx 1884.2$

The distance apart is $1884.2 - 282.5 = 1601.7$, or about 1602 feet.

16. Let t represent the amount to invest in treasure bonds, and c represent the amount to invest in CDs.

$t + c = 20{,}000$

$0.0418t + 0.0542c = 1000$

$-542(t + c = 20{,}000)$

$10{,}000(0.0418t + 0.0542c = 1000)$

$-542t - 542c = -10{,}840{,}000$

$418t + 542c = 10{,}000{,}000$

$-124t = -840{,}000$

$t = 6774$

The couple should invest about \$6774 in treasure bonds.

17. Let x represent the amount of olive oil and y represent the amount of mayonnaise.

$15x + 5y < 75$

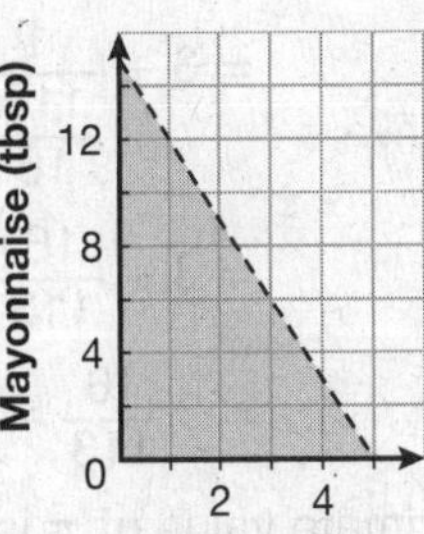

Sample: A point in the shaded area is (3, 5). This means that the dip can have 3 tablespoons of olive oil and 5 tablespoons of mayonnaise.

18. The correlation coefficient only measures the strength and direction of linear relationships. These points do not form a straight line.

19.

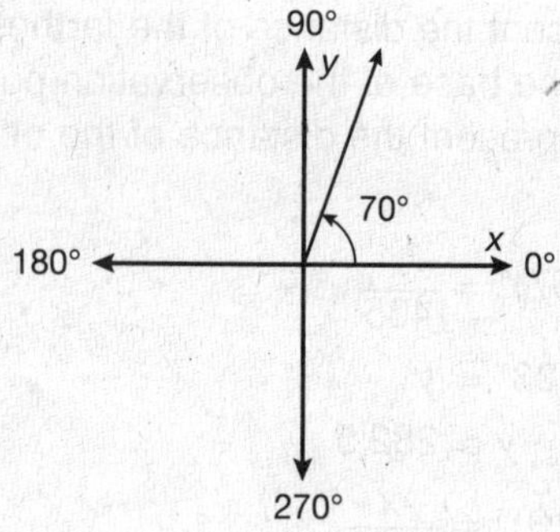

20.

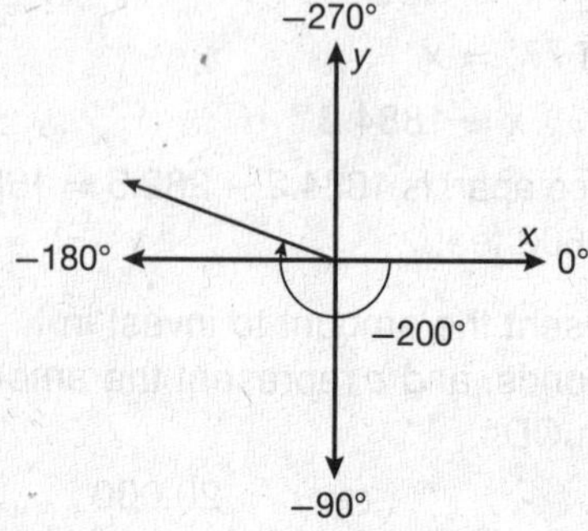

21.

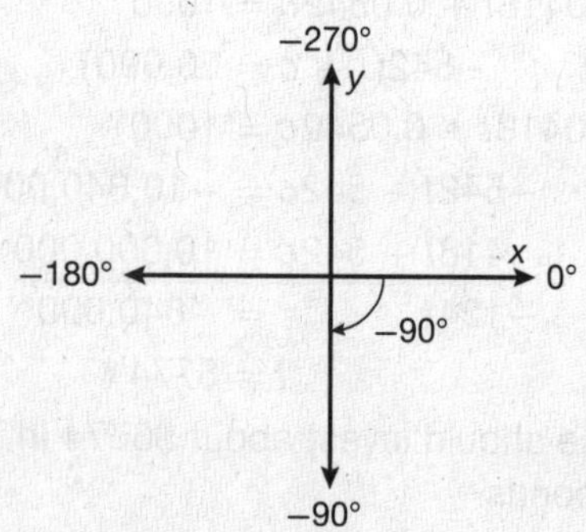

22. $3 + \cfrac{1}{7 + \cfrac{1}{15 + 1}} = 3 + \cfrac{1}{7 + \cfrac{1}{16}}$

$= 3 + \cfrac{1}{\frac{113}{16}}$

$= 3 + \frac{16}{113}$

$= 3\frac{16}{113} \approx 3.1415922$

The approximate value of π is 3.141592654.

23. Sample:

$A = \begin{pmatrix} 10 & -12 \\ 14 & 16 \end{pmatrix}$

$A^{-1} = \frac{1}{10(16) - 14(12)} \begin{pmatrix} 16 & -12 \\ -14 & 10 \end{pmatrix}$

$= \frac{1}{-8} \begin{pmatrix} 16 & -12 \\ -14 & 10 \end{pmatrix}$

$= \begin{pmatrix} -2 & 1.5 \\ 1.75 & -1.25 \end{pmatrix} = B$

$A = \begin{bmatrix} 10 & 12 \\ 14 & 16 \end{bmatrix}$ and $B = \begin{bmatrix} -2 & 1.5 \\ 1.75 & -1.25 \end{bmatrix}$

$\det A = 10(16) - 14(12) = -8$

$\det B = -2(-1.25) - (1.75)(1.5) = -0.125$, which is $-\frac{1}{8}$.

The determinants are reciprocals of each other. That is, their product is 1, which is the determinant of the identity matrix, which in turn is the product of the two original matrices.

24.

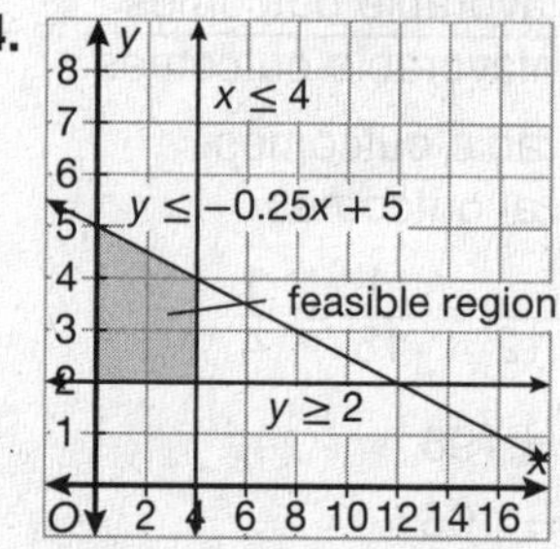

The feasible region is bounded by the points (0, 2), (0, 5), (4, 2), and (4, 4).

25. The graph is a continuous function, since there are no gaps or points of discontinuity, and it passes the vertical line test.

26. a. $P(\text{Florida}) = \frac{\text{favorable outcomes}}{\text{total outcomes}}$

$= \frac{18{,}089{,}888}{299{,}398{,}484} \approx 6\%$

b. $\text{odds in favor} = \frac{\text{favorable outcomes}}{\text{unfavorable outcomes}}$

$= \frac{18{,}089{,}888}{299{,}398{,}484 - 18{,}089{,}888}$

$= \frac{18{,}089{,}888}{281{,}308{,}596}$

$\approx \frac{3}{47}$

The odds are about 3 to 47.

27. $P(\text{2 red marbles}) = \frac{\text{ways to get 2 red marbles}}{\text{total outcomes}}$

$= \frac{C(6, 2)}{C(12, 2)} = \cfrac{\frac{6!}{2!(6-2)!}}{\frac{12!}{2!(12-2)!}}$

$= \frac{15}{66} = \frac{5}{22}$

$P(1 \text{ red}, 1 \text{ blue})$

$= \dfrac{\text{ways to get 1 red and 1 blue marble}}{\text{total outcomes}}$

$= \dfrac{C(6, 1) \times C(5, 1)}{C(12, 2)}$

$= \dfrac{\dfrac{6!}{1!(6-1)!} \times \dfrac{5!}{1!(5-1)!}}{\dfrac{12!}{2!(12-2)!}} = \dfrac{30}{66} = \dfrac{5}{11}$

$\frac{5}{11} > \frac{5}{22}$, so it is more likely that 1 red and 1 blue marble will be selected.

28. A graph in the form $y = a(x - h)^2 + k$ opens upward when a is positive and downward when a is negative, and has vertex at (h, k). The parent function $y = x^2$ opens upward and has vertex at (0, 0).
The function $y = -2.5(x - 5)^2 + 2$ opens downward and has vertex (5, 2) so it is shifted 5 units right and 2 units up.
$|a| > 1$, so the graph is narrower than the parent function.

29. Let l represent the length of the playground, and w represent the width.
$l \leq 40$, $w \geq 20$,
$(14 + 25)(2l + 2w) \leq 2500$, or
$78l + 78w \leq 2500$

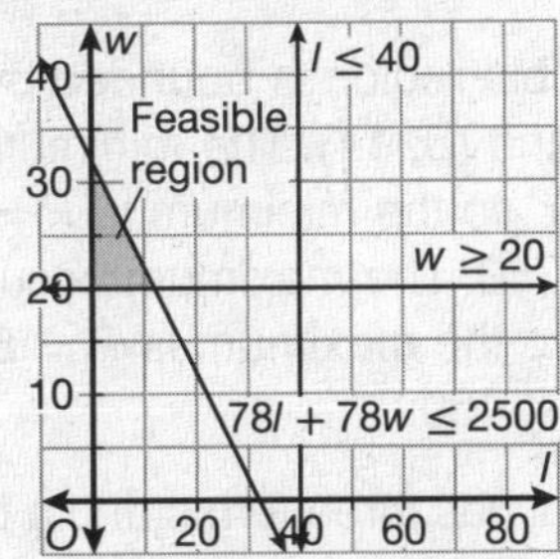

The feasible region is bounded by (0, 32.05), (0, 20), and (12.05, 20).
The maximum area occurs at $w = 12.05$ and $l = 20$, which is $12.05(20) = 241$ square feet.

30. **a.** $f(x)$ rotates (0, 1) 180 degrees clockwise to (0, −1). Then $g(x)$ takes (0, −1) 2 units right to (2, −1).

b. $g(x)$ takes (0, 1) 2 units right to (2, 1). Then $f(x)$ rotates (2, 1) 180 degrees clockwise to (−2, −1).

LESSON 57

Warm Up 57

1. exponential
2. $f(f^{-1}(x)) = x$, Therefore $f(g(x)) = x$
3. $2^{-1} = \dfrac{1}{2^1} = 0.5$
4. In exponential functions of the form $y = ab^x$ $a \neq 0$, $b > 0$, $b \neq 1$, and x is a real number, so the statement is false.

Lesson Practice 57

a. $A = P\left(1 + \frac{r}{n}\right)^{nt}$

$A = 5000\left(1 + \dfrac{0.035}{12}\right)^{12(4)}$

$A = \$5750.20$

b. For continuous compounding the base is e, which is approximately 2.72. After four years, the account will be worth $5000e^{4(0.035)}$ dollars, or \$5751.37.

c. Solve for P.

$$A = Pe^{rt}$$
$$15{,}320 = Pe^{(0.04)(4)}$$
$$15{,}320 = P(1.174)$$
$$13{,}054.84 = P$$

The initial value of the account was \$13,054.84.

d. The function modeling the remainder is exponential decay, $f(t) = b^t$. The half-life is 5730, so $f(5730) = \frac{1}{2}f(0)$. That is, $b^{5730} = \frac{1}{2}b^0 = 0.5$. Therefore $b = \sqrt[5730]{0.5}$ ≈ 0.99988. After 9000 years, the portion remaining is $f(9000) = 0.99988^{9000} \approx 0.34$. The portion of a 10 kg mass that remains is $10(0.34) = 3.4$ kg.

e. Find the value of a in the equation $y = ab^x$

$803 = ab^0$

$803 = a$

Substitute the values at $x = 10$ to find the value of b.

$412 = 803b^{10}$

$b^{10} \approx 0.5130$

$b \approx \sqrt[10]{0.5130} \approx 0.9354$

Calculate the value of y at $x = 15$ and $x = 45$.

$y \approx 803(0.9354)^{15}$ $\quad y \approx 803(0.9354)^{45}$

$\approx 803(0.3672)$ $\quad \approx 803(0.0495)$

≈ 294.9 $\quad \approx 39.77$

f. Find the value of a in the equation $y = ab^x$

$983{,}403 = ab^0 = a$

Substitute the values at $x = 10$ to find the value of b.

$1{,}321{,}045 = 983{,}403b^{10}$

$b^{10} \approx 1.343$

$b \approx \sqrt[10]{1.343} \approx 1.0299$

Calculate the value of y at $x = 20$.

$y \approx 983{,}403(1.0299)^{20}$

$\approx 983{,}403(1.803) \approx 1{,}770{,}000$

The population of Phoenix, Arizona will be approximately 1,770,000 in 2010.

Practice 57

1. $2(4) - (0) + (-1) \stackrel{?}{=} 7$

$7 = 7$

$-3(4) + 5(0) - 3(-1) \stackrel{?}{=} -9$

$-9 = -9$

$4(4) - 2(0) + 2(-1) \stackrel{?}{=} -14$

$14 \neq -14$

(4, 0, −1) is not a solution to the system.

2. $4\sqrt{3} \cdot 3\sqrt{12} \cdot 2\sqrt{3} = 24(3)\sqrt{12}$

$= 72\sqrt{4}\sqrt{3} = 144\sqrt{3}$

3. $3\sqrt{75} - 4\sqrt{48} = 3\sqrt{25}\sqrt{3} - 4\sqrt{16}\sqrt{3}$

$= 15\sqrt{3} - 16\sqrt{3} = -\sqrt{3}$

4. $2\sqrt{5}(5\sqrt{5} - 3\sqrt{15}) = 10\sqrt{25} - 6\sqrt{75}$

$= 50 - 6\sqrt{25 \cdot 3}$

$= 50 - 30\sqrt{3}$

5. $\frac{x}{x-2} \div \frac{6x-2}{3x+6} = \frac{x}{x-2} \cdot \frac{3(x+2)}{2(3x-1)}$

The expression is undefined when $x - 2 = 0$ or when $3x - 1 = 0$.

$x - 2 = 0 \rightarrow x = 2$

$3x - 1 = 0 \rightarrow x = \frac{1}{3}$

6.

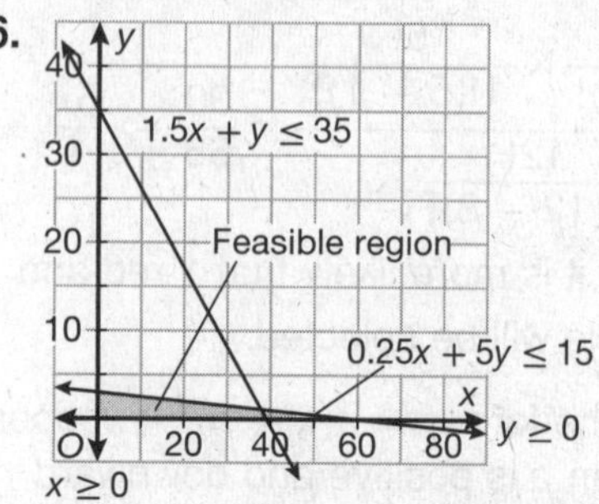

The feasible region is bounded by (0, 3), (23.3, 0), and (22, 1.9). The minimum occurs at (0, 3), so the minimum is $P = 15(0) + 7(3) = 21$. The maximum occurs at (23.3, 0), so the maximum is $P = 15(23.3) + 7(0) = 350$.

7.

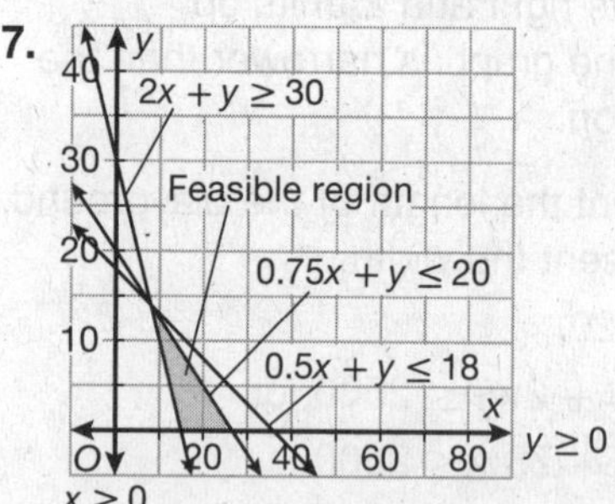

The feasible region is bounded by (15, 0), (36, 0), and (8, 14). The minimum occurs at (15, 0), so the minimum is $P = 50(15) + 75(0) = 750$. The maximum occurs at (8, 14), so the maximum is $P = 50(8) + 75(14) = 1450$.

8. A trinomial has three terms and a binomial has two terms. The sum can result in 1, 2, 3, 4, or 5 terms.

9. The input for x is $g(x)$ so the calculations are correct. However, since $g(0)$ is undefined, the domain of the composite function does not include 0. The student should have mentioned this restriction.

10. a.

x	−3	−2	−1	0	1	2
$f(x)$	−4	10	12	8	4	6

b. The smallest x-interval whose associated portion of the graph contains a relative maximum is the interval from -3 to -1 because the function values increase and then decrease on that interval. The smallest x-interval whose associated portion of the graph contains a relative minimum is the interval from -1 to 1 because the function values decrease and then increase on that interval.

11. $900° - 2(360°) = 180°$
The rotation is two full turns and a half turn.

12. $d = \sqrt{(x_2 - x_1)^2 + (y_2 - y_1)^2}$
$= \sqrt{(0.5 - 1)^2 + (10 - 4)^2}$
$= \sqrt{0.25 + 36} \approx 6.02$
If one unit represents 25 km, then the cities are $6.02 \cdot 25 = 150.5$ km apart.

13. These are individual points, so they are discrete. Since 3 is paired with two different y-values, this is a relation, but not a function.
Answer Choice **D**

14. slope $= \frac{\text{rise}}{\text{run}} = \frac{6}{8} = \frac{3}{4}$
The slope is negative since, it falls. Therefore, the slope is $-\frac{3}{4}$.

15. One way is to graph the points with the intercepts of $2y - x = 6$, $(0, 3)$ and $(-6, 0)$. Connect the points with a dashed line. Choose the test point $(0, 0)$. Because $0 < 6$ is true, the origin is in the region to be shaded, so shade below the line.
The other way to graph the inequality is to first write the inequality in slope–intercept form: $y < \frac{1}{2}x + 3$. Graph the point with the y-intercept $(0, 3)$ and find a second point by moving up one and right two from there. Connect the points with a dashed line. Shade below the line because the symbol is less than.

16. Although 3 can be factored out of the expression, x cannot be factored out because there is no power of x in the constant term. The correct factorization is
$9x^2 - 6x - 15 = 3(3x^2 - 2x - 5)$
$= 3(3x - 5)(x + 1)$

17. This is an increasing function. Therefore it shows exponential growth.

18. This is an decreasing function. Therefore it shows exponential decay.

19. $\tan \theta$ is undefined for 90° and 270°

20. The probability for each quadrant is 1 out of 4 total outcomes.

Quadrant	I	II	III	IV
P(point in that quadrant)	0.25	0.25	0.25	0.25

21. The student used $X = BA^{-1}$ instead of $X = A^{-1}B$. Matrix multiplication is not commutative. The correct solution is
$X = A^{-1}B \begin{bmatrix} 8 & -3 \\ 5 & -2 \end{bmatrix} \cdot \begin{bmatrix} 0 & 2 \\ 1 & 4 \end{bmatrix} = \begin{bmatrix} -3 & 4 \\ -2 & 2 \end{bmatrix}$

22. The x-term in the second equation needs to be $-6x$. So mulitply by -2 to get $3x(-2) = -6x$.
Answer Choice **C**

23. Sample: The fourth diagonal of Pascal's Triangle has the Tetrahedral Numbers. The sum of the numbers in each row in Pascal's Triangle is a power of 2. If the odd and even numbers in Pascal's Triangle are colored using two different colors, the Sierpinski Triangle will be shown.

24. $2x + 3y = 3$
$3y = -2x + 3$
$y = \frac{-2}{3}x + 1$
Plot the y-intercept $(0,1)$. Then move down two units and across three units to $(3, -1)$. Draw a straight line through the two points.

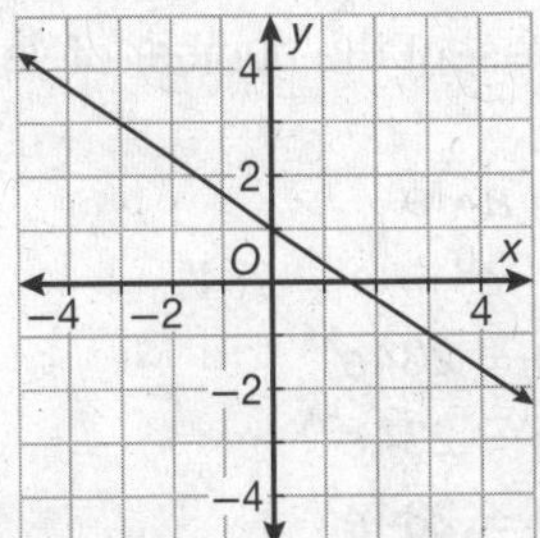

25. $\frac{\sqrt{P}}{\sqrt{R}} = \frac{\sqrt{P}}{\sqrt{R}} \cdot \frac{\sqrt{R}}{\sqrt{R}} = \frac{\sqrt{PR}}{R}$

26. The determinant of the matrix is $3 - (-8) = 11$. The determinant of a single number must be the number itself. (The determinant is not the number's absolute value, as the determinant notation might indicate.)

27.
$$y = ab^x$$
$$2 = ab^0$$
$$a = 2$$
$$18 = 2b^2$$
$$9 = b^2$$
$$b = 3$$
$$y = 2 \cdot 3^x$$
The function is increasing.

28. a.
$$x \le y$$
$$7.5x + 15y \le 300$$

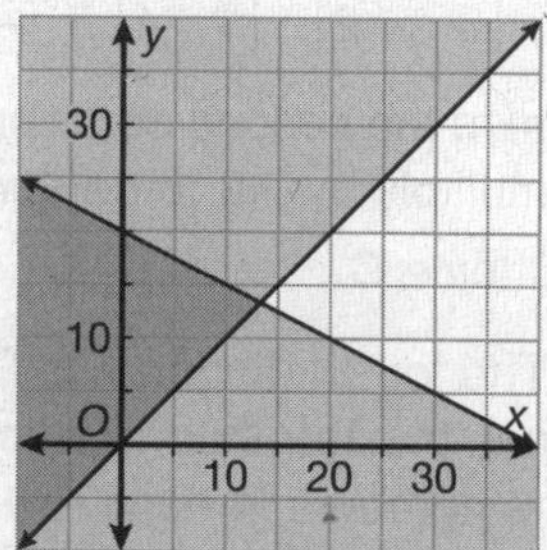

b. For the point of intersection $x = y$, so
$$7.5y + 15y = 300$$
$$22.5y = 300$$
$$y = 13.33$$
$$x = 13.33$$
The intersection is (13.33, 13.33).

c. (13.25, 13.25). It represents 13.25 pounds of salmon and 13.25 pounds of shrimp at a total cost of \$298.13, which is \$1.87 less than the maximum that can be spent.

29. Let t represent the number of years since 1950.
$$I = f(t) = a \cdot e^{kt}$$
$$f(0) = a \cdot e^0 = a = 234$$
$$f(t) = 234e^{kt}$$
$$f(5) = 234e^{5k}$$
$$373 = 234e^{5k}$$
$$1.594 = e^{5k}$$
$$\ln(1.594) = 5k$$
$$0.466 = 5k$$
$$k = 0.0933$$
$$I = 234e^{0.0933t}$$
Substitute 60 for t.
$$I = 234e^{0.0933(60)}$$
$$= 63{,}377$$
Therefore this model predicts that 63,377 billion dollars will be invested.

30. Using a graphing calculator, the y-intercept is 1.

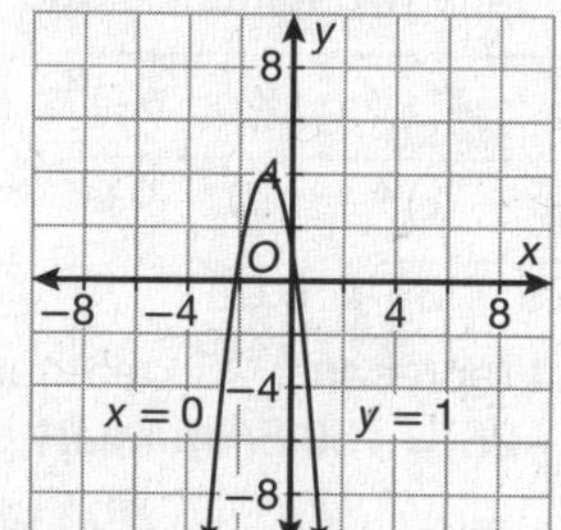

LESSON 58

Warm Up 58

1. constant
2. $x^2 + 2x + 1 = (x + 1)(x + 1)$
   $= (x + 1)^2$
3. Perfect squares, such as 1, 4, 9, 16, and so on have square roots that are whole numbers. Therefore, the statement is true.

Lesson Practice 58

a.
$$x^2 - 2x + 1 = 36$$
$$(x - 1)(x - 1) = 36$$
$$(x - 1)^2 = 36$$
$$x - 1 = \pm\sqrt{36}$$
$$x - 1 = \pm 6$$
$$x - 1 = 6 \text{ or } x - 1 = -6$$
$$x = 7 \qquad x = -5$$

b.
$$x^2 + 16x + 64 = 6$$
$$(x + 8)(x + 8) = 6$$
$$(x + 8)^2 = 6$$
$$x + 8 = \pm\sqrt{6}$$
$$x = -8 \pm \sqrt{6}$$
$$x = -8 + \sqrt{6} \text{ or } x = -8 - \sqrt{6}$$

c. $x^2 - 20x + \left(\frac{-20}{2}\right)^2 = x^2 - 20x + 100$

$= (x - 10)^2$

d. $x^2 + 26x - 2 = 0$

$x^2 + 26x = 2$

$x^2 + 26x + \left(\frac{26}{2}\right)^2 = 2 + \left(\frac{26}{2}\right)^2$

$x^2 + 26x + 169 = 2 + 169$

$(x + 13)^2 = 171$

$x + 13 = \pm\sqrt{171}$

$x = -13 \pm 3\sqrt{19}$

e. Substitute 4 for h and solve for t.

$4 = -16t^2 + 20t$

$0 = -16t^2 + 20t - 4$

$0 = -4(4t^2 - 5t + 1)$

$0 = -4(4t - 1)(t - 1)$

$0 = 4t - 1$ or $0 = t - 1$

$t = \frac{1}{4} = 0.25$ or $t = 1$ second

Practice 58

1. $2y - 2x = 8 \rightarrow 2y - 2x = 8$

$-2(y + x = -2) \rightarrow \underline{-2y - 2x = 4}$

$-4x = 12$

$x = -3$

$y + (-3) = -2$

$y = 1$

The solution is $(-3, 1)$.

2. $y - 2x = 1$

$y = -2$

Substitute the second equation into the first.

$-2 - 2x = 1$

$-2x = 1 + 2$

$-2x = 3$

$x = -\frac{3}{2}$

The solution is $\left(-\frac{3}{2}, -2\right)$.

3. $2(3x + 2y = 12) \rightarrow 6x + 4y = 24$

$5x - 4y = 8 \rightarrow \underline{5x - 4y = 8}$

$11x = 32$

$x = \frac{32}{11}$

Substitute for x.

$5\left(\frac{32}{11}\right) - 4y = 8$

$-4y = 8 - \frac{160}{11}$

$-4y = -\frac{72}{11}$

$y = \frac{18}{11}$

The solution is $\left(\frac{32}{11}, \frac{18}{11}\right)$.

4. $-3 < d + 2$

$-3 - 2 < d$

$-5 < d$

$d + 2 < 12$

$d < 10$

So, $-5 < d < 10$

5. $-4 \le 4x - 8 < 12$

$-4 + 8 \le 4x - 8 + 8 < 12 + 8$

$4 \le 4x < 20$

$\frac{4}{4} \le \frac{4}{4}x < \frac{20}{4}$

$1 \le x < 5$

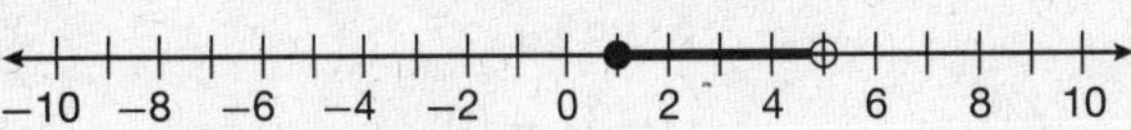

6. $y = \frac{1}{x}$

$xy = 1$

An inverse variation has the form $xy = k$. This is an inverse variation.

7. If $a = 0$, the equation is $z = \frac{1}{xy}$. This is a joint variation.

8. $x^2 - 8x + 16 = 3$

$(x - 4)(x - 4) = 3$

$(x - 4)^2 = 3$

$x - 4 = \pm\sqrt{3}$

$x = 4 \pm \sqrt{3}$

9. $x^2 + 26x + 169 = 81$

$(x + 13)(x + 13) = 81$

$(x + 13)^2 = 81$

$x + 13 = \pm\sqrt{81}$

$x + 13 = \pm 9$

$x = -13 + 9$ or $x = -13 - 9$

$x = -4$ or $x = -22$

10. The graphs can be written in the form $y = a(x - h)^2 + k$ to compare.

$y = -4.9(x + 0)^2 + 4$

$y = -16(x + 0)^2 + 1.2$

Since the absolute value of a is less in the first equation, the graph of $y = -4.9x^2 + 4$ is wider than the graph of $y = -16x^2 + 1.2$. The vertex of the graph in the first equation is (0, 4) and the vertex of the graph in the second equation is (0, 1.2). This represents a vertical shift of 2.8 units for $y = -16x^2 + 1.2$.

11. The points are discrete since they are not connected. The points are a relation, but not a function, since the x-value 1 is paired with two different y-values. Sam could change (1, 2) to (x, 2), where $x \neq 1, 2$, or 5. This would make his example a discrete function.

12.

$$\begin{array}{r} x^2 + 2x - 3 \\ x - 2\overline{)x^3 + 0x^2 - 7x + 3} \\ \underline{-(x^3 - 2x^2)} \\ 2x^2 - 7x + 3 \\ \underline{-(2x^2 - 4x)} \\ -3x + 3 \\ \underline{-(-3x + 6)} \\ -3 \end{array}$$

$x^3 - 7x + 3 \div x - 2 = x^2 + 2x - 3 - \dfrac{3}{x - 2}$

Answer Choice **C**

13. a. Isolate the binomial by adding 97 to both sides.

b. $\left(\dfrac{104}{2}\right)^2 = 2704$

c. $x^2 + 104x + 2704 = (x + 52)^2$

d.
$$x^2 + 104x - 97 = 4$$
$$x^2 + 104x = 101$$
$$x^2 + 104x + 2704 = 101 + 2704$$
$$(x + 52)^2 = 2805$$
$$x + 52 = \pm\sqrt{2805}$$
$$x = -52 \pm \sqrt{2805}$$

14. The third angle is $180 - (90 + 42) = 48°$.

$\sin 42° = \dfrac{x}{32}$

$x = 32(\sin 42°)$

$x \approx 21.4$

$\cos 48° = \dfrac{x}{32}$

$x = 32(\cos 48°)$

$x \approx 21.4$

15. Compounding is monthly, so the rate is $\frac{1}{12}$ of 2.4% or 0.24%. Each month the value is multiplied by 1.0024. one year consist of 12 months. So the account will have a value of $1850(1.0024)^{12}$ dollars.

16.
$$x^2 - 42x + 441 = 2$$
$$(x - 21)^2 = 2$$
$$x - 21 = \pm\sqrt{2}$$
$$x = 21 \pm \sqrt{2}$$

Answer Choice **C**

17. Let W represent one dimension, and L represent the other.

$2W + L = 80$

18. Multiply the first terms in each binomial $2x(3x)$, then multiply the outer two terms $2x(-6)$, then multiply the inner two terms $8(3x)$, and then multiply the last two terms $8(-6)$. Combine any like terms to simplify.

19. $-1 \leq r \leq 1$ and the points get closer to forming a line as $|r|$ approaches 1.

20.
$$P(\text{3 vowels}) = \frac{5}{26} \times \frac{5}{26} \times \frac{5}{26}$$
$$= \frac{125}{17{,}576} \approx 0.71\%$$

21. $A = \dfrac{bh}{2}$

$$72x^2 - 98 = \frac{(12x + 14)h}{2}$$
$$144x^2 - 196 = (12x + 14)h$$
$$\frac{144x^2 - 196}{12x + 14} = h$$
$$\frac{(12x - 14)(12x + 14)}{12x + 14} = h$$
$$12x - 14 \text{ ft} = h$$

22. The fence divides the equilateral triangle into two right triangles, so the fence is a leg of the right triangle, and its height. The fence also bisects the base of the equilateral triangle. The length of the fence is

$200^2 = a^2 + 100^2$

$$40{,}000 = a^2 + 10{,}000$$
$$30{,}000 = a^2$$
$$173.21 \approx a$$

The fence is 173.21 m long.

Each brother owns $\frac{173.21(100)}{2} = 8660.5 \text{ m}^2$ of land.

23.

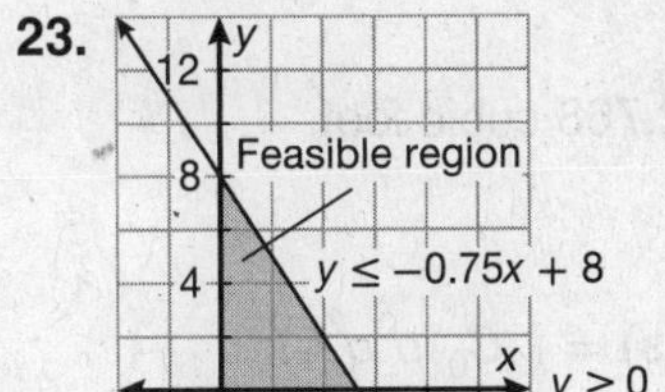

The region is bounded by (0, 0), (0, 8), (10.67, 0).

24. The variable y should have canceled out, so there is no solution.

25.
$$T = 2\pi\sqrt{\frac{l}{9.8}}$$
$$T^2 = \left(2\pi\sqrt{\frac{l}{9.8}}\right)^2$$
$$T^2 = 4\pi^2\frac{l}{9.8}$$
$$\frac{9.8T^2}{4\pi^2} = l$$

26. a. $f(t) = b^t$.

The half-life is 245,000 so $f(245{,}000) = \frac{1}{2}f(0)$.

$$b^{245{,}000} = \frac{1}{2}b^0 = 0.5$$

Therefore, $b = \sqrt[245{,}000]{0.5} \approx 0.9999971708$

The portion remaining can be represented by $f(t) = a(0.999997)^t$

b. $f(182{,}000) = 150(0.9999971708)^{182{,}000}$
≈ 90 grams

27. $f(x) = 3x$, $g(x) = 3x + 2$
$g(f(x)) = 3(3x) + 2$
$g(f(x)) = 9x + 2$

28. His friend is correct because the negative sign is not part of the radicand. The square root of 81 is 9, and the opposite of 9 is −9.

29. Multiply both the numerator and the denominator by $\frac{(\sqrt[3]{5})^2}{(\sqrt[3]{5})^2}$.

30. Substitute 0 for h and solve for t.

$$0 = -16t^2 + 880t + 70.7$$
$$16t^2 - 880t = 70.7$$
$$t^2 - \left(\frac{880}{16}\right)t = \frac{70.7}{16}$$
$$t^2 - 55t = 4.41875$$
$$t^2 - 55t + 756.25 = 4.41875 + 756.25$$
$$(t - 27.5)^2 = 760.66875$$
$$t - 27.5 = \pm 27.58$$
$$t = 27.5 \pm 27.58$$

Ignoring the negative solution, because time cannot be negative $t \approx 55.1$ s.

LESSON 59

Warm Up 59

1. exponent

2. $\frac{x^2y^4}{x^{-1}y^3} = x^{2-(-1)}y^{4-3} = x^3y$

3.
$$\sqrt{x} = 4$$
$$(\sqrt{x})^2 = 4^2$$
$$x = 16$$

Lesson Practice 59

a. $a^{\frac{1}{n}} = \sqrt[n]{a}$

In this case, $a = 7$ and $n = 7$.

$7^{\frac{1}{7}} = \sqrt[7]{7}$

b. $a^{\frac{m}{n}} = \sqrt[n]{a^m}$

In this case, $a = 4$, $m = 5$, and $n = 3$.

$4^{\frac{5}{3}} = \sqrt[3]{4^5}$

c.
$$\sqrt[6]{64x^{18}} = \sqrt[6]{2^6 \cdot x^6 \cdot x^6 \cdot x^6}$$
$$= \sqrt[6]{2^6} \cdot \sqrt[6]{x^6} \cdot \sqrt[6]{x^6} \cdot \sqrt[6]{x^6}$$
$$= 2 \cdot x \cdot x \cdot x$$
$$= 2x^3$$

d.
$$\sqrt[3]{\frac{x^{24}}{6}} = \frac{\sqrt[3]{x^{24}}}{\sqrt[3]{6}}$$
$$= \frac{\sqrt[3]{(x^8)^3}}{\sqrt[3]{6}}$$
$$= \frac{x^8}{\sqrt[3]{6}}$$

$= \frac{x^8}{\sqrt[3]{6}} \cdot \frac{\sqrt[3]{6}}{\sqrt[3]{6}} \cdot \frac{\sqrt[3]{6}}{\sqrt[3]{6}}$

$= \frac{x^8\sqrt[3]{36}}{6}$

e. $49^{-\frac{5}{4}} \cdot 49^{\frac{3}{4}} = 49^{-\frac{5}{4}+\frac{3}{4}}$

$= 49^{-\frac{2}{4}}$

$= 49^{-\frac{1}{2}}$

$= \frac{1}{49^{\frac{1}{2}}}$

$= \frac{1}{\sqrt{49}}$

$= \frac{1}{7}$

f. $\frac{15^{\frac{17}{6}}}{15^{\frac{5}{6}}} = 15^{\frac{17}{6}-\frac{5}{6}}$

$= 15^{\frac{12}{6}}$

$= 15^2$

$= 225$

g. $\left(625^{\frac{1}{16}}\right)^4 = 625^{\frac{1}{16}\times 4}$

$= 625^{\frac{4}{16}}$

$= 625^{\frac{1}{4}}$

$= \sqrt[4]{625}$

$= \sqrt[4]{5^4}$

$= 5$

h. $(1024 \cdot 32)^{\frac{1}{5}} = 1024^{\frac{1}{5}} \cdot 32^{\frac{1}{5}}$

$= \sqrt[5]{1024}\,\sqrt[5]{32}$

$= 4 \cdot 2$

$= 8$

i. $x^{\frac{1}{9}} = 3$

$\left(x^{\frac{1}{9}}\right)^9 = 3^9$

$x = 19{,}683$

j. $x^{\frac{7}{6}} = 128$

$\left(x^{\frac{7}{6}}\right)^{\frac{6}{7}} = 128^{\frac{6}{7}}$

$x = \left(\sqrt[7]{128}\right)^6$

$x = (2)^6$

$x = 64$

k. $x^{\frac{5}{2}} = 4$

$x^{\frac{5}{2}\cdot\frac{2}{5}} = 4^{\frac{2}{5}}$

$x = \sqrt[5]{4^2}$

$x = \sqrt[5]{16}$

l. Substitute 32 for y and solve for x.

$32 = \sqrt[3]{x}$

$32 = x^{\frac{1}{3}}$

$32^3 = x^{\frac{1}{3}\cdot\frac{3}{1}}$

$32{,}768 = x$

The volume is 32,768 cubic feet.

Practice 59

1. $P(\text{exactly 0 heads}) = ({}_3C_0)p^0q^{3-0}$

$({}_3C_0)p^0q^3 = (1)\left(\frac{1}{2}\right)^0\left(\frac{1}{2}\right)^3$

$= \frac{1}{8}$

2. $3\sqrt{\frac{7}{5}} + 2\sqrt{\frac{5}{7}} = 3\frac{\sqrt{7}}{\sqrt{5}} + 2\frac{\sqrt{5}}{\sqrt{7}}$

$= 3\frac{\sqrt{7}}{\sqrt{5}} \cdot \frac{\sqrt{5}}{\sqrt{5}} + 2\frac{\sqrt{5}}{\sqrt{7}} \cdot \frac{\sqrt{7}}{\sqrt{7}}$

$= 3\frac{\sqrt{35}}{5} + 2\frac{\sqrt{35}}{7}$

$= 3\frac{\sqrt{35}}{5} \cdot \frac{7}{7} + 2\frac{\sqrt{35}}{7} \cdot \frac{5}{5}$

$= \frac{21\sqrt{35}}{35} + \frac{10\sqrt{35}}{35}$

$= \frac{31\sqrt{35}}{35}$

3. $\frac{2}{5\sqrt{18}} = \frac{2}{5\sqrt{9}\sqrt{2}}$

$= \frac{2}{15\sqrt{2}}$

$= \frac{2}{15\sqrt{2}} \cdot \frac{\sqrt{2}}{\sqrt{2}}$

$= \frac{2\sqrt{2}}{30}$

$= \frac{\sqrt{2}}{15}$

4. $\sqrt{\frac{2}{3}} + \sqrt{\frac{3}{2}} = \frac{\sqrt{2}}{\sqrt{3}} + \frac{\sqrt{3}}{\sqrt{2}}$

$= \frac{\sqrt{2}}{\sqrt{3}} \cdot \frac{\sqrt{3}}{\sqrt{3}} + \frac{\sqrt{3}}{\sqrt{2}} \cdot \frac{\sqrt{2}}{\sqrt{2}}$

$$= \frac{\sqrt{6}}{3} + \frac{\sqrt{6}}{2}$$
$$= \frac{\sqrt{6}}{3} \cdot \frac{2}{2} + \frac{\sqrt{6}}{2} \cdot \frac{3}{3}$$
$$= \frac{2\sqrt{6}}{6} + \frac{3\sqrt{6}}{6} = \frac{5\sqrt{6}}{6}$$

5. $x^2 + 3x + \left(\frac{3}{2}\right)^2 = x^2 + 3x + \left(\frac{9}{4}\right)$
$$= \left(x + \frac{3}{2}\right)^2$$

6. $x^2 - 14x + \left(\frac{14}{2}\right)^2 = x^2 - 14x + 49$
$$= (x - 7)^2$$

7. $2x + y = 4$
$$y = -2x + 4$$
The slope, m, of the perpendicular line will be the opposite reciprocal of -2, which is $\frac{1}{2}$. Substitute the slope, $\frac{1}{2}$, and the point $(-2, -1)$ into the point-slope formula.
$$y - y_1 = m(x - x_1)$$
$$y - (-1) = \frac{1}{2}(x - (-2))$$
$$y + 1 = \frac{1}{2}x + 1$$
$$y = \frac{1}{2}x$$

8. $a^{\frac{1}{n}} = \sqrt[n]{a}$
In this case, $a = 27$ and $n = 3$.
$$27^{\frac{1}{3}} = \sqrt[3]{27}$$

9. $a^{\frac{m}{n}} = \sqrt[n]{a^m}$
In this case, $a = 16$, $m = 3$, and $n = 4$.
$$16^{\frac{3}{4}} = \sqrt[4]{16^3}$$

10. $a^{\frac{1}{n}} = \sqrt[n]{a}$
In this case, $a = 64$ and $n = 6$.
$$64^{\frac{1}{6}} = \sqrt[6]{64}$$

11. a. $(a + b)^2 = (a + b)(a + b)$
$$= a(a) + a(b) + b(a) + b(b)$$
$$= a^2 + 2ab + b^2$$
b. $(a - b)^2 = (a - b)(a - b)$
$$= a(a) + a(-b) + (-b)(a) + (-b)(-b)$$
$$= a^2 - 2ab + b^2$$

12. Let d represent the distance, and l represent the length of the string.
$$d = l \cdot 2^{-\frac{n}{12}}$$
$$d = 66 \cdot 2^{-\frac{2}{12}} = 66 \cdot 2^{-\frac{1}{6}}$$
$$d = \frac{66}{2^{\frac{1}{6}}} = \frac{66}{\sqrt[6]{2}}$$
$$d = \frac{66}{\sqrt[6]{2}} \cdot \frac{\sqrt[6]{2}}{\sqrt[6]{2}} \cdot \frac{\sqrt[6]{2}}{\sqrt[6]{2}} \cdot \frac{\sqrt[6]{2}}{\sqrt[6]{2}} \cdot \frac{\sqrt[6]{2}}{\sqrt[6]{2}} \cdot \frac{\sqrt[6]{2}}{\sqrt[6]{2}}$$
$$d = \frac{66\sqrt[6]{32}}{2} = 33\sqrt[6]{32} \approx 58.8 \text{ cm}$$

13. $x > -4$

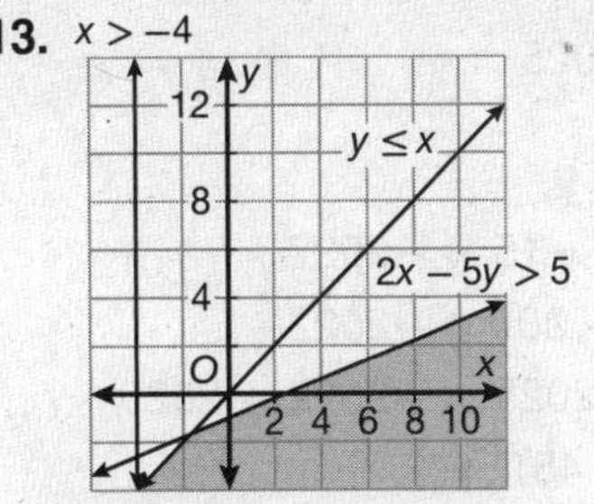

Answer Choice **A**

14.

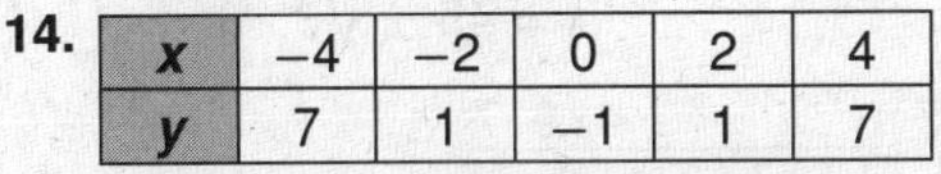

x	−4	−2	0	2	4
y	7	1	−1	1	7

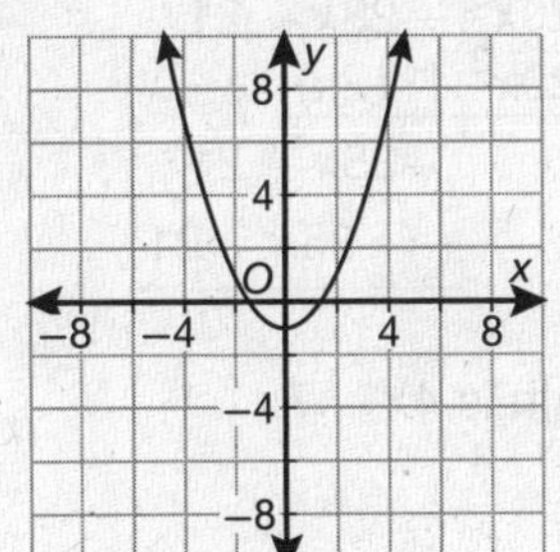

15.

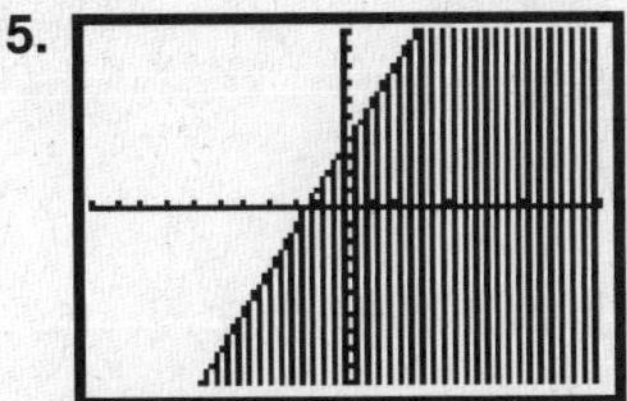

Sample: (4, 0) is a solution not on the boundary line and (4, 11) is a solution that is on the boundary line.

16. In order for $\sqrt[4]{-256}$ to have a real root there must be some value b such that $-256 = b^4$. If b is positive then $b^4 = b \cdot b \cdot b \cdot b$ is positive. If b is negative then $b^4 = -b \cdot -b \cdot -b \cdot -b =$ $b^2 \cdot b^2$ is also positive. Therefore there is no way to achieve a negative value when raising

a number to an even power.

17. $x - d$ would be a common factor, so the numerator would have the value $(x - d)(x + d)$. This means that $|a| = |d|$.

18. $(4 \times 8) \div 4 = 8$ tiles are needed for the picture. There are 8 tiles to be taken 8 at a time. Order matters so this is a permutation. $P(8, 8) = 8! = 40{,}320$

19. a. Isolate the binomial by adding 15 to each side.

b. $\left(\frac{-90}{2}\right)^2 = 2025$

c. $(x - 45)^2$

d.
$$\begin{aligned} x^2 - 90x - 15 &= -2037 \\ x^2 - 90x &= -2022 \\ x^2 - 90x + 2025 &= -2022 + 2025 \\ (x - 45)^2 &= 3 \\ x - 45 &= \pm\sqrt{3} \\ x &= 45 \pm \sqrt{3} \end{aligned}$$

20.
$$\begin{array}{r} 4x - 7 \\ 5x + 3\overline{)20x^2 - 23x - 21} \\ \underline{-(20x^2 + 12x)} \\ -35x - 21 \\ \underline{-(-35x - 21)} \\ 0 \end{array}$$

The length is $4x - 7$.

21. $2\pi r = C$

$r = \frac{C}{2\pi}$

Substitute 44 for C.

$r = \frac{44}{2\pi} = \frac{22}{\pi} \approx 7$

The radius is about 7 inches.

22. $A = lw$, $P = 2(l + w)$

Dimensions	1 by 6	4 by 4	2 by 9	3 by 10	1 by 1	2 by 3	5 by 5
Area (unit²)	6	16	18	30	1	6	25
Perimeter (unit)	14	16	22	26	4	10	20

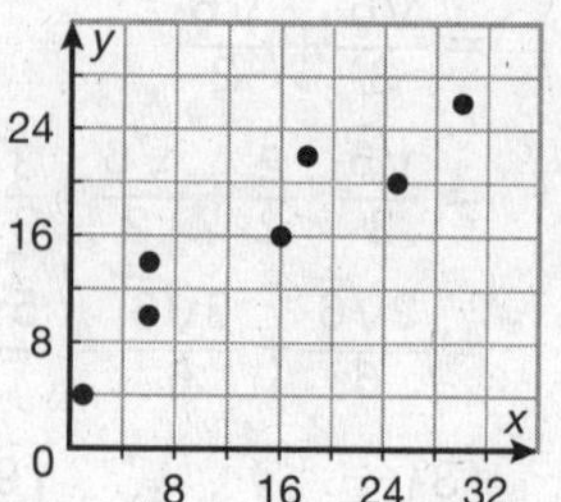

There is a fairly strong positive correlation.

23. Let x represent the number of years since 1900.

Find the value of a in the equation $y = ab^x$

$150 = ab^0$

$150 = a$

Substitute the values at $x = 10$ to find the value of b.

$100 = 150b^{10}$

$b^{10} = \frac{2}{3}$

$b = \sqrt[10]{\frac{2}{3}}$

$b \approx 0.96$

Calculate the value of y at $x = 50$.

$y \approx 150(0.96)^{50}$

$\approx 150(0.13)$

≈ 19.5 thousand

The population of humpback whales in 1950 was approximately 19,500.

24. The tangent of the angle is the ratio of the opposite side to the adjacent side, which is 3 to 4 or 0.75.

25. The probability is $\frac{1}{5} \times \frac{1}{4} \times \frac{1}{3} = \frac{1}{60} \approx 1.7\%$

Answer Choice **C**

26. The line joining the point and its x-coordinate makes an angle of 90° with the x-axis. So, the triangle formed is a right triangle. The line $y = x$ makes an angle of 45° with the x-axis. So, the triangle formed is a 45°-45°-90° right triangle. All 45°-45°-90° triangles are similar.

27. A conditional probability is the probability of an event occurring given that another event has already occurred. For example, suppose a bag has 5 red and 10 yellow chips. The probability of a yellow chip is $\frac{10}{15} = \frac{2}{3}$. But if a yellow chip was already picked, there are only 9 yellow chips and 14 chips in all, so the probability of selecting a yellow chip, given that one was already picked, is $\frac{9}{14}$.

28. $\frac{3}{\sqrt{5}} = \frac{3}{\sqrt{5}} \cdot \frac{2\sqrt{2}}{2\sqrt{2}} = \frac{6\sqrt{2}}{2\sqrt{10}}$

$\frac{3\sqrt{5}}{2\sqrt{2}} = \frac{3\sqrt{5}}{2\sqrt{2}} \cdot \frac{\sqrt{5}}{\sqrt{5}} = \frac{15}{2\sqrt{10}}$

$\frac{6}{\sqrt{10}} = \frac{6}{\sqrt{10}} \cdot \frac{2}{2} = \frac{12}{2\sqrt{10}}$

$\frac{6\sqrt{2}}{2\sqrt{10}} < \frac{12}{2\sqrt{10}} < \frac{15}{2\sqrt{10}}$

So

$\frac{3}{\sqrt{5}} < \frac{6}{\sqrt{10}} < \frac{3\sqrt{5}}{2\sqrt{2}}$

29. The composition $m(n(t)) = (t^{-2})^{-3} = t^6$. Although the domain of this function might be all real numbers, the domain of the composite is limited to the domain of the first function, $n(t)$, which is only positive real numbers.

30. $180° - 15° = 165°$

$15° - 360° = -345°$

LESSON 60

Warm Up 60

1. permutation

2. ${}_8C_3 = \frac{8!}{3!(8-3)!} = \frac{8 \times 7 \times 6 \times \cancel{5!}}{3 \times 2 \times \cancel{5!}} = 56$

3. $P(\text{odd}) = \frac{\text{favorable outcomes}}{\text{total outcomes}} = \frac{3}{6} = \frac{1}{2}$

Lesson Practice 60

a. odd = {1, 3, 5},

Greater than 5 = {6}.

The two sets have no outcomes in common, therefore, the events are mutually exclusive.

b. Even = {2, 4, 6}

Divisible by 3 = {3, 6}. The two sets intersect at 6, therefore the events are inclusive.

c. It is possible to select a green marble with an odd number. The events are inclusive and the formula is $P(A) + P(B) - P(A \text{ and } B)$. Let A be the event that the marble is green and B the event that the marble has an odd number.

$$P(A) = \frac{10}{20} = \frac{1}{2},\ P(B) = \frac{10}{20} = \frac{1}{2}$$

$$P(A \text{ and } B) = \frac{6}{20} = \frac{3}{10}$$

$$P(A \text{ or } B) = P(A) + P(B) - P(A \text{ and } B)$$

$$P(A \text{ or } B) = \frac{1}{2} + \frac{1}{2} - \frac{3}{10} = \frac{7}{10} = 0.7$$

d. It is not possible to select an orange marble with a number that is less than 6. The events are mutually exclusive and the formula is $P(A) + P(B)$. Let A be the event that the marble is orange and B the event that the marble has a number that is less than 6.

$$P(A) = \frac{10}{20} = \frac{1}{2},\ P(B) = \frac{5}{20} = \frac{1}{4}$$

$$P(A \text{ or } B) = P(A) + P(B)$$

$$P(A \text{ or } B) = \frac{1}{2} + \frac{1}{4} = \frac{3}{4} = 0.75$$

e. Since the outcome of flipping the coin does not affect the outcome of rolling the cube, the events are independent.

f. Since the tile is not replaced,it affects the outcome for the second draw. The events are dependent.

g. Since the objects are replaced, the events are independent. Let A_1 be the probability of a marble on the first draw, A_2 be the probability of a block on the second draw, and A_3 be the probability of a marble on the third draw.

$$A_1 = \frac{12}{19},\ A_2 = \frac{7}{19},\ A_3 = \frac{12}{19}$$

$$P(A_1, A_2, \text{ and } A_3) = P(A_1) \cdot P(A_2) \cdot P(A_3)$$

$$= \frac{12}{19} \cdot \frac{7}{19} \cdot \frac{12}{19}$$

$$= \frac{1008}{6859} \approx 0.1470$$

h. The birth of a female does not affect the sex of the other children, so the events are independent. Let A_1 be the probability of a birth of a female, A_2 be the probability of a birth of a female next, A_3 be the probability of a female next, and A_4 be the probability of not having a female (having a male).

$A_1 = 0.488$, $A_2 = 0.488$, $A_3 = 0.488$, $A_4 = 0.512$

$P(A_1, A_2, A_3, \text{ and } A_4)$

$= P(A_1) \cdot P(A_2) \cdot P(A_3) \cdot P(A_4)$

$= 0.488 \cdot 0.488 \cdot 0.488 \cdot 0.512$

$= 0.0595$

Practice 60

1. The slope, m, of the perpendicular line will have the opposite reciprocal slope, $-\frac{1}{3}$. Substitute the slope, $-\frac{1}{3}$ and the point (2, 2) into the point-slope formula.

$y - y_1 = m(x - x_1)$

$y - 2 = -\frac{1}{3}(x - 2)$

$y - 2 = -\frac{1}{3}x + \frac{2}{3}$

$y = -\frac{1}{3}x + \frac{8}{3}$

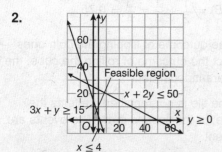

2. $3x + y \geq 15$, $x + 2y \leq 50$, $y \geq 0$, $x \leq 4$; Feasible region

The feasible region is bounded by (0, 15), (0, 25), (4, 3), and (4, 23).

The minimum value occurs at (4, 3).

$P = 111(4) + 95(3) = 729$

The maximum value occurs at (4, 23).

$P = 111(4) + 95(23) = 2629$

3. $d = \sqrt{(x_2 - x_1)^2 + (y_2 - y_1)^2}$

$= \sqrt{(-3 - 4)^2 + (-5 - (-2))^2}$

$= \sqrt{(-7)^2 + (-3)^2}$

$= \sqrt{58}$

4. $$\begin{array}{r|rrrr} 5 & 1 & 0 & 0 & -7 \\ & & 5 & 25 & 125 \\ \hline & 1 & 5 & 25 & 118 \end{array}$$

$= x^2 + 5x + 25 + \frac{118}{x - 5}$

5. $$\begin{array}{r|rrrr} -1 & 1 & 3 & 7 & 5 \\ & & -1 & -2 & -5 \\ \hline & 1 & 2 & 5 & 0 \end{array}$$

$= x^2 + 2x + 5$

6. $$\begin{array}{r} x^2 - x + 1 \\ x + 1\overline{)x^3 + 0x^2 + 0x + 2} \\ \underline{-(x^3 + x^2)} \\ -x^2 + 0x + 2 \\ \underline{-(-x^2 - x)} \\ x + 2 \\ \underline{-(x + 1)} \\ 1 \end{array}$$

$= x^2 - x + 1 + \frac{1}{x + 1}$

7. $$\begin{array}{r} x^3 - x^2 + x - 1 \\ x + 1\overline{)x^4 + 0x^3 + 0x^2 + 0x - 2} \\ \underline{-(x^4 + x^3)} \\ -x^3 + 0x^2 + 0x - 2 \\ \underline{-(-x^3 - x^2)} \\ x^2 + 0x - 2 \\ \underline{-(x^2 + x)} \\ -x - 2 \\ \underline{-(-x - 1)} \\ -1 \end{array}$$

$= x^3 - x^2 + x - 1 - \frac{1}{x + 1}$

8. It is not possible to select a black block with a number greater than 21. The events are mutually exclusive and the formula is $P(A) + P(B)$. Let A be the event of a black block and B the event of a number greater than 21.

$P(A) = \frac{19}{44}$, $P(B) = \frac{23}{44}$

$P(A \text{ or } B) = P(A) + P(B)$

$P(A \text{ or } B) = \frac{19}{44} + \frac{23}{44} = \frac{42}{44} = 0.9545$

Answer Choice **B**

9. $3 \leq 1 + 2$ is true

$3 > -(1) + 4$ is false

(1, 3) is not a solution.

10. If there is no remainder, then $(x + d)$ is a factor of $ax^2 + bx + c$ and $x + d = 0$. Solving for $x + d = 0$ results in $x = -d$ (one of the x-intercepts). So, the parabola intersects the x-axis at $(-d, 0)$.

11. a. $A \cdot T = \begin{bmatrix} 2 & 0 \\ 0 & 2 \\ 0 & 0 \end{bmatrix} \cdot \begin{bmatrix} 3 & 3 \\ -3 & 3 \end{bmatrix}$

$= \begin{bmatrix} 2(3) + 0(-3) & 2(3) + 0(3) \\ 0(3) + 2(-3) & 0(3) + 2(3) \\ 0(3) + 0(-3) & 0(3) + 0(3) \end{bmatrix}$

$= \begin{bmatrix} 6 & 6 \\ -6 & 6 \\ 0 & 0 \end{bmatrix}$

b. The vertices of the triangle are (6, 6), (−6, 6), and (0, 0).

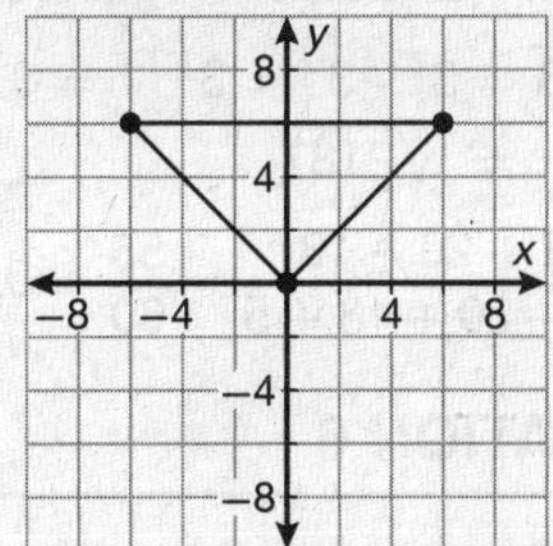

c. Area of original triangle $= \dfrac{2(2)}{2} = 2$

Area of transformed triangle $= \dfrac{6(12)}{2} = 36$

d. The determinant of matrix T is $3(3) - (-3)(3) = 18$. The area is multiplied by 18, the determinant of T.

12. $\cos 30° = \dfrac{x}{16}$

$\dfrac{\sqrt{3}}{2} = \dfrac{x}{16}$

$2x = 16\sqrt{3}$

$x = 8\sqrt{3} \approx 14$ inches

13. a. The result of the number cube does not affect the result of the coin. Therefore, the events are independent.

b. $P(<5) = \dfrac{4}{6} = \dfrac{2}{3} \approx 0.67$

c. $P(\text{heads}) = \dfrac{1}{2} = 0.5$

d. $P(<5, \text{heads}) = P(<5) \cdot (\text{heads})$

$= \dfrac{2}{3} \times \dfrac{1}{2} = \dfrac{1}{3} \approx 0.33$

14. Let x be the weight of the total compound.

Amount of sodium chloride $= 0.7x$

Amount of sodium chloride $= x - 660$

$0.7x = x - 660$

$-0.3x = -660$

$x = 2200$

The total compound weighed 2200 g.

15. $t = \sqrt{\dfrac{2(110)}{9.8}} = \dfrac{\sqrt{220}}{\sqrt{9.8}}$

$= \dfrac{\sqrt{220}}{\sqrt{9.8}} \cdot \dfrac{\sqrt{9.8}}{\sqrt{9.8}}$

$= \dfrac{\sqrt{2156}}{9.8} = \dfrac{2\sqrt{539}}{9.8}$

$= \dfrac{\sqrt{539}}{4.9} \approx 4.7$

It takes about 4.7 s.

16.

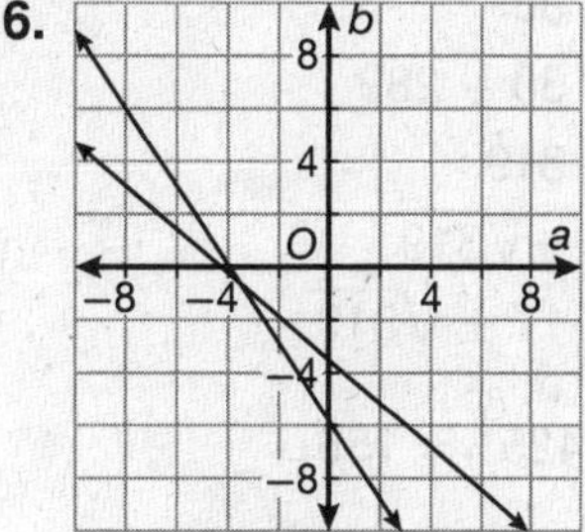

The solution is about (−3, −1).

17. The divisor is always a polynomial of degree 1 in a synthetic division. Here, the polynomial of the divisor is of degree 2, so long division or another method must be used.

18. The events are dependent because the probability of the sum being greater than 5 changes with the knowledge that one of the cubes is showing 2.

19. Surface area $= 2(2x)(2x) + 2(x)(2x) + 2(x)(2x)$ and

volume $= 2x(2x)x$. So

$\dfrac{S}{V} = \dfrac{2(2x)(2x) + 2(x)(2x) + 2(x)(2x)}{2x(2x)x}$

$= \dfrac{8x^2 + 4x^2 + 4x^2}{4x^3}$

$$= \frac{16x^2}{4x^3} = \frac{4}{x}$$

20. Substitue 0 for h and solve for t.

$0 = -42t^2 + 90t$

$0 = -2t(21t - 45)$

$-2t = 0$ or $21t - 45 = 0$

$t = 0$ or $\quad t = 2.1$

The object will return to the surface in approximately 2.1 s.

21. The hypotenuse is the longest side.

22. If equation 1 is multiplied by 3, equation 2 by −4, and equation 3 by 12, the same equation results. Therefore, the lines coincide, so the system has infinitely many solutions and is consistent.

Answer Choice **D**

23. In the third line, 289 was added to the left side of the equation, but not to the right side. The correct solution is

$x^2 - 34x - 15 = 15$

$x^2 - 34x = 30$

$x^2 - 34x + 289 = 30 + 289$

$(x - 17)^2 = 319$

$x - 17 = \pm\sqrt{319}$

$x = 17 \pm \sqrt{319}$

24. S.D. $= \left(425^{\frac{5}{3}}\right)^{\frac{1}{2}} = 425^{\frac{5}{6}} \approx 155$

25.

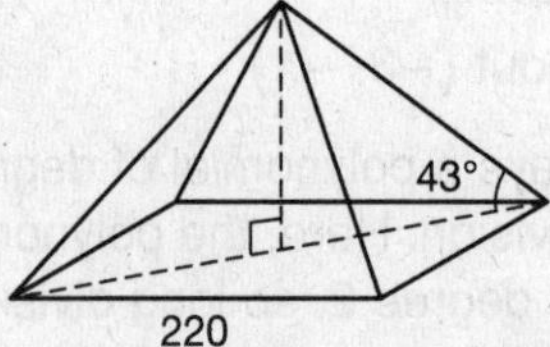

The diagonal of the base is the hypotenuse of a 45-45-90 triangle, so its length is $220\sqrt{2}$.

The base of the right triangle is $220\sqrt{2} \div 2 = 110\sqrt{2}$.

$\cos 43° = \dfrac{110\sqrt{2}}{x}$

$x = \dfrac{110\sqrt{2}}{\cos 43°}$

≈ 212.7

The edge of the pyramid is about 212.7 m long.

26. $y = ab^t$

$\frac{1}{4}a = ab^3$

$\frac{1}{4} = b^3$

$b \approx 0.63$

$y = a(0.63)^4$

$y \approx a(0.157)$

About 15.7%

27. Using a graphing calculator, the values in the table results in $r \approx 0.41$. Exchanging the x- and y-values results in the same r-value.

28. For the first month $f(x) = x + 0.05x = 1.05x$. For the second month $g(x) = x - 0.05x = 0.95x$. The composite function $g(f(x)) = 0.95(1.05x) = 0.9975x$. Therefore, more has been lost than has been gained.

29. $\sqrt{3} \cdot \sqrt[5]{3} = 3^{\frac{1}{2}} \cdot 3^{\frac{1}{5}} = 3^{\frac{1}{2}+\frac{1}{5}} = 3^{\frac{7}{10}} = \sqrt[10]{3^7}$

$= \sqrt[10]{2187}$

30. $P = \dfrac{22 + 20 + 13}{22 + 20 + 13 + 5} = \dfrac{55}{60} \approx 0.917$ or 91.7%

INVESTIGATION 6

1.

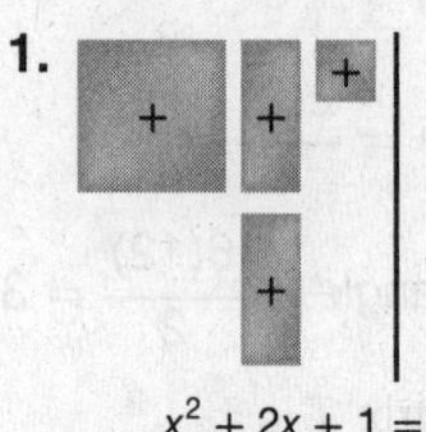

$x^2 + 2x + 1 = 0$

2.

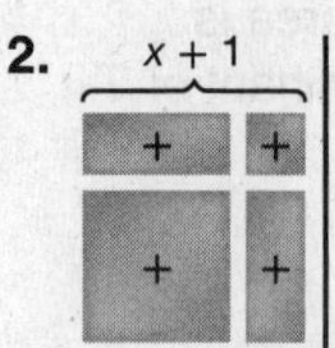

$(x + 1)^2 = 0$

3. a.

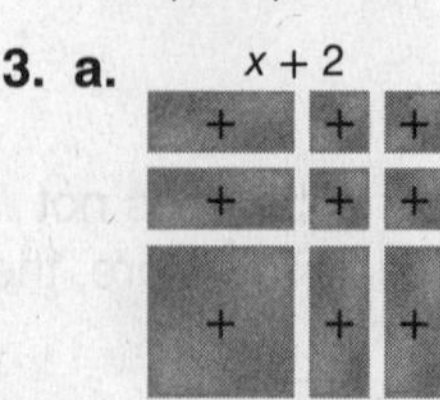

$(x + 2)^2$

b. $x + 3$

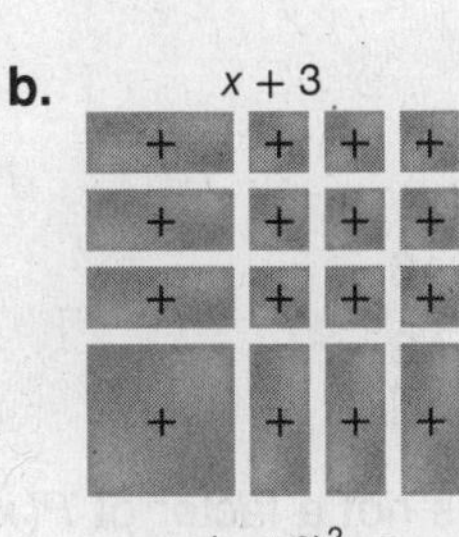

$(x + 3)^2$

c. $x + 4$

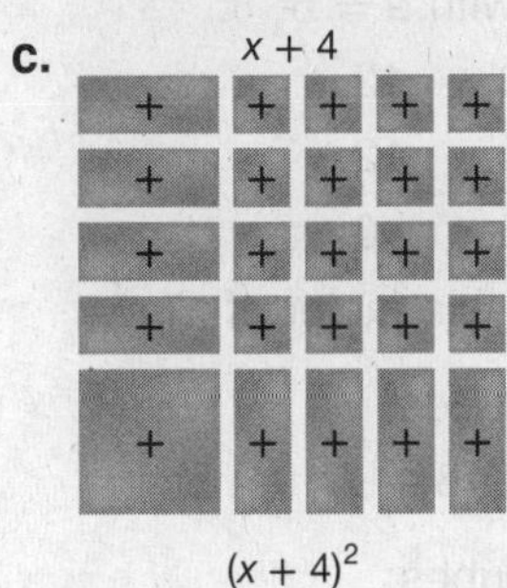

$(x + 4)^2$

4.

Perfect Square	b	c
$(x + 1)^2$	2	1
$(x + 2)^2$	4	4
$(x + 3)^2$	6	9
$(x + 4)^2$	8	16

5. $\left(\frac{b}{2}\right)^2 = c$

6. a. There should be a vertical line, one x^2 tile, three x tiles, and one unit tile on the left and nothing on the right. The tiles should be arranged so there are three x tiles on either side of the squared tile, so its obvious that eight unit tiles are missing.

b. eight unit tiles

c. $x^2 + 6x + 9 = 8$

$(x + 3)^2 = 8$

d. $x = -3 \pm \sqrt{8} = -3 \pm 2\sqrt{2}$

7. $x^2 + \frac{b}{a}x + \frac{c}{a} = 0$

8. Subtract the constant term from each side of each equation.

$$x^2 + \frac{b}{a}x = -\frac{c}{a}$$

9. Find the amount needed to complete the square.

$$\left(\frac{b}{2a}\right)^2$$

10. Add the amount determined in problem 9 to both sides of the equation.

$$x^2 + \frac{b}{a}x + \left(\frac{b}{2a}\right)^2 = -\frac{c}{a} + \left(\frac{b}{2a}\right)^2$$

11. Write the left side as the square of a binomial.

$$\left(x + \frac{b}{2a}\right)^2 = -\frac{c}{a} + \frac{b^2}{4a^2}$$

12. Simplify the right side of the equation.

$$\left(x + \frac{b}{2a}\right)^2 = \frac{b^2 - 4ac}{4a^2}$$

13. Apply the Square Root Property.

$$x + \frac{b}{2a} = \pm\sqrt{\frac{b^2 - 4ac}{4a^2}}$$

14. Simplify the right side of the equation.

$$x + \frac{b}{2a} = \pm\frac{\sqrt{b^2 - 4ac}}{2a}$$

15. Solve for x:

$$x = \frac{-b \pm \sqrt{b^2 - 4ac}}{2a}$$

16. Solve the quadratic equation $2x^2 + 6x - 3 = 0$ by substituting the values for a, b, and c.

$$x = \frac{-6 \pm \sqrt{6^2 - 4(2)(-3)}}{2(2)}$$
$$= \frac{-6 \pm \sqrt{36 + 24}}{4}$$
$$= \frac{-6 \pm \sqrt{60}}{4}$$
$$= \frac{-6 \pm 2\sqrt{15}}{4}$$
$$= \frac{-3 \pm \sqrt{15}}{2}$$

Investigation Practice 6

a. perfect square

b. not a perfect square

c. perfect square

d. $x^2 + 4x + 1 = 0$

$$x^2 + 4x = -1$$
$$x^2 + 4x + 4 = -1 + 4$$
$$(x + 2)^2 = 3$$
$$x + 2 = \pm\sqrt{3}$$
$$x = -2 \pm \sqrt{3}$$

$$x = \frac{-4 \pm \sqrt{4^2 - 4(1)(1)}}{2(1)}$$
$$= \frac{-4 \pm \sqrt{16 - 4}}{2}$$
$$= \frac{-4 \pm \sqrt{12}}{2}$$
$$= \frac{-4 \pm 2\sqrt{3}}{2}$$
$$= -2 \pm \sqrt{3}$$

e. $x^2 + 6x + 2 = 0$

$$x^2 + 6x = -2$$
$$x^2 + 6x + 9 = -2 + 9$$
$$(x + 3)^2 = 7$$
$$x + 3 = \pm\sqrt{7}$$
$$x = -3 \pm \sqrt{7}$$

$$x = \frac{-6 \pm \sqrt{6^2 - 4(1)(2)}}{2(1)}$$
$$= \frac{-6 \pm \sqrt{36 - 8}}{2}$$
$$= \frac{-6 \pm \sqrt{28}}{2} = \frac{-6 \pm 2\sqrt{7}}{2} = -3 \pm \sqrt{7}$$

LESSON 61

Warm Up 61

1. linear binomial
2. terms do not have a GCF except 1; false
3. Synthetic division with $a = 1$:

$$\begin{array}{r|rrr} 1 & 4 & -2 & 5 \\ & & 4 & 2 \\ \hline & 4 & 2 & 7 \end{array}$$

Quotient $= 4x + 2$, R 7

$$\frac{4x^2 - 2x + 5}{x - 1} = 4x + 2 + \frac{7}{x - 1}$$

Lesson Practice 61

a. Synthetic division with $a = -3$:

$$\begin{array}{r|rrrr} -3 & 3 & 19 & 32 & 16 \\ & & -9 & -30 & -6 \\ \hline & 3 & 10 & 2 & 10 \end{array}$$

$P(-3) \neq 0$, so $x + 3$ is not a factor of $P(x)$.

b. Synthetic division with $a = 6$:

$$\begin{array}{r|rrrr} 6 & 4 & -33 & 56 & -12 \\ & & 24 & -54 & 12 \\ \hline & 4 & -9 & 2 & 0 \end{array}$$

$P(6) = 0$, so $x - 6$ is a factor of $P(x)$.

c. Difference of two cubes:

$64 - h^3 = (4 - h)(16 + 4h + h^2)$

d. Difference of two cubes:

$s^6t^{12} - 125r^3$
$= (s^2t^4)^3 - (5r)^3$
$= (s^2t^4 - 5r)\left((s^2t^4)^2 + (s^2t^4)(5r) + (5r)^2\right)$
$= (s^2t^4 - 5r)(s^4t^8 + 5rs^2t^4 + 25r^2)$

e. First factor out GCF, x^4. Then factor sum of two cubes:

$$\frac{8}{27}x^7 + x^4 = x^4\left(\frac{8}{27}x^3 + 1\right)$$
$$= x^4\left(\frac{2}{3}x + 1\right)\left(\frac{4}{9}x^2 - \frac{2}{3}x + 1\right)$$

f. $xy - 9y + 5x - 45 = (xy - 9y) + (5x - 45)$
$= y(x - 9) + 5(x - 9)$
$= (y + 5)(x - 9)$

g. $4m^2n + 12m^2 - n - 3$
$= (4m^2n + 12m^2) + (-n - 3)$
$= 4m^2(n + 3) + (-1)(n + 3)$
$= (4m^2 - 1)(n + 3)$
$= (2m - 1)(2m + 1)(n + 3)$

h. $x^5 + 12x^4 + 36x^3 + 5x^2 + 60x + 180$
$= (x^5 + 12x^4 + 36x^3) + (5x^2 + 60x + 180)$
$= x^3(x^2 + 12x + 36) + 5(x^2 + 12x + 36)$
$= (x^3 + 5)(x^2 + 12x + 36)$
$= (x^3 + 5)(x + 6)^2$

i. Length $x - 15$ is a factor of Polynomial for volume:

$$\begin{array}{r|rrrr} 15 & 1 & 5 & -600 & 4500 \\ & & 15 & 300 & -4500 \\ \hline & 1 & 20 & -300 & 0 \end{array}$$

Volume factors as
$(x - 15)(x^2 + 20x - 300)$
$= (x - 15)(x - 10)(x + 30)$

Practice 61

1.

x	−5	−5	−5
y	−2	0	3

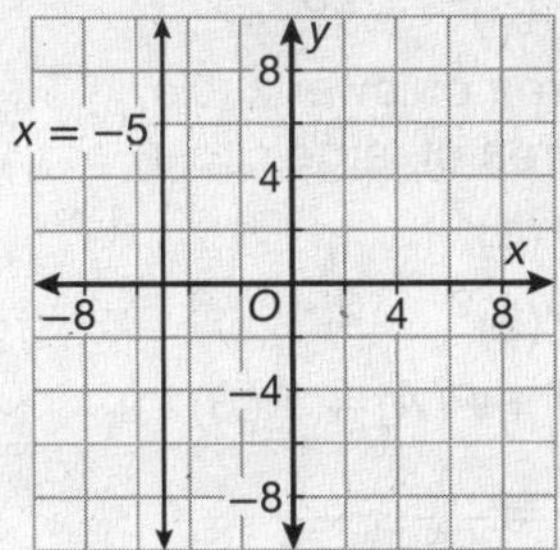

2.

x	−2	0	3
y	−8	−4	2

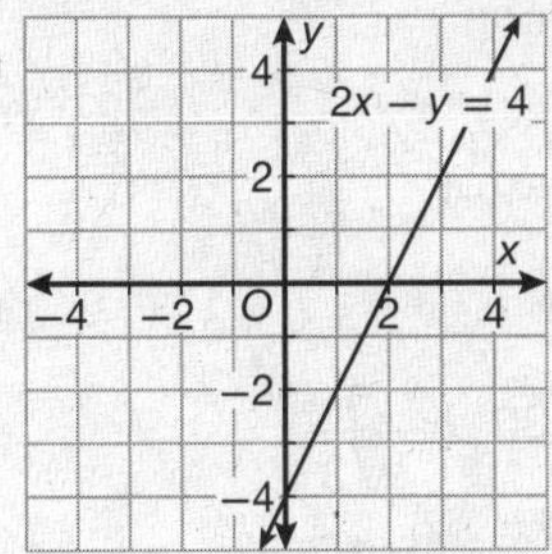

3.

x	−2	0	3
y	5	3	0

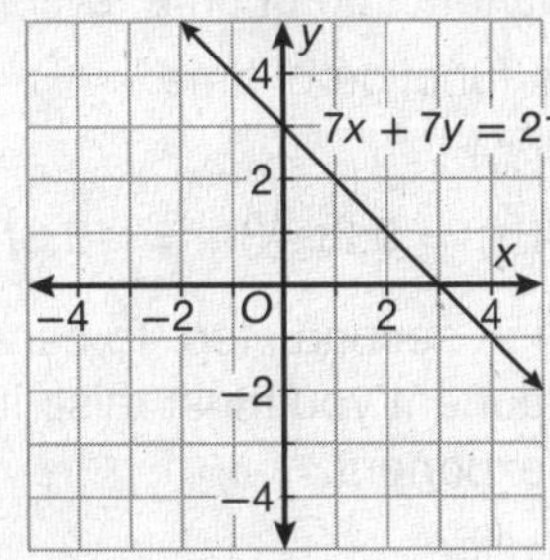

4. x-intercept:

$$5x - 4y + 7z = 21$$
$$5x - 4(0) + 7(0) = 21$$
$$5x = 21$$
$$x = 4.2$$

x-intercept is (4.2, 0, 0).

y-intercept:

$$5x - 4y + 7z = 21$$
$$5(0) - 4y + 7(0) = 21$$
$$-4y = 21$$
$$y = -5.25$$

y-intercept is (0, −5.25, 0).

z-intercept:

$$5x - 4y + 7z = 21$$
$$5(0) - 4(0) + 7z = 21$$
$$7z = 21$$
$$z = 3$$

z-intercept is (0, 0, 3).

5. $-16^{-\frac{1}{2}} = -\frac{1}{16^{\frac{1}{2}}} = -\frac{1}{\sqrt{16}} = -\frac{1}{4}$

6. $27^{-\frac{1}{3}} = \frac{1}{27^{\frac{1}{3}}} = \frac{1}{\sqrt[3]{27}} = \frac{1}{3}$

7. $9^{\frac{3}{2}} = \left(9^{\frac{1}{2}}\right)^3 = (\sqrt{9})^3 = 3^3 = 27$

8. $y = \frac{2}{3}x - 3$

Interchange variables:

$$y = \frac{2}{3}x - 3$$
$$x = \frac{2}{3}y - 3$$
$$x + 3 = \frac{2}{3}y$$
$$\frac{3}{2}(x + 3) = y$$
$$\frac{3}{2}x + \frac{9}{2} = y$$

Inverse is $y = \frac{3}{2}x + \frac{9}{2}$.

9. $y = 5x + 15$

Interchange variables:

$$x = 5y + 15$$
$$x - 15 = 5y$$
$$\frac{x - 15}{5} = y$$

$\frac{1}{5}x - 3 = y$

Inverse is $y = \frac{1}{5}x - 3$.

10. $K(L(u)) = K(-13) = 17$ because $K(u) = 17$ for any value of u. Similarly, $L(K(u)) = L(17) = -13$.

11. 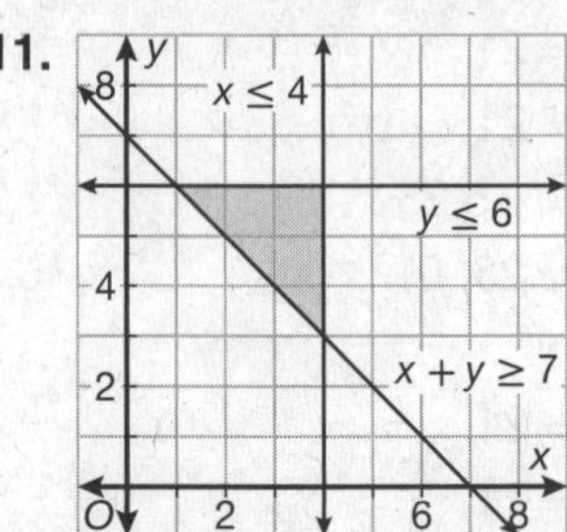

Vertices are (4, 3), (1, 6), (4, 6).

x	y	P = 4x + 3y
4	3	4(4) + 3(3) = 25
1	6	4(1) + 3(6) = 22
4	6	4(4) + 3(6) = 34

P is minimized at (1, 6), with minimum value 22.

12. $A = Pe^{rt}$

$= 980e^{0.07(9)}$

≈ 1840.06

She will have \$1840.06.

13. # of tornados in 1st 6 months

$= 59 + 395 + 258 = 712$

Total # of tornados

$= 59 + 395 + 258 + 151 + 160 + 82$

$= 1105$

P(tornado in 1st 6 months)

$= \frac{\text{\# of favorable outcomes}}{\text{total \# of outcomes}}$

$= \frac{712}{1105}$

≈ 0.644 or about 64.4%

14. In both, first factors have cube root of each term, separated by the same sign between terms in original expression. Also, in both, second factors have square of each term in first factor as well as the products of two terms in first factor, and sign before products is the oposite of the sign separating terms in original expression.

15. 0%; Sample: points fall from left to right when r-value is negative. So the line of best fit also falls from left to right, making slope of line negative.

16. Let A be event that point lies within upper circle and B be event that Point lies within lower circle. Events are mutually exclusive, so $P(A \text{ or } B) = P(A) + P(B)$.

$P(A) = \frac{\text{area of upper circle}}{\text{area of large circle}}$

$= \frac{\pi(3)^2}{\pi(5)^2} = \frac{9}{25}$

$P(A) = \frac{\text{area of lower circle}}{\text{area of large circle}}$

$= \frac{\pi(1)^2}{\pi(5)^2} = \frac{1}{25}$

$P(A \text{ or } B) = P(A) + P(B)$

$= \frac{9}{25} + \frac{1}{25}$

$= \frac{10}{25} = \frac{2}{5}$

17. 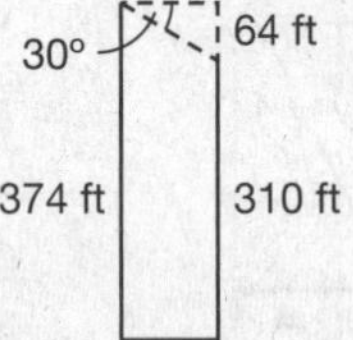

$\frac{64}{x} = \tan 30° = \frac{1}{\sqrt{3}}$

$x = 64\sqrt{3} \approx 111$

Distance is about 111 ft.

18. Shadow as function of distance: $s(d) = 0.2d$

Distance as function of time: $d(t) = -3t$

Shadow as function of time:

$s(t) = s(d(t))$

$= s(-3t) = 0.2(-3t) = -0.6t$

19. no; Error is in second step. To cancel a rational exponent you must raise it to the reciprocal exponent.

Correct solution:

$x^{\frac{3}{8}} = 3 \rightarrow \left(x^{\frac{3}{8}}\right)^{\frac{8}{3}} = 3^{\frac{8}{3}}$

$\rightarrow x^1 = 3^{\frac{8}{3}} \rightarrow x = \sqrt[3]{6561}$

20. $P(\text{black}) = \frac{3}{4}$, $P(\text{white}) = \frac{1}{4}$

$P(\text{black 5 times}) = ({}_8C_5)P^5q^3$

$= ({}_8C_5)\left(\frac{3}{4}\right)^5\left(\frac{1}{4}\right)^3$

$= 56\left(\frac{3^5}{4^8}\right)$

≈ 0.21 or 21%

21. Set coefficients of x equal to each other and solve for c:

$b = 2c \rightarrow c = \frac{b}{2} \rightarrow c^2 = \left(\frac{b}{2}\right)^2$

22. feasible region labeled $x \geq 0$, $y \geq 0$, $y \leq -0.75x + 8$

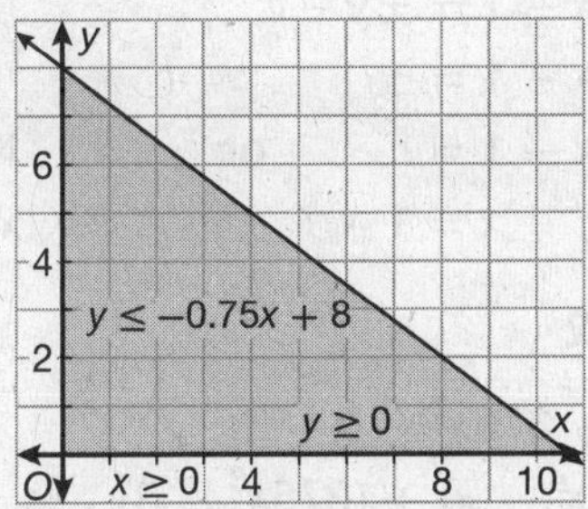

Region is bounded by vertices (0, 0), (0, 8), (10.67, 0).

23. Set of Points is closest to forming a line when r is closest to 1 or −1. Correct choice is **A.**

24. Let A be event that worker carpools and B be event that worker uses public transportation. Events are mutually exclusive, so

$P(A \text{ or } B) = P(A) + P(B)$

$= 0.1067 + 0.0466$

$= 0.1533$ or 15.33%

25. Sample: When $b < 1$, curve asymptotically approaches 0 for large positive x. As you move to the left, the curve rises very quickly. When $b > 1$, the opposite is true; curve asymptotically approaches 0 on the left, and rises quickly on the right. The closer b is to 1, the flatter the graph.

26. a. Product of Powers Property; Sample: By order of operations you must evaluate powers and roots before performing multiplication and division.

b. $\frac{5^{\frac{3}{5}} \cdot 5^{\frac{3}{5}}}{5^{\frac{4}{5}}} = \frac{5^{\frac{3}{5}+\frac{3}{5}}}{5^{\frac{4}{5}}} = \frac{5^{\frac{6}{5}}}{5^{\frac{4}{5}}}$

c. Quotient of Powers Property

d. $\frac{5^{\frac{6}{5}}}{5^{\frac{4}{5}}} = 5^{\frac{6}{5}-\frac{4}{5}} = 5^{\frac{2}{5}}$

e. $5^{\frac{2}{5}} = (5^2)^{\frac{1}{5}} = \sqrt[5]{25}$

27. Determine MN:

$\frac{LM}{MN} = \sin 45° = \frac{1}{\sqrt{2}}$

$LM\sqrt{2} = MN$

$MN = \frac{15}{\sqrt{2}}\sqrt{2} = 15$

Correct choice is **C.**

28. a. $x^2 - 275 - 11x + 25x$

$= x^2 - 11x + 25x - 275$

$= (x^2 - 11x) + (25x - 275)$

$= x(x - 11) + 25(x - 11)$

$= (x + 25)(x - 11)$

b. Area $= (x + 25)(x - 11)$

$= (50 + 25)(50 - 11)$

$= (75)(39) = 2925$

Area is 2925 in.^{2}

29.

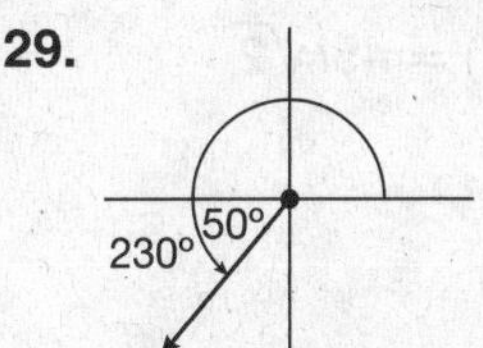

$230° - 180° = 50°$

Reference angle for 230° is 50°.

30. $(3d + 6f) + (d^2 + 2df)$

$= 3(d + 2f) + d(d + 2f)$

$= (3 + d)(d + 2f)$

and $(3d + d^2) + (6f + 2df)$

$= d(3 + d) + 2f(3 + d)$

$= (3 + d)(d + 2f)$

LESSON 62

Warm Up 62

1. real

2. $(5 + 3x) - (6 - 2x) = 5 + 3x - 6 + 2x$
$= 5 - 6 + 3x + 2x$
$= (5 - 6) + (3 + 2)x$
$= -1 + 5x$

3. $5x^2 - 125 = 0$
$5(x^2 - 25) = 0$
$5(x + 5)(x - 5) = 0$
$x + 5 = 0$ or $x - 5 = 0$
$x = -5$ or $x = 5$

4. $\sqrt{150} = \sqrt{25 \cdot 6} = \sqrt{25} \cdot \sqrt{6} = 5\sqrt{6}$

Lesson Practice 62

a. $\frac{1}{2}\sqrt{-100} = \frac{1}{2}\sqrt{100 \cdot (-1)}$
$= \frac{1}{2}\sqrt{100}\sqrt{-1}$
$= \frac{1}{2} \cdot 10 \cdot i = 5i$

b. $3\sqrt{-450} = 3\sqrt{225 \cdot 2 \cdot (-1)}$
$= 3\sqrt{225}\sqrt{2}\sqrt{-1}$
$= 3 \cdot 15 \cdot \sqrt{2}(i) = 45i\sqrt{2}$

c. $0 = 196 + x^2$
$-196 = x^2$
$\pm\sqrt{-196} = x$
$x = \pm 14i$

Check:

$0 = 196 + x^2$	$0 = 196 + x^2$
$0 \stackrel{?}{=} 196 + (14i)^2$	$0 \stackrel{?}{=} 196 + (-14i)^2$
$0 \stackrel{?}{=} 196 + 196(i)^2$	$0 \stackrel{?}{=} 196 + 196(i)^2$
$0 \stackrel{?}{=} 196 + 196(-1)$	$0 \stackrel{?}{=} 196 + 196(-1)$
$0 = 0$ ✓	$0 = 0$ ✓

d. $-6x^2 = 216$
$\frac{-6x^2}{-6} = \frac{216}{-6}$
$x^2 = -36$
$x = \pm\sqrt{-36}$
$x = \pm 6i$

e. $(-2 + i) + (14 + 4i) = (-2 + 14) + (1 + 4)i$
$= 12 + 5i$

f. $(10 - 6i) - (-4 + 3i)$
$= (10 - (-4)) + (-6 - 3)i$
$= 14 - 9i$

g. $(x + 9)^2 = -9$
$x + 9 = \pm\sqrt{-9}$
$x + 9 = \pm 3i$
$x + 9 = 3i$ or $x + 9 = -3i$
$x = -9 + 3i$ $\quad$ $x = -9 - 3i$

h. $x^2 - 2x + 2 = 0$
$x^2 - 2x + 1 = -1$
$(x - 1)^2 = -1$
$x - 1 = \pm\sqrt{-1}$
$x - 1 = \pm i$
$x - 1 = i$ or $x - 1 = -i$
$x = 1 + i$ $\quad$ $x = 1 - i$

Practice 62

1. $125x^4 + 375x^3 - x - 3$
$= (125x^4 - x) + (375x^3 - 3)$
$= x(125x^3 - 1) + 3(125x^3 - 1)$
$= (x + 3)(125x^3 - 1)$
$= (x + 3)((5x)^3 - (1)^3)$
$= (x + 3)(5x - 1)((5x)^2 + (5x) + 1)$
$= (x + 3)(5x - 1)(25x^2 + 5x + 1)$

2. $64x^{12} - 125y^9 = (4x^4)^3 - (5y^3)^3$
$= (4x^4 - 5y^3)((4x^4)^2 + (4x^4)(5y^3) + (5y^3)^2)$
$= (4x^4 - 5y^3)(16x^8 + 20x^4y^3 + 25y^6)$

3. $a + \frac{a}{b} = \frac{ab}{b} + \frac{a}{b} = \frac{ab + a}{b}$

4. $\frac{ax^2}{m^2p} - c + \frac{2}{m} = \frac{ax^2}{m^2p} - \frac{m^2p(c)}{m^2p} + \frac{mp(2)}{mp(m)}$
$= \frac{ax^2 - m^2pc + 2mp}{m^2p}$

5. $-\frac{gh^2}{x^3} + xh + \frac{g^2h^2}{gx^3}$
$= -\frac{gh^2}{x^3} + xh + \frac{g \cdot gh^2}{gx^3}$
$= -\frac{gh^2}{x^3} + xh + \frac{gh^2}{x^3} = xh$

6. $35x^7y^5m - 7x^5m^2y^2 + 14y^7x^4m^2$
$= 7 \cdot 5 \cdot x^4 \cdot x^3 \cdot y^2 \cdot y^3 \cdot m - 7 \cdot x^4 \cdot x \cdot m \cdot m \cdot y^2 + 7 \cdot 2 \cdot y^2 \cdot y^5 \cdot x^4 \cdot m \cdot m$
$= 7x^4y^2m(5x^3y^3 - xm + 2y^5m)$

7. $6x^2ym^5 - 2x^2ym + 4xym$
$= 2 \cdot 3 \cdot x \cdot x \cdot y \cdot m \cdot m^4 - 2 \cdot x \cdot x \cdot y \cdot m + 2 \cdot 2 \cdot x \cdot y \cdot m$
$= 2xym(3xm^4 - x + 2)$

8. $\frac{1}{81^{\frac{-3}{4}}} = 81^{\frac{3}{4}}$
$= \left(81^{\frac{1}{4}}\right)^3$
$= (\sqrt[4]{81})^3 = 3^3 = 27$

9. $(-27)^{\frac{-2}{3}} = \frac{1}{(-27)^{\frac{2}{3}}}$
$= \frac{1}{\left((-27)^{\frac{1}{3}}\right)^2}$
$= \frac{1}{(\sqrt[3]{-27})^2}$
$= \frac{1}{(-3)^2} = \frac{1}{9}$

10. $\frac{1}{-3^{-2}} = -3^2 = -9$

11. $P(\text{walk}) = 0.15$, $P(\text{don't walk}) = 0.85$
$P(\text{2 out of 5 walk}) = ({}_5C_2)p^2q^3$
$= ({}_5C_2)(0.15)^2(0.85)^3$
$= 10(0.15)^2(0.85)^3$
≈ 0.14 or 14%

12. Interchange variables:
$x = \frac{1}{5}y^3 + 6$
$x - 6 = \frac{1}{5}y^3$
$5(x - 6) = y^3$
$\sqrt[3]{5(x - 6)} = y$
Inverse is $y = \sqrt[3]{5(x - 6)}$.

13. Odds in favor of rolling a 3
$= \frac{\text{\# of outcomes for rolling 3}}{\text{\# of outcomes for not rolling 3}} = \frac{1}{5}$
Odds in favor are 1 to 5.

14. $5 + 0i = 5 + 0 = 5$ is real. Correct choice is **C**.

15. $\frac{1}{1 + \frac{1}{x+1}} = \frac{1}{\frac{x+1}{x+1} + \frac{1}{x+1}}$
$= \frac{1}{\left(\frac{x+2}{x+1}\right)} = \frac{x+1}{x+2}$

16. $(4 - 2i) + (6 - 6i) = (4 + 6) + (-2 - 6)i$
$= 10 - 8i$
Sum of currents is $(10 - 8i)$.

17. Probability can be written as $\frac{1}{2}$, where 1 is the number of favorable outcomes and 2 is the total number of outcomes, meaning there are $2 - 1 = 1$ unfavorable outcomes. The odds in favor of an event is the ratio of the number of favorable to unfavorable outcomes, which is 1 to 1.

18. $h = -16t^2 + 80t + 180.4$
$200 = -16t^2 + 80t + 180.4$
$16t^2 - 80t - 180.4 + 200 = 0$
$16t^2 - 80t + 19.6 = 0$
$t^2 - 5t + 1.225 = 0$
Use quadratic formula:
$t = \frac{5 \pm \sqrt{25 - 4(1)(1.225)}}{2}$
$t = \frac{5 \pm \sqrt{20.1}}{2}$
$t = \frac{5 - \sqrt{20.1}}{2}$ or $t = 5 + \frac{\sqrt{20.1}}{2}$
$t \approx 0.3$ $\quad t \approx 4.7$
Times: ≈ 0.3 s and ≈ 4.7 s

19. inclusive; Both 4 and 6 are greater than 3 and multiples of 2.

20. $V(x) = x^3 - 6x^2 + 8x + 5x^2 - 30x + 40$
$= x(x^2 - 6x + 8) + 5(x^2 - 6x + 8)$
$= (x + 5)(x^2 - 6x + 8)$
$= (x + 5)(x - 2)(x - 4)$
$V(x) = (x + 5)(x - 2)(x - 4)$
$V(10) = (10 + 5)(10 - 2)(10 - 4)$
$= (15)(8)(6) = 720$
Volume is 720 ft^3.

21. An angle is coterminal with 225° if it differs by a multiple of 360°.
A 585° − 225° = 360°

B $-135° - 225° = -360° = -1(360°)$

C $935° - 225° = 710°$; not a multiple of 360°

D $-495° - 225° = -720° = -2(360°)$

Only choice is **C**.

22. a. $N(P) = P + 0.015P = 1.015P$

b. $N(N(P)) = N(1.015P)$
$= 1.015(1.015P)$
$= 1.015^2P$

$N(N(N(P))) = N(1.015^2P)$
$= 1.015(1.015^2P)$
$= 1.015^3P$
$\approx 1.046P$

23. $2x^5 - x^4 - 2x + 1$
$= x^4(2x - 1) - (2x - 1)$
$= (x^4 - 1)(2x - 1)$
$= (x^2 + 1)(x^2 - 1)(2x - 1)$
$= (x^2 + 1)(x + 1)(x - 1)(2x - 1)$

The y-values are the same for each x-value; it means the graphs are the same so the factorization is correct.

24. Sample: Positive root of $\sqrt[6]{64}$ is 2 because $2^6 = 2 \cdot 2 \cdot 2 \cdot 2 \cdot 2 \cdot 2 = 4 \cdot 4 \cdot 4 = 64$, but $(-2)^6 = -2 \cdot -2 \cdot -2 \cdot -2 \cdot -2 \cdot -2 = 4 \cdot 4 \cdot 4 = 64$ also.

25. Length $x + 4$ is a factor of the Polynomial for volume:

-4	2	7	-14	-40
		-8	4	40
	2	-1	-10	0

Volume factors as
$(x + 4)(2x^2 - x - 10)$
$= (x + 4)(x + 2)(2x - 5)$

Missing dimension: $2x - 5$

26. Substitute points into $y = b^x + k$:

$y = b^x + k$
$-3 = b^3 + k \quad (1)$
$0 = b^5 + k \quad (2)$

Multiply (1) by -1 and add vertically to eliminate k:

$3 = -b^3 - k$
$\underline{0 = b^5 + k}$
$3 = b^5 - b^3$
$3 = b^2(b^3 - 1)$

Since 3 and b^2 are positive,

$b^3 - 1 > 0$
$b^3 > 1$
$b > 1$

So, equation models exponential growth.

27. Triangles with congruent corresponding angles are similar, not necessarily congruent.

28.
$p = -0.04d^2 + 0.4d$
$0.8 = -0.04d^2 + 0.4d$
$0.04d^2 - 0.4d + 0.8 = 0$
$25(0.04d^2 - 0.4d + 0.8) = 25(0)$
$d^2 - 10d + 20 = 0$

Use quadratic formula:

$d = \frac{10 \pm \sqrt{100 - 4(20)}}{2}$

$d = \frac{10 \pm \sqrt{20}}{2}$

$d = 5 - \sqrt{5}$ or $d = 5 + \sqrt{5}$
$d \approx 3$ $\quad d \approx 7$

Ignore answer > 5: Clerk should work 3 days.

29.
$x^2 = -121$
$(11i)^2 \stackrel{?}{=} -121$
$121(i)^2 \stackrel{?}{=} -121$
$121(-1) \stackrel{?}{=} -121$
$-121 = -121$ ✓

and

$x^2 = -121$
$(-11i)^2 \stackrel{?}{=} -121$
$121(i)^2 \stackrel{?}{=} -121$
$121(-1) \stackrel{?}{=} -121$
$-121 = -121$ ✓

30. Let x be number of minutes and y be number of cell phones.

Cost per month under CP is $0.1(x - 2000) + 20y$.

Cost per month under MP is $0.07(x - 1200) + 25y$.

Constraints: $x \geq 500y$, $y \geq 12$

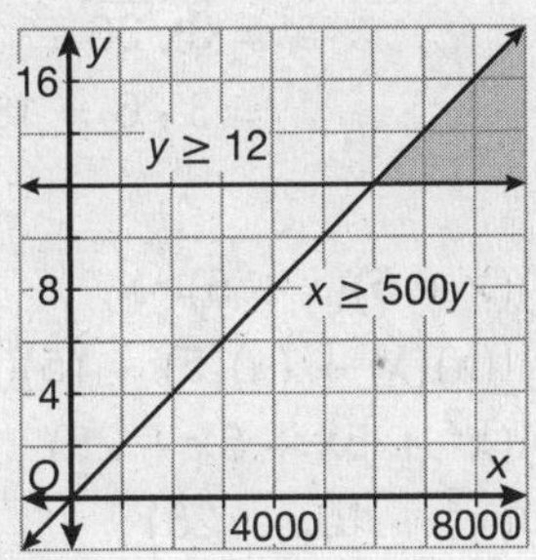

Lower left vertex: (6000, 12)

Cost under CP at $x = 6000$, $y = 12$ is:

$0.1(x - 2000) + 20y$

$= 0.1(6000 - 2000) + 20(12)$

$= 400 + 240 = 640$

Cost under MP at $x = 6000$, $y = 12$ is:

$0.07(x - 1200) + 25y$

$= 0.07(6000 - 1200) + 25(12)$

$= 336 + 300 = 636$

The Continental Plan is \$640 per month, and the Metropolitan Plan is \$636 per month. The Metropolitan Plan has a higher start-up fee, but long term offers the better deal if the company stays with the plan for at least a year.

LESSON 63

Warm Up 63

1. radius
2. $a^2 + b^2 = c^2$

   $1^2 + 1^2 = c^2$

   $2 = c^2$

   $c = \sqrt{2}$
3. 

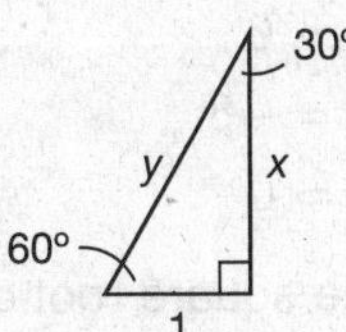

$\tan 30^\circ = \frac{1}{x}$ $\qquad$ $\cos 60^\circ = \frac{1}{y}$

$\frac{1}{\sqrt{3}} = \frac{1}{x}$ $\qquad$ $\frac{1}{2} = \frac{1}{y}$

$x = \sqrt{3}$ $\qquad$ $y = 2$

Lesson Practice 63

a. $\cancel{150^\circ}\left(\frac{\pi \text{ radians}}{\cancel{180^\circ}}\right) = \frac{5\pi}{6}$ radians

b. $\left(-\frac{4\pi}{3}\cancel{\text{radians}}\right)\left(\frac{180^\circ}{\cancel{\pi \text{ radians}}}\right) = -240^\circ$

c. Terminal side of 315° passes through $\left(\frac{\sqrt{2}}{2}, -\frac{\sqrt{2}}{2}\right)$ on unit circle.

$\cos 315^\circ = \frac{\sqrt{2}}{2}$

d. Terminal side of $\frac{3\pi}{4}$ passes through $\left(-\frac{\sqrt{2}}{2}, \frac{\sqrt{2}}{2}\right)$ on unit circle.

$\tan \frac{3\pi}{4} = \frac{\frac{\sqrt{2}}{2}}{-\frac{\sqrt{2}}{2}} = \frac{\sqrt{2}}{2} \cdot \left(-\frac{2}{\sqrt{2}}\right) = -1$

e. Reference angle → (exact) sin, cos, tan of 210°

Measure of reference angle is 210° − 180° = 30°.

$\sin 30^\circ = \frac{1}{2}$, $\cos 30^\circ = \frac{\sqrt{3}}{2}$, $\tan 30^\circ =$

$\frac{\frac{1}{2}}{\frac{\sqrt{3}}{2}} = \frac{1}{2} \cdot \frac{2}{\sqrt{3}} = \frac{1}{\sqrt{3}}$

$= \frac{1}{\sqrt{3}} \cdot \frac{\sqrt{3}}{\sqrt{3}} = \frac{\sqrt{3}}{3}$

In Quad. II, sin θ is negative:

$\sin 210^\circ = -\frac{1}{2}$

In Quad. II, cos θ is negative:

$\cos 210^\circ = -\frac{\sqrt{3}}{2}$

In Quad. II, tan θ is positive:

$\tan 210^\circ = \frac{\sqrt{3}}{3}$

f. $s = r\theta$

$s_1 = 8.5 \cdot \frac{4\pi}{3}$

$= \frac{34\pi}{3} \approx 35.6$ m

g. $\cancel{135^\circ}\left(\frac{\pi \text{ radians}}{\cancel{180^\circ}}\right) = \frac{3\pi}{4}$ radians

$s = r\theta$

$s_2 = 8 \cdot \frac{3\pi}{4}$

$= 6\pi \approx 18.8$ in.

h. In 25 min, minute hand makes $\frac{25}{60} = \frac{5}{12}$ of a complete rotation, so $\theta = \frac{5}{12} \cdot 2\pi = \frac{5\pi}{6}$.

$s = r\theta$

$= 15 \cdot \frac{5\pi}{6}$

$= \frac{25\pi}{2} \approx 39$ cm

Practice 63

1. $\dfrac{\frac{1}{x} + \frac{4}{y}}{3 + \frac{1}{xy}} = \dfrac{xy\left(\frac{1}{x} + \frac{4}{y}\right)}{xy\left(3 + \frac{1}{xy}\right)}$

$= \dfrac{\frac{xy}{x} + \frac{4xy}{y}}{3xy + \frac{xy}{xy}} = \dfrac{y + 4x}{3xy + 1}$

2. $\dfrac{\frac{4}{x} - 3}{\frac{7}{x} + 2} = \dfrac{x\left(\frac{4}{x} - 3\right)}{x\left(\frac{7}{x} + 2\right)} = \dfrac{\frac{4x}{x} - 3x}{\frac{7x}{x} + 2x} = \dfrac{4 - 3x}{7 + 2x}$

3. $\dfrac{x + \frac{1}{x^2}}{x^2 - \frac{2}{x^2}} = \dfrac{x^2\left(x + \frac{1}{x^2}\right)}{x^2\left(x^2 - \frac{2}{x^2}\right)}$

$= \dfrac{x^3 + \frac{x^2}{x^2}}{x^4 - \frac{2 \cdot x^2}{x^2}}$

$= \dfrac{x^3 + 1}{x^4 - 2}$

4. Not binomial: More than two outcomes.

5. Two outcomes (match/no match), probabilities the same for each flip; therefore, binomial

6. $5\sqrt{45} - 2\sqrt{75} + 2\sqrt{108}$

$= 5\sqrt{9 \cdot 5} - 2\sqrt{25 \cdot 3} + 2\sqrt{36 \cdot 3}$

$= 5\sqrt{9}\sqrt{5} - 2\sqrt{25}\sqrt{3} + 2\sqrt{36}\sqrt{3}$

$= 5 \cdot 3\sqrt{5} - 2 \cdot 5\sqrt{3} + 2 \cdot 6\sqrt{3}$

$= 15\sqrt{5} + (-10 + 12)\sqrt{3}$

$= 15\sqrt{5} + 2\sqrt{3}$

7. $3\sqrt{12}(4\sqrt{3} - 3\sqrt{3}) = 3\sqrt{12}(\sqrt{3})$

$= 3\sqrt{36}$

$= 3 \cdot 6 = 18$

8. $(x + 5)^3$

$= (x + 5)(x + 5)(x + 5)$

$= (x + 5)[(x)(x) + (x)(5) + (5)(x) + (5)(5)]$

$= (x + 5)(x^2 + 5x + 5x + 25)$

$= (x + 5)(x^2 + 10x + 25)$

$= x(x^2) + x(10x) + x(25) + 5(x^2) + 5(10x) + 5(25)$

$= x^3 + 10x^2 + 25x + 5x^2 + 50x + 125$

$= x^3 + 15x^2 + 75x + 125$

9. $(x + 4)^3$

$= (x + 4)(x + 4)(x + 4)$

$= (x + 4)[(x)(x) + (x)(4) + (4)(x) + (4)(4)]$

$= (x + 4)(x^2 + 4x + 4x + 16)$

$= (x + 4)(x^2 + 8x + 16)$

$= x(x^2) + x(8x) + x(16) + 4(x^2) + 4(8x) + 4(16)$

$= x^3 + 8x^2 + 16x + 4x^2 + 32x + 64$

$= x^3 + 12x^2 + 48x + 64$

10. $36x^2 - 36 = 0$

$36(x^2 - 1) = 0$

$x^2 - 1 = 0$

$(x - 1)(x + 1) = 0$

$x - 1 = 0$ or $x + 1 = 0$

$x = 1$ $\quad x = -1$

11. $24x = -11x^2 - x^3$

$x^3 + 11x^2 + 24x = 0$

$x(x^2 + 11x + 24) = 0$

$x(x + 3)(x + 8) = 0$

$x + 3 = 0$ or $x + 8 = 0$

$x = -3$ $\quad x = -8$

or $x = 0$

12. Step Four. He has taken the square root of the left side but the cube root of the right.

13. $(15 - \sqrt{-4}) + (10 + \sqrt{-1})$

$= (15 - \sqrt{4}\sqrt{-1}) + (10 + \sqrt{-1})$

$= (15 - 2i) + (10 + i)$

$= (15 + 10) + (-2 + 1)i$

$= 25 - i$

14. $a^2 + b^2 = c^2$

$$x^2 + x^2 = 9^2$$
$$2x^2 = 81$$
$$x^2 = \frac{81}{2}$$
$$x = \sqrt{\frac{81}{2}} = \frac{9}{\sqrt{2}} = \frac{9\sqrt{2}}{\sqrt{2}\sqrt{2}}$$
$$= \frac{9\sqrt{2}}{2} \text{ m or} \approx 6.36 \text{ m}$$

15. In 1 hr, object makes $\frac{1}{9.8}$ of a complete rotation, so $\theta = \frac{1}{9.8} \cdot 2\pi = \frac{\pi}{4.9}$.

$$s = r\theta$$
$$= 44{,}365 \cdot \frac{\pi}{4.9}$$
$$\approx 28{,}444 \text{ mi}$$

16. **A** $y = \frac{1}{e^x} = e^{-x}$ **B** $y = 2e^{-x}$

C $y = \frac{2}{e^{2x}} = 2e^{-2x}$ **D** $y = \frac{2.4}{e^{-2x}} = 2.4e^{2x}$

Exponent of e must be positive for exponential growth. Only choice is **D**.

17.

(x – 180) ft
x ft
34°
480 ft
180 ft

$$\frac{x - 180}{480} = \tan 34°$$
$$x - 180 = 480 \tan 34°$$
$$x = 180 + 480 \tan 34°$$
$$\approx 504$$

Height is about 504 ft.

18.

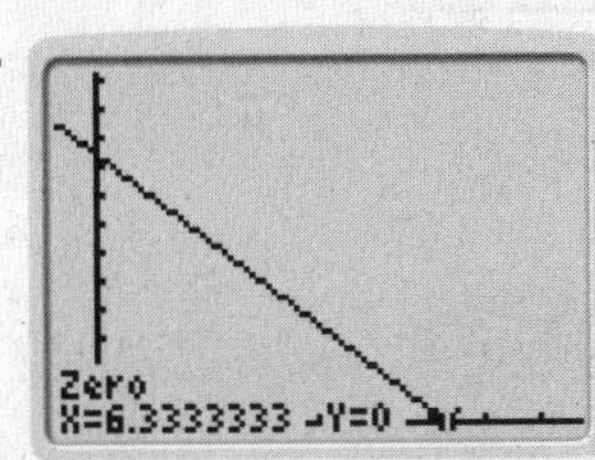

Feasible region is triangle with vertices (0, 0), (0, 9.5), (6.33, 0)

19. $P(H,H,H) = P(H) \cdot P(H) \cdot P(H) = [P(H)]^3$

$P(H,H,H,H) = P(H) \cdot P(H) \cdot P(H) \cdot P(H) = [P(H)]^4$

$P(H,H,H,H,H,H,H)$
$= P(H) \cdot P(H) \cdot P(H) \cdot P(H) \cdot P(H) \cdot P(H) \cdot P(H)$
$= [P(H)]^7$

$P(A_1, A_2, \ldots, A_n) = [P(A)]^n$
where $A = A_1 = A_2 = \ldots = A_n$ are the same event.

20.

$$\frac{\frac{1}{x} + \frac{1}{y}}{1 - \frac{1}{x}} = \frac{xy\left(\frac{1}{x} + \frac{1}{y}\right)}{xy\left(1 - \frac{1}{x}\right)}$$
$$= \frac{\frac{xy}{x} + \frac{xy}{y}}{xy - \frac{xy}{x}} = \frac{y + x}{xy - y} = \frac{x + y}{xy - y}$$

Correct choice is **C**.

21. When adding and subtracting complex numbers, group terms with i in the same way that you group x-terms when adding and subtracting polynomials.

22. Sample:

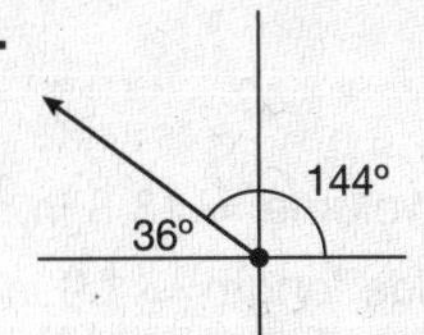

23. a.

$$\theta = \frac{180°(n - 2)}{n}$$
$$= \frac{180°(10 - 2)}{10} = 144°$$

b.

144°
36°

$180° - 144° = 36°$

Reference angle for 144° is 36°.

24. 0.3π is close to $\frac{\pi}{3}$, so

$$\cos(0.3\pi) \approx \cos\left(\frac{\pi}{3}\right) \approx \frac{1}{2}$$

25.

$$h = -42t^2 + 100t$$
$$50 = -42t^2 + 100t$$
$$42t^2 - 100t + 50 = 0$$

$$t = \frac{100 \pm \sqrt{10{,}000 - 4(42)(50)}}{2(42)}$$

$$t = \frac{100 - \sqrt{1600}}{84} \quad \text{Use smaller solution.}$$

$t \approx 0.7$

Object first reaches 50 ft after 0.7 s.

26. Determine condition by setting composite functions equal:

$$f(g(x)) = g(f(x))$$
$$f(cx + d) = g(ax + b)$$
$$a(cx + d) + b = c(ax + b) + d$$
$$acx + ad + b = acx + bc + d$$
$$ad + b = bc + d$$

27. Length $x + 70$ is a factor of polynomial for volume:

−70	1	−20	−4500	126,000
		−70	6300	−126,000
	1	−90	1800	0

Volume factors as

$x^3 - 20x^2 - 4500x + 126{,}000$

$= (x + 70)(x^2 - 90x + 1800)$

$= (x + 70)(x - 30)(x - 60)$

28.

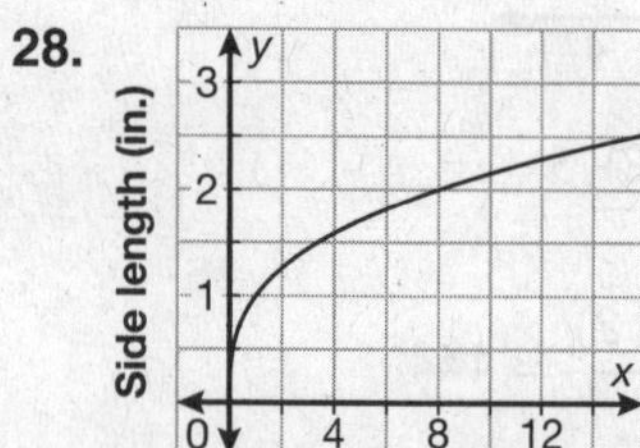

From graph:

$y = 2.4 \rightarrow x \approx 13.8$; volume ≈ 13.8 in.^{3}

$x = 6.9 \rightarrow y \approx 1.9$; side length ≈ 1.9 in.

29. Student used degrees instead of radians.

$$\cancel{60^\circ}\left(\frac{\pi \text{ radians}}{\cancel{180^\circ}}\right) = \frac{\pi}{3} \text{ radians}$$

$$s = r\theta$$

$$s_2 = 10 \cdot \frac{\pi}{3} = \frac{10\pi}{3} \approx 10.5 \text{ m}$$

30. $P(3 \text{ vowels})$

$= P(\text{1st letter is vowel}) \cdot P(\text{2nd letter is vowel}) \cdot P(\text{3rd letter is vowel})$

$$= \frac{5}{26} \cdot \frac{4}{25} \cdot \frac{3}{24}$$

$$= \frac{60}{15{,}600} = \frac{1}{260} \approx 0.0038 \text{ or } 0.38\%$$

LAB 10

Lab Practice 10

1.

```
6log(8)
        5.418539922
```

5.42

2.

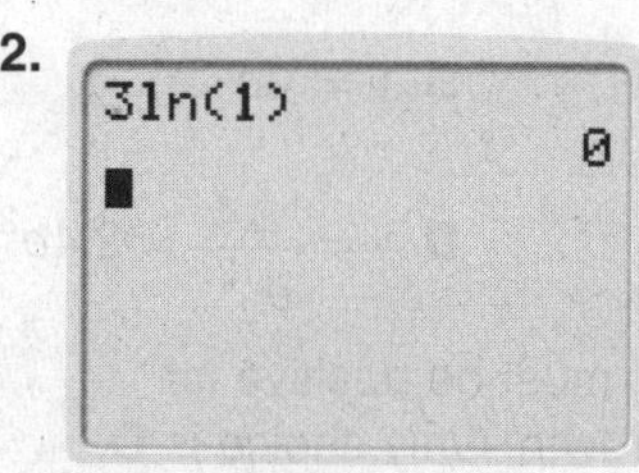

0

3.

1.13

4.

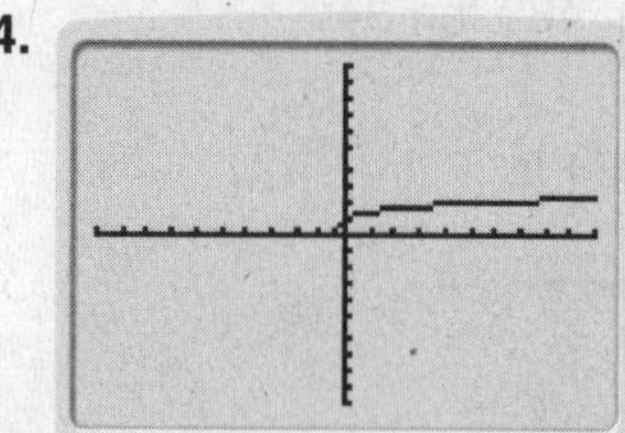

5.

LESSON 64

Warm Up 64

1. exponent
2. $2^3 = 2 \cdot 2 \cdot 2 = 8$
3. $10^x = 100$
   $10^x = (10)^2$
   $x = 2$

Lesson Practice 64

a. $b^x = a \Leftrightarrow \log_b a = x$
   $3^2 = 9 \Leftrightarrow \log_3 9 = 2$
   The logarithmic form is $\log_3 9 = 2$.

b. $4^1 = 4 \Leftrightarrow \log_4 4 = 1$

c. $9^0 = 1 \Leftrightarrow \log_9 1 = 0$

d. $8^{-1} = 0.125 \Leftrightarrow \log_8 0.125 = -1$

e. $\log_{10} 100 = 2 \Leftrightarrow 10^2 = 100$
   The exponential form is $10^2 = 100$.

f. $\log_8 8 = 1 \Leftrightarrow 8^1 = 8$

g. $\log_5 125 = x \Leftrightarrow 5^x = 125$

h. $[H^+] = 0.0000200$ mol/L
   $pH = -\log[H^+]$
   $pH = -\log(0.0000200)$
   $pH \approx 4.7$
   The pH of the rainwater was about 4.7.

Practice 64

1. $f(x) = x^4 - 4x^3 + 2x^2 + 4x - 18$
   Synthetic substitution with $a = 6$:

6	1	−4	2	4	−18
		6	12	84	528
	1	2	14	88	510

   $f(6) = 510$

2. $f(x) = x^4 + 5x^3 - 12x^2 - 4x + 8$
   Synthetic substitution with $a = -7$:

−7	1	5	−12	−4	8
		−7	14	−14	126
	1	−2	2	−18	134

   $f(-7) = 134$

3. Slope of line is
   $$m = \frac{y_2 - y_1}{x_2 - x_1} = \frac{-3 - 5}{-6 - (-2)} = \frac{-8}{-4} = 2$$
   Use the slope-intercept form
   $y - y_1 = m(x - x_1)$
   $y - 5 = 2(x - (-2))$
   $y - 5 = 2x + 4$
   $y - 5 + 5 = 2x + 4 + 5$
   $y = 2x + 9$

4. $a^2 + b^2 = c^2$
   $7^2 + 6^2 \stackrel{?}{=} 8^2$
   $49 + 36 \stackrel{?}{=} 64$
   $85 \neq 64$
   The triangle is not a right triangle.

5. $f(x) = 2x^2 + x - 15$
   $= (x + 3)(2x - 5)$
   The zeros of $f(x)$ are
   $x + 3 = 0$ and $2x - 5 = 0$
   $x = -3$ $\quad 2x = 5$
   $x = \frac{5}{2}$

6. $f(x) = -32x^2 - 28x$
   $= -4x(8x + 7)$
   The zeros of $f(x)$ are
   $x = 0$ and $8x + 7 = 0$
   $8x = -7$
   $x = -\frac{7}{8}$

7. $f(x) = x^2 - 9$
   $= (x - 3)(x + 3)$
   The zeros of $f(x)$ are
   $x - 3 = 0$ and $x + 3 = 0$
   $x = 3$ $\quad x = -3$

8. $5x + 2y < 4$
   $5(0) + 2(-3) \stackrel{?}{<} 4$
   $0 + (-6) \stackrel{?}{<} 4$
   $-6 < 4$
   $(0, -3)$ is a solution.

9. $y - 2x > 6$
   $(-3) - 2(0) \stackrel{?}{>} 6$
   $-3 - 0 \stackrel{?}{>} 6$

$-3 \not> 6$

(0, −3) is not a solution.

10. $16y - 2 \geq x$

$16(-3) - 2 \overset{?}{\geq} 0$

$-48 - 2 \overset{?}{\geq} 0$

$-50 \not\geq 0$

(0, −3) is not a solution.

11. Draw a diagram to represent the situation.

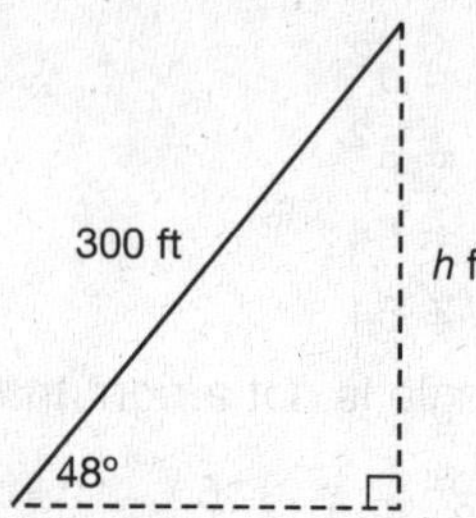

$\sin 48° = \frac{h}{300}$

12. Let point $S\left(\frac{\sqrt{3}}{2}, 0\right)$ be vertically below P on x-axis. Then

$\tan 30° = \frac{RQ}{OR} = \frac{PS}{OS}$

$RQ = OR \tan 30°$

$= 3 \cdot \frac{\sqrt{3}}{3} = \sqrt{3}$

$A = \frac{1}{2}bh$

$= \frac{1}{2}\, OR \cdot RQ$

$= \frac{1}{2} \cdot 3 \cdot \sqrt{3}$

$= \frac{3\sqrt{3}}{2} \approx 2.6$ square units

13. Interchange the variables

$y = 5x - 8$

$x = 5y - 8$

$x + 8 = 5y$

$\frac{x+8}{5} = y$

$y = \frac{x+8}{5}$

$= \frac{x}{5} + \frac{8}{5}$

The inverse is a linear function. Therefore, the domain and range are both all real numbers.

14. Sample: $\log_0 9$ does not exist because there is no power of 0 that equals 9; $\log_1 9$ does not exist because there is no power of 1 that equals 9.

15. Function $f(p) = 1.006p$ gives the population one year after the population is p. The population in 2015 will be the composition of f with itself 15 times, evaluated at 281 million. That is, the population will be $1.006^{15}(281) \approx$ 307 million.

16. **a.** Power of a Quotient Property. By order of operations you must evaluate exponents before multiplying.

b. $\left(\frac{9}{7}\right)^{\frac{1}{4}}\left(\frac{9}{7}\right)^{\frac{1}{4}} = \frac{9^{\frac{1}{4}}}{7^{\frac{1}{4}}} \cdot \frac{9^{\frac{1}{4}}}{7^{\frac{1}{4}}}$

c. Product of Powers Property

d. $\frac{9^{\frac{1}{4}}}{7^{\frac{1}{4}}} \cdot \frac{9^{\frac{1}{4}}}{7^{\frac{1}{4}}} = \frac{9^{\frac{1}{4}+\frac{1}{4}}}{7^{\frac{1}{4}+\frac{1}{4}}} = \frac{9^{\frac{1}{2}}}{7^{\frac{1}{2}}}$

e. $\frac{9^{\frac{1}{2}}}{7^{\frac{1}{2}}} = \frac{\sqrt{9}}{\sqrt{7}} = \frac{3}{\sqrt{7}} = \frac{3\sqrt{7}}{\sqrt{7}\sqrt{7}} = \frac{3\sqrt{7}}{7}$

17. $x^3 - 15x^2 + 56x + 6x^2 - 90x + 336$

$= x(x^2 - 15x + 56) + 6(x^2 - 15x + 56)$

$= (x + 6)(x^2 - 15x + 56)$

$= (x + 6)(x - 7)(x - 8)$

The dimensions are $(x + 6)$, $(x - 7)$, and $(x - 8)$. So the dimensions are 21 ft, 8 ft, and 7 ft.

18. $N(0) = 1$, $N(1) = 3$, $N(2) = 9 = 3^2$, $N(3) = 27 = 3^3, \ldots$

Pattern is $N(x) = 3^x$.

19. $m = \frac{y_2 - y_1}{x_2 - x_1}$

$= \frac{\frac{5}{x} - \frac{1}{3}}{\frac{1}{5} - \frac{3}{x}}$

$= \frac{15x\left(\frac{5}{x} - \frac{1}{3}\right)}{15x\left(\frac{1}{5} - \frac{3}{x}\right)}$

$= \frac{\frac{75x}{x} - \frac{15x}{3}}{\frac{15x}{5} - \frac{45x}{x}}$

$$= \frac{75 - 5x}{3x - 45}$$

$$= \frac{5(15 - x)}{3(x - 15)} = -\frac{5}{3}$$

20. Convert degrees to radians

$$135°\left(\frac{\pi \text{ radians}}{180°}\right) = \frac{3\pi}{4} \text{ radians}$$

$$s = r\theta$$

$$s_1 = 9 \cdot \frac{3\pi}{4} = \frac{27\pi}{4}$$

$$s_2 = 23 \cdot \frac{3\pi}{4} = \frac{69\pi}{4}$$

$$s_2 - s_1 = \frac{69\pi}{4} - \frac{27\pi}{4} = \frac{42\pi}{4} \approx 33 \text{ in.}$$

21. $\dfrac{3}{5 - \sqrt{2}} = \dfrac{3(5 + \sqrt{2})}{(5 - \sqrt{2})(5 + \sqrt{2})}$

$$= \frac{3(5 + \sqrt{2})}{25 - 2}$$

$$= \frac{15 + 3\sqrt{2}}{23}$$

Answer choice **B**

22. $x^2 + 12x + 42 = 0$

$x^2 + 12x = -42$ Isolate the binomial

$x^2 + 12x + 6^2 = -42 + 6^2$ Add square of half the x coefficient 0

$$x^2 + 12x + 36 = -6$$

$$x^2 + 2(6)x + 36 = -6$$

$$(x + 6)^2 = -6$$

$$x + 6 = \pm\sqrt{-6}$$

$$x + 6 = \pm i\sqrt{6}$$

$$x = -6 \pm i\sqrt{6}$$

23. $[H^+] = 0.0000316$ mol/L:

$pH = -\log[H^+]$

$pH = -\log(0.0000316)$

≈ 4.5

The pH of the rainwater was about 4.5

Check:

$-\log(0.0000316) \approx 4.5$

$\log(0.0000316) \approx -4.5$

$10^{-4.5} \approx 0.0000316$

24. The events are dependent because the probability of the sum being a multiple of 2 changes with the knowledge that one of the cubes is showing less than 5.

25. Sample: getting a 7 when rolling a number cube. The probability is 0. There are no favorable outcomes, because 7 is not in sample space.

26.

The value is 2.

27. The x-coordinate is −6, not 6. So, in the final step

$$\cos\theta = \frac{-6}{10} = -0.6.$$

28. $\log_b a = x \Leftrightarrow b^x = a$

$\log_2 16 = x \Leftrightarrow 2^x = 16$

Answer choice **A**

29. Both are equally close to forming a straight line, but −0.45 represents a negative (inverse) correlation, and 0.45 represents a positive (direct) correlation.

30. The intial height $h_0 = 100$ ft, the intial velocity $v_0 = 92$ ft per second, and the final height $h(t) = 0$

$$h = -16t^2 + v_0 + h_0$$

Solve by completing the square

$$0 = -16t^2 + 92t + 100$$

$$16t^2 - 92t = 100$$

$$\frac{16t^2}{16} - \frac{92t}{16} = \frac{100}{16}$$

$$t^2 - 5.75t = 6.25$$

$$t^2 - 5.75t + 8.265625 = 6.25 + 8.265625$$

$$(t - 2.875)^2 = 14.515625$$

$$t - 2.875 = \pm\sqrt{14.515625}$$

$t = 2.875 \pm \sqrt{14.515625}$

$t = 2.875 - \sqrt{14.515625}$ or

$t = 2.875 + \sqrt{14.515625}$
$t \approx -0.9$ or $t \approx 6.7$

Ignoring negative value, coin hits ground at $t \approx 6.7$ s.

LESSON 65

Warm Up 65

1. imaginary

2. $$x^2 - 26x = 13$$
$$x^2 - 26x + 169 = 13 + 169$$
$$x^2 - 26x + 169 = 182$$
$$(x - 13)^2 = 182$$
$$x - 13 = \pm\sqrt{182}$$
$$x = 13 \pm \sqrt{182}$$

3. $3\sqrt{-25} = 3\sqrt{25}\,\sqrt{-1} = 3 \cdot 5 \cdot i = 15i$

4. $b^2 - 4ac = (7)^2 - 4(2)(5) = 49 - 40 = 9$

Lesson Practice 65

a. $3x^2 - 7x + 2 = 0$
$$x = \frac{-b \pm \sqrt{b^2 - 4ac}}{2a}$$
$$= \frac{-(-7) \pm \sqrt{(-7)^2 - 4(3)(2)}}{2(3)}$$
$$= \frac{7 \pm \sqrt{25}}{6}$$
$$= \frac{7}{6} + \frac{5}{6} \text{ and } \frac{7}{6} - \frac{5}{6}$$
$$= 2 \text{ and } \frac{1}{3}$$
The solutions are $\frac{1}{3}$ and 2.

b. $9x^2 + 12x + 4 = 0$
$$x = \frac{-b \pm \sqrt{b^2 - 4ac}}{2a}$$
$$= \frac{-12 \pm \sqrt{(12)^2 - 4(9)(4)}}{2(9)}$$
$$= \frac{-12 \pm \sqrt{0}}{18} = -\frac{2}{3}$$
The solution is $-\frac{2}{3}$.

c. $$x^2 + 5x = -9$$
$$x^2 + 5x + 9 = -9 + 9$$
$$x^2 + 5x + 9 = 0$$
$$x = \frac{-b \pm \sqrt{b^2 - 4ac}}{2a}$$
$$= \frac{-5 \pm \sqrt{5^2 - 4(1)(9)}}{2(1)}$$
$$= \frac{-5 \pm \sqrt{-11}}{2}$$
$$= -\frac{5}{2} \pm \frac{\sqrt{11}}{2}i$$
Solutions are $-\frac{5}{2} + \frac{\sqrt{11}}{2}i$ and $-\frac{5}{2} - \frac{\sqrt{11}}{2}i$.

d. $$-x^2 + \frac{1}{3}x - \frac{1}{9} = 0$$
$$-9\left(-x^2 + \frac{1}{3}x - \frac{1}{9}\right) = 0$$
$$9x^2 - 3x + 1 = 0$$
$$x = \frac{-b \pm \sqrt{b^2 - 4ac}}{2a}$$
$$= \frac{-(-3) \pm \sqrt{(-3)^2 - 4(9)(1)}}{2(9)}$$
$$= \frac{3 \pm \sqrt{-27}}{18}$$
$$= \frac{3 \pm \sqrt{9}\sqrt{3}\sqrt{-1}}{18}$$
$$= \frac{3 \pm 3i\sqrt{3}}{18}$$
$$= \frac{1}{6} \pm \frac{\sqrt{3}}{6}i$$
Solutions are $\frac{1}{6} + \frac{\sqrt{3}}{6}i$ and $\frac{1}{6} - \frac{\sqrt{3}}{6}i$.

e. $8x^2 + 7x - 100 = 0$

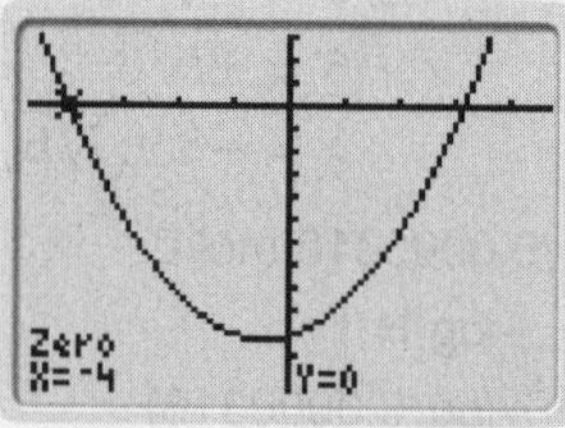

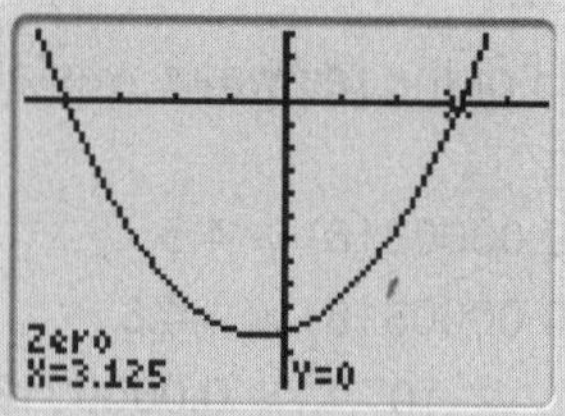

Solutions are −4 and 3.125.

f. The distances traveled by the two hikers are the legs of a right triangle. Let time = h hours. The first hiker will travel $4h$ and the second will travel $(2h - 1)$

$$(4h)^2 + [2(h-1)]^2 = 15^2$$
$$16h^2 + 4(h^2 - 2h + 1) = 225$$
$$16h^2 + 4h^2 - 8h + 4 - 225 = 0$$
$$20h^2 - 8h - 221 = 0$$
$$h = \frac{-b \pm \sqrt{b^2 - 4ac}}{2a}$$
$$h = \frac{-(-8) \pm \sqrt{(-8)^2 - 4(20)(-221)}}{2(20)}$$
$$h = \frac{8 \pm \sqrt{64 + 17680}}{40}$$
$$h = \frac{8 \pm \sqrt{17744}}{40}$$
$$h \approx \frac{8 - 133.2}{40} \approx -3.13$$

This is inadmissible because time cannot be negative.

$$h \approx \frac{8 + 133.2}{40} \approx 3.53 \text{ hours}$$

Practice 65

1. Use the decay function $f(t) = b^t$.

$$f(23) = \frac{1}{2}f(0)$$
$$b^{23} = \frac{1}{2}b^0 = 0.5$$
$$b = \sqrt[23]{0.5} \approx 0.97031$$

After 7 h, portion remaining is

$f(7) \approx 0.97031^7\, f(0) \approx 0.8098 \cdot 360 \approx 291.5$ kg

2. First, divide by $x - 3$. Use synthetic division with $a = 3$.

3	3	12	−15	15
		9	63	144
	3	21	48	159

$$(3x^3 + 12x^2 - 15x + 15) \div (x - 3)$$
$$= 3x^2 + 21x + 48 + \frac{159}{x-3}$$
$$(3x^3 + 12x^2 - 15x + 15) \div (3x - 9)$$
$$= \left(3x^2 + 21x + 48 + \frac{159}{x-3}\right) \div 3$$
$$= \frac{3x^2}{3} + \frac{21x}{3} + \frac{48}{3} + \frac{159}{3(x-3)}$$
$$= x^2 + 7x + 16 + \frac{53}{x-3}$$

3. First, divide by $x + 2$. Use synthetic division with $a = -2$.

−2	2	14	−4	−48
		−4	−20	48
	2	10	−24	0

$$(2x^3 + 14x^2 - 4x - 48) \div (x + 2)$$
$$= 2x^2 + 10x - 24$$
$$(2x^3 + 14x^2 - 4x - 48) \div (2x + 4)$$
$$= x^2 + 5x - 12$$

4. Solve by completing the square

$$x^2 = 7 + 3x$$
$$x^2 - 3x = 7$$
$$x^2 - 3x + \frac{9}{4} = 7 + \frac{9}{4}$$
$$\left(x - \frac{3}{2}\right)^2 = \frac{37}{4}$$
$$x - \frac{3}{2} = \pm\sqrt{\frac{37}{4}}$$
$$x - \frac{3}{2} = \pm\frac{\sqrt{37}}{2}$$
$$x = \frac{3}{2} \pm \frac{\sqrt{37}}{2}$$

5. Solve by completing the square

$$x^2 = -x + 1$$
$$x^2 + x = 1$$
$$x^2 + x + \frac{1}{4} = 1 + \frac{1}{4}$$
$$\left(x + \frac{1}{2}\right)^2 = \frac{5}{4}$$
$$x + \frac{1}{2} = \pm\sqrt{\frac{5}{4}}$$
$$x + \frac{1}{2} = \pm\frac{\sqrt{5}}{2}$$
$$x = -\frac{1}{2} \pm \frac{\sqrt{5}}{2}$$

6. $2\sqrt{3}(5\sqrt{3} - 2\sqrt{6})$

$$= 2\sqrt{3}(5\sqrt{3}) + 2\sqrt{3}(-2\sqrt{6})$$

$= 10\sqrt{9} - 4\sqrt{18}$
$= 10 \cdot 3 - 4 \cdot 3\sqrt{2}$
$= 30 - 12\sqrt{2}$

7. $4\sqrt{63} - 3\sqrt{28} = 4\sqrt{9}\sqrt{7} - 3\sqrt{4}\sqrt{7}$
$= 4 \cdot 3\sqrt{7} - 3 \cdot 2\sqrt{7}$
$= (12 - 6)\sqrt{7}$
$= 6\sqrt{7}$

8. $3\sqrt{2} \cdot 2\sqrt{6} \cdot 3\sqrt{6} = 3 \cdot 2 \cdot 3\sqrt{2}\sqrt{6}\sqrt{6}$
$= 18\sqrt{2} \cdot 6 = 108\sqrt{2}$

9. $P(1 \text{ or } 5) = \dfrac{\#\text{ total outcomes for 1 or 5}}{\text{total \# outcomes}}$
$= \dfrac{2}{6} = \dfrac{1}{3}$

10. The student substituted 37 instead of −37 for b in the first term of the numerator.

$$x = \frac{-b \pm \sqrt{b^2 - 4ac}}{2a}$$
$$= \frac{-(-37) \pm \sqrt{(-37)^2 - 4(4)(9)}}{2(4)}$$
$$= \frac{37 \pm \sqrt{1369 - 144}}{8}$$
$$= \frac{37 \pm \sqrt{1225}}{8}$$
$$= \frac{37 \pm 35}{8}$$

Solutions are $\frac{2}{8} = \frac{1}{4}$ and $\frac{72}{8} = 9$.

11.
1
1 1
1 2 1
1 3 3 1
1 4 6 4 1
1 5 10 10 5 1
1 6 15 20 15 6 1

The 6th row is 1, 6, 15, 20, 15, 6, 1

12. $P(5 \text{ Civil War Qs}) = \left(\frac{7}{20}\right)\left(\frac{6}{19}\right)\left(\frac{5}{18}\right)\left(\frac{4}{17}\right)\left(\frac{3}{16}\right)$
$= \dfrac{2520}{1{,}860{,}480}$
$= \dfrac{7}{5168}$
≈ 0.00135 or 0.135%

13. Possible answer: let $\sin\theta = y$, where (x, y) is on the unit circle and the terminal side of θ passes through (x, y). The terminal side of $\frac{3\pi}{2}$ passes through $(0, -1)$.
Therefore, $\sin\frac{3\pi}{2} = -1$.

14. The slope of line will be the opposite reciprocal of $\frac{1}{3}$:

$$m = -\left(\frac{1}{3}\right)^{-1} = -3$$

Any line $y = mx + b$ with $m = -3$ is perpendicular. Possible answer: $y = -3x + 9$

15. Let x = the opposite side, y = the adjacent side, and h = the hypotenuse in a right triangle with acute angle θ.
Then $\frac{x}{h} = \sin\theta$ and $\frac{y}{h} = \cos\theta$, so if $\sin\theta = \cos\theta$ then $\frac{x}{h} = \frac{y}{h}$ so $x = y$
Therefore the opposite and adjacent sides are congruent. Triangles with equal sine and cosine values must be isosceles right triangles.

16. $\dfrac{x}{3} = \tan 30° = \dfrac{\sqrt{3}}{3}$

$$x = 3 \cdot \frac{\sqrt{3}}{3} = \sqrt{3}$$
$$\frac{3}{y} = \cos 30° = \frac{\sqrt{3}}{2}$$
$$3 \cdot \frac{2}{\sqrt{3}} = y \cdot \frac{\sqrt{3}}{2} \cdot \frac{2}{\sqrt{3}}$$
$$\frac{6}{\sqrt{3}} = y$$
$$y = \frac{6\sqrt{3}}{\sqrt{3}\sqrt{3}}$$
$$= \frac{6\sqrt{3}}{3} = 2\sqrt{3}$$

17. $\dfrac{5}{x} = \tan 30° = \dfrac{\sqrt{3}}{3}$

$$5 \cdot \frac{3}{\sqrt{3}} = x \cdot \frac{\sqrt{3}}{3} \cdot \frac{3}{\sqrt{3}}$$
$$\frac{15}{\sqrt{3}} = x$$
$$x = \frac{15\sqrt{3}}{\sqrt{3}\sqrt{3}}$$
$$= \frac{15\sqrt{3}}{3} = 5\sqrt{3}$$

$$\frac{5}{y} = \sin 30° = \frac{1}{2}$$

$$5 \cdot 2 = y \cdot \frac{1}{2} \cdot 2$$

$$y = 10$$

18. a. $x = \log_b a \Leftrightarrow b^x = a$

$$y = \log_2 \frac{1}{4} \Leftrightarrow 2^y = \frac{1}{4}$$

$$y = -2 \rightarrow 2^y = 2^{-2} = \frac{1}{4} \rightarrow -2 = \log_2 \frac{1}{4}$$

b.

x	$\frac{1}{4}$	$\frac{1}{2}$	1	2	4	8
y such that $2^y = x$	−2	−1	0	1	2	3
$y = \log_2 x$	−2	−1	0	1	2	3

c.

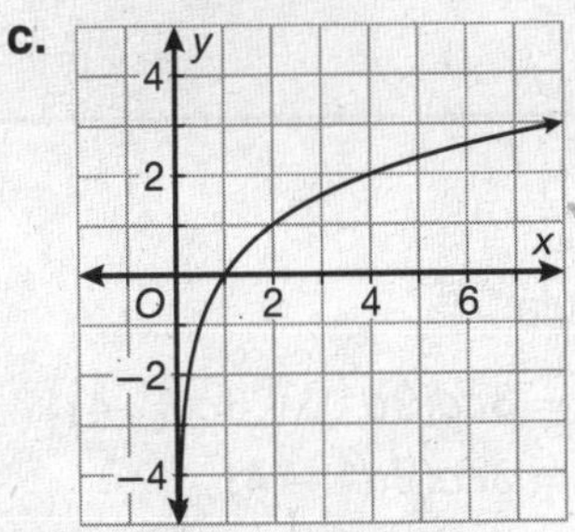

d. $\log_2 6 \approx 2.6$;
Check: $2^{2.6} \approx 6.06$

19. Solve by completing the square:

$$x^2 + 2x + 7 = 8$$
$$x^2 + 2x + 7 - 7 = 8 - 7$$
$$x^2 + 2x = 1$$
$$x^2 + 2x + 1 = 2$$
$$(x + 1)^2 = 2$$
$$x + 1 = \pm\sqrt{2}$$
$$x = -1 \pm \sqrt{2}$$

Answer choice **A**

20. Let x be number of red ribbons, so total length of red ribbons is $3x$. Let y be number of blue ribbons, so total length of blue ribbons is $4y$. Inequality is:

$3x + 4y \geq 60$

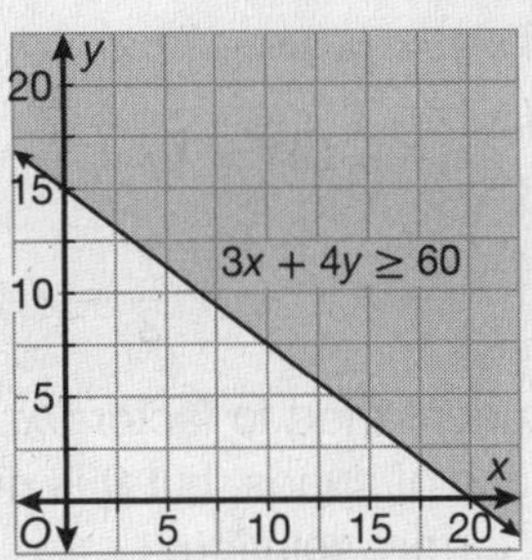

21. a. No. The car could be washed by a hose; it doesn't have to be raining for the car to get wet.

b. True. If the car is outside and dry, it can't be raining.

22. $A = \frac{1}{2}bh$

$$= \frac{1}{2} \cdot 5\sqrt{2} \cdot \frac{1}{\sqrt{3}}$$

$$= \frac{5\sqrt{2}}{2\sqrt{3}}$$

$$= \frac{5\sqrt{2}\sqrt{3}}{2\sqrt{3}\sqrt{3}} = \frac{5\sqrt{6}}{6}$$

The area is $\frac{5\sqrt{6}}{6}$ ft^2.

23. Solve by completing the square:

$$-16t^2 + 160t = 560$$
$$-16t^2 + 160t - 560 = 0$$
$$\frac{-16t^2}{-16} + \frac{160t}{-16} - \frac{560}{-16} = 0$$
$$t^2 - 10t + 35 = 0$$
$$t = \frac{-b \pm \sqrt{b^2 - 4ac}}{2a}$$
$$= \frac{-(-10) \pm \sqrt{(-10)^2 - 4(1)(35)}}{2}$$
$$= \frac{10 \pm \sqrt{100 - 140}}{2}$$
$$= 5 \pm \frac{\sqrt{-40}}{2} = 5 \pm \frac{2i\sqrt{10}}{2} = 5 \pm i\sqrt{10}$$

The time solutions are not real numbers, so the fireworks will never reach the desired height.

24. a. $f(g(x)) = f\left(\frac{1}{3}x + \frac{7}{3}\right)$

$$= 3\left(\frac{1}{3}x + \frac{7}{3}\right) - 7$$

$$= x + 7 - 7 = x$$

b. $g(f(x)) = g(3x - 7)$
$= \frac{1}{3}(3x - 7) + \frac{7}{3}$
$= x - \frac{7}{3} + \frac{7}{3} = x$

25. The student tried to factor $9x^3 - 8$ as a difference of cubes, but 9 is not a perfect cube. Correct solution:
$9x^4 - 63x^3 - 8x + 56$
$9x^3(x - 7) - 8(x - 7)$
$(9x^3 - 8)(x - 7)$
Expression does not factor further.

26. $-16t^2 + 136 = 0$

$$t = \frac{-b \pm \sqrt{b^2 - 4ac}}{2a}$$
$$= \frac{-(0) \pm \sqrt{(0)^2 - 4(-16)(136)}}{2(-16)}$$
$$= \frac{0 \pm \sqrt{8704}}{-32}$$
$$= \pm\frac{\sqrt{256}\sqrt{34}}{32}$$
$$= \pm\frac{16\sqrt{34}}{32}$$
$$= \pm\frac{\sqrt{34}}{2} \approx \pm 2.92$$

Ignoring the negative solution, the time to reach the pool is about 2.92 s.

27. Add any multiple of 360° to 15°:
$15° + n(360°)$
Sample answer: 375°, 735°, −345°

28.

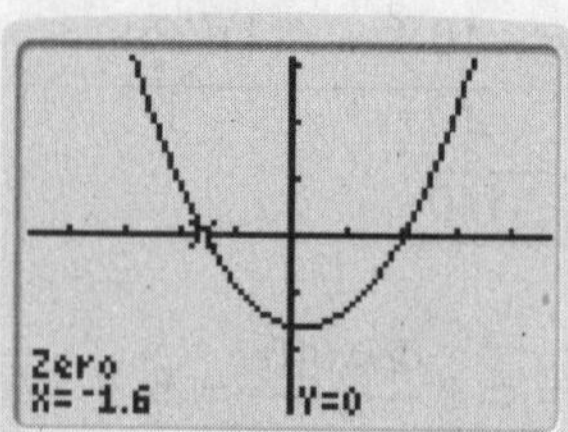

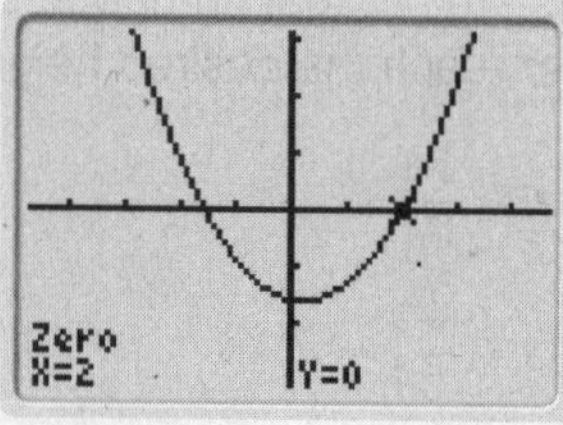

Solutions are −1.6 and 2.

29. $V = \frac{Z^{\frac{2}{3}}}{137}c$

$$= \frac{78^{\frac{2}{3}}}{137}c$$
$$= \frac{\sqrt[3]{78^2}}{137}c$$
$$= \frac{\sqrt[3]{6084}}{137}c$$
$$\approx \frac{18.26}{137}c \approx 0.133c$$

30. $\log_b a = x \Leftrightarrow b^x = a$
$\log_2 1 = 0 \Leftrightarrow 2^0 = 1$
$\log_3 1 = 0 \Leftrightarrow 3^0 = 1$
$\log_{15} 1 = 0 \Leftrightarrow 15^0 = 1$
Property is $b^0 = 1$ for all nonzero values of b

LESSON 66

Warm Up 66

1. quadratic formula

2. $27cd^3 - 12cd = 3cd(9d^2) + 3cd(-4)$
$= 3cd(9d^2 - 4)$
$= 3cd[(3d)^2 - (2)^2]$
$= 3cd(3d - 2)(3d + 2)$

3. $x(x - 4) = 0$
$x = 0$ or $x - 4 = 0$
$x - 4 + 4 = 0 + 4$
$x = 4$

4. Use synthetic division with $a = -7$:

−7	1	8	1	−42
		−7	−7	42
	1	1	−6	0

Remainder is 0, so $x + 7$ is a factor.

5. $x^2 + x + 1 = 0$

$$x = \frac{-b \pm \sqrt{b^2 - 4ac}}{2a}$$
$$= \frac{-1 \pm \sqrt{(1)^2 - 4(1)(1)}}{2}$$
$$= \frac{-1 \pm \sqrt{1 - 4}}{2}$$

$$= \frac{-1 \pm \sqrt{-3}}{2}$$

$$= -\frac{1}{2} \pm \frac{i\sqrt{3}}{2}$$

Lesson Practice 66

a. $x^4 - 3x^3 - 28x^2 = 0$

$x^2(x^2 - 3x - 28) = 0$

$x^2(x - 7)(x + 4) = 0$

$x = 0$ or $x - 7 = 0$ or $x + 4 = 0$

$x = 7$ $\quad x = -4$

b. $18x^3 - 18x = 0$

$18x(x^2 - 1) = 0$

$18x(x - 1)(x + 1) = 0$

$x = 0$ or $x - 1 = 0$ or $x + 1 = 0$

$x = 1$ $\quad x = -1$

c. $2x^3 - 32x^2 + 128x = 0$

$2x(x^2 - 16x + 64) = 0$

$2x(x - 8)^2 = 0$

$x = 0$ or $x - 8 = 0$

$x = 8$

Because x occurs as a factor once, the root of 0 has multiplicity 1. Because $x - 8$ occurs as a factor 2 times, the root of 8 has multiplicity 2.

d. $x^6 + 12x^5 + 27x^4 = 0$

$x^4(x^2 + 12x + 27) = 0$

$x^4(x + 3)(x + 9) = 0$

$x = 0$ or $x + 3 = 0$ or $x + 9 = 0$

$x = -3$ $\quad x = -9$

Because x occurs as a factor 4 times, the root of 0 has multiplicity 4. Because $x + 3$ and $x + 9$ each occur as a factor once, the roots of -3 and -9 have multiplicity 1.

e. By Rational Root Theorem, possible roots are ± 1 and ± 5.

Use synthetic division to test:

$$\begin{array}{r|rrrr} 1 & 1 & -5 & -1 & 5 \\ & & 1 & -4 & -5 \\ \hline & 1 & -4 & -5 & 0 \end{array}$$

Equation can be written as

$(x - 1)(x^2 - 4x - 5) = 0$

$(x - 1)(x - 5)(x + 1) = 0$

Zero Product Property → roots are 1, 5, and -1.

f. By Rational Root Theorem, possible roots are ± 1, ± 2, ± 7, and ± 14.

Use synthetic division to test:

$$\begin{array}{r|rrrr} 1 & 1 & 4 & -5 & -14 \\ & & 1 & 5 & 0 \\ \hline & 1 & 5 & 0 & -14 \end{array}$$

$x - 1$ is not a factor.

$$\begin{array}{r|rrrr} -1 & 1 & 4 & -5 & -14 \\ & & -1 & -3 & 8 \\ \hline & 1 & 3 & -8 & 6 \end{array}$$

$x + 1$ is not a factor.

$$\begin{array}{r|rrrr} 2 & 1 & 4 & -5 & -14 \\ & & 2 & 12 & 14 \\ \hline & 1 & 6 & 7 & 0 \end{array}$$

Equation can be written as

$(x - 2)(x^2 + 6x + 7) = 0$

Solve $x^2 + 6x + 7 = 0$ using quadratic formula:

$$x = \frac{-b \pm \sqrt{b^2 - 4ac}}{2a}$$

$$= \frac{-6 \pm \sqrt{(6)^2 - 4(1)(7)}}{2(1)}$$

$$= \frac{-6 \pm \sqrt{36 - 28}}{2}$$

$$= \frac{-6 \pm \sqrt{8}}{2}$$

$$= -3 \pm \frac{2\sqrt{2}}{2} = -3 \pm \sqrt{2}$$

Equation is

$(x - 2)\left(x - (-3 + \sqrt{2})\right)\left(x - (-3 - \sqrt{2})\right) = 0$

Zero Product Property → roots are 2, $-3 + \sqrt{2}$, and $-3 - \sqrt{2}$.

g.

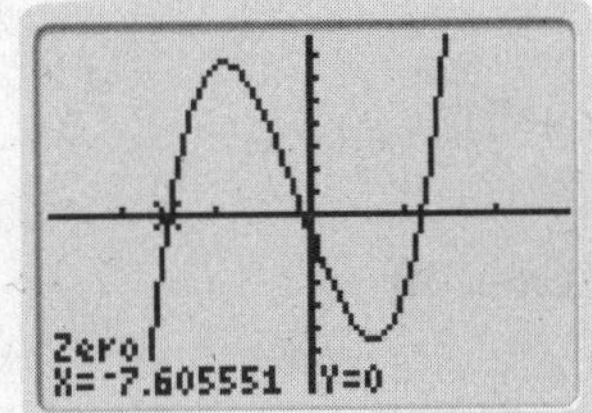

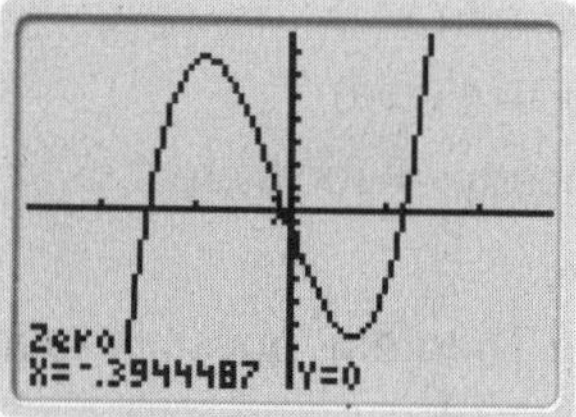

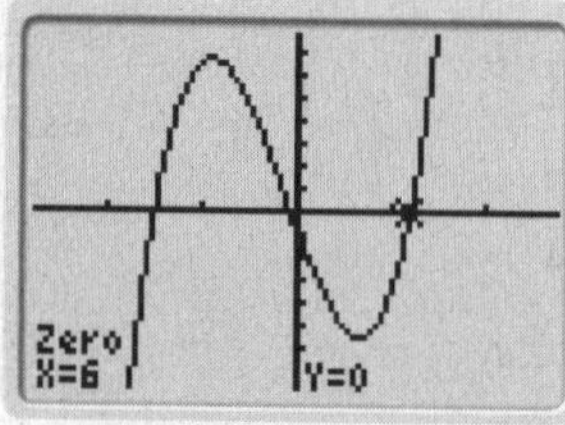

Use synthetic division with $a = 6$:

$$\begin{array}{r|rrrr} 6 & 1 & 2 & -45 & -18 \\ & & 6 & 48 & 18 \\ \hline & 1 & 8 & 3 & 0 \end{array}$$

Equation can be written as

$(x - 6)(x^2 + 8x + 3) = 0$

Solve $x^2 + 8x + 3 = 0$:

$$x = \frac{-b \pm \sqrt{b^2 - 4ac}}{2a}$$

$$= \frac{-8 \pm \sqrt{(8)^2 - 4(1)(3)}}{2(1)}$$

$$= \frac{-8 \pm \sqrt{64 - 12}}{2}$$

$$= \frac{-8 \pm \sqrt{52}}{2}$$

$$= -4 \pm \frac{2\sqrt{13}}{2} = -4 \pm \sqrt{13}$$

Equation is

$(x - 6)\left(x - (-4 + \sqrt{13})\right)\left(x - (-4 - \sqrt{13})\right) = 0$

Zero Product Property → roots are 6, $-4 + \sqrt{13}$, and $-4 - \sqrt{13}$.

h. If x represents length, $x + 3$ represents height and $x - 2$ represents width.

$V = lwh$

$18 = x(x - 2)(x + 3)$

$18 = x^3 + x^2 - 6x$

$0 = x^3 + x^2 - 6x - 18$

Use synthetic division with $a = 3$:

$$\begin{array}{r|rrrr} 3 & 1 & 1 & -6 & -18 \\ & & 3 & 12 & 18 \\ \hline & 1 & 4 & 6 & 0 \end{array}$$

The polynomial factors into

$(x - 3)(x^2 + 4x + 6) = 0$

The roots of $x^2 + 4x + 6 = 0$ must be negative if real, because the x-coefficient is positive. Therefore, length is positive root of original equation, 3 in.

Practice 66

1. $\dfrac{81^{\frac{2}{4}}}{81^{\frac{3}{4}}} = 81^{\frac{2}{4} - \frac{3}{4}} = 81^{-\frac{1}{4}} = \dfrac{1}{81^{\frac{1}{4}}} = \dfrac{1}{\sqrt[4]{81}} = \dfrac{1}{3}$

2. $\dfrac{p - 4px}{p} = \dfrac{p(1) + p(-4x)}{p}$

$= \dfrac{\cancel{p}(1 - 4x)}{\cancel{p}}$

$= 1 - 4x$

3. $\dfrac{4a}{a + 4} + \dfrac{a + 2}{2a} = \dfrac{2a(4a)}{2a(a + 4)} + \dfrac{(a + 2)(a + 4)}{2a(a + 4)}$

$= \dfrac{8a^2 + a^2 + 6a + 8}{2a(a + 4)}$

$= \dfrac{9a^2 + 6a + 8}{2a(a + 4)}$

Numerator will not factor further.

4. $\dfrac{x}{x + 2} + \dfrac{3 + x}{x^2 + 4x + 4} = \dfrac{x}{x + 2} + \dfrac{3 + x}{(x + 2)^2}$

$= \dfrac{x(x + 2)}{(x + 2)^2} + \dfrac{3 + x}{(x + 2)^2}$

$= \dfrac{x^2 + 2x + 3 + x}{(x + 2)^2}$

$= \dfrac{x^2 + 3x + 3}{(x + 2)^2}$

Numerator will not factor further.

5. $(4^6)^{\frac{1}{3}} = 4^{6 \times \frac{1}{3}} = 4^2 = 16$

6. $343^{\frac{1}{3}} \cdot 343^{\frac{1}{3}} = 343^{\frac{1}{3} + \frac{1}{3}}$

$= 343^{\frac{2}{3}}$

$= (\sqrt[3]{343})^2$
$= 7^2 = 49$

7. $P(\text{2 grapes}) = \frac{3}{10} \cdot \frac{2}{9} = \frac{6}{90} = \frac{1}{15}$

8. The line will have the same slope, $m = -\frac{3}{8}$. Use slope-intercept form:

$$y - y_1 = m(x - x_1)$$
$$y - (-3) = -\frac{3}{8}(x - 2)$$
$$y + 3 = -\frac{3}{8}x + \frac{6}{8}$$
$$y + 3 - 3 = -\frac{3}{8}x + \frac{3}{4} - 3$$
$$y = -\frac{3}{8}x - \frac{9}{4}$$

9. a. $V = \pi r^2 h$
$125 = \pi r^2(r + 6)$
$125 = \pi r^3 + 6\pi r^2$
$0 = \pi r^3 + 6\pi r^2 - 125$

b.

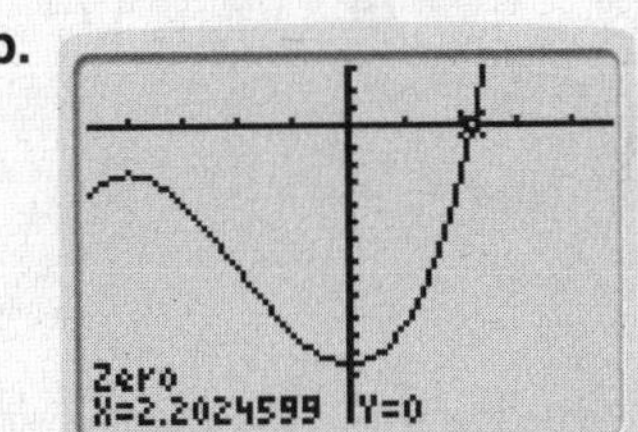

The radius is about 2.2 in.

10. Interchange variables

$$y = 7x^2 + 21$$
$$x = 7y^2 + 21$$
$$7y^2 = x - 21$$
$$y = \sqrt{\frac{x - 21}{7}}$$

Domain: the expression under the radical must be non-negative, so $\frac{x-21}{7} \geq 0$ or $x \geq 21$. Range: positive square root is taken, so $y \geq 0$.

11. $f(x)$ is a linear function; it can be drawn without lifting pencil, so it is continuous. Answer choice **A**

12. Sample: You must add $\left(\frac{b}{2}\right)^2$ because to complete the square, you must divide the coefficient of the middle term, b, and square the result. Additionally, if two things are equal and you change one of them and not the other, then they can no longer be equal. In order for them to stay equal they must both be changed in the exact same way.

13. $p = 0.17$ and $q = 0.83$

$P(\text{8 successes in 50 trials})$
$= ({}_{50}C_8)p^8q^{42}$
$= 536{,}878{,}650(0.17)^8(0.83)^{42}$
≈ 0.1495 or 14.95%

14. $270°$ is $\frac{3}{4}$ of $360°$. The area will be divided into the same proportions. Area of larger sector $= \frac{3}{4}$(area of circle)

$= \frac{3}{4}(\pi 5^2) = \frac{75\pi}{4}$
≈ 58.9 square units

15. Sample: The student wrote the logarithm as the base instead of writing the logarithm as the exponent.

$$\log_b a = x \Leftrightarrow b^x = a$$
$$\log_2 64 = x \Leftrightarrow 2^x = 64$$

16. a. Let x represent the width of the frame.

$$A = lw$$
$$1200 = (2x + 24)(2x + 36)$$
$$1200 = 4x^2 + 120x + 864$$
$$0 = 4x^2 + 120x - 336$$
$$0 = \frac{4x^2}{4} + \frac{120x}{4} - \frac{336}{4}$$
$$0 = x^2 + 30x - 84$$

b. Solve using quadratic formula:

$$x = \frac{-b \pm \sqrt{b^2 - 4ac}}{2a}$$
$$= \frac{-30 \pm \sqrt{(30)^2 - 4(1)(-84)}}{2(1)}$$
$$= \frac{-30 \pm \sqrt{900 + 336}}{2}$$
$$= \frac{-30 \pm \sqrt{1236}}{2}$$
$$= -15 \pm \frac{2\sqrt{309}}{2} = -15 \pm \sqrt{309}$$

Ignoring negative root, the width of the frame is $-15 + \sqrt{309} \approx 2.58$ in.

17. $y = a \cdot e^{kx}$

when $x = 0$, $y = 5$

$y = a = 5$

$y = 5e^{kx}$

when $x = -2$, $y = 125$

$y = 5e^{-2k} = 125$

$e^{-2k} = 25$

$e^{-k} = 25^{\frac{1}{2}} = \sqrt{25} = 5$

$e^{k} = \frac{1}{5}$

$y = 5e^{kx}$

$= 5(e^{k})^{x}$

$= 5\left(\frac{1}{5}\right)^{x}$

The function is decreasing.

18. Rearrange equation to either $3x^2 + 16 = 0$ or $-3x^2 - 16 = 0$. So either $a = 3$, $b = 0$, and $c = 16$ or $a = -3$, $b = 0$, and $c = -16$

19. $s = r\theta$

Radius = 12 in. and distance = 5 ft = 60 in.,

$60 = 12\theta$

$\theta = \frac{60}{12} = 5$ radians

Convert to degrees:

$(5\ \text{radians})\left(\frac{180°}{\pi\ \text{radians}}\right) = \left(\frac{900}{\pi}\right)° \approx 286°$

20. a. $P(\text{Calif.}) = \frac{\#\ \text{outcomes for Calif.}}{\text{total}\ \#\ \text{outcomes}}$

$= \frac{36{,}457{,}549}{299{,}398{,}484}$

≈ 0.12 or 12%

b. odds in favor are about 12% to 88%, or 3 to 22 (dividing by 4%).

21. The 1st, 2nd, and last equations have imaginary solutions.

P(both equations have imaginary solutions)

$= \frac{3}{5} \cdot \frac{2}{4}$

$= \frac{6}{20}$

$= \frac{3}{10}$ or 30%

22. By Transitive Property of Equality

$\frac{\sqrt{3}}{2} = \frac{y}{12}$

$12\left(\frac{\sqrt{3}}{2}\right) = 12\left(\frac{y}{12}\right)$

$y = 6\sqrt{3} \approx 10.392$

23. By Transitive Property of Equality

$\frac{1}{2} = \frac{x}{12}$

$12\left(\frac{1}{2}\right) = 12\left(\frac{x}{12}\right)$

$x = 6$

24. a. Inclusive, because some math textbooks are paperbacks.

b. Total # books = 7 + 3 + 23 + 14 + 6 + 16 + 1 + 4 = 74

P(math or pbk)

$= P(\text{math}) + P(\text{pbk}) - P(\text{math and pbk})$

$= \frac{7 + 3}{74} + \frac{3 + 14 + 16 + 4}{74} - \frac{3}{74}$

$= \frac{10 + 37 - 3}{74}$

$= \frac{44}{74}$

$= \frac{22}{37}$

$P(\text{4 books are math or pbk}) = \left(\frac{22}{37}\right)^4 \approx 0.125$

25. $d = l \cdot 2^{-\frac{n}{12}}$

$= 64 \cdot 2^{-\frac{5}{12}}$

$= 64 \cdot \frac{1}{2^{\frac{5}{12}}}$

$= 64 \cdot \frac{1}{\sqrt[12]{2^5}}$

$= \frac{64}{\sqrt[12]{32}} \approx 47.95$ cm

26. Rearrange terms so that each group of terms has the same ratio. Factor each group into product of a monomial term and a common (polynomial) factor. Combine monomial terms to make the other factor.

27. $P(\text{at least 1 tail}) = 1 - P(4 \text{ heads})$
$$= 1 - \left(\frac{1}{2}\right)^4$$
$$= 1 - \frac{1}{16} = \frac{15}{16}$$

28. Rational Root Theorem → possible rational factors have form $\pm\frac{p}{q}$ where p divides 27 and q divides 2. $\frac{2}{3}$ does not fit this form.
Answer choice **C**

29. Method 1: Find$(f \circ g)(x)$, then substitute -2 for x.
$$(f \circ g)(x) = f(g(x))$$
$$= f(4x^2 + 1)$$
$$= 8(4x^2 + 1) - 6$$
$$= 32x^2 + 8 - 6$$
$$= 32x^2 + 2$$
$$(f \circ g)(-2) = 32(-2)^2 + 2$$
$$= 128 + 2 = 130$$
Method 2: Substitute -2 for x directly.
$$g(-2) = 4(-2)^2 + 1$$
$$= 16 + 1 = 17$$
$$(f \circ g)(-2) = f(g(-2))$$
$$= f(17)$$
$$= 8(17) - 6$$
$$= 136 - 6 = 130$$

30. Possible answer: $\log_0 5$ does not exist because there is no power of 0 that equals 5. $\log_1 5$ does not exist because there is no power of 1 that equals 5.

LESSON 67

Warm Up 67

1. unit circle

2.

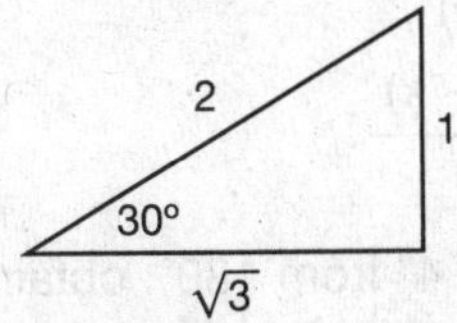

From triangle, $\sin 30° = \frac{1}{2}$

3.

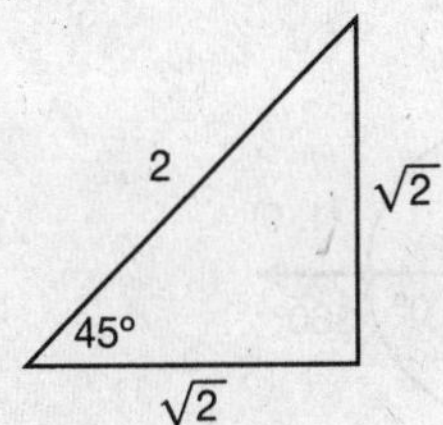

From triangle, $\cos \frac{\pi}{4} = \frac{\sqrt{2}}{2}$

Lesson Practice 67

a. Values of θ between 0 and 2π:
$$\frac{\sqrt{3}}{2} = \cos\frac{\pi}{6} = \cos\frac{11\pi}{6}$$
All values of θ are $\frac{\pi}{6} + 2\pi n$ and $\frac{11\pi}{6} + 2\pi n$.

b. $\frac{5\pi}{6}$ is angle measure between 0 and π whose cosine is $-\frac{\sqrt{3}}{2}$.
$$\text{Cos}^{-1}\left(-\frac{\sqrt{3}}{2}\right) = \frac{5\pi}{6} = 150°$$

c. Domain of inverse sine function is $\{a|-1 \le a \le 1\}$. Since $-\frac{3}{2}$ is not in domain, $\text{Sin}^{-1}\left(-\frac{3}{2}\right)$ is undefined.

d. $2 \sin \theta = -1$
$$\frac{2 \sin \theta}{2} = \frac{-1}{2}$$
$$\sin \theta = -\frac{1}{2}$$

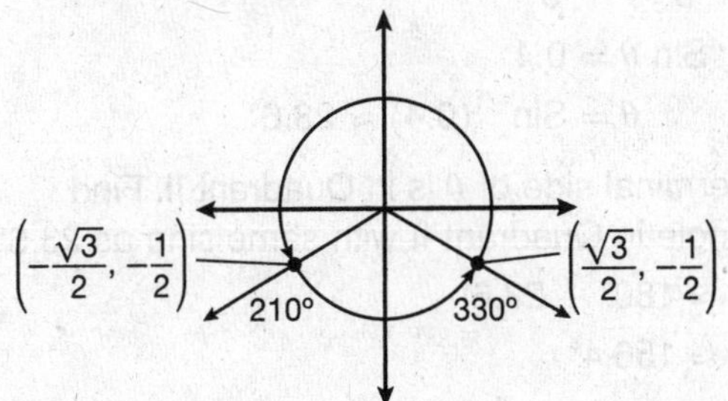

Solutions are 210° and 330°.

e. $-\cos \theta = -1$
$$\cos \theta = 1$$

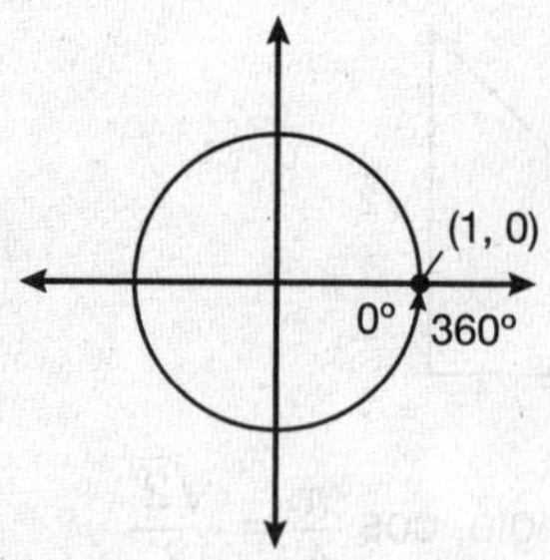

Solutions are 0° and 360.

f. $10\cos\theta - 5 = 0$

$10\cos\theta - 5 + 5 = 0 + 5$

$10\cos\theta = 5$

$\frac{10\cos\theta}{10} = \frac{5}{10}$

$\cos\theta = \frac{1}{2}$

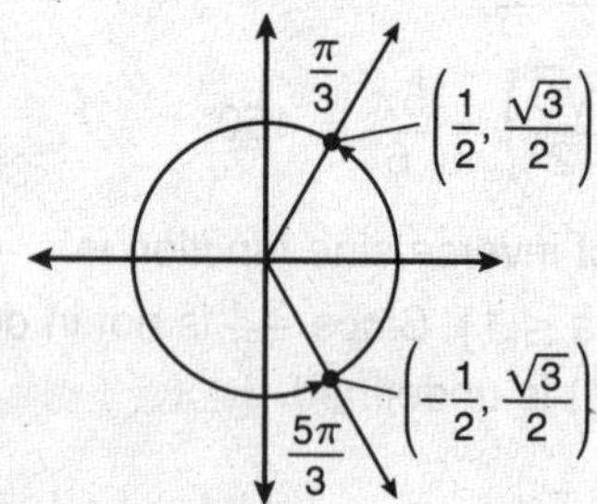

Solutions are $\frac{\pi}{3}$ and $\frac{5\pi}{3}$.

g. $5 \text{ Sin } \theta = 2$

$\frac{5 \text{ Sin } \theta}{5} = \frac{2}{5}$

$\text{Sin } \theta = 0.4$

$\theta = \text{Sin}^{-1}(0.4) \approx 23.6°$

h. Terminal side of θ is in Quadrant II. Find angle in Quadrant II with same sine as 23.6°.

$\theta \approx 180° - 23.6°$

$\approx 156.4°$

i.

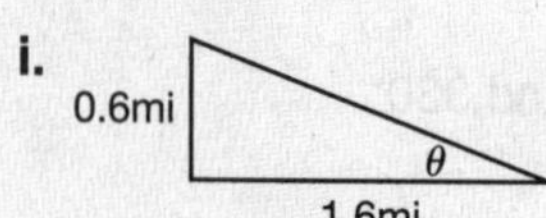

$\text{Tan } \theta = \frac{\text{opp.}}{\text{adj.}}$

$= \frac{0.6}{1.6} = 0.375$

$\theta = \text{Tan}^{-1}(0.375) \approx 21°$

Hikers should head 21° north of west.

Practice 67

1. Add 360° repeatedly until angle becomes positive: $-1787° \rightarrow 13°$. Since this angle is acute, it is the reference angle: 13°.

2. $60\not{°}\left(\frac{\pi \text{ radians}}{180\not{°}}\right) = \frac{\pi}{3}$ radians

3. $125\not{°}\left(\frac{\pi \text{ radians}}{180\not{°}}\right) = \frac{25\pi}{36}$ radians

4. $-240\not{°}\left(\frac{\pi \text{ radians}}{180\not{°}}\right) = -\frac{4\pi}{3}$ radians

5.
$$\begin{array}{r|rrrrr} -3 & 7 & -3 & 1 & 0 & 11 \\ & & -21 & 72 & -219 & 657 \\ \hline & 7 & -24 & 73 & -219 & 668 \end{array}$$

$f(-3) = 668$

6. $x^2 + 6x \rightarrow$

$x^2 + 6x + 3^2 = x^2 + 6x + 9$

$= (x + 3)^2$

7. $\frac{\frac{a}{b}}{\frac{a+b}{b}} = \frac{\not{b}\left(\frac{a}{\not{b}}\right)}{\not{b}\left(\frac{a+b}{\not{b}}\right)} = \frac{a}{a+b}$

8. $\frac{\frac{s}{a+b} + \frac{x}{b}}{\frac{a}{s+x}}$

$= \frac{b(a+b)(s+x)\left(\frac{s}{a+b} + \frac{x}{b}\right)}{b(a+b)(s+x)\left(\frac{a}{s+x}\right)}$

$= \frac{\frac{b\cancel{(a+b)}(s+x)s}{\cancel{(a+b)}} + \frac{\not{b}(a+b)(s+x)x}{\not{b}}}{\frac{b(a+b)\cancel{(s+x)}a}{\cancel{(s+x)}}}$

$= \frac{bs(s+x) + (ax+bx)(s+x)}{ab(a+b)}$

$= \frac{(bs + ax + bx)(s+x)}{ab(a+b)}$

9. Student subtracted 33.4° from 180°, obtaining an angle that terminates in Quadrant II and whose sine is positive. An angle with a negative sine value that satisfies $90° \leq \theta \leq 270°$ terminates in Quadrant III, so 33.4° must be added to 180° to obtain correct answer, 213.4°.

10. $\text{Tan}\theta = \dfrac{\text{opp.}}{\text{adj.}}$

$= \dfrac{45}{8.5}$

$\theta = \text{Tan}^{-1}\left(\dfrac{45}{8.5}\right) \approx 79°$

Maximum angle is about 79°.

11. a.

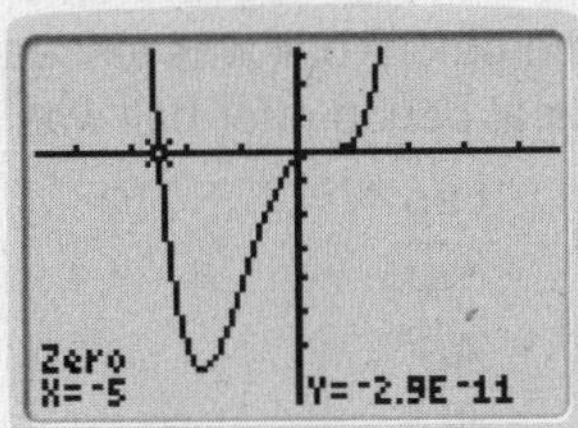

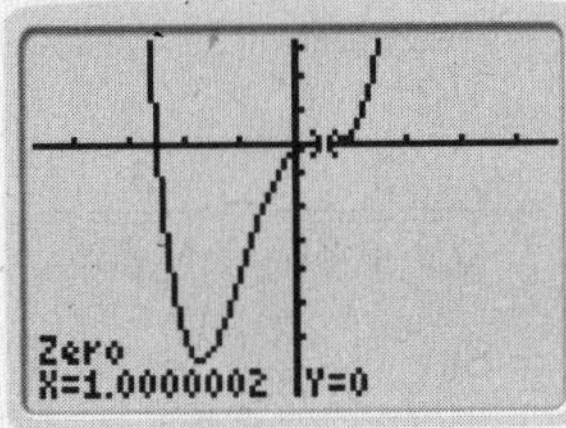

x-intercepts: −5 and 1

b. Use synthetic division with $a = -5$:

−5	1	2	−12	14	−5
		−5	15	−15	5
	1	−3	3	−1	0

Equation factors as:

$(x + 5)(x^3 - 3x^2 + 3x - 1) = 0$

$(x + 5)(x - 1)(x^2 - 2x - 1) = 0$

$(x + 5)(x - 1)^3 = 0$

$x + 5$ divides once, so root −5 has multiplicity 1; $x - 1$ divides 3 times, so root 1 has multiplicity 3

12. Graph feasible region:

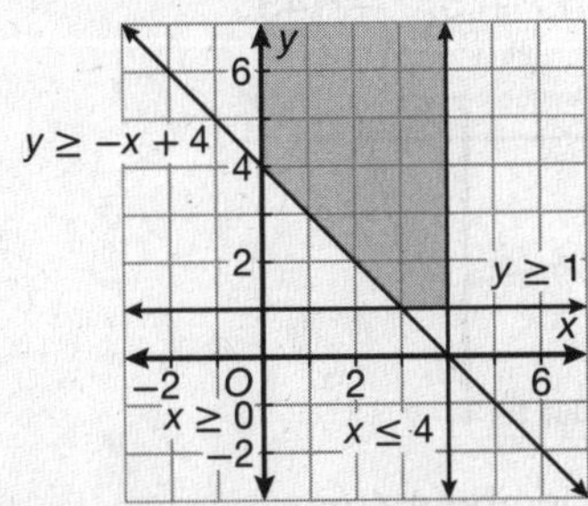

Vertices: (0, 4), (3, 1), (4, 1)

x	y	$P = 4x + 6y$
0	4	$4(0) + 6(4) = 24$
3	1	$4(3) + 6(1) = 18$
4	1	$4(4) + 6(1) = 22$

Minimum of P is 18 at $x = 3$, $y = 1$.

13. $5 + 2x^2 = -3x$

$2x^2 + 3x + 5 = 0$

$x = \dfrac{-b \pm \sqrt{b^2 - 4ac}}{2a}$

$x = \dfrac{-3 \pm \sqrt{3^2 - 4(2)(5)}}{2(2)}$

$x = \dfrac{-3 \pm \sqrt{9 - 40}}{4}$

$x = -\dfrac{3}{4} \pm \dfrac{\sqrt{31}}{4}i$

Correct choice is **D**.

14. 50%; whichever lens she picks, she is equally likely to put it in the correct or the incorrect eye.

15. a. This is a right angle: $x = \frac{\pi}{2}$

b. Angle is $\frac{24}{60} = \frac{2}{5}$ of a full turn:

$(x + y + z) = \dfrac{2}{5}(2\pi) = \dfrac{4\pi}{5}$

c. Hour hand moves through $\frac{2}{5}$ of $\frac{1}{12}$ of a turn, or $\frac{2}{60} = \frac{1}{30}$ of a turn:

$y = \dfrac{1}{30}(2\pi) = \dfrac{\pi}{15}$

d. $z = (x + y + z) - x - y$

$= \dfrac{4\pi}{5} - \dfrac{\pi}{2} - \dfrac{\pi}{15}$

$= \dfrac{6(4\pi)}{6 \cdot 5} - \dfrac{15(\pi)}{15 \cdot 2} - \dfrac{2(\pi)}{2 \cdot 15}$

$= \dfrac{24\pi - 15\pi - 2\pi}{30}$

$= \dfrac{(24 - 15 - 2)\pi}{30} = \dfrac{7\pi}{30}$

16. 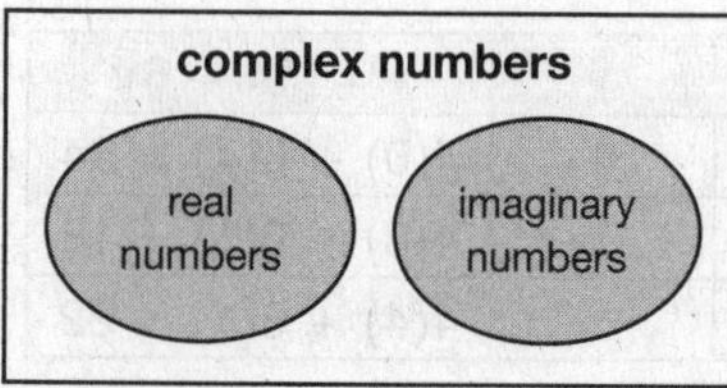

17. Factor by grouping:
$x^3 - 2x^2 + 5x - 10$
$= x^2(x - 2) + 5(x - 2)$
$= (x - 2)(x^2 + 5)$

18. Problem is to maximize $A = xy$ for the constraints $\begin{cases} 2(x + y)(20 + 12) \leq 2000 \\ 0 \leq x \leq 30 \\ y \geq 15 \end{cases}$ or

$$\begin{cases} 64x + 64y \leq 2000 \\ 0 \leq x \leq 30 \\ y \geq 15 \end{cases}$$

Graph feasible region:

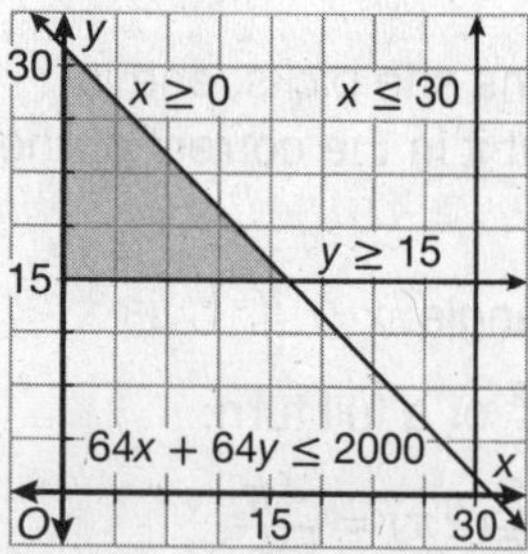

Vertices: (0, 31.25), (0, 15), (16.25, 15)

x	y	$A = xy$
0	31.25	(0)(31.25) = 0
0	15	(0)(15) = 0
16.25	15	(16.25)(15) = 243.75

Maximum of A is 243.75 ft^2 at $x = 16.25$ ft, $y = 15$ ft; cost is \$2000 since this lies on the line $64x + 64y = 2000$.

19. Work is correct. Explanation: Find the probability of each event. The events are independent so use the formula for independent events. Multiply the three probabilities.

20. $\sqrt[3]{\frac{216x^{12}}{4}} = \sqrt[3]{54x^{12}}$
$= \sqrt[3]{27}\sqrt[3]{2}\sqrt[3]{x^{12}}$
$= 3\sqrt[3]{2} \cdot x^{\frac{12}{3}} = 3x^4\sqrt[3]{2}$

Correct choice is **B**.

21. Quotient is a factor of polynomial. Because it is of degree two, it can be solved by using quadratic formula.

22. Sample: In this situation negative time represents time before ball was tossed, and we are looking at period after ball was tossed.

23. $\text{Sin}(m\angle AOB) = \frac{\text{opp}}{\text{hyp}}$
$= \frac{AB}{AO}$
$= \frac{3}{\sqrt{3^3 + 8^2}}$
$= \frac{3}{\sqrt{9 + 64}} = \frac{3}{\sqrt{73}}$
$m\angle AOB = \text{Sin}^{-1}\left(\frac{3}{\sqrt{73}}\right) \approx 20.6°$

24. There are ${}_{10}C_3$ ways to choose 3 athletes from 10. There is only one way to choose the top 3 placers. Therefore

$P(\text{choose top 3}) = \frac{\text{\# outcomes for top 3}}{\text{total \# outcomes}}$
$= \frac{1}{{}_{10}C_3}$

25. $V = \pi r^2 h$
$450 = \pi r^2(r + 5)$
$\frac{450}{\pi} = \frac{\pi r^2(r + 5)}{\pi}$
$143 = r^2(r + 5)$
$143 = r^3 + 5r^2$
$0 = r^3 + 5r^2 - 143$

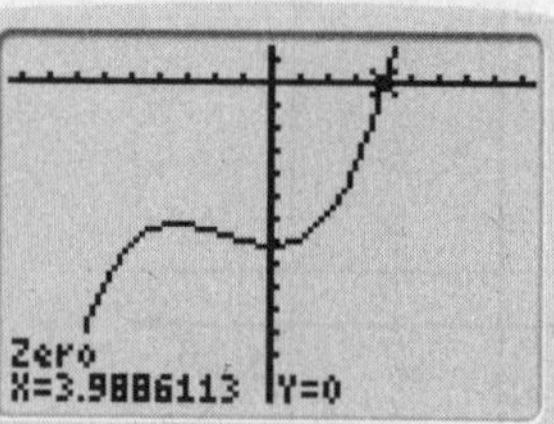

Radius is about 4 cm.

26. In Quadrant I, x and y are both positive, so $\sin\theta = \frac{y}{1}$, $\cos\theta = \frac{x}{1}$, and $\tan\theta = \frac{y}{x}$ are all positive.

In Quadrant II, x is negative and y is positive, so $\sin\theta = \frac{y}{1}$ is positive and $\cos\theta = \frac{x}{1}$ and $\tan\theta = \frac{y}{x}$ are negative.

In Quadrant III, x and y are both negative, so $\sin\theta = \frac{y}{1}$ and $\cos\theta = \frac{x}{1}$ are negative, and $\tan\theta = \frac{y}{x}$ is positive.

In Quadrant IV, x is positive and y is negative, so $\sin\theta = \frac{y}{1}$ and $\tan\theta = \frac{y}{x}$ are negative and $\cos\theta = \frac{x}{1}$ is positive.

27. dependent; The probability of choosing a blue crayon is larger if a yellow crayon was chosen 1st than if a blue crayon was chosen 1st.

28.
$$f(t) = a \cdot e^{kt}$$
$$f(0) = a = 400$$
$$f(3) = 400e^{3k} = 1600$$
$$\frac{400e^{3k}}{400} = \frac{1600}{400}$$
$$e^{3k} = 4$$
$$e^k = e^{\frac{3k}{3}} = \sqrt[3]{4}$$
$$f(t) = 400e^{kt} = 400(e^k)^t = 400(\sqrt[3]{4})^t$$
$$f(10) = 400(\sqrt[3]{4})^{10} \approx 40{,}637$$

After 10 years there would be 40,637 rabbits.

29. Graph feasible region:

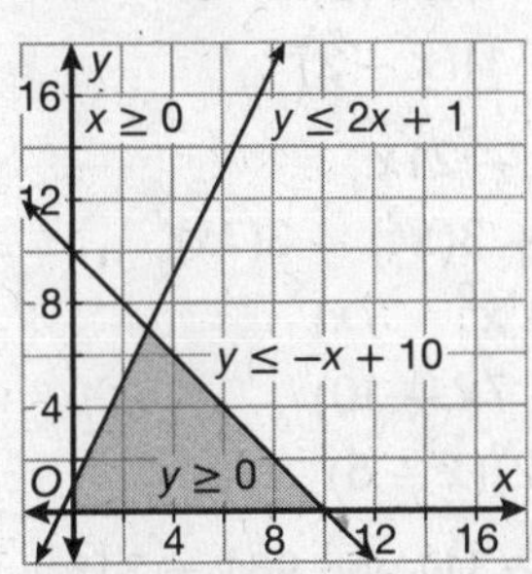

Vertices: (0, 0), (0, 1), (3, 7), (10, 0)

x	y	$P = 5x + 2y$
0	0	$5(0) + 2(0) = 0$
0	1	$5(0) + 2(1) = 2$
3	7	$5(3) + 2(7) = 29$
10	0	$5(10) + 2(0) = 50$

Maximum of P is 50 at $x = 10$, $y = 0$.

30. $-16t^2 + 177 = 0$
$$t = \frac{-b \pm \sqrt{b^2 - 4ac}}{2a}$$
$$= \frac{-(0) \pm \sqrt{0^2 - 4(-6)(177)}}{2(-16)}$$
$$= \pm\frac{\sqrt{64 \cdot 177}}{32}$$
$$= \pm\frac{8\sqrt{177}}{32}$$
$$= \pm\frac{\sqrt{177}}{4}$$

Ignoring negative root, time to fall is $\frac{\sqrt{177}}{4}$ ≈ 3.33 s.

LESSON 68

Warm Up 68

1. dependent

2. $P(\text{3 heads}) = \left(\frac{1}{2}\right)^3$
$$= \frac{1}{2^3}$$
$$= \frac{1}{8}$$
$$= 0.125 \text{ or } 12.5\%$$

3. $P(\text{white or black})$
$$= \frac{\#\text{ outcomes for white or black}}{\text{total }\#\text{ outcomes}}$$
$$= \frac{16 + 4}{8 + 16 + 4}$$
$$= \frac{20}{28}$$
$$= \frac{5}{7}$$
$$\approx 0.714 \text{ or } 71.4\%$$

Lesson Practice 68

a. Let events be A and B.

1,1 2,1 3,1 4,1
1,2 2,2 3,2 4,2
1,3 2,3 3,3 4,3
1,4 2,4 3,4 4,4

1,1 2,1 3,1 4,1
1,2 2,2 3,2 4,2
1,3 2,3 3,3 3,4
1,4 2,4 3,4 4,4

If A occurs, $P(B) = \frac{1}{2}$; if A does not occur, $P(B) = \frac{11}{12}$. Events are dependent.

$$P(A \text{ and } B) = P(A)P(B \mid A)$$
$$= \frac{1}{4} \cdot \frac{1}{2} = \frac{1}{8} = 12.5\%$$

b. Let events be A and B.

1,1 2,1 3,1 4,1
1,2 2,2 3,2 4,2
1,3 2,3 3,3 4,3
1,4 2,4 3,4 4,4

1,1 2,1 3,1 4,1
1,2 2,2 3,2 4,2
1,3 2,3 3,3 4,3
1,4 2,4 3,4 4,4

If A occurs, $P(B) = \frac{9}{12} = \frac{3}{4}$; if A does not occur, $P(B) = \frac{1}{4}$. Events are dependent.

$$P(A \text{ and } B) = P(A)P(B \mid A)$$
$$= \frac{3}{4} \cdot \frac{3}{4} = \frac{9}{16} = 56.25\%$$

c. $\frac{\text{Math}}{\text{all subjects G12}}$:

$$\frac{11}{11 + 26 + 66 + 58} = \frac{11}{161} \approx 6.8\%$$

d. $\frac{\text{G10}}{\text{History all grades}}$:

$$\frac{45}{45 + 19 + 26} = \frac{45}{90} = \frac{1}{2} = 50\%$$

e. Total names $= 237 + 318 = 555$

$P(M, M, M, W, W)$

$$= \frac{237}{555} \cdot \frac{236}{554} \cdot \frac{235}{553} \cdot \frac{318}{552} \cdot \frac{317}{551} \approx 2.6\%$$

f.

	a.m.	p.m.
Acceptable	2634	1859
Unacceptable	32	11

$$\frac{\text{evening}}{\text{unacceptable}}: \frac{1859}{2634 + 1859} \approx 41.4\%$$

Practice 68

1.
$$s^2 - 22 = -112$$
$$s^2 - 22 + 22 = -112 + 22$$
$$s^2 = -90$$
$$s = \pm\sqrt{-90}$$
$$= \pm\sqrt{9}\sqrt{-1}\sqrt{10}$$
$$= \pm 3i\sqrt{10}$$

2. $-3pax + pax^2 + 2pa$
$$= pa(-3x) + pa(x^2) + pa(2)$$
$$= pa(-3x + x^2 + 2)$$
$$= pa(x^2 - 3x + 2)$$
$$= pa(x - 1)(x - 2)$$

3. $30 + 3x^2 - 21x$
$$= 3(10) + 3(x^2) - 3(7x)$$
$$= 3(10 + x^2 - 7x)$$
$$= 3(x^2 - 7x + 10)$$
$$= 3(x - 2)(x - 5)$$

4. a. $62 = 2(31)$ and $961 = 31^2$

b. $x^2 - 62x + 961$
$$= x^2 - 2(x)(31) + 31^2$$
$$= (x - 31)^2$$

c. $x^2 - 62x + 961 = 26$
$$(x - 31)^2 = 26$$
$$x - 31 = \pm\sqrt{26}$$
$$x - 31 + 31 = \pm\sqrt{26} + 31$$
$$x = 31 \pm \sqrt{26}$$

5. Student did not take factor of x into account; 0 is also a root, with multiplicity 1.

6. There are more favorable outcomes than unfavorable outcomes; probability is greater than 50%.

7. $V = s^3$
$= (2b + 5)^3$
$= (2b + 5)((2b)^2 + 2(2b)(5) + 5^2)$
$= (2b + 5)(4b^2 + 20b + 25)$
$= 2b(4b^2 + 20b + 25) + 5(4b^2 + 20b + 25)$
$= 8b^3 + 40b^2 + 50b + 20b^2 + 100b + 125$
$= 8b^3 + 60b^2 + 150b + 125$
Volume is $(8b^3 + 60b^2 + 150b + 125)\text{ cm}^3$.

8. # houses in Nevada = 936,828 + 128,439
= 1,065,267
total # houses = 1,075,521 + 165,918 + 936,828 + 128,439 + 7,088,376 + 819,138 = 10,214,220

$P(\text{Nevada}) = \dfrac{\text{\# houses in Nevada}}{\text{total \# houses}}$

$= \dfrac{1{,}065{,}267}{10{,}214{,}220} \approx 10.4\%$

$\dfrac{\text{Nevada}}{\text{vacant, Nevada}}$:

$\dfrac{128{,}439}{165{,}918 + 128{,}439 + 819{,}138}$

$= \dfrac{128{,}439}{1{,}113{,}495} \approx 11.5\%$

9. $-64^{-\frac{2}{3}} = -\dfrac{1}{64^{\frac{2}{3}}} = -\dfrac{1}{(\sqrt[3]{64})^2} = -\dfrac{1}{4^2} = -\dfrac{1}{16}$

10. $\dfrac{-3}{-9^{-\frac{3}{2}}} = (-3)\left(-9^{\frac{3}{2}}\right)$
$= (-3)\left(-(\sqrt{9})^3\right)$
$= (-3)\left(-(3)^3\right)$
$= (-3)(-27) = 81$

11. $(-8)^{\frac{1}{3}} = \sqrt[3]{-8} = (\sqrt[3]{-1})(\sqrt[3]{8}) = (-1)(2) = -2$

12. $s = r\theta$
$= 4 \cdot \dfrac{\pi}{6}$
$= \dfrac{4\pi}{6}$
$= \dfrac{2\pi}{3} \approx 2.09$ in.

13. Events are mutually exclusive.
P(all red or all white)
$= P(\text{all red}) + P(\text{all white})$
$= \dfrac{30}{40} \cdot \dfrac{29}{39} \cdot \dfrac{28}{38} + \dfrac{10}{40} \cdot \dfrac{9}{39} \cdot \dfrac{8}{38}$
$= \dfrac{24{,}360 + 720}{59{,}280}$
$= \dfrac{25{,}080}{59{,}280} \approx 42.3\%$

14.

14° x 26° 600 m h y

$\dfrac{x}{600} = \tan 14°$ and $\dfrac{y}{600} = \tan 26°$
$h = x + y$
$= 600 \tan 14° + 600 \tan 26°$
≈ 442.2
Height of bridge is about 442.2 m.

15. 1st statement: insert "=", as this makes $P(A \text{ and } B) = P(A)P(B)$
1st statement: insert "≠", as this makes $P(A \text{ and } B) \neq P(A)P(B)$

16. Sample: Both can be used to make predictions, but probability uses all possibilities, whereas statistics uses only observed data.

17. Reference angles are
A 0° − (−30°) = 30°
B 180° − 120° = 60°
C 570° − 360° − 180° = 30°
D 180° − (−150°) = 330°
Correct choice is **B**.

18. Cos 60° = 0.5 ≈ 0.48
Therefore, $\text{Cos}^{-1}(0.48) \approx 60°$

19. Sample: The reference angle is 30°, and cos 30° $= \frac{\sqrt{3}}{2}$. 150° terminates in Quadrant II, and the cosine of any angle terminating in Quadrant II is negative, so cos 150° $= -\frac{\sqrt{3}}{2}$.

20. $3\sqrt{\frac{5}{2}} - 2\sqrt{\frac{2}{5}} = 3\frac{\sqrt{5}}{\sqrt{2}} - 2\frac{\sqrt{2}}{\sqrt{5}}$

$= 3\frac{\sqrt{5}\sqrt{2}}{\sqrt{2}\sqrt{2}} - 2\frac{\sqrt{2}\sqrt{5}}{\sqrt{5}\sqrt{5}}$

$= \frac{3\sqrt{10}}{2} - \frac{2\sqrt{10}}{5}$

$= \frac{5 \cdot 3\sqrt{10}}{5 \cdot 2} - \frac{2 \cdot 2\sqrt{10}}{5 \cdot 2}$

$= \frac{15\sqrt{10} - 4\sqrt{10}}{10}$

$= \frac{11\sqrt{10}}{10}$

21. $3\sqrt{18} + 2\sqrt{50} - \sqrt{98}$

$= 3\sqrt{9}\sqrt{2} + 2\sqrt{25}\sqrt{2} - \sqrt{49}\sqrt{2}$

$= 3 \cdot 3\sqrt{2} + 2 \cdot 5\sqrt{2} - 7\sqrt{2}$

$= (9 + 10 - 7)\sqrt{2} = 12\sqrt{2}$

22. $P(n,N,p) = \frac{N!}{n!(N-n)!}p^n(1-p)^{N-n}$

$P(12,200,0.09) = \frac{200!}{12!188!}(0.09)^{12}(0.91)^{188}$

$\approx 3.44\%$

23. Graph feasible region:

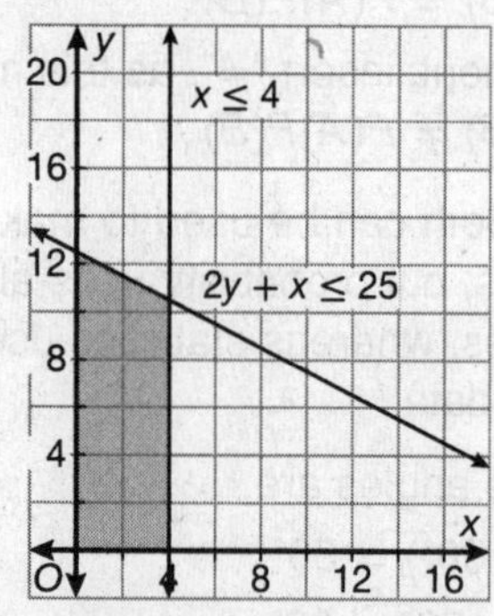

Region is bounded; vertices: (0, 0), (0, 12.5), (4, 0), (4, 10.5).

24. Student forgot to change the sign on "3*i*" when regrouping the terms. Correct solution:

$(7 - 4i) - (2 + 3i)$

$= (7 - 2) + (-4 - 3)i$

$= 5 - 7i$

25. Values between 0 and 2π radians are $\frac{\pi}{6}$ and $\frac{5\pi}{6}$. Therefore, all values are described as in choice **B**.

26.

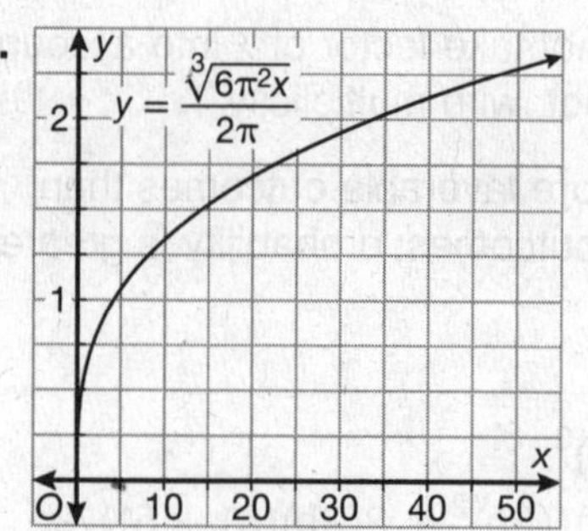

Volume of sphere with radius 2 cm is about 34 cm^3. Radius of sphere with volume 14 cm^3 is about 1.5 cm.

27. Use synthetic division with $a = 8$:

8	12	−36	−432	−384
		96	480	384
	12	60	48	0

Volume factors as:

$(x - 8)(12x^2 + 60x + 48)$

$= 12(x - 8)(x^2 + 5x + 4)$

$= 12(x - 8)(x + 1)(x + 4)$

When $x = 20$, volume is:

$12(x - 8)(x + 1)(x + 4)$

$= 12(20 - 8)(20 + 1)(20 + 4)$

$= 12(12)(21)(24)$

$= 72{,}576 \text{ in.}^3$

28. pH of 0.0001 mol/L and 0.00000001:

$\text{pH} = -\log[\text{H}^+]$ $\quad$ $\text{pH} = -\log[\text{H}^+]$

$= -\log(0.0001)$ $\quad$ $= -\log(0.00000001)$

$= -(-4) = 4$ $\quad$ $= -(-8) = 8$

Check: $10^{-4} = 0.0001$,

$10^{-8} = 0.00000001$

29. Let *x* represent distance driven south by first driver, *y* represent distance driven west by second driver after time *t*. Then $x = 40t$ and $y = 60(t - 1)$. Distance apart is given by

$d^2 = x^2 + y^2$

$= (40t)^2 + [60(t - 1)]^2$

$= 1600t^2 + 3600(t^2 - 2t + 1)$

$= 1600t^2 + 3600t^2 - 7200t + 3600$

$= 5200t^2 - 7200t + 3600$

Solve this equation:

$300^2 = 5200t^2 - 7200t + 3600$

$\frac{90{,}000}{400} = \frac{5200t^2}{400} - \frac{7200t}{400} + \frac{3600}{400}$

$$225 = 13t^2 - 18t + 9$$
$$0 = 13t^2 - 18t - 216$$

Use quadratic formula:

$$t = \frac{-b \pm \sqrt{b^2 - 4ac}}{2a}$$
$$= \frac{-(-18) \pm \sqrt{(-18)^2 - 4(13)(-216)}}{2(13)}$$
$$= \frac{18 \pm \sqrt{324 + 11{,}232}}{26}$$
$$= \frac{9}{13} \pm \frac{\sqrt{11{,}556}}{26}$$
$$= \frac{9}{13} \pm \frac{\sqrt{2889}}{13}$$

Ignoring negative root, time to be 300 mi apart is $\frac{9}{13} + \frac{\sqrt{2889}}{13} \approx 4.8$ h.

30. a. Let events be A and B. If A occurs, $P(B) = 1$. If A does not occur, $P(B)$ changes to $\frac{3}{5}$. Therefore A and B are dependent.

b. $P(A \text{ and } B) = P(A)P(B \mid A)$

$$= \frac{1}{5} \cdot 1 = \frac{1}{5}$$

LESSON 69

Warm Up 69

1. complex number

2. $(3x - 5)(4x + 2)$
$= (3x)(4x) + (3x)(2) + (-5)(4x) + (-5)(2)$
$= 12x^2 + 6x - 20x - 10$
$= 12x^2 - 14x - 10$

3. $\frac{5}{\sqrt{5}} = \frac{\sqrt{5}\,\sqrt{5}}{\sqrt{5}} = \sqrt{5}$

4. $(3 + 2i) + (6 - 8i)$
$= (3 + 6) + (2 + (-8))i$
$= 9 - 6i$

Lesson Practice 69

a. Move 1 unit right and 3 units down.

b. Move 2 units left and 4 units up.

c. Move 3 units left.

d. Move 2 units up.

a–d.

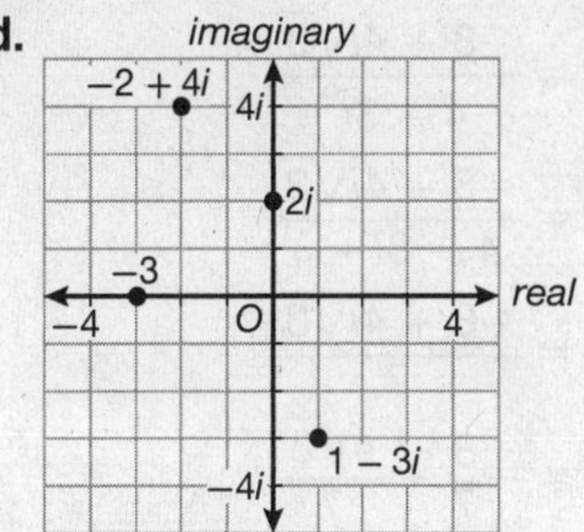

e. $|a + bi| = \sqrt{a^2 + b^2}$
$|7 - 2i| = \sqrt{7^2 + (-2)^2} = \sqrt{49 + 4} = \sqrt{53}$

f. $|-5 + i| = \sqrt{(-5)^2 + 1^2} = \sqrt{25 + 1} = \sqrt{26}$

g. $|10i| = \sqrt{0^2 + 10^2} = \sqrt{100} = 10$

h. $8i(-9 - 5i) = -72i - 40i^2$
$= -72i - 40(-1)$
$= -72i + 40$
$= 40 - 72i$

i. $(2 - 3i)(5 + 9i)$
$= (2)(5) + (2)(9i) + (-3i)(5) + (-3i)(9i)$
$= 10 + 18i - 15i - 27i^2$
$= 10 + 3i - 27(-1)$
$= 10 + 3i + 27$
$= 37 + 3i$

j. $18 \div 4 = 4$ R 2, so $i^{18} = i^2 = -1$

k. $11 \div 4 = 2$ R 3, so $i^{11} = i^3 = -i$
$-3i^{11} = -3(-i) = 3i$

l. $21 \div 4 = 5$ R 1, so $i^{21} = i^1 = i$
$\frac{1}{2}i^{21} = \frac{1}{2}(i) = \frac{1}{2}i$

m. $\frac{3 + 3i}{3i} = \frac{3 + 3i}{3i}\left(\frac{-3i}{-3i}\right)$
$= \frac{-9i - 9i^2}{-9i^2}$
$= \frac{-9i - 9(-1)}{-9(-1)}$
$= \frac{-9i + 9}{9}$
$= 1 - i$

n. $\frac{-4}{2+i\sqrt{3}} = \frac{-4}{2+i\sqrt{3}}\left(\frac{2-i\sqrt{3}}{2-i\sqrt{3}}\right)$

$= \frac{-8+4i\sqrt{3}}{4-3i^2}$

$= \frac{-8+4i\sqrt{3}}{4-3(-1)}$

$= \frac{-8+4i\sqrt{3}}{7}$

$= -\frac{8}{7} + \frac{4\sqrt{3}}{7}i$

Practice 69

1. $f(x) = x^2 + 8x - 3$

$x = \frac{-b \pm \sqrt{b^2 - 4ac}}{2a}$

$= \frac{-8 \pm \sqrt{8^2 - 4(1)(-3)}}{2(1)}$

$= \frac{-8 \pm \sqrt{64+12}}{2}$

$= -4 \pm \frac{\sqrt{76}}{2}$

$= -4 \pm \frac{\sqrt{4}\sqrt{19}}{2}$

$= -4 \pm \sqrt{19}$

2. $f(x) = 3x^2 - 10x + 4$

$x = \frac{-b \pm \sqrt{b^2 - 4ac}}{2a}$

$= \frac{-(-10) \pm \sqrt{(-10)^2 - 4(3)(4)}}{2(3)}$

$= \frac{10 \pm \sqrt{100-48}}{6}$

$= \frac{10}{6} \pm \frac{\sqrt{52}}{2}$

$= \frac{5}{3} \pm \frac{\sqrt{4}\sqrt{13}}{6}$

$= -\frac{5}{3} \pm \frac{\sqrt{13}}{3}$

3. $P(\text{not red}) = P(\text{yellow or green})$

$= \frac{53+30}{53+17+30} = \frac{83}{100}$

4. Quarterly means 4 times per year. Evaluate the equation using $P = 2700$, $n = 4$, $t = 14$, and $r = 0.038$.

$A = P\left(1 + \frac{r}{n}\right)^{nt}$

$= 2700\left(1 + \frac{0.038}{4}\right)^{4 \cdot 14}$

$= 2700(1.0095)^{56}$

≈ 4584.77

The value will be $4548.77.

5. $x^{\frac{1}{7}} = 5$

$\left(x^{\frac{1}{7}}\right)^7 = 5^7$

$x^{\frac{1}{7}\cdot 7} = 5^7$

$x^1 = 78{,}125$

6. $x^{\frac{2}{3}} = 36$

$\left(x^{\frac{2}{3}}\right)^{\frac{3}{2}} = 36^{\frac{3}{2}}$

$x^{\frac{2}{3}\cdot\frac{3}{2}} = \left(\sqrt{36}\right)^3$

$x^1 = 6^3 = 216$

7. To plot, move 5 units right and 1 unit down. This is in Quadrant IV.

Answer choice **D**

8. $x + 6$ is a factor if and only if $P(-6) = 0$, because 0 means there is no remainder. The remainder is 0, so $x + 6$ is a factor.

$$\begin{array}{r|rrrr} -6 & 1 & 3 & -28 & -60 \\ & & -6 & 18 & 60 \\ \hline & 1 & -3 & -10 & 0 \end{array}$$

9. $\frac{1}{4}\sqrt{-256} = \frac{1}{4}\sqrt{256}\sqrt{-1} = \frac{1}{4}\cdot 16i = 4i$

10. $\frac{1}{2}\sqrt{-2500} = \frac{1}{2}\sqrt{2500}\sqrt{-1} = \frac{1}{2}\cdot 50i = 25i$

11. Add multiples of 360°: $-920° \rightarrow -920° + 3(360°) = -920° + 1080° = 160°$. Reference angle is $180° - 160° = 20°$.

12. $(a + bi)(a - bi)$

$= (a)(a) + (a)(-bi) + (bi)(a) + (bi)(-bi)$

$= a^2 - abi + abi - b^2i^2$

$= a^2 - b^2(-1) = a^2 + b^2$

13. Look for angle measure between −90° and 90°

$\sin(-45°) = -\frac{\sqrt{2}}{2}$

$-45° = \text{Sin}^{-1}\left(-\frac{\sqrt{2}}{2}\right)$

In radians, −45° is $-\frac{\pi}{4}$.

14. Sample: The determinant of the matrix is 0, therefore the matrix doesn't have an inverse and would not be able to be decoded.

15. Wheel must turn through a multiple of 360° in total. Multiples of 360° are 360°, 720°, 1080°, 1440°, ... So the additional angle is 1440° − 1370° = 70°

16. The student found $P(\text{Male}|\text{AM})$. The condition is that the person must be male, and there are 24 males. Of those, 16 are in the AM. Probability is $\frac{16}{24} = \frac{2}{3} \approx 66.7\%$.

17. a.

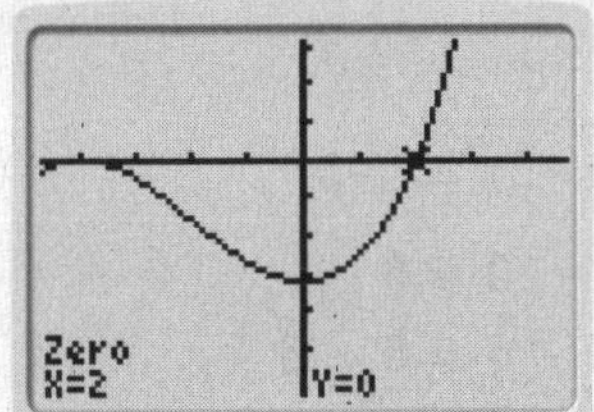

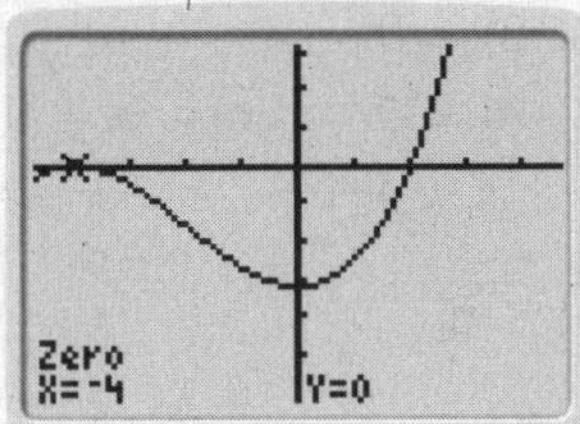

The x-intercepts are −4 and 2.

b. Use synthetic division with $a = 2$

$$\begin{array}{r|rrrr} 2 & 1 & 6 & 0 & -32 \\ & & 2 & 16 & 32 \\ \hline & 1 & 8 & 16 & 0 \end{array}$$

Factor

$f(x) = (x - 2)(x^2 + 8x + 16)$

$= (x - 2)(x + 4)^2$

Since $x - 2$ occurs once, $x = 2$ has multiplicity 1; since $x + 4$ occurs twice, $x = -4$ has multiplicity 2.

18. $P(A \text{ and } B) = P(A)P(B \mid A)$

$\frac{P(A \text{ and } B)}{P(A)} = \frac{P(A)P(B \mid A)}{P(A)}$

$\frac{P(A \text{ and } B)}{P(A)} = P(B \mid A)$

19. $b^x = a \Leftrightarrow \log_b a = x$

$10^x = 0.1 \Leftrightarrow \log_{10} 0.1 = x$

Answer choice **C**

20. $P(A \text{ or } B \text{ or } C) = P(A) + P(B) + P(C) - P(A \text{ and } B) - P(B \text{ and } C) - P(A \text{ and } C) + P(A \text{ and } B \text{ and } C)$

21. a. $f\left(g\left(\frac{1}{2}\right)\right) = \sin\left(\sin^{-1}\left(\frac{1}{2}\right)\right) = \sin\left(\frac{\pi}{6}\right) = \frac{1}{2}$

b. $g\left(f\left(\frac{\pi}{6}\right)\right) = \sin^{-1}\left(\sin\left(\frac{\pi}{6}\right)\right) = \sin^{-1}\left(\frac{1}{2}\right) = \frac{\pi}{6}$

c. When $-1 \le x \le 1$, $f(g(x)) = x$.

When $-\frac{\pi}{2} \le x \le \frac{\pi}{2}$, $g(f(x)) = x$.

22. The error is in the third line. By the Square Root Property,

$x - 22 = \pm\sqrt{121} = \pm 11$

$x = 22 \pm 11$

$x = 11 \text{ or } 33$

23. $9x^2 - 29x + 22 = 0$

$(9x - 11)(x - 2) = 0$

$x = \frac{11}{9} \text{ or } x = 2$

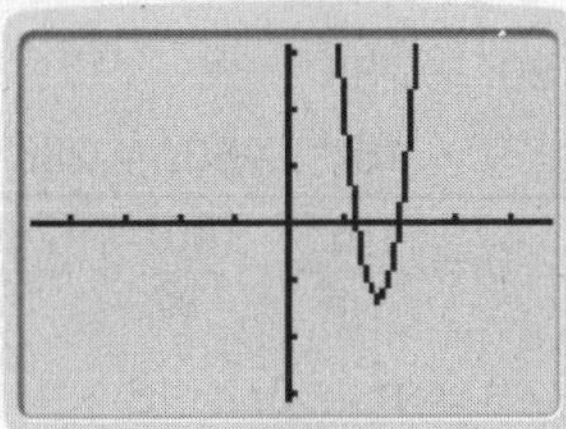

The probability is 0%, because both zeros are positive.

24. 22 ÷ 4 = 5 R 2 and 15 ÷ 4 = 3 R 3, so

$i^{22} + i^{15} = i^2 + i^3$

$= -1 - i$

To plot, move 1 unit left and 1 unit down.

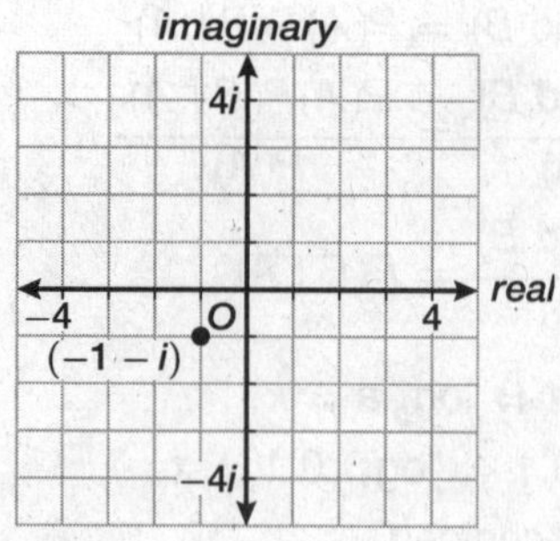

25. 1 h is $\frac{1}{24} \cdot \frac{1}{243} = \frac{1}{5832}$ of a full turn.

$$s = r\theta$$
$$= 3757 \cdot \frac{2\pi}{5832}$$
$$= \frac{3757\pi}{2916} \approx 4.05 \text{ mi}$$

26. Sample: If $b = 1$, then $b^x = 1$ for all values of x. If $b \neq 1$, then b^x has different values, and those values are determined by the values of x.

27. $|a + bi| = \sqrt{a^2 + b^2}$

$$|3 - 4i| = \sqrt{3^2 + (-4)^2}$$
$$= \sqrt{9 + 16}$$
$$= \sqrt{25} = 5$$

28. $|6 + 2i| = \sqrt{6^2 + 2^2}$

$$= \sqrt{36 + 4}$$
$$= \sqrt{40}$$
$$= \sqrt{4}\sqrt{10} = 2\sqrt{10}$$

29. $-16t^2 + 80t = 288$

$$0 = 16t^2 - 80t + 288$$
$$0 = \frac{16t^2}{16^2} - \frac{80t}{16} + \frac{288}{16}$$
$$0 = t^2 - 5t + 18$$

Solve using the quadratic formula

$$t = \frac{-b \pm \sqrt{b^2 - 4ac}}{2a}$$
$$= \frac{-(-5) \pm \sqrt{(-5^2) - 4(1)(18)}}{2(1)}$$
$$= \frac{5 \pm \sqrt{25 - 72}}{2}$$
$$= \frac{5 \pm \sqrt{-47}}{2}$$
$$= \frac{5}{2} \pm \frac{i}{2}\sqrt{47}$$

The time is not a real number, so the football will never reach the top of the dome.

30. $A = \frac{1}{2}bh$

$$= \frac{1}{2}\left(2^{\frac{7}{9}}\right)\left(2^{\frac{11}{9}}\right)$$
$$= \frac{1}{2}\left(2^{\frac{18}{9}}\right)$$
$$= \frac{1}{2}(4) = 2$$

The area of the triangle is 2 cm^2.

LESSON 70

Warm Up 70

1. index
2. $\sqrt{64} = \sqrt{8^2} = 8$
3. $\sqrt[3]{-125} = \sqrt[3]{(-5)^3} = -5$
4. $x^2 + 5x - 30 = 6$

$$x^2 + 5x - 30 - 6 = 6 - 6$$
$$x^2 + 5x - 36 = 0$$
$$(x - 4)(x + 9) = 0$$
$$x - 4 = 0 \quad \text{or} \quad x + 9 = 0$$
$$x = 4 \qquad x = -9$$

5. $(x + 6)^{\frac{1}{2}} = \sqrt{x + 6}$

Lesson Practice 70

a. $\sqrt{2x + 3} = 21$

$$\left(\sqrt{2x + 3}\right)^2 = 21^2$$
$$2x + 3 = 441$$
$$2x + 3 - 3 = 441 - 3$$
$$2x = 438$$
$$\frac{2x}{2} = \frac{438}{2}$$
$$x = 219$$

b. $11 = \sqrt{x - 7} - 2$

$$11 + 2 = \sqrt{x - 7} - 2 + 2$$
$$13 = \sqrt{x - 7}$$
$$13^2 = \left(\sqrt{x - 7}\right)^2$$
$$169 = x - 7$$

$$169 + 7 = x - 7 + 7$$
$$176 = x$$

c. $\sqrt[3]{2x} + 1 = 0$
$$\sqrt[3]{2x} + 1 - 1 = 0 - 1$$
$$\sqrt[3]{2x} = -1$$
$$\left(\sqrt[3]{2x}\right)^3 = (-1)^3$$
$$2x = -1$$
$$\frac{2x}{2} = \frac{-1}{2}$$
$$x = -\frac{1}{2}$$

d. $4\sqrt[3]{3x - 4} = 16$
$$\frac{4\sqrt[3]{3x - 4}}{4} = \frac{16}{4}$$
$$\sqrt[3]{3x - 4} = 4$$
$$\left(\sqrt[3]{3x - 4}\right)^3 = 4^3$$
$$3x - 4 = 64$$
$$3x - 4 + 4 = 64 + 4$$
$$3x = 68$$
$$\frac{3x}{3} = \frac{68}{3}$$
$$x = \frac{68}{3}$$

e. $\sqrt{9x} = \sqrt{5x + 2}$
$$\left(\sqrt{9x}\right)^2 = \left(\sqrt{5x + 2}\right)^2$$
$$9x = 5x + 2$$
$$-5x + 9x = -5x + 5x + 2$$
$$4x = 2$$
$$\frac{4x}{4} = \frac{2}{4}$$
$$x = \frac{1}{2}$$

f. $-\sqrt[3]{2x} = \sqrt[3]{4x + 7}$
$$\left(-\sqrt[3]{2x}\right)^3 = \left(\sqrt[3]{4x + 7}\right)^3$$
$$(-1)^3\left(\sqrt[3]{2x}\right)^3 = \left(\sqrt[3]{4x + 7}\right)^3$$
$$-2x = 4x + 7$$
$$-4x - 2x = -4x + 4x + 7$$
$$-6x = 7$$
$$\frac{-6x}{-6} = \frac{7}{-6}$$
$$x = -\frac{7}{6}$$

g. $\sqrt{3x} + \sqrt[3]{x - 4} - 5 = 0$
$$-\sqrt{3x} + \sqrt{3x} + \sqrt[3]{x - 4} - 5 = -\sqrt{3x}$$
$$\sqrt[3]{x - 4} - 5 = -\sqrt{3x}$$

Graph $Y1 = \sqrt[3]{x - 4} - 5$ and $Y2 = -\sqrt{3x}$

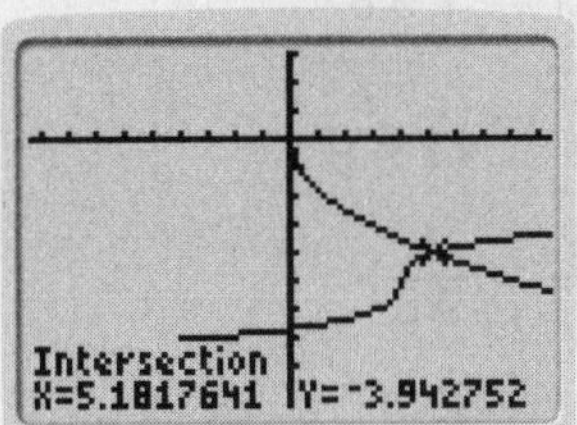

The curves intersect at ≈ 5.18.

h. $\sqrt{-1 - 4x} = \sqrt{x - 11}$
$$\left(\sqrt{-1 - 4x}\right)^2 = \left(\sqrt{x - 11}\right)^2$$
$$-1 - 4x = x - 11$$
$$-1 - 4x + 4x + 11 = x - 11 + 4x + 11$$
$$10 = 5x$$
$$\frac{10}{5} = \frac{5x}{5}$$
$$2 = x$$

Check: $\sqrt{-1 - 4x} = \sqrt{x - 11}$
$$\sqrt{-1 - 4(2)} \stackrel{?}{=} \sqrt{2 - 11}$$
$$\sqrt{-9} \stackrel{?}{=} \sqrt{-9}$$

If imaginary values are discounted, there are no solutions.

i. $x = \sqrt{6 - 5x}$
$$x^2 = \left(\sqrt{6 - 5x}\right)^2$$
$$x^2 = 6 - 5x$$
$$x^2 + 5x - 6 = 0$$
$$(x - 1)(x + 6) = 0$$
$$x = 1, -6$$

Check: $x = \sqrt{6 - 5x}$
$$1 \stackrel{?}{=} \sqrt{6 - 5(1)}$$
$$1 \stackrel{?}{=} \sqrt{1}$$
$$1 = 1$$
$$x = \sqrt{6 - 5x}$$
$$-6 \stackrel{?}{=} \sqrt{6 - 5(-6)}$$
$$-6 \stackrel{?}{=} \sqrt{36}$$
$$-6 \neq 6$$

The solution -6 is extraneous; the only solution is $x = 1$.

j.
$$T = 2\pi\sqrt{\frac{L}{9.8}}$$
$$5 = 2\pi\sqrt{\frac{L}{9.8}}$$
$$\frac{5}{2\pi} = \sqrt{\frac{L}{9.8}}$$
$$\left(\frac{5}{2\pi}\right)^2 = \left(\sqrt{\frac{L}{9.8}}\right)^2$$
$$\frac{25}{4\pi^2} = \frac{L}{9.8}$$
$$9.8\left(\frac{25}{4\pi^2}\right) = L$$
$$6.21 \approx L$$

The length is about 6.21 m.

Practice 70

1.
$$3p^2 + 7 = -9p^2 + 4$$
$$9p^2 + 3p^2 + 7 - 7 = 9p^2 - 9p^2 + 4 - 7$$
$$12p^2 = -3$$
$$\frac{12p^2}{12} = \frac{-3}{12}$$
$$p^2 = -\frac{1}{4}$$
$$p = \pm\sqrt{-\frac{1}{4}}$$
$$= \pm\frac{\sqrt{-1}}{\sqrt{4}}$$
$$= \pm\frac{1}{2}i$$

2.
$$2x^2 + 31 = 9$$
$$2x^2 + 31 - 31 = 9 - 31$$
$$2x^2 = -22$$
$$\frac{2x^2}{2} = \frac{-22}{2}$$
$$x^2 = -11$$
$$x = \pm\sqrt{-11}$$
$$= \pm i\sqrt{11}$$

3. By the Rational Root Theorem, rational roots are ± 1 and ± 5.

Use Synthetic division with $a = 1$.

$$\begin{array}{r|rrrr} 1 & 1 & -7 & 11 & -5 \\ & & 1 & -6 & 5 \\ \hline & 1 & -6 & 5 & 0 \end{array}$$

Equation becomes

$$(x - 1)(x^2 - 6x + 5) = 0$$
$$(x - 1)(x - 1)(x - 5) = 0$$

Since $x - 1$ occurs twice, root $x = 1$ has multiplicity 2. Since $x - 5$ occurs once, root $x = 5$ has multiplicity 1.

4.
$$f(g(x)) = f(x - 2)$$
$$= 3(x - 2) + 1$$
$$= 3x - 6 + 1$$
$$= 3x - 5$$

5. $104 \div 2 = 52$ bought pizza with a credit card.

P(pizza or credit card)

$= P$(pizza) $+ P$(credit card) $- P$(pizza and credit card)

$$= \frac{104}{220} + \frac{82}{220} - \frac{52}{220}$$
$$= \frac{52 + 41 - 26}{110}$$
$$= \frac{67}{110} = 0.61 \approx 61\%$$

6.
$$x^2 = 9x - 7$$
$$x^2 - 9x = 9x - 7 - 9x$$
$$x^2 - 9x = -7$$
$$x^2 - 9x + \left(\frac{9}{2}\right)^2 = -7 + \left(\frac{9}{2}\right)^2$$
$$\left(x - \frac{9}{2}\right)^2 = \frac{53}{4}$$
$$x - \frac{9}{2} = \pm\sqrt{\frac{53}{4}}$$
$$x = \frac{9}{2} \pm \sqrt{\frac{53}{4}}$$

7.
$$-5x - 6 = -x^2$$
$$x^2 - 5x - 6 + 6 = x^2 - x^2 + 6$$
$$x^2 - 5x = 6$$
$$x^2 - 5x + \left(\frac{5}{2}\right)^2 = 6 + \left(\frac{5}{2}\right)^2$$
$$\left(x - \frac{5}{2}\right)^2 = \frac{49}{4}$$
$$x - \frac{5}{2} = \pm\sqrt{\frac{49}{4}}$$
$$x = \frac{5}{2} \pm \frac{7}{2}$$
$$= \frac{12}{2}, -\frac{2}{2}$$
$$= 6, -1$$

8.
$$m = 1.2116\sqrt{h}$$
$$16 = 1.2116\sqrt{h}$$
$$\frac{16}{1.2116} = \sqrt{h}$$
$$\left(\frac{16}{1.2116}\right)^2 = (\sqrt{h})^2$$
$$174 \approx h$$
The height above sea level is about 174 ft.

9. The odds in favor are $x : y$, where x = # of favorable outcomes and y = # of unfavorable outcomes. Therefore
$$\frac{\text{\# fav. outcomes}}{\text{\# unfav. outcomes}} = \frac{x}{y} = \frac{9}{2}$$
Total # of outcomes = $x + y$, so
$$P(\text{event}) = \frac{\text{\# fav. outcomes}}{\text{total \# outcomes}}$$
$$= \frac{x}{x+y}$$
$$= \frac{9}{9+2}$$
$$= \frac{9}{11} \approx 82\%$$

10. $P(-3)$ = remainder on division by $x + 3$. If $x + 3$ is a factor, the remainder is 0.
Answer choice **B**

11.
$$V = \frac{Z^{\frac{2}{3}}}{137}c$$
$$= \frac{(27)^{\frac{2}{3}}}{137}c$$
$$= \frac{(\sqrt[3]{27})^2}{137}c$$
$$= \frac{3^2}{137}c$$
$$= \frac{9}{137}c \approx 0.066c$$

12. Sample: An extraneous solution is not a solution of the original equation, but a solution of an equation that was generated while solving the original equation; it can be formed when both sides of the equation are squared.

13. $43° \approx 45°$ and $\tan 45° = 1$, so $\tan 43° \approx 1$

14. a.
```
(64-82i)(26+31i)
          4206-148i
```

b.
```
-3.7i(2.25+4.5i)
       16.65-8.325i
```

15.
$$5 + (14 - 9i) = (5 + 0i) + (14 - 9i)$$
$$= (5 + 14) + (0 + (-9))i$$
$$= 19 - 9i$$
The sum of the currents is $19 - 9i$ amps.

16. Let x represent experienced workers and y represent inexperienced workers. Problem is to maximize $P = 1.5x + y$ subject to
$$\begin{cases} x + y \le 24 \\ 20x + 15y \le 400 \\ x \ge 0 \\ y \ge 0 \end{cases}$$

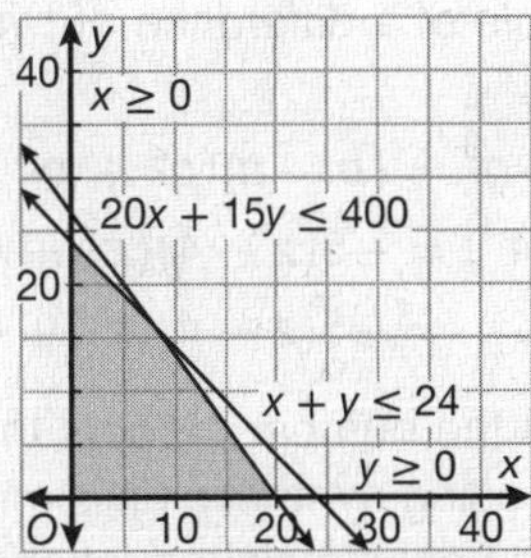

Vertices: (0, 0), (20, 0), (8, 16), (0, 24)

x	y	$P = 1.5x + y$
0	0	$1.5(0) + (0) = 0$
20	0	$1.5(20) + (0) = 30$
8	16	$1.5(8) + (16) = 28$
0	24	$1.5(0) + (24) = 24$

Maximum $P = 30$ is at (20, 0), with 20 experienced and 0 inexperienced workers.

17. a. $(2 + 3i)^{-1} = \dfrac{1}{2 + 3i}$

b. $\frac{1}{2+3i} = \frac{1}{2+3i}\left(\frac{2-3i}{2-3i}\right)$
$= \frac{2-3i}{2^2-(3i)^2}$
$= \frac{2-3i}{4-9i^2}$
$= \frac{2-3i}{4+9}$
$= \frac{2-3i}{13}$

c. $\left(\frac{2-3i}{13}\right)(2+3i) = \frac{(2-3i)(2+3i)}{13}$
$= \frac{2^2-(3i)^2}{13}$
$= \frac{4-9i^2}{13}$
$= \frac{4+9}{13} = 1$

18. $8c^3 + 343 = (2c)^3 + 7^3$ is sum of two cubes. Use model
$p^3 + q^3 = (p+q)(p^2 - pq + q^2)$
$(2c)^3 + 7^3 = (2c+7)((2c)^2 - (2c)(7) + 7^2)$
$= (2c+7)(4c^2 - 14c + 49)$

19. $-5z^3 + 320 = -5(z^3 - 64) = -5(z^3 - 4^3)$ is a multiple of a difference of two cubes. Use model
$p^3 - q^3 = (p-q)(p^2 + pq + q^2)$
$-5(z^3 - 4^3) = -5(z-4)(z^2 + (z)(4) + 4^2)$
$= -5(z-4)(z^2 + 4z + 16)$

20. It reduces the number of roots that must be tested by using synthetic division. Before using it, the polynomial equation must be in standard form and all coefficients must be integers.

21. $\sin\theta = \frac{\text{opp.}}{\text{hyp.}} = \frac{4}{50} = 0.08$
$\theta = \sin^{-1}(0.08) \approx 4.59°$
$4.59° < 4.7°$, so the design satisfies the building code.

22. Interchange variables
$x = 5y^3 - 20$
$x + 20 = 5y^3$
$\frac{x+20}{5} = y^3$
$0.2x + 4 = y^3$
$y = \sqrt[3]{0.2x+4}$
Both relations are functions because they determine y uniquely in terms of x.

23. Use $a = 4$, $b = -11$, and $c = -20$.
$x = \frac{-b \pm \sqrt{b^2 - 4ac}}{2a}$
$= \frac{-(-11) \pm \sqrt{(-11)^2 - 4(4)(-20)}}{2(4)}$
$= \frac{11 \pm \sqrt{121 + 320}}{8}$
$= \frac{11 \pm \sqrt{441}}{8}$
$= \frac{11 \pm 21}{8}$
$x = 4$ or $x = -1.25$

24.

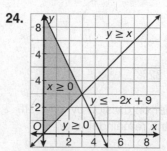

Vertices: (0, 0), (0, 9), (3, 3)

x	y	$P = 4.5x + 2.4y$
0	0	$4.5(0) + 2.4(0) = 0$
3	3	$4.5(3) + 2.4(3) = 20.7$
0	9	$4.5(0) + 2.4(9) = 21.6$

Maximum $P = 21.6$ is at (0, 9).

25. Student wrote $\frac{1}{16}$ as the logarithm, but $\frac{1}{16}$ is not the exponent in the exponential equation. Correct equation is
$b^x = a \Leftrightarrow \log_b a = x$
$4^{-2} = \frac{1}{16} \Leftrightarrow \log_4 \frac{1}{16} = -2$

26. Let G be midpoint of $\overline{AE}$, so that $\triangle AFG$ is a right triangle. Acute angle at F measures $\frac{1}{2}$ of interior angle measure, or
$\frac{1}{2}\left(\frac{(n-2)180}{n}\right) = \frac{1}{2}\left(\frac{(6-2)180°}{6}\right)$

$$= \frac{4 \cdot 180°}{2 \cdot 6}$$
$$= \frac{720°}{12} = 60°$$

$\sin 60° = \frac{AG}{AF}$ and $AE = 2AG$

So $AE = 2AG$
$$= 2AF \sin 60°$$
$$= 2(7)\frac{\sqrt{3}}{2}$$
$$= \frac{14\sqrt{3}}{2}$$
$$= 7\sqrt{3} \approx 12.1 \text{ cm}$$

27. Because the events are inclusive, $P(A)$ includes the overlap of B and $P(B)$ includes the overlap of A, so that the overlap is counted twice.

28. Sale function is $S(x) = x - 0.2x = 0.8x$. Last-day function is $L(x) = x - 0.25x = 0.75x$. Required function is composition
$$L(S(x)) = L(0.8x)$$
$$= 0.75(0.8x)$$
$$= 0.6x$$

29. Solve the equation
$$\sqrt{2x-8} = x - 4$$
$$(\sqrt{2x-8})^2 = (x-4)^2$$
$$2x - 8 = x^2 - 8x + 16$$
$$0 = x^2 - 8x + 16 - 2x + 8$$
$$0 = x^2 - 10x + 24$$
$$0 = (x-4)(x-6)$$
$$x = 4 \text{ or } x = 6$$

Check: $\sqrt{2x-8} = x - 4$
$$\sqrt{2(4)-8} \stackrel{?}{=} 4 - 4$$
$$\sqrt{0} \stackrel{?}{=} 0$$
$$0 = 0$$
$$\sqrt{2x-8} = x - 4$$
$$\sqrt{2(6)-8} \stackrel{?}{=} 6 - 4$$
$$\sqrt{4} \stackrel{?}{=} 2$$
$$2 = 2$$

The solutions are 4 and 6. The rolls are independent, so

$P(\text{solution, solution}) = P(\text{solution}) \cdot P(\text{solution})$
$$= \frac{2}{6} \cdot \frac{2}{6} = \frac{1}{9}$$

30. Total # grapes = 9 + 15 = 24
$$P(G,G,R,R) = \frac{9}{24} \cdot \frac{8}{23} \cdot \frac{15}{22} \cdot \frac{14}{21}$$
$$= \frac{15{,}120}{255{,}024} \approx 5.9\%$$

Answer choice **B**

INVESTIGATION 7

Collecting Data

1. Answers will vary.
2. Answers will vary.
3. Yes
4. 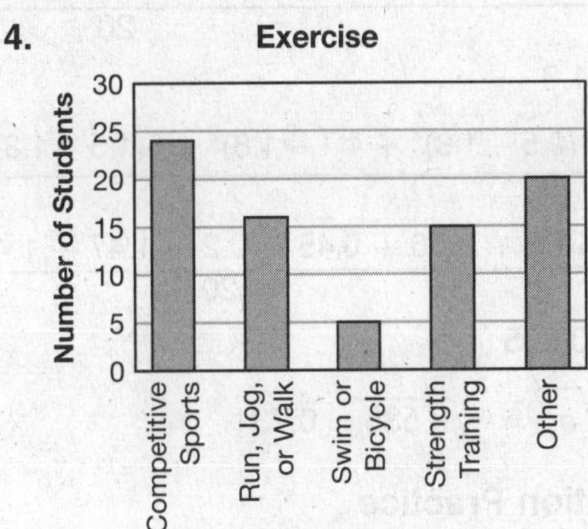

5. 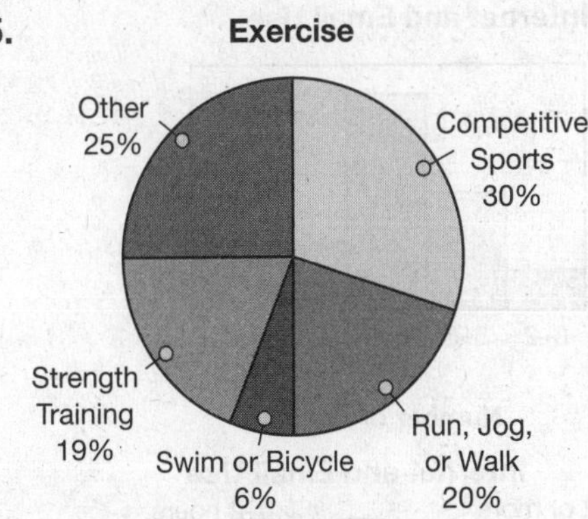

6. Biased; Possible explanation: The phrase "with most high school students" could influence a student to agree. Possible rewrite: Do you think that parents in general give high school students too little freedom to make their own decisions?
7. Biased; Possible explanation: The phrase "unfair policy" could influence a student to not support the policy. Possible rewrite: Do you

support the policy of requiring community service as a high school requirement?

8. Not biased

9. Answers will vary.

10. Systematic because the rule is that “every tenth customer” is surveyed; Not biased

11. Self-selected; Biased; Possible explanation: The request for campaign contributions could result in a set of responses that is not a fair representation of the population.

12. Stratified because a specific number of students are surveyed from each grade; There is no overlap; Not biased

13. Random; Not biased

14. Stratified; Probably biased; Possible explanation: It is not likely that there are approximately equal numbers of registered Democrats, Republicans, and Independents, so choosing 50 of each would probably be significantly out of proportion to their actual numbers.

15. Answers will vary. Check students' work.

16. Population: all sophomores in the school; Sample: stratified, not biased

17. Modes: 1.5, 2.0; Median = 1.75

18. $\overrightarrow{x} = \frac{1(0.5) + 4(1.0) + 5(1.5) + 5(2.0) + 3(2.5) + 1(3.0) + 1(3.5)}{20}$

$\overrightarrow{x} = 1.8$

19. $\sigma^2 = \frac{1(0.5 - 1.8)^2 + 4(1 - 1.8)^2 + 5(1.5 - 1.8)^2 + 5(2 - 1.8) + 3(2.5 - 1.8)^2 + 1(3 - 1.8)^2 + 1(3.5 - 1.8)^2}{20}$

$\sigma^2 = \frac{1.69 + 2.56 + 0.45 + 0.2 + 1.47 + 1.44 + 2.89}{20}$

$\sigma^2 = 0.535$

20. $\sigma = \sqrt{\sigma^2} = \sqrt{0.535} \approx 0.731$

Investigation Practice

a. **Internet and Email Use**

Number of Students: 25, 20, 15, 10, 5, 0

0–2, 3–5, 6–8, 9–11, 12 or more

Number of Hours

Internet and Email Use

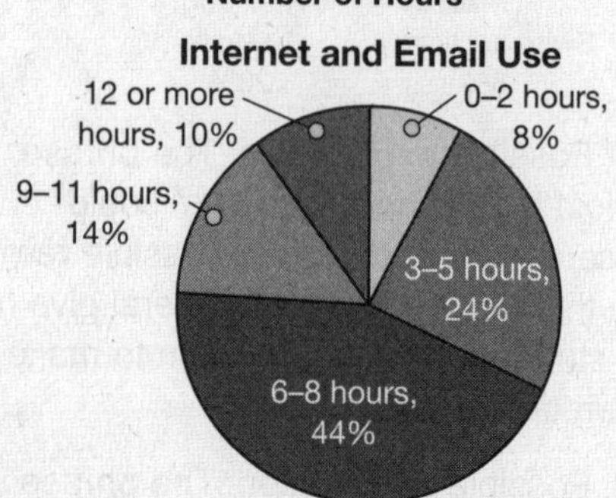

b. Possible answer: There would be no way for a student to give a response such as 2.5 hours.

c. Possible answer: Students who emailed or used the Internet 3 hours per week could be represented in either the 0–3 bar or the 3–6 bar. A similar statement applies for 6, 9, and 12 hours.

d. Not biased

e. Biased; Possible explanation: The phrase “Knowing that teenagers tend to be irresponsible” could influence a student to answer no. Possible rewrite: Should people younger than 18 be allowed to drive without an adult in the vehicle?

f. Not biased

g. Biased; Possible explanation: The first sentence could influence a student to believe that recent climate changes are part of a natural long-term climate cycle rather than global warming caused by humans and therefore cause students to believe that global warming is not a serious problem. Possible rewrite: Do you believe that global warming is a serious problem?

h. Self-selected; Not biased

i. Systematic; Biased; Possible explanation: Residents that live within a half mile of the proposed site could be more likely to not approve than residents who live farther away. The council members want to know if town residents approve, so the sample should be a fair representation of all residents in the town.

j. Stratified; Not biased

k. Random; Not biased

l. All students in the school; Stratified; Not biased

m. Mode = 15; Median = 15; Mean ≈ 15.46

n. $\sigma^2 = \dfrac{1(13-15.46)^2 + 4(14-15.46)^2 + 8(15-15.46)^2 + 7(16-15.46)^2 + 3(17-15.46)^2 + 1(19-15.46)^2}{24}$

$\sigma^2 \approx \dfrac{6.052 + 8.526 + 1.693 + 2.041 + 7.115 + 12.532}{24}$

$\sigma^2 \approx 1.58$

o. $\sigma^2 \approx 1.26$

p. Answers will vary. Check students' work.

LESSON 71

Warm Up 71

1. sine

2. $\sin A = \dfrac{\text{opp}}{\text{hyp}} = \dfrac{14}{50} = \dfrac{7}{25} = 0.28$

3. $\sin x \approx 0.438$

$x \approx 26°$

Lesson Practice 71

a. $\text{Area} = \dfrac{1}{2}cb \sin A$

$\text{Area} = \dfrac{1}{2}(40)(22) \sin 101°$

$\text{Area} \approx 431.9 \text{ m}^2$

b. $\dfrac{\sin 45°}{32} = \dfrac{\sin 19°}{a}$

$a \sin 45° = 32 \sin 19°$

$a = \dfrac{32 \sin 19°}{\sin 45°}$

$a \approx 14.7$

c. $m\angle R = 180° - (36° + 44°)$

$m\angle R = 100°$

$\dfrac{\sin 100°}{9} = \dfrac{\sin 36°}{s}$

$s \sin 100° = 9 \sin 36°$

$s = \dfrac{9 \sin 36°}{\sin 100°}$

$s \approx 5.4$

$\dfrac{\sin 100°}{9} = \dfrac{\sin 44°}{t}$

$t \sin 100° = 9 \sin 44°$

$t = \dfrac{9 \sin 44°}{\sin 100°}$

$t \approx 6.3$

d. $\dfrac{\sin 31°}{14} = \dfrac{\sin A}{10}$

$10 \sin 31° = 14 \sin A$

$\sin A = \dfrac{10 \sin 31°}{14}$

$m\angle A = \sin^{-1}\left(\dfrac{10 \sin 31°}{14}\right)$

$m\angle A \approx 21.6°$

e. $\sin 63° = \dfrac{h}{40}$

$h = 40 \sin 63°$

$h \approx 35.6$

Because 35.6 < 38 < 40, there are two possible triangles,

$\dfrac{\sin 63°}{38} = \dfrac{\sin C}{40}$

$40 \sin 63° = 38 \sin C$

$\sin C = \dfrac{40 \sin 63°}{38}$

$m\angle C = \sin^{-1}\left[\dfrac{40 \sin 63°}{38}\right]$

$m\angle C \approx 69.7°$

$m\angle C \approx 180° - 69.7° \approx 110.3°$

$m\angle C \approx 110.3°$ or $m\angle C \approx 69.7°$

f.

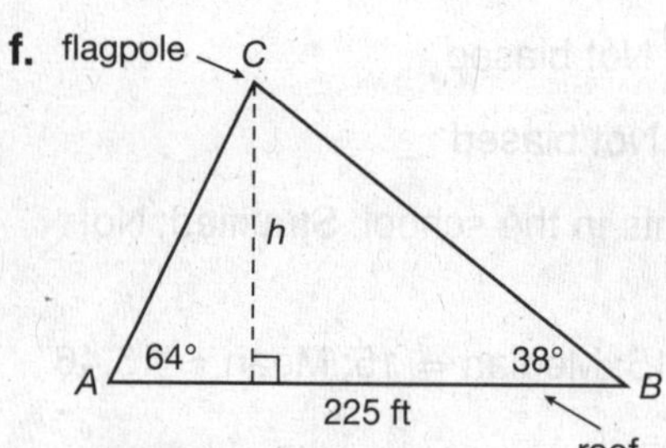

$m\angle C = 180° - (64° + 38°)$

$m\angle R = 78°$

$$\frac{\sin C}{c} = \frac{\sin B}{b}$$

$$\frac{\sin 78°}{225} = \frac{\sin 38°}{b}$$

$$b \sin 78° = 225 \sin 38°$$

$$b = \frac{225 \sin 38°}{\sin 78°}$$

$$b \approx 141.6$$

$$\sin 64° = \frac{h}{141.6}$$

$$h = 141.6 \sin 64°$$

$$h \approx 127.3$$

The distance is about 127.3 ft.

Practice 71

1. $3x(x^2 + 7x - 25) = 0$

so $x = 0$, or

$$x = \frac{-b \pm \sqrt{b^2 - 4ac}}{2a}$$

$$x = \frac{-7 \pm \sqrt{(-7)^2 - 4(1)(-25)}}{2(1)}$$

$$x = \frac{-7 \pm \sqrt{49 + 100}}{2}$$

$$x = \frac{-7 \pm \sqrt{149}}{2}$$

$$x = \frac{-7 + \sqrt{149}}{2} \text{ or } x = \frac{-7 - \sqrt{149}}{2}$$

$x \approx 2.603$ or $x \approx -9.603$

The solutions are $x = 0$, $x \approx 2.603$, or $x \approx -9.603$.

2. $4x(2x^2 + 9x - 45) = 0$

$x = 0$, or

$$x = \frac{-b \pm \sqrt{b^2 - 4ac}}{2a}$$

$$x = \frac{-9 \pm \sqrt{(-9)^2 - 4(2)(-45)}}{2(2)}$$

$$x = \frac{-9 \pm \sqrt{81 + 360}}{4}$$

$$x = \frac{-9 \pm \sqrt{441}}{4}$$

$$x = \frac{-9 + 21}{4} \text{ or } x = \frac{-9 - 21}{4}$$

$x = 3$ or $x = -7.5$

The solutions are $x = 0$, $x = 3$, or $x = -7.5$.

3.

1	5	−10	20	−15
		5	−5	15
	5	−5	15	0

$5x^2 - 5x + 15$

4.

2	4	0	0	0	0	−129
		8	16	32	64	128
	4	8	16	32	64	−1

$$\frac{4x^4 + 8x^3 + 16x^2 + 32x + 64 + \frac{-1}{x-2}}{4}$$

$$= x^4 + 2x^3 + 4x^2 + 8x + 16 - \frac{1}{4(x-2)}$$

5. Whether x is negative or positive, x^2 is always positive. If x is unknown then there is no way to know for sure if it is the positive x or the negative x.

6. $y = -3x$

$x = -3y$ Interchange the variables

$y = -\frac{1}{3}x$

Domain: x is any real number; range: y is any real number

7. (−2, 0), (3, 0), (6, 0)
$P(-2) = (-2)^3 - 7(-2)^2 + 36 = 0$
$P(3) = (3)^3 - 7(3)^2 + 36 = 0$
$P(6) = (6)^3 - 7(6)^2 + 36 = 0$

8. $\begin{cases} x \geq 0 \\ y \geq 0 \\ x + y \leq 40 \\ x > y \end{cases}$ 19 lily bulbs

9. $\sqrt[4]{625x^{28}} = \sqrt[4]{625}\sqrt[4]{x^{28}} = 5x^{(28)\frac{1}{4}} = 5x^7$
Answer Choice **A**

10. $\angle Cuero = 180° - (39° + 65°) = 76°$
$$\frac{\sin 76°}{84} = \frac{\sin 65°}{x}$$
$$x = \frac{84 \sin 65°}{\sin 76°} \approx 78$$
The distance from Mathis to Cuero is about 78 miles.

11. The formula works when the terms are all on the same side of the equation. Using a coefficient of a term that is on the wrong side of the equation will give a value that has the wrong sign, and will ultimately lead to incorrect solutions. Writing the terms in decreasing order makes it less likely that the wrong coefficient will be chosen.

12. $\cos\theta = \frac{adj}{hyp} = \frac{7}{11}$
By Pythagorean Theorem
$opp^2 + adj^2 = hyp^2$
$opp^2 + 7^2 = 11^2$
$opp = \sqrt{121 - 49}$
$opp = 6\sqrt{2}$
$$\sin\theta = \frac{opp}{hyp} = \frac{6\sqrt{2}}{11}$$

13. $3 + 6\sqrt{2}$ because of the Irrational Root Theorem.

14. The 49° angle is not opposite the side labeled x. The angle needed is $180° - 49° - 63° = 68°$
$$\frac{\sin 63°}{16} = \frac{\sin 68°}{x}$$
$$x = \frac{16 \sin 68°}{\sin 63°}$$
$x \approx 16.6$

15. Total number of undefective items during the first shifts $11 - 2 = 9$. The total number of undefective items is:
$9 + 13 + (20 - 4) = 38$
$$\frac{9}{9 + 13 + 16} \approx 23.7\%$$

16. Press Y= to enter the equation $y = \sqrt{3x + 1} - 4 + \sqrt[3]{x}$.
Press GRAPH and then press TRACE to estimate the measure of the root.
≈ 2.12.

17. $y = a\left(\frac{1}{2}\right)^{\frac{t}{7340}}$
$$y = 200\left(\frac{1}{2}\right)^{\frac{10000}{7340}}$$
$y \approx 78g$

18. The student did not adjust the sign. The terminal side of 300° is in Quadrant IV, where the tangent values are negative.
$\tan 300° = -\sqrt{3}$

19. $f(g(x)) = f(-4x)$
$f(g(x)) = 5(-4x)^2$
$f(g(x)) = 5(16x^2)$
$f(g(x)) = 80x^2$

20. Since the hexagon is regular, it is composed of equilateral triangles of side length 2 cm. The apothem of the hexagon is the altitude of the triangle. This apothem forms a special right triangle with hypotenuse 2 cm and base 1 cm. Thus, the apothem is $\sqrt{3}$.

Thus, Area $= 5 \cdot \frac{1}{2}bh = 5\frac{2\sqrt{3}}{2} = 5\sqrt{3}$ cm^2.

21. (6, 0) because $P = 2(6) + (0) = 12$.

22. A radical equation has a variable as a radicand. In this equation, the radicand is the constant 5. Moreover, the equation is a polynomial.

23. $$x - 3\overline{)-x^4 - 7x^3 + 6x^2 - 1}$$ with quotient $-x^3 - 10x^2 - 24x - 72 - \frac{217}{x-3}$

24. $\dfrac{4-8i+2+i}{7+3i+2i}=\dfrac{6-7i}{7+5i}=\dfrac{6-7i}{7+5i}\left(\dfrac{7-5i}{7-5i}\right)$

$=\dfrac{42-30i-49i+35(-1)}{49-25(-1)}$

$=\dfrac{7-79i}{74}$

$=\dfrac{7}{74}-\dfrac{79i}{74}$

25. a. $\dfrac{5-2.5}{1.36}\approx 1.84$

b. $\dfrac{2.5-1}{1.36}\approx 1.10$

c. Darryl

26. $-16t^2+96t=208$

$0=16t^2-96t+208$

$t=\dfrac{-(-96)\pm\sqrt{(-96)^2-4(16)(208)}}{2(16)}$

$t=\dfrac{96\pm\sqrt{9216-13312}}{32}$

$t=\dfrac{96\pm\sqrt{-4096}}{32}$

$t=\dfrac{96\pm 64\sqrt{-1}}{-32}$

$t=3\pm 2i,$

The time is not a real number, so the flare will never reach the bottom of the bridge.

27. 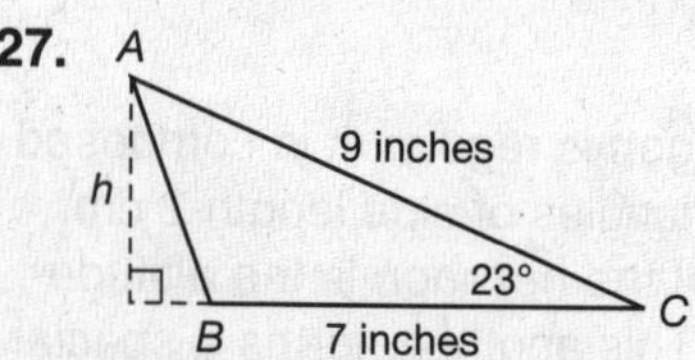

Let height $= h$

$\sin 23° = \dfrac{h}{9}$

$h = 9\sin 23°$

$h \approx 3.52$

Area $\approx \dfrac{7(3.52)}{2}$

$\approx 12.3 \text{ in.}^2$

Answer Choice **A**

28. $\dfrac{2+5i}{i}\cdot\dfrac{i}{i}$

$=\dfrac{2i+5i^2}{i^2}$

$=\dfrac{2i-5}{-1}$

$=5-2i$

29. $7 \div 4 = 1$ R3, so $i^7 = i^3 = -i$

30. $49^{\frac{5}{12}}\cdot 49^{\frac{1}{12}}$

$=49^{\frac{5}{12}+\frac{1}{12}}$

$=49^{\frac{6}{12}}$

$=49^{\frac{1}{2}}$

$=\sqrt{49}$

$=7$

LESSON 72

Warm Up 72

1. base
2. $(2^3)^3 = 2^9 = 512$
3. $2^x \cdot 2^{(x+y)} = 2^{x+(x+y)} = 2^{2x+y}$

Exploration 72

1. $\log_2 4 = 2$

$\log_2 8 = 3$

$\log_2 64 - \log_2 16 = 6 - 4 = 2$

$\log_2 16 - \log_2 2 = 4 - 1 = 3$

2. $\log_2 4 + \log_2 8 = 2 + 3 = 5$

3. $\log_2 32 = x$

$2^x = 32 = 2^5$

So $\log_2 32 = 5$

$\log_2 64 = x$

$2^x = 64 = 2^6$

So $\log_2 64 = 6$

$\log_2 4 + \log_2 8 = 2 + 3 = 5$

$\log_2 2 + \log_2 32 = 1 + 5 = 6$

4. The values are equal.

5. $\log_b(mn) = \log_b(m) + \log_b(n)$

6. $\log_b\left(\frac{m}{n}\right) = \log_b(m) - \log_b(n)$

Lesson Practice 72

a. $10^{\log(3a-1)} = 3a - 1$

b. Let $\ln e^{x+1} = d$
Then $e^d = e^{x+1}$
Then $\ln e^{x+1} = x + 1$

c. Change base to 2 because 32 and 64 are powers of 2.
$\log_{32} 64 = \frac{\log_2 64}{\log_2 32} = \frac{6}{5} = 1.2$
$\log_{32} 64 = 1.2$

d. $\log_2 40 = \log_2(5 \cdot 8)$
$= \log_2 5 + \log_2 8$
$\approx 2.3219 + 3$
≈ 5.3219

e. $\log 1900 = \log(19 \cdot 100)$
$= \log 19 + \log 100$
$\approx 1.2788 + 2$
≈ 3.2788

f. $\log_5 4 = \log_5\left(\frac{60}{15}\right)$ Express 4 as a quotient
$= \log_5 60 - \log_5 15$ Quotient Prop. of Logarithms
$\approx 2.5440 - 1.6826$
≈ 0.8614

g. $\log\left(\frac{11}{10000}\right) = \log 11 - \log 10000$
$\approx 1.0414 - 4$
≈ -2.9586

h. $\log_5 125^4 = 4\log_5 125$ Power Prop. of Log.
$= 4 \cdot 3$ $\log_5 125 = 3$ because $5^3 = 125$
$= 12$

i. $\ln\left(\frac{x+2}{2e^2}\right) = \ln(x+2) - \ln 2e^2$
$= \ln(x+2) - (\ln 2 + \ln e^2)$
$= \ln(x+2) - (\ln 2 + 2\ln e)$
$= \ln(x+2) - (\ln 2 + 2(1))$
$= \ln(x+2) - \ln 2 - 2$

j. $6.6 = \frac{2}{3}\log\left(\frac{E}{10^{11.8}}\right)$
$\frac{3}{2}(6.6) = \log\left(\frac{E}{10^{11.8}}\right)$
$9.9 = \log E - \log 10^{11.8}$ Quot. Prop. of Log.
$9.9 = \log E - 11.8$ Inverse Prop. of Log. and Exp.
$9.9 + 11.8 = \log E$
$21.7 = \log E$
So
$10^{21.7} = E$
$E \approx 5.01 \times 10^{21}$
The energy released was 5.01×10^{21} ergs.

Practice 72

1. $d = \sqrt{(x_2 - x_1)^2 + (y_2 - y_1)^2}$
$d = \sqrt{(6 - (-3))^2 + (0 - (-3))^2}$
$d = \sqrt{9^2 + 3^2}$
$d = \sqrt{90}$
$d = 3\sqrt{10}$

2. $y - y_1 = m(x - x_1)$
$y - (-5) = \frac{2}{5}(x - 3)$
$y + 5 = \frac{2}{5}x - \frac{6}{5}$
$y = \frac{2}{5}x - \frac{6}{5} - \frac{25}{5}$
$y = \frac{2}{5}x - \frac{31}{5}$

3. $4\sqrt{3} \cdot 5\sqrt{2} \cdot 6\sqrt{12} = 4 \cdot 5 \cdot 6\sqrt{36}\sqrt{2}$
$= 720\sqrt{2}$
$= 720\sqrt{2}$

4. $4\sqrt{63} - 3\sqrt{28} = 4\sqrt{9}\sqrt{7} - 3\sqrt{7}\sqrt{4}$
$= 12\sqrt{7} - 6\sqrt{7}$
$= 6\sqrt{7}$

5. Exponential and logarithmic operations are inverse operations.

6. $\tan\theta = \frac{47}{8}$
$\theta = \tan^{-1}(5.875)$
$\theta \approx 80°$

7. Quarterly means four times per year.

$$A = P\left(1 + \frac{r}{n}\right)^{nt}$$

where $P = \$2500$, $r = 0.064$, $n = 4$ and $t = 10$.

$$A = 2500\left(1 + \frac{0.064}{4}\right)^{(10)(4)}$$
$$= 2500(1.016)^{40}$$

8. $|3 + i| = \sqrt{3^2 + 1^2} = \sqrt{9 + 1} = \sqrt{10}$

9. Since $y \geq 0$ and $0 \leq x \leq 15$, we test the lower bounds for x and y:

$3(0) + 4(0) = 0 \leq 75$;

when $x = 0$, $3y + 4(0) = 3y \leq 75$, $y = 25$;

when $y = 0$, $3(0) + 4x = 4(15) = 60 \leq 75$ since the largest possible x-value is 15; and

when $x = 15$, $3y + 4(15) = 3y + 60 \leq 75$, $3y \leq 15$, so $y = 5$.

Region is bounded by: (0, 0), (0, 25), (15, 0), (15, 5).

10. $\frac{\sin 65°}{102} = \frac{\sin 47°}{e}$

$$e = \frac{102 \sin 47°}{\sin 65°}$$
$$e \approx 82.3$$
$$m\angle F = 180° - (47° + 65°) = 68°$$
$$\frac{\sin 65°}{102} = \frac{\sin 68°}{f}$$
$$f = \frac{102 \sin 68°}{\sin 65°}$$
$$f \approx 104.3$$

11.

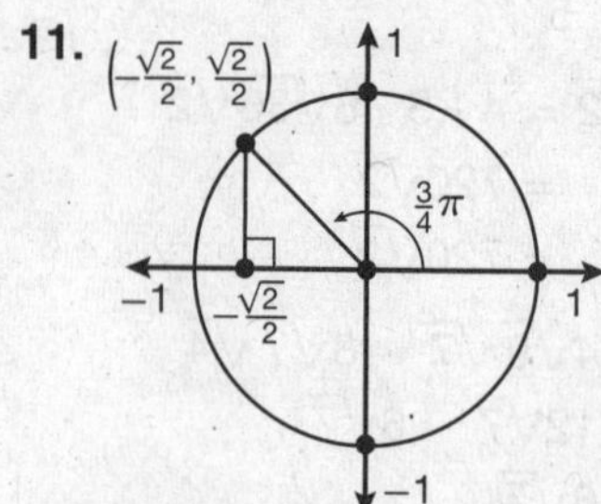

The angle $\frac{3}{4}\pi = 135°$ which creates an isosceles right triangle with the other two angle measures being 45° because the terminal arm of 135° creates a 45° angle with the x-axis in the 3rd quadrant.

By Pythagorean Theorem

$$x^2 + x^2 = 1^2$$
$$2x^2 = 1$$
$$x^2 = \frac{1}{2}$$
$$\sqrt{x^2} = \sqrt{\frac{1}{2}}$$
$$x = \frac{1}{\sqrt{2}}$$
$$x = \frac{\sqrt{2}}{2}$$

$\left(-\frac{\sqrt{2}}{2}, \frac{\sqrt{2}}{2}\right)$ Answer Choice **A**

12. Let x be the number of hours. The distances traveled are the two legs of a right triangle.

$$(50x)^2 + (40(x - 2))^2 = 450^2$$
$$2500x^2 + 1600(x - 2)^2 = 202{,}500$$
$$2500x^2 + 1600(x^2 - 4x + 4) = 202{,}500$$
$$2500x^2 + 1600x^2 - 6400x + 6400 = 202{,}500$$
$$4100x^2 - 6400x - 196{,}100 = 0$$
$$41x^2 - 64x - 1961 = 0$$
$$x = \frac{-b \pm \sqrt{b^2 - 4ac}}{2a}$$
$$x = \frac{-(-64) \pm \sqrt{(-64)^2 - 4(41)(-1961)}}{2(41)}$$
$$x = \frac{64 \pm \sqrt{4096 + 321{,}604}}{82}$$
$$x = \frac{64 \pm 570.7}{82}$$

Ignoring the negative solution.

$$x = \frac{64 + 570.7}{82} \approx 7.7 \text{ hours}$$

13. **a.** $y = 2210(1.06)^x$

b. $x = 2210(1.06)^y$

$$\log_{1.06} x = \log_{1.06}(2210(1.06)^y)$$
$$\log_{1.06} x = \log_{1.06} 2210 + \log_{1.06} 1.06^y$$
$$\log_{1.06} x - \log_{1.06} 2210 = \log_{1.06} 1.06^y$$
$$\log_{1.06} \frac{x}{2210} = y$$

c. $y = 2210(1.06)^x$

$$3000 = 2210(1.06)^x$$
$$\frac{3000}{2210} = 1.06^x$$
$$x \approx 5.2$$

It will take about 5.2 years.

14. The probability of selecting the second item given the condition that the first item was selected is different from what it would be if the first item were never selected. Because there is one fewer item to choose from, the denominator is one less than it would otherwise be.

15. $5^{\log_5 x} = x$

Answer Choice **B**

16. The distance traveled in 45 min is three-quarters of the circumference.

$\frac{3}{4}2\pi(20) = 30\pi$

≈ 94

The distance is about 94 inches.

17. $\begin{pmatrix} -2 & 1 & 4 \\ -5 & 7 & -1 \\ 8 & -3 & 1 \end{pmatrix}\begin{pmatrix} x \\ y \\ z \end{pmatrix} = \begin{pmatrix} -24 \\ -36 \\ 43 \end{pmatrix}$

Solution is (5, −2, −3)

18. This is a valid conclusion if we know that the triangle is a right triangle, but we have no information about the measures of the internal angles of the triangle.

19. Sine ratio:

$\sin 28° = \frac{x}{15}$

$x = 15\sin 28°$

$x \approx 7.042$

Law of Sines:

$\frac{\sin 28°}{x} = \frac{\sin 90°}{15} = \frac{1}{15}$

$x = 15\sin 28°$

$x \approx 7.042$

20. $(6 - 3i) + (5 + 4i) = 6 + 5 - 3i + 4i = 11 + i$

21. $(8 + 20i) - (-8 + 12i) = 8 + 8 + 20i - 12i$
$= 16 + 8i$

22. Use the distance formula to find the side lengths. Then use the inverse sine function to find one angle of the triangle. Use the side lengths and the appropriate included angle. The area is 30 square units.

23. $\begin{pmatrix} 16 & 8 \\ 2 & 0 \end{pmatrix}^{-1} = \frac{1}{ad - bc}\begin{pmatrix} d & -b \\ -c & a \end{pmatrix}$

$= \frac{1}{0 - 16}\begin{pmatrix} 0 & -8 \\ -2 & 16 \end{pmatrix}$

$= \begin{pmatrix} 0 & \frac{1}{2} \\ \frac{1}{8} & -1 \end{pmatrix} = \begin{pmatrix} 0 & 0.5 \\ 0.125 & -1 \end{pmatrix}$

24. Add the real terms and add the complex terms. Given a real number 3 and a complex number $(5 + 6i)$, the real terms are 3 and 5 and the complex terms are $0i$ and $6i$.

$3 + (5 + 6i) = 3 + 5 + 0i + 6i = 8 + 6i$

25. $m = 1.2\sqrt{h}$

$12.4 = 1.2\sqrt{h}$

$\frac{12.4}{1.2} = \sqrt{h}$

so $h \approx (10.3)^2 = 107$

26. $(-2 + 3i) + (5 + i) = 3 + 4i$

Draw the parallelogram with vertices $(-2, 3i)$, $(0, 0)$ and $(5, i)$. The missing vertex is $(3, 4i)$.

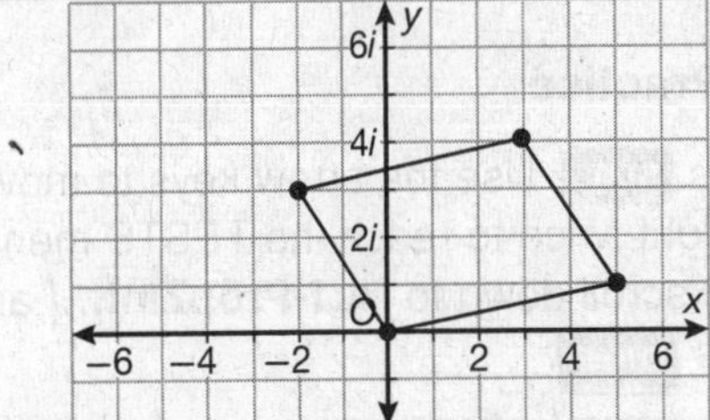

27. Isaiah squared 16 instead of dividing 16 by 2 and then squaring 8.

28. $r = 7$

29. $y - 2x = -3 \rightarrow y = -3 + 2x$

Substitute for y

$2(-3 + 2x) - x = 6$

$-6 + 4x - x = 6$

$3x = 12$

$x = 4$

Sub for x into either equation.

$2y - 4 = 6$

$2y = 6 + 4$

$y = 5$

The solution is (4, 5).

30. $3x = 12 - 2y \rightarrow x = 4 - \frac{2}{3}y$

Substitute for x into the second equation

$$8x - 2y = 10$$

$$8(4 - \tfrac{2}{3}y) - 2y = 10$$

$$32 - \frac{16}{3}y - 2y = 10$$

$$32 - 10 = \frac{16}{3}y + \frac{6}{3}y$$

$$22 = \frac{22}{3}y$$

$$22 \cdot \frac{3}{22} = y$$

$$y = 3$$

Then substitute for y in either equation.

$$8x - 2(3) = 10$$

$$8x = 10 + 6$$

$$8x = 16$$

$$x = 2$$

The solution is (2, 3).

LAB 11

Lab 11 Practice

a. Press STAT. Use the arrow keys to move to the right twice to reach the TESTS menu. Then scroll down to [**A:1-PropZInt...**] and press ENTER.

Press 4, 5, 0 and then ENTER to enter x. Press 3, 6, 5, 5, and then ENTER to enter n. Press •, 9, 7 and press ENTER to enter the confidence interval. Press ENTER for a second time.

Answer: (0.11132, 0.13491)

b. Press STAT. Use the arrow keys to move to the right twice to reach the TESTS menu. Scroll down to [**7:ZInterval...**] and press ENTER. Use the arrow keys to move to the left to **Stats** and press ENTER.

Enter 5, 7, 4, 4 for σ. Enter 3, 8, 5, 7, 6 for x. Enter 4, 3, for n and lastly enter •, 9, 5 for the C-interval. Scroll down to **Calculate** and press ENTER.

Answer: (36,859, 40,293)

c. Press STAT. Use the arrow keys to move to the right twice to reach the TESTS menu. Then scroll down to [**8:TInterval...**] and press ENTER. Use the arrow keys to move to the left to **Stats** and press ENTER.

Enter 5, 1, 0 for x. Enter 1, 1, 5 for Sx. Enter 3, 3 for n, and enter •, 9, 5 for C-interval. Scroll down to **Calculate** and press ENTER.

Answer: (469.22, 550.78)

LESSON 73

Warm Up 73

1. proportion

2. $\frac{24}{b} = \frac{33}{66}$

$$b = \frac{24 \cdot 66}{33}$$

$$b = 48$$

3. $n = \frac{pq}{s}$

$$n = \frac{16 \cdot 32}{8}$$

$$n = 64$$

Lesson Practice 73

a. Population: all the parents and guardians of students in that school. Sample: the parents and guardians the principal actually spoke to.

b. Population: all customers who shop at the store. Sample: the customers who answer the survey.

c. Yes, systematic sample.

d. No, students not on the soccer team did not have a chance.

e. Cassie, Drew, Aaron, Steven, and Jarvis.

f. The question is written in a confusing manner; students may think the question is saying something that it is not.

g. Viewers who do not have cell phones will not be represented in the sample. Viewers who feel strongly about the issue may text their response several times.

h. Write and solve the capture-recapture problem.

$\frac{38}{50} = \frac{43}{n}$

$n \approx 57$

About 57 chipmunks because on the second day, 12 chipmunks were found untagged and 38 were tagged on the first day.

Practice 73

1. $10^7 = 10{,}000{,}000$

2. $6^3 = 216$

3. 45°-45°-90° triangles are all similar because they are all right triangles and isosceles triangles. As such, the ratios of corresponding sides will always be the same with two such triangles.

4. AAS; one triangle since the given angles imply the measure of the remaining internal angle and because the side measure ensures that there can only be one triangle.

5. $6x(x^2 + x - 20) = 0$

$6x(x + 5)(x - 4) = 0$

$x = 0, \quad x = -5, \text{ and } x = 4$

6. $2x(x^2 + 9x - 52) = 0$

$2x(x + 13)(x - 4) = 0$

$x = 0, \quad x = -13, \text{ and } x = 4$

7. Because the roots are represented in the form $\pm\frac{p}{q}$, the possible roots are ±1, ±2, and ±4.

$\frac{1}{6} \approx 16.7\%$

8. $-x^2 + 6x = -12$

$x^2 - 6x = 12$

$x^2 - 6x + 9 = 12 + 9$

$(x - 3)^2 = 21$

$x - 3 = \pm\sqrt{21}$

$x = 3 \pm \sqrt{21}$

9. $-4 = -x^2 - 3x$

$x^2 + 3x = 4$

$x^2 + 3x + 2.25 = 4 + 2.25$

$(x + 1.5)^2 = 6.25$

$x + 1.5 = \sqrt{6.25}$

$x = -1.5 \pm 2.5$

$x = -1.5 - 2.5 \text{ or } x = -1.5 + 2.5$

$x = -4 \text{ or } x = 1$

10. Population: all customers of the grocery stores that sell this company's product. Sample: those customers who were surveyed in the stores. People who shop for food online and have it delivered are not represented.

11. a. $(f \circ g)(x) = f(g(x)) = f(3x) = 3x - 6$

$(g \circ f)(x) = g(f(x)) = g(x - 6)$

$= 3(x - 6) = 3x - 18$

b. $(f \circ g)(-1) = 3(-1) - 6 = -9$

$(g \circ f)(-1) = 3(-1) - 18 = -21$

12. 1^x does not equal 10 for any value of x because for all x, $1^x = 1$.

13. Since $\pi = 180°$, $\frac{6(180°)}{4} = 270°$

14. Since $\pi = 180°$, $\frac{2(180°)}{3} = 120°$

15. $\tan\theta = \frac{\text{opp}}{\text{adj}}$

$\tan\theta = \frac{950}{1500}$

$\theta = 32°$

The camper should head 32 degrees west of south.

16. The question is biased because verb "agree" is used to imply that the correct answer would be to agree that junk food should not be sold in high school vending machines.

Possible rewrite: Should junk food be sold in high school vending machines?

17. $x = \frac{-b \pm \sqrt{b^2 - 4ac}}{2a}$

$x = \frac{-(-7) \pm \sqrt{(-7)^2 - 4(3)(-2)}}{2(3)}$

$$x = \frac{7 \pm \sqrt{49 + 24}}{6}$$

$$x = \frac{7 \pm \sqrt{73}}{6}$$

Answer Choice **C**

18. A conditional probability is a probability of an event given that another event has already occurred. For example, randomly selecting a female student from a high school, given that the student is in the 11th grade.

19. $\frac{12}{12 + 17} = \frac{x}{305}$

$$x = \frac{12 \cdot 305}{29}$$

$$x = 126$$

About 126 students are athletes.

20. No; the error is in the second line. When dealing with equations, whatever operation is done on one side of the equation must also be done on the other side of the equation. In the second line, the left side must also be taken to the exponent 7.

$$x^{\frac{1}{7}} = 2$$

$$(x^{\frac{1}{7}})^7 = 2^7$$

$$x^{\frac{1}{7} \cdot 7} = 128$$

$$x = 128$$

21. $\tan(180° + \theta) = \tan\theta = 2.42$

$$\theta = 67.5°$$

$$\theta = 67.5° + 180° = 247.5°$$

22. $M = \frac{2}{3}\log\left(\frac{E}{10^{11.8}}\right)$

$$8.0 = \frac{2}{3}\log\left(\frac{E}{10^{11.8}}\right)$$

$$\frac{3}{2}(8.0) = \log\left(\frac{E}{10^{11.8}}\right)$$

$$12 = \log E - \log 10^{11.8}$$

$$12 = \log E - 11.8$$

$$23.8 = \log E$$

$$10^{23.8} = E$$

$$E = 6.31 \times 10^{23} \text{ ergs.}$$

23. a. The equation is a perfect square because half of 30 is 15, and 15 squared is 225.

b. $x^2 + 30x + 225 = (x + 15)^2$

c. $(x + 15)^2 = 13$

$$x + 15 = \pm\sqrt{13}$$

$$x = -15 \pm\sqrt{13}$$

24. The student applied the Product Property of Logarithms incorrectly. Correct expression:

$\ln 4e^3 = \ln 4 + \ln e^3 = \ln 4 + 3$

25. We have that an exponential growth of a population is given by $f(t) = a \cdot e^{kt}$, where a is the initial amount, k is the growth rate and t is the time elapsed.

$$f(50) = 529 \cdot e^{50k} = 2771$$

$$e^{50k} = \frac{2771}{529}$$

$$e^{50k} = 5.23...$$

$$\ln e^{50k} = \ln 5.23...$$

$$50k = 1.65...$$

$$k = 0.331...$$

$P(t) = 529e^{0.0331t}$, where t is the number of years since 1900.

$$P(110) = 529e^{0.0331(110)}$$

$$= 529e^{3.643...}$$

$$= 20{,}214$$

20,214 thousands of people in 2010.

26.

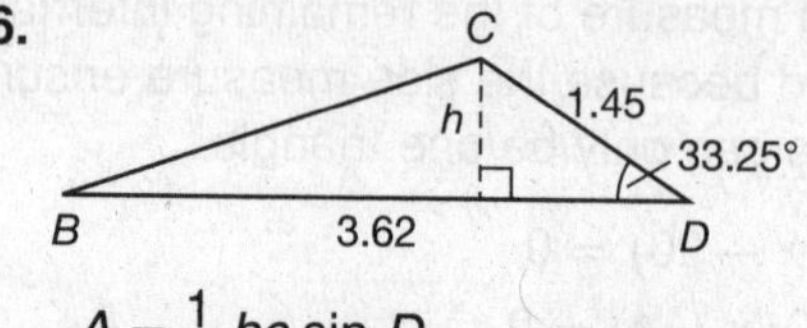

$$A = \frac{1}{2} bc \sin D$$

$$= \frac{1}{2}(1.45)(3.62)\sin(33.25°)$$

$$\approx \frac{1}{2}(1.45)(3.62)(0.54829)$$

$$\approx 1.44 \text{ square units}$$

27. The area of the large circle $= \pi 30^2 = 900\pi$. The area of the small circle $= \pi 15^2 = 225\pi$. The area of the unshaded region $= 2(225\pi) = 450\pi$.

450π equals half 900π, so the probability of the point being randomly chosen inside the shaded region is 50%.

28. $x = \sqrt{-14x - 45}$
$$x^2 = -14x - 45$$
$$x^2 + 14x = -45$$
$$x^2 + 14x + 49 = -45 + 49$$
$$(x + 7)^2 = 4$$
$$x + 7 = \pm 2$$
$$x = -7 \pm 2$$
Both solutions are extraneous; Answer Choice **A**

29. It is similar because it is also a Cartesian plane as you move both up and down and left and right. It is different because both axes in the *xy*-plane represent real numbers but the vertical axis in the complex plane represents the imaginary numbers.

30. The lines are parallel so the slope is the same.
$$y - y_1 = m(x - x_1)$$
$$y - 5 = -\frac{3}{2}(x - 1)$$
$$y - 5 = -\frac{3}{2}x + \frac{3}{2}$$
$$y = -\frac{3}{2}x + \frac{3}{2} + 5$$
$$y = -\frac{3}{2}x + \frac{13}{2}$$

LESSON 74

Warm Up 74

1. roots or solutions

2. $x = \dfrac{-b \pm \sqrt{b^2 - 4ac}}{2a}$
$$x = \frac{-(-4) \pm \sqrt{(-4)^2 - 4(2)(25)}}{2(2)}$$
$$x = \frac{4 \pm \sqrt{16 - 200}}{4}$$
$$x = \frac{4 \pm \sqrt{-184}}{4}$$
$$x = \frac{4 \pm i\sqrt{46 \cdot 4}}{4}$$
$$x = \frac{4 \pm 2i\sqrt{46}}{4}$$
$$x = 1 + \frac{1}{2}i\sqrt{46}$$
$$x = 1 - \frac{1}{2}i\sqrt{46}$$

3. Two roots.

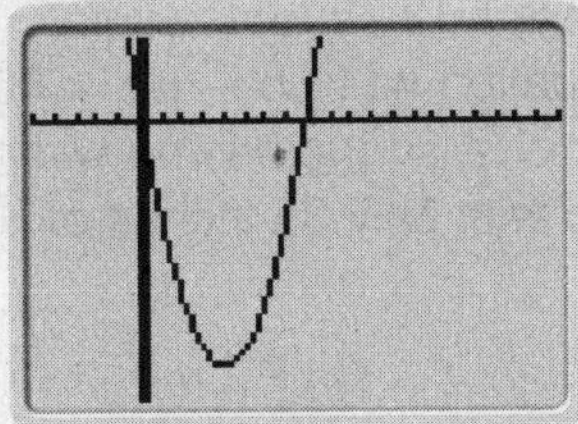

4. $f(x) = (x - 4)^2 + 3$
$$f(x) = x^2 - 8x + 16 + 3$$
$$f(x) = x^2 - 8x + 19$$

Lesson Practice 74

a. $16 + x^2 = 8x$
$$x^2 - 8x + 16 = 0$$
$$b^2 - 4ac = (-8)^2 - 4(1)(16) = 64 - 64 = 0$$
One real root.

b. $2x^2 + 12x + 23 = 0$
$$b^2 - 4ac = (12)^2 - 4(2)(23) = 144 - 184 < 0$$
Two complex roots.

c. $3x^2 - x = 14$
$$3x^2 - x - 14 = 0$$
$$b^2 - 4ac = (-1)^2 - 4(3)(-14) = 1 + 168 > 0$$
Two real roots.

d. $-16x^2 + 40x = 22$
$$16x^2 - 40x + 22 = 0$$
$$b^2 - 4ac = (-40)^2 - 4(16)(22) = 1600 - 1408 = 192$$
The discriminant is 192. Since it is positive, the equation $-16x^2 + 40x = 22$ has two real solutions, which are the times the ball would be at these heights.

e. $w(140 - w) = 4900$
$$140w - w^2 = 4900$$
$$w^2 - 140w + 4900 = 0$$
$$b^2 - 4ac = (-140)^2 - 4(1)(4900) = 19{,}600 - 19{,}600 = 0$$
The discriminant is 0. Since it is 0, the equation $w(140 - w) = 4900$ has exactly one solution which is the width needed.

f. $w(17.5 - w) = 80$

$17.5w - w^2 = 80$

$w^2 - 17.5w + 80 = 0$

$b^2 - 4ac = (-17.5)^2 - 4(1)(80)$

$= 306.25 - 320 = -13.75$

The discriminant is -13.75. Since it is negative, the equation $w(17.5 - w) = 80$ has no real solutions, so there is no width that can be used with only 35 inches of framing material.

g. $y = -16x^2 + vx + h$

$y = -16x^2 + 140x$

$275 = -16x^2 + 140x$

$16x^2 - 140x + 275 = 0$

$b^2 - 4ac = (-140)^2 - 4(16)(275)$

$= 19{,}600 - 17{,}600 = 2000 > 0$

Since the discriminant is positive, the firework set off by the first technician will reach a height 275 feet above the ground.

$y = -16x^2 + vx + h$

$y = -16x^2 + 120x + 15$

$275 = -16x^2 + 120x + 15$

$16x^2 - 120x + 260 = 0$

$b^2 - 4ac = (-120)^2 - 4(16)(260)$

$= 14{,}400 - 16{,}640 = -2240 < 0$

The discriminant is negative so the firework set off by the second technician does not achieve a height of 275 feet.

Practice 74

1.

-1	1	0	0	0	-2
	↓	-1	1	-1	1
	1	-1	1	-1	(−1)

$-1 = -(x + 1) \cdot \frac{1}{x+1}$, so the answer is $x^3 - x^2 + x - 1 - \frac{1}{x+1}$.

2.

5	1	0	0	-2
	↓	5	25	125
	1	5	25	(123)

$123 = (x - 5) \cdot \frac{123}{x-5}$, so the answer is $x^2 + 5x + 25 + \frac{123}{x-5}$.

3. For x between 0 and 1, the value $y = e^x$ is greatest, followed by $y = x$, $y = x^2$ and $y = x^3$ in that order. At $x = 1$, $y = e^x$ achieves a value of e while the polynomial functions all intersect at (1, 1). For $x > 1$, $y = x$ maintains a constant growth rate which is lower than the other functions. $y = x^3$ will always have a higher growth rate than $y = x^2$ because $x^3 > x^2$ for all x. Initially, $y = e^x$ has a lower growth rate than the polynomials of degree 2 and 3 but eventually, $y = e^x$ will have a greater growth rate than both $y = x^3$ and $y = x^2$.

4. $y = -5x^2 + 32x + 1$

$58 = -5x^2 + 32x + 1$

$0 = -5x^2 + 32x - 57$

$b^2 - 4ac = (32)^2 - 4(-5)(-57)$

$= 1024 - 1140 = -116 < 0$

The discriminant is -116 so there are no solutions. The flare does not reach the height of 58 meters.

5. $1696 = V = \pi r^2 h = \pi r^2(r + 9) = \pi(r^3 + 9r^2)$

$r^3 + 9r^2 = \frac{1696}{\pi} \approx 540$

$0 = r^3 + 9r^2 - 540$

6. Coterminal angles $= \theta + 360°\, n$, where n is an integer.

$40° = 400° + 360°(-1)$ and

$-320° = 400° + 360°(-2)$.

7. A. $x - 4$ is not a factor because

$P(4) = (4)^3 + 9(4)^2 + 2(4) - 48$

$= 64 + 144 + 8 - 48 = 168$

8. $5 + 13 + 20 + 2 = 40$

$\frac{5}{40} \cdot \frac{20}{39} \approx 6.4\%$

9. $1700 = 85(I)^{12}$

$\frac{1700}{85} = (I)^{12}$

$20 = (I)^{12}$

$\sqrt[12]{20} = I$

$I \approx 1.284$

$85(1.284)^{130} \approx 1.10 \times 10^{16}$

10. The solutions are rational if the discriminant is a perfect square. The solutions are irrational when the discriminant is positive and not a perfect square.

11. $2(3i) = 6i = 0 + 6i$

12. Let d be the diameter.

$10(d\pi) = 10(25\pi) = 250\pi$ inches.

$\frac{250\pi}{12} \approx 65.4$ feet.

The car travels 65 feet.

13. $\sqrt{9x} + 11 = 14$

$\sqrt{9x} = 14 - 11$

$\sqrt{9x} = 3$

$9x = 3^2$

$x = 1$

14. $-4\sqrt{x} - 6 = -20$

$-4\sqrt{x} = -20 + 6$

$-4\sqrt{x} = -14$

$\sqrt{x} = \frac{-14}{-4}$

$x = \frac{14^2}{4^2}$

$x = \frac{196}{16}$

$x = 12\frac{1}{4}$

15. Exact answers can only be found when the solutions are rational. If the solutions are irrational, they can only be estimated. They cannot be found at all if the solutions are complex numbers.

16. $E = I(Z)$

$265 - 135i = (26 - 30i)Z$

$\frac{265 - 135i}{26 - 30i} = Z$

$Z = \frac{265 - 135i}{26 - 30i} \cdot \frac{26 + 30i}{26 + 30i}$

$Z = \frac{265(26) + 265(30i) - 135i(26) - 135i(30i)}{26^2 - (30i)^2}$

$Z = \frac{6890 + 7950i - 3510i + 4050}{676 + 900}$

$Z = \frac{10{,}940 + 4440i}{1576}$

$Z = \frac{10{,}940}{1576} + \frac{4440i}{1576}$

$Z = \frac{2735}{394} + \frac{555}{197}i$ ohms.

17. $m\angle Y = 180° - (70° + 40°) = 70°$

Then $\triangle XYZ$ is an isosceles triangle.

$z = y = 33$ cm.

$\frac{\sin 70°}{33} = \frac{\sin 40°}{x}$

$x = \frac{33 \sin 40°}{\sin 70°}$

$x \approx 22.6$

Perimeter $\approx 22.6 + 33 + 33 \approx 88.6$ cm.

18. Student A made the error. The real terms of complex numbers are not added to the complex terms because they are not like terms. The real terms are added only to the real terms and the imaginary terms are added only to the imaginary terms.

19. Somerset, Lincoln, Knox, Androscoggin, and Penobscot because you sift through consecutive two-digit numbers and note down the first five counties whose corresponding two-digit number you find.

20. Convenience sampling caters to the biased preferences of the person conducting the survey.

Answer Choice **C**

21. $\frac{1}{2} \cdot \frac{1}{2} = \frac{1}{4}$

22. Exponential and logarithmic operations are inverse operations.

23. $3y^5 - 48y^3 = 3y^3(y^2 - 16)$

$= 3y^3(y - 4)(y + 4)$

24. $x^3 + x^2 + x + 1 = (x^3 + x^2) + (x + 1)$

$= x^2(x + 1) + 1(x + 1)$

$= (x + 1)(x^2 + 1)$

25. a. $16x^2 = 25$

$16x^2 - 25 = 0.$

b. $b^2 - 4ac = 0^2 - 4(16)(-25) = 1600$

c. Because the discriminant is positive, there are two real solutions.

d. $x = \dfrac{-b \pm \sqrt{b^2 - 4ac}}{2a}$

$x = \dfrac{-0 \pm \sqrt{1600}}{2(16)}$

$x = \pm\dfrac{40}{32}$

Then $x = 1.25$ and $x = -1.25$.

26. Using the special case triangle with hypotenuse $\sqrt{2}$ and side lengths 1,

$\dfrac{1}{\sqrt{2}} = \dfrac{x}{120} = \dfrac{y}{130}$.

$x = \dfrac{120}{\sqrt{2}} \approx 84.9$

$y = \dfrac{130}{\sqrt{2}} \approx 91.9$

Then each leg is about 85 to 92 cm long.

27. $x^2 = 16$

$x^3 = 64$

$x^4 = 256$

$x^5 = 1024$

There are extraneous solutions when both sides are raised to the second and fourth powers. Raising both sides to an even power could generate extraneous solutions.

28. a. $f(g(1)) = \text{Tan}(\text{Tan}^{-1}(1)) = \text{Tan}\left(\frac{\pi}{4}\right) = 1$.

$g\left(f\left(\frac{\pi}{4}\right)\right) = \text{Tan}^{-1}\left(\text{Tan}\left(\frac{\pi}{4}\right)\right) = \text{Tan}^{-1}(1) = \frac{\pi}{4}$.

b. $f(g(x)) = x$.

c. $f^{-1}(f(x)) = f(f^{-1}(x)) = x$.

29. a. $\dfrac{64}{64 + 81} = \dfrac{64}{145} \approx 45\%$

b. $\dfrac{64}{64 + 52 + 82} = \dfrac{64}{198} \approx 33\%$

30. In the second factor, the sign of the second term is the opposite of the sign between the terms in the first factor.

LESSON 75

Warm Up 75

1. inverse.

2. True.

3. All real numbers.

Lesson Practice 75

a. The domain of $y = \sqrt{3x - 2}$ is $x \geq \frac{2}{3}$ because $3\left(\frac{2}{3}\right) - 2 = 0$.

The range is $y \geq 0$.

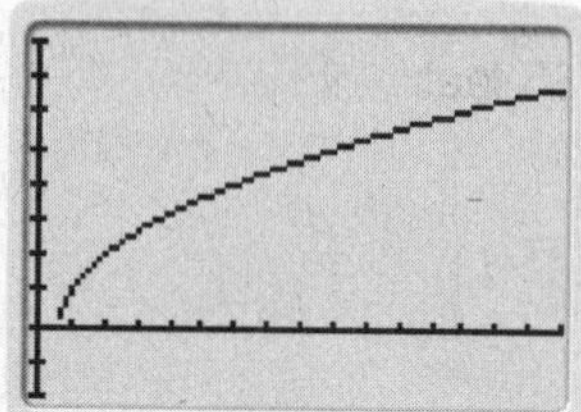

$x = \sqrt{3y + 2}$

$x^2 = 3y - 2$

$y = \dfrac{x^2 + 2}{3}$

The inverse is $y = \frac{1}{3}x^2 + \frac{2}{3}$.

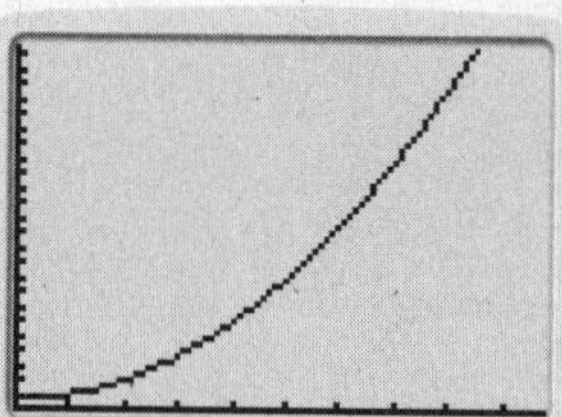

The domain is $x \geq 0$ and the range is $y \geq \frac{2}{3}$.

b. The domain of $y = (4x + 9)^{\frac{1}{2}}$ is $x \geq -\frac{9}{4}$ because $4\left(-\frac{9}{4}\right) + 9 = 0$

The range is $y \geq 0$.

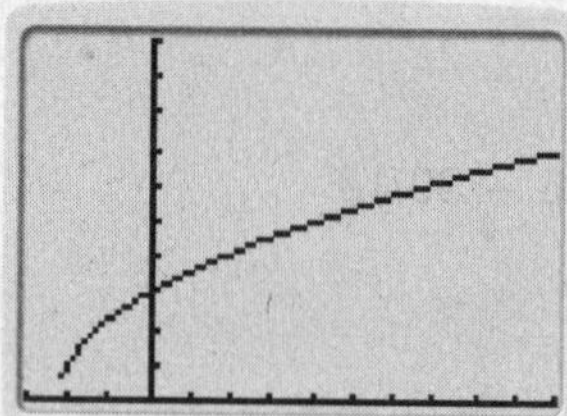

$x = (4y + 9)^{\frac{1}{2}}$

$x^2 = 4y + 9$

$4y = x^2 - 9$

The inverse is $y = \frac{1}{4}x^2 - \frac{9}{4}$, which is graphed below.

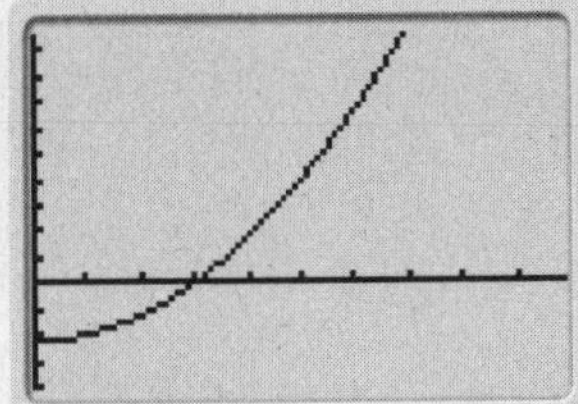

The domain of the inverse is $x \geq 0$ and the range is $y \geq -\frac{9}{4}$.

c. $y = \sqrt[3]{4x + 3}$

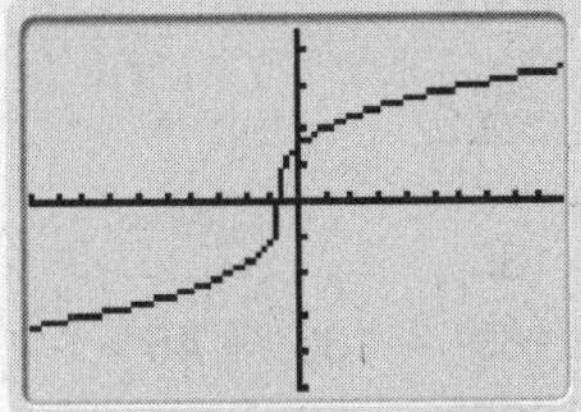

$$x = \sqrt[3]{4y + 3}$$
$$x^3 = 4y + 3$$
$$4y = x^3 - 3$$

The inverse is $y = \frac{1}{4}x^3 - \frac{3}{4}$.

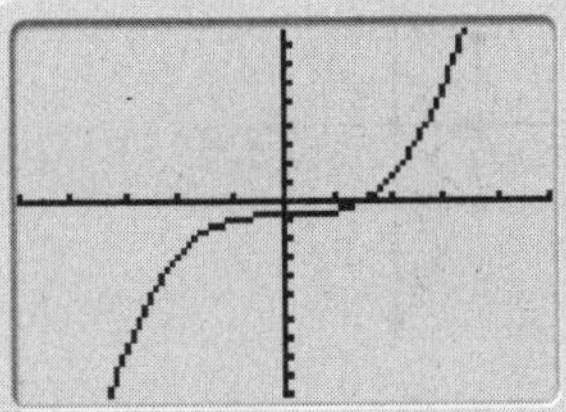

d. The graph of $y = (5x - 4)^{\frac{1}{3}} + 7$

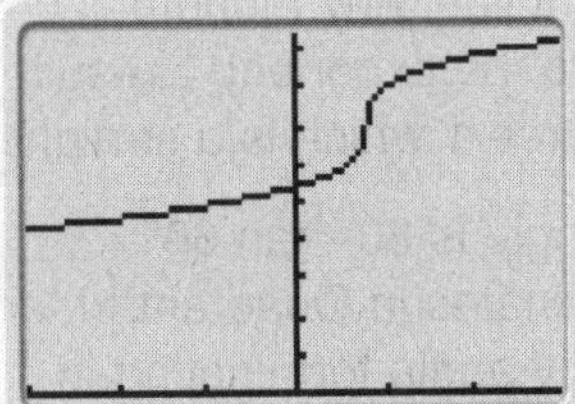

$$x = (5y - 4)^{\frac{1}{3}} + 7$$
$$x - 7 = (5y - 4)^{\frac{1}{3}}$$
$$(x - 7)^3 = 5y - 4$$
$$5y = (x - 7)^3 + 4$$

The inverse is $y = \frac{1}{5}(x - 7)^3 + \frac{4}{5}$ and its graph is.

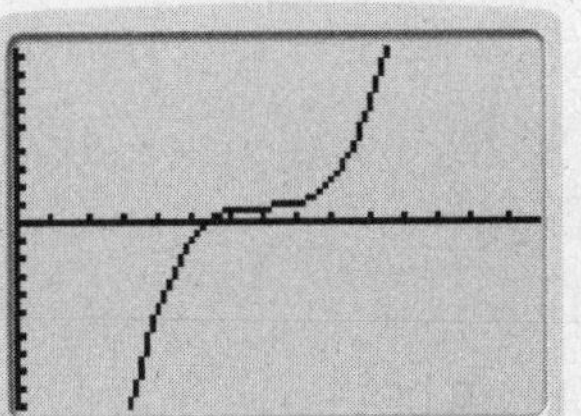

e. $f(x) = \sqrt{3x - 1} + \sqrt[3]{4x + 9}$

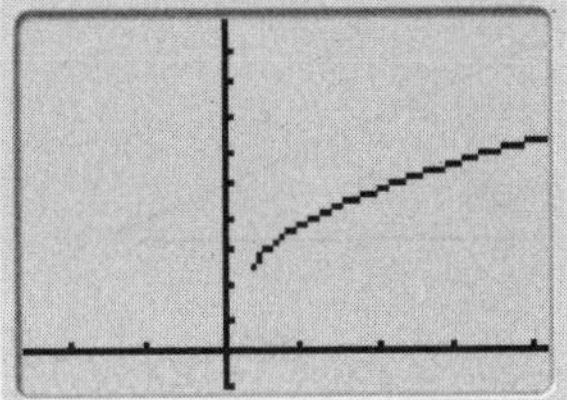

$\sqrt{3x - 1}$ is only defined for $x \geq \frac{1}{3}$, and since $\sqrt[3]{4x + 9}$ is defined for all x, $f(x)$ is defined only for $x \geq \frac{1}{3}$. Thus, the domain is $x \geq \frac{1}{3}$.

Since

$$f\left(\frac{1}{3}\right) = \sqrt{3 \cdot \frac{1}{3} - 1} + \sqrt[3]{4 \cdot \frac{1}{3} + 9} = 0$$

$+ \sqrt[3]{\frac{4}{3} + \frac{27}{3}} = \sqrt[3]{\frac{31}{3}}$, the range is $y \geq \sqrt[3]{\frac{31}{3}}$.

f. $y = \dfrac{\sqrt{6^2 + (x - 7)^2}}{4}$

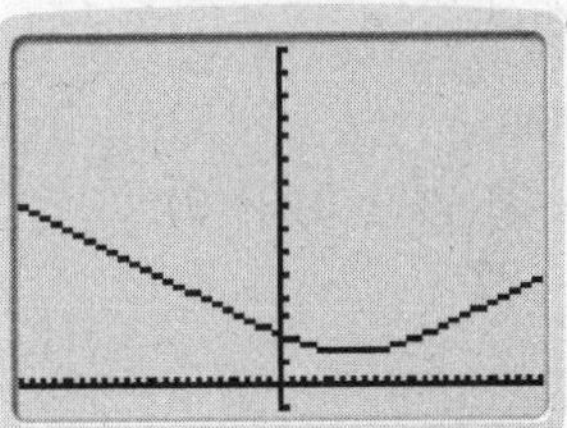

$$3 = \frac{\sqrt{6^2 + (x - 7)^2}}{4}$$
$$12 = \sqrt{6^2 + (x - 7)^2}$$
$$144 = 6^2 + (x - 7)^2$$
$$144 - 36 = (x - 7)^2$$
$$108 = (x - 7)^2$$
$$\pm\sqrt{108} = x - 7$$
$$x = \pm\sqrt{108} + 7$$

The function intersects $y = 3$ at $\left(-\sqrt{108} + 7, 3\right)$ and $\left(\sqrt{108} + 7, 3\right)$

Practice 75

1. $\sin 120° = \frac{h}{7}$

$h = 7\sin 120°$

$h \approx 6.06$

$\text{Area} = \frac{bh}{2} \approx \frac{(11)(6.06)}{2} \approx 33.3$

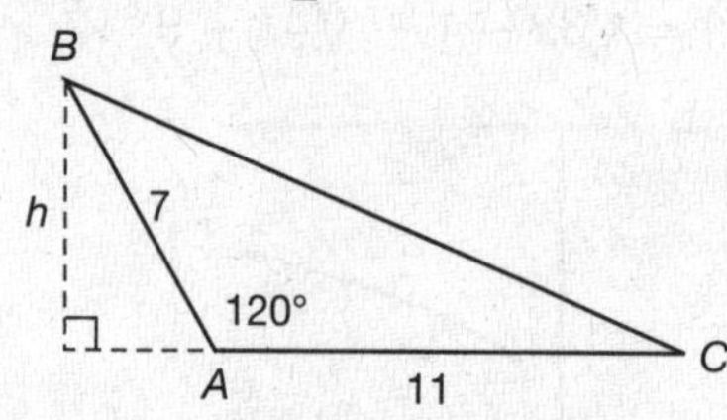

2. $0 = 2x^3 - 4x^2 + 2x = 2x(x^2 - 2x + 1)$
$= 2x(x - 1)^2$

Then $x = 0$ with multiplicity of 1 and $x = 1$ with multiplicity of 2.

3. $\frac{a}{3} = ae^{-0.119t}$

$\frac{a}{3 \cdot a} = \frac{ae^{-0.119t}}{a}$

$\frac{1}{3} = e^{-0.119t}$

$\ln\left(\frac{1}{3}\right) = \ln\left(e^{-0.119t}\right)$

$-1.099 \approx -0.119t$

$t \approx 9.2$ hours.

4. **a.** Switch variables

$x = (y - 3)(y^2 + 3y + 9)$

$x = y^3 - 27$

$x + 27 = y^3$

$y = \sqrt[3]{x + 27}$

b. The domain and the range are the set of all real numbers.

5. Student B made the error. The radicand is the sum of the squares, not the difference of the squares.

6. $y = -4.9x^2 + 45x + 1$

$93 = -4.9x^2 + 45x + 1$

$0 = -4.9x^2 + 45x - 92$

$b^2 - 4ac = 45^2 - 4(-4.9)(-92)$

$= 2025 - 1803.2 = 221.8 > 0$

The discriminant is 221.8 so there are two real solutions. Thus, a piece of confetti will reach the top of the statue.

7. $r = \sqrt{\frac{A}{\pi}}$

$9 = \sqrt{\frac{A}{\pi}}$

$81 = \frac{A}{\pi}$

$A = 81\pi$

$A \approx 254.5$ square inches.

8. $2\cos\theta + \sqrt{2} = 0$

$2\cos\theta = -\sqrt{2}$

$\cos\theta = -\frac{\sqrt{2}}{2}$

$\theta = 135°$

$\alpha = 180° - 135° = 45°$

$135° + 2(45°) = 225°$

$\cos 225° = -\frac{\sqrt{2}}{2}$

Answer Choice **D**; $\{135°, 225°\}$.

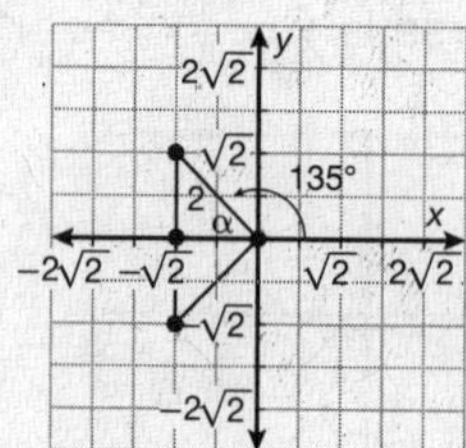

9. It is a monomial of degree n or a constant function. Any constant function taken to the exponent $\frac{1}{n}$ results in a constant function which is a straight line. Any monomial of degree n taken to the exponent $\frac{1}{n}$ results in a monomial of degree 1 which is a straight line.

10. The reference angle is 60°. $\tan 60° = \sqrt{3}$, 240° terminates in Quadrant III, and the tangent of any angle terminating in Quadrant III is positive, so $\tan 240° = \sqrt{3}$.

11. $\frac{18}{18 + 5 + 3} \approx 69.2\%$.

12. **a.** $\tan 60° = \frac{y}{8}$

$y = 8 \tan 60°$

$y = 8\sqrt{3}$

$\cos 60° = \dfrac{8}{x}$

$x = \dfrac{8}{\cos 60°}$

$x = 16$

b. $\sin 60° = \dfrac{AD}{8}$

$AD = 8 \sin 60°$

$AD = 4\sqrt{3}$

$\cos 60° = \dfrac{DC}{8}$

$DC = 8 \cos 60°$

$DC = 4$

13. Triangulation is the process of finding a certain distance when the angles formed from the imaginary line connecting two fixed points a known distance apart and the lines from the fixed points to the object are known.

14. Let V be volume, A_b be the area of the base and h be height.

$V = A_b h$

$6x^3 + 69x^2 + 3x - 330 = A_b(x + 11)$

$A_b = \dfrac{(6x^3 + 69x^2 + 3x - 330)}{(x + 11)}$

−11	6	69	3	−330
	↓	−66	−33	330
	6	3	−30	0

$A_b = 6x^2 + 3x - 30.$

15. $\left(-1 + \sqrt{-9}\right) - \left(-1 - \sqrt{-64}\right)$

$= \left(-1 + i\sqrt{9}\right) - \left(-1 - i\sqrt{64}\right)$

$= -1 + 3i + 1 + 8i = 11i.$

16. $t = \dfrac{-b \pm \sqrt{b^2 - 4ac}}{2a}$

$t = \dfrac{-50 \pm \sqrt{50^2 - 4(-16)(10)}}{2(-16)}$

$t = \dfrac{-50 \pm \sqrt{2500 + 640}}{-32}$

$t = \dfrac{-50 + \sqrt{3140}}{-32} \approx -0.189$

This is inadmissible because time cannot be negative.

$t = \dfrac{-50 - \sqrt{3140}}{-32} \approx 3.31$ seconds.

17. Yes,

$P(6) = 6^3 - 10(6^2) + 19(6) + 30$

$= 216 - 360 + 114 + 30 = 0$

18. No,

$P(4) = 3(4^3) - 2(4^2) - 61(4) - 20$

$= 192 - 32 - 244 - 20 = -104 \neq 0$

19. For root r, the multiplicity of r, is the number of times the factor $x - r$ occurs when the polynomial in the polynomial equation, when written in standard form, is completely factored.

20. $\log_{10} 100{,}000 = 5$

$10^5 = 100{,}000.$

21. $\log_4 1024 = 5$

$4^5 = 1024.$

22. Student B incorrectly takes the fourth root of x on the left side of the equation while raising the right side to the fourth power.

23.

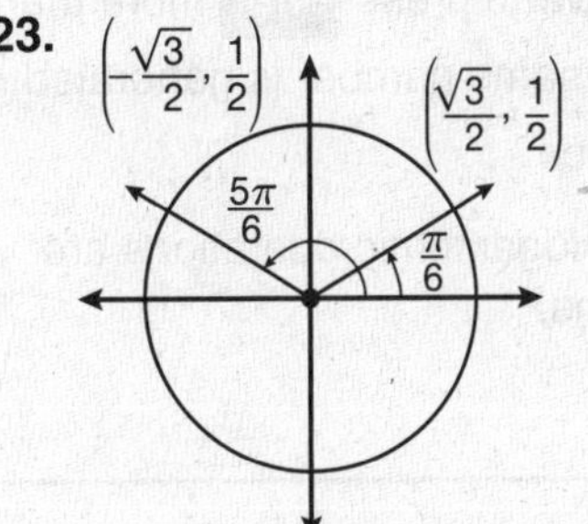

Using the y-coordinates of the points on the unit circle, $\sin \frac{\pi}{6} = \frac{1}{2}$. Therefore, because sin is a periodic function, $\sin^{-1}\left(\frac{1}{2}\right) = \frac{\pi}{6} + 2\pi n$, where n is an integer.

Also, using the unit circle, $\sin \frac{5\pi}{6} = \frac{1}{2}$. Therefore, $\sin^{-1}\left(\frac{1}{2}\right) = \frac{5\pi}{6} + 2\pi n$, where n is an integer.

24. There are 10 integers that are multiples of 10 between 1 and 100. There are 40 numbers larger than 60 between 1 and 100.

$\dfrac{10}{100} \cdot \dfrac{40}{100} = \dfrac{1}{10} \cdot \dfrac{2}{5} = \dfrac{1}{25}$

The probability is $\frac{1}{25}$.

25. The correct choice is **D**, because a negative discriminant results in two complex solutions.

26. $\log_6 \frac{5}{8} = \frac{\log \frac{5}{8}}{\log 6} \approx \frac{-0.204}{0.778} \approx -0.263$

27. $\log_6 40 = \frac{\log 40}{\log 6} \approx \frac{1.602}{0.778} = 2.059$

28. $x^2 + 8x = -25$

$x^2 + 8x + 25 = 0$

$x = \frac{-b \pm \sqrt{b^2 - 4ac}}{2a}$

$x = \frac{-8 \pm \sqrt{8^2 - 4(1)(25)}}{2(1)}$

$x = \frac{-8 \pm \sqrt{64 - 100}}{2}$

$x = \frac{-8 \pm \sqrt{-36}}{2}$

$x = \frac{-8 \pm 6i}{2}$

$x = -4 \pm 3i$, the correct choice is **C**.

29. a. Answers will vary. See student work.

b. You would have to press ENTER more than 3 times if the same number is generated more than once.

30. Exponential and logarithmic operations are inverse operations.

LESSON 76

Warm Up 76

1. factor

2. $2x^2 - 12x = 2x(x - 6)$

3. $x = \frac{-b \pm \sqrt{b^2 - 4ac}}{2a}$ with $a = 5$, $b = -12$, and $c = 13$

$x = \frac{12 \pm \sqrt{12^2 - 4(5)(13)}}{2(5)}$

$x = \frac{12 \pm \sqrt{144 - 260}}{10}$

$x \approx \frac{12 \pm 10.77i}{10}$

$x \approx 1.2 + 1.077i$ or $1.2 - 1.077i$

Lesson Practice 76

a. For $0 = 4x(2x - 7)(x + 9)$:

$4x = 0 \quad 2x - 7 = 0 \quad x + 9 = 0$

$x = 0 \quad x = \frac{7}{2} \quad x = -9$

b. For $0 = 7x^3 - 8x^2 + 3x$:

$0 = x(7x^2 - 8x + 3)$

$x = 0$, and the remaining zeros are complex.

c. For $0 = -9x^3 + 11x^2 + 4x$:

$0 = x(-9x^2 + 11x + 4)$

$x = 0$, and using the quadratic formula for $-9x^2 + 11x + 4 = 0$:

$x = \frac{-b \pm \sqrt{b^2 - 4ac}}{2a}$

$x = \frac{-11 \pm \sqrt{11^2 - 4(-9)(4)}}{2(-9)}$

$x = \frac{-11 \pm \sqrt{121 + 144}}{-18}$

$x \approx \frac{-11 \pm 16.2788}{-18}$

$x \approx 1.5155$ or $x \approx -0.2933$.

d. $0 = (x + 4)(x^2 - 4x - 10)$

$x + 4 = 0$ or $x^2 - 4x - 10 = 0$

$x = -4$, and using the quadratic formula for $x^2 - 4x - 10 = 0$:

$x = \frac{-b \pm \sqrt{b^2 - 4ac}}{2a}$

$x = \frac{4 \pm \sqrt{(-4)^2 - 4(1)(-10)}}{2(1)}$

$x = \frac{4 \pm \sqrt{16 + 40}}{2}$

$x \approx \frac{4 \pm 7.4833}{2}$

$x \approx 5.7417$ or $x \approx -1.7417$

e. $0 = (x - 12)(4x^2 - 7x + 5)$

$x - 12 = 0$ or $4x^2 - 7x + 5 = 0$

$x = 12$, and the remaining zeros are complex.

f. $0 = 4x^4 - 6x^3 + 3x^2 - 7x$

$0 = x(4x^3 - 6x^2 + 3x - 7)$

$x = 0$, and graphing the cubic function to identify additional roots:

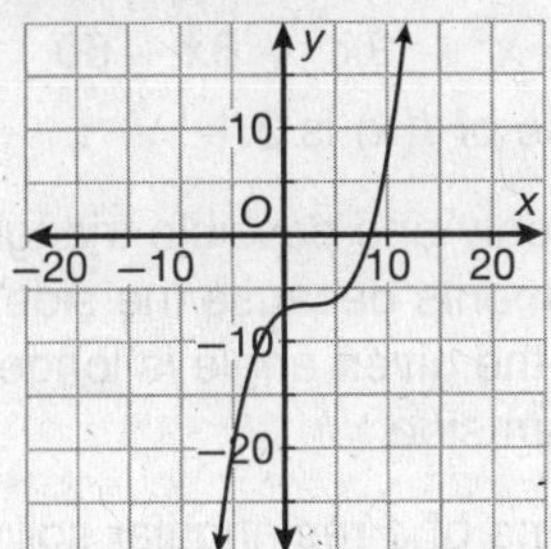

The only other root is 1.6757.

g. $h = -4.9t^2 + 18t + 35$. Finding when the ball hits the ground means solving for t when $h = 0$. $0 = -4.9t^2 + 18t + 35$. Using the quadratic formula:

$$t = \frac{-b \pm \sqrt{b^2 - 4ac}}{2a}$$

$$t = \frac{-18 \pm \sqrt{18^2 - 4(-4.9)(35)}}{2(-4.9)}$$

$$t = \frac{-18 \pm \sqrt{324 + 686}}{-9.8}$$

$$t \approx \frac{-18 \pm 31.78}{-9.8}$$

$t \approx -1.41$ or 5.08

Select the positive quantity. Therefore, the ball will hit the ground approximately 5.08 seconds after it was thrown.

Practice 76

1. $f(g(x)) = (x + 1)^2 - 4$

$= x^2 + 2x - 3$

$= (x + 3)(x - 1)$

The roots of this function will occur when $(x + 3)(x - 1) = 0$ or at $x = -3$ and $x = 1$.

2. For the inverse, interchange x and y, and solve for y:

$x = -2y^5 - 10$

$\frac{x + 10}{-2} = y^5$

$y = \sqrt[5]{-0.5x - 5}$

3. Since $V = s^3$ for a cube of side length s, $s = \sqrt[3]{V}$ or $s = \sqrt[3]{\frac{x^3}{3} - 9}$.

The new length of each side of the cube is $s = \sqrt[3]{\frac{x^3}{3} - 9}$.

4. $\sin(270°) = -1$, $\cos(270°) = 0$, and $\tan(270°)$ is undefined.

5. For the inverse, interchange x and y, and solve for y:

$x = 4y^2 + 12$

$x - 12 = 4y^2$

$\frac{x - 12}{4} = y^2$

$y = \pm\sqrt{0.25x - 3}$

6. $x^3 - 6x^2 + 11x - 6$ factors to $(x - 3)(x - 1)(x - 2)$. Therefore, $(x - 4)$ is not a factor, and the correct answer is **A**.

7. $y^2 = (x + 1)^2 + (x + 2)^2$

$y^2 = x^2 + 2x + 1 + x^2 + 4x + 4$

$y^2 = 2x^2 + 6x + 5$

$y = \sqrt{2x^2 + 6x + 5}$

When $x = 2$, the triangle is a 3-4-5 Pythagorean triple triangle.

8. Since the relationship between the period and the length of the pendulum is a radical involving a square root, in order for the period to double, the length of the pendulum would need to increase by a factor of 4 (as $\sqrt{4} = 2$).

9. 3 breeding pairs of rats = 6 rats in total. As well, 6300% means $\frac{6300}{100}$ or 63 as the growth factor for the year. With time in years, the function to model the population after t years is $y = 6 \cdot 63^t$.

10. The reporter took a sample of the population who were at the basketball game, thus potentially skewing the results toward people in the population that would be in favor of a new and improved stadium. The reporter should not apply the findings of this sample to the whole population.

11. First rearrange into $P(x) = 2x^3 + x^2 - 72x - 36 = 0$. By the RRT, all possible rational roots will be of the form $\frac{\text{(factor of } -36)}{\text{(factor of 2)}}$. The only option that fits these conditions is 9. Therefore, the correct answer is **B**.

12. a. $60 = 10\log\frac{I}{I_o}$, so $6 = \log\frac{I}{I_o}$. Rearranging, we obtain:

$$10^6 = \frac{I}{10^{-12}} \text{ so } I = 10^6 \times 10^{-12}$$
$$= 10^{-6} \text{ or } 0.000001.$$

The intensity of a sound of 60 decibels is 0.000001 watt per square meter.

b. $120 = 10\log\frac{I}{I_o}$, so $12 = \log\frac{I}{I_o}$.
Rearranging, we obtain:

$$10^{12} = \frac{I}{10^{-12}} \text{ so } I = 10^{12} \times 10^{-12}$$
$$= 10^0 \text{ or } 1.$$

The intensity of a sound with a loudness of 120 decibels is 1 watt per square meter.

c. From a. and b., we have

$10^6 = \frac{I_1}{I_o}$ or $I_1 = 10^6 I_o$ and

$10^{12} = \frac{I_2}{I_o}$ or $I_2 = 10^{12} I_o$. Dividing these two expressions will give us our factor:

$$\frac{I_2}{I_1} = \frac{10^{12} I_o}{10^6 I_o} = 10^6 \text{ or } 1{,}000{,}000.$$

When the loudness doubles, the intensity increases by a factor of 1,000,000.

13. There are 5 thoroughbreds, 6 quarter horses, and 21 horses in total. To find the probability:

$$\left(\frac{5}{21}\right)\left(\frac{6}{20}\right) = \frac{30}{420}$$
$$\approx 0.0714 \text{ or } 7.14\%.$$

The probability of one thoroughbred and one quarter horse being chosen is about 7.14%.

14. a. $0 = (x - 5)(x^2 - 12) + (x - 5)(-3x - x)$

$0 = (x - 5)[(x^2 - 12) + (-4x)]$

$0 = (x - 5)(x^2 - 4x - 12)$

$0 = (x - 5)(x - 6)(x + 2)$

$x - 5 = 0, \quad x - 6 = 0, \quad x + 2 = 0$

$x = 5 \quad x = 6 \quad x = -2$

b. Three x-intercepts

c. $f(x) = (x - 5)(x^2 - 12) + (x - 5)(-3x - x)$

$f(x) = (x - 5)(x^2 - 4x - 12)$

$f(x) = x^3 - 4x^2 - 12x - 5x^2 + 20x + 60$

$f(x) = x^3 - 9x^2 + 8x + 60$

Degree of $f(x)$ is 3.

15. There is only one possible triangle for these measurements because the side that is opposite the given angle is longer than the other given side.

16. The volume of a rectangular solid can be found using $V = lwh$. The volume is given by the expression $x^3 - 2x^2 - 40x - 64$, and given the length of $x - 8$, we are given a factor of the expression. We can find the other factors by first performing the polynomial division:

$$\begin{array}{r} x^2 + 6x + 8 \\ x - 8 \overline{) x^3 - 2x^2 - 40x - 64} \\ \underline{-(x^3 - 8x^2)} \\ 6x^2 - 40x \\ \underline{-(6x^2 - 48x)} \\ 8x - 64 \\ \underline{-(8x - 64)} \\ 0 \end{array}$$

Therefore,

$x^3 - 2x^2 - 40x - 64 = (x - 8)(x^2 + 6x + 8)$
$= (x - 8)(x + 2)(x + 4)$

17.

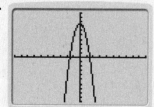

By the display on the graphing calculator, the function crosses the x-axis twice, therefore there are two real solutions.

18. The expression on the left side was not properly squared. $(x - 2)^2 = x^2 - 4x + 4$, not $x^2 - 4$.

19. $h = -16t^2 + 96t + 180.4$. The object will hit the ground when $h = 0$, so we need to solve $0 = -16t^2 + 96t + 180.4$ using the quadratic:

$$t = \frac{-b \pm \sqrt{b^2 - 4ac}}{2a}$$

$$t = \frac{-96 \pm \sqrt{96^2 - 4(-16)(180.4)}}{2(-16)}$$

$$t = \frac{-96 \pm \sqrt{20761.6}}{-32}$$

$$t \approx \frac{-96 \pm 144.09}{-32}$$

$t \approx 7.5$ and -1.5

We eliminate the negative solution and therefore we have a solution of $t \approx 7.5$ seconds.

20. In a 30-60-90 triangle, $\cos 60° = 0.5$. This means that $\cos^{-1}(0.5) = 60°$. The question asks for $\cos^{-1}(0.48)$, which means that the angle must be slightly larger than 60°. An estimate for the angle would be 61°.

21. The student did not rewrite the equation into $ax^2 + bx + c = 0$ (standard form). Therefore, the student is using $b = 5$ instead of $b = -1$ and $c = -1$ instead of $c = 5$.

$$x = \frac{-b \pm \sqrt{b^2 - 4ac}}{2a}$$

$$x = \frac{(-1) \pm \sqrt{-1^2 - 4(6)(5)}}{2(6)}$$

$$x = \frac{1 \pm \sqrt{1 - 120}}{12}$$

$$x = \frac{1 \pm \sqrt{119}\, i}{12}$$

The correct answer is $\frac{1}{12} \pm \frac{\sqrt{119}}{12}i$.

22. $\tan 31° = \frac{\text{height}}{25}$, therefore,

height $= 25 \tan 31° \approx 15$ ft

The tree is about 15 ft tall.

23. If $2\iota\sqrt{2}$ is the square root of -8, then squaring it should produce the result of -8:

$(2\iota\sqrt{2})^2 = 2^2(\iota)^2(\sqrt{2})^2$

$= 4(-1)(2) = -8$

24. $C(t) = 300e^{-0.42t}$

$70 = 300e^{-0.42t}$

$\frac{7}{30} = e^{-0.42t}$

$\ln\left(\frac{7}{30}\right) = -0.42t$

$$t = \frac{\ln\left(\frac{7}{30}\right)}{-0.42}$$

$t \approx 3.46$ hours

There will be 70 mg of medication in the patient's bloodstream after 3.46 hours.

25. If $f(x)$ has n zeros and $g(x)$ has m zeros, the only way for $f(x) \cdot g(x)$ to have $(m + n)$ zeros is when the zeros for each function are unique.

26. There are three odd numbers on a six-sided number cube. This means that the probability of rolling an odd number on one roll is $\frac{1}{2}$. Doing this on four consecutive rolls means that the probability would be $\left(\frac{1}{2}\right)^4 = \frac{1}{16}$. The probability of Mark rolling an odd number four times is $\frac{1}{16}$.

27. For $3x(2x - 9)(x + 5) = 0$:

$3x = 0$, $2x - 9 = 0$, and $x + 5 = 0$

$x = 0$, $x = \frac{9}{2}$, $x = -5$

28. There are two desired outcomes and $\binom{36}{5}$ total outcomes. Therefore, the probability can be found by calculating:

$$\text{Probability} = \frac{2}{\binom{36}{5}} = \frac{2}{\frac{36!}{31!5!}} = \frac{2}{376{,}992} = \frac{1}{188{,}496} \approx 0.000005$$

The probability of the teacher picking either the first 5 or the last 5 slides is about 0.000005.

29. $b^2 - 4ac = (-8)^2 - 4(1)(16) = 0$, therefore there is one real solution.

30. $b^2 - 4ac = (7)^2 - 4(1)(11) = 5$, therefore there are two real solutions.

LESSON 77

Warm Up 77

1. cosine
2. $\cos 45° = \frac{x}{5}$, so $x = 5 \cos 45° \approx 3.5$
3. Since $\cos 60° = 0.5$, $\cos A \approx 0.454$ will yield an angle that is a little larger than 60°. A good estimate of the angle would be 63°.
4. $m\angle C = 180° - 95° - 20° = 65°$. To find b, we can now use the Law of Sines:

$$\frac{b}{\sin 20°} = \frac{14}{\sin 65°}$$
$$b = \frac{14 \sin 20°}{\sin 65°} = 5.28$$
$$b \approx 5.28$$

Lesson Practice 77

a. $c^2 = a^2 + b^2 - 2ab \cos C$
$$c^2 = 13^2 + 20^2 - 2(13)(20)\cos 27°$$
$$c^2 \approx 105.67$$
$$c \approx 10.3$$

b. $e^2 = d^2 + f^2 - 2df \cos E$
$$e^2 = 35^2 + 80^2 - 2(35)(80)\cos 112°$$
$$e^2 \approx 9722.797$$
$$e \approx 98.6$$

$m\angle F$ can be found using the Law of Sines:

$$\frac{\sin F}{35} = \frac{\sin 112°}{98.6}$$
$$\sin F = \frac{35 \sin 112°}{98.6}$$
$$\sin F \approx 0.329$$
$$m\angle F \approx \sin^{-1}(0.329)$$
$$m\angle F \approx 19°$$

The final angle can be found using the property of the sum of the angles in a triangle:

$$112° + 19° + m\angle D = 180°$$
$$131 + m\angle D = 180°$$
$$m\angle D = 180° - 131°$$
$$m\angle D = 49°$$

c. $c^2 = a^2 + b^2 - 2ab\cos C$
$$18^2 = 30^2 + 14^2 - 2(30)(14)\cos C$$
$$324 = 1096 - 840 \cos C$$
$$-772 = -840 \cos C$$
$$\cos C = \frac{-772}{-840}$$
$$m\angle C \approx 23.2°$$

d. $g^2 = f^2 + h^2 - 2fh \cos G$
$$5^2 = 9.2^2 + 10.1^2 - 2(9.2)(10.1)\cos G$$
$$25 = 186.65 - 185.84 \cos G$$
$$-161.65 = -185.84 \cos G$$
$$\cos G = \frac{-161.65}{-185.84}$$
$$m\angle G \approx 29.6°$$

e. Using Heron's formula:
$s = \frac{1}{2}(4 + 15 + 12) = \frac{31}{2}$. We can now find the area:

$$A = \sqrt{\frac{31}{2}\left(\frac{31}{2} - 4\right)\left(\frac{31}{2} - 15\right)\left(\frac{31}{2} - 12\right)}$$
$$= \sqrt{\frac{4991}{16}}$$
$$\approx 17.7 \text{ in.}^2$$

f. The angle between the two vectors is $(75° + 60°) = 135°$. We can now use the Law of Cosines to find the separation distance of the two ships.

$$c^2 = a^2 + b^2 - 2ab \cos C$$
$$c^2 = 22^2 + 40^2 - 2(22)(40)\cos 135°$$
$$c^2 \approx 3328.5$$
$$c \approx 57.69 \text{ mi}$$

At a speed of 14 mph, the first boat will take $\frac{57.69}{14} \approx 4.1$ hours to reach the second boat.

Practice 77

1. $\left|x - 1\frac{3}{4}\right| = \frac{3}{8}$. To find the minimum safe thickness, we solve:

$$-\left(x - 1\frac{3}{4}\right) = \frac{3}{8}$$
$$x - 1\frac{3}{4} = -\frac{3}{8}$$
$$x = -\frac{3}{8} + \frac{7}{4}$$
$$x = -\frac{3}{8} + \frac{14}{8}$$

$$x = \frac{11}{8}$$

$$x = 1\frac{3}{8} \text{ in.}$$

2. $\log_3 2187 = 7$

3. $\log_{12} 144 = 2$

4. $7r^2 - 5 = 2r + 9r^2$

$7r^2 - 9r^2 - 2r - 5 = 0$

$-2r^2 - 2r - 5 = 0$ or $2r^2 + 2r + 5 = 0$

The discriminant can now be found using $a = 2$, $b = 2$, and $c = 5$:

$b^2 - 4ac$

$= (2)^2 - 4(2)(5)$

$= 4 - 40$

$= -36$

Therefore, there are two imaginary solutions.

5. $6 \ln x + 4 \ln y$

$= \ln x^6 + \ln y^4$

$= \ln x^6y^4$

6. $\ln 40 + 2 \ln \frac{1}{2} + \ln x$

$= \ln 40 + \ln\left(\frac{1}{2}\right)^2 + \ln x$

$= \ln 40 + \ln\left(\frac{1}{4}\right) + \ln x$

$= \ln\left(40 \times \frac{1}{4} \times x\right)$

$= \ln(10x)$

7. The student is correct because when isolating C in $-2abc\cos C$, we will divide by $-2bc$, which is negative.

8. $\tan 60° = \frac{x}{8}$ or $x = 8\tan 60° = 8\sqrt{3}$

$\cos 60° = \frac{8}{y}$ or $y = \frac{8}{\cos 60°} = 16$

9. $y = \left((x^3 + 2x^2 + 4)^{\frac{1}{3}}\right)^{\frac{1}{4}}$ so

$y = (x^3 + 2x^2 + 4)^{\frac{1}{12}}$

Therefore, the correct answer is **A**.

10. $\dfrac{\binom{334}{4}}{\binom{563}{4}} = \dfrac{509{,}267{,}001}{4{,}141{,}754{,}540} \approx 0.1229$ or $\approx 12.3\%$

The probability that all four students are freshmen is about 12.3%.

11. First, use the formula for the distance between two points to find the length of each side of the triangle:

$\sqrt{64 + 144}$ ≈ 14.42 $\quad \sqrt{81 + 16}$ ≈ 9.85 $\quad \sqrt{1 + 64}$ ≈ 8.06

Then, use Heron's formula to find s:

$s = \frac{1}{2}(14.42 + 9.85 + 8.06) = 16.165$. We can now find the area:

$A = \sqrt{16.165(16.165 - 14.42)(16.165 - 9.85)(16.165 - 8.06)}$

$= \sqrt{16.165(1.745)(6.315)(8.015)} \approx 38$

12. $N = \frac{n}{m}M$ or $N = \frac{nM}{m}$

13. The student should have calculated $-2i^2$ to be 2. Therefore, $4 + 7i - 2i^2 = 4 + 7i + 2$ or $6 + 7i$.

14. AC and CA are not equivalent because matrix multiplication is not commutative.

15. $y = \frac{2}{9}x + b$. Substituting the given point for x and y, we can calculate the value of b:

$-3 = \frac{2}{9}(5) + b$

$-\frac{27}{9} - \frac{10}{9} = b$

$b = -\frac{37}{9}$

So, $y = \frac{2}{9}x - \frac{37}{9}$

16. Since $i^{18} = (i^2)^9$

$= (-1)^9$

$= -1$ (which is not 1), the correct answer is **A.**

17. Use Heron's formula to find s:
$s = \frac{1}{2}(14 + 15 + 21) = 25$. We can now find the area:

$A = \sqrt{25(25 - 14)(25 - 15)(25 - 21)}$
$= \sqrt{25(11)(10)(4)}$
$\approx 104.9 \text{ ft}^2$

The area of the triangle is about 104.9 ft^2.

18. The terminal arm of the angle is in the second quadrant where only sine and cosecant are positive. As well, the terminal arm containing $(-5, 5)$ makes a 45° angle to the x-axis, so:

$\sin\theta = \frac{\sqrt{2}}{2}$ $\quad \csc\theta = \sqrt{2}$

$\cos\theta = -\frac{\sqrt{2}}{2}$ $\quad \sec\theta = -\sqrt{2}$

$\tan\theta = -1$ $\quad \cot\theta = -1$

19. a. $V = x^2(x + 8)$
$325 = x^2(x + 8)$ or $x^3 + 8x^2 - 325 = 0$

b. $325 = 5 \times 5 \times 13$. Using this information, the possible rational roots are $\pm1, \pm5, \pm13, \pm25, \pm65, \pm325$.

c. When $x = 5$, $(5)^3 + 8(5)^2 - 325 = 0$, therefore $x = 5$ is a factor. The length of one side of the base is 5 inches.

20. The student's mistake was forgetting to distribute the negative sign into the bracket $(6x + 5)$ after factoring.

21. $x = \frac{-0 \pm \sqrt{0^2 - 4(1)(4)}}{2(1)} = \pm 2i.$

22. Answer will vary. Check students' work. Sample answer is $f(x) = g(x) = x^2 + 9$.

23. To check using a graphing calculator, create a graph of the equations $y = \sqrt{6 + x}$ and $y = \sqrt{2x - 1}$, and find their point of intersection. The x-value of the intersection point will be the solution. In this case, $x = 7$ is the solution.

24. $M = \frac{2}{3}\log\left[\frac{E}{10^{11.8}}\right]$

For the 7.7 earthquake:

$$7.7 = \frac{2}{3}\log\left[\frac{E}{10^{11.8}}\right]$$

$$\frac{7.7 \times 3}{2} = \log\left[\frac{E}{10^{11.8}}\right]$$

$$11.55 = \log\left[\frac{E}{10^{11.8}}\right]$$

$$10^{11.55} = \frac{E}{10^{11.8}}$$

$$E = 10^{11.55} \times 10^{11.8}$$
$$= 10^{23.35} \text{ or } 2.24 \times 10^{23} \text{ ergs}$$

For the 8.3 earthquake:

$$8.3 = \frac{2}{3}\log\left[\frac{E}{10^{11.8}}\right]$$

$$\frac{8.3 \times 3}{2} = \log\left[\frac{E}{10^{11.8}}\right]$$

$$12.45 = \log\left[\frac{E}{10^{11.8}}\right]$$

$$10^{12.45} = \frac{E}{10^{11.8}}$$

$$E = 10^{12.45} \times 10^{11.8}$$
$$= 10^{24.25} \text{ or } 1.78 \times 10^{24} \text{ ergs}$$

The energy released by the 1906 earthquake was between $10^{23.35}$ or 2.24×10^{23} ergs and $10^{24.25}$ or 1.78×10^{24} ergs.

25.

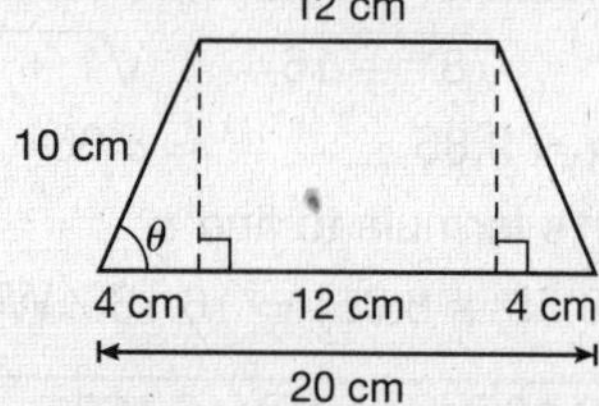

The right triangles at the sides of the isosceles trapezoid have a hypotenuse of 10 cm and an adjacent side of 4 cm. We can find the angle using the cosine ratio:

$\cos\theta = \frac{4}{10}$
$\theta \approx 66.4°$

The measure of the base angle is about 66.4°.

26. $x^2 - 24x - 423 + 18x$
$= x(x - 24) + 18(x - 24)$
$= (x + 18)(x - 24)$

27. These events are independent, meaning that they are mutually exclusive.

28. The value will be negative because the parabola never crosses the x-axis, meaning that the function has no x-intercepts and the related equation has no solutions.

29. There are 7 dogs in total, 4 of which are sheepdogs. The probability that the farmer is taking a walk with a sheepdog is $\frac{4}{7}$.

30. Rearranging: $x^2 - 2x - 5 = 0$.

$$x = \frac{-b \pm \sqrt{b^2 - 4ac}}{2a}$$
$$x = \frac{2 \pm \sqrt{2^2 - 4(1)(-5)}}{2(1)}$$
$$x = \frac{2 \pm \sqrt{4 + 20}}{2}$$
$$x = \frac{2 \pm \sqrt{24}}{2}$$
$$x = \frac{2 \pm 2\sqrt{6}}{2}$$
$$x = 1 \pm \sqrt{6}$$

LESSON 78

Warm Up 78

1. quadratic formula
2. $5x^2 - 3x + 5 = 0$

$$x = \frac{-b \pm \sqrt{b^2 - 4ac}}{2a}$$
$$x = \frac{3 \pm \sqrt{3^2 - 4(5)(5)}}{2(5)}$$
$$x = \frac{3 \pm \sqrt{9 - 100}}{10}$$
$$x = \frac{3 \pm \sqrt{-91}}{10}$$
$$x \approx 0.3 \pm 0.9539i$$

3.

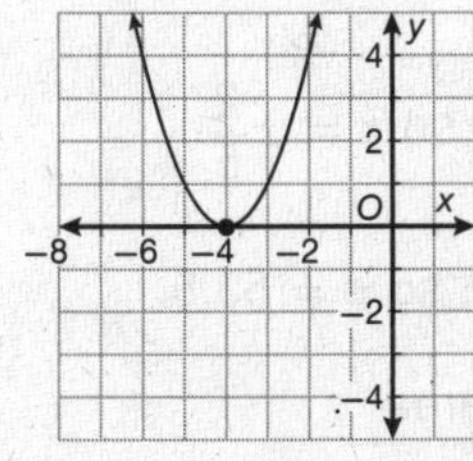

From the graph, we can see that the function touches the x-axis at $x = -4$. This is the only zero of the function.

Lesson Practice 78

a.
$$100x^2 = 1$$
$$100x^2 - 1 = 0$$
$$(10x + 1)(10x - 1) = 0$$
$$x = \pm\frac{1}{10}$$

b.
$$6x^2 - 150 = 0$$
$$x^2 - 25 = 0$$
$$(x + 5)(x - 5) = 0$$
$$x = \pm 5$$

c.
$$18x^3 - 32x = 0$$
$$2x(9x^2 - 16) = 0$$
$$2x(3x + 4)(3x - 4) = 0$$
$$x = 0,\ x = \pm\frac{4}{3}$$

d.
$$16x^4 - 1 = 0$$
$$(4x^2 - 1)(4x^2 + 1) = 0$$
$$(2x + 1)(2x - 1)(4x^2 + 1) = 0$$
$$4x^2 = -1$$
$$x = \pm\frac{1}{2} \qquad x = \pm\frac{1}{2}i$$

e.

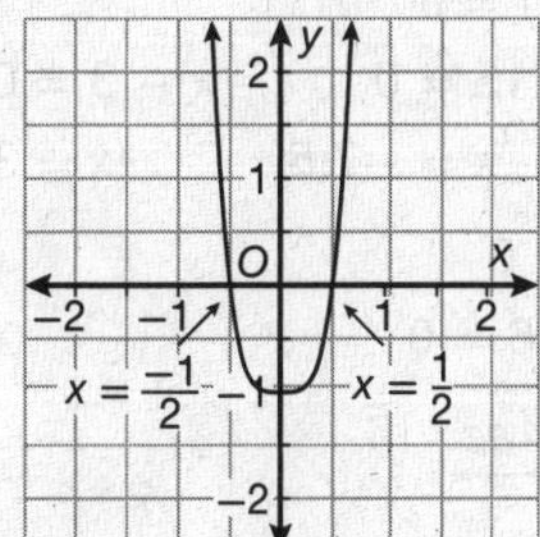

From the graph, we can see that the two real roots are $\pm\frac{1}{2}$.

f.
$$(x+8)^2 - (6x-1)^2 = 0$$
$$(x+8+6x-1)(x+8-6x+1) = 0$$
$$(7x+7)(-5x+9) = 0$$
$$7x+7=0 \quad -5x+9=0$$
$$x=-1 \quad x=\frac{9}{5}$$

g. Since the object is dropped, and not thrown, $v_0 = 0$. The formula becomes:
$h(t) = -4.9t^2 + 62.5$
The object hits the ground when $h(t) = 0$
so: $0 = -4.9t^2 + 62.5$
$4.9t^2 - 62.5 = 0$

$$49t^2 - 625 = 0 = (7t+25)(7t-25)$$

$$t = \pm\frac{25}{7}$$

Since time is measured from $t = 0$, we ignore the negative root. The object hits the ground about 3.57 seconds after it is dropped.

Practice 78

1. $c^2 = a^2 + b^2 - 2ab\cos C$

$n^2 = 3^2 + 13^2 - 2(3)(13)\cos 36°$

$n^2 \approx 114.897$

$n \approx 10.7$

2. Answers will vary. Check students' work. Sample answer: $(-164° - 360°) = -524°$
$(-164° + 360°) = 196°$

3. $4x(2x+15)(x-3) = 0$

$4x = 0 \quad 2x+15=0 \quad x-3=0$

$x = 0 \quad x=-7.5 \quad x=3$

4. $2x(x^2 - 4x + 6) = 0$

$x = 0 \quad x^2 - 4x + 6 = 0$

$$x = \frac{-b \pm \sqrt{b^2-4ac}}{2a}$$

$$x = \frac{4 \pm \sqrt{4^2 - 4(1)(6)}}{2(1)}$$

$$x = \frac{4 \pm \sqrt{16-24}}{2}$$

$$x = \frac{4 \pm \sqrt{-8}}{2}$$

$$x = \frac{4 \pm 2\sqrt{2}i}{2}$$

$$x = 2 \pm \sqrt{2}i$$

5. $(2x+1)(x+4) = 0$

$2x+1=0 \quad x+4=0$

$x=-0.5 \quad x=-4$

6. $3x(x^2-4) = 0$

$3x(x+2)(x-2) = 0$

$x = 0 \quad x = 2, -2$

7. Using the 1, 2, $\sqrt{3}$ triangle:

$$\frac{\sqrt{3}}{2} = \frac{\sqrt{15}}{\text{hypotenuse}}$$

$\sqrt{3}$ hypotenuse $= 2\sqrt{15}$

hypotenuse $= 2\sqrt{5}$

The scale can be found by calculating the ratio of this hypotenuse to the hypotenuse of the larger triangle:

$$\frac{14\sqrt{5}}{2\sqrt{5}} = 7$$

Therefore, the correct answer is **C**.

8. a. $\left[\frac{3}{4}x^2 + \frac{3}{8}x + 1 = 0\right] \times 8$

$6x^2 + 3x + 8 = 0$

b. $x = \dfrac{-b \pm \sqrt{b^2-4ac}}{2a}$

$$x = \frac{-3 \pm \sqrt{3^2 - 4(6)(8)}}{2(4)}$$

$$x = \frac{-3 \pm \sqrt{9-192}}{12}$$

$$x = \frac{-3 \pm \sqrt{-183}}{12}$$

$$x = -\frac{1}{4} \pm \frac{\sqrt{183}}{12}i$$

9. If both sides are multiplied by 10, we obtain $25x^2 - 4 = 0$, which can then be solved using factoring:
$(5x-2)(5x+2) = 0$, so $x = \pm\frac{2}{5}$.

10. $s = \frac{1}{2}(34 + 25 + 48)$, so $s = 53.5$.

We can now find the area:

$$A = \sqrt{53.5(53.5-34)(53.5-25)(53.5-48)}$$

$= \sqrt{53.5(19.5)(28.5)(5.5)}$

$A \approx 404$

Therefore, the correct answer is **B**.

11. 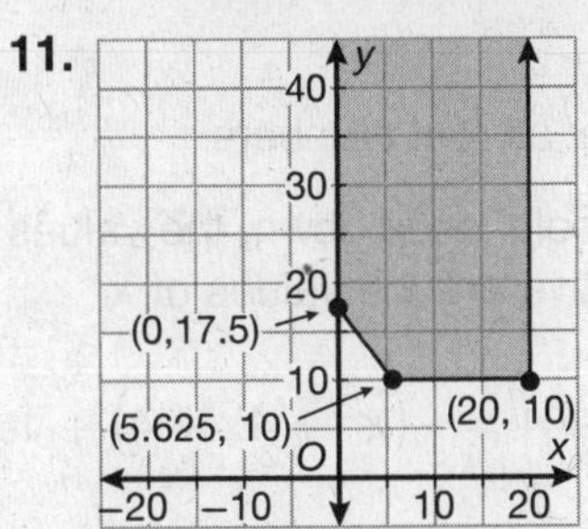

The feasible region for the inequalities is the unbounded region with vertices (20, 10), (5.625, 10), and (0, 17.5).

12. The +2 in $y = 3^x + 2$ moves the function $y = 3^x$ up 2 units, not to the right 2 units. Eric graphed $y = 3^{x-2}$ instead.

13. a. The product of powers should be applied first. The expression within the bracket must be simplified first.

b. We then apply the Power of a Power Property.

c. $\left(5^{\frac{1}{2}} \cdot 5^{\frac{2}{7}}\right)^{\frac{2}{11}}$

$= \left(5^{\frac{7}{14}} \cdot 5^{\frac{4}{14}}\right)^{\frac{2}{11}}$

$= \left(5^{\frac{11}{14}}\right)^{\frac{2}{11}}$

$= 5^{\frac{11}{14} \times \frac{2}{11}}$

$= 5^{\frac{1}{7}}$

$= \sqrt[7]{5}$

14. The total number of people surveyed is 113,126. The number that are either male or have a computer is 39,475 + 20,583 + 30,461 = 90,519. The probability is then $\frac{90,519}{113,126} =$ 0.8002.

15.

$$\begin{array}{r|rrr} -2 & 4 & 7 & 10 \\ & & -8 & 2 \\ \hline & 4 & -1 & 12 \end{array}$$

Therefore, $\dfrac{4x^2 + 7x + 10}{x + 2} = 4x - 1 + \dfrac{12}{x + 2}$.

16.

$$\begin{array}{r|rrr} 5 & 2 & -6 & -12 \\ & & 10 & 20 \\ \hline & 2 & 4 & 8 \end{array}$$

Therefore, $\dfrac{2x^2 - 6x - 12}{x - 5} = 2x + 4 + \dfrac{8}{x - 5}$.

17. Excluded values: $10 - 2x = 0$ means $2x = 10$ or $x = 5$.

Simplifying:

$\dfrac{2x - 10}{10 - 2x} = -\dfrac{(10 - 2x)}{10 - 2x} = -1$

18. If $a = 0$ and $b = 0$, then $a + bi = 0 + 0i = 0$, which is a real number.

19. Answers will vary. Check students' work. Sample answer: Define the inverse sine function as $\sin^{-1} a = \theta$ where $\sin \theta = a$.

20. $6 = 1.2116\sqrt{h}$ means that

$h = \left(\dfrac{6}{1.2116}\right)^2 \approx 24.5$ ft

21. Since all values graphed would be the same distance from the origin, the shape will be a circle, with the common distance representing the radius of the circle.

22. a. Ways of choosing three triangles from a sample of 5, without replacement is $5 \times 4 \times 3 = 60$. There are two ways for the desired outcome to occur: 30-60-90, 45-45-90, and 20-20-140, or 45-45-90, 30-60-90, and 20-20-140. Therefore, the probability of the event $= \frac{2}{60} = \frac{1}{30}$ or $\approx 3.3\%$.

b. 0%, since there are only 2 right triangles.

c. $\dfrac{3}{5} \cdot \dfrac{2}{4} \cdot \dfrac{1}{3} = \dfrac{1}{10} = 10\%$

23. To simplify, you must rationalize the denominator to remove the root from the denominator. Therefore, Alex is correct. Robert multiplied by the conjugate of the numerator instead.

24. Being dropped means $v_o = 0$, therefore, $h(t) = -0.8t^2 + 20$. When the object hits the moon's surface, $h(t) = 0$, so $0 = -0.8t^2 + 20$. Multiplying by 5, we obtain: $0 = -4t^2 + 100$. Using difference of squares:

$4t^2 - 100 = 0$

$(2t + 10)(2t - 10) = 0$

$t = \frac{\pm 10}{2} = \pm 5$

(Notice that the solution of $t = -5$ is ignored due to time starting at $t = 0$.) The object would take 5 seconds to fall.

25. Use Heron's formula to find s: $s = \frac{1}{2}(12 + 16 + 18) = 23$. We can now find the area:

$A = \sqrt{23(23 - 12)(23 - 16)(23 - 18)}$

$= \sqrt{23(11)(7)(5)}$

$A \approx 94.1 \text{ ft}^2$

The area is about 94.1 ft^2.

26. For $P = 2x + 5y$ to be a maximum, we need to look at the region bounded by $x \geq 0$, $y \geq 0$, $y \geq 1.5x + 1$, and $y \geq -x + 6$. The point of intersection of $y = 1.5x + 1$ and $y = -x + 6$:

$1.5x + 1 = -x + 6$

$2.5x = 5$ or $x = 2$.

When $x = 2$, $y = -2 + 6$, or 4.

Therefore, the point of intersection is (2, 4), and this point will maximize $P = 2x + 5y$ at a value of $2(2) + 5(4) = 24$.

27. Assuming that $f(x)$ and $g(x)$ are not equal, there are at least four roots for the multiplication of the two functions.

28. $w(20 - w) = 600$ means that $20w - w^2 = 600$ or $w^2 - 20w + 600 = 0$.

For this:

$b^2 - 4ac = (20)^2 - 4(1)(600) = -2000$.

Since the discriminant is negative, there are no real solutions, which means that the requirements cannot be met.

29. $\log_7 19 = \frac{\log_{10} 19}{\log_{10} 7} \approx 1.513$

30. $\log_6\left(\frac{24}{5}\right) = \frac{\log_{10}\left(\frac{24}{5}\right)}{\log_{10} 6} \approx 0.875$

LESSON 79

Warm Up 79

1. vertical line test

2. Domain and range: all real numbers.

3. Because the parabola faces down, the values for which it is positive are the values of x between the roots.

$f(x) = -(x + 2)^2 + 1 = -(x^2 + 4x + 4) + 1$

$= -x^2 - 4x - 3$.

$0 = -x^2 - 4x - 3 = x^2 + 4x + 3$

$= (x + 3)(x + 1)$

The roots are -1, -3 so $f(x)$ is positive for all $x \in \mathbb{R}$ such that $-1 < x < 3$.

4. $y - y_1 = m(x - x_1)$

$y - 200 = 3(x - 50)$

$y - 200 = 3x - 150$

$y = 3x + 50$

Lesson Practice 79

a. The domain of the function is divided into three different intervals:

6 and under: $x < 6$

Ages 7 to 18: $7 \leq x \leq 18$

over age 18: $x > 18$

For the interval $x < 6$, the range is 10. For the interval $7 \leq x \leq 18$, the range is 20. For the interval $x > 18$, the range is 25. The graph of the function is a step function.

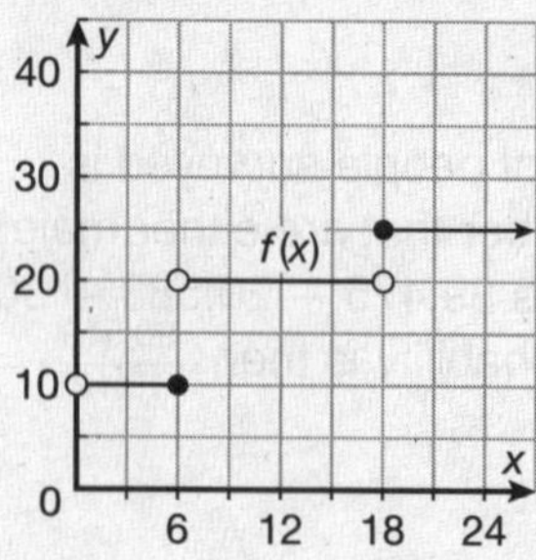

b. When $x = -3$, $f(x) = 2x + 2$, so $f(-3) = 2(-3) + 2 = -4$.

When $x = 10$, $f(x) = x^2 + 4$, so $f(10) = 10^2 + 4 = 104$.

c. The function is a step function comprised of two linear pieces that are represented by line segments on the graph. For $x < 0$, the graph is the line segment $y = -1$. For $x \geq 0$, the graph is the line segment $y = 4$. The function rule is:

$$f(x) = \begin{cases} -1, & \text{if } x < 0 \\ 4, & \text{if } x \geq 0. \end{cases}$$

d. The function is comprised of three linear pieces. Use a table of values to graph each piece of the function.

x	$x+1$	1	4
0	1		
1	2	1	
2		1	4
3			4
4			4

Plot the points (0, 1) and (1, 2) and draw a ray whose endpoint is (1, 2). Plot open circles at points (1, 1) and (2, 1) and draw a line segment connecting the circles. Plot the point (2, 4), (3, 4) and (4, 4) and draw a ray whose endpoint is (2, 4).

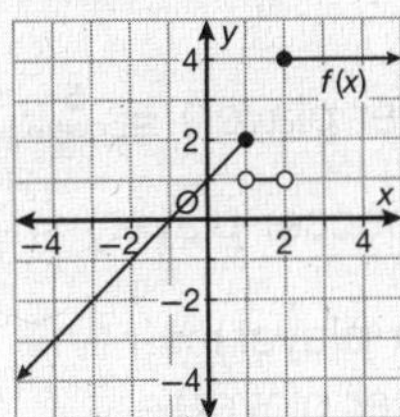

e. The information represents a step function. The function rule is:

$$f(x) = \begin{cases} 50x & \text{if } 0 \leq x \leq 3 \\ 150 + 25\,(x-3) & \text{if } x > 3. \end{cases}$$

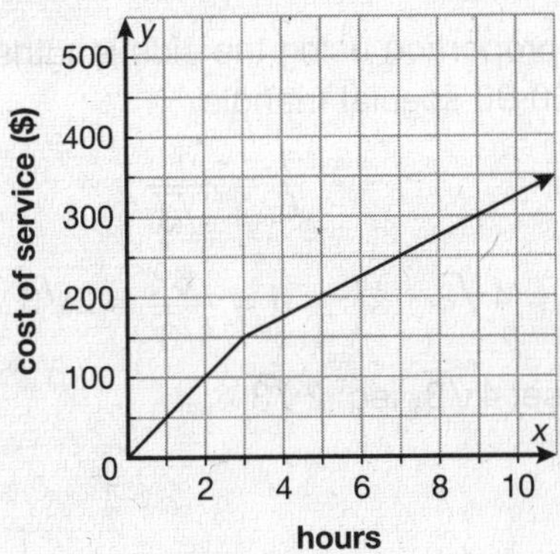

Practice 79

1. Keeping the first marble out of the bag affects the probability of picking the next marble because the sample space has one less outcome. Whereas $P(\text{purple})$ would be $\frac{7}{10}$ if the events were independent, it is now $\frac{7}{9}$. So $P(\text{white then purple}) = \frac{3}{10} \cdot \frac{7}{10} = \frac{21}{90}$.

2. $$\begin{aligned} \sqrt[3]{x} - 10 &= -3 \\ \sqrt[3]{x} &= 7 \\ x &= 7^3 \\ x &= 343 \end{aligned}$$

3. $$\begin{aligned} \sqrt[3]{x-3} + 2 &= 4 \\ \sqrt[3]{x-3} &= 2 \\ x - 3 &= 2^3 \\ x - 3 &= 8 \\ x &= 11 \end{aligned}$$

4. Either the lengths of all three sides or the lengths of two sides and the included angle.

5. $$\begin{aligned} x^4 - 81 &= 0 \\ (x^2)^2 - (9)^2 &= 0 \\ (x^2 + 9)(x^2 - 9) &= 0 \\ (x^2 + 9)(x + 3)(x - 3) &= 0 \end{aligned}$$
$(x^2 + 9) = 0$ or $(x + 3) = 0$ or $(x - 3) = 0$
$x^2 = -9$
$x = \pm\sqrt{-9}$
$x = \pm 3i \qquad x = -3 \qquad x = 3$
The complex roots are $-3i$ and $3i$.
The real roots are -3 and 3.

6. $$\begin{aligned} 12x &= 9x^2 + 4 \\ 9x^2 - 12x + 4 &= 0 \\ (3x - 2)^2 &= 0 \\ (3x - 2) &= 0 \\ x &= \frac{2}{3} \end{aligned}$$
The root is $\frac{2}{3}$.

7. $$\begin{aligned} 8x^3 - 392x &= 0 \\ 8x(x^2 - 49) &= 0 \\ 8x(x + 7)(x - 7) &= 0 \end{aligned}$$
The roots are -7, 0 and 7.

8. **a.** Volume $= A_b h$, where A_b is the area of the base and h is the height of the prism.

$64\sqrt{6} = (4 \cdot 4)h$

$\frac{64\sqrt{6}}{16} = h$

$h = 4\sqrt{6}$

The height of the prism is $4\sqrt{6}$ ft.

b.

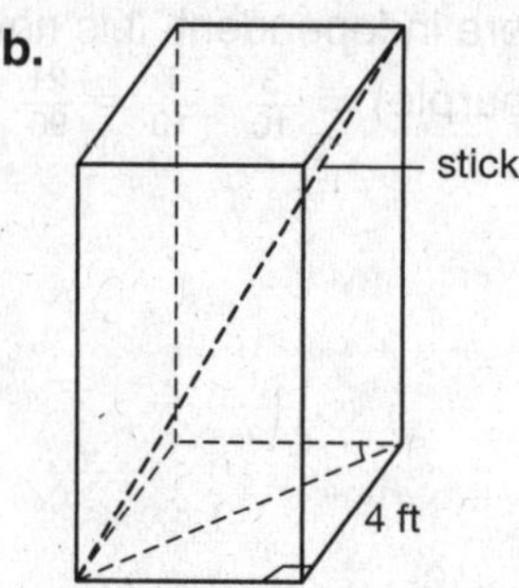

Let a be the diagonal of the square base.

$4^2 + 4^2 = a^2$

$32 = a^2$

$a = \sqrt{32}$

Let r be the diagonal of the prism.

$(\sqrt{32})^2 + (4\sqrt{6})^2 = r^2$

$32 + 16 \cdot 6 = r^2$

$\sqrt{128} = r$

$\sqrt{64 \cdot 2} = r$

$r = 8\sqrt{2}$

The longest stick that can fit inside the box is $8\sqrt{2}$ ft.

c. Using the cosine trigonometry ratio we can solve for the angle between the stick and the vertical face of the box.

$\cos\theta = \frac{4\sqrt{6}}{8\sqrt{2}}$

$\cos\theta = \frac{4\sqrt{2}\sqrt{3}}{8\sqrt{2}}$

$\cos\theta = \frac{\sqrt{3}}{2}$

$\theta = 30°$

The angle it forms is 30°.

9. Yes, it is a binomial experiment because there are 40 trials and only 2 possible outcomes, 2 or not a 2. Each trial is independent of the next and the probability of success is the same from trial to trial.

10. a. $(f \circ g)(x) = f(g(x))$

$= f((x^2))$

$= 2(x^2)$

$= 2x^2$

$(g \circ f)(x) = g(f(x))$

$= g(2x)$

$= (2x)^2$

$= 4x^2$

b. $(f \circ g)(2) = 2x^2$

$= 2(2)^2$

$= 8$

$(g \circ f)(2) = 4x^2$

$= 4(2)^2$

$= 16.$

11. The correct choice is **D** because the two points shown in the graph satisfy the equation.

12. $2^{\frac{1}{3}} \cdot 4^{\frac{1}{6}} \cdot 8^{\frac{1}{9}}$

$= 2^{\frac{1}{3}} \cdot (2^2)^{\frac{1}{6}} \cdot (2^3)^{\frac{1}{9}}$

$= 2^{\frac{1}{3}} \cdot 2^{\frac{1}{3}} \cdot 2^{\frac{1}{3}}$

$= 2^{\frac{1}{3}+\frac{1}{3}+\frac{1}{3}}$

$= 2^1 = 2$

13. $P(\text{left handed AND soccer player}) = \frac{5}{65}$,

$P(\text{left handed}) = \frac{12}{65}$, $P(\text{soccer player}) = \frac{43}{65}$.

$P(\text{left handed OR soccer player}) =$
$P(\text{left handed}) + P(\text{soccer player}) -$
$P(\text{left handed AND soccer player})$

$= \frac{12}{65} + \frac{43}{65} - \frac{5}{65} = \frac{50}{65} = \frac{10}{13}$

So the probability that one of the students on the trip is a soccer player or is left handed is $\frac{10}{13}$.

14. Set up a proportion using the side lengths for a 30-60-90 special triangle.

$\frac{h}{6} = \frac{2}{\sqrt{3}}$ $\qquad$ $\frac{l}{6} = \frac{1}{\sqrt{3}}$

$h = \frac{12}{\sqrt{3}} = 4\sqrt{3}$ $\qquad$ $l = \frac{6}{\sqrt{3}} = 2\sqrt{3}$

hypotenuse: $4\sqrt{3}$, leg: $2\sqrt{3}$

15. $(fg)(x) = (3x - 5)(x + 4)$
$= 3x^2 + 12x - 5x - 20$
$= 3x^2 + 7x - 20$

16. Press Y=, then enter 2, X,T,θ,n, ^, 2, +, X,T,θ,n, −, 4. Then press GRAPH. Press TRACE to scroll along the graph of the function to the roots.
Answer: −1.686, 1.186

17. The angle measure must be in radians before using the formula.
$A = \frac{1}{2}(6)^2\left(\frac{2\pi}{9}\right) \approx 12.6 \text{ cm}^2$

18. For the first sample, 2-digit numbers are found in the table. For the second sample, 3-digit numbers are found.

19. If a is even, $i^a = \pm 1$. There are 6 even numbers from 20 to 30.
So the $P(i^a = \pm 1) = \frac{6}{11} \approx 54.5\%$.

20. A step function is a piece-wise function that is constant for each interval. This function is not constant for $x < -2$.

21. By the Rational Root Theorem the possible roots are:
$$\frac{\pm 1, \pm 2, \pm 4, \pm 8}{\pm 1, \pm 3}$$
$= \pm\frac{1}{3}, \pm\frac{2}{3}, \pm 1, \pm\frac{4}{3}, \pm 2, \pm\frac{8}{3}, \pm 4, \pm 8.$

Test roots. Begin with integers, and you will find that the roots are −1, −2, and $\frac{4}{3}$.
$3(-1)^3 + 5(-1)^2 - 6(-1) - 8$
$= -3 + 5 + 6 - 8 = 0$
$3(-2)^3 + 5(-2)^2 - 6(-2) - 8$
$= -24 + 20 + 12 - 8 = 0$
$3\left(\frac{4}{3}\right)^3 + 5\left(\frac{4}{3}\right)^2 - 6\left(\frac{4}{3}\right) - 8$
$= \frac{64}{9} + \frac{80}{9} - 8 - 8 = 0$

22. This is a piecewise function consisting of two linear functions. Let x represents the number of items being delivered. For $0 \le x \le 10$, the cost of delivery is a constant \$25. For $x \ge 11$, that is to say for every item exceeding the first ten, an additional \$5 will be charged per item. So the piecewise function for the cost is as follows:
$$C(x) = \begin{cases} 25, & \text{if } 0 \le x \le 10 \\ 5(x - 10) + 25, & \text{if } x > 10. \end{cases}$$

23. The range of the inverse sine function includes $-\frac{\pi}{2}$ and $\frac{\pi}{2}$, and the range of the inverse tangent function does not include these two values. Sine values exist for $-\frac{\pi}{2}$ and $\frac{\pi}{2}$, but tangent values do not exist for these two values.

24. $b^2 - 4ac = (-4)^2 - 4(1)(-c)$
$= 16 + 4c$
$= 4(4 + c)$

a. For $c > -4$, the equation has two real solutions.

b. For $c = -4$, the equation has one real solution.

c. For $c < -4$, the equation has two imaginary solutions.

25. $b^2 - 4ac = (-10)^2 - 4(-4)(c)$
$= 100 + 16c$
$= 16(6.25 + c)$

a. For $c > -6.25$, the equation has two real solutions.

b. For $c = -6.25$, the equation has one real solution.

c. For $c < -6.25$, the equation has two imaginary solutions.

26. Keeping the first and the second penny out of the purse affects the probability of picking the next marble because the sample space has one less outcome each time.
$\frac{10}{18} \cdot \frac{9}{17} \cdot \frac{8}{16} = \frac{10}{2} \cdot \frac{1}{17} \cdot \frac{1}{2}$
$= \frac{10}{68} \approx 14.7\%$

The correct choice is **B**.

27. $\frac{1}{2}bc \sin A = \frac{1}{2}ac \sin B = \frac{1}{2}ab \sin C$

$2(\frac{1}{2}bc \sin A) = 2(\frac{1}{2}ac \sin B)$

$= 2(\frac{1}{2}ab \sin C)$

$\frac{bc \sin A}{abc} = \frac{ac \sin B}{abc} = \frac{ab \sin C}{abc}$

$\frac{\sin A}{a} = \frac{\sin B}{b} = \frac{\sin C}{c}$

28. $A^{-1} = \frac{1}{ad - bc}\begin{bmatrix} d & -b \\ -c & a \end{bmatrix}$

$A^{-1} = \frac{1}{1(-6) - (-1)(4)}\begin{bmatrix} -6 & 1 \\ -4 & 1 \end{bmatrix}$

$A^{-1} = \frac{1}{-2}\begin{bmatrix} -6 & 1 \\ -4 & 1 \end{bmatrix}$

$A^{-1} = \begin{bmatrix} 3 & -\frac{1}{2} \\ 2 & -\frac{1}{2} \end{bmatrix}$

29. Lift $= kv^2$, however it is given that weight of the plane is equal to the force of lift. So,

Weight of the plane $= kv^2$

$\frac{\text{Weight of the plane}}{k} = v^2$

$v = \sqrt{\frac{\text{Weight of the plane}}{k}}$

30. When $x = -3$, $f(x) = 3x - 1$, so

$f(-3) = 3(-3) - 1 = -10$.

When $x = 4$, $f(x) = 1 - x$, so

$f(4) = 1 - 4 = -3$.

LESSON 80

Warm Up 80

1. mean
2. True
3. False.

The mean of the first set of data is

$\bar{x} = \frac{1 + 3 + 5 + 7 + 10}{5} = 5.2.$

The standard deviation of the first set of data is

$$\sigma = \sqrt{\frac{(1 - 5.2)^2 + (3 - 5.2)^2 + (5 - 5.2)^2 + (7 - 5.2)^2 + (10 - 5.2)^2}{5}}$$

$$\sigma = \sqrt{\frac{17.64 + 4.84 + 0.04 + 3.24 + 23.04}{5}}$$

$\sigma \approx 9.76.$

The mean of the second set of data is

$\bar{x} = \frac{3 + 4 + 5 + 6 + 7}{5} = 5.$

The standard deviation of the second set of data is

$$\sigma = \sqrt{\frac{(3 - 5)^2 + (4 - 5)^2 + (5 - 5)^2 + (6 - 5)^2 + (7 - 5)^2}{5}}$$

$$\sigma = \sqrt{\frac{4 + 1 + 0 + 1 + 4}{5}}$$

$\sigma \approx 1.41.$

4. mean $= \frac{1+2+87}{3} = 30$ and the median is 2.

Lesson Practice 80

a. About 99.7% of the data lie with 3 standard deviations of the mean. So, the boundary of the range can be given by

mean ± 3(standard deviation)

$300 - 3(18) = 246$

$300 + 3(18) = 354$

99.7% of the data falls between 246 and 354.

b. 95% of the scores are between 264 and 336. Because the data is distributed symmetrically about the mean, about half of 95%, or 47.5%, of the scores are between 264 and 300.

c. 95% of the scores are between 264 and 336, and 68% of the scores are between 282 and 318. Because the data is distributed symmetrically about the mean, about half of 95%, or 47.5%, of the scores are between 300 and 336 and about half of 68%, or 34%, of the scores are between 282 and 300. So, about 34% + 47.5% = 81.5% of the scores are between 282 and 336.

d. 68% of the scores are between 282 and 318. Because the data is distributed symmetrically about the mean, about half of 68%, or 34%, of the scores are between 300 and 318. And 50% of the scores are below the mean. So, about 100% − 50% − 34% = 16% of the scores are greater than 318.

e. Find the z-score, the standardized weight.

$$z\text{-score} = \frac{12 - 12.2}{0.08} = -2.5$$

The standardized weight is −2.5; the hammer is 2.5 standard deviations below the mean.

f. Find the z-score, the standardized weight.

$$z\text{-score} = \frac{12.3 - 12.2}{0.08} = 1.25$$

The standardized weight is 1.25; the hammer is 1.25 standard deviations above the mean.

g. Standardize each score. The student with the greater standardized score did better.

Student A: $z\text{-score} = \frac{445 - 450}{12} \approx -0.417$

Student B: $z\text{-score} = \frac{170 - 175}{15} \approx -0.333$

Student B has the greater standardized score and did better compared to the rest of their class than did student A.

Practice 80

1. Interchange the variables to find the inverse of $y = x^2 - 7$.

$$x = y^2 - 7$$
$$y^2 = x + 7$$
$$y = \pm\sqrt{x+7}$$

The inverse is not a function because it does not pass the vertical line test. For every $x > -7$, y has exactly two real values.

2. Find how many deviations 80 and 96 are away from the mean. $88 - 80 = 8$, $96 - 88 = 8$, and $8 \div 4 = 2$. The scores are two standard deviations away from the mean, so about 95% of the scores are between 80 and 96.

3. Keeping the first ace out of the deck affects the probability of picking the next ace because the sample space has one less outcome. Whereas $P(\text{ace})$ would be $\frac{4}{52}$ if the events were independent, it is now $\frac{3}{51}$. So $P(\text{ace then ace}) = \frac{4}{52} \cdot \frac{3}{51} = \frac{12}{2652} = \frac{1}{221}$.

4. Population growth is modeled by an exponential growth function. That is the population at time t is modeled by $f(t) = a \cdot e^{kt}$, where a is the initial population (400,000) and k is the growth rate.

$$f(3) = 1{,}200{,}000$$
$$f(3) = 400{,}000e^{3k} = 1{,}200{,}000$$
$$e^{3k} = 3$$
$$3k = \ln(3)$$
$$k = \frac{\ln(3)}{3}$$
$$f(8) = 400{,}000 \cdot e^{8k}$$
$$= 400{,}000 \cdot e^{8\left(\frac{\ln(3)}{3}\right)}$$
$$\approx 7{,}488{,}302$$

5. $z\text{-score} = \frac{37 - 43}{2} = -3$

6. The position forms the 45-45-90 special triangle. Solve for s, the perpendicular distance using the Pythagorean Theorem for

45-45-90 special triangle, $2s^2 = c^2$, where c is 18.7 million kilometers.

$2s^2 = 18.7^2$

$s = \sqrt{\frac{18.7^2}{2}}$

$s \approx 13.2$

So, it's about 13.2 million kilometers.

7. $x = 2$, $y = 9$, $r = \sqrt{2^2 + 9^2} = \sqrt{85}$

$\sin\theta = \frac{y}{r} = \frac{9}{\sqrt{85}} = \frac{9\sqrt{85}}{85}$

$\csc\theta = \frac{r}{y} = \frac{\sqrt{85}}{9}$

$\cos\theta = \frac{x}{r} = \frac{2}{\sqrt{85}} = \frac{2\sqrt{85}}{85}$

$\sec\theta = \frac{r}{x} = \frac{\sqrt{85}}{2}$

$\tan\theta = \frac{y}{x} = \frac{9}{2}$

$\cot\theta = \frac{x}{y} = \frac{2}{9}$

8. $a = 0$ because there is no real term in the imaginary unit, and $b = 1$ because the numerical coefficient of i is 1.

9. $\frac{13^{\frac{1}{3}} \cdot 13^{\frac{1}{4}}}{13^{\frac{1}{12}} \cdot 13^{\frac{1}{2}}} = \frac{13^{\frac{4}{12}} \cdot 13^{\frac{3}{12}}}{13^{\frac{1}{12}} \cdot 13^{\frac{6}{12}}} = \frac{13^{\frac{4}{12}+\frac{3}{12}}}{13^{\frac{1}{12}+\frac{6}{12}}}$

$= \frac{13^{\frac{7}{12}}}{13^{\frac{7}{12}}} = 13^{\frac{7}{12}-\frac{7}{12}} = 1.$

10. The correct choice is **C** because $180° = \pi$, and half of that is $\frac{180°}{2} = 90° = \frac{\pi}{2}$.

11. $1.64 = \sqrt{\frac{1.7k}{36}}$

$1.64^2 = \frac{1.7k}{36}$

$(2.6896)(36) = 1.7k$

$98.83 = 1.7k$

$k \approx 57$

12. a. $3^y = \frac{1}{9}$, $y = -2$

b. $-2, -1, 0, 1, 2$

c.

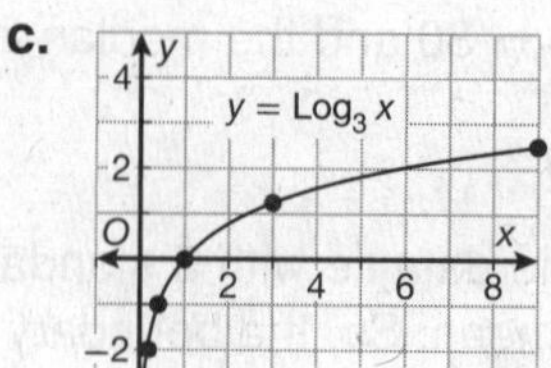

13. Pythagorean Theorem: $x^2 + y^2 = 75^2$, Perimeter of the Triangle: $x + y = 168 - 75 = 93$

$y = 93 - x$

$x^2 + (93 - x)^2 = 75^2$

$x^2 + 8649 - 186x + x^2 = 5625$

$2x^2 - 186x + 8649 - 5625 = 0$

$2x^2 - 186x + 3024 = 0$

$x = \frac{-b \pm \sqrt{b^2 - 4ac}}{2a}$

$x = \frac{-(-186) \pm \sqrt{(-186)^2 - 4(2)(3024)}}{2(2)}$

$x = \frac{186 \pm \sqrt{34596 - 24192}}{4}$

$x = \frac{186 \pm 102}{4}$

So, the legs are 72 inches and 21 inches.

14. $16x^4 - 16$ is the difference of two squares; it can be written as $(4x^2)^2 - (4)^2$.

15. The student used $\frac{q}{p}$ instead of $\frac{p}{q}$:

$\frac{\pm 1, \pm 2, \pm 4}{\pm 1, \pm 2} = \pm\frac{1}{2}, \pm 1, \pm 2, \pm 4.$

16. a. $53.6 \approx 69.033 \cos\theta$

$\cos\theta \approx \frac{53.6}{69.033}$

$\theta \approx 39°$

b. $l_1 \approx 69.033 \cos 0°$

$l_1 \approx 69.033(1)$

$l_1 \approx 69.033$

$l_2 \approx 69.033 \cos 66°$

$l_2 \approx 28.07$

$69.033 - 28.07 \approx 41$ miles.

17. The probability of every possible group of n individuals is not the same. For instance, the probability of selecting a group that consists of half the people in one cluster and half the people in another cluster is 0.

18. Keeping the first yellow pencil of the box affects the probability of picking the next yellow because the sample space has one less outcome. Whereas P(yellow) would be $\frac{8}{16}$ if the events were independent, it is now $\frac{7}{15}$.

So $P(\text{yellow then yellow}) = \frac{8}{16} \cdot \frac{7}{15}$

$= \frac{56}{240} \approx 23.33\%.$

19. $P(\text{Discriminant} = 0, \text{ given Discriminant} \geq 0)$

$= \frac{P(\text{Discriminant} = 0 \text{ AND Discriminant} \geq 0)}{P(\text{Discriminant} \geq 0)}$

$= \frac{\left(\frac{1}{6}\right)}{\left(\frac{4}{6}\right)} = \frac{1}{4} = 25\%$

20. $E = I(Z)$

$= (40 - 36i)(8 + 3i)$

$= 320 + 120i - 288i - 108i^2$

$= 320 - 168i + 108$

$= 428 - 168i$

21. Using the Sine Law.

$\frac{\sin 104°}{5\frac{1}{4}} = \frac{\sin 22°}{x}$

$x = \frac{\frac{21}{4}\sin 22°}{\sin 104°}$

$x \approx 2.03$ in.

So, the distance from Danville to South Boston is $2.03 \times 13.5 = 27.4$ miles.

22. For very large values of x, $y \approx x$ because $\sqrt{x^2 + 200} \approx \sqrt{x^2}$. Similarly, functions of the form $y = \sqrt{x^n + c}$ will approximate $y = x$ for very large values of x because $\sqrt{x^n} \approx \sqrt{x^n + c}$ for very large values of x.

23. Students should conclude that this is true.

24. **B**, because **B** has the smallest absolute value.

25. $y = 3^x$ and $y = \log_3 x$

26. When standardizing a data value selected from a normally distributed set of data, $z < 0$ when the mean is greater than the data value, and $z > 0$ when the mean is less than the data value.

27. Using Heron's Formula.

$s \approx \frac{8 + 3.5 + 6}{2} \approx 8.75$

$A = \sqrt{s(s - a)(s - b)(s - c)}$

$\approx \sqrt{8.75(0.75)(5)(2.75)} \approx 9.5$

28. $f(x) = \begin{cases} 2x, & \text{if } 0 < x < 12 \\ 1.75x, & \text{if } 12 \leq x \leq 24 \\ 1.5x, & \text{if } x > 24. \end{cases}$

29. When $x = \frac{1}{2}$, $f(x) = x^2$, $f\left(\frac{1}{2}\right) = \left(\frac{1}{2}\right)^2 = \frac{1}{4}$.

When $x = -10$, $f(x) = 7$, $f(-10) = 7$.

30. When $x = \frac{1}{2}$, $f(x) = \frac{1}{2}$, $f\left(\frac{1}{2}\right) = \frac{1}{2}$.

When $x = -10$, $f(x) = \frac{1}{2}$, $f(-10) = \frac{1}{2}$.

INVESTIGATION 8

1. 1 unit.

2.

x	$f(x) = -2x^2 + 2x + 24$
0.5	$f(0.5) = -2(0.5)^2 + 2(0.5) + 24 = 24.5$
1.5	$f(1.5) = -2(1.5)^2 + 2(1.5) + 24 = 22.5$
2.5	$f(2.5) = -2(2.5)^2 + 2(2.5) + 24 = 16.5$
3.5	$f(3.5) = -2(3.5)^2 + 2(3.5) + 24 = 6.5$

3. $24.5(1) + 25.5(1) + 16.5(1) + 6.5(1) = 73$ square units.

4.

x	$f(x) = -2x^2 + 2x + 24$
0.25	$f(0.25) = -2(0.25)^2 + 2(0.25) + 24 = 24.375$
0.75	$f(0.75) = -2(0.75)^2 + 2(0.75) + 24 = 24.375$
1.25	$f(1.25) = -2(1.25)^2 + 2(1.25) + 24 = 23.375$
1.75	$f(1.75) = -2(1.75)^2 + 2(1.75) + 24 = 21.375$
2.25	$f(2.25) = -2(2.25)^2 + 2(2.25) + 24 = 18.375$
2.75	$f(2.75) = -2(2.75)^2 + 2(2.75) + 24 = 14.375$
3.25	$f(3.25) = -2(3.25)^2 + 2(3.25) + 24 = 9.375$
3.75	$f(3.75) = -2(3.75)^2 + 2(3.75) + 24 = 3.375$

$0.5(24.75 + 24.375 + 23.375 + 21.375 + 18.375 + 14.375 + 9.375 + 3.375) = 69.5$
69.5 square units.

5. The estimated area is greater than the actual area.

6. Yes, if the widths of the rectangles are smaller with more rectangles created, then the estimated area will be more accurate.

7. It represents the width of the rectangle.

8.

i	x	$f(x) = 0.5x^3 - x^2 + 2$
1	0.25	$f(0.25) = 1.95$
2	0.75	$0.5(0.75)^3 - (0.75)^2 + 2 \approx 1.65$
3	1.25	$0.5(1.25)^3 - (1.25)^2 + 2 \approx 1.41$
4	1.75	$0.5(1.75)^3 - (1.75)^2 + 2 \approx 1.62$
5	2.25	$0.5(2.25)^3 - (2.25)^2 + 2 \approx 2.63$
6	2.75	$0.5(2.75)^3 - (2.75)^2 + 2 \approx 4.84$
7	3.25	$0.5(3.25)^3 - (3.25)^2 + 2 \approx 8.60$
8	3.75	$0.5(3.75)^3 - (3.75)^2 + 2 \approx 14.30$

9. Using the formula from Question 6.

Total Area $= 0.5\left(\sum_{i=1}^{8} f(x_i)\right)$

$\approx 0.5(1.95 + 1.65 + 1.41 + 1.62 + 2.63 + 4.84 + 8.60 + 14.30)$

≈ 18.50 square units

Investigation 8 Practice

a.

x	$(y) = -x^2 + 5x + 7$
0.5	$f(0.5) = -(0.5)^2 + 5(0.5) + 7 = 9.25$
1.5	$f(1.5) = -(1.5)^2 + 5(1.5) + 7 = 12.25$
2.5	$f(2.5) = -(2.5)^2 + 5(2.5) + 7 = 13.25$
3.5	$f(3.5) = -(3.5)^2 + 5(3.5) + 7 = 12.25$
4.5	$f(4.5) = -(4.5)^2 + 5(4.5) + 7 = 9.25$

Total Area $= \left(\sum_{i=1}^{5} f(x_i)\right)$

$= (9.25 + 12.25 + 13.25 + 12.25 + 9.25)$

$= 56.25$ square units

b. Total Area $= \left(\sum_{i=1}^{10} f(x_i)\right)$

c.

i	x	$f(x) = -x^3 + 11x^2 + 7x + 1$
1	0.5	$-(0.5)^3 + 11(0.5)^2 + 7(0.5) + 1 \approx 7.125$
2	1.5	$-(1.5)^3 + 11(1.5)^2 + 7(1.5) + 1 \approx 32.875$
3	2.5	$-(2.5)^3 + 11(2.5)^2 + 7(2.5) + 1 \approx 71.625$
4	3.5	$-(3.5)^3 + 11(3.5)^2 + 7(3.5) + 1 \approx 117.375$
5	4.5	$-(4.5)^3 + 11(4.5)^2 + 7(4.5) + 1 \approx 164.125$
6	5.5	$-(5.5)^3 + 11(5.5)^2 + 7(5.5) + 1 \approx 205.875$
7	6.5	$-(6.5)^3 + 11(6.5)^2 + 7(6.5) + 1 \approx 236.625$
8	7.5	$-(7.5)^3 + 11(7.5)^2 + 7(7.5) + 1 \approx 250.375$
9	8.5	$-(8.5)^3 + 11(8.5)^2 + 7(8.5) + 1 \approx 241.125$
10	9.5	$-(9.5)^3 + 11(9.5)^2 + 7(9.5) + 1 \approx 202.875$

Total Area $= \left(\sum_{i=1}^{10} f(x_i)\right)$

$= (7.125 + 32.875 + 71.625 + 117.375 + 164.125 + 205.875 + 236.625 + 250.375$
$+ 241.125 + 202.875)$

$= 1530$ square units

LESSON 81

Warm Up 81

1. base
2. Product Prop. of Logarithms
   $\log xy = \log x + \log y$
3. Quotient Prop. of Logarithms
   $\log\frac{x}{y} = \log x - \log y$
4. $b^x = a \Leftrightarrow \log_b a = x$
   $9^2 = 81 \Leftrightarrow \log_9 81 = 2$
   Answer Choice **C**

Lesson Practice 81

a. Let $e^{\ln(3d-1)} = c$. Then

$e^x = a \Leftrightarrow \ln a = x$

$e^{\ln(3d-1)} = c \Leftrightarrow \ln c = \ln(3d-1)$

Therefore,

$c = 3d - 1$

$e^{\ln(3d-1)} = 3d - 1$

b. Let $\ln e^{u^3+u} = d$. Then

$\ln a = x \Leftrightarrow e^x = a$

$\ln e^{u^3+u} = d \Leftrightarrow e^d = e^{u^3+u}$

Therefore,

$d = u^3 + u$

$\ln e^{u^3+u} = u^3 + u$

c. $\ln 4e = \ln 4 + \ln e$ Product Prop.

$= \ln 4 + 1$ $\quad \ln e = 1$ because $e^1 = e$

d. $\ln\frac{2x}{e} = \ln 2x - \ln e$ Quotient Prop.

$= \ln 2 + \ln x - \ln e$ Product Prop.

$= \ln 2 + \ln x - 1$ $\quad \ln e = 1$ because $e^1 = e$

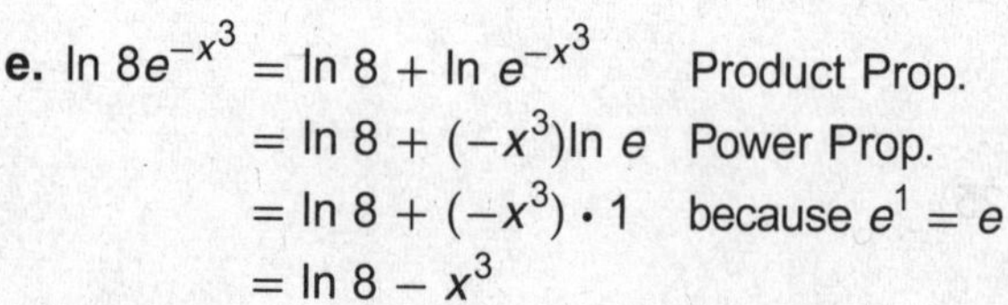

e. $\ln 8e^{-x^3} = \ln 8 + \ln e^{-x^3}$ Product Prop.
$= \ln 8 + (-x^3)\ln e$ Power Prop.
$= \ln 8 + (-x^3) \cdot 1$ because $e^1 = e$
$= \ln 8 - x^3$

f. $\ln\left(\frac{5e^2}{v^3}\right)^3 = 3\ln\left(\frac{5e^2}{v^3}\right)$ Power Prop.
$= 3(\ln 5e^2 - \ln v^3)$ Quot. Prop.
$= 3(\ln 5 + \ln e^2 - \ln v^3)$ Prod. Prop.
$= 3(\ln 5 + 2\ln e - 3\ln v)$ Power Prop.
$= 3(\ln 5 + 2(1) - 3\ln v)$
$= 3\ln 5 + 6 - 9\ln v$

g. Find the decay constant.

$N(t) = N_0e^{-kt}$
$0.5 = 1 \cdot e^{-k(42.3)}$
$\ln 0.5 = \ln e^{-k(42.3)}$
$= -42.3k$
$k = \frac{\ln 0.5}{-42.3} \approx 0.0164$

Write the decay function and solve for t.

$N(t) = N_0e^{-0.0164t}$
$5 = 200e^{-0.0164t}$
$\ln 5 = \ln 200e^{-0.0164t}$
$\ln 5 = \ln 200 + \ln e^{-0.0164t}$
$\ln 5 = \ln 200 - 0.0164t$
$0.0164t = \ln 200 - \ln 5$
$= \ln\frac{200}{5} = \ln 40$
$t = \frac{\ln 40}{0.0164} \approx 225$

It will take about 225 min for 200 mg of chromium-49 to decay to 5 mg.

Practice 81

1. Interchange the variables.

$x = y^2 + 3$
$x - 3 = y^2 + 3 - 3$
$x - 3 = y^2$
$y = \pm\sqrt{x - 3}$

The relation is a function; the inverse is not a function, since there are two possible y-values for any $x > 3$.

2. $z\text{-score} = \frac{x - \text{mean}}{\text{standard deviation}}$
$= \frac{36.8 - 35}{0.5}$
$= \frac{1.8}{0.5} = 3.6$

3. Radicand must be ≥ 0, so domain is $x + 2 \geq 0$ or $x \geq -2$.
$\sqrt{x+2} \geq 0 \rightarrow -4\sqrt{x+2} \leq 0$, so range is $y \leq 0$.

4. Radicand must be ≥ 0, so domain is $x \geq 0$.
$\sqrt{x} \geq 0 \rightarrow \frac{1}{2}\sqrt{x} \geq 0$, so range is $y \geq 0$.

5. $\ln 14e = \ln 14 + \ln e$ Product Prop.
$= \ln 14 + 1$ because $e^1 = e$

6. $\sin(m(\angle C)) = \frac{7.9}{15.8} = \frac{1}{2}$
$m(\angle C) = 30°$

7. Sample: Exponential and logarithmic operations are inverse operations.

8. Domain of $r(u)$ is $\{6, 8\}$. Since $r(6) = 6 - 3 = 3$ and $r(8) = 8 - 3 = 5$, range of $r(u)$ is $\{3, 5\}$. This is a subset of the domain of $p(u)$, so the domain of $p(r(u))$ is identical to domain of $r(u)$, or $\{6, 8\}$. Since

$p(r(6)) = p(3)$
$= 2(3) + 5$
$= 6 + 5 = 11$

and

$p(r(8)) = p(5)$
$= 2(5) + 5$
$= 10 + 5 = 15$,

range of $p(r(u))$ is $\{11, 15\}$.

9.

−9	6	51	−27	0
		−54	27	0
	6	−3	0	0

Remainder is 0, so $x + 9$ is a factor.

10. $Z_2 = (Z_1)^2 + 0.5$
$= (0.3 + 0.8i)^2 + 0.5$
$= 0.3^2 + 2(0.3)(0.8i) + (0.8i)^2 + 0.5$
$= 0.09 + 0.48i + 0.64i^2 + 0.5$
$= 0.09 + 0.48i + 0.64(-1) + 0.5$

$= 0.09 + 0.48i - 0.64 + 0.5$

$= -0.05 + 0.48i$

11. Although the numbers go up to 60, there are only 40 balls, so $P(D)$ is incorrect. Also, probabilities should be added, not multiplied.

12. a. Let x represent frame width. Photo plus frame have length $x + 7 + x = 2x + 7$ inches and width $x + 5 + x = 2x + 5$ inches. Therefore,

$$A = lw$$
$$50 = (2x + 7)(2x + 5)$$
$$50 = 4x^2 + 10x + 14x + 35$$
$$50 = 4x^2 + 24x + 35$$
$$0 = 4x^2 + 24x - 15$$

b. Use the quadratic formula:

$$x = \frac{-b \pm \sqrt{b^2 - 4ac}}{2a}$$
$$= \frac{-24 \pm \sqrt{24^2 - 4(4)(-15)}}{2(4)}$$
$$= \frac{-24 \pm \sqrt{576 + 240}}{8}$$
$$= \frac{-24 \pm \sqrt{816}}{8}$$
$$= -3 \pm \frac{\sqrt{16}\sqrt{51}}{8}$$
$$= -3 \pm \frac{4\sqrt{51}}{8}$$
$$= -3 \pm \frac{\sqrt{51}}{2}$$
$$x = -3 + \frac{\sqrt{51}}{2} \approx 0.57 \text{ or}$$
$$x = -3 - \frac{\sqrt{51}}{2} \approx -6.57$$

Ignoring the negative solution, the frame is about 0.57 in. wide.

13.
$$2d^2 = 8 + 10d$$
$$\frac{2d^2}{2} = \frac{8}{2} + \frac{10d}{2}$$
$$d^2 = 4 + 5d$$
$$d^2 - 5d = 4$$
$$d^2 - 5d + \left(\frac{5}{2}\right)^2 = 4 + \left(\frac{5}{2}\right)^2$$
$$\left(d - \frac{5}{2}\right)^2 = 4 + \frac{25}{4}$$
$$\left(d - \frac{5}{2}\right)^2 = \frac{16 + 25}{4} = \frac{41}{4}$$
$$d - \frac{5}{2} = \pm\frac{\sqrt{41}}{4}$$
$$d = \frac{5}{2} \pm \frac{\sqrt{41}}{2}$$

14.
$$-3x^2 + 18x = -30$$
$$\frac{-3x^2}{-3} + \frac{18x}{-3} = \frac{-30}{-3}$$
$$x^2 - 6x = 10$$
$$x^2 - 6x + (3)^2 = 10 + (3)^2$$
$$(x - 3)^2 = 10 + 9 = 19$$
$$x - 3 = \pm\sqrt{19}$$
$$x = 3 \pm \sqrt{19}$$

15. $P(\text{vacant} \mid \text{Idaho})$

$$= \frac{\text{\# vacant houses in Idaho}}{\text{\# houses in Idaho}}$$
$$= \frac{67{,}148}{548{,}555 + 67{,}148}$$
$$= \frac{67{,}148}{615{,}703} \approx 10.91\%$$

16.
$$\frac{(120x^2 - 60x - 240)\text{ ft}}{\cancel{1\text{ min}}} \cdot \frac{\cancel{1\text{ min}}}{60\text{ s}}$$
$$= \left(\frac{120x^2}{60} - \frac{60x}{60} - \frac{240}{60}\right) \cdot \text{ft/s}$$
$$= (2x^2 - x - 4) \cdot \frac{\text{ft}}{\text{s}}$$

17.
$$2x^2 = 50$$
$$\frac{2x^2}{2} = \frac{50}{2}$$
$$x^2 = 25$$
$$x = \pm\sqrt{25} = \pm 5$$
$$x = 5, -5$$

Answer Choice **C**

18. Sample: The question only gives the negative side of a new shopping mall. Possible re-write: "A new shopping mall will give local jobless people jobs and bring more money to our community. Do you want a new shopping mall in our area?"

19. $\sqrt{3x} + 7 = 9$

$\sqrt{3x} + 7 - 7 = 9 - 7$

$\sqrt{3x} = 2$

$3x = 2^2 = 4$

$x = \frac{4}{3}$

Answer Choice **B**

20. Sample: First function: $x = e^{\frac{1}{2}}$ and $y = \frac{1}{2}$; taking natural logarithm of x, $\ln x = \ln e^{\frac{1}{2}} = \frac{1}{2} = y$, so function could be $y = \ln x$.

Inverse function: $x = \frac{1}{2}$ and $y = e^{\frac{1}{2}}$, so $y = e^x$. Since these functions are inverses of each other, they are the correct functions.

21. $w(190 - w) = 9025$

$190w - w^2 = 9025$

$0 = w^2 - 190w + 9025$

Discriminant

$b^2 - 4ac = (-190)^2 - 4(1)(9025)$

$= 36{,}100 - 36{,}100 = 0$

The discriminant is zero, so there is one real solution. The rancher has just enough material.

22. Find the decay constant.

$N(t) = N_0 e^{-kt}$

$0.5 = 1 \cdot e^{-k(5730)}$

$\ln 0.5 = \ln e^{-k(5730)}$

$= -5730k$

$k = \frac{\ln 0.5}{-5730} \approx 0.00012097$

After 51% has decayed, 49% remains. Write decay function, solve for t:

$N(t) = N_0 e^{-0.00012097t}$

$0.49 = 1e^{-0.00012097t}$

$\ln 0.49 = \ln e^{-0.00012097t}$

$\ln 0.49 = -0.00012097t$

$t = \frac{\ln 0.49}{-0.00012097} \approx 5897$

It will take about 5897 years for 51% of the initial amount to decay.

23. Sample: There are many angles that have any given trigonometric function value.

24. $N(t) = N_0 e^{-kt}$

$N(t) = N_0 e^{-0.0974t}$

$0.3 = 1 \cdot e^{-0.0974t}$

$\ln 0.3 = \ln e^{-0.0974t}$

$\ln 0.3 = -0.0974t$

$t = \frac{\ln 0.3}{-0.0974} \approx 12.36$

25. $V = lwh$

$300 = (2x)(x)(1)$

$300 = 2x^2$

$\frac{300}{2} = \frac{2x^2}{2}$

$150 = x^2$

$x = \pm\sqrt{150} \approx \pm 12.25$

Ignoring the negative root, the dimensions are $1 \times 12.25 \times 2(12.25)$ or $1 \times 12.25 \times 24.50$.

26. $P(\text{integer} > 2)$

$= \frac{\text{\# outcomes for 3, 4, 5, ..., 10}}{\text{total \# outcomes}}$

$= \frac{8}{10} = 0.8$

$P(\text{integer} > 2\text{, 5 times}) = [P(\text{integer} > 2)]^5$

$= (0.8)^5 = 0.32768 = 32.768\%$

27. $c^2 = b^2 + d^2 - 2bd \cos C$

$c^2 = 34.729^2 + 21.65^2$

$-2(34.729)(21.65) \cos(125.37°)$

$c \approx 50.451$

28. mean − 3(s.d.) = 42 − 3(2.2) = 42 − 6.6 = 35.4 in.

mean − 2(s.d.) = 42 − 4.4 = 37.6 in.

mean − 1(s.d.) = 42 − 2.2 = 39.8 in.

mean + 1(s.d.) = 42 + 2.2 = 44.2 in.

mean + 2(s.d.) = 42 + 4.4 = 46.4 in.

mean + 3(s.d.) = 42 + 6.6 = 48.6 in.

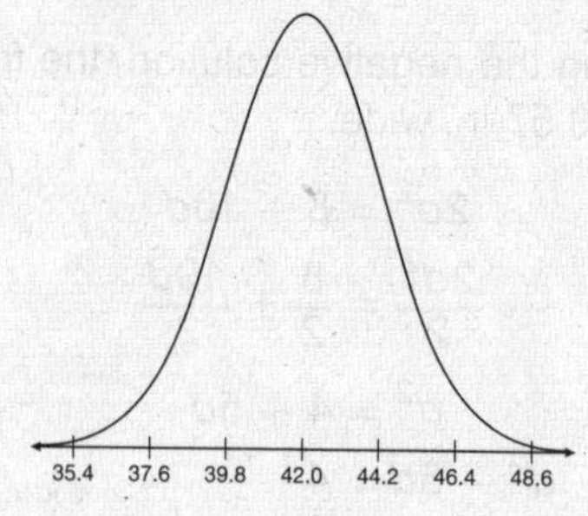

29. $\text{Cos}\,\frac{\pi}{6} = \frac{\sqrt{3}}{2}$

$\text{Cos}^{-1}\left(\frac{\sqrt{3}}{2}\right) = \frac{\pi}{6}$ or 30°

30. Use *z*-score to determine number of s.d.'s of 22 above or below mean:

$z\text{-score} = \frac{x - \text{mean}}{\text{standard deviation}}$

$= \frac{22 - 26}{2} = \frac{-4}{2} = -2$

22 is 2 s.d.'s below mean. 50% of results are above the mean and $\frac{95\%}{2} = 47.5\%$ of results are between 22 and the mean. So 50% + 47.5% = 97.5% of results are above 22.

LESSON 82

Warm Up 82

1. transformation (or *shift* or *translation*)
2. False. $f(x - 1)$ is a shift of 1 unit right.
3. True. $f(x) + 1$ is a shift of 1 unit up.
4. $\sin\frac{\pi}{6} = 0.5$; Answer Choice **B**

Lesson Practice 82

a.

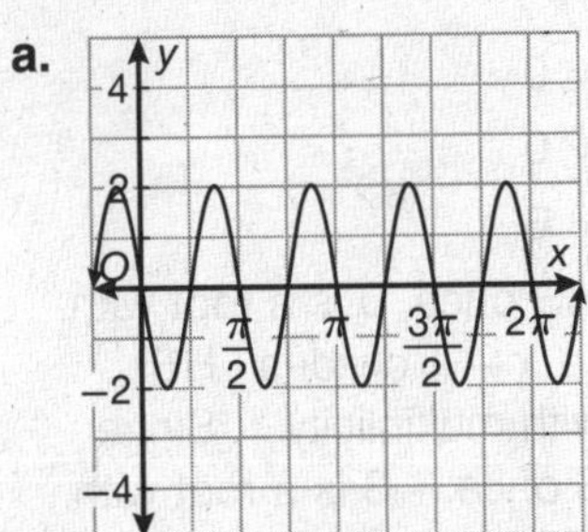

Amplitude: 2; Period: $\frac{\pi}{2}$

b.

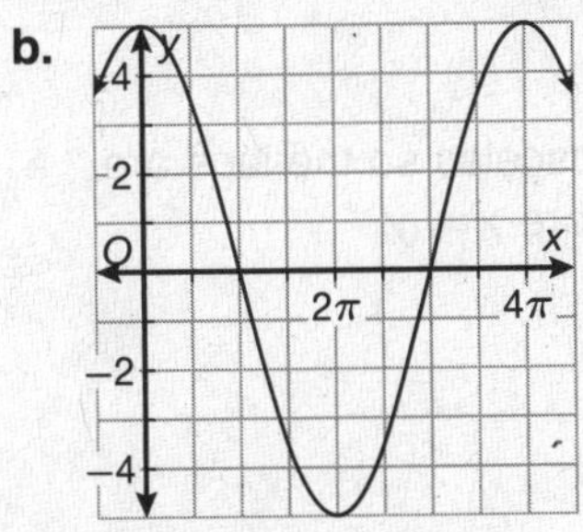

Amplitude: 5; Period: 4π

c. The amplitude is four times the base function and the period is half the base function.

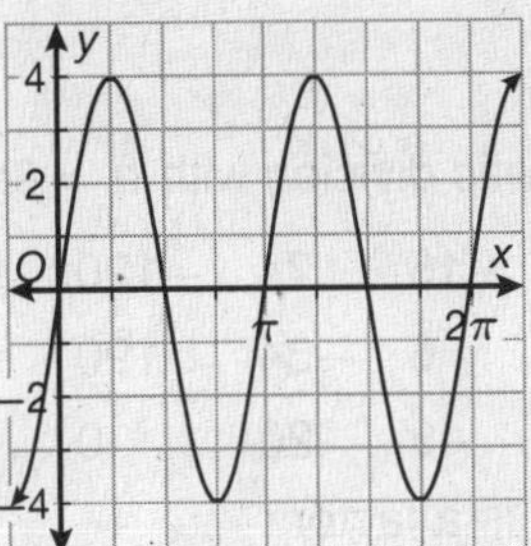

d. The amplitude is negative three times the base function and the period is four times the base function.

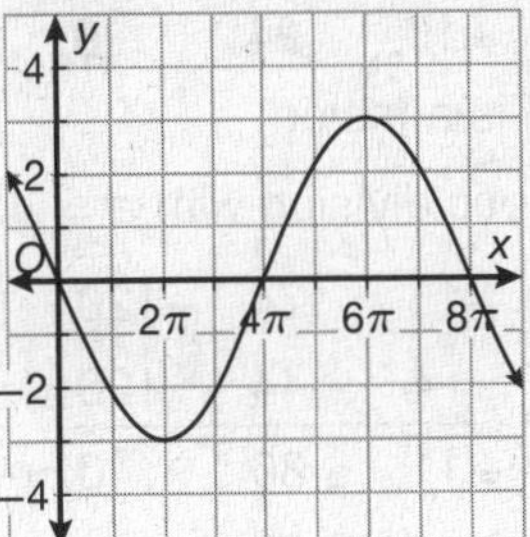

e. The amplitude is three times the base function and the period is half the base function.

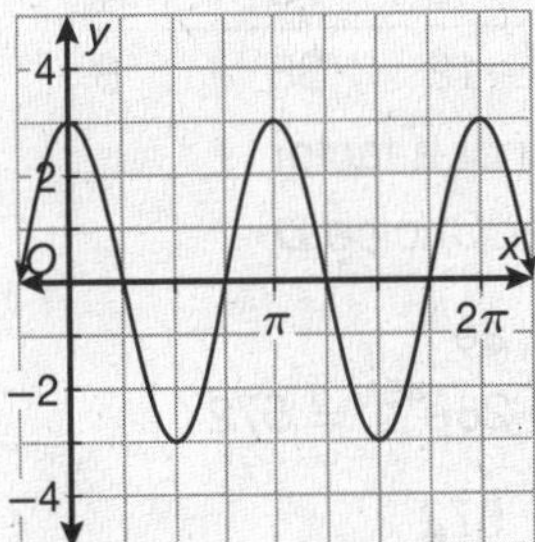

f. The amplitude is negative three times the base function and the period is four times the base function.

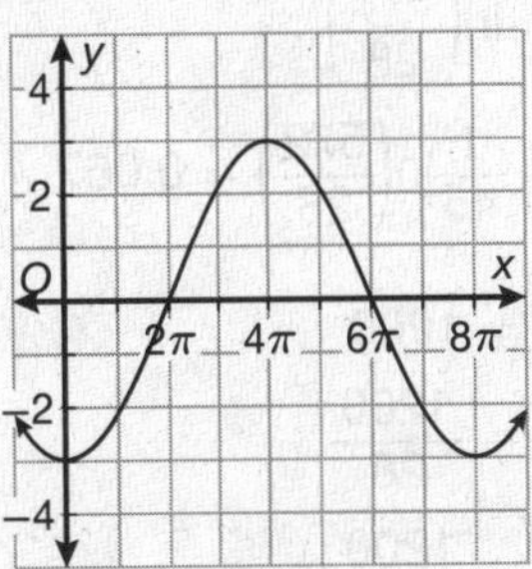

g. The amplitude is two times the base function.
$y = 2 \cos x$

Practice 82

1. A synthetic division with $a = 6$:

$$\begin{array}{r|rrrr} 6 & 1 & -15 & 74 & -120 \\ & & 6 & -54 & 120 \\ \hline & 1 & -9 & 20 & 0 \end{array}$$

$x - 6$ is a factor

B synthetic division with $a = 5$:

$$\begin{array}{r|rrrr} 5 & 1 & -15 & 74 & -120 \\ & & 5 & -50 & 120 \\ \hline & 1 & -10 & 24 & 0 \end{array}$$

$x - 5$ is a factor

C synthetic division with $a = 4$:

$$\begin{array}{r|rrrr} 4 & 1 & -15 & 74 & -120 \\ & & 4 & -44 & 120 \\ \hline & 1 & -11 & 30 & 0 \end{array}$$

$x - 4$ is a factor

D synthetic division with $a = 3$:

$$\begin{array}{r|rrrr} 3 & 1 & -15 & 74 & -120 \\ & & 3 & -36 & 114 \\ \hline & 1 & -12 & 38 & 6 \end{array}$$

$x - 3$ not a factor

Answer Choice **D**

2. $f(t) = ae^{kt}$

$f(45) = 28e^{45k} = 572$

$$\frac{28e^{45k}}{28} = \frac{572}{28}$$

$$e^{45k} = \frac{572}{28}$$

$$45k = \ln\left(\frac{572}{28}\right)$$

$$k = \frac{1}{45}\ln\left(\frac{572}{28}\right) \approx 0.067$$

So,

$$28e^{0.067t} = 1200$$

$$\frac{28e^{0.067t}}{28} = \frac{1200}{28}$$

$$e^{0.067t} = \frac{1200}{28}$$

$$0.067t = \ln\left(\frac{1200}{28}\right)$$

$$t = \frac{1}{0.067}\ln\left(\frac{1200}{28}\right) \approx 56$$

It takes about 56 min for the colony to grow to 1200.

3. Amplitude is $|a| = |-2| = 2$.

Period is $\frac{2\pi}{b} = \frac{2\pi}{1} = 2\pi$.

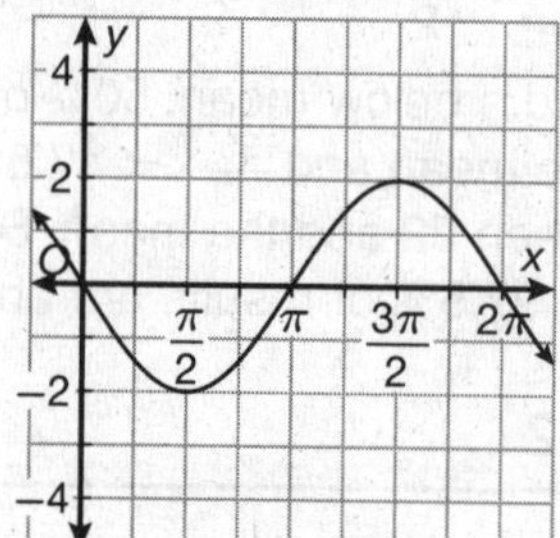

4.

Zero
X=-1
Y=0

Solution is $x = -1$

5. $x^3 + 2x^2 - 3x = 0$

$x(x^2 + 2x - 3) = 0$

$x(x - 1)(x + 3) = 0$

Since x divides LHS once, 0 is a root with multiplicity 1. Since $x - 1$ divides LHS once, 1 is a root with multiplicity 1. Since $x + 3$ divides LHS once, -3 is a root with multiplicity 1.

6. By Pythagorean Theorem

$a^2 + b^2 = c^2$

$x^2 + y^2 = 21^2$

The triangle is isosceles so the legs are congruent, therefore $x = y$.

$2x^2 = 441$

$$x^2 = \frac{441}{2}$$

$$x = \pm\sqrt{\frac{441}{2}}$$

$$= \pm\frac{21}{\sqrt{2}}$$

$$= \pm\frac{21\sqrt{2}}{\sqrt{2}\sqrt{2}} = \pm\frac{21\sqrt{2}}{2}$$

Ignoring the negative solution, $x = y = \frac{21\sqrt{2}}{2}$.

7. $\ln\left(\frac{4x^2}{e^3}\right)^3 = 3\ln\left(\frac{4x^2}{e^3}\right)$ Power Prop. of Log

$= 3(\ln 4x^2 - \ln e^3)$ Quot. Prop. of Log

$= 3(\ln 4 + \ln x^2 - \ln e^3)$ Prod. Prop. of Log

$= 3(\ln 4 + 2\ln x - 3\ln e)$ Power Prop. of Log

$= 3(\ln 4 + 2\ln x - 3)$ because $\ln e = 1$

$= 3\ln 4 + 6\ln x - 9$

8. $A = \frac{1}{2}ac \sin B$

$= \frac{1}{2}(9)(11) \sin 124°$

≈ 41.0

The area is about 41.0 square units.

9. $A = \frac{1}{2}bc \sin A$

$= \frac{1}{2}(13)(7)\sin 68°$

≈ 42.2

The area is about 42.2 square units.

10. a.
$$V = \frac{1}{3}Bh$$
$$108 = \frac{1}{3}(x^2)(x + 3)$$
$$3 \cdot 108 = 3 \cdot \frac{1}{3}(x^2)(x + 3)$$
$$324 = x^2(x + 3)$$
$$324 = x^3 + 3x^2$$
$$324 - 324 = x^3 + 3x^2 - 324$$
$$0 = x^3 + 3x^2 - 324$$

b. Use a graphing calculator:

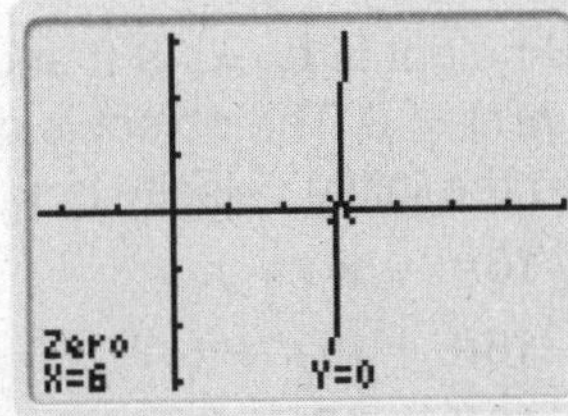

Side length is 6 units.

11. The middle 68% of scores lie within 1 s.d. of the mean, which is between 168.8 − 8.9 = 159.9 cm and 168.8 + 8.9 = 177.7 cm.

12.
$$\text{pH} = -\log[\text{H}^+]$$
$$\text{pH} = 6$$
$$6 = -\log[\text{H}^+]$$
$$-6 = \log[\text{H}^+]$$
$$10^{-6} = [\text{H}^+]$$
$$0.000001 = [\text{H}^+]$$
$$\text{pH} = 8$$
$$8 = -\log[\text{H}^+]$$
$$-8 = \log[\text{H}^+]$$
$$10^{-8} = [\text{H}^+]$$
$$0.00000001 = [\text{H}^+]$$

The range of concentration of hydrogen ions is 0.00000001 to 0.000001 Mol/L.

13. The student interpreted $\text{Cos}^{-1}(0.8)$ as a reciprocal instead of as an inverse trigonometric function value. Correct solution: $\theta = \text{Cos}^{-1}(0.8) \approx 0.64$ radian.

14. $f(x) = 12x^3 + 4x^2 - 2x$

$= 2x(6x^2 + 2x - 1)$

One root is $x = 0$. Use the quadratic formula

$$x = \frac{-b \pm \sqrt{b^2 - 4ac}}{2a}$$
$$= \frac{-2 \pm \sqrt{2^2 - 4(6)(-1)}}{2(6)}$$
$$= \frac{-2 \pm \sqrt{4 + 24}}{12}$$
$$= \frac{-2 \pm \sqrt{28}}{12}$$
$$= \frac{-2 \pm 2\sqrt{7}}{12}$$
$$= \frac{-1 \pm \sqrt{7}}{6}$$

The roots are 0, $\frac{-1 + \sqrt{7}}{6}$, and $\frac{-1 - \sqrt{7}}{6}$.

15. $f(x) = (x - 2)(x^2 + 6) - (x - 2)(7x + 4)$

$= (x - 2)[(x^2 + 6) - (7x + 4)]$

$= (x - 2)(x^2 + 6 - 7x - 4)$

$= (x - 2)(x^2 - 7x + 2)$

One root is $x = 2$. Use the quadratic formula

$$x = \frac{-b \pm \sqrt{b^2 - 4ac}}{2a}$$

$$\frac{-(-7) \pm \sqrt{(-7)^2 - 4(1)(2)}}{2(1)}$$

$$= \frac{7 \pm \sqrt{49 - 8}}{2}$$

$$= \frac{7 \pm \sqrt{41}}{2}$$

The roots are 2, $\frac{7 + \sqrt{41}}{2}$, and $\frac{7 - \sqrt{41}}{2}$.

16. Total # of cars $= 16 + 14 + 9 + 6 = 45$

$$P(\text{5 gold cars}) = \frac{14}{45} \cdot \frac{13}{44} \cdot \frac{12}{43} \cdot \frac{11}{42} \cdot \frac{10}{41}$$

$$= \frac{240{,}240}{146{,}611{,}080}$$

$$\approx 0.0016 \text{ or } 0.16\%$$

The probability is 0.16%.

17.

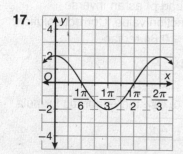

18. $P(\text{2 tails, once}) = P(\text{tail}) \cdot P(\text{tail})$

$$= \frac{1}{2} \cdot \frac{1}{2} = \frac{1}{4}$$

$P(\text{2 tails, 5 times}) = [P(\text{2 tails, once})]^5$

$$= \left(\frac{1}{4}\right)^5$$

$$= \frac{1}{1024} \approx 0.001$$

Answer Choice **C**

19. Sample: If $b = 2$ and $c = 3$, then $bi(ci) = 2i(3i) = 6i^2 = 6(-1) = -6$. If $b = -2$ and $c = 3$, then $bi(ci) = -2i(3i) = -6i^2 = -6(-1) = 6$.

20. Solve the capture=recapture problem.

$$\frac{\text{\# tagged on 2nd visit}}{\text{\# captured on 2nd visit}} = \frac{\text{\# tagged}}{\text{total \# of animals}}$$

$$\frac{n-1}{n-1} = \frac{n}{N}$$

$$1 = \frac{n}{N}$$

$$N = n$$

The population is about n animals.

21. $2(3i) = 6i = 0 + 6i$

22. $-4(5i) = -20i = 0 - 20i$

23. Sample: Exponential and logarithmic operations are inverse operations.

24. Draw a diagram.

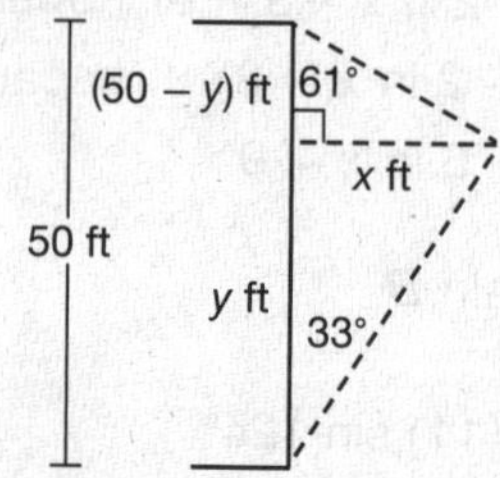

Let y be as shown.

South end: $\tan 33° = \frac{x}{y}$

$$y = \frac{x}{\tan 33°}$$

North end: $\tan 61° = \frac{x}{50 - y}$

$$50 - y = \frac{x}{\tan 61°}$$

$$y = 50 - \frac{x}{\tan 61°}$$

Substitute for y from the first equation.

$$\frac{x}{\tan 33°} = 50 - \frac{x}{\tan 61°}$$

$$x \tan 61° = 50 \tan 33° \tan 61° - x \tan 33°$$

$$x \tan 61° + x \tan 33° = 50 \tan 33° \tan 61°$$

$$x(\tan 61° + \tan 33°) = 50 \tan 33° \tan 61°$$

$$x = \frac{50 \tan 33° \tan 61°}{\tan 61° + \tan 33°}$$

$$x \approx 23.88$$

The flagpole is about 23.88 ft away.

25. The initial height is $h_0 = 49$ ft and final height is $h(t) = 0$. The object is dropped, not thrown, so the initial velocity is $v_0 = 0$.

$$h(t) = -16t^2 + v_0 t + h_0$$

$$0 = -16t^2 + (0)t + (49)$$

$$0 = -16t^2 + 49$$

$$16t^2 = 49$$

$$\frac{16t^2}{16} = \frac{49}{16}$$
$$t^2 = \frac{49}{16}$$
$$t = \pm\sqrt{\frac{49}{16}}$$
$$= \pm\frac{7}{4} = \pm 1.75$$

Ignoring the negative solution, it takes 1.75 s for the object to hit the ground.

26. a. $5x - 3x^2 = 10$
$$5x - 3x^2 - 10 = 10 - 10$$
$$-3x^2 + 5x - 10 = 0$$

b. $b^2 - 4ac = (5)^2 - 4(-3)(-10)$
$$= 25 - 120 = -95$$

c. The discriminant is negative, so there are two complex solutions.

27. $T = 2\pi\sqrt{\frac{L}{9.8}}$
$$4 = 2\pi\sqrt{\frac{L}{9.8}}$$
$$\frac{4}{2\pi} = \frac{2\pi}{2\pi}\sqrt{\frac{L}{9.8}}$$
$$\frac{2}{\pi} = \sqrt{\frac{L}{9.8}}$$
$$\frac{L}{9.8} = \left(\frac{2}{\pi}\right)^2 = \frac{4}{\pi^2}$$
$$L = 9.8 \cdot \frac{4}{\pi^2} \approx 3.97$$

The length is about 3.97 m.

28. Period of $y = 3\cos(2x)$: $\frac{2\pi}{2} = \pi$

Cycles in 2π: $\frac{2\pi}{\pi} = 2$

29. Sample: First add the side lengths and divide the sum by two. Then find the difference between this value, s, and each of the three sides. Next, find product of these three differences and the value of s. Finally, take the square root of this product.

30. Find the decay constant.
$$N(t) = N_0e^{-kt}$$
$$0.5 = 1 \cdot e^{-k(73.1)}$$
$$\ln 0.5 = \ln e^{-k(73.1)}$$
$$\ln 0.5 = -73.1k$$
$$k = \frac{\ln 0.5}{-73.1} \approx 0.00948$$

Write the decay function and solve for t.
$$N(t) = N_0e^{-0.00948t}$$
$$0.7 = 1 \cdot e^{-0.00948t}$$
$$\ln 0.7 = \ln e^{-0.00948t}$$
$$\ln 0.7 = -0.00948t$$
$$t = \frac{\ln 0.7}{-0.00948} \approx 37.6$$

The decay will take about 37.6 h.

LESSON 83

Warm Up 83

1. FOIL
2. Negative factor pairs for 12 are $(-1)(-12)$, $(-2)(-6)$, and $(-3)(-4)$. Factor pair $(-3)(-4)$ sums to -7. Therefore, $x^2 - 7x + 12 = (x - 3)(x - 4)$
3. $(2x + 4)(x - 5)$
$$= (2x)(x) + (2x)(-5) + (4)(x) + (4)(-5)$$
$$= 2x^2 - 10x + 4x - 20$$
$$= 2x^2 - 6x - 20$$

Lesson Practice 83

a. Write the roots as solutions of two equations.

$x = -7$ or $x = 3$

$x + 7 = 0$ or $x - 3 = 0$

Sample:

$(x + 7)(x - 3) = 0$ Converse of Zero Prod. Prop.

$x^2 + 4x - 21 = 0$

b. Write the roots as solutions of two equations.

$x = 2$ or $x = 3$

$x - 2 = 0$ or $x - 3 = 0$

Sample:

$(x - 2)(x - 3) = 0$

$x^2 - 5x + 6 = 0$

Add a constant factor to find the other equations.

$2(x-2)(x-3)=0 \qquad 3(x-2)(x-3)=0$

$2(x^2-5x+6)=0 \qquad 3(x^2-5x+6)=0$

$2x^2-10x+12=0 \qquad 3x^2-15x+18=0$

c. Treat the single root of $x=-5$ as two identical roots.

$x=-5$ or $\quad x=-5$

$x+5=0$ or $x+5=0$

Sample:

$(x+5)(x+5)=0$

$x^2+10x+25=0$

d. Treat the single root of $x=4$ as two identical roots.

$x=4$ or $\quad x=4$

$x-4=0$ or $x-4=0$

Sample:

$(x-4)(x-4)=0$

$x^2-8x+16=0$

Add a constant factor to find the other equations.

$\frac{1}{2}(x-4)(x-4)=0 \qquad -(x-4)(x-4)=0$

$\frac{1}{2}(x^2-8x+16)=0 \qquad -(x^2-8x+16)=0$

$\frac{1}{2}x^2-4x+8=0 \qquad -x^2+8x-16=0$

e. Write the roots as the solution to one equation. Sample:

$x=1\pm 4i$

$x-1=\pm 4i$

$x-1=\pm\sqrt{-16}$

$(x-1)^2=-16$

$x^2-2x+1=-16$

$x^2-2x+17=0$

f. Write the roots as the solution to one equation. Sample:

$x=\pm 7i$

$x=\pm\sqrt{-49}$

$x^2=-49$

$x^2+49=0$

Add a constant factor to find the other equations.

$x^2+49=0 \qquad x^2+49=0$

$\frac{1}{7}(x^2+49)=\frac{1}{7}(0) \qquad -(x^2+49)=-(0)$

$\frac{1}{7}x^2+7=0 \qquad -x^2-49=0$

g. Understand: An arch is parabolic. A parabola's function can be determined given the vertex and the coordinates of another point.

Plan: Set x-intercepts at (0, 0) and (50, 0) to represent the bases. The x-coordinate of the vertex is halfway between them and the y-coordinate is the height, so vertex is at (25, 30).

Solve: Use the vertex form of the quadratic function. Substitute $h=25$ and $k=30$; substitute for x-intercepts and solve for a.

$y=a(x-h)^2+k$

$y=a(x-25)^2+30$

$0=a(0-25)^2+30$

$0=625a+30$

$-30=625a$

$\frac{-30}{625}=a$

$-0.048=a$

Therefore,

$y=-0.048(x-25)^2+30$

$y=-0.048(x^2-50x+625)+30$

$y=-0.048x^2+2.4x-30+30$

$y=-0.048x^2+2.4x$

Check: Graph the function on a graphing calculator.

Practice 83

1. $(8\cdot 216)^{\frac{1}{3}}=(8)^{\frac{1}{3}}(216)^{\frac{1}{3}}$

$=2\cdot 6=12$

2. $\frac{6^{\frac{14}{9}}}{6^{\frac{6}{9}}}=6^{\frac{14}{9}-\frac{6}{9}}$

$=6^{\frac{8}{9}}$

$=\sqrt[9]{6^8}\approx 4.92$

3. Total # of crayons = 3 + 5 + 8 + 2 = 18

P(1 purple, 2 red, 1 green)

$= \frac{3}{18} \cdot \frac{5}{17} \cdot \frac{4}{16} \cdot \frac{8}{15}$

$= \frac{480}{73{,}440} \approx 0.0065$ or 0.65%

4. $32z^5 - 2z$

$= 2z(16z^4 - 1)$

$= 2z((4z^2)^2 - 1^2)$

$= 2z(4z^2 - 1)(4z^2 + 1)$

$= 2z((2z)^2 - 1^2)(4z^2 + 1)$

$= 2z(2z - 1)(2z + 1)(4z^2 + 1)$

5. $a^5b^2 - a^2b^4 + 2a^4b - 2ab^3 + a^3 - b^2$

$= a^2b^2(a^3 - b^2) + 2ab(a^3 - b^2) + (a^3 - b^2)$

$= (a^2b^2 + 2ab + 1)(a^3 - b^2)$

$= \left[(ab)^2 + 2(ab)(1) + 1^2\right](a^3 - b^2)$

$= (ab + 1)^2(a^3 - b^2)$

6. a. Mutually exclusive; any given male client cannot be both younger than 36 and older than 75.

b. P(male under 36 or male over 75)

$= \frac{\text{\# outcomes for event}}{\text{total \# outcomes}}$

$= \frac{39 + 47}{39 + 45 + 54 + 47 + 41 + 52 + 40 + 56}$

$= \frac{86}{374} \approx 0.23$ or 23%

c. P(3 clients male under 36 or male over 75)

$= [P(\text{male under 36 or male over 75})]^3$

$\approx 0.23^3 \approx 0.01$ or 1%

7. Method 1: $(f \circ g)(x) = f(g(x))$

$= f(3x)$

$= 2(3x) + 5$

$= 6x + 5$

$(f \circ g)(4) = 6(4) + 5$

$= 24 + 5 = 29$

Method 2: $g(4) = 3(4) = 12$

$(f \circ g)(4) = f(g(4))$

$= f(12)$

$= 2(12) + 5$

$= 24 + 5 = 29$

8. Equation $x = \frac{-b}{2a}$ is the axis of symmetry, which passes through vertex of the parabola. The vertex has x-coordinate $\frac{-b}{2a}$. The expression $\pm\frac{\sqrt{b^2 - 4ac}}{2a}$ shows that the zeros are the same distance from axis of symmetry.

9. $\log_{20} 20^{a-b} = (a - b)\log_{20} 20$

$= (a - b) \cdot 1$

$= a - b$

Answer Choice **A**

10.

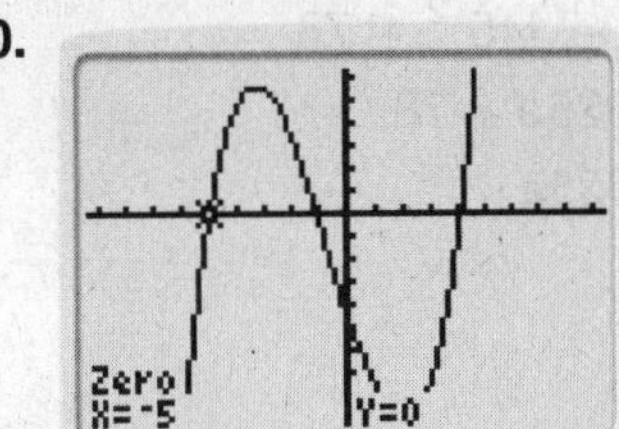

One root is −5. Use synthetic division with $a = -5$:

−5	2	4	−39	−45
		−10	30	45
	2	−6	−9	0

Equation factors as

$(x + 5)(2x^2 - 6x - 9) = 0$

Use the quadratic formula.

$x = \frac{-b \pm \sqrt{b^2 - 4ac}}{2a}$

$= \frac{-(-6) \pm \sqrt{(-6)^2 - 4(2)(-9)}}{2(2)}$

$= \frac{6 \pm \sqrt{36 + 72}}{4}$

$= \frac{6 \pm \sqrt{108}}{4}$

$= \frac{6 \pm \sqrt{36}\sqrt{3}}{4}$

$= \frac{6 \pm 6\sqrt{3}}{4}$

$= \frac{3 \pm 3\sqrt{3}}{2}$

The solutions are −5, $\frac{3 + 3\sqrt{3}}{2}$, and $\frac{3 - 3\sqrt{3}}{2}$.

11. If mn is odd, then m and n are each odd. Therefore, the domain and range are all real numbers.

12. Set x-intercepts at (0, 0) and (290, 0); vertex at (145, 78). Use the vertex form of the quadratic function. Substitute $h = 145$ and $k = 78$; substitute for x-intercepts and solve for a:

$$y = a(x - h)^2 + k$$
$$y = a(x - 145)^2 + 78$$
$$0 = a(0 - 145)^2 + 78$$
$$0 = 21{,}025a + 78$$
$$-78 = 21{,}025a$$
$$-\frac{78}{21{,}025} = a$$

Therefore,

$$y = -\frac{78}{21{,}025}(x - 145)^2 + 78$$
$$y = -\frac{78}{21{,}025}(x^2 - 2(145)(x) + 145^2) + 78$$
$$y = -\frac{78}{21{,}025}(x^2 - 290x + 21{,}025) + 78$$
$$y = -\frac{78}{21{,}025}x^2 + \frac{156}{145}x - 78 + 78$$
$$y \approx -0.0037x^2 + 1.076x$$

13. Possible estimate: $\text{Sin}^{-1}(0.02) \approx 1°$. Possible explanation: 0.02 is close to 0 and $\text{Sin}^{-1}(0) = 0°$. $\text{Sin}^{-1}(0.02)$ is the measure of an angle that terminates in Quadrant I, so angle measure must be positive.

14. $E = I(Z)$
$$= (24 - 28i)(5 + i)$$
$$= 120 + 24i - 140i - 28i^2$$
$$= 120 - 116i - 28(-1)$$
$$= 120 - 116i + 28$$
$$= 148 - 116i$$

The voltage is $(148 - 116i)$ V.

15. Sample: $x^4 - 625$ is difference of two squares. It can be written as $(x^2)^2 - (25)^2$.

16. Prism A:

$$d = \sqrt{l^2 + w^2 + h^2}$$
$$9.1 = \sqrt{7^2 + 3^2 + h^2}$$
$$9.1^2 = 7^2 + 3^2 + h^2$$
$$82.81 = 49 + 9 + h^2$$
$$82.81 - 49 - 9 = h^2$$
$$24.81 = h^2$$
$$h = \sqrt{24.81} \quad \text{(ignore negative root)}$$
$$\approx 5.0$$

Prism B:

$$d = \sqrt{l^2 + w^2 + h^2}$$
$$10.2 = \sqrt{8^2 + 2^2 + h^2}$$
$$10.2^2 = 8^2 + 2^2 + h^2$$
$$104.04 = 64 + 4 + h^2$$
$$104.04 - 64 - 4 = h^2$$
$$36.04 = h^2$$
$$h = \sqrt{36.04} \quad \text{(ignore negative root)}$$
$$\approx 6.0$$

Prism B is higher by about 1 in.

17. When you know the lengths of two sides and the measure of the included angle, or when you know the lengths of the three sides.

18. First 4 two-digit numbers that match labeled numbers are 15, 22, 13, and (ignoring repeat of 22) 11. These correspond to New York, Georgia, Rhode Island, and New Hampshire.

19. **a.**
$$-18x^2 - 84x = 98$$
$$-18x^2 - 84x - 98 = 0$$

b. $-2(9x^2 + 42x + 49) = 0$

c. $b^2 - 4ac = (42)^2 - 4(9)(49)$
$$= 1764 - 1764 = 0$$

Since discriminant is zero, there is one real solution.

20. Let the slower satellite orbit at distance r, and the faster one at distance R.

$$a = \frac{v^2}{r} = \frac{(5v)^2}{R}$$
$$\frac{v^2}{r} = \frac{25v^2}{R}$$
$$v^2R = 25v^2r$$
$$\frac{v^2R}{v^2} = \frac{25v^2r}{v^2}$$
$$R = 25r$$

The faster satellite is 25 times farther from the Earth's center.

21. 80 cannot be subtracted from 116. 116 should be subtracted from each side, and then both sides should be divided by −80.

Correct solution:

$$7.5^2 = 4^2 + 10^2 - 2(4)(10)\cos C$$
$$56.25 = 116 - 80\cos C$$
$$-116 + 56.25 = -116 + 116 - 80\cos C$$
$$-59.75 = -80\cos C$$
$$\frac{-59.75}{-80} = \frac{-80\cos C}{-80}$$
$$0.746875 = \cos C$$
$$\cos^{-1}(0.746875) = m\angle C$$
$$m\angle C \approx 41.7^\circ$$

22.
$$x = 7 \quad \text{or} \quad x = 7$$
$$x - 7 = 7 - 7 \quad\quad x - 7 = 7 - 7$$
$$x - 7 = 0 \quad \text{or} \quad x - 7 = 0$$
$$(x - 7)(x - 7) = 0$$

Answer Choice **C**

23. Student B incorrectly recalled that sin x has period π.

24. $A = \frac{1}{2}ac \sin B$

$= \frac{1}{2}(19)(8)\sin(75^\circ) \approx 73.4$

The area is about 73.4 square units.

25.
$$A = Pe^{rt}$$
$$2P = Pe^{r(10)}$$
$$2 = e^{10r}$$
$$\ln 2 = 10r$$
$$r = \frac{\ln 2}{10} \approx 0.0693 \text{ or } 6.93\%$$

The annual interest rate will be 6.93%.

26. $x = 0 \Rightarrow f(x) = x + 2$

$f(0) = 0 + 2 = 2$

$x = 2 \Rightarrow f(x) = x + 2$

$f(2) = 2 + 2 = 4$

27. $x = 0 \Rightarrow f(0) = 12$

$x = 2 \Rightarrow f(2) = 20$

28. Use the expression for the period.

$$\pi = \frac{2\pi}{b}$$
$$b = \frac{2\pi}{\pi} = 2$$

Answer Choice **D**

29. a. The roots are complex, not real, so the function never crosses the x-axis. Therefore probability = 0 or 0%.

b. x-coordinate of vertex is average of the roots:

$$x = \frac{(4 - 5i) + (4 + 5i)}{2}$$
$$= \frac{(4 + 4) + (5 - 5)i}{2}$$
$$= \frac{8}{2} = 4$$

Therefore probability = 1 or 100%.

30.
$$x = 6 \quad \text{or} \quad x = -2$$
$$x - 6 = 0 \quad \text{or} \quad x + 2 = 0$$

Sample:

$$(x - 6)(x + 2) = 0$$
$$x^2 - 4x - 12 = 0$$

LESSON 84

Warm Up 84

1. rational

2. $4x^2 = 2 \cdot 2 \cdot x^2 \cdot y^0$ and $6x^3y = 2 \cdot 3 \cdot x^3 \cdot y^1$

LCM $= 2 \cdot 2 \cdot 3 \cdot x^3 \cdot y^1 = 12x^3y$

3.
$$\frac{5}{3x + 6} + \frac{x}{x + 2} = \frac{5}{3(x + 2)} + \frac{x}{x + 2}$$
$$= \frac{5}{3(x + 2)} + \frac{3 \cdot x}{3(x + 2)}$$
$$= \frac{5 + 3x}{3(x + 2)}$$

4.
$$\frac{3x^2}{x^2 - 8x + 16} = \frac{3x^2}{(x - 4)^2}$$

and

$$\frac{2}{5x^2 - 15x - 20} = \frac{2}{5(x^2 - 3x - 4)}$$
$$= \frac{2}{5(x - 4)(x + 1)}$$

LCD is LCM of denominators, $5(x - 4)^2(x + 1)$.

Answer Choice **D**

5. $\dfrac{x^2+4x-12}{6x-12} = \dfrac{(x-2)(x+6)}{6(x-2)}$

$= \dfrac{x+6}{6}$

Lesson Practice 84

a. $\dfrac{2x-2}{3x} = \dfrac{5}{2}$

$4x - 4 = 15x$

$-4 = 11x$

$x = \dfrac{-4}{11}$

b. $\dfrac{30}{x} = \dfrac{x+4}{2}$

$60 = x^2 + 4x$

$0 = x^2 + 4x - 60$

$0 = (x+10)(x-6)$

$x + 10 = 0$ and $x - 6 = 0$

$x = -10$ $x = 6$

c. $\dfrac{3x}{x+3} = -1$

Clear the fraction.

$(x+3)\left(\dfrac{3x}{x+3}\right) = -1(x+3)$

$3x = -x - 3$

$x + 3x = x - x - 3$

$4x = -3$

$x = -\dfrac{3}{4}$

Solution does not make denominator 0. Solution is $x = -\frac{3}{4}$.

d. $5 - \frac{4}{x} = x$

Clear the fraction.

$x\left(5 - \frac{4}{x}\right) = x(x)$

$5x - 4 = x^2$

$0 = x^2 - 5x + 4$

$0 = (x-1)(x-4)$

$x - 1 = 0$ or $x - 4 = 0$

$x = 1$ or $x = 4$

Both $x = 1$ and $x = 4$ are solutions since neither is a restricted value.

e. $\dfrac{8x}{x-1} - \dfrac{x+33}{x^2+2x-3} = 9$

$\dfrac{8x}{x-1} - \dfrac{x+33}{(x-1)(x+3)} = 9$

The LCD is $(x-1)(x-3)$.

$(x-1)(x+3)\left(\dfrac{8x}{x-1}\right)$

$-(x-1)(x+3)\left(\dfrac{x+33}{(x-1)(x+3)}\right)$

$(x+3)8x - (x+33) = 9(x-1)(x+3)$

$8x^2 + 24x - x - 33 = 9(x^2 + 2x - 3)$

$8x^2 + 23x - 33 = 9x^2 + 18x - 27$

$0 = 9x^2 - 8x^2 + 18x - 23x - 27 + 33$

$0 = x^2 - 5x + 6$

$0 = (x-2)(x-3)$

$x - 2 = 0$ or $x - 3 = 0$

$x = 2$ $x = 3$

Both $x = 2$ and $x = 3$ are solutions since neither is a restricted value.

f. $\dfrac{3x}{x^2-1} = \dfrac{4}{x}$

$\dfrac{3x}{(x-1)(x+1)} = \dfrac{4}{x}$

The LCD is $x(x-1)(x+1)$.

$x(x-1)(x+1)\left(\dfrac{3x}{(x-1)(x+1)}\right)$

$= x(x-1)(x+1)\left(\dfrac{4}{x}\right)$

$x(3x) = 4(x-1)(x+1)$

$3x^2 = 4x^2 - 4$

$0 = 4x^2 - 3x^2 - 4$

$0 = x^2 - 4$

$0 = (x-2)(x+2)$

$x - 2 = 0$ or $x + 2 = 0$

$x = 2$ $x = -2$

Both $x = 2$ and $x = -2$ are solutions since neither is a restricted value.

g. Use $r = \frac{d}{t}$. Let t represent time on pavement, so $5 - t$ is time on dirt.

$\dfrac{6}{5-t} = \dfrac{3}{4} \cdot \dfrac{18}{t}$

$\dfrac{6}{5-t} = \dfrac{27}{2t}$

$2t(5-t)\left(\dfrac{6}{5-t}\right) = 2t(5-t)\left(\dfrac{27}{2t}\right)$

$$2t(6) = (5 - t)(27)$$
$$12t = 135 - 27t$$
$$39t = 135$$
$$t = \frac{45}{13} \approx 3.46$$

The biker spent about 3.46 h on pavement and 5 − 3.46 = 1.54 h on dirt

Practice 84

1. θ is between 360° and 720°, so has the same reference angle as 504° − 360° = 144°. Therefore reference angle is 180° − 144° = 36°.

2.

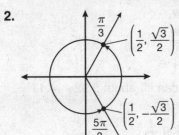

From unit circle, values of $\cos^{-1}\left(\frac{1}{2}\right)$ between 0 and 2π are $\frac{\pi}{3}$ and $\frac{5\pi}{3}$. All values have form $\frac{\pi}{3} + 2\pi n$, $\frac{5\pi}{3} + 2\pi n$, where n is an integer.

3.

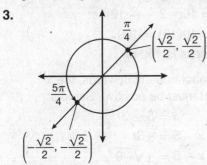

From unit circle, values of $\tan^{-1}(1)$ between 0 and 2π are $\frac{\pi}{4}$ and $\frac{5\pi}{4}$. All values have form $\frac{\pi}{4} + 2\pi n$, $\frac{5\pi}{4} + 2\pi n$, where n is an integer.

4. Possible response is about 10 square units.

5. $x^2 - x + c = 0$

The discriminant is

$b^2 - 4ac = (-1)^2 - 4(1)c = 1 - 4c$

a. If there are two real solutions

$$b^2 - 4ac > 0$$
$$1 - 4c > 0$$
$$1 > 4c$$
$$0.25 > c$$

Two real solutions: $c < 0.25$

b. If there is one real solutions

$$b^2 - 4ac = 0$$
$$1 - 4c = 0$$
$$1 = 4c$$
$$0.25 = c$$

One real solution: $c = 0.25$

c. If there are two complex solutions

$$b^2 - 4ac < 0$$
$$1 - 4c < 0$$
$$1 < 4c$$
$$0.25 < c$$

Two complex solutions: $c > 0.25$

6. $x^2 - 24x \rightarrow x^2 - 24x + \left(\frac{24}{2}\right)^2$

$$= x^2 - 24x + 12^2$$
$$= x^2 - 24x + 144$$
$$= (x - 12)^2$$

7.
$$z = \frac{x - \text{mean}}{\sigma}$$
$$-1.4 = \frac{x - 60}{12}$$
$$-1.4(12) = x - 60$$
$$-16.8 = x - 60$$
$$-16.8 + 60 = x - 60 + 60$$
$$43.2 = x$$

8. Use Heron's formula.

$$s = \frac{1}{2}(a + b + c)$$
$$= \frac{1}{2}(34 + 44 + 27)$$
$$= \frac{1}{2}(105) = 52.5$$
$$A = \sqrt{s(s - a)(s - b)(s - c)}$$
$$= \sqrt{52.5(52.5 - 34)(52.5 - 44)(52.5 - 27)}$$
$$= \sqrt{52.5(18.5)(8.5)(25.5)}$$
$$= \sqrt{210{,}518.4375} \approx 459$$

The enclosed area is about 459 mi^2.

9.

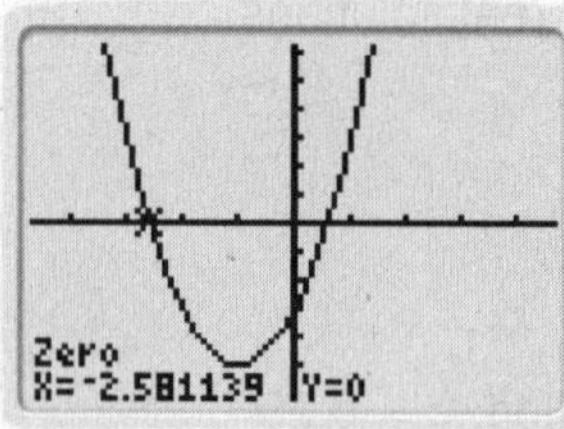

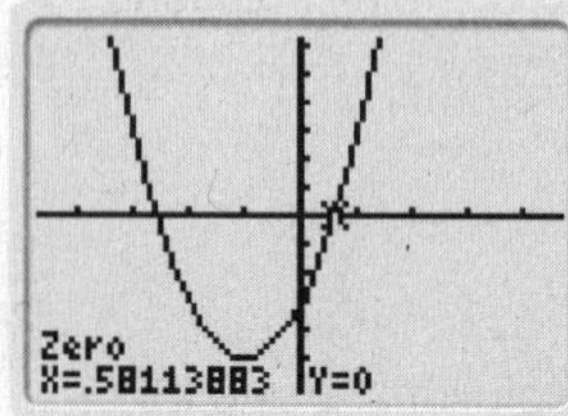

The solutions are −2.581 and 0.581.

10. Exponential and logarithmic operations are inverse operations, so $e^{\ln 4x^2} = 4x^2$.
Answer Choice **D**

11. $P(\text{Texas} \mid \text{occupied})$

$$= \frac{\text{\# occupied houses in Texas}}{\text{total \# occupied houses}}$$

$$= \frac{8{,}109{,}388}{2{,}905{,}071 + 8{,}109{,}388 + 814{,}028}$$

$$= \frac{8{,}109{,}388}{11{,}828{,}487} \approx 0.6856 \text{ or } 68.56\%$$

The probability is 68.65%.

12. Sample: Multiply both sides by 2 to get $x^2 - 4 = 0$, then factor and solve.

13. Student A made the error. The value of b in $|a + bi|$ is −1, not 0.

14. $x = 7$ or $x = 7$

$x - 7 = 0$ or $x - 7 = 0$

Sample:

$(x - 7)(x - 7) = 0$

$x^2 - 14x + 49 = 0$

15. First rope:

$$d = \frac{\sqrt{15w}}{\pi}$$

$$3 = \frac{\sqrt{15w}}{\pi}$$

$$3\pi = \sqrt{15w}$$

$$(3\pi)^2 = 15w$$

$$9\pi^2 = 15w$$

$$\frac{9\pi^2}{15} = \frac{15w}{15}$$

$$w \approx 5.92$$

Second rope:

$$d = \frac{\sqrt{15w}}{\pi}$$

$$2.5 = \frac{\sqrt{15w}}{\pi}$$

$$2.5\pi = \sqrt{15w}$$

$$(2.5\pi)^2 = 15w$$

$$6.25\pi^2 = 15w$$

$$\frac{6.25\pi^2}{15} = \frac{15w}{15}$$

$$w \approx 4.11$$

The first rope can lift about 5.92 − 4.11 = 1.81 tons more.

16. $L(I) = 10 \log \frac{I}{I_0}$

$$L(0.01) = 10 \log \frac{0.01}{10^{-12}}$$

$$= 10(\log 0.01 - \log 10^{-12})$$

$$= 10(-2 - (-12))$$

$$= 10(10) = 100$$

The loudness is 100 db.

17. If the parabola opens upwards, the x^2 coefficient must be positive. Sample:

$$x = 5 \pm 3i$$

$$x - 5 = \pm 3i$$

$$x - 5 = \pm\sqrt{-9}$$

$$(x - 5)^2 = -9$$

$$x^2 - 10x + 25 = -9$$

$$x^2 - 10x + 34 = 0$$

If the parabola opens downwards, the x^2 coefficient must be negative. Sample:

$$x^2 - 10x + 34 = 0$$

$$-\frac{1}{2}(x^2 - 10x + 34) = -\frac{1}{2}(0)$$

$$-\frac{1}{2}x^2 + 5x - 17 = 0$$

18. In voluntary response sampling respondents select themselves, so the sample is non-random.
Answer Choice **B**

19. $2 + \frac{1}{x} = 4$

$x\left(2 + \frac{1}{x}\right) = x(4)$

$2x + 1 = 4x$

$1 = 2x$

$x = \frac{1}{2}$

$x = \frac{1}{2}$ is a solution since it is not a restricted value.

20. $\frac{2}{x+2} + \frac{8}{x-2} = \frac{14}{x^2 - 4}$

$\frac{2}{x+2} + \frac{8}{x-2} = \frac{14}{(x-2)(x+2)}$

The LCD is $(x - 2)(x + 2)$.

$(x-2)(x+2)\left(\frac{2}{x+2} + \frac{8}{x-2}\right)$

$= (x-2)(x+2)\left(\frac{14}{(x-2)(x+2)}\right)$

$2(x - 2) + 8(x + 2) = 14$

$2x - 4 + 8x + 16 = 14$

$10x + 12 = 14$

$10x = 2$

$x = \frac{1}{5}$

$x = \frac{1}{5}$ is a solution since it is not a restricted value.

21. $\frac{-6}{x-3} = 1$

$(x-3)\left(\frac{-6}{x-3}\right) = (x-3)(1)$

$-6 = x - 3$

$-3 = x$

$x = -3$ is a solution since it is not a restricted value.

22. Value will be positive because the parabola crosses the x-axis twice, meaning that the function has two x-intercepts and the related equation has two solutions.

23. $x = 6$ or $x = -1$

$x - 6 = 0$ or $x + 1 = 0$

Sample:

$(x - 6)(x + 1) = 0$

$x^2 - 5x - 6 = 0$

24. P(player or left handed)

$= P$(player) $+ P$(left handed)

$-P$(player and left handed)

$= \frac{58}{70} + \frac{8}{70} - \frac{6}{70}$

$= \frac{58 + 8 - 6}{70}$

$= \frac{60}{70} \approx 0.86$

The probability is 0.86.

25. Because the domain has a lower limit, n is an even number.

26. The periods are $\frac{2\pi}{a}$ and $\frac{2\pi}{b}$. Period of $f(x)$ is $\frac{1}{4}$ of period of $g(x)$, so

$\frac{2\pi}{a} = \frac{1}{4} \cdot \frac{2\pi}{b} = \frac{2\pi}{4b}$

$2\pi(4b) = 2\pi(a)$

$4b = a$

27. $V = 3x^3 + 5x^2 - 12x$

$= x(3x^2 + 5x - 12)$

Positive factor pair for 3 is (1)(3); factor pairs for -12 are $(1)(-12)$, $(-1)(12)$, $(2)(-6)$, $(-2)(6)$, $(3)(-4)$, and $(-3)(4)$. Since $(1)(-4) + (3)(3) = 5$, the volume factors as $V = x(x + 3)(3x - 4)$

The dimensions are x by $(x + 3)$ by $(3x - 4)$.

28. $f(x) = \begin{cases} 3.50x, & \text{if } x < 12 \\ 3.00x, & \text{if } 12 \le x \le 24 \\ 2.50x & \text{if } x > 24 \end{cases}$

x	$f(x) = 3.50x$	$f(x) = 3.00x$	$f(x) = 2.50x$
0	0		
12	42	36	
24		72	60
36			90

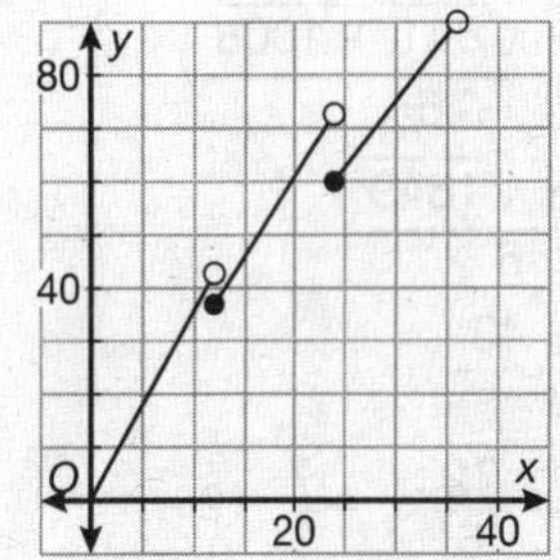

29. Step 1: Use the Law of Cosines to determine RS.
$RS^2 = ST^2 + RT^2 - 2(ST)(RT)\cos T$
$RS^2 = 8.9^2 + 12.2^2 - 2(8.9)(12.2)\cos 78°$
$RS^2 = 228.05 - 217.16\cos 78°$
$RS^2 \approx 182.9$
$RS \approx 13.5$
Step 2: Use the Law of Sines to determine $m\angle S$.
$$\frac{RS}{\sin T} = \frac{RT}{\sin S}$$
$$\frac{13.5}{\sin 78°} = \frac{12.2}{\sin S}$$
$13.5 \sin S = 12.2 \sin 78°$
$$\sin S = \frac{12.2 \sin 78°}{13.5}$$
$\sin S \approx 0.884$
$m\angle S \approx 62°$

30. It would not clear the second fraction, where the denominator is $(x + 5)(x + 5)$. The LCD is $(x + 2)(x + 5)(x + 5)$, so both sides of the equation should be multiplied by that.

LESSON 85

Warm Up 85

1. difference of squares
2. $16x^4 - 81 = (4x^2)^2 - 9^2$
$= (4x^2 - 9)(4x^2 + 9)$
$= [(2x)^2 - 3^2](4x^2 + 9)$
$= (2x - 3)(2x + 3)(4x^2 + 9)$
3. $$x = \frac{-b \pm \sqrt{b^2 - 4ac}}{2a}$$
$$= \frac{-(-29) \pm \sqrt{(-29)^2 - 4(3)(-84)}}{2(3)}$$
$$= \frac{29 \pm \sqrt{841 + 1008}}{6}$$
$$= \frac{29 \pm \sqrt{1849}}{6}$$
$$= \frac{29 \pm 43}{6}$$
$$= \frac{-14}{6}, \frac{72}{6} = -\frac{7}{3}, 12$$

Lesson Practice 85

a. Since $8 = 2^3$, this is a difference of cubes
$x^3 - 8 = 0$
$x^3 - 2^3 = 0$
$(x - 2)(x^2 + 2x + 4) = 0$
Find the discriminant.
$b^2 - 4ac = (2)^2 - 4(1)(4)$
$= 4 - 16 = -12$
$\longrightarrow$ complex roots
The polynomial has one root, $x = 2$.

b. Since $125 = 5^3$, this is a sum of cubes.
$x^3 + 125 = 0$
$x^3 + 5^3 = 0$
$(x + 5)(x^2 - 5x + 25) = 0$
Find the discriminant.
$b^2 - 4ac = (-5)^2 - 4(1)(25)$
$= 25 - 100 = -75$
$\longrightarrow$ complex roots
The polynomial has one root, $x = -5$.

c. This is a difference of cubes.
$x^9 - 512 = 0$
$(x^3)^3 - 8^3 = 0$
$(x^3 - 8)((x^3)^2 + 8x^3 + 64) = 0$
The factor $(x^3 - 8)$ is also a difference of cubes.
$(x^3 - 2^3)(x^6 + 8x^3 + 64) = 0$
$(x - 2)(x^2 + 2x + 4)(x^6 + 8x^3 + 64) = 0$
Graph the quadratic and degree-6 factors.

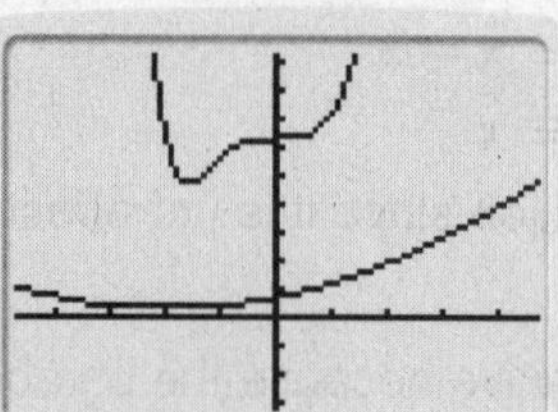

The equation has one root, $x = 2$.

d. This is a difference of cubes.
$x^6 - 729 = 0$
$(x^2)^3 - 9^3 = 0$
$(x^2 - 9)((x^2)^2 + 9x^2 + 81) = 0$
$(x^2 - 3^2)(x^4 + 9x^2 + 81) = 0$
$(x - 3)(x + 3)(x^4 + 9x^2 + 81) = 0$

Graph the quartic factor:

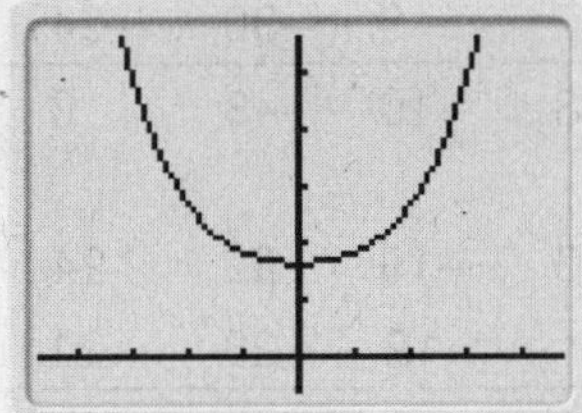

The equation has two roots, $x = -3$ and $x = 3$.

e. $5x^3 + 2x - 1 = 0$

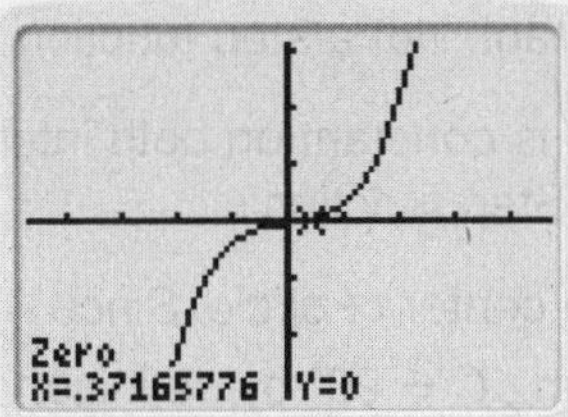

The equation has one root, $x \approx 0.3717$.

f. $4x^3 - 4x^2 + 9x - 9 = 0$

By Rational Root Theorem, p-values are ±1, ±3, ±9; q-values are ±1, ±2, ±4. So

$$\frac{p}{q} \in \{1, -1, 3, -3, 9, -9, \frac{1}{2}, -\frac{1}{2}, \frac{3}{2}, -\frac{3}{2}, \frac{9}{2}, -\frac{9}{2}, \frac{1}{4}, -\frac{1}{4}, \frac{3}{4}, -\frac{3}{4}, \frac{9}{4}, -\frac{9}{4}\}$$

Use synthetic division to test roots.

$$\begin{array}{r|rrrr} 1 & 4 & -4 & 9 & -9 \\ & & 4 & 0 & 9 \\ \hline & 4 & 0 & 9 & 0 \ \checkmark \end{array}$$

$$4x^3 - 4x^2 + 9x - 9 = 0$$
$$(x - 1)(4x^2 + 9) = 0$$

The quadratic does not factor, so the equation has one root, $x = 1$.

g. $x^4 - 2x^3 - 27x + 54 = 0$

By Rational Root Theorem, p-values are ±1, ±2, ±3, ±6, ±9, ±18, ±27, ±54; q-values are ±1. So

$$\frac{p}{q} \in \{\pm1, \pm2, \pm3, \pm6, \pm9, \pm18, \pm27, \pm54\}$$

First root that yields a factor:

$$\begin{array}{r|rrrrr} 2 & 1 & -2 & 0 & -27 & 54 \\ & & 2 & 0 & 0 & -54 \\ \hline & 1 & 0 & 0 & -27 & 0 \ \checkmark \end{array}$$

$$x^4 - 2x^3 - 27x + 54 = 0$$
$$(x - 2)(x^3 - 27) = 0$$
$$(x - 2)(x - 3)(x^2 + 3x + 9) = 0$$

The quadratic does not factor, so roots are $x = 2$ and $x = 3$.

h. $4x^3 + 4x^2 - 29x + 21 = 0$

By Rational Root Theorem, p-values are ±1, ±3, ±7, ±21; q-values are ±1, ±2, ±4. So

$$\frac{p}{q} \in \{\pm1, \pm3, \pm7, \pm21, \pm\frac{1}{2}, \pm\frac{3}{2}, \pm\frac{7}{2}, \pm\frac{21}{2}, \pm\frac{1}{4}, \pm\frac{3}{4}, \pm\frac{7}{4}, \pm\frac{21}{4}$$

First root that yields a factor:

$$\begin{array}{r|rrrr} 1 & 4 & 4 & -29 & 21 \\ & & 4 & 8 & -21 \\ \hline & 4 & 8 & -21 & 0 \ \checkmark \end{array}$$

$$4x^3 + 4x^2 - 29x + 21 = 0$$
$$(x - 1)(4x^2 + 8x - 21) = 0$$

For quadratic, use quadratic formula:

$$x = \frac{-b \pm \sqrt{b^2 - 4ac}}{2a}$$
$$= \frac{-8 \pm \sqrt{8^2 - 4(4)(-21)}}{2(4)}$$
$$= \frac{-8 \pm \sqrt{64 + 336}}{8}$$
$$= \frac{-8 \pm \sqrt{400}}{8}$$
$$= \frac{-8 \pm 20}{8}$$
$$= \frac{-28}{8}, \frac{12}{8}$$
$$= -\frac{7}{2}, \frac{3}{2}$$

The roots of the equation are 1, $-\frac{7}{2}$, and $\frac{3}{2}$.

i.

$$0.05x^3 - 1.3x^2 + 9.6x - 14.4 = 0$$
$$20(0.05x^3 - 1.3x^2 + 9.6x - 14.4) = 20(0)$$
$$x^3 - 26x + 192x - 288 = 0$$

By Rational Root Theorem, p-values are ± 1, ± 2, ± 3, ± 4, ± 6, ...; q-values are ± 1. So $\frac{p}{q} \in \{\pm 1, \pm 2, \pm 3, \pm 4, \pm 6, \ldots\}$

First root that yields a factor:

2	1	−26	192	−288
		2	−48	288
	1	−24	144	0

$x^3 - 26x + 192x - 288 = 0$

$(x - 2)(x^2 - 24x + 144) = 0$

$(x - 2)(x^2 - 2(12)x + 12^2) = 0$

$(x - 2)(x - 12)^2 = 0$

The roots are $x = 2$ and 12.

Practice 85

1. Use the quadratic formula.

$$x = \frac{-b \pm \sqrt{b^2 - 4ac}}{2a}$$

$$= \frac{-7 \pm \sqrt{7^2 - 4(6)(-1)}}{2(6)}$$

$$= \frac{-7 \pm \sqrt{73}}{12} \approx -1.2953, 0.1287$$

2. $y = x^4 - 27x$

$y = x(x^3 - 27) = x(x^3 - 3^3)$

$y = x(x - 3)(x^2 + 3x + 9)$

Find the discriminant

$b^2 - 4ac = 3^2 - 4(1)(9)$

$= 9 - 36$

$= -27$

The only roots are $x = 0$ and 3.

3. Check by synthetic division.

A

−2/3	3	−19	22	24	X
		−2	−14	−24	
	3	−21	36	0	

B

2/3	3	−19	22	24	✓
		2	−34/3	64/9	
	3	−17	32/3	280/9	

C

3	3	−19	22	24	X
		9	−30	−24	
	3	−10	−8	0	

D

4	3	−19	22	24	X
		12	−28	−24	
	3	−7	−6	0	

Answer Choice **B**

4. On interval $x \geq 1$, function is $x + 1$ which is not constant. Not a step function

5. Function is constant on both intervals of domain. Step function

6. Let O be center of circle. Since $m\angle A = m\angle C = 90°$ by definition of tangent, we can solve for $m\angle O$.

$m\angle A + m\angle B + m\angle C + m\angle O = 360°$

$90° + 60° + 90° + m\angle O = 360°$

$m\angle O = 120°$

$\triangle OAB$ is a special triangle (30-60-90), so

$\frac{OA}{AB} = \tan 30°$

$\frac{OA}{10} = \frac{1}{\sqrt{3}}$

$OA = \frac{10}{\sqrt{3}} = \frac{10\sqrt{3}}{3}$

$\widehat{AC}$ subtends an angle of 120° or $\frac{2\pi}{3}$ and radius is $OA = \frac{10\sqrt{3}}{3}$. Therefore

$s = r\theta$

$= \frac{10\sqrt{3}}{3} \cdot \frac{2\pi}{3} = \frac{20\pi\sqrt{3}}{9} \approx 12.1$ cm

7. The ball is dropped, so $v_0 = 0$.

$h(t) = -0.8t^2 + v_0 t + h_0$

$0 = -0.8t^2 + (0)t + 125$

$0 = -0.8t^2 + 125$

$t^2 = \frac{125}{0.8} = 156.25$

$t = 12.5$ seconds

8. Student did not use total # of females in denominator. Correct solution:

$$P(AM \mid \text{female}) = \frac{\text{\# of females AM}}{\text{total \# of females}}$$

$$= \frac{4}{4 + 12}$$
$$= \frac{4}{16} = \frac{1}{4} \text{ or } 25\%$$

9. $T = 2\pi\sqrt{\frac{L}{9.8}}$

$$1.5 = 2\pi\sqrt{\frac{L}{9.8}}$$
$$\frac{1.5}{2\pi} = \sqrt{\frac{L}{9.8}}$$
$$\left(\frac{1.5}{2\pi}\right)^2 = \frac{L}{9.8}$$
$$L = 9.8 \cdot \left(\frac{1.5}{2\pi}\right)^2 \approx 0.56$$

The length is about 0.56 m.

10. $P(3 \text{ tails}) = P(\text{tail}) \cdot P(\text{tail}) \cdot P(\text{ tail})$
$$= \frac{1}{2} \cdot \frac{1}{2} \cdot \frac{1}{2} = \frac{1}{8} \text{ or } 12.5\%$$

11. Sample: To derive an equation given two complex roots, you write a single equation, isolate the imaginary part, and square both sides. To derive an equation from two real roots, you write two equations and use converse of Zero Product Property.

12. Calculate the angle at the lighthouse.

$$m\angle A + m\angle B + m\angle C = 180°$$
$$59° + 34° + m\angle C = 180°$$
$$93° + m\angle C = 180°$$
$$m\angle C = 87°$$

Use the Law of Sines.

$$\frac{\sin A}{a} = \frac{\sin B}{b} = \frac{\sin C}{c}$$
$$\frac{\sin 59°}{a} = \frac{\sin 34°}{b} = \frac{\sin 87°}{320}$$

So

$$320 \sin 59° = a \sin 87°$$
$$\frac{320 \sin 59°}{\sin 87°} = a$$
$$a \approx 274.67$$

and

$$320 \sin 34° = b \sin 87°$$
$$\frac{320 \sin 34°}{\sin 87°} = b$$
$$b \approx 179.19$$

Ship B is about $274.67 - 179.19 \approx 95.5$ yd farther from the lighthouse than Ship A.

13. Student omitted $x = 0$ as one of the solutions.

14.
$$M = \frac{2}{3} \log\left(\frac{E}{10^{11.8}}\right)$$
$$9.5 = \frac{2}{3} \log\left(\frac{E}{10^{11.8}}\right)$$
$$9.5 = \frac{2}{3}(\log E - \log 10^{11.8})$$
$$9.5 = \frac{2}{3}(\log E - 11.8)$$
$$\frac{3}{2}(9.5) = \log E - 11.8$$
$$14.25 = \log E - 11.8$$
$$26.05 = \log E$$
$$10^{26.05} = E$$
$$1.12 \quad 10^{26} \approx E$$

The energy released was about 1.12 10^{26} erg.

15.

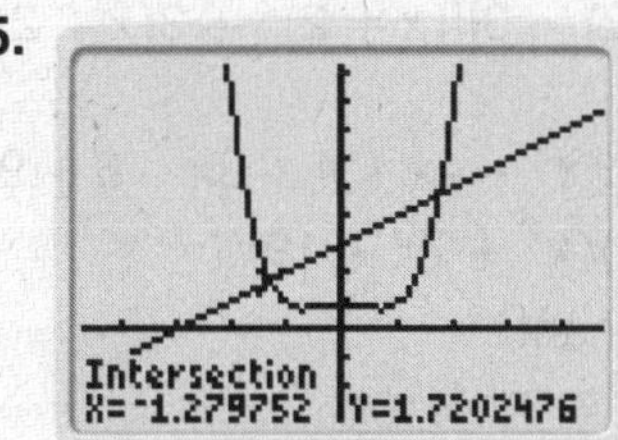

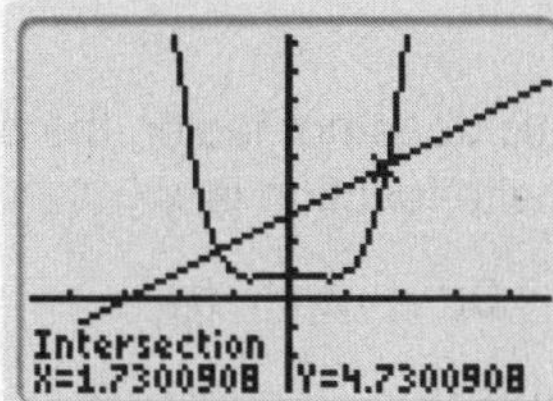

The solutions are $x \approx -1.28$ and 1.73.

16. In voluntary response sampling individuals choose whether or not to be part of the sample. Answering questionnaires and online surveys are ways in which people choose to be part of a sample. They do not qualify as probability samples because the probability of an individual being part of the sample is unknown.

17. a. $83 = 86 - 3 = \text{mean} - 1 \text{ s.d.}$

$89 = 86 + 3 = \text{mean} + 1 \text{ s.d.}$

68% of scores lie within 1 s.d. of mean, or between 83 and 89.

b. Subtract from 100%, since these are all the other scores: 100% − 68% = 32%.

c. For a normal distribution the number of scores that are less than 83 equals the number of scores greater than 89, or exactly half of all scores are less than 83 or greater than 89:

$\frac{1}{2}(32\%) = 16\%$.

18. Restricted values are where each denominator is zero. $5 \neq 0$; $x + 5 = 0 \longrightarrow x = -5$; $3x^2 = 0 \longrightarrow x = 0$

19. Restricted values are where each denominator is zero. $3 \neq 0$; $x - 1 = 0 \longrightarrow x = 1$

20. Possible estimate:

$$b^2 - 4ac \approx (1)^2 - 4(45)(-4)$$
$$\approx 1 + 720 \approx 721$$

Accept answers between 700 and 800.

21.
$$f(g(x)) = f(x + 2)$$
$$= (x + 2)^3 - 27$$
$$= [(x + 2) - 3][(x + 2)^2 + 3(x + 2) + 9]$$
$$= (x - 1)(x^2 + 4x + 4 + 3x + 6 + 9)$$
$$= (x - 1)(x^2 + 7x + 19)$$

Find the discriminant.

$$b^2 - 4ac = (7)^2 - 4(1)(19)$$
$$= 49 - 76$$
$$= -27$$

Since the quadratic does not factor, the only root of the composite function is $x = 1$.

22.
$$h = -4.9t^2 + v_0t + h_0$$
$$4.9t^2 - v_0t = h_0 - h$$
$$\frac{4.9t^2}{4.9} - \frac{v_0t}{4.9} = \frac{h_0 - h}{4.9}$$
$$t^2 - \frac{v_0t}{4.9} = \frac{h_0 - h}{4.9}$$

Completing the square:

$$t^2 - \frac{v_0t}{4.9} + \left(\frac{1}{2} \cdot \frac{v_0}{4.9}\right)^2$$
$$= \frac{h_0 - h}{4.9} + \left(\frac{1}{2} \cdot \frac{v_0}{4.9}\right)^2$$
$$\left(t - \frac{v_0}{9.8}\right)^2 = \frac{h_0 - h}{4.9} + \left(\frac{v_0}{9.8}\right)^2$$
$$t - \frac{v_0}{9.8} = \pm\sqrt{\frac{h_0 - h}{4.9} + \left(\frac{v_0}{9.8}\right)^2}$$
$$t = \frac{v_0}{9.8} \pm \sqrt{\frac{h_0 - h}{4.9} + \frac{v_0^2}{96.04}}$$

23.
$$f(g(h(x))) = f(g(x^2 - 2))$$
$$= f((x^2 - 2) - 5)$$
$$= f(x^2 - 7)$$
$$= 3(x^2 - 7)$$
$$= 3x^2 - 21$$

24. The Law of Cosines, because two sides and the included angle are known. There is not enough information for the Law of Sines.

25. a.
$$P(\text{all 10 acceptable}) = [P(\text{acceptable})]^{10}$$
$$= (0.9)^{10}$$
$$\approx 0.35 \text{ or } 35\%$$

b.
$$P(n \text{ acceptable}) = 0.1$$
$$[P(\text{acceptable})]^n = 0.1$$
$$0.9^n = 0.1$$
$$\log 0.9^n = \log 0.1$$
$$n \log 0.9 = \log 10^{-1} = -1$$
$$\frac{n \log 0.9}{\log 0.9} = \frac{-1}{\log 0.9}$$
$$n = -\frac{1}{\log 0.9} \approx 21.85$$

Rounding up, the probability will be 10% or less for 22 or more samples.

26. self-selected; biased; The population is unfairly represented because only those listening to the station know of the survey.

27. To left of y-axis, graph is straight line with slope −1 through (0, 0). To right of y-axis, graph is horizontal line $y = 3$.

Answer Choice **D**

28.
$$x^3 - 729 = 0$$
$$x^3 - 9^3 = 0$$
$$(x - 9)(x^2 + 9x + 81) = 0$$

Find the discriminant.

$$b^2 - 4ac = 9^2 - 4(1)(81)$$
$$= 81 - 324$$
$$= -243$$

So the only root is $x = 9$.

29. Rational Root Theorem: p-values are ±1, ±2, ±3, ±6, ±9, ±18; q-values are ±1; so
$\frac{p}{q} \in \{\pm1, \pm2, \pm3, \pm6, \pm9, \pm18\}$

First root that yields a factor:

$$\begin{array}{r|rrrrr} 3 & 1 & -13 & 55 & -81 & 18 \\ & & 3 & -30 & 75 & -18 \\ \hline & 1 & -10 & 25 & -6 & 0 \checkmark \end{array}$$

The equation factors as
$(x - 3)(x^3 - 10x^2 + 25x - 6) = 0$
For cubic factor, p-values are ±1, ±2, ±3, ±6; q-values are ±1; so
$\frac{p}{q} \in \{\pm1, \pm2, \pm3, \pm6\}$

First root that yields a factor:

$$\begin{array}{r|rrrr} 6 & 1 & -10 & 25 & -6 \\ & & 6 & -24 & 6 \\ \hline & 1 & -4 & 1 & 0 \end{array}$$

Equation now factors as
$(x - 3)(x - 6)(x^2 - 4x + 1) = 0$
For the quadratic, use the quadratic formula.

$$x = \frac{-b \pm \sqrt{b^2 - 4ac}}{2a}$$
$$= \frac{-(-4) \pm \sqrt{(-4)^2 - 4(1)(1)}}{2(1)}$$
$$= \frac{4 \pm \sqrt{16 - 4}}{2}$$
$$= \frac{4 \pm \sqrt{12}}{2}$$
$$= \frac{4 \pm 2\sqrt{3}}{2}$$
$$= 2 \pm \sqrt{3}$$
The roots of equation are 3, 6, and $2 \pm \sqrt{3}$.

30.

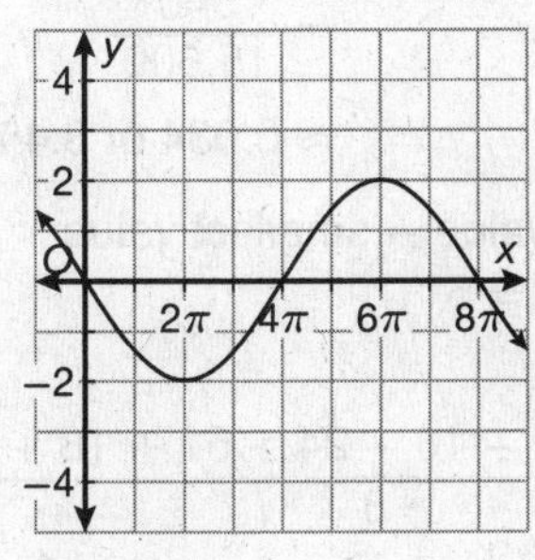

LESSON 86

Warm Up 86

1. periodic
2. Amplitude is $|a| = 5$.
3. Period is $\frac{2\pi}{b} = \frac{2\pi}{2} = \pi$.

Lesson Practice 86

a. right π units

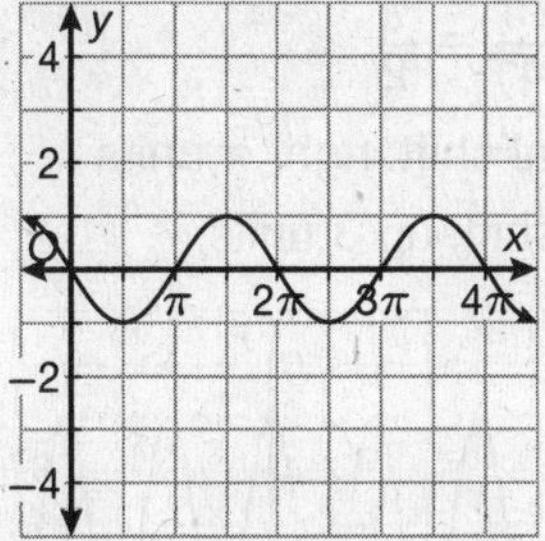

b. left 2π units

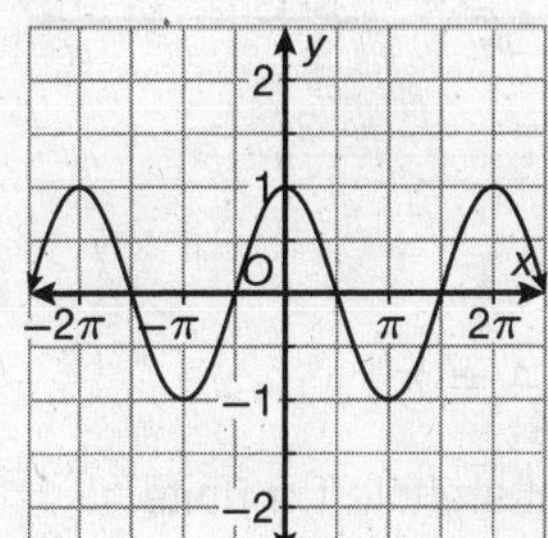

c. 3 units down

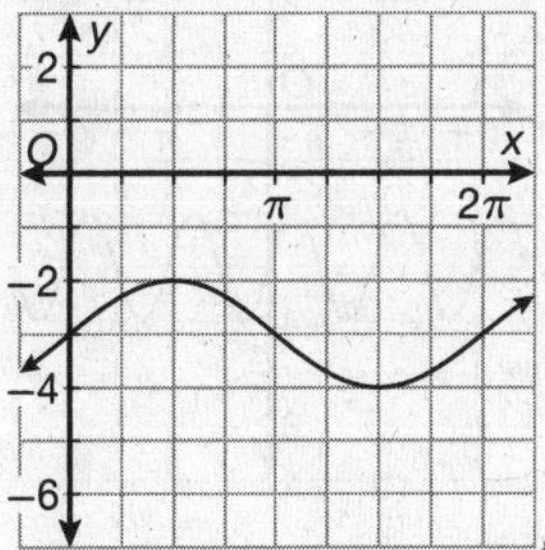

d. 2 units up

e. left π units and 2 units down

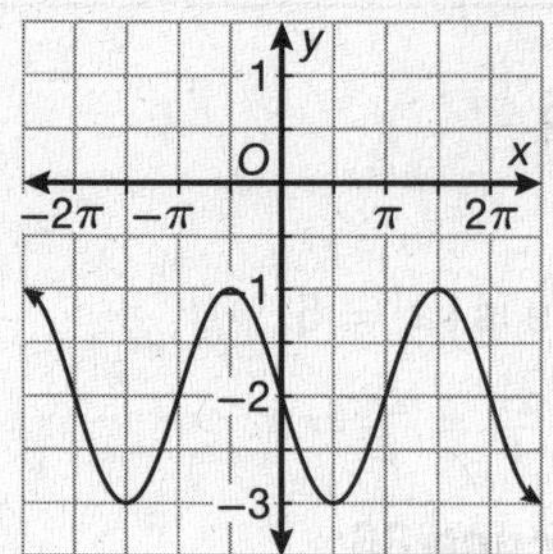

f. Amplitude: 2

Period: $\frac{2\pi}{4} = \frac{\pi}{2}$

Horizontal shift: right π units

Vertical shift: up 3 units

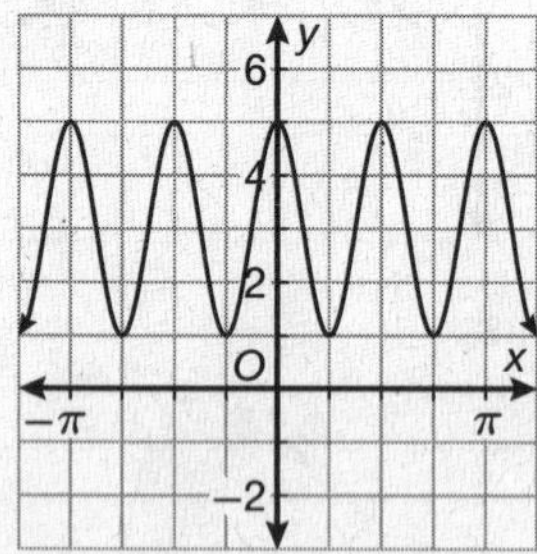

g. Amplitude: 1

Period: $\frac{2\pi}{2} = \pi$

Horizontal shift: left π units

Vertical shift: down 3 units

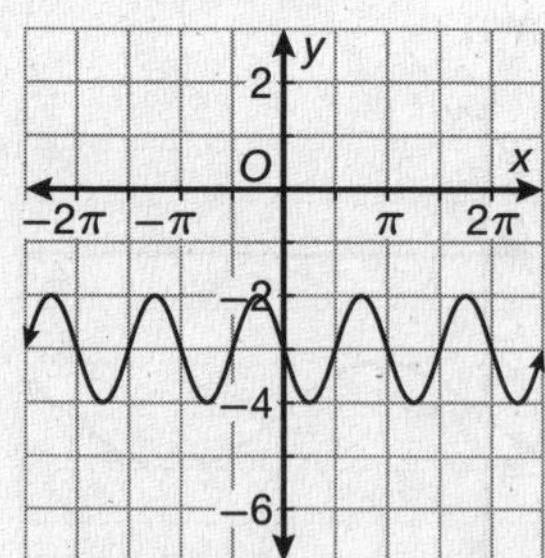

Practice 86

1. Deck has 52 cards; 12 are face cards and 36 are number cards.

$$P\text{(face card, then number card)} = \frac{12}{52} \cdot \frac{36}{51}$$
$$= \frac{432}{2652}$$
$$= \frac{36}{221}$$
$$\approx 0.16 \text{ or } 16\%$$

2. $\sqrt[3]{8x^3 - 1} = 2x - 1$

$$8x^3 - 1 = (2x - 1)^3$$
$$8x^3 - 1 = 8x^3 - 12x^2 + 6x - 1$$
$$0 = -12x^2 + 6x$$
$$0 = -6x(2x - 1)$$
$$x = 0 \quad \text{or} \quad 2x - 1 = 0$$
$$2x - 1 + 1 = 0 + 1$$
$$2x = 1$$
$$x = \frac{1}{2}$$

3. $\sqrt[3]{12x - 5} - \sqrt[3]{8x + 15} = 0$

$$\sqrt[3]{12x - 5} = \sqrt[3]{8x + 15}$$
$$12x - 5 = 8x + 15$$
$$4x = 20$$
$$x = 5$$

4. $x^3 + 12x^2 + 36x = 0$

$$x(x^2 + 12x + 36) = 0$$
$$x(x^2 + 2(6)x + 6^2) = 0$$
$$x(x + 6)^2 = 0$$
$$x = 0 \quad \text{or} \quad x + 6 = 0$$
$$x = -6$$

Factor x divides cubic once, so root $x = 0$ has multiplicity 1. Factor $x + 6$ divides cubic twice, so root $x = -6$ has multiplicity 2.

5. Period is $\frac{2\pi}{b} = \frac{2\pi}{\frac{\pi}{2}} = \frac{2(2\pi)}{2\left(\frac{\pi}{2}\right)} = \frac{4\pi}{\pi} = 4.$

6. Order is not specified, so there are $3! = 6$ possible orders.

$$P(\text{2 tanzanite} + \text{1 sapphire}) = 6\left(\frac{6}{26} \cdot \frac{5}{25} \cdot \frac{3}{24}\right)$$
$$= \frac{540}{15{,}600}$$
$$\approx 0.034 \text{ or } 3.4\%$$

7. Range = largest value − smallest value

$$= 67 - 16 = 51$$

Mean is

$$\overline{x} = \frac{35 + 67 + 21 + 16 + 24 + 51 + 18 + 32}{8}$$
$$= \frac{264}{8} = 33$$

Standard deviation is

$$\sigma = \sqrt{\frac{(35-33)^2 + (67-33)^2 + (21-33)^2 + (16-33)^2 + (24-33)^2 + (51-33)^2 + (18-33)^2 + (32-33)^2}{8}}$$

$$= \sqrt{\frac{2224}{8}} = \sqrt{278} \approx 16.7$$

8. Amplitude: $|a| = |3| = 3$

Period: $\frac{2\pi}{2} = \pi$

9. For Law of Sines, two angles and one side or two sides and a non-included angle must be given. Only choice for which this is not true is answer choice **D**

10. It will be positive if it is greater than the mean and negative if it is less than the mean.

11. $s = \frac{a+b+c}{2}$

$= \frac{12.7 + 12.7 + 12.7}{2}$

$= 19.05$

$A = \sqrt{s(s-a)(s-b)(s-c)}$

$= \sqrt{19.05(19.05 - 12.7)^3}$

$= \sqrt{19.05(6.35)^3} \approx 69.8$

The area of the triangle is about 69.8 cm^2.

12. $y = \cos(2x) + 2$ is shifted up 2.

Answer Choice **A**

13. a. $P = 2l + 2w$

$52 = 2l + 2w$

$\frac{52}{2} = \frac{2l}{2} + \frac{2w}{2}$

$26 = l + w$

$26 - w = l$

b. $lw = 169$

$(26 - w)w = 169$

$26w - w^2 = 169$

$-w^2 + 26w - 169 = 0$

c. $b^2 - 4ac = (26)^2 - 4(-1)(-169)$

$= 676 - 676 = 0$

A discriminant of zero means there is one solution to the equation and one width that gives an area of 169 square units and a perimeter of 52 units.

14. The hypothesis is false. It is possible to find a cubic with 3 real roots, two of which are irrational; for example,

$f(x) = x^3 + 4x^2 + 2x$ has roots $x = 0, -2 \pm \sqrt{2}$.

15. $f(x) = \sqrt{x-4} + 3$

$x - 4 \geq 0, \quad y \geq \sqrt{4-4} + 3$

$x \geq 4 \quad y \geq 3$

The domain of $f(x)$ is $x \geq 4$ and the range is $y \geq 3$.

The inverse of the function $y = (x-3)^2 + 4$ is also a function, so the domain of $f^{-1}(x)$ is $x \geq 3$ and the range is $y \geq 4$.

16. $x^2 + 30x$

$\longrightarrow x^2 + 30x + \left(\frac{30}{2}\right)^2$

$= x^2 + 30x + 15^2$

$= x^2 + 30x + 225$

$= (x + 15)^2$

17. Substitute $a = 3.77$, $v_0 = 20$, $h_0 = 35$, and $h = 0$:

$h = -\frac{1}{2}at^2 + v_0t + h_0$

$0 = -\frac{1}{2}(3.77)t^2 + 20t + 35$

$0 = -1.885t^2 + 20t + 35$

Use a graphing calculator.

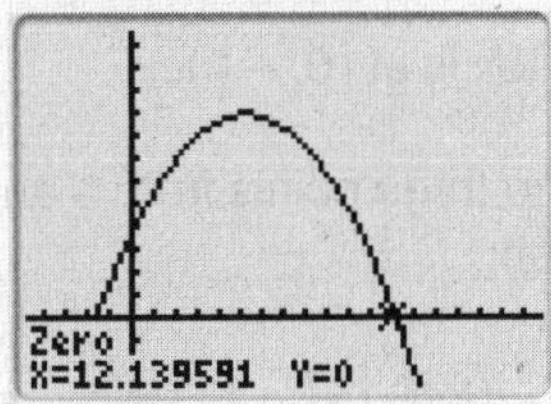

Ignoring the negative root, it takes about 12.14 s.

18. $\frac{2}{x} = \frac{1}{y} + \frac{1}{z}$

$\frac{2}{7.5} = \frac{1}{6} + \frac{1}{z}$

$\frac{2}{7.5} - \frac{1}{6} = \frac{1}{z}$

$\frac{4(2)}{4(7.5)} - \frac{5(1)}{5(6)} = \frac{1}{z}$

$$\frac{8-5}{30} = \frac{1}{z}$$

$$\frac{3}{30} = \frac{1}{z}$$

$$\frac{1}{10} = \frac{1}{z}$$

$$z = 10$$

19. $N(t) = N_0e^{-kt}$

$0.5 = 1 \cdot e^{-k(46)}$

$\ln 0.5 = \ln e^{-k(46)}$

$\ln 0.5 = -46k$

$k = \dfrac{\ln 0.5}{-46} \approx 0.015$

20. a. The roots are solutions of the equation

$$\frac{1}{4}x^2 - \frac{9}{4} = 0$$

$$\left(\frac{x}{2}\right)^2 - \left(\frac{3}{2}\right)^2 = 0$$

$$\left(\frac{x}{2} - \frac{3}{2}\right)\left(\frac{x}{2} + \frac{3}{2}\right) = 0$$

$\dfrac{x}{2} - \dfrac{3}{2} = 0$ or $\dfrac{x}{2} + \dfrac{3}{2} = 0$

$\dfrac{x}{2} = \dfrac{3}{2}$ $\qquad$ $\dfrac{x}{2} = -\dfrac{3}{2}$

$x = 3$ $\qquad$ $x = -3$

So the graph intersects the x-axis at $(-3, 0)$ and $(3, 0)$.

b. The vertex is at minimum of function, which is at $x = 0$, since $x \neq 0 \Rightarrow \frac{1}{4}x^2 > 0$.

Minimum value is $\frac{1}{4}(0)^2 - \frac{9}{4} = -\frac{9}{4}$,

so vertex is at $\left(0, -\frac{9}{4}\right)$.

c. Use the three points from *a* and *b* to graph function:

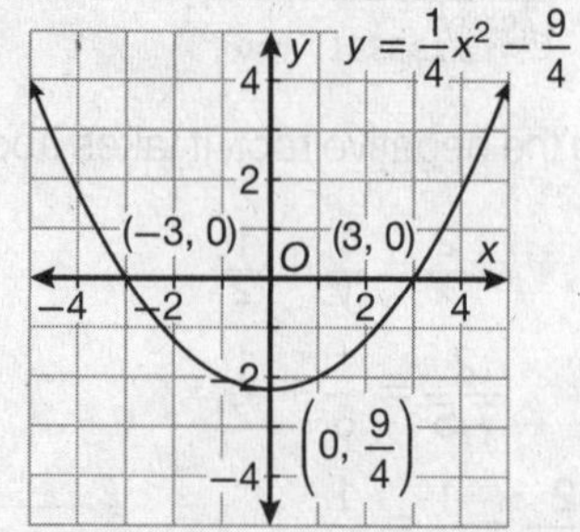

21. Jake graphed $f(x) = -x$ for $x < 0$, instead of $f(x) = x$.

22. a. Each year the population is 95% of the previous year.

$y = 150(0.95)^x$

b. $x = 150(0.95)^y$

$\dfrac{x}{150} = 0.95^y$

$y = \log_{0.95}\dfrac{x}{150}$

c. $y > \log_{0.95}\dfrac{100}{150}$

$y > \dfrac{\log \frac{100}{150}}{\log 0.95}$

$y > 7.904$

about 7.9 years

23. Each wheel must complete a whole number of cycles. Therefore, $4m = 9n$. Least positive integers are $m = 9$ and $n = 4$, so squares are back in sync after $4(9) = 9(4) = 36$ s.

24.

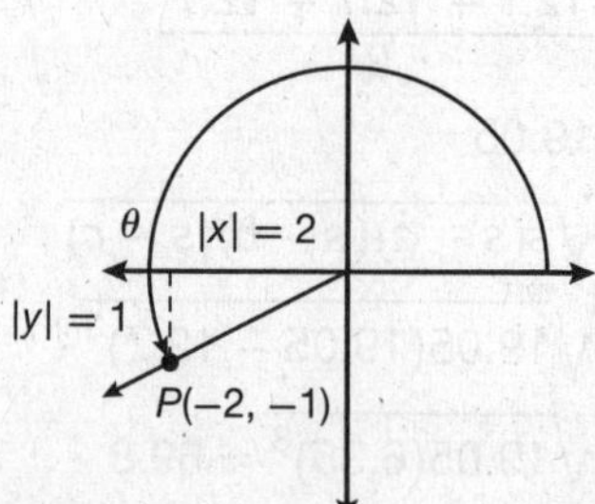

r is the hypotenuse of a right triangle, so

$$r = \sqrt{x^2 + y^2}$$
$$= \sqrt{(-2)^2 + (-1)^2}$$
$$= \sqrt{4 + 1} = \sqrt{5}$$

$$\sin\theta = \frac{y}{r} = \frac{-1}{\sqrt{5}} = \frac{-1\sqrt{5}}{\sqrt{5}\sqrt{5}} = -\frac{\sqrt{5}}{5}$$

$$\cos\theta = \frac{x}{r} = \frac{-2}{\sqrt{5}} = \frac{-2\sqrt{5}}{\sqrt{5}\sqrt{5}} = -\frac{2\sqrt{5}}{5}$$

$$\tan\theta = \frac{y}{x} = \frac{-1}{-2} = \frac{1}{2}$$

$$\csc\theta = \frac{1}{\sin\theta} = -\frac{5}{\sqrt{5}} = -\sqrt{5}$$

$$\sec\theta = \frac{1}{\cos\theta} = -\frac{5}{2\sqrt{5}} = -\frac{\sqrt{5}}{2}$$

$$\cot\theta = \frac{1}{\tan\theta} = 2$$

25. Converse of Zero-Product Property states that if $a = 0$ or $b = 0$ then the product $ab = 0$. It can be used to write a quadratic equation given its two roots.

26. First 6 two-digit numbers (ignoring any repeats) that match labeled numbers are 01, 06, 04, 08, 05, 13. These correspond to Barnstable, Franklin, Dukes, Hampshire, Essex, Suffolk.

27. The interior term $\sin(x)$ has a range of -1 to 1, the maximum value of $\sin(\sin(x))$ is $\sin\left(\sin\left(\frac{\pi}{2}\right)\right) = \sin(1) = 0.84$.

28.
$$x^3 - 216 = 0$$
$$x^3 - 6^3 = 0$$
$$(x-6)(x^2+6x+36) = 0$$
Find the discriminant:
$$b^2 - 4ac = (6)^2 - 4(1)(36)$$
$$= 36 - 144$$
$$= -108$$
The discriminant is negative, so the only root is $x = 6$.

29.
$$x^9 + 125 = 0$$
$$(x^3)^3 + 5^3 = 0$$
$$(x^3+5)((x^3)^2 + 5x^3 + 25) = 0$$
$$\left(x^3 + (\sqrt[3]{5})^3\right)(x^6 + 5x^3 + 25) = 0$$
$$(x + \sqrt[3]{5})\left(x^2 + x\sqrt[3]{5} + (\sqrt[3]{5})^2\right)$$
$$(x^6 + 5x^3 + 25) = 0$$
Use a graphing calculator to check the quadratic and degree-6 terms:

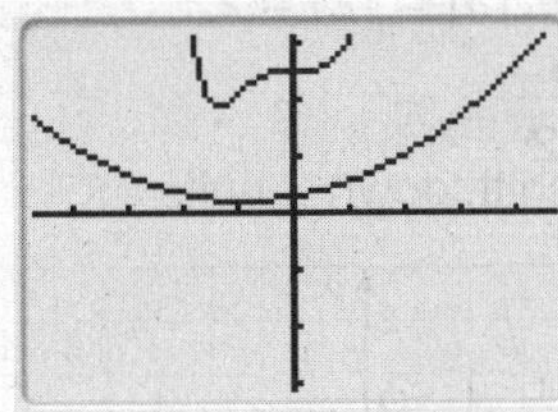

These terms do not factor, so only root is $x = -\sqrt[3]{5}$.

30.
$$d = \sqrt{(x_2-x_1)^2 + (y_2-y_1)^2}$$
$$= \sqrt{(5-2)^2 + (4-(-1))^2}$$
$$= \sqrt{3^2 + 5^2}$$
$$= \sqrt{9+25} = \sqrt{34}$$

LESSON 87

Warm Up 87

1. natural

2.
$$\ln(exy) = \ln e + \ln x + \ln y$$
$$= 1 + \ln x + \ln y$$

3.
$$\ln\left(\frac{x}{ey}\right) = \ln x - \ln(ey)$$
$$= \ln x - (\ln e + \ln y)$$
$$= \ln x - 1 - \ln y$$

4.
$$\log_b x = \frac{\log x}{\log b}$$
$$\log_7 100 = \frac{\log 100}{\log 7} = \frac{2}{\log 7}$$

Lesson Practice 87

a.
$$\log_6(36x)^2 = 2 \cdot \log_6(36x)$$
$$= 2(\log_6 36 + \log_6 x)$$
$$= 2(2 + \log_6 x)$$
$$= 4 + 2\log_6 x$$
when $x = 216$
$$\log_6(36x)^2 = 4 + 2\log_6 216$$
$$= 4 + 2 \cdot 3 = 4 + 6 = 10$$

b.
$$\ln(10e)^3 = 3 \cdot \ln(10e)$$
$$= 3(\ln 10 + \ln e)$$
$$= 3(\ln 10 + 1)$$
$$\approx 3(2.303 + 1) \approx 9.908$$

c.
$$\log_7(5x)^3 = 3 \cdot \log_7(5x)$$
$$= 3\left(\frac{\log 5x}{\log 7}\right)$$
$$= 3\left(\frac{\log 5 + \log x}{\log 7}\right)$$
when $x = 5$
$$\log_7(5x)^3 = 3\left(\frac{\log 5 + \log 5}{\log 7}\right)$$
$$= 3\left(\frac{2\log 5}{\log 7}\right)$$
$$= 3\left(\frac{1.39794}{0.8451}\right)$$
$$= 4.9625$$

d. $\log_8(11x)^2 = 2 \cdot \log_8(11x)$

$= 2\left(\frac{\ln(11x)}{\ln 8}\right)$

$= 2\left(\frac{\ln 11 + \ln x}{\ln 8}\right)$

when $x = 10$

$\log_8(11x)^2 = 2\left(\frac{\ln 11 + \ln 10}{\ln 8}\right)$

$\approx 2\left(\frac{2.39790 + 2.30259}{2.07944}\right)$

≈ 4.5209

e. $5^{3x} = 20$

$\log_5 5^{3x} = \log_5 20$

$3x \log_5 5 = \log_5 20$

$3x = \frac{\log_5 20}{\log_5 5}$

$x = \frac{1}{3} \cdot \frac{\log_5 20}{\log_5 5}$

$x \approx 0.6205$

f. $R = \log\left(\frac{I}{I_0}\right)$

$R = \log\left(\frac{10^{7.1} \cdot I_0}{I_0}\right) = \log(10^{7.1}) = 7.1$

Practice 87

1. Total number of cups = 12 + 12 + 20 = 44

$P(\text{green, blue}) = \frac{20}{44} \cdot \frac{12}{44} = \frac{240}{1936}$

$= \frac{15}{121} \approx 0.124$ or 12.4%

2. $\frac{8 + 2i}{1 + 3i} = \frac{(8 + 2i)(1 - 3i)}{(1 + 3i)(1 - 3i)}$

$= \frac{(8)(1) + (8)(-3i) + (2i)(1) + (2i)(-3i)}{(1)(1) + (1)(-3i) + (3i)(1) + (3i)(-3i)}$

$= \frac{8 - 24i + 2i - 6i^2}{1 - 9i^2}$

$= \frac{8 - 24i + 2i - 6(-1)}{1 - 9(-1)}$

$= \frac{14 - 22i}{10}$

$= \frac{7}{5} - \frac{11}{5}i$

3. $i^{22} + i^{15} = i^{5(4)+2} + i^{3(4)+3}$

$= (i^4)^5 i^2 + (i^4)^3 i^3$

$= 1^5(-1) + 1^3(-i)$

$= -1 - i$

4. Domain of $f \circ g$ = range of g = all real numbers. Therefore, the domain of $f \circ g$ is all real numbers and the range of $f \circ g$ = range of f, which is all real numbers greater or equal to one.

5. $y = \left(\sqrt{x^2 + 3x + 2}\right)^{\frac{1}{3}}$

$= \sqrt[3]{\sqrt{x^2 + 3x + 2}}$

Answer Choice **C**

6. a. Product of Powers Property. The division bar acts as grouping symbols for the numerator and in the denominator. By the order of operations you must first perform operations within any grouping symbols.

b. Quotient of Powers Property

c. $\frac{13^{\frac{2}{3}} \cdot 13^{\frac{1}{4}}}{13^{\frac{1}{12}} \cdot 13^{\frac{1}{2}}} = \frac{13^{\frac{2}{3}+\frac{1}{4}}}{13^{\frac{1}{12}+\frac{1}{2}}}$

$= \frac{13^{\frac{8}{12}+\frac{3}{12}}}{13^{\frac{1}{12}+\frac{6}{12}}}$

$= \frac{13^{\frac{11}{12}}}{13^{\frac{7}{12}}}$

$= 13^{\frac{11}{12}-\frac{7}{12}}$

$= 13^{\frac{4}{12}} = 13^{\frac{1}{3}}$

7. Amplitude: $|a| = |2| = 2$

Period: $\frac{2\pi}{2} = \pi$

Vertical shift: down 3 units

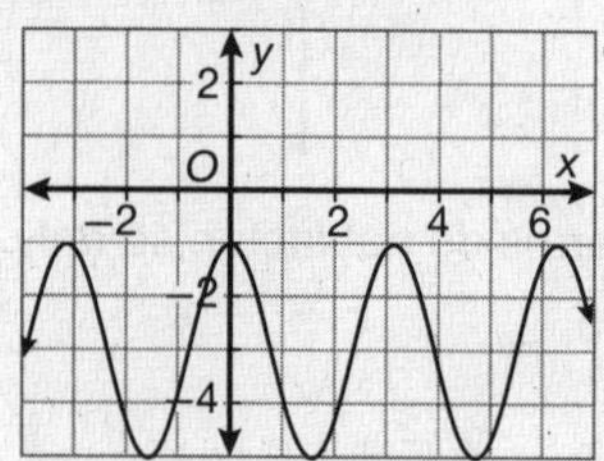

8. $\sin 30° = \frac{\text{opp.}}{\text{hyp.}} = \frac{1}{2}$

$\cos 30° = \frac{\text{adj.}}{\text{hyp.}} = \frac{\sqrt{3}}{2}$

$$\tan 30° = \frac{\text{opp.}}{\text{adj.}} = \frac{1}{\sqrt{3}} = \frac{\sqrt{3}}{\sqrt{3}\sqrt{3}} = \frac{\sqrt{3}}{3}$$

9. Since the missing angle is also 45°, this is an isosceles triangle, so opp. = adj. = 5

$$\sin 45° = \frac{\text{opp.}}{\text{hyp.}} = \frac{5}{5\sqrt{2}} = \frac{1}{\sqrt{2}} = \frac{\sqrt{2}}{\sqrt{2}\sqrt{2}} = \frac{\sqrt{2}}{2}$$

$$\cos 45° = \frac{\text{adj.}}{\text{hyp.}} = \frac{5}{5\sqrt{2}} = \frac{\sqrt{2}}{2}$$

$$\tan 45° = \frac{\text{opp.}}{\text{adj.}} = \frac{5}{5} = 1$$

10. $x = 0$ is a root of **D** but not of **A**, **B**, or **C**.
Answer Choice **D**

11. Total # of songs = 16 + 20 + 18 = 54

P(2 current hits, 2 eighties hits)

$$= \frac{18}{54} \cdot \frac{17}{53} \cdot \frac{16}{52} \cdot \frac{15}{51}$$

$$= \frac{73{,}440}{7{,}590{,}024} \approx 0.0097 \text{ or } 0.97\%$$

12. $R = \log \frac{I}{I_0}$

$10^R = \frac{I}{I_0}$

$I = I_0 \cdot 10^R$

If $R = 7$

$I = I_0 \cdot 10^7 = 10{,}000{,}000 I_0$

The intensity is 10,000,000 that of a zero level earthquake.

13. Let r represent the radius of the circle. By Pythagorean Theorem

$(2r)^2 = x^2 + x^2$

$4r^2 = 2x^2$

$r^2 = \frac{2x^2}{4}$

$r = \sqrt{\frac{2x^2}{4}}$

$= \frac{x\sqrt{2}}{2}$

The area of the triangle is

$A_v = \frac{1}{2}bh = \frac{1}{2}(x)(x) = \frac{1}{2}x^2$

The area of the circle is

$A_e = \pi r^2$

$= \pi\left(\frac{x\sqrt{2}}{2}\right)^2 = \frac{2\pi x^2}{4} = \frac{1}{2}\pi x^2$

Therefore,

$$P(\text{point inside } V) = \frac{A_v}{A_e} = \frac{\frac{1}{2}x^2}{\frac{1}{2}\pi x^2} = \frac{1}{\pi} \approx 0.318 \text{ or } 31.8\%$$

14. $100^{2x} = 1000$

$\log 100^{2x} = \log 1000$

$2x \log 100 = \log 1000$

$2x(2) = 3$

$4x = 3$

$x = \frac{3}{4}$

15. Let x represent weight in ounces (x cannot be negative).

$$f(x) = \begin{cases} 0.41 & 0 \le x \le 1 \\ 0.58 & 1 < x \le 2 \\ 0.75 & 2 < x \le 3 \\ 0.92 & 3 < x \le 3.5 \end{cases}$$

16. The student applied Quotient Property of Logarithms incorrectly.

Correct expression:

$\ln \frac{5e}{x^2} = \ln(5e) - \ln x^2$

$= \ln 5 + \ln e - 2 \ln x$

$= \ln 5 - 2 \ln x + 1$

17. $f(x) = x^3 - a^3 = (x - a)(x^2 + ax + a^2)$

$g(x) = x^3 - b^3 = (x - b)(x^2 + bx + b^2)$

$f(x) \cdot g(x) = (x - a)(x^2 + ax + a^2)(x - b)(x^2 + bx + b^2)$

If $f(x) \cdot g(x)$ only crosses x-axis at one point, roots at $x = a$ and b must coincide, so that $a = b$.

18. Middle 99.7% lies within 3 s.d.'s of the mean, or between

mean − 3(s.d.) = 4.85 − 3(0.068) = 4.646 g

and

mean + 3(s.d.) = 4.85 + 3(0.068) = 5.054 g

19. Given line has slope 2, so required line has slope $m = -\frac{1}{2}$. Use point-slope formula.

$$y - y_1 = m(x - x_1)$$
$$y - (-8) = -\frac{1}{2}(x - 2)$$
$$y + 8 = -\frac{1}{2}x + 1$$
$$y + 8 - 8 = -\frac{1}{2}x + 1 - 8$$
$$y = -\frac{1}{2}x - 7$$

20. Put the equation in standard form

$$w(410 - w) = 50{,}000$$
$$410w - w^2 = 50{,}000$$
$$0 = w^2 - 410w + 50{,}000$$

Find the discriminant.

$$b^2 - 4ac = (-410)^2 - 4(1)(50{,}000)$$
$$= 168{,}100 - 200{,}000$$
$$= -31{,}900$$

There are no real solutions, so the farmer does not have enough material.

21. **a.** The student did not distribute the multiplier 4 to both terms.

b. $\log_7(2x)^4 = 4 \cdot \log_7(2x)$
$= 4 \cdot (\log_7 2 + \log_7 x)$
$= 4 \log_7 2 + 4 \log_7 x$

22. $\ln e^{7x} = 7x \cdot \ln e = 7x \cdot 1 = 7x$

23. $\ln e^{x+4} = (x + 4)\ln e = (x + 4)(1) = x + 4$

24. First sphere:

$$r = \sqrt{\frac{S}{4\pi}}$$
$$20 = \sqrt{\frac{S_1}{4\pi}}$$
$$20^2 = \frac{S_1}{4\pi}$$
$$400 = \frac{S_1}{4\pi}$$
$$S_1 = 400(4\pi) = 1600\pi$$

Second sphere:

$$r = \sqrt{\frac{S}{4\pi}}$$
$$15 = \sqrt{\frac{S_2}{4\pi}}$$
$$15^2 = \frac{S_2}{4\pi}$$
$$225 = \frac{S_2}{4\pi}$$
$$S_2 = 225(4\pi) = 900\pi$$

The surface area of first sphere is $1600\pi - 900\pi = 700\pi$ in.^{2} greater.

25. Amplitude is $a = 10$; period is $\frac{2\pi}{b} = 2$, so $b = \frac{2\pi}{2} = \pi$. Function is $y = a\cos(bx)$ $= 10\cos(\pi x)$.

26. First clear fractions by finding the LCD. This may require factoring. Then multiply both sides of equation by the LCD. This will eliminate the fractions. Solve resulting equation.

27.
$$1000^{6x} = 10$$
$$\log 1000^{6x} = \log 10$$
$$6x \log 1000 = 1$$
$$6x(3) = 1$$
$$18x = 1$$
$$x = \frac{1}{18}$$

28.
$$100^{3x} = 10$$
$$\log 100^{3x} = \log 10$$
$$3x \log 100 = 1$$
$$3x(2) = 1$$
$$6x = 1$$
$$x = \frac{1}{6}$$

29. Sample: Exponential and logarithmic operations are inverse operations.

30. Period $= \frac{2\pi}{b} = \frac{2\pi}{3}$

LESSON 88

Warm Up 88

1. least common denominator

2. $2x + 3 = x - 17$
$$x + 3 = -17$$
$$x = -17 - 3$$
$$x = -20$$

3. $x = \frac{-b \pm \sqrt{b^2 - 4ac}}{2a}$

$x = \frac{-(-35) \pm \sqrt{(-35)^2 - 4(4)(-50)}}{2(4)}$

$x = \frac{35 \pm \sqrt{1225 - (-800)}}{8}$

$x = \frac{35 \pm \sqrt{1225 + 800}}{8}$

$x = \frac{35 \pm \sqrt{2025}}{8}$

$x = \frac{35 \pm 45}{8}$

$x = 10$ or

$x = -\frac{10}{8} = -\frac{5}{4}$

4. Test each factor using the factor-root theorem.

A $x - 6$
$3(6^4) - 6(6^3) + 6(6^2) + 3(6) - 30 \neq 0$

B $x + 6$
$3((-6)^4) - 6((-6)^3) + 6((-6)^2) + 3(-6) - 30 \neq 0$

C $3x - 6 = 3(x - 2)$
$3(2^4) - 6(2^3) + 6(2^2) + 3(2) - 30$
$= 3(16) - 6(8) + 6(4) + 6 - 30 = 0$

D $3x + 6 = 3(x + 2)$
$3((-2)^4) - 6((-2)^3) + 6((-2)^2) + 3(-2) - 30 \neq 0$

Answer Choice **C**

5. $\sqrt[4]{x^8} \cdot \sqrt[3]{x^4} = (x^8)^{\frac{1}{4}}(x^4)^{\frac{1}{3}} = x^2 x^{\frac{4}{3}} = x^{2+\frac{4}{3}}$
$= x^{3+\frac{1}{3}} = x^3\sqrt[3]{x}$

Lesson Practice 88

a. $P = 2l + 2w$
$P - 2l = 2w$
$w = \frac{P - 2l}{2}$

b. $A = \pi R^2 - \pi r^2$
$A + \pi r^2 = \pi R^2$
$\frac{A + \pi r^2}{\pi} = R^2$
$R = \sqrt{\frac{A + \pi r^2}{\pi}}$

c. $S = \pi r^2 + \pi rl$
$4\pi S = 4\pi^2 r^2 + 4\pi^2 rl$
$\pi^2 l^2 + 4\pi S = 4\pi^2 r^2 + 4\pi^2 rl + \pi^2 l^2$
$\pi^2 l^2 + 4\pi S = (2\pi r + \pi l)^2$
$\sqrt{\pi^2 l^2 + 4\pi S} = 2\pi r + \pi l$
$-\pi l + \sqrt{\pi^2 l^2 + 4\pi S} = 2\pi$
$r = \frac{-\pi l + \sqrt{\pi^2 l^2 + 4\pi S}}{2\pi}$

d. $f = \frac{d_1 d_2}{d_1 - d_2}$
$f(d_1 - d_2) = d_1 d_2$
$fd_1 - fd_2 = d_1 d_2$
$fd_1 = d_1 d_2 + fd_2$
$fd_1 - d_1 d_2 = fd_2$
$d_1(f - d_2) = fd_2$
$d_1 = \frac{fd_2}{f - d_2}$

e. $d = \sqrt{l^2 + w^2 + h^2}$
$d^2 = l^2 + w^2 + h^2$
$h^2 = d^2 - l^2 - w$
$h = \sqrt{d^2 - l^2 - w^2}$

f. $S = 4\pi r^2$
$r^2 = \frac{S}{4\pi}$
$r = \sqrt{\frac{S}{4\pi}}$
$r = \sqrt{\frac{197{,}000{,}000}{4\pi}} \approx 3960$ mi

Practice 88

1. $5^3 = 125$
$\log_5 125 = 3$

2. $20^3 = 8000$
$\log_{20} 8000 = 3$

3. Using the factor-root theorem, we can test possible $\pm\frac{p}{q}$ values,
$= (-1)^3 + 8(-1)^2 - 23(-1) - 30$
$= -1 + 8 + 23 - 30 = 0$

$$\begin{array}{r|rrrr} -1 & 1 & 8 & -23 & -30 \\ & & -1 & -7 & 30 \\ \hline & 1 & 7 & -30 & 0 \end{array}$$

$= x^3 + 8x^2 - 23x - 30$
$= (x + 1)(x^2 + 7 - 30)$
$= (x + 1)(x - 3)(x + 10)$

Then $x = -1$, $x = 3$ or $x = -10$.

4. $6x^3 + 12x^2 - 18x = 0$
$6x(x^2 + 2x - 3) = 0$
$6x(x + 3)(x - 1) = 0$
$x = -3$, $x = 0$ or $x = 1$

5. $(1 - 9i)(1 - 4i)(4 - 3i)$
$= (1 - 4i - 9i + 36i^2)(4 - 3i)$
$= (1 - 13i - 36)(4 - 3i)$
$= (-35 - 13i)(4 - 3i)$
$= -140 + 105i - 52i + 39i^2$
$= -140 + 53i - 39$
$= -179 + 53i$

6. $(3 + 2i) + (5 - i) + 6i = 3 + 2i + 5 - i + 6i$
$= 8 + 7i$

7. Sample: The function $f(x)$ that takes 3 to e^3 is $y = e^x$. Its inverse is $y = \ln x$.

8. $pH = -\log[H^+]$
$1 = -\log[H^+]$
$-1 = \log[H^+]$
$H^+ = 10^{-1}$

The hydrogen ion concentration is 0.1 mole per liter.

9. $\log_2(8 \cdot 16)^2 = \log_2(128)^2$
$= 2\log_2 128$
$= 2 \cdot 7$
$= 14$

Answer Choice **C**

10. Write and solve a capture-recapture proportion.

$\frac{68}{130} = \frac{75}{n}$

$68n = 9750$

$n \approx 143$

There are about 143 fish in the pond.

The probability that a randomly chosen fish was tagged on the first day is

$P = \frac{75}{143} \approx 0.524$ or 52.4%

11. If you solve $A = \frac{1}{2}h(b_1 + b_2)$ for h, the result is $h = \frac{2A}{b_1 + b_2}$.

12. Finding the discriminant indicates whether the equation has 2 real roots, 1 real root, or 2 complex roots. If the discriminant is negative, there are two complex roots (i.e. no real roots). If the discriminant is 0, then there is only one real root. If the discriminant is positive, then there are two real roots. Furthermore, if the discriminant is a perfect square, then the equation can be solved by factoring and need not require the quadratic formula.

13. $S = 2\pi r^2 + 2\pi rh$
$2S = 4\pi r^2 + 4\pi rh$
$\pi h^2 + 2S = 4\pi r^2 + 4\pi rh + \pi h^2$
$\pi h^2 + 2S = \pi(4r^2 + 4rh + h^2)$
$\pi h^2 + 2S = \pi(2r + h)^2$
$\frac{\pi h^2 + 2S}{\pi} = (2r + h)^2$
$\pm\sqrt{\frac{\pi h^2 + 2S}{\pi}} = 2r + h$
$\pm\sqrt{\frac{\pi h^2 + 2S}{\pi} \cdot \frac{\pi}{\pi}} = 2r + h$
$\pm\sqrt{\frac{\pi(\pi h^2 + 2S)}{\pi^2}} = 2r + h$
$\frac{\pm\sqrt{\pi(\pi h^2 + 2S)}}{\pi} = 2r + h$
$-h \pm \frac{\sqrt{\pi(\pi h^2 + 2S)}}{\pi} = 2r$
$\frac{-\pi h \pm \sqrt{\pi(\pi h^2 + 2S)}}{\pi} = 2r$
$\frac{-\pi h \pm \sqrt{\pi(\pi h^2 + 2S)}}{2\pi} = r$

14. $\frac{5}{9}(F - 32) = C$

$\frac{9}{5} \cdot \frac{5}{9}(F - 32) = \frac{9}{5}C$

$$F - 32 = \frac{9}{5}C$$

$$F = \frac{9}{5}C + 32$$

15. $\frac{\text{New length}}{\text{Old length}} = \frac{1}{2} = \sqrt{1 - \frac{v^2}{c^2}}$

$$\left(\frac{1}{2}\right)^2 = 1 - \frac{v^2}{c^2}$$

$$\frac{1}{4} = 1 - \frac{v^2}{c}$$

$$\frac{1}{4} - 1 = -\frac{v^2}{c^2}$$

$$-\frac{3}{4} = -\frac{v^2}{c^2}$$

$$\frac{3}{4} = \frac{v^2}{c^2}$$

$$\sqrt{\frac{3}{4}} = \frac{v}{c}$$

$$\frac{\sqrt{3}}{2} = \frac{v}{c}$$

$$v = \frac{c}{2}\sqrt{3}$$

16. $\frac{2}{3x+15} + \frac{1}{3} + \frac{x}{x+5} = \frac{4}{9}$

$$\frac{2}{3(x+5)} + \frac{x}{x+5} = \frac{4}{9} - \frac{3}{9}$$

$$\frac{2}{3(x+5)} + \frac{3}{3} \cdot \frac{x}{x+5} = \frac{1}{9}$$

$$\frac{2}{3(x+5)} + \frac{3x}{3(x+5)} = \frac{1}{9}$$

$$\frac{2+3x}{3(x+5)} = \frac{1}{9}$$

$$9(2+3x) = 3(x+5)$$

$$18 + 27x = 3x + 15$$

$$27x - 3x = 15 - 18$$

$$24x = -3$$

$$x = -\frac{3}{24}$$

$$x = -0.125$$

Answer Choice **A**

17. The triangle is a special 45-45-90 triangle. The base is the hypotenuse so the legs of the triangle are $\frac{x+1}{\sqrt{2}}$. The area of the square is x^2 and the area of the triangle is $\frac{1}{2}\left(\frac{x+1}{\sqrt{2}}\right)^2$.

$$\frac{1}{2}\left(\frac{x+1}{\sqrt{2}}\right)^2 = x^2$$

$$\frac{1}{2} \cdot \frac{(x+1)^2}{2} = x^2$$

$$(x+1)^2 = 4x^2$$

$$x + 1 = 2x$$

$$1 = x$$

18. a. $\log_2(6x)^2 = \frac{\ln(6x)^2}{\ln 2} = \frac{2 \ln 6x}{\ln 2}$

b. $\frac{2 \ln 6}{\ln 2} \approx 5.17$

19. Heron's formula is $A = \sqrt{s(s-a)(s-b)(s-c)}$, where $s = \frac{1}{2}(a+b+c)$; the student used the wrong value for s. s is half the perimeter or 12.

$$A = \sqrt{12(12-3)(12-11)(12-10)}$$

$$= \sqrt{12(9)(1)(2)}$$

$$= \sqrt{216}$$

≈ 14.7 square units

20. The amplitude is $\frac{1}{2}$, and the period is $\frac{2\pi}{2} = \pi$.

21. The amplitude is $\frac{2}{3}$, and the period is $\frac{2\pi}{4} = \frac{\pi}{2}$.

22. $x^2 - 62 = 0$

$$(x + \sqrt{62})(x - \sqrt{62}) = 0$$

$$x = \pm\sqrt{62} \approx \pm 8.$$

23. $\log_6 \frac{24}{5} = \frac{\log_{10} \frac{24}{5}}{\log_{10} 6} \approx 0.875$

24. $f(x) = \begin{cases} 50 & \text{, if } 0 < x \leq 4 \\ 50 + 15(x-4), & \text{if } 4 < x \end{cases}$

25. Shifted right $\frac{\pi}{2}$ radians.

26. a. $\frac{70 - 100}{15} = -2$ and $\frac{130 - 100}{15} = 2$

The scores are within 2 standard deviations of the mean, so 95% of people have an IQ between 70 and 130.

b. $\frac{150 - 100}{15} = \frac{50}{15} = 3.3$ standard deviations

27. Since the function goes through the origin, there is no horizontal shift. The value of the

function at $\frac{\pi}{2}$ is 1 so the amplitude is 1. Since the function achieves a root at $\frac{2\pi}{5}$, the function must be of the form $y = \sin 5x$.

28. $x = -2.58$ or $x = 1.002$

$x + 2.58 = 0$ or $x - 1.002 = 0$

Sample:

$$(x + 2.58)(x - 1.002) = 0$$
$$x^2 - 1.002x + 2.58x - 2.5851 = 0$$
$$x^2 + 1.578x - 2.58516 = 0$$

Press Y= and enter $(x + 2.58)(x - 1.002)$. Then press GRAPH and once the graph appears, press TRACE. Scroll along the function to check for the correct roots.

29. The student failed to raise both sides of the equation to the power 2.

$$(x + 7)^{\frac{1}{2}} = 5$$
$$[(x + 7)^{\frac{1}{2}}]^2 = 5^2$$
$$x + 7 = 25$$
$$x = 18$$

30. a. $z = \frac{x - \overline{x}}{\sigma}$

$$z\sigma = x - \overline{x}$$
$$x = z\sigma + \overline{x}$$

b. $x = z\sigma + \overline{x}$

$$= (-2)(5.5) + 76$$
$$= -11 + 76$$
$$= 65$$

LESSON 89

Warm Up 89

1. boundary line
2. $y < 2x + 5$

   if $x = 0$, $2(0) + 5 = 5 > 5$ is a contradictory statement. So (0, 5) is not a solution for $5 < 2x + 5$.
3. $24x^2 - 14x = 3$

$$24x^2 - 14x - 3 = 0$$
$$x = \frac{-b \pm \sqrt{b^2 - 4ac}}{2a}$$
$$x = \frac{-(-14) \pm \sqrt{(-14)^2 - 4(24)(-3)}}{2(24)}$$
$$x = \frac{14 \pm \sqrt{484}}{48}$$
$$x = \frac{14 \pm 22}{48}$$
$$x = \frac{3}{4} \text{ and } x = -\frac{1}{6}$$

Lesson Practice 89

a. Find the vertex.

$$x = -\frac{b}{2a} = -\frac{8}{2(1)} = -4$$
$$y = (-4)^2 + 8(-4) + 7 = -9$$

Vertex is (−4, −9).

Find the x-intercepts.

$$0 = x^2 + 8x + 7$$
$$0 = (x + 1)(x + 7)$$
$$x = -1 \text{ or } 7$$

x-intercepts are −1 and 7.

Draw the parabola with a solid line and shade above the curve since the greater than or equal symbol is used.

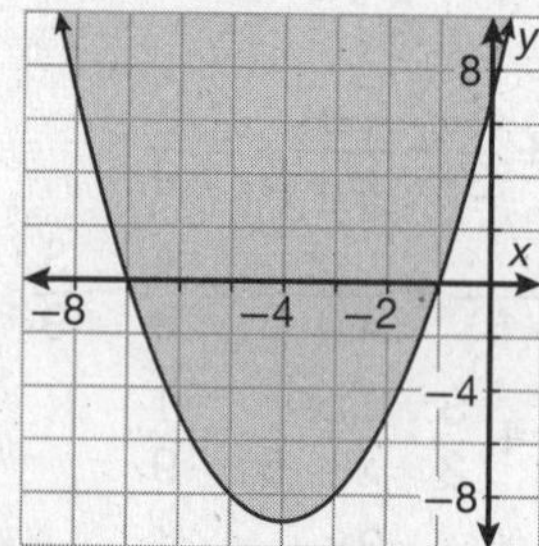

b. Press Y= and enter $-x^2 + 2x + 11$ for Y1 and enter −4 for Y2. Then press GRAPH and press TRACE to scroll up and down the graph to find the x-values for which $-x^2 + 2x + 11 < -4$.

Answer: $x < -3$ or $x > 5$

c. Press Y= and enter $x^2 - 8x + 26$ for Y1 and enter 14 for Y2. Then press GRAPH and press TRACE to scroll up and down the graph to find the x-values for which $x^2 - 8x + 26 \leq 14$.

Answer: $2 \leq x \leq 6$

d.
$$x^2 + 8x < 9$$
$$x^2 + 8x - 9 = 0$$
$$(x + 9)(x - 1) = 0$$

The critical values are −9 and 1.

Interval	Test value	Is the value a solution?
$x \le -9$	-10	$(-10)^2 + 8(-10) = 100 - 80 = 20 \nless 9$, no
$-9 < x < 1$	0	$0^2 + 8(0) = 0 < 9$, yes
$1 \le x$	2	$2^2 + 8(2) = 20 \nless 9$, no

The solutions are $-9 < x < 1$.

e. $2x^2 - 9x - 1 \ge 4$

$2x^2 - 9x - 1 = 4$

$2x^2 - 9x - 5 = 0$

$(2x + 1)(x - 5) = 0$

The critical values are $-\frac{1}{2}$ and 5.

Interval	Test value	Is the value a solution?
$x \le -\frac{1}{2}$	-1	$2(-1)^2 - 9(-1) - 1 = 10 \ge 4$, yes
$-\frac{1}{2} < x < 5$	0	$2(0)^2 - 9(0) - 1 = -1 \ngeq 4$, no
$5 \le x$	6	$2(6)^2 - 9(6) - 1 = 17 \ge 4$, yes

The solutions are $x \le -\frac{1}{2}$ and $5 \le x$.

f. Answers may vary. Sample: (0, –5) is a solution and (3, 0) is not.

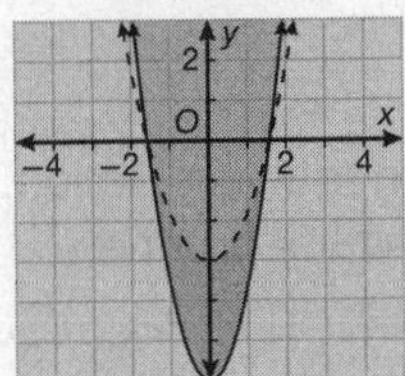

g. The answer is the solution of $3000 \le -16x^2 + 720x - 1950$

$3000 = -16x^2 + 720x - 1950$

$0 = -16x^2 + 720x - 4950$

$0 = -8x^2 + 360 - 2475$

$$x = \frac{-b \pm \sqrt{b^2 - 4ac}}{2a}$$

$$x = \frac{-360 \pm \sqrt{(360)^2 - 4(-8)(-2475)}}{2(-8)}$$

$$x = \frac{-360 \pm \sqrt{129600 - 79200}}{-16}$$

$$x \approx \frac{-360 \pm 224.5}{-16}$$

$x \approx 36.5$ and $x \approx 8.5$

Interval	Test value	Is the value a solution?
$x < 8.5$	8	$-16(8)^2 + 720(8) - 1950 = 2786 < 3000$ no
$8.5 < x < 36.5$	10	$-16(10)^2 + 720(10) - 1950 = 3650 > 3000$ yes
$36.5 < x$	37	$-16(37)^2 + 720(37) - 1950 = 2786 < 3000$ no

There must be between 9 and 36 people inclusive.

Practice 89

1. Using the special triangles, we know $\tan 60° = \frac{\sqrt{3}}{1} = \sqrt{3}$.

Then $\tan^{-1}(\sqrt{3}) = 60° = \frac{\pi}{3}$.

2. $3x^2 - 13x > 10$

$3x^2 - 13x = 10$

$3x^2 - 13x - 10 = 0$

$(3x + 2)(x - 5) = 0$

The critical values are $x = -\frac{2}{3}$ and $x = 5$.

Interval	Test value	Is the value a solution?
$x > 5$	6	$3(6)^2 - 13(6) = 30 > 10$, yes
$5 \ge x \ge -\frac{2}{3}$	0	$3(0)^2 - 13(0) = 0 < 10$, no
$-\frac{2}{3} > x$	-1	$3(-1)^2 - 13(-1) = 16 > 10$, yes

The solutions are $x < -\frac{2}{3}$ or $x > 5$.

3. $5x^2 - 6x - 2 < 0$

$5x^2 - 6x - 2 = 0$

$$x = \frac{-(-6) \pm \sqrt{(-6)^2 - 4(5)(-2)}}{2(5)}$$

$$x = \frac{6 \pm \sqrt{36 + 40}}{10}$$

$x \approx 1.5$ or -0.3.

The critical values are $x \approx 1.5$ and $x \approx -0.3$.

Interval	Test value	Is the value a solution?
$x > 1.5$	2	$5(2)^2 - 6(2) - 2 = 6 > 0$, no
$1.5 > x > -0.3$	0	$5(0)^2 - 6(0) - 2 = -2 < 0$, yes
$-0.3 > x$	-1	$5(-1)^2 - 6(-1) - 2 = 9 > 0$, no

The solutions are $1.5 > x > -0.3$.

4. $\frac{150°}{180°} = \frac{\theta}{\pi}$

$\theta = \frac{150°\pi}{180°}$

$\theta = \frac{5\pi}{6}$

arc length $= r\theta = 12\left(\frac{5\pi}{6}\right) = 10\pi \approx 31.4$ ft

$\frac{\text{area of sector}}{\text{area of circle}} = \frac{150°}{360°}$

$\frac{\text{area of sector}}{\pi(12^2)} = \frac{150}{360}$

area of sector $= \frac{150 \times 144\pi}{360}$

area of sector ≈ 188 ft^2

5. Total number of items $= 5 + 13 + 20 + 2 = 40$

Probability =

$\frac{5}{40} \cdot \frac{20}{39} + \frac{20}{40} \cdot \frac{5}{39} = \frac{5}{2} \cdot \frac{1}{39} + \frac{1}{2} \cdot \frac{5}{39}$

$= \frac{5}{78} + \frac{5}{78}$

$= \frac{10}{78}$

$\approx 12.8\%$

6. Firstly, the student's answer is not a quadratic equation. It also has no real roots.

An equation with a root 9 is

$(x - 9)(x - 9) = 0$

$x^2 - 18x + 81 = 0$

7. Determine the domain for each relation. Then use the graph to write the function for each domain.

8. A quadratic with one real root always has a discriminant of zero. Answer Choice **C**

9. $\theta = \frac{\pi}{2}$ because a horizontal shift of the cosine function to the left by $\frac{\pi}{2}$ results in the sine function.

10. $y = -2\sqrt[3]{x+5} + 5$

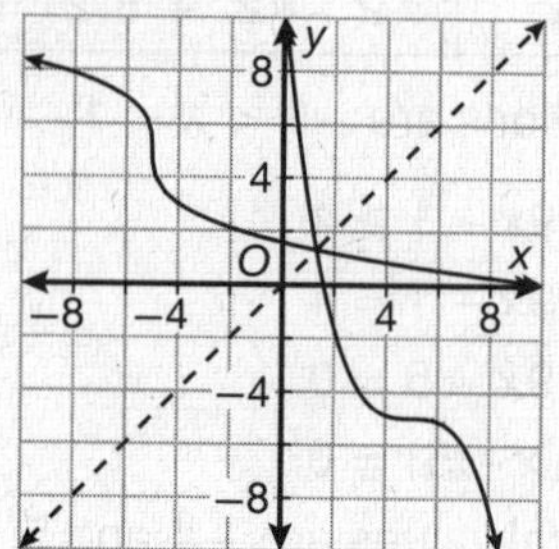

11. Sample: The graph of $y = x^2 - 4x + 7$ is always above the graph of $y = -5$.

12. Acceleration $a = 3.59$, initial speed $v_0 = 35$, and initial height $h_0 = 100$.

$h = -\frac{1}{2}at^2 + v_0t + h_0$

$0 = -\frac{1}{2}(3.59)t^2 + 35t + 100$

$0 = -1.795t^2 + 35t + 100$

$x = \frac{-35 \pm \sqrt{35^2 - 4(-1.795)(100)}}{2(-1.795)}$

$x \approx \frac{-35 \pm 44}{-3.59}$

$x \approx 22$ or $x \approx -2.5$

Ignoring the negative solution, the ball will take 22 s to hit the ground.

13. $A = \pi r^2$

$r^2 = \frac{A}{\pi}$

$r = \pm\sqrt{\frac{A}{\pi}}$

If A is the area of a circle, then only the solution $r = \sqrt{\frac{A}{\pi}}$ represents a possible value for the radius because it is positive; the other solution is negative.

14. The lengths of the sides of the triangle are all different so it is a scalene triangle.

$c^2 = a^2 + b^2 - 2ab \cos C$

$50^2 = 46^2 + 22^2 - 2(46)(22)\cos C$

$2500 = 2600 - 2024 \cos C$

$-100 = -2024 \cos C$
$0.0494 = \cos C$
$87° \approx C$
$b^2 = a^2 + c^2 - 2ac \cos B$
$22^2 = 46^2 + 50^2 - 2(46)(50) \cos B$
$484 = 4616 - 4600 \cos B$
$-4132 = -4600 \cos B$
$0.8983 \approx \cos B$
$26° \approx B$
$180 - (87 + 26) = 67°$

The three angles are acute, so the triangle is an acute scalene triangle.

15. 95% of the data lies within 2 standard deviations from the mean. This range is 62 lb to 74 lb.

Answer Choice **B**

16. $m\angle M = 180° - (93° + 12°) = 75°$

$\frac{\sin 75°}{16} = \frac{\sin 12°}{a}$

$a = \frac{16 \sin 12°}{\sin 75°}$

$a \approx 3.4$

$\frac{\sin 75°}{16} = \frac{\sin 93°}{p}$

$p = \frac{16 \sin 93°}{\sin 75°}$

$p \approx 16.5$

17. Graph both functions.

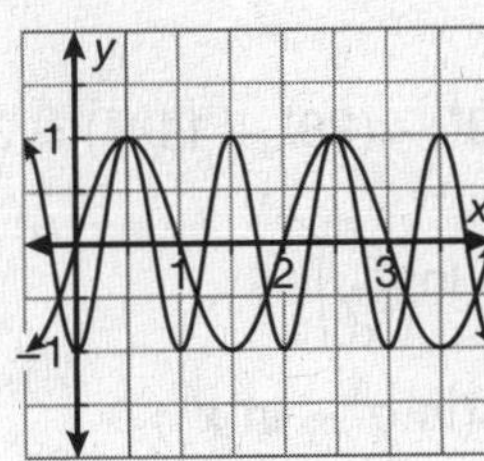

Both weights will reach the top of their movement at 0.5 and 2.5 seconds.

$2.5 - 0.5 = 2$ seconds

18. a. Worker A: $\frac{1}{3}$, Worker B: $\frac{1}{4}$

b. Worker A: $\frac{1}{3}h$, Worker B: $\frac{1}{4}h$

c. $\frac{1}{3}h + \frac{1}{4}h = 1$

$\frac{4h}{12} + \frac{3h}{12} = 1$

$\frac{7h}{12} = 1$

$7h = 12$

$h \approx 1.7$ hours

It will take the workers about 1.7 hours to paint a room together.

19. $A = Pe^{rt}$
$2P = Pe^{0.06t}$
$2 = e^{0.06t}$
$\ln 2 = \ln e^{0.06t}$
$0.693 = 0.06t$
$t \approx 11.6$ years

20. $A = Pe^{rt}$
$A = 3000e^{(0.045)(5)}$
$A = 3000e^{0.225}$
$A = \$3756.97$

The account will have \$3756.97 in it after 5 years.

21. Student *B* incorrectly wrote the binomial factor as $(x - 1)$ instead of $(x^4 - 1)$.

22. For $h = 0.91$

$\log(w) = 0.8h + 0.4 \pm 0.04$
$\log(w) = 0.8(0.91) + 0.4 \pm 0.04$
$\log(w) = 1.128 \pm 0.04$
$\log(w) = 1.168$ or $\log(w) = 1.088$
$w = 10^{1.168}$ $\quad w = 10^{1.088}$
$w = 14.7$ $\quad w = 12.2$

For $h = 0.93$

$\log(w) = 0.8(0.93) + 0.4 \pm 0.04$
$\log(w) = 1.144 \pm 0.04$
$\log(w) = 1.184$ or $\log(w) = 1.104$
$w = 10^{1.184}$ $\quad w = 10^{1.104}$
$w = 15.3$ $\quad w = 12.7$

For $h = 0.96$

$\log(w) = 0.8(0.96) + 0.4 \pm 0.04$
$\log(w) = 1.168 \pm 0.04$
$\log(w) = 1.208$ or $\log(w) = 1.128$
$w = 10^{1.208}$ $\quad w = 10^{1.128}$
$w = 16.1$ $\quad w = 13.4$

For $h = 0.99$

$\log(w) = 0.8(0.99) + 0.4 \pm 0.04$
$\log(w) = 1.192 \pm 0.04$

$\log(w) = 1.232$ or $\log(w) = 1.152$

$w = 10^{1.232}$ $w = 10^{1.152}$

$w = 17.1$ $w = 14.2$

For $h = 1.01$

$\log(w) = 0.8(1.01) + 0.4 \pm 0.04$

$\log(w) = 1.208 \pm 0.04$

$\log(w) = 1.248$ or $\log(w) = 1.168$

$w = 10^{1.248}$ $w = 10^{1.168}$

$w = 17.7$ $w = 14.7$

h (m)	w (kg)
0.91	12.2–14.7
0.93	12.7–15.3
0.96	13.4–16.1
0.99	14.2–17.1
1.01	14.7–17.7

23. Sample: The sample is not a probability sample because the questioner does not talk to the consumers who walk in to the station, nor does he question people on bikes, motorcycles, or ones using only the convenience station.

24. $5 - \sqrt{x+7} = 3$

$\sqrt{x+7} = 5 - 3$

$\sqrt{x+7} = 2$

$x + 7 = 4$

$x = -3$

25. $\sqrt{x+2} = 2 - \sqrt{x}$

$(\sqrt{x+2})^2 = (2 - \sqrt{x})^2$

$x + 2 = 4 - 4\sqrt{x} + x$

$2 = 4 - 4\sqrt{x}$

$4\sqrt{x} = 4 - 2$

$4\sqrt{x} = 2$

$16x = 4$

$x = \frac{1}{4}$

26. Press Y= and enter $x^2 + 7.56x - 40$ for Y1 and enter -23.4 for Y2. Then press GRAPH and press TRACE to scroll up and down the graph to find the x-values for which $x^2 + 7.56x - 40 > -23.4$.

Answer: $x < -9.34$ or $x > 1.78$

27. Initial height $h_0 = 44.1$, and initial velocity $v_0 = 0$ because the object is dropped not thrown.

$h(t) = -4.9t^2 + v_0 t + h_0$

$0 = -4.9t^2 + (0)t + 44.1$

$4.9t^2 = 44.1$

$t^2 = 9$

$t = 3$

It will take 3 s for the object to hit the ground.

28. $a^2 + b^2 = c^2$

$b^2 = c^2 - a^2$

$b = \sqrt{c^2 - a^2}$

$b = \sqrt{(150)^2 - (90)^2}$

$b = \sqrt{14{,}400}$

$b = 120$

The cliff is 120 m high.

29. Law of Cosines

$c^2 = 6^2 + 8^2 - 2(6)(8)\cos 114°$

$c^2 \approx 36 + 64 + 39$

$c \approx \sqrt{139}$

$c \approx 11.8$

Law of Sines

$\frac{\sin 114°}{11.8} = \frac{\sin B}{6}$

$\sin B = \frac{6 \sin 114°}{11.8}$

$\sin B \approx 0.465$

$m\angle B \approx 28°$

$m\angle A \approx 180° - (28° + 114°) \approx 38°$

30. $\ln\left(\frac{e^5}{x^7}\right)^4 = 4\ln\left(\frac{e^5}{x^7}\right)$

$= 4(\ln e^5 - \ln x^7)$

$= 4(5 - 7\ln x)$

$= 20 - 28\ln x$

LESSON 90

Warm Up 90

1. periodic
2. Period $= \frac{2\pi}{b} = \frac{2\pi}{3}$
3. Period $= \frac{2\pi}{b} = \frac{2\pi}{4} = \frac{\pi}{2}$

Lesson Practice 90

a.

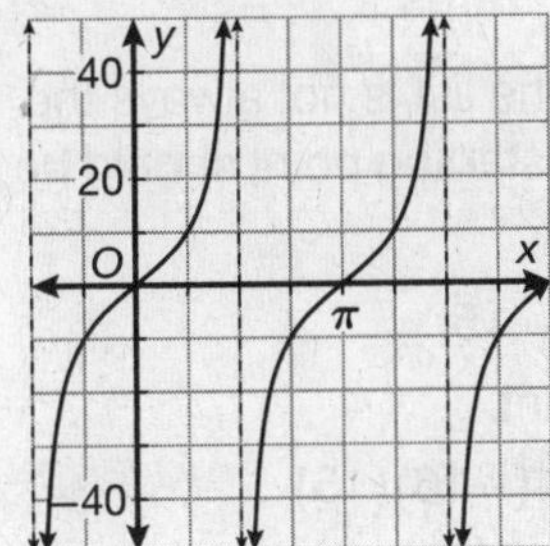

b.

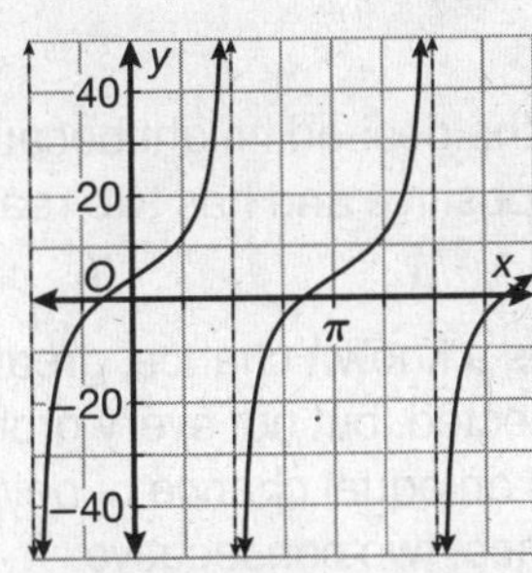

period $= \pi$

c. Period: $\frac{\pi}{6}$; Asymptotes: $x = \frac{\pi}{12} + n\frac{\pi}{6}$

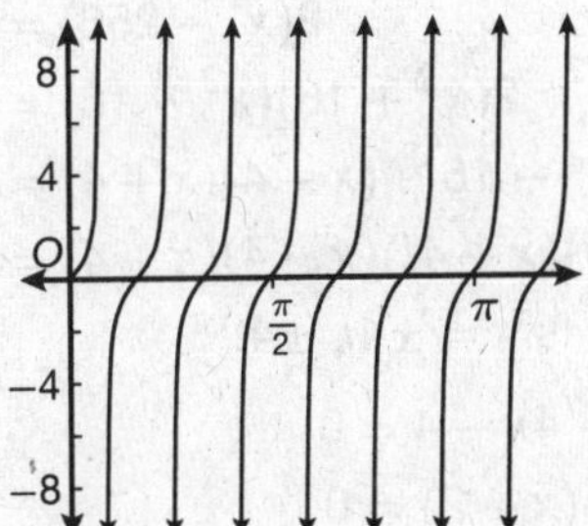

The period $= \frac{\pi}{6}$ whereas the period of the parent function is π. The function is not defined at $\frac{\pi}{12} + \frac{\pi}{6}n$, where n is an integer.

d.

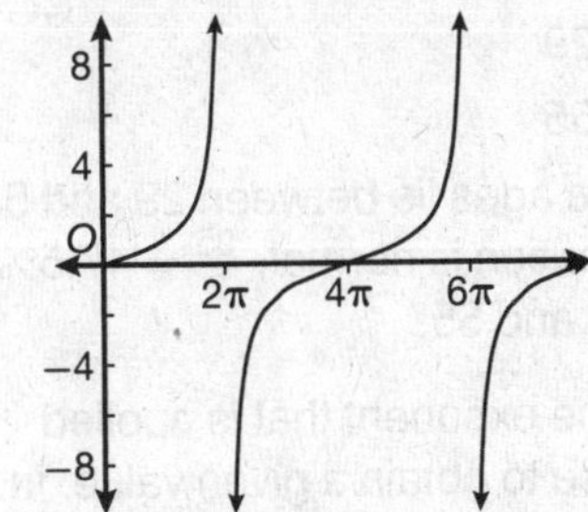

The period is $\frac{\pi}{\frac{1}{4}} = 4\pi$ whereas the period of the parent function is π. The function is not defined at $2\pi + 4\pi n$, where n is an integer.

e.

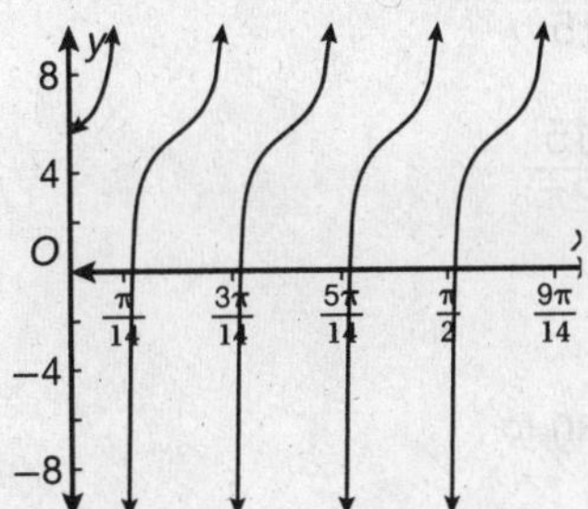

The period is $\frac{\pi}{7}$ and the function is not defined at $\frac{\pi}{14} + \frac{\pi}{7}n$, where n is an integer.

f.

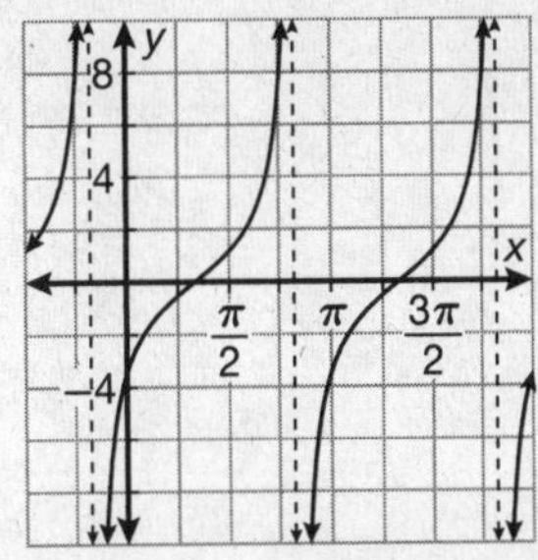

$$\frac{\pi}{3} + \frac{\pi}{2} = \frac{2\pi + 3\pi}{6} = \frac{5\pi}{6}$$

The period is π and the function is not defined at $\frac{5\pi}{6} + \pi n$, where n is an integer. The function is shifted to the right by $\frac{\pi}{3}$.

Practice 90

1. Use the side length of 52.8 miles as the base of the triangle. Denote the height, h, of the triangle as the altitude from Crystal City to the base.

$$\sin 57^\circ = \frac{h}{12.2}$$
$$h = 12.2 \sin 57^\circ$$
$$h = 10.2$$

$$\text{Area} = \frac{bh}{2} = \frac{(52.8)(10.2)}{2} \approx 270 \text{ mi}^2$$

2. $6 = (5x + 3)(x - 2)$
$6 = 5x^2 - 10x + 3x - 6$
$0 = 5x^2 - 7x - 12$
$0 = (5x - 12)(x + 1)$
$x = \frac{12}{5}$ or $x = -1$

Ignoring the negative solution, $x = \frac{12}{5}$. The circumference of the end of the cylinder will be equal to the length $5x + 3$. So

$5\left(\frac{12}{5}\right) + 3 = 15$

$r = \frac{15}{2\pi}$

3. $\tan\varphi = \frac{h_1}{w}$

$h_1 = w\tan\varphi$

$w = \frac{h_1}{\tan\varphi}$

$\tan\theta = \frac{h_2}{w}$

$h_2 = w\tan\theta$

$w = \frac{h_2}{\tan\theta}$

$\frac{h_1}{\tan\varphi} = \frac{h_2}{\tan\theta}$

$h_1\tan\theta = h_2\tan\varphi$

$\tan\theta = \frac{h_2\tan\varphi}{h_1}$

$\theta = \tan^{-1}\left((\tan\varphi)\cdot\frac{h_2}{h_1}\right)$

4. $\frac{3}{8}\cdot\frac{2}{7} = \frac{6}{56} = \frac{3}{28}$

5. $13^{\frac{3}{11}} = (13^3)^{\frac{1}{11}} = \sqrt[11]{13^3}$

6. $22^{\frac{5}{9}} = (22^5)^{\frac{1}{9}} = \sqrt[9]{22^5}$

7.

-10	1	18	95	150
		-10	-80	-150
	1	8	15	0

$x^3 + 18x^2 + 95x + 150$
$= (x + 10)\,(x^2 + 8x + 15)$
$= (x + 10)(x + 3)(x + 5)$

8. $0 = 7x(x^2 + 4x - 12) = 7x(x + 6)(x - 2)$
Then $x = 0$, $x = -6$, or $x = 2$.

9. $8.0 = \frac{2}{3}\log\left(\frac{E}{10^{11.8}}\right)$

$8\cdot\frac{3}{2} = \log\left(\frac{E}{10^{11.8}}\right)$

$12 = \log E - \log 10^{11.8}$

$12 = \log E - 11.8$

$23.8 = \log E$

$E = 10^{23.8}$

$E \approx 6.31\times 10^{23}$ ergs

10. The first name on the list is not always the starting point. The starting point should be chosen randomly.

11. $y = -16x^2 + 45x + 15$
Find the discriminant.
$b^2 - 4ac = 45^2 - 4(-16)(15)$
$= 2025 + 960$
$= 2985$
The ball will reach the desired height because the discriminant is positive and has two real solutions.

12. Every individual has a known chance, greater than 0, of being selected, but not every group of n individuals has an equal chance of being selected. For instance, two consecutive individuals will not be in the same sample.

13. $2x^4 - 512 = 0$
$2(x^4 - 256) = 0$
$2(x^2 + 16)(x^2 - 16) = 0$
$2(x^2 - 16i^2)(x - 4)(x + 4) = 0$
$2(x - 4i)(x + 4i)(x - 4)(x + 4) = 0$
Solution is $x = \pm 4i, \pm 4$.

14. $3x^2 + 4x - 4 = 0$
$(3x - 2)(x + 2) = 0$
$x = -2$ or $\frac{2}{3}$.

15. We know that 95% of the ages lie within two standard deviations from the mean.
$42 - 2(6.5) = 29$
$42 + 2(6.5) = 55$
Then 95% of the ages lie between 29 and 55. Since the distribution is normal, $\frac{95}{2} = 47.5\%$ are between 42 and 55.

16. A logarithm is the exponent that is applied to a specific base to obtain a given value. In the equation $x = e^y$, y is the exponent that is applied to the base e to obtain the value x. Therefore, y is the logarithm of x, using base e. That is, y is the natural logarithm of x.

17. The phase shift is $\frac{\pi}{4}$ to the left.

18. Multiply both sides of the equation by a non-zero constant.

19. Gene can paint $\frac{1}{8}$ of a room in an hour. In 5 hours, he paints $\frac{5}{8}$ of the room. Chandra painted $\frac{3}{8}$ of the room in 5 hours. Then, if x is Chandra's time,

$$5 = \frac{3}{8}x$$
$$x = \frac{40}{3}$$
$$x = 13\frac{1}{3}.$$

Chandra can paint a room in $13\frac{1}{3}$ hours.

20. An odd function because $\tan(-x) = -\tan(x)$.

21. $\tan\theta = \dfrac{y_2 - y_1}{x_2 - x_1}$

22. Given a quadratic inequality, bring all terms to one side and provisionally assume equality to equal zero. Solve for the x-values that are roots for this equation. These x-values represent critical values for the inequality. Arbitrarily choose an x-value from each interval created by the critical value. Test to see if the arbitrarily chosen x-values are solutions for the inequality. If an x-value is a solution, all the x-values in the interval it was chosen from are solutions for the inequality.

23. $A = \frac{1}{2}bh$

$2A = bh$

$b = \dfrac{2A}{h}$

Answer Choice **A**

24. $\log_2(x)^3 = \dfrac{\ln x^3}{\ln 2} = 3\dfrac{\ln x}{\ln 2}$

when $x = 1$

$\log_2(x)^3 = 3\dfrac{\ln 1}{\ln 2} = 3\dfrac{0}{\ln 2} = 0$

25. Press Y= and enter $0.000013x^4 - 0.00255x^3 + 0.13505x^2 - 0.51x + 0.5$

Then press GRAPH. Press CALC and choose **2: zero** follow the instructions on screen. An error will result because there are no real roots.

26.
$$x^2 - 2x \geq 8$$
$$x^2 - 2x = 8$$
$$x^2 - 2x - 8 = 0$$
$$(x-4)(x+2) = 0$$

The critical values are $x = 4$ and $x = -2$.

Interval	Test value	Is it a solution?
$x < -2$	-3	$(-3)^2 - 2(-3) = 15 \geq 8$, yes
$-2 < x < 4$	0	$0^2 - 2(0) = 0 \ngeq 8$, no
$4 < x$	5	$5^2 - 2(5) = 15 \geq 8$, yes

The solutions are $x \leq -2$ and $4 \leq x$.

27.
$$x^2 - 15x + 50 < 0$$
$$x^2 - 15x + 50 = 0$$
$$(x-10)(x-5) = 0$$

The critical values are $x = 10$ and $x = 5$.

Interval	Test value	Is a solution?
$x < 5$	0	$0^2 - 15(0) + 50 = 50 > 0$, no
$5 < x < 10$	6	$6^2 - 15(6) + 50 = -4 < 10$, yes
$10 < x$	11	$11^2 - 15(11) + 50 = 6 > 0$, no

The solutions are $5 < x < 10$.

28. Period $= \dfrac{2\pi}{b} = \dfrac{2\pi}{\frac{1}{\sqrt{5}-1}} = 2\pi(\sqrt{5} - 1)$

29. $-\sin\left(\frac{\pi}{2}x\right)$ is the reflection of $\sin\left(\frac{\pi}{2}x\right)$ in the x-axis. Thus, the amplitude is 1. The period is $2\pi \div \frac{\pi}{2} = 4$.

30.
$$x = 8 \pm 5i$$
$$x - 8 = \pm\sqrt{-25}$$
$$(x-8)^2 = -25$$
$$x^2 - 16x + 64 + 25 = 0$$
$$x^2 - 16x + 89 = 0$$

INVESTIGATION 9

1. a. $0.50 + 0.10(5) = 1.00$

b. $0.50 + 0.10(5.25) \approx 0.50 + 0.10(5) = 1.00$

c. $0.50 + 0.10(0.25) \approx 0.50 + 0.10(0) = 0.50$

2. Yes; although 30 seconds is rounded down to 0 minutes, there is a still a connection fee.

3. No; $5\frac{1}{4}$ rounded down to the nearest whole number is 5 minutes.

4.

x	$f(x)$
$0 < x < 1$	0.50
$1 \le x < 2$	$0.50 + 0.10(1) = 0.60$
$2 \le x < 3$	$0.50 + 0.10(2) = 0.70$
$3 \le x < 4$	$0.50 + 0.10(3) = 0.80$
$4 \le x < 5$	$0.50 + 0.10(4) = 0.90$
$5 \le x < 6$	$0.50 + 0.10(5) = 1.00$

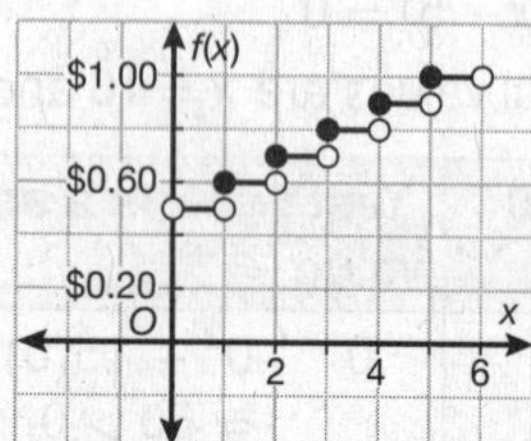

5. a. $f(x) = 0.10x + 0.50$

b. Replace the variable, x, with $[x]$.

c. $f(x) = 0.10[x] + 0.50$

d. Press MODE and scroll down to the fourth line to "Dot". Then press ENTER. Press Y=; then press MATH scroll right to the tab NUM, and then scroll down to "int(" and press ENTER. Enter $0.10[x] + 0.50$.

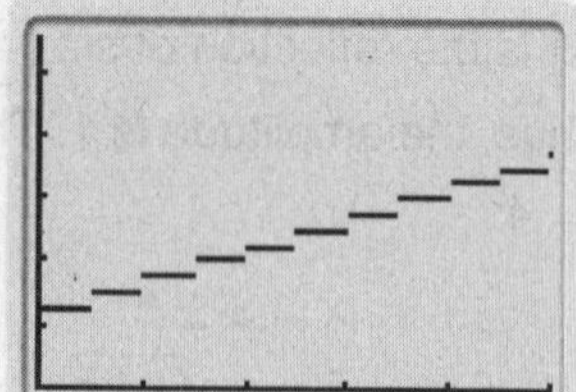

6.

x	$f(x)$
$0 < x \le 1$	6
$1 < x \le 2$	$6(2) = 12$
$2 < x \le 3$	$6(3) = 18$
$3 < x \le 4$	$6(4) = 24$
$4 < x \le 5$	$6(5) = 30$
$5 < x \le 6$	36

a.

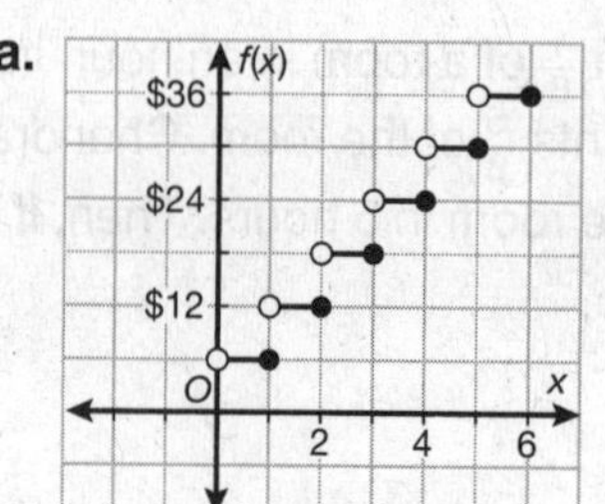

b. $12, $12, $6

c. $6

Investigation Practice 9

a. $f(x) = 0.03\lceil x \rceil$

b. domain: $x > 0$

c. least integer function; the number of ounces is rounded up to the nearest ounce.

d.

x	$f(x)$
$0 < x \le 1$	0.03
$1 < x \le 2$	0.06
$2 < x \le 3$	0.09
$3 < x \le 4$	0.12
$4 < x \le 5$	0.15
$5 < x \le 6$	0.18

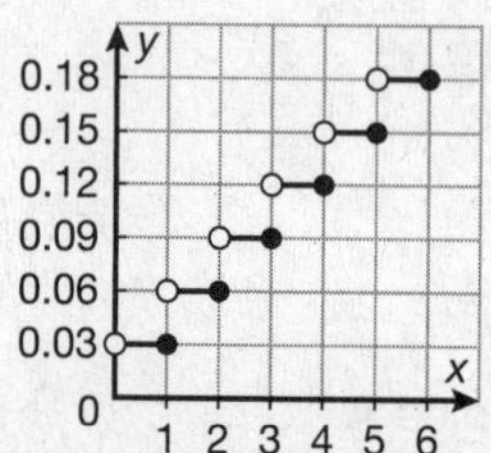

x	$f(x)$
$-2 < x \le -1$	-2
$-1 < x \le 0$	0
$0 < x \le 1$	2

e. $f(x) = 2\lceil x \rceil$

f. least integer function

LAB 13

a. 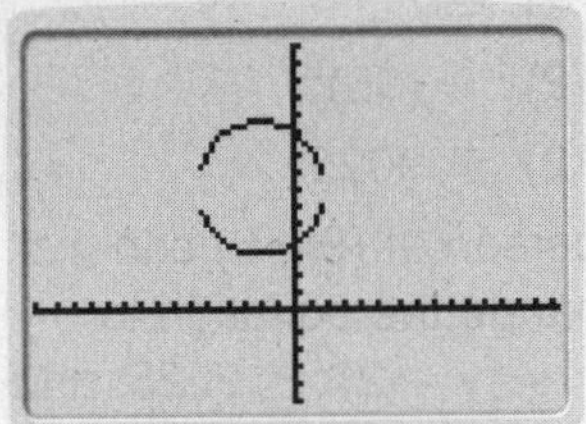

b. 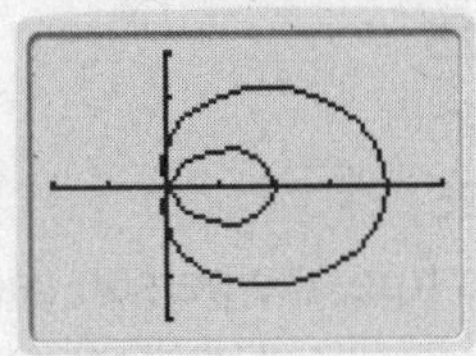

LESSON 91

Warm Up 91

1. radius

2. $d = \sqrt{(x_2 - x_1)^2 + (y_2 - y_1)^2}$
$= \sqrt{(-10 - 3)^2 + (7 - 5)^2}$
$= \sqrt{(-13)^2 + (2)^2}$
$= \sqrt{169 + 4}$
$= \sqrt{173}$

3. The unit circle centered at the origin has a radius of 1, so it can pass through points that are 1 unit from (0, 0), which does not include (1, 1). The statement is false.

Lesson Practice 91

a. $36 = r^2$, so $r = 6$
Step 1: Plot the center (0, 0).
Step 2: Locate the points 6 units above, below, left, and right of the center.
Step 3: Sketch a circle that passes through the four points.

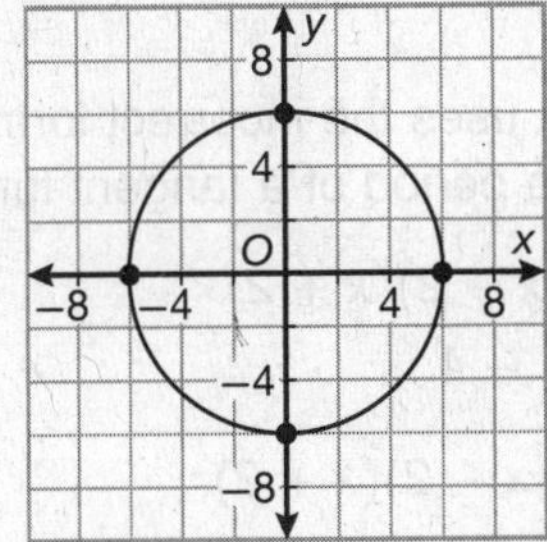

b. Solve for y. Then graph each of the two resulting functions.
$x^2 + y^2 = 25$
$y^2 = 25 - x^2$
$y = \pm\sqrt{25 - x^2}$

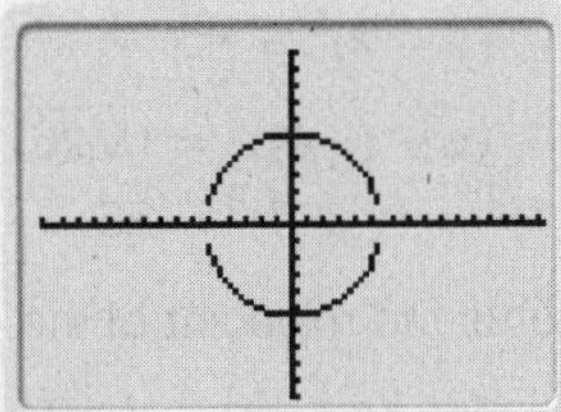

c. $r = \sqrt{4} = 2$.
Plot the center (5, 3). Then locate the points 2 units above, below, left, and right of the center. Sketch a circle that passes through these four points.

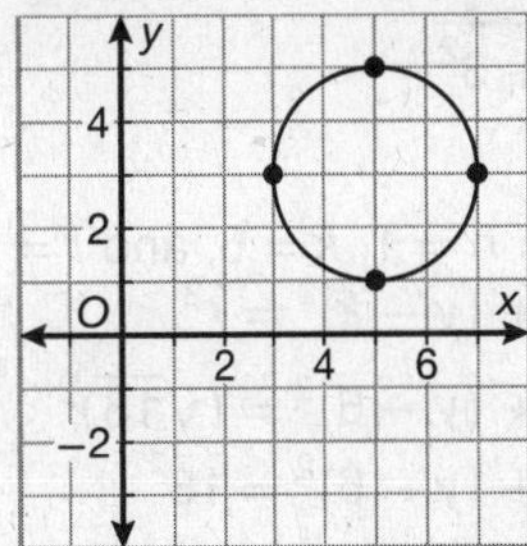

d. Solve for y. Then graph each of the two resulting functions.
$(x + 8)^2 + (y - 1)^2 = 22$
$(y - 1)^2 = 22 - (x + 8)^2$
$y - 1 = \pm\sqrt{22 - (x + 8)^2}$
$y = \pm\sqrt{22 - (x + 8)^2} + 1$

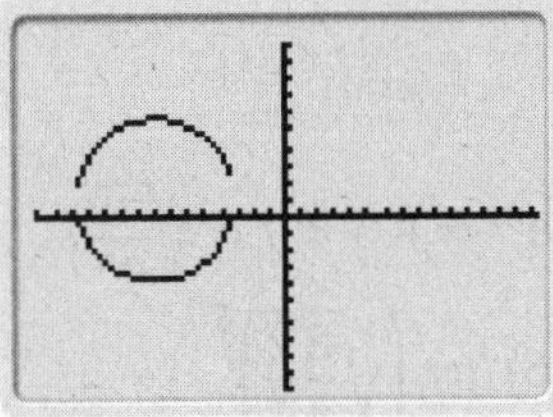

e. Substitute $h = 6$, $k = -7$, and $r = 9$ in $(x - h)^2 + (y - k)^2 = r^2$.
$(x - 6)^2 + (y - (-7))^2 = 9^2$
$(x - 6)^2 + (y + 7)^2 = 81$

f. $r = \sqrt{(x_2 - x_1)^2 + (y_2 - y_1)^2}$

$= \sqrt{(8 - 7)^2 + (1 - (-4))^2}$

$= \sqrt{1^2 + 5^2}$

$= \sqrt{26}$

Substitute $h = 7$, $k = -4$, and $r = \sqrt{26}$ in $(x - h)^2 + (y - k)^2 = r^2$.

$(x - 7)^2 + (y - (-4))^2 = (\sqrt{26})^2$

$(x - 7)^2 + (y + 4)^2 = 26$

g. The center is the midpoint of the diameter.

$M = \left(\frac{x_1 + x_2}{2}, \frac{y_1 + y_2}{2}\right) = \left(\frac{-2 + 4}{2}, \frac{3 + 9}{2}\right)$

$= (1, 6)$

Find the distance between the center and either point on the circle to get the radius.

$r = \sqrt{(4 - 1)^2 + (9 - 6)^2}$

$= \sqrt{3^2 + 3^2}$

$= \sqrt{18}$

Substitute $h = 1$, $k = 6$, and $r = \sqrt{18}$ in $(x - h)^2 + (y - k)^2 = r^2$.

$(x - 1)^2 + (y - 6)^2 = (\sqrt{18})^2$

$(x - 1)^2 + (y - 6)^2 = 18$

h. Let the Sun be at (0, 0).

$C = \pi d$

$421 = \pi d$

$d \approx 134.01$

$r \approx 134.01 \div 2$, or 67

Substitute $r = 67$ in $x^2 + y^2 = r^2$.

$x^2 + y^2 = (67)^2$

$x^2 + y^2 = 4489$

Practice 91

1. Substitute $r = 4.5$ in $r = \sqrt[3]{\frac{3V}{4\pi}}$.

$(4.5)^3 = \left(\sqrt[3]{\frac{3V}{4\pi}}\right)^3$

$91.125 = \frac{3V}{4\pi}$

$91.125(4\pi) = 3V$

$\frac{91.125(4\pi)}{3} = V$

$381.7 \approx V$

2. The center of the circle is (0, 2), and $r = 95$. Substitute $h = 0$, $k = 2$, and $r = 95$ in $(x - h)^2 + (y - k)^2 = r^2$.

$(x - 0)^2 + (y - 2)^2 = (95)^2$

$x^2 + (y - 2)^2 = 9025$

To show that a person at (94, 6) can pick up the signal, change the equation to the inequality $x^2 + (y - 2)^2 \leq 9025$, and substitute 94 for x and 6 for y.

$94^2 + (6 - 2)^2 \overset{?}{\leq} 9025$

$8836 + 16 \overset{?}{\leq} 9025$

$8852 \leq 9025$

Since the inequality is true, the person can pick up the signal.

3. $\left(\frac{-5}{2}\right)^2 - 2 = \frac{25}{4} - 2 = \frac{17}{4}$

4. $\frac{\sin B}{b} = \frac{\sin C}{c}$

$\frac{\sin B}{16} = \frac{\sin 104°}{25}$

$\sin B = \frac{16 \sin 104°}{25}$

$\sin B \approx 0.62$

$\sin^{-1} 0.62 \approx 38.4$

$m\angle B \approx 38.4°$

$m\angle A = 180° - (104° + 38.4°) = 37.6°$

$\frac{\sin A}{a} = \frac{\sin C}{c}$

$\frac{\sin 37.6°}{a} = \frac{\sin 104°}{25}$

$25 \sin 37.6° = a \sin 104°$

$\frac{25 \sin 37.6°}{\sin 104°} = a$

$15.7 \approx a$

5. $s = r\theta$

$s = 42\left(\frac{\pi}{8}\right)$

$= \frac{42\pi}{8} \approx 16.5$

6. Student A uses the incorrect formula for finding the period of a tangent function.

7. a. $y = 1(x - 2)(x + 2)$

$y = x^2 - 4$

b. $y = \frac{1}{2}(x - 2)(x + 2)$

$$y = \frac{1}{2}(x^2 - 4)$$
$$= \frac{1}{2}x^2 - 2$$

c. $y = -1(x - 2)(x + 2)$
$y = -1(x^2 - 4)$
$= -x^2 + 4$

d.

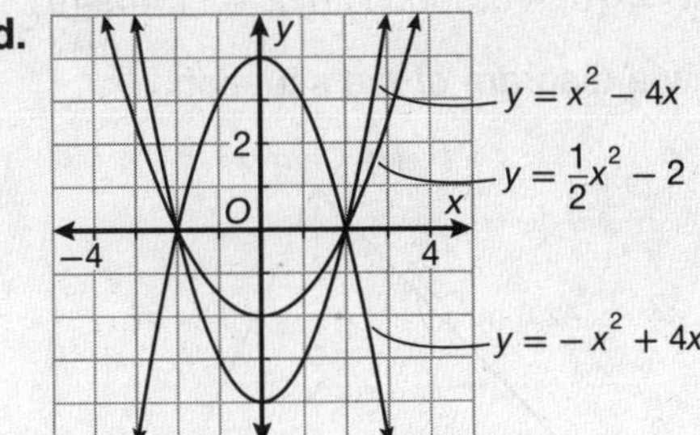

e. An infinite number

8. Multiples of 5 = 5, 10, 15...100
There are 20 multiples of 5.
$P(\text{multiple of } 5) = \frac{20}{100} = 0.2$

9. $110° = 110\frac{\pi}{180} = \frac{11\pi}{18}$
$s = r\theta$
$s = 8\left(\frac{11\pi}{18}\right)$
$= \frac{88\pi}{18} \approx 15.4$

10. The center is (h, k), so in Quadrant II, h will be negative and k will be positive.

11. The function rule is a radical expression that contains a variable in the radicand.

12. The center is the midpoint of the diameter.
$M = \left(\frac{x_1 + x_2}{2}, \frac{y_1 + y_2}{2}\right)$
$= \left(\frac{-2 + 4}{2}, \frac{-1+(-1)}{2}\right) = (1, -1)$
Find the distance between the center and either point on the circle to get the radius.
$r = \sqrt{(4 - 1)^2 + (-1 - (-1))^2}$
$= \sqrt{3^2 + 0^2}$
$= \sqrt{9} = 3$
Substitute $h = 1$, $k = -1$, and $r = 3$ in $(x - h)^2 + (y - k)^2 = r^2$.
$(x - 1)^2 + (y - (-1))^2 = (3)^2$
$(x - 1)^2 + (y + 1)^2 = 9$

13. Substitute 12 for o and 8 for i.
$\frac{1}{f} = \frac{1}{12} + \frac{1}{8}$
$\frac{1}{f} = \frac{2}{24} + \frac{3}{24}$
$\frac{1}{f} = \frac{5}{24}$
$5f = 24$
$f = 4.8$

14. In standard form, one side of the equation derived from the identical roots is a perfect square trinomial.

15. The sample is a self-selected sample, since the coaches can choose whether or not to respond.

16.
$x = 7 \pm 3i$
$x - 7 = \pm 3i$
$x - 7 = \pm\sqrt{-9}$
$(x - 7)^2 = -9$
$x^2 - 14x + 49 = -9$
$x^2 - 14x + 58 = 0$

17.
$f(x) = 15x^3 + 3x^2 - 6x$
$= 3x(5x^2 + x - 2)$
$0 = 3x(5x^2 + x - 2)$
$5x^2 + x - 2 = 0$ or $3x = 0$
If $5x^2 + x - 2 = 0$,
$x = \frac{-1 \pm \sqrt{1^2 - 4(5)(-2)}}{2(5)} = \frac{-1 \pm \sqrt{41}}{10}$
If $3x = 0$, $x = 0$
So, $x = 0$ or $x = \frac{-1 \pm \sqrt{41}}{10}$

18. $(x + 1)(4x^2 + 4) - (x + 1)(2x - 3) = 0$
$(x + 1)(4x^2 + 4 - (2x - 3)) = 0$
$(x + 1)(4x^2 - 2x + 7) = 0$
$x + 1 = 0$ or $4x^2 - 2x + 7 = 0$
If $4x^2 - 2x + 7 = 0$
$x = \frac{-(-2) \pm \sqrt{(-2)^2 - 4(4)(7)}}{2(4)} = \frac{2 \pm \sqrt{-108}}{8}$

If $x + 1 = 0$, $x = -1$.
The only real root is $x = -1$.

19. The graph of $f(x)g(x)$ is identical to the graph of $h(x)$, but it is not defined at $(2n + 1)\frac{\pi}{2}$, for integer values of n.

20. Period $= \frac{\pi}{b} = \frac{\pi}{12}$

The function is undefined where $\cos(12x) = 0$

$12x = \frac{\pi}{2}$

$x = \frac{\pi}{24} + \frac{\pi}{12}n$

21. Draw a diagram of the situation.

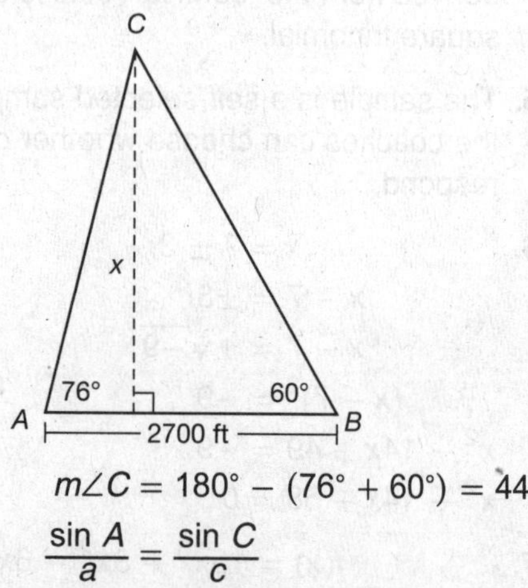

$m\angle C = 180° - (76° + 60°) = 44°$

$\frac{\sin A}{a} = \frac{\sin C}{c}$

$\frac{\sin 76°}{a} = \frac{\sin 44°}{2700}$

$a = \frac{2700 \sin 76°}{\sin 44°}$

$a \approx 3771.35$

$\sin 60° = \frac{x}{3771.35}$

$3771.35 \sin 60° = x$

$3266 \approx x$

22. Solve for y. Graph each of the two resulting functions.

$(x - 1)^2 + (y + 9)^2 = 7$

$(y + 9)^2 = 7 - (x - 1)^2$

$y + 9 = \pm\sqrt{7 - (x - 1)^2}$

$y = -9 \pm \sqrt{7 - (x - 1)^2}$

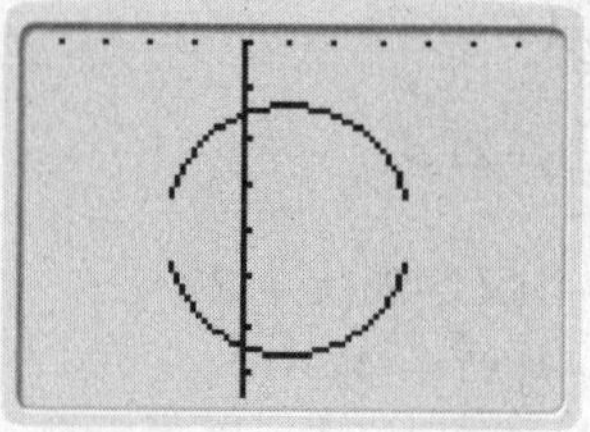

y-int. $= (0, -6.55051), (0, -11.44949)$

23. Draw a diagram of the situation.

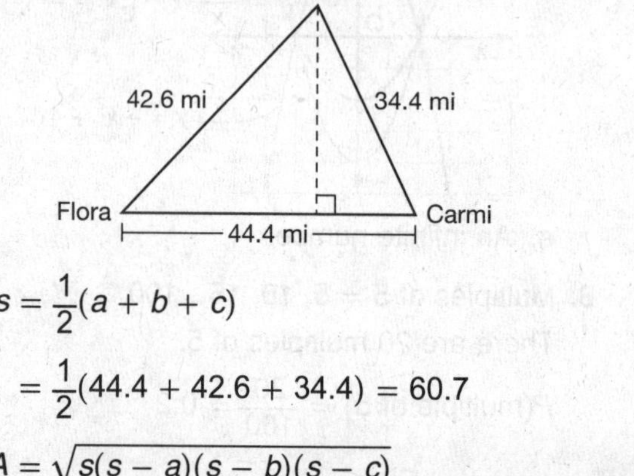

$s = \frac{1}{2}(a + b + c)$

$= \frac{1}{2}(44.4 + 42.6 + 34.4) = 60.7$

$A = \sqrt{s(s - a)(s - b)(s - c)}$

$= \sqrt{60.7(60.7 - 44.4)(60.7 - 42.6)(60.7 - 34.4)}$

$= \sqrt{60.7(16.3)(18.1)(26.3)}$

≈ 686

The area is about 686 square miles.

24. The student who took the reading test has z-score $= \frac{27 - 21.3}{6} = 0.95$, so their reading test is 0.95 standard deviations above the mean. Student who took the math test has z-score $= \frac{24 - 20.7}{5} = 0.66$, so their standard deviation is 0.66 standard deviations above the mean. Therefore, the student who took the reading test performed better.

25. When $x = -0.4$, $f(x) = 8$, so $f(-0.4) = 8$.
When $x = 0$, $f(x) = 8$, so $f(0) = 8$.
When $x = 6$, $f(x) = 3(6) - 1 = 17$, so $f(6) = 17$.

26. $\ln e^{x^2} = d$

$e^{x^2} = e^d$

$x^2 = d$

So, $\ln e^{x^2} = x^2$

Answer Choice **B**

27. $(x^3)^3 - a^3 = (x^3 - a)((x^3)^2 + ax^3 + a^2)$
$= (x^3 - a)(x^6 + ax^3 + a^2)$

The only root is $(x^3 - a)$.

$x^3 = a$

$x = \sqrt[3]{a}$

28. $d^2 = x^2 + x^2$

$d = \sqrt{2x^2}$

$r = \frac{\sqrt{2x^2}}{2}$

$A_{circle} = \pi\left(\frac{\sqrt{2x^2}}{2}\right)^2 = \pi\left(\frac{2x^2}{4}\right) = \frac{2\pi x^2}{4}$

$A_{triangle} = \frac{x(x)}{2} = \frac{x^2}{2}$

$P(\text{not inside triangle}) = 1 - \frac{\frac{x^2}{2}}{\frac{2\pi x^2}{4}}$

$= 1 - \left(\frac{x^2}{2}\right)\left(\frac{4}{2\pi x^2}\right)$

$= 1 - \frac{1}{\pi} \approx 0.682$

29. If you solve $F = \frac{9}{5}C + 32$ for C, the result is $C = \frac{5}{9}(F - 32)$.

30.

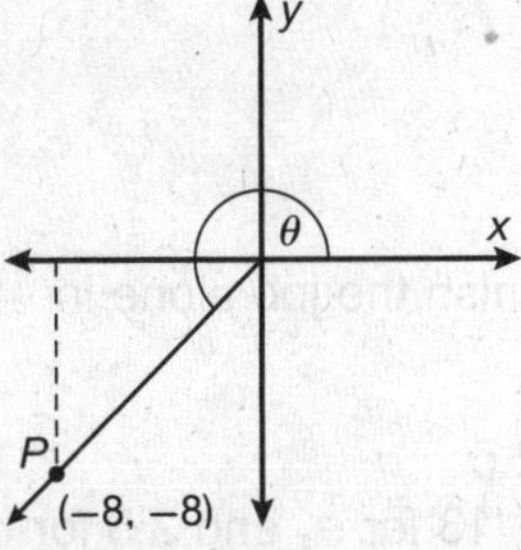

$|x| = 8$, $|y| = 8$

Find the value of r.

$r = \sqrt{x^2 + y^2}$

$r = \sqrt{(-8)^2 + (-8)^2}$

$r = \sqrt{64 + 64}$

$= \sqrt{128}$

$= 8\sqrt{2}$

Use the values of x, y and r to find the values of sine, cosine and tangent of θ.

$\sin\theta = \frac{-8}{8\sqrt{2}} = -\frac{1}{\sqrt{2}} = \frac{-\sqrt{2}}{2}$

$\cos\theta = \frac{-8}{8\sqrt{2}} = \frac{-\sqrt{2}}{2}$ $\tan\theta = \frac{-8}{-8} = 1$

$\csc\theta = \frac{1}{\sin\theta} = -\sqrt{2}$

$\sec\theta = \frac{1}{\cos\theta} = -\sqrt{2}$ $\cot\theta = \frac{1}{\tan\theta} = 1$

LESSON 92

Warm Up 92

1. domain

2. $18 = 6 + 2(n - 1)$

$18 = 6 + 2n - 2$

$18 = 4 + 2n$

$14 = 2n$

$7 = n$

3. True

Exploration 92

Step 1:

Month	1	2	3	4	5
Total Number of DVDs	8	11	14	17	20

Step 2: The total number of DVDs is 3 more than the previous month.

Step 3: $20 + 3 = 23$, $23 + 3 = 26$, $26 + 3 = 29$

Step 4: discrete function; natural numbers

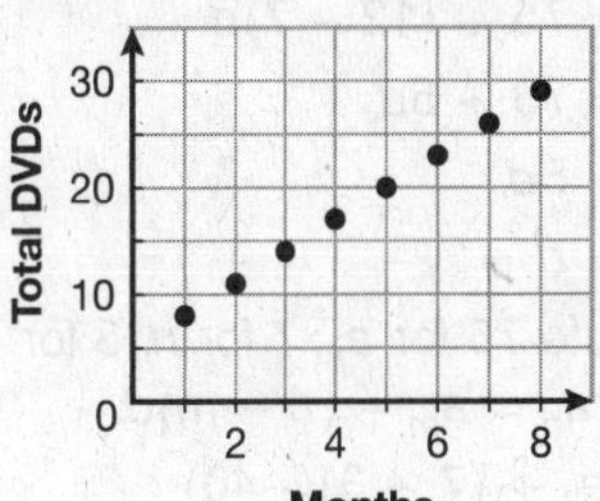

Lesson Practice 92

a. $d = 11\frac{3}{4} - 11 = \frac{3}{4}$

$11\frac{3}{4} + d = 11\frac{3}{4} + \frac{3}{4} = 12\frac{1}{2}$

$12\frac{1}{2} + d = 12\frac{1}{2} + \frac{3}{4} = 13\frac{1}{4}$

$13\frac{1}{4} + d = 13\frac{1}{4} + \frac{3}{4} = 14$

b. $d = -94 - (-103) = 9$
Substitute 44 for n, -121 for a_1 and 9 for d in $a_n = a_1 + (n - 1)d$.
$a_{44} = -121 + (44 - 1)9$
$a_{44} = -121 + 387$
$a_{44} = 266$

c. $d = 0.38 - 0.56 = -0.18$
Substitute 33 for n, 0.56 for a_1 and -0.18 for d in $a_n = a_1 + (n - 1)d$.
$a_{33} = 0.56 + (33 - 1)(-0.18)$
$a_{33} = 0.56 + 32(-0.18)$
$a_{33} = -5.2$

d. Substitute 63 for a_n, 7 for n, 33 for a_m, and 3 for m in $a_n = a_m + (n - m)d$.
$63 = 33 + (7 - 3)d$
$63 = 33 + 4d$
$30 = 4d$
$7.5 = d$
Substitute 33 for a_n, 3 for n, and 7.5 for d in $a_n = a_1 + (n - 1)d$.
$33 = a_1 + (3 - 1)7.5$
$33 = a_1 + 2(7.5)$
$33 = a_1 + 15$
$18 = a_1$

e. Substitute -125 for a_n, 12 for n, 75 for a_m, and 7 for m in $a_n = a_m + (n - m)d$.
$-125 = 75 + (12 - 7)d$
$-125 = 75 + 5d$
$-200 = 5d$
$-40 = d$
Substitute 75 for a_n, 7 for n, 3 for m, and -40 for d in $a_n = a_m + (n - m)d$.
$75 = a_3 + (7 - 3)(-40)$
$75 = a_3 + 4(-40)$
$75 = a_3 - 160$
$235 = a_3$

f. Substitute 36,420 for a_n, 13 for n, 31,975 for a_m, and 6 for m in $a_n = a_m + (n - m)d$.
$36{,}420 = 31{,}975 + (13 - 6)d$
$36{,}420 = 31{,}975 + 7d$
$4445 = 7d$
$635 = d$
Substitute 36,420 for a_n, 13 for n, and 635 for d in $a_n = a_1 + (n - 1)d$.
$36{,}420 = a_1 + (13 - 1)635$
$36{,}420 = a_1 + 7620$
$28{,}800 = a_1$
The starting salary was $28,800.

Practice 92

1. Sample: 1, 2, 4, 7, 11, 16; since there is no common difference between two consecutive terms.

2. Let r_h = rate the homeowner rakes and bags the leaves. Let r_c = rate the children rake and bag the leaves. Since the homeowner can finish 1 yard in 5 hours, $r_h = \frac{1}{5}$. The children alone can finish the job in t hours, $r_c = \frac{1}{t}$. The homeowner and children together finish one yard in 3 hours, $r_h + r_c = \frac{1}{3}$. Substitute $\frac{1}{5}$ for r_h and $\frac{1}{t}$ for r_c.
$\frac{1}{5} + \frac{1}{t} = \frac{1}{3}$
$\frac{1}{t} = \frac{1}{3} - \frac{1}{5} = \frac{5}{15} - \frac{3}{15} = \frac{2}{15}$
$\frac{1}{t} = \frac{2}{15}$
$1(15) = 2t$
$\frac{15}{2} = t$
$7.5 = t$
The children can finish the job alone in 7.5 hours.

3. $d = 15.5 - 13 = 2.5$
Substitute 40 for n, 13 for a_1 and 2.5 for d in $a_n = a_1 + (n - 1)d$.
$a_{40} = 13 + (40 - 1)(2.5)$
$a_{40} = 13 + 97.5$
$a_{40} = 110.5$
Answer Choice **C**

4. Since $y = (x - 3)^2$
$x = (y - 3)^2$
$\sqrt{x} = y - 3$
$\sqrt{x} + 3 = y$
The domain is $x \geq 0$. The range is $y \geq 3$.

5. Using the unit circle:

$$-1 = \cos(\pi)$$
$$\cos^{-1}(-1) = \pi = 180°$$

6. When graphed, the data is single-peaked, bell-shaped, and symmetric about the mean. 68% of the data is within one standard deviation of the mean, 95% of the data is within two standard deviations of the mean, and 99.7% of the data is within three standard deviations of the mean.

7. The center is the midpoint of the diameter.

$$M = \left(\frac{x_1 + x_2}{2}, \frac{y_1 + y_2}{2}\right) = \left(\frac{-4+5}{2}, \frac{-3+2}{2}\right)$$
$$= (0.5, -0.5)$$
$$r = \sqrt{(x_2 - x_1)^2 + (y_2 - y_1)^2}$$
$$= \sqrt{(5 - 0.5)^2 + (2 - (-0.5))^2}$$
$$= \sqrt{20.25 + 6.25}$$
$$= \sqrt{26.5}$$

Substitute $h = 0.5$, $k = -0.5$, and $r = \sqrt{26.5}$ in $(x - h)^2 + (y - k)^2 = r^2$.

$$(x - 0.5)^2 + (y - (-0.5))^2 = (\sqrt{26.5})^2$$
$$(x - 0.5)^2 + (y + 0.5)^2 = 26.5$$

8. Substitute $h = 2$, $k = -9$, and $r = 3$ in $(x - h)^2 + (y - k)^2 = r^2$.

$$(x - 2)^2 + (y - (-9))^2 = (3)^2$$
$$(x - 2)^2 + (y + 9)^2 = 9$$

9. No. The strata are not mutually exclusive. A triangle can be both right and isosceles, or right and scalene.

10. Let v_o be the speed of the outer satellite, and v_i be the speed of the inner satellite.

$$\frac{v_i^2}{r} = \frac{v_o^2}{2r}$$
$$rv_o^2 = 2rv_i^2$$
$$v_o^2 = 2v_i^2$$
$$\sqrt{v_o^2} = \sqrt{2v_i^2}$$
$$v_o = \sqrt{2}v_i$$

The speed of the outer satellite is $\sqrt{2}$ times the speed of the inner satellite.

11. $(3 + i)(1 - 4i) = 3 - 12i + i - 4i^2$

$$= 3 - 11i - 4i^2$$
$$= 3 - 11i - 4(-1)$$
$$= 3 - 11i + 4$$
$$= 7 - 11i$$

12. To use the Law of Cosine either the measure of two sides and the included angle, or the measure of three sides are needed. The triangle in **C** does not meet the requirements.

Answer Choice **C**

13. a. $N(t) = N_o e^{-kt}$

$$0.5 = 1e^{-k(6)}$$
$$\ln 0.5 = \ln e^{-k(6)}$$
$$\ln 0.5 = -6k$$
$$k = \frac{\ln 0.5}{-6} \approx 0.11552$$
$$N(t) = N_o e^{-0.11552t}$$
$$0.2 = 1e^{-0.11552t}$$
$$\ln 0.2 = \ln e^{-0.11552t}$$
$$\ln 0.2 = -0.11552t$$
$$t = \frac{\ln 0.2}{-0.11552} \approx 13.93$$

b.

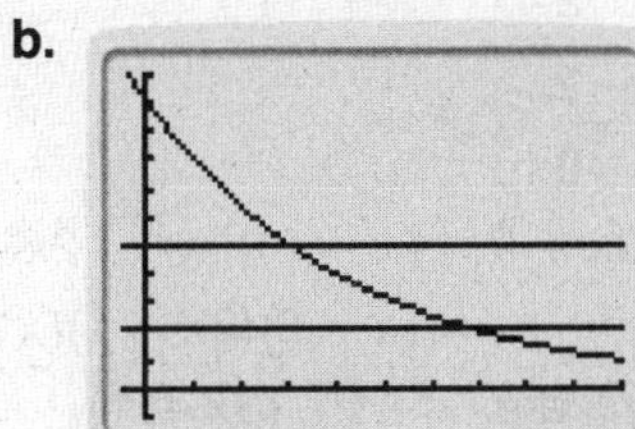

c. The graph of y_1 intersects the graph of y_2 at approximately (6, 0.5), representing the fact that 50% of an initial amount remains after about 6 hours. The graph of y_1 intersects the graph of y_3 at approximately (13.93, 0.2), representing the fact that 20% of an initial amount remains after about 13.93 hours.

14. $f(x) = \begin{cases} 75 & x \le 4 \\ 75 + 25(x - 4) & x > 4 \end{cases}$

15. $d = 21 - 4 = 17$

Substitute 17 for n, 4 for a_1 and 17 for d in $a_n = a_1 + (n - 1)d$.

$$a_{17} = 4 + (17 - 1)17$$
$$a_{17} = 4 + 272$$
$$a_{17} = 276$$

16. $x = \dfrac{-b \pm \sqrt{b^2 - 4ac}}{2a}$

$= \dfrac{-5 \pm \sqrt{5^2 - 4(4)(-1)}}{2(4)}$

$= \dfrac{-5 \pm \sqrt{41}}{8}$

$x \approx 0.1754$ or -1.4254

17. $0 = x^4 - 16$

$0 = (x^2 - 4)(x^2 + 4)$

$0 = (x - 2)(x + 2)(x^2 + 4)$

$x - 2 = 0, x = 2$

$x + 2 = 0, x = -2$

$x^2 + 4 = 0$

$x = \sqrt{-4}$

The roots are $x = 2$ and $x = -2$.

18. Possible rational roots are

$\pm\frac{1}{3}, \pm1, \pm2, \pm\frac{2}{3}$

Test $x - 2$ as a factor.

$$\begin{array}{r|rrrr} 2 & 3 & -8 & 3 & 2 \\ & & 6 & -4 & -2 \\ \hline & 3 & -2 & -1 & 0 \end{array}$$

$3x^3 - 8x^2 + 3x + 2 = (x - 2)(3x^2 - 2x - 1)$

$= (x - 2)(3x + 1)(x - 1)$

The dimensions are $(x - 2)$, $(3x + 1)$, and $(x - 1)$.

19. The first term is 30, and 5 hours later is the sixth term, which is 359. The speed is the same each hour, which is d.

$a_6 = a_1 + (6 - 1)d$

$359 = 30 + 5d$

$329 = 5d$

$65.8 = d$

20.

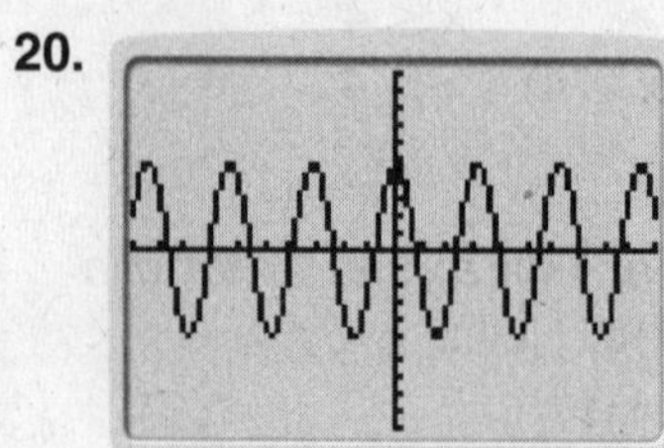

Period $= \dfrac{2\pi}{b} = \dfrac{2\pi}{2} = \pi$

Phase shift $= 3\pi$

21. $\log_5(125x)^2 = 2(\log_5 125 + \log_5 5)$

$= 2(3 + 1) = 8$

22. Compounding is monthly, so the rate is $\frac{1}{12}$ of 2.7% or 0.225%. Each month the value is multiplied by 1.00225. Seven years consist of 84 months. So the account will have a value of $1500(1.00225)^{84}$ dollars, or $1811.68 in seven years.

23. The critical values are the values that separate a number line into regions that contain solutions and regions that do not contain solutions. They are the intersection points of the graph on the left side of the inequality and the graph on the right side of the inequality.

24. $6t^2 + 5 = 2t^2 + 1$

$4t^2 = -4$

$t^2 = -1$

$t = \pm\sqrt{-1}$

$t = \pm i$

25. $-1(x^2 - 8x + 7 = 0) \rightarrow -x^2 + 8x - 7 = 0$

$2(x^2 - 8x + 7 = 0) \rightarrow 2x^2 - 16x + 14 = 0$

Multiplying the given equation by an integer results in the equations

$-x^2 + 8x - 7 = 0$ and $2x^2 - 16x + 14 = 0$.

26. $11^4 = 14{,}641$

$\log_{11} 14{,}641 = 4$

27. $\log_9 729 = 3$

$9^3 = 729$

28. $r = \sqrt{(x_2 - x_1)^2 + (y_2 - y_1)^2}$

$= \sqrt{(-14 - (-14))^2 + (-1 - 2)^2}$

$= \sqrt{0^2 + (-3)^2}$

$= \sqrt{9} = 3$

Substitute $h = -14$, $k = -1$, and $r = 3$ in $(x - h)^2 + (y - k)^2 = r^2$.

$(x - (-14))^2 + (y - (-1))^2 = (3)^2$

$(x + 14)^2 + (y + 1)^2 = 9$

29. A discriminant of 0 means that nothing is added or subtracted from $-b$, meaning there is one real solution, $\frac{-b}{2a}$.

30. $4x^2 = -12x + 4$

$4x^2 + 12x = 4$

$$x^2 + 3x = 1$$
$$x^2 + 3x + \left(\frac{3}{2}\right)^2 = 1 + \left(\frac{3}{2}\right)^2$$
$$x^2 + 3x + \frac{9}{4} = 1 + \frac{9}{4}$$
$$\left(x + \frac{3}{2}\right)^2 = \frac{13}{4}$$
$$x + \frac{3}{2} = \pm\sqrt{\frac{13}{4}}$$
$$x = -\frac{3}{2} \pm \frac{\sqrt{13}}{2}$$

LESSON 93

Warm Up 93

1. base
2. The base is the quantity that is being multiplied repeatedly. The base is 1.022.
3. The base is the quantity that is being multiplied repeatedly. The base is 1 + 0.04

Lesson Practice 93

a. $49^{2y} = 343^{2y+3}$
$$49^{2y} = (7^2)^{2y} = 7^{4y}$$
$$343^{2y+3} = (7^3)^{2y+3} = 7^{6y+9}$$
$$7^{4y} = 7^{6y+9}$$
$$4y = 6y + 9$$
$$-2y = 9$$
$$y = -4.5$$

b. $3^r = 9^5$
$$3^r = (3^2)^5$$
$$3^r = 3^{10}$$
$$r = 10$$

c. $25^t = \frac{1}{25}$
$$25^t = 25^{-1}$$
$$t = -1$$

d. $45 = 2.3^{2x}$
$$\log 45 = \log 2.3^{2x}$$
$$\log 45 = 2x \log 2.3$$
$$\frac{\log 45}{2 \log 2.3} = x$$
$$x \approx 2.29$$

e. $3e^{2c+1} = 432$
$$\ln 3e^{2c+1} = \ln 432$$
$$\ln 3 + \ln e^{2c+1} = \ln 432$$
$$\ln 3 + 2c + 1 = \ln 432$$
$$2c = \ln 432 - \ln 3 - 1$$
$$2c \approx 3.9698$$
$$c \approx 1.98$$

f. The first year stock is \$1.50, the next year stock is \$3.00, the following year is \$6.00, and so on. The stock is $1.50(2)^{n-1}$ on year n.
$$1.50(2)^{n-1} > 90$$
$$\log[1.50(2)^{n-1}] > \log 90$$
$$\log 1.50 + \log(2)^{n-1} > \log 90$$
$$\log(2)^{n-1} > \log 90 - \log 1.50$$
$$(n-1)\log 2 > \log 90 - \log 1.50$$
$$n - 1 > \frac{\log 90 - \log 1.50}{\log 2}$$
$$n - 1 > 5.91$$
$$n > 6.91$$
6.91 years after Dec. 31, 2007 is sometime in 2013.

g. The price on week n is $325(1 - 0.06)^n$ or $325(0.94)^n$.
$$325(0.94)^n < 200$$
$$\log[325(0.94)^n] < \log 200$$
$$\log 325 + \log(0.94)^n < \log 200$$
$$\log(0.94)^n < \log 200 - \log 325$$
$$n \log(0.94) < \log 200 - \log 325$$
$$n > \frac{\log 200 - \log 325}{\log 0.94}$$
$$n > 7.85$$
In week 8 the price will be below 200.

h. $A = P\left(1 + \frac{r}{n}\right)^{nt}$
$$1.5P = P\left(1 + \frac{0.048}{12}\right)^{12t}$$
$$1.5 = (1.004)^{12t}$$
$$\log 1.5 = \log(1.004)^{12t}$$
$$\log 1.5 = 12\, t \log(1.004)$$
$$\frac{\log 1.5}{12 \log(1.004)} = t \approx 8.46$$
It will take about 8.46 years.

Practice 93

1. The population is all of the customers who order take-out, and the sample is the people who call the number.

2. $1.4 = 1.06^x$
$\log 1.4 = \log(1.06)^x$
$\log 1.4 = x \log(1.06)$
$\frac{\log 1.4}{\log 1.06} = x$
Answer Choice **D**

3. Substitute 0 for $h(t)$, 0 for v_o, and 14.4 for h_o.
$0 = -4.9t^2 + 0t + 14.4$
$4.9t^2 = 14.4$
$t^2 \approx 2.939$
$t \approx \pm\sqrt{2.939}$
$t \approx \pm 1.71$
Since time cannot be negative, it will take 1.71 seconds.

4. Substitute 19 for a_1, 13 for n, 127 for a_n, and 9 for d in $a_n = a_1 + (n - 1)d$.
$127 \stackrel{?}{=} 19 + (13 - 1)9$
$127 \stackrel{?}{=} 19 + 108$
$127 = 127$

5. Substitute 6 for a_1, 20 for n, and 4 for d in $a_n = a_1 + (n - 1)d$.
$a_{20} = 6 + (20 - 1)4$
$a_{20} = 6 + 76$
$a_{20} = 82$

6. The domain and range is set of all real numbers.

7. $y = \sqrt{x + 1} + 8$
The domain is $x \geq -1$, and the range is $y \geq 8$.

8. $d = 6.5 - 4 = 2.5$
$9 + d = 9 + 2.5 = 11.5$
$11.5 + d = 11.5 + 2.5 = 14$
$14 + d = 14 + 2.5 = 16.5$

9. $C = \pi d$
$942.5 = \pi d$
$300 \approx d$
$r = 300 \div 2 = 150$
$x^2 + y^2 = (150)^2$
$x^2 + y^2 = 22{,}500$

10. $4^{3x-6} = 32^{x+4}$
$(2^2)^{3x-6} = (2^5)^{x+4}$
$2^{6x-12} = 2^{5x+20}$
$6x - 12 = 5x + 20$
$x = 32$

11. One way is to enter the left side of the expression for Y_1, the right side of the expression for Y_2, and find the point(s) of intersection. The other way is to set the right side equal to 0 by subtracting $(x - 1)$ from both sides, entering the new left side for Y_1 and finding the zeros.

12.

period $= \frac{\pi}{b} = \frac{\pi}{2}$

undefined values: $\frac{\pi}{4} - \frac{3}{2} + \frac{\pi}{2}n$

phase shift $= \frac{3}{2}$

13. $-16x^2 + 40 > 20$
$-16x^2 > -20$
$x^2 < 1.25$
$x < \sqrt{1.25}$
$x < 1.12$
Between 0 and 1.12 s.

14. Each year the value is 84% of the previous year's value. The value at the end of t years can be represented by $y = 18{,}500(0.84)^t$. Enter the equation into Y_1 into the calculator. Let $y_2 = 2000$. Graph the functions and find the point of intersection.

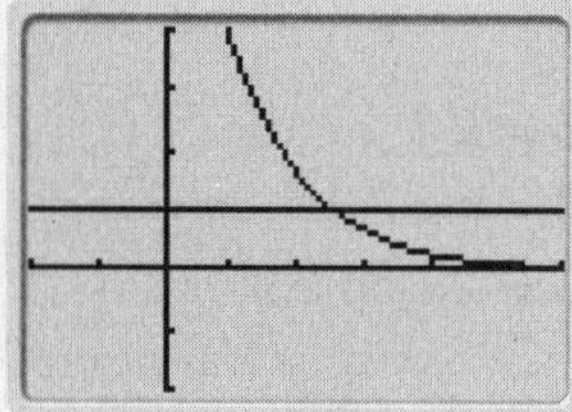

It will be in the year 2020.

15. a. $S = \frac{\theta R^2 - \theta r^2}{2}$

b. $S = \frac{\theta R^2 - \theta r^2}{2}$

$2S = \theta R^2 - \theta r^2$

$2S = \theta(R^2 - r^2)$

$\frac{2S}{R^2 - r^2} = \theta$

c. $\theta = \frac{2S}{R^2 - r^2}$

$\theta = \frac{2(200)}{25^2 - 10^2}$

$\theta = \frac{400}{525} = 0.76$ radians

$0.76 \times \frac{180}{\pi} \approx 44°$

16. a. The student switched the numerator and denominator in the change of base formula.

b. $\log_8(3x) = \frac{\ln 3x}{\ln 8}$

$\frac{\ln 3x}{\ln 8} = \frac{\ln 3 + \ln x}{\ln 8}$

17.

$\frac{c}{a}$	a	b	c
		c	$\frac{c}{a}(b + c)$
	a	$b + c$	0

If $x - \frac{c}{a}$ is a factor, then

$\frac{c}{a}(b + c) + c = 0$

$\frac{bc}{a} + \frac{c^2}{a} + c = 0$

$bc + c^2 + ac = 0$

$b + c + a = 0$

18. period $= \frac{2\pi}{b}$

A period $= \frac{2\pi}{b} = \frac{2\pi}{2\pi} = 1$

B period $= \frac{2\pi}{b} = \frac{2\pi}{\pi} = 2$

C period $= \frac{2\pi}{b} = \frac{2\pi}{1} = 2\pi$

D period $= \frac{2\pi}{b} = \frac{2\pi}{\frac{1}{2}} = 4\pi$

Answer Choice **C**

19. It would take $2 \times 73.1 = 146.2$ hours for 1 gram to decay to 0.25 gram, so it would take slightly less than 146.2 hours for 1 gram to decay to 0.26 gram. So, it would take about 145 hours.

20. $\sin \theta = 0.95$

$\theta = \sin^{-1}(0.95)$

$\theta = 71.8°$

21. $\cos \theta = -0.181$

$\theta = \cos^{-1}(-0.181)$

$\theta = 100.4°$

$360° - 100.4° = 259.6°$

22. Domain = all real numbers.

Range = $\{0, 3\}$

23. Domain = $x > 0$

Range = $0 < x \leq 10$

24. Set one side of the equation equal to 0.

$3x^4 = 12x^3 - 9x^2 + 6x$

$3x^4 - 12x^3 + 9x^2 - 6x = 0$

Identify the monomial factor.

$3x(x^3 - 4x^2 + 3x - 2) = 0$

$3x = 0$, so $x = 0$

Graph the Y1 $= x^3 - 4x^2 + 3x - 2$ to identify additional roots.

$x^3 - 4x^2 + 3x - 2 = 0$, so $x = 3.27$

$x = 0, 3.27$

25. Set one side of the equation equal to 0.

$x^3 = 2x^4 - 5x^2 + 4x$

$0 = 2x^4 - x^3 - 5x^2 + 4x$

Identify the monomial factor:

$x(2x^3 - x^2 - 5x + 4)$

Graph Y1 $= 2x^3 - x^2 - 5x + 4$ to identify additional roots.

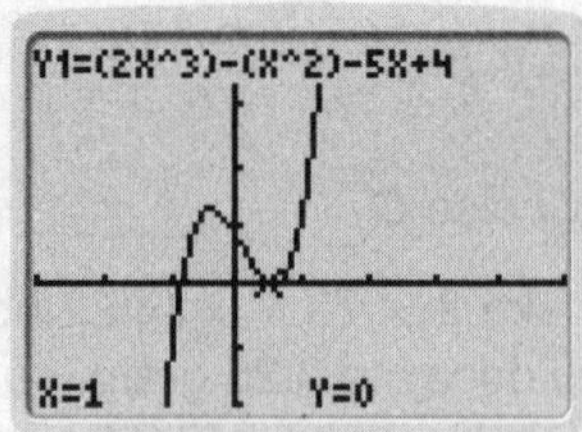

Divide $2x^3 - x^2 - 5x + 4$ by $(x - 1)$ to find the quadratic factor.

$0 = x(x - 1)(2x^2 + x - 4)$

$x = 0$ or

$(x - 1) = 0$, so $x = 1$, or

$0 = 2x^2 + x - 4$, so

$$x = \frac{-b \pm \sqrt{b^2 - 4ac}}{2a}$$

$$= \frac{-1 \pm \sqrt{1^2 - 4(2)(-4)}}{2(2)}$$

$$= \frac{-1 \pm \sqrt{33}}{4}$$

$$x = 0,\ 1,\ \frac{-1 \pm \sqrt{33}}{4}$$

26. The left side of $(cx - ca)(dx - db) = 0$ can be factored and the equation written as $c(x - a)\ d(x - b) = 0$, where cd is a real number not equal to zero. Using the Zero-Product Property, both equations have roots of a and b.

27. $N(t) = N_o e^{-kt}$

$0.6 = 1e^{-0.6372t}$

$0.6 = e^{-0.6372t}$

The decay function is $0.6 = e^{-0.6372t}$.

Solving for t.

$0.6 = e^{-0.6372t}$

$\ln 0.6 = \ln e^{-0.6372t}$

$\ln 0.6 = -0.6372t$

$$t = \frac{\ln 0.6}{-0.6372}$$

$t \approx 0.802$

28. $x = -5$, so $x + 5 = 0$

$x = 4$, so $x - 4 = 0$

$(x + 5)(x - 4) = 0$

$x^2 + x - 20 = 0$

29. $x^4 - 81 = (x^2 - 9)(x^2 + 9)$

$= (x - 3)(x + 3)(x^2 + 9)$

$x + 3 = 0,\ x = -3$

$x - 3 = 0,\ x = 3$

$x^2 + 9 = 0$

$x^2 = -9$

$x = \pm\sqrt{-9}$

$x = \pm 3i$

The student left out the complex roots, $3i$ and $-3i$.

30. 14.7 ounces is $15.5 - 14.7 = 0.8$, which is $0.8 \div 0.4 = 2$ standard deviations below the mean. This value lies within $5\% \div 2$, or 2.5% of the data. Therefore the probability is 2.5% or 0.025.

LESSON 94

Warm Up 94

1. least common denominator

2. Graph Y1 $= \frac{2x}{x + 5} - 14$ and find the zeros.

$x = -5.8\overline{3}$

3. $x^2 + 10x = -16$

$x^2 + 10x + 16 = 0$

$(x + 8)(x + 2) = 0$

$x + 8 = 0$ or $x + 2 = 0$

$x = -8$ or $x = -2$

The critical values are -8 and -2. These values separate the number line into $x > -2$, $-8 < x < -2$, and $x < -8$. Test a point in each region to see whether it contains the solution.

$0^2 + 10(0) < -16$ false

$(-5)^2 + 10(-5) < -16$ true

$(-10)^2 + 10(-10) < -16$ false

The solution is $-8 < x < -2$.

Lesson Practice 94

a. $\frac{7}{x + 4} \le 3$

Case 1: The LCD is positive. The LCD is $x + 4$. Since it is positive $x + 4 > 0$, so $x > -4$.

$$\frac{7}{x + 4} \le 3$$

$$\frac{7}{x+4}(x+4) \le 3(x+4)$$
$$7 \le 3x + 12$$
$$-5 \le 3x$$
$$-\frac{5}{3} \le x$$

The solution must satisfy both $x > -4$ and $x \ge -\frac{5}{3}$. Therefore $x \ge -\frac{5}{3}$.

Case 2: The LCD is negative. The LCD is $x + 4$. Since it is negative, $x + 4 < 0$, so $x < -4$.

$$\frac{7}{x+4} \le 3$$
$$\frac{7}{x+4}(x+4) \ge 3(x+4)$$
$$7 \ge 3x + 12$$
$$-5 \ge 3x$$
$$-\frac{5}{3} \ge x$$

The solution must satisfy both $x < -4$ and $x \le -\frac{5}{3}$. Therefore, $x < -4$.
So, $x < -4$ or $x \ge -\frac{5}{3}$.

b. The right side is already 0. Find the boundary points.
Factor to find the values that make either the numerator or denominator 0.

$$\frac{x-8}{(x+5)(x+2)} \ge 0$$

The numerator is 0 when $x = 8$. The denominator is 0 when $x = -5$ or $x = -2$.

The boundary points are 8, −2, and −5. This gives four intervals to test. Use < or > for the asymptotes of −5 and −2. These values are restricted because they make the fraction undefined.

Interval	Test Value	Is the test value a solution
$x \ge 8$	10	$\frac{10-8}{10^2+7(10)+10} \ge 0$ $\frac{2}{180} \ge 0$ True
$8 \ge x > -2$	0	$\frac{0-8}{0^2+7(0)+10} \ge 0$ $\frac{-8}{10} \ge 0$ False
$-2 > x > -5$	−4	$\frac{-4-8}{(-4)^2+7(-4)+10} \ge 0$ $6 \ge 0$ True
$x < -5$	−10	$\frac{-10-8}{(-10)^2+7(-10)+10} \ge 0$ $\frac{-18}{40} \ge 0$ False

The value of x is a solution when $x \ge 8$ or $-2 > x > -5$.

c. The right side is already 0. Find the boundary points. The numerator is 0 when $x = -1$. The denominator is 0 when $x = 4$. The boundary points are −1 and 4. This gives three intervals to test.

	$x > 4$	$-1 < x < 4$	$x < -1$
Test Point	5	0	−2
Numerator $x + 1$	+	+	−
Denominator $x - 4$	+	−	−
Value of Rational Expression	+	−	+

The value of x is the solution $-1 < x < 4$.

d. The right side is already 0. Find the boundary points. The numerator is 0 when $x = -8$. The denominator is 0 when $x = 2$, $x = 5$, or $x = -1$. The boundary points are −8, −1, 2, or 5. This gives five intervals to test.

	$x > 5$	$2 < x < 5$	$-1 < x < 2$	$-8 < x < -1$	$x < -8$
Test Point	10	3	0	−5	−10
$x + 8$	+	+	+	+	−
$x - 2$	+	+	−	−	−
$x - 5$	+	−	−	−	−
$x + 1$	+	+	+	−	−
Value of Rational Expression	+	−	+	−	+

The value of x is the solution $x < -8$, $-1 \leq x < 2$, $x > 5$.

e. Graph $Y1 = \frac{x}{x+6}$ and $Y2 = -2$. Look for where the first graph is at or above the line. The entire left part of the rational expression is above the line. This occurs for all x-values to the left of the asymptote of $x = -6$, so one part of the solution is $x < -6$.

Use the intersect command to find where the right part of the graph is above the line. The intersection is $x \geq -4$.

The solution is $x < -6$ or $x \geq -4$.

f. The cost per student is $\frac{75}{x}$ where x is the number of students.

Solve $\frac{75}{x} \leq 6.25$.

Graph $Y1 = \frac{75}{x}$, and $Y2 = 6.25$.

Find the point of intersection: (12, 6.25). Therefore, 12 or more students must participate.

Practice 94

1. $x = \dfrac{-2 \pm \sqrt{2^2 - 4(1)(4)}}{2(1)}$

$= \dfrac{-2 \pm \sqrt{-12}}{2}$

$= -1 \pm i\sqrt{3}$

2. $x = \dfrac{-(-1) \pm \sqrt{(-1)^2 - 4(1)(12)}}{2(1)}$

$= \dfrac{-1 \pm \sqrt{-47}}{2}$

$= \dfrac{-1 \pm i\sqrt{47}}{2}$

3. $P = 2l + 2w$

$2l = P - 2w$

$l = \dfrac{P - 2w}{2}$

4. a. $\dfrac{x^2 - 3x - 18}{x^2 - 16} \leq 0$

$\dfrac{(x-6)(x+3)}{(x-4)(x+4)} \leq 0$

b. The numerator is 0 when $x = 6$, or $x = -3$. The denominator is 0 when $x = 4$, and $x = -4$. The critical values are −4, −3, 4, and 6. The intervals are $x < -4$, $-4 < x \leq -3$, $-3 \leq x < 4$, $4 < x \leq 6$, $x \geq 6$.

c. This gives five intervals to test.

	$x < -4$	$-4 < x \leq -3$	$-3 \leq x < 4$	$4 < x \leq 6$	$x \geq 6$
Test Point	−10	−3.5	0	5	10
$x + 3$	−	−	+	+	+
$x - 6$	−	−	−	−	+
$x - 4$	−	−	−	+	+
$x + 4$	−	+	+	+	+
Value of Rational Expression	+	−	+	−	+

The solution is $-4 < x \leq -3$ or $4 < x \leq 6$.

5. 5 feet 6 inches = 5.5 feet, 3 inches = 0.25 feet.

$z\text{-score} = \dfrac{5.5 - 6}{0.25} = -2$

6. $(4x^2 - 4x + 1) - (16x^2 - 24x + 9) = 0$

$4x^2 - 4x + 1 - 16x^2 + 24x - 9 = 0$

$-12x^2 + 20x - 8 = 0$

$x = \dfrac{-b \pm \sqrt{b^2 - 4ac}}{2a}$

$= \dfrac{-20 \pm \sqrt{20^2 - 4(-12)(-8)}}{2(-12)}$

$= \dfrac{-20 \pm \sqrt{16}}{-24}$

$= \dfrac{-20 \pm 4}{-24}$

$= \frac{-16}{-24} = \frac{2}{3}$ or $\frac{-24}{-24} = 1$

Answer Choice **B**

7. The cost per county is $\frac{1{,}000{,}000}{x}$.

The equation is $\frac{1{,}000{,}000}{x} < 6500$.

Graph Y1 $= \frac{1{,}000{,}000}{x}$, and Y2 $= 6500$.

Find the point of intersection: (153.8, 6500).
$154 \le x$

The maximum number of counties is 254.
$x \le 254$.

The solution is $154 \le x \le 254$.

8. The probability of rolling each number on a number cube is the same. The bars on the histogram would be about the same height, and not bell-shaped.

9. The critical values are the boundary points of each interval. These values occur at either a zero or an asymptote, so they occur where either the numerator or denominator is 0. In the given inequality, this happens three times, and three boundary points divide a number line into four intervals.

10. Each leg of the triangle, a and b, is $(200 - 92) \div 2 = 54$. Find $\angle C$.

$$c^2 = a^2 + b^2 - 2ab\cos C$$
$$92^2 = 54^2 + 54^2 - 2(54)(54)\cos C$$
$$8464 = 5832 - 5832\cos C$$
$$2632 = -5832\cos C$$
$$-0.4513 = \cos C$$
$$C = 116.83°$$

11. Comparing the equation $A = P\left(1 + \frac{r}{n}\right)^{nt}$ to $500\left(1 + \frac{0.04}{12}\right)^{12t}$ $P = 500$, $r = 0.04$, and $n = 12$. Compounding daily is 365 times per year, so replace n with 365. The equation is $500\left(1 + \frac{0.04}{365}\right)^{365t}$.

12. $\angle B = (180° - (67° + 32°)) = 81°$

$$\frac{\sin B}{b} = \frac{\sin C}{c}$$
$$\frac{\sin 81°}{31} = \frac{\sin 67°}{c}$$
$$0.0319 = \frac{\sin 67°}{c}$$
$$28.9 = c$$

13. log(0.5) is negative, so the inequality symbol should be reversed. The correct step is

$$n\log(0.5) < \log 2 - \log 20$$
$$n > \frac{\log 2 - \log 20}{\log 0.5}$$

14. The equation is $-16t^2 + 35x + 15 = 0$.

$$t = \frac{-35 \pm \sqrt{35^2 - 4(-16)(15)}}{2(-16)}$$
$$= \frac{-35 \pm \sqrt{2185}}{-32}$$
$$\approx \frac{-35 \pm 46.7}{-32}$$
$$\approx -0.37 \text{ or } 2.6$$

Time cannot be negative, so $t \approx 2.6$ s.

15. $-1.25x^2 + 66x - 720 \ge 100$
Graph Y1 $= -1.25x^2 + 66x - 720$ and Y2 $= 100$. Find the x-values for which the first graph has greater y-values than the second.
The solution is $x = 20$ to $x = 32$

16.
$$y = 1100(1 + 0.065)^t$$
$$1500 = 1100(1 + 0.065)^t$$
$$\frac{1500}{1100} = (1.065)^t$$
$$\frac{15}{11} = (1.065)^t$$
$$\log\left(\frac{15}{11}\right) = \log(1.065)^t$$
$$\log\left(\frac{15}{11}\right) = t\log(1.065)$$
$$\frac{\log\left(\frac{15}{11}\right)}{\log 1.065} = t$$
$$t \approx 4.93$$

17. The possible outcomes are

2,2 4,2 6,2 8,2
2,4 4,4 6,4 8,4
2,6 4,6 6,6 8,6
2,8 4,8 6,8 8,8

Of the possible spins, only 6, 2 and 6, 4 have 6 as the first spin and a sum of 10 or less. The probability is $\frac{2}{16} = \frac{1}{8}$.

18. **A** period $= \frac{\pi}{b} = \frac{\pi}{2}$

B period $= \frac{\pi}{b} = \frac{\pi}{2\pi} = \frac{1}{2}$

C period $= \frac{\pi}{b} = \frac{\pi}{1} = \pi$

D period $= \frac{\pi}{b} = \frac{\pi}{\frac{1}{2}} = 2\pi$

Answer Choice **D**

19. Using the graphing calculator, the 6th term is −5, and the 15th term is −41.

20. $x = -1$, so $(x + 1) = 0$, and $x = 5$, so $(x - 5) = 0$.

$(x + 1)(x - 5) = 0$

$x^2 - 4x - 5 = 0$

The parabola opens up for $x^2 - 4x - 5 = 0$. For the parabola to open down ax^2 has to be negative. The parabola opens down for $-1(x^2 - 4x - 5 = 0)$ or $-x^2 + 4x + 5 = 0$.

21. It will be positive when the common difference is positive, and it will be negative when the common difference is negative.

22. period $= \frac{2\pi}{b} = \frac{2\pi}{1} = 2\pi$

Amplitude = 3

23. The radius is $28 \div 2 = 14$. Substitute $h = 6$, $k = 2$, and $r = 14$ into $(x - h)^2 + (y - k)^2 = r^2$.

$(x - 6)^2 + (y - 2)^2 = 14^2$

$(x - 6)^2 + (y - 2)^2 = 196$

24. The bold numbers are the selected numbers.
60**2016**0482898240870 5**17**91346815762212
5650 89337 53603 73597 04633

The numbers correspond to Tanela, Luke, and Cassie.

25.

$$f = \frac{1}{\frac{1}{d_1} + \frac{1}{d_2}}$$

$$f = \frac{1}{\frac{1}{d_1} + \frac{1}{d_2}} \cdot \frac{d_1 d_2}{d_1 d_2}$$

$$f = \frac{d_1 d_2}{\frac{d_1 d_2}{d_1} + \frac{d_1 d_2}{d_2}}$$

$$f = \frac{d_1 d_2}{d_2 + d_1}$$

$f(d_2 + d_1) = d_1 d_2$

$fd_2 + fd_1 = d_1 d_2$

$fd_1 = d_1 d_2 - fd_2$

$fd_1 = d_2(d_1 - f)$

$\frac{fd_1}{d_1 - f} = d_2$

26. Let L_1 = the original length and L_2 = the shorter length. Set $2\pi\sqrt{\frac{L_2}{9.8}}$ equal to $\frac{1}{2}\left(2\pi\sqrt{\frac{L_1}{9.8}}\right)$ and solve for L_2.

$$2\pi\sqrt{\frac{L_2}{9.8}} = \frac{1}{2}\left(2\pi\sqrt{\frac{L_1}{9.8}}\right)$$

$$\sqrt{\frac{L_2}{9.8}} = \frac{1}{2}\left(\sqrt{\frac{L_1}{9.8}}\right)$$

$$\frac{L_2}{9.8} = \left(\frac{1}{2}\right)^2 \frac{L_1}{9.8}$$

$$L_2 = \left(\frac{1}{2}\right)^2 L_1$$

$$L_2 = \frac{1}{4}L_1 = \frac{L_1}{4}$$

27. $N(t) = N_o e^{-kt}$

$0.5 = 1\, e^{-k(4.5)}$

$\ln 0.5 = \ln e^{-k(4.5)}$

$\ln 0.5 = -4.5k$

$k = \frac{\ln 0.5}{-4.5} \approx 0.15403$

$N(t) = N_o e^{-0.15403t}$

$0.99 = 1\, e^{-0.15403t}$

$\ln 0.99 = \ln e^{-0.15403t}$

$\ln 0.99 = -0.15403t$

$t = \frac{\ln 0.99}{-0.15403} \approx 0.065$

It will take 0.065 billion years, or 65,000,000 million years.

28 When $x = 2$, $\frac{\log 2}{\log 2} = 1$, (2, 1). When $x = 4$, $\frac{\log 4}{\log 2} = 2$, (4, 2)

29. $4x(7x - 3)(6x + 1) = 0$

$4x = 0, x = 0$

$7x - 3 = 0, x = \frac{3}{7}$

$6x + 1 = 0, x = -\frac{1}{6}$

30. $16x^3 - 24x^2 + 6x = 2x(8x^2 - 12x + 3)$

$2x = 0, x = 0$

$8x^2 - 12x + 3 = 0$

$$x = \frac{-(-12) \pm \sqrt{(-12)^2 - 4(8)(3)}}{2(8)}$$

$$= \frac{12 \pm \sqrt{48}}{16}$$

$$= \frac{3 \pm \sqrt{3}}{4}$$

Lesson Practice 95

a. Use synthetic division to test if $r(7) = 0$. Divide $P(x)$ by $(x - 7)$.

7	2	−43	75	1765	−857	−22,542	−30,240
		14	−203	−896	6083	36,582	98,280
	2	−29	−128	869	5226	14,040	68,040

The remainder is not 0, so $x = 7$ is not a root.

b. Use synthetic division to test if $r(7) = 0$. Divide $P(x)$ by $(x - 7)$.

7	9	−101	195	622	−621	−1565	−1947	2772	2940
		63	−266	−497	875	1778	1491	−3192	−2940
	9	−38	−71	125	254	213	−456	−420	0

The remainder is 0, so $x = 7$ is a root.

c. By the Rational Root Theorem $p = 6$, $q = 1$ the possible rational roots are ± 1, ± 2, ± 3, ± 6.

Use synthetic division to check roots

1	1	4	1	−6
		1	5	6
	1	5	6	0

$P(x) = (x - 1)(x^2 + 5x + 6)$

Factor the quadratic.

$P(x) = (x - 1)(x + 2)(x + 3)$

The roots are −3, −2, and 1.

d. Use synthetic division to find $r(2)$.

2	−16	40	0
		−32	16
	−16	8	16

$r(2) = 16$, so the height is 16 feet.

LESSON 95

Warm Up 95

1. factor

2.

2	6	−5	−34	40
		12	14	−40
	6	7	−20	0

The remainder is 0, so the polynomial is divisible by $(x - 2)$.

3.

2	20	−53	−122	56
		40	−26	−296
	20	−13	−148	−240

The remainder is not 0, so the polynomial is not divisible by $(x - 2)$.

Practice 95

1. $x - \frac{6}{x} = 1$

$x\left(x - \frac{6}{x}\right) = 1(x)$

$x^2 - 6 = x$

$x^2 - x - 6 = 0$

$(x - 3)(x + 2)$

$x = 3, x = -2$

2. $\frac{x^2 + x - 6}{x + 1} = 0$

$\frac{x^2 + x - 6}{x + 1}(x + 1) = 0(x + 1)$

$x^2 + x - 6 = 0$

$(x + 3)(x - 2) = 0$

$x = -3, x = 2$

3. $\frac{7x}{3x + 2} = 2$

$\frac{7x}{3x + 2}(3x + 2) = 2(3x + 2)$

$7x = 6x + 4$

$x = 4$

4. As x increases, y increases, therefore the graph models growth.

5. The denominator must be greater than 0, $x > 0$.

$\frac{1}{x^3} \geq 5$

$1 \geq 5x^3$

$\frac{1}{5} \geq x^3$

$\sqrt[3]{\frac{1}{5}} \geq \sqrt[3]{x^3}$

$0.585 \geq x$

The solution is $0 < x \leq 0.585$.

6. $\frac{3}{8} = \frac{x}{12}$

$8x = 36$

$x = 4.5$

7. Student B incorrectly uses 4 instead of −4 to divide in the synthetic division.

8. The three middle intervals $-6 \leq x < -2$, $-2 < x < 3$, and $3 < x \leq 4$, because they contain the asymptotes of −2 and 3. These values make the inequality undefined.

9. a. $y_1 = 1{,}998{,}000(1.0521)^t$

b. $y_2 = 3{,}406{,}000(1.0036)^t$

c.

$$y_1 = y_2$$

$$1{,}998{,}000(1.0521)^t = 3{,}406{,}000(1.0036)^t$$

$$\log 1{,}998{,}000 + \log(1.0521)^t = \log 3{,}406{,}000 + \log(1.0036)^t$$

$$\log 1{,}998{,}000 + t\log(1.0521) = \log 3{,}406{,}000 + t\log(1.0036)$$

$$\log 1{,}998{,}000 - \log 3{,}406{,}000 = t\log(1.0036) - t\log(1.0521)$$

$$\log 1{,}998{,}000 - \log 3{,}406{,}000 = t(\log 1.0036 - \log 1.0521)$$

$$\frac{\log 1{,}998{,}000 - \log 3{,}406{,}000}{\log 1.0036 - \log 1.0521} = t$$

$$11.30 \approx t$$

The predicted year is just over 11 years from 2000, which is 2011 or 2012, depending on the month the 2000 census was taken.

10. $2\ln e^x = 2x \ln e$

$= 2x \cdot 1$

$= 2x$

11. $x \cdot \ln e^3 = 3x \ln e$

$= 3x \cdot 1$

$= 3x$

12. $\frac{4}{16} = \frac{6}{n}$

$4n = 96$

$n = 24$

13. The largest angle is opposite the longest side. Let $a = 125$, $b = 182$, and $c = 211$.

$c^2 = a^2 + b^2 - 2ab \cos C$

$211^2 = 125^2 + 182^2 - 2(125)(182) \cos C$

$44{,}521 = 15{,}625 + 33{,}124 - 45{,}500 \cos C$

$-4228 = -45{,}500 \cos C$

$0.09292 = \cos C$

$C = 84.7°$

14. Domain = all real numbers

Range = all positive real numbers.

15. $z\text{-score} = \frac{182 - 174.1}{7} \approx 1.13$

16. $z\text{-score} = \frac{10.25 - 13}{0.625} \approx -4.4$

17. A polynomial that is the result of adding or subtracting polynomials can have any degree less than or equal to the polynomial with the greatest degree. Possible examples: $P_1 = 5x^3 + x$ has degree 3, $P_2 = -x^2 - 2 + 1$ has degree 2, and $P_3 = -5x^3 - x - 2$ has degree 3. The degree of $P_1 + P_2$ is 3 and the degree of $P_1 + P_3$ is 0.

18. Let x represent the width and $x + 15$ represent the length.

$$x(x + 15) = 100$$
$$x^2 + 15x = 100$$
$$x^2 + 15x - 100 = 0$$
$$(x - 5)(x + 20) = 0$$
$$x = 5 \text{ or } x = -20$$

The width cannot be negative, so the width is 5 meters and the length is 5 + 15 = 20 meters.

19. **A**

5	48	212	−1098	−5298	1174	22,350	18,900
		240	2260	5810	2560	18,670	205,100
	48	452	1162	512	3734	41,020	224,000

B

5	48	644	2754	2154	−12,974	−30,750	−18,900
		240	4420	35,870	190,120	885,730	4,274,900
	48	884	7174	38,024	177,146	854,980	4,256,900

C

5	48	868	6282	23,238	46,274	46,950	18,900
		240	5540	59,110	411,740	2,290,070	11,685,100
	48	1108	11,822	82,348	458,014	2,337,020	11,704,000

D

5	48	−268	−818	4282	6254	−14,790	−18,900
		240	−140	−4790	−2540	18,570	18,900
	48	−28	−958	−508	3714	3780	0

Answer Choice **D**

20. **A** $2 \cdot 9 \cdot 5 = 2 \cdot 5 \cdot 9$ shows the Commutative Property of Multiplication
B $(2 \cdot 9) \cdot 5 = 2 \cdot (9 \cdot 5)$ shows the Associative Property of Multiplication
Answer Choice **D**

21. Since $P(0) = 0$ and $P(-4) = 0$, two of the factors are x and $x + 4$. A possible polynomial that fits these parameters is $x(x + 4)$ or $x^2 + 4x$.

Dividing this polynomial by $x - 2$

2	1	4	0
		2	12
	1	6	12

The result is $P(2) = 12$. The desired result is $P(2) = 20$. Since $20 = 12\left(\frac{20}{12}\right)$, multiply $x^2 + 4x$ by $\frac{20}{12}$.

$$\frac{20}{12}(x^2 + 4x) = \frac{5}{3}(x^2 + 4x) = \frac{5}{3}x^2 + \frac{20}{3}x.$$

22. $\ln (8x)^3 + \ln e\left(\frac{2x}{3}\right)$

$3 \ln (8x) + \ln e + \ln 2 + \ln x - \ln 3$

$3 \ln 8 + 4 \ln x + 1 + \ln 2 - \ln 3$

23. **a.** Sample:

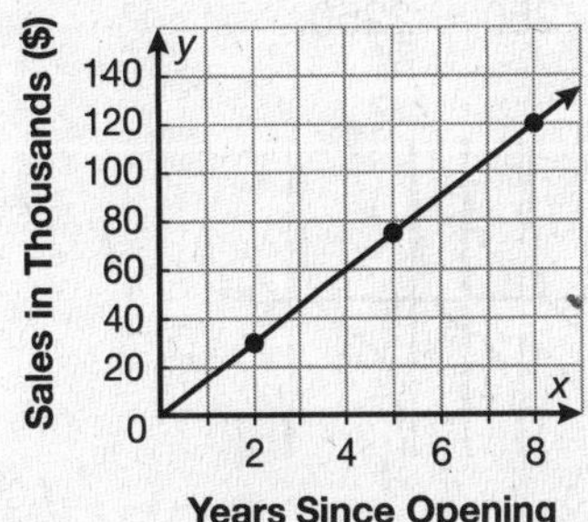

b. Extend the line to $x = 15$ and read the y-value. The y-value is about 225,000. The total sales is about 225,000.

24. The student incorrectly distributes the negative sign to the constant term.

25. 4 hours later is $n = 5$. Substitute 30 for a_1, 5 for n, and 242 for a_n to find d in $a_n = a_1 + (n - 1)d$.

$242 = 30 + (5 - 1)d$

$242 = 30 + 4d$

$212 = 4d$

$53 = d$

The speed is 53 mph.

26. $\frac{\sin B}{b} = \frac{\sin C}{c}$

$\frac{\sin 56°}{14} = \frac{\sin C}{7}$

$\frac{7 \sin 56°}{14} = \sin C$

$0.414519 = \sin C$

$C \approx 24.5°$

$\angle A \approx 180° - (24.5° + 56°) \approx 99.5°$

$\frac{\sin B}{b} = \frac{\sin A}{a}$

$\frac{\sin 56°}{14} = \frac{\sin 99.5}{a}$

$\frac{14 \sin 99.5°}{\sin 56°} = a$

$16.7 \approx a$

27. Substitute $h = 3$, $k = 8$, and $r = 4$ into $(x - h)^2 + (y - k)^2 = r^2$.

$(x - 3)^2 + (y - 8)^2 = 4^2$

$(x - 3)^2 + (y - 8)^2 = 16$

28. Sample: Think of 18 months as 20 months −2 months. Write an expression for the savings in 18 months: 125(20 − 2). Use the Distributive Property: 125(20) − 125(2) = 2500 − 250 = 2250.

29.

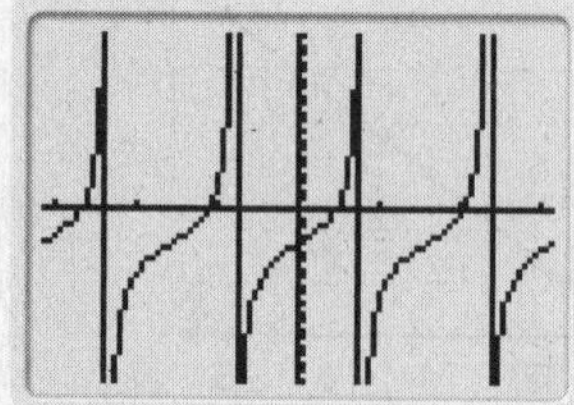

period $= \frac{\pi}{2}$

Undefined values $= \frac{\pi}{4} + \pi + n\frac{\pi}{2}$

phase shift $= \pi$.

30. If −3 is the root then $(x + 3)$ and $(x + 3)$ are the factors.

$(x + 3)(x + 3) = 0$

$x^2 + 6x + 9 = 0$

One possible answer: $x^2 + 6x + 9 = 0$

LESSON 96

Warm Up 96

1. sine
2. −1
3. 0

Lesson Practice 96

a. $x = r\cos\theta = 3\cos\pi = 3(-1) = -3$

$y = r\sin\theta = 2\sin\pi = 2(0) = 0$

$(-3, 0)$

b. $x = r\cos\theta = 1\cos\frac{2\pi}{3} = 1\left(-\frac{1}{2}\right) = -\frac{1}{2}$

$y = r\sin\theta = 1\sin\frac{2\pi}{3} = 1\left(\frac{\sqrt{3}}{2}\right) = \frac{\sqrt{3}}{2}$

$\left(-\frac{1}{2}, \frac{\sqrt{3}}{2}\right)$

c. $\tan\theta = \frac{y}{x} = \frac{-2}{2\sqrt{3}} = -\frac{1}{\sqrt{3}}$, and θ terminates in Quadrant IV, so one value of θ is $\frac{11\pi}{6}$.

$r^2 = x^2 + y^2 = (2\sqrt{3})^2 + (-2)^2$

$= 16$

$r = 4$

One ordered pair is $\left(4, \frac{11\pi}{6}\right)$.

d. $\tan\theta = \frac{y}{x} = \frac{0}{-4} = 0$, and θ terminates on the negative x-axis so one value of θ is π.

$r^2 = x^2 + y^2 = (-4)^2 + (0)^2$

$= 16$

$r = 4$

One ordered pair is $(4, \pi)$.

e. The graph consists of all points 3 units from the pole, so it is the circle with the pole as center and radius 3.

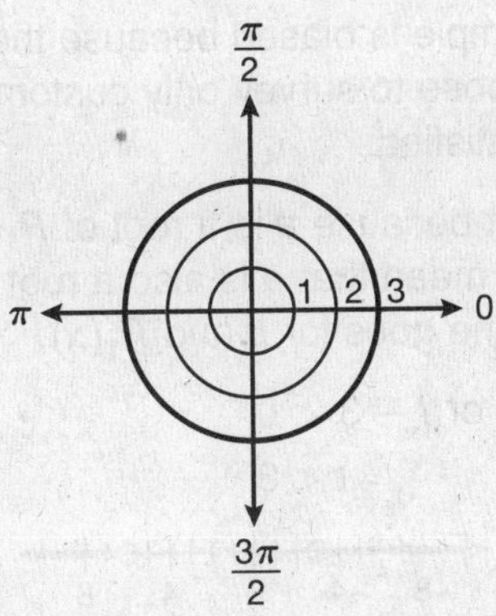

Check. Convert the polar equation to a Cartesian equation.

$$r = 3$$
$$r^2 = 9$$
$$x^2 + y^2 = 9$$

f. The graph consists of all points on the line that makes an angle of $\frac{3\pi}{4}$ radians with the positive *x*-axis.

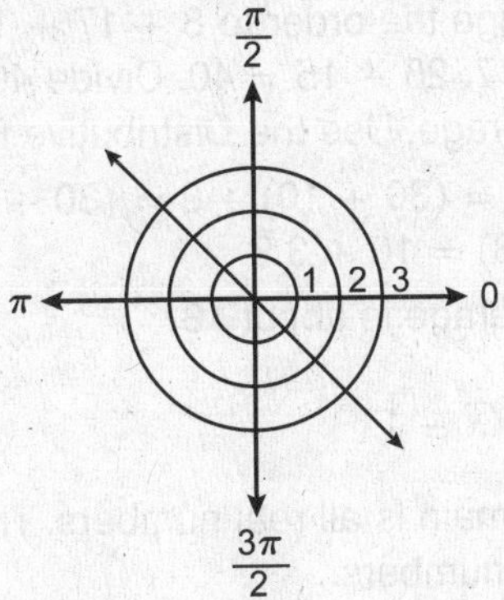

Check. Convert the polar equation to a Cartesian equation.

$$\theta = \frac{3\pi}{4}$$
$$\tan\theta = \tan\frac{3\pi}{4} = -1$$
$$\frac{y}{x} = -1$$
$$y = -x$$

$y = -x$ is the Cartesian equation of the line through any point (x, y) and the origin with slope -1. That is the same line because $\tan\theta = \tan\frac{3\pi}{4} = -1$.

g. Use the following window:
$\theta\text{ min} = 0$, $\theta\text{ max} = 8\pi$, $\theta\text{ step} = \frac{\pi}{24}$, $X\text{ min} = -36$, $X\text{ max} = 36$, $Y\text{ min} = -24$, $Y\text{ max} = 24$

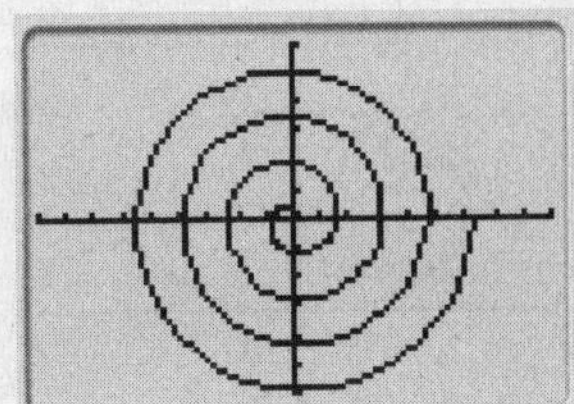

h. Use the following window:
$\theta\text{ min} = 0$, $\theta\text{ max} = 2\pi$, $\theta\text{ step} = \frac{\pi}{24}$, $X\text{ min} = -1$, $X\text{ max} = 3$, $Y\text{ min} = -2$, $Y\text{ max} = 2$

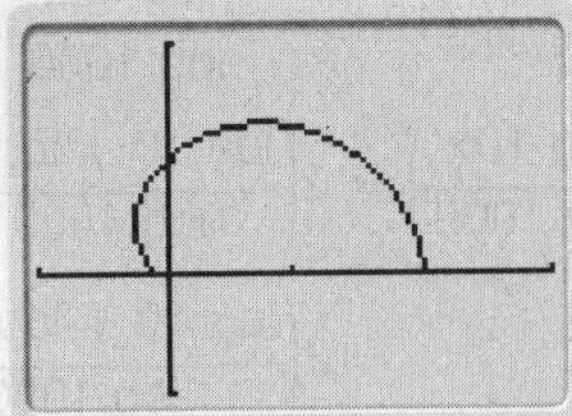

i. Use the following window:
$\theta\text{ min} = 0$, $\theta\text{ max} = 2\pi$, $\theta\text{ step} = \frac{\pi}{24}$, $X\text{ min} = -4$, $X\text{ max} = 4$, $Y\text{ min} = -6$, $Y\text{ max} = 10$

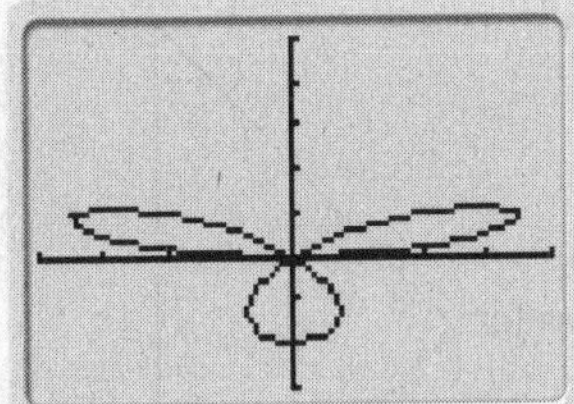

j. The boundary is a circle with radius 2 and center (0, 2).

$$(x - 0)^2 + (y - 2)^2 = 2^2$$
$$x^2 + y^2 - 4y + 4 = 4$$
$$x^2 + y^2 - 4y = 0$$
$$r^2 - 4r\sin\theta = 0$$
$$r(r - 4\sin\theta) = 0$$
$$r - 4\sin\theta = 0$$
$$r = 4\sin\theta$$

The polar equation is $r = 4\sin\theta$. Graph the polar equation on a calculator.
Use the following window:

$\theta\text{ min} = 0$, $\theta\text{ max} = 4\pi$, $\theta\text{ step} = \frac{\pi}{24}$, $X\text{ min} = -3$, $X\text{ max} = 3$, $Y\text{ min} = -2$, $Y\text{ max} = 5$

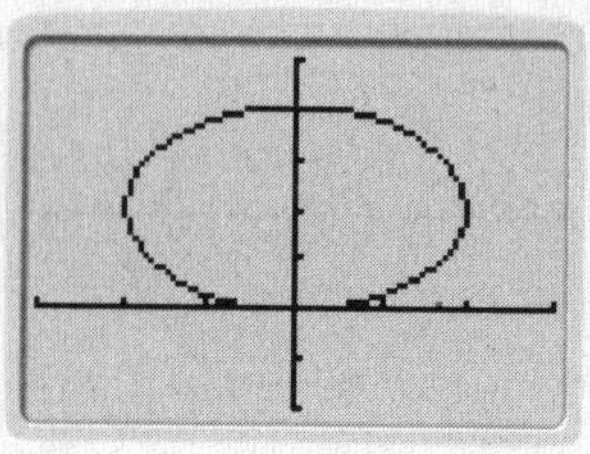

Practice 96

1. a. $\log_{1000}(10x)^2 = 2 \cdot \log_{1000}(10x)$

$$2 \cdot \log_{1000}(10x) = 2\frac{\log 10x}{\log 1000}$$

b. $$2\left(\frac{\log 10x}{\log 1000}\right) = 2\left(\frac{\log 10 + \log x}{\log 1000}\right)$$

$$= 2\left(\frac{\log 10 + \log 100}{\log 1000}\right)$$

$$= 2\left(\frac{1 + 2}{3}\right) = 2$$

2. Draw a diagram of the situation.

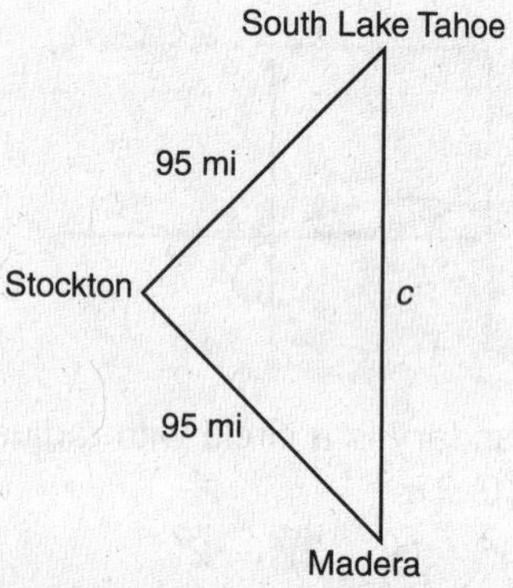

Use the Pythagorean Theorem.

$$a^2 + b^2 = c^2$$
$$95^2 + 95^2 = c^2$$
$$18{,}050 = c^2$$
$$\sqrt{18{,}050} = c$$
$$134 \approx c$$

The distance is about 134 miles due north.

3. $x = r\cos\theta = -3\cos\frac{\pi}{2} = -3(0) = 0$

$y = r\sin\theta = -3\sin\frac{\pi}{2} = -3(1) = -3$

$(0, -3)$

4. The sample is biased because the drivers can choose to survey only customers that were satisfied.

5. No. Just because a is a root of $P_1(x)$ it doesn't mean that a is also a root of $P_2(x)$. The same goes for b and $P_1(x)$.

6. $3t > 18$ or $t - 3 < 0$

$t > 6 \qquad t < 3$

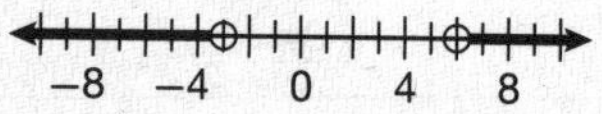

7. $-(h - 2) > 7$ or $-8 \geq -2h$

$-h + 2 > 7 \qquad 4 \leq h$

$-h > 5$

$h < -5$

8. Sample: Find the sum 8 + 15 + 17. Use the Commutative Property of Addition to change the order to 8 + 17 + 15. Add 8 and 17. 25 + 15 = 40. Divide 40 by 3 to get the average. Use the Distributive Property: $40 \div 3 = (30 + 10) \div 3 = (30 \div 3) + (10 \div 3) = 10 + 3.\overline{3}$
The average is about 13.

9. $y = \frac{3}{4}\sqrt[3]{x} - 1$

The domain is all real numbers. The range is all real numbers.

10. $x + 2$ cannot be negative, so the domain is $x \geq -2$. Then the range is $f(x) \geq \sqrt[3]{-2 - 1}$ or $f(x) \geq \sqrt[3]{-3}$

11. The equation is $3 = -16t^2 + 40x + 4$ or $0 = -16t^2 + 40x + 1$.

$$t = \frac{-40 \pm \sqrt{(40)^2 - 4(-16)(1)}}{2(-16)}$$

$$= \frac{-40 \pm \sqrt{1664}}{-32}$$

$= \dfrac{-40 \pm 8\sqrt{26}}{-32}$

$= \dfrac{-5 \pm \sqrt{26}}{-4}$

≈ -0.024 or 2.5

Time cannot be negative, so $t = 2.5$ s.

12. $c^2 = a^2 + b^2 - 2ab\cos C$

$c^2 = 14^2 + 8^2 - 2(14)(8)\cos 84°$

$c^2 = 260 - 23.414$

$c \approx 15.4$

13. $A = P + Prt$

$A - P = Prt$

$\dfrac{A - P}{Pr} = t$

$\dfrac{2P - P}{0.05P} = t$

$\dfrac{P(2 - 1)}{0.05P} = t$

$\dfrac{(2 - 1)}{0.05} = t$

$20 = t$

It will take 20 years.

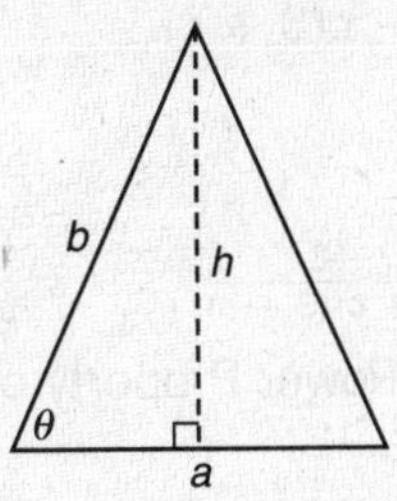

$\sin\theta = \dfrac{h}{b}$

$b\sin\theta = h$

The area of a triangle is $\frac{1}{2}bh$. Substitute a for the base and $b\sin\theta$ for the height.

$A = \dfrac{1}{2}ab\sin\theta$

15. The circle with (−5, 4) and radius 3 has $h = -5$, $k = 4$ and $r = 3$ in the equation $(x - h)^2 + (y - k)^2 = r^2$.

Answer Choice **D**

16. The arch is parabolic. Set the x-intercepts at (0, 0) and (60, 0) to represent the bases. The x-coordinate of the vertex is halfway between them at 30. The y-coordinate is the height. The vertex is at (30, 50). Substitute this point into $y = a(x - h)^2 + k$, then solve for a.

$0 = a(0 - 30)^2 + 50$

$-50 = a(900)$

$-0.05556 \approx a$

The function is $y \approx -0.05556(x - 30)^2 + 50$

$= -0.05556(x^2 - 60x + 900) + 50$

$= -0.05556x^2 + 3.33x - 50 + 50$

$= -0.056x^2 + 3.33x$

17. The factors of 1 are ±1. The factors of 128 are ±1, ±2, ±4, ±8, ±16, ±32, ±64, ±128.

Test roots with synthetic division.

$$\begin{array}{r|rrrrrrrrrr} 1 & 1 & 0 & -1 & -8 & -16 & 8 & 16 & 128 & 0 & -128 \\ & & 1 & 1 & 0 & -8 & -24 & -16 & 0 & 128 & 128 \\ \hline & 1 & 1 & 0 & -8 & -24 & -16 & 0 & 128 & 128 & 0 \end{array}$$

$x - 1$ is a factor.

$$\begin{array}{r|rrrrrrrrr} -1 & 1 & 1 & 0 & -8 & -24 & -16 & 0 & 128 & 128 \\ & & -1 & 0 & 0 & 8 & 16 & 0 & 0 & -128 \\ \hline & 1 & 0 & 0 & -8 & -16 & 0 & 0 & 128 & 0 \end{array}$$

$x + 1$ is a factor.

$$\begin{array}{r|rrrrrrrr} 2 & 1 & 0 & 0 & -8 & -16 & 0 & 0 & 128 \\ & & 2 & 4 & 8 & 0 & -32 & -64 & -128 \\ \hline & 1 & 2 & 4 & 0 & -16 & -32 & -64 & 0 \end{array}$$

$x - 2$ is a factor

$$\begin{array}{r|rrrrrrr} -2 & 1 & 2 & 4 & 0 & -16 & -32 & -64 \\ & & -2 & 0 & -8 & 16 & 0 & 64 \\ \hline & 1 & 0 & 4 & -8 & 0 & -32 & 0 \end{array}$$

$x + 2$ is a factor

$$\begin{array}{r|rrrrrr} 4 & 1 & 0 & 4 & -8 & 0 & -32 \\ & & 4 & 16 & 80 & 288 & 1152 \\ \hline & 1 & 4 & 20 & 72 & 288 & 1120 \end{array}$$

$x - 4$ is not a factor.

$$\begin{array}{r|rrrrrr} -4 & 1 & 0 & 4 & -8 & 0 & -32 \\ & & -4 & 16 & -80 & 352 & -1408 \\ \hline & 1 & -4 & 20 & -88 & 352 & -1440 \end{array}$$

$x + 4$ is not a factor.

All other possibilities will have a remainder.

18. $c\left(\frac{1}{a}+\frac{1}{b}\right)=\frac{1}{c}(c)$

$c\left(\frac{1}{a}+\frac{1}{b}\right)=1$

$c=\dfrac{1}{\frac{1}{a}+\frac{1}{b}}$

$c=\dfrac{1}{\frac{b}{ab}+\frac{a}{ab}}$

$c=\dfrac{1}{\frac{a+b}{ab}}$

$c=\dfrac{ab}{a+b}$

19. $f(x)=0.15x^3-2.85x^2+14.85x-12.15$
$=0.15(x^3-19x^2+99x-81)$

Factors of 1 and −81

$1=\pm1,\ 81=\pm1,\pm3,\pm9,\pm27,\pm81$

$\frac{p}{q}=\pm1,\pm3,\pm9,\pm27,\pm81$

Test if 1 is a root.

$$\begin{array}{r|rrrr} 1 & 1 & -19 & 99 & -81 \\ & & 1 & -18 & 81 \\ \hline & 1 & -18 & 81 & 0 \end{array}$$

$x-1$ is a factor

$f(x)=0.15x^3-2.85x^2+14.85x-12.15$
$=0.15(x-1)(x^2-18x+81)$
$=0.15(x-1)(x-9)^2$

The roots are $x=1$ and $x=9$.

20.

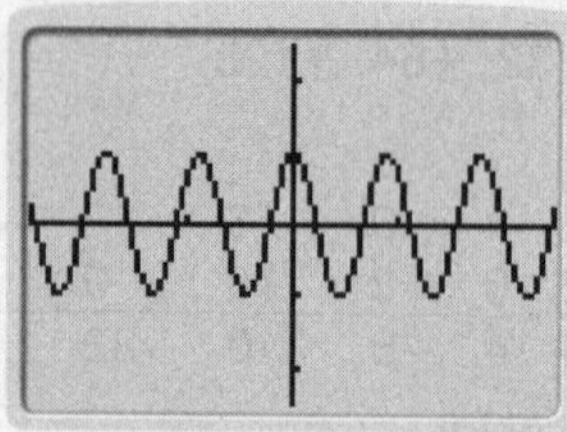

The period is $\frac{2\pi}{b}=\frac{2\pi}{7}$. The period of the parent function is 2π.

21. **A** $(0)\le-(0)^2+4(0)+8$ True
$(0)<-3(0)+1$ True
(0, 0) is a solution

B $(-3)\le-(0)^2+4(0)+8$ True
$(-3)<-3(0)+1$ True
(0, −3) is a solution

C $(-6)\le-(1)^2+4(1)+8$ True
$(-6)<-3(1)+1$ True
(1, −6) is a solution

D $(-2)\le-(2)^2+4(2)+8$ True
$(-2)<-3(2)+1$ False
(2, −2) is not a solution

Answer Choice **D**

22. $f(g(x))=\tan(5(3x+5)+5)$
$f(g(x))=\tan(15x+30)$

$\text{Period}=\frac{\pi}{b}=\frac{\pi}{15}$

23. Rate with current is $(3+c)$ and rate against current is $(3-c)$.

$t_1=\frac{d}{r}=\frac{7}{3+c}$

$t_2=\frac{d}{r}=\frac{7}{3-c}$

$T=t_1+t_2=\frac{7}{3+c}+\frac{7}{3-c}$

$=\frac{7(3-c)}{3+c(3-c)}+\frac{7(3+c)}{3-c(3+c)}$

$=\frac{21-7c}{3+c(3-c)}+\frac{21+7c}{3-c(3+c)}$

$=\frac{42}{(3+c)(3-c)}$

The inequality is $7>\frac{42}{(3+c)(3-c)}$.

24. The student applied the Power Property of Logarithms incorrectly.

$\ln(ex)^3=3\cdot\ln ex$
$=3(\ln e+\ln x)$
$=3+3\ln x$

25. Sample answer: Any point with coordinates (r,θ) also has coordinates $(-r,\theta+\pi)$.

26. Substitute 450 for a_1, n for 52 and 50 for d.

$a_n=a_1+(n-1)d$
$a_{52}=450+(52-1)50$
$a_{52}=450+(51)50$
$a_{52}=3000$

27. $4x^3-36x=0$
$4x(x^2-9)=0$
$4x(x-3)(x+3)$

$x = 0,\ x = 3,\ x = -3$

The student omitted 3 as one of the solutions.

28. $(a - b)(a + b) = a(a) + a(b) - b(a) - b(b)$
$= a^2 + ab - ab - b^2$
$= a^2 - b^2$

29. They are alike because they are both the same distance away from the mean. They are different because -0.5 is below the mean and 0.5 is above the mean.

30. The boundary is a circle with radius 6 and center $(-6, 0)$.

$$(x - (-6))^2 + (y - 0)^2 = 6^2$$
$$(x + 6)^2 + (y - 0)^2 = 36$$
$$x^2 + 12x + 36 + y^2 = 36$$
$$x^2 + y^2 + 12x = 0$$
$$r^2 + 12\,r\cos\theta = 0$$
$$r(r + 12\cos\theta) = 0$$
$$r + 12\cos\theta = 0$$
$$r = -12\cos\theta$$

The polar equation is $r = -12\cos\theta$. Graph the polar equation on a calculator.

Use the following window:

θ min $= 0$, θ max $= 2\pi$, θ step $= \frac{\pi}{24}$, X min $= -18$, X max $= 5$, Y min $= -7$, Y max $= 7$

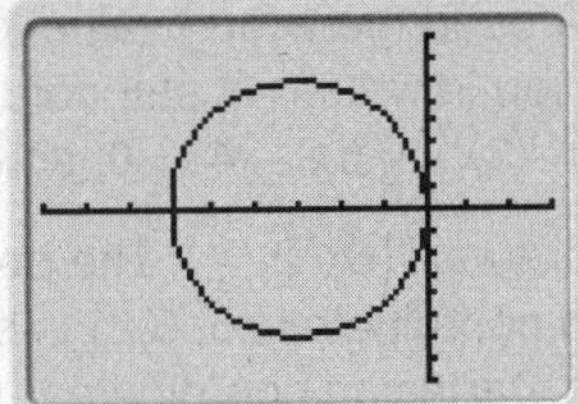

LESSON 97

Warm Up 97

1. term
2. False; the first difference is not constant.
3. $5(-3)^4 = 5(-3)(-3)(-3)(-3) = 405$

Lesson Practice 97

a. Divide a term by its previous term, $\frac{0.2}{2} = \frac{1}{10}$. Then, find the next three terms by multiplying $\frac{1}{10}$, so $r = 0.1$.

$0.002(0.1) = 0.0002$
$0.0002(0.1) = 0.00002$
$0.00002(0.1) = 0.000002$

b. Divide a term by its previous term, $\frac{-40}{-200} = \frac{1}{5}$. Then, find the next three terms by multiplying $\frac{1}{5}$, so $r = \frac{1}{5}$.

$$-\frac{8}{5}\left(\frac{1}{5}\right) = -\frac{8}{25}$$
$$-\frac{8}{25}\left(\frac{1}{5}\right) = -\frac{8}{125}$$
$$-\frac{8}{125}\left(\frac{1}{5}\right) = -\frac{8}{625}$$

c. Find r: $-5 \div 1 = -5$. Then, use the formula $a_n = a_1 r^{n-1}$.

$$a_9 = -1(-5)^{9-1}$$
$$= -1(-5)^8$$
$$= -5^8 = -390{,}625$$

d. Find r: $4 \div 16 = \frac{1}{4}$. Then, use the formula $a_n = a_1\, r^{n-1}$.

$$a_9 = 16\left(\frac{1}{4}\right)^{11-1}$$
$$= 4^2\left(\frac{1}{4}\right)^{10}$$
$$= \frac{1}{4^8} = \frac{1}{65{,}536}$$

e. Use the formula $a_n = a_m\, r^{n-m}$.

$$a_8 = \frac{5}{4}\left(-\frac{1}{2}\right)^{8-4}$$
$$= \frac{5}{2^2}\left(-\frac{1}{2}\right)^4$$
$$= \frac{5}{2^6} = \frac{5}{64}$$

f. Use the formula $a_n = a_m\, r^{n-m}$, and solve for r.

$$a_6 = a_3\, r^{6-3}$$
$$8192 = 128r^3$$
$$r = \sqrt[3]{\frac{8192}{128}}$$
$$r = \sqrt[3]{\frac{16^3 \times 2}{4^3 \times 2}}$$
$$r = \frac{16}{4} = 4$$

Now, find a_1. Use either of the known terms.

$128 = a_1 (4)^{3-1}$

$128 = 16a_1$

$a_1 = 8$

g. Use the formula $a_n = a_m r^{n-m}$, and solve for r.

$a_6 = a_4 r^{6-4}$

$96 = 24r^2$

$r = \sqrt{\frac{96}{24}}$

$r = \sqrt{4} = \pm 2$

Now, find a_9. Use either of the known terms.

$a_9 = a_6 (\pm 2)^{9-6}$

$a_9 = 96(\pm 2)^3$

$a_9 = \pm 768$

h. The salaries each year form a geometric sequence where $r = 1.0425$. Substitute 10 for n, 35,890 for a_1, and 1.0425 for r in $a_n = a_1 r^{n-1}$.

$a_{10} = 35{,}890(1.0425)^{10-1}$

$a_{10} = 52{,}198.50$

The employee's salary in the 10th year will be \$52,198.50.

Practice 97

1. Solve for h.

$V = \pi r^2 h$

$h = \frac{V}{\pi r^2}$

2. The question is biased because it leads students to vote for the more popular candidate. The survey shouldn't focus on characteristics such as appearance or popularity, but should focus on each candidate's qualifications.

3. Let $d = \log_8 x$. Then $8^d = 8^{\log_8 x}$, so $d = \log_8 x$. Therefore, $8^{\log_8 x} = x$.

4. $\log_3 81^x = \log_3(3^{4x})$. Therefore, $\log_3 81^x = 4x$.

5. a. The price of the car forms a geometric sequence where $r = 0.85$. Substitute 18,900 for a_1 and 0.85 for r. So, $a_n = 18{,}900(0.85)^{n-1}$.

b. Substitute 6 for n.

$a_6 = 18{,}900(0.85)^{6-1}$

$= 8386.03$

The value of the car in year 6 is \$8386.03.

6. Find $\left(\frac{b}{2}\right)^2$ for $x^2 + 18x + 36 = 0$.

$\left(\frac{18}{2}\right)^2 = 81$. So, $45 = 81 - 36$ needs to be added to both sides to make it a perfect square.

7. When 4 is subtracted from both sides, the square root equals a negative number.

8. $\begin{bmatrix} -6 & 2 \\ -1 & -3 \end{bmatrix} + \begin{bmatrix} 11 & 2 \\ 8 & 3 \end{bmatrix} = \begin{bmatrix} 5 & 4 \\ 7 & 0 \end{bmatrix}$

9. $\begin{bmatrix} 11 & 2 \\ 8 & 3 \end{bmatrix} - 3\begin{bmatrix} -6 & 2 \\ -1 & -3 \end{bmatrix} = \begin{bmatrix} 29 & -4 \\ 11 & 12 \end{bmatrix}$

10. Divide a term by its previous term, $\frac{6}{2} = 3$. Then, use the formula $a_n = a_1 r^{n-1}$.

$a_n = a_1 r^{n-1}$

$a_{15} = 2(3)^{15-1}$

$= 9{,}565{,}938$

11. Student A used the wrong value for c. When the equation is written in standard form, it becomes $-3x^2 + 6x - 4 = 0$, so $c = -4$.

12. Sample answer: $\left(6\sqrt{2}, \frac{\pi}{4}\right)$; The point with Cartesian coordinates (6, 6.2) is close to the point with Cartesian coordinates (6, 6), which has $\left(6\sqrt{2}, \frac{\pi}{4}\right)$ as polar coordinates.

13. $x^2 - 24x + 150 = 0$

$x = \frac{-(-24) \pm \sqrt{(-24)^2 - 4(1)(150)}}{2(1)}$

$x = 12 \pm i\sqrt{6}$

The rectangle does not exist because there is no real number for the length, x.

14. Sample answer: $\theta = \frac{\pi}{4}$

15. discrete, discontinuous function

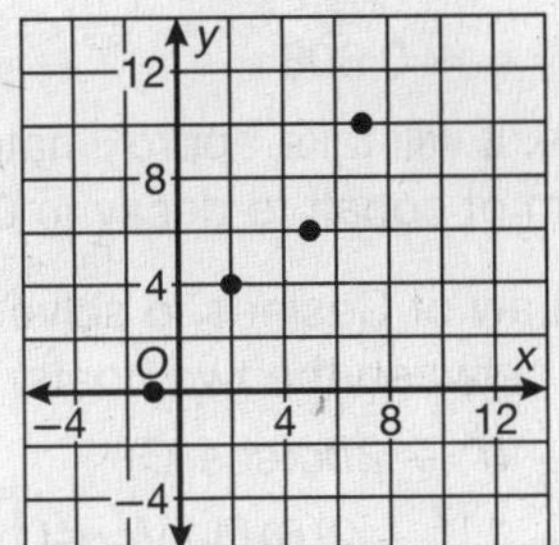

16. To find the inverse, interchange x and y.

$$y = \frac{1}{3}\sqrt{x} - 4$$

$$x = \frac{1}{3}\sqrt{y} - 4$$

$$x + 4 = \frac{1}{3}\sqrt{y}$$

$$3(x + 4) = \sqrt{y}$$

$$y = (3(x + 4))^2$$

$$y = 9(x^2 + 8x + 16)$$

$$y = 9x^2 + 72x + 144$$

Keep in mind that $y > 0$.

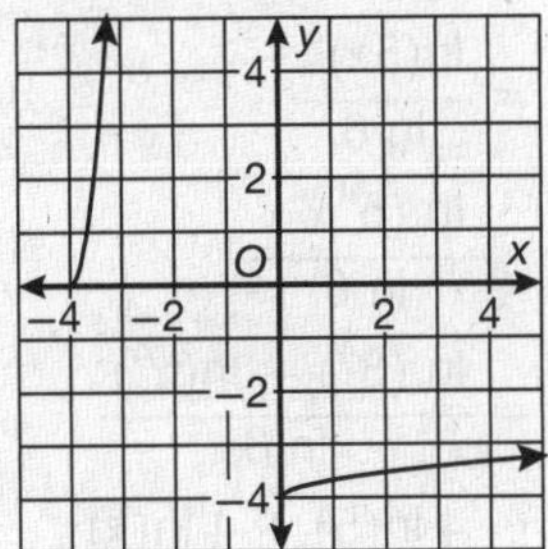

17. Recall that $t = \frac{d}{v}$, where t is time, d is distance, and v is speed.

Let r represent the speed limit during the day. Then, $r - 5$ is the speed limit at night.

Total time = time during day + time during night

$$= \frac{\text{distance during day}}{\text{time during day}} + \frac{\text{distance during night}}{\text{time during night}}$$

$$8 = \frac{350}{r} + \frac{195}{r - 5}$$

Solve for r.

$$8 = \frac{350(r - 5) + 195r}{r(r - 5)}$$

$$8r(r - 5) = 545r - 1750$$

$$8r^2 - 40r = 545r - 1750$$

$$8r^2 - 585r + 1750 = 0$$

Use the quadratic formula.

$$r = \frac{-b \pm \sqrt{b^2 - 4ac}}{2a}$$

$$r = \frac{585 \pm \sqrt{(-585)^2 - 4(8)(1750)}}{2(8)}$$

$$r = \frac{585 \pm 535}{16}$$

$$r = 70$$

The smaller value is discarded because it will make the speed at night negative. Therefore, the speed limit during the day is 70 mph.

18. Divide the 4th term by the 2nd term to solve for r. The correct answer is **D**.

$$\frac{a_4}{a_2} = \frac{a_1 r^{4-1}}{a_1 r^{2-1}}$$

$$\frac{1}{16} = r^2$$

$$r = \sqrt{\frac{1}{16}}$$

$$r = \pm\frac{1}{4}$$

19. If $(x - 1)$ is a factor:

$$\begin{array}{r|ccc} 1 & a & b & c \\ & & a & a+b \\ \hline & a & a+b & a+b+c \end{array}$$

$$\begin{array}{cc} d & e \\ a+b+c & a+b+c+d \\ \hline a+b+c+d & 0 \end{array}$$

Since $(x - 1)$ is a factor, synthetic division by 1 will yield a 0 remainder, therefore $a + b + c + d + e = 0$.

20. Find the LCM of the two numbers, 3 and 5. LCM of 3 and 5 is 15.

The lowest common multiple signifies when the two wheels are back in sync. Answer: 15 seconds.

21. $-67 - (-62) = -5$, the common difference is -5.

22. Solve each equation for y, and graph the solution region.

$$4y + 12 > x^2$$

$$4y > x^2 - 12 \qquad -\frac{1}{2}x \geq y$$

$$y > \frac{1}{4}x^2 - 3 \qquad y \leq -\frac{1}{2}x$$

$y \geq -2$ means the region is above and including the horizontal line $y = -2$

Sample: (0, 0) and (1, 2)

23. Recall that period $= \frac{2\pi}{b}$. Since $\frac{2\pi}{\left(\frac{2}{7}\right)} = 7\pi$, the correct answer is **B.**

24. Amplitude $= 0.5$, period $= \frac{2\pi}{2} = \pi$

25. Since 95% of the values fall between 12 and 18, and the data is symmetric about the mean, 15, 47.5% of the data is between 15 and 18. Therefore, 2.5% of values are above 18.

26. If $x = -0.4$, $f(x) = 9 - 5x$, so
$f(-0.4) = 9 - 5(-0.4) = 11$
If $x = 0$, $f(x) = 2$, so $f(-0.4) = 2$
If $x = 6$, $f(x) = x^3 - x$,
so $f(6) = (6)^3 - 6 = 210$

27. Using the natural decay function $N(t) = N_0e^{-kt}$, where k is the rate of decay.
Given:
$N(0) = N_0e^{-0k} = N_0 = 1$ gram
$N(5.3) = N_0e^{-5.3k} = 0.5$ gram
Solve for the rate of decay k.

$$\frac{N(5.3)}{N(0)} = \frac{N_0e^{-5.3k}}{N_0e^{-0k}} = \frac{0.5}{1}$$

$$e^{-5.3k} = 0.5$$
$$-5.3k = \ln 0.5$$
$$k = -\frac{\ln 0.5}{5.3}$$
$$\approx 0.13078$$

Solve for t when $N(t) = 0.9$

$$1e^{-tk} = 0.9$$
$$1e^{-0.13078t} = 0.9$$
$$-0.13078t = \ln 0.9$$
$$t \approx -\frac{\ln 0.9}{0.13078}$$
$$\approx 0.806$$

Therefore, it will take approximately 0.8 year for 1 gram of cobalt to decay to 0.9 gram.

28. Use the Law of Cosines to solve for the distance between the two boats.
$c^2 = a^2 + b^2 - 2bc(\cos C)$
$c^2 = 6^2 + 11^2 - 2(6)(11)(\cos(15° + 65°))$
$c^2 = 36 + 121 - 132 \cos 80°$
$c \approx \sqrt{134.08}$
≈ 11.58 miles
Traveling at 8 mph, it will take about $\frac{11.58}{8} = 1.4$ hours, or 1 hour and 24 minutes.

29. From the endpoints of the diameter, we can determine the radius and the center of the circle to be 6 and $(-4, -2)$ respectively. Therefore, the equation for the circle is
$(x - h)^2 + (y - k)^2 = r^2$
$(x + 4)^2 + (y + 2)^2 = 36.$

30. Use the change of base formula.

$$\log_6(5x)^4 = \frac{\ln(5x)^4}{\ln 6}$$
$$= \frac{\ln(5^4x^4)}{\ln 6}$$
$$= \frac{\ln(5^4) + \ln(x^4)}{\ln 6}$$
$$= \frac{4\ln(5) + 4\ln(x)}{\ln 6}$$

Then, evaluate when $x = 3$.

$$\frac{4\ln(5) + 4\ln(3)}{\ln 6} x \approx 6.05$$

LESSON 98

Warm Up 98

1. circle
2. A circle of radius 5 centered at (1, 1)
3. (7, 0) and (– 7, 0)
4. $c^2 = 13^2 - 5^2 = 169 - 25 = 144$
   $c = \pm 12$
   The correct answer is **A.**

5. $c^2 = 4^2 - 3^2 = 16 - 9 = 7$
$c = \pm\sqrt{7}$

Lesson Practice 98

a. $a = 5$ because the vertices are (5, 0) and (−5, 0)
$b = 2$ because the co-vertices are (0, −2) and (0, 2)
Use the following form since the major axis is horizontal.
$$\frac{(x-h)^2}{a^2} + \frac{(y-k)^2}{b^2} = 1$$
$$\frac{x^2}{5^2} + \frac{y^2}{2^2} = 1$$

b. $$\frac{16x^2}{576} + \frac{36y^2}{576} = 1$$
$$\frac{x^2}{36} + \frac{y^2}{16} = 1$$
$$\frac{x^2}{6^2} + \frac{y^2}{4^2} = 1$$
$a = 6$; $b = 4$; $c = \sqrt{6^2 - 4^2} = 2\sqrt{5}$
center: (0, 0)
vertices: (−6, 0), (6, 0)
co-vertices: (0, 4), (0, −4)
foci: $(-2\sqrt{5}, 0)(2\sqrt{5}, 0)$
e: $\frac{c}{a} = \frac{2\sqrt{5}}{6} = \frac{\sqrt{5}}{3}$

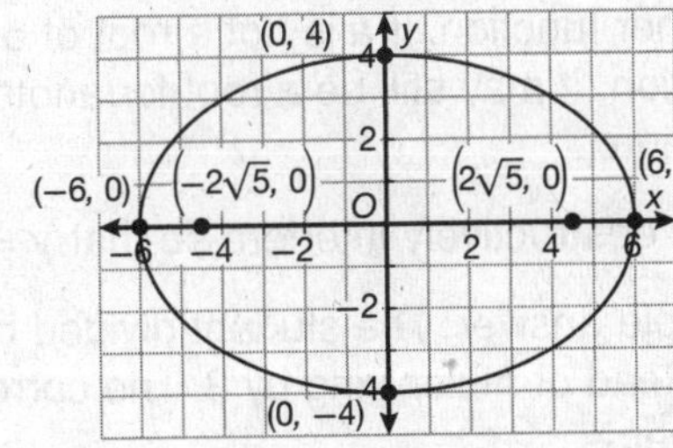

c. $$\frac{9(x-2)^2}{576} + \frac{64(y-5)^2}{576} = 1$$
$$\frac{(x-2)^2}{64} + \frac{(y-5)^2}{9} = 1$$
$$\frac{(x-2)^2}{8^2} + \frac{(y-5)^2}{3^2} = 1$$
$a = 8$; $b = 3$; $c = \sqrt{8^2 - 3^2} = \sqrt{55}$
center: (2, 5)
vertices: $(2 \pm 8, 5)$
(10, 5), (−6, 5)
co-vertices: $(2, 5 \pm 3)$
(2, 8), (2, 2)
foci: $(2 + \sqrt{55}, 5)(2 - \sqrt{55}, 5)$
e: $\frac{c}{a} = \frac{\sqrt{55}}{8}$

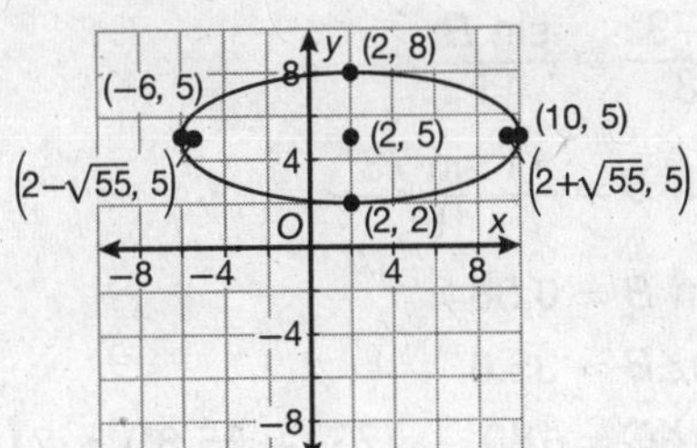

d. $$e = \sqrt{1 - \frac{b^2}{a^2}}$$
$$0.093 = \sqrt{1 - \frac{b^2}{a^2}}$$
$$0.008649 = 1 - \frac{b^2}{a^2}$$
$$0.991351 = \frac{b^2}{a^2}$$
$$\frac{b}{a} = 0.9957$$
$$b = 0.9957a$$
$$\frac{x^2}{1^2} + \frac{y^2}{0.9957^2} = 1$$

Practice 98

1. Press **2nd**, then press **x^{-1}**. Scroll to **EDIT**, and press **ENTER**. Enter the dimensions of the matrix and the elements for each entry. Then, press **2nd** and **MODE**. Press **2nd** and **x^{-1}**. Scroll to **MATH** and press **ENTER** when **1: det(** is highlighted. Then, press **2nd** and **x^{-1}**. Under the **NAMES** tab, highlight [A], and press **ENTER**. Close the brackets, and press **ENTER**.
Determinant = 250

2. There are an infinite number, one for every possible orientation of an ellipse that also crosses that point.

3. $c = \sqrt{a^2 - b^2} = \sqrt{15^2 - 10^2} = \sqrt{225 - 100}$
≈ 11.2

$\sqrt{10^2 + 11.2^2} + \sqrt{(-10)^2 + (-11.2)^2}$
$= \sqrt{100 + 125} + \sqrt{100 + 125}$
$= \sqrt{225} + \sqrt{225}$
$= 30$

4. $\frac{\sin 73°}{18} = \frac{\sin B}{11}$

$\sin B = \frac{11 \sin 73°}{18}$

$\sin B = 0.584$

$m\angle B \approx 35.8°$

$m\angle C = 180° - (73° + 35.8°) \approx 71.2°$

$\frac{\sin 73°}{18} = \frac{\sin 71.2°}{c}$

$c = \frac{18 \sin 71.2°}{\sin 73°}$

$c \approx 17.8$

5. $2x^2 + 3y^2 = 6$

$\frac{2x^2}{6} + \frac{3y^2}{6} = 1$

$\frac{x^2}{(\sqrt{3})^2} + \frac{y^2}{(\sqrt{2})^2} = 1$

6. Let x be the side length of the square base.

$V = l \times w \times h$
$28 = (x)(x)(x + 5)$
$28 = x^2 (x + 5)$
$0 = x^3 + 5x^2 - 28$
$2^3 + 5(2)^2 - 28 = 8 + 20 - 28 = 0$
$x = 2$
height $= 2 + 5 = 7$

7. $(4c \times d) + (16 \times (2 + 5c)) = 4cd + 80c + 32$

8. $1 - 0.00089 = 0.99911$
$a_8 = a_1(r)^{n-1}$
$a_8 = 582{,}049(0.99911)^{8-1} = 578{,}433$

9. $\log(w) = 0.8h + 0.4 \pm 0.04$
$\log(w) - 0.4 \pm 0.04 = 0.8h$

$h = \frac{\log(w) - 0.4 \pm 0.04}{0.8}$

$h = \frac{\log(40) - 0.4 \pm 0.04}{0.8}$

$h = 1.45\ m$ and $h = 1.55\ m$

The child is between 1.45 m and 1.55 m tall.

10. First, isolate for y,
$5y = -3x - 35$

$y = \frac{-3}{5}x - 7$

Plot the y-intercept (0, −7). Then, since the slope is negative, rise negatively (i.e., move down by 3 units), and run 5 units to the right. Plot that point. Connect the points, and the resulting line is the graph of the function.

11. The student divided in the wrong order:

$r = \frac{10}{30} = \frac{1}{3}$

12. Amplitude = 6; Period $= \frac{2\pi}{8} = \frac{\pi}{4}$

13. $f(x) = (x + 8)(3x^2 - 6) - (x + 8)(11x - 4)$
$f(x) = (x + 8)(3x^2 - 6 - 11x + 4)$
$f(x) = (x + 8)(3x^2 - 11x - 2)$
$x = -8$ or

$x = \frac{-b \pm \sqrt{b^2 - 4ac}}{2a}$

$x = \frac{-(-11) \pm \sqrt{(-11)^2 - 4(3)(-2)}}{2(3)}$

$x = \frac{11 \pm \sqrt{145}}{6}$

14. No; a root of one function may be a root of another function. If a is not a root of one function, it may still be a root for another function.

15. They destructively interfere so that $y = 0$.

16. Sample answer: The student divided by 3 instead of multiplying by 3. The correct answer is

$V = \frac{1}{3}\pi r^3$

$3V = \pi r^3$

$\frac{3V}{\pi} = r^3$

$r = \sqrt[3]{\frac{3V}{\pi}}$

17. $$\frac{(x^{-2}yp)^{-3}(x^0yp)^2}{(2x^2)^{-2}} = \frac{x^6y^{-3}p^{-3}x^0y^2p^2}{2^{-2}x^{-4}}$$
$$= \frac{x^6y^{-1}p^{-1}}{\frac{1}{4}x^{-4}}$$
$$= \frac{(4x^{10})}{yp}$$

18. $$-\frac{3x^2y}{xx} + \frac{2x^{-2}x^4}{y^{-1}x^2} - \frac{5xy^2}{xy} =$$
$$-3y + 2y - 5y = -6y$$

19. a. $$(12 + x)(9 + x) < 300$$
$$108 + 12x + 9x + x^2 < 300$$
$$x^2 + 21x + 108 < 300$$

b. $$x^2 + 21x + 108 - 300 < 0$$
$$x^2 + 21x - 192 < 0$$
$$x = \frac{-b \pm \sqrt{b^2 - 4ac}}{2a}$$
$$x = \frac{-21 \pm \sqrt{21^2 - 4(1)(-192)}}{2(1)}$$
$$x = \frac{-21 + 34.8}{2}$$
$$x = 6.9$$

Between 0 feet and about 6.9 feet

20. For $\theta = 2\pi n$ for integer values of n.

21. $f(3)$ is undefined because f is not defined for values greater than or equal to 3.

$f(0) = 0^2 - 5 = -5$

22. $f(3) = (3) = 3$, $f(0) = \frac{1}{2}$

23. $0 = (x + 5i)(x - 5i) = x^2 - (5i)^2 = x^2 + 25$

24. $$x^3 + 10x^2 + 17x - 28 = 0$$
$$1^3 + 10(1)^2 + 17(1) - 28 = 0$$
$$1 + 10 + 17 - 28 = 0$$

$$\begin{array}{r|rrrr} 1 & 1 & 10 & 17 & -28 \\ & & 1 & 11 & 28 \\ \hline & 1 & 11 & 28 & 0 \end{array}$$

$$0 = (x - 1)(x^2 + 11x + 28)$$
$$0 = (x - 1)(x + 4)(x + 7)$$
$x = 1$, $x = -4$, and $x = -7$

25. $$x^3 - 343 = 0$$
$$(x - 7)(x^2 + 7x + 49) = 0$$
$$b^2 - 4ac = 7^2 - 4(1)(49) = -147.$$

Since the discriminant is negative, there are no other real roots than $x = 7$.

26. $$\frac{x^2 + 5x - 6}{x^2 - 12x + 32} = \frac{(x + 6)(x - 1)}{(x - 8)(x - 4)}$$

Since there are four critical values, −6, 1, 8, and 4, there will be five intervals for which a point needs to be checked to see if it is a solution.

The correct answer is **C**.

27. $$\frac{\frac{1}{2} - \frac{4}{15}}{\frac{5}{6} + \frac{1}{9}} = \frac{\frac{15}{30} - \frac{8}{30}}{\frac{15}{18} + \frac{2}{18}} = \frac{\frac{7}{30}}{\frac{17}{18}}$$
$$= \frac{7}{30} \cdot \frac{18}{17} = \frac{126}{510} = \frac{21}{85}$$

28. $$\frac{\frac{1}{x+1} - \frac{1}{x-1}}{\frac{x}{x^2 - 1}}$$
$$= \left(\frac{x - 1}{(x - 1)(x + 1)} - \frac{x + 1}{(x - 1)(x + 1)}\right)$$
$$\div \frac{x}{(x + 1)(x - 1)}$$
$$= \left(\frac{x - 1 - x - 1}{(x - 1)(x + 1)}\right) \cdot \frac{(x + 1)(x - 1)}{x}$$
$$= -\frac{2}{x}$$

29. The LCD is the LCM of the denominators, so every denominator can be divided into it. Both sides of the equation are multiplied by the LCD, so every term is multiplied by the LCD. The denominator divides out with all or some of the factors in the LCD. Any remaining terms are multiplied by the numerator. What remains is an equation without fractions.

30. $r = 3$ represents a circle of radius 3. Points inside which are at least 1 unit from the pole are outside the concentric circle with radius 1. The probability is the ratio of the area of the annulus between the circles to the area of the larger circle.

$$p = \frac{(3)^2\pi - (1)^2\pi}{(3)^2\pi} = \frac{9 - 1}{9} = \frac{8}{9}$$

LESSON 99

Warm Up 99

1. real part
2. false
3. $d = \sqrt{(3 - (-2))^2 + (7 - 3)^2} = \sqrt{25 + 16} \approx 6.4$

Lesson Practice 99

a. $\begin{bmatrix} 10 \\ 5 \end{bmatrix}$; $10 + 5i$

b. $\begin{bmatrix} -12 \\ -36 \end{bmatrix}$; $-12 - 36i$

c. $\begin{bmatrix} 5 \\ 4 \end{bmatrix} + \begin{bmatrix} -6 \\ 4 \end{bmatrix} = \begin{bmatrix} -1 \\ 8 \end{bmatrix}$

d. $\begin{bmatrix} -10 \\ 7 \end{bmatrix} - \begin{bmatrix} -3 \\ 9 \end{bmatrix} = \begin{bmatrix} -7 \\ -2 \end{bmatrix}$

e. $\begin{bmatrix} -10 \\ 7 \end{bmatrix} \cdot \begin{bmatrix} -3 \\ 9 \end{bmatrix} = (-10)(-3) + (7)(9)$

$= 30 + 63 = 93$

f. $\theta = \text{arc cos}\left(\dfrac{x_1x_2 + y_1y_2}{\sqrt{x_1^2 + y_1^2}\sqrt{x_2^2 + y_2^2}}\right)$

$\theta = \text{arc cos}\left(\dfrac{(-8)(9) + (12)(-12)}{\sqrt{(-8)^2 + (12)^2}\sqrt{(9)^2 + (-12)^2}}\right)$

$\theta = \text{arc cos}\left(\dfrac{-216}{\sqrt{208}\sqrt{225}}\right)$

$\theta = \text{arc cos}\left(\dfrac{-216}{216.33307}\right)$

$\theta = 176.82°$

g. $\begin{bmatrix} 0 \\ 600 \end{bmatrix} + \begin{bmatrix} -30 \cos 40° \\ -30 \sin 40° \end{bmatrix} \approx \begin{bmatrix} -22.98 \\ 580.7 \end{bmatrix}$

$\sqrt{(-22.98)^2 + (580.7)^2} \approx 580.26$

$\theta \approx \text{arc cos}\left(\dfrac{-22.98}{580.7}\right)$

$\theta \approx 87.73°$ NNE

Practice 99

1. The student did not check the answer in the original equation. 4 is an extraneous solution because it does not make the original equation true. The equation has no solutions. Additionally, the student should also recognize after the second step that −2 cannot result from the square root of a real number.

2. None. A figure with an eccentricity of zero is a circle.

3. Sample answer: Exponential and logarithmic operations are inverse operations.

4. a. $\dfrac{5}{9} = \dfrac{20}{x}$

b. $x = \dfrac{180}{5} = 36$ oz

c. $\dfrac{5}{9} = \dfrac{20}{36}$

$20 \times 9 \Rightarrow 5(36) = 9(20) \Rightarrow 180 = 180$

5. $A = x(x + 10) + \frac{1}{2}[x + (x + 10)]\left(\frac{1}{2}x\right)$

$A = x^2 + 10x + \frac{1}{4}x(2x + 10)$

$A = x^2 + 10x + \frac{1}{2}x^2 + \frac{5}{2}x$

$A = \frac{3}{2}x^2 + \frac{25}{2}x$

6. $\frac{1}{4} \cdot \frac{2}{4} = \frac{2}{16} = 12.5\%$

7. $f(-0.4) = (-0.4) - (-0.4)^2 = -0.56$

$f(0) = (0) - (0)^2 = 0$

$f(6) = -(6) - 8 = -14$

8. In the numerator, the mean should be subtracted from the data value, not the other way around.

$z = \dfrac{15 - 20}{4} = -\dfrac{5}{4} = -1.25$

9. $RS^2 = 20^2 + 17^2 - 2(20)(17)\cos 38°$

$RS^2 = 689 - 535.85$

$RS = 12.375$

$\dfrac{\sin 38°}{12.375} = \dfrac{\sin(m\angle S)}{20}$

$\sin(m\angle S) = \dfrac{20 \sin 38°}{12.375}$

$m\angle S = 84.3°$

10. quintic, quartic, cubic, quadratic, linear, and constant

11. 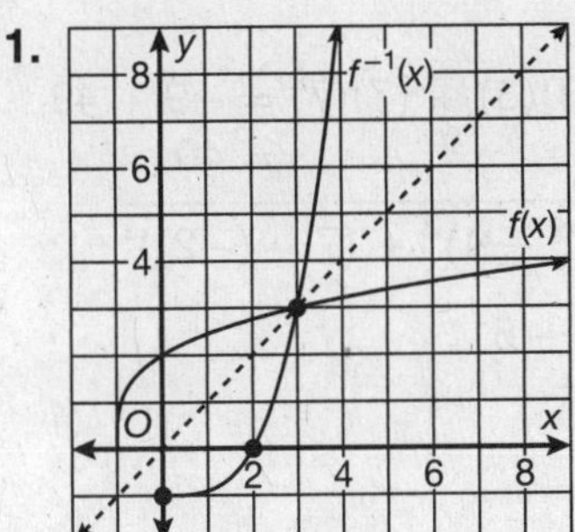

12. a. 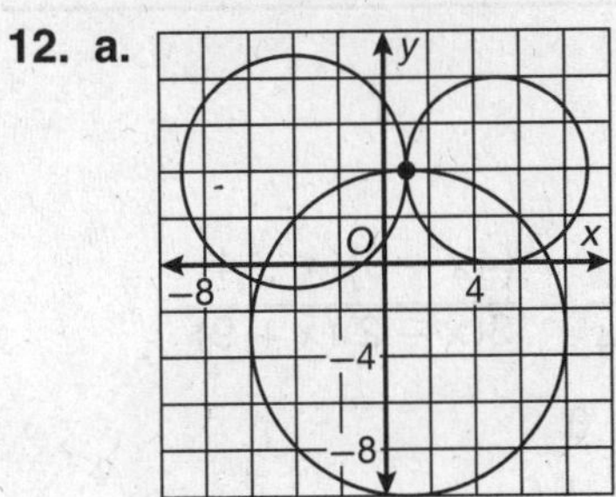

b. (1, 4)

13. Population: all seniors in the class meeting; sample: the 40 polled seniors

14.
$$y \approx a(x-h)^2 + k$$
$$y \approx a(x-144)^2 + 105$$
$$0 \approx a(288-144)^2 + 105$$
$$-105 \approx 20{,}736a$$
$$a \approx -0.005\ldots$$
$$y \approx -0.005(x-144)^2 + 105$$
$$y \approx -0.005(x^2 - 288x + 20{,}736) + 105$$
$$y \approx -0.005x^2 + 1.458x$$

15. $d = 10\log\frac{I}{I_o}$
$$d = 10\log\frac{(2.3\times10^9)I_o}{I_o}$$
$$d = 10\log 2.3\times10^9$$
$$d = \log(2.3\times10^9)^{10}$$
$$d = \frac{\ln(2.3\times10^9)^{10}}{\ln 10}$$
$$d\ln 10 = 10\ln(2.3\times10^9)$$
$$2.303d = 215.56$$
$$d \approx 93.62 \text{ decibels}$$
The decibel level is 93.62.

16. $\frac{3}{x+5} = \frac{2}{x+5}$
$$2x + 10 = 3x + 15$$
$x = -5$; this is not a solution for the equation because it makes both rational expressions undefined.

17. The sample is random and unbiased. Each student has an equal chance of being selected.

18. Yes, if the inequality has no solutions, or if the solution is all real numbers, then the graphs of the left and right sides of the inequality will not intersect.

19. -6; $12(-6) + 1 = -71$

20. Press 2nd and x^{-1}. Scroll to the EDIT tab and press ENTER. When the screen shows MATRIX A, enter "3 × 3", and then enter the elements of the matrix.

Then, press 2nd and x^{-1}. Press ENTER, and then press x^{-1}, followed by ENTER.
$$\begin{pmatrix} -2 & 6 & -1 \\ -4 & 9 & -1 \\ 3 & -7 & 1 \end{pmatrix}$$

21. $\begin{bmatrix}6\\8\end{bmatrix}\cdot\begin{bmatrix}2\\7\end{bmatrix} = (6)(2) + (8)(7) = 12 + 56 = 68$

22. $\tan\theta = \frac{-3\sqrt{3}}{-3}$
$$\tan\theta = \sqrt{3}$$
$$\theta = 60° \text{ or } \theta = 60° + 180° = 240°$$
$$\theta = \frac{\pi}{3} \text{ or } \theta = \frac{4\pi}{3}$$
$$r^2 = (-3)^2 + (-3\sqrt{3})^2$$
$$r^2 = 36$$
$$r = 6$$
The correct answer is **D**.

23.
$$6^2 = 36$$
$$(-5)^2 = 25$$
$$\frac{x^2}{36} + \frac{y^2}{25} = 1$$

24. $3\frac{2}{5}x - 4\frac{1}{10}x = 2\frac{1}{4}$
$$\frac{17}{5}x - \frac{41}{10}x = \frac{9}{4}$$

$$\frac{34x - 41x}{10} = \frac{9}{4}$$

$$\frac{-7x}{10} = \frac{9}{4}$$

$$90 = -28x$$

$$x = -\frac{45}{14}$$

25. $0.02(p - 2) = 0.03(2p - 6)$

$0.02p - 0.04 = 0.06p - 0.18$

$-0.04 + 0.18 = 0.06p - 0.02p$

$0.14 = 0.04p$

$p = 3.5$

26. We should test the possible values $\pm\frac{1}{2}, \pm1, \pm\frac{3}{2}, \pm2, \pm3, \pm4, \pm6, \pm12$.

$2(2)^3 - 3(2)^2 - 8(2) + 12 = 16 - 12 - 16 + 12 = 0$

2	2	−3	−8	12
		4	2	−12
	2	1	−6	0

$0 = (x - 2)(2x^2 + x - 6)$

$$x = \frac{-b \pm \sqrt{b^2 - 4ac}}{2a}$$

$$x = \frac{-1 \pm \sqrt{1^2 - 4(2)(-6)}}{2(2)}$$

$$x = \frac{-1 \pm 7}{4}$$

$x = 1.5$, $x = -2$, and $x = 2$

27. $3xy^2m + \frac{4}{x} = 3xy^2m\left(\frac{x}{x}\right) + \frac{4}{x} = \frac{3x^2y^2m + 4}{x}$

28. $\frac{5x^2}{pm} - 4 + \frac{c}{p^2m} = \frac{5x^2}{pm}\left(\frac{p}{p}\right) - 4\left(\frac{p^2m}{p^2m}\right) + \frac{c}{p^2m}$

$= \frac{5x^2p - 4p^2m + c}{p^2m}$

29. Magnitude of $A = \sqrt{(-3)^2 + 7^2} = \sqrt{9 + 49}$
$= 7.62$

Magnitude of $B = \sqrt{3^2 + 7^2} = \sqrt{9 + 49}$
$= 7.62$

$$\theta = \arccos\left(\frac{(3)(-3) + (7)(7)}{\sqrt{(-3)^2 + 7^2}\,\sqrt{3^2 + 7^2}}\right)$$

$$\theta = \arccos\left(\frac{-9 + 49}{\sqrt{58}\,\sqrt{58})}\right)$$

$$\theta = \arccos\left(\frac{40}{58}\right)$$

$\theta = 46.4°$

$\begin{bmatrix}-3\\7\end{bmatrix} \cdot \begin{bmatrix}3\\7\end{bmatrix} = (-3)(3) + (7)(7) = -9 + 49$
$= 40$

30. distance $= \sqrt{(-3 - 4)^2 + (7 - (-2))^2}$

$= \sqrt{49 + 81}$

$= \sqrt{130}$

LESSON 100

Warm Up 100

1. polynomial

2. $\frac{4x^2 - 11x - 20}{3x^2 + 21x - 54} = \frac{(4x + 5)(x - 4)}{3(x - 2)(x + 9)}$

3. $7x^2 + 3x - 4 \neq 0$

$(7x - 4)(x + 1) \neq 0$

$x \neq \frac{4}{7}$ and $x \neq -1$

Lesson Practice 100

a. $x^2 - 4x - 5 = 0$

$(x - 5)(x + 1) = 0$

$x - 5 = 0$ and $x + 1 = 0$

$x = 5$ $\quad$ $x = -1$

b. $x + 3 = 0$

$x = -3$

c. A vertical asymptote can be found at each point that would make a factor of the denominator zero and cannot be cancelled by a factor in the numerator. In this case there is a vertical asymptote at $x = -3$ and $x = 5$

d. Since $x + 5$ is a factor of the numerator and denominator there is a hole at $x = -5$. Since $x - 6$ is a factor twice in the denominator but only once in the numerator, there is a vertical asymptote at $x = -6$

e. degree numerator = degree denominator

Horizontal asymptote: $y = \frac{6}{2} = 3$

f. degree numerator > degree denominator; no horizontal asymptotes

g. Vertical asymptotes occurs where $x - 2 = 0$.

Vertical asymptote: $x = 2$

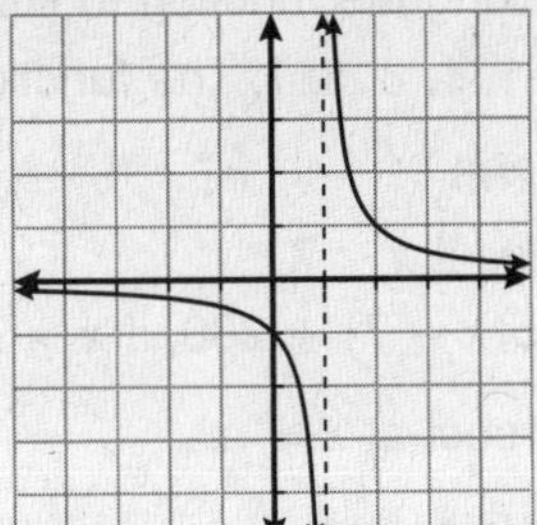

h. Vertical asymptotes occurs where $x^3 - x = 0$.

$x(x + 1)(x - 1) = 0$

Vertical asymptotes: $x = 0$, $x = -1$, $x = 1$

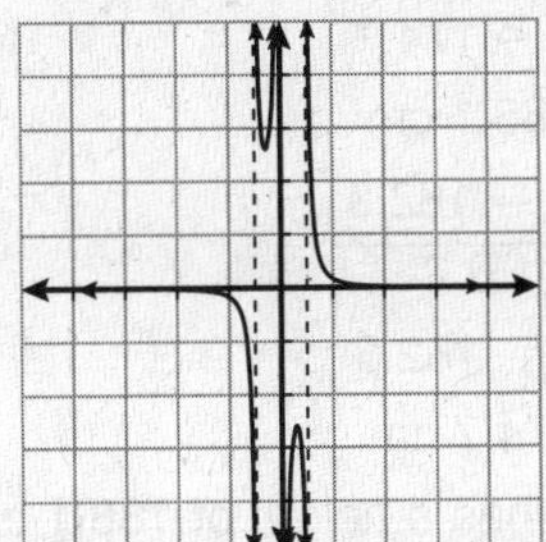

i. Factor the numerator and the denominator

$$y = \frac{x^2 - 2x - 15}{x^2 + 5x + 6} = \frac{(x-5)\cancel{(x+3)}}{(x+2)\cancel{(x+3)}}$$

Hole at $x = -3$. $(-3, 8)$

Vertical Asymptote where $(x + 2) = 0$: $x = -2$

Horizontal Asymptote: $y = \frac{1}{1} = 1$ because degree of numerator equal to degree of denominator. x-intercept where $(x - 5) = 0$: $x = 5$ $(5, 0)$

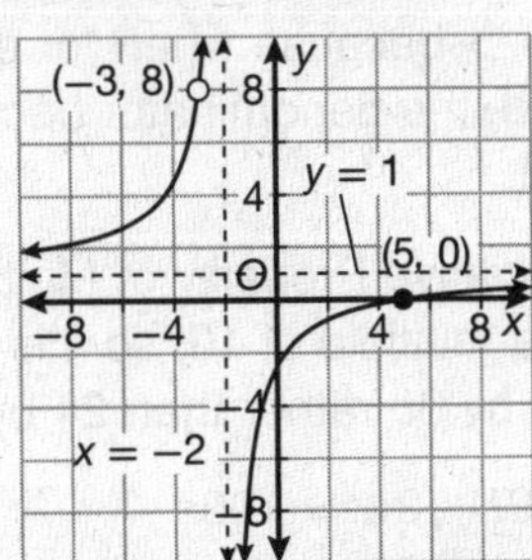

j. $y = \frac{x^2 - 2x - 15}{x^3 - 9x} = \frac{(x-5)\cancel{(x+3)}}{x(x-3)\cancel{(x+3)}}$

Hole at $x = -3$. $\left(-3, -\frac{4}{9}\right)$

Vertical Asymptote where $x = 0$ and $(x - 3) = 0$: $x = 0$ and $x = 3$

Horizontal Asymptote: $y = 0$ because degree of denominator greater than degree of numerator.

x-intercept where $(x - 5) = 0$: $x = (5, 0)$

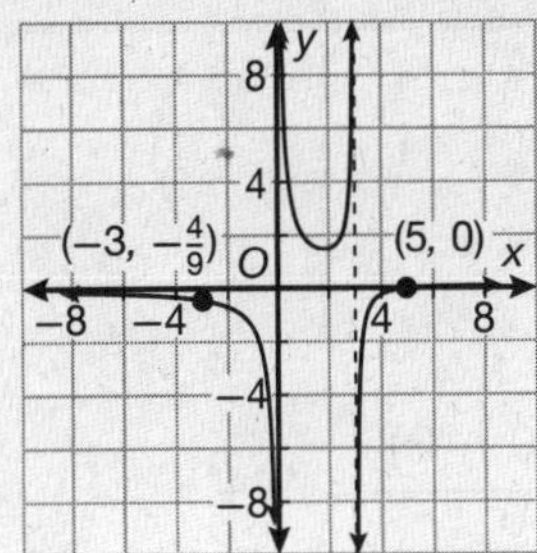

Practice 100

1.

$$x = 4 + \frac{5}{x}$$
$$x - 4 = \frac{5}{x}$$
$$x(x - 4) = 5$$
$$x^2 - 4x - 5 = 0$$
$$(x - 5)(x + 1) = 0$$
$$x = 5, -1$$

2.

$$-x^2 - 2x - 1 > 2$$
$$-1(x^2 + 2x + 1) > 2$$
$$-1(x + 1)^2 > 2$$

$(x + 1)^2$ will always be positive for all x, and the coefficient -1 will always make it a negative number. There is no negative number greater than 2. Thus, there are no solutions.

3. Student B mistakenly transposes the x and y terms in the numerator.

4.

$$y - y_1 = m(x - x_1)$$
$$y - 10 = 7(x - 6)$$
$$y = 7x - 42 + 10$$
$$y = 7x - 32$$

5.

$$(x - 5)^2 + (y + 12)^2 = 13^2$$
$$x^2 - 10x + 25 + y^2 + 24y + 144 = 169$$
$$x^2 + y^2 - 10x + 24y = 0$$
$$r^2 - 10(r\cos\theta) + 24(r\sin\theta) = 0$$
$$r(r - 10\cos\theta + 24\sin\theta) = 0,\ r \neq 0$$
$$r - 10\cos\theta + 24\sin\theta = 0$$
$$r = 10\cos\theta - 24\sin\theta$$

Press MODE, and be sure that the settings are attuned to radian measures and the function setting is "Pol". Then, press Y=, and enter the equation of the function.

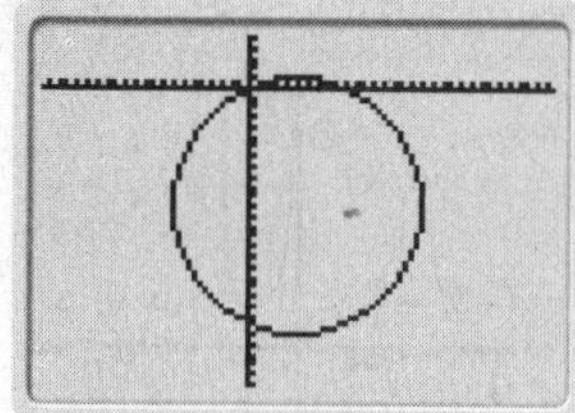

6. a. $\frac{180(10-2)}{10} = 144°$

b. $180 - 144 = 36°$

7. $V(x) = (x + 20)(x - 4)(x + 7)$
$V(x) = (x + 20)(x^2 + 3x - 28)$
$V(x) = x^3 + 23x^2 + 32x - 560$

$$\begin{array}{r|rrrr} 20 & 1 & 23 & 32 & -560 \\ & & 20 & 860 & 17,840 \\ \hline & 1 & 43 & 892 & 17,280 \end{array}$$

$V(20) = 17,280$.

8. $f(x) = \begin{cases} 9, \text{ if } x < 0 \\ -4, \text{ if } x \geq 5. \end{cases}$

9. $f(x) = \begin{cases} x, \text{ if } x < 0 \\ x^2 + 2, \text{ if } x \geq 0 \end{cases}$

10. The correct answer is **D** because

$y = \frac{x^2 - 16}{x^2 - 11x + 28} = \frac{(x+4)(x-4)}{(x-4)(x-7)}$
$= \frac{x+4}{x-7}$

The asymptote is $x = 7$.

11. a. The y-values decrease to 0.

b. The y-values increase.

12. Yes; Sample answer: Let $P_1 = 3x^2 - x - 2$ and $P_2 = -3x^2 - x - 2$. Then, $P_1 + P_2 = -2x - 4$ and $P_1 - P_2 = 6x^2$.

13. Press Y=, and enter $2x + 3$ as the function. Press GRAPH, and then press TRACE to scroll along the function to find the range. Range: −1, 1, 3, 5, 7. The function is discrete.

14. $7 \cdot 38 = 266$

$f(x) = \begin{cases} 38x, \text{ if } x \leq 7 \\ 35(x - 7) + 266, \text{ if } x > 7 \end{cases}$

15. They intersect at $x = a$.

16. Let x be the height of a man with a z-score of 2, and let y be the height of a woman with a z-score of 2.

$2 = \frac{x - 174.1}{7}$
$14 = x - 174.1$
$x = 188.1$ cm
$2 = \frac{y - 162.3}{6.2}$
$12.4 = y - 162.3$
$y = 174.7$ cm

The man has a height of 188.1 cm, and the woman has a height of 174.7 cm.

17. $4331.87 = \frac{2\pi}{a}$
$4331.87a = 2\pi$
$a = \frac{2\pi}{4331.87}$
$a = 0.0015$
$y = \sin(0.0015x)$

18. Student A made the error. The critical values obtained from the denominator should have < or > because when "or equal to" is included, the denominator becomes undefined.

19. The Associative Property of Multiplication; (6)(5) is a multiple of 10, so it is easier to multiply 4 by 30 rather than 24 by 5.

20. $2l + 2w = 100$
$2l = 100 - 2w$
$l = \frac{100 - 2w}{2}$
$l = 50 - w$
$A = (50 - w)w$
$A = 50w - w^2$
$450 \leq 50w - w^2$

$$450 = 50w - w^2$$
$$w^2 - 50w + 450 = 0$$
$$x = \frac{-b \pm \sqrt{b^2 - 4ac}}{2a}$$
$$x = \frac{-(-50) \pm \sqrt{(-50)^2 - 4(1)(450)}}{2(1)}$$
$$x = \frac{50 \pm 26.5}{2}$$
$x = 11.8$, $x = 38.2$

Interval	x-value	Is it a solution?
$x < 38.2$	39	$50(39) - 39^2 = 429 < 450$, no.
$11.8 < x < 38.2$	12	$50(12) - 12^2 = 456 > 450$, yes.
$11.8 < x$	0	$50(0) - 0^2 = 0 < 450$, no.

21. $y = \frac{\sin x}{\cos(x - \theta)} = \frac{\sin x}{\cos x} = \tan x$

$x \neq \frac{1}{2}\pi + \pi n$, for all integer n. Then, the function is not periodic when

$\theta = \frac{1}{2}\pi + \pi n = \frac{\pi + 2\pi n}{2} = (2n + 1)\frac{\pi}{2}$.

22. $\frac{2\pi}{0.001} = 2000\pi$

$y = 100 \cos(2000\pi x)$

23. $2\sqrt{3}(5\sqrt{3} - 2\sqrt{6}) = 10\sqrt{3}\sqrt{3} - 4\sqrt{3}\sqrt{6}$
$= 10(3) - 4\sqrt{18}$
$= 30 - 4\sqrt{9}\sqrt{2}$
$= 30 - 12\sqrt{2}$

24. $2\sqrt{3} \cdot 3\sqrt{6} \cdot 5\sqrt{12} = (2)(3)(5)\sqrt{3}\sqrt{6}\sqrt{12}$
$= 30\sqrt{216}$
$= 30\sqrt{36}\sqrt{6}$
$= 180\sqrt{6}$

25. Sample answer: The goal is to isolate the y-variable, so first subtract $(x - 5)^2$ from both sides of the equation. To undo the square on the left, take the square root of both sides, remembering both the positive and negative root on the right. Isolate y by adding 5 to each side. Graph both functions.

26. $\frac{1}{R_T} = \frac{1}{R_1} + \frac{1}{R_2}$

$\frac{1}{R_T} = \frac{1}{R} + \frac{1}{2R + 1}$

$\frac{1}{R_T} = \frac{2R + 1}{R(2R + 1)} + \frac{R}{R(2R + 1)}$

$\frac{1}{R_T} = \frac{3R + 1}{R(2R + 1)}$

$R_T(3R + 1) = R(2R + 1)$

$R_T = \frac{R(2R + 1)}{3R + 1}$

27.
$$\begin{array}{r|rrr} 1 & 1 & 5 & -6 \\ & & 1 & 6 \\ \hline & 1 & 6 & 0 \end{array}$$
$(x^4 + 5x^3 - 6x^2) \div (x - 1) = x^3 + 6x^2$

28.
$$\begin{array}{r|rrrr} 3 & 1 & -20 & 123 & -216 \\ & & 3 & -51 & 216 \\ \hline & 1 & -17 & 72 & 0 \end{array}$$
$(x^4 - 20x^3 + 123x^2 - 216x) \div (x - 3) = x^3 - 17x^2 + 72x$

29. $\begin{bmatrix} 10 \\ 6 \end{bmatrix} + \begin{bmatrix} 4 \\ 5 \end{bmatrix} = \begin{bmatrix} 10 + 4 \\ 6 + 5 \end{bmatrix} = \begin{bmatrix} 14 \\ 11 \end{bmatrix}$

30. $\begin{bmatrix} 10 \\ 4 \end{bmatrix} - \begin{bmatrix} 3 \\ 14 \end{bmatrix} = \begin{bmatrix} 10 - 3 \\ 4 - 14 \end{bmatrix} = \begin{bmatrix} 7 \\ -10 \end{bmatrix}$

INVESTIGATION 10

1. The graph of $r = \sin\theta$ is the unit circle translated up the length of the radius. The graph of $r = \cos\theta$ is the unit circle translated right the length of the radius.
2. The circles are smaller than the parent circle and translated to the right. As a decreased the size of the circle decreased.
3. The circles are larger than the parent circle and translated up. As a increased the size of the circle increased.
4. The value of r increases as θ increases.
5. The curvature of the spiral increased.
6. The curvature of the spiral decreased.
7. The coefficient a determines the curvature of the spiral, and b is the translation of the graph along the horizontal axis.

8. The number of petals is twice the value of b.

9. The number of petals equals the value of b.

10. b is half the number of petals. $b = 10$

11. b is odd so the number of petals equals b. 19 petals

12. The length of the petals increases.

13. The length of the petals decreases.

14. a circle

15. an ellipse

16. a parabola

17. the radius of a circle

18.

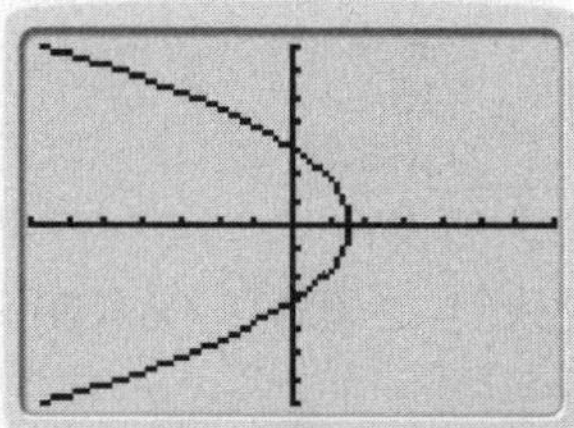

$r = \pm\dfrac{3}{1 + \cos\theta}$

19.

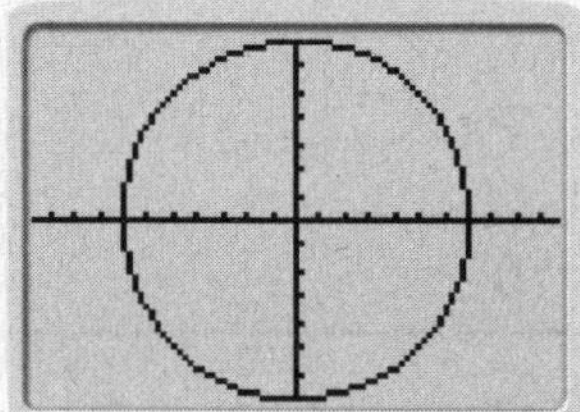

$r = \pm 7$ or $r = 14 \sin\theta$

20.

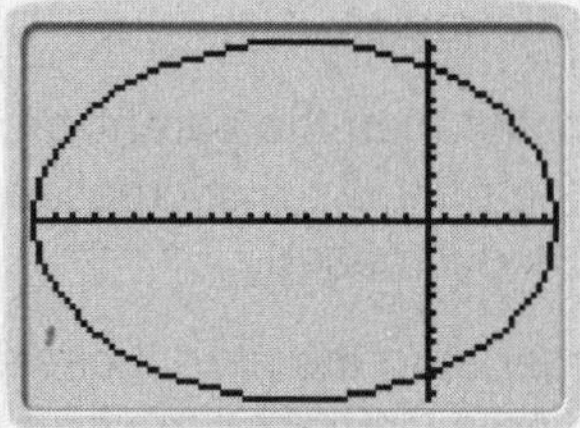

Sample answer: $\dfrac{10}{1 + 5\cos\theta}$

Investigation Practice

a. Sample: $r = 3 \sin\theta$

b. The curvature of the spiral decreased.

c. $r = \sin(8\theta)$

d. $r = \sin(9\theta)$

e. Sample: $r = 4 \sin(3\theta)$

f. The value of e is between 0 and 1 so the conic section is an ellipse

g. The value of e is 1 so the conic section is a parabola

LESSON 101

Warm Up 101

1. coefficient

2. $f(x) = 2x^3 - x + 5$
$f(-2) = 2(-2)^3 - (-2) + 5$
$= 2(-8) - (-2) + 5$
$= -16 + 2 + 5 = -9$

3. $g(x) = x^3 + 3x^2 + 2x$
$= x(x^2 + 3x + 2)$
$= x(x + 1)(x + 2)$
$x = 0$ or $x + 1 = 0$ or $x + 2 = 0$
$x + 1 - 1 = 0 - 1$ $\quad x + 2 - 2 = 0 - 2$
$x = -1$ $\quad x = -2$

4. $x - 2(3x - 1)$
$= x - 2(3x) - 2(-1)$
$= x - 6x + 2$
$= -5x + 2$

5. $3y^2(-3y) = -3 \cdot 3 \cdot y^2 \cdot y = -9y^{2+1} = -9y^3$

Lesson Practice 101

a. $f(x) = x^4 + 6x - 8$
The leading coefficient is 1 (since $x^4 = 1x^4$) and the degree is 4. The leading coefficient is positive and the degree is even.
Therefore, as $x \longrightarrow +\infty$, $f(x) \longrightarrow +\infty$, and as $x \longrightarrow -\infty$, $f(x) \longrightarrow +\infty$.

b. $g(x) = -2x^5 + 3x^4 - x$
The leading coefficient is -2 (negative) and degree is 5 (odd). Therefore, as $x \longrightarrow -\infty$, $g(x) \longrightarrow +\infty$, and as $x \longrightarrow +\infty$, $g(x) \longrightarrow -\infty$.

c. $f(x)$ is of odd degree with a negative leading coefficient.

d. $g(x)$ is of odd degree with a negative leading coefficient.

e. $f(x) = x^3 - 2x^2 - 5x + 6$

Use Rational Root Theorem p-values: ±1, ±2, ±3, ±6; q-values: ±1; so $\frac{p}{q} \in \{\pm1, \pm2, \pm3, \pm6\}$

First root that yields a factor:

$$\begin{array}{r|rrrr} 1 & 1 & -2 & -5 & 6 \\ & & 1 & -1 & -6 \\ \hline & 1 & -1 & -6 & 0 \end{array}$$

$$\begin{aligned} f(x) &= (x-1)(x^2 - x - 6) \\ &= (x-1)(x-3)(x+2) \end{aligned}$$

The real zeros are 1, 3, and −2. These are the x-intercepts.

x	−2	−1	0	1	2	3
y	0	8	6	0	−4	0

The y-intercept is 6.

The degree is odd and the leading coefficient is positive, so $x \longrightarrow +\infty$, $f(x) \longrightarrow \infty$, and as $x \longrightarrow -\infty$, $f(x) \longrightarrow -\infty$.

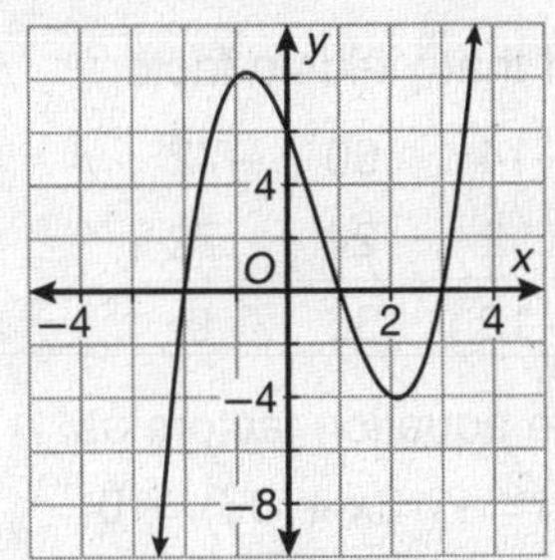

f. $g(x) = x^4 - 4x^3 + 3x + 8$

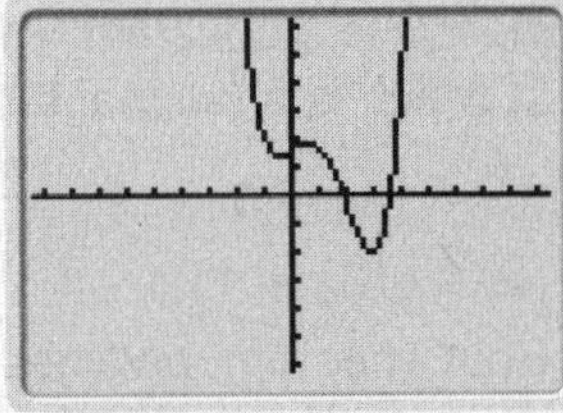

The graph appears to have two local minima and one local maximum.

Press **2nd** **TRACE** to access **CALC** menu. Choose **3:Minimum**.

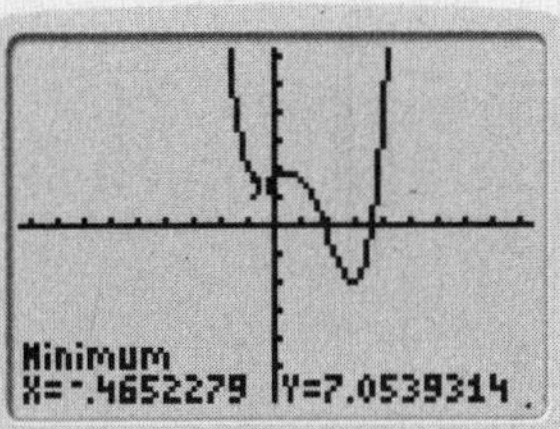

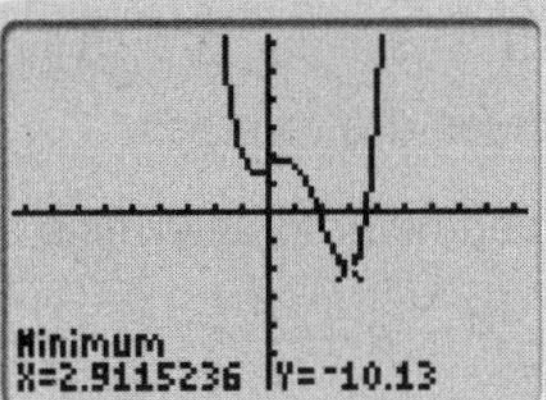

The local minima are about 7.0539 and −10.13.

Press **2nd** **TRACE** to access **CALC** menu. Choose **4:Maximum**.

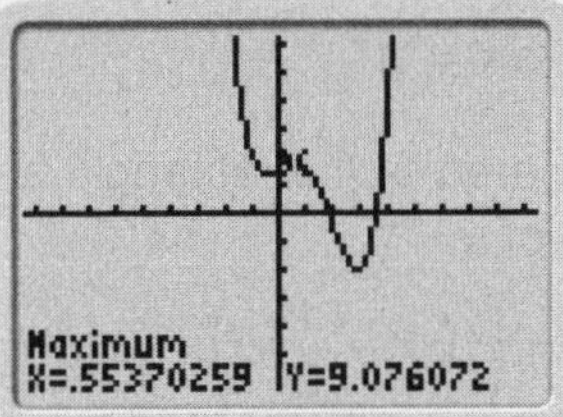

The local maximum is about 9.0761.

g. $V = x(8 - 2x)(10 - 2x)$

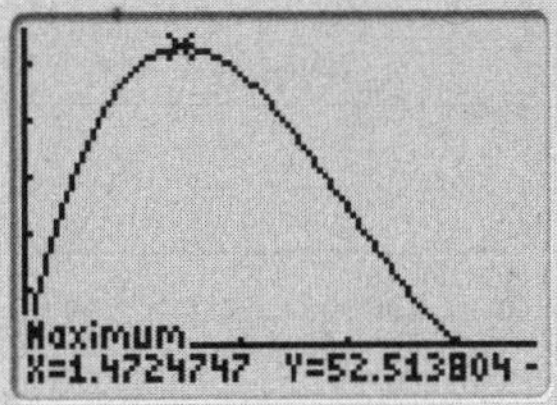

The graph has a local maximum of about 52.5 when $x \approx 1.47$. Therefore, the maximum possible volume is about 52.5 ft^3.

Practice 101

1. Determine the products.

$$AL = \begin{bmatrix} 2 & 7 \\ -1 & -2 \end{bmatrix} \begin{bmatrix} -\frac{2}{3} & -\frac{7}{3} \\ \frac{1}{3} & \frac{2}{3} \end{bmatrix}$$

$$= \begin{bmatrix} -\frac{4}{3} + \frac{7}{3} & -\frac{14}{3} + \frac{14}{3} \\ \frac{2}{3} - \frac{2}{3} & \frac{7}{3} - \frac{4}{3} \end{bmatrix} = \begin{bmatrix} 1 & 0 \\ 0 & 1 \end{bmatrix}$$

$$LA = \begin{bmatrix} -\frac{2}{3} & -\frac{7}{3} \\ \frac{1}{3} & \frac{2}{3} \end{bmatrix}\begin{bmatrix} 2 & 7 \\ -1 & -2 \end{bmatrix}$$

$$= \begin{bmatrix} -\frac{4}{3}+\frac{7}{3} & -\frac{14}{3}+\frac{14}{3} \\ \frac{2}{3}-\frac{2}{3} & \frac{7}{3}-\frac{4}{3} \end{bmatrix} = \begin{bmatrix} 1 & 0 \\ 0 & 1 \end{bmatrix}$$

The matrices are inverses.

2. Use the perimeter to determine a in terms of x.

$$P = a + \frac{1}{2}(\pi x) + a + \frac{1}{2}(\pi x)$$

$$200 = 2a + \pi x$$

$$\frac{200}{2} = \frac{2a}{2} + \frac{\pi x}{2}$$

$$100 = a + \frac{1}{2}\pi x$$

$$100 - \frac{1}{2}\pi x = a$$

Find the area of the rectangle as a function of x.

$$A = ax = \left(100 - \frac{1}{2}\pi x\right)x$$

Graph the area function to determine maximum.

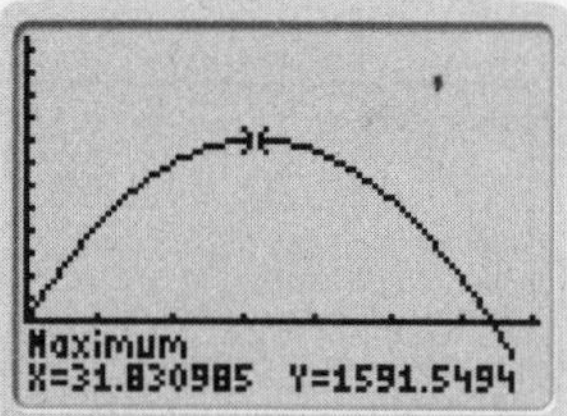

The graph has a local maximum of about 1592 when $x \approx 31.8$. Therefore, the maximum possible area is about 1592 in^2.

3. $$A = P\left(1 + \frac{r}{n}\right)^{nt}$$

$$1800 = 1000\left(1 + \frac{0.06}{12}\right)^{12t}$$

$$1.8 = (1 + 0.005)^{12t}$$

$$\log 1.8 = \log(1.005)^{12t}$$

$$\log 1.8 = 12t \log 1.005$$

$$12t = \frac{\log 1.8}{\log 1.005}$$

$$12t \approx 117.85$$

$$t \approx 9.82 \text{ years}$$

It takes about 9.82 years.

4. The student did not test regions and chose the wrong region for solutions.

Correct solution: Use test values −7, 0, and 3:

$$x^2 + 4x - 12 > 0 \qquad x^2 + 4x - 12 > 0$$

$$(-7)^2 + 4(-7) - 12 \overset{?}{>} 0 \qquad (0)^2 + 4(0) - 12 \overset{?}{>} 0$$

$$49 - 28 - 12 \overset{?}{>} 0 \qquad 0 + 0 - 12 \overset{?}{>} 0$$

$$9 > 0 \qquad -12 \not> 0$$

$$x^2 + 4x - 12 > 0$$

$$(3)^2 + 4(3) - 12 \overset{?}{>} 0$$

$$9 + 12 - 12 \overset{?}{>} 0$$

$$9 > 0$$

The solutions are $x < -6$ or $x > 2$.

5. $$0.1x^3 - 1.4x^2 + 6.0x - 7.2 = 0$$

$$10(0.1x^3 - 1.4x^2 + 6.0x - 7.2) = 10(0)$$

$$x^3 - 14x^2 + 60x - 72 = 0$$

By the Rational Root Theorem: p-values: ±1, ±2, ±3, ±4, ±6, ...; q-values: ±1; so $\frac{p}{q} \in \{\pm1, \pm2, \pm3, \pm4, \pm6, \ldots\}$

First root that yields a factor:

2	1	−14	60	−72
		2	−24	72
	1	−12	36	0

Therefore equation factors as

$$(x - 2)(x^2 - 12x + 36) = 0$$

$$(x - 2)(x - 6)^2 = 0$$

The roots are $x = 2$ and 6.

6. $xy = k$, where k is a constant. This means that $y = \frac{k}{x}$, which is a rational function.

7. $6x^3 - 12x^2 - 18x + 6$

$= 6(x^3 - 2x^2 - 3x + 1)$

Rational Root Theorem: p-values, q-values, and therefore possible rational roots are ±1.

1	1	−2	−3	1
		1	−1	−4
	1	−1	−4	−3

−1	1	−2	−3	1
		−1	3	0
	1	−3	0	1

Expression does not factor

8. $x^2 - 64 = x^2 - 8^2$

$= (x - 8)(x + 8)$

9. $W = \overrightarrow{F} \cdot \overrightarrow{d}$

$= |\overrightarrow{F}||\overrightarrow{d}|\cos\theta$

$= (25)(10)\cos 45°$

$= 250 \cos 45° \approx 176.78$

The work exerted is about 176.78 J.

10. $x^2 = 25$ $\quad$ $y + 4 = 16$

$x = \pm\sqrt{25}$ $\quad$ $y + 4 - 4 = 16 - 4$

$= \pm 5$ $\quad$ $y = 12$

$1 = z + 2$

$1 - 2 = x + 2 - 2$

$-1 = z$

Finally, substitute for y

$\frac{y}{2} = x + 1$

$\frac{12}{2} = x + 1$

$6 - 1 = x + 1 - 1$

$5 = x$

Solution is $x = 5$, $y = 12$, $z = -1$.

11. For $x = -3$, $f(x) = -12$, so $f(-3) = -12$.
For $x = 4$, $f(x) = 7x$, so $f(4) = 7(4) = 28$.

12. There are 31 choices for flavor, 2 choices for topping, and 2 choices for syrup. Total # of choices $= 31 \cdot 2 \cdot 2 = 124$

13. The 100th term is -3 because the common ratio is -1, so every even-numbered term is -3.

14. Use vertex form with $h = \frac{65}{2} = 32.5$ and $k = 45$.

$y = a(x - h)^2 + k$

$y = a(x - 32.5)^2 + 45$

The graph passes through (0, 0).

$0 = a(0 - 32.5)^2 + 45$

$0 = 1056.25a + 45$

$-45 = 1056.25a$

$a = \frac{-45}{1056.25} \approx -0.043$

The function is therefore

$y \approx -0.043(x - 32.5)^2 + 45$

15. z-score for 25.9 is

$z = \frac{x - \text{mean}}{\text{s.d.}}$

$= \frac{25.9 - 34}{2.7}$

$= \frac{-8.1}{2.7} = -3$

25.9 is 3 s.d.'s below the mean. The middle 99.7% of data are within 3 s.d.'s of mean, so 0.15% are below 25.9.

16. Heron's formula is

$A = \sqrt{s(s - a)(s - b)(s - c)}$

where

$s = \frac{1}{2}(a + b + c)$

$= \frac{1}{2}(14 + 19 + 21)$

$= \frac{1}{2}(54) = 27$

$A = \sqrt{s(s - a)(s - b)(s - c)}$

$= \sqrt{27(27 - 14)(27 - 19)(27 - 21)}$

$= \sqrt{27(13)(8)(6)}$

$= \sqrt{16{,}848} \approx 129.8$

The area is about 129.8 m^2.

17. a.

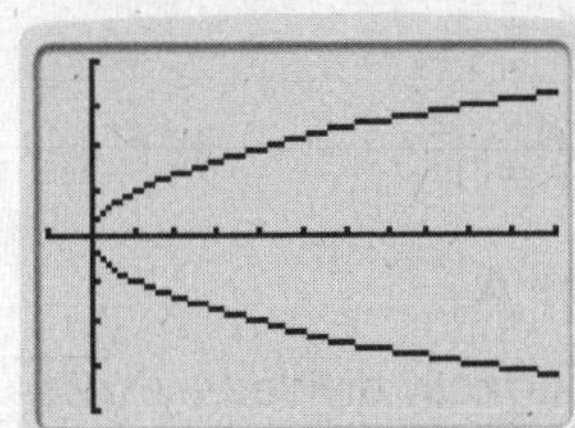

b. Sample: Parabola

c. $r = \frac{\cos\theta}{\sin^2\theta}$

$r\sin^2\theta = \cos\theta$

$r^2\sin^2\theta = r\cos\theta$

$(r\sin\theta)^2 = r\cos\theta$

Let $r\sin\theta = y$ and $r\cos\theta = x$,

$y^2 = x$

d. Interchange the variables: the equation is the inverse of $y = x^2$.

18. $\begin{bmatrix} 3 & 2 & 3 \\ 2 & 3 & 2 \\ 3 & 1 & 3 \end{bmatrix}\begin{bmatrix} 6 \\ 3 \\ 1 \end{bmatrix}$

$= \begin{bmatrix} 3(6) + 2(3) + 3(1) \\ 2(6) + 3(3) + 2(1) \\ 3(6) + 1(3) + 3(1) \end{bmatrix}$

$= \begin{bmatrix} 18 + 6 + 3 \\ 12 + 9 + 2 \\ 18 + 3 + 3 \end{bmatrix} = \begin{bmatrix} 27 \\ 23 \\ 24 \end{bmatrix}$

The most points were scored in game #9.

19. $\log 3x^4 = \log 3 + \log x^4$

$= \log 3 + 4 \log x$

20.

x	1	2	3	4
y	4	2	$1\frac{1}{3}$	1
xy	4	4	4	4

Since xy is constant, the relationship is an inverse variation. Answer Choice **C**

21. Substitute values for x and y.

$$\frac{x^2}{4^2} + \frac{y^2}{7^2} = 1$$

$$\frac{(-7)^2}{4^2} + \frac{(0)^2}{7^2} \stackrel{?}{=} 1$$

$$\frac{49}{4} + \frac{0}{7} \stackrel{?}{=} 1$$

$$\frac{49}{4} \neq 1$$

Answer Choice **A**

22. Student A incorrectly divided by $\sqrt{2+1}$ instead of $\frac{1}{\sqrt{2+1}}$.

23. If the LCD includes a variable and one of the fractions has the variable in the numerator, but not in the denominator, the variables will be multiplied together when both sides are multiplied by the LCD because they will not divide out. For example,

$$\frac{5}{x} + \frac{x}{3} = 10$$

$$3x\left(\frac{5}{x}\right) + 3x\left(\frac{x}{3}\right) = 3x(10)$$

$$15 + 3x^2 = 30x$$

$$3x^2 - 30x + 15 = 0$$

24. Given $\log_b x$, use x as new log argument in numerator with new base a: $\log_a x$. Use b as new log argument in denominator with new base a: $\log_a b$. This can be used in the same manner with natural logarithms.

25. $y = a\tan(bx + c)$

$= a\tan\left(b\left(x + \frac{c}{b}\right)\right)$

$= a\tan\left(b\left(x - \left(-\frac{c}{b}\right)\right)\right)$

Period $= \frac{\pi}{b}$; phase shift $= -\frac{c}{b}$

26. $\frac{f(x)}{f(g(x))} = \frac{x-1}{f(x^2-1)}$

$= \frac{x-1}{(x^2-1)-1}$

$= \frac{x-1}{x^2-2}$

$= \frac{x-1}{x^2-\left(\sqrt{2}\right)^2}$

$= \frac{x-1}{(x-\sqrt{2})(x+\sqrt{2})}$

Since there are no common factors in the numerator and denominator, the vertical asymptotes are at $x = \sqrt{2}$ and $x = -\sqrt{2}$.

27. $P(x) = x^3 - 10x^2 + 19x + 30$

Use synthetic division with $a = 6$.

$$\begin{array}{r|rrrr} 6 & 1 & -10 & 19 & 30 \\ & & 6 & -24 & -30 \\ \hline & 1 & -4 & -5 & 0 \end{array}$$

$P(6) = R(6) = 0$. By Remainder Theorem, $x - 6$ is a factor.

28. $P(x) = (x-6)(x^2 - 4x - 5)$

$= (x-6)(x-5)(x+1)$

29. $y < -5x + 3$

$1 \stackrel{?}{<} -5(1) + 3$

$1 \stackrel{?}{<} -5 + 3$

$1 \not< -2$

(1, 1) is not a solution.

30. All the functions are in standard form except

$h(x) = -3x^3 - 3x^4 + x^5$
$= x^5 - 3x^4 - 3x^3$

$f(x)$, $g(x)$, and $h(x)$ all have odd degree and a positive leading coefficient, but $k(x)$ has odd degree and a negative leading coefficient. Therefore the end behavior of $k(x)$ is different.

LESSON 102

Warm Up 102

1. base

2. $\log_3 9 = \log_3 3^2 = 2 \log_3 3 = 2(1) = 2$

3. true, by Product Property of Logarithms

4. false

$\log a - \log(a - 6) = \log \dfrac{a}{a-6}$
$\neq \log[a - (a - 6)]$

5. $\log_b a = y \Leftrightarrow b^y = a$

$\log_x x = 1 \Leftrightarrow x^1 = x$

Lesson Practice 102

a. $\log_3(x - 1) = 2$

$3^{\log_3(x-1)} = 3^2$ use 3 as a base for both sides

$x - 1 = 9$
$x - 1 + 1 = 9 + 1$
$x = 10$

b. $\log_{125} x^3 = 4$

$3 \log_{125} x = 4$ Power Prop. of Log.

$\dfrac{3 \log_{125} x}{3} = \dfrac{4}{3}$

$\log_{125} x = \dfrac{4}{3}$

$x = 125^{\frac{4}{3}}$

$x = (5^3)^{\frac{4}{3}}$

$x = 5^4 = 625$

c. $\log x + \log(x + 9) = 1$

$\log[x(x + 9)] = 1$ Prod. Prop. of Log.

$x(x + 9) = 10^1$

$x^2 + 9x = 10$
$x^2 + 9x - 10 = 0$
$(x - 1)(x + 10) = 0$
$x - 1 = 0$ or $x + 10 = 0$
$x - 1 + 1 = 0 + 1$ $\quad x + 10 - 10 = 0 - 10$
$x = 1$ $\quad x = -10$

$x = -10$ is not a solution because log is not defined for negative numbers. The solution is $x = 1$.

d. $\log 45x - \log 3 \geq 1$

$\log\left(\dfrac{45x}{3}\right) \geq 1$ Quotient Prop. of Log.

$\log 15x \geq 1$

$10^{\log 15x} \geq 10^1$

$15x \geq 10$

$\dfrac{15x}{15} \geq \dfrac{10}{15}$

$x \geq \dfrac{2}{3}$

e. Enter $\log x - \log 2$ as Y1 and $\log 75$ as Y2. Find x-value of point of intersection:

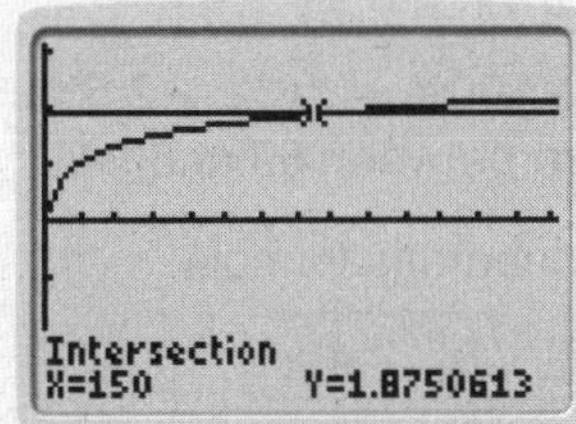

Find x-value for which Y1 = Y2.

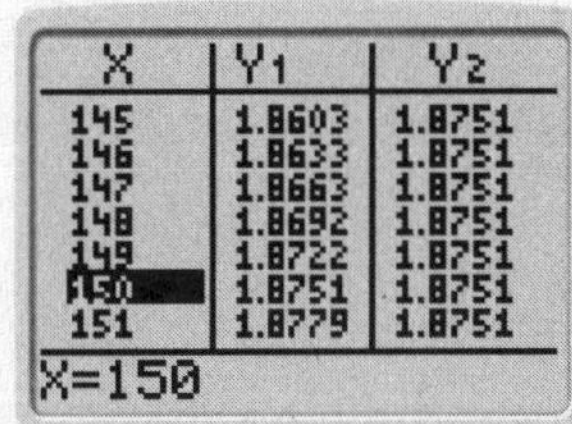

X	Y1	Y2
145	1.8603	1.8751
146	1.8633	1.8751
147	1.8663	1.8751
148	1.8692	1.8751
149	1.8722	1.8751
150	1.8751	1.8751
151	1.8779	1.8751

X=150

The solution is $x = 150$.

$\log x - \log 2 = \log 75$

f. If the population is 10,000,000 then $y = 10{,}000$.

$3875 + 1876 \ln t = y$

$3875 + 1876 \ln t = 10{,}000$

$1876 \ln t = 6125$

$\ln t = \dfrac{6125}{1876}$

$\ln t \approx 3.265$

$t \approx e^{3.265} \approx 26.2$

If $t = 10$ represents 1950, then $t = 0$ is 1940.
$t \approx 26.2$ represents $1940 + 26.2 = 1966.2$.
The population reached 10,000,000 in 1966.

Practice 102

1. z-score for 69:

$$z = \frac{x - \text{mean}}{\text{s.d.}}$$

$$= \frac{69 - 74}{5} = -\frac{5}{5} = -1$$

Middle 68% of scores are within 1 s.d. of mean, so $\frac{100\% - 68\%}{2} = \frac{32\%}{2} = 16\%$ of scores are below $74 - 5 = 69$.

z-score for 84:

$$z = \frac{x - \text{mean}}{\text{s.d.}}$$

$$= \frac{84 - 74}{5} = \frac{10}{5} = 2$$

Middle 95% of scores are within 2 s.d.'s of mean, so $\frac{100\% - 95\%}{2} = \frac{5\%}{2} = 2.5\%$ of scores are above $74 + 2(5) = 84$.

Therefore $100\% - 16\% - 2.5\% = 81.5\%$ of scores are between 69 and 84.

2. Use the quadratic formula.

$$x = \frac{-b \pm \sqrt{b^2 - 4ac}}{2a}$$

$$= \frac{-5 \pm \sqrt{5^2 - 4(4)(-1)}}{2(4)}$$

$$= \frac{-5 \pm \sqrt{25 + 16}}{-8}$$

$$= \frac{-5 \pm \sqrt{41}}{8}$$

$x \approx -1.4254$ or $x \approx 0.1754$

3. $y = x^4 - 16$

$= (x^2)^2 - 4^2$

$= (x^2 - 4)(x^2 + 4)$

$= (x^2 - 2^2)(x^2 + 4)$

$= (x - 2)(x + 2)(x^2 + 4)$

The roots are $x = 2$ and -2.

4. $-4.4 + 12.6 \ln t = y$

If $y = 30\%$

$-4.4 + 12.6 \ln t = 30$

$12.6 \ln t = 34.4$

$$\ln t = \frac{34.4}{12.6}$$

$\ln t \approx 2.73$

$t \approx e^{2.73} \approx 15.3$

If $t = 5$ represents 1935, then $t = 0$ is 1930. $1930 + 15.3 = 1945.3$, so union membership reached 30% in 1945.

5. The graph is decreasing as x moves through 4 toward $+\infty$. Therefore, as $x \rightarrow +\infty$, $P(x) \rightarrow -\infty$. Degree is odd, so as $x \rightarrow -\infty$, $P(x) \rightarrow +\infty$.

6. Let r represent the speed limit inside a business or residential district; then the speed limit outside the district is $2r$. Use the formula $v = \frac{d}{t} \rightarrow t = \frac{d}{v}$.

time inside + time outside = 2

$$\frac{12.5}{r} + \frac{75}{2r} = 2$$

$$(2r)\left(\frac{12.5}{r} + \frac{75}{2r}\right) = (2r)(2)$$

$25 + 75 = 4r$

$100 = 4r$

$25 = r$

The speed limit inside a business or residential district is 25 mi/hr.

7. $$P(\text{outside ellipse}) = \frac{A_{\text{ellipse}} - A_{\text{circle}}}{A_{\text{ellipse}}}$$

$$= \frac{\pi ab - \pi a^2}{\pi ab}$$

$$= \frac{\pi a(b - a)}{\pi a(b)}$$

$$= \frac{b - a}{b}$$

8. A is at the origin, so $A = A(0, 0)$ is one set of polar coordinates.

$B = B(4, 12)$ in Cartesian coordinates: $\tan\theta = \frac{y}{x} = \frac{12}{4} = 3$, and θ terminates in Quad. I, so one value of θ is $\tan^{-1} 3$.

$r^2 = x^2 + y^2$

$= (4)^2 + (12)^2$

$= 16 + 144 = 160$

$r = \sqrt{160} = \sqrt{16}\sqrt{10} = 4\sqrt{10}$

$B = B(4\sqrt{10}, \tan^{-1} 3)$ is the second set of polar coordinates.

$C = C(14, 12)$ in Cartesian coordinates: $\tan \theta = \frac{y}{x} = \frac{12}{14} = \frac{6}{7}$, and θ terminates in Quad. I, so one value of θ is $\tan^{-1}\left(\frac{6}{7}\right)$.

$$r^2 = x^2 + y^2$$
$$= (14)^2 + (12)^2$$
$$= 196 + 144 = 340$$
$$r = \sqrt{340} = \sqrt{4}\sqrt{85} = 2\sqrt{85}$$

$C = C(2\sqrt{85}, \tan^{-1}\left(\frac{6}{7}\right))$ is the third set of polar coordinates.

$D = D(18, 0)$ in Cartesian coordinates: one value of θ is 0, and $r = 18$.

$D = D(18, 0)$ is the final set of polar coordinates.

9. The vectors must have same magnitude and opposite directions.

10. $|T| = \begin{vmatrix} -6 & -2 \\ 11 & -3 \end{vmatrix}$

$$= (-6)(-3) - (-2)(11)$$
$$= 18 + 22 = 40$$

$$T^{-1} = \frac{1}{40}\begin{bmatrix} -3 & 2 \\ -11 & -6 \end{bmatrix}$$

$$= \begin{bmatrix} \frac{-3}{40} & \frac{2}{40} \\ \frac{-11}{40} & \frac{-6}{40} \end{bmatrix} = \begin{bmatrix} -\frac{3}{40} & \frac{1}{20} \\ -\frac{11}{40} & -\frac{3}{20} \end{bmatrix}$$

11. Surface area of cylinder $= 2\pi rh + 2\pi r^2$.
Volume of cylinder $= \pi r^2 h$.

$$f(r,h) = \frac{2\pi rh + 2\pi r^2}{\pi r^2 h}$$
$$= \frac{\pi r(2h + 2r)}{\pi r(rh)}$$
$$= \frac{2h + 2r}{rh}$$

The asymptotes are at $h = 0$ and $r = 0$.

12. Use the Law of Cosines:

$$c^2 = a^2 + b^2 - 2ab \cos C$$
$$CL^2 = JC^2 + JL^2 - 2(JC)(JL)\cos J$$
$$CL^2 = 28^2 + 37^2 - 2(28)(37)\cos 18°$$
$$CL^2 \approx 784 + 1369 - 2072(0.9511) \approx 182.4$$
$$CL \approx \sqrt{182.4} \approx 13.5$$

The distance from Carlinville to Litchfield is about 13.5 mi.

13. $S = 4\pi r^2$

$$\frac{S}{4\pi} = \frac{4\pi r^2}{4\pi} = r^2$$
$$\pm\sqrt{\frac{S}{4\pi}} = r$$

Solving the surface area formula for r yields two possible solutions, one negative and one positive. The radius cannot be negative.

$$V = \frac{4}{3}\pi r^3$$
$$\frac{3}{4\pi}V = \frac{3}{4\pi} \cdot \frac{4}{3}\pi r^3 = r^3$$
$$\sqrt[3]{\frac{3V}{4\pi}} = r$$

Solving the volume formula for r yields only a positive solution, which is a possible solution for the radius.

14. Sample: To solve $4^x = 100$, take logs of both sides, obtaining the equivalent equation $\log 4^x = \log 100$. Then apply the Power Property of Logarithms and the fact that $\log 100 = 2$, obtaining the equivalent equation $x \log 4 = 2$.

15. The population is all residents in the town; the sample is 80 dog owners surveyed.

16. $\log 5x + \log 2 = 4$

$$\log[(5x)(2)] = 4$$
$$\log 10x = 4$$
$$\log 10 + \log x = 4$$
$$1 + \log x = 4$$
$$\log x = 4 - 1 = 3$$
$$x = 10^3 = 1000$$

Answer Choice **A**

17. $\log_4(4x + 7) = \log_4 11x$

$$4^{\log_4(4x+7)} = 4^{\log_4 11x}$$
$$4x + 7 = 11x$$
$$7 = 7x$$
$$1 = x$$

18. a. Enter $9\left(\frac{2}{3}\right)^{x-1}$ for Y1. Access **TABLE** and arrow down to 14 in the X-column. Find corresponding value of Y1.

b. Sample: Enter $9\left(\frac{2}{3}\right)^{x-1}$ for Y1. Press **2nd** **TRACE** to access **CALC** menu and choose **1:value** Type in 14 for the x-value and press **ENTER**. The y-value is displayed.

c.

X	Y1
8	.52675
9	.35117
10	.23411
11	.15607
12	.10405
13	.06937
14	.04624

X=14

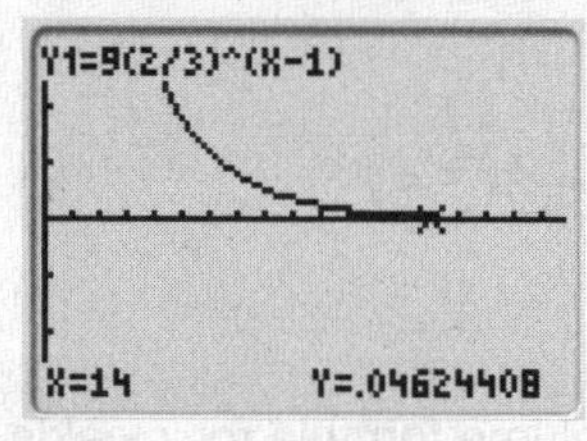

$y \approx 0.0462$

19. Amplitude $= a = 3$.

Period $= \frac{2\pi}{b} = \frac{2\pi}{\frac{1}{2}} = \frac{4\pi}{1} = 4\pi$

20. Substitute $h = 0$, $h_0 = 2000$, and $v_0 = 200$.

$h = -1.885t^2 + v_0t + h_0$

$0 = -1.885t^2 + 200t + 2000$

Use the quadratic formula.

$$t = \frac{-b \pm \sqrt{b^2 - 4ac}}{2a}$$

$$= \frac{-200 \pm \sqrt{200^2 - 4(-1.885)(2000)}}{2(-1.885)}$$

$$= \frac{-200 \pm \sqrt{40{,}000 + 15{,}080}}{-3.77}$$

$$= \frac{200 \pm \sqrt{55{,}080}}{3.77}$$

$$\approx \frac{200 \pm 234.7}{3.77}$$

Ignore the negative solution.

$$t \approx \frac{434.7}{3.77} \approx 115.3$$

The landing takes about 115.3 seconds.

21. The student chose the degree of the first term, not the term with the greatest degree. The degree is 4.

22. a.

$$(x - h)^2 + (y - k)^2 = r^2$$
$$(x - (-1))^2 + (y - (-3))^2 = 12^2$$
$$(x + 1)^2 + (y + 3)^2 = 144$$

b. Sample: Change the equation to an inequality $(x + 1)^2 + (y + 3)^2 \le 144$ and substitute $(11, -2)$ for x and y.

$$(11 + 1)^2 + (-2 + 3)^2 \overset{?}{\le} 144$$
$$(12)^2 + (1)^2 \overset{?}{\le} 144$$
$$144 + 1 \overset{?}{\le} 144$$
$$145 \not\le 144$$

Since the inequality is false, the building was not in affected area.

23. a. $AB = \begin{bmatrix} 10 & 1 \\ 4 & 10 \end{bmatrix}\begin{bmatrix} 11 & 4 \\ 16 & 11 \end{bmatrix}$

$= \begin{bmatrix} 110 + 16 & 40 + 11 \\ 44 + 160 & 16 + 110 \end{bmatrix}$

$= \begin{bmatrix} 126 & 51 \\ 204 & 126 \end{bmatrix}$

b. $BA = \begin{bmatrix} 11 & 4 \\ 16 & 11 \end{bmatrix}\begin{bmatrix} 10 & 1 \\ 4 & 10 \end{bmatrix}$

$= \begin{bmatrix} 110 + 16 & 11 + 40 \\ 160 + 44 & 16 + 110 \end{bmatrix}$

$= \begin{bmatrix} 126 & 51 \\ 204 & 126 \end{bmatrix}$

c. Yes, $\begin{bmatrix} 126 & 51 \\ 204 & 126 \end{bmatrix} = \begin{bmatrix} 126 & 51 \\ 204 & 126 \end{bmatrix}$.

24. Sample:

$$x = 6 \pm 2i$$
$$x - 6 = \pm 2i$$
$$x - 6 = \pm\sqrt{-4}$$
$$(x - 6)^2 = -4$$
$$x^2 - 12x + 36 = -4$$
$$x^2 - 12x + 36 + 4 = -4 + 4$$
$$x^2 - 12x + 40 = 0$$

25. $y = \frac{x^2 + 3x - 4}{x - 2}$

$y = \frac{(x - 1)(x + 4)}{x - 2}$

Since there are no common factors in the numerator and denominator, there is one vertical asymptote, at $x = 2$.

26. $\dfrac{(x-h)^2}{a^2}+\dfrac{(y-k)^2}{b^2}=1$

$\dfrac{(x-0)^2}{(4)^2}+\dfrac{(y-0)^2}{(6)^2}=1$

$\dfrac{x^2}{16}+\dfrac{y^2}{36}=1$

27. Use synthetic division with $a = 2$.

$$\begin{array}{r|rrrr} 2 & 1 & 0 & 0 & -6 \\ & & 2 & 4 & 8 \\ \hline & 1 & 2 & 4 & 2 \end{array}$$

$(x^3 - 6) \div (x - 2) = x^2 + 2x + 4 + \dfrac{2}{x-2}$

28. Use synthetic division with $a = -1$.

$$\begin{array}{r|rrrr} -1 & 1 & 3 & 7 & 5 \\ & & -1 & -2 & -5 \\ \hline & 1 & 2 & 5 & 0 \end{array}$$

$(x^3 + 3x^2 + 7x + 5) \div (x + 1) = x^2 + 2x + 5$

29. $d = \sqrt{(x_2 - x_1)^2 + (y_2 - y_1)^2}$

$= \sqrt{(3-(-2))^2 + (4-5)^2}$

$= \sqrt{5^2 + (-1)^2}$

$= \sqrt{25+1} = \sqrt{26}$

30. $4\begin{bmatrix} 2 & 1 \\ -6 & 3.5 \end{bmatrix} - 3\begin{bmatrix} 0 & 0.4 \\ 8 & -2 \end{bmatrix}$

$= \begin{bmatrix} 8 & 4 \\ -24 & 14 \end{bmatrix} - \begin{bmatrix} 0 & 1.2 \\ 24 & -6 \end{bmatrix}$

$= \begin{bmatrix} 8-0 & 4-1.2 \\ -24-24 & 14-(-6) \end{bmatrix} = \begin{bmatrix} 8 & 2.8 \\ -48 & 20 \end{bmatrix}$

LESSON 103

Warm Up 103

1. reciprocal
2. Period $= \dfrac{\pi}{b} = \dfrac{\pi}{1} = \pi$
3. Asymptotes are where

$\tan(2x) = 0$

$2x = \dfrac{\pi}{2} + n\pi$

$x = \dfrac{\pi}{4} + n\dfrac{\pi}{2}$

4. The graph is a vertical stretch of the parent function $y = \cos x$.

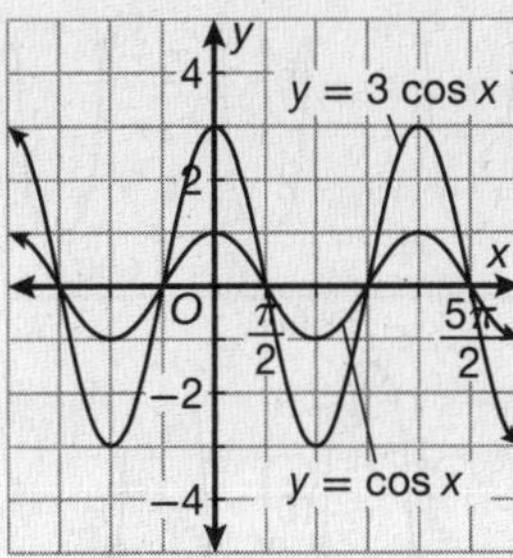

Lesson Practice 103

a. $y = 2\csc(x)$ has period 2π and asymptotes at $\sin x = 0$, or $x = n\pi$.

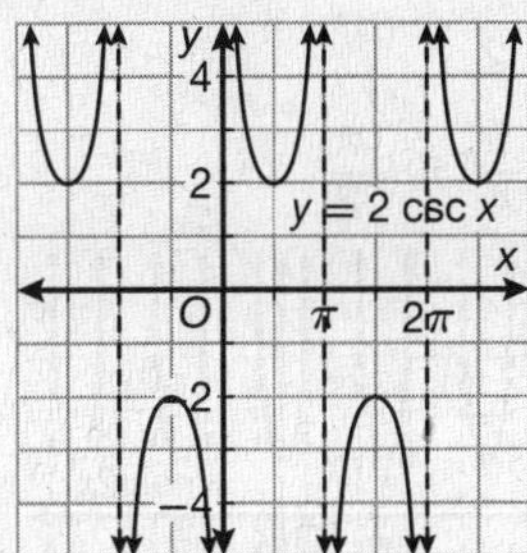

b. $y = \csc\left(\frac{1}{2}x\right)$ has period $\frac{2\pi}{\frac{1}{2}} = 4\pi$, and asymptotes at

$\sin\left(\frac{1}{2}x\right) = 0$

$\dfrac{1}{2}x = n\pi$

$x = 2n\pi$

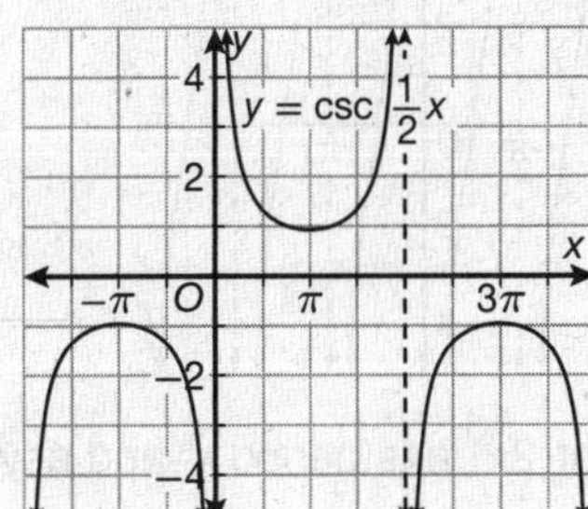

c. $y = 3\sec(x)$ has period 2π and asymptotes at $\cos x = 0$, or $x = \frac{\pi}{2} + n\pi$.

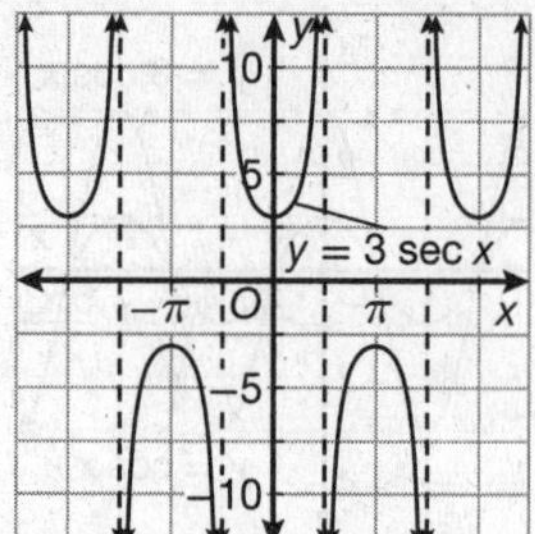

d. $y = \sec(2x)$ has period $\frac{2\pi}{2} = \pi$ and asymptotes at

$$\cos 2x = 0$$

$$2x = \frac{\pi}{2} + n\pi$$

$$x = \frac{\pi}{4} + n\frac{\pi}{2}$$

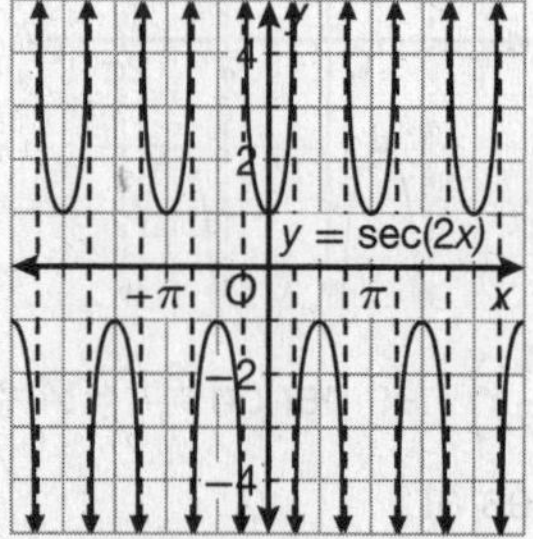

e. $y = 4\cot(x)$ has period π and asymptotes at $\tan x = 0$, or $x = n\pi$.

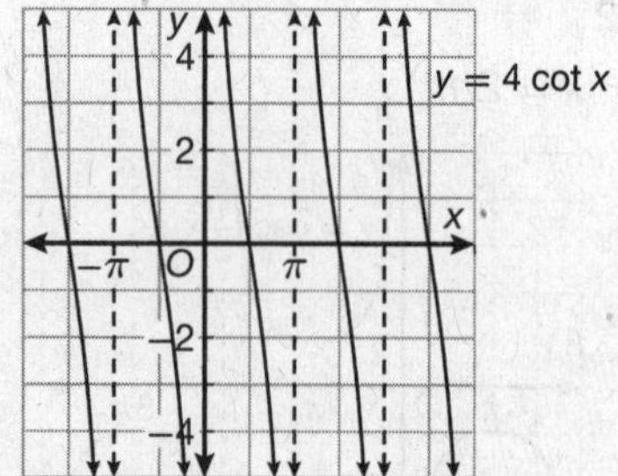

f. $y = \frac{1}{4}\cot(2x)$ has period $\frac{\pi}{2}$ and asymptotes at $x = \frac{n\pi}{2}$

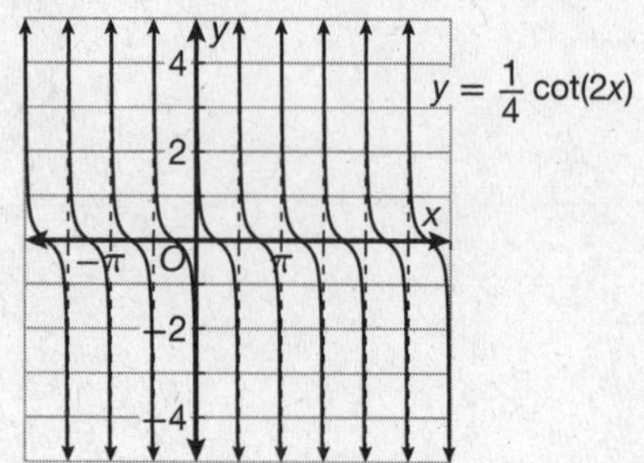

g. Enter Y1 $= \frac{\left(\frac{4}{5}\right)}{\sin(X)}$; press ZOOM and select **7:Z Trig**.

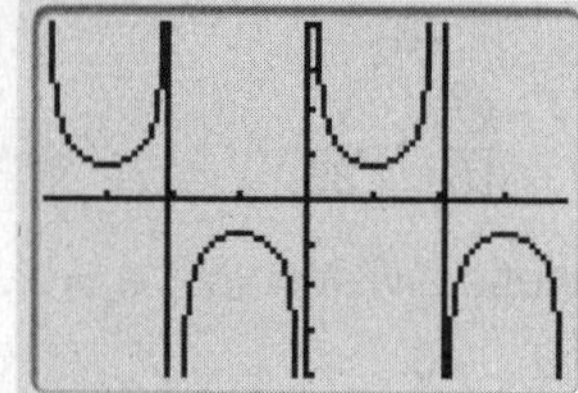

h. Use the cotangent function:

$$\cot x = \frac{\text{adj.}}{\text{opp.}} = \frac{y}{22{,}000}$$

$$22{,}000 \cot x = y$$

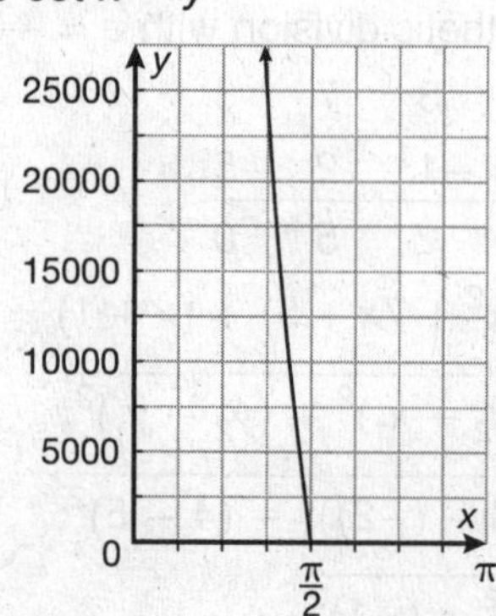

Practice 103

1. Enter Y1 $= \frac{3}{\cos(2X)}$; press ZOOM and select **7:Z Trig**.

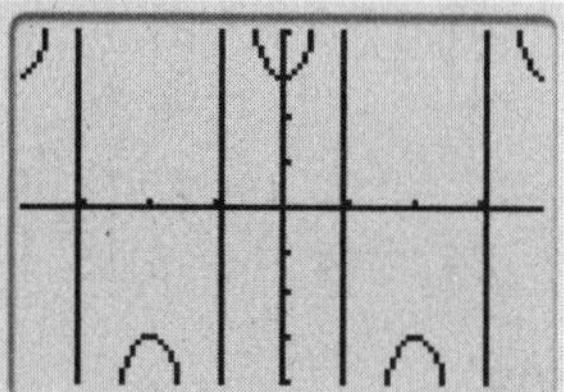

2. a.

$$V = \frac{\pi(r^2 + rR + R^2)h}{3}$$

$$3V = \pi(r^2 + rR + R^2)h$$

$$\frac{3V}{\pi(r^2 + rR + R^2)} = \frac{\pi(r^2 + rR + R^2)h}{\pi(r^2 + rR + R^2)}$$

$$\frac{3V}{\pi(r^2 + rR + R^2)} = h$$

b. $h = \frac{3V}{\pi(r^2 + rR + R^2)}$

$$h = \frac{3(500)}{\pi((4)^2 + (4)(5) + (5)^2)}$$

$$= \frac{1500}{\pi(16 + 20 + 25)} = \frac{1500}{\pi(61)} \approx 7.83$$

The minimum height is about 7.9 cm.

3. $A(x) = 96x - 3x^2$

Use a graphing calculator to graph $A(x)$ and determine its maximum.

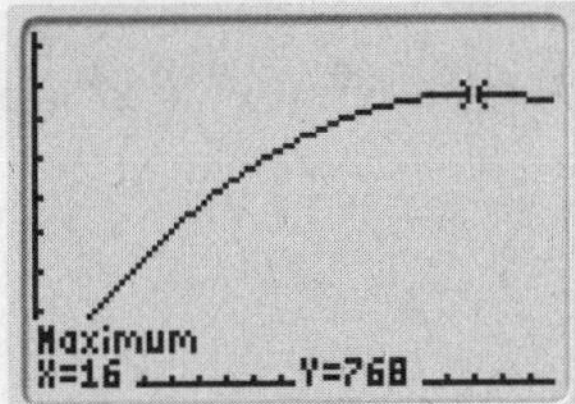

The maximum area is 768 ft^2.

4. $x = r\cos\theta$ $\quad$ $y = r\sin\theta$

$= 5\cos\left(-\frac{\pi}{4}\right)$ $\quad$ $= 5\sin\left(-\frac{\pi}{4}\right)$

$= 5 \cdot \frac{\sqrt{2}}{2} = \frac{5\sqrt{2}}{2}$ $\quad$ $= 5\left(-\frac{\sqrt{2}}{2}\right) = -\frac{5\sqrt{2}}{2}$

Answer Choice **C**

5. $a_n = a_1(r)^{n-1}$

$a_6 = 12{,}765{,}427(1.0052)^5 \approx 13{,}100{,}798$

6. There are 5 choices for each digit, and so $5^4 = 625$ choices for pass code.

7. Use a graphing calculator to graph $Y1 = -1.5X^2 + 80X - 600$ and determine where profit function is positive.

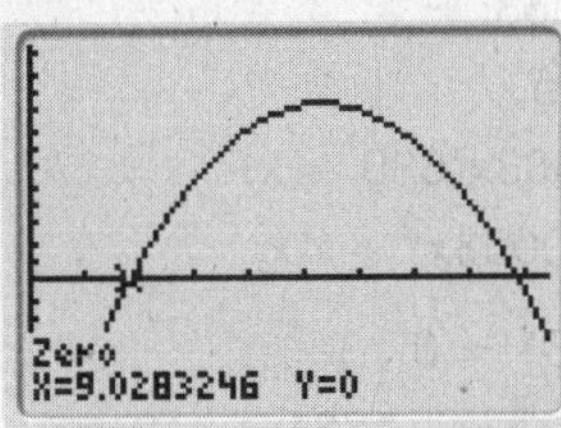

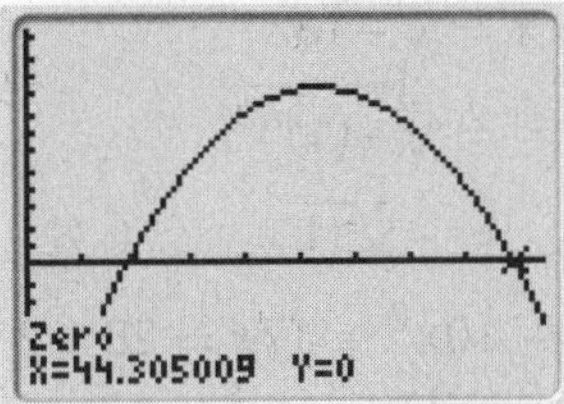

Profit is earned from \$10 to \$44 inclusive. Graph Y2 = 200 and determine intersections with Y1.

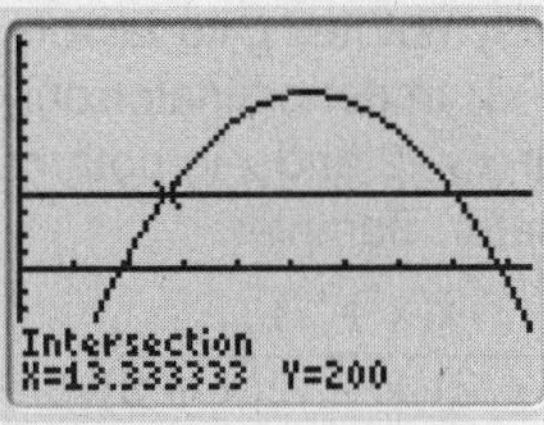

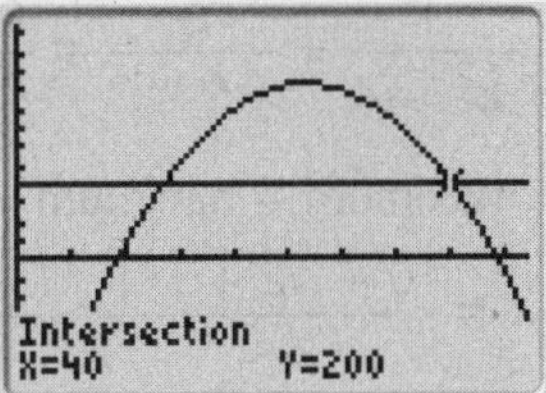

At least \$200 profit will be earned from \$14 to \$40 inclusive.

8. Solve the second equation for x.

$x + 4y = 2$

$x = 2 - 4y$

Substitute for x into the first equation and solve for y.

$2x + 5y = 7$

$2(2 - 4y) + 5y = 7$

$4 - 8y + 5y = 7$

$4 - 3y = 7$

$-3y = 3$

$y = -1$

Substitute for y in the second equation.

$x + 4y = 2$

$x + 4(-1) = 2$

$x = 6$

The solution is $(6, -1)$.

9. For $\overrightarrow{A} = a + bi$ and $\overrightarrow{B} = c + di$, consider the real and imaginary parts as horizontal and vertical components, respectively. Then

$\overrightarrow{A} \cdot \overrightarrow{B} = [a \quad b]\begin{bmatrix} c \\ d \end{bmatrix} = ac + bd$

10. Sample: The common difference is $19 - 15 = 4$. Using arithmetic sequence formula,

$a_n = a_1 + (n-1)d$

$a_n = 3 + (n-1)(4)$

$a_n = 3 + 4n - 4$

$a_n = 4n - 1$

This is the same as $y = 4x - 1$, where 4 is the slope.

11. Vertical asymptotes give factors of $(x-7)$ and $(x+3)$ in denominator only. Holes give factors of $x+2$ and x in both numerator and denominator. Sample:

$$y = \frac{x(x+2)}{x(x+2)(x-7)(x+3)}$$

12. $$\frac{1}{x^2-4} + \frac{3}{4x+8} = \frac{6}{x}$$

$$\frac{1}{(x-2)(x+2)} + \frac{3}{4(x+2)} = \frac{6}{x}$$

The LCD is $4x(x-2)(x+2)$.

Answer Choice **C**

13. Let $P_1(x) = x^6 + x^5 + x^4$ and $P_2(x) = x^3 + x^2 + x$.

Then

$P_1(x) + P_2(x) = x^6 + x^5 + x^4 + x^3 + x^2 + x.$

14. Range = maximum − minimum = 20 − 6 = 14

Mean is $\bar{x} = \dfrac{10+12+7+11+20+7+8+6+9}{9}$

$$= \frac{90}{9} = 10$$

Standard deviation is

$$\sigma = \sqrt{\frac{(10-10)^2 + (12-10)^2 + (7-10)^2 + (11-10)^2 + (20-10)^2 + (7-10)^2 + (8-10)^2 + (6-10)^2 + (9-10)^2}{9}}$$

$$= \sqrt{\frac{144}{9}} = \sqrt{16} = 4$$

15. Equation is

$\frac{x^2}{a^2} + \frac{y^2}{b^2} = 1$, where b = semi-minor axis = 2.

Substitute this value and $e = 0.92$ into formula for eccentricity:

$$e = \sqrt{1 - \frac{b^2}{a^2}}$$

$$0.92 = \sqrt{1 - \frac{2^2}{a^2}}$$

$$0.92^2 = 1 - \frac{4}{a^2}$$

$$\frac{4}{a^2} = 1 - 0.92^2 = 1 - 0.8464 = 0.1536$$

$$\frac{4}{0.1536} = a^2$$

$$a = \sqrt{\frac{4}{0.1536}} \approx 5.1$$

The equation is $\dfrac{x}{5.1^2} + \dfrac{y}{2^2} \approx 1.$

16. Graph passes through (0, 0), (315, 630) (vertex), and (630, 0). Use the vertex form of a quadratic function.

$y = a(x-h)^2 + k$

Substitute $h = 315$ and $k = 630$. Then substitute for an x-intercept and solve for a.

$y = a(x-315)^2 + 630$

$0 = a(0-315)^2 + 630$

$0 = 315^2 a + 630$

$a = \dfrac{630}{315^2}$

$a \approx 0.0063$

Therefore,

$y \approx 0.0063x(630 - x)$

$y \approx -0.0063x^2 + 4x$

17. $$x^9 + 1331 = 0$$

$$x^9 = -1331$$

$$x = \sqrt[9]{-1331}$$

$$= \sqrt[9]{-(11)^3}$$

$$= -\sqrt[3]{11}$$

18. $$x^3 + 10x^2 + 17x = 28$$

$$x^3 + 10x^2 + 17x - 28 = 0$$

Use Rational Root Theorem p-values are ±1, ±2, ±4, ±7, ±14, ±28; q-values are ±1; so

$\frac{p}{q} \in \{\pm1, \pm2, \pm4, \pm7, \pm14, \pm28\}$

First root that yields a factor:

$$\begin{array}{r|rrrr} 1 & 1 & 10 & 17 & -28 \\ & & 1 & 11 & 28 \\ \hline & 1 & 11 & 28 & 0 \end{array}$$

The LHS of the equation factors as

$(x - 1)(x^2 + 11x + 28)$

$= (x - 1)(x + 4)(x + 7)$

$x - 1 = 0$ or $x + 4 = 0$

$x = 1$ $\quad x = -4$

or

$x + 7 = 0$

$x = -7$

The roots are $x = 1$, $x = -4$, and $x = -7$.

19. $\tan\theta = \frac{\text{opp.}}{\text{adj.}} = \frac{h}{d}$

$\theta = \tan^{-1}\left(\frac{h}{d}\right)$

20. Use synthetic division with $a = 4$.

$$\begin{array}{r|rrrr} 4 & 2 & -3 & 1 & -5 \\ & & 8 & 20 & 84 \\ \hline & 2 & 5 & 21 & 79 \end{array}$$

$P(4) = r(4) = 79$

21. Period $= \frac{\pi}{|b|} = \frac{\pi}{\frac{2}{3}} = \frac{3\pi}{2}$ and asymptotes are at $x = \frac{n\pi}{|b|} = \frac{n\pi}{\frac{2}{3}} = \frac{3n\pi}{2}$ where n is an integer.

22. a. $N(t) = N_0e^{-kt}$

$0.5 = 1 \cdot e^{-k(68)}$

$\ln 0.5 = -68k$

$k = \frac{\ln 0.5}{-68} \approx 0.0102$

b. $N(t) = N_0e^{-0.0102t}$

$7 = 10e^{-0.0102t}$

$\ln 7 = \ln 10 - 0.0102t$

$0.0102t = \ln 10 - \ln 7$

$t = \frac{\ln 10 - \ln 7}{0.0102} \approx 35.0$

It takes about 35.0 s for 10 g to decay to 7 g.

23. The student used the square of the radius instead of the radius. The radius is the square root of 4, or 2.

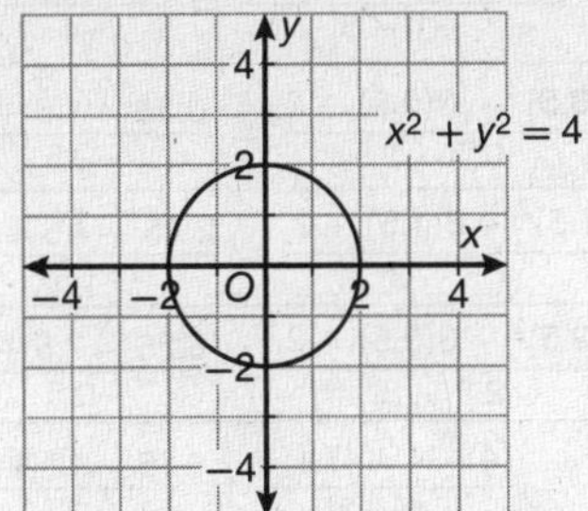

24. Sample: The student solved $\log(x + 5) = 4$.

25. Yes. Possible justification: $\log x^2 = 2$ has solutions 10 and −10.

26. $\frac{48}{\sqrt{3}} = \frac{48\sqrt{3}}{\sqrt{3}\sqrt{3}} = \frac{48\sqrt{3}}{3} = 16\sqrt{3}$

27. $\sqrt{108} + \sqrt{12} + \sqrt{112}$

$= \sqrt{36}\sqrt{3} + \sqrt{4}\sqrt{3} + \sqrt{16}\sqrt{7}$

$= 6\sqrt{3} + 2\sqrt{3} + 4\sqrt{7}$

$= (6 + 2)\sqrt{3} + 4\sqrt{7}$

$= 8\sqrt{3} + 4\sqrt{7}$

28. For $x \le 6$, $y = 35$.

For $x > 6$,

$y = 7(\#\text{ items over } 6) + 35$

$= 7(x - 6) + 35$

Therefore

$$y = \begin{cases} 35 & x \le 6 \\ 7(x - 6) + 35 & x > 6 \end{cases}$$

29. LHS $= \frac{x^2 - 3x + 2}{x - 3} = \frac{(x - 1)(x - 2)}{x - 3}$ has zeros at $x = 1$ and 2 and an asymptote at $x = 3$. RHS has a zero at $x = 0$. Use test values −1, 0.5, 1.5, 2.5, and 4.

x	$\frac{x^2 - 3x + 2}{x - 3}$
-1	$\frac{(-1)^2 - 3(-1) + 2}{-1 - 3} = \frac{1 + 3 + 2}{-4} = -1.5$
0.5	$\frac{(0.5)^2 - 3(0.5) + 2}{0.5 - 3} = \frac{0.25 - 1.5 + 2}{-2.5} = -0.3$
1.5	$\frac{(1.5)^2 - 3(1.5) + 2}{1.5 - 3} = \frac{2.25 - 4.5 + 2}{-1.5} \approx 0.167$
2.5	$\frac{(2.5)^2 - 3(2.5) + 2}{2.5 - 3} = \frac{6.25 - 7.5 + 2}{-0.5} = -1.5$
4	$\frac{(4)^2 - 3(4) + 2}{4 - 3} = \frac{16 - 12 + 2}{1} = 6$

Inequality is true for all test values except $x = 4$. Therefore the solution is $x < 3$.

30. $\cot(x) = \frac{\text{adj.}}{\text{opp.}} = \frac{y}{8000}$

$8000 \cot(x) = y$

LESSON 104

Warm Up 104

1. Transformations
2. Since $f(x - h)$ transforms the function h units to the right, then $g(x) = f(x + 2)$ will be $f(x)$ shifted two units left.

   $g(x) = f(x + 2)$

   $= |x + 2|$
3. Quadrant I, since the domain and the range only consist of positive values.

Lesson Practice 104

a. Compare the equation $h(x)$ to that of $f(x)$. The equation for $h(x)$ adds 10 to each value of $f(x)$.

$y = h(x) = \sqrt{x} + 10 = f(x) + 10$

The graph of $h(x)$ will have the same shape as $f(x)$ only it will be shifted up 10 units.

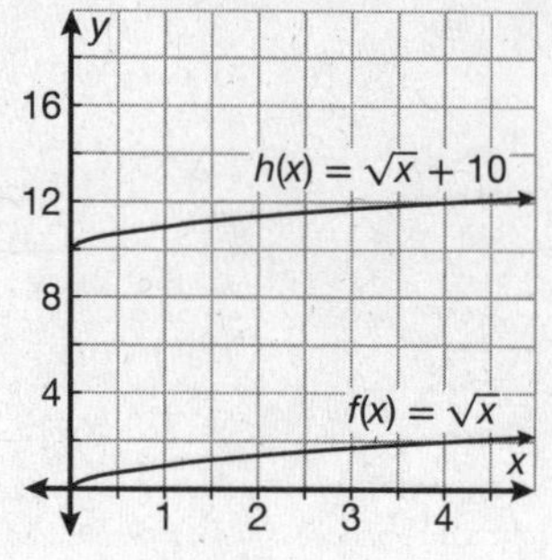

b. Compare the equation $h(x)$ to that of $f(x)$. The equation for $h(x)$ subtracts 1 from each value of x.

$y = h(x) = \sqrt{x - 1} = f(x - 1)$

The graph of $h(x)$ will have the same shape as $f(x)$ only it will be shifted right 1 unit.

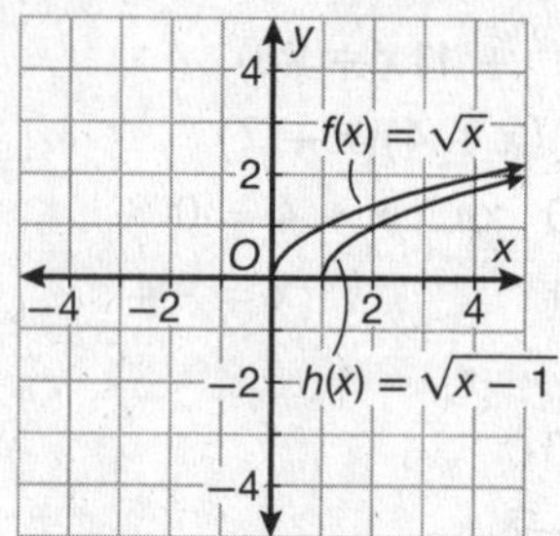

c. Compare the equation $h(x)$ to that of $f(x)$. The equation for $h(x)$ is the opposite of each value of $f(x)$.

$y = h(x) = -\sqrt{x} = -f(x)$

The graph of $h(x)$ will have the same shape as $f(x)$ only it will be a reflection about the x-axis.

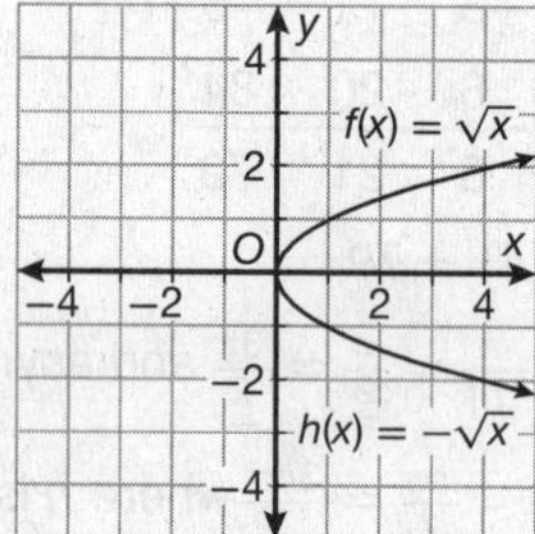

d. Compare the equation $h(x)$ to that of $f(x)$. The equation for $h(x)$ multiplies each value $f(x)$ by 4.

$y = h(x) = 4\sqrt{x} = 4f(x)$

$h(x)$ is obtained by vertically stretching $f(x)$ by a factor of 4.

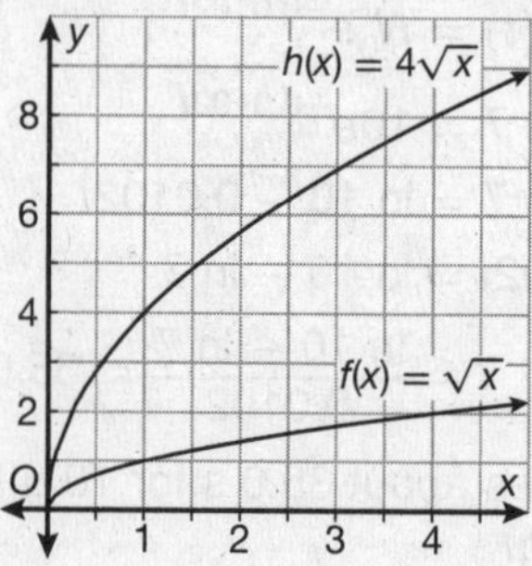

e. Horizontal Shifts: Since 2 is being added to the expression under the radical, this will shift $f(x)$ 2 units to the right.

Vertical Stretching or Compressing: Since $f(x)$ is multiplied by $\frac{1}{5}$, there is a vertical compression by a factor of 5.

Reflections: there is no vertical reflection, but there is a horizontal reflection across the y-axis because the coefficient of x changes.

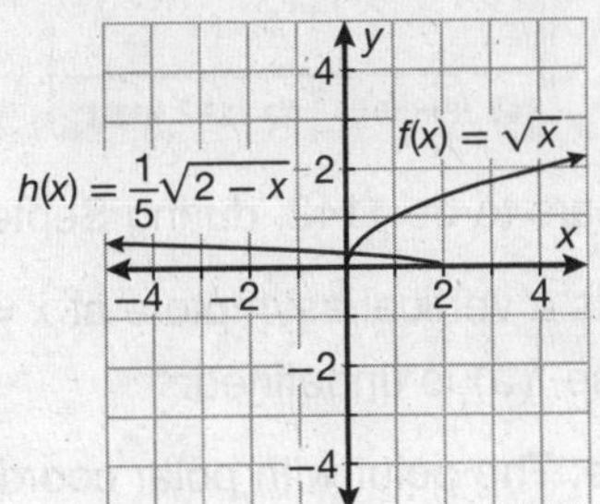

f. Compare the equation $g(x)$ to that of $f(x)$. The equation for $g(x)$ subtracts 4 from each value of $f(x)$.

$y = g(x) = 5^x - 4 = f(x) - 4$

The graph of $h(x)$ will have the same shape as $f(x)$ only it will be shifted down 4 units.

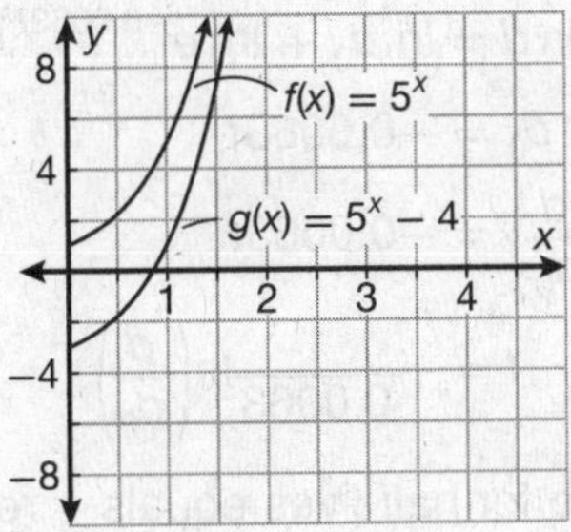

g. Compare the equation $g(x)$ to that of $f(x)$. The equation for $g(x)$ adds 6 to each value of x.

$y = g(x) = 5^{x+6} = f(x + 6)$

The graph of $h(x)$ will have the same shape as $f(x)$ only it will be shifted left 6 units.

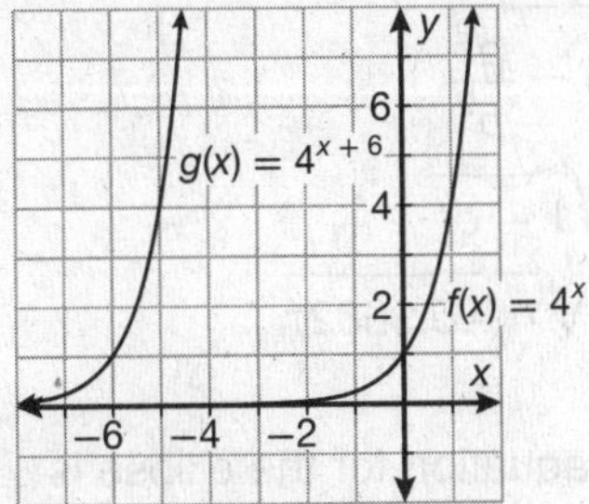

h. Compare the equation $g(x)$ to that of $f(x)$. The equation for $g(x)$ is the opposite of each value of $f(x)$.

$y = g(x) = -10^x = -f(x)$

The graph of $h(x)$ will have the same shape as $f(x)$ only it will be a reflection about the x-axis.

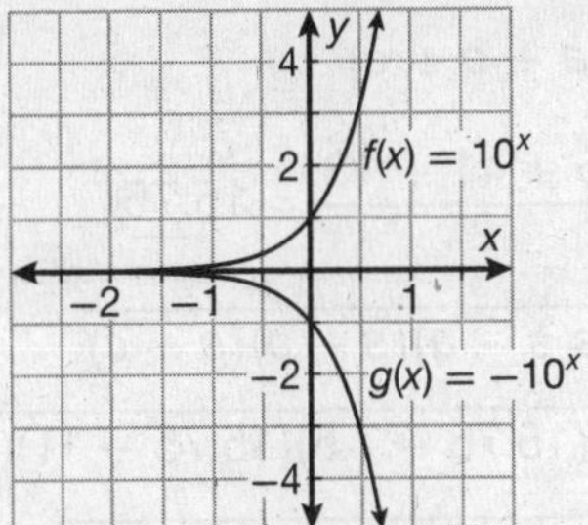

i. Compare the equation $g(x)$ to that of $f(x)$. The equation for $g(x)$ is the opposite of each value of x.

$y = g(x) = 7^{-x} = f(-x)$

The graph of $h(x)$ will have the same shape as $f(x)$ only it will be a reflection about the y-axis.

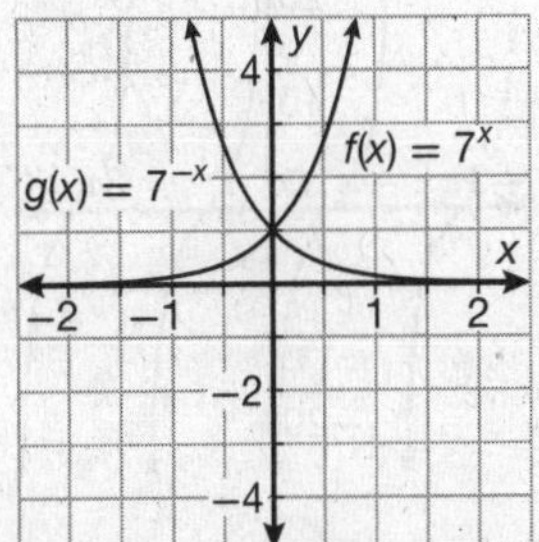

j. Vertical Stretching or Compressing; Since $f(x)$ is multiplied by 2.009, there is a vertical stretch by a factor of 2.009.

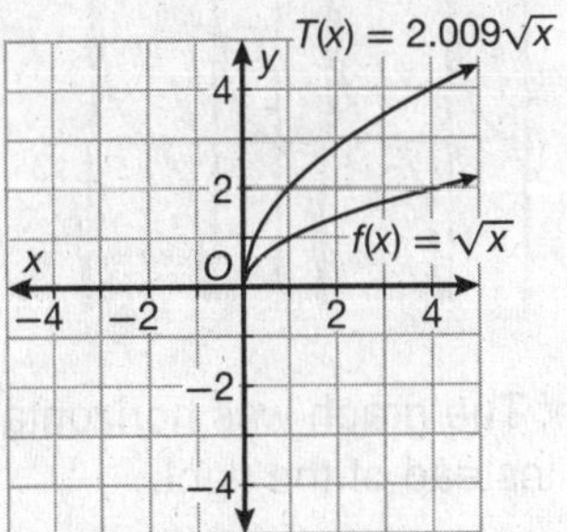

Use the graph to estimate $T(x)$ when $x = 4$.

$T(x) \approx 3.66$, when $x = 4$.

Practice 104

1. $\dfrac{x^2 + 5x + 6}{x^2 - 12x + 32} = \dfrac{(x + 3)(x + 2)}{(x - 4)(x - 8)}$

There are 2 roots in the numerator and 2 roots in the denominator. There will be 5 intervals. Answer Choice **C**

2. Using Heron's Formula.

$$s = \frac{1}{2}(a + b + c)$$
$$= \frac{7.5 + 11 + 13}{2} = 15.75$$
$$A = \sqrt{s(s - a)(s - b)(s - c)}$$
$$= \sqrt{15.75(15.75 - 7.5)(15.75 - 11)(15.75 - 13)}$$
$$= \sqrt{15.75(8.25)(4.75)(2.75)}$$
$$\approx 41.2 \text{ m}^2$$

The area of the triangle is about 41.2 m^2.

3. $y = 4\cot\left(\frac{1}{2}x\right)$ has a period of 2π. The asymptotes occur at $x = 2\pi n$, where n is an integer.

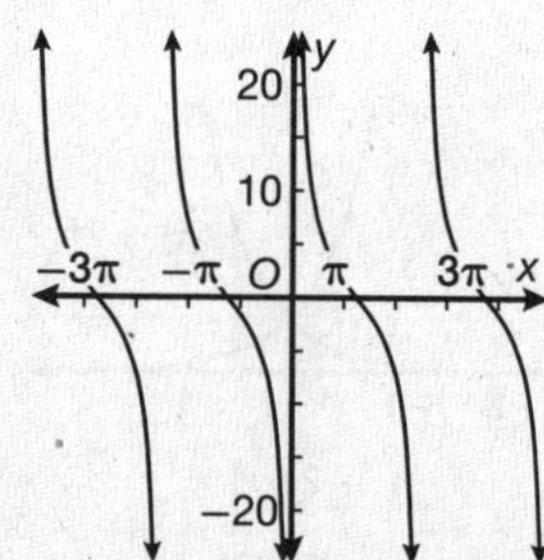

4. $y = \tan(x + b)$ has a period of π. The asymptotes are $\frac{\pi}{2} - 6 + \pi n$, where n is an integer.

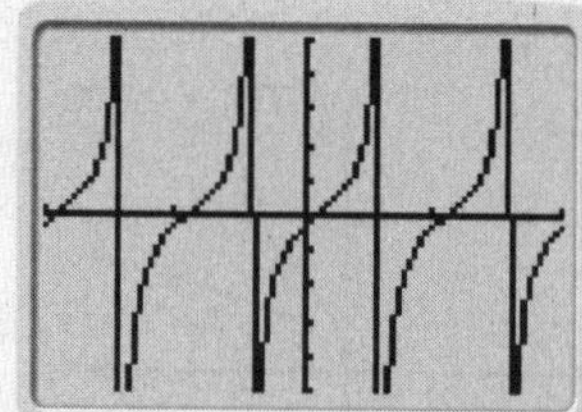

5. Sample: The graph was horizontally shifted to the left instead of the right.

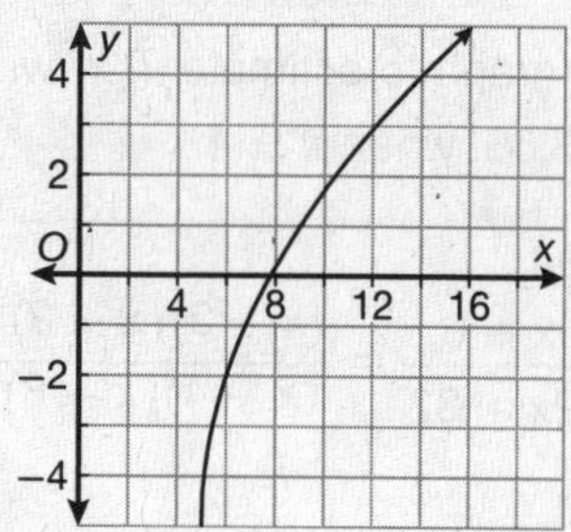

6. Graph the function on the calculator and determine the local minimum.

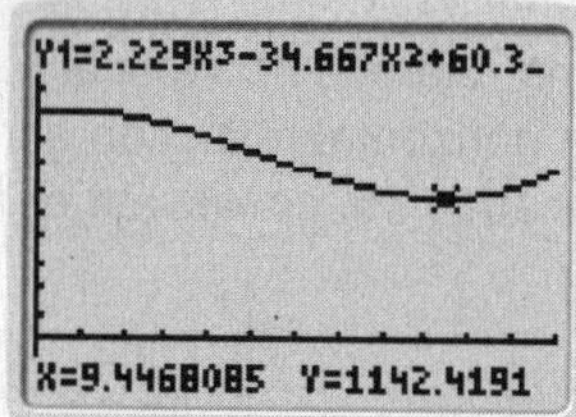

It appears to be 1142, during September.

7. There is a vertical asymptote at $x = a$ because $f(a)$ is undefined.

8. Sample: The point with polar coordinates $(-1, \pi)$ is on the positive x-axis in the Cartesian coordinate system. Correct answer: (1, 0)

9. Solving for t.

$$d = d_0 e^{-0.0063t}$$
$$\ln d = \ln\left(d_0 e^{-0.0063t}\right)$$
$$\ln d = \ln d_0 + \ln\left(e^{-0.0063t}\right)$$
$$\ln d - \ln d_0 = -0.0063t$$
$$\ln\left(\frac{d}{d_0}\right) = -0.0063t$$
$$t = -\frac{1}{0.0063}\ln\left(\frac{d}{d_0}\right)$$

10. The ratio for half-lives equals $\frac{1}{2}$ regardless of time.

11. No, the histogram is not bell-shaped, it is double peaked.

12. $b = 21 - 5 = 16$

Using the formula for eccentricity,

$$e = \sqrt{1 - \frac{a^2}{b^2}}$$
$$a = b\sqrt{1 - e^2}$$
$$a = 16\sqrt{1 - 0.9682^2}$$
$$a \approx 4$$

So the equation for the ellipse is

$$\frac{(x - (-3))^2}{4^2} + \frac{(y - 5)^2}{16^2} = 1$$

13. $\frac{12m^7}{3m^9} = \frac{4 \cdot 3m^7}{m^2 \cdot 3m^7} = \frac{4}{m^2}$, $m \neq 0$.

14. Positive a and negative b, Quadrant IV. Answer Choice **D**

15. Solve the equation for y.

$$6x - 8y = 24$$
$$-8y = -6x + 24$$
$$y = \frac{-6x}{-8} + \frac{24}{-8}$$
$$y = \frac{3}{4}x - 3$$

16. Sample:

$$y = \left(\frac{x-5}{x-5}\right)\left(\frac{1}{x(x+1)(x-3)}\right)$$
$$= \frac{x-5}{x^4 - 7x^3 + 7x^2 + 15x}$$

17. This is a step function since the fee is constant for each interval.

$$C(x) = \begin{cases} 1.30 & \text{if } 0 < x \le 1 \\ 1.64 & \text{if } 1 < x \le 2 \\ 1.98 & \text{if } 2 < x \le 3 \\ \text{undefined} & \text{if } x = \text{otherwise} \end{cases}$$

18. By Pythagorean Theorem the opposite side of the triangle $= \sqrt{72}$. Cosecant is not the reciprocal of cosine, it is the reciprocal of sine.

$$\sin\theta = \frac{\sqrt{72}}{11} = \frac{6\sqrt{2}}{11}$$
$$\csc\theta = \frac{1}{\sin\theta} = \frac{11}{6\sqrt{2}} = \frac{11\sqrt{2}}{12}$$

19. The difference in the employee's salary each year is a fixed constant. Use a linear function to model the employee's salary and solve for a_1, where n is time in years, and d is the constant difference, $a_n = a_1 + (n-1)d$.

$$a_8 = a_1 + (8-1)d \qquad a_{17} = a_1 + (17-1)d$$
$$d = \frac{a_8 - a_1}{7} \qquad d = \frac{a_{17} - a_1}{16}$$

Set the two equation to equal each other.

$$\frac{a_8 - a_1}{7} = \frac{a_{17} - a_1}{16}$$
$$16(a_8 - a_1) = 7(a_{17} - a_1)$$
$$16a_8 - 16a_1 = 7a_{17} - 7a_1$$
$$9a_1 = 16a_8 - 7a_{17}$$
$$a_1 = \frac{16a_8 - 7a_{17}}{9}$$

$a_8 = 42{,}710$ and $a_{17} = 50{,}135$.

$$a_1 = \frac{16(42{,}710) - 7(50{,}135)}{9}$$
$$a_1 = 36{,}935$$

The starting salary was \$36,935.

20. **a.** Solve for E when $M = 6$.

$$M = \frac{2}{3}\log\left(\frac{E}{10^{11.8}}\right)$$
$$6 = \frac{2}{3}\log\left(\frac{E}{10^{11.8}}\right)$$
$$\frac{6 \cdot 3}{2} = \log\left(\frac{E}{10^{11.8}}\right)$$
$$9 = \log\left(\frac{E}{10^{11.8}}\right)$$
$$10^9 = \frac{E}{10^{11.8}}$$
$$E = 10^9 \cdot 10^{11.8}$$
$$E = 10^{9+11.8}$$
$$E = 10^{20.8} \approx 6.3096 \times 10^{20} \text{ ergs}$$

b. Solve for E when $M = 7$.

$$M = \frac{2}{3}\log\left(\frac{E}{10^{11.8}}\right)$$
$$7 = \frac{2}{3}\log\left(\frac{E}{10^{11.8}}\right)$$
$$\frac{7 \cdot 3}{2} = \frac{2}{3}\log\left(\frac{E}{10^{11.8}}\right)$$
$$10.5 = \log\left(\frac{E}{10^{11.8}}\right)$$
$$10^{10.5} = \frac{E}{10^{11.8}}$$
$$E = 10^{10.5} \cdot 10^{11.8}$$
$$E = 10^{10.5+11.8}$$
$$E = 10^{22.3} \approx 1.9953 \times 10^{22} \text{ ergs}$$

c. Divide the answer in b by the answer in a.

$$\frac{10^{22.3}}{10^{20.8}} = 10^{1.5} \approx 31.6$$

21. Solve for P.

$$A = P + Prt$$
$$A = P(1 + rt)$$

$P = \frac{A}{1 + rt}$

Substitute 0.05 for *r*, 10,000 for *A*, and 2 for *t*.

$P = \frac{10{,}000}{1 + (0.05)(2)}$

$P \approx 9090.91$

$9090.91 would have to be invested.

22. $8 - 2 \leq x \leq 8 + 2$
$6 \leq x \leq 10$

23. To vertically shift a graph down, you must subtract a value from each *y*-coordinate of the graph.

24. $-C = -\begin{bmatrix} 2\frac{1}{2} & \frac{1}{2} & -3 \end{bmatrix} = \begin{bmatrix} -2\frac{1}{2} & -\frac{1}{2} & 3 \end{bmatrix}$

25. $\frac{1}{2}C + 4B$

$= \frac{1}{2}\begin{bmatrix} 2\frac{1}{2} & \frac{1}{2} & -3 \end{bmatrix} + 4\begin{bmatrix} 3\frac{1}{2} & -\frac{1}{2} & -\frac{1}{4} \end{bmatrix}$

$= \begin{bmatrix} 1\frac{1}{4} & \frac{1}{4} & -1\frac{1}{2} \end{bmatrix} + [14 \quad -2 \quad -1]$

$= \begin{bmatrix} 15\frac{1}{4} & -1\frac{3}{4} & -2\frac{1}{2} \end{bmatrix}$

26. $\frac{x^2 + 6x + 9}{x^2 - 9} \div (x - 7) = \frac{x^2 + 6x + 9}{x^2 - 9} \cdot \frac{1}{(x - 7)}$

$= \frac{\cancel{(x + 3)}(x + 3)}{\cancel{(x + 3)}(x - 3)(x - 7)}$

$= \frac{(x + 3)}{(x - 3)(x - 7)}$

$x = -3, 3, 7$

27. The second equation is a multiple of the first equation, so there are infinite solutions; the system is consistent and dependent.

28. $7x + 2y = 11 \longrightarrow 14x + 4y = 22$

$-2x + 3y = 29 \longrightarrow -14x + 21y = 203$

$25y = 225$

$y = 9$

substitute for *y*

$7x + 2(9) = 11$

$x = \frac{-7}{7} = -1$

$(-1, 9)$, consistent and independent.

29. Since every value of *x* is subtracted by 8, the phase shift is 8 units to the right.

30. Period $= \frac{2\pi}{b} = \frac{2\pi}{4} = \frac{\pi}{2}$.

The asymptotes can be found by finding the values of *x* that make $-\cos 4x = 0$, and they are $\frac{\pi}{8} + \frac{\pi}{2}n$ where *n* is an integer.

LESSON 105

Warm Up 105

1. common difference
2. $-14, -17, -20$
3. $18 - 11 = 7$

   $a_{14} = 11 + 7(13) = 102$

Lesson Practice 105

a. $\sum_{k=1}^{10} k = 1 + 2 + 3 + 4 + 5 + 6 + 7 + 8 + 9 + 10$
$= 55$

b. $\sum_{k=1}^{4} 5 + 2k$

$= 5 + 2(1) + 5 + 2(2) + 5 + 2(3) + 5 + 2(4)$
$= 40$

c. $\sum_{k=1}^{6} 8k$

d. $\sum_{k=0}^{3} 25 + 3k$

e. $a_n = 5 - 10(n - 1)$

$a_{18} = 5 - 10(18 - 1) = -165$

$S_{18} = \frac{18(5 + (-165))}{2} = -1440$

f. $\sum_{k=1}^{33} 6k$

$6(1) = 6, 6(33) = 198$

$S_{33} = \frac{33(198 + 6)}{2} = 3366$

g. $\sum_{k=1}^{7} 4.5 + 1.5k$

$4.5 + 1.5(1) = 6$

$4.5 + 1.5(7) = 15$

$S_7 = \frac{7(15 + 6)}{2} = 73.5$

Practice 105

1. $P(x) = f(g(x)) = f(x^2 - 5x + 6)$
   $= (x^2 - 5x + 6)^4$
   $P(3) = (3^2 - 5(3) + 6)^4 = (9 - 15 + 6)^4 = 0$

2. $30 - 48 = -18$
   $a_n = 48 - 18(n - 1)$
   $a_{16} = 48 - 18(15) = -222$
   $S_{16} = \frac{16(48 + (-222))}{2} = -1392$

3. The graph is vertically stretched in comparison to the base function. Answer Choice **D**

4. 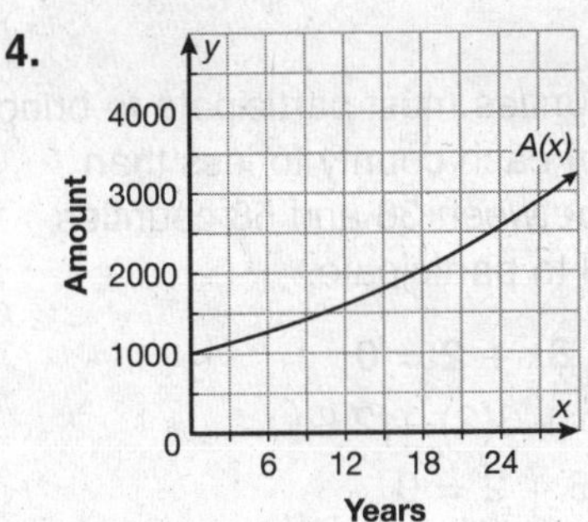

5. $x = 7$ or $x = 7$
   $x - 7 = 0$ or $x - 7 = 0$
   Possible equation:
   $(x - 7)(x - 7) = 0$
   $x^2 - 14x + 49 = 0$

6. $A = lw = x\left(-\frac{1}{4}x^2 + 6\right)$
   $= -\frac{1}{4}x^3 + 6x$

   Press Y= and enter the equation followed by pressing GRAPH. Then press TRACE to scroll along the graph.
   Maximum area ≈ 11.31 square units;
   $x \approx 2.83,\ y = 4$

7. $A = \frac{1}{2}bh = \frac{1}{2}(10)x = 5x$
   $5x \geq 95$
   $x \geq 19$

8. 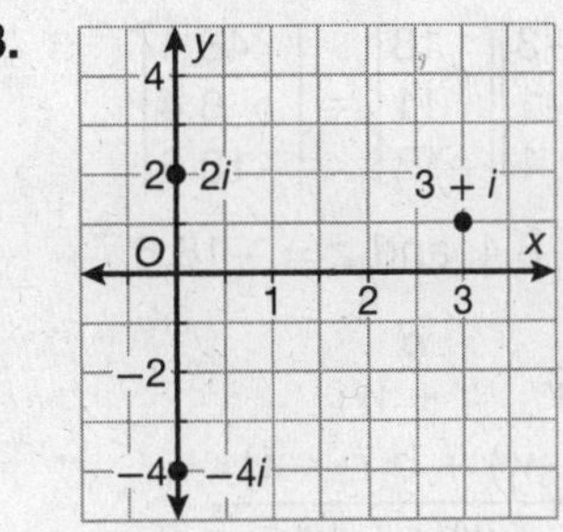

9. $d = \frac{33.2 - 6.2}{18} = 1.5$
   $a_n = 6.2 + 1.5(n - 1)$
   $a_4 = 6.2 + 1.5(4 - 1) = 10.7$

10. The rows of the 3 × 3 matrix represent C.J, Lyle and Avery and the columns represent drinks, sandwiches and snacks. The column matrix represents the costs for the drinks, sandwiches and snacks.

$$\begin{bmatrix} 1 & 3 & 3 \\ 2 & 1 & 4 \\ 2 & 2 & 5 \end{bmatrix}\begin{bmatrix} 1.00 \\ 3.50 \\ 1.50 \end{bmatrix}$$

$$= \begin{bmatrix} 1(1.00) + 3(3.50) + 3(1.50) \\ 2(1.00) + 1(3.50) + 4(1.50) \\ 2(1.00) + 2(3.50) + 5(1.50) \end{bmatrix}$$

$$= \begin{bmatrix} 16.00 \\ 11.50 \\ 16.50 \end{bmatrix}$$

C.J. spent \$16, Lyle spent \$11.50, and Avery spent \$16.50. Avery spent the most money.

11. The system is given by

$$\begin{bmatrix} -3 & 1 \\ 1 & -2 \\ 2 & -2 \end{bmatrix} \quad \begin{bmatrix} -8 & 18 \\ 1 & 11 \\ 5 & -17 \end{bmatrix}$$

Press 2nd and "x^{-1}"; scroll to the right-most tab EDIT and press ENTER. Input the values of the first matrix.
Then press 2nd and MODE. Press 2nd and "x^{-1}"; under the tab "NAME" press ENTER.
Then press "x^{-1}" and ENTER.

$$A^{-1} = \begin{bmatrix} -1.6 & 2.2 & -3 \\ -0.6 & 0.2 & -1 \\ 0.4 & -0.8 & 1 \end{bmatrix}$$

$$\begin{bmatrix} -1.6 & 2.2 & -3 \\ -0.6 & 0.2 & -1 \\ 0.4 & -0.8 & 1 \end{bmatrix}\begin{bmatrix} 18 \\ 11 \\ -17 \end{bmatrix} = \begin{bmatrix} 46.4 \\ 8.4 \\ -18.6 \end{bmatrix}$$

So $x = 46.4$, $y = 8.4$, and $z = -18.6$.

12. a. $t = \frac{d}{r-w} + \frac{d}{r+w}$

$$t = \frac{d(r+w) + d(r-w)}{(r-w)(r+w)}$$
$$t = \frac{d(r+w+r-w)}{(r-w)(r+w)}$$
$$t = \frac{d(2r)}{(r-w)(r+w)}$$
$$d(2r) = t(r-w)(r+w)$$
$$d = \frac{t(r-w)(r+w)}{2r}$$

b. $d = \frac{t(r-w)(r+w)}{2r}$

$$= \frac{14.4(500-100)(500+100)}{2(500)}$$
$$= \frac{14.4(400)(600)}{1000}$$
$$= 3456$$

The distance from London to New York is 3456 mi.

13. Press **2nd** and "STAT"; scroll to the tab **MATH** and then scroll down to **5:sum(** and press **ENTER**. Then press "2nd" and **STAT**; scroll to the tab **"OPS"** and scroll down to **5:seq(** and press **ENTER**. Press "4.25x, x, 1, 100))" and press **ENTER**.

Answer: 21,462.5

14. $a_1 = 8 - 3(1) = 5$

$a_{10} = 8 - 3(10) = -22$

$$\sum_{k=1}^{10} (8 - 3k) = S_{10} = \frac{10(5 + (-22))}{2} = -85$$

15. The student did not multiply both terms on the left-hand side by the LCD.

$$\frac{2}{3x+6} + 4 = \frac{1}{2}$$
$$\frac{2(2)}{2(3x+6)} + \frac{4(2)(3x+6)}{2(3x+6)} = \frac{1}{2}$$
$$\frac{4 + 24x + 48}{6x+12} = \frac{1}{2}$$
$$\frac{24x + 52}{6x+12} = \frac{1}{2}$$
$$2(24x + 52) = 6x + 12$$
$$48x + 104 = 6x + 12$$
$$48x - 6x = 12 - 104$$
$$42x = -92$$
$$x = -\frac{92}{42}$$
$$x = -\frac{46}{21}$$

16. $\frac{500{,}000}{x} < 14{,}000$

$500{,}000 < 14{,}000x$

$\frac{500{,}000}{14{,}000} < x$

$35.7 < x$

At least 36 counties must participate to bring the donation of each county to less than \$14,000. So, between 36 and 58 counties inclusive need to participate.

17. $8x^3 - 18x^2 + 3x + 2 = 0$

$8(2)^3 - 18(2)^2 + 3(2) + 2$

$= 64 - 72 + 6 + 2 = 0$

Use synthetic division with $a = 2$.

2	8	−18	3	2
		16	−4	−2
	8	−2	−1	0

$8x^3 - 18x^2 + 3x + 2 = (x - 2)(8x^2 - 2x - 1)$

$$x = \frac{-b \pm \sqrt{b^2 - 4ac}}{2a}$$
$$x = \frac{-(-2) \pm \sqrt{(-2)^2 - 4(8)(-1)}}{2(8)}$$
$$x = \frac{2 \pm 6}{16}$$

$x = \frac{1}{2}$ and $x = -\frac{1}{4}$

Answer choice **A** because **B**, **C** and **D** have been shown to be roots of the equation.

18. $\log_3(9x)^5 = \log_3(3^2\,x)^5$

$= \log_3(3^{10}\,x^5)$

$= \log_3(3^{10}) + \log_3 x^5$
$= 10 + 5\log_3 x$

when $x = 81$

$\log_3(9x)^5 = 10 + 5\log_3 81$
$= 10 + 5(4) = 30$

19. $\tan\theta = \frac{h}{d}$

$h = d\tan\theta$

20. Find y from the first equation.

$3x - y = 2$
$y = 3x - 2$

Substitute into the second equation.

$6x + 3(3x - 2) = 14$
$6x + 9x - 6 = 14$
$15x = 20$
$x = \frac{4}{3}$

Substitute for x into the first equation.

$3\left(\frac{4}{3}\right) - y = 2$
$4 - y = 2$
$y = 4 - 2$
$y = 2$

The solution is $\left(\frac{4}{3}, 2\right)$.

21. No, there are several x-values that are paired to two different y-values. In other words, it fails the vertical line test since there are several x-values to which two y-values are assigned.

22. Sample: To solve $2(3)^x < 310$, you can take the log of both sides to obtain the equivalent inequality $\log 2(3)^x < \log 310$. Then you can apply the Product Property of Logarithms to obtain the equivalent inequality $\log 2 + \log 3^x < \log 310$. Finally, you can apply the Power Property of Logarithms to obtain the equivalent inequality $\log 2 + x\log 3 < \log 310$.

23. $4 < 3x + 1 \leq 10$

$3 < 3x$ and $3x + 1 \leq 10$
$1 < x$ $\quad 3x \leq 9$
$1 < x$ $\quad x \leq 3$

so $1 < x \leq 3$

24. $y = mx + b$

$y = 5x + 3$

25. First add the numbers together, to get 58.593. Then round to one decimal place, because of significant digits, to get 58.6 in.

26. $y > 4x + 8$

$19 \overset{?}{>} 4(7) + 8$
$19 \overset{?}{>} 28 + 8$
$19 \not> 36$

No, it is not a solution.

27. $f(-2) = 0$, $f(0) = 0$

28. $f(-2) = 15$, $f(0) = -(0)^2 = 0$

29. Since 3.998 is approximately 4, we can substitute 4 for 3.998.

$1 + \log x = 3.998$
$1 + \log x \approx 4,$
$\log x \approx 3$
$x \approx 1000$

30. change of base: $\log_a x = \frac{\log_b x}{\log_b a}$

$\log_8(9x)^2 = \frac{\log(9x)^2}{\log 8} = \frac{2\log(9x)}{\log 8}$

when $x = 4$

$\log_8(9x)^2 = \frac{2\log(9 \cdot 4)}{\log 8} \approx 3.45$

LESSON 106

Warm Up 106

1. multiplicity

2.

−1	15	22	5	−2
		−15	−7	2
	15	7	−2	

Yes, $x + 1$ is a factor; the remaining quadratic is $15x^2 + 7x - 2$.

3. Rational Root Theorem: ±1, ±2, ±3, ±6, ±9, ±18

4. $4x^5 - 8x^4 - 32x^3 = 0$

$4x^3(x^2 - 2x - 8) = 0$
$4x^3(x - 4)(x + 2) = 0$

The roots are $x = 0$, $x = 4$, and $x = -2$.

Lesson Practice 106

a. $x^3 + x^2 - 17x + 15 = 0$

$$\begin{array}{r|rrrr} 1 & 1 & -17 & 15 & 15 \\ & 1 & 2 & -15 & -15 \\ \hline & 1 & 2 & -15 & 0 \end{array}$$

$(x - 1)$ is a factor.

$x^3 + x^2 - 17x + 15$

$= (x - 1)(x^2 + 2x - 15)$

$= (x - 1)(x + 5)(x - 3)$

$x = 1$, $x = 3$ and $x = -5$

b. $x^3 - 2x^2 - 4x + 8 = 0$

$x^2(x - 2) - 4(x - 2) = 0$

$(x - 2)(x^2 - 4) = 0$

$(x - 2)(x - 2)(x + 2) = 0$

$x = 2$ and $x = -2$

c. $x^3 - 7x^2 + 9x + 17 = 0$

$$\begin{array}{r|rrrr} -1 & 1 & -7 & 9 & 17 \\ & & -1 & 8 & -17 \\ \hline & 1 & -8 & 17 & \end{array}$$

$(x + 1)$ is a factor.

$x^3 - 7x^2 + 9x + 17$

$= (x + 1)(x^2 - 8x + 17)$

Use the quadratic formula.

$$x = \frac{-b \pm \sqrt{b^2 - 4ac}}{2a}$$

$$x = \frac{-(-8) \pm \sqrt{(-8)^2 - 4(1)(17)}}{2(1)}$$

$$x = \frac{8 \pm \sqrt{-4}}{2}$$

$$x = \frac{8 \pm 2i}{2}$$

$x = -1$, $x = 4 + i$, and $x = 4 - i$.

d. $x^4 - 8x^3 + 13x^2 + 16x - 30 = 0$

$$\begin{array}{r|rrrrr} 3 & 1 & -8 & 13 & 16 & -30 \\ & & 3 & -15 & -6 & 30 \\ \hline & 1 & -5 & -2 & 10 & \end{array}$$

$(x - 3)$ is a factor.

$x^4 - 8x^3 + 13x^2 + 16x - 30$

$= (x - 3)(x^3 - 5x^2 - 2x + 10)$

$= (x - 3)[x^2(x - 5) - 2(x - 5)]$

$= (x - 3)(x - 5)(x^2 - 2)$

$= (x - 3)(x - 5)(x - \sqrt{2})(x + \sqrt{2})$

So $x = 3$, $x = 5$, $x = -\sqrt{2}$, and $x = \sqrt{2}$.

e. $x^5 - 5x^4 - 5x^3 + 45x^2 - 108 = 0$

$$\begin{array}{r|rrrrrr} 3 & 1 & -5 & -5 & 45 & 0 & -108 \\ & & 3 & -6 & -33 & 36 & 108 \\ \hline & 1 & -2 & -11 & 12 & 36 & \end{array}$$

$(x - 3)$ is a factor.

$x^5 - 5x^4 - 5x^3 + 45x^2 - 108$

$= (x - 3)(x^4 - 2x^3 - 11x^2 + 12x + 36)$

$$\begin{array}{r|rrrrr} -2 & 1 & -2 & -11 & 12 & 36 \\ & & -2 & 8 & 6 & -36 \\ \hline & 1 & -4 & -3 & 18 & \end{array}$$

$(x + 2)$ is a factor.

$(x - 3)(x^4 - 2x^3 - 11x^2 + 12x + 36)$

$= (x - 3)(x + 2)(x^3 - 4x^2 - 3x + 18)$

$$\begin{array}{r|rrrr} -2 & 1 & -4 & -3 & 18 \\ & & -2 & 12 & -18 \\ \hline & 1 & -6 & 9 & \end{array}$$

$(x + 2)$ is a factor.

$(x - 3)(x + 2)(x^3 - 4x^2 - 3x + 18)$

$= (x - 3)(x + 2)(x + 2)(x^2 - 6x + 9)$

$= (x - 3)(x + 2)^2(x^2 - 6x + 9)$

$= (x - 3)(x + 2)^2(x - 3)(x - 3)$

$= (x - 3)^3(x + 2)^2$

So $x = 3$ and $x = -2$.

f. Because both irrational and complex roots come in pairs, there are four roots: $(2 + 3i)$, $(2 - 3i)$, $\sqrt{7}$, and $-\sqrt{7}$. Write the solution as a product of the factors and multiply.

$$P(x) = (x - (2 - 3i))(x - (2 + 3i))(x - \sqrt{7})(x + \sqrt{7})$$
$$P(x) = \left(x^2 - (2 + 3i)x - (2 - 3i)x + (2 + 3i)(2 - 3i)\right)\left(x^2 - (\sqrt{7})^2\right)$$
$$P(x) = \left(x^2 - x(2 + 3i + 2 - 3i) + (4 - 9i^2)\right)(x^2 - 7)$$
$$P(x) = (x^2 - 4x + 13)(x^2 - 7)$$
$$P(x) = x^4 - 7x^2 - 4x^3 + 28x + 13x^2 - 91$$
$$P(x) = x^4 - 4x^3 + 6x^2 + 28x - 91$$

g. Understand: The total volume equals the volume of the cylinder plus the volume of the cone.

Plan: $V = \frac{1}{3}\pi r^2 h + \pi r^2 h$

Solve: $1863\pi = \frac{1}{3}\pi x^2 \cdot x + \pi x^2(20)$

$$5589\pi = \pi x^3 + 60\pi x^2$$
$$5589 = x^3 + 60x^2$$
$$0 = x^3 + 60x^2 - 5589$$

Use a graphing calculator to find the root. Enter the function after pressing Y=; then press GRAPH. Press TRACE to scroll along the graph.

Answer: $r = 9$ feet.

Practice 106

1. $V = \frac{4}{3}\pi r^3 + \pi r^2 h$

$$22.5\pi = \frac{4}{3}\pi r^3 + \pi r^2 8$$
$$22.5 = \frac{4}{3}r^3 + 8r^2$$
$$67.5 = 4r^3 + 24r^2$$
$$0 = 4r^3 + 24r^2 - 67.5$$

Use a graphing calculator to find the root. Enter the function after pressing Y=; then press GRAPH. Press TRACE to scroll along the graph.

Answer: $r = 1.5$ mm. The radius of the vitamin is 1.5 mm.

2. $y = -1202 + 1495 \ln t$

y is the population in 1000s, so $y = 3000$.

$$3000 = -1202 + 1495 \ln t$$
$$4202 = 1495 \ln t$$
$$2.81 = \ln t$$
$$t = e^{2.81}$$
$$t = 16.6$$

$t = 10$ represents 1950, so $t = 0$ is 1940.

$t = 1940 + 16.6 \approx 1957$

The population reached 30,000,000 in 1957.

3. Sample: Both can be solved by finding critical values and using test points to determine which intervals created by the critical values contain the solutions of the inequality. In a quadratic inequality, the greatest number of critical values is two and the greatest number of intervals is three. A rational inequality can have more than two critical values and three intervals.

4. S_9 is the sum of the first 9 terms and a_9 is the value of the 9th term.

5. The student used the wrong values for k. As is, the first term is 13, not 9, so the domain should go from 0 to 4.

$$\sum_{k=0}^{4} 9 + 4k$$

6. Change of base formula:

$$\log_a x = \frac{\log_b x}{\log_b a}$$

So $\log_{12} 5 = \frac{\log 5}{\log 12}$

Answer Choice **B**

7. Period $= 2\pi$. The asymptotes occur at $x = \pi n$, where n is an integer.

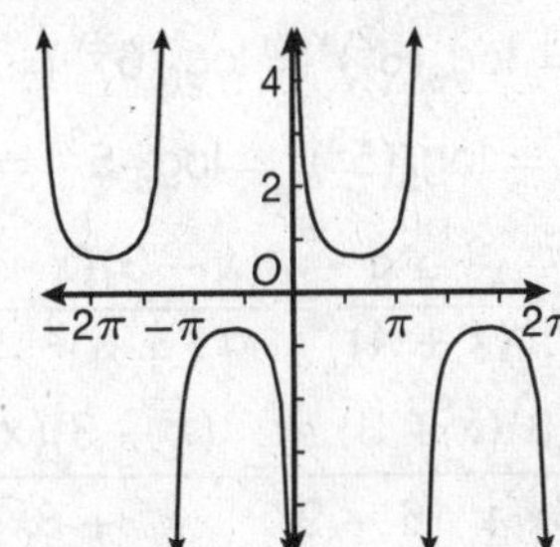

8. 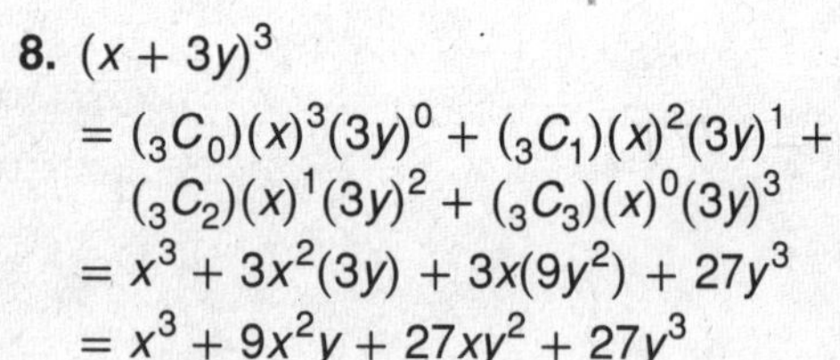

$(x + 3y)^3$
$= ({}_3C_0)(x)^3(3y)^0 + ({}_3C_1)(x)^2(3y)^1 + ({}_3C_2)(x)^1(3y)^2 + ({}_3C_3)(x)^0(3y)^3$
$= x^3 + 3x^2(3y) + 3x(9y^2) + 27y^3$
$= x^3 + 9x^2y + 27xy^2 + 27y^3$

9. 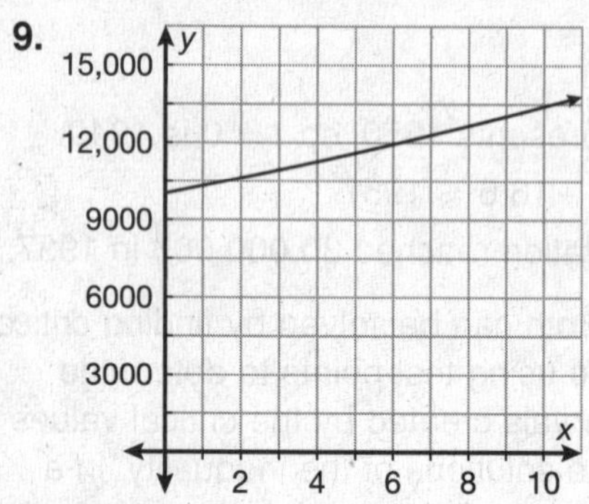

10. diameter $= \sqrt{(-8-2)^2 + (4-4)^2}$
$= \sqrt{100} = 10$

midpoint $= \left(\frac{-8+2}{2}, \frac{4+4}{2}\right) = (-3, 4)$

$(x - (-3))^2 + (y-4)^2 = 5^2$
$(x+3)^2 + (y-4)^2 = 25$

11. The function is a polynomial of degree 4 so it either faces upwards or downwards. The fact that it has a negative y-intercept between -1 and 2 implies that as $x \to -\infty$, $f(x) \to +\infty$. Then the function faces upwards and as $x \to +\infty$, $f(x) \to +\infty$.

12. As a approaches ∞, e approaches 1. No, the figure is not still an ellipse.

13. Every a_n with an odd n is equal to -4.
Answer Choice **B**

14. $f(x) = (x-3)^2 + 6$
$f(x) = x^2 - 6x + 9 + 6$
$y = x^2 - 6x + 15$

15. $\log_6 36^x = \log_6(6^2)^x = \log_6 6^{2x} = 2x$

16. $\log_5 125^x = \log_5(5^3)^x = \log_5 5^{3x} = 3x$

17. $\frac{f(x)}{f(g(x))} = \frac{x^2-9}{f(x+4)} = \frac{(x-3)(x+3)}{(x+4)^2-9}$
$= \frac{(x-3)(x+3)}{x^2+8x+16-9} = \frac{(x-3)(x+3)}{x^2+8x+7}$
$= \frac{(x-3)(x+3)}{(x+7)(x+1)}$

Vertical asymptotes at $x = -1$ and $x = -7$. There are no holes in the function.

18. Enter the function after pressing Y=; then press GRAPH. Press TRACE to scroll along the graph.
The vertex is shifted up 2 units and opens down. Both have the same axis of symmetry.

19. The initial height h_0 is 2000, the initial speed v_0 is 200, and the final height h is zero.
$h = -12.95t^2 + v_0t + h_0$
$0 = -12.95t^2 + 200t + 2000$
$t = \frac{-b \pm \sqrt{b^2 - 4ac}}{2a}$

$t = \frac{-200 \pm \sqrt{200^2 - 4(-12.95)(2000)}}{2(-12.95)}$
$t \approx \frac{-200 \pm 378.95}{-25.9}$
$t \approx 22.35$ seconds
It will take the ship 22.35 s to land.

20. $\frac{6}{x} + \frac{2x}{x+2} = \frac{6(x+2)}{x(x+2)} + \frac{2x(x)}{(x+2)(x)}$
$= \frac{2x^2 + 6x + 12}{x^2 + 2x}$

21. $\frac{\frac{1}{x+5}}{\frac{x}{2}} = \frac{1}{x+5} \cdot \frac{2}{x} = \frac{2}{x^2+5x}$

22. Let $\angle CAD$ be denoted by θ.
$\tan\theta = \frac{60}{100}$
$\theta = \tan^{-1}(0.6)$
$AC^2 = 60^2 + 100^2$
$AC^2 = 3600 + 10000$
$AC = \sqrt{13{,}600}$
$A(0,0)$, $B(60, \frac{\pi}{2})$, $D(100,0)$ and $C(\sqrt{13{,}600}, \tan^{-1} 0.6) \approx (116.62, 31°) \approx \left(116.62, \frac{\pi}{6}\right)$.

23. $P(n, r) = \frac{n!}{(n-r)!} = \frac{9!}{3!}$
$= \frac{9 \times 8 \times 7 \times 6 \times 5 \times 4 \times \cancel{3!}}{\cancel{3!}}$
$= 60{,}480$

24.

Partition	Midpoint	$f(x) = -x^2 + 5x + 5$
$0 \le x < 1$	0.5	$-(0.5)^2 + 5(0.5) + 5 = 7.25$
$1 \le x < 2$	1.5	$-(1.5)^2 + 5(1.5) + 5 = 10.25$
$2 \le x < 3$	2.5	$-(2.5)^2 + 5(2.5) + 5 = 11.25$
$3 \le x < 4$	3.5	$-(3.5)^2 + 5(3.5) + 5 = 10.25$
$4 \le x \le 5$	4.5	$-(4.5)^2 + 5(4.5) + 5 = 7.25$

$A = 7.25(1) + 10.25(1) + 11.25(1) + 10.25(1) + 7.25(1)$

$A = 46.25$

25. $_{26}C_3 = \frac{26!}{3!(26-3)!} = \frac{26 \times 25 \times 24 \times \cancel{23!}}{1 \times 2 \times 3 \times \cancel{23!}}$

$= 2600$

26. 34% of the data lies within the mean and the mean +1 standard deviation. So 34% of the data lies between 46 and 50, and 34% lies between 50 and 54. Then 68% of the data lies between 46 and 54.

27. a. There are 3 roots because it is a cubic polynomial.

b. $x^3 + x = 0$

$x(x^2 + 1) = 0$

0 is a real root.

c. $x^2 = -1$

$x = \pm\sqrt{-1}$

$x = \pm i$

The remaining roots are i and $-i$.

d. 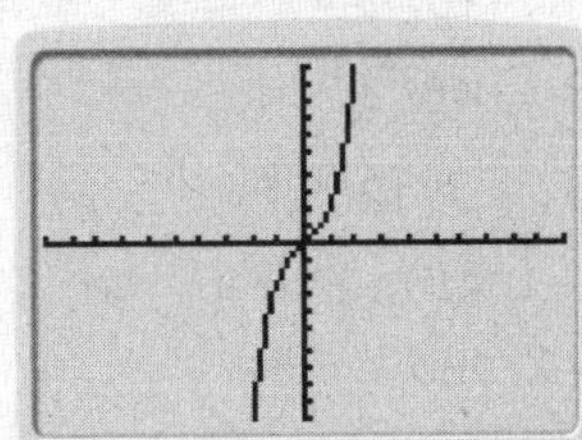

The graph intersects the x-axis at 0, so it has a real root of degree 1 at (0, 0). There are no other x-intercepts, so the remaining two roots are not real.

28. The midpoint of a diameter of a circle is the center of the circle, so first find the midpoint of a segment with those endpoints. The radius is the distance from this center point to any point on the circle, so use the distance formula to find the distance between the center point and either of the two points which are endpoints of the diameter. Write the equation substituting the coordinates of the center point for h and k and the radius for r in $(x - h)^2 + (y - k)^2 = r^2$.

29. $x = -\frac{3}{4}$ $x = 6$ $x = -1$

$x + \frac{3}{4} = 0$ $x - 6 = 0$ $x + 1 = 0$

so

$P(x) = \left(x + \frac{3}{4}\right)(x - 6)(x + 1)$

$P(x) = \left(x + \frac{3}{4}\right)(x^2 - 5x - 6)$

$P(x) = x^3 - 5x^2 - 6x + \frac{3}{4}x^2 - \frac{15}{4}x - \frac{18}{4}$

$P(x) = x^3 - \frac{20}{4}x^2 - \frac{24}{4}x + \frac{3}{4}x^2 - \frac{15}{4}x - \frac{9}{2}$

$P(x) = x^3 - \frac{17}{4}x^2 - \frac{39}{4}x - \frac{9}{2}$

30. A dot product of zero indicates that the two vectors are perpendicular, so $\theta = 90°$.

LESSON 107

Warm Up 107

1. synthetic division

2. $\frac{x^2 - 6x + 9}{x^2 - 9} = \frac{(x-3)^2}{(x+3)(x-3)} = \frac{(x-3)}{(x+3)}$

3. Factor the denominator to find the vertical asymptotes.

$3x^2 - 28x + 32 = (3x - 4)(x - 8)$

So the vertical asymptotes are $x = \frac{4}{3}$ and $x = 8$.

Lesson Practice 107

a. Graph the equation to verify that there is a slant asymptote.

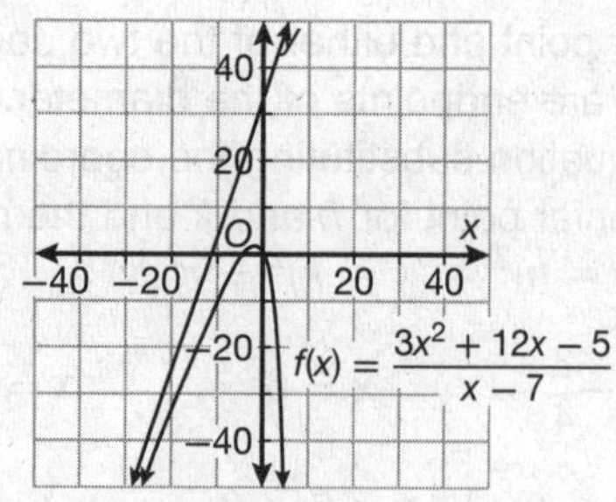

Divide the numerator by the denominator using polynomial division.

$$\begin{array}{r} 3x + 33 \\ (x-7)\overline{)3x^2 + 12x - 5} \\ \underline{-(3x^2 - 21x)} \\ 0 + 33x - 5 \\ \underline{-(33x - 231)} \\ 0 + 226 \end{array}$$

The quotient, without the remainder, is the equation of the slant asymptote.

$y = 3x + 33$, or $y = 3(x + 11)$

b. Graph the equation to verify that there is a slant asymptote.

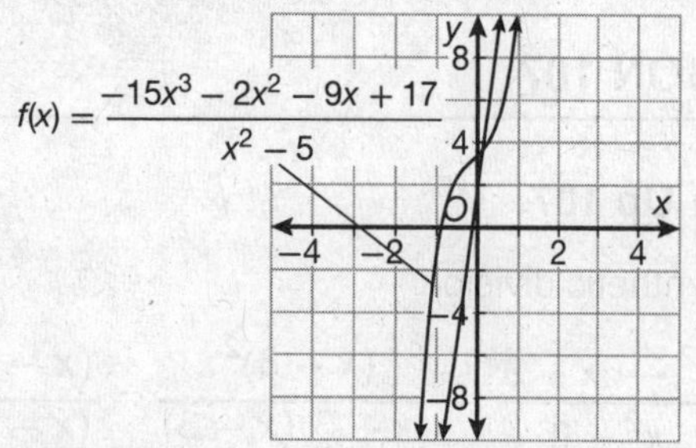

Divide the numerator by the denominator using polynomial division.

$$\begin{array}{r} -15x - 2 \\ x^2 - 5\overline{)-15x^3 - 2x^2 - 9x + 17} \\ \underline{-15x^3 + 0x^2 + 75x} \\ -2x^2 - 84x + 17 \\ \underline{-2x^2 \;\; - 0x + 10} \\ -84x + 7 \end{array}$$

The quotient, without the remainder, is the equation of the slant asymptote.

$y = -15x - 2$, or $y = -(15x + 2)$

c. Factor the numerator and the denominator to find the vertical asymptotes and holes.

$x^8 - 1 = (x^4 - 1)(x^4 + 1)$

$= (x^2 - 1)(x^2 + 1)(x^4 + 1)$

$= (x - 1)(x + 1)(x^2 + 1)(x^4 + 1)$

$x^7 - x^4 - 16x^3 + 16$

$= x^7 - 16x^3 - x^4 + 16$

$= x^3(x^4 - 16) - 1(x^4 - 16)$

$= (x^3 - 1)(x^4 - 16)$

$= (x - 1)(x^2 + x + 1)(x^2 - 4)(x^2 + 4)$

$= (x - 1)(x^2 + x + 1)(x - 2)(x + 2)(x^2 + 4)$

So there is a hole at $x = 1$, since both contain the $(x - 1)$ factor. The asymptotes occur at $x = -2$ and $x = 2$.

Since the numerator is exactly one degree greater than the denominator and the leading term coefficients are both 1, the slant asymptote is $y = x$.

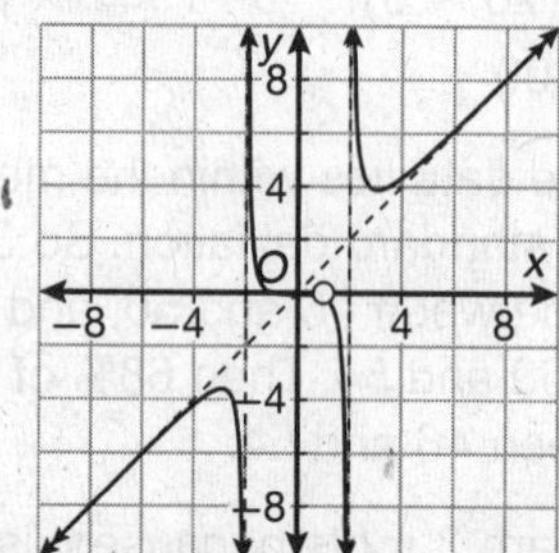

d. Evaluate $f(x)$ for $x = 1313$ and 1484.

$f(1313) = \frac{7500}{0.1(1313) - 25} \approx 70.6$

$f(1484) = \frac{7500}{0.1(1484) - 25} \approx 60.8$

about 70.6 and 60.8 mpg

Practice 107

1. $\frac{4t^3k^7}{8t} \cdot \frac{3k^3}{6t^4k^9} = \frac{12t^3k^{10}}{48t^5k^9}$

$= \frac{k(12t^3k^9)}{4t^2(12t^3k^9)} = \frac{k}{4t^2}$

Substitute $t = 2$, and $k = 5$.

$\frac{k}{4t^2} = \frac{5}{4(2^2)} = \frac{5}{16}$

2. The formula for the sum requires a_1, which is given, and a_{30} which can be found once the common difference, d, is known.

$a_{30} = a_1 + (n - 1)d$

$a_{30} = 101 + (30 - 1)(95 - 101)$

$a_{30} = 101 + (29)(-6)$

$a_{30} = 101 - 174$

$a_{30} = -73$

Use the sum formula.

$$S_n = \frac{n(a_1 + a_n)}{2}$$

$$S_{30} = \frac{30(a_1 + a_{30})}{2} = \frac{30(101 + (-73))}{2}$$

$$S_{30} = 15(101 - 73) = 420$$

3. Sample: The point with polar coordinates $\left(2, \frac{1}{2}\right)$ is close to the point with polar coordinates $\left(2, \frac{\pi}{6}\right)$, which has Cartesian coordinates $\left(\sqrt{3}, 1\right)$.

4. Answer Choice **D**

$$\begin{array}{r} 2x - 4 \\ x + 2\overline{)2x^2 + 0x - 1} \\ \underline{2x^2 + 4x} \\ -4x - 1 \\ \underline{-4x - 8} \\ 7 \end{array}$$

5. Use the Binomial Theorem to calculate the probability that exactly 2 cars were silver.

$$P(\text{exactly 2 silver}) = \binom{4}{2}\left(\frac{1}{6}\right)^2\left(1 - \frac{1}{6}\right)^{4-2}$$

$$= 6\left(\frac{1}{36}\right)\left(\frac{25}{36}\right) \approx 0.12$$

The probability is about 0.12.

6. Use the formula for a geometric sequence.

$$a_6 = a_1 r^{6-1} = 5(-4)^5 = -5120$$

7. They are reflections of each other over the y-axis.

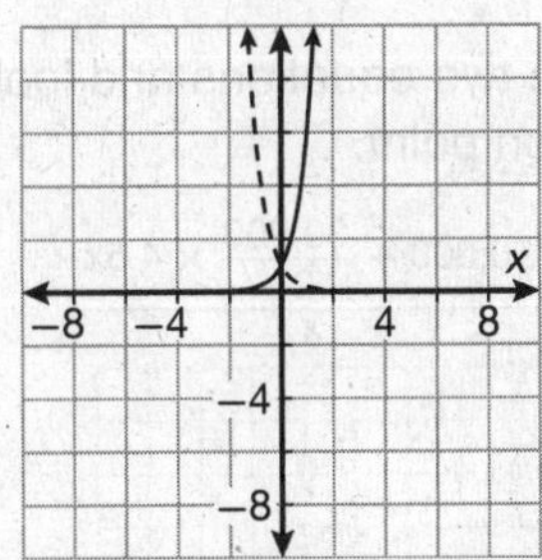

8. In an arithmetic sequence, the numbers added to the previous number must be constant.

9. $-5x^2 + 2y = -5(1)^2 + 2(-1) = -7$

Answer Choice **A**

10. 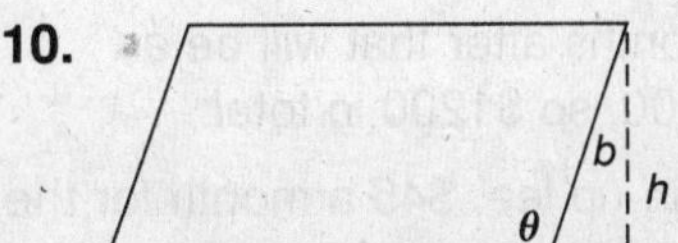

$$\sin\theta = \sin 180 - \theta$$

$$\sin\theta = \frac{\text{h}}{\text{b}}$$

$$h = b\sin\theta$$

$$A = ah = ab\sin\theta$$

11. Use polynomial division.

$$\begin{array}{r} 2.5x^3 - x^2 - 3.5x \\ 2x\overline{)5x^4 - 2x^3 - 7x^2 - 39} \\ \underline{5x^4} \\ -2x^3 \\ \underline{-2x^3} \\ -7x^2 \\ \underline{-7x^2} \end{array}$$

The remainder is −39.

$$(5x^4 - 2x^3 - 7x^2 - 39) \div 2x$$

$$= 2.5x^3 - x^2 - 3.5x - \frac{39}{2x}$$

12. Use polynomial division.

$$\begin{array}{r} 3x + 4 \\ x - 5\overline{)3x^2 - 11x - 26} \\ \underline{3x^2 - 15x} \\ 4x - 26 \\ \underline{4x - 20} \\ -6 \end{array}$$

The remainder is −6.

$$(3x^2 - 11x - 26) \div (x - 5)$$

$$= 3x + 4 - \frac{6}{x - 5}$$

13. The student forgot to add the $0x^2$ entry in his division.

14. Real roots do not come in conjugate pairs, so −4 is not necessarily a root.

15. **a.** You would need to pay the $60 initial sign-up fee, and the 6 months membership, which is $300, then another $45 a month for a year's membership, which is $540, so the total cost will be $900.

b. Another 6 months after that will be an additional \$300, so \$1200 in total.

c. \$60 initial sign-up fee, \$45 a month for the first year, and \$40 a month for the second year, which totals to \$1080

d. \$1080 − \$1200 = \$120.

16. They are similar in that they have the same center point: (0, 7). They are different because their radii are different: $\sqrt{20}$ and $\sqrt{24}$.

17. For even functions $f(-x) = f(x)$.

For this function,

$$f(-x) = \frac{1}{(-x)^2n} = \frac{1}{(-1)^2(x)^2n} = \frac{1}{x^2n} = f(x).$$

18. One way is to find the sign of the value of the numerator and denominator for a test point in each interval. If the signs are the same, the expression is positive in that interval, and if the signs are different, the expression is negative in that interval. Another way is to find the value of each factor in each interval and then determine the sign of the rational expression based on those signs. This method only works if the polynomials are, or can be, factored. If the polynomials cannot be factored, the first method must be used.

19. Evaluate $h(10)$ for Earth and Saturn.

$$h_{Earth}(t) = -\frac{1}{2}g_{Earth}t^2 + v_0t + h_0$$

$$h_{Earth}(t) = -\frac{1}{2}9.81t^2 + v_0t + h_0$$

$$h_{Earth}(10) = -\frac{1}{2}9.81(10^2) + 100(10) + 100$$

$$= 609.5$$

$$h_{Saturn}(t) = -\frac{1}{2}g_{Saturn}t^2 + v_0t + h_0$$

$$h_{Saturn}(t) = -\frac{1}{2}11.08t^2 + v_0t + h_0$$

$$h_{Saturn}(10) = -\frac{1}{2}11.08(10^2) + 100(10) + 100$$

$$= 546$$

The forces of gravity on Earth and Saturn are close in value.

20.

$$p = p_0e^{-ax}$$

$$\ln p = \ln\left(p_0e^{-ax}\right)$$

$$\ln p = \ln p_0 + \ln\left(e^{-ax}\right)$$

$$\ln p - \ln p_0 = -ax$$

$$\ln\left(\frac{p}{p_0}\right) = -ax$$

$$x = -\frac{1}{a}\ln\left(\frac{p}{p_0}\right)$$

21. The population growth forms a geometric sequence. Use the geometric formula and solve for t.

$$p_t = p_m r^{t-m}$$

$$150{,}000{,}000 = 127{,}000{,}000(1.0026)^{t-2000}$$

$$\frac{150}{127} = 1.0026^{t-2000}$$

$$\ln\left(\frac{150}{127}\right) = (t - 2000)\ln(1.0026)$$

$$t = \frac{\ln\left(\frac{150}{127}\right)}{\ln(1.0026)} + 2000$$

$$t \approx 2064.10$$

The population will reach 150,000,000 between 2064 and 2065.

22. Using the formula on the page, the two equations are as follows:

$$y_1 = \frac{20{,}000 + \frac{30{,}000}{20} \times 4.5x}{x}$$

$$y_2 = \frac{40{,}000 + \frac{30{,}000}{40} \times 4.5x}{x}$$

Graph the two equations and look for the intersection point.

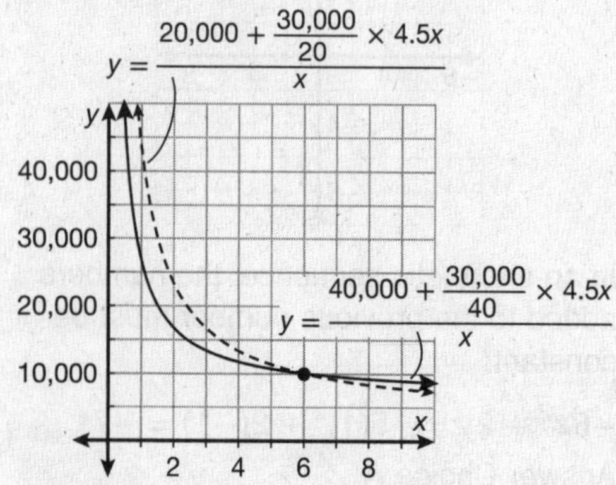

The 40 mpg car becomes a better deal after roughly 6 years.

23. First calculate the magnitude of each vector.

$$\begin{vmatrix}3\\6\end{vmatrix} = \sqrt{3^2 + 6^2} = 3\sqrt{5} \approx 6.71 \qquad \begin{vmatrix}2\\-5\end{vmatrix} = \sqrt{2^2 + (-5)^2} = \sqrt{29} \approx 5.39$$

Then use the dot product formula to calculate the angle between the two vectors.

The dot product is

$$\begin{bmatrix}3\\6\end{bmatrix}\begin{bmatrix}2\\-5\end{bmatrix} = (3)(2) + (6)(-5) = 6 - 30$$

$$= -24 \text{ to find } \theta$$

$$-24 = \begin{vmatrix}3\\6\end{vmatrix}\begin{vmatrix}2\\-5\end{vmatrix} \sin\theta$$

$$-24 \approx 6.71 \times 5.39 \times \cos\theta$$

$$\cos\theta \approx -0.6636$$

$$\theta \approx 131.57°$$

24. $P(n) = 0.5(0.5)^{n-1}$

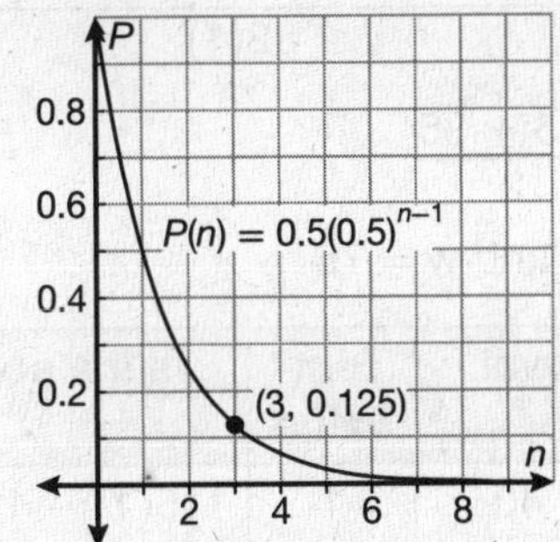

The probability is about 0.125.

25. Sample:

$$y = \frac{P(x)}{(x+1)(x-1)}$$

$$(3x + 1) = \frac{P(x)}{(x+1)(x-1)}$$

$$P(x) = (x+1)(x-1)(3x+1)$$
$$= (x^2 - 1)(3x + 1)$$
$$= 3x^2 + x^2 - 3x - 1$$
$$= 4x^2 - 3x - 1$$

$$y = \frac{4x^2 - 3x - 1}{x^2 - 1}$$

26. $x^2 + 21x - 46 = (x + 23)(x - 2)$

$x = -23$ or 2

27. $x^2 + \frac{5x}{12} - \frac{1}{6}$

Use the quadratic formula.

$$x = \frac{-b \pm \sqrt{b^2 - 4ac}}{2a}$$

$$x = \frac{-\frac{5}{12} \pm \sqrt{\left(\frac{5}{12}\right)^2 - 4(1)\left(-\frac{1}{6}\right)}}{2}$$

$$= \frac{-\frac{5}{12} \pm \sqrt{\left(\frac{25}{144}\right) + \left(\frac{4}{6}\right)}}{2}$$

$$= \frac{-\frac{5}{12} \pm \frac{11}{12}}{2}$$

$$= \frac{-5 \pm 11}{24}$$

$$x = -\frac{2}{3} \text{ or } \frac{1}{4}$$

28. $\frac{1}{5 + \sqrt{6}} \cdot \frac{5 - \sqrt{6}}{5 - \sqrt{6}} = \frac{5 - \sqrt{6}}{25 - 6} = \frac{5 - \sqrt{6}}{19}$

29. $\frac{3 + \sqrt{7}}{2 - \sqrt{10}} \cdot \frac{2 + \sqrt{10}}{2 + \sqrt{10}}$

$$= \frac{6 + 3\sqrt{10} + 2\sqrt{7} + \sqrt{70}}{4 - 10}$$

$$= -\frac{6 + 3\sqrt{10} + 2\sqrt{7} + \sqrt{70}}{6}$$

30. $y = -16x^2 + 134$

Solve $-16x^2 + 134 \geq 50$.

$$-16x^2 + 134 \geq 50$$

$$x \leq \sqrt{\frac{134 - 50}{16}}$$

$$x \leq 2.29$$

The nail will be at least 50 ft above the ground between 0 and 2.29 seconds after the drop.

LESSON 108

Warm Up 108

1. tangent
2. False; it is the cosine.
3. False; it is the sine.

Lesson Practice 108

a. $\sin^2(\theta) + \cos^2(\theta) = 1$

$\sin 60° = \frac{\sqrt{3}}{2}$, $\cos 60° = \frac{1}{2}$

$\left(\frac{1}{2}\right)^2 + \left(\frac{\sqrt{3}}{2}\right)^2 = \frac{1}{4} + \frac{3}{4} = 1$

b. $\sin^2(\theta) + \cos^2(\theta) = 1$

$\cos \pi = -1$, $\sin \pi = 0$

$(0)^2 + (-1)^2 = 1$

c. $\tan^2(98.5) + 1 \approx 44.77157 + 1 \approx 45.77157$,

$\sec^2(98.5) = \frac{1}{\cos^2(98.5)} \approx 45.77157$

d. $\tan^2\left(\frac{5\pi}{4}\right) + 1 = (1)^2 + 1 = 2$,

$\sec^2\left(\frac{5\pi}{4}\right) = \left(-\sqrt{2}\right)^2 = 2$

e. $1 + \cot^2(212) \approx 1 + 2.561 = 3.561$,

$\csc^2(212) \approx 3.561$

f. $\cot^2\left(\frac{\pi}{6}\right) + 1 = \left(\sqrt{3}\right)^2 + 1 = 4$,

$\csc^2\left(\frac{\pi}{6}\right) = (2)^2 = 4$

g. Graph $y_1 = \cot^2(\theta)$ and $y_2 = \csc^2(\theta)$.

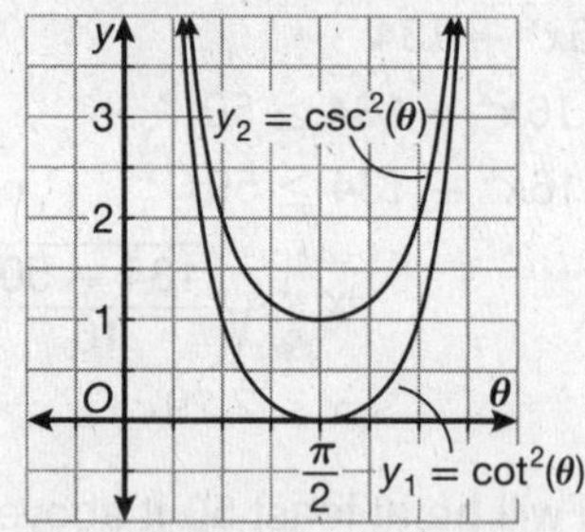

y_2 is y_1 shifted up one unit. Therefore $\csc^2 \theta = 1 + \cot^2 \theta$.

Practice 108

1. $6^5 = 7776$

$\log_6 7776 = 5$

2. $x^3 = 6859$

$\log_x 6859 = 3$

3. $g(f(x)) + 1 = g(\sin(x)) + 1$

$= (\sin x - 1)(\sin x + 1) + 1$

$= \sin^2 x - 1 + 1$

$= \sin^2 x$

4. $2l + 2w = 230$

$2l = 230 - 2w$

$l = 115 - w$

$A = lw$

and $lw \geq 3000$

so

$3000 \leq (115 - w)w$

$3000 \leq 115w - w^2$

$w^2 - 115w + 3000 \leq 0$

$w^2 - 115w + 3000 = 0$

$w = \frac{-b \pm \sqrt{b^2 - 4ac}}{2a}$

$w = \frac{-(-115) \pm \sqrt{(-115)^2 - 4(1)(3000)}}{2(1)}$

$w = \frac{115 \pm 35}{2}$

$w = 40$ and $w = 75$

Interval	Test-value	Is it a solution?
$x < 40$	1	$115(1) - 1^2 = 114 < 3000$, no.
$40 < x < 75$	41	$115(41) - 41^2 = 3034 > 3000$, yes.
$75 < x$	76	$115(76) - 76^2 = 2964 < 3000$, no.

The range of widths is from 40 feet to 75 feet inclusive.

5. To vertically stretch a graph you must multiply each y-coordinate of the graph by a value greater than one.

6. $9 \times 8 \times 7 \times 6 = 3024$

7. $\frac{1}{1 - \frac{1}{1 + \tan^2(\theta)}} = \frac{1}{1 - \frac{1}{1 + \frac{\sin^2(\theta)}{\cos^2(\theta)}}} = \frac{1}{1 - \frac{1}{1 + \frac{\frac{y^2}{r^2}}{\frac{x^2}{r^2}}}}$

$= \frac{1}{1 - \frac{1}{1 + \frac{y^2}{x^2}}} = \frac{1}{1 - \frac{1}{\frac{x^2 + y^2}{x^2}}} = \frac{1}{1 - \frac{x^2}{x^2 + y^2}}$

$$= \frac{1}{\frac{x^2+y^2-x^2}{x^2+y^2}} = \frac{1}{\frac{y^2}{x^2+y^2}} = \frac{x^2+y^2}{y^2} = \frac{x^2}{y^2} + 1$$

$$= \frac{x^2}{r^2} \div \frac{y^2}{r^2} + 1 = \frac{\cos^2(\theta)}{\sin^2(\theta)} + 1 = \cot^2(\theta) + 1$$

$$= \csc^2(\theta)$$

8. linear (degree 1) and constant (degree 0)

9. $S = B + \frac{1}{2}pl$

$S - B = \frac{1}{2}pl$

$2S - 2B = pl$

$l = \frac{2S - 2B}{p}$

Answer Choice **D**

10. $x = -6$ $\quad x = -2$ $\quad x = 1$

$x + 6 = 0$ $\quad x + 2 = 0$ $\quad x - 1 = 0$

Sample:

$f(x) = (x + 6)(x + 2)(x - 1)$

$f(x) = (x^2 + 8x + 12)(x - 1)$

$f(x) = x^3 - x^2 + 8x^2 - 8x + 12x - 12$

$f(x) = x^3 + 7x^2 + 4x - 12$

11. The vertical asymptotes imply that $(x - 2)(x + 2) = x^2 - 4$ must be the denominator of the rational function.

Slant asymptote $\approx \frac{f(x)}{x^2 - 4}$, then

$f(x) = (x^2 - 4)(-2x + 3)$

$f(x) = -2x^3 + 3x^2 + 8x - 12$

Sample: $y = \frac{-2x^3 + 3x^2 + 8x - 12}{x^2 - 4}$

12. $(2x + y)^2$

$= ({}_2C_0)(2x)^2(y)^0 + ({}_2C_1)(2x)^1(y)^1 + ({}_2C_2)(2x)^0(y)^2$

$= 4x^2 + 4xy + y^2$

13. $2(0)^3 - 3(0)^2 - 12(0) = 0$

$2(-2)^3 - 3(-2)^2 - 12(-2)$

$= -16 - 12 + 24 = -4$

Since the values of $x = 0$ and $x = -2$ yield y-values that are less than 7, $(-1, 7)$ is a local maximum.

Answer Choice **A**

14. Yes, the differences between consecutive terms are constant (zero).

15.

4	3	0	6	−1	−22
		12	48	216	860
	3	12	54	215	838

Answer: 838

16. $\frac{23 + 29}{2} = 26$

diameter $= 29 - 23 = 6$

$(x - 26)^2 + (y + 4)^2 = 3^2$

$(x - 26)^2 + (y + 4)^2 = 9$

17. $y = x^5 - 4x^3 - x^2 + 4$

$y = x^3(x^2 - 4) - 1(x^2 - 4)$

$y = (x^3 - 1)(x^2 - 4)$

$y = (x - 1)(x^2 + x + 1)(x - 2)(x + 2)$

For $x^2 + x + 1$, the discriminant $b^2 - 4ac = 1^2 - 4(1)(1) = -3$ is negative.

So the zeros are 1, ±2.

18. $\frac{x+3}{x-6} > 0$ when the numerator and denominator are both positive and when they are both negative.

They are both positive when $x > 6$, and they are both negative when $x < -3$.

So $\frac{x+3}{x-6} > 0$ when $x > 6$ and $x < -3$.

19. a. The polynomial must have a minimum degree of 3 because complex roots come in pairs. For example, this equation will also have $-7i$ as a root because it has $7i$ as a root.

b. $(x - 6)(x - 7i)(x + 7i) = 0$

$(x - 6)(x^2 - 49i^2) = 0$

$(x - 6)(x^2 + 49) = 0$

$x^3 - 6x^2 + 49x - 294 = 0$

c. Sample: $2(x^3 - 6x^2 + 49x - 294) = 0$

$2x^3 - 12x^2 + 98x - 588 = 0$

20.

x	$y = \lvert x - 4 \rvert + 2$
2	4
3	3
4	2
5	3
6	4

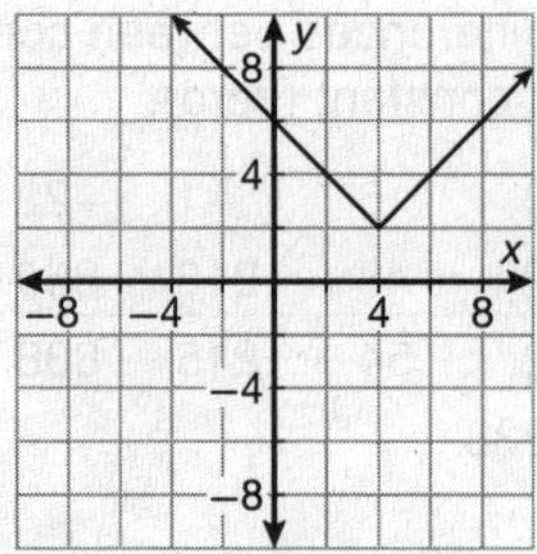

21. $a^2 + b^2 = c^2$

$$b^2 = c^2 - a^2$$

$$b = \sqrt{c^2 - a^2}$$

22. Graph $y = \sin(12t)$ and $y = \sin(28t)$.

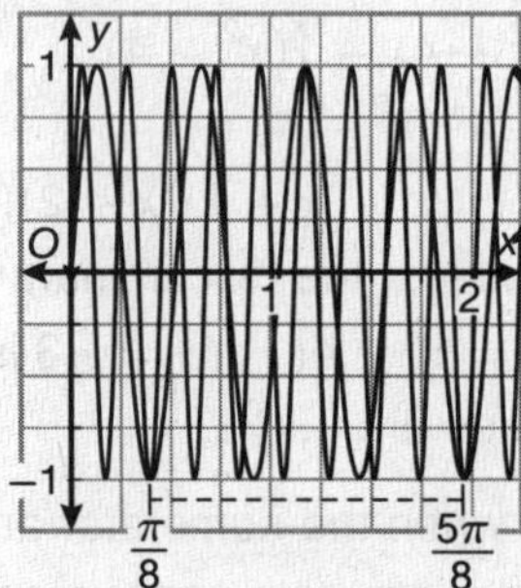

The period of $y = \sin(t)$ is 2π, so

Period of $y = \sin(12t)$ is $\frac{2\pi}{12} = \frac{\pi}{6}$

Period of $y = \sin(28t)$ is $\frac{2\pi}{28} = \frac{\pi}{14}$

Convert fractions to a common denominator $\left(\frac{7\pi}{42} \text{ and } \frac{3\pi}{42}\right)$. The LCM of 7 and 3 is 21, so the period it takes each weight to reach its lowest point at the same time is $\frac{21\pi}{42} = \frac{\pi}{2}$. Every $\frac{\pi}{2}$ seconds.

23. Student A incorrectly distributed the minus sign to the terms of the second complex number.

24. $L(I) = 10 \log \frac{I}{I_0}$

$$40 = 10 \log \frac{I}{10^{-12}}$$

$$4 = \log \frac{I}{10^{-12}}$$

$$10^4 = \frac{I}{10^{-12}}$$

$$I = 10^4 \cdot 10^{-12}$$

$$I = 10^{-8}$$

The intensity is 0.00000001 watt per square meter.

25. $\frac{1}{AB} + \frac{1}{BC} = \frac{5}{32}$

$BC = 4AB$, so

$$\frac{1}{AB} + \frac{1}{4AB} = \frac{5}{32}$$

$$\frac{4}{4AB} + \frac{1}{4AB} = \frac{5}{32}$$

$$\frac{5}{4AB} = \frac{5}{32}$$

$$4AB = 32$$

$$AB = 8$$

26. The student incorrectly converted $\csc^2(x)$ into $(1 - \cos^2 x)$.

27. $63x^3 - 7x = 0$

$$7x(9x^2 - 1) = 0$$

$$7x(3x - 1)(3x + 1) = 0$$

$$x = 0,\ x = \frac{1}{3} \text{ and } x = -\frac{1}{3}$$

28. $4x^3 + 6x^2 - 40x = 0$

$$2x(2x^2 + 3x - 20) = 0$$

$$2x(2x - 5)(x + 4) = 0$$

$$x = 0,\ x = \frac{5}{2}, \text{ and } x = -4$$

29. $m = \frac{y_2 - y_1}{x_2 - x_1}$

$$m = \frac{5 - 4}{0 - (-2)} = \frac{1}{2}$$

$$y - y_1 = m(x - x_1)$$

$$y - 5 = \frac{1}{2}(x - 0)$$

$$y = \frac{1}{2}x + 5$$

30. $y = 2\sec(x)$ has a period of 2π. The asymptotes occur at $x = \frac{\pi}{2} + \pi n$, where n is an integer.

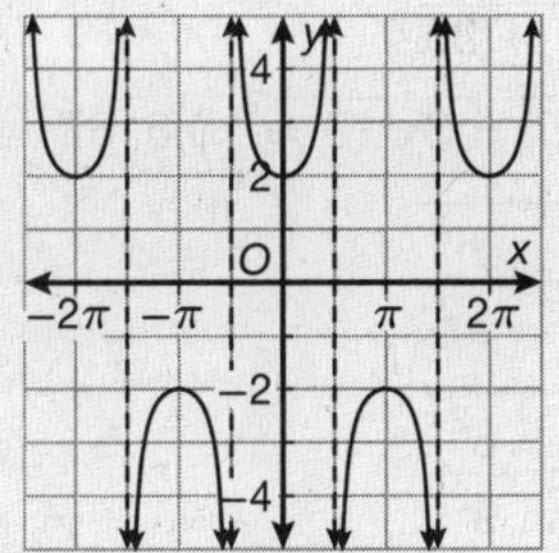

LESSON 109

Warm Up 109

1. completing the square
2. Use the Point-Slope Formula.

$$y - y_1 = m(x - x_1)$$
$$y - (-25) = 3(x - 2)$$
$$y + 25 = 3x - 6$$
$$y = 3x - 31$$

3.
$$2x^2 - 4x + 10 = 0$$
$$2x^2 - 4x = -10$$
$$x^2 - 2x = -5$$
$$x^2 - 2(1)x + (1)^2 = -5 + (1)^2$$
$$(x - 1)^2 = -4$$
$$x - 1 = \pm\sqrt{-4}$$
$$x - 1 = \pm 2i$$
$$x = 1 \pm 2i$$

Lesson Practice 109

a. $\frac{x^2}{6^2} - \frac{y^2}{4^2} = 1$ has horizontal orientation

$a = 6,\ b = 4$

$$c = \sqrt{a^2 + b^2}$$
$$= \sqrt{6^2 + 4^2}$$
$$= \sqrt{36 + 16}$$
$$= \sqrt{52} = 2\sqrt{13} \approx 7.2111$$
$$e = \sqrt{1 + \frac{b^2}{a^2}}$$
$$= \sqrt{1 + \frac{4^2}{6^2}}$$
$$= \sqrt{1 + \frac{16}{36}}$$
$$= \sqrt{\frac{52}{36}} = \sqrt{\frac{13}{9}} = \frac{\sqrt{13}}{3} \approx 1.2019$$

Asymptotes: $y = \pm\frac{b}{a}x$

$$y = \pm\frac{4}{6}x = \pm\frac{2}{3}x$$

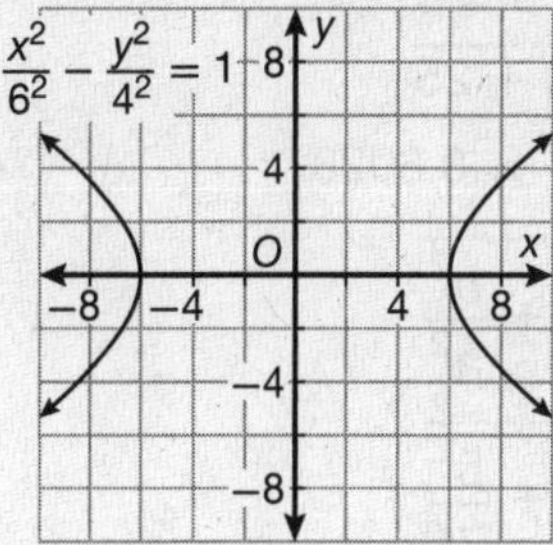

b. $\frac{y^2}{7^2} - \frac{x^2}{5^2} = 1$ has vertical orientation

$a = 7,\ b = 5$

$$c = \sqrt{a^2 + b^2}$$
$$= \sqrt{7^2 + 5^2}$$
$$= \sqrt{49 + 25}$$
$$= \sqrt{74} \approx 8.6023$$
$$e = \sqrt{1 + \frac{b^2}{a^2}}$$
$$= \sqrt{1 + \frac{5^2}{7^2}}$$
$$= \sqrt{1 + \frac{25}{49}}$$
$$= \sqrt{\frac{74}{49}} = \frac{\sqrt{74}}{7} \approx 1.2289$$

Asymptotes: $y = \pm\frac{a}{b}x$

$$y = \pm\frac{7}{5}x$$

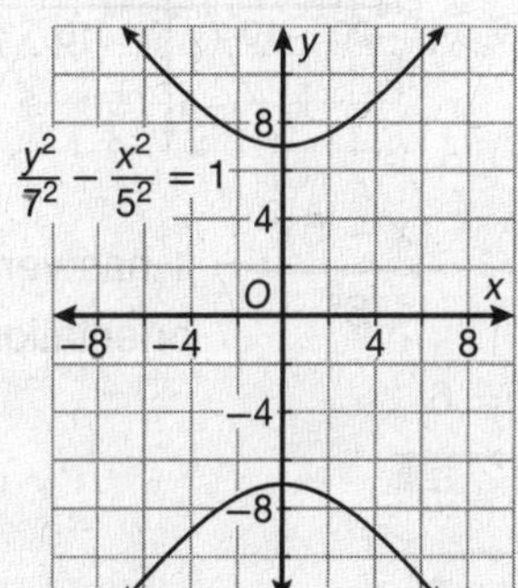

c. $\dfrac{(x-5)^2}{7^2} - \dfrac{(y-4)^2}{5^2} = 1$ has horizontal orientation

$a = 7, b = 5$

$c = \sqrt{a^2 + b^2}$

$= \sqrt{7^2 + 5^2}$

$= \sqrt{49 + 25}$

$= \sqrt{74} \approx 8.6023$

$e = \sqrt{1 + \dfrac{b^2}{a^2}}$

$= \sqrt{1 + \dfrac{5^2}{7^2}}$

$= \sqrt{1 + \dfrac{25}{49}}$

$= \sqrt{\dfrac{74}{49}} = \dfrac{\sqrt{74}}{7} \approx 1.2289$

Calculate the slope values.

$m = \pm\dfrac{b}{a} = \pm\dfrac{5}{7}$

Use point-slope formula for each asymptote. Use (h, k).

$y - y_1 = m(x - x_1)$	$y - y_1 = m(x - x_1)$
$y - 4 = \frac{5}{7}(x - 5)$	$y - 4 = -\frac{5}{7}(x - 5)$
$y - 4 = \frac{5}{7}x - \frac{25}{7}$	$y - 4 = -\frac{5}{7}x + \frac{25}{7}$
$y = \frac{5}{7}x + \frac{3}{7}$	$y = -\frac{5}{7}x + \frac{53}{7}$

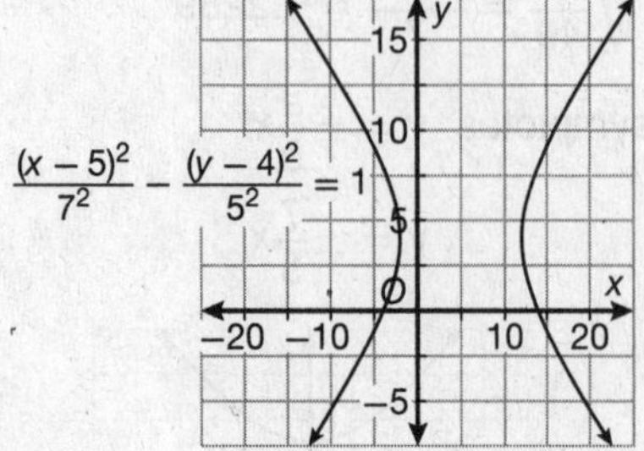

d. $\dfrac{(y-8)^2}{9^2} - \dfrac{(x-5)^2}{6^2} = 1$ has vertical orientation

$a = 9, b = 6$

$c = \sqrt{a^2 + b^2}$

$= \sqrt{9^2 + 6^2}$

$= \sqrt{81 + 36}$

$= \sqrt{117} = 3\sqrt{13} \approx 10.8167$

$e = \sqrt{1 + \dfrac{b^2}{a^2}}$

$= \sqrt{1 + \dfrac{6^2}{9^2}}$

$= \sqrt{1 + \dfrac{36}{81}}$

$= \sqrt{\dfrac{117}{81}} = \sqrt{\dfrac{13}{9}} = \dfrac{\sqrt{13}}{3} \approx 1.2019$

Calculate the slope values:

$m = \pm\dfrac{a}{b} = \pm\dfrac{9}{6} = \pm\dfrac{3}{2}$

Use point-slope formula for each asymptote. Use (h, k).

$y - y_1 = m(x - x_1)$	$y - y_1 = m(x - x_1)$
$y - 8 = \frac{3}{2}(x - 5)$	$y - 8 = -\frac{3}{2}(x - 5)$
$y - 8 = \frac{3}{2}x - \frac{10}{3}$	$y - 8 = -\frac{3}{2}x + \frac{10}{3}$
$y = \frac{3}{2}x + \frac{14}{3}$	$y = -\frac{3}{2}x + \frac{34}{3}$

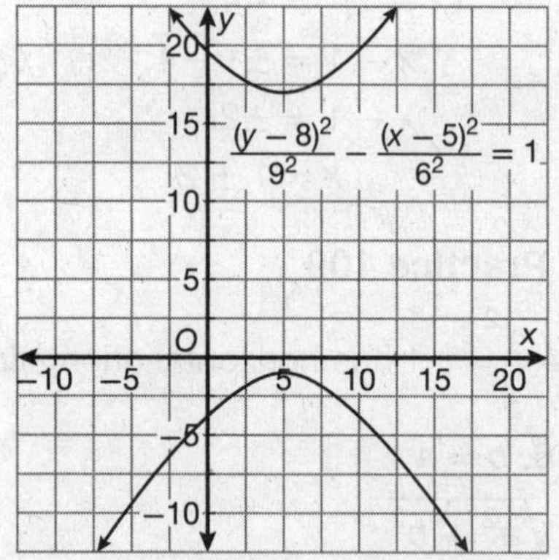

e. $54y - 9y^2 + 4x^2 - 32x - 161 = 0$

$(4x^2 - 32x) - (9y^2 - 54y) - 161 = 0$

$4(x^2 - 8x) - 9(y^2 - 6y) - 161 = 0$

$4(x^2 - 2(4)x + 4^2) - 9(y^2 - 2(3)y + 3^2)$
$-161 - 4(4)^2 + 9(3)^2 = 0$

$4(x-4)^2 - 9(y-3)^2 - 161 - 64 + 81 = 0$

$4(x-4)^2 - 9(y-3)^2 - 144 = 0$

$4(x-4)^2 - 9(y-3)^2 = 144$

$\dfrac{4(x-4)^2}{144} - \dfrac{9(y-3)^2}{144} = \dfrac{144}{144}$

$$\frac{(x-4)^2}{36} - \frac{(y-3)^2}{16} = 1$$
$$\frac{(x-4)^2}{6^2} - \frac{(y-3)^2}{4^2} = 1$$

f. $\sin h^2(x) - \cos h^2(x)$

$$= \left(\frac{e^x - e^{-x}}{2}\right)^2 - \left(\frac{e^x - e^{-x}}{2}\right)^2$$
$$= \frac{1}{4}(e^{2x} - 2e^x e^{-x} + e^{-2x} - e^{2x} - 2e^x e^{-x} - e^{-2x})$$
$$= \frac{1}{4}(-2 - 2)$$
$$= \frac{1}{4}(-4) = -1$$

Practice 109

1. $$\frac{x+4}{x^2 - x - 12} + \frac{2x}{x+3}$$
$$= \frac{x+4}{(x-4)(x+3)} + \frac{2x}{x+3}$$
$$= \frac{(x+4) + (x-4)(2x)}{(x-4)(x+3)}$$
$$= \frac{x + 4 + 2x^2 - 8x}{(x-4)(x+3)}$$
$$= \frac{2x^2 - 7x + 4}{(x-4)(x+3)}$$
$$= \frac{2x^2 - 7x + 4}{x^2 - x - 12}$$

2. $$\frac{\frac{x-1}{x+5}}{\frac{x+6}{x-3}} = \frac{x-1}{x+5} \cdot \frac{x-3}{x+6}$$
$$= \frac{x^2 - 4x + 3}{x^2 + 11x + 30}$$

3. $\tan\theta = \frac{y}{x} = \frac{-5}{-5} = 1$ and θ terminates in Quadrant III, so one value of θ is $\pi + \tan^{-1}(1) = \pi + \frac{\pi}{4} = \frac{5\pi}{4}$.

$$r^2 = x^2 + y^2$$
$$= (-5)^2 + (-5)^2$$
$$= 25 + 25 = 50$$
$$r = \sqrt{50} = 5\sqrt{2}$$

$\left(5\sqrt{2}, \frac{5\pi}{4}\right)$ is one set of polar coordinates.

4. The terminal arm lies along the negative y-axis, so one value of θ is $\frac{3\pi}{2}$.

$$r^2 = x^2 + y^2$$
$$= (0)^2 + (-4)^2$$
$$= 0 + 16 = 16$$
$$r = \sqrt{16} = 4$$

$\left(4, \frac{3\pi}{2}\right)$ is one set of polar coordinates.

5. The asymptote equations imply that $a = b$ and $h = k = 0$. The graph includes (5, 0), so the orientation is horizontal. Write the equation for the hyperbola and substitute known information.

$$\frac{(x-h)^2}{a^2} - \frac{(y-k)^2}{b^2} = 1$$
$$\frac{(5-0)^2}{a^2} - \frac{(0-0)^2}{a^2} = 1$$
$$\frac{25}{a^2} = 1$$
$$25 = a^2$$
$$a = \pm 5$$

Ignoring the negative solution, $a = 5$.

Therefore the equation is $\frac{x^2}{5^2} - \frac{y^2}{5^2} = 1$.

6. $$M \cdot N = \begin{bmatrix} 10 & -3 \\ 3 & -1 \end{bmatrix} \cdot \begin{bmatrix} 1 & -3 \\ 3 & -10 \end{bmatrix}$$
$$= \begin{bmatrix} 10(1) - 3(3) & 10(-3) - 3(-10) \\ 3(1) - 1(3) & 3(-3) - 1(-10) \end{bmatrix}$$
$$= \begin{bmatrix} 10 - 9 & -30 + 30 \\ 3 - 3 & -9 + 10 \end{bmatrix}$$
$$= \begin{bmatrix} 1 & 0 \\ 0 & 1 \end{bmatrix} = I$$

$$N \cdot M = \begin{bmatrix} 1 & -3 \\ 3 & -10 \end{bmatrix} \cdot \begin{bmatrix} 10 & -3 \\ 3 & -1 \end{bmatrix}$$
$$= \begin{bmatrix} 1(10) - 3(3) & 1(-3) - 3(-1) \\ 3(10) - 10(3) & 3(-3) - 10(-1) \end{bmatrix}$$
$$= \begin{bmatrix} 10 - 9 & -3 + 3 \\ 30 - 30 & -9 + 10 \end{bmatrix}$$
$$= \begin{bmatrix} 1 & 0 \\ 0 & 1 \end{bmatrix} = I$$

Therefore M and N are inverses.

7. Sample: The brother's age satisfies $6 \leq x \leq 9$ and $9 \leq x \leq 12$. Lana can buy a size 3 or a size 4. The table does not form a function because there is more than one size for the same age. Therefore the graph will not pass the vertical line test.

8. Sample: As $x \rightarrow \pm\infty$, the absolute value of the highest-degree term becomes much greater than the absolute value of the sum of all the other terms, and the difference between the absolute value of the highest-degree term and the absolute value of the sum of all the other terms increases.

9. Sample: As entered on a calculator, $\log(2) \div 12\log(1.05) = \left(\frac{\log 2}{12}\right)(\log 1.05)$. Possible correct expression: $\log(2) \div (12\log(1.05))$

10. The difference in distances of satellite from each focus should be constant.

11. Any multiple of 2π can be added to θ, so possible coordinates are $(r, \theta + 2n\pi)$, where n is any integer.

12. $\frac{1}{4}\begin{bmatrix}2 & 4\\6 & 8\end{bmatrix} + \begin{bmatrix}-2 & 1\\-\frac{1}{2} & 5\end{bmatrix}$

$= \begin{bmatrix}\frac{1}{2} & 1\\\frac{3}{2} & 2\end{bmatrix} + \begin{bmatrix}-2 & 1\\-\frac{1}{2} & 5\end{bmatrix}$

$= \begin{bmatrix}\frac{1}{2}-2 & 1+1\\\frac{3}{2}-\frac{1}{2} & 2+5\end{bmatrix} = \begin{bmatrix}-\frac{3}{2} & 2\\1 & 7\end{bmatrix}$

13. $\frac{x^2 - x - 12}{x - 2} = 0$

$\frac{(x-4)(x+3)}{x-2} = 0$

$x - 4 = 0$ or $x + 3 = 0$

$x = 4$ $\quad x = -3$

14. Press MODE and select **Radian.** Enter Y1 = $\tan(X)^{-2}$ and Y2 = $\sin(X)^{-2}$; press ZOOM and select **7: ZTrig.**

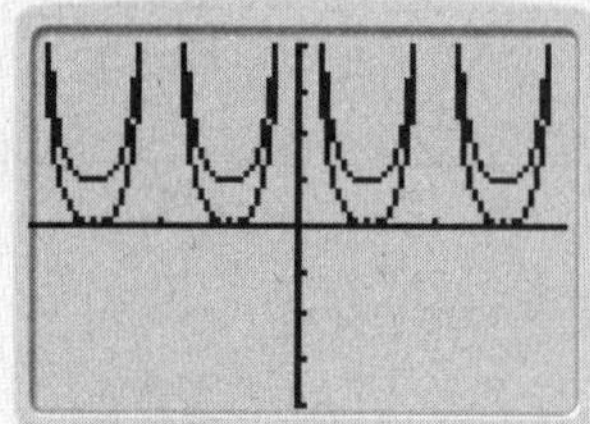

At any given x-coordinate, $y_1 = \cot^2(x)$ is exactly 1 unit below $y_2 = \csc^2(x)$.

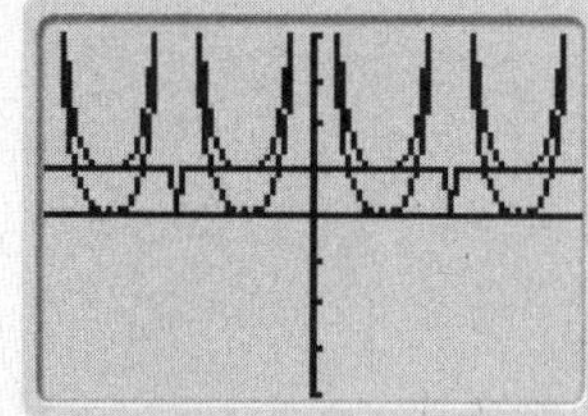

15. $A = lw$

$22 = (3x + 2)(x - 1)$

$22 = (3x)(x) + (3x)(-1) + (2)(x) + (2)(-1)$

$22 = 3x^2 - 3x + 2x - 2$

$0 = 3x^2 - x - 24$

Positive factor pair for 3 is (1)(3); factor pairs for -24 are $(1)(-24)$, $(-1)(24)$, $(2)(-12)$, $(-2)(12)$, $(3)(-8)$, $(-3)(8)$, $(4)(-6)$, and $(-6)(1)$. Since $(1)(8) + (3)(-3) = -1$, right hand side factors as $0 = (x - 3)(3x + 8)$. Ignoring the negative solution, $x = 3$, so

$l = 3x + 2$

$= 3(3) + 2$

$= 9 + 2 = 11$

Since the length of the sheet is the circumference of the cylinder

$2\pi r = l = 11$

$r = \frac{2\pi r}{2\pi} = \frac{11}{2\pi}$

Radius is $\frac{11}{2\pi}$ units.

16. Line perpendicular to $y = 19$ (horizontal) has the form $x = a$ (vertical). Since the line passes through $(6, -5)$, the equation is $x = 6$.

17. For $x = -8$, $f(x) = 2 - x$

$f(-8) = 2 - (-8) = 10$

For $x = 5$, $f(x) = 2 - x$

$f(5) = 2 - (5) = -3$

18. Sample: The student's expression for P contains P. When an equation is solved for a variable correctly, expression for variable cannot contain that variable.

Correct solution:

$$A = P + Prt$$
$$A = P(1 + rt)$$
$$P = \frac{A}{(1 + rt)}$$

19. $$\frac{1}{1 + \tan^2\theta} = \frac{1}{1 + \frac{\sin^2\theta}{\cos^2\theta}}$$
$$= \frac{\cos^2\theta}{\cos^2\theta\left(1 + \frac{\sin^2\theta}{\cos^2\theta}\right)}$$
$$= \frac{\cos^2\theta}{\cos^2\theta + \sin^2\theta}$$
$$= \frac{\cos^2\theta}{1} = \cos^2\theta$$

Answer Choice **D**

20. $$\tan\theta = \frac{\text{opp.}}{\text{adj.}} = \frac{h}{L}$$
$$L\tan\theta = h$$
$$L = \frac{h}{\tan\theta}$$

21. For choice B, the centers are $(1, -2)$ and $(1, -2)$, the radii are $\sqrt{6}$ and $\sqrt{8}$, so the centers are the same but the radii are different.

Answer Choice **B**

22. $$y = 628 + 1842 \ln t$$
$$7000 = 628 + 1842 \ln t$$
$$6372 = 1842 \ln t$$
$$3.459 \approx \ln t$$
$$t \approx e^{3.459} \approx 31.8$$

The population reached 7,000,000 in 1971 or 1972.

23. a. $y = ab^t$

From table, $a = 1{,}267{,}000{,}000$ and $b = 1 + 0.0104 = 1.0104$. Function is $y_1 = 1{,}267{,}000{,}000(1.0104)^t$.

b. From table, $a = 1{,}005{,}000{,}000$ and $b = 1 + 0.0183 = 1.0183$. Function is $y_1 = 1{,}005{,}000{,}000(1.0183)^t$.

c.
$$y_1 = y_2$$
$$1{,}267{,}000{,}000(1.0104)^t = 1{,}005{,}000{,}000(1.0183)^t$$
$$1267(1.0104)^t = 1005(1.0183)^t$$
$$\ln\left(1267(1.0104)^t\right) = \ln\left(1005(1.0183)^t\right)$$
$$\ln 1267 + t\ln 1.0104 = \ln 1005 + t\ln 1.0183$$
$$\ln 1267 - \ln 1005 = t\ln 1.0183 - t\ln 1.0104$$
$$\ln 1267 - \ln 1005 = t(\ln 1.0183 - \ln 1.0104)$$
$$t = \frac{\ln 1267 - \ln 1005}{\ln 1.0183 - \ln 1.0104} \approx 29.7$$

India will overtake China about 29.7 years after 2000, that is, in 2029 or 2030.

24. $$y = \frac{d(t)}{t}$$
$$y = \frac{-4.9t^2 + v_0^t + d_0}{t}$$
$$y = \frac{-4.9t^2 + 65t + 25}{t}$$
$$y = -4.9t + 65 + \frac{25}{t}$$

Slant asymptote equation is $y = -4.9t + 65$.

25. Sample: Both a geometric sequence and an arithmetic sequence are an ordered list of numbers, where each term except the first is generated by performing an operation on the previous term. They are also similar in that the nth term of either can be found by using a formula, given first term and the common difference or common ratio.

26. $f(-x) = \frac{1}{(-x)(2n+1)}$
$= -\frac{1}{x(2n+1)} = -f(x)$

27. Find the sums of first 8 terms and of first 9 terms of the series. Use $a_1 = 16$ and $d = 48 - 16 = 32$.
$a_m = a_1 + (n-1)d$
$a_8 = 16 + (8-1)(32)$
$= 16 + 7(32) = 16 + 224 = 240$
$a_9 = 16 + (9-1)(32)$
$= 16 + 8(32) = 16 + 256 = 272$
$S_8 = 8\left(\frac{16+240}{2}\right) = 8\left(\frac{256}{2}\right) = 1024$
$S_9 = 9\left(\frac{16+272}{2}\right) = 9\left(\frac{288}{2}\right) = 1296$
The height is between 1024 ft and 1296 ft.

28. Excluded values
$x^2 - 49 = 0$
$x^2 = 49$
$x = \pm\sqrt{49} = \pm 7$
$\frac{4x+28}{x^2-49} = \frac{4\cancel{(x+7)}}{(x-7)\cancel{(x+7)}} = \frac{4}{x-7}$

29. Function is $y = (x+4)^3(x-2)(x-6)^2$. Roots at $x = -4$ and 2 have odd multiplicity, so the graph crosses x-axis at $(-4, 0)$ and $(2, 0)$; the root at $x = 6$ has even multiplicity, so the graph just touches x-axis at $(6, 0)$.

30. Asymptote slopes are $m = \pm\frac{b}{a} = \pm\frac{3}{4}$
$b = \frac{3}{4}a$
Suppose foci are at (0, 5) and (0, −5). Then
$c = \sqrt{a^2 + b^2}$
$5 = \sqrt{a^2 + \left(\frac{3}{4}a\right)^2}$
$5^2 = a^2 + \frac{9}{16}a^2$
$25(16) = 16a^2 + 9a^2$
$400 = 25a^2$
$16 = a^2$
$a = \sqrt{16} = 4$

Therefore, $b = \frac{3}{4}(4) = 3$. Possible equation is $\frac{x^2}{4^2} - \frac{y^2}{3^2} = 1$.

LESSON 110

Warm Up 110

1. natural logarithm
2. $\log\frac{(x^2-1)}{x-3}$
$= \log\frac{(x-1)(x+1)}{x-3}$
$= \log(x-1) + \log(x+1) - \log(x-3)$
3. $\log_b x = \frac{\ln x}{\ln b}$
$\log_6 78 = \frac{\ln 78}{\ln 6}$

Lesson Practice 110

a. $f(x)$

x	−2	−1	0	1	2
y	$\frac{1}{9}$	$\frac{1}{3}$	1	3	9

$f^{-1}(x)$

x	$\frac{1}{9}$	$\frac{1}{3}$	1	3	9
y	−2	−1	0	1	2

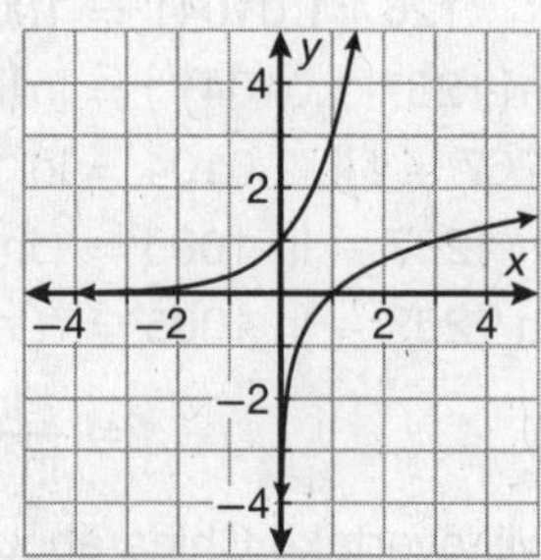

The domain of $f(x) = 3^x$ is all real numbers. The range is $f(x) > 0$. So, the domain of the inverse function $f^{-1}(x) = \log_3 x$ is $x > 0$, and the range $f^{-1}(x)$ is all real numbers.

b.

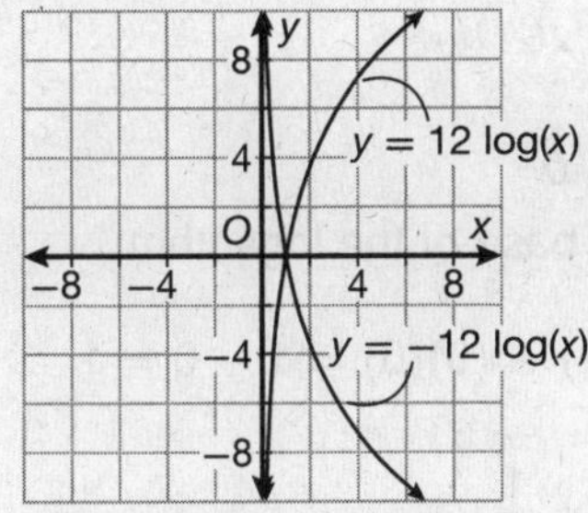

The graphs are reflections of each other in x-axis.

c.

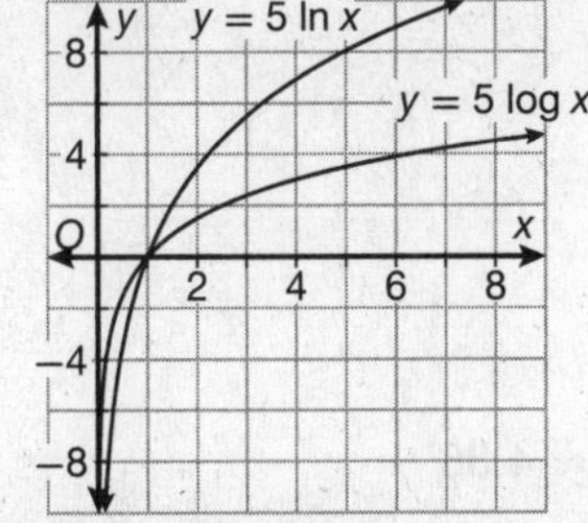

The larger the base, the lower the graph to the right of $x = 1$.

d.

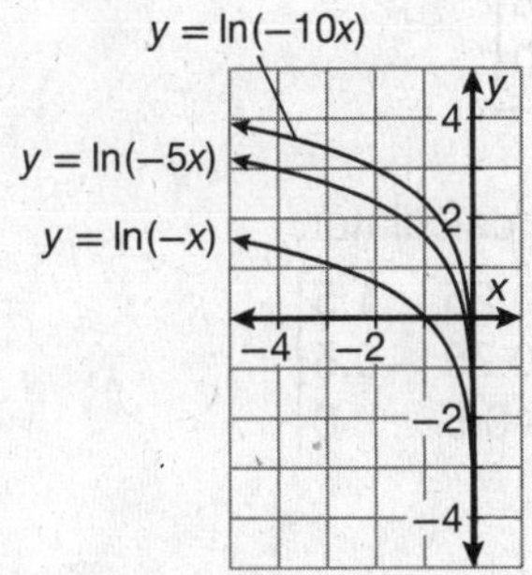

The larger the absolute value of c, the greater the vertical shift up of the graph.

e. $db_2 - db_1 = 10\log\left(\frac{I_2}{I_0}\right) - 10\log\left(\frac{I_1}{I_0}\right)$

$$= 10\log\left(\frac{I_2}{I_0} \Big/ \frac{I_2}{I_0}\right) = 10\log\left(\frac{I_2}{I_1}\right)$$

$$20 - 0 = 10\log\left(\frac{I_2}{I_1}\right)$$

$$20 = 10\log\left(\frac{I_2}{I_1}\right)$$

$$2 = \log\left(\frac{I_2}{I_1}\right)$$

$$10^2 = \frac{I_2}{I_1}$$

$$I_2 = 10^2\, I_1 = 100 I_1$$

The intensity of a whisper is 100 times louder than the threshold of hearing.

Practice 110

1. The polynomial can be partially factored by grouping.

$$y = (12x^{11} - 23x^{10} + 10x^9) - (12x^8 - 23x^7 + 10x^6) - (12x^5 - 23x^4 + 10x^3) + (12x^2 - 23x + 10)$$

$$= x^9(12x^2 - 23x + 10) - x^6(12x^2 - 23x + 10) - x^3(12x^2 - 23x + 10) + (12x^2 - 23x + 10)$$

$$= (x^9 - x^6 - x^3 + 1)(12x^2 - 23x + 10)$$

Use Rational Root Theorem for degree-9 factor: p-values, q-values, and values for $\frac{p}{q}$ are all ±1. Synthetic division with $a = 1$.

1	1	0	0	−1	0	0	−1	0	0	1
		1	1	1	0	0	0	−1	−1	−1
	1	1	1	0	0	0	−1	−1	−1	0

Synthetic division with $a = -1$.

−1	1	0	0	−1	0	0	−1	0	0	1
		−1	1	−1	2	−2	2	−1	1	−1
	1	−1	1	−2	2	−2	1	−1	1	0

So $x = 1$ and -1 are both roots of function.

Determine the roots of the quadratic factor using the quadratic formula.

$$x = \frac{-b \pm \sqrt{b^2 - 4ac}}{2a}$$

$$= \frac{-(-23) \pm \sqrt{(-23)^2 - 4(12)(10)}}{2(12)}$$

$$= \frac{23 \pm \sqrt{529 - 480}}{24}$$

$$= \frac{23 \pm \sqrt{49}}{24}$$

$$= \frac{23 \pm 7}{24}$$

$$= \frac{16}{24}, \frac{30}{24}$$

$$= \frac{2}{3}, \frac{5}{4}$$

The roots of function are -1, 1, $\frac{2}{3}$, and $\frac{5}{4}$.

2. $a_n = a_1 + (n-1)d$
$-54 = -12 + (15-1)d$
$-54 = -12 + 14d$
$-42 = 14d$
$-3 = d$
Answer Choice **B**

3. $16x = 2 - x^2 + y$
$x^2 + 16x - 2 = y$

4. $-9 + 13x = 4x^2 - y$
$y = 4x^2 - 13x + 9$

5. The denominator is zero when
$x^2 + x - 30 = 0$
$(x-5)(x+6) = 0$
$x - 5 = 0$ or $x + 6 = 0$
$x = 5$ $\quad x = -6$

6. a. $V = lwh$
$y = (x)(x-1)(x-2)$
$y = x(x^2 - 3x + 2)$
$y = x^3 - 3x^2 + 2x$

b. The function is cubic, so there are three zeros, at least one is real.

c. $120 = x^3 - 3x^2 + 2x$
$0 = x^3 - 3x^2 + 2x - 120$
By Rational Root Theorem, p-values are $\pm1, \pm2, \pm3, \pm4, \ldots$; q-values are ±1; so
$\frac{p}{q} \in \{\pm1, \pm2, \pm3, \pm4, \ldots\}$
First value that yields a factor is

6	1	−3	2	−120
		6	18	120
	1	3	20	0

Equation factors as
$0 = (x-6)(x^2 + 3x + 20)$
The quadratic factor has no roots, so the only root of the equation is $x = 6$. Therefore, the dimensions are x by $x - 1$ by $x - 2$, or 6 by 5 by 4.

7. $N(t) = \log_b(t)$
$1 = \log_b(t_1)$
$b^1 = t_1$
$b = t_1$
$2 = \log_b(t_2)$
$b^2 = t_2$
$t_2 - t_1 = b^2 - b$
where b is the base of the logarithm.

8. $\begin{vmatrix} 1 & 0 \\ 0 & 1 \end{vmatrix} = (1)(1) - (0)(0) = 1 - 0 = 1$

9. $\frac{1}{f} = \frac{1}{o} + \frac{1}{i}$
$\frac{1}{4} = \frac{1}{48} + \frac{1}{i}$
$\frac{1}{4} - \frac{1}{48} = \frac{1}{i}$
$\frac{12 - 1}{48} = \frac{1}{i}$
$\frac{11}{48} = \frac{1}{i}$
$i = \frac{48}{11} \approx 4.36$
The image distance is about 4.36 cm.

10. $\underbrace{\begin{bmatrix} 1 & 1 & 1 \\ 3 & 3 & 1 \\ 4 & 2 & 1 \end{bmatrix}}_{A} \underbrace{\begin{bmatrix} x \\ y \\ z \end{bmatrix}}_{B} \underbrace{\begin{bmatrix} -2 \\ -18 \\ -20 \end{bmatrix}}_{C}$

Using a graphing calculator:
$A^{-1} = \begin{bmatrix} -0.25 & -0.25 & 1.5 \\ -0.25 & 0.75 & -0.5 \\ 1.5 & -0.5 & 0 \end{bmatrix}$

$X = A^{-1}B = \begin{bmatrix} -5 \\ -3 \\ 6 \end{bmatrix}$
The solution is $x = -5$, $y = -3$, $z = 6$.

11. Number of outfits $= {}_4C_2 \times {}_3C_2 = 6 \times 3 = 18$

12. $y = -82{,}110 + 70{,}059 \ln t$
$100{,}000 = -82{,}110 + 70{,}059 \ln t$
$182{,}110 = 70{,}059 \ln t$
$\ln t = \frac{182{,}110}{70{,}059} \approx 2.60$
$t \approx e^{2.60} \approx 13.5$
The number reached 100,000,000 in 1973.

13. The x term is $ax^2 + cx$.
$ax^2 + cx$

$a\left(x^2 + 2\left(\frac{c}{2a}\right)x + \left(\frac{c}{2a}\right)^2\right)$

$a\left(x + \frac{c}{2a}\right)^2$

14. $f(g(x)) = f\left(\frac{1}{\sqrt{x}}\right)$

$= 12\log\left(\frac{4}{\sqrt{x}}\right)$

$12\log\left(\frac{4}{\sqrt{x}}\right) = 0$

$\frac{4}{\sqrt{x}} = 10^0 = 1$

$\frac{4}{\sqrt{x}} = 1$

$4 = \sqrt{x}$

$x = 4^2 = 16$

15. The equation of a circle located at any point is $(x - h)^2 + (y - k)^2 = r^2$ where h and k are the coordinates of the center. If the center is at the origin

$(x - 0)^2 + (y - 0)^2 = r^2$

$x^2 + y^2 = r^2$

16. $N(t) = N_0 b^t$

$1000 = 800(1.04)^t$

$1.25 = (1.04)^t$

$\log 1.25 = t \log 1.04$

$t = \frac{\log 1.25}{\log 1.04} \approx 5.69$

It will take about 5.69 years for the membership to reach 1000.

17. Use synthetic division with $a = -1$.

−1	1	0	0	0	−1
		−1	1	−1	1
	1	−1	1	−1	0

$(x^4 - 1) \div (x + 1) = x^3 - x^2 + x - 1$

18. Use synthetic division with $a = 5$.

5	1	0	0	−7
		5	25	125
	1	5	25	118

$(x^3 - 7) \div (x - 5) = x^2 + 5x + 25 + \frac{118}{x - 5}$

19. The student used 5 instead of −5 for the y-coordinate.

20. $\csc A = \frac{\text{hyp.}}{\text{opp.}} = \frac{17}{6.4} \approx 2.66$

21. $\sec A = \frac{\text{hyp.}}{\text{adj.}} = \frac{17}{15.8} \approx 1.08$

22. $x^2 + 4x < 5$

$x^2 + 4x - 5 < 0$

$(x - 1)(x + 5) < 0$

The roots of LHS are $x = 1$ and -5. The parabola is not inverted, so the inequality is true between roots; $-5 < x < 1$

Answer Choice **A**

23. Sample: Phase shifts do not affect trigonometric identities. For example, consider $\sin^2 x + \cos^2 x = 1$. Phase shift changes x to $x - \theta$, but letting $y = x - \theta$, $\sin^2(x - \theta) + \cos^2(x - \theta) = \sin^2 y + \cos^2 y = 1$.

24. $V = \frac{1}{3}Bh$

$x^3 + 4x^2 + 4x = \frac{1}{3}B(3x)$

$x^3 + 4x^2 + 4x = Bx$

$x^2 + 4x + 4 = B$

$(x + 2)^2 = B$

Dimensions of base are $x + 2$ by $x + 2$.

25. $f(n) = \frac{\frac{1}{2}n(n + 1)}{n^2}$

$= \frac{\frac{1}{2}(n + 1)}{n}$

$= \frac{\frac{1}{2}n + \frac{1}{2}}{n} = \frac{1}{2} + \frac{1}{2n}$

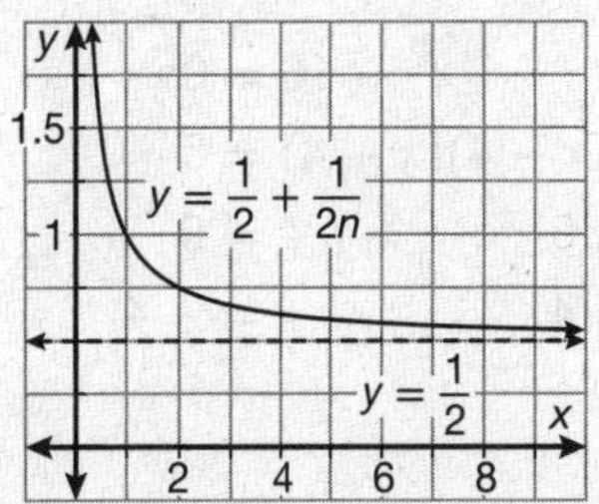

Asymptote is $y = \frac{1}{2}$. As n increases, the ratio approaches $\frac{1}{2}$.

26. Student B divided by $\frac{2}{3}$ incorrectly.

27. $\tan\theta = \frac{h_2}{w}$ and $\tan\varphi = \frac{h_1}{w}$

$$w = \frac{h_2}{\tan\theta} \qquad w = \frac{h_1}{\tan\varphi}$$

Therefore

$$\frac{h_2}{\tan\theta} = \frac{h_1}{\tan\varphi}$$

$$h_2 \tan\varphi = h_1 \tan\theta$$

$$\frac{h_2 \tan\varphi}{h_1} = \tan\theta$$

$$\theta = \tan^{-1}\left(\frac{h_2}{h_1}\tan\varphi\right)$$

28. $f(x) = 0.195x^4 - 5.035x^3 + 6.205x^2 + 338.331x + 10,219$

Use graphing calculator to graph function over domain $0 \le x \le 20$; press 2nd TRACE to access CALC menu and use **4:maximum**.

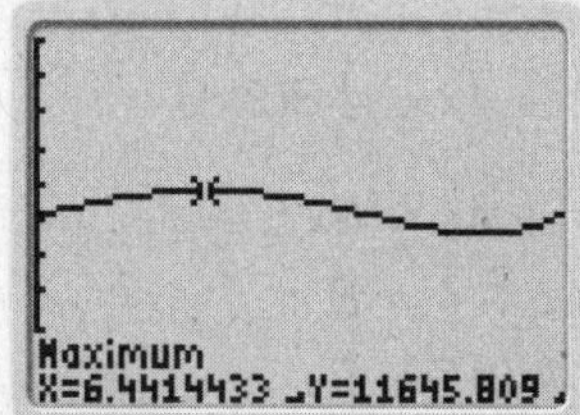

Highest quarterly value is about 11,645.8, at $x \approx 6.44 \approx 6$, or in the 6th quarter (April-June 2000)

29. Factor pairs for -21 are $(1)(-21)$, $(-1)(21)$, $(3)(-7)$, and $(-3)(7)$; $-3 + 7 = 4$, so RHS of equation factors as $0 = (x - 3)(x + 7)$.

Therefore,

$$x - 3 = 0 \quad \text{or} \quad x + 7 = 0$$

$$x = 3 \qquad x = -7$$

30.

$$x^2 - 16 = 0$$

$$(x - 4)(x + 4) = 0$$

$$x - 4 = 0 \quad \text{or} \quad x + 4 = 0$$

$$x = 4 \qquad x = -4$$

INVESTIGATION 11

1. a-f.

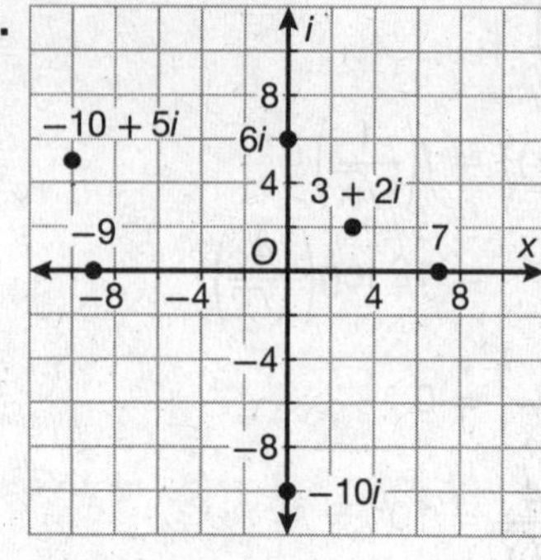

2. a-f.

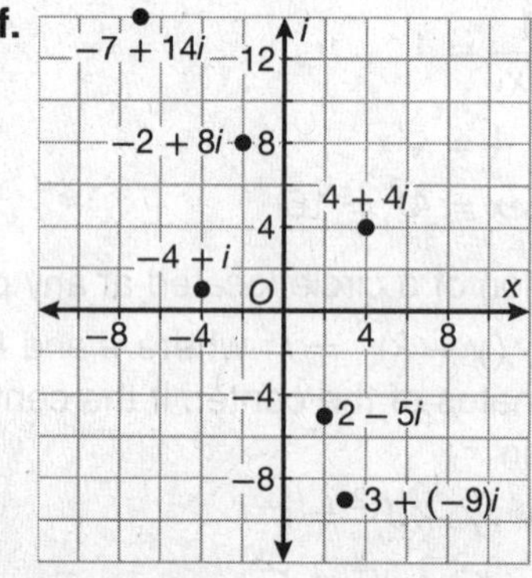

a. $0 \le \theta < 90$

$\tan\theta = \frac{4}{4}$

$\theta = \tan^{-1}(1)$

$\theta = 45°$

b. $90 < \theta \le 180$

$\tan\theta = \frac{-7}{14}$

$\theta = \tan^{-1}(-2)$

$\theta \approx 116.57°$

c. $270 < \theta \le 360$

$\tan\theta = \frac{-9}{3}$

$\theta = \tan^{-1}(-3)$

$\theta \approx 288.43°$

d. $90 < \theta \le 180$

$\tan\theta = \frac{8}{-2}$

$\theta = \tan^{-1}(-4)$

$\theta \approx 104.03°$

e. $270 < \theta \le 360$

$\tan\theta = \frac{-5}{2}$

$\theta = \tan^{-1}(-2.5)$

$\theta \approx 291.80°$

f. $90 < \theta \le 180$

$\tan\theta = \frac{1}{-4}$

$\theta = \tan^{-1}(-0.25)$

$\theta \approx 165.96°$

3.

a	b	$r=\sqrt{a^2+b^2}$
4	4	$\sqrt{16+16}=\sqrt{32}\approx 5.66$
−7	14	$\sqrt{49+196}=\sqrt{245}$ ≈ 15.65
3	−9	$\sqrt{9+81}=\sqrt{90}\approx 9.49$
−2	8	$\sqrt{4+64}=\sqrt{68}\approx 8.25$
2	−5	$\sqrt{4+25}=\sqrt{29}\approx 5.39$
−4	1	$\sqrt{16+1}=\sqrt{17}\approx 4.12$

4. **a.** $r=\sqrt{4^2+(-2)^2}=\sqrt{20}\approx 4.47$

$\theta=\tan^{-1}\left(\frac{-2}{4}\right)\approx -26.57°$.

Since $4-2i$ is in Quadrant IV, 26.57° is a reference angle.

$\theta = 360° - 26.57° = 333.43°$

$z = 4.47\cos(333.43°) + i4.47\sin(333.43°)$

b. $r=\sqrt{(-1)^2+(-1)^2}=\sqrt{2}$

$\theta=\tan^{-1}\left(\frac{-1}{-1}\right)=45°$.

Since $-1-i$ is in Quadrant III, 45° is a reference angle.

$\theta = 180° + 45° = 225°$

$z=\sqrt{2}\cos(225°)+i\sqrt{2}\sin(225°)$

c. $r=\sqrt{3^2+4^2}=\sqrt{25}=5$

$\theta=\tan^{-1}\left(\frac{4}{3}\right)\approx 53.13°$.

Since $3+4i$ is in Quadrant I, 53.13° is θ.

$z = 5\cos(53.13°) + i5\sin(53.13°)$

5. **a.** $7\cos(45°) + i7\sin(45°)$

$= 7\left(\frac{\sqrt{2}}{2}\right) + 7i\left(\frac{\sqrt{2}}{2}\right)$

$= \frac{7\sqrt{2}}{2} + \frac{7\sqrt{2}}{2}i$

b. $10\cos(90°) + 10i\sin(90°)$

$= 10(0) + 10i(1)$

$= 0 + 10i$

c. $5\cos(120°) + 5i\sin(120°)$

$= 5\left(-\frac{1}{2}\right) + 5i\left(\frac{\sqrt{3}}{2}\right)$

$= -\frac{5}{2} + \frac{5\sqrt{3}}{2}i$

$= -2.5 + \frac{5\sqrt{3}}{2}i$

d. Use a calculator to evaluate $17\cos(200°) + 17i\sin(200°)$.

$17\cos(200°) + 17i\sin(200°)$

$= 17(-0.9396) + 17i(-0.3420)$

$= -15.97 - 5.81i$

6.

r	θ	a	b
7	45°	$7\cos 45° \approx 4.95$	$7\sin 45°$ $\approx 4.95°$
10	90°	$10\cos 90° = 0$	$10\sin 90°$ $= 10$
5	120°	$5\cos 120°$ $= -2.5$	$5\sin 120°$ ≈ 4.33
17	200°	$17\cos 200°$ ≈ -15.97	$17\sin 200°$ ≈ -5.81

7. $r=\sqrt{4^2+6^2}=\sqrt{52}\approx 7.21$

$\theta=\tan^{-1}\left(\frac{6}{4}\right)$ in Q. I $\approx 56.31°$

$r=\sqrt{7^2+7^2}=\sqrt{98}\approx 9.90$

$\theta=\tan^{-1}\left(\frac{7}{7}\right)$ in Q. I $= 45°$

$r=\sqrt{(-3)^2+4^2}=\sqrt{25}=5$

$\theta=\tan^{-1}\left(\frac{4}{-3}\right)$ in Q. II $\approx 126.87°$

$r=\sqrt{15^2+0^2}=\sqrt{225}=15$

$\theta = 0°$

$r=\sqrt{0^2+(28)^2}=28$

$\theta = 90°$

$a+bi$	r	θ	Polar Form
$4+6i$	7.21	56.31°	$7.21\cos(56.31°) +$ $7.21\sin(56.31°)i$
$7+7i$	9.90	45°	$9.90\cos(45°) +$ $9.90\sin(45°)i$
$-3+4i$	5	126.87°	$5\cos(126.87°) +$ $5\sin(126.87°)i$
15	15	0°	$15\cos(0°) +$ $15\sin(0°)i$
$28i$	28	90°	$28\cos(90°) +$ $28\sin(90°)i$

8. a. $[7\cos(20°) + i7\sin(20°)]^3$
$= 7^3\cos(3 \cdot 20) + i7^3\sin(3 \cdot 20)$
$= 343(.5) + i343(0.866)$
$= 171.5 + 297.05i$

b. $[3\cos(45°) + i3\sin(45°)]^2$
$= 3^2\cos(2 \cdot 45) + i3^2\sin(2 \cdot 45)$
$= 9(0) + i9(1)$
$= 9i$

c. $[2\cos(120°) + i2\sin(120°)]^4$
$= 2^4\cos(4 \cdot 120) + i2^4\sin(4 \cdot 120)$
$= 16(-0.5) + i16(0.866)$
$= -8 + 13.86i$

d. $[\cos(210°) + i\sin(210°)]^3$
$= 1^3\cos(3 \cdot 210) + i1^3\sin(3 \cdot 210)$
$= 1(0) + i1(-1)$
$= -i$

e. $[4\cos(180°) + i4\sin(180°)]^2$
$= 4^2\cos(4 \cdot 180) + i4^2\sin(4 \cdot 180)$
$= 16(1) + i16(0)$
$= 16$

f. $[2\cos(30°) + i2\sin(30°)]^6$
$= 2^6\cos(6 \cdot 30) + i2^6\sin(6 \cdot 30)$
$= 64(-1) + i64(0)$
$= -64$

9. a. $r = \sqrt{3^2 + 4^2} = \sqrt{25} = 5$
$\theta = \tan^{-1}\left(\frac{4}{3}\right)$ in Q. I $\approx 53.13°$
$r^3 = 5^3 = 125,\ 3\theta \approx 3(53.13°)$
$\approx 159.39°$
$(3 + 4i)^3 \approx 125\cos(159.39°)$
$+ i125\sin(159.39°)$

b. $r = \sqrt{10^2 + (-10)^2} = \sqrt{200}$
≈ 14.14
$\theta = \tan^{-1}\left(\frac{10}{-10}\right)$ in Q. IV = 315°
$r^4 = \left(\sqrt{200}\right)^2 = 40{,}000$
$4\theta = 4(315°) = 1260°$ or $180°$
$(10 - 10i)^4 = 40{,}000\cos(180°)$
$+ i40{,}000\sin(180°)$

c. $r = \sqrt{5^2 + 12^2} = \sqrt{169} = 13,$
$\theta = \tan^{-1}\left(\frac{12}{5}\right)$ in Q. I $\approx 67.38°$
$r^6 = 13^6 = 4{,}826{,}809$
$6\theta \approx 3(67.38°) \approx 404.28°$ or $44.28°$
$(3 + 4i)^3 \approx 4{,}826{,}809\cos(44.28°)$
$+ i4{,}826{,}809\sin(44.28°)$

d. $r = 4,\ \theta = 180°$
$r^8 = 4^8 = 65{,}536,\ 8\theta = 8(180°)$
$= 1440°$ or $0°$
$(-4 + 0i)^8 = 65{,}536\cos(0°)$
$+ i65{,}536\sin(0°)$

e. $r = 7,\ \theta = 90°$
$r^{12} = 7^{12} \approx 1.38 \times 10^{10},$
$12\theta = 12(90°) = 1080°$ or $0°$
$(0 + 7i)^{12} = 1.38 \times 10^{10}\cos(0°)$
$+ i1.38 \times 10^{10}\sin(0°)$

Investigation Practice 11

a. $r = 5 + (-5i)$
$\rightarrow r = \sqrt{5^2 + (-5)^2} = \sqrt{50} \approx 7.07,$
$\theta = \tan^{-1}\left(\frac{-5}{5}\right)$ in Q. IV = 315°
$r = -7 + 10i$
$r = \sqrt{(-7)^2 + 10^2} = \sqrt{149} \approx 12.21,$
$\theta = \tan^{-1}\left(\frac{10}{-7}\right)$ in Q. II $\approx 124.99°$
$r = 0 + 18i \rightarrow r = 18,\ \theta = 90°$
$r = 25 + 0i \rightarrow r = 25,\ \theta = 0°$
$r = -9 + (-3i)$
$\rightarrow r = \sqrt{(-9)^2 + (-3)^2} = \sqrt{90} \approx 9.49,$
$\theta = \tan^{-1}\left(\frac{-3}{-9}\right)$ in Q. III $\approx 198.43°$

$a + bi$	r	θ	Polar Form
$5 + (-5i)$	7.07	315°	$7.07\cos(315°) + i7.07\sin(315°)$
$-7 + 10i$	12.21	124.99°	$12.21\cos(124.99°) + i12.21\sin(124.99°)$
$0 + 18i$	18.00	90°	$18\cos(90°) + i18\sin(90°)$
$25 + 0i$	25.00	0°	$25\cos(0°) + i25\sin(0°)$
$-9 + (-3i)$	9.49	198.43°	$9.49\cos(198.43°) + i9.49\sin(198.43°)$

b. $r = 2 + 7i \longrightarrow |r| = \sqrt{2^2 + 7^2} = \sqrt{53}$
$\approx 7.28,$

$\theta = \tan^{-1}\left(\frac{7}{2}\right)$ in Q. I $\approx 74.055°$

$\longrightarrow r^4 = (\sqrt{53})^4 = 2809,\ 4\theta \approx 4(74.055°)$
$\approx 296.22°$

$\longrightarrow (2 + 7i)^4 = 2809\cos(296.22°) + i2809\sin(296.22°)$

c. $r = 1 - 13i$

$\longrightarrow r = \sqrt{1^2 + (-13)^2} = \sqrt{170} \approx 13.038,$

$\theta = \tan^{-1}\left(\frac{-13}{1}\right)$ in Q. IV $\approx -85.601°$

$\longrightarrow r^7 \approx (13.038)^7 \approx 64{,}057{,}682.83,$

$7\theta \approx 7(-85.601°) \approx -599.207°$ or $120.793°$

$\longrightarrow (1 - 13i)^7 \approx 64{,}057{,}682.83\cos(120.\ 79°) + i64{,}057{,}682.83\sin(120.\ 79°)$

d. $r = 6 + 8i$

$\longrightarrow r = \sqrt{6^2 + 8^2} = \sqrt{100} = 10,$

$\theta = \tan^{-1}\left(\frac{8}{6}\right)$ in Q. I $\approx 53.130°$

$\longrightarrow |r|^8 = 10^8,\ 8\theta \approx 8(53.130°) \approx 425.04°$ or $65.04°$

$\longrightarrow (6 + 8i)^8 \approx 10^8\cos(65.04°) + i10^8\sin(65.04°)$

e. $r = -9 + 0i$

$\longrightarrow r = 9,\ \theta = 180°$

$\longrightarrow r^{12} = 9^{12} \approx 2.824 \times 10^{11},$

$12\ \theta = 12(180°) = 2160°$ or $0°$

$\longrightarrow (-9 + 0i)^{12}$

$\approx 2.824 \times 10^{11}\cos(0°) + i2.824 \times 10^{11}\sin(0°)$

f. $r = 0 + 19i$

$\longrightarrow r = 19,\ \theta = 90°$

$\longrightarrow r^{15} = 19^{15} \approx 1.518 \times 10^{19},$

$15\theta = 15(90°) = 1350°$ or $270°$

$\longrightarrow (0 + 19i)^{15} \approx 1.518 \times 10^{19}\cos(270°) + i1.518 \times 10^{19}\sin(270°)$

LESSON 111

Warm Up 111

1. translation
2. $f(x) + 3 = 5x^2 - x + 1 + 3 = 5x^2 - x + 4$
3. $2 \cdot f(x) = 2(x - 6) = 2x - 12$

Lesson Practice 111

a. $g(x) = x^3 - 1 + 5 = x^3 + 4$

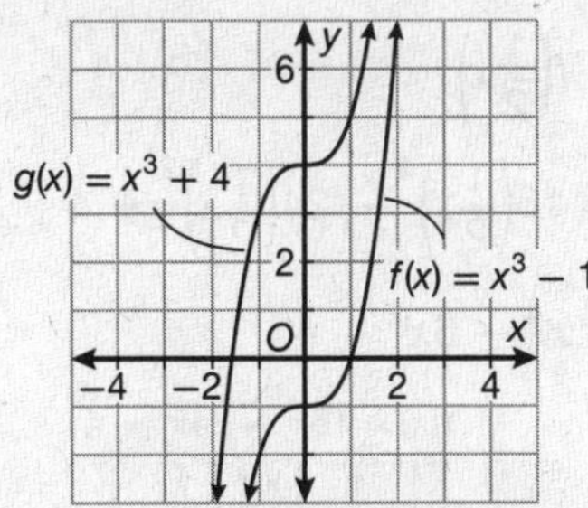

b. $g(x) = (x + 3)^3 - 1$

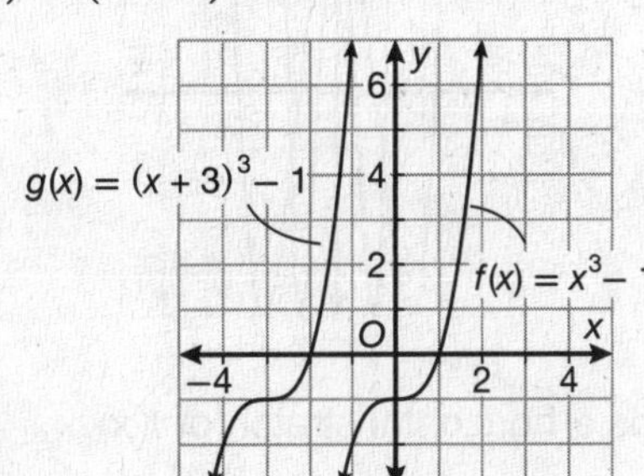

c. $g(x) = -f(x)$
$g(x) = -(x^3 + x^2 - 6x - 1)$
$g(x) = -x^3 - x^2 + 6x + 1$

d. $g(x) = f(-x)$
$g(x) = (-x)^3 + (-x)^2 - 6(-x) - 1$
$g(x) = -x^3 + x^2 + 6x - 1$

e. $g(x) = \frac{1}{4}f(x)$

$g(x) = \frac{1}{4}(16x^4 - 24x^2 + 4)$

$g(x) = 4x^4 - 6x^2 + 1$

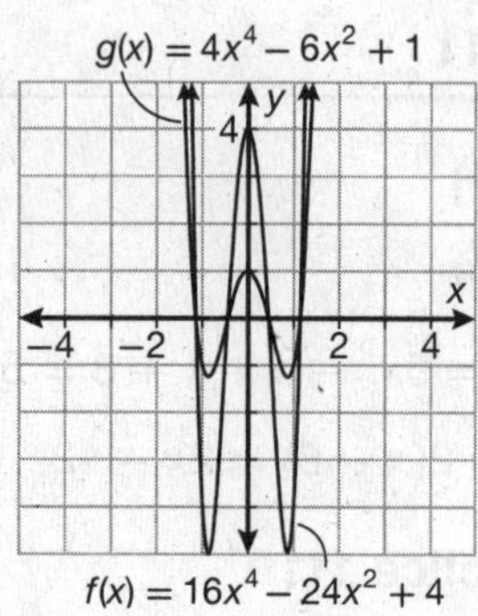

$g(x)$ is a vertical compression of $f(x)$.

f. $g(x) = f\left(\frac{1}{2}x\right)$

$g(x) = 16\left(\frac{1}{2}x\right)^4 - 24\left(\frac{1}{2}x\right)^2 + 4$

$g(x) = x^4 - 6x^2 + 4$

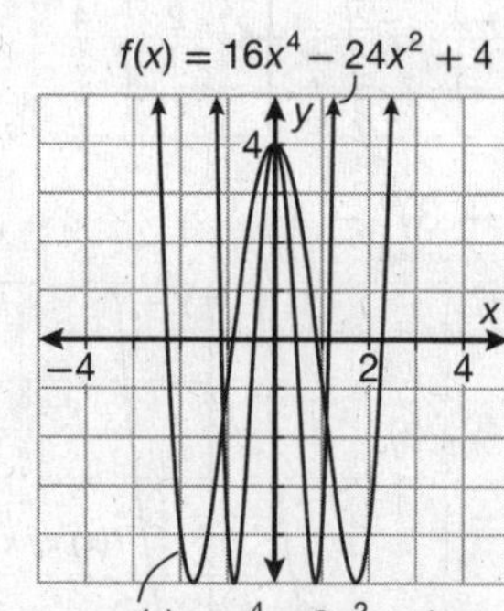

$g(x)$ is a horizontal stretch of $f(x)$.

g. $g(x) = \frac{1}{2}f(x - 3)$

$g(x) = \frac{1}{2}(8(x - 3)^3 - 2)$

$g(x) = 4(x - 3)^3 - 1$

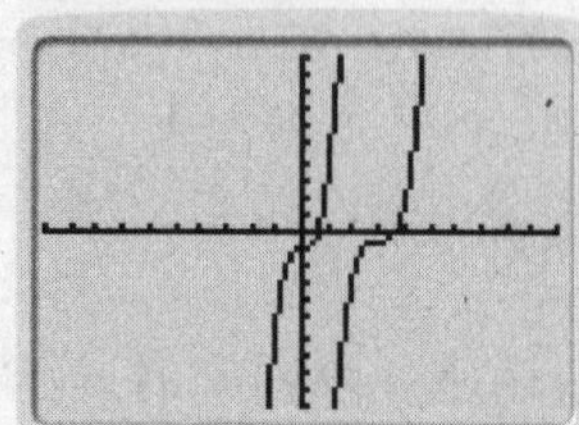

h. $g(x) = -f(x + 4)$

$g(x) = -(8(x + 4)^3 - 2)$

$g(x) = -8(x + 4)^3 + 2$

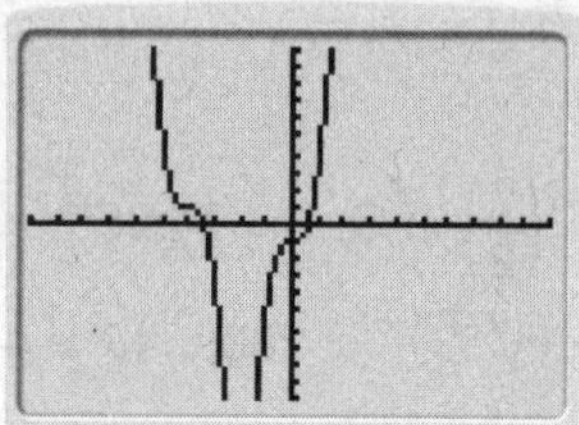

i. $g(t) = (-16t^2 - 15t + 200) - 40$

$g(t) = -16t^2 - 15t + 160$

The graph of $g(t)$ is a vertical shift 40 units down of the graph $h(t)$. If the height of object H is given by $h(t)$ and the height of object G is given by $g(t)$, then object G is 40 feet lower than object H at all times that both objects are in the air.

Practice 111

1. $y - y_1 = m(x - x_1)$

$y - 8 = -4(x - 6)$

$y - 8 = -4x + 24$

$y = -4x + 32$

2. $g(x) = 1.922(x - 1)^4 - 36.769(x - 1)^3 + 132.212(x - 1)^2 + 3558.615(x - 1) - 11.$

The function values of $g(x)$ are the same as those of $f(x)$, but they lag behind by one season. That is, $g(2) = f(1)$, $g(3) = f(2)$, and so on. If no fans had attended in 1996, then $g(x)$ would be the model for the years 1996–2005.

3. $\begin{bmatrix} a \\ 0 \end{bmatrix} \cdot [0 \quad b] = a \cdot 0 + 0 \cdot b = 0$

4. The larger the value of the base, the shorter the height.

Answer Choice **B**

5. $\sqrt{a^2 + b^2} = \sqrt{8^2 + 24^2} \approx 25.3$

$\frac{24}{8} = \tan\theta$

$3 = \tan\theta$

$71.6 \approx \theta$

$|z| = |z|\cos(\theta) + i|z|\sin\theta$

$= 25.3\cos(71.6°) + i25.3\sin(71.6°)$

$(25.3, 71.6°)$

6. $-8 < 4(x + 1)$ and $12 > 4x$

$-2 < x + 1$ $\qquad$ $3 > x$

$-3 < x$

So $-3 < x < 3$

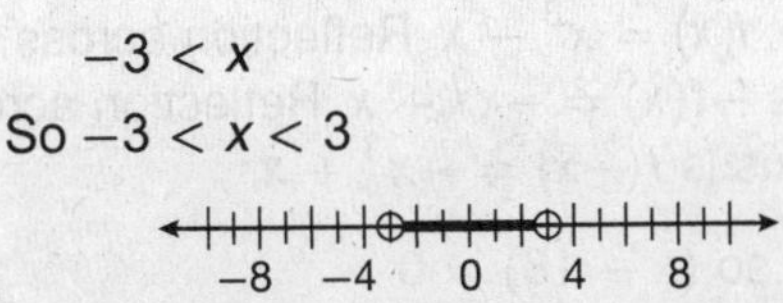

7. The student shaded the wrong region because (0, 0) is a solution. Also the student should have used a dashed line.

8. **A** Period $= \frac{\pi}{b} = \frac{\pi}{1} = \pi$

B Period $= \frac{\pi}{b} = \frac{\pi}{1} = \pi$

C Period $= \frac{\pi}{b} = \frac{\pi}{5}$

D Period $= \frac{\pi}{\frac{1}{5}} = 5\pi$

Answer Choice **C**

9. $1 - \tan h^2(x) \stackrel{?}{=} \frac{1}{\cos h^2(x)}$

$1 - \frac{\sin h^2(x)}{\cos h^2(x)} \stackrel{?}{=} \frac{1}{\cos h^2(x)}$

$\frac{\cos h^2(x)}{\cos h^2(x)} - \frac{\sin h^2(x)}{\cos h^2(x)} \stackrel{?}{=} \frac{1}{\cos h^2(x)}$

$\frac{\cos h^2(x) - \sin h^2(x)}{\cos h^2(x)} = \frac{1}{\cos h^2(x)}$

$\frac{1}{\cos h^2(x)} = \frac{1}{\cos h^2(x)}$

10. $a_n = a_m + (n - m)d$

$24 = 13 + (14 - 3)d$

$24 = 13 + 11d$

$1 = d$

$a_7 = 13 + (7 - 3)1$

$a_7 = 17$

11. $C = \frac{5}{9}(F - 32)$

$\frac{9}{5}C = F - 32$

$\frac{9}{5}C + 32 = F$

Substitute x for both F and C, set the equations equal to each other, and solve.

$\frac{5}{9}(x - 32) = \frac{9}{5}x + 32$

$45\left(\frac{5}{9}(x - 32)\right) = 45\left(\frac{9}{5}x + 32\right)$

$25(x - 32) = 81x + 1440$

$25x - 800 = 81x + 1440$

$-2240 = 56x$

$-40 = x$

So, –40 °C = –40 °F.

12. It would take 9.04 hours for 4 grams to decay to 2 grams, and then another 9.04 hours for 2 grams to decay to 1 gram. This is a total of 18.08 hours.

13. $V = (15x + 2)(4x - 1)(3x + 4)$

$= (60x^2 - 7x - 2)(3x + 4)$

$= 180x^3 + 219x^2 - 34x - 8$

3	180	219	–34	–8
		540	2277	6729
	180	759	2243	6721

$V(3) = 6721$ cubic units.

14. Combining equations 1 and 2, and equations 1 and 3.

$x + 5y - 2z = 1$

$-x - 2y + z = 6$

$3y - z = 7$

$2(x + 5y - 2z = 1) \rightarrow 2x + 10y - 4z = 2$

$-2x - 7y + 3z = 7$

$3y - z = 9$

The resulting equations have the same coefficients but different constants, so there is no solution and the system is inconsistent.

15. Divide the second term by the first term to find the common ratio. Raise the common ratio to the power of $n - 1$, and multiply the result by the first term.

16. $\log_b(\log_b(x))$ has the greater x-intercept because it increases at a slower rate than $\log_b(x)$.

17. **a.** $y = x^2$

$r \sin\theta = (r \cos\theta)^2$

$r \sin\theta = r^2 \cos^2\theta$

$\sin\theta = r \cos^2\theta$

$\frac{\sin\theta}{\cos^2\theta} = r$

b. 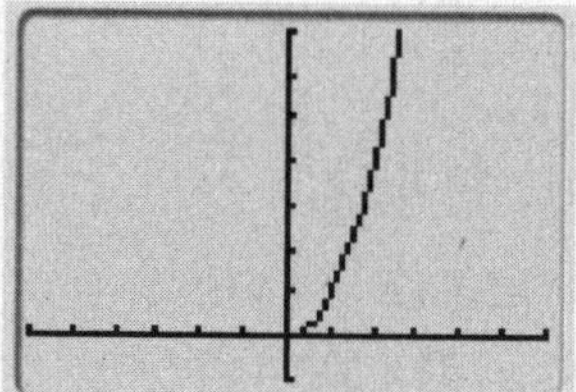

No; The graph of $y = x^2$ lies in Quadrants I and II (and one point is on the origin). When θ min $= 0$, θ max $= \frac{\pi}{2}$ are used as window settings, angles that terminate in Quadrant II are excluded. And, only positive values are obtained for $\sin\theta$ and $\cos^2\theta$. Therefore, only positive values are obtained for $r = \frac{\sin\theta}{\cos^2\theta}$. Therefore, it is not possible to obtain a point in Quadrant II.

c. θ max $= \pi$. This value allows points in Quadrant II.

18. Write the equation in the form $\frac{x^2}{a^2} + \frac{y^2}{b^2} = 1$.

$$5x^2 + 2y^2 = 10$$

$$\frac{5x^2 + 2y^2}{10} = 1$$

$$\frac{x^2}{2} + \frac{y^2}{5} = 1$$

$$\frac{x^2}{(\sqrt{2})^2} + \frac{y^2}{(\sqrt{5})^2} = 1$$

19. 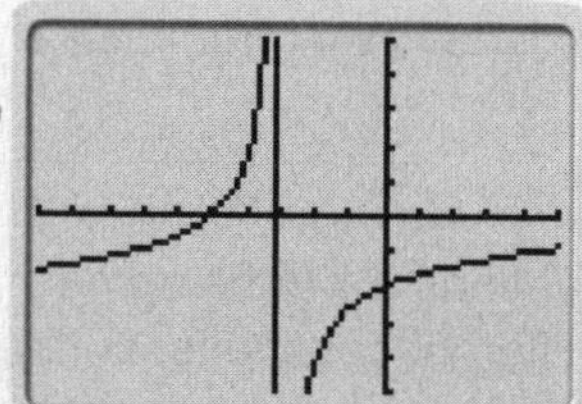

The vertical asymptote is $x = -3$.

20. The solution to $\log x = 3 \log x$ is $x = 1$. Since $\log 1 = 0$, the point of intersection is (1, 0).

21.

−3	1	19	79	−35
		−3	−48	−93
	1	16	31	−128

The remainder is not 0, so $x + 3$ is not a factor of $P(x)$.

22. Sample: $f(x) = x^3 - x$. Reflection across the x-axis is $-f(x) = -x^3 + x$. Reflection across the y-axis is $f(-x) = -x^3 + x$.

23. $x = 18$, so $(x - 18) = 0$

$x = 3$, so $(x - 3) = 0$

$(x - 18)(x - 3) = x^2 - 21x + 54$

24. Find the roots of

$f(g(x)) = (2x - 1)^3 - 125$

$(2x - 1)^3 - 125$

$= ((2x - 1) - 5)((2x - 1)^2 + 5(2x - 1) + 25)$

$= (2x - 6)(4x^2 - 4x + 1 + 10x - 5 + 25)$

$(2x - 6)(4x^2 + 6x + 21)$

$2x - 6 = 0$ or $4x^2 + 6x + 21 = 0$

$2x = 6$

$x = 3$

For $4x^2 + 6x + 21$, the discriminant is $6^2 - 4(4)(21) = -300$, a complex root. The root is $x = 3$.

25. The terms 3 and 1 need to be factored. The possible values of p are ±1, and for q $\pm1, \pm3$. Test roots for $\frac{p}{q} = \left\{1, -1, \frac{1}{3}, -\frac{1}{3}\right\}$.

1	3	2	0	1
		3	5	5
	3	5	5	6

$x - 1$ is not a factor.

−1	3	2	0	1
		−3	1	−1
	3	−1	1	0

$x = -1$ is a root.

$(x + 1)(3x^2 - x + 1)$

Discriminant of $3x^2 - x + 1$ is $(-1)^2 - 4(3)(1) = -11$, so $3x^2 - x + 1$ does not have a real root.

The only root is $x = -1$.

26. $0 = 5x^4 + 2x^3 + x^2$

$0 = x^2(5x^2 + 2x + 1)$

$x^2 = 0$ or $5x^2 + 2x + 1 = 0$

$x = 0$

Discriminant of $5x^2 + 2x + 1$ is $(2)^2 - 4(5)(1) = -16$, so $5x^2 + 2x + 1$ does not have a real root.

27. $\log(12x - 11) = \log(3x + 13)$

$$12x - 11 = 3x + 13$$
$$9x = 24$$
$$x = \frac{24}{9} = \frac{8}{3}$$

28. $\log_2(x - 4) = 6$

$$2^{\log_2(x-4)} = 2^6$$
$$x - 4 = 64$$
$$x = 68$$

29. $z - \text{score} = \dfrac{82.5 - 87}{4.3} \approx -1.05$

30. Each previous event affects the outcome of the following events, so it is a dependent event.

LESSON 112

Warm Up 112

1. cosine
2. In a special right triangle, 30°-60°-90°, the side opposite each angle is 1, $\sqrt{3}$, 2 respectively. Sin 30° $= \frac{\text{opposite}}{\text{hypotenuse}} = \frac{1}{2}$.
3. In a special right triangle, 45°-45°-90°, the side opposite each angle is 1, 1, $\sqrt{2}$ respectively. Tan 45° $= \frac{\text{opposite}}{\text{adjacent}} = \frac{1}{1} = 1$.

Lesson Practice 112

a. $\tan 105° = \tan(60° + 45°)$

$$= \frac{\tan A + \tan B}{1 - \tan A \tan B}$$
$$= \frac{\sqrt{3} + 1}{1 - \sqrt{3}(1)}$$
$$= \frac{\sqrt{3} + 1}{1 - \sqrt{3}}$$
$$= \frac{\sqrt{3} + 1}{1 - \sqrt{3}} \cdot \frac{1 + \sqrt{3}}{1 + \sqrt{3}}$$
$$= \frac{\sqrt{3} + 3 + 1 + \sqrt{3}}{1 - 3}$$
$$= \frac{2\sqrt{3} + 4}{-2} = -\sqrt{3} - 2$$

b. $\cos\frac{11\pi}{12} = \cos\left(\frac{8\pi}{12} + \frac{3\pi}{12}\right) = \cos\left(\frac{2\pi}{3} + \frac{\pi}{4}\right)$

$$= \cos A \cos B - \sin A \sin B$$
$$= -\frac{1}{2}\left(\frac{\sqrt{2}}{2}\right) - \frac{\sqrt{3}}{2}\left(\frac{\sqrt{2}}{2}\right)$$
$$= \frac{-\sqrt{2}}{4} - \frac{\sqrt{6}}{4}$$
$$= \frac{-\sqrt{2} - \sqrt{6}}{4}$$

c. Find cos A and cos B. Sin A is positive so A is in the first quadrant.

$$\sin A = \frac{24}{25}$$
$$x^2 + y^2 = r^2$$
$$x^2 + 24^2 = 25^2$$
$$x = +\sqrt{625 - 576} = 7$$
$$\cos A = \frac{7}{25}$$
$$\tan B = -1$$
$$x = -1,\ y = 1$$
$$x^2 + y^2 = r^2$$
$$(-1)^2 + 1^2 = r^2$$
$$\sqrt{2} = r$$
$$\cos B = \frac{1}{\sqrt{2}},\ \sin B = -\frac{1}{\sqrt{2}}$$

Use the difference identity to find cos($A + B$).

$$\cos(A + B) = \cos A \cos B - \sin A \sin B$$
$$= \frac{7}{25}\left(\frac{1}{\sqrt{2}}\right) - \frac{24}{25}\left(-\frac{1}{\sqrt{2}}\right)$$
$$= \frac{7}{25\sqrt{2}} + \frac{24}{25\sqrt{2}}$$
$$= \frac{31}{25\sqrt{2}}$$
$$= \frac{31}{25\sqrt{2}} \cdot \frac{\sqrt{2}}{\sqrt{2}}$$
$$= \frac{31\sqrt{2}}{50}$$

d. $R_{45°}\begin{bmatrix}\cos 45° & -\sin 45° \\ \sin 45° & \cos 45°\end{bmatrix}\ S = \begin{bmatrix}1 & -2 & 1 \\ 0 & 0 & 3\sqrt{3}\end{bmatrix}$

$$R_{45°} \times S = \begin{bmatrix}\frac{\sqrt{2}}{2} & -\frac{\sqrt{2}}{2} \\ \frac{\sqrt{2}}{2} & \frac{\sqrt{2}}{2}\end{bmatrix} \times \begin{bmatrix}1 & -2 & 1 \\ 0 & 0 & 3\sqrt{3}\end{bmatrix}$$

$$= \begin{bmatrix} \frac{\sqrt{2}}{2} & \frac{\sqrt{2}}{2}(-2) & \frac{\sqrt{2}}{2} + 3\sqrt{3}\left(-\frac{\sqrt{2}}{2}\right) \\ \frac{\sqrt{2}}{2} & \frac{\sqrt{2}}{2}(-2) & \frac{\sqrt{2}}{2} + 3\sqrt{3}\left(\frac{\sqrt{2}}{2}\right) \end{bmatrix}$$

$$= \begin{bmatrix} \frac{\sqrt{2}}{2} & -\sqrt{2} & \frac{\sqrt{2} - 3\sqrt{6}}{2} \\ \frac{\sqrt{2}}{2} & -\sqrt{2} & \frac{\sqrt{2} + 3\sqrt{6}}{2} \end{bmatrix}$$

$A' = \left(\frac{\sqrt{2}}{2}, \frac{\sqrt{2}}{2}\right), B' = \left(-\sqrt{2}, -\sqrt{2}\right)$

$C' = \left(\frac{\sqrt{2} - 3\sqrt{6}}{2}, \frac{\sqrt{2} + 3\sqrt{6}}{2}\right)$

Practice 112

1. $\frac{3}{\sqrt[4]{144}} = \frac{3}{\sqrt[4]{16}\sqrt[4]{9}} = \frac{3}{2\sqrt{3}}$
   $= \frac{3}{2\sqrt{3}}\left(\frac{\sqrt{3}}{\sqrt{3}}\right) = \frac{3\sqrt{3}}{6} = \frac{\sqrt{3}}{2}$

2. $\frac{\sqrt[3]{9}}{\sqrt[5]{27}} = \frac{\sqrt[3]{9}}{\sqrt[5]{27}} \cdot \frac{\sqrt[5]{9}}{\sqrt[5]{9}} = \frac{3\sqrt[15]{3}}{3} = \sqrt[15]{3}$

3. $\frac{2\pi}{b} = \frac{2\pi}{0.017} \approx 365$
   $\frac{2\pi}{b} = \frac{2\pi}{b} \approx 224.63$
   $b \approx 0.028$
   The equation is $y = \sin(0.028x)$

4. There are 3600 seconds in one hour.
   $\frac{30 \text{ hr}}{1} \times \frac{3600 \text{ s}}{1 \text{ hr}} = \frac{30(3600) \text{ s}}{1} = 108{,}000 \text{ s}$

5. $\sin 75° = \sin(30° + 45°)$
   $= \sin 30° \cos 45° + \cos 30° \sin 45°$
   $= \left(\frac{1}{2}\right)\left(\frac{\sqrt{2}}{2}\right) + \left(\frac{\sqrt{3}}{2}\right)\left(\frac{\sqrt{2}}{2}\right)$
   $= \frac{\sqrt{2} + \sqrt{6}}{4}$

6. Using a graphing calculator, there is a real solution of about 1.503 with an odd multiplicity. The remaining solutions are not real.

7. $A = 2x(x) - 3(x - 5)$
   $= 2x^2 - 3x + 15$

8. **A**

3	1	0	0	0	0	0	3	0	0	0	5	−100	13
		3	9	27	81	243	729	2196	6588	19,764	59,292	177,891	533,373
	1	3	9	27	81	243	732	2196	6588	19,764	59,297	177,791	533,386

$P(3) = 533{,}386$

B

3	1	0	0	0	0	0	0	3	0	0	0	0	5	−100	13
		3	9	27	81	243	729	2187	6570	19,710	59,130	177,390	532,170	1,596,525	4,789,275
	1	3	9	27	81	243	729	2190	6570	19,710	59,130	177,390	532,175	1,596,425	4,789,288

$P(3) = 4{,}789{,}288$

C

3	1	0	0	0	0	0	3	0	0	5	−100	13
		3	9	27	81	243	729	2196	6588	19,764	59,307	177,621
	1	3	9	27	81	243	732	2196	6588	19,769	59,207	177,634

$P(3) = 177{,}634$

D

3	1	0	0	0	3	5	0	0	−100	13
		3	9	27	81	252	771	2313	6939	20,517
	1	3	9	27	84	257	771	2313	6839	20,530

$P(3) = 20{,}530$

Answer Choice **A**

9. A hyperbola with a vertical orientation has the form $\frac{(y-k)^2}{a^2} - \frac{(x-h)^2}{b^2} = 1$.

$m = \frac{a}{b}$

$\frac{4}{3} = \frac{a}{b}$

$a = 4$

$b = 3$

The point (h, k) is the point where the asymptotes cross.

$$\frac{4}{3}x - \frac{11}{3} = -\frac{4}{3}x + \frac{29}{3}$$
$$\frac{8}{3}x = \frac{40}{3}$$
$$8x = 40$$
$$x = 5$$

Substitute $x = 5$ into $\frac{4}{3}x - \frac{11}{3} = y$ and solve.

$$y = \frac{4}{3}x - \frac{11}{3}$$
$$= \frac{4}{3}(5) - \frac{11}{3}$$
$$= \frac{20}{3} - \frac{11}{3}$$
$$= \frac{9}{3} = 3$$

The asymptotes cross at (5, 3). $h = 5$, $k = 3$.

$$\frac{(y-k)^2}{a^2} - \frac{(x-h)^2}{b^2} = 1$$
$$\frac{(y-3)^2}{4^2} - \frac{(x-5)^2}{3^2} = 1$$

10. For $x < -4$, $(-5\ -1)$ is negative and the value of the expression is negative. For $-4 < x < 1$, the value of the expression is positive. The solution is $x < -4$ or $1 < x < 5$.

11. Complete the square for each quadratic term, then divide by the constant term to get the equation of an ellipse in standard form.

$$x^2 + 9y^2 - 10x - 18y + 7 = 0$$
$$(x^2 - 10x) + 9(y^2 - 2y) = -7$$
$$(x^2 - 10x + 25) + 9(y^2 - 2y + 1) = -7 + 25 + 9$$
$$(x-5)^2 + 9(y-1)^2 = 27$$
$$\frac{(x-5)^2}{27} + \frac{9(y-1)^2}{27} = \frac{27}{27}$$
$$\frac{(x-5)^2}{(\sqrt{27})^2} + \frac{(y-1)^2}{(\sqrt{3})^2} = 1$$

12. a. This is a vertical compression by a factor of $\frac{1}{4}$. Each point has the same x-coordinate and $\frac{1}{4}$ the y-coordinate as its corresponding point of $f(x)$. Therefore, the turning point is (0, 1) and (4, −7).

b. This is a horizontal stretch by a factor of 4. Each point has 4 times the x-coordinate and the same y-coordinate as its corresponding point of $f(x)$. Therefore, the turning point is (0, 4) and (16, −28).

c. This is a horizontal translation $\frac{1}{4}$ units to the right. Each x-coordinate is $\frac{1}{4}$ greater than the corresponding point of $f(x)$ and each y-coordinate is the same. Therefore, the turning point is $(\frac{1}{4}, 4)$ and $(4\frac{1}{4}, -28)$.

13. $$\frac{6a^2b}{4ab} \cdot \frac{3ab^3}{5a^2b^2} = \frac{18a^3b^4}{20a^3b^3} = \frac{9}{10}b$$
$$= \frac{9}{10}(3) = \frac{27}{10}$$

14. 225 mph × 2 h = 550 mi

268 mph × 3 h = 804 mi

$550 \sin(-30°) + 804 \sin(20°) \approx -275 + 275$
≈ 0

$550 \cos(-30°) + 804 \cos(20°)$
$\approx 476.3 + 755.5 \approx 1231.8$

$\arcsin\left(\frac{0}{1231.8}\right) = 0°$

1231.8 miles due west

15. The graph of $f(x) = x^3 + 1$ should be shifted 4 units left.

16. n is the vertical displacement of the function. For large values of x, the function approaches n.

17. $$y = -4.4 + 12.6 \ln t$$
$$30 = -4.4 + 12.6 \ln t$$
$$34.4 = 12.6 \ln t$$
$$2.73 \approx \ln t$$
$$e^{2.73} \approx t$$
$$15.3 \approx t$$

$t = 5$ represents $1930 + 5 = 1935$, so $t = 15.3$ represents $1930 + 15.3$ or 1945 or 1946.

18. Sketch the graph $A(x) = 50{,}000(1.05)^x$, where the y-intercept is (0, 50,000).

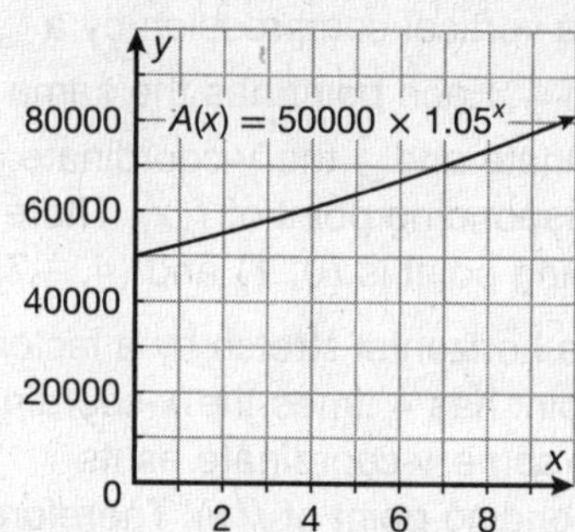

19. The point is r units from the pole, and since r is the directed distance, another point is $(-r, \theta + \pi)$.

20. $\tan(A + B) = \dfrac{\tan A + \tan B}{1 - \tan A \tan B}$

$$= \frac{\frac{1}{2} + \frac{1}{4}}{1 - \frac{1}{2}\left(\frac{1}{4}\right)}$$

$$= \frac{\frac{3}{4}}{\frac{7}{8}}$$

$$= \frac{6}{7}$$

Answer Choice **D**

21. $V_{hemisphere} = \frac{2}{3}\pi r^3$ and $V_{cylinder} = \pi r^2 h$

$$\frac{2}{3}\pi x^3 + \pi x^2(28) = 8550\pi$$

$$\frac{2}{3}\pi x^3 + 28\pi x^2 - 8550\pi = 0$$

$$\frac{2}{3}x^3 + 28x^2 - 8550 = 0$$

Using a graphing calculator it appears that 15 is a root. Check by synthetic division.

15	$\frac{2}{3}$	28	0	−8550
		10	570	8550
	$\frac{2}{3}$	38	570	0

Since the polynomial is cubic there must be two other roots, but the roots are negative. Since radius must be positive, the radius is 15 feet.

22. $\dfrac{1}{x^3 + 4x^2 - 21x} = \dfrac{1}{x(x^2 + 4x - 21)}$

$$= \frac{1}{x(x + 7)(x - 3)}$$

$x = 0, x = -7, x = 3$

23. By the cosine sum identity

$$\cos\frac{2\pi}{5}\cos\frac{3\pi}{5} - \sin\frac{2\pi}{5}\sin\frac{3\pi}{5} =$$

$$\cos\left(\frac{2\pi}{5} + \frac{3\pi}{5}\right) = \cos\pi = -1$$

24. Sub $a_1 = 32$, $d = -2$, $n = 12$ in

$$a_n = a_1 + (n - 1)d$$
$$a_{12} = 32 + (12 - 1)(-2)$$
$$a_{12} = 10$$
$$S_{12} = 12\left(\frac{32 + 10}{2}\right) = 252$$

25. $d = \sqrt{l^2 + w^2 + h^2}$

$$d^2 = l^2 + w^2 + h^2$$
$$d^2 - w^2 - h^2 = l^2$$
$$\sqrt{d^2 - w^2 - h^2} = l$$

26. $m^2 = l^2 + n^2 - 2ln\cos M$

$$m^2 = 29^2 + 24^2 - 2(29)(24)\cos 65°$$
$$m^2 = 1417 - 1392\cos 65°$$
$$m^2 \approx 1417 - 588.3$$
$$m^2 \approx 828.7$$
$$m \approx 28.8$$

27. $x = 0$,

$x = 16, x - 16 = 0$

$x = -9, x + 9 = 0$

$x(x - 16)(x + 9)$

$x(x^2 - 7x - 144)$

$x^3 - 7x^2 - 144x$

28. The salaries each year form a geometric sequence where $r = 1.0275$. Substitute 10 for n, 25,925 for a, and 1.0275 for r in $a_n = a_1^{r-1}$

$$a_n = 25{,}925(1.0275)^{10-1}$$
$$= 33{,}094.46$$

29.

$$\begin{aligned} y + z + w &= 6 \\ -y + 3z - w &= 2 \\ \hline 4z \quad &= 8 \\ z &= 2 \end{aligned}$$

$$-y + 3(2) - w = 2 \rightarrow -y + 6 - w = 2$$
$$2y - (2) + w = 5 \rightarrow \underline{2y - 2 + w = 5}$$
$$y + 4 = 7$$
$$y = 3$$

$$3 + 2 + w = 6$$
$$5 + w = 6$$
$$w = 1$$

30. $\log_{10}(15x)^2 = \log_{10}(15(1))^2$
$$= 2 \cdot \log_{10} 15$$
$$\approx 2 \cdot 1.176$$
$$\approx 2.352$$

LESSON 113

Warm Up 113

1. common ratio
2. Divide a term by a previous term: $10 \div (-2) = -5$. Find the next three terms by multiplying by -5.
   $250(-5) = -1250$, $-1250(-5) = 6250$, $6250(-5) = -31{,}250$
3. $r = \frac{1}{6} \div \frac{2}{3} = \frac{1}{6} \times \frac{3}{2} = \frac{1}{4}$

   Sub. $n = 9$, $a_1 = \frac{2}{3}$, $r = \frac{1}{4}$ into $a_n = a_1 r^{n-1}$

   $$a_9 = \frac{2}{3}\left(\frac{1}{4}\right)^{9-1}$$
   $$a_9 = \frac{2}{3}\left(\frac{1}{65{,}536}\right) = \frac{1}{98{,}304}$$

Lesson Practice 113

a. Substitute 6 for a_1, 10 for n, and $-12 \div 6 = -2$ for r.
$$S_n = a_1\left(\frac{1 - r^n}{1 - r}\right)$$
$$S_{10} = 6\left(\frac{1 - (-2)^{10}}{1 - (-2)}\right)$$
$$S_{10} = 6\left(\frac{1 - 1024}{3}\right)$$
$$S_{10} = 6\left(\frac{-1023}{3}\right) = -2046$$

b. Substitute 1 for k to find a_1.
$$a_1 = 400\left(\frac{1}{4}\right)^{1-1} = 400$$
Substitute 9 for n, and $\frac{1}{4}$ for r.
$$S_n = a_1\left(\frac{1 - r^n}{1 - r}\right)$$
$$S_9 = 400\left(\frac{1 - \left(\frac{1}{4}\right)^9}{1 - \frac{1}{4}}\right)$$
$$S_9 = 400\left(\frac{1 - \frac{1}{262{,}144}}{\frac{3}{4}}\right)$$
$$S_9 = 400\left(\frac{262{,}143}{262{,}144} \cdot \frac{4}{3}\right) \approx 533.33$$

c. Compare r to 1:
$$r = -\frac{25}{15} = -\frac{5}{3}$$
$$\left|-\frac{5}{3}\right| > 1$$
Therefore, the series diverges.

d. Compare r to 1:
$$r = \frac{30}{90} = \frac{1}{3}$$
$$\left|\frac{1}{3}\right| < 1$$
Therefore, the series converges.

e. $r = \frac{140}{700} = \frac{1}{5}$
$$S = \frac{a_1}{1 - r} = \frac{700}{1 - \frac{1}{5}} = \frac{700}{\frac{4}{5}} = 875$$

f. $r = 1.0285$
$$S_n = a_1\left(\frac{1 - r^n}{1 - r}\right)$$
$$S_{20} = 27{,}700\left(\frac{1 - (1.0285)^{20}}{1 - (1.0285)}\right) = 733{,}056.22$$

Practice 113

1. $S = \frac{25}{1 - \frac{4}{5}} = \frac{25}{\frac{1}{5}} = 125$

2. For excluded values $x^2 + 6x = 0$.
$x(x + 6) = 0$ so $x = 0$ or $x + 6 = 0$,
If $x + 6 = 0$, $x = -6$.
The excluded values are $x = 0$, $x = -6$.
$$\frac{x^2 + 4x - 12}{x^2 + 6x} = \frac{\cancel{(x+6)}(x-2)}{x\cancel{(x+6)}} = \frac{x-2}{x}$$

3. $g(x) = (7.300x^3 - 116.411x^2 + 363.122x + 3400) + 100$
$g(x) = 7.300x^3 - 116.411x^2 + 363.122x + 3500$
The function $g(x)$ models what would have been the season attendance if 100,000 more people had attended games each year.

4. $$\frac{\frac{x}{x+2}}{2x + \frac{x}{5}} = \frac{\frac{x}{x+2}}{\frac{10x}{5} + \frac{x}{5}}$$
$$= \frac{\frac{x}{x+2}}{\frac{11x}{5}}$$
$$= \frac{x}{x+2} \cdot \frac{5}{11x}$$
$$= \frac{5}{11x + 22}$$

5. $$\frac{5}{2x^8} + \frac{7}{2x^8} = \frac{12}{2x^8} = \frac{6}{x^8}$$

6. $$\frac{x(y^3 + 6)}{4x + 8} \cdot \frac{x+2}{x^2y^2} \div \frac{y}{x}$$
$$= \frac{\cancel{x}(y^3 + 6)}{4\cancel{(x+2)}} \cdot \frac{\cancel{x+2}}{\cancel{x^2}y^2} \cdot \frac{\cancel{x}}{y}$$
$$= \frac{(y^3 + 6)}{4y^3}$$

7. The wheel travels 360° in 30 minutes, so it travels 12° in one minute.
$$\begin{bmatrix} \cos 12° & -\sin 12° \\ \sin 12° & \cos 12° \end{bmatrix}\begin{bmatrix} 220 \\ 0 \end{bmatrix} = \begin{bmatrix} 220 \cos 12° \\ 220 \sin 12° \end{bmatrix}$$
$$\approx \begin{bmatrix} 215.2 \\ 45.7 \end{bmatrix}$$
The coordinates will be about (215.2, 45.7).

8. $$A = \frac{1}{2}(b_1 + b_2)h$$
$$2A = (b_1 + b_2)h$$
$$\frac{2A}{h} = b_1 + b_2$$
$$\frac{2A}{h} - b_2 = b_1$$

9. The error is leaving off the ± sign after taking the square root of both sides of the equation. Because sin A is positive and $90° < A < 270°$, A terminates in Quadrant II, so the value of $x = -3$. $\cos A = \frac{x}{r} = -\frac{3}{5}$.

10. Joint variation has the form $\frac{y}{xz} = k$, where k is a constant.
$$A = \frac{bh}{2}$$
$$\frac{A}{bh} = \frac{1}{2}$$

11. $x = 4$, so $(x - 4) = 0$
$x = 1$, so $(x - 1) = 0$
$(x - 4)(x - 1) = 0$
$x^2 - 5x + 4 = 0$

12. Draw inequalities (including a quadratic) in which there is no overlap in the shaded regions.
Sample answer:

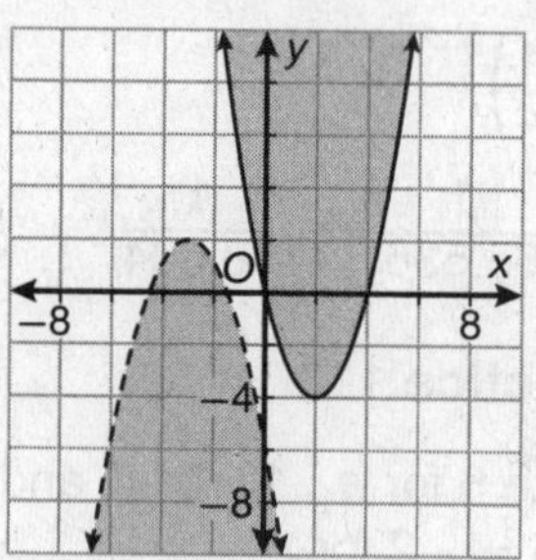

13. $$\bar{x} = \frac{18 + 20 + 14 + 15 + 20 + 17 + 16}{7}$$
$$= \frac{120}{7} \approx 17.1$$
Median: 14, 15, 16, <u>17</u>, 18, 20, 20
The median is 17.
The mode is 20.

14. $\bar{x} = \dfrac{21 + 23 + 22 + 25 + 28 + 31 + 28}{7}$

$= \dfrac{178}{7} \approx 25.4$

Median: 21, 22, 23, $\underline{25}$, 28, 28, 31

The median is 25.

The mode is 28.

15. 

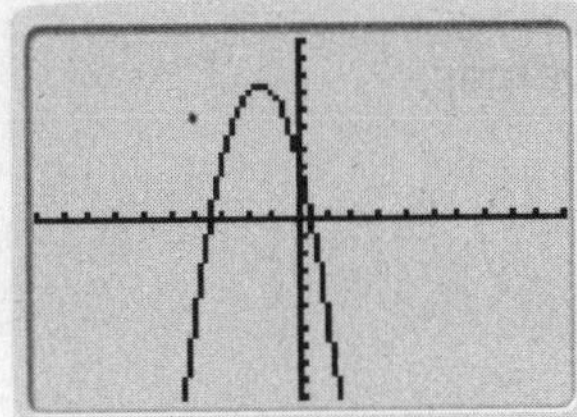

The vertex is $\left(-1\frac{1}{2}, 7\frac{1}{2}\right)$. The axis symmetry is $x = -1\frac{1}{2}$.

16. $2x^2 - 3x - 2 = (2x + 1)(x - 2)$

$x^2 - 4 = (x - 2)(x + 2)$

$\text{LCM} = (2x + 1)(x - 2)(x + 2)$

17. Since the logarithm on each side has the same base, set $25x = 151$ and solve for x.

$\log_2 25x = \log_2 151$

$25x = 151$

$x \approx 6$

18. a. $\dfrac{x^5}{f(g(x))} = \dfrac{x^5}{(x^2 - 1)^2 - 1}$

$= \dfrac{x^5}{x^4 - 2x^2 + 1 - 1}$

$= \dfrac{x^5}{x^4 - 2x^2}$

$= \dfrac{x^3}{x^2 - 2}$

b.

$$\begin{array}{r} x \\ x^2 - 0x - 2\,\overline{)\,x^3 + 0x^2 + 0x + 0} \\ \underline{x^3 + 0x^2 - 2x} \\ 2x \end{array}$$

The slant asymptote is the quotient without the remainder; so it is $y = x$

Asymptotes: $x^2 = 2$, $x = \pm\sqrt{2}$

Hole: $x = 0$

19. Total area $= \sum_{i=1}^{4}\left(\frac{1}{2}x^2 + 4x + 1\right)$

x	$f(x) = \frac{1}{2}x^2 + 4x + 1$
0.5	3.125
1.5	8.125
2.5	14.125
3.5	21.125

$\sum_{i=1}^{4}\left(\frac{1}{2}x^2 + 4x + 1\right) \approx 46.5$

20. Job A: $r = 1.0185$

$S_n = a_1\left(\dfrac{1 - r^n}{1 - r}\right)$

$S_{15} = 31{,}225\left(\dfrac{1 - (1.0185)^{15}}{1 - (1.0185)}\right) = 534{,}173.23$

Job B: $r = 1.0225$

$S_n = a_1\left(\dfrac{1 - r^n}{1 - r}\right)$

$S_{15} = 28{,}995\left(\dfrac{1 - (1.0225)^{15}}{1 - (1.0225)}\right) = 510{,}578.50$

He will make more with Job A. The difference is \$534,173.23 − \$510,578.50 = \$23,594.73.

21. Use the binomial theorem to expand $(a + b)^n$ where $a = n$, $b = 2m$, and $n = 4$.

$(n + 2m)^4$

$= ({}_4C_0)n^4(2m)^0 + ({}_4C_1)n^3(2m)^1 + ({}_4C_2)n^2(2m)^2 + ({}_4C_3)n^1(2m)^3 + ({}_4C_4)n^0(2m)^4$

$= (1)n^4(2m)^0 + (4)n^3(2m)^1 + (6)n^2(2m)^2 + (4)n^1(2m)^3 + (1)n^0(2m)^4$

$= n^4 + 8n^3m + 24n^2m^2 + 32nm^3 + 16m^4$

22. $d = 0.75$

$a_{12} = 3 + (12 - 1)0.75$

$= 11.25$

$S_n = n\left(\dfrac{a_1 + a_n}{2}\right)$

$S_{12} = 12\left(\dfrac{3 + 11.5}{2}\right) = 85.5$

23. $10x - 2y = 16$

$-2y = 16 - 10x$

$y = -8 + 5x$

$5x + 3y = -12$

$$5x + 3(-8 + 5x) = -12$$
$$5x - 24 + 15x = -12$$
$$20x = 12$$
$$x = \frac{12}{20} = \frac{3}{5}$$
$$10\left(\frac{3}{5}\right) - 2y = 16$$
$$-2y = 10$$
$$y = -5$$

24. $r = 1.015$

$$S_n = a_1\left(\frac{1 - r^n}{1 - r}\right)$$
$$393{,}967.18 = a_1\left(\frac{1 - (1.015)^{10}}{1 - (1.015)}\right)$$
$$393{,}967.18 = a_1(10.7027)$$
$$a_1 = 36{,}810$$

25. Period $= \frac{\pi}{b} = \frac{\pi}{2}$

26. $N(t) = N_0e^{-kt}$

$$0.5 = 1e^{-k(16)}$$
$$\ln 0.5 = -16k$$
$$k = \frac{\ln 0.5}{-16}$$
$$\approx 0.04332$$
$$N(t) = N_oe^{-0.04332t}$$
$$0.5 = 2e^{-0.04332t}$$
$$0.25 = e^{-0.04332t}$$

Answer Choice **C**

27. a. Probability $= \frac{A_{small}}{A_{large}} = \frac{\pi x^2}{\pi(x + 2)^2}$

$$= \frac{x^2}{x^2 + 4x + 4}$$

b. $\frac{x^2}{x^2 + 4x + 4} \leq 0.25$

$$x^2 \leq 0.25(x^2 + 4x + 4)$$
$$x^2 \leq 0.25x^2 + x + 1$$
$$x^2 - 0.25x^2 - x - 1 \leq 0$$
$$0.75x^2 - x - 1 \leq 0$$

$$x = \frac{-(-1) \pm \sqrt{(-1)^2 - 4(0.75)(-1)}}{2(0.75)}$$

$$x = \frac{-(-1) \pm \sqrt{4}}{1.5} = 2 \text{ or } -0.6$$

The value of x cannot be zero or less, so $0 < x \leq 2$.

28. **A** Compare r to 1.

$r = \frac{4}{2} = 2$

$|2| > 1$

The series diverges.

B $r = \frac{8}{16} = \frac{1}{2}$

$\left|\frac{1}{2}\right| < 1$

The series converges.

C $r = \frac{15}{3} = 5$

$|5| > 1$

The series diverges.

D $r = \frac{-15}{3} = -5$

$|-5| > 1$

The series diverges.

Answer Choice **B**

29. The difference of the term numbers must be an even number because then the exponent is even and an even root must be taken on each side of the equation.

30. Vector A, which is at a 60° angle is added to vector B which is at a 30° angle.

LESSON 114

Warm Up 114

1. circle
2. $(x - 8)^2 = x^2 - 2(8)x + 8^2 = x^2 - 16x + 64$
3. Discriminant $= b^2 - 4ac = 5^2 - 4(1)(-12)$
$$= 25 - (-48)$$
$$= 73$$

Lesson Practice 114

a. $x^2 + y^2 = 225$ can be written as $(x - 0)^2 + (y - 0)^2 = 15^2$. This equation has the form $(x - h)^2 + (y - k)^2 = r^2$, so the equation represents a circle.

b. $\frac{(x-4)^2}{25} + \frac{y^2}{49} = 1$ can be written as $\frac{(x-4)^2}{5^2} + \frac{(y-0)^2}{7^2} = 1$. This equation has the form $\frac{(x-h)^2}{a^2} + \frac{(y-k)^2}{b^2} = 1$, so the equation represents an ellipse.

c. $A = 5$, $B = 0$, and $C = -4$.
$B^2 - 4AC = 0^2 - 4(5)(-4) = 80$
$B^2 - 4AC > 0$ so the conic section is a hyperbola.

d. $A = 3$, $B = 0$, and $C = 0$.
$B^2 - 4AC = 0^2 - 4(3)(0) = 0$
$B^2 - 4AC = 0$ so the conic section is a parabola.

e.
$$x - 2 = \frac{1}{4}(y+3)^2$$
$$x - 2 = \frac{1}{4}(y^2 + 6y + 9)$$
$$4x - 8 = y^2 + 6y + 9$$
$$0 = y^2 - 4x + 6y + 9 + 8$$
$$y^2 - 4x + 6y + 17 = 0$$

f. $(x-5)^2 + (y+8)^2 = 64$
$x^2 - 10x + 25 + y^2 + 16y + 64 = 64$
$x^2 + y^2 - 10x + 16y + 25 = 0$

g. The path is a circle so use completing the square.
$x^2 + y^2 - 30x - 30y - 175 = 0$
$(x^2 - 30x) + (y^2 - 30y) = 175$
$(x^2 - 30x + 225) + (y^2 - 30y + 225)$
$= 175 + 225 + 225$
$(x-15)^2 + (y-15)^2 = 625$
$(x-15)^2 + (y-15)^2 = 25^2$

Practice 114

1. $X = A^{-1}B = \begin{bmatrix} 1 & 2.5 \\ 0 & -0.5 \end{bmatrix}\begin{bmatrix} 3 & -1 & 0 \\ 6 & 8 & 4 \end{bmatrix}$
$= \begin{bmatrix} 18 & 19 & 10 \\ -3 & -4 & -2 \end{bmatrix}$

2. The function is undefined where $\cos(2x) = 0$
$2x = \frac{\pi}{2}$
$\tan(2x)$ is undefined at $x = \frac{\pi}{4} + n\frac{\pi}{2}$.

3. $\sqrt[3]{-125} = \sqrt[3]{(-5)^3} = -5$

4. $\sqrt[3]{12} \cdot \sqrt[3]{18} = \sqrt[3]{216} = \sqrt[3]{(6)^3} = 6$

5. $g(x) = (0.048x^3 + 0.605x^2 + 5.649x + 45) - 20$
$g(x) = 0.048x^3 + 0.605x^2 + 5.649x + 25$
The function $g(x)$ models a team payroll that was $20,000,000 less each year than that of the first team.

6.
$$m = \frac{y_2 - y_1}{x_2 - x_1} = \frac{5-4}{0-(-2)} = \frac{1}{2}$$
$(y - y_1) = m(x - x_1)$
$(y - 5) = \frac{1}{2}(x - 0)$
$y = \frac{1}{2}x + 5$
y-intercept is 5 or (0, 5).
For x-intercept let $y = 0$.
$0 = \frac{1}{2}x + 5$
$-\frac{1}{2}x = 5$
$x = -10$
The x-intercept is -10 or $(-10, 0)$.

7. To shift $f(x)$ to the right change $f(x)$ to $f(x + a)$ where a is negative.

8. $y = \frac{1^2}{r}$, $y = \frac{2^2}{r}$, $y = \frac{3^2}{r}$, $y = \frac{4^2}{r}$, $y = \frac{5^2}{r}$

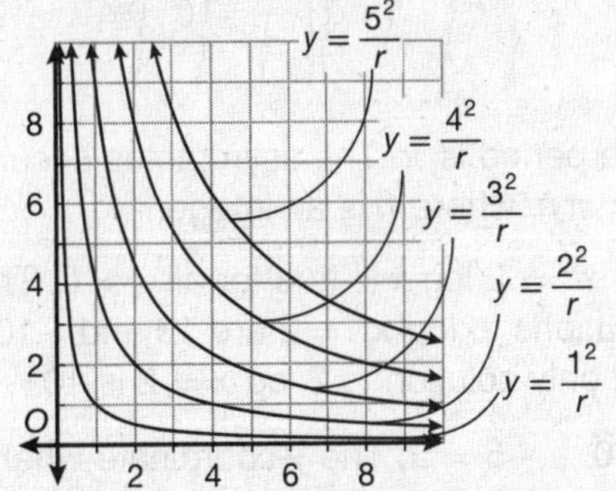

From the graph, acceleration range from $a = 0.5$ to 12.5 occurs at $r = 2$.

9. The graph could be a circle or an ellipse. If $B = 0$ and $A = C$, the conic section is a circle. If either $B \neq 0$ or $A \neq C$, the conic section is an ellipse.

10. The path is a circle so use completing the square.

$x^2 + y^2 - 10x - 10y - 575 = 0$
$(x^2 - 10x) + (y^2 - 10y) = 575$
$(x^2 - 10x + 25) + (y^2 - 10y + 25)$
$= 575 + 25 + 25$
$(x - 5)^2 + (y - 5)^2 = 625$
$(x - 5)^2 + (y - 5)^2 = 25^2$

11. $a_1 = 0.75(1) - 5 = -4.25$
$a_{20} = 0.75(20) - 5 = 10$

$$S_n = n\left(\frac{a_1 + a_n}{2}\right)$$

$$S_{20} = 20\left(\frac{-4.25 + 10}{2}\right) = 57.5$$

12. $\sum_{k=2}^{7}(8 + 5k)$
$= (8 + 5(2)) + (8 + 5(3)) + (8 + 5(4)) + (8 + 5(5)) + (8 + 5(6)) + (8 + 5(7))$
$= 18 + 23 + 28 + 33 + 38 + 43$
$= 183$

13. Graph $y = 6\frac{1}{\tan x}$.

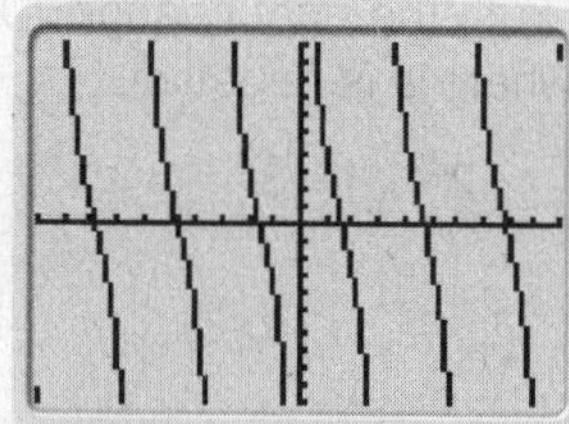

The period is π. The asymptotes occur at $x = \pi n$, where n is an integer.

14. $\log x^2 = 2 \log x$ is true for all $x > 0$. The solutions to $\log x^2 = 2$ are 10 and -10, but the only solution to $2 \log x = 2$ is 10.

15. $-10 \div -5 = 2$. The y-coordinate when the x is 6, is $(-40 \times 2) \times 2 = -160$.

16. $x^2 - 4x - 8y - 84 = 0$
$x^2 - 4x = 8y + 84$
$x^2 - 4x + 4 = 8y + 84 + 4$
$(x - 2)^2 = 8y + 88$
$(x - 2)^2 = 8(y + 11)$
$\frac{1}{8}(x - 2)^2 = (y + 11)$

Answer Choice **B**

17. $4x - 8y + 2z = 10$
$\underline{-3x + y - 2z = 6}$
$x - 7y = 16$

$-3x + y - 2z = 6 \rightarrow -3x + y - 2z = 6$
$-2(-2x + 4y - z = 8) \rightarrow \underline{4x - 8y + 2z = -16}$
$x - 7y = -10$

The resulting equations $x - 7y = 16$ and $x - 7y = -10$ have the same x-and y-coefficients but different constants. Therefore, the system has no solution.

18. One root is 18. Find the other roots.

18	1	−37	406	−1068	−1512
		18	−342	1152	1512
	1	−19	64	84	0

Factor $x^3 - 19x^2 + 64x + 84$

Possible roots are $\pm1, \pm2, \pm3, \pm4, \pm6, \pm7, \pm12, \pm14, \pm21, 28, \pm42, \pm84$.

6	1	−19	64	84
		6	−78	−84
	1	−13	−14	0

$f(x) = x^4 - 37x^3 + 406x^2 - 1068x - 1512$
$= (x - 18)(x - 6)(x^2 - 13x - 14)$
$= (x - 18)(x - 6)(x - 14)(x + 1)$

The roots are 18, 6, 14 and -1. Since the year cannot be negative, the other years are year 6 and year 14.

19. a. $N(t) = N_oe^{-kt}$
$0.5 = 1e^{-k(11.1)}$
$\ln 0.5 = -11.1k$
$k = \frac{\ln 0.5}{-11.1}$
≈ 0.06245

b. $N(t) = N_oe^{-0.06245t}$
$1 = 5e^{-0.06245t}$
$0.2 = e^{-0.06245t}$
$\ln 0.2 = -0.06245t$
$t = \frac{\ln 0.2}{-0.06245} \approx 25.8$

20. Sample: A polynomial function that has exactly n distinct real zeros has exactly n x-intercepts. If there are n x-intercepts, then there are $n - 1$ intervals between consecutive x-intercepts. The graph is continuous and must either increase and then decrease or decrease and then increase in each of those intervals, so it must have exactly one turning point in each of those intervals.

21. $$\begin{aligned} f(g(x)) + 1 &= \frac{1}{\csc^2(x) - 1} + 1 \\ &= \frac{1}{1 + \cot^2(x) - 1} + 1 \\ &= \frac{1}{\cot^2(x)} + 1 \\ &= \tan^2(x) + 1 \\ &= \sec^2(x) \end{aligned}$$

22. $$\begin{aligned} a_n &= a_m + (n - m)d \\ 8 &= 60 + (13 - 9)d \\ 8 &= 60 + 4d \\ -52 &= 4d \\ -13 &= d \\ a_n &= a_1 + (n - 1)d \\ 8 &= a_1 + (13 - 1)(-13) \\ 8 &= a_1 + (-156) \\ 164 &= a_1 \end{aligned}$$

23. **a.** $2\sum_{k=1}^{n}(57(0.3))(0.3)^{k-1} = 2\sum_{k=1}^{n}(17.1)(0.3)^{k-1}$

b. $a_1 = 2(17.1)(0.3)^{1-1} = 34.2$

$S = \frac{a_1}{1 - r} = \frac{34.2}{1 - 0.3} \approx 48.9$

24. The hyperbola has a horizontal orientation.

$\pm\frac{b}{a} = \pm\frac{5}{12}$, $c = 13$, $(h, k) = (4, -5)$

$$\frac{(x - 4)^2}{12^2} - \frac{(y + 5)^2}{5^2} = 1$$

25. **a.** $$\begin{aligned} A &= \pi r^2 \\ \frac{A}{\pi} &= r^2 \\ \sqrt{\frac{A}{\pi}} &= r \end{aligned}$$

$2 : 1 = \sqrt{2} : \sqrt{1} = \sqrt{2} : 1$

26. The series diverges because the absolute value of the common ratio is greater than 1. The series does not have a sum.

27. **A** The terms increase by 16, where k is the domain from 1 to 5. This is an arithmetic series.

B Each term increase by a multiple of 16 plus 2, where k is the domain from 1 to 5. This is an arithmetic series.

C Each term increases exponentially in the domain k, 1 to 5. This is not an arithmetic series.

D Each term increases by a multiple of one-sixteenth, in the domain 1 to 5. This is an arithmetic series.

Answer Choice **C**

28. Probability of glasses is $\frac{1}{3}$.

$$\begin{aligned} P &= ({}_4C_2)p^2q^2 \\ &= ({}_4C_2)\left(\frac{1}{3}\right)^2\left(\frac{2}{3}\right)^2 \\ &= 6\left(\frac{1}{9}\right)\left(\frac{4}{9}\right) \\ &= \frac{8}{27} \approx 0.3 \end{aligned}$$

29. The student incorrectly simplifies the rational terms. It should be as follows:

$$\begin{aligned} 16x^2 + 9y^2 = 144 &\rightarrow \frac{16}{144}x^2 + \frac{9}{144}y^2 \\ &= 1 \rightarrow \frac{x^2}{9} + \frac{y^2}{16} \\ &= 1 \rightarrow \frac{x^2}{3^2} + \frac{y^2}{4^2} = 1 \end{aligned}$$

30. Sample: $(0, \sqrt{2})$; $(0, \sqrt{2})$ is the image point that results when the point (1, 1) is rotated 45° counterclockwise about the origin.

LESSON 115

Warm Up 115

1. radian

2.

Quadrant	sine	cosine	tangent
I	+	+	+
II	+	−	−
III	−	−	+
IV	−	+	−

3. $\sin 105° = \sin(60° + 45°)$

$= \sin 60° \cos 45° + \cos 60° \sin 45°$

$= \frac{\sqrt{3}}{2} \cdot \frac{\sqrt{2}}{2} + \frac{1}{2} \cdot \frac{\sqrt{2}}{2}$

$= \frac{\sqrt{6}}{4} + \frac{\sqrt{2}}{4}$

$= \frac{\sqrt{6} + \sqrt{2}}{4}$

Lesson Practice 115

a. $\cos\theta = \sqrt{1 - \left(\frac{1}{5}\right)^2} = \sqrt{1 - \frac{1}{25}}$

$= \sqrt{\frac{24}{25}} = \frac{2\sqrt{6}}{5}$

$\sin 2\theta = 2 \sin\theta \cos\theta$

$= 2\left(\frac{1}{5}\right)\left(\frac{2\sqrt{6}}{5}\right)$

$= \frac{4\sqrt{6}}{25}$

$\cos 2\theta = 1 - 2\sin^2\theta$

$= 1 - 2\left(\frac{1}{5}\right)^2$

$= \frac{23}{25}$

b. $\cos 2\theta = 1 - \sin 2\theta \tan\theta$

$= 1 - 2\sin\theta\cos\theta\tan\theta$

$= 1 - 2\sin\theta\cos\theta\frac{\sin\theta}{\cos\theta}$

$= 1 - 2\sin^2\theta$

$= \cos 2\theta$

c. $\cot\theta = \frac{\sin 2\theta}{1 - \cos 2\theta}$

$= \frac{2\sin\theta\cos\theta}{1 - (1 - 2\sin^2\theta)}$

$= \frac{2\sin\theta\cos\theta}{2\sin^2\theta}$

$= \frac{\cos\theta}{\sin\theta} = \cot\theta$

d. $\cos 75°$ is in QI so $\cos\left(\frac{150}{2}\right)^\circ$ is positive.

$\cos\left(\frac{150}{2}\right)^\circ = \sqrt{\frac{1 + \cos 150}{2}}$.

The cosine of 150° is $-\sqrt{\frac{3}{2}}$, so

$\cos\left(\frac{150}{2}\right)^\circ = \sqrt{\frac{1 + \left(-\frac{\sqrt{3}}{2}\right)}{2}} = \sqrt{\frac{\frac{2-\sqrt{3}}{2}}{2}}$

$= \frac{\sqrt{2 - \sqrt{3}}}{2}$

e. The tan of $\frac{\pi}{12}$ is located in QI so it is positive.

$\tan\left(\frac{1}{2}\right)\left(\frac{\pi}{6}\right) = \sqrt{\frac{1 - \cos\frac{\pi}{6}}{1 + \cos\frac{\pi}{6}}}$.

The value

of $\cos\frac{\pi}{6} = \frac{\sqrt{3}}{2}$, so

$\tan\left(\frac{1}{2}\right)\left(\frac{\pi}{6}\right) = \sqrt{\frac{1 - \cos\frac{\pi}{6}}{1 + \cos\frac{\pi}{6}}}$

$= \sqrt{\frac{1 - \frac{\sqrt{3}}{2}}{1 + \frac{\sqrt{3}}{2}}}$

$= \sqrt{\frac{\frac{2-\sqrt{3}}{2}}{\frac{2+\sqrt{3}}{2}}}$

$= \sqrt{\frac{2 - \sqrt{3}}{2 + \sqrt{3}}}$

$= \sqrt{\frac{2 - \sqrt{3}}{2 + \sqrt{3}} \cdot \frac{2 - \sqrt{3}}{2 - \sqrt{3}}}$

$= \sqrt{\frac{4 - 4\sqrt{3} + 3}{4 - 3}}$

$= \sqrt{7 - 4\sqrt{3}} = 2 - \sqrt{3}$

f. Sine is positive.

$\sin\frac{\theta}{2} = \sqrt{\frac{1 - \cos\theta}{2}} = \sqrt{\frac{1 - \left(-\frac{7}{9}\right)}{2}} = \sqrt{\frac{\frac{16}{9}}{2}}$

$= \sqrt{\frac{8}{9}} = \frac{2\sqrt{2}}{3}$

Cosine is negative.

$$\cos\frac{\theta}{2} = -\sqrt{\frac{1+\cos\theta}{2}} = -\sqrt{\frac{1+\left(-\frac{7}{9}\right)}{2}}$$

$$= -\sqrt{\frac{\frac{2}{9}}{2}}$$

$$= -\sqrt{\frac{1}{9}} = -\frac{1}{3}$$

Tangent is negative.

$$\tan\frac{\theta}{2} = -\sqrt{\frac{1-\cos\theta}{1+\cos\theta}} = -\sqrt{\frac{1-\left(-\frac{7}{9}\right)}{1+\left(-\frac{7}{9}\right)}}$$

$$= -\sqrt{\frac{\frac{16}{9}}{\frac{2}{9}}}$$

$$= -\sqrt{8} = -2\sqrt{2}$$

g. $x = \frac{1}{32}v^2 \sin 2\theta$

$x = \frac{1}{32}(100)^2 \sin 2(45)^\circ$

$x = (312.5)(2(\sin 45)(\cos 45))$

$x = 625\left(\frac{\sqrt{2}}{2}\right)\left(\frac{\sqrt{2}}{2}\right)$

$x = 312.5$ ft

Practice 115

1. The quotient without the remainder is the equation of the slant asymptote, so the degree of $h(x)$ must be $3m + 1 - 1$, which is $3m$.

2. $x^2 - 9x - 10 = (x - 10)(x + 1)$

3. $4ax + ax^2 - 5a = a(4x + x^2 - 5)$
$= a(x^2 + 4x - 5)$
$= a(x + 5)(x - 1)$

4. The equation is $r = a\sin(b\theta) = 4\sin(5\theta)$ or $-4\sin(5\theta)$.

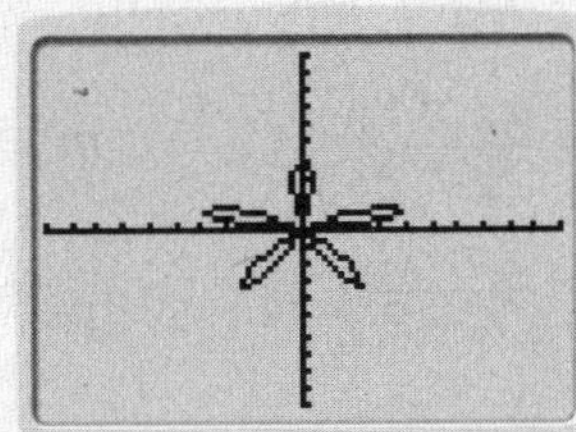

5. a. For 30°:

$x = \frac{1}{32}v^2 \sin 2\theta$

$x = \frac{1}{32}(80)^2 \sin 2(30°)$

$x = (200)(2(\sin 30°)(\cos 30°))$

$x = 400\left(\frac{1}{2}\right)\left(\frac{\sqrt{3}}{2}\right)$

$x \approx 173.2$ ft

For 45°:

$x = \frac{1}{32}v^2 \sin 2\theta$

$x = \frac{1}{32}(80)^2 \sin 2(45°)$

$x = (200)(2(\sin 45°)(\cos 45°))$

$x = 400\left(\frac{\sqrt{2}}{2}\right)\left(\frac{\sqrt{2}}{2}\right)$

$x = 200$ ft

For 70°:

$x = \frac{1}{32}v^2 \sin 2\theta$

$x = \frac{1}{32}(80)^2 \sin 2(70°)$

$x = (200)(2(\sin 70°)(\cos 70°))$

$x = 400(\sin 70)(\cos 70)$

$x = 128.6$ ft

For 90°:

$x = \frac{1}{32}v^2 \sin 2\theta$

$x = \frac{1}{32}(80)^2 \sin 2(90°)$

$x = (200)(2(\sin 90°)(\cos 90°))$

$x = 400(1)(0)$

$x = 0$ ft

So 45° gives the maximum distance.

b. If $\sin 2\theta$ is a fractional value, it will decrease the distance. Because $\sin 2(45°) = 2\sin(45°)\cos(45°) = 1$, this is the only value that will not decrease the distance the ball will be kicked.

6. 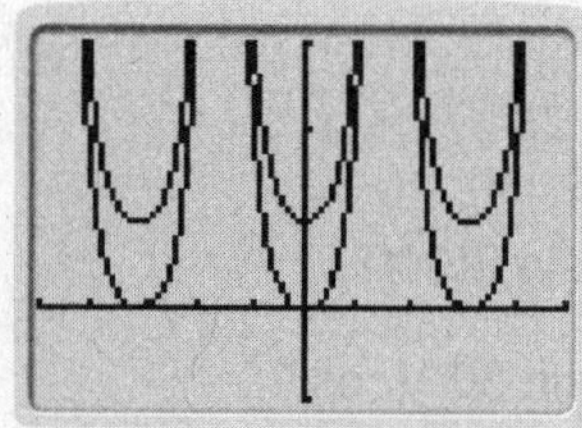

At any given point, $1 + \sec^2(x)\sin^2(x) - \tan^2(x) = 1$. Therefore, $\sec^2(x)\sin^2(x) = \tan^2(x)$.

7. $P(\text{even}) = \frac{\text{favorable outcomes}}{\text{total outcomes}} = \frac{3}{6} = \frac{1}{2}$

8. $16^4 = 65536$
$\log_{16} 65536 = 4$

9. $3^{14} = 4782969$
$\log_3 4782969 = 14$

10. The figure is a circle with radius 4 and the center at the pole of a polar coordinate system.

11. a. $x^2 - 10x - 12y - 95 = 0$
$B^2 - 4AC = 0^2 - 4(1)(0) = 0$. Therefore the conic section is a parabola.

b. $x^2 - 10x - 12y - 95 = 0$

$$x^2 - 10x = 12y + 95$$
$$x^2 - 10x + 25 = 12y + 95 + 25$$
$$(x-5)^2 = 12y + 120$$
$$(x-5)^2 = 12(y+10)$$
$$\frac{1}{12}(x-5)^2 = (y+10)$$

12.
$$\begin{array}{r} 4x^2 + 12x + 28 \\ x^2 - 3x + 2 \overline{)4x^4 + 0x^3 + 0x^2 + 5x - 4} \\ \underline{-(4x^4 - 12x^3 + 8x^2)} \\ 12x^3 - 8x^2 + 5x \\ \underline{-(12x^3 - 36x^2 + 24x)} \\ 28x^2 - 19x - 4 \\ \underline{-(28x^2 - 84x + 56)} \\ 65x - 60 \end{array}$$

The quotient is $4x^2 + 12x + 28 + \frac{65x - 60}{x^2 - 3x + 2}$.

13.
$$\begin{array}{r} x^2 + 5x + 25 \\ x - 5 \overline{)x^3 + 0x^2 + 0x - 2} \\ \underline{-(x^3 - 5x^2)} \\ 5x^2 + 0x \\ \underline{-(5x^2 - 25x)} \\ 25x - 2 \\ \underline{-(25x - 125)} \\ 123 \end{array}$$

The quotient is $x^2 + 5x + 25 + \frac{123}{x-5}$.

14. The exponent in the formula is one less than the value of n.

$$a_8 = 2(-5)^{8-1}$$
$$= 2(-5)^7$$
$$= -156{,}250$$

15. cos 112.5° is in QII so $\cos\frac{225}{2} = -\sqrt{\frac{1 + \cos 225}{2}}$. The cosine of 225° is $-\frac{\sqrt{2}}{2}$, so

$$\cos\frac{225}{2} = -\sqrt{\frac{1 + \left(-\frac{\sqrt{2}}{2}\right)}{2}} = -\sqrt{\frac{\frac{2 - \sqrt{2}}{2}}{2}}$$
$$= -\sqrt{\frac{2 - \sqrt{2}}{4}}$$
$$= -\frac{\sqrt{2 - \sqrt{2}}}{2}$$

16. $\underbrace{\begin{bmatrix} 4 & -1 \\ -7 & -2 \end{bmatrix}}_{A} \underbrace{\begin{bmatrix} x \\ y \end{bmatrix}}_{X} = \underbrace{\begin{bmatrix} 10 \\ -25 \end{bmatrix}}_{B}$

$$X = A^{-1}B = \begin{bmatrix} 0.1\overline{3} & -0.0\overline{6} \\ -0.4\overline{6} & -0.2\overline{6} \end{bmatrix} \begin{bmatrix} 10 \\ -25 \end{bmatrix} = \begin{bmatrix} 3 \\ 2 \end{bmatrix}$$

17. The polynomial has at least one real root and a pair of positive and negative complex roots. The minimum degree is 5.

Answer Choice **C**

18. This is a horizontal orientation. Find the slope.

$$m = \pm\frac{b}{a} = \pm\frac{7}{12}$$

$$m = \frac{y_2 - y_1}{x_2 - x_1} \qquad m = \frac{y_2 - y_1}{x_2 - x_1}$$

$$\frac{7}{12} = \frac{y - 13}{x - 9} \qquad -\frac{7}{12} = \frac{y - 13}{x - 9}$$

$7x - 63 = 12y - 156 \quad -7x + 63 = 12y - 156$

$y = \frac{7}{12}x + \frac{31}{4} \qquad y = -\frac{7}{12}x + \frac{73}{4}$

Answer Choice **B**

19. If the signs of consecutive terms alternate, the common ratio is negative.

20. $\log_8(32x)^4 = 4\log_8(32x)$

$= 4\left(\frac{\ln 32x}{\ln 8}\right)$

$= 4\left(\frac{\ln 32 + \ln x}{\ln 8}\right)$

when $x = 5$

$\log_8(32x)^4 = 4\left(\frac{\ln 32 + \ln 5}{\ln 8}\right)$

$\approx 4\left(\frac{3.4657 + 1.6094}{2.0794}\right) \approx 9.76$

21. $4x^2 + 8x - 21 \geq 0$

Let $4x^2 + 8x - 21 = 0$

$x = \frac{-8 \pm \sqrt{8^2 - 4(4)(-21)}}{2(4)}$

$= \frac{-8 \pm \sqrt{400}}{8}$

$= \frac{-8 \pm 20}{8}$

$x = 1.5$ or -3.5

The critical values are 1.5 and −3.5.

Interval	Test Value	Solution
$x > 1.5$	2	$4(2)^2 + 8(2) - 21 \geq 0$ $11 \geq 0$ true
$-3.5 < x < 1.5$	0	$4(0)^2 + 8(0) - 21 \geq 0$ $-21 \geq 0$ false
$x < -3.5$	−5	$4(-5)^2 + 8(-5) - 21 \geq 0$ $39 \geq 0$ true

Therefore $x \geq 1.5$ or $x \leq -3.5$

22. Graph the equation $A(x) = 15{,}000(1.0225)^x$.

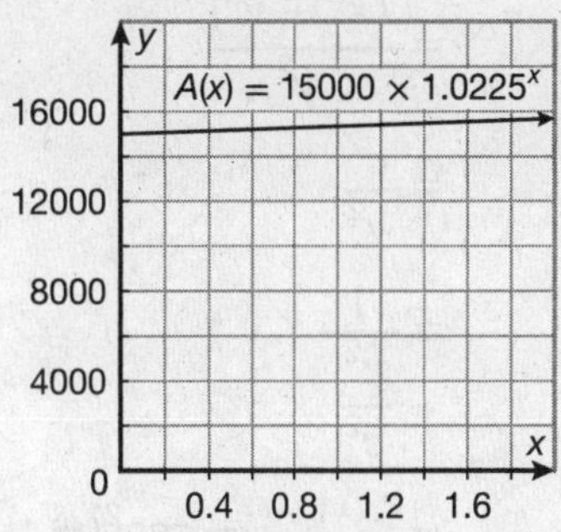

23.

$y = 281{,}000{,}000(1.0124)^t$

$400{,}000{,}000 = 281{,}000{,}000(1.0124)^t$

$1.42349 = (1.0124)^t$

$\log 1.42349 = \log(1.0124)^t$

$\log 1.42349 = t\log(1.0124)$

$\frac{\log 1.42349}{\log 1.0124} = t$

$28.7 \approx t$

The year will be about 28.7 years after 2000, so in the year 2028 or 2029, depending on the start month.

24. a. The equation can be written as $(x - 0)^2 + (y - 2)^2 = 6^2$ so the equation has the general form $(x - h)^2 + (y - k)^2 = r^2$ which represents the equation of a circle.

b. $x^2 + (y - 2)^2 = 36$

$x^2 + y^2 - 4y + 4 = 36$

$x^2 + y^2 - 4y - 32 = 0$

25. $\underbrace{\begin{bmatrix} 4 & 5 & 3 \\ 1 & -3 & 2 \\ -1 & 2 & -1 \end{bmatrix}}_{A} \underbrace{\begin{bmatrix} x \\ y \\ z \end{bmatrix}}_{X} = \underbrace{\begin{bmatrix} 15 \\ -6 \\ 3 \end{bmatrix}}_{B}$

$X = A^{-1}B = \begin{bmatrix} 0.08\overline{3} & -0.91\overline{6} & -1.58\overline{3} \\ 0.08\overline{3} & 0.08\overline{3} & 0.41\overline{6} \\ 0.08\overline{3} & 1.08\overline{3} & 1.41\overline{6} \end{bmatrix} \begin{bmatrix} 15 \\ -6 \\ 3 \end{bmatrix}$

$= \begin{bmatrix} 2 \\ 2 \\ -1 \end{bmatrix}$

Solution is $x = 2$, $y = 2$, and $z = -1$.

26. $1 + \cot^2(\theta) = 1 + \dfrac{x^2}{y^2}$

$$= \frac{(x^2 + y^2)}{y^2}$$

$$= \frac{c^2}{y^2}$$

$$= \frac{1}{\frac{y^2}{c^2}}$$

$$= \frac{1}{\sin^2(\theta)} = \csc^2(\theta)$$

27. The student used the wrong coordinates for the center. Because the formula uses negative signs before h and k, h should be 2 and k should be −9 making the center (2, −9).

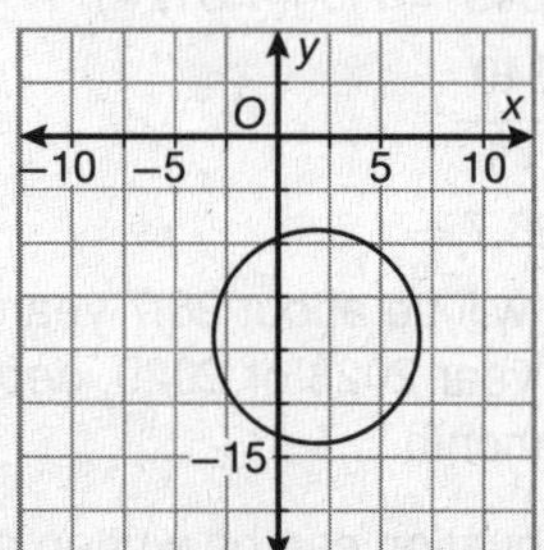

28. Order does not matter so this is a combination.

$${}_{13}C_4 = \frac{13!}{4!(13 - 4)!}$$

$$= \frac{13 \times 12 \times 11 \times 10 \times \not{9}!}{4!\not{9}!} = 715$$

29. Comparing $y = a\log_b(cx)$ and $y = a\log_b(cx - d)$, the horizontal offset is the ratio $\frac{d}{c}$. Therefore the x-intercept is $x = \frac{1}{c} + \frac{d}{c} = \frac{1 + d}{c}$.

30. The graph of this function would extend to the left and right without end, so the domain is the set of real numbers. The asymptote is the line $y = 3$, since as x decreases without bound, y approaches 3. The range is the set of real numbers greater than 3.

LAB 14

1.

$R^2 = 0.577$;
$y = -0.042x^3 + 0.770x^2 - 3.383x + 5.999$

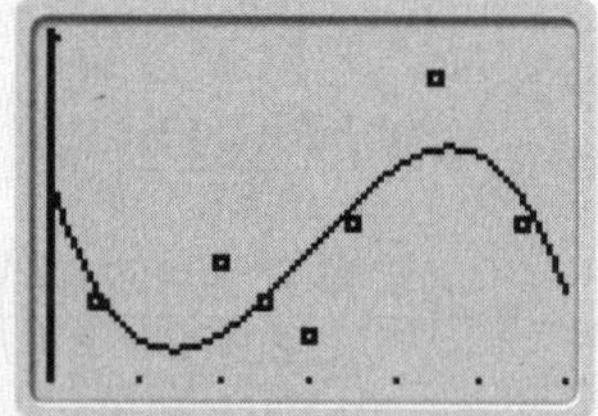

2.

LnReg
y=a+blnx
a=.2119524366
b=.9165977454
r²=.9694129695
r=.9845877155

$R^2 = 0.969$; $y = 0.212 + 0.917\ \ln(x)$

LESSON 116

Warm Up 116

1. correlation

2. $\frac{5}{8} \div \frac{5}{6} = \frac{5}{8} \times \frac{6}{5} = \frac{3}{4}$

3. The parent graph is $y = b^x$ where $0 < b < 1$, and since this graph, $y = ab^x$, is a reflection of the parent graph over the x-axis, $a < 0$. The y-intercept is (0, −2), so only **A** fits the criteria. Answer Choice **A**

4. $6(3a + b = -5) \longrightarrow 18a + 6b = -30$
$2a - 6b = 30 \longrightarrow \quad 2a - 6b = 30$

$$20a \quad = 0$$
$$a = 0$$

$$2(0) - 6b = 30$$
$$-6b = 30$$
$$b = -5$$

The solution is $a = 0$, $b = -5$.

Lesson Practice 116

a. First differences: 4 3 4 0 1
Second differences: −1 1 −4 1
$y \approx -0.482x^2 + 0.018x + 19.96$

b. First differences: −17 −16 3 15 14
Second differences: 1 19 12 −1
Third differences: 18 −7 −13
Fourth differences: −25 −6
$y \approx -0.0000646x^4 + 0.0088x^3 - 0.35x^2 + 3.62x + 32.83$

c. Ratios between consecutive y-values is 1.46, 1.49, 1.48, 1.47, 1.48 or about 1.5.
$y \approx 77.41(1.478)^x$

d. The population increases less as the years increase. Enter the data into a graphing calculator and choose **LnReg** to get a natural logarithmic function in the form $y = a + b\ln(x)$.
$y \approx -30.94 + 41.5\ln(x)$

e. Compare the R^2 values. The value for quartic is greatest. The equation is $y \approx -0.0000822x^4 + 0.0039x^3 - 0.067x^2 + 0.51x - 0.175$.
To estimate the population in 2003, find the value for $x = 11$, which is about 1,340,000.

Practice 116

1. First differences: −1733 −275 −233 −1765
Second differences: 1458 42 −1532
Third differences: −1416 −1574
$y \approx -1.993x^3 - 0.063x^2 - 0.967x + 1.54$
When x is 3, $y \approx -56$, which changes to about −60 for a quartic function.

2. a. $\sum_{k=1}^{n} 2(45(0.25))(0.25)^{k-1}$

$= \sum_{k=1}^{n} 2(11.25)(0.25)^{k-1}$

b. $a_1 = \sum_{k-1}^{n} 2(11.25)(0.25)^{1-1} = 22.5$

$S = \dfrac{a_1}{1-r} = \dfrac{22.5}{1-0.25} = 30$

c. $45 + 30 = 75$ m.
The total distance traveled is 75 m.

3. All numbers greater than 25 up to 50 are either even or odd. There are 25 such numbers, so there are 25 outcomes.

4. $y = x^9 - 8x^6 - x^3 + 8$.
Possible factors are ±1, ±2, ±4, ±8.

```
1 | 1  0  0  -8   0   0  -1   0   0   8
  |    1  1   1  -7  -7  -7  -8  -8  -8
    1  1  1  -7  -7  -7  -8  -8  -8   0

-1| 1  1  1  -7  -7  -7  -8  -8  -8
  |   -1  0  -1   8  -1   8   0   8
    1  0  1  -8   1  -8   0  -8   0

2 | 1  0  1  -8   1  -8   0  -8
  |    2  4  10   4  10   4   8
    1  2  5   2   5   2   4   0

-2| 1  2  5   2   5   2   4
  |   -2  0 -10  16 -42  80
    1  0  5  -8  21 -40  84
```

−2 is not a root.
The roots are −1, 1, and 2.

5. a. R^2 values in order from greatest to least: quartic, cubic, quadratic, exponential, linear, logarithmic.

b. The estimate for the quartic model is 1.54 million.

6. $\sqrt{15} \cdot \sqrt{5} = \sqrt{3}\sqrt{5} \cdot \sqrt{5} = 5\sqrt{3}$

7. $\sqrt{175} - \sqrt{63} + \sqrt{20}$
$= \sqrt{25}\sqrt{7} - \sqrt{9}\sqrt{7} + \sqrt{4}\sqrt{5}$
$= 5\sqrt{7} - 3\sqrt{7} + 2\sqrt{5}$
$= 2\sqrt{7} + 2\sqrt{5}$

8. $a_n = a_m + (n-m)d$
$33 = a_5 + (21-5)(-9)$
$33 = a_5 + (-144)$
$177 = a_5$

9. The student forgot to distribute $\csc\theta$ to $\cos^2\theta - \sin^2\theta$. The correct response is as follows:
$\cot\theta\cos\theta - \sin\theta = \cos 2\theta\csc\theta$
$= (\cos^2\theta \sin^2\theta)\left(\dfrac{1}{\sin\theta}\right)$
$= \dfrac{\cos^2\theta}{\sin\theta} - \dfrac{\sin^2\theta}{\sin\theta}$

$$= \frac{\cos\theta}{\sin\theta}(\cos\theta) - \sin\theta$$
$$= \cot\theta(\cos\theta) - \sin\theta$$
$$\cot\theta\cos\theta - \sin\theta = \cot\theta\cos\theta - \sin\theta$$

10. $\frac{x+9}{3x} \div \frac{3x+27}{x} = \frac{x+9}{3x} \times \frac{x}{3(x+9)}$

$$= \frac{x(x+9)}{9x(x+9)} = \frac{1}{9}$$

The value is always $\frac{1}{9}$ no matter what value of x is substituted, since x has been eliminated. So, if $x = 7$

$$\frac{7(7+9)}{9(7)(7+9)} = \frac{1}{9}$$

11. Point $C(0, 0)$ is the rotation point, so C' is also $(0, 0)$.

$$\begin{bmatrix} \cos 25° & -\sin 25° \\ \sin 25° & \cos 25° \end{bmatrix}\begin{bmatrix} 3 & -3 \\ 4 & 4 \end{bmatrix}$$
$$= \begin{bmatrix} 3\cos 25° - 4\sin 25° & -3\cos 25° - 4\sin 25° \\ 3\sin 25° + 4\cos 25° & -3\sin 25° + 4\cos 25° \end{bmatrix}$$
$$\approx \begin{bmatrix} 1.03 & -4.41 \\ 4.89 & 2.36 \end{bmatrix}$$

The image is $A'(1.03, 4.89)$, $B'(-4.41, 2.36)$, $C'(0, 0)$.

12. $y \le \frac{2}{3}x - 5$

$-3 \le \frac{2}{3}(3) - 5$

$-3 \le 2 - 5$

$-3 \le -3$

True. Therefore $(3, -3)$ is a solution.

13. $y < 9x - 3$

$-6 < 9(-2) - 3$

$-6 < -21$

False. Therefore $(-2, -6)$ is not a solution.

14. Only reflections; the end behavior is determined only by the sign of the coefficient and the degree of the highest-degree term. None of the transformations can change the degree, and only a reflection can change the sign of the coefficient.

15. This is a horizontal orientation of a hyperbola, where $a = 4$, $b = 3$ and $c = 5$. The lens would be placed at the focus $(c, 0)$ which is $(5, 0)$.

16. The equation of a parabola contains one squared term. This equation has two squared terms, so the equation is not a parabola.

17. Possible root: ± 2. Use synthetic division.

$$\begin{array}{r|rrrrrr} 2 & 12 & -49 & 49 & -96 & 392 & -392 \\ & & 24 & -50 & -2 & -196 & 392 \\ \hline & 12 & -25 & -1 & -98 & 196 & 0 \end{array}$$

2 is a root.

$12x^5 - 49x^4 + 49x^3 - 96x^2 + 392x - 392$
$= (x - 2)(12x^4 - 25x^3 - x^2 - 98x + 196)$.

Using a graphing calculator the other roots are $\frac{7}{3}$ and $\frac{7}{4}$.

18. Possible root: ± 1. Use synthetic division.

$$\begin{array}{r|rrrrrrrrrrrrrrr} 1 & 1 & 0 & -1 & -1 & 0 & 1 & 0 & 0 & 0 & -1 & 0 & 1 & 1 & 0 & -1 \\ & & 1 & 1 & 0 & -1 & -1 & 0 & 0 & 0 & 0 & -1 & -1 & 0 & 1 & 1 \\ \hline & 1 & 1 & 0 & -1 & -1 & 0 & 0 & 0 & 0 & -1 & -1 & 0 & 1 & 1 & 0 \end{array}$$

$$\begin{array}{r|rrrrrrrrrrrrrr} -1 & 1 & 1 & 0 & -1 & -1 & 0 & 0 & 0 & 0 & -1 & -1 & 0 & 1 & 1 \\ & & -1 & 0 & 0 & 1 & 0 & 0 & 0 & 0 & 0 & 1 & 0 & 0 & -1 \\ \hline & 1 & 0 & 0 & -1 & 0 & 0 & 0 & 0 & 0 & -1 & 0 & 0 & 1 & 0 \end{array}$$

± 1 are roots.

$x^{14} - x^{12} - x^{11} + x^9 - x^5 + x^3 + x^2 - 1$
$= (x - 1)(x + 1)(x^{12} - x^9 - x^3 + 1)$. There are no other roots.

19. **A** $x^2 - 12x + 35 = (x - 7)(x - 5)$, $x \neq 7$, or 5

B $x^2 - 14x + 48 = (x - 6)(x - 8)$, $x \neq 6$, or 8

C $x^2 - x - 30 = (x - 6)(x + 5)$, $x \neq 6$, or -5

D $x^2 + x - 30 = (x + 6)(x - 5)$, $x \neq -6$, or 5

Answer Choice **C**

20. $C = 2\pi r = 20\pi$, so $r = 10$

Substitute $r = 10$, $h = 5$, and $k = -1$ into $(x - h)^2 + (y - k)^2 = r^2$

$(x - 5)^2 + (y - (-1))^2 = 10^2$

$(x - 5)^2 + (y + 1)^2 = 100$

21. The student probably identified the leading coefficient as -1 instead of 1. The correct response should be: as $x \to +\infty$, $f(x) \to +\infty$, and as $x \to -\infty$, $f(x) \to +\infty$.

22. First differences: 1.25 0.94 1.16 0.95

Second differences −0.31 0.22 −0.21

Using a graphing calculator, $R^2 \approx 0.9942$ and the function is $y \approx -0.117x^2 + 1.79x - 6.8$.

When $x = 6$, $y \approx -0.28$

23. $y = 0.485x^3 - 362x^2 + 89{,}889x - 7{,}379{,}874$ and $220 \le x \le 280$.

$45{,}000 = 0.485x^3 - 362x^2 + 89{,}889x - 7{,}379{,}874$

$0.485x^3 - 362x^2 + 89{,}889x - 7{,}424{,}874 = 0$

Using a graphing calculator, the roots are about 228, 253, and 265.

24. $\sin\theta$ is positive.

$$\sin\frac{\theta}{2} = \sqrt{\frac{1-\cos\theta}{2}} = \sqrt{\frac{1-\left(-\frac{1}{4}\right)}{2}} = \sqrt{\frac{5}{8}}$$

$$= \frac{2\sqrt{10}}{8} = \frac{\sqrt{10}}{4}$$

Answer Choice **B**

25. $\frac{125}{x} < 7.5$

$125 < 7.5x$

$x > 16.7$

Therefore, it would take 17 members.

26. To vertically compress a graph, you must multiply each *y*-coordinate of the graph by a value between zero and one.

27. Interchange the variables.

$y = 4x^2 + 24$

$x = 4y^2 + 24$

$x - 24 = 4y^2$

$\frac{x-24}{4} = y^2$

$\sqrt{\frac{x-24}{4}} = y$

$\frac{\sqrt{x-24}}{2} = y$

or $y = \frac{1}{2}\sqrt{x-24}$

28. Possible roots: ±1, ±3, ±5. Use synthetic division to test.

$$\begin{array}{r|rrrr} 1 & 1 & 7 & 7 & -15 \\ & & 1 & 8 & 15 \\ \hline & 1 & 8 & 15 & 0 \end{array}$$

$x = 1$ is a root. Since the equation is cubic there are two other roots.

$x^3 + 7x^2 + 7x - 15 = (x-1)(x^2 + 8x + 15)$

$= (x-1)(x+3)(x+5)$

29. Possible roots: ±1, ±2, ±3, ±4, ±6, ±7, ±12, ±14, ±21, ±28, ±42, ±84. Using a graphing calculator, one root is 4.

$$\begin{array}{r|rrrrr} 4 & 1 & 3 & -25 & 9 & -84 \\ & & 4 & 28 & 12 & 84 \\ \hline & 1 & 7 & 3 & 21 & 0 \end{array}$$

$x = 4$ is a root.

$x^4 + 3x^3 - 25x^2 + 9x - 84 = (x-4)(x^3 + 7x^2 + 3x + 21)$

Possible roots of $x^3 + 7x^2 + 3x + 21$ are ±1, ±3, ±7. Using a graphing calculator, one root is −7.

$$\begin{array}{r|rrrr} -7 & 1 & 7 & 3 & 21 \\ & & -7 & 0 & -21 \\ \hline & 1 & 0 & 3 & 0 \end{array}$$

$x = -7$ is a root.

$x^4 + 3x^3 - 25x^2 + 9x - 84$

$= (x-4)(x+7)(x^2 + 3)$

30. Substitute $a_1 + (n-1)d$ for a_n in $S_n = n\left(\frac{a_1 + a_n}{2}\right)$.

$$S_n = n\left(\frac{(a_1 + (a_1 + (n-1)d)}{2}\right)$$

$$= n\left(\frac{2a_1 + (n-1)d}{2}\right)$$

The formula can be used to find the sum of the first *n* terms, given the number of terms, the first term, and the common ratio. It is not necessary to know the value of the *n*th term.

LESSON 117

Warm Up 117

1. parabola

2. false

3. 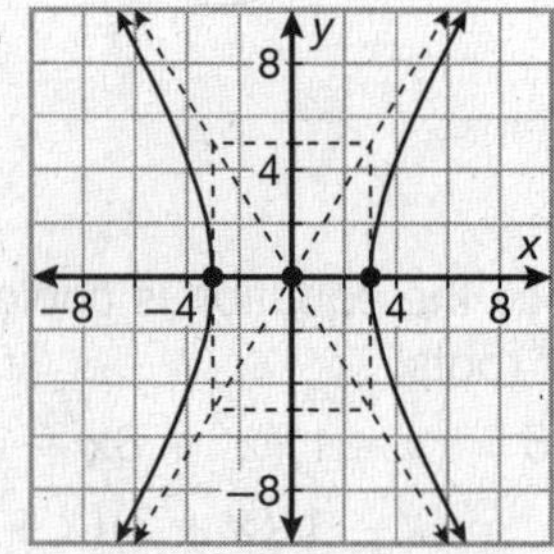

Lesson Practice 117

a. $x^2 - y^2 = 48$

$x = 7y$

Substitute $x = 7y$ into the first equation.

$x^2 - y^2 = 48$

$(7y)^2 - y^2 = 48$

$49y^2 - y^2 = 48$

$48y^2 = 48$

$y^2 = 1$

$y = \pm 1$

Substitute -1 and 1 into the second equation.

$x = 7(1) = 7$

$x = 7(-1) = -7$

The solutions are (7, 1) and (−7, −1).

b. $x^2 + y^2 = 16 \rightarrow \quad x^2 + y^2 = 16$

$x^2 - 2y^2 = 1 \rightarrow -x^2 + 2y^2 = -1$

$3y^2 = 15$

$y = \pm\sqrt{5}$

$x^2 + (\pm\sqrt{5})^2 = 16$

$x^2 + 5 = 16$

$x = \pm\sqrt{11}$

The solutions are $(-\sqrt{11}, -\sqrt{5})$, $(-\sqrt{11}, \sqrt{5})$, $(\sqrt{11}, -\sqrt{5})$, and $(\sqrt{11}, \sqrt{5})$

c. Graph each equation and find the points of intersection.

Rewrite the first equation.

$y + 2 = 2x \rightarrow y = 2x - 2$

Plot the point with the y-intercept, (0, −2) and move up 2, and right 1 to plot another point.

Rewrite the second equation.

$xy = 24$

$y = \frac{24}{x}$

x	$y = \frac{24}{x}$	x	$y = \frac{24}{x}$
−12	−2	2	12
−6	−4	6	4
−2	−12	12	2

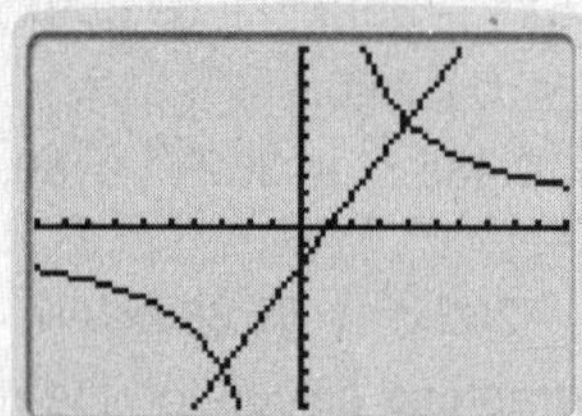

The graphs intersect at (−3, −8) and (4, 6).

d. Solve each equation for y.

$y^2 - x^2 = 36 \qquad 2x + y = -1.5$

$y^2 = 36 + x^2 \qquad y = -2x - 1.5$

$y = \pm\sqrt{36 + x^2}$

Press Y= and enter the three functions $y = \sqrt{36 + x^2}$, $y = -\sqrt{36 + x^2}$ and $y = -2x - 1.5$.

Press GRAPH and then press TRACE to scroll along the graphs to find the solutions.The solutions are (−4.5, 7.5) and (2.5, −6.5).

e. $3x + 4y = 12$

$3x = -4y + 12$

$x = -\frac{4}{3}y + 4$

Substitute for x.

$9x^2 + 16y^2 = 144$

$9\left(-\frac{4}{3}y + 4\right)^2 + 16y^2 = 144$

$9\left(\frac{16}{9}y^2 - \frac{32}{3}y + 16\right) + 16y^2 = 144$

$16y^2 - 96y + 144 + 16y^2 = 144$

$32y^2 - 96y = 0$

$32y(y - 3) = 0$

$y = 0, 3$

Substitute for y.

$3x + 4(0) = 12 \qquad 3x + 4(3) = 12$

$3x = 12 \qquad 3x + 12 = 12$

$x = 4 \qquad 3x = 0$

$x = 0$

The solutions are (0, 3) and (4, 0). The paths will cross at (0, 3) and (4, 0).

Practice 117

1. $a < 0$ and $b > 0$

2. $A = \frac{1}{2}d_1d_2$

$2A = d_1d_2$

$d_1 = \frac{2A}{d_2}$

3. Quarterly means 4 times per year, so

$i = \frac{0.08}{4} = 0.02$

$A = P(1 + i)^{nt}$

$A = 2000(1 + 0.02)^{30\cdot4}$

$= 2000(1.02)^{120}$

$= \$21{,}530.33$

\$21,530.33 will be in the account after 30 years.

4. Answer Choice **A**

5. $P(x) = x^3 + 2x^2 - 13x + 10$

$P(1) = 1^3 + 2(1)^2 - 13(1) + 10 = 0$

$$\begin{array}{r|rrrr} 1 & 1 & 2 & -13 & 10 \\ & & 1 & 3 & -10 \\ \hline & 1 & 3 & -10 & \end{array}$$

$P(x) = (x - 1)(x^2 + 3x - 10)$

$= (x - 1)(x + 5)(x - 2)$

$Q(x) = x^3 - 2x^2 + x = x(x^2 - 2x + 1)$

$= x(x - 1)^2$

$R(x) = 3x^3 + 48x = 3x(x^2 + 16)$

$x^2 = -16$, there are no more real roots

$S(x) = 2x^3 - 32x = 2x(x^2 - 16)$

$= 2x(x - 4)(x + 4)$

$T(x) = x^3 - 7x^2 + 4x - 28$

$= x^2(x - 7) + 4(x - 7)$

$= (x - 7)(x^2 + 4)$

$x^2 = -4$, there are no more real roots

Two of the five functions have exactly one x-intercept. Probability $= \frac{2}{5} = 40\%$. Odds are 2 to 3.

6. $\log_7 5^3 = 3 \log_7 5$

7. $\log_5 42 - \log_5 7 = \log_5 \frac{42}{7} = \log_5 6$

8. The correlation coefficient is r and it only measures the strength of a linear regression. R^2 values measure the strength of nonlinear regressions.

9. $$\begin{array}{r|rrrr} -2 & 3 & -4 & -28 & -16 \\ & & -6 & 20 & 16 \\ \hline & 3 & -10 & -8 & \end{array}$$

$x + 2$ is a factor of $P(x)$.

$Q(x) = 3x^2 - 10x - 8$

10. Press Y= and enter the function. Then press GRAPH.

Continuous, $y \leq 3$

11. $d = \frac{140 - 55}{20 - 3} = 5$

$a_n = a_0 + 5(n - 1)$

$a_3 = a_0 + 5(3 - 1)$

$55 = a_0 + 10$

$45 = a_0$

$a_6 = 45 + 5(6 - 1) = 70$

12. $2x + y = 7$

$y = -2x + 7$

Substitute for y.

$4x^2 + y^2 = 25$

$4x^2 + (-2x + 7)^2 = 25$

$4x^2 + 4x^2 - 28x + 49 = 25$

$8x^2 - 28x + 24 = 0$

$4(2x^2 - 7x + 6) = 0$

$4(2x - 3)(x - 2) = 0$

$x = \frac{3}{2}$ and $x = 2$

Substitute for x.

$2\left(\frac{3}{2}\right) + y = 7$ | $2(2) + y = 7$

$y = 7 - 3$ | $y = 7 - 4$

$y = 4$ | $y = 3$

The two planes could collide at (1.5, 4) or (2, 3).

13. If the LCD includes a variable, then the value of that variable is unknown. It could be positive or negative.

14. $40 \cdot \frac{\pi}{180°} = \frac{2}{9}\pi$

$30° \le x \le 40°$

$\frac{\pi}{6} \le x \le \frac{2}{9}\pi$

$0.5236 \le x \le 0.6981$

15. The terms form a line; the partial sums form a curve.

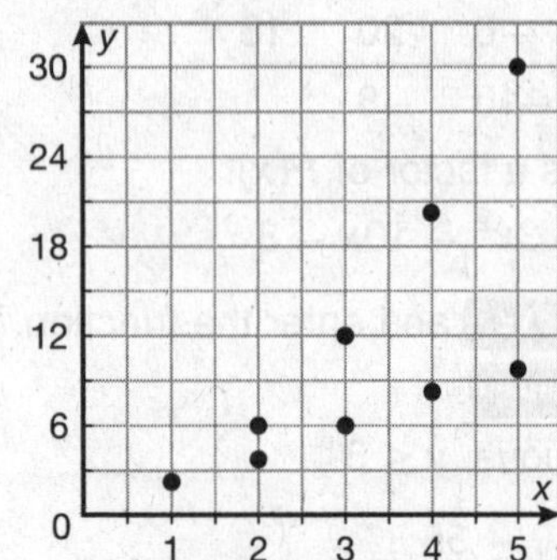

16. **A** $\frac{x^2}{2^2} + \frac{y^2}{5^2} = \frac{0^2}{2^2} + \frac{5^2}{5^2} = 1$

B $\frac{x^2}{2^2} + \frac{y^2}{5^2} = \frac{2^2}{2^2} + \frac{0^2}{5^2} = 1$

C $\frac{x^2}{2^2} + \frac{y^2}{5^2} = \frac{5^2}{2^2} + \frac{0^2}{5^2} = \frac{25}{4} \neq 1$

D $\frac{x^2}{2^2} + \frac{y^2}{5^2} = \frac{(-2)^2}{2^2} + \frac{0^2}{5^2} = 1$

Answer Choice **C**

17. a. $200 = x^2 + 4xh$

$200 - x^2 = 4xh$

$h = \frac{200 - x^2}{4x}$

b. $V = x^2h$

$V = x^2\left(\frac{200 - x^2}{4x}\right) = \frac{-x^3 + 200x}{4}$

c. Press Y= and then enter the function. Press GRAPH and then TRACE to scroll along the function to determine the maximum volume.

maximum volume $\approx 272.17 \text{ in.}^3$

$x \approx 8.16$ in.

so,

$V = x^2h$

$272.17 = (8.16)^2h$

$h = \frac{272.17}{(8.16)^2}$

$h \approx 4.09$ in.

18. The maximum number of points of intersection of a line and a circle is two.

19. $f(x)$ is reflected in the y-axis and shifted 3.5 units to the left.

Then $g(x) = \sqrt{-(x + 3.5)} = \sqrt{-x - 3.5}$

20. a. hyperbola and ellipse

b. There could be up to four solutions since each half of the hyperbola could intersect the ellipse at two points.

c. $x^2 - y^2 = 15 \rightarrow \quad -9x^2 + 9y^2 = -135$

$9x^2 + 16y^2 = 160 \rightarrow 9x^2 + 16y^2 = 160$

$25y^2 = 25$

$y = \pm 1$

Substitute for y.

$x^2 - (\pm 1)^2 = 15$

$x^2 = 16$

$x = \pm 4$

The solutions are $(-4, -1)$, $(-4, 1)$, $(4, -1)$, and $(4, 1)$.

d. $x^2 - y^2 = 15$

$x^2 - 15 = y^2$

$y = \pm\sqrt{x^2 - 15}$

$9x^2 + 16y^2 = 160$

$16y^2 = 160 - 9x^2$

$y^2 = \frac{160 - 9x^2}{16}$

$y = \pm\sqrt{\frac{160 - 9x^2}{16}}$

The equations entered would be

$y = -\sqrt{\frac{160 - 9x^2}{16}}$, $y = \sqrt{\frac{160 - 9x^2}{16}}$,

$y = -\sqrt{x^2 - 15}$, and $y = \sqrt{x^2 - 15}$.

21. slope $= -\frac{1}{-\frac{1}{2}} = 2$

$y - y_1 = m(x - x_1)$

$y - 7 = 2(x - 1)$

$y - 7 = 2x - 2$

$y = 2x - 2 + 7$

$y = 2x + 5$

22. $r = \frac{l}{1 + e\sin(\theta)}$

$r = \frac{2}{1 + 2\sin(\theta)}$

Since the eccentricity is larger than 1, the conic is a hyperbola.

23. Press STAT and under the EDIT tab, highlight the first option **1: Edit** and press ENTER. Input the data provided in the table. Then press STAT and scroll to the CALC tab and then scroll down to **4: LinReg(*ax*+*b*)** and press ENTER. Then press 2nd and 1. Then press , followed by 2nd and 2. Finally press ENTER. Answer: $y = 4.2x - 2$.

24. $x = \frac{1}{32}v^2 \sin 2\theta$

$x = \frac{1}{32}(481)^2 \sin 2(85°)$

$x = \frac{1}{32}(481)^2(2\sin(85°)\cos(85°))$

$x \approx 1255.48$ feet

25. $\log_5 625 = \log_5 5^4 = 4$

26. $\log_5(5x + 9) = \log_5 6x$

$6x = 5x + 9$

$6x - 5x = 9$

$x = 9$

27. Student A factored incorrectly because $9x^2 + 30x + 25 \neq (3x + 5)(3x + 6)$.

28. The degree is odd and the leading coefficient is negative, so $f(x) \to +\infty$ as $x \to -\infty$ and $f(x) \to -\infty$ as $x \to +\infty$

29. 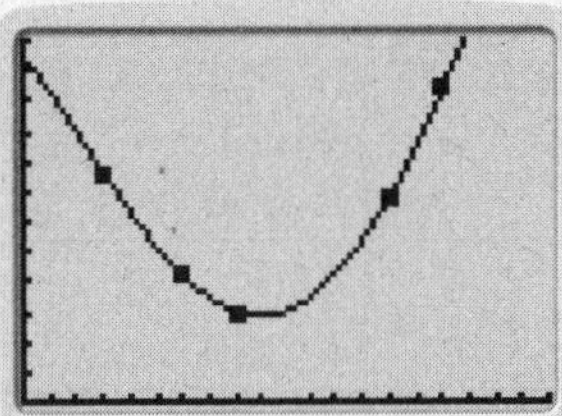

A quartic function appears to fit the data. Press STAT and under the EDIT tab, highlight the first option **1: Edit** and press ENTER. Input the data provided in the table. Then press STAT and scroll to the CALC tab, and then scroll down to 7: **QuartReg** and press ENTER. Then press 2nd and 1. Then press , followed by 2nd and 2. Finally, press ENTER.

Answer:

$y \approx -0.002x^4 + 0.083x^3 - 0.484x^2 - 5.74x + 57.5$

30. $16 - 9 = 7$, $30 - 23 = 7$, so the sequence is an arithmetic sequence, with $d = 7$.

$a_n = 2 + 7(n - 1)$

$a_{18} = 2 + 7(18 - 1) = 121$

$S_n = \frac{n(a_n + a_1)}{2}$

$S_{18} = \frac{18(121 + 2)}{2} = 1107$

LESSON 118

Warm Up 118

1. probability
2. true
3. The sample is every teen interviewed, the population is every teen in the county.

Lesson Practice 118

a. The sample size of four dermatologists is too small to be trusted as accurate.

b. Students will tend to round their heights. Also, because they are still growing, they may not know their current height, and either give their height from their last check up, or just guess it. Last, since the answer is being given orally, in front of their peers, they may lie and say they are taller than they are.

c. Because the second balloon is twice as wide as well as twice as high as the first, a reader just looking at the size of the balloons may think there were four times as many balloons ordered for the second party than the first, when it was really about twice as many.

d. No, correlation is not causation. It could be that individuals that make more money can afford to visit a dentist more often.

Practice 118

1. $a_n = 20 + 10(n - 1)$
$a_{16} = 20 + 10(16 - 1) = 170$
$S_{16} = \frac{16(20 + 170)}{2} = \$1520$

2. $36(1)^4 - 27(1)^3 - 13(1)^2 + 3(1) + 1 = 0$
Use synthetic division to factor.
$$\begin{array}{r|rrrrr} 1 & 36 & -27 & -13 & 3 & 1 \\ & & 36 & 9 & -4 & -1 \\ \hline & 36 & 9 & -4 & -1 & \end{array}$$
$36x^4 - 27x^3 - 13x^2 + 3x + 1$
$= (x - 1)(36x^3 + 9x^2 - 4x - 1)$
$= (x - 1)[9x^2(4x + 1) - 1(4x + 1)]$
$= (x - 1)(4x + 1)(9x^2 - 1)$
$= (x - 1)(4x + 1)(3x - 1)(3x + 1)$
$x = 1, -\frac{1}{4}, \pm\frac{1}{3}$

3. $80(1)^4 - 64(1)^3 - 21(1)^2 + 4(1) + 1 = 0$
Use synthetic division to factor.
$$\begin{array}{r|rrrrr} 1 & 80 & -64 & -21 & 4 & 1 \\ & & 80 & 16 & -5 & -1 \\ \hline & 80 & 16 & -5 & -1 & \end{array}$$
$80x^4 - 64x^3 - 21x^2 + 4x + 1$
$= (x - 1)(80x^3 + 16x^2 - 5x - 1)$
$= (x - 1)[16x^2(5x + 1) - 1(5x + 1)]$
$= (x - 1)(5x + 1)(16x^2 - 1)$
$= (x - 1)(5x + 1)(4x - 1)(4x + 1)$
$x = 1, -\frac{1}{5}, \pm\frac{1}{4}$

4. The graph is misleading because the values on the vertical axis start just below the lowest value, making the differences in prices between the Model A vehicles and the Model B vehicles appear greater than they actually are. A salesperson for Model B might have made the graph to get customers from a neighboring Model A dealership to buy his vehicles instead.

5. a. Since a tangent ratio is being used, the internal angle is that of a right triangle. Since $\tan\theta = \frac{opp}{adj}$, we have the two legs of the right triangle which we can use to find the hypotenuse.
$5^2 + 12^2 = h^2$
$25 + 144 = h^2$
$h = \sqrt{169}$
$h = 13$
$\cos\theta = \frac{12}{13}$

b. Sine is in QI so it is positive.
$\sin\frac{\theta}{2} = \sqrt{\frac{1 - \cos\theta}{2}}$
$\sin\frac{\theta}{2} = \sqrt{\frac{1 - \frac{12}{13}}{2}}$
$\sin\frac{\theta}{2} = \sqrt{\frac{1}{26}}$
$\sin\frac{\theta}{2} = \frac{1}{\sqrt{26}} = \frac{\sqrt{26}}{26}$

6. $2l + 2w = 82$
$l = \frac{82 - 2w}{2}$
$l = 41 - w$
$A = lw$
$250 > (41 - w)w$
$250 > 41w - w^2$
$w^2 - 41w + 250 > 0$
$w = \frac{-b \pm \sqrt{b^2 - 4ac}}{2a}$
$w = \frac{-(-41) \pm \sqrt{(-41)^2 - 4(1)(250)}}{2(1)}$
$w = \frac{41 \pm \sqrt{681}}{2}$
$w = 33.5$ and $w = 7.5$

Interval	Test value	Is it a solution?
$0 < w < 7.5$	7	$41(7) - 7^2 = 238 < 250$, yes
$7.5 < w < 33.5$	8	$41(8) - 8^2 = 264 > 250$, no
$33.5 < w$	34	$41(34) - 34^2 = 238 < 250$ yes

The solutions are $0 < w < 7.5$ or $33.5 < w < 41$.

7. $\frac{4}{3}x + 11 < y$

$\frac{4}{3}(-6) + 11 \stackrel{?}{<} 10$

$-8 + 11 \stackrel{?}{<} 10$

yes, it is a solution.

8. Since $f(x)$ has holes at $\pm c$, $g(x)$ and $h(x)$ both have $(x - c)$ and $(x + c)$ as factors. Then $h(x) = j(x)(x^2 - c^2)$ for any $j(x)$.

9. Use a graphing calculator to input the data. Press STAT and under the tab EDIT press ENTER right away. Enter the x-values under **L1** and the y-values under **L2**. Calculate the R^2 value by pressing STAT and under tab CALC, find the appropriate regression.
Linear regression has $R^2 = 0.792$
Quadratic regression has $R^2 = 0.959$
Cubic regression has $R^2 = 0.998$
Quartic regression has $R^2 = 1$
Exponential regression has $R^2 = 0.692$
Logarithmic regression has $R^2 = 0.979$
probability $= \frac{2}{6} = 33.3\%$

10. Yes, irrational roots come in pairs, so there would be three conjugate pairs of irrational roots.

11. $\sin 2\theta = -\frac{\sqrt{15}}{8}$; $\cos 2\theta = -\frac{7}{8}$. You do not need to find the value of $\sin \theta$ because once $\cos 2\theta$ is found you can solve for $\sin \theta$ in the $\cos 2\theta$ identity and then substitute it and solve for $\sin 2\theta$ in the $\cos 2\theta$ identity.

12. a. Using a graphing calculator, press STAT and ENTER to input the data. Press STAT and under the tab CALC scroll to **0:ExpReg** and enter **L1**, **L2**. Then press ENTER.
$y \approx 1.3(1.03)^x$
$1.3(1.03)^{125} \approx \$0.52$

b. Using a graphing calculator, press STAT and ENTER to input the data. Press STAT and under the tab CALC scroll to **7:QuartReg** and enter **L1**, **L2**. Then press ENTER.
$y \approx -0.000000014x^4 + 0.0000033x^3 - 0.00018x^2 + 0.002x + 0.03$
$- 0.000000014(125)^4 + 0.0000033(125)^3 - 0.00018(125)^2 + 0.002(125) + 0.03$
$\approx -3.42 + 6.45 - 2.81 + 0.25 + 0.03$
$\approx \$0.51$

c. Possible answer: \$0.51 because the R^2 value for the quartic value, 0.984, is greater than for the exponential model, 0.890, although predicting beyond the given domain is not very trustworthy to begin with.

13. The student did not consider the sign between the two terms. The sign is positive, so the graph is an ellipse.

14. The correct answer is **B**. Reporting the mean would be misleading because the outlier, in skewing the data, may produce a mean that is either larger than all other data points or smaller than all other data points. Similarly, reporting the range would be misleading as the outlier would represent an endpoint that is significantly farther than the rest of the data.
Answer Choice **B**

15. A limit is the number that the partial sums of a geometric series approaches. It is considered the sum of an infinite geometric series when the absolute value of the common ratio of the series is less than one.

16. The leading coefficient is 1 and the degree is 4. Since the leading coefficient is positive, the graph opens facing up, then
$f(x) \to +\infty$ as $x \to -\infty$ and $f(x) \to +\infty$ as $x \to +\infty$

17. A circle and a line can only have two points of intersection. A hyperbola and a circle can have up to 4 points of intersection. A circle and an ellipse can have up to 4 points of intersection. Finally, two parabolas could be identical and have infinitely many points of intersection.
Answer Choice **A**

18. To rotate P to P' a rotation of 60° is needed.

$$\begin{pmatrix} \cos\theta & -\sin\theta \\ \sin\theta & \cos\theta \end{pmatrix}\begin{pmatrix} x \\ y \end{pmatrix} = \begin{pmatrix} x' \\ y' \end{pmatrix}$$

$$\begin{pmatrix} \cos 60° & -\sin 60° \\ \sin 60° & \cos 60° \end{pmatrix}\begin{pmatrix} -3 \\ 0 \end{pmatrix}$$

$$= \begin{pmatrix} -3\cos 60° - (0)\sin 60° \\ -3\sin 60° + (0)\cos 60° \end{pmatrix}$$

$$= \begin{pmatrix} -1.50 \\ -2.60 \end{pmatrix}$$

$p' = (-1.50, -2.60)$

19. The question leads people to say "yes" because it gives a safety claim, a positive impact of the new light. No mention of possible negative impacts is given.

20. a. As viewed from the ground level, the cone looks like a triangle.

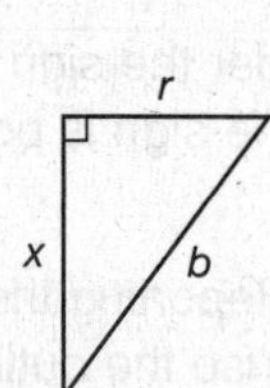

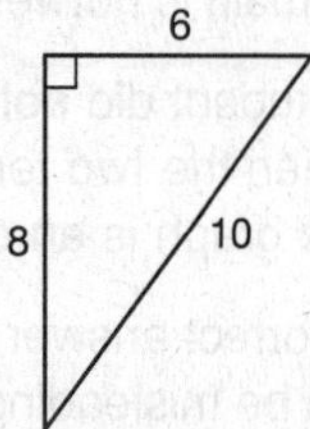

As the height decreases, the radius decreases.

$$\frac{x}{8} = \frac{r}{6}$$

$$r = \frac{6x}{8} = \frac{3}{4}x$$

$$V(x) = \frac{1}{3}\pi r^2 h$$

$$V(x) = \frac{1}{3}\pi\left(\frac{3}{4}x\right)^2 x$$

$$V(x) = \frac{1}{3}\pi\,\frac{9}{16}x^2 x$$

$$V(x) = \frac{3\pi}{16}x^3$$

b. $V(2x) = \frac{3\pi}{16}(2x)^3$

$$V(2x) = \frac{3\pi}{16}(8x^3)$$

$$V(2x) = \frac{3\pi}{2}x^3$$

$g(x)$ is a horizontal compression of $V(2x)$ since $2 > 1$. The cylinder's volume is multiplied by 8 when the height of the water is doubled.

21.

$$\begin{array}{r|rrrr} -2 & 1 & -11 & 14 & 80 \\ & & -2 & 26 & -80 \\ \hline & 1 & -13 & 40 & \end{array}$$

$(x^4 - 11x^3 + 14x^2 + 80x) \div (x + 2)$
$= x^3 - 13x^2 + 40x$

22.

$$\begin{array}{r|rrrr} 1 & 1 & 0 & -57 & 56 \\ & & 1 & 1 & -56 \\ \hline & 1 & 1 & -56 & \end{array}$$

$(x^3 - 57x + 56) \div (x - 1) = x^2 + x - 56$

23. $(-3)^4 - 2(-3)^3 - 14(-3)^2 - 2(-3) - 15$

Use synthetic division to check -3 as a root.

$= 81 + 54 - 126 + 6 - 15 = 0$

$$\begin{array}{r|rrrrr} -3 & 1 & -2 & -14 & -2 & -15 \\ & & -3 & 15 & -3 & 15 \\ \hline & 1 & -5 & 1 & -5 & \end{array}$$

$x^4 - 2x^3 - 14x^2 - 2x - 15$
$= (x + 3)(x^3 - 5x^2 + x - 5)$
$= (x + 3)[(x^2(x - 5) + 1(x - 5))]$
$= (x + 3)(x - 5)(x^2 + 1)$
$x = -3$, $x = 5$ and $x = \pm\sqrt{1} = \pm i$

24. $f(g(x)) = \tan(3x - 2) = \tan\left(3\left(x - \frac{2}{3}\right)\right)$

Since the function is horizontally compressed by a factor of 3, the period is $\frac{\pi}{3}$.

25. Press Y= and then enter the function as **Y1**. Then press GRAPH; press TRACE to determine the vertex and axis of symmetry.

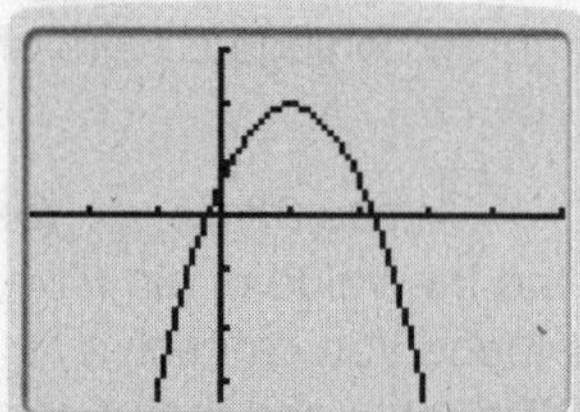

Vertex: (1, 6); Axis of symmetry: $x = 1$.

26. The student wrote the coordinates in the wrong order. The solution is (5, 3).

27. $2(1)^7 - (1)^6 - 15(1)^5 + 18(1)^4 - 2(1)^3 + (1)^2 + 15(1) - 18$
$= 2 - 1 - 15 + 18 - 2 + 1 + 15 - 18 = 0$

Use synthetic division to test 1 as a root.

$$\begin{array}{r|rrrrrrrr} 1 & 2 & -1 & -15 & 18 & -2 & 1 & 15 & -18 \\ & & 2 & 1 & -14 & 4 & 2 & 3 & 18 \\ \hline & 2 & 1 & -14 & 4 & 2 & 3 & 18 & \end{array}$$

$(x - 1)$ is a root.

$2x^7 - x^6 - 15x^5 + 18x^4 - 2x^3 + x^2 + 15x - 18$
$= (x - 1)(2x^6 + x^5 - 14x^4 + 4x^3 + 2x^2 + 3x + 18).$

$2(-1)^6 + (-1)^5 - 14(-1)^4 + 4(-1)^3$
$+ 2(-1)^2 + 3(-1) + 18$
$= 2 - 1 - 14 - 4 + 2 - 3 + 18 = 0$

−1	2	1	−14	4	2	3	18
		−2	1	13	−17	15	−18
	2	−1	−13	17	−15	18	

$(x+1)$ is a root.
$2x^7 - x^6 - 15x^5 + 18x^4 - 2x^3 + x^2$
$+ 15x - 18$
$= (x-1)(x+1)(2x^5 - x^4 - 13x^3 + 17x^2$
$- 15x + 18)$.
$2(2)^5 - (2)^4 - 13(2)^3 + 17(2)^2 - 15(2) + 18$
$= 64 - 16 - 104 + 68 - 30 + 18 = 0$

2	2	−1	−13	17	−15	18
		4	6	−14	6	−18
	2	3	−7	3	−9	

$x - 2$ is a root.
$2x^7 - x^6 - 15x^5 + 18x^4 - 2x^3 + x^2$
$+ 15x - 18$
$= (x-1)(x+1)(x-2)(2x^4 + 3x^3 - 7x^2$
$+ 3x - 9)$.
$2(-3)^4 + 3(-3)^3 - 7(-3)^2 + 3(-3) - 9$
$= 162 - 81 - 63 - 9 - 9 = 0$

−3	2	3	−7	3	−9
		−6	9	−6	9
	2	−3	2	−3	

$(x+3)$ is a root.
$2x^7 - x^6 - 15x^5 + 18x^4 - 2x^3 + x^2 + 15x - 18$
$= (x-1)(x+1)(x-2)(x+3)(2x^3 - 3x^2$
$+ 2x - 3)$
$= (x-1)(x+1)(x-2)(x+3)[x^2(2x-3)$
$+ 1(2x-3)]$
$= (x-1)(x+1)(x-2)(x+3)(2x-3)$
$(x^2 + 1)$
The real roots are $x = \pm 1, 2, -3$ and $\frac{3}{2}$.

28. At any point x, $\sec^2 x - \tan^2 x = 1$ coincides with $1 + \tan^2 x = \sec^2 x$. Additionally, $1 + \tan^2 x = \sec^2 x$ implies that $\sec^2 x$ is the function $\tan^2 x$ shifted up by one unit. A vertical of length 1 should intersect both graphs for all x.

29. 13 diamonds + three 4's (excluding the 4 of diamonds) = 16 possible outcomes.

30. $4! \cdot 6! = (4 \times 3 \times 2 \times 1)(6 \times 5 \times 4 \times 3 \times 2 \times 1)$
$= 17{,}280$

LESSON 119

Warm Up 119

1. identity

2.
$x^2 - 9 = 8x$
$x^2 - 8x - 9 = 0$
$(x-9)(x+1) = 0$
$x = 9$ or -1
$x = 9$ is the only positive solution.

3. $\sin^2 \theta + \cos^2 \theta = 1$

4. $\sin \theta = \dfrac{1}{\csc \theta}$

Lesson Practice 119

a. Solve for θ.
$8 \sin \theta + 1 = 4 \sin \theta - 1$
$4 \sin \theta = -2$
$\sin \theta = -\frac{1}{2}$
$\theta = \frac{7\pi}{6} + 2\pi n, \frac{11\pi}{6} + 2\pi n$

b. Solve for $0° \le x < 360°$.
$4 \cos^2 x = 4 \cos x - 1$
$4 \cos^2 x - 4 \cos x + 1 = 0$
$(2 \cos x - 1)(2 \cos x - 1) = 0$
$\cos x = \frac{1}{2}$
$x = 60°, 300°$

c. Solve for $-\frac{\pi}{2} < z < \frac{\pi}{2}$
$3 \tan^2 z - \tan z - 3 = 0$
$\tan z = \dfrac{1 \pm \sqrt{(-1)^2 - 4(3)(-3)}}{2(3)}$
$\tan z = \dfrac{1 \pm \sqrt{37}}{6}$
$\tan z = -0.8471$ or 1.1804
$z = -0.70$ or 0.87

d. Solve for $0° \le \theta \le 360°$.

$$1 - \cos^2\theta + 3\sin\theta = \sin\theta - 1$$
$$(1 - \cos^2\theta) + 3\sin\theta = \sin\theta - 1$$
$$\sin^2\theta + 3\sin\theta - \sin\theta + 1 = 0$$
$$\sin^2\theta + 2\sin\theta + 1 = 0$$
$$(\sin\theta + 1)^2 = 0$$
$$\sin\theta = -1$$
$$\theta = 270°$$

e. Graph $y = \sin\theta - \frac{1}{2}$ and $y = 2\sin\theta + \frac{1}{2}$ in the same viewing window for $0 \le \theta \le 2\pi$. Find the intersection of the two graphs using the calc menu.

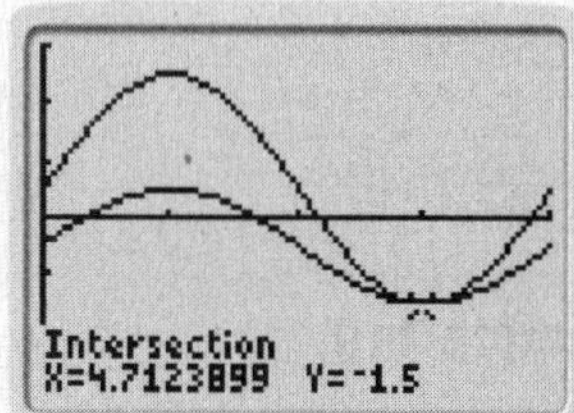

Between $0 \le \theta \le 2\pi$ the graphs only intersect at one point, $\theta \approx 4.712$.

f. Substitute 125 for $P(t)$.

$$P(t) = 250\cos\left(\frac{\pi}{6}(t+6)\right) + 250$$
$$125 = 250\cos\left(\frac{\pi}{6}(t+6)\right) + 250$$
$$-125 = 250\cos\left(\frac{\pi}{6}(t+6)\right)$$
$$-\frac{125}{250} = \cos\left(\frac{\pi}{6}(t+6)\right)$$
$$-\frac{1}{2} = \cos\left(\frac{\pi}{6}(t+6)\right)$$
$$\frac{2\pi}{3} = \frac{\pi}{6}(t+6) \qquad -\frac{2\pi}{3} = \frac{\pi}{6}(t+6)$$
$$4 = t+6 \quad \text{or} \quad -4 = t+6$$
$$t = 2 \qquad t = 10$$

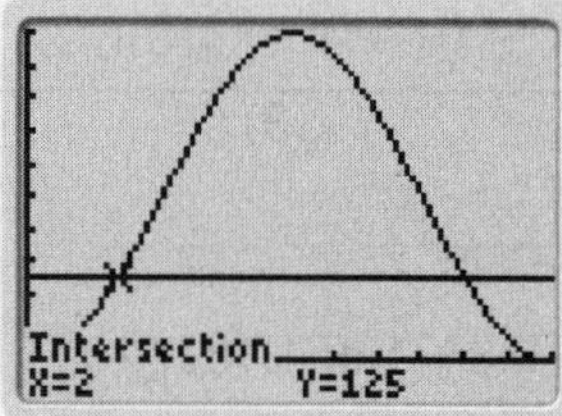

Therefore, in February the population of birds will first reach 125 birds.

Practice 119

1. The least degree is 4 because each of those roots has a conjugate pair.

2. Sample: An equation need not be true for any values of the variable, but an identity must be true for all values of the variable.

3. Solve for t.

$$N = N_0(r)^t$$
$$800 = 600(1.05)^t$$
$$\frac{4}{3} = (1.05)^t$$
$$\ln\left(\frac{4}{3}\right) = t\ln(1.05)$$
$$t = \frac{\ln\left(\frac{4}{3}\right)}{\ln(1.05)}$$
$$t \approx 5.896$$

It will take approximately 6 years for there to be 800 students.

4. **a.** Since there are no xy terms and the leading x and y terms are both of degree 2, the boundary is a circle.

b. $x^2 + y^2 - 8x - 40y - 209 = 0$

$$x^2 - 8x + y^2 - 40y = 209$$

completing the squares

$$(x^2 - 8x + 16) + (y^2 - 40x + 400)$$
$$= 209 + 16 + 400$$
$$(x-4)^2 + (y-20)^2 = 25^2$$

5. $${}_{16}C_{12} = \frac{16!}{12!(16-12)!}$$
$$= \frac{16 \times 15 \times 14 \times 13 \times 12!}{12! \times 4 \times 3 \times 2 \times 1} = 1820$$

6. Graph the two equations using the graphing calculator.

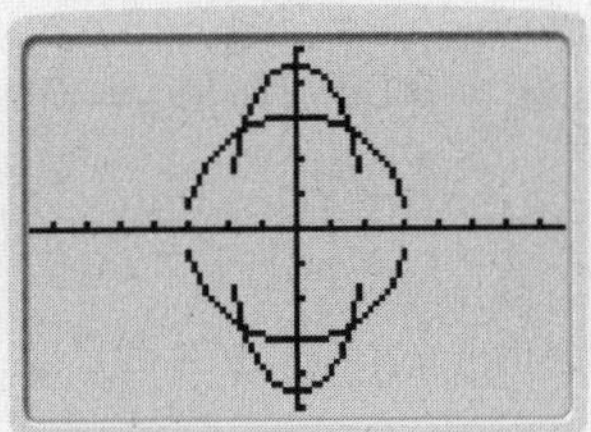

Use the TRACE option to locate all four intersecting points.

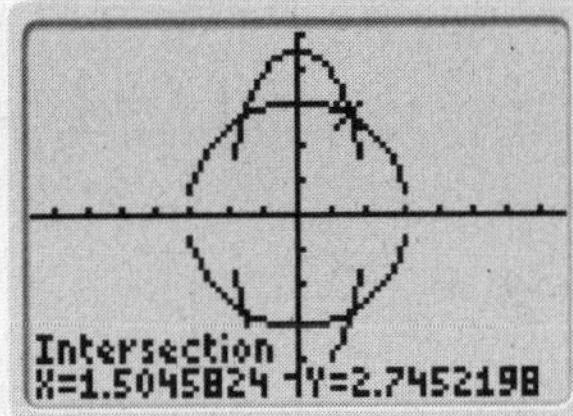

The four intersecting points are approximately (1.50, 2.75), (–1.50, 2.75), (1.50, –2.75), and (–1.50, –2.75).

7. New moon:

$$\cos\left(\frac{\pi}{14}t\right) = -1$$

$$\frac{\pi}{14}t = \cos^{-1}(-1)$$

$$\frac{\pi}{14}t = \pi$$

$$t = 14$$

So, the next new moon will occur 14 days from now.

Solar Eclipse: Yes, a solar eclipse is possible because the moon will be on the line between the earth and the sun after $11\frac{2}{3}$ days (within 3 days of the new moon on day 14).

8. Sample: An open question allows for people to write whatever they want without limiting their replies. It allows for answers that the surveyor may not have thought of. The drawback of an open question is that there may be too many replies to easily analyze the data. A closed question can make analyzing easier, but it may exclude valid options, forcing people to choose answers they don't want.

9. Divide a term by the previous term to find the ratio.

$\frac{2}{14} = \frac{1}{7}$, so $r = \frac{1}{7}$. Multiply the sequence by $r = \frac{1}{7}$ to obtain the next 3 terms.

$\frac{2}{49}, \frac{2}{343}, \frac{2}{2401}$

10. The perspective makes the heights misleading. It looks like the lowest population occurred in year 3 but it was actually lowest in year 1.

11. First express $(6 - 7i)$ in terms of $(\cos\theta + i\sin\theta)$

$(6 - 7i) = \sqrt{85}(\cos 310.6° + i\sin 310.6°)$

Use DeMoivre's Theorem.

$(\cos\theta + i\sin\theta)^n = \cos(n\theta) + i\sin(n\theta)$

$(6 - 7i)^3$

$= \left(\sqrt{85}\,(\cos 310.6° + i\sin 310.6°)\right)^3$

$= \left(\sqrt{85}\right)^3\left(\cos(3(310.6°)) + i\sin(3(310.6°))\right)$

$\approx 783.7(\cos 931.8° + i\sin 931.8°)$

$\approx 783.7(\cos 221.8° + i\sin 221.8°)$

12.

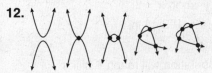

13. Solve by using the identity $\sin 2\theta = 2\sin\theta\cos\theta$.

if $\sin 2\theta = \sin\theta$

then $2\sin\theta\cos\theta = \sin\theta$

$2\cos\theta = 1$, if $\sin\theta \neq 0$

$$\cos\theta = \frac{1}{2}$$

$$\theta = \frac{\pi}{3}, \frac{5\pi}{3}$$

If $\sin\theta = 0$, then $\sin\theta = 0$, or π.

So $\theta = 0, \frac{\pi}{3}, \pi, \frac{5\pi}{3}$.

Answer Choice **C**

14. Enter the data from the table into the graphing calculator.

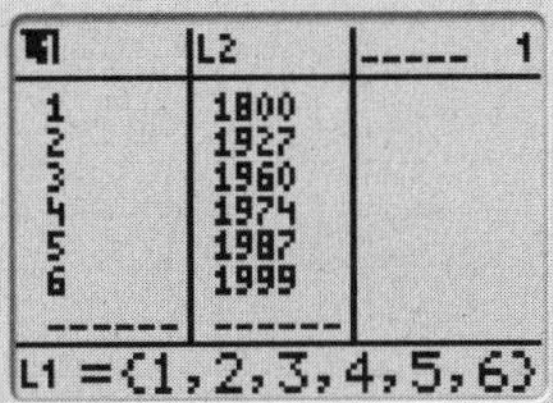

Select and perform a natural logarithm regression on the data.

Record the equation for the curve of best fit.

LnReg
y=a+blnx
a=1824.405882
b=106.4809176
r²=.9217216471
r=.9600633558

$y \approx 1824.4 + 106.48\ \ln(x)$.

Solve for y when $x = 8$.

$y \approx 1824.4 + 106.48\ \ln(8)$

≈ 2045.8

So the population will reach 8 billion sometime in 2045

15. Each year's rent can be represented by the formula for geometric sequence.

$R_k = 850(1.02)^{k-1}$, so the total cost will be the summation of all R_k for $k \in \{1, 2, 3, ..., 10\}$.

$$R_{total} = \sum_{k=1}^{10} R_k = \sum_{k=1}^{10} 850(1.02)^{k-1} = 9307.26$$

16. Only **B** has a constant ratio. Answer Choice **B**

17. Substitute 255 for v and 45° for θ.

$$x = \frac{1}{32}v^2 \sin 2\theta$$

$$= \frac{1}{32}(255)^2 \sin(90°)$$

$$\approx 2032.03 \text{ ft}$$

18. Sample:

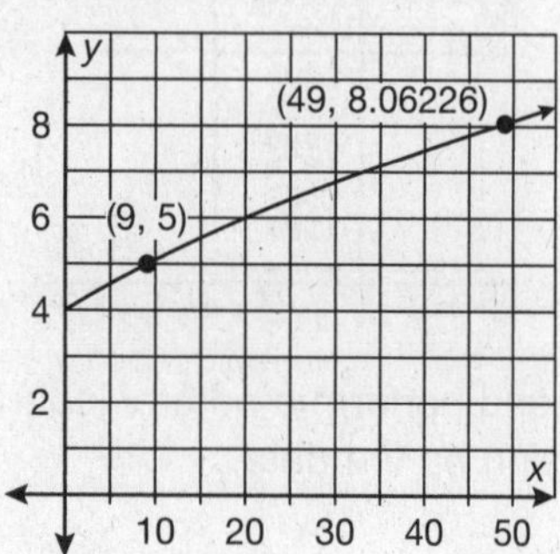

hypotenuse = 5 cm, leg = 3 cm;
hypotenuse = 8.06 cm, leg = 7 cm

19. Sample: $y = \dfrac{x^2 + 2x - 1}{x - 1}$.

20. $f(x) = 12\log(4x)$, $g(x) = \dfrac{x+2}{x^4 - 1}$

Solve for x when $f(g(x)) = 0$,

$$f(g(x)) = 12\log\left(4\left(\frac{x+2}{x^4-1}\right)\right)$$

$$0 = 12\log\left(4\left(\frac{x+2}{x^4-1}\right)\right)$$

$$1 = 4\left(\frac{x+2}{x^4-1}\right)$$

$$x^4 - 1 = 4x + 8$$

$$x^4 - 4x - 9 = 0$$

Graph this equation on the calculator and look for x-intercepts.

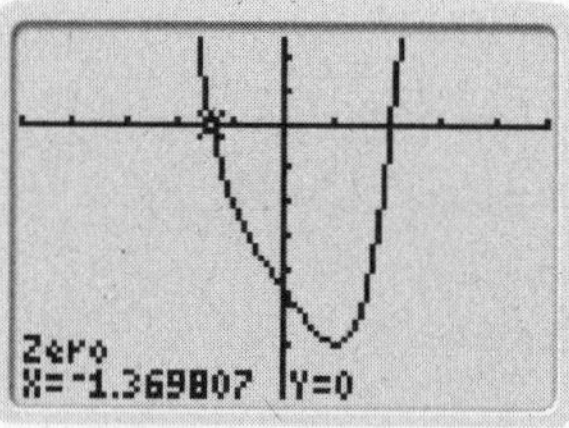

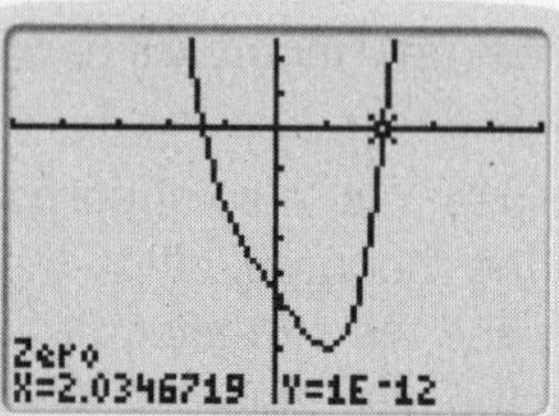

$x = -1.3698, 2.0347$

21. Solve for t.

$$50 = e^{-0.200064t+4.0073} + 30$$

$$20 = e^{-0.200064t+4.0073}$$

$$\ln 20 = -0.200064t + 4.0073$$

$$t = \frac{\ln 20 - 4.0073}{-0.200064}$$

$$t \approx 5.06 \text{ minutes}$$

It will take about 5.06 minutes.

22. $\log 2x + \log 4 \neq \log(2x + 4)$.

Correct solution:

$$\log 2x + \log 4 = 3$$

$$\log 8x = 3$$

$$8x = 10^3$$

$$x = \frac{1000}{8} = 125$$

23. First find the 40th term.

$$a_n = a_1 + d(n-1)$$

$$a_{40} = -160 + 8(40-1)$$

$$a_{40} = 152$$

Then find the sum of the first 40 terms.

$$S_{40} = \frac{40(a_1 + a_{40})}{2}$$

$$S_{40} = 20(-160 + 152)$$

$$= 20(-8) = -160$$

24. List all the possible roots.

$$\frac{p}{q} \in \left\{\frac{\pm1, \pm2}{\pm1, \pm2, \pm3, \pm6}\right\}$$

Test each root out and you will find that

$$x = \pm1, -\frac{1}{3}$$

25. List all the possible roots.

$$\frac{p}{q} \in \left\{\frac{\pm1, \pm2, \pm4, \pm8, \pm16}{\pm1, \pm3, \pm5, \pm15}\right\}$$

Test each root out and you will find that

$$x = \pm2, \frac{2}{5}, \frac{2}{3}$$

26. $5\sqrt[3]{48} - \sqrt[3]{750} = 5\sqrt[3]{2^3 \times 6} - \sqrt[3]{5^3 \times 6}$

$$= (5 \times 2)\sqrt[3]{6} - 5\sqrt[3]{6}$$

$$= 10\sqrt[3]{6} - 5\sqrt[3]{6}$$

$$= 5\sqrt[3]{6}$$

27. $\frac{\sqrt[4]{36} \cdot \sqrt[4]{9}}{\sqrt[4]{4}} = \frac{\sqrt[4]{2^2 3^2} \cdot \sqrt[4]{3^2}}{\sqrt[4]{2^2}}$

$$= \sqrt[4]{2^{2-2} 3^{2+2}}$$

$$= \sqrt[4]{3^4} = 3$$

28. **a.** Solve for *z*.

$$3\tan^2 z + 2\tan z - 1 = 0$$

$$(3\tan z - 1)(\tan z + 1) = 0$$

$$\tan z = \frac{1}{3} \quad \text{or} \quad -1$$

$$z = 18.43° \quad \text{or} \quad -45°$$

b. none

29. The stubs he finds on the floor are not random sample, they are a convenience sample because the stubs are those that are convenient to use. People who attend certain types of movies may be more likely to toss their stubs on the floor, rather than tossing them in the trash can, or taking them home.

30. The data in the table appears to be exponential. Perform the exponential regression on the calculator and obtain the correlation coefficient to verify.

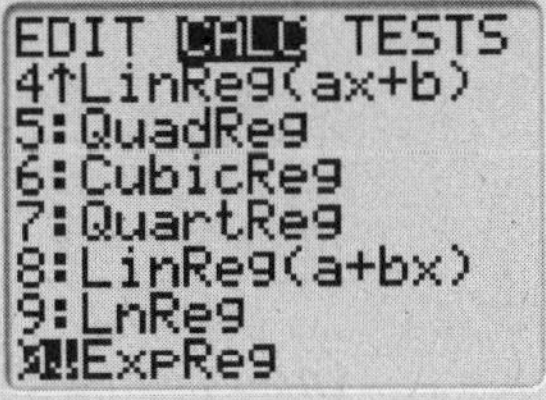

$r^2 = 0.9999925$, almost a perfect fit.

INVESTIGATION 12

1. Sample:

For $n = 10$

$$1 + 2 + 3 + 4 + 5 + 6 + 7 + 8 + 9 + 10 = 55$$

$$\frac{10(10+1)}{2} = 55$$

For $n = 20$

$$1 + 2 + 3 + \ldots + 20 = 210$$

$$\frac{20(20+1)}{2} = 210$$

For $n = 30$

$$1 + 2 + 3 + \ldots + 30 = 465$$

$$\frac{30(30+1)}{2} = 465$$

2. As *n* gets larger in value, the number of calculations is still the same.

3. $a_1 = 1$

$$\sum_{k=1}^{1} k = \frac{1(1+1)}{2} = 1$$

$$\sum_{k=1}^{1} k = a_1 \text{ true}$$

4. $\sum_{k=1}^{m} k = \frac{m(m+1)}{2}$

5. $a_{m+1} = m + 1$

$$\left(\sum_{k=1}^{m} k\right) + a_{m+1} = \frac{m(m+1)}{2} + (m+1)$$
$$= \frac{m^2+m}{2} + \frac{2m+2}{2}$$
$$= \frac{m^2+3m+2}{2}$$
$$= \frac{(m+1)(m+2)}{2}$$

6. $\sum_{k=1}^{m+1} k = \frac{(m+1)((m+1)+1)}{2}$

$$= \frac{(m+1)(m+2)}{2}$$

$$\sum_{k=1}^{m+1} k = \left(\sum_{k=1}^{m} k\right) + a_{m+1}$$

7. Yes, it is true by the process of mathematical induction.

8. $a_k = 2k$

9. $\sum_{k=1}^{n} 2k$

10. Use the summation formula for an arithmetic sequence.

$$\sum_{k=1}^{n} 2k = \frac{n(a_1 + a_n)}{2}$$
$$= \frac{n(2+2n)}{2}$$
$$= \frac{2n(1+n)}{2} = n(n+1)$$

11. Sample:

$2 + 4 + 6 + 8 + 10 + 12 + 14 + 16 + 18 + 20 = 110$

$10(10 + 1) = 110$

For $n = 20$, $n = 30$, check students' work.

12. a. $a_1 = 2(1) = 2$

$$\sum_{k=1}^{1} 2k = 1(1+1) = 2$$

$$\sum_{k=1}^{1} 2k = a_1 \text{ true}$$

b. $\sum_{k=1}^{m} 2k = m(m+1)$

c. $a_{m+1} = 2(m+1)$

$$\left(\sum_{k=1}^{m} 2k\right) + a_{m+1} = m(m+1) + 2(m+1)$$
$$= m^2 + m + 2m + 2$$
$$= m^2 + 3m + 2$$

$$\sum_{k=1}^{m+1} 2k = (m+1)((m+1)+1)$$
$$= (m+1)(m+2)$$
$$= m^2 + 3m + 2$$

$$\sum_{k=1}^{m+1} 2k = \left(\sum_{k=1}^{m} 2k\right) + a_{m+1}$$

Therefore, the formula works for all values of n.

Investigation Practice

a. Find the first five sums.

$S_1 = 1$

$S_2 = 1 + 3 = 4$

$S_3 = 1 + 3 + 5 = 9$

$S_4 = 1 + 3 + 5 + 7 = 16$

$S_5 = 1 + 3 + 5 + 7 + 9 = 25$

b. $a_k = 2k - 1$

c. $\sum_{k=1}^{n} 2k - 1$

d. Use the summation formula for an arithmetic sequence.

$$\sum_{k=1}^{n} 2k - 1 = \frac{n(a_1 + a_n)}{2}$$
$$= \frac{n(1 + (2n-1))}{2}$$
$$= \frac{n(2n)}{2} = n^2$$

e. $a_1 = 2(1) - 1 = 1$

$$\sum_{k=1}^{1} 2k - 1 = (1)^2 = 1$$

$$\sum_{k=1}^{1} 2k - 1 = a_1 \text{ true}$$

f. $\sum_{k=1}^{m} 2k - 1 = m^2$

g. $a_{m+1} = 2(m+1) - 1 = 2m + 1$

$$\sum_{k=1}^{m} 2k - 1 = m^2 \text{, by assumption}$$

$$\sum_{k=1}^{m+1} 2k - 1 = \left(\sum_{k=1}^{m} 2k - 1\right) + a_{m+1}$$

$$= (m^2) + (2m + 1)$$

$$= (m + 1)^2$$

Therefore, the formula works for all values of *n*.

h. Use mathematical induction

Check base case. $a_1 = 3(1) = 3$

$$\sum_{k=1}^{1} 3k = \frac{3(1)(1+1)}{2} = 3$$

$$\sum_{k=1}^{1} 3k = a_1 \text{ true}$$

Assume true up to *m*.

$$\sum_{k=1}^{m} 3k = \frac{3m(m+1)}{2}$$

Show that $\sum_{k=1}^{m+1} 3k = \left(\sum_{k=1}^{m} 3k\right) + a_{m+1}$

$a_{m+1} = 3(m+1) = 3m + 3$

$$\left(\sum_{k=1}^{m} 3k\right) + a_{m+1} = \frac{3m(m+1)}{2} + 3m + 3$$

$$= \frac{3m^2 + 3m}{2} + \frac{6m + 6}{2}$$

$$= \frac{3m^2 + 9m + 6}{2}$$

$$= \frac{3(m^2 + 3m + 2)}{2}$$

$$= \frac{3(m+1)(m+2)}{2}$$

$$\sum_{k=1}^{m+1} 3k = \frac{3(m+1)((m+1)+1)}{2}$$

$$= \frac{3(m+1)(m+2)}{2}$$

$$\sum_{k=1}^{m+1} 3k = \left(\sum_{k=1}^{m} 3k\right) + a_{m+1}$$

Therefore, the formula is true.

i. This formula does not hold for the first case.

$a_1 = 5(1) = 5$

$$\sum_{k=1}^{1} 5k = \frac{1(1+1)}{5} = \frac{2}{5}$$

$$5 \neq \frac{2}{5}$$

The correct formula is

$$\sum_{k=1}^{n} 5k = \frac{n(a_1 + a_n)}{2}$$

$$= \frac{n(5 + 5n)}{2} = \frac{5n(n+1)}{2}$$

j. Sample: The LCM of 3 and 5 is 15. To find the formula for the sum of consecutive numbers divisible by 3 and 5, find the formula for the sum of consecutive numbers divisible by 15: $\sum_{k=1}^{n} 15k = \frac{n(15n + 15)}{2} = \frac{15n(n+1)}{2}$

Check base case

$a_1 = 15(1) = 15$

$$\sum_{k=1}^{1} 15k = \frac{15(1)(1+1)}{2} = 15$$

$$\sum_{k=1}^{1} 15k = a_1 \text{ true}$$

Assume true up to *m*.

$$\sum_{k=1}^{m} 15k = \frac{15m(m+1)}{2}$$

Show that $\sum_{k=1}^{m+1} 15k = \left(\sum_{k=1}^{m} 15k\right) + a_{m+1}$

$a_{m+1} = 15(m+1) = 15m + 15$

$$\left(\sum_{k=1}^{m} 15k\right) + a_{m+1} = \frac{15m(m+1)}{2} + 15m + 15$$

$$= \frac{15m^2 + 15m}{2} + \frac{30m + 30}{2}$$

$$= \frac{15m^2 + 45m + 30}{2}$$

$$= \frac{15(m^2 + 3m + 2)}{2}$$

$$= \frac{15(m+1)(m+2)}{2}$$

$$\sum_{k=1}^{m+1} 15k = \frac{15(m+1)((m+1)+1)}{2}$$

$$= \frac{15(m+1)(m+2)}{2}$$

$$\sum_{k=1}^{m+1} 15k = \left(\sum_{k=1}^{m} 15k\right) + a_{m+1}$$

Therefore, the formula is true.

APPENDIX LESSONS

Appendix Lesson Practice 1

a. $A = \frac{b(2h)}{2} = 2\left(\frac{bh}{2}\right)$. The area is doubled.

b. $A = (3h)\left(\frac{3b_1 + 3b_2}{2}\right) = 9\left[h\left(\frac{b_1 + b_2}{2}\right)\right]$.

The new area is nine times the original area.

c. $SA = 6\left(\frac{x}{5}\right)^2 = 6\frac{x^2}{25} = \frac{1}{25}(6x^2)$

$V = \left(\frac{x}{5}\right)^3 = \frac{x^3}{125} = \frac{1}{125}x^3$

The surface area is $\frac{1}{25}$ the original surface area. The volume is $\frac{1}{125}$ the original volume.

d. $V = \frac{1}{3}\pi r^2(4h) = 4\left(\frac{1}{3}\pi r^2 h\right)$

The volume is quadrupled.

e. $V = \frac{4}{3}\pi(3r)^3 = \frac{4}{3}\pi(27r^3) = 27\left(\frac{4}{3}\pi r^3\right)$

The new volume is 27 times the volume of the original sphere.

f. $V = \frac{l}{2} \times w \times \frac{h}{2} = \frac{1}{4}(l \times w \times h)$

The volume is $\frac{1}{4}$ the original volume.

g. $V = \pi\left(\frac{d}{2}\right)^2 h = \frac{\pi}{4}d^2 h$

$V = \pi\left(\frac{2d}{2}\right)^2 h = \pi d^2 h$

The volume of the larger pool is four times the volume of the smaller pool.

Appendix Lesson Practice 2

a.

A11

	A	B	C	D
1		2007	2008	
2	Terrace Box	30	31.5	
3	Upper Reserved	10	10.5	
4	Upper Box	20	21	
5	Club Box	55	57.75	
6	Field Box	40	42	
7	Lower Box	40	42	
8				

b.

A13

	A	B	C	D	E
1		2007	2008	Amount of Increase	
2	Terrace Box	30	31.5	1.5	
3	Upper Reserved	10	10.5	0.5	
4	Upper Box	20	21	1	
5	Club Box	55	57.75	2.75	
6	Field Box	40	42	2	
7	Lower Box	40	42	2	
8					

c. $2(31.5) = \$63$

d.

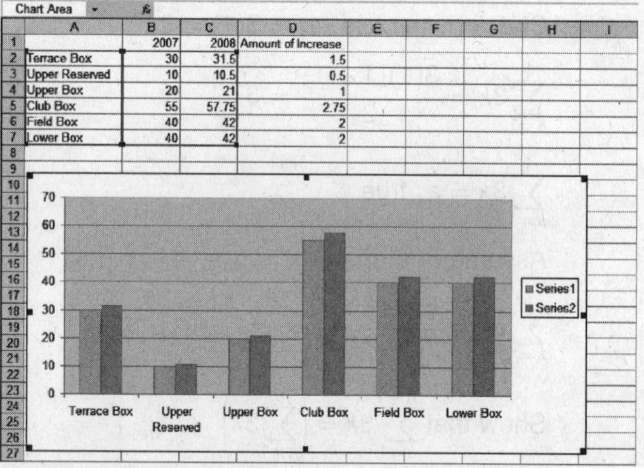

Chart Area

	A	B	C	D	E	F	G	H	I
1		2007	2008	Amount of Increase					
2	Terrace Box	30	31.5	1.5					
3	Upper Reserved	10	10.5	0.5					
4	Upper Box	20	21	1					
5	Club Box	55	57.75	2.75					
6	Field Box	40	42	2					
7	Lower Box	40	42	2					

Appendix Lesson Practice 3

a. $\frac{201.2 - 200}{200} = 0.006 = 0.6\%$

b. $\frac{180 - 178}{180} \approx 0.011 \approx 1.1\%$

c. $86.2 - 85 = 1.2$, $86.4 - 85.0 = 1.4$

Group A has greater precision.

d. $\frac{10.1 - 10.0}{10.0} \approx 0.01 \approx 1\%$

e. $123.5 \text{ g} \leq x < 124.5 \text{ g}$

f. $123.95 \text{ g} \le x < 124.05 \text{ g}$

g. $56 \times 0.05 = 2.8,\ 53.2 \le x \le 58.8$
Yes, it is acceptable.

h. $\frac{5}{8} + \frac{1}{64} = \frac{41}{64}, \frac{5}{8} - \frac{1}{64} = \frac{39}{64}$
Yes, it is acceptable.

i. Most accurate: 35.5 g; Next most accurate: 34.8 g; Least accurate: 35 g
Equally precise: 34.8 g and 35.5 g; Least precise: 35 g

Appendix Lesson Practice 4

a. $\frac{108 - 80}{399 - 309} = \frac{180 - 108}{y}$

$\frac{28}{90} = \frac{72}{y}$

$28y = 6480$

$y = 231.43$

$399 + 231.43 = 630.43$

A rug with an area of 108 ft^2 would be priced at \$630.43.

$\frac{54 - 24}{199 - 99} = \frac{35 - 24}{x}$

$\frac{30}{100} = \frac{11}{x}$

$30x = 1100$

$x = 36.67$

$99 + 36.7 = 135.67$

A rug with an area of 35 ft^2 would be priced at \$135.67.

b. Press STAT and ENTER to input the data. Then, press STAT and scroll to the CALC tab. Scroll down to **4:Lin Reg(ax+b)**, and press ENTER. Enter **L1,L2** followed by pressing ENTER.
The best-fit linear regression of the data is $y \approx 38.55x - 27.79$.
We use interpolation since 4 is within the range of x-values.

$y \approx 38.55x - 27.79$

$y \approx 38.55(4) - 27.79$

$y \approx 126.41$ miles

c. Press STAT and ENTER to input the data. Then, press STAT and scroll to the CALC tab. Try the various regression models (e.g., linear, cubic, logarithmic) to find the best r-value. Quartic regression works best; Highlight **7:QuartReg** and enter **L1,L2** followed by pressing ENTER.
The best regression model is

$y \approx -0.539x^4 + 14.460x^3 - 134.835x^2 + 477.646x + 622.379$

Since the year 2009 is outside of the range of x-values, we use extrapolation.

$y \approx -0.539x^4 + 14.460x^3 - 134.835x^2 + 477.646x + 622.379$

$y \approx -0.539(12)^4 + 14.460(12)^3 - 134.835(12)^2 + 477.646(12) + 622.379$

$y \approx -11176.7 + 24986.9 - 19416.2 + 5731.8 + 622.379$

$y \approx 748$

Appendix Lesson Practice 5

a.
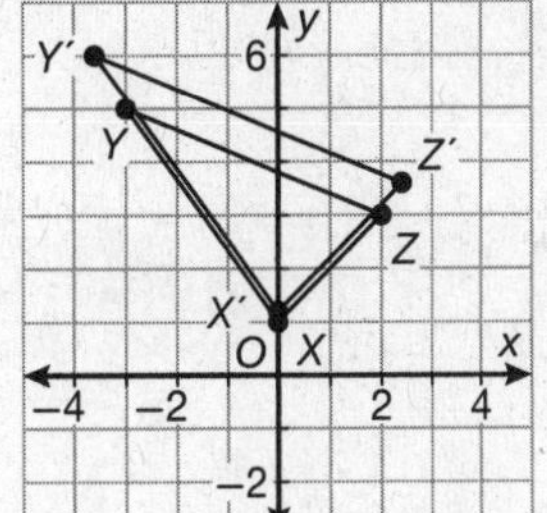

b.
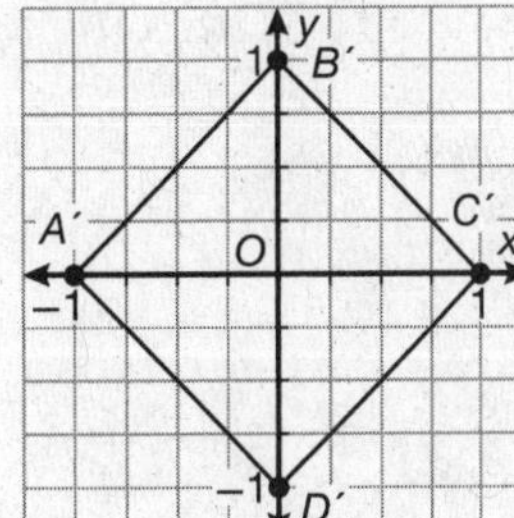

c. The length of $\overline{QT}$ is 6 units and the length of $\overline{Q'T'}$ is 18 units. Therefore, the scale factor is $18 \div 6 = 3$.

d. $\left(4\left(\frac{1}{2}\right), 3\left(\frac{1}{2}\right)\right) = (2, 1.5)$

$\left(1\left(\frac{1}{2}\right), -2\left(\frac{1}{2}\right)\right) = (0.5, -1)$

$\left(7\left(\frac{1}{2}\right), -2\left(\frac{1}{2}\right)\right) = (3.5, -1)$

The co-ordinates are (2, 1.5), (0.5, −1) and (3.5, −1).

e. $\frac{7.5}{3} = 2.5$; a scale factor of 2.5

When enlarging on a copy machine, 250% should be used.

Appendix Lesson Practice 6

a. Neither

b. Polygon

c. Neither

d. Polyhedron

e. 8 faces (2 hexagons, 6 rectangles), 18 edges

f. 10 faces (2 octagons, 8 rectangles), 24 edges

g.

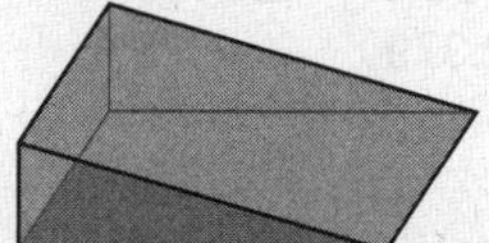

h.

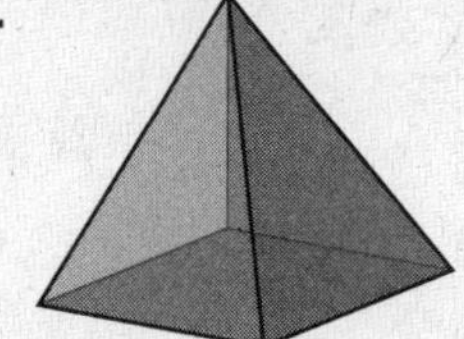

i.

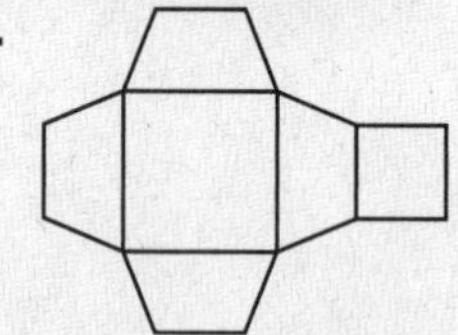

j.

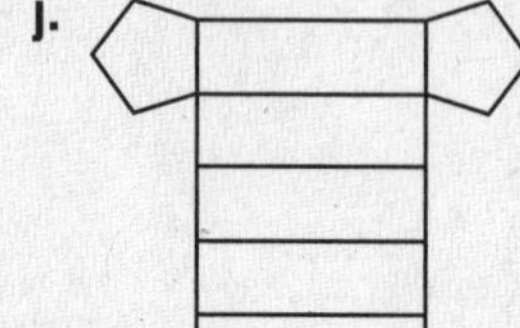

k. $SA = 2(5 \cdot 2) + 2(10 \cdot 5) + 2(10 \cdot 2)$
$= 160$ square units

Appendix Lesson Practice 7

a. $0.00000004 = 4 \times 10^{-8}$

b. $354{,}000{,}000{,}000{,}000 = 3.54 \times 10^{14}$

c. $9.9 \times 10^{-5} = 0.000099$

d. $6.02 \times 10^{9} = 6{,}020{,}000{,}000$

e. $1.04 \times 10^{12} = 1{,}040{,}000{,}000{,}000$

f. $(3.25 \times 10^{-5}) + (4.14 \times 10^{-3})$
$= 0.0000325 + 0.00414$
$= 0.0041725$

g. $(6.022 \times 10^{23}) \times 8.15$
$= (10^{23} \times 6.022) \times 8.15$
$= 10^{23} \times (6.022 \times 8.15)$
$= 10^{23} \times 49.0793$
$= 10^{23} \times (4.90793 \times 10)$
$= 4.90793 \times 10^{24}$

h. $\frac{1.024 \times 10^{26}}{5.974 \times 10^{24}} = 0.171 \times 10^{2} \approx 17$

About 17 times

i. Let x be the diameter of the Earth.

$0.95x = 1.2 \times 10^{4}$

$x = \frac{1.2 \times 10^{4}}{0.95}$

$x \approx 1.26 \times 10^{4}$

$x \approx 12{,}600$ km

j. An atom is about 10^{-13} km in size

$10^{-13} \times (5 \times 10^{10}) = 5 \times 10^{-3} = 0.005$ km

SKILLS BANK

Skills Bank Lesson 1

a. $38 \times 82 \approx 40 \times 80 = 3200$

b. $8320 - 94 \approx 8320 - 100 = 8220$

c. $0.078 \div 2 \approx 0.080 \div 2 = 0.04$

d. $0.042 + 0.78 \approx 0.04 + 0.80 = 0.84$

e. $618 \cdot 68 \approx 600 \cdot 70 = 42{,}000$

f. $3958 \div 492 \approx 4000 \div 500 = 8$

g. $906 + 378 \approx 900 + 378 = 1278$

h. $439 \times 87 \approx 400 \times 90 = 36{,}000$

i. $4023 \times 50 \approx 4000 \times 50 = 200{,}000$

j. $9387 - 1959 \approx 9387 - 2000 = 7387$

k. $8374 + 3305 + 91 \approx 8400 + 3300 + 100$
$= 11{,}800$

l. $948 - 298 \approx 948 - 300 = 648$

m. $402 \div 95 \approx 400 \div 100 = 4$

n. $6306 \div 928 \approx 6300 \div 900 = 7$

o. $38 \times 5820 \approx 40 \times 6000 = 240{,}000$

p. $4503 - 581 \approx 4600 - 600 = 4000$

q. $298 \times 682 \approx 300 \times 700 = 210{,}000$

r. $4.982 - 0.593 \approx 4.982 - 0.600 = 4.382$

Skills Bank Lesson 2

a. $42 + 19 + 8 = (42 + 8) + 19$
$= 50 + 19 = 69$

b. $8 \times 71 = (8 \times 70) + (8 \times 1)$
$= 560 + 8 = 568$

c. $63 - 28 = 65 - 30 = 35$

d. $75 + 17$
$75 + 20 = 95$
$95 - 3 = 92$

e. $6 \times 12 \times 5 = 6 \times (5 \times 12)$
$= 6 \times 60 = 360$

f. $514 - 298 = 516 - 300 = 216$

g. $3.2 + 2.5 + 4.5 = 3.2 + (2.5 + 4.5)$
$= 3.2 + 7 = 10.2$

h. $4 \times 241 = (4 \times 240) + (4 \times 1)$
$= 960 + 4 = 964$

i. $7 \times 81 = (7 \times 80) + (7 \times 1)$
$= 560 + 7 = 567$

j. $45 + 92$
$50 + 92 = 142$
$142 - 5 = 137$

k. $138 - 29 = 139 - 30 = 109$

l. $32 + 78$
$32 + 80 = 112$
$112 - 2 = 110$

m. $949 + 111$
$950 + 111 = 1061$
$1061 - 1 = 1060$

n. $7 \times 26 = (7 \times 25) + (7 \times 1)$
$= 175 + 7 = 182$

o. $14 + 91 + 6 = (14 + 6) + 91$
$= 20 + 91 = 111$

p. $2 \times 18 \times 5 = (2 \times 5) \times 18$
$= 10 \times 18 = 180$

q. $482 - 197 = 485 - 200 = 285$

r. $4 \times 3 \times 15 = (4 \times 15) \times 3$
$= 60 \times 3 = 180$

s. $77 + 48$
$77 + 50 = 127$
$127 - 2 = 125$

t. $2 \times 7 \times 25 \times 2 = (2 \times 25) \times 7 \times 2$
$= (50 \times 2) \times 7$
$= 100 \times 7 = 700$

u. $57 + 245$
$60 + 245 = 305$
$305 - 3 = 302$

v. $8 \times 32 = (8 \times 30) + (8 \times 2)$
$= 240 + 16 = 256$

w. $92 - 47 = 95 - 50$
$= 45$

x. $14 \times 7 = (10 \times 7) + (4 \times 7)$
$= 70 + 28 = 98$

Skills Bank Lesson 3

a. $3^2 = 3 \cdot 3 = 9$

b. $9^0 = 1$

c. $17^1 = 17$

d. $5^4 = 5 \cdot 5 \cdot 5 \cdot 5 = 625$

e. $-1^5 = -(1 \cdot 1 \cdot 1 \cdot 1 \cdot 1) = -1$

f. $0^8 = 0 \cdot 0 \cdot 0 \cdot 0 \cdot 0 \cdot 0 \cdot 0 \cdot 0 = 0$

g. $(-4)^3 = (-4) \cdot (-4) \cdot (-4) = -64$

h. $-8^1 = -8$

i. $(-2)^6 = (-2) \cdot (-2) \cdot (-2) \cdot (-2) \cdot (-2) \cdot (-2)$
$= 64$

j. $-5^0 = -1$

k. $(3x)^2 = (3x) \cdot (3x) = 9x^2$

l. $(-3)^3 + 4^2 = ((-3) \cdot (-3) \cdot (-3)) + (4 \cdot 4)$
$= -11$

m. $(-3)^3 - (-3)^2 =$
$((-3) \cdot (-3) \cdot (-3)) - ((-3) \cdot (-3)) = -36$

n. $(-x)^4 + (2x)^2$
$= ((-x) \cdot (-x) \cdot (-x) \cdot (-x)) + ((2x)(2x))$
$= x^4 + 4x^2$

o. $-7^0 + (-2)^2 = -1 + ((-2) \cdot (-2)) = 3$

p. $(-9)^1 + (-9)^0 = (-9) + 1 = -8$

q. $7^3 + (-7)^3$
$= (7 \cdot 7 \cdot 7) + ((-7) \cdot (-7) \cdot (-7)) = 0$

r. $7 - 8^1 = 7 - 8 = -1$

s. $11^3 = 11 \cdot 11 \cdot 11$

t. $-6^7 = -(6 \cdot 6 \cdot 6 \cdot 6 \cdot 6 \cdot 6 \cdot 6)$

u. $(-13)^5$
$= (-13) \cdot (-13) \cdot (-13) \cdot (-13) \cdot (-13)$

v. $-(-2)^3 = -((-2) \cdot (-2) \cdot (-2))$

w. $4^8 = 4 \cdot 4 \cdot 4 \cdot 4 \cdot 4 \cdot 4 \cdot 4 \cdot 4$

x. $(-5)^2 = (-5) \cdot (-5)$

Skills Bank Lesson 4

a. $\begin{array}{r} 4.6 \\ +\ 3.92 \\ \hline 8.52 \end{array}$

b. $\begin{array}{r} 2.5 \\ \times\ 1.5 \\ \hline 3.75 \end{array}$

c. $0.08\overline{)2.4}$
$(0.08 \times 100)\overline{)(2.4 \times 100)}$
$\begin{array}{r} 30 \\ 8\overline{)240} \\ -240 \\ \hline 0 \end{array}$

d. $\begin{array}{r} 3.05 \\ -1.6 \\ \hline 1.45 \end{array}$

e. $\begin{array}{r} 4.9 \\ \times\ 2.27 \\ \hline 11.123 \end{array}$

f. $\begin{array}{r} 3.6 \\ +\ 4.12 \\ \hline 7.72 \end{array}$

g. $\begin{array}{r} 0.105 \\ -\ 0.06 \\ \hline 0.045 \end{array}$

h. $0.36\overline{)0.054}$
$(0.36 \times 100)\overline{)(0.054 \times 100)}$
$\begin{array}{r} 0.15 \\ 36\overline{)5.40} \\ -36 \\ \hline 180 \\ -180 \\ \hline 0 \end{array}$

i. $\begin{array}{r} 0.2 \\ \times\ 3.8 \\ \hline 0.76 \end{array}$

j. $\begin{array}{r} 2.4 \\ +\ 8.03 \\ \hline 10.43 \end{array}$

k. $0.04\overline{)60}$
$(0.04 \times 100)\overline{)(60 \times 100)}$
$\begin{array}{r} 1500 \\ 4\overline{)6000} \\ -6000 \\ \hline 0 \end{array}$

l. $\begin{array}{r} 5.25 \\ \times\ 8 \\ \hline 42.00 \end{array}$

m. $\begin{array}{r} 0.98 \\ +\ 0.35 \\ \hline 1.33 \end{array}$

n. $1.4\overline{)4.074}$

$(1.4 \times 10)\overline{)(4.074 \times 10)}$

$$\begin{array}{r} 2.91 \\ 14\overline{)40.74} \\ -28 \\ \hline 127 \\ -126 \\ \hline 14 \\ -14 \\ \hline 0 \end{array}$$

o. $\begin{array}{r} 3.6 \\ \times\ 0.4 \\ \hline 1.44 \end{array}$

p. $\begin{array}{r} 6.52 \\ -\ 2.74 \\ \hline 3.78 \end{array}$

q. $\begin{array}{r} 4.872 \\ -\ 0.084 \\ \hline 4.788 \end{array}$

r. $\begin{array}{r} 32.4 \\ \times\ 18.9 \\ \hline 612.36 \end{array}$

s. $0.04\overline{)2.334}$

$(0.04 \times 100)\overline{)(2.334 \times 100)}$

$$\begin{array}{r} 58.35 \\ 4\overline{)233.4} \\ -20 \\ \hline 33 \\ -32 \\ \hline 14 \\ -12 \\ \hline 20 \\ -20 \\ \hline 0 \end{array}$$

t. $\begin{array}{r} 3.1 \\ +\ 4.82 \\ \hline 7.92 \end{array}$

Skills Bank Lesson 5

a. $\frac{1}{2} > 0.3$

b. $0.65 = \frac{13}{20}$

c. $-3 < -\frac{45}{20}$

d. $\frac{2}{5} > 25\%$

e. $17.5\% = \frac{7}{40}$

f. $\frac{6}{5} < 1.5$

g. $\frac{3}{4} > \frac{5}{8}$

h. $1 = 100\%$

i. $-\frac{15}{7} < -2$

j. $1.27 < \frac{37}{13}$

k. $\frac{23}{40} = 0.575$

l. $0.87 > 75\%$

m. $\frac{2}{17} < 17\%$

n. $23\% > \frac{5}{28}$

o. $-\frac{14}{23} < -0.45$

p. $0.034 < 34\%$

q. 0.6

1.4

$30\% = 0.3$

$\frac{15}{21} \approx 0.71$

0.3, 0.6, 0.71, 1.4

30%, 0.6, $\frac{15}{21}$, 1.4

r. −5

$-\frac{27}{7} \approx -3.86$

−0.01

−0.45

−5, −3.86, −0.45, −0.01

−5, $-\frac{27}{7}$, −0.45, −0.01

s. 0.7

$40\% = 0.4$

$\frac{3}{5} = 0.6$

$\frac{1}{8} = 0.125$

0.125, 0.4, 0.6, 0.7

$\frac{1}{8}$, 40%, $\frac{3}{5}$, 0.7

t. 0.56

0.65

$55\% = 0.55$

$\frac{2}{3} \approx 0.67$

0.55, 0.56, 0.65, 0.67

55%, 0.56, 0.65, $\frac{2}{3}$

u. 1.7

$50\% = 0.50$

$\frac{46}{90} \approx 0.51$

0.05

0.05, 0.50, 0.51, 1.7

0.05, 50%, $\frac{46}{90}$, 1.7

v. -1.5

$-\frac{63}{20} = -3.15$

$-\frac{57}{40} = -1.425$

-2.3

$-3.15, -2.3, -1.5, -1.425$

$-\frac{63}{20}, -2.3, -1.5, -\frac{57}{40}$

Skills Bank Lesson 6

a. $\frac{2}{5} + \frac{1}{10} = \frac{4}{10} + \frac{1}{10} = \frac{5}{10} = \frac{1}{2}$

b. $\frac{3}{8} - \frac{1}{5} = \frac{15}{40} - \frac{8}{40} = \frac{7}{40}$

c. $\frac{1}{6} \cdot \frac{4}{5} = \frac{1 \times 4}{6 \times 5} = \frac{4}{30} = \frac{2}{15}$

d. $\frac{5}{6} \div \frac{1}{8} = \frac{5}{6} \times \frac{8}{1} = \frac{5 \times 8}{6 \times 1} = \frac{40}{6} = 6\frac{2}{3}$

e. $\frac{7}{9} - \frac{3}{5} = \frac{35}{45} - \frac{27}{45} = \frac{8}{45}$

f. $\frac{11}{12} \times \frac{3}{55} = \frac{11 \times 3}{12 \times 55} = \frac{33}{660} = \frac{1}{20}$

g. $\frac{7}{15} + \frac{2}{3} = \frac{7}{15} + \frac{10}{15} = \frac{17}{15} = 1\frac{2}{15}$

h. $\frac{12}{17} \div \frac{3}{8} = \frac{12}{17} \times \frac{8}{3} = \frac{12 \times 8}{17 \times 3} = \frac{96}{51} = 1\frac{15}{17}$

i. $\frac{7}{8} \times \frac{1}{3} = \frac{7 \times 1}{8 \times 3} = \frac{7}{24}$

j. $6 \div \frac{3}{4} = 6 \times \frac{4}{3} = \frac{24}{3} = 8$

k. $\frac{5}{8} + \frac{4}{5} = \frac{25}{40} + \frac{32}{40} = \frac{57}{40} = 1\frac{17}{40}$

l. $6\frac{1}{8} - 2\frac{5}{6} = \frac{49}{8} - \frac{17}{6} = \frac{147}{24} - \frac{68}{24}$

$= \frac{79}{24} = 3\frac{7}{24}$

m. $1\frac{2}{3} \times 6\frac{1}{8} = \frac{5}{3} \times \frac{49}{8} = \frac{5 \times 49}{3 \times 8} = \frac{245}{24} = 10\frac{5}{24}$

n. $7\frac{3}{8} \div 6 = \frac{59}{8} \times \frac{1}{6} = \frac{59 \times 1}{8 \times 6} = \frac{59}{48} = 1\frac{11}{48}$

o. $10 - 3\frac{7}{12} = \frac{120}{12} - \frac{43}{12} = \frac{77}{12} = 6\frac{5}{12}$

p. $5\frac{1}{4} + 8\frac{7}{8} = \frac{21}{4} + \frac{71}{8} = \frac{42}{8} + \frac{71}{8}$

$= \frac{113}{8} = 14\frac{1}{8}$

q. $\frac{8}{19} - \frac{7}{38} + \frac{3}{19} = \frac{16}{38} - \frac{7}{38} + \frac{6}{38} = \frac{15}{38}$

r. $\frac{14}{26} \cdot \frac{13}{49} \cdot \frac{7}{10} = \frac{14 \cdot 13 \cdot 7}{26 \cdot 49 \cdot 10} = \frac{1274}{12{,}740} = \frac{1}{10}$

s. $2\frac{2}{5} + 9\frac{1}{5} - 7\frac{3}{5} = \frac{12}{5} + \frac{46}{5} - \frac{38}{5} = \frac{20}{5} = 4$

Skills Bank Lesson 7

a. $5 + 12 = 17$

b. $48 \div -6 = -8$

c. $7(-5) = -35$

d. $1.6 \cdot -2 = -3.2$

e. $32 \div 4 = 8$

f. $4.3 + (-8.1) = 4.3 - 8.1 = -3.8$

g. $4 - 9 = -5$

h. $(-2) \cdot (-9) = 18$

i. $-42 + -12 = -42 - 12 = -54$

j. $-12 \times 4 = -48$

k. $-540 \div -0.9 = 600$

l. $100 - (-4) = 100 + 4 = 104$

m. $-10 \times -14 = 140$

n. $-81 \div 9 = -9$

o. $-6 + 13 = 7$

p. $16 - (-3) = 16 + 3 = 19$

Skills Bank Lesson 8

a. $\frac{x}{10} = \frac{5}{100}$

b. $\frac{19}{x} = \frac{57}{12}$

$19 \cdot 12 = 57 \cdot x$

$228 = 57x$

$\frac{228}{57} = \frac{57x}{57}$

$4 = x$

c. $0.11 \times 14 = 1.54$

d. $3 \div 80 = 0.0375$

$0.0375 \times 100\% = 3.75\%$

e. $7 \cdot 108 \stackrel{?}{=} 9 \cdot 84$

$756 = 756$

True

f. $81 \div 300 = 0.27$

$0.27 \times 100\% = 27\%$

g. $88 \times 0.25 = 22$

h. $23 \cdot 50 = 46 \cdot x$

$1150 = 46x$

$\frac{1150}{46} = \frac{46x}{46}$

$25 = x$

Skills Bank Lesson 9

a. $d = rt$

$d = (7)(6)$

$d = 42$

The distance is 42 miles.

b. $d = rt$

$(34.3) = (3.5)t$

$\frac{34.3}{3.5} = \frac{3.5t}{3.5}$

$9.8 = t$

The time is 9.8 hours.

c. $d = rt$

$312 = r(6.25)$

$\frac{312}{6.25} = \frac{6.25r}{6.25}$

$50 \approx r$

Mark's rate was 50 miles per hour.

d. $d = r_1t_1 + r_2t_2$

$d = (6)(0.5) + (5)(0.5)$

$d = 3 + 2.5$

$d = 5.5$

The runners will be 5.5 miles apart.

e. $t_1 + t_2 = 2.5$

$t_1 = 2.5 - t_2$

$d_1 = r_1t_1$

$d_2 = r_2t_2$

$d_1 = 9(2.5 - t_2)$

$d_1 = 22.5 - 9t_2$

$d_2 = 6t_2$

$d_2 = d_1$

$6t_2 = 22.5 - 9t_2$

$0 = 22.5 - 15t_2$

$15t_2 = 22.5$

$t_2 = 1.5$

$t_1 = 2.5 - 1.5 = 1.0$

$d = r_1t_1 + r_2t_2$

$d = (9)(1.0) + (6)(1.5)$

$d = 18$

The runner ran a total of 18 miles.

Skills Bank Lesson 10

a–o.

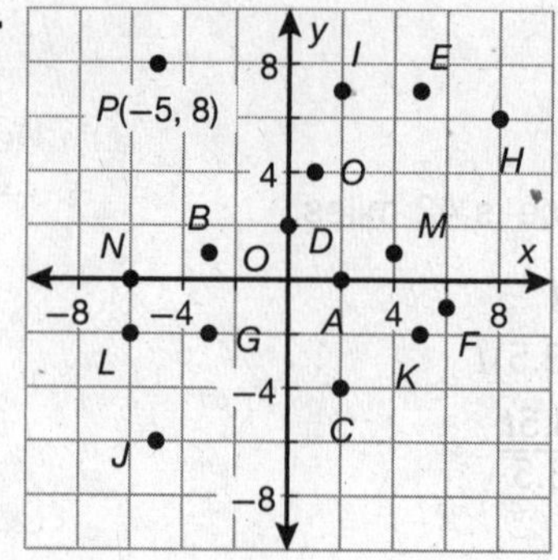

p. (−4, 2)

q. (0, −4)

r. (2, 3)

s. (6, −7)

t. (−7, −1)

u. (2, 6)

v. (4, 0)

w. (−3, −5)

x. (−5, 8)

Skills Bank Lesson 11

a.

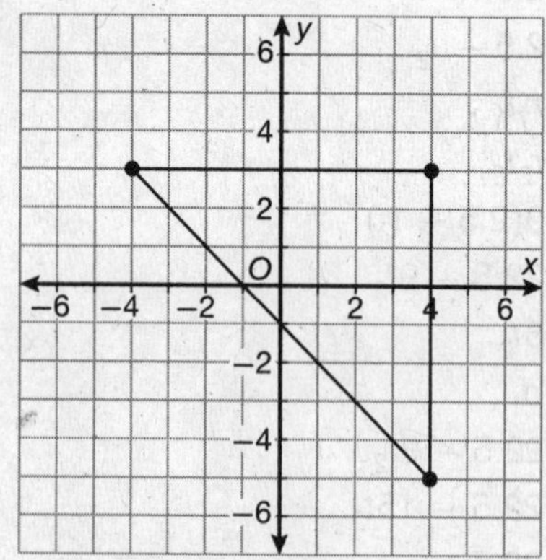

Right isosceles triangle

b.

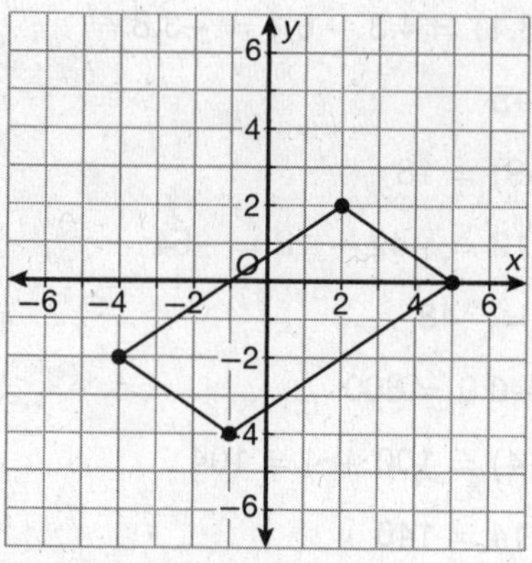

Parallelogram

c.

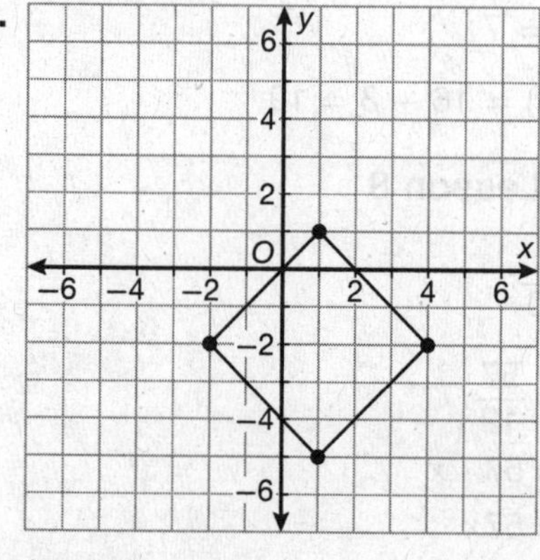

(1, −5)

d. $\left(\frac{x_1 + x_2}{2}, \frac{y_1 + y_2}{2}\right)$

$= \left(\frac{0 + 3}{2}, \frac{(-4) + (-7)}{2}\right)$

$= \left(\frac{3}{2}, \frac{-11}{2}\right)$

$= (1.5, -5.5)$

$d = \sqrt{(x_1 - x_2)^2 + (y_1 - y_2)^2}$

$d = \sqrt{(0 - 3)^2 + ((-4) - (-7))^2}$

$d = \sqrt{(-3)^2 + (3)^2}$

$d = \sqrt{9 + 9}$

$d = \sqrt{18} = 3\sqrt{2}$

e.

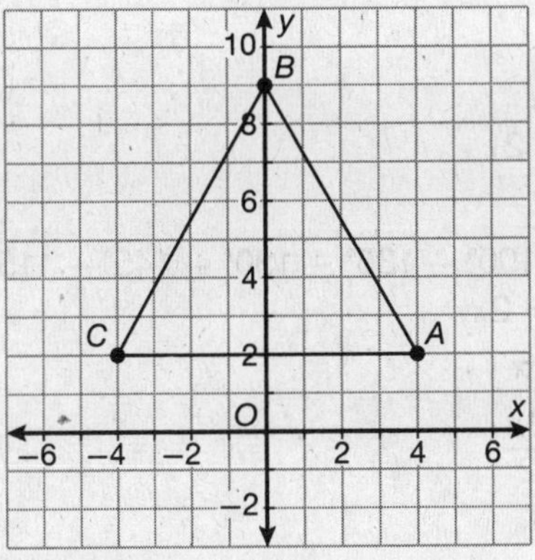

Isosceles

f. $d = \sqrt{(x_1 - x_2)^2 + (y_1 - y_2)^2}$

$d = \sqrt{((-1) - 2)^2 + ((1) - 6)^2}$

$d = \sqrt{9 + 25}$

$d = \sqrt{34}$

$d = \sqrt{(2 - 5)^2 + (6 - 1)^2}$

$d = \sqrt{9 + 25}$

$d = \sqrt{34}$

$d = \sqrt{(5 - 2)^2 + (1 - (-4))^2}$

$d = \sqrt{9 + 25}$

$d = \sqrt{34}$

$d = \sqrt{(2 - (-1))^2 + ((-4) - 1)^2}$

$d = \sqrt{9 + 25}$

$d = \sqrt{34}$

The length of each side is $\sqrt{34}$, so the quadrilateral is a rhombus.

g. $\left(\frac{x_1 + x_2}{2}, \frac{y_1 + y_2}{2}\right)$

$= \left(\frac{(-8) + (-3)}{2}, \frac{1 + 13}{2}\right)$

$= \left(\frac{-11}{2}, \frac{14}{2}\right) = (-5.5, 7)$

The center of the circle is $(-5.5, 7)$.

$d = \sqrt{(x_1 - x_2)^2 + (y_1 - y_2)^2}$

$d = \sqrt{((-8) - (-3))^2 + (1 - 13)^2}$

$d = \sqrt{(-5)^2 + (-12)^2}$

$d = \sqrt{25 + 144}$

$d = \sqrt{169}$

$d = 13$

$r = \frac{13}{2}$

$A = \pi r^2 = \pi\left(\frac{13}{2}\right)^2 = \frac{169\pi}{4}$

The area of the circle is $= \frac{169\pi}{4}$.

h. $\left(\frac{x_1 + x_2}{2}, \frac{y_1 + y_2}{2}\right)$

$= \left(\frac{4 + 0}{2}, \frac{3 + 9}{2}\right) = \left(\frac{4}{2}, \frac{12}{2}\right)$

$= (2, 6)$

$d = \sqrt{(x_1 - x_2)^2 + (y_1 - y_2)^2}$

$d = \sqrt{(2 - (-4))^2 + (6 - 2)^2}$

$d = \sqrt{(6)^2 + (4)^2}$

$d = \sqrt{36 + 16}$

$d = \sqrt{52}$

Skills Bank Lesson 12

a. 4

b. 1

c. 6

d. Alternate exterior

e. Alternate interior

f. Corresponding

g. $m\angle 3 = m\angle 8 = m\angle 1 = m\angle 6 = 135°$

$m\angle 2 = m\angle 4 = m\angle 5 = m\angle 7 = 45°$

Skills Bank Lesson 13

a. 45°

b. 131°

c. 80°

d. 100°

e. 72°

f. 77°

g. 55°

h. 170°

i. 33°

Skills Bank Lesson 14

a. $90° - 30° = 60°$

b. $90° - 88° = 2°$

c. $90° - 17° = 73°$

d. $90° - 47° = 43°$

e. $180° - 19° = 161°$

f. $180° - 122° = 58°$

g. $180° - 163° = 17°$

h. $180° - 81° = 99°$

i. $\angle TMR$

j. $\angle AMB$; $\angle BMZ$

k. $m\angle RMS + m\angle SMD = 180°$

$(7x + 8) + (3x + 12) = 180$

$7x + 3x + 8 + 12 = 180$

$10x + 20 = 180$

$10x + 20 - 20 = 180 - 20$

$10x = 160$

$\frac{10x}{10} = \frac{160}{10}$

$x = 16$

l. $4x = 2x + 70$

$4x - 2x = 2x - 2x + 70$

$2x = 70$

$\frac{2x}{2} = \frac{70}{2}$

$x = 35$

Skills Bank Lesson 15

a. Polygon, quadrilateral, parallelogram, rhombus

b. Polygon, triangle, right triangle, scalene triangle

c. Polygon, quadrilateral, trapezoid

d. Polygon, pentagon

e. $n = 5$

$180°(5 - 2)$

$= 540°$

f. $n = 8$

$180°(8 - 2)$

$= 1080°$

$1080° - 100° - 135° - 130° - 145° - 115° - 105° = 2x$

$350° = 2x$

$\frac{350°}{2} = \frac{2x}{2}$

$175° = x$

g. $n = 10$

$180°(10 - 2)$

$= 1440°$

$1440° \div 10 = 144°$

Skills Bank Lesson 16

a. $C = 2\pi r$

$14 = 2\pi r$

$\frac{14}{2\pi} = r$

$2.23 \approx r$

$V = \pi r^2 h$

$= \pi \cdot (2.23)^2 \cdot 7$

$\approx 109.18 \text{ m}^3$

The volume of the cylinder is 109.18 m^3.

b. $V = \frac{4}{3}\pi r^3$

$113.1 = \frac{4}{3}\pi r^3$

$\frac{3}{4} \cdot \frac{113.1}{\pi} = r^3$

$27 \approx r^3$

$\sqrt[3]{27} = r$

$3 = r$

The radius of the sphere is 3 in.

c. $SA = B + \frac{1}{2}Pl$

$= 15 \cdot 15 + \frac{1}{2} \cdot 15 \cdot 4 \cdot 23$

$= 225 + 690$

$= 915 \text{ cm}^2$

The surface area of the pyramid is 915 cm^2.

d. $SA = 2\pi r(r + h)$
$= 2 \cdot \pi \cdot 3(3 + 11)$
$= 263.9 \text{ cm}^2$

e. $V = Bh$
$= 5.89 \cdot 2.4 \cdot 3$
$= 42.41 \text{ m}^3$

f. $V = \frac{1}{3}Bh$
$32 = \frac{1}{3} \cdot 12 \cdot h$
$32 = 4 \cdot h$
$\frac{32}{4} = \frac{4h}{4}$
$8 \text{ in.} = h$
The height of the pyramid is 8 in.

g. $V = \frac{1}{3}Bh$
$= \frac{1}{3} \cdot 27 \cdot 7$
$= 63 \text{ ft}^3$
The volume of the pyramid is 63 ft^3.

h. $SA = 2\pi r(r + h)$
$96\pi = 2\pi r(r + 8)$
$96\pi = 2\pi r^2 + 16\pi r$
$\frac{96\pi}{2\pi} = \frac{2\pi r^2 + 16\pi r}{2\pi}$
$48 = r^2 + 8r$
$0 = r^2 + 8r - 48$
$0 = (r + 12)(r - 4)$
$r = -12; r = 4$
Since the radius cannot be negative, the radius of the cylinder is 4 cm.

i. $V = \pi r^2 h$
$= \pi \cdot 9^2 \cdot 9$
$= 729\pi \text{ cm}^3$
$V = \frac{4}{3}\pi r^3$
$= \frac{4}{3} \cdot \pi \cdot 9^3$
$= 972\pi \text{ cm}^3$
The sphere's volume is $\frac{4}{3}$ of the cylinder's volume.

Skills Bank Lesson 17

a. $A = \frac{1}{2}bh$
$= \frac{1}{2} \cdot 7 \cdot 24$
$= 84 \text{ m}^2$

b. $A = bh$
$= 2.5 \cdot 0.9$
$= 2.25 \text{ in.}^2$

c. $A = bh$
$= 8 \cdot 19$
$= 152 \text{ cm}^2$

d. $A = bh + bh$
$= 10 \cdot 2 + 2 \cdot 4$
$= 28 \text{ ft}^2$

e. $A = bh + 2bh + 2 \cdot \frac{1}{2}bh$
$= 18 \cdot 10 + 2 \cdot 6 \cdot 2 + 2 \cdot \frac{1}{2} \cdot 4 \cdot 2$
$= 212 \text{ cm}^2$

f. $A = bh + \pi r^2$
$= 32 \cdot 32 + \pi \cdot 16^2$
$\approx 1827.84 \text{ mm}^2$

g. $A = bh + \frac{1}{2}bh$
$= 10 \cdot 3 + \frac{1}{2} \cdot 10 \cdot 4$
$= 50 \text{ in.}^2$

Skills Bank Lesson 18

a. $r = R\cos\left(\frac{180°}{n}\right)$
$R = \frac{7}{\cos\left(\frac{180°}{6}\right)}$
$R \approx 8.08$
$s = 2R\sin\left(\frac{180°}{n}\right)$
$s \approx 2 \cdot 8.08 \cdot \sin\left(\frac{180°}{6}\right)$
$s \approx 8.08 \text{ m}$

b. $r = R\cos\left(\frac{180°}{n}\right)$

$r = 10 \cdot \cos\left(\frac{180°}{3}\right)$

$r = 5$ ft

c. $l = 2r$

$l = 10$ cm

d. $r = R\cos\left(\frac{180°}{n}\right)$

$r = 30 \cdot \cos\left(\frac{180°}{10}\right)$

$r \approx 28.53$ in.

e. $s = 2R\sin\left(\frac{180°}{n}\right)$

$R = \dfrac{4}{2\sin\left(\frac{180°}{7}\right)}$

$R \approx 4.61$

$r = R\cos\left(\frac{180°}{n}\right)$

$r \approx 4.61 \cdot \cos\left(\frac{180°}{7}\right)$

$r \approx 4.15$ m

Skills Bank Lesson 19

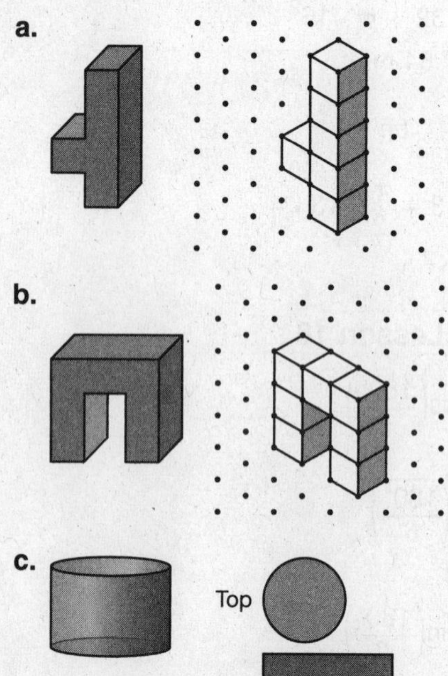

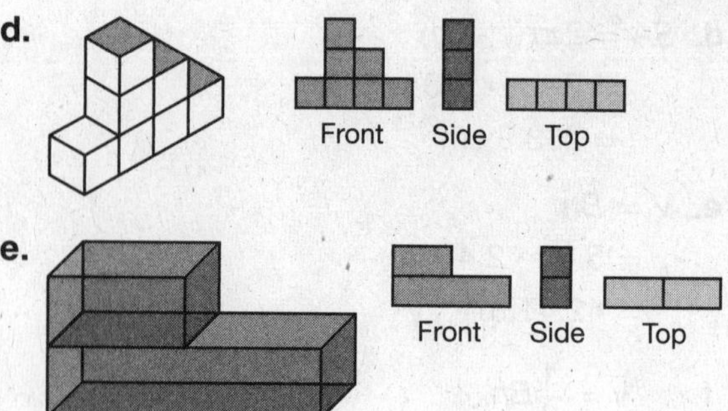

Skills Bank Lesson 20

a. 1, 4, 7, 10; add 3; 13

b. 4, 6, 8, 10, 12; add 2; 14

c. 1, 5, 9; add 4; 13

Skills Bank Lesson 21

a.

Stems	Leaves
0	9
1	2, 5, 5, 8, 9
2	0, 2, 2, 3, 5, 5, 7, 9
3	1, 5
4	
5	6, 8

b.

Stems	Leaves
6	2, 4, 8
7	0, 0, 3, 5, 9, 9, 9
8	1, 2, 3, 3, 6, 8
9	0, 0, 0, 0, 2, 4, 6, 8, 9
10	0

c. **i.** 19

ii. 83

iii. 121

iv. 102

v. 106

Skills Bank Lesson 22

a. School Population by Grade

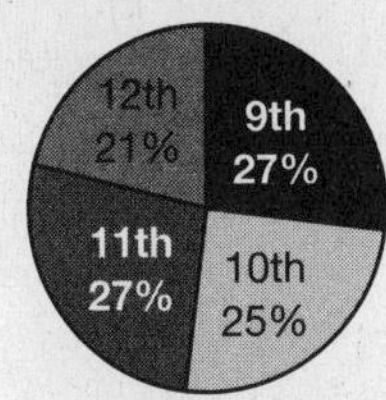

b. **Number of Songs Downloaded**

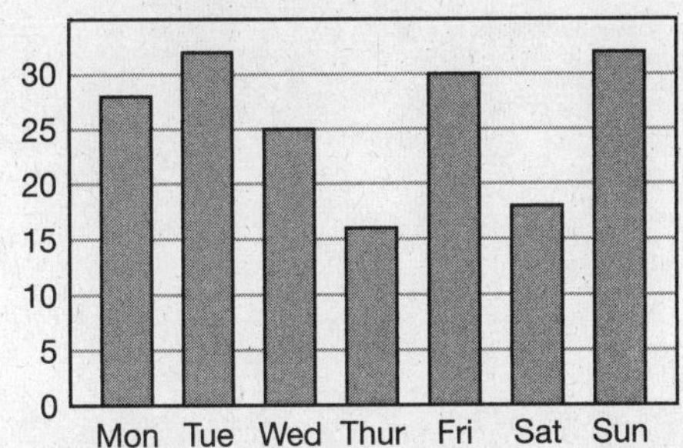

c. $(x + 3)(x + 2)(x + 1) \stackrel{?}{=} x^3 + 6x^2 + 11x + 6$

$(x + 3)(x + 2)(x + 1) = (x^2 + 3x + 2x + 6)(x + 1)$

$= (x^2 + 5x + 6)(x + 1) = x^3 + 5x^2 + 6x + x^2 + 5x + 6$

$x^2 + 6x^2 + 11x + 6 = x^3 + 6x^2 + 11x + 6$

True

d. $(x + 7)(x - 4) \stackrel{?}{=} (x + 2)(x + 1)$

$(x + 7)(x - 4) = x^2 + 7x - 4x - 28 = x^2 + 3x - 28$

$(x + 2)(x + 1) = x^2 + 2x + x + 2 = x^2 + 3x + 2$

$x^2 + 3x - 28 \neq x^2 + 3x + 2$

$-28 \neq 2$

False

e.

Conclusion	Justification
MQPN is a parallelogram.	Given
$MP \cong MP$	Reflexive Property
$MQ \parallel PN$; $QP \parallel MN$	Definition of Parallelogram
$\angle QMP \cong \angle MPN$; $\angle QPM \cong \angle PMN$	Alternate Interior Angles are Congruent
$\Delta MQP \cong \Delta PNM$	Angle-Side-Angle Congruence Theorem

Skills Bank Lesson 23

a. $(x + 5)^2 \stackrel{?}{=} x^2 + 25$

$(x + 5)(x + 5) = x^2 + 10x + 25$

$x^2 + 10x + 25 \neq x^2 + 25$

$(x + 5)^2 \neq x^2 + 25$

False

b. $x(x - 3) + 5x - 9 \stackrel{?}{=} (x + 1)^2 - 10$

$x(x - 3) + 5x - 9 = x^2 - 3x + 5x - 9$

$= x^2 + 2x - 9$

$(x + 1)^2 - 10 = x^2 + 2x + 1 - 10$

$= x^2 + 2x - 9$

$x^2 + 2x - 9 = x^2 + 2x - 9$

True

Skills Bank Lesson 24

a.

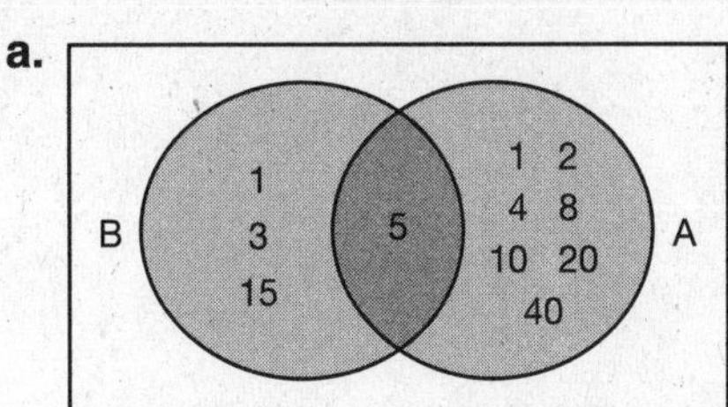

b.

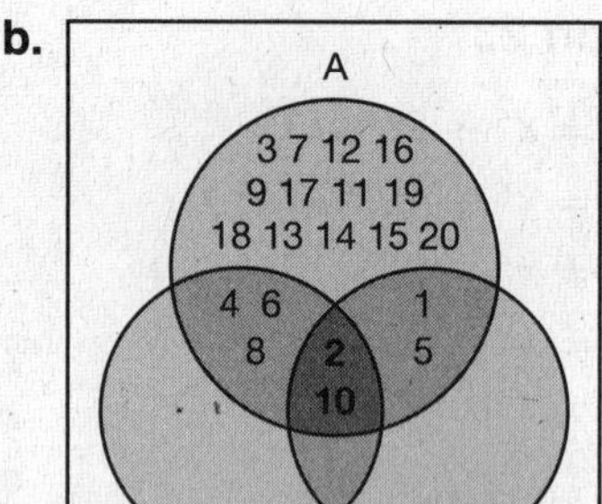
A
3 7 12 16
9 17 11 19
18 13 14 15 20
4 6
8
2
10
1
5
C
B

c.

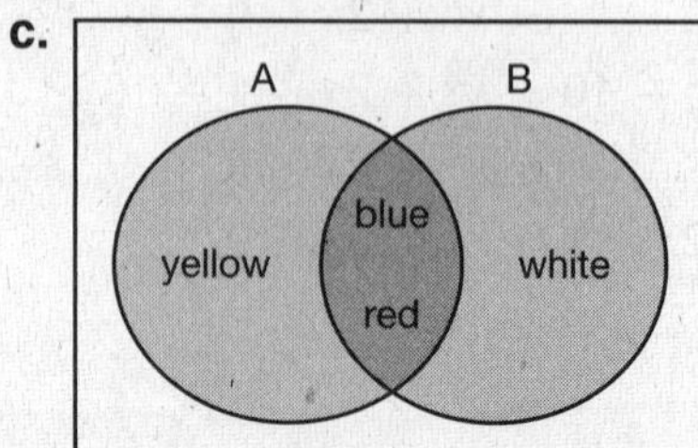
A
B
yellow
blue
red
white

d.

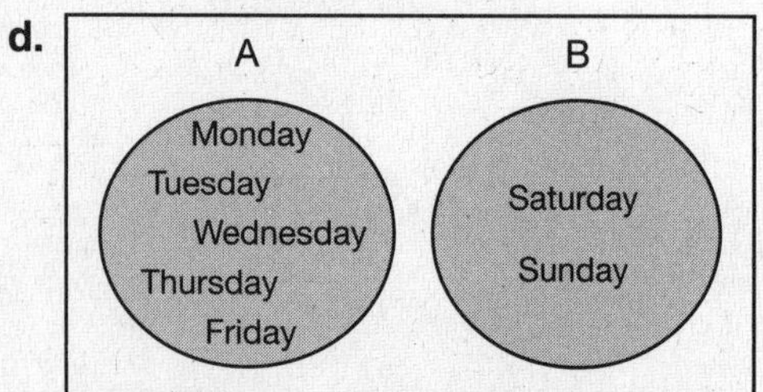
A
B
Monday
Tuesday
Wednesday
Thursday
Friday
Saturday
Sunday

e.

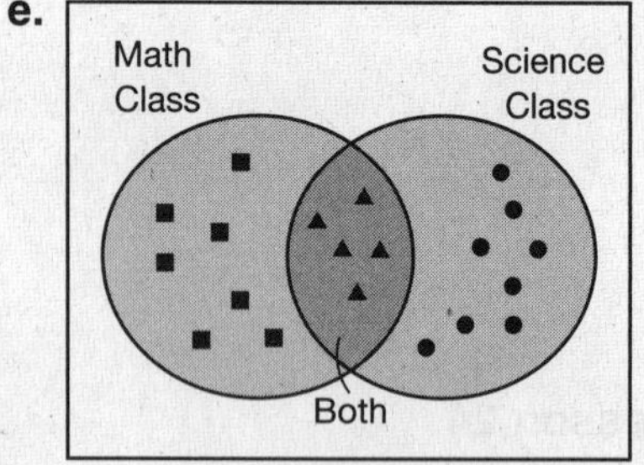
Math
Class
Science
Class
Both

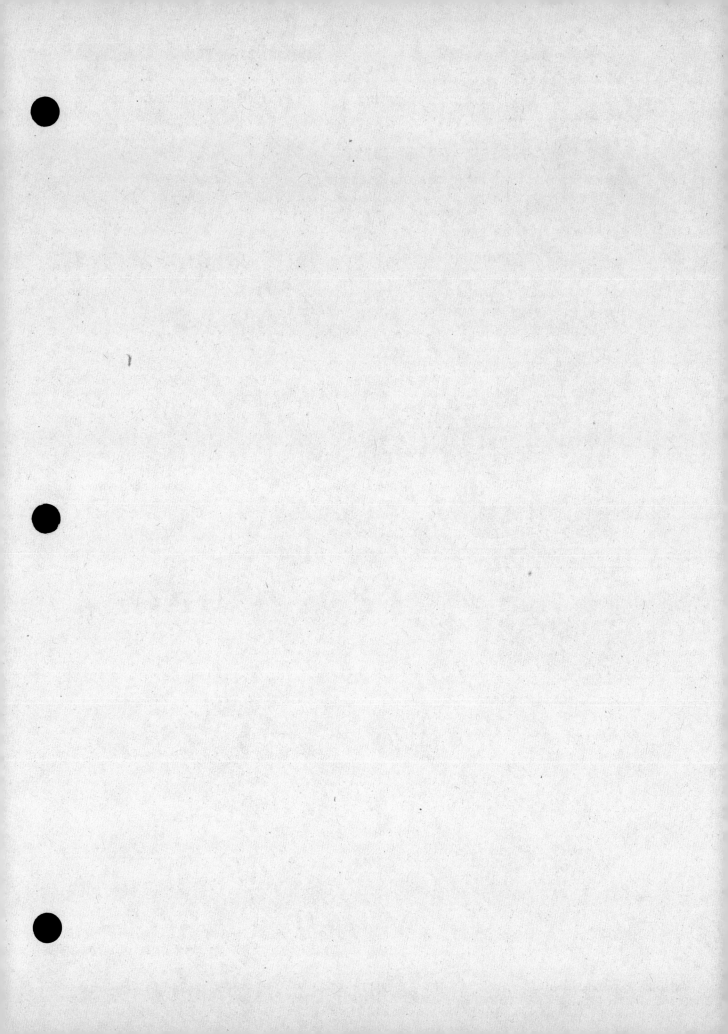